SAS/STAT® User's Guide, Version 6, Fourth Edition
Volume 2

SAS Institute Inc.
SAS Circle □ Box 8000
Cary, NC 27512-8000

The correct bibliographic citation for this manual is as follows: SAS Institute Inc., *SAS/STAT® User's Guide, Version 6, Fourth Edition, Volume 2*, Cary, NC: SAS Institute Inc., 1989. 846 pp.

SAS/STAT® User's Guide, Version 6, Fourth Edition, Volume 2

The SAS® System is an integrated system of software providing complete control over data management, analysis, and presentation. Base SAS software is the foundation of the SAS System. Products within the SAS System include SAS/ACCESS® SAS/AF® SAS/ASSIST® SAS/DMI® SAS/ETS® SAS/FSP® SAS/GRAPH® SAS/IML® SAS/IMS-DL/I® SAS/OR® SAS/QC® SAS/REPLAY-CICS® SAS/SHARE® SAS/STAT® SAS/CPE™ SAS/DB2™ and SAS/SQL-DS™software. Other SAS Institute products are SYSTEM 2000® Data Management Software, with basic SYSTEM 2000, CREATE™ Multi-User™ QueX™ Screen Writer™ and CICS interface software; NeoVisuals® software; JMP™ and JMP IN™ software; SAS/RTERM® software; SAS/C® and SAS/CX™ Compilers. *SAS Communications® SAS Training® SAS Views® and the SASware Ballot®* are published by SAS Institute Inc. Plink86® and Plib86® are registered trademarks of Phoenix Technologies Ltd. All other trademarks above are registered trademarks or trademarks, as indicated by their mark, of SAS Institute Inc.

A footnote must accompany the first use of each Institute registered trademark or trademark and must state that the referenced trademark is used to identify products or services of SAS Institute Inc.

The Institute is a private company devoted to the support and further development of its software and related services.

MXG® is a registered trademark of Merrill Consultants.

Doc SS1, Ver 111.2121589

Contents

CHAPTERS

24 The GLM Procedure 891

25 The LIFEREG Procedure 997

26 The LIFETEST Procedure .1027

27 The LOGISTIC Procedure .1071

28 The NESTED Procedure 1127

29 The NLIN Procedure 1135

30 The NPAR1WAY Procedure 1195

31 The ORTHOREG Procedure 1211

32 The PLAN Procedure 1221

33 The PRINCOMP Procedure 1241

34 The PRINQUAL Procedure .1265

35 The PROBIT Procedure 1324

36 The REG Procedure 1351

37 The RSREG Procedure 1457

38 The SCORE Procedure 1479

39 The STEPDISC Procedure .1493

40 The TRANSREG Procedure 1511

41 The TREE Procedure 1613

42 The TTEST Procedure 1633

43 The VARCLUS Procedure .1641

44 The VARCOMP Procedure .1661

APPENDIX

1 Special SAS Data Sets 1675

Index I-1

Tables

30.1 Comparison of PROC NPAR1WAY with Nonparametric Tests . .1196

36.1 Formulas and Definitions for Options Available Only with
SELECTION=RSQUARE, ADJRSQ, or CP 1369

40.1 PROC TRANSREG Matrix Table 1549

A1.1 SAS/STAT Procedures and Types of Data Sets 1677

Chapter 24

The GLM Procedure

ABSTRACT   893
INTRODUCTION   893
  PROC GLM Features   893
  PROC GLM Contrasted with Other SAS Procedures   894
  Using PROC GLM Interactively   894
  Specification of Effects   895
    Types of Effects   895
    The Bar Operator   897
  PROC GLM for Multiple Regression   898
  PROC GLM for Unbalanced ANOVA   898
SPECIFICATIONS   900
  PROC GLM Statement   902
  ABSORB Statement   903
  BY Statement   904
  CLASS Statement   904
  CONTRAST Statement   905
  ESTIMATE Statement   907
  FREQ Statement   908
  ID Statement   908
  LSMEANS Statement   908
  MANOVA Statement   910
    MANOVA Examples   912
  MEANS Statement   913
  MODEL Statement   917
  OUTPUT Statement   920
    OUTPUT Examples   922
  RANDOM Statement   922
  REPEATED Statement   923
    Syntax Details   924
    REPEATED Examples   926
  TEST Statement   926
  WEIGHT Statement   927
DETAILS   928
  Parameterization of GLM Models   928
    Intercept   928
    Regression Effects   928
    Main Effects   928
    Crossed Effects   928
    Nested Effects   929
    Continuous-Nesting-Class Effects   930
    Continuous-by-Class Effects   930
    General Effects   930
    Degrees of Freedom   931
  Hypothesis Testing in GLM   932

Example   932
Estimability   933
Type I Tests   934
Type II Tests   935
Type III and Type IV Tests   936
Absorption   937
Specification of ESTIMATE Expressions   939
A Check for Estimability   941
Comparisons of Means   941
Pairwise Comparisons   942
Comparing All Treatments to a Control   945
Multiple-Stage Tests   946
Bayesian Approach   947
Recommendations   948
Least-Squares Means   948
Multivariate Analysis of Variance   949
Repeated Measures Analysis of Variance   951
Organization of Data for Repeated Measures Analysis   951
Hypothesis Testing in Repeated Measures Analysis   953
Transformations Used in Repeated Measures Analysis of Variance   955
CONTRAST transformation   955
POLYNOMIAL transformation   956
HELMERT transformation   956
MEAN transformation   957
PROFILE transformation   957
Expected Mean Squares for Random Effects   958
Missing Values   959
Computational Resources   960
Memory   960
CPU time   961
Computational Method   961
Output Data Sets   961
OUT= Data Set Created by the OUTPUT Statement   961
OUT= Data Set Created by the LSMEANS Statement   962
OUTSTAT= Data Set   963
Printed Output   963
EXAMPLES   964
Example 1:   Balanced Data from Randomized Complete Block with
            Means Comparisons and Contrasts   964
Example 2:   Regression with Mileage Data   969
Example 3:   Unbalanced ANOVA for Two-Way Design with
            Interaction   972
Example 4:   Analysis of Covariance   973
Example 5:   Three-Way Analysis of Variance with Contrasts   976
Example 6:   Multivariate Analysis of Variance   978
Example 7:   Repeated Measures Analysis of Variance   982
Example 8:   Mixed Model Analysis of Variance Using the RANDOM
            Statement   986
Example 9:   Analyzing a Doubly-multivariate Repeated Measures
            Design   988
REFERENCES   993

ABSTRACT

The GLM procedure uses the method of least squares to fit general linear models. Among the statistical methods available in PROC GLM are regression, analysis of variance, analysis of covariance, multivariate analysis of variance, and partial correlation.

INTRODUCTION

PROC GLM analyzes data within the framework of **G**eneral **L**inear **M**odels, hence the name GLM. GLM handles classification variables, which have discrete levels, as well as continuous variables, which measure quantities. Thus GLM can be used for many different analyses including

- simple regression
- multiple regression
- analysis of variance (*ANOVA*), especially for unbalanced data
- analysis of covariance
- response-surface models
- weighted regression
- polynomial regression
- partial correlation
- multivariate analysis of variance (*MANOVA*)
- repeated measures analysis of variance.

PROC GLM Features

The following list summarizes the features in PROC GLM:

- When more than one dependent variable is specified, GLM automatically groups together those variables that have the same pattern of missing values within the data set or within a BY group. This ensures that the analysis for each dependent variable brings into use all possible observations.
- GLM can be used interactively. After specifying and running a model, a variety of statements can be executed without GLM recomputing the model parameters or sums of squares.
- GLM allows you to specify any degree of interaction (crossed effects) and nested effects. It also provides for polynomial, continuous-by-class, and continuous-nesting-class effects.
- Through the concept of estimability, GLM can provide tests of hypotheses for the effects of a linear model regardless of the number of missing cells or the extent of confounding. GLM prints the sum of squares (SS) associated with each hypothesis tested and, upon request, the form of the estimable functions employed in the test. GLM can produce the general form of all estimable functions.
- The MANOVA statement allows you to specify both the hypothesis effects and the error effect to use for a multivariate analysis of variance.
- GLM can create an output data set containing a wide variety of diagnostic measures and all of the original variables. In addition, GLM can create an output data set containing sums of squares and crossproducts and results of canonical analyses performed using the MANOVA statement. Also, GLM can save values, standard errors, and covariances of least-squares means by creating an output data set in the LSMEANS statement.

- The REPEATED statement allows you to specify effects in the model that represent repeated measurements on the same experimental unit and for the same response, and it provides both univariate and multivariate tests of hypotheses.
- The RANDOM statement allows you to specify random effects in the model; expected mean squares are printed for each Type I, Type II, Type III, Type IV, and contrast mean square used in the analysis. Upon request, F tests using appropriate mean squares or linear combinations of mean squares as error terms are performed.
- The ESTIMATE statement allows you to specify an **L** vector for estimating a linear function of the parameters **Lβ**.
- The CONTRAST statement allows you to specify a contrast vector or matrix for testing the hypothesis that **Lβ**=0. When specified, the CONTRASTs are also incorporated into analyses using the MANOVA and REPEATED statements.

PROC GLM Contrasted with Other SAS Procedures

As described above, GLM can be used for many different analyses and has many special features not available in other SAS procedures. However, for some types of analyses, other procedures are available. As discussed in **PROC GLM for Multiple Regression** and **PROC GLM for Unbalanced ANOVA** later in this chapter, sometimes these other procedures are more efficient than GLM. The following procedures perform some of the same analyses as GLM:

ANOVA   performs analysis of variance for balanced designs. ANOVA is generally more efficient than GLM for these models.

NESTED   performs analysis of variance and estimates variance components for nested random models. NESTED is generally more efficient than GLM for these models.

NPAR1WAY   performs nonparametric one-way analysis of rank scores. This can also be done using PROC RANK and PROC GLM.

REG   performs general-purpose regression. REG allows several MODEL statements and gives additional regression diagnostics, especially for detection of collinearity.

RSREG   builds quadratic response-surface regression models and performs canonical and ridge analysis. RSREG is generally recommended for data from a response surface experiment.

TTEST   compares the means of two groups of observations. Also, tests for equality of variances for the two groups. TTEST is usually more efficient than GLM for this type of data.

VARCOMP   estimates variance components for a general linear model.

Using PROC GLM Interactively

PROC GLM can be used interactively. After you specify a model with a MODEL statement and run GLM with a RUN statement, a variety of statements can be executed without reinvoking GLM.

The **SPECIFICATIONS** section describes which statements can be used interactively. These interactive statements can be executed singly or in groups by following the single statement or group of statements with a RUN statement. Note that the MODEL statement cannot be repeated; PROC GLM allows only one MODEL statement.

If you use GLM interactively, you can end the GLM procedure with a DATA step, another PROC step, an ENDSAS statement, or with a QUIT statement. The syntax of the QUIT statement is

```
quit;
```

When you are using GLM interactively, additional RUN statements do not end the procedure but tell GLM to execute additional statements.

When a WHERE statement is used with GLM, it should appear before the first RUN statement. See **Changes and Enhancements** earlier in this book for a summary of using the WHERE statement with SAS/STAT software, and see base SAS documentation for details on this statement.

When a BY statement is used with GLM, interactive processing is not possible; that is, once the first RUN statement is encountered, processing proceeds for each BY group in the data set, and no further statements are accepted by the procedure.

Interactivity is also disabled when there are different patterns of missing values among the dependent variables. For details, see **Missing Values** later in this chapter.

Specification of Effects

Each term in a model, called an *effect*, is a variable or combination of variables. Effects are specified with a special notation using variable names and operators. There are two kinds of variables: *classification* (or *class*) *variables* and *continuous variables*. There are two primary operators: *crossing* and *nesting*. A third operator, the *bar operator*, is used to simplify effect specification.

In an analysis-of-variance model, independent variables must be variables that identify classification levels. In the SAS System these are called *class variables* and are declared in the CLASS statement. (They may also be called *categorical*, *qualitative*, *discrete*, or *nominal variables*.) Class variables may be either *numeric* or *character*. The values of a class variable are called *levels*. For example, the class variable SEX has the levels "male" and "female."

In a model, an independent variable that is not declared in the CLASS statement is assumed to be continuous. Continuous variables, which must be numeric, are used for response variables and covariates. For example, the heights and weights of subjects are continuous variables.

Types of Effects

There are seven different types of effects used in GLM. In the following list, assume that A, B, C, D, and E are class variables and X1, X2, and Y are continuous variables:

- Regressor effects are specified by writing continuous variables by themselves: X1 X2.
- Polynomial effects are specified by joining two or more continuous variables with asterisks: X1*X1 X1*X2.
- Main effects are specified by writing class variables by themselves: A B C.
- Crossed effects (interactions) are specified by joining class variables with asterisks: A*B B*C A*B*C.

- Nested effects are specified by following a main effect or crossed effect with a class variable or list of class variables enclosed in parentheses. The main effect or crossed effect is nested within the effects listed in parentheses:

     B(A)   C(B A)   D*E(C B A) .

In the examples above, B(A) is read "B nested within A."
- Continuous-by-class effects are written by joining continuous variables and class variables with asterisks: X1*A.
- Continuous-nesting-class effects consist of continuous variables followed by a list of class variables enclosed in parentheses: X1(A)   X1*X2(A B).

One example of the general form of an effect involving several variables is

     X1*X2*A*B*C(D E)   .

This example contains crossed continuous terms by crossed classification terms nested within multiple class variables. The continuous list comes first, followed by the crossed list, followed by the nested list in parentheses. Note that no asterisks appear within the nested list or immediately before the left parenthesis. For details on how the design matrix and parameters are defined with respect to the effects specified in this section, see **Parameterization of GLM Models** later in this chapter.

The MODEL statement and several other statements use these effects. Some examples of MODEL statements using various kinds of effects are shown below. A, B, and C represent class variables; and Y1, Y2, X1, and X2 represent continuous variables.

Specification	Kind of Model
`model y=x1;`	simple regression
`model y=x1 x2;`	multiple regression
`model y=x1 x1*x1;`	polynomial regression
`model y1 y2=x1 x2;`	multivariate regression
`model y=a;`	one-way *ANOVA*
`model y=a b c;`	main effects model
`model y=a b a*b;`	factorial model (with interaction)
`model y=a b(a) c(b a);`	nested model
`model y1 y2=a b;`	multivariate analysis of variance (*MANOVA*)
`model y=a x1;`	analysis-of-covariance model
`model y=a x1(a);`	separate-slopes model
`model y=a x1 x1*a;`	homogeneity-of-slopes model

The Bar Operator

You can shorten the specification of a factorial model using the bar operator. For example, one way of writing the model for a full three-way factorial is

```
proc glm;
   class a b c;
   model y=a b c a*b a*c b*c a*b*c;
run;
```

Another way of writing the model for a full 3 way factorial is

```
proc glm;
   class a b c;
   model y=a|b|c;
run;
```

When the bar (|) is used, the right- and left-hand sides become effects, and the cross of them becomes an effect. Multiple bars are permitted. The expressions are expanded from left to right, using rules 2–4 given in Searle (1971, p. 390):

- Multiple bars are evaluated left to right. For instance, A | B | C is evaluated as follows:

$$A \mid B \mid C \rightarrow \{A \mid B\} \mid C$$
$$\rightarrow \{A \; B \; A*B\} \mid C$$
$$\rightarrow A \; B \; A*B \; A*C \; B*C \; A*B*C$$

- Crossed and nested groups of variables are combined. For example, A(B) | C(D) generates A*C(B D), among other terms.
- Duplicate variables are removed. For example, A(C) | B(C) generates A*B(CC), among other terms, and the extra C is removed.
- Effects are discarded if a variable occurs on both the crossed and nested sides of an effect. For instance, A(B) | B(D E) generates A*B(B D E), but this effect is eliminated immediately.

You can also specify the maximum number of variables involved in any effect that results from bar evaluation by specifying that maximum number, preceded by an @ sign, at the end of the bar effect. For example, the specification A | B | C@2 would result in only those effects that contain 2 or fewer variables: in this case A B A*B C A*C and B*C.

Additional examples of using the bar and at operators are

A | C(B)	is equivalent to	A C(B) A*C(B)
A(B) | C(B)	is equivalent to	A(B) C(B) A*C(B)
A(B) | B(D E)	is equivalent to	A(B) B(D E)
A | B(A) | C	is equivalent to	A B(A) C A*C B*C(A)
A | B(A) | C@2	is equivalent to	A B(A) C A*C
A | B | C | D@2	is equivalent to	A B A*B C A*C B*C D A*D B*D C*D

PROC GLM for Multiple Regression

In multiple regression, the values of a dependent variable (also called a response variable) are described or predicted in terms of one or more independent or explanatory variables. The statements

```
proc glm;
   model dependent=independents;
```

can be used to describe a multiple regression model in GLM. The REG procedure provides additional statistics for multiple regression and is often more efficient than GLM for these models.

PROC GLM for Unbalanced *ANOVA*

The ANOVA procedure should be used whenever possible for analysis of variance because ANOVA processes data more efficiently than GLM. However, GLM should be used in most unbalanced situations, that is, models where there are unequal numbers of observations for the different combinations of CLASS variables specified in the MODEL statement.

Here is an example of a 2×2 factorial model. The data are shown in a table and then read into a SAS data set:

```
                    A
              1        2

         ┌─────────┬─────────┐
         │  12     │  20     │
      1  │         │         │
         │  14     │  18     │
  B      ├─────────┼─────────┤
         │  11     │  17     │
      2  │         │         │
         │   9     │         │
         └─────────┴─────────┘
```

```
title 'Analysis of Unbalanced 2-by-2 Factorial';
data exp;
   input a $ b $ y @@;
   cards;
A1 B1 12 A1 B1 14 A1 B2 11 A1 B2 9
A2 B1 20 A2 B1 18 A2 B2 17
;
```

Note that there is only one value for the second levels of A and B. Since one cell contains a different number of values from the other cells in the table, this is an unbalanced design and GLM should be used. The statements needed for this two-way factorial model are

```
proc glm;
   class a b;
   model y=a b a*b;
run;
```

The results from PROC GLM are shown in **Output 24.1**.

Output 24.1 Analyzing a Two-Way Factorial

```
                    Analysis of Unbalanced 2-by-2 Factorial                    1

                      General Linear Models Procedure
                         Class Level Information

                      Class    Levels    Values

                      A           2      A1 A2

                      B           2      B1 B2


              Number of observations in data set = 7
```

```
                    Analysis of Unbalanced 2-by-2 Factorial                    2

                      General Linear Models Procedure

Dependent Variable: Y
```

Source	DF	Sum of Squares	Mean Square	F Value	Pr > F
Model	3	91.71428571	30.57142857	15.29	0.0253
Error	3	6.00000000	2.00000000		
Corrected Total	6	97.71428571			

R-Square	C.V.	Root MSE	Y Mean
0.938596	9.801480	1.41421356	14.42857143

Source	DF	Type I SS	Mean Square	F Value	Pr > F
A	1	80.04761905	80.04761905	40.02	0.0080
B	1	11.26666667	11.26666667	5.63	0.0982
A*B	1	0.40000000	0.40000000	0.20	0.6850

Source	DF	Type III SS	Mean Square	F Value	Pr > F
A	1	67.60000000	67.60000000	33.80	0.0101
B	1	10.00000000	10.00000000	5.00	0.1114
A*B	1	0.40000000	0.40000000	0.20	0.6850

Four types of estimable functions of parameters are available for testing hypotheses in GLM. For data with no missing cells, the Type III and Type IV estimable functions are the same and test the same hypotheses that would be tested if the data were balanced.

Using a significance level of 5% ($\alpha = 0.05$), the Type III results on this printout indicate a significant A effect but no significant B effect or A*B interaction.

SPECIFICATIONS

Although there are numerous statements and options available in GLM, many applications use only a few of them. Often you can find the features you need by looking at an example or by quickly scanning through this section. The statements available in GLM are

PROC GLM <*options*>;   must precede MODEL statement
    CLASS *variables*;

    MODEL *dependents*=*independents* < / *options*>;   required statement

    ABSORB *variables*;
    BY *variables*;
    FREQ *variable*;   must appear before
    ID *variables*;   the first RUN statement
    WEIGHT *variable*;

    CONTRAST *'label'* effect values
        < . . . effect values>
        < / *options*>;
    ESTIMATE *'label'* effect values
        <. . . effect values>
        < / *options*>;
    LSMEANS *effects* < / *options*>;
    MANOVA <H=*effects* INTERCEPT | _ALL_>
        <E=*effect*>
        <M=*equation*, . . . ,*equation*
            | (*row-of-matrix*, . . . ,*row-of-matrix*)>
        <MNAMES=*names*>   can appear
        <PREFIX=*name*> < / *options*>;   after the
    MEANS *effects* < / *options*>;   MODEL statement
    OUTPUT <OUT=*SAS-data-set*>   and can be used
        keyword=*names*   interactively
        <. . . *keyword*=*names*>;
    RANDOM *effects* < / *options*>;
    REPEATED *factor-name* *levels*
        <(*level-values*)> <*transformation*>
        <, . . . ,*factor-name* *levels*
        <(*level-values*)> <*transformation*>>
        < / *options*>;
    TEST <H=*effects*> E=*effect* < / *options*>;

To use PROC GLM, the PROC GLM and MODEL statements are required. If your model contains classification effects, the classification variables must be listed in a CLASS statement, and the CLASS statement must appear before the MODEL statement. In addition, if you use a CONTRAST statement in combination with a MANOVA, RANDOM, REPEATED, or TEST statement, the CONTRAST statement must be entered first in order for the CONTRAST to be included in the MANOVA, RANDOM, REPEATED, or TEST analysis.

The following table summarizes the positional requirements for the statements in the GLM procedure.

Statement	Must Appear Before the	Must Appear After the
ABSORB	first RUN statement	
BY	first RUN statement	
CLASS	MODEL statement	
CONTRAST	MANOVA, REPEATED, or RANDOM statements	MODEL statement
ESTIMATE		MODEL statement
FREQ	first RUN statement	
ID	first RUN statement	
LSMEANS		MODEL statement
MANOVA		CONTRAST or MODEL statements
MEANS		MODEL statement
MODEL	CONTRAST, ESTIMATE, LSMEANS, or MEANS statements	CLASS
RANDOM		CONTRAST or MODEL statements
REPEATED		CONTRAST, MODEL, or TEST statements
TEST	MANOVA or REPEATED statements	MODEL
WEIGHT	first RUN statement	

The following list summarizes the function of each statement (other than the PROC GLM statement) in the GLM procedure:

ABSORB	absorbs classification effects in a model.
BY	processes BY groups.
CLASS	declares classification variables.
CONTRAST	constructs and tests linear functions of the parameters.
ESTIMATE	estimates linear functions of the parameters.
FREQ	specifies a frequency variable.
ID	identifies observations on printed output.
LSMEANS	computes least-squares (marginal) means.
MANOVA	performs a multivariate analysis of variance.
MEANS	requests that means be printed and compared.
MODEL	defines the model to be fit.
OUTPUT	requests an output data set containing diagnostics for each observation.
RANDOM	declares certain effects to be random and computes expected mean squares.
REPEATED	performs multivariate and univariate repeated measures analysis of variance.
TEST	constructs tests using the sums of squares for effects and the error term you specify.
WEIGHT	specifies a variable for weighting observations.

The rest of this section gives detailed syntax information for each of the statements above, beginning with the PROC GLM statement. The remaining statements are covered in alphabetical order.

PROC GLM Statement

PROC GLM <*options*>;

The PROC GLM statement starts the GLM procedure. The following options can be used in the PROC GLM statement:

DATA=*SAS-data-set*
  names the SAS data set used by GLM. By default, GLM uses the most recently created SAS data set.

MANOVA
  requests the multivariate mode of eliminating observations with missing values. If any of the dependent variables have missing values, the procedure eliminates that observation from the analysis. MANOVA is useful if you use GLM in interactive mode and plan to perform a multivariate analysis.

MULTIPASS
  requests that PROC GLM reread the input data set when necessary, instead of writing the necessary values of dependent variables to a utility file. This option decreases disk space usage at the expense of increased execution times, and is only useful in rare situations.

NOPRINT
  suppresses all printed output. NOPRINT is useful when you want only to create one or more output data sets with the procedure.

ORDER=DATA | FORMATTED | FREQ | INTERNAL
> specifies the sorting order for the levels of the classification variables (specified in the CLASS statement). This ordering determines which parameters in the model correspond to each level in the data, so the ORDER= option may be useful when you use CONTRAST or ESTIMATE statements. The table below shows how GLM interprets values of ORDER= option.

Value of ORDER=	Levels Sorted By
DATA	order of appearance in the input data set
FORMATTED	external formatted value
FREQ	descending frequency count; levels with the most observations come first in the order
INTERNAL	internal value

> By default, ORDER=FORMATTED. For FORMATTED and INTERNAL, the sort order is machine-dependent. For more information on sorting order, see the chapter on the SORT procedure in *SAS Procedures Guide, Version 6, Third Edition*, and "Rules of the SAS Language" in *SAS Language: Reference, Version 6, First Edition*.

OUTSTAT=*SAS-data-set*
> names an output data set that will contain sums of squares, degrees of freedom, *F* statistics, and probability levels for each effect in the model, as well as for each CONTRAST statement used. If you use the CANONICAL option in the MANOVA statement and do not use a M= specification in the MANOVA statement, the data set also contains results of the canonical analysis. See **Output Data Sets** later in this chapter for more information.

ABSORB Statement

> **ABSORB** *variables*;

Absorption is a computational technique that provides a large reduction in time and memory requirements for certain types of models. The *variables* are one or more variables in the input data set.

For a main-effect variable that does not participate in interactions, you can absorb the effect by naming it in an ABSORB statement. This means that the effect can be adjusted out before the construction and solution of the rest of the model. This is particularly useful when the effect has a large number of levels.

Several variables can be specified, in which case each one is assumed to be nested in the preceding variable in the ABSORB statement.

When you use the ABSORB statement, the data set (or each BY group) must be sorted by the variables in the ABSORB statement. GLM cannot produce predicted values or create an output data set of diagnostic values if ABSORB is used. If the ABSORB statement is used, it must appear before the first RUN statement or it is ignored.

When you use an ABSORB statement and also use the INT option in the MODEL statement, the procedure ignores the option.

When you use an ABSORB statement and also use the INT option in the MODEL statement, the procedure ignores the option except that the procedure prints the uncorrected total sum of squares (SS) instead of the corrected total SS.

See **Absorption** later in this chapter for more information.

BY Statement

BY *variables*;

A BY statement can be used with PROC GLM to obtain separate analyses on observations in groups defined by the BY variables. When a BY statement appears, the procedure expects the input data set to be sorted in order of the BY variables. The *variables* are one or more variables in the input data set.

If your input data set is not sorted in ascending order, use one of the following alternatives:

- Use the SORT procedure with a similar BY statement to sort the data.
- Use the BY statement options NOTSORTED or DESCENDING in the BY statement for the GLM procedure. As a cautionary note, the NOTSORTED option does not mean that the data are unsorted, but rather means that the data are arranged in groups (according to values of the BY variables) and that these groups are not necessarily in alphabetical or increasing numeric order.
- Use the DATASETS procedure (in base SAS software) to create an index on the BY variables.

Since sorting the data changes the order that GLM reads observations, this can affect the sorting order for the levels of the classification variables if you have specified ORDER=DATA in the PROC GLM statement. This, in turn, will affect specifications in CONTRAST and ESTIMATE statements.

For more information on the BY statement, see the discussion in *SAS Language: Reference*. For more information on the DATASETS procedure, see the discussion in *SAS Procedures Guide*.

When a BY statement is used with PROC GLM, interactive processing is not possible; that is, once the first RUN statement is encountered, processing proceeds for each BY group in the data set, and no further statements are accepted by the procedure. If the BY statement appears after the first RUN statement, it is ignored.

When both a BY and an ABSORB statement are used, observations must be sorted first by the variables in the BY statement, and then by the variables in the ABSORB statement.

CLASS Statement

CLASS *variables*;

The CLASS statement names the classification variables to be used in the analysis. Typical class variables are TRTMENT, SEX, RACE, GROUP, and REP. If the CLASS statement is used, it must appear before the MODEL statement.

Classification variables can be either character or numeric. The procedure uses only the first 16 characters of a character variable.

Class levels are determined from the formatted values of the CLASS variables. Thus, you can use formats to group values into levels. See the discussion of the FORMAT procedure in *SAS Procedures Guide*, and the discussions for the FORMAT statement and SAS formats in *SAS Language: Reference*.

CONTRAST Statement

> **CONTRAST** *'label' effect values;*
> **CONTRAST** *'label' INTERCEPT values;*
> **CONTRAST** *'label' effect values <. . . effect values> < / options>;*

The CONTRAST statement provides a mechanism for obtaining custom hypothesis tests. This is achieved by specifying an **L** vector or matrix for testing the univariate hypothesis **Lβ** =0 or the multivariate hypothesis **LβM** =0. Thus, to use this feature you must be familiar with the details of the model parameterization that PROC GLM uses. For more information, see **Parameterization of GLM Models** later in this chapter.

There is no limit to the number of CONTRAST statements, but they must appear after the MODEL statement. In addition, if you use a CONTRAST statement and a MANOVA, REPEATED, or TEST statement, appropriate tests for contrasts are carried out as part of the MANOVA, REPEATED, or TEST analysis. If you use a CONTRAST statement and a RANDOM statement, the expected mean square of the contrast is printed. As a result of these additional analyses, the CONTRAST statement must appear before the MANOVA, REPEATED, RANDOM, or TEST statements.

In the CONTRAST statement,

label identifies the contrast on the printout. A label is required for every contrast specified. Labels can be up to 20 characters long, and must be enclosed in single quotes.

effect | INTERCEPT

 identifies an effect that appears in the MODEL statement. INTERCEPT can be used as an effect when an intercept is fitted in the model. You do not need to include all effects that are in the MODEL statement.

values are constants that are elements of the **L** vector associated with the effect.

The following options are available in the CONTRAST statement and are specified after a slash:

E

 prints the entire **L** vector.

E=*effect*

 specifies an error term, which must be one of the effects in the model. The procedure uses this effect as the denominator in *F* tests in univariate analysis. In addition, if you use a MANOVA or REPEATED statement, the procedure uses the effect specified by E= as the basis of the **E** matrix. By default, the procedure uses the error mean square (MSE) as an error term.

ETYPE=*n*

 specifies the type (1, 2, 3, or 4) of the E= effect. If E= is specified and ETYPE= is not, the procedure uses the highest type computed in the analysis.

SINGULAR=*number*

 tunes the estimability checking. If ABS(**L**−**LH**)>C*number* for any row in the contrast, then **L** is declared nonestimable. **H** is the (**X′X**)⁻**X′X** matrix, and C is ABS(**L**) except for rows where **L** is zero, and then it is 1. The default for SINGULAR= is 1E−4. Values for SINGULAR= must be between 0 and 1.

As stated above, the CONTRAST statement allows you to perform custom hypothesis tests. If the hypothesis is testable in the univariate case, $SS(H_0: \mathbf{L}\boldsymbol{\beta} = 0)$ is computed as

$$(\mathbf{Lb})'(\mathbf{L}(\mathbf{X'X})^{-}\mathbf{L'})^{-1}(\mathbf{Lb})$$

where $\mathbf{b} = (\mathbf{X'X})^{-}\mathbf{X'y}$. This is the SS printed on the analysis-of-variance table.

For multivariate testable hypotheses, the usual multivariate tests are performed using

$$\mathbf{H} = \mathbf{M'}(\mathbf{Lb})'(\mathbf{L}(\mathbf{X'X})^{-}\mathbf{L'})^{-1}(\mathbf{Lb})\mathbf{M}$$

The **L** matrix should be of full row rank. However, if it is not, the degrees of freedom associated with the hypotheses are reduced to the row rank of **L**. The SS computed in this situation are equivalent to the SS computed using an **L** matrix with any row deleted that is a linear combination of previous rows.

Multiple-degree-of-freedom hypotheses can be specified by separating the rows of the **L** matrix with commas, as shown below. For example, for the model

```
proc glm;
   class a b;
   model y=a b;
run;
```

with A at five levels and B at two levels, the parameter vector is

$$(\mu \quad \alpha_1 \ \alpha_2 \ \alpha_3 \ \alpha_4 \ \alpha_5 \ \beta_1 \ \beta_2) \quad .$$

To test the hypothesis that the pooled A linear and A quadratic effect is zero, you can use the following **L** matrix:

$$\mathbf{L} = \begin{bmatrix} 0 & -2 & -1 & 0 & 1 & 2 & 0 & 0 \\ 0 & 2 & -1 & -2 & -1 & 2 & 0 & 0 \end{bmatrix}$$

The corresponding CONTRAST statement is

```
contrast 'A LINEAR & QUADRATIC'
         a -2 -1  0  1 2,
         a  2 -1 -2 -1 2;
```

If the first level of A is a control level and you want a test of control versus others, you can use this statement:

```
contrast 'CONTROL VS OTHERS'  a -1 .25 .25 .25 .25;
```

See the discussion of the ESTIMATE statement below and **Specification of ESTIMATE Expressions** later in this chapter for rules on specification, construction, distribution, and estimability in the CONTRAST statement.

ESTIMATE Statement

ESTIMATE *'label' effect values;*
ESTIMATE *'label'* INTERCEPT *values;*
ESTIMATE *'label' effect values* < *. . . effect values*> < / *options*>;

The ESTIMATE statement can be used to estimate linear functions of the parameters by multiplying the vector **L** by the parameter estimate vector **b** resulting in **Lb**. All of the elements of the **L** vector may be given, or if only certain portions of the **L** vector are given, the remaining elements are constructed by GLM from the context (in a manner similar to rule 4 discussed in the **Least-Squares Means** section).

The linear function is checked for estimability. The estimate **Lb**, where $b=(X'X)^-X'y$, is printed along with its associated standard error, $\sqrt{L(X'X)^-L's^2}$, and *t*-test.

There is no limit to the number of ESTIMATE statements, but they must appear after the MODEL statement. In the ESTIMATE statement,

label identifies the contrast on the printout. A label is required for every contrast specified. Labels can be up to 20 characters long, and must be enclosed in single quotes.

effect | INTERCEPT

identifies an effect that appears in the MODEL statement. INTERCEPT can be used as an effect when an intercept is fitted in the model. You do not need to include all effects that are in the MODEL statement.

values are constants that are the elements of the **L** vector associated with the preceding effect. For example,

```
estimate 'A1 VS A2' A  1 -1;
```

forms an estimate that is the difference between the parameters estimated for the first and second levels of the CLASS variable A.

The following options can appear in the ESTIMATE statement after a slash:

DIVISOR=*number*
specifies a value by which to divide all coefficients so that fractional coefficients can be entered as integer numerators, for example,

```
estimate '1/3(A1+A2) - 2/3A3' a 1 1 -2 / divisor=3;
```

instead of

```
estimate '1/3(A1+A2) - 2/3A3' a .33333 .33333 -.66667;
```

E
prints the entire **L** vector.

SINGULAR=*number*
tunes the estimability checking. If ABS(**L**−**LH**)>C*number*, then the **L** is declared nonestimable. **H** is the $(X'X)^-X'X$ matrix, and C is ABS(**L**) except for rows where **L** is zero, and then it is 1. The default for SINGULAR= is 1E−4. Values for SINGULAR= must be between 0 and 1.

See also **Specification of ESTIMATE Expressions** later in this chapter.

FREQ Statement

FREQ *variable*;

The FREQ statement names a variable that provides frequencies for each observation in the DATA= data set. Specifically, if *n* is the value of the FREQ variable for a given observation, then that observation is used *n* times.

The analysis produced using a FREQ statement reflects the expanded number of observations. For example, means and total degrees of freedom reflect the expanded number of observations. You could produce the same analysis (without the FREQ statement) by first creating a new data set that contained the expanded number of observations. For example, if the value of the FREQ variable is 5 for the first observation, the first 5 observations in the new data set would be identical. Each observation in the old data set would be replicated n_i times in the new data set, where n_i is the value of the FREQ variable for that observation.

If the value of the FREQ variable is missing or is less than one, the observation is not used in the analysis. If the value is not an integer, only the integer portion is used.

If the FREQ statement is used, it must appear before the first RUN statement or it is ignored.

ID Statement

ID *variables*;

When predicted values are requested as a MODEL statement option, values of the variables given in the ID statement are printed beside each observed, predicted, and residual value for identification. Although there are no restrictions on the length of ID variables, GLM may truncate the number of values printed in order to print on one line. GLM prints a maximum of five ID variables.

If the ID statement is used, it must appear before the first RUN statement or it is ignored.

LSMEANS Statement

LSMEANS *effects* < / *options*>;

Least-squares means are computed for each *effect* listed in the LSMEANS statement.

Least-squares estimates of marginal means (LSMs) are to unbalanced designs as class and subclass arithmetic means are to balanced designs. LSMs are simply estimators of the class or subclass marginal means that would be expected had the design been balanced. For further information, see **Least-Squares Means** later in this chapter.

Least-squares means can be computed for any effect involving class variables as long as the effect is in the model. Any number of LSMEANS statements can be used, but they must appear after the MODEL statement. The statements below give an example.

```
proc glm;
   class a b;
   model y=a b a*b;
   lsmeans a b a*b;
run;
```

Least-squares means are printed for each level of the A, B, and A*B effects.
The following options can appear in the LSMEANS statement after a slash:

COV
:   includes covariances in the output data set specified in the OUT=
    option in the LSMEANS statement. If you omit OUT=, the COV option
    has no effect. When you specify the COV option, you can specify only
    one effect in the LSMEANS statement.

E
:   prints the estimable functions used to compute the LSM.

E=effect
:   specifies an effect in the model to use as an error term. The procedure
    uses the mean square for the effect when calculating standard errors
    (requested with the STDERR option) and probabilities (requested with
    the STDERR, PDIFF, or TDIFF options). Unless STDERR, PDIFF or TDIFF
    is specified, the E= option is ignored. By default, if you specify STDERR,
    PDIFF, or TDIFF, and do not specify E=, the procedure uses the error
    MS for calculating standard errors and probabilities.

ETYPE=n
:   specifies the type (1, 2, 3, or 4) of the E= effect. If E= is specified and
    ETYPE= is not, the highest type computed in the analysis is used.

NOPRINT
:   suppresses the printed output from the LSMEANS statement. This option
    is useful when an output data set is created with the OUT= option in
    the LSMEANS statement.

OUT=SAS-data-set
:   creates an output data set that contains the values, standard errors, and,
    optionally, the covariances (see the COV option above) of the least-
    squares means. For more information, see **Output Data Sets** later in this
    chapter.

PDIFF
:   prints all possible probability values for the hypotheses
    H_0: LSM(i)=LSM(j).

SINGULAR=number
:   tunes the estimability checking. If ABS($\mathbf{L}-\mathbf{LH}$)>C*number for any row,
    then the **L** is declared nonestimable. **H** is the $(\mathbf{X'X})^{-}\mathbf{X'X}$ matrix, and C is
    ABS(**L**) except for rows where **L** is zero, and then it is 1. The default for
    SINGULAR= is 1E−4. Values for SINGULAR= must be between 0 and
    1.

STDERR
:   prints the standard error of the LSM and the probability level for the
    hypothesis H_0: LSM=0.

TDIFF
:   prints the t values for the hypotheses H_0: LSM(i)=LSM(j) and the
    corresponding probabilities.

MANOVA Statement

MANOVA;
MANOVA <H=*effects* | INTERCEPT | _ALL_> <E=*effect*> < / *options*>;
MANOVA <H=*effects* | INTERCEPT | _ALL_> <E=*effect*>
    <M=*equation*, . . . ,*equation* | (*row-of-matrix*, . . . ,*row-of-matrix*)>
    <MNAMES=*names*> <PREFIX=*name*> < / *options*>;

If the MODEL statement includes more than one dependent variable, additional multivariate statistics can be requested with the MANOVA statement.

When a MANOVA statement appears before the first RUN statement, GLM enters a multivariate mode with respect to the handling of missing values; observations with missing independent or dependent variables are excluded from the analysis. If you want to use this mode of handling missing values and do not need any multivariate analyses, specify the MANOVA option in the PROC GLM statement.

If you use both the CONTRAST and MANOVA statements, the MANOVA statement must appear after the CONTRAST statement.

The terms below are specified in the MANOVA statement:

H=*effects* | INTERCEPT | _ALL_

specifies effects in the preceding model to use as hypothesis matrices. For each **H** matrix (the SSCP matrix associated with that effect), the H= specification prints the characteristic roots and vectors of $E^{-1}H$ (where **E** is the matrix associated with the error effect), Hotelling-Lawley trace, Pillai's trace, Wilks' criterion, and Roy's maximum root criterion with approximate *F* statistic. Use the keyword INTERCEPT to print tests for the intercept. To print tests for all effects listed in the MODEL statement, use the keyword _ALL_ in place of a list of effects. For background and further details, see **Multivariate Analysis of Variance** later in this chapter.

E=*effect*   specifies the error effect. If you omit the E= specification, GLM uses the error SSCP (residual) matrix from the analysis.

<M= *equation*, . . . ,*equation* | (*row-of-matrix*, . . . ,*row-of-matrix*)>
specifies a transformation matrix for the dependent variables listed in the MODEL statement. The equations in the M= specification are of the form

$$c_1*dependent\text{-}variable \pm c_2*dependent\text{-}variable \pm c_n*dependent\text{-}variable$$

where the c_i values are coefficients for the various *dependent-variables*. If the value of a given c_i is 1, it may be omitted; in other words, 1*Y is the same as Y. Equations should involve two or more dependent variables. For sample syntax, see **MANOVA Examples** later in this section.

Alternatively, you can input the transformation matrix directly by entering the elements of the matrix with commas separating the rows, and parentheses surrounding the matrix. When this alternate form of input is used, the number of elements in each row must equal the number of dependent variables. Although these combinations actually represent the columns of the **M** matrix, they are printed by rows.

When you include an M= specification, the analysis requested in the MANOVA statement is carried out for the variables defined by the equations in the specification, not the original dependent variables. If M= is omitted, the analysis is performed for the original dependent variables in the MODEL statement.

If an M= specification is included without either the MNAMES= or PREFIX= option, the variables are labeled MVAR1, MVAR2, and so forth by default. For further information, see **Multivariate Analysis of Variance** later in this chapter.

MNAMES=*names*   provides names for the variables defined by the equations in the M= specification. Names in the list correspond to the M= equations or the rows of the M matrix (as it is entered).

PREFIX=*name*   is an alternative means of identifying the transformed variables defined by the M= specification. For example, if you specify PREFIX=DIFF, the transformed variables are labeled DIFF1, DIFF2, and so forth.

The following options can appear in the MANOVA statement after a slash:

CANONICAL
   prints a canonical analysis of the **H** and **E** matrices (transformed by the **M** matrix, if specified) instead of the default printout of characteristic roots and vectors.

ETYPE=*n*
   specifies the type (1, 2, 3, or 4) of the **E** matrix. You need this option if you use the E= specification (rather than residual error) and you want to specify the type of SS used for the effect. If an ETYPE=*n*, the corresponding test must have been performed in the MODEL statement, either by options SS*n*, E*n*, or the default Type I and Type III. By default, the procedure uses an ETYPE= value corresponding to the highest type (largest *n*) used in the analysis.

HTYPE=*n*
   specifies the type (1, 2, 3, or 4) of the **H** matrix. See the ETYPE= option for more details.

ORTH
   requests that the transformation matrix in the M= specification of the MANOVA statement be orthonormalized by rows before the analysis.

PRINTE
   prints the **E** matrix. If the E matrix is the error SSCP (residual) matrix from the analysis, the partial correlations of the dependent variables given the independent variables are also printed.

   For example, the statement

```
manova / printe;
```

   prints the error SSCP matrix and the partial correlation matrix computed from the error SSCP matrix.

PRINTH
   prints the **H** matrix (the SSCP matrix) associated with each effect specified by the H= specification.

SUMMARY
produces analysis-of-variance tables for each dependent variable. When
no **M** matrix is specified, a table is printed for each original dependent
variable from the MODEL statement; with an **M** matrix other than the
identity, a table is printed for each transformed variable defined by the
M matrix.

MANOVA Examples

The following statements give several examples of using a MANOVA statement.

```
proc glm;
   class a b;
   model y1-y5=a b(a);
   manova h=a e=b(a) / printh printe htype=1 etype=1;
   manova h=b(a) / printe;
   manova h=a e=b(a) m=y1-y2,y2-y3,y3-y4,y4-y5
         prefix=diff;
   manova h=a e=b(a) m=(1 -1  0  0  0,
                        0  1 -1  0  0,
                        0  0  1 -1  0,
                        0  0  0  1 -1) prefix=diff;
run;
```

Since this MODEL statement requests no options for type of sums of squares,
GLM uses Type I and Type III. The first MANOVA statement specifies A as the
hypothesis effect and B(A) as the error effect. As a result of PRINTH, the procedure prints the **H** matrix associated with the A effect; and, as a result of PRINTE,
the procedure prints the **E** matrix associated with the B(A) effect. HTYPE=1 specifies a Type I **H** matrix, and ETYPE=1 specifies a Type I **E** matrix.

The second MANOVA statement specifies B(A) as the hypothesis effect. Since
no error effect is specified, GLM uses the error SSCP matrix from the analysis as
the **E** matrix. The PRINTE option prints this **E** matrix. Since the **E** matrix is the error
SSCP matrix from the analysis, the partial correlation matrix computed from this
matrix is also printed.

The third MANOVA statement requests the same analysis as the first MANOVA
statement, but the analysis is carried out for variables transformed to be successive differences between the original dependent variables. PREFIX=DIFF labels
the transformed variables as DIFF1, DIFF2, DIFF3, and DIFF4.

Finally, the fourth MANOVA statement has the identical effect as the third, but
it uses an alternative form of the M= specification. Instead of specifying a set
of equations, the fourth MANOVA statement specifies rows of a matrix of coefficients for the five dependent variables.

As a second example of the use of the M= specification, consider the following:

```
proc glm;
   class group;
   model dose1-dose4=group;
   manova h=group m=-3*dose1-dose2+dose3+3*dose4,
                   dose1-dose2-dose3+dose4,
                   -dose1+3*dose2-3*dose3+dose4
            mnames=linear quadrtic cubic / printe;
run;
```

The M= specification gives a transformation of the dependent variables DOSE1 through DOSE4 into orthogonal polynomial components, and the MNAMES= option labels the transformed variables LINEAR, QUADRTIC, and CUBIC, respectively. Since the PRINTE option is specified and the default residual matrix is used as an error term, the partial correlation matrix of the orthogonal polynomial components is also printed.

MEANS Statement

MEANS *effects* < / *options*>;

For any effect that appears on the right-hand side of the model and that does not contain any continuous variables, GLM can compute means of all continuous variables in the model. However, these means are not adjusted for effects in the model; for adjusted means, see the LSMEANS statement. If you use a WEIGHT statement, GLM computes weighted means.

You can use any number of MEANS statements, provided they appear after the MODEL statement. For more information, see **Comparisons of Means** later in this chapter. For example, suppose A and B each have two levels, then,

```
proc glm;
   class a b;
   model y=a b a*b;
   means a*b;
run;
```

Means and standard deviations are printed for each of the four combinations of levels for A*B. For the model

```
model y=a x a*x;
```

where X is a continuous variable, the effects X and A*X cannot be used in the MEANS statement.

The options that perform multiple comparison tests and specify details for these tests apply only to main effect terms in the model. For example, if your model contains the effects A, B, and A*B, and you request Duncan's test with the DUNCAN option, the test is performed on the main effect means (A and B). If you use a WEIGHT statement, GLM computes weighted means and then uses the weighted means as if they were unweighted means when performing multiple comparison tests. The statistical interpretation of such tests is not well understood. See **Comparisons of Means** later in this chapter for formulas. The table below summarizes categories of options in the MEANS statement.

Task	Available options
Modify printed output	DEPONLY
Perform multiple comparison test	BON DUNCAN DUNNETT DUNNETTL DUNNETTU GABRIEL GT2 LSD REGWF REGWQ SCHEFFE SIDAK SMM SNK T TUKEY WALLER
Specify additional details for multiple comparison tests	ALPHA= CLDIFF CLM E= ETYPE= HTYPE= KRATIO= LINES NOSORT

The options that can be specified in the MODEL statement are described below.

ALPHA=p
> gives the level of significance for comparisons among the means. By default, ALPHA=0.05. With the DUNCAN option, you may only specify values of 0.01, 0.05, or 0.1. For other options that perform multiple comparison tests, you may use values between 0.0001 and 0.9999.

BON
> performs Bonferroni t-tests of differences between means for all main effect means in the MEANS statement. See the CLDIFF and LINES options for a discussion of how the procedure displays results.

CLDIFF
> presents results of the BON, GABRIEL, SCHEFFE, SIDAK, SMM, GT2, T, LSD, and TUKEY options as confidence intervals for all pairwise differences between means. CLDIFF is the default for unequal cell sizes unless DUNCAN, REGWF, REGWQ, SNK, or WALLER is specified.

CLM
> presents results of the BON, GABRIEL, SCHEFFE, SIDAK, SMM, T, and LSD options as confidence intervals for the mean of each level of the variables specified in the MEANS statement.

DEPONLY

prints only means for the dependent variable means. By default, GLM prints means for all continuous variables, including independent variables.

DUNCAN

performs Duncan's multiple-range test on all main effect means given in the MEANS statement. See the LINES option for a discussion of how the procedure displays results.

DUNNETT<*(formatted-control-values)*>

performs Dunnett's two-tailed *t*-test, testing if any treatments are significantly different from a single control for all main effects means in the MEANS statement.

To specify which level of the effect is the control, enclose the formatted value in quotes in parentheses after the keyword. If more than one effect is specified in the MEANS statement, you can use a list of control values within the parentheses. By default, the first level of the effect is used as the control, for example,

```
means a / dunnett('CONTROL');
```

where CONTROL is the formatted control value of A. As another example,

```
means a b c / dunnett('CNTLA' 'CNTLB' 'CNTLC');
```

where CNTLA, CNTLB, and CNTLC are the formatted control values for A, B, and C, respectively.

DUNNETTL<*(formatted-control-value)*>

performs Dunnett's one-tailed *t*-test, testing if any treatment is significantly smaller than the control. Control level information is specified as described above for the DUNNETT option.

DUNNETTU<*(formatted-control-value)*>

performs Dunnett's one-tailed *t*-test, testing if any treatment is significantly larger than the control. Control level information is specified as described above for the DUNNETT option.

E=*effect*

specifies the error mean square used in the multiple comparisons. By default, GLM uses the residual mean square (MS). The effect specified with the E= option must be a term in the model; otherwise, the procedure uses the residual MS.

ETYPE=*n*

specifies the type of mean square for the error effect. When E=*effect* is specified, you may need to indicate which type (1, 2, 3, or 4) of MS is to be used. The *n* value must be one of the types specified or implied by the MODEL statement. The default MS type is the highest type used in the analysis.

GABRIEL

performs Gabriel's multiple-comparison procedure on all main effect means in the MEANS statement. See the CLDIFF and LINES options for discussions of how the procedure displays results.

GT2
see the SMM option below.

HTYPE=*n*
gives the MS type for the hypothesis MS. The HTYPE= option is needed only when the WALLER option is specified. The default HTYPE= value is the highest type used in the model.

KRATIO=*value*
gives the type1/type2 error seriousness ratio for the Waller-Duncan test. Reasonable values for KRATIO are 50, 100, 500, which roughly correspond for the two-level case to ALPHA levels of 0.1, 0.05, and 0.01. By default, the procedure uses the default value of 100.

LINES
presents results of the BON, DUNCAN, GABRIEL, REGWF, REGWQ, SCHEFFE, SIDAK, SMM, GT2, SNK, T, LSD, TUKEY, and WALLER options by listing the means in descending order and indicating nonsignificant subsets by line segments beside the corresponding means. The LINES option is appropriate for equal cell sizes, for which it is the default. LINES is also the default if DUNCAN, REGWF, REGWQ, SNK, or WALLER is specified, or if there are only two cells of unequal size. If the cell sizes are unequal, the harmonic mean of the cell sizes is used, which may lead to somewhat liberal tests if the cell sizes are highly disparate. LINES cannot be used in combination with the DUNNETT, DUNNETTL, or DUNNETTU options. In addition, the procedure has a restriction that no more than 24 overlapping groups of means can exist. If a mean belongs to more than 24 groups, the procedure issues an error message. You can either reduce the number of levels of the variable, or use a multiple comparison test that allows the CLDIFF option rather than the LINES option.

LSD
see the T option below.

NOSORT
prevents the means from being sorted into descending order when CLDIFF or CLM is specified.

REGWF
performs the Ryan-Einot-Gabriel-Welsch multiple *F* test on all main effect means in the MEANS statement. See the LINES option for a discussion of how the procedure displays results.

REGWQ
performs the Ryan-Einot-Gabriel-Welsch multiple-range test on all main effect means in the MEANS statement. See the LINES option for a discussion of how the procedure displays results.

SCHEFFE
performs Scheffe's multiple-comparison procedure on all main effect means in the MEANS statement. See the CLDIFF and LINES options for discussions of how the procedure displays results.

SIDAK

performs pairwise *t*-tests on differences between means with levels adjusted according to Sidak's inequality for all main effect means in the MEANS statement. See the CLDIFF and LINES options for discussions of how the procedure displays results.

SMM

GT2

performs pairwise comparisons based on the studentized maximum modulus and Sidak's uncorrelated-*t* inequality, yielding Hochberg's GT2 method when sample sizes are unequal, for all main effect means in the MEANS statement. See the CLDIFF and LINES options for discussions of how the procedure displays results.

SNK

performs the Student-Newman-Keuls multiple range test on all main effect means in the MEANS statement. See the LINES option for a discussion of how the procedure displays results.

T

LSD

performs pairwise *t*-tests, equivalent to Fisher's least-significant-difference test in the case of equal cell sizes, for all main effect means in the MEANS statement. See the CLDIFF and LINES options for discussions of how the procedure displays results.

TUKEY

performs Tukey's studentized range test (HSD) on all main effect means in the MEANS statement. See the CLDIFF and LINES options for discussions of how the procedure displays results.

WALLER

performs the Waller-Duncan *k*-ratio *t*-test on all main effect means in the MEANS statement. See the KRATIO= and HTYPE= options for information on controlling details of the test, and the LINES option for a discussion of how the procedure displays results.

MODEL Statement

MODEL *dependents=independents* < / *options*>;

The MODEL statement names the dependent variables and independent effects. The syntax of effects is described in the introductory section **Specification of Effects**. If no independent effects are specified, only an intercept term is fit.

The table below summarizes options available in the MODEL statement .

Task	Options
Print tests for the intercept	INTERCEPT
Omit the intercept parameter from model	NOINT
Obtain additional printouts	SOLUTION TOLERANCE
Suppress univariate tests and output	NOUNI
Print estimable functions	E E1 E2 E3 E4
Control hypothesis tests performed	SS1 SS2 SS3 SS4
Print confidence intervals	ALPHA= CLI CLM
Print predicted and residual values	P
Print intermediate calculations	INVERSE XPX
Tune sensitivity	SINGULAR= ZETA=

The options that can be specified in the MODEL statement are described below.

ALPHA=0.01 | 0.05 | 0.10
> specifies the alpha level for confidence intervals. By default, ALPHA=0.05.

CLI
> prints confidence limits for individual predicted values for each observation. CLI should not be used with CLM; it is ignored if CLM is also specified.

CLM
> prints confidence limits for a mean predicted value for each observation.

E
> prints the general form of all estimable functions.

E1
> prints the Type I estimable functions for each effect in the model and computes the corresponding sums of squares (SS).

E2

> prints the Type II estimable functions for each effect in the model and computes the corresponding SS.

E3

> prints the Type III estimable functions for each effect in the model and computes the corresponding SS.

E4

> prints the Type IV estimable functions for each effect in the model and computes the corresponding SS.

INTERCEPT
INT

> prints the hypothesis tests associated with the intercept as an effect in the model. By default, the procedure includes the intercept in the model, but does not print associated tests of hypotheses. Except for printing the uncorrected total SS instead of the corrected total SS, INT is ignored when you use an ABSORB statement.

INVERSE
I

> prints the inverse or the generalized inverse of the **X'X** matrix.

NOINT

> omits the intercept parameter from the model.

NOUNI

> suppresses printing of univariate statistics. You typically use the NOUNI option with a multivariate or repeated measures analysis of variance when you do not need the standard univariate output. The NOUNI option in a MODEL statement does not affect the univariate output produced by the REPEATED statement.

P

> prints observed, predicted, and residual values for each observation that does not contain missing values for independent variables. The Durbin-Watson statistic is also printed when P is specified. The PRESS statistic is also printed if either CLM or CLI is specified.

SINGULAR=*number*

> tunes the sensitivity of the regression routine to linear dependencies in the design. If a diagonal pivot element is less than C*number* as GLM sweeps the **X'X** matrix, the associated design column is declared to be linearly dependent with previous columns, and the associated parameter is zeroed.
>
> The C value adjusts the check to the relative scale of the variable. C is equal to the corrected SS for the variable, unless the corrected SS is 0, in which case C is 1. If NOINT is specified but the ABSORB option is not, GLM uses the uncorrected SS instead.
>
> The default value of SINGULAR=, $1E-7$, may be too small, but this value is necessary in order to handle the high-degree polynomials used in the literature to compare regression routines.

SOLUTION

> prints a solution to the normal equations (parameter estimates). SOLUTION is useful when you use a CLASS statement; by default, GLM prints a solution when a CLASS statement is not used.

SS1

> prints the sum of squares (SS) associated with Type I estimable functions for each effect. These are also printed by default.

SS2

prints the SS associated with Type II estimable functions for each effect.

SS3

prints the SS associated with Type III estimable functions for each effect to be printed. These are also printed by default.

SS4

prints the SS associated with Type IV estimable functions for each effect.

TOLERANCE

prints the tolerances used in the SWEEP routine The tolerances are of the form C/USS or C/CSS, as described in the discussion of the SINGULAR= option above. The tolerance value for the intercept is not divided by its uncorrected SS.

XPX

prints the $\mathbf{X'X}$ crossproducts matrix.

ZETA=value

tunes the sensitivity of the check for estimability for Type III and Type IV functions. Any element in the estimable function basis with an absolute value less than ZETA= is set to zero. The default value for ZETA= is 1E−8, which suffices for all *ANOVA*-type models.

Although it is possible to generate data for which this absolute check can be defeated, the check suffices in most practical examples. Additional research needs to be performed to make this check relative rather than absolute.

OUTPUT Statement

OUTPUT <OUT=*SAS-data-set*> *keyword=names*
        <. . . *keyword=names*>;

The OUTPUT statement creates a new SAS data set that saves diagnostic measures calculated after fitting the model. At least one specification of the form *keyword=names* is required.

All the variables in the original data set are included in the new data set, along with variables created in the OUTPUT statement. These new variables contain the values of a variety of diagnostic measures that are calculated for each observation in the data set. If you want to create a permanent SAS data set, you must specify a two-level name (see "SAS Files" in *SAS Language: Reference* and "Introduction to DATA STEP Processing" in *SAS Language and Procedures: Usage, Version 6, First Edition* for (more information on permanent SAS data sets).

Details on the specifications in the OUTPUT statement are given below.

keyword=names   specifies the statistics to include in the output data set and gives names to the new variables that contain the statistics. Specify a keyword for each desired statistic (see the following list of keywords), an equal sign, and the variable or variables to contain the statistic.

In the output data set, the first variable listed after a keyword in the OUTPUT statement contains that statistic for the first dependent variable listed in the MODEL statement; the second variable contains the statistic for the second dependent variable in the MODEL statement, and so on. The list of variables following the equal sign can be shorter than the list of dependent variables in the MODEL statement. In this case, the procedure creates the new names in order of the dependent variables in the MODEL statement. See **OUTPUT Examples** later in this section.

The keywords allowed and the statistics they represent are as follows:

COOKD	Cook's D influence statistic.
COVRATIO	standard influence of observation on covariance of betas.
DFFITS	standard influence of observation on predicted value.
H	leverage, $x_i(\mathbf{X'X})^{-1}x_i'$.
L95	lower bound of a 95% confidence interval for an individual prediction. This includes the variance of the error, as well as the variance of the parameter estimates. For the corresponding upper bound, see U95.
L95M	lower bound of a 95% confidence interval for the expected value (mean) of the dependent variable. For the corresponding upper bound, see U95M.
PREDICTED | P	predicted values.
PRESS	residual for the ith observation that results from dropping the ith observation from the parameter estimates. This is the residual divided by $(1-h)$ where h is the leverage above.
RESIDUAL | R	residuals, calculated as ACTUAL−PREDICTED.
RSTUDENT	a studentized residual with the current observation deleted.
STDI	standard error of the individual predicted value.
STDP	standard error of the mean predicted value.
STDR	standard error of the residual.
STUDENT	studentized residuals, the residual divided by its standard error.
U95M	upper bound of a 95% confidence interval for the expected value (mean) of the dependent variable. For the corresponding lower bound, see L95M.
U95	upper bound of a 95% confidence interval for an individual prediction. For the corresponding lower bound, see L95.

OUT=*SAS-data-set*

> gives the name of the new data set. By default, the procedure uses the DATA*n* convention to name the new data set.

See **Influence Diagnostics** in Chapter 36, "The REG Procedure", and Chapter 1, "Introduction to Regression Procedures," for details on the calculation of these statistics.

OUTPUT Examples

The statements below show the syntax for creating an output data set with a single dependent variable.

```
proc glm;
   class a b;
   model y=a b a*b;
   output out=new p=yhat r=resid stdr=eresid;
run;
```

These statements create an output data set named NEW. In addition to all the variables from the original data set, NEW contains the variable YHAT, whose values are predicted values of the dependent variable Y; the variable RESID, whose values are the residual values of Y; and the variable ERESID, whose values are the standard errors of the residuals.

The statements below show a situation with five dependent variables.

```
proc glm;
   by group;
   class a;
   model y1-y5=a x(a);
   output out=pout predicted=py1-py5;
run;
```

Data set POUT contains five new variables, PY1 through PY5. PY1's values are the predicted values of Y1; PY2's values are the predicted values of Y2; and so on.

For more information on the data set produced by the OUTPUT statement, see **Output Data Sets** later in this chapter.

RANDOM Statement

> **RANDOM** *effects* < / *options*>;

The RANDOM statement specifies which effects in the model are random. When you use a RANDOM statement, GLM always prints the expected value of each Type III, Type IV, or contrast MS used in the analysis. Since the estimable function basis is not automatically calculated for Type I and Type II sums of squares, the E1 (for Type I) or E2 (for Type II) option must be specified in the MODEL statement in order for the RANDOM statement to produce expected mean squares for Type I or Type II sums of squares. GLM only uses the information pertaining to expected mean squares when you specify the TEST option of the RANDOM statement (see below). Since other features in GLM assume that all effects are fixed, all other tests and all estimability checks are based on a fixed effects model, even when you use a RANDOM statement.

You can use as many RANDOM statements as you want, provided that they appear after the MODEL statement. If you use a CONTRAST statement with a RANDOM statement and you want to obtain the expected mean squares for the contrast hypothesis, you must enter the CONTRAST statement before the RANDOM statement.

The list of effects in the RANDOM statement should contain one or more of the pure classification effects (main effects, crossed effects, or nested effects) specified in the MODEL statement. The levels of each effect specified are assumed to be normally and independently distributed with common variance. Levels in different effects are assumed to be independent.

The following options can appear in the RANDOM statement after a slash:

Q
> provides a complete printout of all quadratic forms in the fixed effects that appear in the expected mean squares. For some designs, large mixed-level factorials, for example, Q may generate a substantial amount of output.

TEST
> performs hypothesis tests for each effect specified in the model, using appropriate error terms as determined by the expected mean squares.

GLM does not automatically declare interactions to be random when the effects in the interaction are declared random. For example,

```
random a b / test;
```

does not produce the same expected mean squares or tests as

```
random a b a*b / test;
```

To ensure correct tests, all random interactions and random main effects need to be listed in the RANDOM statement.

See **Expected Mean Squares for Random Effects** later in this chapter for more information on the calculation of expected mean squares and the tests that are produced by the TEST option. See Chapter 2, "Introduction to Analysis-of-Variance Procedures," and Chapter 44, "The VARCOMP Procedure," for more information on random effects.

REPEATED Statement

> **REPEATED** factor-name;
> **REPEATED** factor-name <levels <(level-values)>>
>   <transformation> < / options>;
> **REPEATED** factor-name levels, <factor-name levels>;
> **REPEATED** factor-name levels <(level-values)> <transformation>
>   <, . . . , factor-name levels<(level-values)> <transformation>>
>   < / options>;

When values of the dependent variables in the MODEL statement represent repeated measurements on the same experimental unit, the REPEATED statement allows you to test hypotheses about the measurement factors (often called *within-subject factors*) as well as the interactions of within-subject factors with independent variables in the MODEL statement (often called *between-subject factors*). The REPEATED statement provides multivariate and univariate tests as well as hypothesis tests for a variety of single-degree-of-freedom contrasts. There is no limit to the number of within-subject factors that can be specified.

The REPEATED statement handles repeated measures designs with one repeated response variable. It does not handle doubly-multivariate repeated measures designs, triply-multivariate repeated measures designs, and so on. In other words, the variables on the left-hand side of the equation in the MODEL statement must represent one repeated response variable. This does not mean that only one factor can be listed in the REPEATED statement. For example, one repeated response variable (hemoglobin count) might be measured 12 times (implying variables Y1 to Y12 on the left-hand side of the equal sign in the MODEL statement), with the associated within-subject factors treatment and time (implying two factors listed in the REPEATED statement). See **REPEATED Examples** later in this section for an example of how GLM handles this case. Designs with two or more repeated response variables can, however, be handled with appropriate MANOVA statements. See **Example 9** later in this chapter for an example of analyzing a doubly-multivariate repeated measures design.

When a REPEATED statement appears, the GLM procedure enters a multivariate mode of handling missing values. If any values for variables corresponding to each combination of the within-subject factors are missing, the observation is excluded from the analysis.

If you use a CONTRAST or TEST statement with a REPEATED statement, you must enter the CONTRAST or TEST statement before the REPEATED statement. The simplest form of the REPEATED statement requires only a *factor-name*. With two repeated factors, you must specify the *factor-name* and number of levels (*levels*) for each factor. Optionally, you can specify the actual values for the levels (*level-values*), a *transformation* that defines single-degree-of-freedom contrasts, and *options* for additional analyses and printed output. When more than one within-subject factor is specified, the *factor-names* (and associated level and transformation information) must be separated by a comma in the REPEATED statement. These terms are described below.

Syntax Details

The terms below are specified in the REPEATED statement:

factor-name names a factor to be associated with the dependent variables. The name should not be the same as any variable name that already exists in the data set being analyzed and should conform to the usual conventions of SAS variable names.

levels gives the number of levels associated with the factor being defined. When there is only one within-subject factor, the number of levels is equal to the number of dependent variables. In this case, *levels* is optional. When more than one within-subject factor is defined, however, *levels* is required, and the product of the levels of all the factors must equal the number of dependent variables in the MODEL statement.

(level-values) gives values that correspond to levels of a repeated-measures factor. These values are used to label output and as spacings for constructing orthogonal polynomial contrasts. The number of values specified must correspond to the number of levels for that factor in the REPEATED statement. Enclose the *level-values* in parentheses.

The following *transformation* keywords define single-degree-of-freedom contrasts for factors specified in the REPEATED statement. Since the number of contrasts generated is always one less than the number of levels of the factor, you have some control over which contrast is omitted from the analysis by which transformation you select. By default, the procedure uses the CONTRAST transformation.

CONTRAST <(*ordinal-reference-level*)>

> generates contrasts between levels of the factor and a reference level. By default, the procedure uses the last level; you can optionally specify a reference level in parentheses after the keyword CONTRAST. The reference level corresponds to the ordinal value of the level rather than the level value specified. For example, to generate contrasts between the first level of a factor and the other levels, use

> `contrast(1)`

HELMERT   generates contrasts between each level of the factor and the mean of subsequent levels.

MEAN <(*ordinal-reference-level*)>

> generates contrasts between levels of the factor and the mean of all other levels of the factor. Specifying a reference level eliminates the contrast between that level and the mean. Without a reference level, the contrast involving the last level is omitted. See the CONTRAST transformation above for an example.

POLYNOMIAL   generates orthogonal polynomial contrasts. Level values, if provided, are used as spacings in the construction of the polynomials; otherwise, equal spacing is assumed.

PROFILE   generates contrasts between adjacent levels of the factor.

The following options can appear in the REPEATED statement after a slash:

CANONICAL
   performs a canonical analysis of the **H** and **E** matrices corresponding to the transformed variables specified in the REPEATED statement.

HTYPE=*n*
   specifies the type of the **H** matrix used in the multivariate tests and the type of sums of squares used in the univariate tests. See the HTYPE= option in the specifications for the MANOVA statement for further details.

NOM
   prints only the results of the univariate analyses.

NOU
   prints only the results of the multivariate analyses.

PRINTE
   prints the **E** matrix for each combination of within-subject factors, as well as partial correlation matrices for both the original dependent variables and the variables defined by the transformations specified in the REPEATED statement. In addition, the PRINTE option provides sphericity tests for each set of transformed variables. If the requested transformations are not orthogonal, the PRINTE option also provides a sphericity test for a set of orthogonal contrasts.

PRINTH
   prints the **H** (SSCP) matrix associated with each multivariate test.

PRINTM

prints the transformation matrices that define the contrasts in the analysis. GLM always prints the **M** matrix so that the transformed variables are defined by the rows, not the columns, of the **M** matrix on the printout. In other words, GLM actually prints **M'**.

PRINTRV

prints the characteristic roots and vectors for each multivariate test.

SUMMARY

produces analysis-of-variance tables for each contrast defined by the within-subject factors. Along with tests for the effects of the independent variables specified in the MODEL statement, a term labeled MEAN tests the hypothesis that the overall mean of the contrast is zero.

REPEATED Examples

When specifying more than one factor, list the dependent variables in the MODEL statement so that the within-subject factors defined in the REPEATED statement are nested; that is, the first factor defined in the REPEATED statement should be the one with values that change least frequently. For example, assume three treatments are administered at each of four times, for a total of twelve dependent variables on each experimental unit. If the variables are listed in the MODEL statement as Y1 through Y12, then the following REPEATED statement:

```
proc glm;
    classes group;
    model y1-y12=group / nouni;
    repeated trt 3, time 4;
run;
```

implies the following structure:

DEP VARIABLE	Y1	Y2	Y3	Y4	Y5	Y6	Y7	Y8	Y9	Y10	Y11	Y12
value of TRT	1	1	1	1	2	2	2	2	3	3	3	3
value of TIME	1	2	3	4	1	2	3	4	1	2	3	4

The REPEATED statement always produces a table like the one above. For more information, see **Repeated Measures Analysis of Variance** later in this chapter.

TEST Statement

TEST <H=*effects*> E=*effect*</ *options*>;

Although an F value is computed for all SS in the analysis using the residual MS as an error term, you may request additional F tests using other effects as error terms. You need a TEST statement when a nonstandard error structure (as in a split-plot) exists. However, in most unbalanced models with nonstandard error structures, most mean squares are not independent and do not have equal expectations under the null hypothesis.

GLM does not check any of the assumptions underlying the F statistic. **When you specify a TEST statement, you assume sole responsibility for the validity of the F statistic produced**. To help validate a test, you can use the RANDOM statement and inspect the expected mean squares, or you can use the TEST option of the RANDOM statement.

You may use as many TEST statements as you want, provided they appear after the MODEL statement.

The following terms are specified in the TEST statement:

H=*effects*   specifies which effects in the preceding model are to be used as hypothesis (numerator) effects.

E=*effect*   specifies one, and only one, effect to use as the error (denominator) term. The E= specification is required.

By default, the SS type for all hypothesis SS and error SS is the highest type computed in the model. If the hypothesis type or error type is to be another type that was computed in the model, you should specify one or both of the following options after a slash:

ETYPE=*n*

specifies the type of SS to use for the error term. The type must be a type computed in the model (n=1, 2, 3, or 4).

HTYPE=*n*

specifies the type of SS to use for the hypothesis. The type must be a type computed in the model (n=1, 2, 3, or 4).

The following example illustrates the TEST statement with a split-plot model:

```
proc glm;
   class a b c;
   model y=a  b(a) c a*c b*c(a);
   test h=a e=b(a)/ htype=1 etype=1;
   test h=c a*c e=b*c(a) / htype=1 etype=1;
run;
```

WEIGHT Statement

WEIGHT *variable;*

When a WEIGHT statement is used, a weighted residual sum of squares

$$\Sigma_i w_i(y_i - \hat{y}_i)^2$$

is minimized, where w_i is the value of the variable specified in the WEIGHT statement, y_i is the observed value of the response variable, and $\hat{y}_i$ is the predicted value of the response variable.

The observation is used in the analysis only if the value of the WEIGHT statement variable is greater than zero.

The WEIGHT statement has no effect on degrees of freedom or number of observations, but is used by the MEANS statement when calculating means and performing multiple comparison tests (as described in the section on the MEANS statement earlier in this chapter). The normal equations used when a WEIGHT statement is present are

$$\beta = (X'WX)^- X'WY$$

where **W** is a diagonal matrix consisting of the values of the variable specified in the WEIGHT statement.

If the weights for the observations are proportional to the reciprocals of the error variances, then the weighted least-squares estimates are BLUE (best linear unbiased estimators).

If the WEIGHT statement is used, it must appear before the first RUN statement or it is ignored.

DETAILS

Parameterization of GLM Models

GLM constructs a linear model according to the specifications in the MODEL statement. Each effect generates one or more columns in a design matrix **X**. This section shows precisely how **X** is built.

Intercept

All models automatically include a column of 1s to estimate an intercept parameter μ. You can use the NOINT option to suppress the intercept.

Regression Effects

Regression effects (covariates) have the values of the variables copied into the design matrix directly. Polynomial terms are multiplied out and then installed in **X**.

Main Effects

If a class variable has m levels, GLM generates m columns in the design matrix for its main effect. Each column is an indicator variable for a given level. The order of the columns is the sort order of the values of their levels and can be controlled with the ORDER= option of the PROC GLM statement, for example,

data			A		B		
A	B	μ	A1	A2	B1	B2	B3
1	1	1	1	0	1	0	0
1	2	1	1	0	0	1	0
1	3	1	1	0	0	0	1
2	1	1	0	1	1	0	0
2	2	1	0	1	0	1	0
2	3	1	0	1	0	0	1

There are more columns for these effects than there are degrees of freedom for them; in other words, GLM is using an over-parameterized model.

Crossed Effects

First, GLM reorders the terms to correspond to the order of the variables in the CLASS statement; thus, B*A becomes A*B if A precedes B in the CLASS statement. Then GLM generates columns for all combinations of levels that occur in the data. The order of the columns is such that the rightmost variables in the cross index faster than the leftmost variables. Empty columns (that would contain all zeros) are not generated.

data			A		B			A*B					
A	B	μ	A1	A2	B1	B2	B3	A1B1	A1B2	A1B3	A2B1	A2B2	A2B3
1	1	1	1	0	1	0	0	1	0	0	0	0	0
1	2	1	1	0	0	1	0	0	1	0	0	0	0
1	3	1	1	0	0	0	1	0	0	1	0	0	0
2	1	1	0	1	1	0	0	0	0	0	1	0	0
2	2	1	0	1	0	1	0	0	0	0	0	1	0
2	3	1	0	1	0	0	1	0	0	0	0	0	1

In the above matrix, main-effects columns are not linearly independent of crossed-effect columns; in fact, the column space for the crossed effects contains the space of the main effect.

Nested Effects

Nested effects are generated in the same manner as crossed effects. Hence the design columns generated by the following statements are the same (but the ordering of the columns is different):

    model y=a b(a);   (B nested within A)

and

    model y=a a*b;   (omitted main effect for B).

The nesting operator in GLM is more a notational convenience than an operation distinct from crossing. Nested effects are characterized by the property that the nested variables never appear as main effects. The order of the variables within nesting parentheses is made to correspond to the order of these variables in the CLASS statement. The order of the columns is such that variables outside the parentheses index faster than those inside the parentheses, and the rightmost nested variables index faster than the leftmost variables.

data			A		B(A)					
A	B	μ	A1	A2	B1A1	B2A1	B3A1	B1A2	B2A2	B3A2
1	1	1	1	0	1	0	0	0	0	0
1	2	1	1	0	0	1	0	0	0	0
1	3	1	1	0	0	0	1	0	0	0
2	1	1	0	1	0	0	0	1	0	0
2	2	1	0	1	0	0	0	0	1	0
2	3	1	0	1	0	0	0	0	0	1

Continuous-Nesting-Class Effects

When a continuous variable nests with a class variable, the design columns are constructed by multiplying the continuous values into the design columns for the class effect.

data			A		X(A)	
X	A	μ	A1	A2	X(A1)	X(A2)
21	1	1	1	0	21	0
24	1	1	1	0	24	0
22	1	1	1	0	22	0
28	2	1	0	1	0	28
19	2	1	0	1	0	19
23	2	1	0	1	0	23

This model estimates a separate slope for **X** within each level of A.

Continuous-by-Class Effects

Continuous-by-class effects generate the same design columns as continuous-nesting-class effects. The two models are made different by the presence of the continuous variable as a regressor by itself, as well as a contributor to a compound effect.

data			X	A		X*A	
X	A	μ	X	A1	A2	X*A1	X*A2
21	1	1	21	1	0	21	0
24	1	1	24	1	0	24	0
22	1	1	22	1	0	22	0
28	2	1	28	0	1	0	28
19	2	1	19	0	1	0	19
23	2	1	23	0	1	0	23

Continuous-by-class effects are used to test the homogeneity of slopes. If the continuous-by-class effect is nonsignificant, the effect can be removed so that the response with respect to **X** is the same for all levels of the class variables.

General Effects

An example that combines all the effects is

    X1*X2*A*B*C(D E)   .

The continuous list comes first, followed by the crossed list, followed by the nested list in parentheses.

The sequencing of parameters is not important to learn unless you contemplate using the CONTRAST or ESTIMATE statements to compute some function of the parameter estimates.

Effects may be retitled by GLM to correspond to ordering rules. For example, B*A(E D) may be retitled A*B(D E) to satisfy the following:

- Class variables that occur outside parentheses (crossed effects) are sorted in the order they appear in the CLASS statement.
- Variables within parentheses (nested effects) are sorted in the order they appear in a CLASS statement.

The sequencing of the parameters generated by an effect can be described by which variables have their levels indexed faster:

- Variables in the crossed part index faster than variables in the nested list.
- Within a crossed or nested list, variables to the right index faster than variables to the left.

For example, suppose a model includes four effects—A, B, C, and D—each having two levels, 1 and 2. If the CLASS statement is

```
class a b c d;
```

then the order of the parameters for the effect B*A(C D), which is retitled A*B(C D), is

$$A_1B_1C_1D_1 \rightarrow A_1B_2C_1D_1 \rightarrow A_2B_1C_1D_1 \rightarrow A_2B_2C_1D_1 \rightarrow A_1B_1C_1D_2 \rightarrow$$

$$A_1B_2C_1D_2 \rightarrow A_2B_1C_1D_2 \rightarrow A_2B_2C_1D_2 \rightarrow A_1B_1C_2D_1 \rightarrow A_1B_2C_2D_1 \rightarrow$$

$$A_2B_1C_1D_2 \rightarrow A_2B_2C_2D_1 \rightarrow A_1B_1C_2D_2 \rightarrow A_1B_2C_2D_2 \rightarrow A_2B_1C_2D_2 \rightarrow$$

$$A_2B_2C_2D_2 \quad .$$

Note that first the crossed effects B and A are sorted in the order that they appear in the CLASS statement so that A precedes B in the parameter list. Then, for each combination of the nested effects in turn, combinations of A and B appear. B moves fastest because it is rightmost in the cross list. Then A moves next fastest. D moves next fastest. C is the slowest since it is leftmost in the nested list.

When numeric levels are used, levels are sorted by their character format, which may not correspond to their numeric sort sequence. Therefore, it is advisable to include a format for numeric levels or to use the ORDER=INTERNAL option in the PROC GLM statement to ensure that levels are sorted by their internal values.

Degrees of Freedom

For models with class variables, there are more design columns constructed than there are degrees of freedom for the effect. Thus, there are linear dependencies among the columns. In this event, the parameters are not estimable; there is an infinite number of least-squares solutions. GLM uses a generalized (g2) inverse to obtain values for the estimates. The solution values are not printed unless the SOLUTION option is specified in the MODEL statement. The solution has the characteristic that estimates are zero whenever the design column for that parameter is a linear combination of previous columns. (Strictly termed, the solution values should not be called estimates.) With this full parameterization, hypothesis tests are constructed to test linear functions of the parameters that are estimable.

Other procedures (such as PROC CATMOD) reparameterize models to full rank using certain restrictions on the parameters. GLM does not reparameterize, making the hypotheses that are commonly tested more understandable. See Goodnight (1978) for additional reasons for not reparameterizing.

GLM does not actually construct the design matrix **X**; rather, the procedure constructs directly the crossproduct matrix **X′X**, which is made up of counts, sums, and crossproducts.

Hypothesis Testing in GLM

See Chapter 9, "The Four Types of Estimable Functions," for a complete discussion of the four standard types of hypothesis tests.

Example

To illustrate the four types of tests and the principles upon which they are based, consider a two-way design with interaction based on these data:

		B	
		1	2
A	1	23.5 23.7	28.7
	2	8.9	5.6 8.9
	3	10.3 12.5	13.6 14.6

Invoke GLM and ask for all the estimable functions options to examine what GLM can test. The code below is followed by the summary *ANOVA* table from the printout. See **Output 24.2**.

```
data example;
   input a b y aa;
   cards;
1 1 23.5   1 1 23.7   1 2 28.7   2 1   8.9   2 2   5.6
2 2   8.9   3 1 10.3   3 1 12.5   3 2 13.6   3 2 14.6
;

proc glm;
   class a b;
   model y=a b a*b / e e1 e2 e3 e4;
run;
```

Output 24.2 Summary *ANOVA* Table from PROC GLM

```
                              The SAS System
                       General Linear Models Procedure

Dependent Variable: Y

Source              DF       Sum of Squares      Mean Square     F Value     Pr > F

Model                5        520.47600000      104.09520000       49.66     0.0011

Error                4          8.38500000        2.09625000

Corrected Total      9        528.86100000

                  R-Square             C.V.         Root MSE                   Y Mean

                  0.984145         9.633022       1.44784322              15.03000000
```

The following sections show the general form of estimable functions and discuss the four standard tests, their properties, and abbreviated printouts for the two-way crossed example.

Estimability

Output 24.3 is the general form of estimable functions for the example. In order to be testable, a hypothesis must be able to fit within the framework printed here.

Output 24.3 General Form of Estimable Functions

```
                              The SAS System

                       General Linear Models Procedure
                     General Form of Estimable Functions

Effect            Coefficients

INTERCEPT         L1

A        1        L2
         2        L3
         3        L1-L2-L3

B        1        L5
         2        L1-L5

A*B      1 1      L7
         1 2      L2-L7
         2 1      L9
         2 2      L3-L9
         3 1      L5-L7-L9
         3 2      L1-L2-L3-L5+L7+L9
```

If a hypothesis is estimable, the Ls in the above scheme can be set to values that match the hypothesis. All the standard tests in GLM can be shown in the format above, with some of the Ls zeroed and some set to functions of other Ls.

The following sections show how many of the hypotheses can be tested by comparing the model sum-of-squares regression from one model to a submodel. The notation used is

$$SS(Beffects \mid Aeffects) = SS(Beffects, Aeffects) - SS(Aeffects)$$

where SS(*Aeffects*) denotes the regression model sum of squares for the model consisting of *Aeffects*. This notation is equivalent to the reduction notation defined by Searle (1971) and summarized in Chapter 9, "The Four Types of Estimable Functions."

Type I Tests

Type I sums of squares, also called *sequential sums of squares*, are the incremental improvement in error SS as each effect is added to the model. They can be computed by fitting the model in steps and recording the difference in SSE at each step.

Source	Type I SS
A	$SS(A \mid \mu)$
B	$SS(B \mid \mu, A)$
A*B	$SS(A*B \mid \mu, A, B)$

Type I SS are printed by default because they are easy to obtain and can be used in various hand calculations to produce SS values for a series of different models. The Type I hypotheses have the following properties:

- Type I SS for all effects add up to the model SS. None of the other SS types have this property, except in special cases.
- Type I hypotheses can be derived from rows of the Forward-Dolittle transformation of **X'X** (a transformation that reduces **X'X** to an upper triangular matrix by row operations).
- Type I SS are statistically independent from each other if the residual errors are independent and identically normally distributed.
- Type I hypotheses depend on the order in which effects are specified in the MODEL.
- Type I hypotheses are uncontaminated by effects preceding the effect being tested; however, the hypotheses usually involve parameters for effects following the tested effect in the model. For example, in the model

```
y=a b;
```

the Type I hypothesis for B does not involve A parameters, but the Type I hypothesis for A does involve B parameters.
- Type I hypotheses are functions of the cell counts for unbalanced data; the hypotheses are not usually the same hypotheses that are tested if the data are balanced.
- Type I SS are useful for polynomial models where you want to know the contribution of a term as though it had been made orthogonal to preceding effects. Thus, Type I SS correspond to tests of the orthogonalized polynomials.

The Type I estimable functions and associated tests for the example are shown in **Output 24.4**. (This combines output from several pages of actual printout.)

Output 24.4   Type I Estimable Functions and Associated Tests

```
                                      The SAS System
                              General Linear Models Procedure

Type I Estimable Functions for: A      Type I Estimable Functions for: B      Type I Estimable Functions for: A*B

Effect          Coefficients           Effect         Coefficients            Effect         Coefficients

INTERCEPT       0                      INTERCEPT      0                        INTERCEPT      0

A        1      L2                     A       1      0                        A       1      0
         2      L3                             2      0                                2      0
         3      -L2-L3                         3      0                                3      0

B        1      0.1667*L2-0.1667*L3    B       1      L5                       B       1      0
         2      -0.1667*L2+0.1667*L3           2      -L5                              2      0

A*B    1 1      0.6667*L2             A*B    1 1      0.2857*L5               A*B    1 1      L7
       1 2      0.3333*L2                    1 2      -0.2857*L5                     1 2      -L7
       2 1      0.3333*L3                    2 1      0.2857*L5                      2 1      L9
       2 2      0.6667*L3                    2 2      -0.2857*L5                     2 2      -L9
       3 1      -0.5*L2-0.5*L3               3 1      0.4286*L5                      3 1      -L7-L9
       3 2      -0.5*L2-0.5*L3               3 2      -0.4286*L5                     3 2      L7+L9


         Source              DF         Type I SS          Mean Square       F Value        Pr > F
         A                    2       494.03100000       247.01550000        117.84         0.0003
         B                    1        10.71428571        10.71428571          5.11         0.0866
         A*B                  2        15.73071429         7.86535714          3.75         0.1209
```

Type II Tests

The Type II tests can also be calculated by comparing the error SS for subset models. The Type II SS are the reduction in error SS due to adding the term after all other terms have been added to the model except terms that contain the effect being tested. An effect is contained in another effect if it can be derived by deleting terms in the latter effect. For example, A and B are both contained in A*B. For this model

Source	Type II SS
A	SS(A | μ,B)
B	SS(B | μ,A)
A*B	SS(A*B | μ,A,B)

Type II SS have the following properties:

- Type II SS do not necessarily sum up to the model SS.
- The hypothesis for an effect does not involve parameters of other effects except for containing effects (which it must involve to be estimable).
- Type II SS are invariant to the ordering of effects in the model.
- For unbalanced designs, Type II hypotheses for effects that are contained in other effects are not usually the same hypotheses that are tested if the data are balanced. The hypotheses are generally functions of the cell counts.

The Type II estimable functions and associated tests for the example are shown in **Output 24.5**. (Again, this combines output from several pages of actual printout.)

Output 24.5 Type II Estimable Functions and Associated Tests

```
                                    The SAS System
                             General Linear Models Procedure

Type II Estimable Functions for: A     Type II Estimable Functions for: B      Type II Estimable Functions for: A*B

Effect          Coefficients           Effect          Coefficients            Effect          Coefficients

INTERCEPT       0                      INTERCEPT       0                       INTERCEPT       0

A        1      L2                     A        1      0                       A        1       0
         2      L3                              2      0                                2       0
         3      -L2-L3                          3      0                                3       0

B        1      0                      B        1      L5                      B        1       0
         2      0                               2      -L5                              2       0

A*B    1 1      0.619*L2+0.0476*L3     A*B    1 1      0.2857*L5               A*B    1 1       L7
       1 2      0.381*L2-0.0476*L3            1 2      -0.2857*L5                     1 2       -L7
       2 1      -0.0476*L2+0.381*L3           2 1      0.2857*L5                      2 1       L9
       2 2      0.0476*L2+0.619*L3            2 2      -0.2857*L5                     2 2       -L9
       3 1      -0.5714*L2-0.4286*L3          3 1      0.4286*L5                      3 1       -L7-L9
       3 2      -0.4286*L2-0.5714*L3          3 2      -0.4286*L5                     3 2       L7+L9

                             General Linear Models Procedure

         Source         DF         Type II SS          Mean Square          F Value          Pr > F

         A              2          499.12028571        249.56014286         119.05           0.0003
         B              1          10.71428571         10.71428571          5.11             0.0866
         A*B            2          15.73071429         7.86535714           3.75             0.1209
```

Type III and Type IV Tests

Type III and Type IV SS, sometimes referred to as *partial sums of squares*, are considered by many to be the most desirable. These SS cannot in general be computed by comparing model SS from several models using GLM's parameterization. (However, they can sometimes be computed by reduction for methods that reparameterize to full rank.) In GLM they are computed by constructing an estimated hypothesis matrix **L** and then computing the SS associated with the hypothesis **Lβ**=0. As long as there are no missing cells in the design, Type III and Type IV SS are the same.

The following are properties of Type III and Type IV SS:

- The hypothesis for an effect does not involve parameters of other effects except for containing effects (which it must involve to be estimable).
- The hypotheses to be tested are invariant to the ordering of effects in the model.
- The hypotheses are the same hypotheses that are tested if there are no missing cells. They are not functions of cell counts.
- The SS do not normally add up to the model SS.

The SS are constructed from the general form of estimable functions. Type III and Type IV tests are different only if the design has missing cells. In this case, the Type III tests have an orthogonality property, while the Type IV tests have a balancing property. These properties are discussed in Chapter 9, "The Four Types of Estimable Functions." For this example, Type IV tests are identical to the Type III tests that are shown in **Output 24.6**. (This combines output from several pages of actual printout.)

Output 24.6 Type III Estimable Functions and Associated Tests

```
                              The SAS System
                        General Linear Models Procedure


Type III Estimable Functions for: A    Type III Estimable Functions for: B    Type III Estimable Functions for: A*B

Effect          Coefficients           Effect          Coefficients           Effect          Coefficients

INTERCEPT       0                      INTERCEPT       0                      INTERCEPT       0

A      1   L2                          A      1   0                          A      1   0
       2   L3                                 2   0                                 2   0
       3   -L2-L3                              3   0                                 3   0

B      1   0                           B      1   L5                         B      1   0
       2   0                                  2   -L5                                2   0

A*B  1 1   0.5*L2                      A*B  1 1   0.3333*L5                  A*B  1 1   L7
     1 2   0.5*L2                           1 2   -0.3333*L5                      1 2   -L7
     2 1   0.5*L3                           2 1   0.3333*L5                       2 1   L9
     2 2   0.5*L3                           2 2   -0.3333*L5                      2 2   -L9
     3 1   -0.5*L2-0.5*L3                   3 1   0.3333*L5                       3 1   -L7-L9
     3 2   -0.5*L2-0.5*L3                   3 2   -0.3333*L5                      3 2   L7+L9


      Source         DF        Type III SS      Mean Square      F Value     Pr > F

      A               2       479.10785714     239.55392857      114.28      0.0003
      B               1         9.45562500       9.45562500        4.51      0.1009
      A*B             2        15.73071429       7.86535714        3.75      0.1209
```

Absorption

Absorption is a computational technique used to reduce computing resource needs in certain cases. The classic use of absorption occurs when a blocking factor with a large number of levels is a term in the model.

For example, the statements

```
proc glm;
    absorb herd;
    class a b;
    model y=a b a*b;
run;
```

are equivalent to

```
proc glm;
    class herd a b;
    model y=herd a b a*b;
run;
```

with the exception that the Type II, Type III, or Type IV SS for HERD are not computed when HERD is absorbed.

Several effects may be absorbed at one time. For example, these statements

```
proc glm;
    absorb herd cow;
    class a b;
    model y=a b a*b;
run;
```

are equivalent to

```
proc glm;
   class herd cow a b;
   model y=herd cow(herd) a b a*b;
run;
```

When you use absorption, the size of the **X'X** matrix is a function only of the effects in the MODEL statement. The effects being absorbed do not contribute to the size of the **X'X** matrix.

For the example above, A and B could be absorbed:

```
proc glm;
   absorb a b;
   class herd cow;
   model y=herd cow(herd);
run;
```

Although the sources of variation in the results are listed as

```
a b(a) herd cow(herd)
```

all types of estimable functions for HERD and COW(HERD) are free of A, B, and A*B parameters.

To illustrate the savings in computing using the ABSORB statement, GLM was run on generated data with 1147 degrees of freedom in the model with these statements:

```
data a;
   length herd cow trtment 4;
   do herd=1 to 40;
      n=1+ranuni(1234567)*60;
      do cow=1 to n;
         do trtment=1 to 3;
            do rep=1 to 2;
               y=herd / 5+cow / 10+trtment+rannor(1234567);
               output;
            end;
         end;
      end;
   end;
   drop n;

proc glm;
   class herd cow trtment;
   model y=herd cow(herd) trtment;
run;
```

This analysis would have required over six megabytes of memory for the **X'X** matrix had GLM solved it directly. However, in the statements below, GLM only needs a 4×4 matrix for the intercept and treatment because the other effects are absorbed.

```
proc glm;
   absorb herd cow;
   class trtment;
   model y=trtment;
run;
```

These statements produce the printout shown in **Output 24.7**.

Output 24.7 Absorption of Effects

```
                              The SAS System                                1

                        General Linear Models Procedure
                           Class Level Information

                         Class     Levels    Values

                         TRTMENT      3       1 2 3


              Number of observations in data set = 6876
```

```
                              The SAS System                                2

                        General Linear Models Procedure
```

Dependent Variable: Y

Source	DF	Sum of Squares	Mean Square	F Value	Pr > F
Model	1147	52049.89684153	45.37916028	44.17	0.0001
Error	5728	5884.55787530	1.02733203		
Corrected Total	6875	57934.45471683			

R-Square	C.V.	Root MSE	Y Mean
0.898427	12.48196	1.01357389	8.12031348

Source	DF	Type I SS	Mean Square	F Value	Pr > F
HERD	39	36230.70919772	928.99254353	904.28	0.0001
COW(HERD)	1106	11375.42905347	10.28519806	10.01	0.0001
TRTMENT	2	4443.75859037	2221.87929518	2162.77	0.0001

Source	DF	Type III SS	Mean Square	F Value	Pr > F
TRTMENT	2	4443.75859037	2221.87929518	2162.77	0.0001

Specification of ESTIMATE Expressions

For this example of the regression model

```
model y=x1 x2 x3;
```

the associated parameters are β_0, β_1, β_2, and β_3 (where β_0 represents the intercept). To estimate $3\beta_1 + 2\beta_2$, you need the following **L** vector:

$$\mathbf{L} = (0\ 3\ 2\ 0) \quad .$$

The corresponding ESTIMATE statement is

```
estimate '3B1+2B2'  x1 3  x2 2;
```

To estimate $\beta_0 + \beta_1 - 2\beta_3$ you need this **L** vector:

$$\mathbf{L} = (1\ 1\ 0\ -2) \quad .$$

The corresponding ESTIMATE statement is

```
estimate 'B0+B1-2B3' intercept 1 x1 1 x3 -2;
```

Now consider models involving class variables such as

```
model y=a b a*b;
```

with the associated parameters:

$$(\mu \; \alpha_1 \; \alpha_2 \; \alpha_3 \; \beta_1 \; \beta_2 \; \alpha\beta_{11} \; \alpha\beta_{12} \; \alpha\beta_{21} \; \alpha\beta_{22} \; \alpha\beta_{31} \; \alpha\beta_{32}) \; .$$

To estimate the least-squares mean for α_1, you need the following **L** vector:

$$\mathbf{L} = (1 \mid 1 \; 0 \; 0 \mid 0.5 \; 0.5 \mid \; 0.5 \; 0.5 \; 0 \; 0 \; 0 \; 0)$$

and you could use this ESTIMATE statement:

```
estimate 'LSM(A1)' intercept 1 a 1 b 0.5 0.5 a*b 0.5 0.5;
```

Note in the above statement that only one element of **L** is specified following the A effect, even though A has three levels. Whenever the list of constants following an effect name is shorter than the effect's number of levels, zeros are used as the remaining constants. In the event that the list of constants is longer than the number of levels for the effect, the extra constants are ignored, and a warning message is printed.

To estimate the A linear effect in the model above, assuming equally spaced levels for A, the following **L** can be used:

$$\mathbf{L} = (0 \mid -1 \; 0 \; 1 \mid 0 \; 0 \mid \; -0.5 \; -0.5 \; 0 \; 0 \; 0.5 \; 0.5) \; .$$

The ESTIMATE statement for the above **L** is written as

```
estimate 'A LINEAR' a -1 0 1;
```

If the elements of **L** are not specified for an effect that contains a specified effect, then the elements of the specified effect are equitably distributed over the levels of the higher-order effect. In addition, if the intercept is specified in an ESTIMATE or CONTRAST statement, it is distributed over all classification effects that are not contained by any other specified effect. The distribution of lower-order coefficients to higher-order effect coefficients follows the same general rules as in the LSMEANS statement and is similar to that used to construct Type IV **L**s. In the previous example, the -1 associated with α_1 is divided by the number of $\alpha\beta_{1j}$ parameters; then each $\alpha\beta_{1j}$ coefficient is set to -1/number of $\alpha\beta_{1j}$. The 1 associated with α_3 is distributed among the $\alpha\beta_{3j}$ parameters in a similar fashion. In the event that an unspecified effect contains several specified effects, only that specified effect with the most factors in common with the unspecified effect is used for distribution of coefficients to the higher-order effect.

Numerous syntactical expressions for the ESTIMATE statement were considered, including many that involved specifying the effect and level information associated with each coefficient. For models involving higher-level effects, the requirement of specifying level information would lead to very bulky specifications. Consequently, the simpler form of the ESTIMATE statement described above was implemented. The syntax of this ESTIMATE statement puts a burden on you to know a priori the order of the parameter list associated with each effect. You can use the ORDER= option of the PROC GLM statement to ensure that the levels of the classification effects are sorted appropriately. When you first begin to use this statement, use the E option to make sure that the actual **L** constructed is the one you envisioned.

A Check for Estimability

Each **L** is checked for estimability using the relationship: **L**=**LH** where
H= $(X'X)^-X'X$. The **L** vector is declared nonestimable, if for any i

$$\text{ABS}(L_i-(LH)_i) > \begin{cases} 1E-4 & \text{if } L_i = 0 \text{ or} \\ 1E-4*\text{ABS}(L_i) & \text{otherwise.} \end{cases}$$

Continued fractions (like 1/3) should be specified to at least six decimal places, or the DIVISOR parameter should be used.

Comparisons of Means

When comparing more than two means, an *ANOVA F* test tells you if the means are significantly different from each other, but it does not tell you which means differ from which other means. Multiple comparison methods (also called *mean separation tests*) give you more detailed information about the differences among the means. A variety of multiple comparison methods are available with the MEANS statement in the ANOVA and GLM procedures.

By *multiple comparisons* we mean more than one comparison among three or more means. There is a serious lack of standardized terminology in the literature on comparison of means. Einot and Gabriel (1975), for example, use the term *multiple comparison procedure* to mean what we define below as a *step-down multiple-stage test*. Some methods for multiple comparisons have not yet been given names, such as those referred to below as REGWQ and REGWF. When reading the literature, you may need to determine what methods are being discussed based on the formulas and references given.

When you interpret multiple comparisons, remember that failure to reject the hypothesis that two or more means are equal should not lead you to conclude that the population means are in fact equal. Failure to reject the null hypothesis implies only that the difference between population means, if any, is not large enough to be detected with the given sample size. A related point is that nonsignificance is nontransitive: given three sample means, the largest and smallest may be significantly different from each other, while neither is significantly different from the middle one. Nontransitive results of this type occur frequently in multiple comparisons.

Multiple comparisons can also lead to counter-intuitive results when the cell sizes are unequal. Consider four cells labeled A, B, C, and D, with sample means in the order A>B>C>D. If A and D each have two observations, and B and C each have 10,000 observations, then the difference between B and C may be significant, while the difference between A and D is not.

Confidence intervals may be more useful than significance tests in multiple comparisons. Confidence intervals show the degree of uncertainty in each comparison in an easily interpretable way; they make it easier to assess the practical significance of a difference, as well as the statistical significance; and they are less likely to lead nonstatisticians to the invalid conclusion that nonsignificantly different sample means imply equal population means.

The formulas shown in the rest of this section are used both when you use a WEIGHT statement and (as is more common) when you do not. In the more common situation of omitting a WEIGHT statement, GLM computes unweighted means and computes the statistics as shown in the formulas. The multiple comparison tests were developed for this situation, and the statistical behavior of these tests is well-understood. In the less common situation of using a WEIGHT statement, GLM computes weighted means and uses the weighted means in the formulas shown. The statistical behavior here is not well-understood, since the multiple comparison tests were designed for the situation of unweighted means.

Pairwise Comparisons

The simplest approach to multiple comparisons is to do a t-test on every pair of means (the T option in the MEANS statement). For the ith and jth means you can reject the null hypothesis that the population means are equal if

$$|\bar{y}_i - \bar{y}_j| / s \sqrt{1/n_i + 1/n_j} \geq t(\alpha;v)$$

where $\bar{y}_i$ and $\bar{y}_j$ are the means, n_i and n_j are the number of observations in the two cells, s is the root mean square error based on v degrees of freedom, α is the significance level, and $t(\alpha;v)$ is the two-tailed critical value from a Student's t distribution. If the cell sizes are all equal to, say, n, the above formula can be rearranged to give

$$|\bar{y}_i - \bar{y}_j| \geq t(\alpha;v)\, s \sqrt{2/n}$$

the value of the right-hand side being Fisher's least significant difference (LSD).

There is a problem with repeated t-tests, however. Suppose there are ten means and each t-test is performed at the 0.05 level. There are $10(10-1)/2=45$ pairs of means to compare, each with a 0.05 probability of a type 1 error (a false rejection of the null hypothesis). The chance of making at least one type 1 error is much higher than 0.05. It is difficult to calculate the exact probability, but you can derive a pessimistic approximation by assuming the comparisons are independent, giving an upper bound to the probability of making at least one type 1 error (the experimentwise error rate) of

$$1 - (1 - 0.05)^{45} = 0.90 \quad .$$

The actual probability is somewhat less than 0.90, but as the number of means increases, the chance of making at least one type 1 error approaches 1.

If you decide to control the individual type 1 error rates for each comparison, you are controlling the comparisonwise error rate. On the other hand, if you want to control the overall type 1 error rate for all the comparisons, you are controlling the experimentwise error rate. It is up to you to decide whether to control the comparisonwise error rate or the experimentwise error rate, but there are many situations in which the experimentwise error rate should be held to a small value. Statistical methods for making two or more inferences while controlling the probability of making at least one type 1 error are called *simultaneous inference methods* (Miller 1981), although Einot and Gabriel (1975) use the term *simultaneous test procedure* in a much more restrictive sense.

It has been suggested that the experimentwise error rate can be held to the α level by performing the overall *ANOVA F* test at the α level and making further comparisons only if the *F* test is significant, as in Fisher's protected LSD. This assertion is false if there are more than three means (Einot and Gabriel 1975). Consider again the situation with ten means. Suppose that one population mean differs from the others by a sufficiently large amount that the power (probability of correctly rejecting the null hypothesis) of the *F* test is near 1 but that all the other population means are equal to each other. There will be $9(9-1)/2=36$ t-tests of true null hypotheses, with an upper limit of 0.84 on the probability of at least one type 1 error. Thus, you must distinguish between the experimentwise error rate under the complete null hypothesis, in which all population means are equal, and the experimentwise error rate under a partial null hypothesis, in which some means are equal but others differ. The following abbreviations are used in the discussion below:

CER   comparisonwise error rate

EERC   experimentwise error rate under the complete null hypothesis

EERP   experimentwise error rate under a partial null hypothesis

MEER   maximum experimentwise error rate under any complete or partial null hypothesis.

A preliminary F test controls the EERC but not the EERP or the MEER.

The MEER can be controlled at the α level by setting the CER to a sufficiently small value. The Bonferroni inequality (Miller 1981) has been widely used for this purpose. If

$$CER = \alpha/c$$

where c is the total number of comparisons, then the MEER is less than α. Bonferroni t-tests (the BON option) with MEER $<\alpha$ declare two means to be significantly different if

$$|\bar{y}_i - \bar{y}_j| \,/\, s\sqrt{1/n_i + 1/n_j} \geq t(\varepsilon;v)$$

where $\varepsilon = \alpha/(k(k-1)/2)$ for comparison of k means. If the cell sizes are equal, the test simplifies to

$$|\bar{y}_i - \bar{y}_j| \geq t(\varepsilon;v)\, s\sqrt{2/n} \ .$$

Sidak (1967) has provided a tighter bound, showing that

$$CER = 1 - (1 - \alpha)^{1/c}$$

also ensures MEER $\leq \alpha$ for any set of c comparisons. A Sidak t-test (Games 1977), provided by the SIDAK option, is thus given by

$$|\bar{y}_i - \bar{y}_j| \,/\, s\sqrt{1/n_i + 1/n_j} \geq t(\varepsilon;v)$$

where $\varepsilon = 1-(1-\alpha)^{1/(k(k-1)/2)}$ for comparison of k means. If the sample sizes are equal, the test simplifies to

$$|\bar{y}_i - \bar{y}_j| \geq t(\varepsilon;v)\, s\sqrt{2/n} \ .$$

You can use the Bonferroni additive inequality and the Sidak multiplicative inequality to control the MEER for any set of contrasts or other hypothesis tests, not just pairwise comparisons. The Bonferroni inequality can provide simultaneous inferences in any statistical application requiring tests of more than one hypothesis. Other methods discussed below for pairwise comparisons can also be adapted for general contrasts (Miller 1981).

Scheffe (1953, 1959) proposed another method to control the MEER for any set of contrasts or other linear hypotheses in the analysis of linear models, including pairwise comparisons, obtained with the SCHEFFE option. Two means are declared significantly different if

$$|\bar{y}_i - \bar{y}_j| / s \sqrt{1/n_i + </n_j} \geq \sqrt{(k-1)F(\alpha;k-1,v)}$$

or, for equal cell sizes,

$$|\bar{y}_i - \bar{y}_j| \geq s \sqrt{(k-1)F(\alpha;k-1,v)(2/n)}$$

where $F(\alpha;k-1,v)$ is the α-level critical value of an F distribution with $k-1$ numerator degrees of freedom and v denominator degrees of freedom.

Scheffe's test is compatible with the overall *ANOVA F* test in that Scheffe's method never declares a contrast significant if the overall F test is nonsignificant. Most other multiple comparison methods can find significant contrasts when the overall F is nonsignificant and therefore suffer a loss of power when used with a preliminary F test.

Scheffe's method may be more powerful than the Bonferroni or Sidak methods if the number of comparisons is large relative to the number of means. For pairwise comparisons, Sidak t-tests are generally more powerful.

Tukey (1952, 1953) proposed a test designed specifically for pairwise comparisons based on the studentized range, sometimes called the "honestly significant difference test," that controls the MEER when the sample sizes are equal. Tukey (1953) and Kramer (1956) independently proposed a modification for unequal cell sizes. The Tukey or Tukey-Kramer method is provided by the TUKEY option. This method has fared extremely well in Monte Carlo studies (Dunnett 1980). In addition, Hayter (1984) gives a proof that the Tukey-Kramer procedure controls the MEER. The Tukey-Kramer method is more powerful than the Bonferroni, Sidak, or Scheffe methods for pairwise comparisons. Two means are considered significantly different by the Tukey-Kramer criterion if

$$|\bar{y}_i - \bar{y}_j| / s \sqrt{(1/n_i + 1/n_j)/2} \geq q(\alpha;k,v)$$

where $q(\alpha;k,v)$ is the α-level critical value of a studentized range distribution of k independent normal random variables with v degrees of freedom. For equal cell sizes, Tukey's method rejects the null hypothesis of equal population means if

$$|\bar{y}_i - \bar{y}_j| \geq q(\alpha;k,v) s / \sqrt{n} \quad .$$

Hochberg (1974) devised a method (the GT2 or SMM option) similar to Tukey's, but it uses the studentized maximum modulus instead of the studentized range and employs Sidak's (1967) uncorrelated-t inequality. It was proved to hold the MEER at a level not exceeding α with unequal sample sizes. It is generally less powerful than the Tukey-Kramer method and always less powerful than Tukey's test for equal cell sizes. Two means are declared significantly different if

$$|\bar{y}_i - \bar{y}_j| / s \sqrt{1/n_i + 1/n_j} \geq m(\alpha;c,v)$$

where $m(\alpha;c,v)$ is the α-level critical value of the studentized maximum modulus distribution of c independent normal random variables with v degrees of freedom and $c=k(k-1)/2$. For equal cell sizes, the test simplifies to

$$|\bar{y}_i - \bar{y}_j| \geq m(\alpha;c,v)\, s\, \sqrt{2/n} \quad .$$

Gabriel (1978) proposed another method (the GABRIEL option) based on the studentized maximum modulus for unequal cell sizes that rejects if

$$|\bar{y}_i - \bar{y}_j|\, /s\!\left(1/\sqrt{2n_i} + 1/\sqrt{2n_j}\right) \geq m(\alpha;k,v) \quad .$$

For equal cell sizes, Gabriel's test is equivalent to Hochberg's GT2 method. For unequal cell sizes, Gabriel's method is more powerful than GT2 but may become liberal with highly disparate cell sizes (see also Dunnett 1980). Gabriel's test is the only method for unequal sample sizes that lends itself to a convenient graphical representation. Assuming $\bar{y}_i > \bar{y}_j$, the above inequality can be rewritten as

$$\bar{y}_i - m(\alpha;k,v)\, s/\sqrt{2n_i} \geq \bar{y}_j + m(\alpha;k,v)\, s/\sqrt{2n_j} \quad .$$

The expression on the left does not depend on j, nor does the expression on the right depend on i. Hence, you can form what Gabriel calls an (l,u)-interval around each sample mean and declare two means to be significantly different if their (l,u)-intervals do not overlap.

Comparing All Treatments to a Control

One special case of means comparison is that in which the only comparisons that need to be tested are between a set of new treatments and a single control. In this case, you can achieve better power by using a method that is restricted to test only comparisons to the single control mean. Dunnett (1955) proposed a test for this situation which declares a mean significantly different from the control if

$$|\bar{y}_i - \bar{y}_0| \geq d(\alpha;k,v,\rho)\, s\, \sqrt{1/n_i + 1/n_0}$$

where $\bar{y}_0$ is the control mean, and $d(\alpha;k,v,\rho)$ is the critical value of the "many-one t statistic" (Miller 1981; Krishnaiah and Armitage 1966) for k means to be compared to a control, with v degrees of freedom and correlation ρ. The correlation term arises because each of the treatment means is being compared to the same control. When the number of observations for the control is different from that of the treatments, but all the treatments have the same number of observations, then the correlation between the comparisons is $n_t/(n_0+n_t)$, where n_0 is the sample size of the control, and n_t is the sample size of each of the treatments. For example, in the case where all sample sizes (both control and treatment) are equal, the correlation between any two comparisons of treatments to control is $1/2$. If the treatments do not have the same number of observations, then the correlation is calculated using the harmonic mean of the sample sizes of the treatments as their "common" sample size. Dunnett's test holds the MEER to a level not exceeding the stated α.

Multiple-Stage Tests

You can use all of the methods discussed so far to obtain simultaneous confidence intervals (Miller 1981). By sacrificing the facility for simultaneous estimation, it is possible to obtain simultaneous tests with greater power using multiple-stage tests (MSTs). MSTs come in both step-up and step-down varieties (Welsch 1977). The step-down methods, which have been more widely used, are available in SAS/STAT software.

Step-down MSTs first test the homogeneity of all of the means at a level γ_k. If the test results in a rejection, then each subset of $k-1$ means is tested at level γ_{k-1}; otherwise, the procedure stops. In general, if the hypothesis of homogeneity of a set of p means is rejected at the γ_p level, then each subset of $p-1$ means is tested at the γ_{p-1} level; otherwise, the set of p means is considered not to differ significantly and none of its subsets are tested. The many varieties of MSTs that have been proposed differ in the levels γ_p and the statistics on which the subset tests are based. Clearly, the EERC of a step-down MST is not greater than γ_k, and the CER is not greater than γ_2, but the MEER is a complicated function of γ_p, $p=2, \ldots, k$.

MSTs can be used with unequal cell sizes, but the resulting operating characteristics are undesirable, so only the balanced case is considered here. With equal sample sizes, the means can be arranged in ascending or descending order, and only contiguous subsets need be tested. It is common practice to report the results of an MST by writing the means in such an order and drawing lines parallel to the list of means spanning the homogeneous subsets. This form of presentation is also convenient for pairwise comparisons with equal cell sizes.

The best known MSTs are the Duncan (the DUNCAN option) and Student-Newman-Keuls (the SNK option) methods (Miller 1981). Both use the studentized range statistic and, hence, are called *multiple range tests*. Duncan's method is often called the "new" multiple range test despite the fact that it is one of the oldest MSTs in current use. The Duncan and SNK methods differ in the γ_p values used. For Duncan's method they are

$$\gamma_p = 1 - (1 - \alpha)^{p-1}$$

whereas the SNK method uses

$$\gamma_p = \alpha \quad .$$

Duncan's method controls the CER at the α level. Its operating characteristics appear similar to those of Fisher's unprotected LSD or repeated t-tests at level α (Petrinovich and Hardyck 1969). Since repeated t-tests are easier to compute, easier to explain, and applicable to unequal sample sizes, Duncan's method is not recommended. Several published studies (for example, Carmer and Swanson 1973) have claimed that Duncan's method is superior to Tukey's because of greater power without considering that the greater power of Duncan's method is due to its higher type 1 error rate (Einot and Gabriel 1975).

The SNK method holds the EERC to the αlevel but does not control the EERP (Einot and Gabriel 1975). Consider ten population means that occur in five pairs such that means within a pair are equal, but there are large differences between pairs. Making the usual sampling assumptions and also assuming that the sample sizes are very large, all subset homogeneity hypotheses for three or more means are rejected. The SNK method then comes down to five independent tests, one for each pair, each at the α level. Letting α be 0.05, the probability of at least one false rejection is

$$1 - (1 - 0.05)^5 = 0.23 \quad .$$

As the number of means increases, the MEER approaches 1. Therefore, the SNK method cannot be recommended.

A variety of MSTs that control the MEER have been proposed, but these methods are not as well known as those of Duncan and SNK. An approach developed by Ryan (1959, 1960), Einot and Gabriel (1975), and Welsch (1977) sets

$$\gamma_p = 1 - (1 - \alpha)^{p/k} \quad \text{for } p < k - 1$$
$$= \alpha \quad\quad\quad\quad \text{for } p \geq k - 1 \quad.$$

You can use either range or F statistics, leading to what we call the REGWQ and REGWF methods, respectively, after the authors' initials. Assuming the sample means have been arranged in descending order from $\bar{y}_1$ through $\bar{y}_k$, the homogeneity of means $\bar{y}_i , \ldots , \bar{y}_j , i<j$, is rejected by REGWQ if

$$\bar{y}_i - \bar{y}_j \geq q(\gamma_p;p,\nu)s / \sqrt{n}$$

or by REGWF if

$$n(\Sigma \bar{y}_u^2 - (\Sigma \bar{y}_u)^2 / k) / (p - 1)s^2 \geq F(\gamma_p;p - 1,\nu)$$

where $p=j-i+1$ and the summations are over $u = i, \ldots , j$ (Einot and Gabriel 1975).

REGWQ and REGWF appear to be the most powerful step-down MSTs in the current literature (for example, Ramsey 1978). REGWF has the advantage of being compatible with the overall *ANOVA F* test in that REGWF rejects the complete null hypothesis if and only if the overall F test does so since the latter is identical to the first step in REGWF. Use of a preliminary F test decreases the power of all the other multiple comparison methods discussed above except for Scheffe's test.

Other multiple comparison methods proposed by Peritz (Marcus, Peritz, and Gabriel 1976; Begun and Gabriel 1981) and Welsch (1977) are still more powerful than the REGW procedures. These methods have not yet been implemented in SAS/STAT software.

Bayesian Approach

Waller and Duncan (1969) and Duncan (1975) take an approach to multiple comparisons that differs from all the methods discussed above in minimizing the Bayes risk under additive loss rather than controlling type 1 error rates. For each pair of population means μ_i and μ_j, null (H_0^{ij}) and alternative (H_a^{ij}) hypotheses are defined:

$$H_0^{ij}: \mu_i - \mu_j \leq 0$$

$$H_a^{ij}: \mu_i - \mu_j > 0 \quad.$$

For any i,j pair, let d_0 indicate a decision in favor of H_0^{ij} and d_a indicate a decision in favor of H_a^{ij}, and let $\delta = \mu_i - \mu_j$. The loss function for the decision on the i,j pair is

$$L(d_0 \mid \delta) = 0 \quad \text{if } \delta \leq 0$$
$$ = \delta \quad \text{if } \delta > 0$$

$$L(d_a \mid \delta) = -k\delta \quad \text{if } \delta \leq 0$$
$$ = 0 \qquad \text{if } \delta > 0$$

where k represents a constant that you specify rather than the number of means. The loss for the joint decision involving all pairs of means is the sum of the losses for each individual decision. The population means are assumed to have a normal prior distribution with unknown variance, the logarithm of the variance of the means having a uniform prior distribution. For the i,j pair, the null hypothesis is rejected if

$$\bar{y}_i - \bar{y}_j \geq t_B s \sqrt{2/n}$$

where t_B is the Bayesian t value (Waller and Kemp 1975) depending on k, the F statistic for the one-way ANOVA, and the degrees of freedom for F. The value of t_B is a decreasing function of F, so the Waller-Duncan test becomes more liberal as F increases.

Recommendations

In summary, if you want to control the CER, the recommended methods are repeated t-tests or Fisher's unprotected LSD (the T or LSD option). If you want to control the MEER, do not need confidence intervals, and have equal cell sizes, then the REGWF and REGWQ methods are recommended. If you want to control the MEER and need confidence intervals or have unequal cell sizes, then the Tukey or Tukey-Kramer methods (the TUKEY option) are recommended. If you agree with the Bayesian approach and Waller and Duncan's assumptions, you should use the Waller-Duncan test (the WALLER option).

Least-Squares Means

Simply put, least-squares means, or *population marginal means*, are the expected value of class or subclass means that you would expect for a balanced design involving the class variable with all covariates at their mean value. This informal concept is explained further in Searle, Speed, and Milliken (1980).

To construct a least-squares mean (LSM) for a given level of a given effect, construct a set of Xs according to the following rules and use them in the linear model with the parameter estimates to yield the value of the LSM:

1. Hold all covariates (continuous variables) to their mean value.
2. Consider effects contained by the given effect. Give the Xs for levels associated with the given level a value of 1. Make the other Xs equal to 0. (See Chapter 9, "The Four Types of Estimable Functions," for a definition of containing.)
3. Consider the given effect. Make the X associated with the given level equal to 1. Set the Xs for the other levels to 0.
4. Consider the effects that contain the given effect. If these effects are not nested within the given effect, then for the columns associated with the given level, use $1/k$, where k is the number of such columns. If these effects are nested within the given effect, then for the columns

associated with the given level, use $1/k_1k_2$, where k_1 is the number of nested levels within this combination of nested effects, and k_2 is the number of such combinations. For the other columns use 0.

5. Consider the other effects not yet considered. If there are no nested factors, then use $1/j$, where j is the number of levels in the effect. If there are nested factors, use $1/j_1j_2$, where j_1 is the number of nested levels within a given combination of nested effects, and j_2 is the number of such combinations.

The consequence of these rules is that the sum of the Xs within any classification effect is 1. This set of Xs forms a linear combination of the parameters that is checked for estimability before it is evaluated.

For example, consider the following model:

```
proc glm;
    class a b c;
    model y=a b a*b c x;
    lsmeans a b a*b c;
run;
```

Assume A has 3 levels, B has 2, and C has 2, and assume that every combination of levels of A and B exists in the data. Assume also that X is a continuous variable with an average of 12.5. Then the least-squares means are computed by the following linear combinations of the parameter estimates:

	μ	A 1	A 2	A 3	B 1	B 2	A*B 11	A*B 21	A*B 31	A*B 12	A*B 22	A*B 32	C 1	C 2	X
LSM( )	1	1/3	1/3	1/3	1/2	1/2	1/6	1/6	1/6	1/6	1/6	1/6	1/2	1/2	12.5
LSM(A1)	1	1	0	0	1/2	1/2	1/2	0	0	1/2	0	0	1/2	1/2	12.5
LSM(A2)	1	0	1	0	1/2	1/2	0	1/2	0	0	1/2	0	1/2	1/2	12.5
LSM(A3)	1	0	0	1	1/2	1/2	0	0	1/2	0	0	1/2	1/2	1/2	12.5
LSM(B1)	1	1/3	1/3	1/3	1	0	1/3	1/3	1/3	0	0	0	1/2	1/2	12.5
LSM(B2)	1	1/3	1/3	1/3	0	1	0	0	0	1/3	1/3	1/3	1/2	1/2	12.5
LSM(AB11)	1	1	0	0	1	0	1	0	0	0	0	0	1/2	1/2	12.5
LSM(AB12)	1	1	0	0	0	1	0	0	0	1	0	0	1/2	1/2	12.5
LSM(AB21)	1	0	1	0	1	0	0	1	0	0	0	0	1/2	1/2	12.5
LSM(AB22)	1	0	1	0	0	1	0	0	0	0	1	0	1/2	1/2	12.5
LSM(AB31)	1	0	0	1	1	0	0	0	1	0	0	0	1/2	1/2	12.5
LSM(AB32)	1	0	0	1	0	1	0	0	0	0	0	1	1/2	1/2	12.5
LSM(C1)	1	1/3	1/3	1/3	1/2	1/2	1/6	1/6	1/6	1/6	1/6	1/6	1	0	12.5
LSM(C2)	1	1/3	1/3	1/3	1/2	1/2	1/6	1/6	1/6	1/6	1/6	1/6	0	1	12.5

Multivariate Analysis of Variance

If you fit several dependent variables to the same effects, you may want to make tests jointly involving parameters of several dependent variables. Suppose you have p dependent variables, k parameters for each dependent variable, and n observations. The models can be collected into one equation:

$$\mathbf{Y} = \mathbf{X}\boldsymbol{\beta} + \boldsymbol{\varepsilon}$$

where $\mathbf{Y}$ is $n \times p$, $\mathbf{X}$ is $n \times k$, $\boldsymbol{\beta}$ is $k \times p$, and $\boldsymbol{\varepsilon}$ is $n \times p$. Each of the p models can be estimated and tested separately. However, you may also want to consider the joint distribution, and test the p models simultaneously.

For multivariate tests, you need to make some assumptions about the errors. With p dependent variables, there are $n \times p$ errors that are independent across observations but not across dependent variables. Assume

$$\text{vec}(\varepsilon) \sim N(\mathbf{0}, \mathbf{I}_n \otimes \Sigma)$$

where $\text{vec}(\varepsilon)$ strings ε out by rows , $\otimes$ denotes Kronecker product multiplication, and Σ is $p \times p$. Σ can be estimated by

$$\mathbf{S} = (\mathbf{e}'\mathbf{e}) / (n - r) = (\mathbf{Y} - \mathbf{Xb})'(\mathbf{Y} - \mathbf{Xb}) / (n - r)$$

where $\mathbf{b} = (\mathbf{X}'\mathbf{X})^-\mathbf{X}'\mathbf{Y}$, r is the rank of the $\mathbf{X}$ matrix, and $\mathbf{e}$ is the matrix of residuals.

If $\mathbf{S}$ is scaled to unit diagonals, the values in $\mathbf{S}$ are called *partial correlations of the Ys adjusting for the Xs*. This matrix can be printed by GLM if PRINTE is specified as a MANOVA option.

The multivariate general linear hypothesis is written:

$$\mathbf{L\beta M} = 0 \quad .$$

You can form hypotheses for linear combinations across columns, as well as across rows of $\boldsymbol{\beta}$.

The MANOVA statement of the GLM procedure tests special cases where $\mathbf{L}$ is for Type I, Type II, Type III, or Type IV tests, and $\mathbf{M}$ is the $p \times p$ identity matrix. These tests are joint tests that the Type I, Type II, Type III, or Type IV hypothesis holds for all dependent variables in the model and are often sufficient to test all hypotheses of interest.

When these special cases are not appropriate, you can specify your own $\mathbf{L}$ and $\mathbf{M}$ matrices by using the CONTRAST statement (which is used by MANOVA when the CONTRAST statement appears before the MANOVA statement) and the M= specification of the MANOVA statement, respectively. Another alternative is to use a REPEATED statement, which automatically generates a variety of $\mathbf{M}$ matrices useful in repeated measures analysis of variance. See the section on the REPEATED statement and **Repeated Measures Analysis of Variance** later in this chapter for more information.

One useful way to think of a MANOVA analysis with an $\mathbf{M}$ matrix other than the identity is as an analysis of a set of transformed variables defined by the columns of the $\mathbf{M}$ matrix. You should note, however, that GLM always prints the $\mathbf{M}$ matrix so that the transformed variables are defined by the rows, not the columns, of the $\mathbf{M}$ matrix on the printout.

All multivariate tests carried out by GLM first construct the matrices $\mathbf{H}$ and $\mathbf{E}$ that correspond to the numerator and denominator of a univariate F test.

$$\mathbf{H} = \mathbf{M}'(\mathbf{Lb})'(\mathbf{L}(\mathbf{X}'\mathbf{X})^-\mathbf{L}')^{-1}(\mathbf{Lb})\mathbf{M} \qquad \mathbf{E} = \mathbf{M}'(\mathbf{Y}'\mathbf{Y} - \mathbf{b}'(\mathbf{X}'\mathbf{X})\mathbf{b})\mathbf{M} \quad .$$

The diagonal elements of $\mathbf{H}$ and $\mathbf{E}$ correspond to the hypothesis and error SS for univariate tests. When the $\mathbf{M}$ matrix is the identity matrix (the default), these tests are for the original dependent variables on the left-hand side of the MODEL statement. When an $\mathbf{M}$ matrix other than the identity is specified, the tests are for transformed variables defined by the columns of the $\mathbf{M}$ matrix. (The $\mathbf{M}$ matrix is always printed when the M= option is specified in the MANOVA statement.) These tests can be studied by requesting the SUMMARY option, which produces univariate analyses for each original or transformed variable.

Four test statistics, all functions of the eigenvalues of $\mathbf{E}^{-1}\mathbf{H}$ (or $(\mathbf{E}+\mathbf{H})^{-1}\mathbf{H}$), are constructed:

- Wilks' lambda=det($\mathbf{E}$)/det($\mathbf{H}+\mathbf{E}$)
- Pillai's trace=trace($\mathbf{H}(\mathbf{H}+\mathbf{E})^{-1}$)
- Hotelling-Lawley trace=trace($\mathbf{E}^{-1}\mathbf{H}$)
- Roy's maximum root=λ, largest eigenvalue of $\mathbf{E}^{-1}\mathbf{H}$.

All four are reported with F approximations. For further details on these four statistics, see **Multivariate Tests** in Chapter 1, "Introduction to Regression Procedures."

Repeated Measures Analysis of Variance

When several measurements are taken on the same experimental unit (person, plant, machine, and so on), the measurements tend to be correlated with each other. When the measurements represent qualitatively different things, such as weight, length, and width, this correlation is taken into account by use of multivariate methods, such as multivariate analysis of variance. When the measurements can be thought of as responses to levels of an experimental factor of interest, such as time, treatment, or dose, the correlation can be taken into account by performing a repeated measures analysis of variance.

PROC GLM provides both univariate and multivariate tests for repeated measures for one response. For an overall reference on univariate repeated measures, see Winer (1971). The multivariate approach is covered in Cole and Grizzle (1966). For a discussion of the relative merits of the two approaches, see LaTour and Miniard (1983).

Organization of Data for Repeated Measures Analysis

In order to deal efficiently with the correlation of repeated measures, GLM uses the multivariate method of specifying the model, even if only a univariate analysis is desired. In some cases, data may already be entered in the univariate mode, that is, each repeated measure listed as a separate observation along with a variable that represents the experimental unit (subject) on which measurement was taken. Consider the following data set OLD:

SUBJ	GROUP	TIME	Y
1	1	1	15
1	1	2	19
1	1	3	25
2	1	1	21
2	1	2	18
2	1	3	17
1	2	1	14
1	2	2	12
1	2	3	16
2	2	1	11
2	2	2	20
2	2	3	21
.			
.			
.			
10	3	1	14
10	3	2	18
10	3	3	16

Notice how there are three observations for each subject, corresponding to measurements taken at time 1, 2, and 3. These data could be analyzed using the following statements:

```
proc glm data=old;
   classes group subj time;
   model y=group subj(group) time group*time;
   test h=group e=subj(group);
run;
```

However, a more complete and efficient repeated measures analysis could be performed using data set NEW:

```
GROUP        Y1      Y2      Y3
   1         15      19      25
   1         21      18      17
   2         14      12      16
   2         11      20      21
                      .
                      .
                      .
   3         14      18      16
```

In NEW, the three measurements for a subject are all in one observation. For example, 15, 19, and 25 are the measurements for subject 1 for time 1, 2, and 3. For these data, the statements for a repeated measures analysis (assuming default options) would be

```
proc glm data=new;
   class group;
   model y1-y3=group / nouni;
   repeated time;
run;
```

To convert the univariate form of repeated measures data to the multivariate form, you can use a program like the following:

```
proc sort data=old;
   by group subj;
run;

data new(keep=y1-y3 group);
   array yy(3)  y1-y3;
   do time=1 to 3;
      set old;
      by group subj;
      yy(time)=y;
      if last.subj then return;
   end;
run;
```

Alternatively, you could use PROC TRANSPOSE to achieve the same results with a program like this one:

```
proc sort data=old;
   by group subj;
run;
```

```
proc transpose out=new(rename=(_1=y1 _2=y2 _3=y3));
  by group subj;
  id time;
run;
```

See discussions in the *SAS Language: Reference, Version 6, First Edition* and *SAS Language and Procedures: Usage, Version 6, First Edition* for more information on rearrangement of data sets.

Hypothesis Testing in Repeated Measures Analysis

In repeated measures analysis of variance, the effects of interest are

- between-subject effects (such as GROUP in the previous example)
- within-subject effects (such as TIME in the previous example)
- interactions between the two types of effects (such as GROUP*TIME in the previous example).

Repeated measures analyses are distinguished from other multivariate analyses because of interest in testing hypotheses about the within-subject effects and the within-subject-by-between-subject interactions.

For tests that involve only between-subjects effects, both the multivariate and univariate approaches give rise to the same tests. These tests are provided for all effects in the MODEL statement, as well as for any CONTRASTs specified. The *ANOVA* table for these tests is labeled "Tests of Hypotheses for Between Subjects Effects" on the GLM printout. These tests are constructed by first adding together the dependent variables in the model. Then an analysis of variance is performed on the sum divided by the square root of the number of dependent variables. For example, the statements

```
model y1-y3=group;
repeated time;
```

give a one-way analysis of variance using $Y1+Y2+Y3/\sqrt{3}$ as the dependent variable for performing tests of hypothesis on the between-subject effect GROUP. Tests for between-subject effects are tests of the hypothesis $\mathbf{L\beta M} = 0$, where $\mathbf{M}$ is simply a vector of 1s.

For within-subject effects and for within-subject-by-between-subject interaction effects, the univariate and multivariate approaches yield different tests. These tests are provided for the within-subject effects, and the interactions between these effects and the other effects in the MODEL statement, as well as for any CONTRASTs specified. The univariate tests are labeled "Univariate Tests of Hypotheses for Within Subject Effects" on the GLM printout. Results for multivariate tests are labeled "Repeated Measures Analysis of Variance" on the GLM printout.

The multivariate tests provided for within-subjects effects and interactions involving these effects are Wilks' Lambda, Pillai's Trace, Hotelling-Lawley Trace, and Roy's maximum root. For further details on these four statistics, see **Multivariate Tests** in Chapter 1, "Introduction to Regression Procedures." As an example, the statements

```
model y1-y3=group;
repeated time;
```

produce multivariate tests for the within-subject effect TIME and the interaction TIME*GROUP.

The multivariate tests for within-subject effects are produced by testing the hypothesis $\mathbf{L\beta M} = 0$, where the $\mathbf{L}$ matrix is the usual matrix corresponding to Type I, Type II, Type III, or Type IV hypotheses tests, and the $\mathbf{M}$ matrix is one of several matrices that you can specify in the REPEATED statement. The only assumption required for valid tests is that the dependent variables in the model have a multivariate normal distribution with a common covariance matrix across the between-subject effects.

The univariate tests for within-subject effects and interactions involving these effects require some assumptions for the probabilities provided by the ordinary *F* tests to be correct. Specifically, these tests require certain patterns of covariance matrices, known as Type H covariances (Huynh and Feldt 1970). Data with these patterns in the covariance matrices are said to satisfy the Huynh-Feldt condition. You can test this assumption (and the Huynh-Feldt condition) by applying a sphericity test (Anderson 1958) to any set of variables defined by an orthogonal contrast transformation. Such a set of variables is known as a set of orthogonal components. When you use the PRINTE option of the REPEATED statement, this sphericity test is applied both to the transformed variables defined by the REPEATED statement and to a set of orthogonal components if the specified transformation was not orthogonal. It is the test applied to the orthogonal components that is important in determining if your data have Type H covariance structure. When there are only two levels of the within-subject effect, there is only one transformed variable, and a sphericity test cannot be applied, nor is one needed. The sphericity test is labeled "Test for Sphericity" on the GLM printout.

If your data satisfy the assumptions above, use the usual *F* tests to test univariate hypotheses for the within-subject effects and associated interactions.

If your data do not satisfy the assumption of Type H covariance, an adjustment to numerator and denominator degrees of freedom can be used. Two such adjustments, based on a degrees of freedom adjustment factor known as ε (epsilon) (Box 1954), are provided in PROC GLM. Both adjustments estimate ε and then multiply the numerator and denominator degrees of freedom by this estimate before determining significance levels for the *F* tests. Significance levels associated with the adjusted tests are labeled "Adj Pr > F" on the GLM printout. The first adjustment, initially proposed for use in data analysis by Greenhouse and Geisser (1959), is labeled "Greenhouse-Geisser Epsilon" and represents the maximum-likelihood estimate of Box's ε factor. Significance levels associated with adjusted *F* tests are labeled "G-G" on the printout. Huynh and Feldt (1976) have shown that the G-G estimate tends to be biased downward (that is, too conservative), especially for small samples, and have proposed an alternative estimator that is constructed using unbiased estimators of the numerator and denominator of Box's ε. Huynh and Feldt's estimator is labeled "Huynh-Feldt Epsilon" on the GLM printout, and the significance levels associated with adjusted *F* tests are labeled "H-F." Although ε must be in the range of 0 to 1, the H-F estimator can be outside this range. When the H-F estimator is greater than 1, a value of 1 is used in all calculations for probabilities, and the H-F probabilities are not adjusted. In summary, if your data do not meet the assumptions, use adjusted *F* tests. However, in cases where the sphericity test is dramatically rejected ($p \leq 0.0001$), all these univariate tests should be interpreted cautiously.

The univariate sums of squares for hypotheses involving within-subject effects can be easily calculated from the **H** and **E** matrices corresponding to the multivariate tests described in **Multivariate Analysis of Variance** earlier in this chapter. If the **M** matrix is orthogonal, the univariate sums of squares is calculated as the trace (sum of diagonal elements) of the appropriate **H** matrix; if it is not orthogonal, GLM calculates the trace of the **H** matrix that would result from an orthogonal **M** matrix transformation. The appropriate error term for the univariate *F* tests is constructed in a similar way from the error SSCP matrix and is labeled Error(*factorname*), where *factorname* indicates the **M** matrix that was used in the transformation.

When the design specifies more than one repeated measures factor, GLM computes the **M** matrix for a given effect as the direct (Kronecker) product of the **M** matrices defined by the REPEATED statement if the factor is involved in the effect or a vector of 1s if the factor is not involved. The test for the main effect of a repeated-measures factor is constructed using an **L** matrix that corresponds to a test that the mean of the observation is zero. Thus, the main effect test for repeated measures is a test that the means of the variables defined by the **M** matrix are all equal to zero, while interactions involving repeated-measures effects are tests that the between-subjects factors involved in the interaction have no effect on the means of the transformed variables defined by the **M** matrix. In addition, you can specify other **L** matrices to test hypotheses of interest by using the CONTRAST statement, which is used by REPEATED whenever it is present. To see which combinations of the original variables the transformed variables represent, you can specify the PRINTM option in the REPEATED statement. This option prints **M'**, which is labeled as "M" in the GLM printout. The tests produced are the same for any choice of transformation (**M**) matrix specified in the REPEATED statement; however, depending on the nature of the repeated measurements being studied, a particular choice of transformation matrix, coupled with the CANONICAL or SUMMARY options, can provide additional insight into the data being studied.

Transformations Used in Repeated Measures Analysis of Variance

As mentioned in the specifications of the REPEATED statement, several different **M** matrices can be generated automatically, based on the transformation that you specify in the REPEATED statement. Remember that both the univariate and multivariate tests that GLM performs are unaffected by the choice of transformation; the choice of transformation is only important when you are trying to study the nature of a repeated measures effect, particularly with the CANONICAL and SUMMARY options. If one of these matrices does not meet your needs for a particular analysis, you may want to use the M= option of the MANOVA statement to perform the tests of interest.

The following sections describe the transformations available in the REPEATED statement, provide an example of the **M** matrix that is produced, and give guidelines for the use of the transformation. As in the GLM printout, the printed matrix is labeled "M". This is the **M'** matrix.

CONTRAST transformation   This is the default used by the REPEATED statement. It is useful when one level of the repeated measures effect can be thought of as a control level against which the others are compared. For example, if five drugs are administered to each of several animals and the first drug is a control or placebo, the statements

```
proc glm;
   model d1-d5= / nouni;
   repeated drug 5 contrast(1) / summary printm;
run;
```

produce the following **M** matrix:

$$\mathbf{L} = \begin{bmatrix} -1 & 1 & 0 & 0 & 0 \\ -1 & 0 & 1 & 0 & 0 \\ -1 & 0 & 0 & 1 & 0 \\ -1 & 0 & 0 & 0 & 1 \end{bmatrix}$$

When you examine the analysis of variance tables produced by the SUMMARY option, you can tell which of the drugs differed significantly from the placebo.

POLYNOMIAL transformation   This transformation is useful when the levels of the repeated measure represent quantitative values of a treatment, such as dose or time. If the levels are unequally spaced, *level values* can be specified in parentheses after the number of levels in the REPEATED statement. For example, if five levels of a drug corresponding to 1, 2, 5, 10 and 20 milligrams are administered to different treatment groups, represented by GROUP, the statements

```
proc glm;
   class group;
   model r1-r5=group / nouni;
   repeated dose 5 (1 2 5 10 20) polynomial / summary printm;
run;
```

produce the following **M** matrix:

$$\mathbf{M} = \begin{bmatrix} -0.4250 & -0.3606 & -0.1674 & 0.1545 & 0.7984 \\ 0.4349 & -0.2073 & -0.3252 & -0.7116 & 0.3946 \\ -0.4331 & 0.1366 & 0.7253 & -0.5108 & 0.0821 \\ 0.4926 & -0.7800 & 0.3743 & -0.0936 & 0.0066 \end{bmatrix}$$

The SUMMARY option in this example provides univariate *ANOVAs* for the variables defined by the rows of the above **M** matrix. In this case, they represent the linear, quadratic, cubic, and quartic trends for dose and are labeled DOSE.1, DOSE.2, DOSE.3, and DOSE.4, respectively.

HELMERT transformation   Since the HELMERT transformation compares a level of a repeated measure to the mean of subsequent levels, it is useful when interest lies in the point at which responses cease to change. For example, if four levels of a repeated measures factor represent responses to treatments administered over time to males and females, the statements

```
proc glm;
   class sex;
   model resp1-resp4=sex / nouni;
   repeated trtmnt 4 helmert / canon printm;
run;
```

produce the following **M** matrix:

$$M = \begin{bmatrix} 1 & -0.33333 & -0.33333 & -0.33333 \\ 0 & 1 & -0.50000 & -0.50000 \\ 0 & 0 & 1 & -1 \end{bmatrix}$$

To determine the point at which the treatment effect reaches a plateau, you can examine the canonical coefficients based on the **H** and **E** matrices corresponding to the main effect of TRTMNT and conclude that the plateau was reached when these coefficients became small.

MEAN transformation   This transformation can be useful in the same types of situations that the CONTRAST transformation is useful. For the statements in the CONTRAST section above, if you substitute

```
repeated drug 5 mean / printm;
```

for the REPEATED statement in that example, the following **M** matrix is produced:

$$M = \begin{bmatrix} 1 & -0.25 & -0.25 & -0.25 & -0.25 \\ -0.25 & 1 & -0.25 & -0.25 & -0.25 \\ -0.25 & -0.25 & 1 & -0.25 & -0.25 \\ -0.25 & -0.25 & -0.25 & 1 & -0.25 \end{bmatrix}$$

As with the CONTRAST transformation, if you want to omit a level other than the last, you can specify it in parentheses after the keyword MEAN in the REPEATED statement.

PROFILE transformation   When a repeated measure represents a series of factors administered over time, but a polynomial response is unreasonable, a profile transformation may prove useful. As an example, consider a training program in which four different methods are employed to teach students at several different schools. The repeated measure is the score on tests administered after each of the methods is completed. The statements

```
proc glm;
   class school;
   model t1-t4=school / nouni;
   repeated method 4 profile / summary nom printm;
run;
```

produce the following **M** matrix:

$$L = \begin{bmatrix} 1 & -1 & 0 & 0 \\ 0 & 1 & -1 & 0 \\ 0 & 0 & 1 & -1 \end{bmatrix}$$

To determine the point at which an improvement in test scores takes place, the analyses of variance for the transformed variables representing the differences between adjacent tests can be examined. These analyses are requested by the SUMMARY option in the REPEATED statement, and the variables are labeled METHOD.1, METHOD.2, and METHOD.3.

Expected Mean Squares for Random Effects

The RANDOM statement in GLM declares one or more effects in the model to be random rather than fixed. By default, GLM prints the coefficients of the expected mean squares for all terms in the model. In addition, when the TEST option in the RANDOM statement is specified, it determines what tests are appropriate, and provides F ratios and probabilities for these tests.

The expected mean squares are computed as follows. Consider the model

$$Y = X_0\beta_0 + X_1\beta_1 + \ldots + X_k\beta_k + \varepsilon$$

where β_0 represents the fixed effects, and $\beta_1, \beta_2, \ldots, \varepsilon$ represent the random effects. Random effects are assumed to be normally and independently distributed. For any L in the row space of

$$X = (X_0 \mid X_1 \mid X_2 \mid \ldots \mid X_k)$$

then

$$E(SS_L) = \beta_0'C_0'C_0\beta_0 + SSQ(C_1)\sigma_1^2 + SSQ(C_2)\sigma_2^2 + \ldots + SSQ(C_k)\sigma_k^2 + \text{rank}(L)\sigma_\varepsilon^2$$

where C is of the same dimensions as L and partitioned as the X matrix. In other words,

$$C = (C_0 \mid C_1 \mid \ldots \mid C_k) \quad .$$

Furthermore, $C=ML$, where M is the inverse of the lower triangular Cholesky decomposition matrix of $L(X'X)^-L'$. SSQ(A) is defined as tr($A'A$).

For the model in the MODEL statement below

```
model y=a b(a) c a*c;
random b(a);
```

with B(A) declared as random, the expected mean square of each effect is printed as

$$\text{Var(Error)} + \textit{constant}*\text{Var(B(A))} + Q(A,C,A*C) \quad .$$

If any fixed effects appear in the expected mean square of an effect, the letter Q followed by the list of fixed effects in the expected value is printed. The actual numeric values of the quadratic form (**Q** matrix) can be printed using the Q option.

To determine appropriate means squares for testing the effects in the model, the TEST option in the RANDOM statement performs the following:

1. First, it forms a matrix of coefficients of the expected mean squares of those effects which were declared to be random.
2. Next, for each effect in the model, it determines the combination of these expected mean squares which will produce an expectation that includes all the terms in the expected mean square of the effect of interest except the one corresponding to the effect of interest. For example, if the expected mean square of an effect A*B is

$$Var(Error) + 3*Var(A) + Var(A*B)$$

GLM determines the combination of other expected mean squares in the model that will have expectation

$$Var(Error) + 3*Var(A) .$$

3. If the above criterion is met by the expected mean square of a single effect in the model (as is often the case in balanced designs), the F test is formed directly. In this case, the mean square of the effect of interest is used as the numerator, the mean square of the single effect whose expected mean square satisfies the criterion is used as the denominator, and the degrees of freedom for the test are simply the usual model degrees of freedom.
4. When more than one mean square must be combined to achieve the appropriate expectation, an approximation is employed to determine the appropriate degrees of freedom (Satterthwaite 1946). When effects other than the effect of interest are listed after the Q in the printout, tests of hypotheses involving the effect of interest are not valid unless all other fixed effects involved in it are assumed to be zero. When tests such as these are performed by using the TEST option in the RANDOM statement, a note is printed reminding you that further assumptions are necessary for the validity of these tests. Remember that although the tests are not valid unless these assumptions are made, this does not provide a basis for these assumptions to be true. The particulars of a given experiment must be examined to determine if the assumption is reasonable.

See Goodnight and Speed (1978), Milliken and Johnson (1984, chap. 22 and chap. 23), and Hocking (1985) for further theoretical discussion.

Missing Values

For an analysis involving one dependent variable, GLM uses an observation if values are present for that dependent variable and all the variables used in independent effects.

For an analysis involving multiple dependent variables without the MANOVA or REPEATED statement, or without the MANOVA option in the PROC GLM statement, a missing value in one dependent variable does not eliminate the observation from the analysis of other nonmissing dependent variables. For an analysis with the MANOVA or REPEATED statement, or with the MANOVA option in the PROC GLM statement, GLM requires values for all dependent variables to be present for an observation before the observation can be used in the analysis.

During processing, GLM groups the dependent variables on their missing values across observations so that sums and crossproducts can be collected in the most efficient manner.

If your data have different patterns of missing values among the dependent variables, interactivity is disabled. This could occur when some of the variables in your data set have missing values and

- you do not use the MANOVA option in the PROC ANOVA statement
- you do not use a MANOVA or REPEATED statement before the first RUN statement.

Computational Resources

Memory

For large problems, most of the memory resources are required for holding the **X'X** matrix of the sums and crossproducts. The **Parameterization of GLM Models** section earlier in this chapter describes how columns of the **X** matrix are allocated for various types of effects. For each level that occurs in the data for a combination of class variables in a given effect, a row and column for **X'X** is needed.

An example illustrates the calculation. Suppose A has 20 levels, B has 4, and C has 3. Then consider the model

```
proc glm;
  class a b c;
    model y1 y2 y3=a b a*b c a*c b*c a*b*c x1 x2;
run;
```

The **X'X** matrix (bordered by **X'Y** and **Y'Y**) can have as many as 425 rows and columns:

1	for the intercept term
20	for A
4	for B
80	for A*B
3	for C
60	for A*C
12	for B*C
240	for A*B*C
2	for X1 and X2 (continuous variables)
3	for Y1, Y2, and Y3 (dependent variables).

The matrix has 425 rows and columns only if all combinations of levels occurred for each effect in the model. For m rows and columns, $8*m^2$ bytes are needed for crossproducts. In this case, $8*425^2$ is 1,445,000 bytes. To convert to K units, divide by 1024 to get 1411K.

The required memory grows as the square of the number of columns of **X** and **X'X**; most is for the A*B*C interaction. Without A*B*C, you have 185 columns and need 268K for **X'X**. Without either A*B*C or A*B, you need 86K. If A is recoded to have ten levels, then the full model has only 220 columns and requires 378K.

The second time that a large amount of memory is needed is when Type III, Type IV, or contrast sums of squares are being calculated. This memory requirement is a function of the number of degrees of freedom of the model being analyzed and the maximum degrees of freedom for any single source. Let RANK equal the sum of the model degrees of freedom, MAXDF be the maximum number of degrees of freedom for any single source, and NY be the number of dependent variables in the model. Then the memory requirement in bytes is

$$8 * \frac{\text{RANK}*(\text{RANK} + 1)}{2} + \text{NY}*\text{RANK} + \frac{\text{MAXDF}*(\text{MAXDF} + 1)}{2} + \text{NY}*\text{MAXDF} \ .$$

Unfortunately, these quantities are not available when the $\mathbf{X'X}$ matrix is being constructed, so GLM may occasionally request additional memory even after you have increased the memory allocation available to the program.

If you have a large model that will exceed the memory capacity of your computer, these are your options:

- cut out terms, especially high-level interactions
- cut down the number of levels for variables with many levels
- use the ABSORB statement for parts of the model that are large
- use the REPEATED statement for repeated measures variables
- use PROC ANOVA or PROC REG rather than PROC GLM, if your design allows.

CPU time

For large problems, two operations consume a lot of CPU time: the collection of sums and crossproducts and the solution of the normal equations.

The time required for collecting sums and crossproducts is difficult to calculate because it is a complicated function of the model. For a model with m columns and n rows (observations) in $\mathbf{X}$, the worst case occurs if all columns are continuous variables, involving $n{*}m^2/2$ multiplications and additions. If the columns are levels of a classification, then only m sums may be needed, but a significant amount of time may be spent in look-up operations. Solving the normal equations requires time for approximately $m^3/2$ multiplications and additions.

Suppose you know that Type IV sums of squares will be appropriate for the model you are analyzing (for example, if your design has no missing cells). You can specify the SS4 option in your MODEL statement, which saves CPU time by requesting the Type IV sums of squares instead of the more computationally burdensome Type III sums of squares. This proves especially useful if you have a factor in your model that has many levels and is involved in several interactions.

Computational Method

Let $\mathbf{X}$ represent the $n{\times}p$ design matrix. (When effects containing only class variables are involved, the columns of $\mathbf{X}$ corresponding to these effects contain only 0s and 1s. No reparameterization is made.) Let $\mathbf{Y}$ represent the $n{\times}1$ vector of dependent variables.

The normal equations $\mathbf{X'X\beta}=\mathbf{X'Y}$ are solved using a modified sweep routine that produces a generalized (g2) inverse $(\mathbf{X'X})^-$ and a solution $\mathbf{b}=(\mathbf{X'X})^-\mathbf{X'y}$ (Pringle and Raynor 1971).

For each effect in the model, a matrix $\mathbf{L}$ is computed such that the rows of $\mathbf{L}$ are estimable. Tests of the hypothesis $\mathbf{L\beta}=0$ are then made by first computing

$$SS(\mathbf{L\beta} = 0) = (\mathbf{Lb})'(\mathbf{L}(\mathbf{X'X})^-\mathbf{L'})^{-1}(\mathbf{Lb})$$

then computing the associated F value using the mean squared error.

Output Data Sets

OUT= Data Set Created by the OUTPUT Statement

The OUTPUT statement produces an output data set that contains the following:

- all original data from the SAS data set input to GLM
- the new variables corresponding to the diagnostic measures specified with statistics keywords in the OUTPUT statement (PREDICTED=, RESIDUAL=, and so on).

With multiple dependent variables, a name can be specified for any of the diagnostic measures for each of the dependent variables in the order in which they occur in the MODEL statement.

For example, suppose the input data set A contains the variables Y1, Y2, Y3, X1, and X2. Then you can use the following statements:

```
proc glm data=a;
   model y1 y2 y3=x1;
   output p=y1hat y2hat y3hat r=y1resid l95m=y1lcl u95m=y1ucl;
run;
```

The output data set contains Y1, Y2, Y3, X1, X2, Y1HAT, Y2HAT, Y3HAT, Y1RESID, Y1LCL, and Y1UCL. X2 is output even though it was not used by GLM. Although predicted values are generated for all three dependent variables, residuals are output for only the first dependent variable.

When any independent variable in the analysis is missing for an observation, then all new variables that correspond to diagnostic measures are missing for the observation in the output data set.

When a dependent variable in the analysis is missing for an observation, then some new variables that correspond to diagnostic measures are missing for the observation in the output data set, and some are still available. Specifically, in this case, the new variables that correspond to COOKD, COVRATIO, DFFITS, PRESS, R, RSTUDENT, STDR, and STUDENT are missing in the output data set. The variables corresponding to H, L95, L95M, P, STDI, STDP, U95, and U95M are not missing in this case.

OUT= Data Set Created by the LSMEANS Statement

The OUT= option in the LSMEANS statement produces an output data set that contains

- the unformatted values of each classification variable specified in any effect in the LSMEANS statement.
- a new variable, LSMEAN, which contains the least square mean for the specified levels of the classification variables.
- a new variable, STDERR, which contains the standard error of the least square mean.

The covariances among the least square means are also output when the COV option is specified along with the OUT= option. In this case, only one effect may be specified in the LSMEANS statement, and the following variables are included in the output data set:

- new variables, COV1, COV2, . . . , COVn, where n is the number of levels of the effect specified in the LSMEANS statement. These variables contain the covariances of each least squares mean with each other least squares mean.
- a new variable, NUMBER, which provides an index for each observation to identify the covariances which correspond to that observation. The covariances for the observation with NUMBER equal to n can be found in the variable COV n.

OUTSTAT= Data Set

The OUTSTAT= option in the PROC GLM statement produces an output data set that contains

- the BY variables, if any.
- _TYPE_, a new character variable. _TYPE_ may take the values SS1, SS2, SS3, SS4, or CONTRAST, corresponding to the various types of sums of squares generated, or the values CANCORR, STRUCTUR, or SCORE, if a canonical analysis is performed through the MANOVA statement and no M= matrix is specified.
- _SOURCE_, a new character variable. For each observation in the data set, _SOURCE_ contains the name of the model effect or contrast label from which the corresponding statistics are generated.
- _NAME_, a new character variable. For each observation in the data set, _NAME_ contains the name of one of the dependent variables in the model, or in the case of canonical statistics, the name of one of the canonical variables (CAN1, CAN2, and so forth).
- four new numeric variables: SS, DF, F, and PROB, containing sums of squares, degrees of freedom, F values, and probabilities, respectively, for each model or contrast sum of squares generated in the analysis. For observations resulting from canonical analyses, these variables have missing values.
- if there is more than one dependent variable, then variables with the same names as the dependent variables represent
  - for _TYPE_='SS1', 'SS2', 'SS3', 'SS4', or 'CONTRAST', the crossproducts of the hypothesis matrices
  - for _TYPE_='CANCORR', the canonical correlations for each variable
  - for _TYPE_='STRUCTUR', the coefficients of the total structure matrix
  - for _TYPE_='SCORE', the raw canonical score coefficients.

The output data set can be used to perform special hypothesis tests (for example, with the IML procedure in SAS/IML software), to reformat output, to produce canonical variates (through PROC SCORE), or to rotate structure matrices (through PROC FACTOR).

Printed Output

The GLM procedure produces the following printed output by default:

1. The overall analysis-of-variance table breaks down the Total Sum of Squares for the dependent variable
2. into the portion attributed to the Model
3. and the portion attributed to Error.
4. The Mean Square term is the
5. Sum of Squares divided by the
6. degrees of freedom (DF).
7. The Mean Square for Error is an estimate of σ^2, the variance of the true errors.
8. The F Value is the ratio produced by dividing the Mean Square for the Model by the Mean Square for Error. It tests how well the model as a whole (adjusted for the mean) accounts for the dependent variable's behavior. An F test is a joint test to determine that all parameters except the intercept are zero.
9. A small significance probability, $Pr > F$, indicates that some linear function of the parameters is significantly different from zero.
10. R-Square, R^2, measures how much variation in the dependent variable can be accounted for by the model. R^2, which can range from 0 to 1, is

the ratio of the sum of squares for the model divided by the sum of squares for the corrected total. In general, the larger the value of R^2, the better the model's fit.

11. C.V., the coefficient of variation, which describes the amount of variation in the population, is 100 times the standard deviation estimate of the dependent variable, Root MSE, divided by the Mean. The coefficient of variation is often a preferred measure because it is unitless.

12. Root MSE estimates the standard deviation of the dependent variable (or equivalently, the error term) and equals the square root of the Mean Square for Error.

13. Mean is the sample mean of the dependent variable.

These tests are used primarily in analysis-of-variance applications:

14. The Type I SS measures incremental sums of squares for the model as each variable is added.

15. The Type III SS is the sum of squares that results when that variable is added last to the model.

16. The F Value and Pr > F values for Type III tests, where each effect is adjusted for every other effect.

These items are used primarily in regression applications:

17. The Estimates for the model Parameters (the intercept and the coefficients).

18. T for H_0: Parameter=0 is the Student's t value for testing the null hypothesis that the parameter (if it is estimable) equals zero.

19. The significance level, Pr > |T|, is the probability of getting a larger value of t if the parameter is truly equal to zero. A very small value for this probability leads to the conclusion that the independent variable contributes significantly to the model.

20. The Std Error of Estimate is the standard error of the estimate of the true value of the parameter.

Other portions of output are discussed in the examples below.

EXAMPLES

Example 1:   Balanced Data from Randomized Complete Block with Means Comparisons and Contrasts

Since these data are balanced, you can obtain the same answer more efficiently using the ANOVA procedure; however, GLM presents the results in a slightly different way. Notice that since the data are balanced, the Type I and Type III SS are the same and equal the ANOVA SS.

First, the standard analysis is shown followed by an analysis that uses the SOLUTION option and includes MEANS and CONTRAST statements. The ORDER=DATA option in the second PROC GLM statement is used so that the ordering of coefficients in the CONTRAST statement can correspond to the ordering in the input data. The SOLUTION option requests a printout of the parameter estimates, which are only printed by default if there are no CLASS variables. A MEANS statement is used to request a printout of the means with two multiple comparison procedures requested. In experiments with well-understood treatment levels, CONTRAST statements are preferable to a blanket means comparison method. The following statements produce **Output 24.8** and **Output 24.9**:

```
/*---------------SNAPDRAGON EXPERIMENT---------------*/
/* As reported by Stenstrom, 1940, an experiment was */
/* undertaken to investigate how snapdragons grew in */
/* various soils. Each soil type was used in three   */
/* blocks.                                           */
/*---------------------------------------------------*/
data plants;
   input type $ @;
   do block=1 to 3;
      input stemleng @;
      output;
      end;
   cards;
CLARION  32.7 32.3 31.5
CLINTON  32.1 29.7 29.1
KNOX     35.7 35.9 33.1
O'NEILL  36.0 34.2 31.2
COMPOST  31.8 28.0 29.2
WABASH   38.2 37.8 31.9
WEBSTER  32.5 31.1 29.7
;

proc glm;
   class type block;
   model stemleng=type block;
run;

proc glm order=data;
   class type block;
   model stemleng=type block / solution;

   /*-type-order-----------------clrn-cltn-knox-onel-cpst-wbsh-wstr */
contrast 'COMPOST VS OTHERS'  type -1  -1  -1  -1   6  -1  -1;
contrast 'RIVER SOILS VS.NON' type -1  -1  -1  -1   0   5  -1,
                              type -1   4  -1  -1   0   0  -1;
contrast 'GLACIAL VS DRIFT'   type -1   0   1   1   0   0  -1;
contrast 'CLARION VS WEBSTER' type -1   0   0   0   0   0   1;
contrast 'KNOX VS ONEILL'     type  0   0   1  -1   0   0   0;
run;

   means type / waller regwq;
run;
```

Output 24.8 Standard Analysis for Randomized Complete Block

```
                              The SAS System                                    1
                       General Linear Models Procedure
                          Class Level Information
          Class    Levels   Values
          TYPE        7     CLARION CLINTON COMPOST KNOX O'NEILL WABASH WEBSTER
          BLOCK       3     1 2 3


               Number of observations in data set = 21
```

```
                              The SAS System                                    2
                       General Linear Models Procedure

Dependent Variable: STEMLENG
Source              ⑥ DF      ⑤ Sum of Squares    ④ Mean Square   ⑧ F Value   ⑨ Pr > F
Model                   8     ② 142.18857143        17.77357143    10.80       0.0002
Error                  12     ③  19.74285714      ⑦ 1.64523810
Corrected Total        20     ①  161.93142857

           R-Square              C.V.            Root MSE          STEMLENG Mean
        ⑩ 0.878079          ⑪ 3.939745         ⑫ 1.28266835       ⑬ 32.55714286


Source              DF         Type I SS          Mean Square       F Value      Pr > F
TYPE                 6      ⑭ 103.15142857        17.19190476       10.45        0.0004
BLOCK                2         39.03714286        19.51857143    ⑯ 11.86      ⑯ 0.0014

Source              DF         Type III SS        Mean Square       F Value      Pr > F
TYPE                 6      ⑮ 103.15142857        17.19190476       10.45        0.0004
BLOCK                2         39.03714286        19.51857143       11.86        0.0014
```

This analysis shows that the stem length is significantly different for the different soil types. In addition, there are significant differences in stem length between the three blocks in the experiment.

Output 24.9   Randomized Complete Block with Means Comparisons and Contrasts

```
                              The SAS System                                      3

                      General Linear Models Procedure
                         Class Level Information
           Class    Levels    Values

           TYPE        7      CLARION CLINTON KNOX O'NEILL COMPOST WABASH WEBSTER

           BLOCK       3      1 2 3


                   Number of observations in data set = 21
```

```
                              The SAS System                                      4

                      General Linear Models Procedure

   Dependent Variable: STEMLENG

   Source              DF      Sum of Squares      Mean Square    F Value    Pr > F

   Model                8       142.18857143       17.77357143      10.80    0.0002

   Error               12        19.74285714        1.64523810

   Corrected Total     20       161.93142857

                 R-Square               C.V.            Root MSE        STEMLENG Mean

                 0.878079            3.939745          1.28266835          32.55714286


   Source              DF          Type I SS         Mean Square    F Value    Pr > F

   TYPE                 6       103.15142857        17.19190476      10.45    0.0004
   BLOCK                2        39.03714286        19.51857143      11.86    0.0014

   Source              DF        Type III SS         Mean Square    F Value    Pr > F

   TYPE                 6       103.15142857        17.19190476      10.45    0.0004
   BLOCK                2        39.03714286        19.51857143      11.86    0.0014

   Contrast            DF        Contrast SS         Mean Square    F Value    Pr > F
```
Ⓐ
```
   COMPOST VS OTHERS     1        29.24198413        29.24198413      17.77    0.0012
   RIVER SOILS VS.NON    2        48.24694444        24.12347222      14.66    0.0006
   GLACIAL VS DRIFT      1        22.14083333        22.14083333      13.46    0.0032
   CLARION VS WEBSTER    1         1.70666667         1.70666667       1.04    0.3285
   KNOX VS ONEILL        1         1.81500000         1.81500000       1.10    0.3143
```

	Parameter		Ⓐ17 Estimate	Ⓐ18 T for H0: Parameter=0	Ⓐ19 Pr > |T|	Ⓐ20 Std Error of Estimate
Ⓑ	INTERCEPT		29.35714286 B	34.96	0.0001	0.83970354
	TYPE	CLARION	1.06666667 B	1.02	0.3285	1.04729432
		CLINTON	-0.80000000 B	-0.76	0.4597	1.04729432
		KNOX	3.80000000 B	3.63	0.0035	1.04729432
		O'NEILL	2.70000000 B	2.58	0.0242	1.04729432
		COMPOST	-1.43333333 B	-1.37	0.1962	1.04729432
		WABASH	4.86666667 B	4.65	0.0006	1.04729432
		WEBSTER	0.00000000 B	.	.	.
	BLOCK	1	3.32857143 B	4.85	0.0004	0.68561507
		2	1.90000000 B	2.77	0.0169	0.68561507
		3	0.00000000 B	.	.	.

```
   NOTE: The X'X matrix has been found to be singular and a generalized inverse was used to solve the normal equations.  Estimates
         followed by the letter 'B' are biased, and are not unique estimators of the parameters.
```

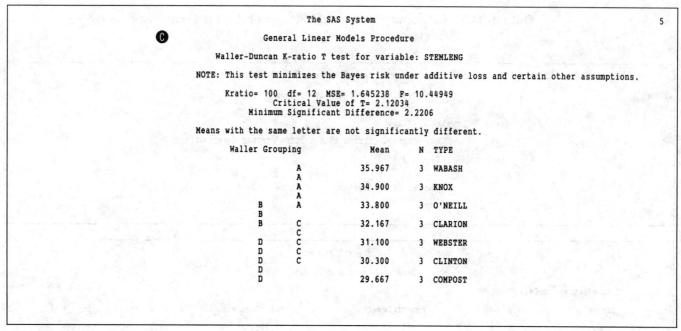

```
                              The SAS System                                    5
     C                General Linear Models Procedure

              Waller-Duncan K-ratio T test for variable: STEMLENG

  NOTE: This test minimizes the Bayes risk under additive loss and certain other assumptions.

          Kratio= 100  df= 12  MSE= 1.645238  F= 10.44949
                    Critical Value of T= 2.12034
                 Minimum Significant Difference= 2.2206

       Means with the same letter are not significantly different.

            Waller Grouping              Mean    N  TYPE

                         A              35.967    3  WABASH
                         A
                         A              34.900    3  KNOX
                         A
                  B      A              33.800    3  O'NEILL
                  B
                  B      C              32.167    3  CLARION
                         C
                  D      C              31.100    3  WEBSTER
                  D      C
                  D      C              30.300    3  CLINTON
                  D
                  D              29.667    3  COMPOST
```

```
                              The SAS System                                    6

                      General Linear Models Procedure

        Ryan-Einot-Gabriel-Welsch Multiple Range Test for variable: STEMLENG

         NOTE: This test controls the type I experimentwise error rate.

                   Alpha= 0.05  df= 12  MSE= 1.645238

Number of Means       2         3         4         5         6         7
Critical Range   2.987665 3.2838329 3.4396257 3.5402242 3.5177193 3.6653735

       Means with the same letter are not significantly different.

            REGWQ Grouping               Mean    N  TYPE

                         A              35.967    3  WABASH
                         A
                  B      A              34.900    3  KNOX
                  B      A
                  B      A   C          33.800    3  O'NEILL
                  B          C
                  B      D   C          32.167    3  CLARION
                  D          C
                  D      C              31.100    3  WEBSTER
                  D
                  D              30.300    3  CLINTON
                  D
                  D              29.667    3  COMPOST
```

The circled letters on the printout correspond to the descriptions below:

A. The section of output labeled "Contrast" shows the result of the CONTRAST statements. The contrast label, the degrees of freedom for the contrast, the Contrast SS, Mean Square, F Value, and Pr > F are shown for each contrast requested. In this example, the contrasts show that at the 5% significance level:

- the stem length of plants grown in compost soil is significantly different from the stem length of plants grown in other soils
- the stem length of plants grown in river soils is significantly different from the stem length of those grown in non-river soils

- the stem length of plants grown in glacial soils (CLARION and WEBSTER) is significantly different from the stem length of those grown in drift soils (KNOX and O'NEILL).
- stem lengths for CLARION and WEBSTER are not significantly different
- stem lengths for KNOX and O'NEILL are not significantly different.

B. The section of output labeled "Parameter" gives estimates for the parameters and results of *t*-tests about the parameters. The B following the parameter estimates means the estimates are biased and do not represent a unique solution to the normal equations.

C. The final two pages of output give results of the Waller-Duncan and REGWQ multiple comparison procedures. For each test, notes and information pertinent to the test are given on the printout. The TYPE means are arranged from highest to lowest. Means with the same letter are not significantly different.

Example 2:   Regression with Mileage Data

A car is tested for gas mileage at various speeds to determine at what speed the car achieves the greatest gas mileage. A quadratic response surface is fit to the experimental data. The following statements produce **Output 24.10** and **Output 24.11**:

```
    /*-----------GASOLINE MILEAGE EXPERIMENT-------------*/
data mileage;
   input mph mpg @@;
   cards;
20 15.4 30 20.2 40 25.7 50 26.2 50 26.6 50 27.4 55  . 60 24.8
;

proc glm;
   model mpg=mph mph*mph / p clm;
   output out=pp p=mpgpred r=resid;
run;
proc plot data=pp;
   plot mpg*mph='A' mpgpred*mph='P' / overlay;
run;
```

Output 24.10   Performing a Regression Analysis with PROC GLM

```
                        The SAS System                                    1
                  General Linear Models Procedure
                 Number of observations in data set = 8

NOTE: Due to missing values, only 7 observations can be used in this analysis.
```

```
                                    The SAS System                                          2
                              General Linear Models Procedure

        Dependent Variable: MPG

        Source              DF        Sum of Squares      Mean Square     F Value      Pr > F

        Model                2        111.80861827        55.90430913      77.96       0.0006

        Error                4          2.86852459         0.71713115

        Corrected Total      6        114.67714286

                          R-Square               C.V.              Root MSE              MPG Mean

                          0.974986             3.564553            0.84683596          23.75714286


        Source              DF          Type I SS         Mean Square     F Value      Pr > F

        MPH                  1         85.64464286        85.64464286     119.43       0.0004
        MPH*MPH              1         26.16397541        26.16397541      36.48       0.0038

        Source              DF         Type III SS        Mean Square     F Value      Pr > F

        MPH                  1         41.01171219        41.01171219      57.19       0.0016
        MPH*MPH              1         26.16397541        26.16397541      36.48       0.0038


                                                       T for H0:
        Parameter                   Estimate          Parameter=0      Pr > |T|      Std Error of
                                                                                       Estimate

        INTERCEPT                 -5.985245902            -1.88          0.1334       3.18522249
        MPH                        1.305245902             7.56          0.0016       0.17259876
        MPH*MPH                   -0.013098361            -6.04          0.0038       0.00216852


        Observation      Observed        Predicted        Residual     Lower 95% CL    Upper 95% CL
                          Value            Value                         for Mean        for Mean

              1         15.40000000      14.88032787      0.51967213    12.69704271     17.06361303
              2         20.20000000      21.38360656     -1.18360656    20.01729041     22.74992270
              3         25.70000000      25.26721311      0.43278689    23.87461925     26.65980698
              4         26.20000000      26.53114754     -0.33114754    25.44574892     27.61654616
              5         26.60000000      26.53114754      0.06885246    25.44574892     27.61654616
              6         27.40000000      26.53114754      0.86885246    25.44574892     27.61654616
              7   *          .           26.18073770          .         24.88681059     27.47466482
              8         24.80000000      25.17540984     -0.37540984    23.05957840     27.29124127

        * Observation was not used in this analysis


              Sum of Residuals                       0.00000000
              Sum of Squared Residuals               2.86852459
              Sum of Squared Residuals - Error SS   -0.00000000
              Press Statistic                       23.18107335
              First Order Autocorrelation           -0.54376613
              Durbin-Watson D                        2.94425592
```

This output shows that both the linear and quadratic terms in the regression model are significant. The model fits well, with an R^2 of 0.97. The estimated equation is

$$MPG = -5.9852 + 1.3052*MPH - 0.0131*MPH*MPH \quad .$$

The section labeled "Observation" shows the results of requesting the P and CLM options. For each observation, the observed, predicted, and residual values are shown. In addition, the 95% confidence limits for a mean predicted value are shown for each observation. Note that the observation with a missing value for MPH was not used in the analysis, but predicted and confidence limit values are shown.

The final portion of output gives some additional information on the residuals. The Press statistic gives the sum of squares of predicted residual errors, as described in Chapter 1, "Introduction to Regression Procedures." The First Order Autocorrelation and the Durbin-Watson D statistic, which tests for the presence of first-order autocorrelation, are also given. **Output 24.11** shows the actual and predicted values for the data.

Output 24.11   Plot of Mileage Data

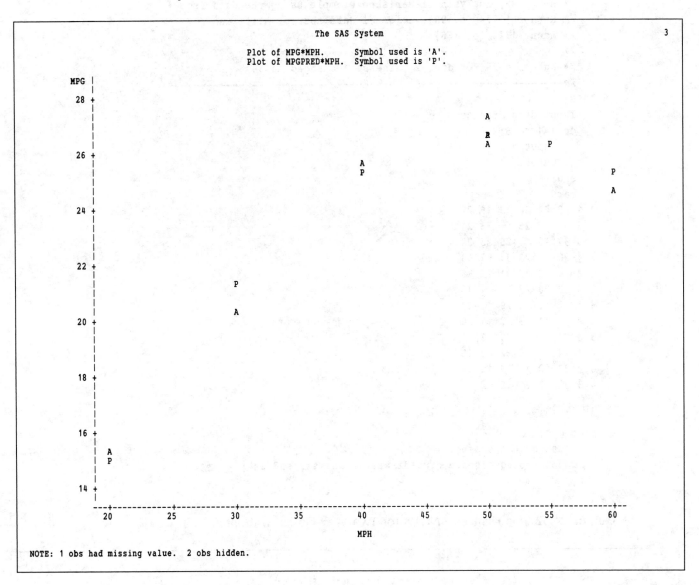

Example 3:   Unbalanced *ANOVA* for Two-Way Design with Interaction

This example uses data from Kutner (1974) to illustrate a two-way analysis of variance. The original data source is Afifi and Azen (1972). These statements produce **Output 24.12**:

```
/*-----------------------------------------------------------------*/
/* A two-way analysis-of-variance example using the data from */
/* Kutner (1974, p. 98). Original data source: Afifi and      */
/* Azen (1972, p. 166).                                       */
/*                                                            */
/* Kutner's 24 for drug 2, disease 1 changed to 34 .          */
/*-----------------------------------------------------------------*/
data a;
   input drug disease @;
   do i=1 to 6;
      input y @;
      output;
   end;
   cards;
1 1 42 44 36 13 19 22
1 2 33  . 26  . 33 21
1 3 31 -3  . 25 25 24
2 1 28  . 23 34 42 13
2 2  . 34 33 31  . 36
2 3  3 26 28 32  4 16
3 1  .  .  1 29  . 19
3 2  . 11  9  7  1 -6
3 3 21  1  .  9  3  .
4 1 24  .  9 22 -2 15
4 2 27 12 12 -5 16 15
4 3 22  7 25  5 12  .
;

proc glm;
   class drug disease;
   model y=drug disease drug*disease / ss1 ss2 ss3 ss4;
run;
```

Output 24.12   Unbalanced *ANOVA* for Two-Way Design with Interaction

```
                              The SAS System                              1

                        General Linear Models Procedure
                          Class Level Information

                        Class     Levels    Values

                        DRUG         4      1 2 3 4

                        DISEASE      3      1 2 3


                   Number of observations in data set = 72

        NOTE: Due to missing values, only 58 observations can be used in this analysis.
```

```
                               The SAS System                                        2
                          General Linear Models Procedure

Dependent Variable: Y

Source              DF        Sum of Squares       Mean Square     F Value      Pr > F

Model               11         4259.33850575      387.21259143        3.51      0.0013

Error               46         5080.81666667      110.45253623

Corrected Total     57         9340.15517241

          R-Square                 C.V.              Root MSE                   Y Mean

          0.456024              55.66750           10.50964016               18.87931034


Source              DF             Type I SS         Mean Square     F Value      Pr > F

DRUG                 3         3133.23850575      1044.41283525        9.46      0.0001
DISEASE              2          418.83374069       209.41687035        1.90      0.1617
DRUG*DISEASE         6          707.26625931       117.87770988        1.07      0.3958

Source              DF            Type II SS         Mean Square     F Value      Pr > F

DRUG                 3         3063.43286350      1021.14428783        9.25      0.0001
DISEASE              2          418.83374069       209.41687035        1.90      0.1617
DRUG*DISEASE         6          707.26625931       117.87770988        1.07      0.3958

Source              DF           Type III SS         Mean Square     F Value      Pr > F

DRUG                 3         2997.47186048       999.15728683        9.05      0.0001
DISEASE              2          415.87304632       207.93652316        1.88      0.1637
DRUG*DISEASE         6          707.26625931       117.87770988        1.07      0.3958

Source              DF            Type IV SS         Mean Square     F Value      Pr > F

DRUG                 3         2997.47186048       999.15728683        9.05      0.0001
DISEASE              2          415.87304632       207.93652316        1.88      0.1637
DRUG*DISEASE         6          707.26625931       117.87770988        1.07      0.3958
```

This analysis shows a significant difference among the four drugs. The DISEASE effect and the DRUG*DISEASE interaction are not significant.

Example 4:   Analysis of Covariance

Analysis of covariance combines some of the features of regression and analysis of variance. Typically, a continuous variable (the covariate) is introduced into the model of an analysis-of-variance experiment.

Data in the following example were selected from a larger experiment on the use of drugs in the treatment of leprosy (Snedecor and Cochran 1967, p. 422).

Variables in the study are

> DRUG   two antibiotics (A and D) and a control (F)
>
> X   a pre-treatment score of leprosy bacilli
>
> Y   a post-treatment score of leprosy bacilli.

Ten patients were selected for each treatment (DRUG), and six sites on each patient were measured for leprosy bacilli.

The covariate (a pre-treatment score) is included in the model for increased precision in determining the effect of drug treatments on the post-treatment count of bacilli.

The code below creates the data set, performs an analysis of covariance with GLM, and creates an output data set that contains least-squares means. These statements produce **Output 24.13**.

```
      /* From Snedecor and Cochran (1967, p.422) */
data drugtest;
   input drug $ x y @@;
   cards;
A 11  6  A  8  0  A  5  2  A 14  8  A 19 11
A  6  4  A 10 13  A  6  1  A 11  8  A  3  0
D  6  0  D  6  2  D  7  3  D  8  1  D 18 18
D  8  4  D 19 14  D  8  9  D  5  1  D 15  9
F 16 13  F 13 10  F 11 18  F  9  5  F 21 23
F 16 12  F 12  5  F 12 16  F  7  1  F 12 20
;

proc glm;
   class drug;
   model y=drug x / solution;
   lsmeans drug / stderr pdiff cov out=adjmeans;
run;

proc print data=adjmeans;
run;
```

Output 24.13 Analysis of Covariance

```
                                  The SAS System                                    1

                         General Linear Models Procedure
                             Class Level Information

                       Class     Levels     Values
                       DRUG         3        A D F


                 Number of observations in data set = 30
```

```
                                  The SAS System                                    2

                         General Linear Models Procedure

Dependent Variable: Y

Source              DF       Sum of Squares        Mean Square       F Value       Pr > F

Model                3         871.49740304        290.49913435        18.10        0.0001

Error               26         417.20259696         16.04625373

Corrected Total     29        1288.70000000

                R-Square                 C.V.              Root MSE              Y Mean

                0.676261             50.70604            4.00577754          7.90000000
```

(continued on next page)

(continued from previous page)

Source	DF	Type I SS	Mean Square	F Value	Pr > F
DRUG	2	(A) 293.60000000	146.80000000	9.15	0.0010
X	1	577.89740304	577.89740304	36.01	0.0001

Source	DF	Type III SS	Mean Square	F Value	Pr > F
DRUG	2	(B) 68.55371060	34.27685530	2.14	0.1384
X	1	577.89740304	577.89740304	36.01	0.0001

Parameter		Estimate	T for H0: Parameter=0	Pr > |T|	Std Error of Estimate
INTERCEPT		-0.434671164 B	-0.18	0.8617	2.47135356
DRUG	A	-3.446138280 B	-1.83	0.0793	1.88678065
	D	-3.337166948 B	-1.80	0.0835	1.85386642
	F	0.000000000 B	.	.	.
X		0.987183811	6.00	0.0001	0.16449757

NOTE: The X'X matrix has been found to be singular and a generalized inverse was used to solve the normal equations.   Estimates followed by the letter 'B' are biased, and are not unique estimators of the parameters.

The SAS System   3

General Linear Models Procedure
Least Squares Means

DRUG	(C) Y LSMEAN	(D) Std Err LSMEAN	Pr > |T| H0:LSMEAN=0	(E) Pr > |T| H0: LSMEAN(i)=LSMEAN(j) i/j 1		
				1	2	3
A	6.7149635	1.2884943	0.0001	1 .	0.9521	0.0793
D	6.8239348	1.2724690	0.0001	2 0.9521	.	0.0835
F	10.1611017	1.3159234	0.0001	3 0.0793	0.0835	.

NOTE: To ensure overall protection level, only probabilities associated with pre-planned comparisons should be used.

The SAS System   4

OBS	_NAME_	DRUG	LSMEAN	STDERR	NUMBER	COV1	COV2	COV3
1	Y	A	6.7150	1.28849	1	1.66022	0.02844	-0.08403
2	Y	D	6.8239	1.27247	2	0.02844	1.61918	-0.04299
3	Y	F	10.1611	1.31592	3	-0.08403	-0.04299	1.73165

The circled letters on the printout correspond to the descriptions that follow:

A. The Type I SS for DRUG gives the between-drug sums of squares that would be obtained for the analysis-of-variance model Y=DRUG.

B. Type III SS for DRUG gives the DRUG SS adjusted for the covariate.

C. The LSMEANS printed are the same as adjusted means (means adjusted for the covariate).

D. The STDERR option in the LSMEANS statement causes the standard error of the least-squares means and the probability of getting a larger *t* value under the hypothesis H_0: LSM=0 to be printed.

E. Specifying the PDIFF option causes all probability values for the hypothesis H_0: LSM(I)=LSM(J) to be printed.

Example 5:   Three-Way Analysis of Variance with Contrasts

This example uses data from Cochran and Cox (1957, p. 176) to illustrate a three-way factorial design with replication, two uses of the CONTRAST statement, and the OUTSTAT= data set that GLM can create. The object of the study is to determine the effects of electric current on denervated muscle.

The variables are

REP   the replicate number, 1 or 2

TIME   the length of time the current was applied to the muscle, ranging from 1 to 4

CURRENT   the level of electric current applied, ranging from 1 to 4

NUMBER   the number of treatments per day, ranging from 1 to 3

Y   the weight of the denervated muscle.

The code below produces **Output 24.14**:

```
data one;
  do rep=1 to 2;
    do time=1 to 4;
      do current=1 to 4;
        do number=1 to 3;
          input y aa;
          output;
        end;
      end;
    end;
  end;
  cards;
72 74 69 61 61 65 62 65 70 85 76 61
67 52 62 60 55 59 64 65 64 67 72 60
57 66 72 72 43 43 63 66 72 56 75 92
57 56 78 60 63 58 61 79 68 73 86 71
46 74 58 60 64 52 71 64 71 53 65 66
44 58 54 57 55 51 62 61 79 60 78 82
53 50 61 56 57 56 56 56 71 56 58 69
46 55 64 56 55 57 64 66 62 59 58 88
;

proc glm outstat=summary;
  class rep current time number;
  model y=rep current|time|number;
  contrast 'TIME IN CURRENT 3'
    time 1 0 0 -1 current*time 0 0 0 0 0 0 0 0 1 0 0 -1,
    time 0 1 0 -1 current*time 0 0 0 0 0 0 0 0 0 1 0 -1,
    time 0 0 1 -1 current*time 0 0 0 0 0 0 0 0 0 0 1 -1;
  contrast 'CURR 1 VS. CURR 2' current 1 -1;
run;

proc print data=summary;
run;
```

The first CONTRAST statement examines the effects of TIME within level 3 of CURRENT. Note that since there are three degrees of freedom, it is necessary to specify three rows in the CONTRAST statement, separated by commas. Since the parameterization that PROC GLM uses is determined in part by the ordering of the variables in the CLASS statement, CURRENT was specified before TIME so that the TIME parameters would be nested within the CURRENT*TIME parameters; thus, the CURRENT*TIME parameters in each row are simply the TIME parameters of that row within the appropriate level of CURRENT.

The second CONTRAST statement isolates a single degree of freedom effect corresponding to the difference between the first two levels of CURRENT. You can use such a contrast in a large experiment where certain preplanned comparisons are important, but you want to take advantage of the additional error degrees of freedom available when all levels of the factors are considered.

Output 24.14 Three-Way Analysis of Variance with Contrasts

```
                              The SAS System                                    1

                       General Linear Models Procedure
                          Class Level Information

                    Class     Levels    Values

                    REP          2      1 2

                    CURRENT      4      1 2 3 4

                    TIME         4      1 2 3 4

                    NUMBER       3      1 2 3


               Number of observations in data set = 96
```

```
                              The SAS System                                    2

                       General Linear Models Procedure

Dependent Variable: Y

Source                DF      Sum of Squares       Mean Square     F Value     Pr > F

Model                 48      5782.91666667       120.47743056       1.77      0.0261

Error                 47      3199.48958333        68.07424645

Corrected Total       95      8982.40625000

            R-Square              C.V.             Root MSE              Y Mean

            0.643805           13.05105           8.25071188          63.21875000


Source                DF          Type I SS        Mean Square     F Value     Pr > F
REP                    1       605.01041667       605.01041667        8.89      0.0045
CURRENT                3      2145.44791667       715.14930556       10.51      0.0001
TIME                   3       223.11458333        74.37152778        1.09      0.3616
CURRENT*TIME           9       298.67708333        33.18634259        0.49      0.8756
NUMBER                 2       447.43750000       223.71875000        3.29      0.0461
CURRENT*NUMBER         6       644.39583333       107.39930556        1.58      0.1747
TIME*NUMBER            6       367.97916667        61.32986111        0.90      0.5023
CURRENT*TIME*NUMBER   18      1050.85416667        58.38078704        0.86      0.6276
```

(continued on next page)

(continued from previous page)

Source	DF	Type III SS	Mean Square	F Value	Pr > F
REP	1	605.01041667	605.01041667	8.89	0.0045
CURRENT	3	2145.44791667	715.14930556	10.51	0.0001
TIME	3	223.11458333	74.37152778	1.09	0.3616
CURRENT*TIME	9	298.67708333	33.18634259	0.49	0.8756
NUMBER	2	447.43750000	223.71875000	3.29	0.0461
CURRENT*NUMBER	6	644.39583333	107.39930556	1.58	0.1747
TIME*NUMBER	6	367.97916667	61.32986111	0.90	0.5023
CURRENT*TIME*NUMBER	18	1050.85416667	58.38078704	0.86	0.6276

Contrast	DF	Contrast SS	Mean Square	F Value	Pr > F
TIME IN CURRENT 3	3	34.83333333	11.61111111	0.17	0.9157
CURR 1 VS. CURR 2	1	99.18750000	99.18750000	1.46	0.2334

The SAS System

OBS	_NAME_	_SOURCE_	_TYPE_	DF	SS	F	PROB
1	Y	ERROR	ERROR	47	3199.49	.	.
2	Y	REP	SS1	1	605.01	8.8875	0.00454
3	Y	CURRENT	SS1	3	2145.45	10.5054	0.00002
4	Y	TIME	SS1	3	223.11	1.0925	0.36159
5	Y	CURRENT*TIME	SS1	9	298.68	0.4875	0.87562
6	Y	NUMBER	SS1	2	447.44	3.2864	0.04614
7	Y	CURRENT*NUMBER	SS1	6	644.40	1.5777	0.17468
8	Y	TIME*NUMBER	SS1	6	367.98	0.9009	0.50231
9	Y	CURRENT*TIME*NUMBER	SS1	18	1050.85	0.8576	0.62757
10	Y	REP	SS3	1	605.01	8.8875	0.00454
11	Y	CURRENT	SS3	3	2145.45	10.5054	0.00002
12	Y	TIME	SS3	3	223.11	1.0925	0.36159
13	Y	CURRENT*TIME	SS3	9	298.68	0.4875	0.87562
14	Y	NUMBER	SS3	2	447.44	3.2864	0.04614
15	Y	CURRENT*NUMBER	SS3	6	644.40	1.5777	0.17468
16	Y	TIME*NUMBER	SS3	6	367.98	0.9009	0.50231
17	Y	CURRENT*TIME*NUMBER	SS3	18	1050.85	0.8576	0.62757
18	Y	TIME IN CURRENT 3	CONTRAST	3	34.83	0.1706	0.91574
19	Y	CURR 1 VS. CURR 2	CONTRAST	1	99.19	1.4570	0.23344

The output above shows significant main effects for REP, CURRENT, and NUMBER. None of the interactions are significant, nor are the contrasts significant.

Example 6:   Multivariate Analysis of Variance

Using data from A. Anderson, Oregon State University, this example illustrates a multivariate analysis of variance. See **Output 24.15**.

```
/*---------MULTIVARIATE ANALYSIS OF VARIANCE-------*/
/* Data from A. Anderson, Oregon State University. */
/* Four different response variables are measured. */
/* The hypothesis to be tested is that sex does     */
/* not affect any of the four responses.            */
/*-------------------------------------------------*/
data skull;
   input sex $ length basilar zygomat postorb @@;
   cards;
M 6460 4962 3286 1100 M 6252 4773 3239 1061 M 5772 4480 3200 1097
M 6264 4806 3179 1054 M 6622 5113 3365 1071 M 6656 5100 3326 1012
M 6441 4918 3153 1061 M 6281 4821 3133 1071 M 6606 5060 3227 1064
M 6573 4977 3392 1110 M 6563 5025 3234 1090 M 6552 5086 3292 1010
M 6535 4939 3261 1065 M 6573 4962 3320 1091 M 6537 4990 3309 1059
M 6302 4761 3204 1135 M 6449 4921 3256 1068 M 6481 4887 3233 1124
M 6368 4824 3258 1130 M 6372 4844 3306 1137 M 6592 5007 3284 1148
M 6229 4746 3257 1153 M 6391 4834 3244 1169 M 6560 4981 3341 1038
```

```
M 6787 5181 3334 1104 M 6384 4834 3195 1064 M 6282 4757 3180 1179
M 6340 4791 3300 1110 M 6394 4879 3272 1241 M 6153 4557 3214 1039
M 6348 4886 3160  991 M 6534 4990 3310 1028 M 6509 4951 3282 1104
F 6287 4845 3218  996 F 6583 4992 3300 1107 F 6518 5023 3246 1035
F 6432 4790 3249 1117 F 6450 4888 3259 1060 F 6379 4844 3266 1115
F 6424 4855 3322 1065 F 6615 5088 3280 1179 F 6760 5206 3337 1219
F 6521 5011 3208  989 F 6416 4889 3200 1001 F 6511 4910 3230 1100
F 6540 4997 3320 1078 F 6780 5259 3358 1174 F 6336 4781 3165 1126
F 6472 4954 3125 1178 F 6476 4896 3148 1066 F 6276 4709 3150 1134
F 6693 5177 3236 1131 F 6328 4792 3214 1018 F 6661 5104 3395 1141
F 6266 4721 3257 1031 F 6660 5146 3374 1069 F 6624 5032 3384 1154
F 6331 4819 3278 1008 F 6298 4683 3270 1150
;

proc glm;
   class sex;
   model length basilar zygomat postorb=sex;
   manova h=sex / printe printh;
   title 'MULTIVARIATE ANALYSIS OF VARIANCE';
run;
```

Output 24.15   Multivariate Analysis of Variance

```
                         MULTIVARIATE ANALYSIS OF VARIANCE                               1

                          General Linear Models Procedure
                             Class Level Information

                          Class    Levels   Values

                          SEX         2      F M


                    Number of observations in data set = 59
```

```
                         MULTIVARIATE ANALYSIS OF VARIANCE                               2

                          General Linear Models Procedure
```

Dependent Variable: LENGTH

Source	DF	Sum of Squares	Mean Square	F Value	Pr > F
Model	1	47060.93163052	47060.93163052	1.59	0.2119
Error	57	1683039.20396301	29527.00357830		
Corrected Total	58	1730100.13559353			

R-Square	C.V.	Root MSE	LENGTH Mean
0.027201	2.662355	171.83423285	6454.22033898

Source	DF	Type I SS	Mean Square	F Value	Pr > F
SEX	1	47060.93163052	47060.93163052	1.59	0.2119

Source	DF	Type III SS	Mean Square	F Value	Pr > F
SEX	1	47060.93163052	47060.93163052	1.59	0.2119

MULTIVARIATE ANALYSIS OF VARIANCE

General Linear Models Procedure

3

Dependent Variable: BASILAR

Source	DF	Sum of Squares	Mean Square	F Value	Pr > F
Model	1	23985.10578405	23985.10578405	1.02	0.3174
Error	57	1343555.19930095	23571.14384739		
Corrected Total	58	1367540.30508500			

	R-Square	C.V.	Root MSE	BASILAR Mean
	0.017539	3.122939	153.52896745	4916.16949153

Source	DF	Type I SS	Mean Square	F Value	Pr > F
SEX	1	23985.10578405	23985.10578405	1.02	0.3174

Source	DF	Type III SS	Mean Square	F Value	Pr > F
SEX	1	23985.10578405	23985.10578405	1.02	0.3174

MULTIVARIATE ANALYSIS OF VARIANCE

General Linear Models Procedure

4

Dependent Variable: ZYGOMAT

Source	DF	Sum of Squares	Mean Square	F Value	Pr > F
Model	1	66.95272806	66.95272806	0.01	0.9045
Error	57	262647.62354317	4607.85304462		
Corrected Total	58	262714.57627124			

	R-Square	C.V.	Root MSE	ZYGOMAT Mean
	0.000255	2.082299	67.88116856	3259.91525424

Source	DF	Type I SS	Mean Square	F Value	Pr > F
SEX	1	66.95272806	66.95272806	0.01	0.9045

Source	DF	Type III SS	Mean Square	F Value	Pr > F
SEX	1	66.95272806	66.95272806	0.01	0.9045

MULTIVARIATE ANALYSIS OF VARIANCE

General Linear Models Procedure

5

Dependent Variable: POSTORB

Source	DF	Sum of Squares	Mean Square	F Value	Pr > F
Model	1	192.91266643	192.91266643	0.06	0.8132
Error	57	195162.71445222	3423.90727109		
Corrected Total	58	195355.62711865			

	R-Square	C.V.	Root MSE	POSTORB Mean
	0.000987	5.359188	58.51416300	1091.84745763

Source	DF	Type I SS	Mean Square	F Value	Pr > F
SEX	1	192.91266643	192.91266643	0.06	0.8132

Source	DF	Type III SS	Mean Square	F Value	Pr > F
SEX	1	192.91266643	192.91266643	0.06	0.8132

(continued on next page)

(continued from previous page)

Ⓐ   E = Error SS&CP Matrix

	LENGTH	BASILAR	ZYGOMAT	POSTORB
LENGTH	1683039.204	1430839.7517	386107.03613	74382.903263
BASILAR	1430839.7517	1343555.1993	324249.61888	38106.472028
ZYGOMAT	386107.03613	324249.61888	262647.62354	33070.588578
POSTORB	74382.903263	38106.472028	33070.588578	195162.71445

MULTIVARIATE ANALYSIS OF VARIANCE   6

General Linear Models Procedure
Multivariate Analysis of Variance

Ⓑ

Partial Correlation Coefficients from the Error SS&CP Matrix / Prob > |r|

DF = 56	LENGTH	BASILAR	ZYGOMAT	POSTORB
LENGTH	1.000000	0.951516	0.580729	0.129786
	0.0001	0.0001	0.0001	0.3315
BASILAR	0.951516	1.000000	0.545840	0.074417
	0.0001	0.0001	0.0001	0.5788
ZYGOMAT	0.580729	0.545840	1.000000	0.146069
	0.0001	0.0001	0.0001	0.2739
POSTORB	0.129786	0.074417	0.146069	1.000000
	0.3315	0.5788	0.2739	0.0001

MULTIVARIATE ANALYSIS OF VARIANCE   7

General Linear Models Procedure
Multivariate Analysis of Variance

Ⓒ   H = Type III SS&CP Matrix for SEX

	LENGTH	BASILAR	ZYGOMAT	POSTORB
LENGTH	47060.931631	33597.044862	1775.0655644	3013.0797874
BASILAR	33597.044862	23985.105784	1267.2285765	2151.0533958
ZYGOMAT	1775.0655644	1267.2285765	66.952728063	113.64871005
POSTORB	3013.0797874	2151.0533958	113.64871005	192.91266643

Ⓓ   Characteristic Roots and Vectors of: E Inverse * H, where
         H = Type III SS&CP Matrix for SEX   E = Error SS&CP Matrix

Characteristic Root	Percent	Characteristic Vector V'EV=1			
		LENGTH	BASILAR	ZYGOMAT	POSTORB
0.0452508453	100.00	-0.00181900	0.00111840	0.00115382	-0.00005517
0.0000000000	0.00	-0.00177193	0.00249294	-0.00105296	0.00049855
0.0000000000	0.00	-0.00063453	0.00075834	0.00181151	0.00038762
0.0000000000	0.00	0.00000267	-0.00019018	-0.00026194	0.00223311

Ⓔ Manova Test Criteria and Exact F Statistics for the Hypothesis of no Overall SEX Effect
         H = Type III SS&CP Matrix for SEX   E = Error SS&CP Matrix

                    S=1   M=1   N=26

Statistic	Value	F	Num DF	Den DF	Pr > F
Wilks' Lambda	0.95670815	0.6109	4	54	0.6566
Pillai's Trace	0.04329185	0.6109	4	54	0.6566
Hotelling-Lawley Trace	0.04525085	0.6109	4	54	0.6566
Roy's Greatest Root	0.04525085	0.6109	4	54	0.6566

The output above first gives the univariate analyses for each of the dependent variables. These analyses can be supressed using the NOUNI option in the MODEL statement. These analyses show SEX is not significant for any single variable.

The circled letters on the printout correspond to the descriptions below:

A. This portion of output is the result of the PRINTE option in the MANOVA statement. This portion shows elements of the error matrix, also called the Error Sums of Squares and Crossproducts matrix. The diagonal elements of this matrix are the error sums of squares from the corresponding univariate analyses.

B. This portion is also produced as a result of the PRINTE option, and shows the partial correlation matrix associated with the E matrix. In this example, it appears that LENGTH and BASILAR are highly correlated ($r=0.95$). Also, it appears that POSTORB is not correlated with LENGTH, BASILAR, and ZYGOMAT ($r=0.13$, 0.07, and 0.15, respectively).

C. The PRINTH option produces the SSCP matrix for SEX (the H=specification in the MANOVA statement). Since the Type III SS are the highest level SS produced by GLM by default, and since the HTYPE= option is not used, the SSCP matrix for SEX gives the type III **H** matrix. The diagonal elements of this matrix are the model sums of squares from the corresponding univariate analyses.

D. The characteristic roots and vectors of $\mathbf{E}^{-1}\mathbf{H}$ are shown. Note that the Type III **H** matrix is used.

E. The Manova Test Criteria are printed as a result of the MANOVA statement. This section shows four test statistics and their associated probabilities. In this example, all four tests give the same result, although this is not always the case. Notice how the probability levels for the multivariate tests differ from the univariate levels. This section of output identifies the **H** and **E** matrices used in the statistical tests.

Example 7:   Repeated Measures Analysis of Variance

This example uses data from Cole and Grizzle (1966) to illustrate a commonly occurring repeated measures *ANOVA* design. Sixteen dogs were randomly assigned to four groups. (One animal is removed from the analysis due to a missing value for one dependent variable.) Dogs in each group received either morphine or trimethaphan (variable DRUG) and had either depleted or intact histamine levels (variable DEPL) before receiving the drugs. The dependent variable is the blood concentration of histamine at 0, 1, 3, and 5 minutes after injection of the drug. Logarithms were applied to these concentrations to minimize correlation between the mean and the variance of the data.

These SAS statements perform both univariate and multivariate repeated measures analyses and produce **Output 24.16**:

```
data dogs;
   input drug $ depl $ hist0 hist1 hist3 hist5;
   lhist0=log(hist0); lhist1=log(hist1);
   lhist3=log(hist3); lhist5=log(hist5);
   cards;
MORPHINE N  .04  .20  .10  .08
MORPHINE N  .02  .06  .02  .02
MORPHINE N  .07 1.40  .48  .24
MORPHINE N  .17  .57  .35  .24
MORPHINE Y  .10  .09  .13  .14
MORPHINE Y  .12  .11  .10  .
```

```
MORPHINE Y  .07  .07  .06  .07
MORPHINE Y  .05  .07  .06  .07
TRIMETH  N  .03  .62  .31  .22
TRIMETH  N  .03 1.05  .73  .60
TRIMETH  N  .07  .83 1.07  .80
TRIMETH  N  .09 3.13 2.06 1.23
TRIMETH  Y  .10  .09  .09  .08
TRIMETH  Y  .08  .09  .09  .10
TRIMETH  Y  .13  .10  .12  .12
TRIMETH  Y  .06  .05  .05  .05
;

proc glm;
    class drug depl;
    model lhist0--lhist5=drug depl drug*depl / nouni;
    repeated time 4 (0 1 3 5) polynomial / summary;
run;
```

The NOUNI option in the MODEL statement suppresses the individual
ANOVAs for the original dependent variables. These analyses are usually of no
interest in a repeated measures analysis. The POLYNOMIAL option in the
REPEATED statement indicates that the transformation used to implement the
repeated measures analysis is an orthogonal polynomial transformation, and the
SUMMARY option requests that the univariate analyses for the orthogonal polynomial contrast variables be printed. The parenthetical numbers (0 1 3 5) determine the spacing of the orthogonal polynomials used in the analysis.

Output 24.16   Repeated Measures Analysis of Variance

```
                          The SAS System                                    1
                    General Linear Models Procedure
                       Class Level Information

            Class    Levels    Values

            DRUG        2       MORPHINE TRIMETH

            DEPL        2       N Y


        Number of observations in data set = 16

NOTE: Observations with missing values will not be included in this analysis.  Thus, only 15 observations can be
      used in this analysis.
```

The SAS System   2

General Linear Models Procedure
Repeated Measures Analysis of Variance
Repeated Measures Level Information

Ⓐ Dependent Variable   LHIST0   LHIST1   LHIST3   LHIST5

Level of TIME   0   1   3   5

Ⓑ Manova Test Criteria and Exact F Statistics for the Hypothesis of no TIME Effect
H = Type III SS&CP Matrix for TIME   E = Error SS&CP Matrix

S=1   M=0.5   N=3.5

Statistic	Value	F	Num DF	Den DF	Pr > F
Wilks' Lambda	0.11097706	24.0326	3	9	0.0001
Pillai's Trace	0.88902294	24.0326	3	9	0.0001
Hotelling-Lawley Trace	8.01087137	24.0326	3	9	0.0001
Roy's Greatest Root	8.01087137	24.0326	3	9	0.0001

Manova Test Criteria and Exact F Statistics for the Hypothesis of no TIME*DRUG Effect
H = Type III SS&CP Matrix for TIME*DRUG   E = Error SS&CP Matrix

S=1   M=0.5   N=3.5

Statistic	Value	F	Num DF	Den DF	Pr > F
Wilks' Lambda	0.34155984	5.7832	3	9	0.0175
Pillai's Trace	0.65844016	5.7832	3	9	0.0175
Hotelling-Lawley Trace	1.92774470	5.7832	3	9	0.0175
Roy's Greatest Root	1.92774470	5.7832	3	9	0.0175

Manova Test Criteria and Exact F Statistics for the Hypothesis of no TIME*DEPL Effect
H = Type III SS&CP Matrix for TIME*DEPL   E = Error SS&CP Matrix

S=1   M=0.5   N=3.5

Statistic	Value	F	Num DF	Den DF	Pr > F
Wilks' Lambda	0.12339988	21.3112	3	9	0.0002
Pillai's Trace	0.87660012	21.3112	3	9	0.0002
Hotelling-Lawley Trace	7.10373567	21.3112	3	9	0.0002
Roy's Greatest Root	7.10373567	21.3112	3	9	0.0002

The SAS System   3

General Linear Models Procedure
Repeated Measures Analysis of Variance

Manova Test Criteria and Exact F Statistics for the Hypothesis of no TIME*DRUG*DEPL Effect
H = Type III SS&CP Matrix for TIME*DRUG*DEPL   E = Error SS&CP Matrix

S=1   M=0.5   N=3.5

Statistic	Value	F	Num DF	Den DF	Pr > F
Wilks' Lambda	0.19383010	12.4775	3	9	0.0015
Pillai's Trace	0.80616990	12.4775	3	9	0.0015
Hotelling-Lawley Trace	4.15915732	12.4775	3	9	0.0015
Roy's Greatest Root	4.15915732	12.4775	3	9	0.0015

```
                                    The SAS System                                        4
        (C)
                             General Linear Models Procedure
                            Repeated Measures Analysis of Variance
                       Tests of Hypotheses for Between Subjects Effects

        Source           DF        Type III SS        Mean Square     F Value     Pr > F

        DRUG              1          5.99336243         5.99336243       2.71      0.1281
        DEPL              1         15.44840703        15.44840703       6.98      0.0229
        DRUG*DEPL         1          4.69087508         4.69087508       2.12      0.1734

        Error            11         24.34683348         2.21334850
```

```
                                    The SAS System                                        5
        (D)
                             General Linear Models Procedure
                            Repeated Measures Analysis of Variance
                    Univariate Tests of Hypotheses for Within Subject Effects

                                                                           Adjusted  Pr > F
        Source        DF      Type III SS      Mean Square   F Value   Pr > F    G - G     H - F

        TIME           3       12.05898677       4.01966226    53.44    0.0001   0.0001    0.0001
        TIME*DRUG      3        1.84429514       0.61476505     8.17    0.0003   0.0039    0.0008
        TIME*DEPL      3       12.08978557       4.02992852    53.57    0.0001   0.0001    0.0001
        TIME*DRUG*DEPL 3        2.93077939       0.97692646    12.99    0.0001   0.0005    0.0001

        Error(TIME)   33        2.48238887       0.07522391

                           Greenhouse-Geisser Epsilon = 0.5694
                              Huynh-Feldt Epsilon = 0.8475
```

```
                                    The SAS System                                        6
        (E)
                             General Linear Models Procedure
                            Repeated Measures Analysis of Variance
                           Analysis of Variance of Contrast Variables

                 TIME.N represents the nth degree polynomial contrast for TIME

        Contrast Variable: TIME.1

        Source           DF        Type III SS        Mean Square     F Value     Pr > F

        MEAN              1          2.00963483         2.00963483      34.99      0.0001
        DRUG              1          1.18069076         1.18069076      20.56      0.0009
        DEPL              1          1.36172504         1.36172504      23.71      0.0005
        DRUG*DEPL         1          2.04346848         2.04346848      35.58      0.0001

        Error            11          0.63171161         0.05742833

        Contrast Variable: TIME.2

        Source           DF        Type III SS        Mean Square     F Value     Pr > F

        MEAN              1          5.40988418         5.40988418      57.15      0.0001
        DRUG              1          0.59173192         0.59173192       6.25      0.0295
        DEPL              1          5.94945506         5.94945506      62.86      0.0001
        DRUG*DEPL         1          0.67031587         0.67031587       7.08      0.0221

        Error            11          1.04118707         0.09465337

        Contrast Variable: TIME.3

        Source           DF        Type III SS        Mean Square     F Value     Pr > F

        MEAN              1          4.63946776         4.63946776      63.04      0.0001
        DRUG              1          0.07187246         0.07187246       0.98      0.3443
        DEPL              1          4.77860547         4.77860547      64.94      0.0001
        DRUG*DEPL         1          0.21699504         0.21699504       2.95      0.1139

        Error            11          0.80949018         0.07359002
```

The circled letters on the output correspond to the descriptions below:

A. This portion of output gives information on the repeated measures effect. In this example, the within-subject (within-DOG) effect is TIME, which has the levels 0, 1, 3, and 5.

B. This section of output gives multivariate analyses for within-subject effects and related interactions. For the example, the TIME effect is significant. In addition, the TIME*DRUG*DEPL interaction is significant. This means the effect of TIME on the blood concentration of histamine is different for the four DRUG*DEPL combinations studied.

C. This section gives tests of hypotheses for between-subject (between-DOG) effects. This section tests the hypotheses that the different DRUGs, DEPLs and their interaction have no effects on the dependent variables, while ignoring the within-DOG effects. From this analysis, there is a significant between-DOG effect for DEPL. The interaction and the main effect for DRUG are not significant.

D. This section gives univariate analyses for within-subject (within-DOG) effects and related interactions. For the example, the results are the same as for the multivariate analyses. This is not always the case. In addition, before the univariate analyses are used to make conclusions about the data, the result of the sphericity test should be examined. This test is given by the PRINTE option in the REPEATED statement and is not shown here. If the sphericity test is rejected, use the adjusted G-G or H-F probabilities. See **Repeated Measures Analysis of Variance** earlier in this chapter for more information.

E. This section of output is produced by the SUMMARY option in the REPEATED statement. If the POLYNOMIAL option had not been used, a similar section would have been printed using the default CONTRAST transformation.

   This section shows the linear, quadratic, and cubic trends for TIME, labeled as TIME.1, TIME.2, and TIME.3, respectively. In each case, the Source labeled MEAN gives a test for the respective trend.

Example 8:   Mixed Model Analysis of Variance Using the RANDOM Statement

Milliken and Johnson (1984) present an example of an unbalanced mixed model. Three machines, which were considered as a fixed effect, and six employees, which were considered a random effect, were studied. Each employee operated each machine for either one, two, or three different times. The dependent variable was an overall rating, which took into account the number and quality of components produced.

   The following statements form the data set and perform a mixed model analysis of variance by requesting the TEST option in the RANDOM statement. Note that the MACHINE*PERSON interaction is declared as a random effect; in general, when an interaction involves a random effect, it too should be declared as random. The results of the analysis are shown in **Output 24.17**.

```
data machine;
   input machine person rating ðð;
   cards;
1 1 52.0   1 2 51.8   1 2 52.8   1 3 60.0   1 4 51.1   1 4 52.3
1 5 50.9   1 5 51.8   1 5 51.4   1 6 46.4   1 6 44.8   1 6 49.2
2 1 64.0   2 2 59.7   2 2 60.0   2 2 59.0   2 3 68.6   2 3 65.8
2 4 63.2   2 4 62.8   2 4 62.2   2 5 64.8   2 5 65.0   2 6 43.7
2 6 44.2   2 6 43.0   3 1 67.5   3 1 67.2   3 1 66.9   3 2 61.5
```

```
3 2 61.7   3 2 62.3   3 3 70.8   3 3 70.6   3 3 71.0   3 4 64.1
3 4 66.2   3 4 64.0   3 5 72.1   3 5 72.0   3 5 71.1   3 6 62.0
3 6 61.4   3 6 60.5
;

proc glm;
   class machine person;
   model rating=machine person machine*person;
   random person machine*person / test;
run;
```

The TEST option in the RANDOM statement requests that GLM determine the appropriate F tests based on PERSON and MACHINE*PERSON being treated as random effects. As you can see in the output, this requires that a linear combination of mean squares be constructed to test both the MACHINE and PERSON hypotheses; thus, F tests using Satterthwaite approximations are used.

Output 24.17   Mixed Model Analysis of Variance

```
                            The SAS System                                  1

                    General Linear Models Procedure
                         Class Level Information

             Class    Levels    Values

             MACHINE     3      1 2 3

             PERSON      6      1 2 3 4 5 6


        Number of observations in data set = 44
```

```
                            The SAS System                                  2

                    General Linear Models Procedure

Dependent Variable: RATING

Source            DF       Sum of Squares     Mean Square    F Value     Pr > F

Model             17       3061.74333333     180.10254902    206.41      0.0001

Error             26         22.68666667       0.87256410

Corrected Total   43       3084.43000000

          R-Square            C.V.            Root MSE         RATING Mean

          0.992645          1.560754         0.93411140        59.85000000


Source            DF          Type I SS      Mean Square    F Value     Pr > F

MACHINE            2       1648.66472222     824.33236111    944.72      0.0001
PERSON             5       1008.76358308     201.75271662    231.22      0.0001
MACHINE*PERSON    10        404.31502803      40.43150280     46.34      0.0001

Source            DF        Type III SS      Mean Square    F Value     Pr > F

MACHINE            2       1238.19762557     619.09881279    709.52      0.0001
PERSON             5       1011.05383401     202.21076680    231.74      0.0001
MACHINE*PERSON    10        404.31502803      40.43150280     46.34      0.0001
```

```
                               The SAS System                                    3
                        General Linear Models Procedure

Source          Type III Expected Mean Square

MACHINE         Var(Error) + 2.137 Var(MACHINE*PERSON) + Q(MACHINE)

PERSON          Var(Error) + 2.2408 Var(MACHINE*PERSON) + 6.7224 Var(PERSON)

MACHINE*PERSON  Var(Error) + 2.3162 Var(MACHINE*PERSON)
```

```
                               The SAS System                                    4
                        General Linear Models Procedure
                 Tests of Hypotheses for Mixed Model Analysis of Variance

Dependent Variable: RATING


       Source: MACHINE
       Error: 0.9226*MS(MACHINE*PERSON) + 0.0774*MS(Error)

                               Denominator    Denominator
               DF    Type III MS        DF            MS     F Value    Pr > F
                2   619.09881279     10.04    37.370383818     16.567    0.0007

       Source: PERSON
       Error: 0.9674*MS(MACHINE*PERSON) + 0.0326*MS(Error)

                               Denominator    Denominator
               DF    Type III MS        DF            MS     F Value    Pr > F
                5    202.2107668     10.01    39.143708026      5.166    0.0133

       Source: MACHINE*PERSON
       Error: MS(Error)

                               Denominator    Denominator
               DF    Type III MS        DF            MS     F Value    Pr > F
               10    40.431502803       26     0.8725641026     46.336    0.0001
```

Example 9: Analyzing a Doubly-multivariate Repeated Measures Design

This example shows how to analyze a doubly-multivariate repeated measures design by using PROC GLM with a MANOVA statement. Each of two responses, Y1 and Y2, is measured three times for each subject (at pre, post, and follow-up). Each subject received one of three treatments; A, B, or the control. By defining different M matrices in the MANOVA statement, the TIME*TRT interaction, and TRT and TIME effects are tested. The statements below produce **Output 24.18**.

```
/*--------------------------------------------------------------*/
/*   prey1 is the "pre" measure for y1                          */
/*   psty1 is the "post" measure for y1                         */
/*   foly1 is the "follow-up" measure for y1                    */
/*   prey2 is the "pre" measure for y2                          */
/*   psty2 is the "post" measure for y2                         */
/*   foly2 is the "follow-up" measure for y2                    */
/*--------------------------------------------------------------*/
data exam9;
   input trt $ reps prey1 psty1 foly1 prey2 psty2 foly2;
   cards;
TRTA  1  3  13   9   0   0   9
TRTA  2  0  14  10   6   6   3
TRTA  3  4   6  17   8   2   6
TRTA  4  7   7  13   7   6   4
```

```
TRTA 5  3 12 11  6 12  6
TRTA 6 10 14  8 13  3  8
TRTB 1  9 11 17  8 11 27
TRTB 2  4 16 13  9  3 26
TRTB 3  8 10  9 12  0 18
TRTB 4  5  9 13  3  0 14
TRTB 5  0 15 11  3  0 25
TRTB 6  4 11 14  4  2  9
CONT 1 10 12 15  4  3  7
CONT 2  2  8 12  8  7 20
CONT 3  4  9 10  2  0 10
CONT 4 10  8  8  5  8 14
CONT 5 11 11 11  1  0 11
CONT 6  1  5 15  8  9 10
;

proc glm data=exam9;
  class trt;
  model prey1 psty1 foly1 prey2 psty2 foly2=trt / nouni;

  /* Set up test for trt effect                   */
manova h=trt m=prey1+psty1+foly1,
          prey2+psty2+foly2;

  /*------------------------------------------------------------------*/
  /* The same test could have been produced by specifying the   */
  /* M matrix in the following form:  m= (1 1 1 0 0 0,          */
  /*                               0 0 0 1 1 1)          */
  /*                                             */
  /* Notice that the transformation matrices are block diagonal */
  /* Each block consists of the contrasts that test the effect  */
  /* of one dependent variable.                         */
  /*------------------------------------------------------------------*/


  /* Set up test for time effect (repeated measure)         */
manova h=intercept m=prey1-psty1,
          prey1-foly1,
          prey2-psty2,
          PREY2-FOLY2/SUMMARY ;

  /*------------------------------------------------------------------*/
  /* The same test could have been produced by specifying the   */
  /* M matrix in the following form:  m= (1 -1  0 0  0  0,     */
  /*                        1  0 -1 0  0  0,      */
  /*                        0  0  0 1 -1  0,      */
  /*                        0  0  0 1  0 -1)      */
  /*                                             */
  /*------------------------------------------------------------------*/
```

```
        /* Set up test for trt*time interaction              */
    manova h=trt      m=prey1-psty1,
                prey1-foly1,
                prey2-psty2,
                prey2-foly2;
      /*----------------------------------------------------------------*/
      /* The same test could have been produced by specifying the   */
      /* M matrix in the following form: m= (1 -1 0 0 0 0,       */
      /*                          1 0 -1 0 0 0,     */
      /*                          0 0 0 1 -1 0,     */
      /*                          0 0 0 1 0 -1)     */
      /*                                  */
      /* Note: same M matrix for above manova, but different      */
      /* H= effect, simultaneously testing trt differences and     */
      /* time differences                         */
      /*----------------------------------------------------------------*/
    run;
```

```
                              The SAS System                                1

                        General Linear Models Procedure
                           Class Level Information

                   Class     Levels    Values
                   TRT          3      CONT TRTA TRTB


                Number of observations in data set = 18
```

```
                              The SAS System                                2

                        General Linear Models Procedure
                       Multivariate Analysis of Variance

                    M Matrix Describing Transformed Variables
```

	PREY1	PSTY1	FOLY1	PREY2	PSTY2	FOLY2
MVAR1	1	1	1	0	0	0
MVAR2	0	0	0	1	1	1

The SAS System   3

General Linear Models Procedure
Multivariate Analysis of Variance

Characteristic Roots and Vectors of: E Inverse * H, where
H = Type III SS&CP Matrix for TRT   E = Error SS&CP Matrix

Variables have been transformed by the M Matrix

Characteristic Root	Percent	Characteristic Vector V'EV=1	
		MVAR1	MVAR2
0.3769877999	98.53	0.02368613	0.02356288
0.0056287968	1.47	0.04843467	-0.01362490

Manova Test Criteria and F Approximations for the Hypothesis of no Overall TRT Effect
on the variables defined by the M Matrix Transformation
H = Type III SS&CP Matrix for TRT   E = Error SS&CP Matrix

S=2   M=-0.5   N=6

Statistic	Value	F	Num DF	Den DF	Pr > F
Wilks' Lambda	0.72215797	1.2372	4	28	0.3178
Pillai's Trace	0.27937444	1.2178	4	30	0.3240
Hotelling-Lawley Trace	0.38261660	1.2435	4	26	0.3172
Roy's Greatest Root	0.37698780	2.8274	2	15	0.0908

NOTE: F Statistic for Roy's Greatest Root is an upper bound.
NOTE: F Statistic for Wilks' Lambda is exact.

The SAS System   4

General Linear Models Procedure
Multivariate Analysis of Variance

M Matrix Describing Transformed Variables

	PREY1	PSTY1	FOLY1	PREY2	PSTY2	FOLY2
MVAR1	1	-1	0	0	0	0
MVAR2	1	0	-1	0	0	0
MVAR3	0	0	0	1	-1	0
MVAR4	0	0	0	1	0	-1

The SAS System   5

General Linear Models Procedure
Multivariate Analysis of Variance

Characteristic Roots and Vectors of: E Inverse * H, where
H = Type III SS&CP Matrix for INTERCEPT   E = Error SS&CP Matrix

Variables have been transformed by the M Matrix

Characteristic Root	Percent	Characteristic Vector V'EV=1			
		MVAR1	MVAR2	MVAR3	MVAR4
6.1066236155	100.00	-0.00157729	0.04081620	-0.04210209	0.03519437
0.0000000000	0.00	-0.04976412	0.04507459	-0.00985156	-0.00851229
0.0000000000	0.00	-0.00344451	0.01402404	0.05079843	0.00343091
0.0000000000	0.00	-0.04518163	-0.00683849	-0.00437561	0.04176456

(continued on next page)

(continued from previous page)

Manova Test Criteria and Exact F Statistics for the Hypothesis of no Overall INTERCEPT Effect
on the variables defined by the M Matrix Transformation
H = Type III SS&CP Matrix for INTERCEPT   E = Error SS&CP Matrix

S=1   M=1   N=5

Statistic	Value	F	Num DF	Den DF	Pr > F
Wilks' Lambda	0.14071380	18.3199	4	12	0.0001
Pillai's Trace	0.85928620	18.3199	4	12	0.0001
Hotelling-Lawley Trace	6.10662362	18.3199	4	12	0.0001
Roy's Greatest Root	6.10662362	18.3199	4	12	0.0001

The SAS System   6

General Linear Models Procedure
Multivariate Analysis of Variance

Dependent Variable: MVAR1

Source	DF	Type III SS	Mean Square	F Value	Pr > F
INTERCEPT	1	512.00000000	512.00000000	22.65	0.0003
Error	15	339.00000000	22.60000000		

Dependent Variable: MVAR2

Source	DF	Type III SS	Mean Square	F Value	Pr > F
INTERCEPT	1	813.38888889	813.38888889	32.87	0.0001
Error	15	371.16666667	24.74444444		

Dependent Variable: MVAR3

Source	DF	Type III SS	Mean Square	F Value	Pr > F
INTERCEPT	1	68.05555556	68.05555556	3.49	0.0814
Error	15	292.50000000	19.50000000		

Dependent Variable: MVAR4

Source	DF	Type III SS	Mean Square	F Value	Pr > F
INTERCEPT	1	800.00000000	800.00000000	26.43	0.0001
Error	15	454.00000000	30.26666667		

The SAS System   7

General Linear Models Procedure
Multivariate Analysis of Variance

M Matrix Describing Transformed Variables

	PREY1	PSTY1	FOLY1	PREY2	PSTY2	FOLY2
MVAR1	1	-1	0	0	0	0
MVAR2	1	0	-1	0	0	0
MVAR3	0	0	0	1	-1	0
MVAR4	0	0	0	1	0	-1

```
                              The SAS System                                    8

                      General Linear Models Procedure
                      Multivariate Analysis of Variance

                 Characteristic Roots and Vectors of: E Inverse * H, where
                 H = Type III SS&CP Matrix for TRT    E = Error SS&CP Matrix

                    Variables have been transformed by the M Matrix

   Characteristic   Percent                    Characteristic Vector  V'EV=1
       Root
                                     MVAR1         MVAR2         MVAR3         MVAR4

     2.1265190526    84.20       -0.02780329    0.02023561   -0.03439916    0.05466141
     0.3990560890    15.80       -0.04526733   -0.00757601    0.03858928    0.00609866
     0.0000000000     0.00       -0.00632222    0.04530926    0.02107407    0.00000000
     0.0000000000     0.00        0.04086655   -0.03770033    0.03677926    0.00648754


        Manova Test Criteria and F Approximations for the Hypothesis of no Overall TRT Effect
             on the variables defined by the M Matrix Transformation
             H = Type III SS&CP Matrix for TRT    E = Error SS&CP Matrix

                          S=2      M=0.5     N=5
      Statistic                 Value         F       Num DF    Den DF    Pr > F

      Wilks' Lambda            0.22861451   3.2744       8        24      0.0115
      Pillai's Trace           0.96538785   3.0325       8        26      0.0151
      Hotelling-Lawley Trace   2.52557514   3.4727       8        22      0.0097
      Roy's Greatest Root      2.12651905   6.9112       4        13      0.0033

         NOTE: F Statistic for Roy's Greatest Root is an upper bound.
              NOTE: F Statistic for Wilks' Lambda is exact.
```

REFERENCES

Afifi, A.A. and Azen, S.P. (1972), *Statistical Analysis: A Computer-Oriented Approach*, New York: Academic Press, Inc.

Anderson, T.W. (1958), *An Introduction to Multivariate Statistical Analysis*, New York: John Wiley & Sons, Inc.

Begun, J.M. and Gabriel, K.R. (1981), "Closure of the Newman-Keuls Multiple Comparisons Procedure," *Journal of the American Statistical Association*, 76, 374.

Belsley, D.A., Kuh, E., and Welsch, R.E. (1980), *Regression Diagnostics*, New York: John Wiley & Sons, Inc.

Box, G.E.P. (1954), "Some Theorems on Quadratic Forms Applied in the Study of Analysis of Variance Problems. II, Effects of Inequality of Variance and of Correlation Between Errors in the Two-Way Classification," *Annals of Mathematical Statistics, 25*, 484–498.

Carmer, S.G. and Swanson, M.R. (1973), "Evaluation of Ten Pairwise Multiple Comparison Procedures by Monte-Carlo Methods," *Journal of the American Statistical Association*, 68, 66–74.

Cochran, W.G. and Cox, G.M. (1957), *Experimental Designs*, 2d edition. New York: John Wiley & Sons, Inc.

Cole, J.W.L. and Grizzle, J.E. (1966), "Applications of Multivariate Analysis of Variance to Repeated Measures Experiments," *Biometrics*, 22, 810–828.

Draper, N.R. and Smith, H. (1966), *Applied Regression Analysis*, New York: John Wiley & Sons, Inc.

Duncan, D.B. (1975), "*t*-Tests and Intervals for Comparisons Suggested by the Data," *Biometrics*, 31, 339–359.

Dunnett, C.W. (1955), "A Multiple Comparisons Procedure for Comparing Several Treatments with a Control," *Journal of the American Statistical Association*, 50, 1096–1121.

Dunnett, C.W. (1980), "Pairwise Multiple Comparisons in the Homogeneous Variance, Unequal Sample Size Case," *Journal of the American Statistical Association*, 75, 789–795.

Einot, I. and Gabriel, K.R. (1975), "A Study of the Powers of Several Methods of Multiple Comparisons," *Journal of the American Statistical Association*, 70, 351.

Freund, R.J., Littell, R.C., and Spector, P.C. (1986), *SAS System for Linear Models, 1986 Edition*, Cary, NC: SAS Institute Inc.

Gabriel, K.R. (1978), "A Simple Method of Multiple Comparisons of Means," *Journal of the American Statistical Association*, 73, 364.

Games, P.A. (1977), "An Improved *t* Table for Simultaneous Control on *g* Contrasts," *Journal of the American Statistical Association*, 72, 531–534.

Goodnight, J.H. (1976), "The New General Linear Models Procedure," *Proceedings of the First International SAS Users' Conference*, Cary, NC: SAS Institute Inc.

Goodnight, J.H. (1978), *Tests of the Hypotheses in Fixed-Effects Linear Models*, SAS Technical Report R-101, Cary, NC: SAS Institute Inc.

Goodnight, J.H. (1979), "A Tutorial on the Sweep Operator," *American Statistician*, 33, 149–158. (Also available as *The Sweep Operator: Its Importance in Statistical Computing*, SAS Technical Report R-106.)

Goodnight, J.H. and Harvey, W.R. (1978), *Least-Squares Means in the Fixed-Effects General Linear Models*, SAS Technical Report R-103, Cary, NC: SAS Institute Inc.

Goodnight, J.H. and Speed, F.M. (1978), *Computing Expected Mean Squares*, SAS Technical Report R-102, Cary, NC: SAS Institute Inc.

Graybill, F.A. (1961), *An Introduction to Linear Statistical Models, Volume I*, New York: McGraw-Hill Book Co.

Greenhouse, S.W. and Geisser, S. (1959), "On Methods in the Analysis of Profile Data," *Psychometrika*, 32, 95–112.

Harvey, W.R. (1975), *Least-squares Analysis of Data with Unequal Subclass Numbers*, USDA Report ARS H-4.

Hayter, A.J. (1984), "A Proof of the Conjecture that the Tukey-Kramer Method is Conservative." *The Annals of Statistics*, 12, 61-75.

Heck, D.L. (1960), "Charts of Some Upper Percentage Points of the Distribution of the Largest Characteristic Root," *Annals of Mathematical Statistics*, 31, 625–642.

Hochberg, Y. (1974), "Some Conservative Generalizations of the T-Method in Simultaneous Inference," *Journal of Multivariate Analysis*, 4, 224–234.

Hocking, R.R. (1976), "The Analysis and Selection of Variables in a Linear Regression," *Biometrics*, 32, 1–50.

Hocking, R.R. (1985), *The Analysis of Linear Models*, Belmont, CA: Brooks/Cole Publishing Co.

Huynh, H. and Feldt, L. S. (1970), "Conditions under Which Mean Square Ratios in Repeated Measurements Designs Have Exact F-Distributions," *Journal of the American Statistical Association*, 65, 1582–1589.

Huynh, H. and Feldt, L.S. (1976), "Estimation of the Box Correction for Degrees of Freedom from Sample Data in the Randomized Block and Split Plot Designs," *Journal of Educational Statistics*, 1, 69-82.

Kennedy, W.J., Jr. and Gentle, J.E. (1980), *Statistical Computing*, New York: Marcel Dekker, Inc.

Kramer, C.Y. (1956), "Extension of Multiple Range Tests to Group Means with Unequal Numbers of Replications," *Biometrics*, 12, 307–310.

Krishnaiah, P.R. and Armitage, J.V. (1966), "Tables for Multivariate *t* Distribution," *Sankhya, Series B*, 31–56.

Kutner, M.H. (1974), "Hypothesis Testing in Linear Models (Eisenhart Model)," *American Statistician*, 28, 98–100.

LaTour, S.A. and Miniard, P.W. (1983), "The Misuse of Repeated Measures Analysis in Marketing Research," *Journal of Marketing Research*, XX, 45–57.

Marcus, R., Peritz, E., and Gabriel, K.R. (1976), "On Closed Testing Procedures with Special Reference to Ordered Analysis of Variance," *Biometrika*, 63, 655–660.

Miller, R.G., Jr. (1981), *Simultaneous Statistical Inference*, New York: Springer-Verlag.

Milliken, G.A. and Johnson, D.E. (1984), *Analysis of Messy Data, Volume I: Designed Experiments*, Belmont, CA: Lifetime Learning Publications.

Morrison, D.F. (1976), *Multivariate Statistical Methods*, 2d Edition, New York: McGraw-Hill Book Co.

Petrinovich, L.F. and Hardyck, C.D. (1969), "Error Rates for Multiple Comparison Methods: Some Evidence Concerning the Frequency of Erroneous Conclusions," *Psychological Bulletin*, 71, 43–54.

Pillai, K.C.S. (1960), *Statistical Tables for Tests of Multivariate Hypotheses*, Manila: The Statistical Center, University of the Philippines.

Pringle, R.M. and Raynor, A.A. (1971), *Generalized Inverse Matrices with Applications to Statistics*, New York: Hafner Publishing Co.

Ramsey, P.H. (1978), "Power Differences Between Pairwise Multiple Comparisons," *Journal of the American Statistical Association*, 73, 363.

Rao, C.R. (1965), *Linear Statistical Inference and Its Applications*, New York: John Wiley & Sons, Inc.

Ryan, T.A. (1959), "Multiple Comparisons in Psychological Research," *Psychological Bulletin*, 56, 26–47.

Ryan, T.A. (1960), "Significance Tests for Multiple Comparison of Proportions, Variances, and Other Statistics," *Psychological Bulletin*, 57, 318–328.

Satterthwaite, F. E. (1946), "An Approximate Distribution of Estimates of Variance Components," *Biometrics Bulletin*, 2, 110–114.

Schatzoff, M. (1966), "Exact Distributions of Wilks' Likelihood Ratio Criterion," *Biometrika*, 53, 347–358.

Scheffe, H. (1953), "A Method for Judging All Contrasts in the Analysis of Variance," *Biometrika*, 40, 87–104.

Scheffe, H. (1959), *The Analysis of Variance*, New York: John Wiley & Sons, Inc.

Searle, S.R. (1971), *Linear Models*, New York: John Wiley & Sons, Inc.

Searle, S.R., Speed, F.M., and Milliken, G.A. (1980), "Populations Marginal Means in the Linear Model: An Alternative to Least Squares Means," *The American Statistician*, 34, 216–221.

Searle, S.R. (1987), *Linear Models for Unbalanced Data*, New York: John Wiley & Sons, Inc.

Sidak, Z. (1967), "Rectangular Confidence Regions for the Means of Multivariate Normal Distributions," *Journal of the American Statistical Association*, 62, 626–633.

Snedecor, G.W. and Cochran, W.G. (1967), *Statistical Methods*, Ames, IA: Iowa State University Press.

Steel, R.G.D. and Torrie, J.H. (1960), *Principles and Procedures of Statistics*, New York: McGraw-Hill Book Co.

Tukey, J.W. (1952), "Allowances for Various Types of Error Rates," Unpublished IMS address, Chicago, IL.

Tukey, J.W. (1953), "The Problem of Multiple Comparisons," Unpublished manuscript.

Waller, R.A. and Duncan, D.B. (1969), "A Bayes Rule for the Symmetric Multiple Comparison Problem," *Journal of the American Statistical Association*, 64, 1484–1499, and (1972) "Corrigenda," 67, 253–255.

Waller, R.A. and Kemp, K.E. (1976), "Computations of Bayesian t-Values for Multiple Comparisons," *Journal of Statistical Computation and Simulation*, 75, 169–172.

Welsch, R.E. (1977), "Stepwise Multiple Comparison Procedures," *Journal of the American Statistical Association*, 72, 359.

Winer, B. J. (1971), *Statistical Principles in Experimental Design*, 2d Edition, New York: McGraw-Hill Book Co.

Chapter 25

The LIFEREG Procedure

ABSTRACT 997
INTRODUCTION 998
SPECIFICATIONS 999
  PROC LIFEREG Statement 1000
  BY Statement 1001
  CLASS Statement 1001
  MODEL Statement 1002
  OUTPUT Statement 1006
  WEIGHT Statement 1008
DETAILS 1008
  Missing Values 1008
  Main Effects 1008
  Computational Method 1008
  Model Specifications 1009
  Distributions Allowed 1010
    Exponential 1010
    Gamma 1010
    Loglogistic 1011
    Lognormal 1011
    Weibull 1011
  Predicted Values 1011
  OUTEST= Data Set 1012
  Computational Resources 1013
  Printed Output 1013
EXAMPLES 1014
  Example 1: Motorette Failure 1014
  Example 2: VA Lung Cancer Data 1016
  Example 3: Tobit Analysis 1024
REFERENCES 1025

ABSTRACT

The LIFEREG procedure fits parametric models to failure time data that may be right-, left-, or interval-censored. The models for the response variable consist of a linear effect composed of the covariables together with a random disturbance term. The distribution of the random disturbance can be taken from a class of distributions that includes the extreme value, normal and logistic distributions, and, by using a log transformation, exponential, Weibull, lognormal, loglogistic, and gamma distributions.

More explicitly, the model assumed for the response y is

$$y = X\beta + \sigma\varepsilon$$

where **y** is the vector of response values, often the log of the failure times, **X** is a matrix of covariates or independent variables, **β** is a vector of unknown regression parameters, σ is an unknown scale parameter, and **ε** is a vector of errors assumed to come from a known distribution (such as the standard normal distribution). In general, the distribution may depend on additional shape parameters. These models are equivalent to accelerated failure time models when the log of the response is the quantity being modeled. The effect of the covariates in an accelerated failure time model then is to change the scale, but not the location, of a baseline distribution of failure times.

The parameters are estimated by maximum likelihood using a Newton-Raphson algorithm. The estimates of the standard errors of the parameter estimates are computed from the inverse of the observed information matrix.

INTRODUCTION

The accelerated failure time model assumes that the effect of independent variables on an event-time distribution is multiplicative on the event time. Usually, the scale function is $\exp(\mathbf{x}'\boldsymbol{\beta})$, where **x** is the vector of covariate values and **β** is a vector of unknown parameters. Thus, if T_0 is an event time sampled from the baseline distribution corresponding to values of zero for the covariates, then the accelerated failure time model specifies that if the vector of covariates had been **x**, the event time would have been $T = \exp(\mathbf{x}'\boldsymbol{\beta})T_0$. If $y = \log(T)$ and $y_0 = \log(T_0)$, then

$$y = \mathbf{x}'\boldsymbol{\beta} + y_0 \quad .$$

This is a linear model with y_0 playing the role of the error term.

In terms of survival or exceedance probabilities, this model is

$$\text{Prob}(T > t \mid \mathbf{x}) = \text{Prob}(T_0 > \exp(-\mathbf{x}'\boldsymbol{\beta})t)$$

where the probability on the left-hand side of the equal sign is evaluated given the value **x** for the covariates, and the right-hand side is computed using the baseline probability distribution but at a scaled value of the argument. The right-hand side of the equation represents the value of the baseline Survival Distribution Function evaluated at $\exp(-\mathbf{x}'\boldsymbol{\beta})t$.

Usually, an intercept parameter and a scale parameter are allowed in the model above. In terms of the original untransformed event times, the effects of the intercept term and the scale term are to scale the event time and power the event time, respectively. That is, if

$$\log(T) = \mu + \sigma\log(T_0)$$

then

$$T = \exp(\mu)T_0^{\sigma} \quad .$$

Although it is possible to fit these models to the original response variable using the NOLOG option, it is more common to model the log of the response variable. Because of this log transformation, zero values for the observed failure times are not allowed unless the NOLOG option is specified. Similarly, small values for the observed failure times lead to large negative values for the transformed response. The parameter estimates for the normal distribution are sensitive to large negative values, and care must be taken that the fitted model is not unduly influenced by them. Likewise, values that are extremely large even after the log transformation will have a strong influence in fitting the extreme value (Weibull) and normal distributions. You should examine the residuals and check the effects of removing observations with large residuals or extreme values of covariates on the model parameters. The logistic distribution gives robust parameter estimates in the sense that the estimates have a bounded influence function.

The standard errors of the parameter estimates are computed from large sample normal approximations using the observed information matrix. In small samples, these approximations may be poor. See Lawless (1982) for additional discussion and references. Better confidence intervals can sometimes be constructed by transforming the parameters. For example, it is often the case that large sample theory is more accurate for $\log(\sigma)$ than σ. Therefore, it may be more accurate to construct confidence intervals for $\log(\sigma)$ and transform these into confidence intervals for σ. The parameter estimates and their estimated covariance matrix are available in an output SAS data set and can be used to construct additional tests or confidence intervals for the parameters. Alternatively, tests of parameters can be based on log likelihood ratios. See Cox and Oakes (1984) for a discussion of the merits of some possible test methods including score, Wald, and likelihood ratio tests. It is believed that likelihood ratio tests are generally more reliable in small samples than tests based on the information matrix.

The log likelihood function is computed using the log of the failure time as a response. This log likelihood differs from the log likelihood obtained using the failure time as the response by an additive term of $\Sigma\log(t_i)$, where the sum is over the noncensored failure times. This term does not depend on the unknown parameters and does not affect parameter or standard error estimates. However, many published values of log likelihoods use the failure time as the basic response variable and hence differ by the above additive term from the value computed by the LIFEREG procedure.

The classic Tobit model (Tobin 1958) also fits into this class of models, but with data usually censored on the left. The data considered by Tobin in his original paper came from a survey of consumers where the response variable was the ratio of expenditures on durable goods to the total disposable income. The two independent variables were the age of the head of household and the ratio of liquid assets to total disposable income. Because many observations in this data set had a value of zero for the response variable, the model fit by Tobin was

$$\mathbf{y} = \max(\mathbf{x}'\boldsymbol{\beta} + \boldsymbol{\varepsilon}, 0)$$

which is a regression model with left-censoring.

SPECIFICATIONS

The following statements are available in PROC LIFEREG:

PROC LIFEREG <*options*>;   must precede **MODEL** statement

MODEL *response=independents*   required statement
        < / *options*>;

BY *variables*;
CLASS *variables*;   optional
OUTPUT <OUT=*SAS-data-set*> <*options*>;   statements
WEIGHT *variable*;

The PROC LIFEREG statement invokes the procedure. The MODEL statement is required and specifies the variables used in the regression part of the model as well as the distribution used for the error, or random, component of the model. Only main effects can be specified in the MODEL statements. Interaction terms involving CLASS variables, allowed in the GLM procedure, are not available in LIFEREG. Initial values can be specified in the MODEL statement. If no initial values are specified, the starting estimates are obtained by ordinary least squares. The CLASS statement determines which independent variables are treated as categorical. The WEIGHT statement identifies a variable whose values are used to weight the observations. Observations with zero or negative weights are not used to fit the model although predicted values can be computed for them. The OUTPUT statement creates an output data set containing predicted values and residuals.

PROC LIFEREG Statement

PROC LIFEREG <*options*>;

The PROC LIFEREG statement invokes the procedure. The following options can appear in the PROC LIFEREG statement; they are described below in alphabetic order.

Task	Option
write estimated covariance matrix to OUTEST= data set	COVOUT
name the input SAS data set	DATA=
suppress printed output	NOPRINT
specify ordering of levels for CLASS variables	ORDER=
name an output data set containing parameter estimates	OUTEST=

COVOUT
    writes the estimated covariance matrix to the OUTEST= data set if convergence is attained.

DATA=*SAS-data-set*
    names the input SAS data set used by LIFEREG. By default, the most recently created SAS data set is used.

NOPRINT
    suppresses the printing of output.

ORDER=DATA | FORMATTED | FREQ | INTERNAL
    specifies the sorting order for the levels of the classification variables (specified in the CLASS statement). This ordering determines which parameters in the model correspond to each level in the data. The table below shows how LIFEREG interprets values of ORDER=.

Value of ORDER=	Levels Sorted by
DATA	order of appearance in the input data set
FORMATTED	formatted value
FREQ	descending frequency count; levels with the most observations come first in the order
INTERNAL	unformatted value

By default, ORDER=FORMATTED. For FORMATTED and INTERNAL, the sort order is machine dependent. For more information on sorting order, see the chapter on the SORT procedure in the *SAS Procedures Guide, Version 6, Third Edition*, and "Rules of the SAS Language" in *SAS Language: Reference, Version 6, First Edition*.

OUTEST=*SAS-data-set*
  names an output SAS data set containing the parameter estimates, the maximized log likelihood and, optionally, the estimated covariance matrix. See **OUTEST= Data Set** later in this chapter for a detailed description of the contents of the OUTEST= data set. This data set is not created if class variables are used.

BY Statement

BY *variables*;

A BY statement can be used with PROC LIFEREG to obtain separate analyses on observations in groups defined by the BY variables. When a BY statement appears, the procedure expects the input data set to be sorted in order of the BY variables.

If your input data set is not sorted in ascending order, use one of the following alternatives:

- Use the SORT procedure with a similar BY statement to sort the data.
- Use the BY statement options NOTSORTED or DESCENDING in the BY statement for the LIFEREG procedure. As a cautionary note, the NOTSORTED option does not mean that the data are unsorted, but rather means that the data are arranged in groups (according to values of the BY variables) and that these groups are not necessarily in alphabetical or increasing numeric order.
- Use the DATASETS procedure (in base SAS software) to create an index on the BY variables.

For more information on the BY statement, see the discussion in *SAS Language: Reference*. For more information on the DATASETS procedure, see the discussion in the *SAS Procedures Guide*.

CLASS Statement

CLASS *variables*;

Variables that are classification variables rather than quantitative numeric variables must be listed in the CLASS statement. For each independent variable listed in the CLASS statement, indicator variables are generated for the levels assumed by the CLASS variable. If you use a CLASS statement, you cannot output parameter estimates to a SAS data set.

MODEL Statement

<label>: **MODEL** response<*censor(list)>=independents <options>;

<label>: **MODEL** (lower,upper)=independents< / options>;

<label>: **MODEL** events/trials=independents< / options>;

Multiple MODEL statements can be used with one invocation of the LIFEREG procedure. The optional *label* is used to label the model estimates in the output SAS data set. The response can be specified in one of the ways listed above.

The first MODEL syntax shown above allows for right-censoring. The variable *response* is possibly right-censored. If the *response* variable can be right-censored, then a second variable, denoted *censor* above, must appear after *response* with a list of parenthesized values, separated by commas or blanks, to indicate censoring. That is, if the *censor* variable takes on a value given in the list, the *response* is a right-censored value; otherwise, it is an observed value.

The second MODEL syntax shown specifies two variables, *lower* and *upper*, that contain values of the endpoints of the censoring interval. If the two values are the same (and not missing), it is assumed that there is no censoring and the actual response value was observed. If the *lower* value is missing, then the *upper* value is used as a left-censored value. If the *upper* value is missing, then the *lower* value is taken as a right-censored value. If both values are present and the *lower* value is less than the *upper* value, it is assumed that the values specify a censoring interval. If the *lower* value is greater than the *upper* value or both values are missing, then the observation is not used in the analysis, although predicted values can still be obtained if none of the covariates is missing. The table below summarizes the ways of specifying censoring.

lower	upper	Comparison	Interpretation
not missing	not missing	equal	no censoring
not missing	not missing	lower<upper	censoring interval
missing	not missing		upper used as left-censoring value
not missing	missing		lower used as right-censoring value
not missing	not missing	lower>upper	observation not used
missing	missing		observation not used

The third MODEL syntax specifies two variables that contain count data for a binary response. The value of the first variable, *events*, is the number of successes. The value of the second variable, *trials*, is the number of tries. The values of both *events* and (*trials*−*events*) must be nonnegative, and *trials* must be positive for the response to be valid. The values of the two variables do not need to be integers and are not modified to be integers.

The variables following the equal sign are the covariates in the model. No higher order effects, such as interactions, are allowed in the covariables list; only variable names are allowed to appear in this list. However, a class variable can be used as a main effect, and indicator variables will be generated for the class levels.

Examples of three valid MODEL statements are

a: `model time*flag(1,3)=temp;`

b: `model (start, finish)=;`

c: `model r/n=dose;`

MODEL statement A indicates that the response is contained in a variable named TIME and that, if the variable FLAG takes on the values 1 or 3, the observation is right-censored. The independent variable is TEMP, which could be a class variable. MODEL statement B indicates that the response is known to be in the interval between the values of the variables START and FINISH and that there are no covariates except for a default intercept term. MODEL statement C indicates a binary response with the variable R containing the number of responses and the variable N containing the number of trials.

The following options can appear in the MODEL statement; they are explained following the table in alphabetic order.

Task	Option
Model specification	
specify distribution type for failure time	DISTRIBUTION=
request no log transformation of response	NOLOG
initial estimate for intercept term	INTERCEPT=
hold intercept term fixed	NOINT
initial estimates for regression parameters	INITIAL=
initialize scale parameter	SCALE=
hold scale parameter fixed	NOSCALE
initialize first shape parameter	SHAPE1=
hold first shape parameter fixed	NOSHAPE1
Model fitting	
set convergence criterion	CONVERGE=
set maximum iterations	MAXITER=
set tolerance for testing singularity	SINGULAR=
Printing	
print estimated correlation matrix	CORRB
print estimated covariance matrix	COVB
print iteration history, final gradient, and second derivative matrix	ITPRINT

CONVERGE=*value*
>   sets the convergence criterion. The iterations are considered to have converged when the maximum change in the parameter estimates between Newton-Raphson steps is less than the value specified. The change is a relative change if the parameter is greater than 0.01 in absolute value; otherwise, it is an absolute change. By default, CONVERGE=0.001.

CORRB
>   prints the estimated correlation matrix of the parameter estimates.

COVB

prints the estimated covariance matrix of the parameter estimates.

DISTRIBUTION=*distribution-type*
DIST=*distribution-type*
D=*distribution-type*

specifies the distribution type assumed for the failure time. By default, LIFEREG fits a Type one extreme value distribution when the log of the response is modeled. The scale parameter for the extreme value distribution is related to a Weibull shape parameter and the intercept is related to the Weibull variance. When NOLOG is specified, LIFEREG models the untransformed response with an extreme value distribution as the default. See **Distributions Allowed** later in this chapter for descriptions of the distributions.

Valid values for *distribution-type* are as follows:

EXPONENTIAL	the exponential distribution, which is treated as a restricted Weibull distribution.
GAMMA	a gamma distribution.
LLOGISTIC	a loglogistic distribution.
LNORMAL	a lognormal distribution.
LOGISTIC	a logistic distribution (equivalent to LLOGISTIC with NOLOG specified).
NORMAL	a normal distribution (equivalent to LNORMAL with NOLOG specified).
WEIBULL	a Type one extreme value distribution fit to the log of the response unless NOLOG is specified. (When NOLOG is specified, an extreme value distribution is fit to the raw data.)

INITIAL=*values*

sets initial values for the regression parameters. This option can be helpful in the case of convergence difficulty. The values listed are used to initialize the regression coefficients for the covariates specified in the MODEL statement. The intercept parameter is initialized with the INTERCEPT= option and is not included here. The values are assigned to the variables in the MODEL statement in the same order as they are listed in the MODEL statement. Note that a class variable requires $k-1$ values when the class variable takes on k different levels. The order of the class levels is determined by the ORDER= option. If there is no intercept term, the first class variable requires k initial values. If a BY statement is used, all class variables must take on the same number of levels in each BY group, or no meaningful initial values can be specified. The INITIAL option can be specified as shown below.

Type of List	Specification
list separated by blanks	initial=3 4 5
list separated by commas	initial=3,4,5
x to y	initial=3 to 5
x to y by z	initial=3 to 5 by 1
combination of above	initial=1,3 to 5,9

By default, LIFEREG computes initial estimates with ordinary least squares. See **Computational Methods** later in this chapter for details.

INTERCEPT=*value*

initializes the intercept term to *value*. By default, the intercept is initialized by an ordinary least-squares estimate.

ITPRINT

prints the iteration history, the final evaluation of the gradient, and the final evaluation of the negative of the second derivative matrix, that is, the negative of the Hessian.

MAXITER=*value*

sets the maximum allowable number of iterations during the model estimation. By default, MAXITER=50.

NOINT

holds the intercept term fixed. Because of the usual log transformation of the response, the intercept parameter is usually a scale parameter for the untransformed response.

NOLOG

requests that no log transformation of the response variable be performed. By default, LIFEREG models the log of the response variable.

NOSCALE

holds the scale parameter fixed. Note that if the log transformation has been applied to the response, the effect of the scale parameter is a power transformation of the original response. If no SCALE= value is specified, the scale parameter is fixed at the value 1.

NOSHAPE1

holds the first shape parameter, SHAPE1, fixed. If no SHAPE= value is specified, SHAPE1 is fixed at a value that depends on the distribution type.

SCALE=*value*

initializes the scale parameter to *value*. Note that with a log transformation, the exponential model is the same as a Weibull model with the scale parameter fixed at the value 1.

SHAPE1=*value*

initializes the first shape parameter to *value*. If the specified distribution does not depend on this parameter, then this option has no effect. See **Distributions Allowed** later in this chapter for descriptions of the parameterizations of the distributions.

SINGULAR=*value*

sets the tolerance for testing singularity of the information matrix and the crossproducts matrix for the initial least-squares estimates. Roughly, the test requires that a pivot be at least this number times the original diagonal value. By default, SINGULAR=1E-12.

OUTPUT Statement

OUTPUT <OUT=*SAS-data-set*> *keyword=name* < ... *keyword=name* >;

The OUTPUT statement creates a new SAS data set containing statistics calculated after fitting the model. At least one specification of the form *keyword=name* is required.

All variables in the original data set are included in the new data set, along with the variables created as options to the OUTPUT statement. These new variables contain fitted values and estimated quantiles. If you want to create a permanent SAS data set, you must specify a two-level name. (See "SAS Files" in *SAS Language: Reference, Version 6, First Edition*, and "Introduction to DATA Step Processing" in *SAS Language and Procedures: Usage, Version 6, First Edition*, for more information on permanent SAS data sets.) Each OUTPUT statement applies to the preceding MODEL statement. See **Example 1** and **Example 2** for illustrations of the OUTPUT statement.

Details on the specifications in the OUTPUT statement are given below.

keyword=name   specifies the statistics to include in the output data set and gives names to the new variables. Specify a keyword for each desired statistic, an equal sign, and the variable to contain the statistic.

The keywords allowed and the statistics they represent are as follows:

CENSORED

names an indicator variable to signal censoring. The variable takes on the value 1 if the observation was censored; otherwise, it is 0.

CDF

names a variable to contain the estimates of the cumulative distribution function evaluated at the observed response. See **Predicted Values** later in this chapter for more information.

CONTROL

names a variable in the input data set to control the estimation of quantiles. See **Example 1** for an illustration. If the variable named has the value of 1, estimates for all the values listed in the QUANTILE= list are computed for that observation in the input data set; otherwise, no estimates are computed. If no CONTROL= variable is specified, all quantiles are estimated for all observations. If the response variable in the MODEL statement is binomial, then this option has no effect.

PREDICTED
P

names a variable to contain the quantile estimates. If the response variable in the corresponding model statement is binomial, then this variable contains the estimated probabilities, $1-F(-\mathbf{x}'\mathbf{b})$.

QUANTILES
QUANTILE
Q

>gives a list of values for which quantiles are calculated. The values must be between 0 and 1, noninclusive. For each value, a corresponding quantile is estimated. This option is not used if the response variable in the corresponding MODEL statement is binomial. The QUANTILES option can be specified as follows:

Type of List	Specification
list separated by blanks	.2 .4 .6 .8
list separated by commas	.2,.4,.6,.8
x to y	.2 to .8
x to y by z	.2 to .8 by .1
combination of above	.1,.2 to .8 by .2

>By default, QUANTILES=.5.
>When the response is not binomial, a numeric variable, _PROB_, is added to the OUTPUT data set whenever the QUANTILES= option is specified. The variable _PROB_ gives the probability value for the quantile estimates. These are the values taken from the QUANTILES= list above and are given as values between 0 and 1, not as values between 0 and 100.

STD_ERR
STD

>names a variable to contain the estimates of the standard errors of the estimated quantiles or x'b. If the response used in the MODEL statement is a binomial response, then these are the standard errors of x'b. Otherwise, they are the standard errors of the quantile estimates. These estimates can be used to compute confidence intervals for the quantiles. However, if the model is fit to the log of the event time, better confidence intervals can usually be computed by transforming the confidence intervals for the log response. See **Example 1** later in this chapter for such a transformation.

XBETA

>names a variable to contain the computed value of x'b, where x is the covariate vector and b is the vector of parameter estimates.

OUT=*SAS-data-set*

>names the new data set. By default, the procedure uses the DATA*n* convention to name the new data set.

WEIGHT Statement

WEIGHT *variable*;

If you want to use weights for each observation in the input data set, place the weights in a variable in the data set and specify the name in a WEIGHT statement. The values of the WEIGHT variable can be nonintegral and are not truncated. Observations with nonpositive or missing values for the weight variable do not contribute to the analysis. The WEIGHT variable multiplies the contribution to the log likelihood for each observation.

DETAILS

Missing Values

Any observation with missing values for the dependent variable is not used in the model estimation unless it is one and only one of the values in an interval specification. Also, if one of the independent variables or the censoring variable is missing, the observation is not used. For any observation to be used in the estimation of a model, only the variables needed in that model have to be nonmissing. Predicted values are computed for all observations with no missing independent variable values. If the censoring variable is missing, the CENSORED= variable in the OUT= data set is also missing.

Main Effects

Unlike the GLM procedure, only main effect terms are allowed in the model specification. For numeric variables, this is a linear term equal to the value of the variable, unless the variable appears in the CLASS statement. For variables listed in the CLASS statement, PROC LIFEREG creates indicator variables (variables taking the values 0 or 1) for every level of the variable except the last level. The levels are ordered according to the ORDER= option. If there is no intercept term, the first class variable has indicator variables created for all levels including the last level. Estimates of a main effect depend on other effects in the model and therefore are adjusted for the presence of other effects in the model.

Computational Method

An initial ordinary least-squares calculation ignoring the censoring information is performed to compute the starting values for the parameter estimates and also to estimate the rank of the design matrix **X**. The INITIAL= option of the MODEL statement can be used to override these starting values. Columns of **X** that are judged linearly dependent on other columns have the corresponding parameters set to zero. The test for linear dependence is controlled by the SINGULAR= option in the MODEL statement. Variables are included in the model in the order listed in the MODEL statement with the non-class variables included in the model before any class variables.

The log likelihood function is maximized by means of a ridge-stabilized Newton-Raphson algorithm.

A composite chi-square test statistic is computed for each class variable, testing whether there is any effect from any of the levels of the variable. This statistic is computed as a quadratic form in the appropriate parameter estimates using the corresponding submatrix of the asymptotic covariance matrix estimate. The asymptotic covariance matrix is computed as the inverse of the observed information matrix. Note that if the NOINT option is specified and class variables are used, the first class variable contains a contribution from an intercept term.

Model Specifications

Suppose there are n observations from the model $y = X\beta + \sigma\varepsilon$, where X is an $n \times k$ matrix of covariate values, y is a vector of responses, and ε is a vector of errors with survival distribution function S, cumulative distribution function F, and probability density function f. That is, $S(t) = PROB(\varepsilon_i > t)$, $F(t) = PROB(\varepsilon_i \leq t)$, and $f(t) = d\, F(t)/dt$, where ε_i is a component of the error vector. Then, if all the responses are observed, the log likelihood, L, can be written as

$$L = \Sigma \log(f(w_i)/\sigma) \quad \text{where } w_i = (y_i - x_i'\beta)/\sigma \quad .$$

If some of the responses are left-, right-, or interval-censored, the log likelihood can be written as

$$L = \Sigma \log(f(w_i)/\sigma) + \Sigma \log(S(w_i)) + \Sigma \log(F(w_i)) + \Sigma \log(F(w_i) - F(v_i))$$

with the first sum over uncensored observations, the second sum over right-censored observations, the third sum over left-censored observations, the last sum over interval-censored observations, and $v_i = (z_i - x_i'\beta)/\sigma$, where z_i is the lower end of a censoring interval.

If the response is specified in the binomial format, *events/trials*, then the log likelihood function is

$$L = \Sigma r_i \log(P_i) + (n_i - r_i)\log(1 - P_i)$$

where r_i is the number of events and n_i is the number of trials for the ith observation. In this case, $P_i = 1 - F(-x_i'\beta)$. For the symmetric distributions, logistic and normal, this is the same as $F(x_i'\beta)$. Additional information on censored and limited dependent variable models can be found in Kalbfleisch and Prentice (1980) and Maddala (1983).

The estimated covariance matrix of the parameter estimates is computed as the negative inverse of I, the information matrix of second derivatives of L with respect to the parameters evaluated at the final parameter estimates. If I is not positive definite, a positive definite submatrix of I is inverted, and the remaining rows and columns of the inverse are set to zero. If some of the parameters, such as the scale and intercept, are restricted, the corresponding elements of the estimated covariance matrix are set to zero. The standard error estimates for the parameter estimates are taken as the square roots of the corresponding diagonal elements.

For restrictions placed on the intercept, scale, and shape parameters, one-degree-of-freedom Lagrange Multiplier test statistics are computed. These statistics are computed as

$$\chi^2 = g^2/V$$

where g is the derivative of the log likelihood with respect to the restricted parameter at the restricted maximum and

$$V = I_{11} - I_{12} I_{22}^{-1} I_{21}$$

where the 1 subscripts refer to the restricted parameter and the 2 subscripts refer to the unrestricted parameters. The information matrix is evaluated at the restricted maximum. These statistics are asymptotically distributed as chi squares with one degree of freedom under the null hypothesis that the restrictions are valid, provided that some regularity conditions are satisfied. See Rao (1973,

p. 418) for a more complete discussion. It is possible for these statistics to be missing if the observed information matrix is not positive definite. Higher degree-of-freedom tests for multiple restrictions are not currently computed.

In **Example 2** later in this chapter, a Weibull model and an exponential model are both fit to the same data. The exponential distribution is equivalent to a restricted Weibull distribution. A Lagrange multiplier test statistic is computed to test this constraint. Notice that this test statistic is comparable to the Wald test statistic for testing that the scale is one. The Wald statistic is the result of squaring the difference of the estimate of the scale parameter from one and dividing this by the square of its estimated standard error.

Distributions Allowed

The baseline distributions allowed are listed below. For each distribution, the baseline survival distribution function (S) and the probability density function (f) are listed for the additive random disturbance. These distributions apply when the log of the response is modeled (this is the default analysis). The corresponding survival distribution function (G) and its density function (g) are given for the untransformed baseline distribution. For example, under the heading **Weibull**, S(w) and f(w) are the baseline survival distribution function and the probability density function for the extreme value distribution (the log of the response), while G(t) and g(t) are the survival distribution function and probability distribution function of a Weibull distribution (using the untransformed response).

The chosen baseline functions define the meaning of the intercept, scale, and shape parameters. Only the gamma distribution has a free shape parameter in the parameterizations given below. Notice that some of the distributions do not have mean zero, and that σ is not in general the standard deviation of the baseline distribution. Additionally, it is worth mentioning that for the Weibull distribution, the accelerated failure time model is also a proportional-hazards model, but that the parameterization for the covariates differs by a multiple of the scale parameter from the parameterization commonly used for the proportional hazards model.

Exponential

$$S(w) = \exp(-\exp(w - \mu))$$
$$f(w) = \exp(w - \mu)\exp(-\exp(w - \mu))$$

$$G(t) = \exp(-\alpha t)$$
$$g(t) = \alpha\exp(-\alpha t)$$

where $\exp(-\mu) = \alpha$.

Gamma

(with $\mu = 0$, $\sigma = 1$)

$$S(w) = \Gamma(1/\delta^2, \exp(\delta w)/\delta^2)/\Gamma(1/\delta^2) \qquad \text{if } \delta > 0$$
$$S(w) = 1 - \Gamma(1/\delta^2, \exp(\delta w)/\delta^2)/\Gamma(1/\delta^2) \qquad \text{if } \delta < 0$$
$$f(w) = |\delta|(\exp(\delta w)/\delta^2)^{(1/\delta^2)}\exp(-\exp(\delta w)/\delta^2)/\Gamma(1/\delta^2)$$

$$G(t) = \Gamma(1/\delta^2, t^\delta/\delta^2)/\Gamma(1/\delta^2) \qquad \text{if } \delta > 0$$
$$G(t) = 1 - \Gamma(1/\delta^2, t^\delta/\delta^2)/\Gamma(1/\delta^2) \qquad \text{if } \delta < 0$$
$$g(t) = |\delta|(t^\delta/\delta^2)^{(1/\delta^2)}\exp(-t^\delta/\delta^2)/(t\Gamma(1/\delta^2))$$

where $\Gamma(a)$ denotes the complete gamma function, $\Gamma(a,z)$ denotes the incomplete gamma function, and δ is a free shape parameter. The δ parameter is referred to as SHAPE1 by LIFEREG.

Loglogistic

$$S(w) = 1/(1 + \exp((w - \mu)/\sigma))$$
$$f(w) = \exp((w - \mu)/\sigma)/(1 + \exp((w - \mu)/\sigma))^2 \sigma$$

$$G(t) = 1/(1 + \alpha t^\gamma)$$
$$g(t) = \alpha \gamma t^{\gamma-1}/(1 + \alpha t^\gamma)^2$$

where $\gamma = 1/\sigma$ and $\alpha = \exp(-\mu/\sigma)$.

Lognormal

$$S(w) = 1 - \Phi((w - \mu)/\sigma)$$
$$f(w) = \exp(-(w - \mu)^2/2\sigma^2)/(\sqrt{2\pi}\,\sigma)$$

$$G(t) = 1 - \Phi((\log(t) - \mu)/\sigma)$$
$$g(t) = \exp(-(\log(t) - \mu)^2/2\sigma^2)/(\sqrt{2\pi}\,\sigma t)$$

where Φ is the cumulative distribution function for the normal distribution.

Weibull

$$S(w) = \exp(-\exp((w - \mu)/\sigma))$$
$$f(w) = \exp((w - \mu)/\sigma)\exp(-\exp((w - \mu)/\sigma))/\sigma$$

$$G(t) = \exp(-\alpha t^\gamma)$$
$$g(t) = \gamma \alpha t^{\gamma-1}\exp(-\alpha t^\gamma)$$

where $\sigma = 1/\gamma$ and $\alpha = \exp(-\mu/\sigma)$.

Again note that the expected value of the baseline log response is, in general, not zero, and that the distributions are not symmetric in all cases. Thus for a given set of covariates, **x**, the expected value of the log response is not always **x'β**.

Some relations among the distributions are as follows:

- The gamma with SHAPE1=1 is a Weibull distribution.
- The gamma with SHAPE1=0 is a lognormal distribution.
- The Weibull with SCALE=1 is an exponential distribution.

Predicted Values

For a given set of covariates, **x**, the pth quantile of the log response, y_p, is given by

$$y_p = \mathbf{x'\beta} + \sigma w_p$$

where w_p is the pth quantile of the baseline distribution. The estimated quantile is computed by replacing the unknown parameters with their estimates, including any shape parameters on which the baseline distribution might depend. The estimated quantile of the original response is obtained by taking the exponential of the estimated log quantile unless the NOLOG option was specified in the preceding MODEL statement. The standard errors of the quantile estimates are computed using the estimated covariance matrix of the parameter estimates and a Taylor series expansion of the quantile estimate. The standard error is computed as

$$STD = \sqrt{\mathbf{z}'\mathbf{V}\mathbf{z}}$$

where $\mathbf{V}$ is the estimated covariance matrix of the parameter vector $(\boldsymbol{\beta}',\sigma,\boldsymbol{\delta})'$, and $\mathbf{z}$ is the vector

$$\mathbf{z} = \begin{bmatrix} \mathbf{x} \\ \hat{w}_p \\ \hat{\sigma}\partial w_p/\partial\boldsymbol{\delta} \end{bmatrix}$$

where $\boldsymbol{\delta}$ is the vector of the shape parameters. Unless the NOLOG option is specified, this standard error estimate is converted into a standard error estimate for $\exp(y_p)$ as $\exp(\hat{y}_p)STD$. It may be more desirable to compute confidence limits for the log response and convert them back to the original response variable than to use the standard error estimates for $\exp(y_p)$ directly. See **Example 1** later in this chapter for a 90 percent confidence interval of the response constructed by exponentiating a confidence interval for the log response.

The variable, CDF, is computed as

$$CDF_i = F((y_i - \mathbf{x}_i'\mathbf{b})/\hat{\sigma})$$

where F is the baseline cumulative distribution function.

OUTEST= Data Set

The OUTEST= data set contains parameter estimates and the log likelihood for the specified models. A set of observations is created for each MODEL statement specified. You can use a label in the MODEL statement to distinguish between the estimates for different MODEL statements. If the COVOUT option is specified, the OUTEST= data set also contains the estimated covariance matrix of the parameter estimates. Note that if the LIFEREG procedure does not converge, the parameter estimates are set to missing in the OUTEST= data set.

The OUTEST= data set is not created if there are any CLASS variables in any models. If created, this data set contains each variable used as a dependent or independent variable in any MODEL statement. One observation consists of parameter values for the model with the dependent variable having the value −1. If the COVOUT option is specified, there are additional observations containing the rows of the estimated covariance matrix. For these observations the dependent variable contains the parameter estimate for the corresponding row variable. The variables listed below are also added to the data set:

MODEL   a character variable of length 8 containing the label of the MODEL statement, if present, or blank otherwise

NAME   a character variable of length 8 containing the name of the dependent variable for the parameter estimates observations or the name of the row for the covariance matrix estimates

TYPE   a character variable of length 8 containing the type of the observation, either 'PARMS' for parameter estimates or 'COV' for covariance estimates

DIST   a character variable of length 8 containing the name of the distribution modeled

_LNLIKE _   a numeric variable containing the last computed value of the log likelihood

INTERCEP   a numeric variable containing the intercept parameter estimates and covariances

_SCALE _   a numeric variable containing the scale parameter estimates and covariances

_SHAPE1 _   a numeric variable containing the first shape parameter estimates and covariances if the specified distribution has additional shape parameters.

Any BY variables specified are also added to the OUTEST= data set.

Computational Resources

Let p be the number of parameters estimated in the model. Then, the minimum working space (in bytes) needed is

$$16p^2 + 100p \quad .$$

However, if sufficient space is available, the input data set is also kept in memory; otherwise, the input data set is reread for each evaluation of the likelihood function and its derivatives, with the resulting execution time of the procedure substantially increased.

Let n be the number of observations used in the model estimation. Then, each evaluation of the likelihood function and its first and second derivatives requires $O(np^2)$ multiplications and additions, n individual function evaluations for the log density or log distribution function, and n evaluations of the first and second derivatives of the function. The calculation of each updating step from the gradient and Hessian requires $O(p^3)$ multiplications and additions. The $O(v)$ notation means that for large values of the argument, v, $O(v)$ is approximately a constant times v.

Printed Output

For each model, PROC LIFEREG prints

1. the name of the Data Set
2. the name of the Dependent Variable
3. the name of the Censoring Variable
4. the Censoring Value(s) that indicates a censored observation
5. the number of Noncensored and Censored Values
6. the final estimate of the maximized Log Likelihood
7. the iteration history and the Last Evaluation of the Gradient and Hessian if the ITPRINT option was specified (not shown).

For each independent variable in the model, the LIFEREG procedure prints

8. the name of the Variable
9. the degrees of freedom (DF) associated with the variable in the model
10. the Estimate of the parameter
11. the standard error (Std Err) estimate from the observed information matrix
12. an approximate chi-square statistic for testing that the parameter is zero (the class variables also have an overall chi-square test statistic computed that precedes the individual level parameters)

13. the probability of a larger chi-square value (Pr>Chi)
14. the Label of the variable or, if the variable is a class level, the Value of the class variable.

If there were constrained parameters in the model, such as the scale or intercept, then LIFEREG prints

15. a Lagrange Multiplier test for the constraint.

EXAMPLES

Example 1:   Motorette Failure

This example fits a Weibull model and a log normal model to the example given in Kalbfleisch and Prentice (1980, p. 5). An output data set called MODELS is specified to contain the parameter estimates. By default, the natural log of the variable TIME is used by the procedure as the response. After this log transformation, the Weibull model is fit using the extreme value baseline distribution, and the lognormal is fit using the normal baseline distribution. Since the extreme value and normal distributions do not contain any shape parameters, the variable SHAPE1 is missing in the MODELS data set. An additional output data set, OUT, is requested. It contains the predicted quantiles and their standard errors for values of the covariate corresponding to TEMP=130 and 150. This is done with the CONTROL variable, which is set to 1 for only two observations. Using the standard error estimates obtained from the output data set, approximate 90 percent confidence limits are then created in a subsequent DATA step for the log response. To do this, first the logs of the predicted values are obtained because the values of the P= variable in the OUT= data set are in the same units as the untransformed response variable, TIME. Next, the standard errors of the quantiles of the log(TIME) are approximated (using a Taylor series approximation) by the standard deviation of TIME divided by the mean value of TIME. These confidence limits are then converted back to the original scale by the exponential function.

The following statements produce **Output 25.1**:

```
title 'Motorette Failures With Operating Temperature as a Covariate';
data motors;
   input time censor temp @@;
   if _N_=1 then
      do;
         temp=130;
         time=.;
         control=1;
         z=1000/(273.2+temp);
         output;
         temp=150;
         time=.;
         control=1;
         z=1000/(273.2+TEMP);
         output;
      end;
   if temp>150;
   control=0;
   z=1000/(273.2+temp);
   output;
   cards;
```

```
8064 0 150 8064 0 150 8064 0 150 8064 0 150 8064 0 150
8064 0 150 8064 0 150 8064 0 150 8064 0 150 8064 0 150
1764 1 170 2772 1 170 3444 1 170 3542 1 170 3780 1 170
4860 1 170 5196 1 170 5448 0 170 5448 0 170 5448 0 170
 408 1 190  408 1 190 1344 1 190 1344 1 190 1440 1 190
1680 0 190 1680 0 190 1680 0 190 1680 0 190 1680 0 190
 408 1 220  408 1 220  504 1 220  504 1 220  504 1 220
 528 0 220  528 0 220  528 0 220  528 0 220  528 0 220
;

proc lifereg outest=models covout;
   a: model time*censor(0)=z;
   b: model time*censor(0)=z / dist=lnormal;
         output out=out quantiles=.1 .5 .9 std=std p=predtime
         control=control;
run;

proc print data=models;
   id _model_;
   title 'fitted models';
run;

data out1;
   set out;
   ltime=log(predtime);
   stde=std/predtime;
   upper=exp(ltime+1.64*stde);
   lower=exp(ltime-1.64*stde);

proc print;
   id temp;
   title 'quantile estimates and confidence limits';
run;
```

Output 25.1   Motorette Failure: PROC LIFEREG

```
                  Motorette Failures With Operating Temperature as a Covariate                    1

                                        Lifereg  Procedure

❶    Data Set         =WORK.MOTORS
 ❷   Dependent Variable=Log(TIME)
❸    Censoring Variable=CENSOR
  ❹  Censoring Value(s)=      0
     Noncensored Values=      17  Right Censored Values=      13 ❺
     Left Censored Values=   0  Interval Censored Values=    0
     Observations with Missing Values=   2


❻    Log Likelihood for WEIBULL -22.95148315
```

```
                    Motorette Failures With Operating Temperature as a Covariate                    2

                                      Lifereg  Procedure
          ⓼      ⓽      ⓾        ⑪          ⑫       ⑬       ⑭
        Variable  DF   Estimate  Std Err  ChiSquare  Pr>Chi  Label/Value

        INTERCPT   1  -11.89122  1.965507  36.6019   0.0001  Intercept
        Z          1   9.03834032 0.905993 99.52392  0.0001
        SCALE      1   0.36128138 0.079501                   Extreme value scale parameter
```

```
                    Motorette Failures With Operating Temperature as a Covariate                    3

                                      Lifereg  Procedure

        Data Set            =WORK.MOTORS
        Dependent Variable=Log(TIME)
        Censoring Variable=CENSOR
        Censoring Value(s)=      0
        Noncensored Values=     17  Right Censored Values=     13
        Left Censored Values=    0  Interval Censored Values=   0
        Observations with Missing Values=    2


        Log Likelihood for LNORMAL -24.47381031
```

```
                    Motorette Failures With Operating Temperature as a Covariate                    4

                                      Lifereg  Procedure

        Variable  DF   Estimate  Std Err  ChiSquare  Pr>Chi  Label/Value

        INTERCPT   1  -10.470563  2.77192  14.26851  0.0002  Intercept
        Z          1   8.3220835  1.284124 42.00011  0.0001
        SCALE      1   0.6040344  0.110729                   Normal scale parameter
```

```
                                         fitted models                                              5

    _MODEL_   _NAME_   _TYPE_   _DIST_   _LNLIKE_   INTERCEP    TIME       Z      _SCALE_  _SHAPE1_

       A      TIME     PARMS    WEIBULL  -22.9515  -11.8912   -1.0000   9.03834   0.36128     .
       A      INTERCPT COV      WEIBULL  -22.9515    3.8632  -11.8912  -1.77878   0.03448     .
       A      Z        COV      WEIBULL  -22.9515   -1.7788    9.0383   0.82082  -0.01488     .
       A      SCALE    COV      WEIBULL  -22.9515    0.0345    0.3613  -0.01488   0.00632     .
       B      TIME     PARMS    LNORMAL  -24.4738  -10.4706   -1.0000   8.32208   0.60403     .
       B      INTERCPT COV      LNORMAL  -24.4738    7.6835  -10.4706  -3.55566   0.03267     .
       B      Z        COV      LNORMAL  -24.4738   -3.5557    8.3221   1.64897  -0.01285     .
       B      SCALE    COV      LNORMAL  -24.4738    0.0327    0.6040  -0.01285   0.01226     .
```

```
                              quantile estimates and confidence limits                              6

 TEMP  TIME  CENSOR  CONTROL      Z     _PROB_  PREDTIME      STD      LTIME    STDE     UPPER      LOWER

 130    .      0        1     2.48016   0.1    12033.19    5482.34    9.3954   0.45560  25402.68   5700.09
 130    .      0        1     2.48016   0.5    26095.68   11359.45   10.1695   0.43530  53285.36  12779.95
 130    .      0        1     2.48016   0.9    56592.19   26036.90   10.9436   0.46008 120349.65  26611.42
 150    .      0        1     2.36295   0.1     4536.88    1443.07    8.4200   0.31808   7643.71   2692.83
 150    .      0        1     2.36295   0.5     9838.86    2901.15    9.1941   0.29487  15957.38   6066.36
 150    .      0        1     2.36295   0.9    21336.97    7172.34    9.9682   0.33615  37029.72  12294.62
```

Example 2: VA Lung Cancer Data

This example uses data presented in Kalbfeisch and Prentice (1980,
Appendix 1). The response is the survival time in days of a group of lung cancer
patients. The covariates are type of cancer cell (CELL), type of therapy (THER-
APY), prior therapy (PRIOR), age in years (AGE), time in months from diagnosis
to entry into the trial (DIAGTIME), and a measure of the overall status of the
patient at entry into the trial (KPS). The first three variables are taken to be class

variables, although only CELL has more than two levels. The censored values are given as negative, and a censoring indicator (CENSOR) is created. Before beginning any modeling, you should do preliminary investigations of the data with graphic and other descriptive methods. However, this chapter concentrates only on the use of the LIFEREG procedure, and the following does not constitute a complete analysis of the data.

Models are fit to the survival time using the Weibull, lognormal, and loglogistic baseline distributions. The exponential distribution is also fit. The Lagrange multiplier test arising from this model tests whether the exponential model is adequate relative to the Weibull model. An output data set containing predicted values from the Weibull model is also created. The OUTPUT statement must immediately follow the desired MODEL statement.

The following statements produce **Output 25.2**:

```
title 'VA Lung Cancer Data from Appendix I of K&P';
data valung;
   drop check x4 m;
   retain therapy cell;
   infile cards column=column;
   length prior  $ 3 check  $ 1;
   label t='Failure or Censoring Time'
         kps='Karnofsky Performance Status'
         diagtime='Months Till Randomization'
         age='Age in Years'
         prior='Prior Treatment?'
         cell='Cell Type'
         therapy='Type of Treatment';
   m=column;
   input check $ @@;
   if m>column then m=1;
   if check='s' or check='t' then  input @m therapy $ cell $;
   else input @m t kps diagtime age x4 @@;
   if t>.;
   censor=(t<0);
   t=abs(t);
   if x4=10 then prior='yes';
   else prior='no';
   cards;
standard squamous
  72 60  7 69  0   411 70  5 64 10    228 60  3 38  0
 126 60  9 63 10   118 70 11 65 10     10 20  5 49  0
  82 40 10 69 10   110 80 29 68  0    314 50 18 43  0
-100 70  6 70  0    42 60  4 81  0      8 40 58 63 10
 144 30  4 63  0   -25 80  9 52 10     11 70 11 48 10
standard small
  30 60  3 61  0   384 60  9 42  0      4 40  2 35  0
  54 80  4 63 10    13 60  4 56  0   -123 40  3 55  0
 -97 60  5 67  0   153 60 14 63 10     59 30  2 65  0
 117 80  3 46  0    16 30  4 53 10    151 50 12 69  0
  22 60  4 68  0    56 80 12 43 10     21 40  2 55 10
  18 20 15 42  0   139 80  2 64  0     20 30  5 65  0
  31 75  3 65  0    52 70  2 55  0    287 60 25 66 10
  18 30  4 60  0    51 60  1 67  0    122 80 28 53  0
  27 60  8 62  0    54 70  1 67  0      7 50  7 72  0
  63 50 11 48  0   392 40  4 68  0     10 40 23 67 10
```

```
    standard adeno
      8 20 19 61 10    92 70 10 60  0    35 40  6 62  0
    117 80  2 38  0   132 80  5 50  0    12 50  4 63 10
    162 80  5 64  0     3 30  3 43  0    95 80  4 34  0
    standard large
    177 50 16 66 10   162 80  5 62  0   216 50 15 52  0
    553 70  2 47  0   278 60 12 63  0    12 40 12 68 10
    260 80  5 45  0   200 80 12 41 10   156 70  2 66  0
   -182 90  2 62  0   143 90  8 60  0   105 80 11 66  0
    103 80  5 38  0   250 70  8 53 10   100 60 13 37 10
    test squamous
    999 90 12 54 10   112 80  6 60  0   -87 80  3 48  0
   -231 50  8 52 10   242 50  1 70  0   991 70  7 50 10
    111 70  3 62  0     1 20 21 65 10   587 60  3 58  0
    389 90  2 62  0    33 30  6 64  0    25 20 36 63  0
    357 70 13 58  0   467 90  2 64  0   201 80 28 52 10
      1 50  7 35  0    30 70 11 63  0    44 60 13 70 10
    283 90  2 51  0    15 50 13 40 10
    test small
     25 30  2 69  0  -103 70 22 36 10    21 20  4 71  0
     13 30  2 62  0    87 60  2 60  0     2 40 36 44 10
     20 30  9 54 10     7 20 11 66  0    24 60  8 49  0
     99 70  3 72  0     8 80  2 68  0    99 85  4 62  0
     61 70  2 71  0    25 70  2 70  0    95 70  1 61  0
     80 50 17 71  0    51 30 87 59 10    29 40  8 67  0
    test adeno
     24 40  2 60  0    18 40  5 69 10   -83 99  3 57  0
     31 80  3 39  0    51 60  5 62  0    90 60 22 50 10
     52 60  3 43  0    73 60  3 70  0     8 50  5 66  0
     36 70  8 61  0    48 10  4 81  0     7 40  4 58  0
    140 70  3 63  0   186 90  3 60  0    84 80  4 62 10
     19 50 10 42  0    45 40  3 69  0    80 40  4 63  0
    test large
     52 60  4 45  0   164 70 15 68 10    19 30  4 39 10
     53 60 12 66  0    15 30  5 63  0    43 60 11 49 10
    340 80 10 64 10   133 75  1 65  0   111 60  5 64  0
    231 70 18 67 10   378 80  4 65  0    49 30  3 37  0
    ;

proc lifereg;
   class prior therapy cell;
   model t*censor(1)=kps age diagtime prior cell therapy
                   / dist=weibull;
   output out=out cdf=f p=pred censored=flag;
   model t*censor(1)=kps age diagtime prior cell therapy
                   / dist=exponential;
   model t*censor(1)=kps age diagtime prior cell therapy
                   / dist=lnormal;
   model t*censor(1)=kps age diagtime prior cell therapy
                   / dist=llogistic;
run;

proc print;
run;
```

Output 25.2   VA Lung Cancer Data: PROC LIFEREG

```
                    VA Lung Cancer Data from Appendix I of K&P                      1

                               Lifereg  Procedure
                           Class Level Information

                    Class    Levels    Values

                    PRIOR      2       no yes

                    CELL       4       adeno large small squamous

                    THERAPY    2       standard test

                        Number of observations used = 137
```

```
                    VA Lung Cancer Data from Appendix I of K&P                      2

                               Lifereg  Procedure

Data Set         =WORK.VALUNG
Dependent Variable=Log(T)      Failure or Censoring Time
Censoring Variable=CENSOR
Censoring Value(s)=      1
Noncensored Values=  128  Right Censored Values=      9
Left Censored Values=  0  Interval Censored Values=   0


Log Likelihood for WEIBULL -196.1386213
```

```
                    VA Lung Cancer Data from Appendix I of K&P                      3

                               Lifereg  Procedure

Variable  DF   Estimate   Std Err  ChiSquare  Pr>Chi Label/Value

INTERCPT   1  2.98959332  0.709345  17.7627   0.0001 Intercept
KPS        1  0.0300683   0.004828  38.78887  0.0001 Karnofsky Performance Status
AGE        1  0.00609918  0.008553  0.508475  0.4758 Age in Years
DIAGTIME   1 -0.0004688   0.008361  0.003144  0.9553 Months Till Randomization

PRIOR      1                        0.042763  0.8362 Prior Treatment?
           1  0.04389765  0.212279  0.042763  0.8362 no
           0      0          0         .        .    yes


CELL       3                        22.02965  0.0001 Cell Type
           1 -1.1327251   0.257598  19.3359   0.0001 adeno
           1 -0.3976808   0.254749  2.436927  0.1185 large
           1 -0.8261846   0.246312  11.2508   0.0008 small
           0      0          0         .        .    squamous


THERAPY    1                        1.495897  0.2213 Type of Treatment
           1  0.22852267  0.186844  1.495897  0.2213 standard
           0      0          0         .        .    test

SCALE      1  0.92811528  0.061545                   Extreme value scale parameter
```

```
                    VA Lung Cancer Data from Appendix I of K&P                      4

                               Lifereg  Procedure
                           Class Level Information

                    Class    Levels    Values

                    PRIOR      2       no yes

                    CELL       4       adeno large small squamous

                    THERAPY    2       standard test

                        Number of observations used = 137
```

```
                        VA Lung Cancer Data from Appendix I of K&P                    5

                                  Lifereg  Procedure

Data Set        =WORK.VALUNG
Dependent Variable=Log(T)     Failure or Censoring Time
Censoring Variable=CENSOR
Censoring Value(s)=      1
Noncensored Values=   128  Right Censored Values=      9
Left Censored Values=   0  Interval Censored Values=   0


Log Likelihood for EXPONENT -196.7463712
```

```
                        VA Lung Cancer Data from Appendix I of K&P                    6

                                  Lifereg  Procedure

      Variable DF   Estimate  Std Err  ChiSquare  Pr>Chi Label/Value

      INTERCPT  1 2.91956338 0.752159  15.06666   0.0001 Intercept
      KPS       1 0.03062403 0.005108  35.94997   0.0001 Karnofsky Performance Status
      AGE       1 0.00610766 0.009161   0.444531  0.5049 Age in Years
      DIAGTIME  1 -0.000297  0.00897    0.001097  0.9736 Months Till Randomization

      PRIOR     1                       0.04757   0.8273 Prior Treatment?
                1 0.04948165 0.226871   0.04757   0.8273 no
                0     0        0                 .    .   yes


      CELL      3                      18.82178   0.0003 Cell Type
                1 -1.113121 0.275825   16.28611   0.0001 adeno
                1 -0.3772196 0.272626   1.914497  0.1665 large
                1 -0.8202445 0.262111   9.793045  0.0018 small
                0     0        0                 .    .   squamous


      THERAPY   1                       1.221858  0.2690 Type of Treatment
                1 0.21956529 0.198634   1.221858  0.2690 standard
                0     0        0                 .    .   test
 15   SCALE     0     1        0                          Extreme value scale parameter
               Lagrange Multiplier ChiSquare for Scale  1.37717 Pr>Chi is 0.2406.
```

```
                        VA Lung Cancer Data from Appendix I of K&P                    7

                                  Lifereg  Procedure
                                Class Level Information

            Class     Levels   Values

            PRIOR       2      no yes

            CELL        4      adeno large small squamous

            THERAPY     2      standard test

                 Number of observations used = 137
```

```
                        VA Lung Cancer Data from Appendix I of K&P                    8

                                  Lifereg  Procedure

Data Set        =WORK.VALUNG
Dependent Variable=Log(T)     Failure or Censoring Time
Censoring Variable=CENSOR
Censoring Value(s)=      1
Noncensored Values=   128  Right Censored Values=      9
Left Censored Values=   0  Interval Censored Values=   0


Log Likelihood for LNORMAL -195.2222289
```

```
                    VA Lung Cancer Data from Appendix I of K&P                    9

                              Lifereg  Procedure

        Variable  DF   Estimate  Std Err  ChiSquare  Pr>Chi Label/Value

        INTERCPT  1   1.3969047 0.687131   4.132892  0.0421 Intercept
        KPS       1   0.03729538 0.004842  59.33226  0.0001 Karnofsky Performance Status
        AGE       1   0.01278756 0.008899   2.064662  0.1507 Age in Years
        DIAGTIME  1  -0.0012385 0.009704    0.016288  0.8984 Months Till Randomization

        PRIOR     1                         0.221982  0.6375 Prior Treatment?
                  1   0.10667088 0.226406   0.221982  0.6375 no
                  0            0        0          .       . yes


        CELL      3                        12.55481   0.0057 Cell Type
                  1  -0.6542245 0.283856   5.312008   0.0212 adeno
                  1   0.11875999 0.280177   0.17967   0.6717 large
                  1  -0.6065537 0.249295   5.919868   0.0150 small
                  0            0        0         .        . squamous


        THERAPY   1                         0.792061  0.3735 Type of Treatment
                  1   0.16910486  0.19001   0.792061  0.3735 standard
                  0            0        0          .       . test

        SCALE     1   1.05982287 0.066337                    Normal scale parameter
```

```
                    VA Lung Cancer Data from Appendix I of K&P                    10

                              Lifereg  Procedure
                            Class Level Information

              Class    Levels    Values

              PRIOR       2      no yes

              CELL        4      adeno large small squamous

              THERAPY     2      standard test

                    Number of observations used = 137
```

```
                    VA Lung Cancer Data from Appendix I of K&P                    11

                              Lifereg  Procedure

        Data Set         =WORK.VALUNG
        Dependent Variable=Log(T)     Failure or Censoring Time
        Censoring Variable=CENSOR
        Censoring Value(s)=      1
        Noncensored Values=  128  Right Censored Values=      9
        Left Censored Values=  0  Interval Censored Values=   0


        Log Likelihood for LLOGISTC -192.5298424
```

```
                    VA Lung Cancer Data from Appendix I of K&P                    12

                              Lifereg  Procedure

        Variable  DF   Estimate  Std Err  ChiSquare  Pr>Chi Label/Value

        INTERCPT  1   1.833792  0.697812   6.905944  0.0086 Intercept
        KPS       1   0.03606026 0.004484  64.67655  0.0001 Karnofsky Performance Status
        AGE       1   0.008546  0.008921   0.917646  0.3381 Age in Years
        DIAGTIME  1   0.00210661 0.010269  0.04208   0.8375 Months Till Randomization

        PRIOR     1                         0.233315  0.6291 Prior Treatment?
                  1   0.10200928 0.211187   0.233315  0.6291 no
                  0            0        0          .       . yes
```

(continued on next page)

(continued from previous page)

CELL	3			16.09257	0.0011	Cell Type
	1	-0.7425488	0.272132	7.445421	0.0064	adeno
	1	0.01662671	0.26956	0.003805	0.9508	large
	1	-0.7079773	0.249254	8.067793	0.0045	small
	0	0	0	.	.	squamous
THERAPY	1			0.24333	0.6218	Type of Treatment
	1	0.08846214	0.179333	0.24333	0.6218	standard
	0	0	0	.	.	test
SCALE	1	0.57900028	0.042955			Logistic scale parameter

VA Lung Cancer Data from Appendix I of K&P   13

OBS	THERAPY	CELL	PRIOR	T	KPS	DIAGTIME	AGE	CENSOR	_PROB_	PRED	F	FLAG
1	standard	squamous	no	72	60	7	69	0	0.5	171.316	0.23845	0
2	standard	squamous	yes	411	70	5	64	0	0.5	215.021	0.75169	0
3	standard	squamous	no	228	60	3	38	0	0.5	142.068	0.68460	0
4	standard	squamous	yes	126	60	9	63	0	0.5	157.918	0.41927	0
5	standard	squamous	yes	118	70	11	65	0	0.5	215.729	0.30360	0
6	standard	squamous	no	10	20	5	49	0	0.5	45.592	0.12644	0
7	standard	squamous	yes	82	40	10	69	0	0.5	89.733	0.46688	0
8	standard	squamous	no	110	80	29	68	0	0.5	307.496	0.20466	0
9	standard	squamous	no	314	50	18	43	0	0.5	107.672	0.88877	0
10	standard	squamous	no	100	70	6	70	1	0.5	232.935	0.24324	1
11	standard	squamous	no	42	60	4	81	0	0.5	184.584	0.13119	0
12	standard	squamous	yes	8	40	58	63	0	0.5	84.584	0.05315	0
13	standard	squamous	no	144	30	4	63	0	0.5	67.106	0.79362	0
14	standard	squamous	yes	25	80	9	52	1	0.5	269.442	0.05209	1
15	standard	squamous	yes	11	70	11	48	0	0.5	194.481	0.03090	0
16	standard	small	no	30	60	3	61	0	0.5	71.551	0.23792	0
17	standard	small	no	384	60	9	42	0	0.5	63.542	0.99189	0
18	standard	small	no	4	40	2	35	0	0.5	33.479	0.06784	0
19	standard	small	yes	54	80	4	63	0	0.5	126.419	0.24210	0
20	standard	small	no	13	60	4	56	0	0.5	69.369	0.10783	0
21	standard	small	no	123	40	3	55	1	0.5	37.805	0.91550	1
22	standard	small	no	97	60	5	67	1	0.5	74.148	0.60380	1
23	standard	small	yes	153	60	14	63	0	0.5	68.962	0.80519	0
24	standard	small	no	59	30	2	65	0	0.5	29.762	0.76517	0
25	standard	small	no	117	80	3	46	0	0.5	119.138	0.49326	0
26	standard	small	yes	16	30	4	53	0	0.5	26.448	0.33190	0
27	standard	small	no	151	50	12	69	0	0.5	55.384	0.87029	0
28	standard	small	no	22	60	4	68	0	0.5	74.637	0.16962	0
29	standard	small	yes	56	80	12	43	0	0.5	111.483	0.28115	0
30	standard	small	yes	21	40	2	55	0	0.5	36.198	0.31990	0
31	standard	small	no	18	20	15	42	0	0.5	19.033	0.47937	0
32	standard	small	no	139	80	2	64	0	0.5	133.025	0.51652	0
33	standard	small	no	20	30	5	65	0	0.5	29.720	0.36388	0
34	standard	small	no	31	75	3	65	0	0.5	115.103	0.15519	0
35	standard	small	no	52	70	2	55	0	0.5	93.220	0.30896	0
36	standard	small	yes	287	60	25	66	0	0.5	69.874	0.95826	0
37	standard	small	no	18	30	4	60	0	0.5	28.841	0.34104	0
38	standard	small	no	51	60	1	67	0	0.5	74.287	0.37010	0
39	standard	small	no	122	80	28	53	0	0.5	122.886	0.49730	0
40	standard	small	no	27	60	8	62	0	0.5	71.820	0.21460	0
41	standard	small	no	54	70	1	67	0	0.5	100.346	0.29920	0
42	standard	small	no	7	50	7	72	0	0.5	56.539	0.07040	0
43	standard	small	no	63	50	11	48	0	0.5	48.749	0.59898	0
44	standard	small	no	392	40	4	68	0	0.5	40.905	0.99963	0
45	standard	small	yes	10	40	23	67	0	0.5	38.566	0.14947	0
46	standard	adeno	yes	8	20	19	61	0	0.5	15.025	0.29635	0
47	standard	adeno	no	92	70	10	60	0	0.5	70.469	0.60300	0
48	standard	adeno	no	35	40	6	62	0	0.5	28.997	0.57213	0
49	standard	adeno	no	117	80	2	38	0	0.5	83.548	0.63077	0
50	standard	adeno	no	132	80	5	50	0	0.5	89.766	0.65012	0
51	standard	adeno	yes	12	50	4	63	0	0.5	37.751	0.18259	0
52	standard	adeno	no	162	80	5	64	0	0.5	97.767	0.69710	0
53	standard	adeno	no	3	30	3	43	0	0.5	19.145	0.08980	0
54	standard	adeno	no	95	80	4	34	0	0.5	81.458	0.55872	0
55	standard	large	yes	177	50	16	66	0	0.5	79.737	0.80537	0
56	standard	large	no	162	80	5	62	0	0.5	201.429	0.42198	0

VA Lung Cancer Data from Appendix I of K&P   14

OBS	THERAPY	CELL	PRIOR	T	KPS	DIAGTIME	AGE	CENSOR	_PROB_	PRED	F	FLAG
57	standard	large	no	216	50	15	52	0	0.5	76.532	0.87997	0
58	standard	large	no	553	70	2	47	0	0.5	136.275	0.95650	0
59	standard	large	no	278	60	12	63	0	0.5	110.707	0.84576	0
60	standard	large	yes	12	40	12	68	0	0.5	59.867	0.11545	0
61	standard	large	no	260	80	5	45	0	0.5	181.590	0.63956	0
62	standard	large	yes	200	80	12	41	0	0.5	169.047	0.56431	0
63	standard	large	no	156	70	2	66	0	0.5	153.018	0.50723	0

(continued on next page)

(continued from previous page)

OBS	THERAPY	CELL	PRIOR	T	KPS	DIAGTIME	AGE	CENSOR	_PROB_	PRED	F	FLAG
64	standard	large	no	182	90	2	62	1	0.5	272.469	0.36158	1
65	standard	large	no	143	90	8	60	0	0.5	268.410	0.29651	0
66	standard	large	no	105	80	11	66	0	0.5	205.824	0.28512	0
67	standard	large	no	103	80	5	38	0	0.5	174.000	0.32563	0
68	standard	large	yes	250	70	8	53	0	0.5	134.903	0.74008	0
69	standard	large	yes	100	60	13	37	0	0.5	90.373	0.53839	0
70	test	squamous	yes	999	90	12	54	0	0.5	292.746	0.92582	0
71	test	squamous	no	112	80	6	60	0	0.5	235.551	0.26739	0
72	test	squamous	no	87	80	3	48	1	0.5	219.235	0.22591	1
73	test	squamous	yes	231	50	8	52	1	0.5	87.030	0.86252	1
74	test	squamous	no	242	50	1	70	0	0.5	101.821	0.82824	0
75	test	squamous	yes	991	70	7	50	0	0.5	156.943	0.99358	0
76	test	squamous	no	111	70	3	62	0	0.5	176.770	0.34285	0
77	test	squamous	yes	1	20	21	65	0	0.5	37.993	0.01367	0
78	test	squamous	no	587	60	3	58	0	0.5	127.711	0.97228	0
79	test	squamous	no	389	90	2	62	0	0.5	322.687	0.57163	0
80	test	squamous	no	33	30	6	64	0	0.5	53.673	0.33662	0
81	test	squamous	no	25	20	36	63	0	0.5	38.942	0.34948	0
82	test	squamous	no	357	70	13	58	0	0.5	171.703	0.78243	0
83	test	squamous	no	467	90	2	64	0	0.5	326.648	0.63897	0
84	test	squamous	yes	201	80	28	52	0	0.5	212.496	0.47943	0
85	test	squamous	no	1	50	7	35	0	0.5	82.017	0.00599	0
86	test	squamous	no	30	70	11	63	0	0.5	177.186	0.09722	0
87	test	squamous	yes	44	60	13	70	0	0.5	130.892	0.19276	0
88	test	squamous	no	283	90	2	51	0	0.5	301.748	0.47631	0
89	test	squamous	yes	15	50	13	40	0	0.5	80.698	0.10694	0
90	test	small	no	25	30	2	69	0	0.5	24.266	0.51117	0
91	test	small	yes	103	70	22	36	1	0.5	62.632	0.69415	1
92	test	small	no	21	20	4	71	0	0.5	18.168	0.55524	0
93	test	small	no	13	30	2	62	0	0.5	23.252	0.30959	0
94	test	small	no	87	60	2	60	0	0.5	56.614	0.66754	0
95	test	small	yes	2	40	36	44	0	0.5	26.508	0.04191	0
96	test	small	yes	20	30	9	54	0	0.5	21.124	0.47977	0
97	test	small	no	7	20	11	66	0	0.5	17.565	0.22682	0
98	test	small	no	24	60	8	49	0	0.5	52.791	0.25655	0
99	test	small	no	99	70	3	72	0	0.5	82.241	0.57107	0
100	test	small	no	8	80	2	68	0	0.5	108.463	0.04092	0
101	test	small	no	99	85	4	62	0	0.5	121.416	0.42668	0
102	test	small	no	61	70	2	71	0	0.5	81.779	0.39675	0
103	test	small	no	25	70	2	70	0	0.5	81.282	0.17682	0
104	test	small	no	95	70	1	61	0	0.5	76.977	0.58084	0
105	test	small	no	80	50	17	71	0	0.5	44.506	0.72851	0
106	test	small	yes	51	30	87	59	0	0.5	20.997	0.83527	0
107	test	small	no	29	40	8	67	0	0.5	32.290	0.46063	0
108	test	adeno	no	24	40	2	60	0	0.5	22.836	0.51871	0
109	test	adeno	yes	18	40	5	69	0	0.5	23.056	0.41190	0
110	test	adeno	no	83	99	3	57	1	0.5	132.107	0.34301	1
111	test	adeno	no	31	80	3	39	0	0.5	66.855	0.26128	0
112	test	adeno	no	51	60	5	62	0	0.5	42.119	0.57337	0

VA Lung Cancer Data from Appendix I of K&P   15

OBS	THERAPY	CELL	PRIOR	T	KPS	DIAGTIME	AGE	CENSOR	_PROB_	PRED	F	FLAG
113	test	adeno	yes	90	60	22	50	0	0.5	37.168	0.83427	0
114	test	adeno	no	52	60	3	43	0	0.5	37.546	0.62638	0
115	test	adeno	no	73	60	3	70	0	0.5	44.267	0.69524	0
116	test	adeno	no	8	50	5	66	0	0.5	31.951	0.14436	0
117	test	adeno	no	36	70	8	61	0	0.5	56.468	0.34738	0
118	test	adeno	no	48	10	4	81	0	0.5	10.522	0.97146	0
119	test	adeno	no	7	40	4	58	0	0.5	22.538	0.17851	0
120	test	adeno	no	140	70	3	63	0	0.5	57.296	0.83717	0
121	test	adeno	no	186	90	3	60	0	0.5	102.647	0.73158	0
122	test	adeno	yes	84	80	4	62	0	0.5	73.585	0.55041	0
123	test	adeno	no	19	50	10	42	0	0.5	27.536	0.37169	0
124	test	adeno	no	45	40	3	69	0	0.5	24.113	0.74272	0
125	test	adeno	no	80	40	4	63	0	0.5	23.236	0.92765	0
126	test	large	no	52	60	4	45	0	0.5	79.228	0.35618	0
127	test	large	yes	164	70	15	68	0	0.5	117.242	0.63032	0
128	test	large	yes	19	30	4	39	0	0.5	29.660	0.34882	0
129	test	large	no	53	60	12	66	0	0.5	89.717	0.32505	0
130	test	large	no	15	30	5	63	0	0.5	35.859	0.23740	0
131	test	large	yes	43	60	11	49	0	0.5	77.443	0.30769	0
132	test	large	yes	340	80	10	64	0	0.5	154.914	0.80147	0
133	test	large	no	133	75	1	65	0	0.5	140.716	0.47914	0
134	test	large	no	111	60	5	64	0	0.5	88.921	0.58532	0
135	test	large	yes	231	70	18	67	0	0.5	116.365	0.76567	0
136	test	large	no	378	80	4	65	0	0.5	163.315	0.81951	0
137	test	large	no	49	30	3	37	0	0.5	30.629	0.68336	0

Example 3: Tobit Analysis

The data set below mimics the data used by Tobin and includes 20 observations with a response variable DURABLE, which is left-censored at zero, and two independent variables, AGE and LQTY.

The following statements produce **Output 25.3**:

```
title 'Estimation of Tobit Model for Durable Goods Expenditures';
data tobit;
   input durable age lqty ₔₔ;
   if durable=0 then lower=.;
   else lower=durable;
   label durable='Durable Goods Purchase'
      age='Age in Years'
      lqty='Liquidity Ratio Times 1000';
cards;
 0.0 57.7 236    0.0 59.8 216    10.4 46.8 207    0.0 39.9 219
 0.7 50.9 283    0.0 44.3 284    0.0 58.0 249    0.0 33.4 240
 0.0 48.5 207    3.7 45.1 221    0.0 58.9 246    3.5 48.1 266
 0.0 41.7 220    0.0 51.7 275    0.0 40.0 277    6.1 46.1 214
 0.0 47.7 238    3.0 50.0 269    1.5 34.1 231    0.0 53.1 251
;

proc lifereg;
  model (lower,durable)=age lqty / d=normal;
run;
```

Output 25.3 Tobit Analysis

```
              Estimation of Tobit Model for Durable Goods Expenditures        1

                              Lifereg  Procedure

       Data Set          =WORK.TOBIT
       Dependent Variable=LOWER
       Dependent Variable=DURABLE    Durable Goods Purchase
       Noncensored Values=    7  Right Censored Values=    0
       Left Censored Values= 13  Interval Censored Values=  0


       Log Likelihood for NORMAL -28.92596097
```

```
              Estimation of Tobit Model for Durable Goods Expenditures        2

                              Lifereg  Procedure

       Variable  DF   Estimate  Std Err  ChiSquare  Pr>Chi Label/Value

       INTERCPT  1 15.2771208  16.03272  0.907964  0.3407 Intercept
       AGE       1 -0.1340075  0.218931  0.374664  0.5405 Age in Years
       LQTY      1 -0.0451356  0.058269  0.600026  0.4386 Liquidity Ratio Times 1000
       SCALE     1  5.56935051 1.728145                   Normal scale parameter
```

REFERENCES

Cox, D.R. (1972), "Regression Models and Life Tables (with discussion)," *Journal of the Royal Statistical Society*, Series B, 34, 187–220.

Cox, D.R. and Oakes, D. (1984), *Analysis of Survival Data*, London: Chapman and Hall.

Elandt-Johnson, R.C. and Johnson, N.L. (1980), *Survival Models and Data Analysis*, New York: John Wiley & Sons, Inc.

Gross, A.J. and Clark, V.A. (1975), *Survival Distributions: Reliability Applications in the Biomedical Sciences*, New York: John Wiley & Sons, Inc.

Kalbfleisch, J.D. and Prentice, R.L. (1980), *The Statistical Analysis of Failure Time Data*, New York: John Wiley & Sons, Inc.

Lawless, J.E. (1982), *Statistical Models and Methods for Lifetime Data*, New York: John Wiley & Sons, Inc.

Lee, E.T. (1980), *Statistical Methods for Survival Data Analysis*, Belmont, CA: Lifetime Learning Publications.

Maddala, G.S. (1983) *Limited-Dependent and Qualitative Variables in Econometrics*, New York: Cambridge University Press.

Rao, C.R. (1973), *Linear Statistical Inference and Its Applications*, New York: John Wiley & Sons, Inc.

Tobin, J. (1958), "Estimation of Relationships for Limited Dependent Variables," *Econometrica*, 26, 24–36.

1026

Chapter 26

The LIFETEST Procedure

ABSTRACT   1027
INTRODUCTION   1028
  Survival Distribution   1028
  Comparison of Survival Curves   1028
  Assessment of the Dependence of Survival Time on Covariates   1034
SPECIFICATIONS   1037
  PROC LIFETEST Statement   1038
  BY Statement   1041
  FREQ Statement   1042
  ID Statement   1042
  STRATA Statement   1042
  TEST Statement   1043
  TIME Statement   1043
DETAILS   1043
  Missing Values   1043
  Computational Formulas   1044
    Product-Limit Method   1044
    Life Table Method   1044
    Interval Determination   1045
    Confidence Limits Added to the Output Data Set   1046
    Tests for Equality of Survival Curves across Strata   1046
      Log rank test and Wilcoxon test   1046
      Likelihood ratio test   1046
    Rank Tests for the Association of Survival Time with Covariates   1046
  Output Data Sets   1048
    OUTSURV= Data Set   1048
    OUTTEST= Data Set   1049
  Computer Resources   1049
    Memory Requirements   1049
  Printed Output   1050
EXAMPLES   1052
  Example 1: Product-Limit Estimates and Tests of Association for the VA
         Lung Cancer Data   1052
  Example 2: Life Table Estimates for Males with Angina Pectoris   1062
REFERENCES   1068

ABSTRACT

The LIFETEST procedure can be used with data that may be right-censored to compute nonparametric estimates of the survival distribution and to compute rank tests for association of the response variable with other variables. The survival estimates are computed within defined strata levels, and the rank tests are pooled over the strata and are therefore adjusted for strata differences. Additionally, statistics testing homogeneity over strata are computed.

Throughout the chapter, the terms *failure time* and *survival time* are used interchangeably. *Event times* are uncensored survival times.

INTRODUCTION

A common feature of lifetime or survival data is the presence of right-censored observations due either to withdrawal of experimental units or termination of the experiment. For such observations it is only known that the lifetime exceeded the given value. The exact lifetime remains unknown. Such data cannot be analyzed by ignoring the censored observations because, among other considerations, the longer-lived units are generally more likely to be censored. The analysis methodology must correctly use the censored observations as well as the noncensored observations.

Survival Distribution

Usually, a first step in the analysis of survival data is the estimation of the distribution of the failure times. The survival distribution function (SDF), also known as the survival function, is used to describe the lifetimes of the population of interest. The SDF evaluated at t is the probability that an experimental unit from the population will have a lifetime exceeding t, that is

$$S(t) = \text{Prob}(T > t)$$

where $S(t)$ denotes the survival function and T is the lifetime of a randomly selected experimental unit. The LIFETEST procedure can compute estimates of the survival function either by the product-limit method (also called the Kaplan-Meier method) or the life table method. See **Computational Formulas** for a brief description of the estimators or see one of the books listed in **REFERENCES** at the end of this chapter for a more complete description of these methods.

Some functions closely related to the SDF are the cumulative distribution function (CDF), the probability density function (PDF), and the hazard function. The CDF, denoted $F(t)$, is defined as $1 - S(t)$ and is the probability that a lifetime does not exceed t. The PDF, denoted $f(t)$, is defined as the derivative of $F(t)$, and the hazard function, denoted $h(t)$, is defined as $f(t)/S(t)$. If the life table method is chosen, the estimates of the probability density function and the hazard function can also be computed. Printer plots of these estimates can be produced as well as data sets containing the estimates. The output data set can be used to produce graphical plots of the estimates.

Comparison of Survival Curves

An important task in the analysis of survival data is the comparison of survival curves. It is of interest to determine whether two or more samples could have arisen from identical survival functions. The LIFETEST procedure provides two rank tests and a likelihood ratio test for testing the homogeneity of survival functions across strata. The rank tests are censored-data generalizations of the Savage (exponential scores) test and the Wilcoxon test. The generalized Savage test is also known as the *log rank test*, while the generalized Wilcoxon test is simply referred to as the Wilcoxon test. The likelihood ratio test is based on an underlying exponential model, whereas the rank tests are not.

The following example illustrates the use of PROC LIFETEST. The data, taken from Kalbfleisch and Prentice (1980), represent the lifetimes in days of two groups of rats (distinguished by a pretreatment regimen) following exposure to the carcinogen DMBA. The right-censored observations are indicated by giving the censoring times as a negative sign.

The following statements produce **Output 26.1**:

```
title 'Lifetimes of Rats Exposed to DMBA';
data cancer;
    label days='days from exposure to death'
          group='pre-treatment group';
    input days @@;
    censored=(days < 0);
    days=abs(days);
    if _n_>19 then group='pretrt1';
    else group='pretrt2';
    cards;
143 164 188 188 190 192 206 209 213 216
220 227 230 234 246 265 304  -216  -244
142 156 163 198 205 232 232 233 233 233 239
240 261 280 280 296 296 323 -204 -344
;

proc lifetest plots=(s,ls,lls);
    time days*censored(1);
    strata group;
run;
```

The PLOTS= option in the PROC LIFETEST statement is used to request a plot of the estimated survival function against time (by specifying S), a plot of the negative log of the estimated survival function against time (by specifying LS), and a plot of the log of the negative log of the estimated survival function against log time (by specifying LLS). The LS and LLS plots provide an empirical check of the appropriateness of the exponential model and the Weibull model, respectively, for the survival data (Kalbfleisch and Prentice, 1980, Chapter 2). If the exponential model is appropriate, the LS plot should be approximately linear through the origin. If the Weibull model is appropriate, the LLS plot should be approximately linear. Since there are more than one stratum, the LLS plot may also be used to check the proportional hazards model assumption. Under this assumption, the LLS plots should be approximately parallel across strata. The estimates are product-limit estimates by default. The TIME statement indicates that the time variable is DAYS and that if the variable CENSORED has the value 1, the observation is right-censored. The STRATA statement indicates that the data are to be divided into strata based on the values of the variable GROUP. The SDF estimates are thus computed within strata, but the printer plots are superimposed on one plot.

Output 26.1   Comparing Survival Curves with PROC LIFETEST

```
                     Lifetimes of Rats Exposed to DMBA                      1

                          The LIFETEST Procedure

                      Product-Limit Survival Estimates
                             GROUP = pretrt1

                                        Survival
                                        Standard    Number    Number
           DAYS     Survival   Failure    Error     Failed     Left

          0.000     1.0000       0          0          0        21
        142.000     0.9524     0.0476     0.0465       1        20
        156.000     0.9048     0.0952     0.0641       2        19
        163.000     0.8571     0.1429     0.0764       3        18
        198.000     0.8095     0.1905     0.0857       4        17
        204.000*       .          .          .         4        16
        205.000     0.7589     0.2411     0.0941       5        15
        232.000        .          .          .         6        14
        232.000     0.6577     0.3423     0.1053       7        13
        233.000        .          .          .         8        12
        233.000        .          .          .         9        11
        233.000        .          .          .        10        10
        233.000     0.4554     0.5446     0.1114      11         9
        239.000     0.4048     0.5952     0.1099      12         8
        240.000     0.3542     0.6458     0.1072      13         7
        261.000     0.3036     0.6964     0.1031      14         6
        280.000        .          .          .        15         5
        280.000     0.2024     0.7976     0.0902      16         4
        296.000        .          .          .        17         3
        296.000     0.1012     0.8988     0.0678      18         2
        323.000     0.0506     0.9494     0.0493      19         1
        344.000*       .          .          .        19         0
                            * Censored Observation


            Quantiles  75%  280.000    Mean               240.795
                       50%  233.000    Standard Error      11.206
                       25%  232.000

NOTE: The last observation was censored so the estimate of the mean is biased.
```

```
                     Lifetimes of Rats Exposed to DMBA                      2

                          The LIFETEST Procedure

                      Product-Limit Survival Estimates
                             GROUP = pretrt2

                                        Survival
                                        Standard    Number    Number
           DAYS     Survival   Failure    Error     Failed     Left

          0.000     1.0000       0          0          0        19
        143.000     0.9474     0.0526     0.0512       1        18
        164.000     0.8947     0.1053     0.0704       2        17
        188.000        .          .          .         3        16
        188.000     0.7895     0.2105     0.0935       4        15
        190.000     0.7368     0.2632     0.1010       5        14
        192.000     0.6842     0.3158     0.1066       6        13
        206.000     0.6316     0.3684     0.1107       7        12
        209.000     0.5789     0.4211     0.1133       8        11
        213.000     0.5263     0.4737     0.1145       9        10
        216.000     0.4737     0.5263     0.1145      10         9
        216.000*       .          .          .        10         8
        220.000     0.4145     0.5855     0.1145      11         7
        227.000     0.3553     0.6447     0.1124      12         6
        230.000     0.2961     0.7039     0.1082      13         5
        234.000     0.2368     0.7632     0.1015      14         4
        244.000*       .          .          .        14         3
        246.000     0.1579     0.8421     0.0934      15         2
        265.000     0.0789     0.9211     0.0728      16         1
        304.000     0          1.0000       0         17         0
                            * Censored Observation


            Quantiles  75%  234.000    Mean               218.757
                       50%  216.000    Standard Error       9.403
                       25%  190.000
```

(continued on next page)

(continued from previous page)

Summary of the Number of Censored and Uncensored Values

GROUP	Total	Failed	Censored	%Censored
pretrt1	21	19	2	9.5238
pretrt2	19	17	2	10.5263
Total	40	36	4	10.0000

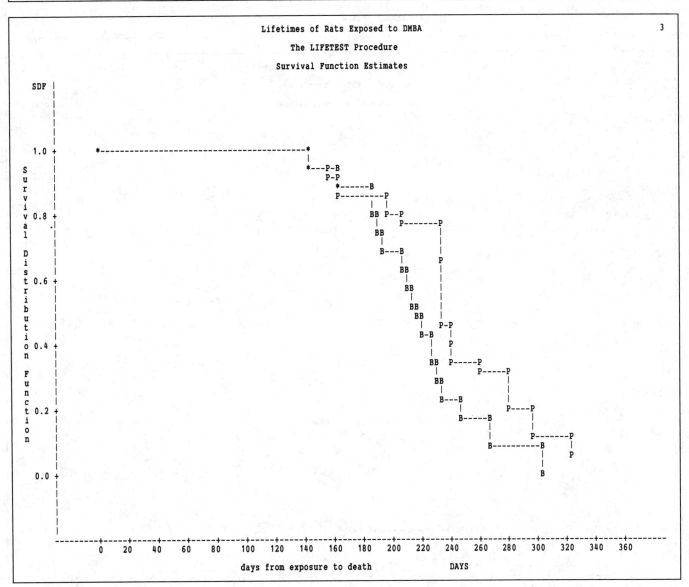

Lifetimes of Rats Exposed to DMBA

The LIFETEST Procedure

Survival Function Estimates

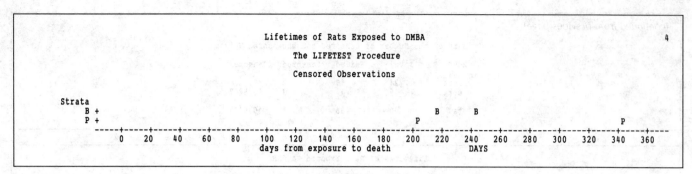

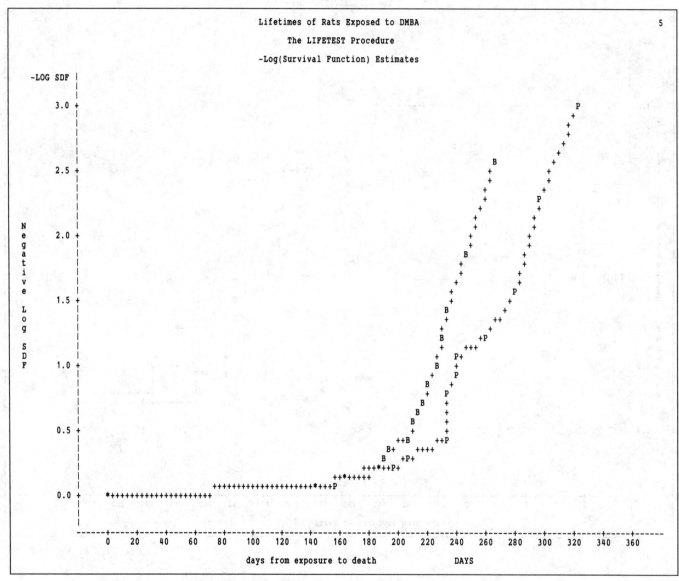

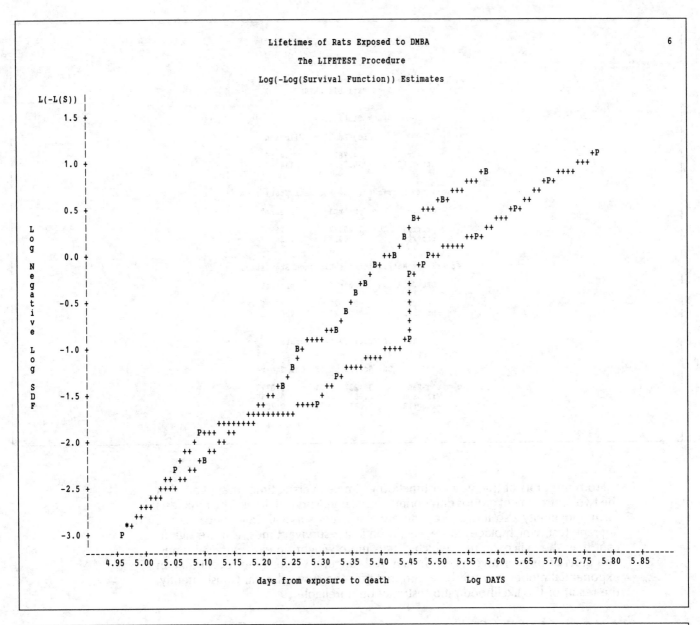

```
                        Lifetimes of Rats Exposed to DMBA                         8

                             The LIFETEST Procedure

                 Testing Homogeneity of Survival Curves over Strata
                                Time Variable DAYS


                                 Rank Statistics

                     GROUP        Log-Rank      Wilcoxon

                     pretrt1       -4.7625       -114.00
                     pretrt2        4.7625        114.00


             Covariance Matrix for the Log-Rank Statistics

                 GROUP         pretrt1        pretrt2

                 pretrt1       7.26327       -7.26327
                 pretrt2      -7.26327        7.26327


            Covariance Matrix for the Wilcoxon Statistics

                 GROUP         pretrt1        pretrt2

                 pretrt1       4902.22       -4902.22
                 pretrt2      -4902.22        4902.22


                    Test of Equality over Strata

                                              Pr >
              Test       Chi-Square    DF   Chi-Square

              Log-Rank      3.1227      1     0.0772
              Wilcoxon      2.6510      1     0.1035
              -2Log(LR)     0.0775      1     0.7807
```

From the plots of the survival function estimates versus time, it appears that the two pretreatment groups differ primarily at larger survival times. The rank tests for homogeneity also indicate a difference at larger survival times because the log rank test, which places more weight on larger survival times, is more significant than the Wilcoxon test, which places more weight on early survival times. The plots of the negative log of the survival function versus time reveal that an exponential model may not be appropriate for the survival data. Consequently, the result of the likelihood ratio test may be unreliable.

Assessment of the Dependence of Survival Time on Covariates

Often there are additional variables called covariates that may be related to the failure time. These variables can either be used to define strata and the resulting SDF estimates visually compared, or they can be used to construct statistics that test for association between the covariates and the lifetime variable. The LIFETEST procedure can compute two such test statistics: censored data linear rank statistics based on the exponential scores and based on the Wilcoxon scores. The corresponding tests are known as the log rank test and the Wilcoxon test, respectively. These tests are computed by pooling over any defined strata, thus adjusting for the stratum variables. Except for a difference in the treatment of ties, these two rank tests are the same as those used to test for homogeneity over strata.

Consider the following set of data presented in Cox and Oakes (1984). The data consist of the survival times in weeks and white blood cell counts for two groups of leukemia patients, one group with AG positive and the other group with AG negative. The LIFETEST procedure computes tests of the association between the log of the white blood cell count and survival time, pooled over the two groups. Tests for the equality of the survival curves of the two groups of patients are also provided.

The following statements produce **Output 26.2**:

```
title 'Relation of Log White Blood Count and Lifetime';
data wbc;
    input wbc t @@;
    if _n_<18 then group='AG+';
    else group='AG-';
    lwbc=log(wbc);
    cards;
 2.3  65    .75 156    4.3 100    2.6 134    6.0  16 10.5 108
10.0 121  17.0    4    5.4  39    7.0 143    9.4  56 32.0  26
35.0  22 100.0    1 100.0    1  52.0    5 100.0  65
 4.4  56   3.0   65    4.0  17    1.5    7    9.0  16  5.3  22
10.0   3  19.0    4   27.0    2  28.0    3  31.0   8 26.0   4
21.0   3  79.0   30  100.0    4 100.0 43
;

proc lifetest notable;
    time t;
    strata group;
    test lwbc;
run;
```

The NOTABLE option in the PROC LIFETEST statement suppresses the printing of the tables of SDF estimates. The STRATA statement indicates that the variable GROUP defines stratum levels. The TIME statement specifies that the variable T contains the failure times. (Note that there is no censoring of the data.) The TEST statement requests rank tests for the association of LWBC with the TIME variable, T.

Output 26.2   Using PROC LIFETEST with Covariates

```
              Relation of Log White Blood Count and Lifetime                        1

                          The LIFETEST Procedure

        Summary of the Number of Censored and Uncensored Values

             GROUP     Total    Failed   Censored  %Censored

             AG+         17        17        0       0.0000
             AG-         16        16        0       0.0000

             Total       33        33        0       0.0000
```

Relation of Log White Blood Count and Lifetime   2

The LIFETEST Procedure

Testing Homogeneity of Survival Curves over Strata
Time Variable T

Rank Statistics

GROUP	Log-Rank	Wilcoxon
AG+	-6.7034	-128.00
AG-	6.7034	128.00

Covariance Matrix for the Log-Rank Statistics

GROUP	AG+	AG-
AG+	5.31858	-5.31858
AG-	-5.31858	5.31858

Covariance Matrix for the Wilcoxon Statistics

GROUP	AG+	AG-
AG+	2927.69	-2927.69
AG-	-2927.69	2927.69

Test of Equality over Strata

Test	Chi-Square	DF	Pr > Chi-Square
Log-Rank	8.4487	1	0.0037
Wilcoxon	5.5962	1	0.0180
-2Log(LR)	11.9401	1	0.0005

Relation of Log White Blood Count and Lifetime   3

The LIFETEST Procedure

Rank Tests for the Association of T with Covariates
Pooled over Strata

Univariate Chi-Squares for the WILCOXON Test

Variable	Test Statistic	Standard Deviation	Chi-Square	Pr > Chi-Square
LWBC	-11.7337	3.9816	8.6848	0.0032

Covariance Matrix for the WILCOXON Statistics

Variable	LWBC
LWBC	15.8531

Forward Stepwise Sequence of Chi-Squares for the WILCOXON Test

Variable	DF	Chi-Square	Pr > Chi-Square	Chi-Square Increment	Pr > Increment
LWBC	1	8.6848	0.0032	8.6848	0.0032

Univariate Chi-Squares for the LOG RANK Test

Variable	Test Statistic	Standard Deviation	Chi-Square	Pr > Chi-Square
LWBC	-19.4051	7.1221	7.4237	0.0064

(continued on next page)

(continued from previous page)

```
                   Covariance Matrix for the LOG RANK Statistics
                            Variable        LWBC

                            LWBC          50.7236


            Forward Stepwise Sequence of Chi-Squares for the LOG RANK Test
                                      Pr >        Chi-Square       Pr >
        Variable    DF   Chi-Square   Chi-Square   Increment     Increment
        LWBC         1     7.4237      0.0064        7.4237        0.0064
```

Here, the results of two sets of hypothesis tests are presented. The first section, titled "Testing Homogeneity of Survival Curves over Strata," compares the survival curves between the two groups of patients. The next section, titled "Rank Tests for the Association of T with Covariates," tests the association between the survival time and the log of the white blood counts. All three tests for homogeneity indicate that the survival functions for the two groups of patients are different. Both the log rank test and the Wilcoxon test provide evidence that the lifetime of leukemia patients is negatively related to the log of their white blood cell counts.

SPECIFICATIONS

The following statements can be used with the LIFETEST procedure:

PROC LIFETEST <*options*>;   must precede TIME statement

TIME *variable* <**censor(list)* >;   required statement

BY *variables*;
FREQ *variable*;
ID *variables*;   optional statements
STRATA *variable* <(list)* >
        < ... variable <(list)>>;
TEST *variables*;

The PROC LIFETEST statement invokes the procedure. All statements but the TIME statement are optional, and there is no required order for the statements following the PROC LIFETEST statement. The TIME statement is used to specify the variables that define the survival time and censoring indicator. The STRATA statement specifies a variable or set of variables defining the strata for the analysis. The TEST statement gives a list of numeric covariates to be tested for their association with the response survival time. Each variable is tested individually, and a joint test statistic is also computed. The ID statement provides a list of variables whose values are used to identify observations on the printout of the product-limit estimates of the survival function. When only the TIME statement appears, no strata are defined, and no tests of homogeneity are performed.

PROC LIFETEST Statement

PROC LIFETEST <*options*>;

The PROC LIFETEST statement invokes the procedure. The following options can appear in the PROC LIFETEST statement. They are described following the table (in alphabetic order). If no options are requested, PROC LIFETEST computes and prints product-limit estimates of the survival distribution within each stratum and tests the equality of the survival functions across strata.

Tasks	Option
Name input/output data sets	
name the input SAS data set	DATA=
name an output data set to contain survival estimates and confidence limits	OUTSURV=
name an output data set to contain rank test statistics for association of survival time with covariates	OUTTEST=
Specify model	
set confidence level for survival estimates	ALPHA=
give interval endpoints for life table calculations	INTERVALS=
set maximum value of time variable for plots	MAXTIME=
specify method to compute survival function	METHOD=
allow missing values to be a stratum level	MISSING
give number of intervals for LIFE TABLE estimates	NINTERVAL=
set tolerance for testing singularity of covariance matrix of rank test statistics	SINGULAR=
give width of intervals for LIFE TABLE estimates	WIDTH=
Control printing	
define characters used for plot axes	FORMCHAR(1,2,7,9)=
suppress printing of output	NOPRINT
suppress printing of survival function estimates	NOTABLE
plot estimates versus time (or log(time))	PLOTS=

ALPHA=*value*

gives a number between .0001 and .9999 that sets the confidence level for the confidence intervals for the survival distribution estimates. The confidence level for the interval is 1−ALPHA. For example, ALPHA=.05 requests a 95 percent confidence interval for the SDF at each time point. By default, ALPHA=.05.

DATA=*SAS-data-set*

names the SAS data set used by PROC LIFETEST. By default, the most recently created SAS data set is used.

FORMCHAR(1,2,7,9)=*'string'*

defines the characters used for constructing the vertical and horizontal axes of the plots. The string should be four characters long. The first and second characters define the vertical and horizontal bars, respectively, which are also used in drawing the *steps* of the product-limit survival function. The third character defines the tick mark for the axes and the fourth character defines the lower left corner of the plot. If the FORMCHAR option in PROC LIFETEST is not specified, the value supplied, if any, with the system option FORMCHAR= will be used. The default is FORMCHAR(1,2,7,9)=' | -+-'. Any character or hexadecimal string can be used to customize the plot appearance. For printing on a PC screen or a printer with IBM graphics character set (1 or 2), use

    formchar(1,2,7,9)='B3C4C5C0'x

or system option

    formchar='B3C4DAC2BFC3C5B4C0C1D9'x

See "The PLOT Procedure" in the *SAS Procedures Guide, Version 6, Third Edition*, or see discussion of the FORMCHAR= system option in *SAS Language: Reference, Version 6, First Edition* for further information.

INTERVALS=*values*
gives a list of interval endpoints for the life table calculations. These endpoints must all be nonnegative numbers. The initial interval is assumed to start at zero, whether or not zero is specified in the list. The interval below an endpoint does not contain the endpoint, while the interval above the endpoint contains the endpoint. When this option is used with the product-limit method, it reduces the number of survival estimates displayed by printing only the estimates for the smallest time within each specified interval. The INTERVALS= option can be specified in any of the following ways:

Type of List	Specification
list separated by blanks	intervals=1 3 5 7
list separated by commas	intervals=1,3,5,7
x to y	intervals=1 to 7
x to y by z	intervals=1 to 7 by 1
combination of the above	intervals=1,3 to 5,7

For example, the specification INTERVALS=5,10 to 30 by 10 produces the set of intervals {[0,5), [5,10), [10,20), [20,30), [30,∞)}.

MAXTIME=*value*
gives the maximum value of the time variable allowed on the printer plots so that outlying points do not determine the scale of the time axis of the plots. This parameter only affects the printed plots and has no effect on the calculations.

METHOD=*type*
specifies the method used to compute the survival function estimates. Valid values for *type* are as follows:

PL | KM
specifies that product-limit (or Kaplan-Meier) estimates be computed.

ACT | LIFE | LT
specifies that life table (or actuarial) estimates be computed.

By default, LIFETEST uses product-limit estimates.

MISSING
> allows missing values for numeric variables and blank values for character variables as valid stratum levels. See **Missing Values** later in this chapter for details. By default, LIFETEST does not use observations with missing values for any stratum variables.

NINTERVAL=_value_
> gives the number of intervals used to compute the life table estimates of the survival function. This parameter is overridden by the WIDTH= option or the INTERVALS= option. When NINTERVAL= is specified, LIFETEST tries to find an interval that will result in round numbers for the endpoints. Consequently, the number of intervals may be different from the number requested. Use the INTERVALS= option to exactly control the interval endpoints. See **Computational Formulas** later in this chapter for details of computing the width of the time intervals. By default, NINTERVAL=10.

NOPRINT
> suppresses the printing of output. This is useful when only an output data set is needed.

NOTABLE
> suppresses the printing of survival function estimates. Only the summary of the number of censored and uncensored values, plots (if requested), and test results will be printed.

OUTSURV=_SAS-data-set_
OUTS=_SAS-data-set_
> creates an output SAS data set to contain the estimates of the survival function and corresponding confidence limits for all strata. See **Output Data Sets** later in this chapter for more information on the contents of the OUTSURV= data set.

OUTTEST=_SAS-data-set_
OUTT=_SAS-data-set_
> creates an output SAS data set to contain the overall chi-square test statistic for association with failure time for the variables in the TEST statement, the values of the univariate rank test statistics for each variable in the TEST statement, and the estimated covariance matrix of the univariate rank test statistics. See **Output Data Sets** for more information on the contents of the OUTTEST= data set.

PLOTS=(_type_ <, . . . ,_type_>)
> produces printer plots of the estimates against time or log(time). Valid values for _type_ are:
>
> > **SURVIVAL | S**
> > > specifies a plot of the estimated SDF versus time.
> >
> > **LOGSURV | LS**
> > > specifies a plot of the $-\log$(estimated SDF) versus time.
> >
> > **LOGLOGS | LLS**
> > > specifies a plot of the $\log(-\log$(estimated SDF)) versus log(time).
> >
> > **HAZARD | H**
> > > requests a plot of the estimated hazard function versus time.
> >
> > **PDF | P**
> > > requests a plot of the estimated probability density function versus time.

Parentheses are required in specifying the printer plots. For example,

```
plots = (s)
```

requests a plot of the estimated survival function, and

```
plots = (s, h)
```

requests a plot of the estimated survival function and a plot of the estimated hazard function.

SINGULAR=*value*

sets the tolerance for testing singularity of the covariance matrix for the rank test statistics. The test requires that a pivot for sweeping a covariance matrix be at least this number times a norm of the matrix. By default, SINGULAR=1E-12.

WIDTH=*value*

sets the width of the intervals used in the life table calculation of the survival function. This parameter is overridden by the INTERVALS= option.

BY Statement

BY *variables*;

A BY statement can be used with PROC LIFETEST to obtain separate analyses on observations in groups defined by the BY variables. For large data sets, it is more efficient to use the BY statement than the STRATA statement for defining strata. However, if the BY statement is used to define strata, no pooling over strata for testing the association of survival time with covariates is done and no tests for homogeneity across BY groups are done.

Interval size is computed separately for each BY group. When intervals are determined by default, they might be different for each BY group. To make intervals the same for each BY group, use the INTERVALS= option on the PROC LIFETEST statement.

When a BY statement appears, the procedure expects the input data set to be sorted in order of the BY variables. If your input data set is not sorted in ascending order, use one of the following alternatives:

- Use the SORT procedure with a similar BY statement to sort the data.
- Use the BY statement options NOTSORTED or DESCENDING in the BY statement for the LIFETEST procedure. As a cautionary note, the NOTSORTED option does not mean that the data are unsorted, but rather means that the data are arranged in groups (according to values of the BY variables) and that these groups are not necessarily in alphabetical or increasing numeric order.
- Use the DATASETS procedure (in base SAS software) to create an index on the BY variables.

For more information on the BY statement, see the discussion in *SAS Language: Reference, Version 6, First Edition*.

FREQ Statement

FREQ *variable*;

The *variable* in the FREQ statement identifies a variable containing the frequency of occurrence of each observation. PROC LIFETEST treats each observation as if it appeared *n* times, where *n* is the value of the FREQ variable for the observation. The FREQ statement is useful for producing life tables when the data are already in the form of a summary data set. If not an integer, the frequency value is truncated to an integer. If the frequency value is less than one, the observation is not used.

ID Statement

ID *variables*;

The ID variable values are used to label the observations of the product-limit survival function estimates. They are not used for any other purpose. SAS format statements can be used to format the values of the ID variables.

STRATA Statement

The STRATA statement indicates which variables determine strata levels for the computations. The strata are formed according to the nonmissing values of the designated strata variables. The MISSING option can be used to allow missing values as a valid stratum level.

The form of the STRATA statement is

STRATA *variable* <(list)>< ... *variable* <(list)>>;

where *variable* is a variable whose values are to determine the stratum levels, and *list* is a list of endpoints for a numeric variable. The values for *variable* can be formatted or unformatted. If the variable is character, or if the variable is numeric and no list appears, then the strata are defined by the unique values of the strata variable. More than one variable can be specified in the STRATA statement, and each numeric variable may be followed by a list. The interval below an endpoint does not include the endpoint, while the interval above the endpoint contains the endpoint. The corresponding strata are formed by the combination of levels. If a variable is numeric and is followed by a list, then the levels for that variable correspond to the intervals defined by the list. The STRATA statement can have any of the following forms:

Type of List	Specification
list separated by blanks	`strata age(5 10 20 30)`
list separated by commas	`strata age(5,10,20,30)`
x to y	`strata age(5 to 10)`
x to y by z	`strata age(5 to 30 by 10)`
combination of the above	`strata age(5,10 to 50 by 10)`

For example, the specification

```
strata age(5,20 to 50 by 10) sex;
```

indicates the following levels for the AGE variable:

{(-∞,5), [5,20), [20,30), [30,40), [40,50), [50,∞)}

This statement also specifies that the age strata be further subdivided by SEX groups. In this example there would be 6 age groups by 2 sex groups, forming a total of 12 strata.

The specification of several variables (for example, A B C) is equivalent to the A*B*C... syntax of the FREQ procedure TABLES statement. The number of strata levels usually grows very rapidly with the number of strata variables, so you must be cautious when specifying the STRATA list.

TEST Statement

   TEST *variables*;

The TEST statement gives a list of numeric covariates you want tested for association with the failure time.

Two sets of rank statistics are computed (see **Assessment of the Dependence of Survival Time on Covariates** earlier in this chapter.) These rank statistics and their variances are pooled over all strata. Univariate (marginal) test statistics are printed for each of the covariates.

Additionally, a sequence of test statistics for joint effects of covariates is printed. The first element of the sequence is the largest univariate test statistic. Other variables are then added on the basis of the largest increase in the joint test statistic. The process is continued until all the variables have been added or the remaining variables are linearly dependent on the previously added variables. See **Computational Formulas** later in this chapter for more information.

TIME Statement

   TIME *variable*   <**censor(list)*>;

The TIME statement is required. It is used to indicate the failure time variable, where *variable* is the name of the failure time variable that can be optionally followed by an asterisk, the name of the censoring variable (which must be numeric), and a parenthetical list of values that correspond to right-censoring. The censoring values should be nonmissing values. For example, the statement

```
time t*flag(1,2);
```

identifies the variable T as containing the values of the event or censored time. If the variable FLAG has value 1 or 2, the corresponding value of T is a right-censored value and not an observed failure time.

DETAILS

Missing Values

Any observation with a missing value for the failure time or the censoring variable, if a censoring variable is listed, is not used in the analysis. If a stratum variable value is missing, survival function estimates are computed for the strata labeled by the missing value, but these data are not used in any rank tests. However, the

MISSING option can be used to request that missing values be treated as valid stratum values. If any variable specified in the TEST statement has a missing value, that observation is not used in the calculation of the rank statistics.

Computational Formulas

Product-Limit Method

Let $t_1 < t_2 < \ldots < t_k$ represent the distinct event times. For each $i = 1, \ldots, k$ let n_i be the number of surviving units, the size of the risk set, just prior to t_i. Let d_i be the number of units that fail at t_i, and let $s_i = n_i - d_i$.

The product-limit estimate of the SDF at t_i is the cumulative product

$$\hat{S}(t_i) = \Pi_{j=1}^{i}(1 - d_j / n_j) \quad .$$

Notice that the estimator is defined to be right continuous; that is, the events at t_i are included in the estimate of $S(t_i)$. The corresponding estimate of the standard error is computed using Greenwood's formula (see Kalbfleish and Prentice 1980) as

$$\hat{\sigma}(\hat{S}(t_i)) = \hat{S}(t_i) \sqrt{\Sigma_{j=1}^{i} d_j / (n_j s_j)} \quad .$$

The first sample quartile of the survival time distribution is given by

$$q_{.25} = \min\{t: 1 - \hat{S}(t) \geq .25\} \quad .$$

The second and third sample quartiles are calculated in a similar manner.

The estimated mean survival time is

$$\hat{\mu} = \Sigma_{i=1}^{k} \hat{S}(t_{i-1})(t_i - t_{i-1})$$

where t_0 is defined to be zero. If the last observation is censored, this sum under-estimates the mean. The standard error of $\hat{\mu}$ is estimated as

$$\hat{\sigma}(\hat{\mu}) = \sqrt{(m/m-1)\Sigma_{i=1}^{k-1} A_i^2 d_i / (n_i s_i)}$$

where

$$A_i = \Sigma_{j=i}^{k-1} \hat{S}(t_j)(t_{j+1} - t_j) \quad \text{and} \quad m = \Sigma_{j=1}^{k} d_j \quad .$$

Life Table Method

The life table estimates are computed by counting the numbers of censored and uncensored observations that fall into each of the time intervals $[t_{i-1}, t_i)$, $i = 1, 2, \ldots, k+1$, where $t_0 = 0$ and $t_{k+1} = \infty$. Let n_i be the number of units entering the interval $[t_{i-1}, t_i)$, and let d_i be the number of events occurring in the interval. Let $b_i = t_i - t_{i-1}$, and let $n'_i = n_i - w_i/2$, where w_i is the number of units censored in the interval. n'_i is known as the *effective sample size* of the interval $[t_{i-1}, t_i)$. Let t_{mi} denote the midpoint of $[t_{i-1}, t_i)$.

The conditional probability of an event in $[t_{i-1}, t_i)$ is estimated by

$$\hat{q}_i = d_i / n'_i$$

and its estimated standard error is

$$\hat{\sigma}(\hat{q}_i) = \sqrt{\hat{q}_i\,\hat{p}_i/n_i'}$$

where $\hat{p}_i = 1 - \hat{q}_i$.

The estimate of the survival function at t_i is

$$\hat{S}(t_i) = \Pi_{j=1}^{i}\,(1 - \hat{q}_j)$$

and its estimated standard error is

$$\hat{\sigma}(\hat{S}(t_i)) = \hat{S}(t_i)\,\sqrt{\Sigma_{j=1}^{i}\,\hat{q}_j/(n_j'\,\hat{p}_j)} \quad .$$

The density function at t_{mi} is estimated by

$$\hat{f}(t_{mi}) = \hat{S}(t_{i-1})\,\hat{q}_i\,/\,b_i$$

and its estimated standard error is

$$\hat{\sigma}(\hat{f}(t_{mi})) = \hat{f}(t_{mi})\,\sqrt{\Sigma_{j=1}^{i-1}\hat{q}_j\,/(n_j'\,\hat{p}_j) + \hat{p}_i\,/(n_i'\,\hat{q}_i)} \quad .$$

The estimated hazard function at t_{mi} is

$$\hat{h}(t_{mi}) = 2\hat{q}_i/(b_i(1 + \hat{p}_i))$$

and its estimated standard error is

$$\hat{\sigma}(\hat{h}(t_{mi})) = \hat{h}(t_{mi})\,\sqrt{(1 - (b_i\hat{h}(t_{mi})/2)^2)\,/(n_i'\,\hat{q}_i)} \quad .$$

Let $[t_{j-1}, t_j)$ be the interval in which $\hat{S}(t_{j-1}) \geq \hat{S}(t_i)/2 > \hat{S}(t_j)$. The median residual lifetime at t_i is estimated by

$$\hat{M}_i = t_{j-1} - t_i + b_j(S(t_{j-1}) - S(t_i)/2)/(S(t_{j-1}) - S(t_j))$$

and the corresponding standard error is estimated by

$$\hat{\sigma}(\hat{M}_i) = \hat{S}(t_i)/(2\,\hat{f}(t_{mj})\,\sqrt{n_i'}\,) \quad .$$

Interval Determination

If you want to determine the intervals exactly, use the INTERVALS= options in the PROC LIFETEST statement to specify the interval endpoints. Use the WIDTH= option to specify the width of the intervals, thus indirectly determining the number of intervals. If neither the INTERVALS= option nor the WIDTH= option are specified in the life table estimation, the number of intervals is determined by the NINTERVAL= option. The width of the time intervals is 2, 5, or 10 times an integer (possibly negative integer) power of 10. Let $c = \log10(\text{maximum event or censored time/number of intervals})$, and let b be the largest integer not exceeding c. Let $d = 10^{c-b}$ and let

$$a = 2*I(d \leq 2) + 5*I(2 < d \leq 5) + 10*I(d > 5)$$

with I being the indicator function. The width is then given by

$$\text{width} = a*10^b \quad .$$

By default, NINTERVAL=10.

Confidence Limits Added to the Output Data Set

The upper confidence limits (UCL) and the lower confidence limits (LCL) for the distribution estimates for both the product-limit and life table methods are computed as

$$UCL = \hat{\lambda} + z_{\alpha/2}\hat{\sigma}$$
$$LCL = \hat{\lambda} - z_{\alpha/2}\hat{\sigma}$$

where $\hat{\lambda}$ is the estimate (either the survival function, the density, or the hazard function), $\hat{\sigma}$ is the corresponding estimate of the standard error, and $z_{\alpha/2}$ is the critical value for the normal distribution. That is, $\Phi(-z_{\alpha/2})=\alpha/2$, where Φ is the CDF for the standard normal distribution. The value of α can be specified with the ALPHA= option.

Tests for Equality of Survival Curves across Strata

Log rank test and Wilcoxon test   The rank statistics used to test homogeneity between the strata (see Kalbfleish and Prentice 1980) have the form of a $c \times 1$ vector $\mathbf{v}=(v_1, v_2, \ldots, v_c)'$ with

$$v_j = \Sigma_{i=1}^{k} w_i(d_{ij} - n_{ij}d_i/n_i)$$

where c is the number of strata, and the estimated covariance matrix, $\mathbf{V}=(V_{jl})$, is given by

$$V_{jl} = \Sigma_{i=1}^{k} w_i^2(n_i n_{il}\delta_{jl} - n_{ij}n_{il})d_i s_i/(n_i^2(n_i - 1))$$

where i labels the distinct event times, δ_{jl} is 1 if $j=l$ and 0 otherwise, n_{ij} is the size of the risk set in the jth stratum at the ith event time, d_{ij} is the number of events in the jth stratum at the ith time, $n_i=\Sigma_{j=1}^{c}n_{ij}$, $d_i= \Sigma_{j=1}^{c}d_{ij}$, and $s_i=n_i-d_i$. The term v_j can be interpreted as a weighted sum of observed minus expected numbers of failure under the null hypothesis of identical survival curves. The weight w_i is 1 for the log rank test and n_i for the Wilcoxon test. The overall test statistic for homogeneity is $\mathbf{v}'\mathbf{V}^-\mathbf{v}$, where $\mathbf{V}^-$ denotes a generalized inverse of $\mathbf{V}$. This statistic is treated as having a chi-square distribution with degrees of freedom equal to the rank of $\mathbf{V}$ for the purposes of computing an approximate probability level.

Likelihood ratio test   The likelihood ratio test statistic (see Lawless 1982, section 6.3) for homogeneity assumes that the data in the various strata are exponentially distributed and tests that the scale parameters are equal. The test statistic is computed as

$$Z = 2(N \log(T/N) - \Sigma_{j=1}^{c} N_j \log(T_j / N_j))$$

where N_j is the total number of events in the jth stratum, $N=\Sigma_{j=1}^{c}N_j$, T_j is the total time on test in the jth stratum, and $T=\Sigma_{j=1}^{c}T_j$. The approximate probability value is computed by treating Z as having a chi-square distribution with $c-1$ degrees of freedom.

Rank Tests for the Association of Survival Time with Covariates

The rank tests for the association of covariates are more general cases of the rank tests for homogeneity. A good discussion of these tests can be found in Kalbfleisch and Prentice (1980). In this section the index α will be used to label all observations, $\alpha = 1, 2, \ldots, n$, and the indices i, j will range only over the observations that correspond to events, $i, j = 1, 2, \ldots, k$. The ordered event times will be denoted as $t_{(i)}$, the corresponding vectors of covariates will be denoted $\mathbf{z}_{(i)}$, and the ordered times, both censored and event times, will be denoted t_α.

The rank test statistics have the form

$$\mathbf{v} = \Sigma_{\alpha=1}^{n} \, c_{\alpha,\delta_\alpha} \mathbf{z}_\alpha$$

where n is the total number of observations, c_{α,δ_α} are rank scores, which can be either log rank or Wilcoxon rank scores, δ_α is 1 if the observation is an event and 0 if the observation is censored, and $\mathbf{z}_\alpha$ is the vector of covariates from the TEST statement for the αth observation. Notice that the scores, c_{α,δ_α}, depend on the censoring pattern and that the summation is over all observations.

The log rank scores are

$$c_{\alpha,\delta_\alpha} = \Sigma_{(j:t_{(j)} \le t_\alpha)} \, (1/n_j) - \delta_\alpha$$

and the Wilcoxon scores are

$$c_{\alpha,\delta_\alpha} = 1 - (1 + \delta_\alpha)\Pi_{(j:t_{(j)} \le t_\alpha)} \, n_j / (n_j + 1)$$

where n_j is the number at risk just prior to $t_{(j)}$.

The estimates used for the covariance matrix of the log rank statistics are

$$\mathbf{V} = \Sigma_{i=1}^{k} \, \mathbf{V}_i / n_i$$

where $\mathbf{V}_i$ is the corrected sum of squares and crossproducts matrix for the risk set at time $t_{(i)}$, that is,

$$\mathbf{V}_i = \Sigma_{(\alpha:t_\alpha \ge t_{(i)})} \, (\mathbf{z}_\alpha - \bar{\mathbf{z}}_i)'(\mathbf{z}_\alpha - \bar{\mathbf{z}}_i)$$

where

$$\bar{\mathbf{z}}_i = \Sigma_{(\alpha:t_\alpha \ge t_{(i)})} \, \mathbf{z}_\alpha / n_i \quad .$$

The estimate used for the covariance matrix of the Wilcoxon statistics is

$$\mathbf{V} = \Sigma_{i=1}^{k} \, (a_i (1 - a_i^*)(2\mathbf{z}_{(i)}\mathbf{z}_{(i)}' + \mathbf{S}_i) - (a_i^* - a_i)(a_i\mathbf{x}_i\mathbf{x}_i' + \Sigma_{j=i+1}^{k} \, a_j(\mathbf{x}_i\mathbf{x}_j' + \mathbf{x}_j\mathbf{x}_i')))$$

where

$$a_i = \Pi_{j=1}^{i} \, n_j / (n_j + 1)$$

$$a_i^* = \Pi_{j=1}^{i} \, (n_j + 1) / (n_j + 2)$$

$$\mathbf{S}_i = \Sigma_{(\alpha:t_{(i+1)} > t_\alpha > t_{(i)})} \, \mathbf{z}_\alpha \mathbf{z}_\alpha'$$

$$\mathbf{x}_i = 2\mathbf{z}_{(i)} + \Sigma_{(\alpha:t_{(i+1)} > t_\alpha > t_{(i)})} \, \mathbf{z}_\alpha \quad .$$

In the case of tied failure times, the statistics $\mathbf{v}$ are computed as averaged over the possible orderings of the tied failure times. The covariance matrices are also averaged over the tied failure times. Averaging the covariance matrices over the tied orderings gives functions with appropriate symmetries for the tied observations; however, the actual variances of the $\mathbf{v}$ statistics would be smaller than the estimates above. Unless the proportion of ties is large, it is unlikely that this will be a problem.

The univariate tests for each covariate are formed from each component of **v** and the corresponding diagonal element of **V** as v_i^2/V_{ii}. These statistics are treated as coming from a chi-square distribution for calculation of probability values.

The statistic $\mathbf{v'V^-v}$ is computed by sweeping each pivot of the **V** matrix in the order of greatest increase to the statistic. The corresponding sequence of partial statistics is tabulated. Sequential increments for including a given covariate and the corresponding probabilities are also included in the same table. These probabilities are calculated as the tail probabilities of a chi-square distribution with one degree of freedom. Because of the selection process, these probabilities should not be interpreted as *p*-values.

If desired for data screening purposes, the output data set requested by the OUTTEST= option can be treated as a sum of squares and crossproducts matrix and processed by the REG procedure using METHOD=RSQUARE. Then, the sets of variables of a given size can be found that give the largest test statistics. **Example 1** illustrates this process.

Output Data Sets

OUTSURV= Data Set

The OUTSURV= option in the LIFETEST statement creates an output data set containing survival estimates. It contains

- any BY variables specified.
- any STRATA variables specified, their values coming from either their original values or the midpoints of the stratum intervals if endpoints are used to define strata (semi-infinite intervals are labeled by their finite endpoint).
- _STRTUM_, a numeric variable that numbers the strata.
- the time variable with the same name as is used on the TIME statement. For the product-limit estimates, it contains the observed failure or censored times; for the life table estimates, it contains the lower endpoints of the time intervals.
- SURVIVAL, a variable containing the survival function estimates.
- SDF_LCL, a variable containing the lower endpoint of the survival confidence interval.
- SDF_UCL, a variable containing the upper endpoint of the survival confidence interval.

If the estimation uses the product-limit method, then the data set also contains

- _CENSOR_, an indicator variable that has a value 1 for a censored observation and a value 0 for an event observation.

If the estimation uses the life table method, then the data set also contains

- MIDPOINT, a variable containing the value of the midpoint of the time interval.
- PDF, a variable containing the density function estimates.
- PDF_LCL, a variable containing the lower endpoint of the PDF confidence interval.
- PDF_UCL, a variable containing the upper endpoint of the PDF confidence interval.
- HAZARD, a variable containing the hazard estimates.
- HAZ_LCL, a variable containing the lower endpoint of the hazard confidence interval.

- HAZ_UCL, a variable containing the upper endpoint of the hazard confidence interval.

Each survival function contains an initial observation with the value 1 for the SDF and the value 0 for the time. The output data set contains an observation for each distinct failure time if the product-limit method was used or an observation for each time interval if the life table method was used. The product-limit survival estimates are defined so as to be right continuous; that is, the estimates at a given time include the factor for the failure events that occurred at that time.

Labels are assigned to all the variables in the output data set except the BY variable and the STRATA variable. To obtain the labels, use the LABEL option in the PROC PRINT statement.

OUTTEST= Data Set

The OUTTEST= option in the LIFETEST statement creates an output data set containing the rank statistics for testing the association of failure time with covariates. It contains

- any BY variables
- _TYPE_, a character variable of length 8 that labels the type of rank test, either "LOG RANK" or "WILCOXON"
- _NAME_, a character variable of length 8 that labels the rows of the covariance matrix and the test statistics
- the TIME variable, containing the overall test statistic in the observation that has _NAME_ equal to the name of the time variable and the univariate test statistics under their respective covariates.
- all variables listed in the TEST statement.

The output is in the form of a symmetric matrix formed by the covariance matrix of the rank statistics bordered by the rank statistics and the overall chi-square statistic. If the value of _NAME_ is the name of a variable in the TEST statement, the observation contains a row of the covariance matrix and the value of the rank statistic in the time variable. If the value of _NAME_ is the name of the TIME variable, then the observation contains the values of the rank statistics in the variables from the TEST list and the value of the overall chi-square test statistic in the TIME variable.

Two complete sets of statistics labeled by the _TYPE_ variable are output, one for the log rank test and one for the Wilcoxon test.

Computer Resources

The data are first read and sorted into strata. If the data were originally sorted by failure time and censoring state, with smaller failure times coming first and event values preceding censored values in cases of ties, the data can be processed by strata without additional sorting. Otherwise, the data are read into memory by strata and sorted.

Memory Requirements

For a given BY group, define

N	the total number of observations
V	the number of STRATA variables
C	the number of covariates listed on the TEST statement
L	total length of the ID variables in bytes

S number of strata

n maximum number of observations within strata

b $12+8C+L$

$m1$ $(112+16V)*S$

$m2$ $50*b*S$

$m3$ $(50+n)*(b+4)$

$m4$ $8(C+4)^2$

$m5$ $20N+8S*(S+4)$.

The memory, in bytes, required to process the BY-group is at least

$$m1 + max(m2,m3) + m4.$$

The test of equality of survival functions across strata requires additional memory ($m5$ bytes). However, if this additional memory is not available, PROC LIFETEST skips the test for equality of survival functions and finishes the other computations. Additional memory is required for the PLOTS= option. Temporary storage of $16n$ bytes is required to store the product-limit estimates for plotting. Each plot produced can require up to 10K memory for a 60 line pagesize.

Printed Output

For each stratum, the LIFETEST procedure prints the following:

1. the values of the stratum variables if the STRATA statement is used.

Items 2 through 12 are printed when product-limit estimates are requested:

2. the observed event or censored times
3. the estimate of the Survival function
4. the estimate of the cumulative distribution function of the Failure time
5. the standard error estimate of the estimated survival function
6. the number of event times that have been observed
7. the number of event or censored times which remain to be observed
8. the frequency of the observed event or censored times if the FREQ statement is used (not shown)
9. the values of the ID variables if the ID statement is used
10. the sample Quartiles of the survival times
11. the estimated Mean survival time
12. the estimated Standard Error of the estimated mean

Items 13 through 27 are printed when life table estimates are requested:

13. time intervals into which the failure and censored times are distributed; each interval is from the lower limit, up to but not including the upper limit. If the upper limit is infinity, the missing value is printed
14. the number of events that occur in the interval
15. the Number of Censored observations that fall into the interval
16. the Effective Sample Size for the interval
17. the estimate of Conditional Probability of events (Failures) in the interval
18. the Standard Error of the estimated conditional probability of events
19. the estimate of the Survival function at the beginning of the interval
20. the estimate of the cumulative distribution function of the Failure time at the beginning of the interval
21. the standard error estimate of the estimated survival function

22. the estimate of the Median Residual Lifetime, which is the amount of time elapsed before reducing the number of at-risk units to one-half. This is also known as the *median future lifetime* in Johnson and Johnson (1980).
23. the estimated standard error of the estimated median residual lifetime
24. the density function estimated at the midpoint of the interval
25. the Standard Error estimate of the estimated density
26. the Hazard rate estimated at the midpoint of the interval
27. the Standard Error estimate of the estimated hazard.

The following results, summarized over all strata, are printed:

28. a summary of the number of censored and event times
29. a table of rank statistics for testing homogeneity over strata. For each stratum, the log rank statistic can be interpreted as the difference between the observed number of failures and the expected number of failures under the null hypothesis of identical survival function.
30. the Covariance Matrix for the Log-Rank Statistics for testing homogeneity over strata
31. the Covariance Matrix for the Wilcoxon Statistics for testing homogeneity over strata
32. the approximate chi-square statistic for the log rank test, computed as a quadratic form of the log rank statistics (see **Computational Formulas** earlier in this chapter)
33. the approximate chi-square statistic for the Wilcoxon test
34. the likelihood ratio test for homogeneity over strata based on the exponential distribution.

If plots are requested, then printer plots may be generated for

35. the estimated Survival Function against Failure Time
36. the −Log(estimated Survival Function) against Failure Time
37. the Log(−Log(estimated Survival Function)) against log(failure time)
38. censored observations for each stratum if the product-limit estimation method was used.

Note that an asterisk in a plot indicates multiple points.

If the life table estimation method is requested, then plots may also be generated for

39. the estimated Hazard against Failure Time
40. the estimated Density against Failure Time

If the TEST statement is specified then the following statistics are printed:

41. the univariate Wilcoxon statistics
42. the Standard Deviations of the Wilcoxon statistics
43. the corresponding approximate Chi-Square statistics
44. the approximate probability values of the univariate chi-square statistics
45. the Covariance Matrix for the Wilcoxon Statistics
46. the sequence of partial Chi-Square statistics for the Wilcoxon test in the order of the greatest increase to the overall test statistic
47. the approximate probability values of the partial chi-square statistics
48. the Chi-Square Increments for including the given covariate
49. the probability values of the Chi-Square Increments. (See **Computational Formulas** earlier in this chapter for a warning concerning these probabilities.)
50. the univariate log rank statistics
51. the Standard Deviations of the log rank statistics

52. the corresponding approximate Chi-Square statistics
53. the approximate probability values of the univariate chi-square statistics
54. the Covariance Matrix for the LOG RANK Statistics
55. the sequence of partial Chi-Square statistics for the log rank test in the order of the greatest increase to the overall test statistic
56. the approximate probability values of the partial chi-square statistics
57. the Chi-Square Increments for including the given covariate
58. the probability values of the chi-square increments. (See **Computational Formulas** earlier in this chapter for a warning concerning these probabilities.)

EXAMPLES

Example 1:   Product-Limit Estimates and Tests of Association for the VA Lung Cancer Data

This example uses the data presented in Appendix I of Kalbfleisch and Prentice (1980). The response is the survival time in days of a group of lung cancer patients. The covariates are type of cancer cell (CELL), type of therapy (THERAPY), prior therapy (PRIOR), age in years (AGE), time in months from diagnosis to entry into the trial (DIAGTIME), and a measure of the overall status of the patient at entry into the trial (KPS). An indicator variable for therapy type (TREAT) is created in the program.

Because of a few large survival times, a MAXTIME of 600 is used to set the scale of the time axis. An output data set named TEST containing the rank test matrices is requested. The rank tests using the log rank scores are then passed to the RSQUARE method in the REG procedure to find the sets of variables that yield the largest chi-square test statistics.

For example, KPS generates the largest univariate test statistic, KPS and AGE generate a larger test statistic than any other pair, and so on, thus revealing the entry order of the covariates in the LIFETEST procedure's table of partial sequence of chi-squares.

The following statements produce **Output 26.3**:

```
    /* data from Kalbfleisch and Prentice (1980, pp 223-224) */
data valung;
    drop check m;
    retain therapy cell;
    infile cards column=column;
    length check $ 1;
    label t='failure or censoring time'
        kps='karnofsky index'
        diagtime='months till randomization'
        age='age in years'
        prior='prior treatment?'
        cell='cell type'
        therapy='type of treatment'
        treat='treatment indicator';
    m=column;
    input check $ @@;
    if m>column then m=1;
    if check='s'|check='t' then input @m therapy $ cell $ ;
    else input @m t kps diagtime age prior @@;
    if t>.;
    censor=(t<0);
```

```
   t=abs(t);
   treat=(therapy='test');
   cards;
standard squamous
 72 60  7 69  0    411 70  5 64 10    228 60  3 38  0    126 60  9 63 10
118 70 11 65 10     10 20  5 49  0     82 40 10 69 10    110 80 29 68  0
314 50 18 43  0   -100 70  6 70  0     42 60  4 81  0      8 40 58 63 10
144 30  4 63  0    -25 80  9 52 10     11 70 11 48 10
standard small
 30 60  3 61  0    384 60  9 42  0      4 40  2 35  0     54 80  4 63 10
 13 60  4 56  0   -123 40  3 55  0    -97 60  5 67  0    153 60 14 63 10
 59 30  2 65  0    117 80  3 46  0     16 30  4 53 10    151 50 12 69  0
 22 60  4 68  0     56 80 12 43 10     21 40  2 55 10     18 20 15 42  0
139 80  2 64  0     20 30  5 65  0     31 75  3 65  0     52 70  2 55  0
287 60 25 66 10     18 30  4 60  0     51 60  1 67  0    122 80 28 53  0
 27 60  8 62  0     54 70  1 67  0      7 50  7 72  0     63 50 11 48  0
392 40  4 68  0     10 40 23 67 10
standard adeno
  8 20 19 61 10     92 70 10 60  0     35 40  6 62  0    117 80  2 38  0
132 80  5 50  0     12 50  4 63 10    162 80  5 64  0      3 30  3 43  0
 95 80  4 34  0
standard large
177 50 16 66 10    162 80  5 62  0    216 50 15 52  0    553 70  2 47  0
278 60 12 63  0     12 40 12 68 10    260 80  5 45  0    200 80 12 41 10
156 70  2 66  0   -182 90  2 62  0    143 90  8 60  0    105 80 11 66  0
103 80  5 38  0    250 70  8 53 10    100 60 13 37 10
test squamous
999 90 12 54 10    112 80  6 60  0    -87 80  3 48  0   -231 50  8 52 10
242 50  1 70  0    991 70  7 50 10    111 70  3 62  0      1 20 21 65 10
587 60  3 58  0    389 90  2 62  0     33 30  6 64  0     25 20 36 63  0
357 70 13 58  0    467 90  2 64  0    201 80 28 52 10      1 50  7 35  0
 30 70 11 63  0     44 60 13 70 10    283 90  2 51  0     15 50 13 40 10
test small
 25 30  2 69  0   -103 70 22 36 10     21 20  4 71  0     13 30  2 62  0
 87 60  2 60  0      2 40 36 44 10     20 30  9 54 10      7 20 11 66  0
 24 60  8 49  0     99 70  3 72  0      8 80  2 68  0     99 85  4 62  0
 61 70  2 71  0     25 70  2 70  0     95 70  1 61  0     80 50 17 71  0
 51 30 87 59 10     29 40  8 67  0
test adeno
 24 40  2 60  0     18 40  5 69 10    -83 99  3 57  0     31 80  3 39  0
 51 60  5 62  0     90 60 22 50 10     52 60  3 43  0     73 60  3 70  0
  8 50  5 66  0     36 70  8 61  0     48 10  4 81  0      7 40  4 58  0
140 70  3 63  0    186 90  3 60  0     84 80  4 62 10     19 50 10 42  0
 45 40  3 69  0     80 40  4 63  0
test large
 52 60  4 45  0    164 70 15 68 10     19 30  4 39 10     53 60 12 66  0
 15 30  5 63  0     43 60 11 49 10    340 80 10 64 10    133 75  1 65  0
111 60  5 64  0    231 70 18 67 10    378 80  4 65  0     49 30  3 37  0
;
```

```
title 'VA Lung Cancer Data from Appendix I of Kalbfleisch & Prentice';
proc lifetest plots=(s,ls,lls) outtest=test maxtime=600;
   time t*censor(1);
   id therapy;
   strata cell;
   test age prior diagtime kps treat;
run;

proc print data=test;
   title 'Rank Tests for the Association of Time with Covariates';
run;

data rsq; set test;
   if _type_='LOG RANK';
   _type_='cov';

proc reg data=rsq(type=cov);
   model t=age prior diagtime kps treat / selection=rsquare;
   title 'All Possible Subsets of Covariables for the log rank Test';
run;
```

Output 26.3 Producing Product-Limit Estimates and Tests of Association

```
          VA Lung Cancer Data from Appendix I of Kalbfleisch & Prentice                    1

                            The LIFETEST Procedure

                         Product-Limit Survival Estimates
                               CELL = adeno
```

	T	Survival	Failure	Survival Standard Error	Number Failed	Number Left	THERAPY
	0.000	1.0000	0	0	0	27	
	3.000	0.9630	0.0370	0.0363	1	26	standard
	7.000	0.9259	0.0741	0.0504	2	25	test
	8.000	.	.	.	3	24	standard
	8.000	0.8519	0.1481	0.0684	4	23	test
	12.000	0.8148	0.1852	0.0748	5	22	standard
	18.000	0.7778	0.2222	0.0800	6	21	test
	19.000	0.7407	0.2593	0.0843	7	20	test
	24.000	0.7037	0.2963	0.0879	8	19	test
	31.000	0.6667	0.3333	0.0907	9	18	test
	35.000	0.6296	0.3704	0.0929	10	17	standard
	36.000	0.5926	0.4074	0.0946	11	16	test
	45.000	0.5556	0.4444	0.0956	12	15	test
	48.000	0.5185	0.4815	0.0962	13	14	test
	51.000	0.4815	0.5185	0.0962	14	13	test
	52.000	0.4444	0.5556	0.0956	15	12	test
	73.000	0.4074	0.5926	0.0946	16	11	test
	80.000	0.3704	0.6296	0.0929	17	10	test
	83.000*	.	.	.	17	9	test
	84.000	0.3292	0.6708	0.0913	18	8	test
	90.000	0.2881	0.7119	0.0887	19	7	test
	92.000	0.2469	0.7531	0.0850	20	6	standard
	95.000	0.2058	0.7942	0.0802	21	5	standard
	117.000	0.1646	0.8354	0.0740	22	4	standard
	132.000	0.1235	0.8765	0.0659	23	3	standard
	140.000	0.0823	0.9177	0.0553	24	2	test
	162.000	0.0412	0.9588	0.0401	25	1	standard
	186.000	0	1.0000	0	26	0	test

```
                              * Censored Observation


             Quantiles  75%  92.000     Mean             65.556
                        50%  51.000     Standard Error   10.127
                        25%  19.000
```

VA Lung Cancer Data from Appendix I of Kalbfleisch & Prentice   2

The LIFETEST Procedure

Product-Limit Survival Estimates
CELL = large

T	Survival	Failure	Survival Standard Error	Number Failed	Number Left	THERAPY
0.000	1.0000	0	0	0	27	
12.000	0.9630	0.0370	0.0363	1	26	standard
15.000	0.9259	0.0741	0.0504	2	25	test
19.000	0.8889	0.1111	0.0605	3	24	test
43.000	0.8519	0.1481	0.0684	4	23	test
49.000	0.8148	0.1852	0.0748	5	22	test
52.000	0.7778	0.2222	0.0800	6	21	test
53.000	0.7407	0.2593	0.0843	7	20	test
100.000	0.7037	0.2963	0.0879	8	19	standard
103.000	0.6667	0.3333	0.0907	9	18	standard
105.000	0.6296	0.3704	0.0929	10	17	standard
111.000	0.5926	0.4074	0.0946	11	16	test
133.000	0.5556	0.4444	0.0956	12	15	test
143.000	0.5185	0.4815	0.0962	13	14	standard
156.000	0.4815	0.5185	0.0962	14	13	standard
162.000	0.4444	0.5556	0.0956	15	12	standard
164.000	0.4074	0.5926	0.0946	16	11	test
177.000	0.3704	0.6296	0.0929	17	10	standard
182.000*	.	.	.	17	9	standard
200.000	0.3292	0.6708	0.0913	18	8	standard
216.000	0.2881	0.7119	0.0887	19	7	standard
231.000	0.2469	0.7531	0.0850	20	6	test
250.000	0.2058	0.7942	0.0802	21	5	standard
260.000	0.1646	0.8354	0.0740	22	4	standard
278.000	0.1235	0.8765	0.0659	23	3	standard
340.000	0.0823	0.9177	0.0553	24	2	test
378.000	0.0412	0.9588	0.0401	25	1	test
553.000	0	1.0000	0	26	0	standard

* Censored Observation

Quantiles	75%	231.000	Mean	170.506
	50%	156.000	Standard Error	25.098
	25%	53.000		

VA Lung Cancer Data from Appendix I of Kalbfleisch & Prentice   3

The LIFETEST Procedure

Product-Limit Survival Estimates
CELL = small

T	Survival	Failure	Survival Standard Error	Number Failed	Number Left	THERAPY
0.000	1.0000	0	0	0	48	
2.000	0.9792	0.0208	0.0206	1	47	test
4.000	0.9583	0.0417	0.0288	2	46	standard
7.000	.	.	.	3	45	standard
7.000	0.9167	0.0833	0.0399	4	44	test
8.000	0.8958	0.1042	0.0441	5	43	test
10.000	0.8750	0.1250	0.0477	6	42	standard
13.000	.	.	.	7	41	standard
13.000	0.8333	0.1667	0.0538	8	40	test
16.000	0.8125	0.1875	0.0563	9	39	standard
18.000	.	.	.	10	38	standard
18.000	0.7708	0.2292	0.0607	11	37	standard
20.000	.	.	.	12	36	standard
20.000	0.7292	0.2708	0.0641	13	35	test
21.000	.	.	.	14	34	standard
21.000	0.6875	0.3125	0.0669	15	33	test
22.000	0.6667	0.3333	0.0680	16	32	standard
24.000	0.6458	0.3542	0.0690	17	31	test
25.000	.	.	.	18	30	test
25.000	0.6042	0.3958	0.0706	19	29	test
27.000	0.5833	0.4167	0.0712	20	28	standard
29.000	0.5625	0.4375	0.0716	21	27	test
30.000	0.5417	0.4583	0.0719	22	26	standard
31.000	0.5208	0.4792	0.0721	23	25	standard
51.000	.	.	.	24	24	standard
51.000	0.4792	0.5208	0.0721	25	23	test
52.000	0.4583	0.5417	0.0719	26	22	standard
54.000	.	.	.	27	21	standard
54.000	0.4167	0.5833	0.0712	28	20	standard
56.000	0.3958	0.6042	0.0706	29	19	standard
59.000	0.3750	0.6250	0.0699	30	18	standard
61.000	0.3542	0.6458	0.0690	31	17	test
63.000	0.3333	0.6667	0.0680	32	16	standard

(continued on next page)

(continued from previous page)

80.000	0.3125	0.6875	0.0669	33	15	test
87.000	0.2917	0.7083	0.0656	34	14	test
95.000	0.2708	0.7292	0.0641	35	13	test
97.000*	.	.	.	35	12	standard
99.000	.	.	.	36	11	test
99.000	0.2257	0.7743	0.0609	37	10	test
103.000*	.	.	.	37	9	test
117.000	0.2006	0.7994	0.0591	38	8	standard
122.000	0.1755	0.8245	0.0567	39	7	standard
123.000*	.	.	.	39	6	standard
139.000	0.1463	0.8537	0.0543	40	5	standard
151.000	0.1170	0.8830	0.0507	41	4	standard
153.000	0.0878	0.9122	0.0457	42	3	standard
287.000	0.0585	0.9415	0.0387	43	2	standard
384.000	0.0293	0.9707	0.0283	44	1	standard
392.000	0	1.0000	0	45	0	standard

VA Lung Cancer Data from Appendix I of Kalbfleisch & Prentice   4

The LIFETEST Procedure

* Censored Observation

Quantiles	75%	99.000	Mean	78.981
	50%	51.000	Standard Error	14.837
	25%	20.000		

VA Lung Cancer Data from Appendix I of Kalbfleisch & Prentice   5

The LIFETEST Procedure

Product-Limit Survival Estimates
CELL = squamous

T	Survival	Failure	Survival Standard Error	Number Failed	Number Left	THERAPY
0.000	1.0000	0	0	0	35	
1.000	.	.	.	1	34	test
1.000	0.9429	0.0571	0.0392	2	33	test
8.000	0.9143	0.0857	0.0473	3	32	standard
10.000	0.8857	0.1143	0.0538	4	31	standard
11.000	0.8571	0.1429	0.0591	5	30	standard
15.000	0.8286	0.1714	0.0637	6	29	test
25.000	0.8000	0.2000	0.0676	7	28	test
25.000*	.	.	.	7	27	standard
30.000	0.7704	0.2296	0.0713	8	26	test
33.000	0.7407	0.2593	0.0745	9	25	test
42.000	0.7111	0.2889	0.0772	10	24	standard
44.000	0.6815	0.3185	0.0794	11	23	test
72.000	0.6519	0.3481	0.0813	12	22	standard
82.000	0.6222	0.3778	0.0828	13	21	standard
87.000*	.	.	.	13	20	test
100.000*	.	.	.	13	19	standard
110.000	0.5895	0.4105	0.0847	14	18	standard
111.000	0.5567	0.4433	0.0861	15	17	test
112.000	0.5240	0.4760	0.0870	16	16	test
118.000	0.4912	0.5088	0.0875	17	15	standard
126.000	0.4585	0.5415	0.0876	18	14	standard
144.000	0.4257	0.5743	0.0873	19	13	standard
201.000	0.3930	0.6070	0.0865	20	12	test
228.000	0.3602	0.6398	0.0852	21	11	standard
231.000*	.	.	.	21	10	test
242.000	0.3242	0.6758	0.0840	22	9	test
283.000	0.2882	0.7118	0.0820	23	8	test
314.000	0.2522	0.7478	0.0793	24	7	standard
357.000	0.2161	0.7839	0.0757	25	6	test
389.000	0.1801	0.8199	0.0711	26	5	test
411.000	0.1441	0.8559	0.0654	27	4	standard
467.000	0.1081	0.8919	0.0581	28	3	test
587.000	0.0720	0.9280	0.0487	29	2	test
991.000	0.0360	0.9640	0.0352	30	1	test
999.000	0	1.0000	0	31	0	test

* Censored Observation

Quantiles	75%	357.000	Mean	230.225
	50%	118.000	Standard Error	48.475
	25%	33.000		

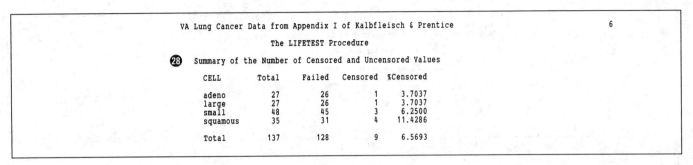

The LIFETEST Procedure

28 Summary of the Number of Censored and Uncensored Values

CELL	Total	Failed	Censored	%Censored
adeno	27	26	1	3.7037
large	27	26	1	3.7037
small	48	45	3	6.2500
squamous	35	31	4	11.4286
Total	137	128	9	6.5693

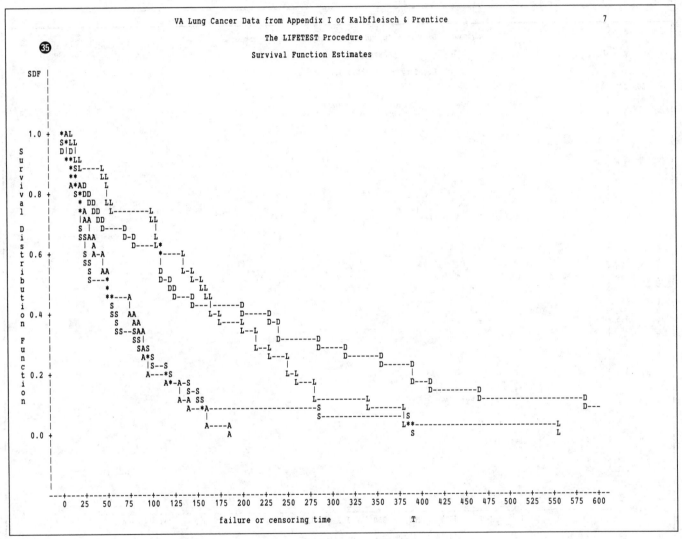

The LIFETEST Procedure

Survival Function Estimates

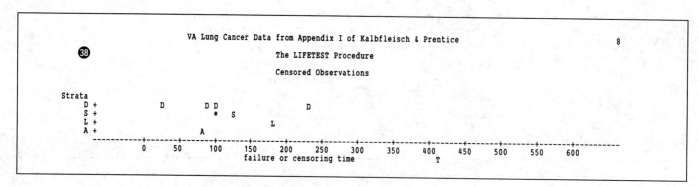

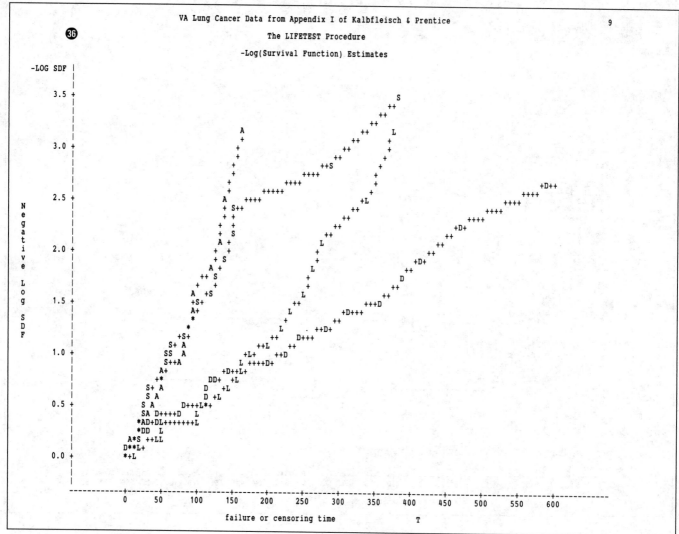

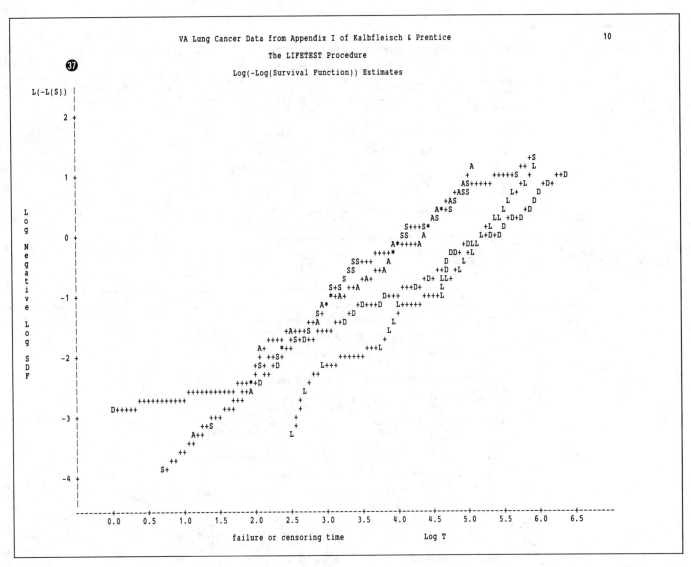

The LIFETEST Procedure

Log(-Log(Survival Function)) Estimates

VA Lung Cancer Data from Appendix I of Kalbfleisch & Prentice   11

The LIFETEST Procedure

Legend for Strata Symbols

A:CELL=adeno L:CELL=large S:CELL=small D:CELL=squamous

VA Lung Cancer Data from Appendix I of Kalbfleisch & Prentice   12

The LIFETEST Procedure

Testing Homogeneity of Survival Curves over Strata
Time Variable T

Rank Statistics

CELL	Log-Rank	Wilcoxon
adeno	10.306	697.0
large	-8.549	-1085.0
small	14.898	1278.0
squamous	-16.655	-890.0

(continued on next page)

(continued from previous page)

㉚ Covariance Matrix for the Log-Rank Statistics

CELL	adeno	large	small	squamous
adeno	12.9662	-4.0701	-4.4087	-4.4873
large	-4.0701	24.1990	-7.8117	-12.3172
small	-4.4087	-7.8117	21.7543	-9.5339
squamous	-4.4873	-12.3172	-9.5339	26.3384

㉛ Covariance Matrix for the Wilcoxon Statistics

CELL	adeno	large	small	squamous
adeno	121188	-34718	-46639	-39831
large	-34718	151241	-59948	-56576
small	-46639	-59948	175590	-69002
squamous	-39831	-56576	-69002	165410

Test of Equality over Strata

Test	Chi-Square	DF	Pr > Chi-Square
㉜ Log-Rank	25.4037	3	0.0001
㉝ Wilcoxon	19.4331	3	0.0002
㉞ -2Log(LR)	33.9343	3	0.0001

VA Lung Cancer Data from Appendix I of Kalbfleisch & Prentice 13

The LIFETEST Procedure

Rank Tests for the Association of T with Covariates
Pooled over Strata

Univariate Chi-Squares for the WILCOXON Test

Variable	㊶ Test Statistic	㊷ Standard Deviation	㊸ Chi-Square	㊹ Pr > Chi-Square	Label
AGE	14.4158	66.7598	0.0466	0.8290	age in years
PRIOR	-26.3997	28.9150	0.8336	0.3612	prior treatment?
DIAGTIME	-82.5069	72.0117	1.3127	0.2519	months till randomization
KPS	856.0	118.8	51.9159	0.0001	karnofsky index
TREAT	-3.1952	3.1910	1.0027	0.3167	treatment indicator

㊺ Covariance Matrix for the WILCOXON Statistics

Variable	AGE	PRIOR	DIAGTIME	KPS	TREAT
AGE	4456.9	-214.7	-343.8	-1153.9	32.0
PRIOR	-214.7	836.1	777.6	-197.1	-4.1
DIAGTIME	-343.8	777.6	5185.7	-1548.2	15.9
KPS	-1153.9	-197.1	-1548.2	14113.4	-24.5
TREAT	32.0	-4.1	15.9	-24.5	10.2

Forward Stepwise Sequence of Chi-Squares for the WILCOXON Test

Variable	DF	㊻ Chi-Square	㊼ Pr > Chi-Square	㊽ Chi-Square Increment	㊾ Pr > Increment	Label
KPS	1	51.9159	0.0001	51.9159	0.0001	karnofsky index
AGE	2	53.5489	0.0001	1.6329	0.2013	age in years
TREAT	3	54.0758	0.0001	0.5269	0.4679	treatment indicator
PRIOR	4	54.2139	0.0001	0.1381	0.7101	prior treatment?
DIAGTIME	5	54.4814	0.0001	0.2674	0.6051	months till randomization

Univariate Chi-Squares for the LOG RANK Test

Variable	㊿ Test Statistic	(51) Standard Deviation	(52) Chi-Square	(53) Pr > Chi-Square	Label
AGE	-40.7383	105.7	0.1485	0.7000	age in years
PRIOR	-19.9435	46.9836	0.1802	0.6712	prior treatment?
DIAGTIME	-115.9	97.9	1.4013	0.2365	months till randomization
KPS	1123.1	170.3	43.4747	0.0001	karnofsky index
TREAT	-4.2076	5.0407	0.6967	0.4039	treatment indicator

VA Lung Cancer Data from Appendix I of Kalbfleisch & Prentice   14

The LIFETEST Procedure

(54) Covariance Matrix for the LOG RANK Statistics

Variable	AGE	PRIOR	DIAGTIME	KPS	TREAT
AGE	11175.4	-301.2	-892.2	-2948.4	119.3
PRIOR	-301.2	2207.5	2010.9	78.6	13.9
DIAGTIME	-892.2	2010.9	9578.7	-2295.3	21.9
KPS	-2948.4	78.6	-2295.3	29015.6	61.9
TREAT	119.3	13.9	21.9	61.9	25.4

Forward Stepwise Sequence of Chi-Squares for the LOG RANK Test

Variable	DF	**(55)** Chi-Square	**(56)** Pr > Chi-Square	**(57)** Chi-Square Increment	**(58)** Pr > Increment	Label
KPS	1	43.4747	0.0001	43.4747	0.0001	karnofsky index
TREAT	2	45.2008	0.0001	1.7261	0.1889	treatment indicator
AGE	3	46.3012	0.0001	1.1004	0.2942	age in years
PRIOR	4	46.4134	0.0001	0.1122	0.7377	prior treatment?
DIAGTIME	5	46.4200	0.0001	0.00665	0.9350	months till randomization

Rank Tests for the Association of Time with Covariates   15

OBS	_TYPE_	_NAME_	T	AGE	PRIOR	DIAGTIME	KPS	TREAT
1	WILCOXON	T	54.48	14.42	-26.40	-82.51	855.98	-3.195
2	WILCOXON	AGE	14.42	4456.87	-214.67	-343.81	-1153.92	31.976
3	WILCOXON	PRIOR	-26.40	-214.67	836.08	777.59	-197.13	-4.138
4	WILCOXON	DIAGTIME	-82.51	-343.81	777.59	5185.69	-1548.22	15.873
5	WILCOXON	KPS	855.98	-1153.92	-197.13	-1548.22	14113.39	-24.520
6	WILCOXON	TREAT	-3.20	31.98	-4.14	15.87	-24.52	10.182
7	LOG RANK	T	46.42	-40.74	-19.94	-115.86	1123.14	-4.208
8	LOG RANK	AGE	-40.74	11175.44	-301.23	-892.24	-2948.45	119.297
9	LOG RANK	PRIOR	-19.94	-301.23	2207.46	2010.85	78.64	13.875
10	LOG RANK	DIAGTIME	-115.86	-892.24	2010.85	9578.69	-2295.32	21.859
11	LOG RANK	KPS	1123.14	-2948.45	78.64	-2295.32	29015.62	61.945
12	LOG RANK	TREAT	-4.21	119.30	13.87	21.86	61.95	25.409

All Possible Subsets of Covariables for the Log-Rank Test   16

N = 10000   Regression Models for Dependent Variable: T

Number in Model	R-square	Variables in Model
1	0.93655158	KPS
1	0.03018749	DIAGTIME
1	0.01500948	TREAT
1	0.00388154	PRIOR
1	0.00319916	AGE
2	0.97373615	KPS TREAT
2	0.94722032	AGE KPS
2	0.94170901	PRIOR KPS
2	0.93822385	DIAGTIME KPS
2	0.04339589	DIAGTIME TREAT
2	0.03554445	AGE DIAGTIME
2	0.03041878	PRIOR DIAGTIME
2	0.01805867	PRIOR TREAT
2	0.01590303	AGE TREAT
2	0.00753586	AGE PRIOR
3	0.99744050	AGE KPS TREAT
3	0.97742399	PRIOR KPS TREAT
3	0.97465738	DIAGTIME KPS TREAT
3	0.95154354	AGE PRIOR KPS
3	0.94809518	AGE DIAGTIME KPS
3	0.94181173	PRIOR DIAGTIME KPS
3	0.04558237	AGE DIAGTIME TREAT
3	0.04380568	PRIOR DIAGTIME TREAT
3	0.03552332	AGE PRIOR DIAGTIME
3	0.01922675	AGE PRIOR TREAT
4	0.99985671	AGE PRIOR KPS TREAT
4	0.99755435	AGE DIAGTIME KPS TREAT
4	0.97743976	PRIOR DIAGTIME KPS TREAT
4	0.95154408	AGE PRIOR DIAGTIME KPS
4	0.04592628	AGE PRIOR DIAGTIME TREAT
5	1.00000000	AGE PRIOR DIAGTIME KPS TREAT

For testing the equality of survival functions across strata, the LIFETEST procedure prints the log rank and Wilcoxon tests and their corresponding covariance matrices. The procedure also prints a table that consists of the approximate chi-square statistics, degrees of freedom, and *p*-values for the log rank, Wilcoxon, and likelihood ratio tests. All three tests indicate strong evidence of a significant difference among the survival curves for the four types of cancer cells.

For testing the association of the covariates with the survival time, the LIFETEST procedure first prints a table of univariate test results, which corresponds to testing the association of each individual covariate with the survival time. The joint covariance matrix of these univariate test statistics is also printed. In computing the overall chi-square statistic, the partial chi-square statistics following a forward stepwise entry approach are tabulated.

Consider the case of the log rank test. Since the univariate test for KPS has the largest chi-square (43.4747 on page 14 of the output) among all the covariates, KPS was entered first. The partial chi-square and the chi-square increment for KPS are the same as the univariate chi-square. Among all the covariates not in the model (AGE, PRIOR, DIAGTIME, TREAT), TREAT has the largest approximate chi-square increment (1.7261) and was entered next. The approximate chi-square for the model containing KPS and TREAT is 43.4747+1.7261=45.2008 with 2 degrees of freedom. AGE is a third covariate to enter. PRIOR is the fourth and DIAGTIME is the fifth. The overall chi-square statistic on the last line of output is the partial chi-square for including all the covariates and has a value of 46.4200 with 5 degrees of freedom.

Example 2:   Life Table Estimates for Males with Angina Pectoris

The data in this example come from Lee (1980) and represent the survival rate of males with angina pectoris. The data are read as number of events and number of withdrawals in each time interval. Life table estimates of the survival curve are requested. Plots of the survival, −log(survival), log(−log(survival)), hazard, and probability density estimates are also printed. No tests for homogeneity are carried out because the data are not stratified.

The following statements produce **Output 26.4**:

```
    /* data from Lee (1980) Statistical Methods for */
    /* Survival Data Analysis p 93                   */
title 'Survival of Males with Angina Pectoris';
data survival;
   keep freq time c;
   retain time -.5;
   input fail withdraw aa;
   time=time+1;
   c=0;
   freq=fail;
   output;
   c=1;
   freq=withdraw;
   output;
   cards;
456    0 226   39 152   22 171   23 135 24 125 107
 83 133   74 102   51  68   42  64   43 45  34  53
 18  33    9  27    6  23    0   0    0 30
;

proc lifetest plots=(s,ls,lls,h,p) intervals=(0 to 15 by 1) method=act;
   time time*c(1);
   freq freq;
run;
```

Output 26.4   Producing life table Estimates

Survival of Males with Angina Pectoris   1

The LIFETEST Procedure

Life Table Survival Estimates

⑬ Interval [Lower, Upper)	**⑭** Number Failed	**⑮** Number Censored	**⑯** Effective Sample Size	**⑰** Conditional Probability of Failure	Conditional Probability Standard Error	**⑱** **⑲** Survival	**⑳** Failure	**㉑** Survival Standard Error	**㉒** Median Residual Lifetime	**㉓** Median Standard Error
0 1	456	0	2418.0	0.1886	0.00796	1.0000	0	0	5.3313	0.1749
1 2	226	39	1942.5	0.1163	0.00728	0.8114	0.1886	0.00796	6.2499	0.2001
2 3	152	22	1686.0	0.0902	0.00698	0.7170	0.2830	0.00918	6.3432	0.2361
3 4	171	23	1511.5	0.1131	0.00815	0.6524	0.3476	0.00973	6.2262	0.2361
4 5	135	24	1317.0	0.1025	0.00836	0.5786	0.4214	0.0101	6.2185	0.1853
5 6	125	107	1116.5	0.1120	0.00944	0.5193	0.4807	0.0103	5.9077	0.1806
6 7	83	133	871.5	0.0952	0.00994	0.4611	0.5389	0.0104	5.5962	0.1855
7 8	74	102	671.0	0.1103	0.0121	0.4172	0.5828	0.0105	5.1671	0.2713
8 9	51	68	512.0	0.0996	0.0132	0.3712	0.6288	0.0106	4.9421	0.2763
9 10	42	64	395.0	0.1063	0.0155	0.3342	0.6658	0.0107	4.8258	0.4141
10 11	43	45	298.5	0.1441	0.0203	0.2987	0.7013	0.0109	4.6888	0.4183
11 12	34	53	206.5	0.1646	0.0258	0.2557	0.7443	0.0111	.	.
12 13	18	33	129.5	0.1390	0.0304	0.2136	0.7864	0.0114	.	.
13 14	9	27	81.5	0.1104	0.0347	0.1839	0.8161	0.0118	.	.
14 15	6	23	47.5	0.1263	0.0482	0.1636	0.8364	0.0123	.	.
15 .	0	30	15.0	0	0	0.1429	0.8571	0.0133	.	.

Evaluated at the Midpoint of the Interval

Interval [Lower, Upper)	**㉔** PDF	**㉕** PDF Standard Error	**㉖** Hazard	Hazard **㉗** Standard Error
0 1	0.1886	0.00796	0.208219	0.009698
1 2	0.0944	0.00598	0.123531	0.008201
2 3	0.0646	0.00507	0.09441	0.007649
3 4	0.0738	0.00543	0.119916	0.009154
4 5	0.0593	0.00495	0.108043	0.009285
5 6	0.0581	0.00503	0.118596	0.010589
6 7	0.0439	0.00469	0.1	0.010963
7 8	0.0460	0.00518	0.116719	0.013545
8 9	0.0370	0.00502	0.10483	0.014659
9 10	0.0355	0.00531	0.112299	0.017301
10 11	0.0430	0.00627	0.155235	0.023602
11 12	0.0421	0.00685	0.17942	0.030646
12 13	0.0297	0.00668	0.149378	0.03511
13 14	0.0203	0.00651	0.116883	0.038894
14 15	0.0207	0.00804	0.134831	0.054919
15 .	.	.	.	.

Summary of the Number of Censored and Uncensored Values

Total	Failed	Censored	%Censored
2418	1625	793	32.7957

Survival of Males with Angina Pectoris   2

The LIFETEST Procedure

NOTE: There were 4 observations with missing values, negative time values or frequency values less than 1.

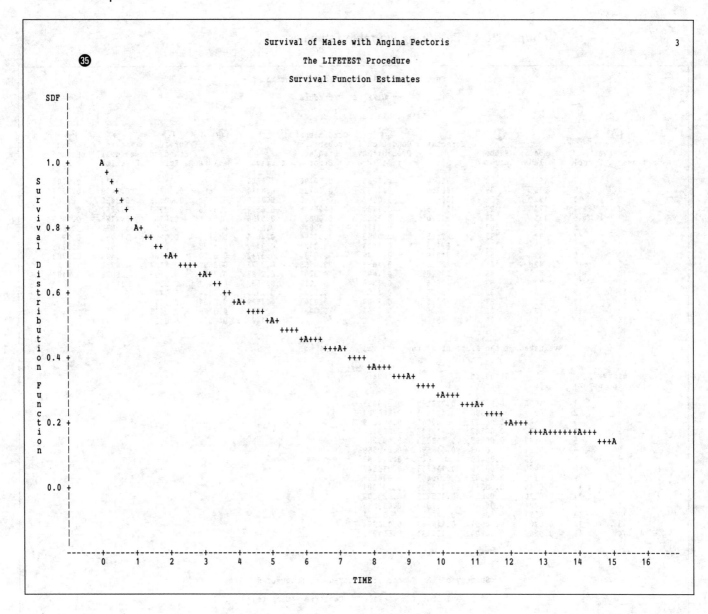

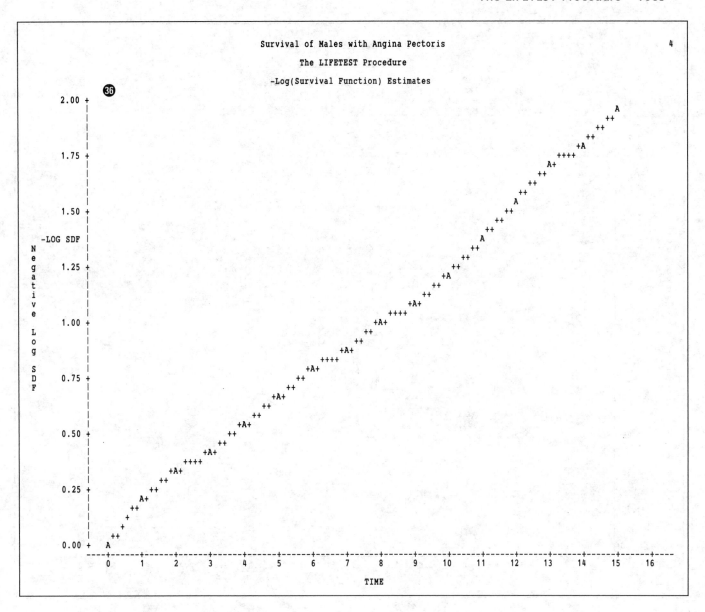

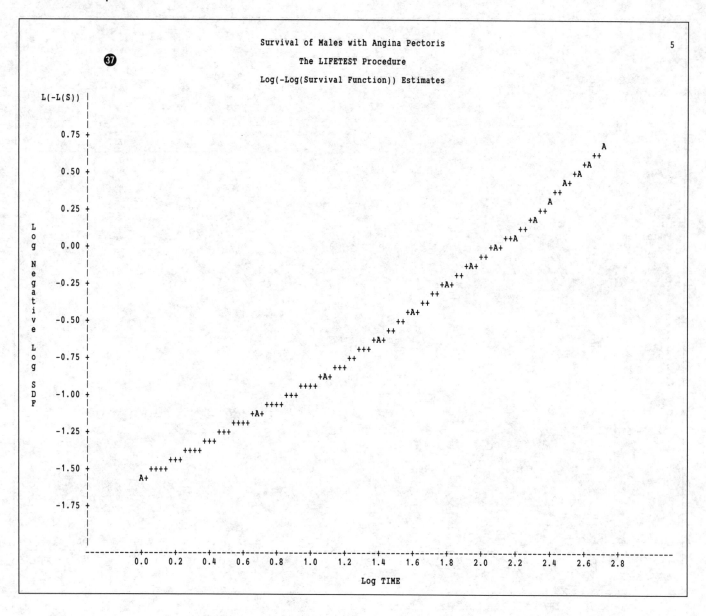

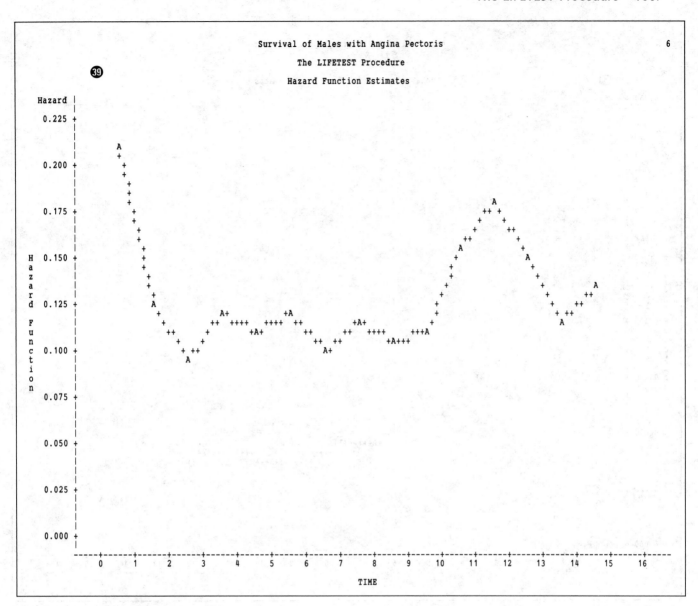

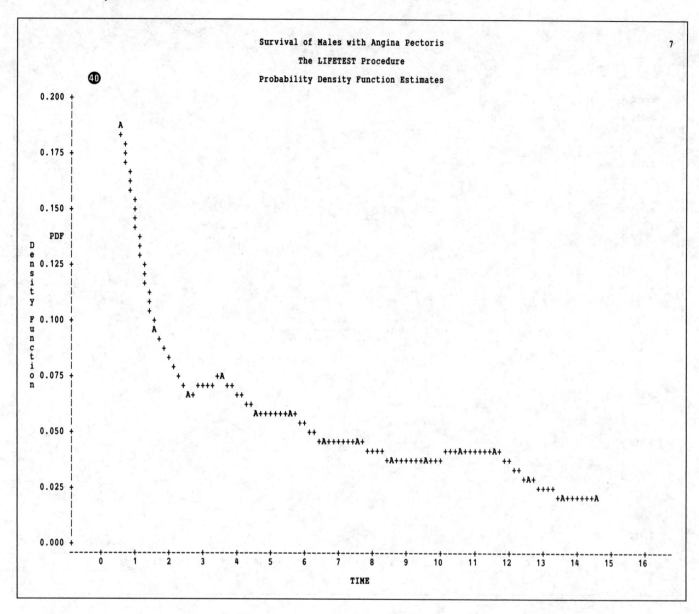

6

As discussed in Lee (1980), the estimated hazard function shows that the death rate is highest in the first year, remains relatively constant from the end of the first year to the end of the tenth year, and is generally higher after the tenth year. One may interpret such an observation as an indication that a patient who has survived the first year has a better chance than a patient who has just been diagnosed.

REFERENCES

Cox, D.R. and Oakes, D. (1984), *Analysis of Survival Data*, London: Chapman and Hall.

Elandt-Johnson, R.C. and Johnson, N.L. (1980), *Survival Models and Data Analysis*, New York: John Wiley & Sons, Inc.

Kalbfleisch, J.D. and Prentice, R.L. (1980), *The Statistical Analysis of Failure Time Data*, New York: John Wiley & Sons, Inc.

Lawless, J.E. (1982), *Statistical Models and Methods for Lifetime Data*, New York: John Wiley & Sons, Inc.

Lee, E.T. (1980), *Statistical Methods for Survival Data Analysis*, Belmont, CA: Lifetime Learning Publications.

Chapter 27

The LOGISTIC Procedure

ABSTRACT   1072
INTRODUCTION   1072
  Response Types and Models   1072
    Binary Response   1072
    Ordinal Response   1073
  Using the LOGISTIC Procedure   1073
    Introductory Example: Analyzing Ingot Data   1074
  Model Selection   1076
SPECIFICATIONS   1077
  PROC LOGISTIC Statement   1077
  BY Statement   1078
  MODEL Statement   1079
  OUTPUT Statement   1084
  WEIGHT Statement   1086
DETAILS   1086
  Missing Values   1086
  Link Functions and the Corresponding Distributions   1086
  Determining Observations for Likelihood Contributions   1087
  Iteratively Reweighted Least Squares (IRLS) Algorithm   1088
  Criteria for Assessing Model Fit   1088
  Score Statistics and Tests   1089
    Residual Chi-Square   1089
    Testing Individual Variables Not in the Model   1090
    Testing the Parallel Lines Assumption   1090
  Rank Correlation between the Observed Responses and Predicted
    Probabilities   1090
  Linear Predictor, Predicted Probability and Confidence Limits   1091
  Classification Table   1091
    Calculation Method   1092
  Regression Diagnostics   1093
    Hat Matrix Diagonal   1093
    Pearson Residual and Deviance Residual   1093
    DFBETAs   1094
    C and CBAR   1094
    DIFDEV and DIFCHISQ   1095
  OUTEST= Output Data Set   1095
    Number of Variables and Number of Observations   1095
    Variables in the Data Set   1095
  OUT= Output Data Set   1096
  Computational Resources   1096
  Printed Output   1096
EXAMPLES   1099
  Example 1:   Multiple-Response Cheese Tasting Experiment   1099
  Example 2:   Stepwise Regression on Cancer Remission Data   1101

Example 3:   Analysis of Vaso-Constriction Data with Regression
            Diagnostics   1109
Example 4:   Poisson Regression   1120
Example 5:   Conditional Logistic Regression for 1–1 Matched Data   1122
REFERENCES   1125

ABSTRACT

The LOGISTIC procedure fits linear logistic regression models for binary or ordinal response data by the method of maximum likelihood. Subsets of explanatory variables can be chosen by various model-selection methods. Regression diagnostics can be displayed for the binary response model. The logit link function in the logistic regression models can be replaced by the normit function or the complementary log-log function.

INTRODUCTION

Binary response variables (for example, success, failure) and ordinal response variables (for example, none, mild, severe) arise in many fields of study. Logistic regression analysis is often used to investigate the relationship between the response probability and the explanatory variables. A thorough discussion of binary response model methodology is given in Cox and Snell (1989). The simplest model for ordinal response data involves parallel lines regression on some appropriately chosen scale. This model has been considered by many researchers. Aitchison and Silvey (1957) and Ashford (1959) employed a probit scale and provided a maximum likelihood analysis; Walker and Duncan (1967) and Cox and Snell (1989) have discussed the use of the log-odds scale. For the log-odds scale, the parallel lines regression model is often referred to as the *proportional odds model*. Several texts that discuss logistic regression are Agresti (1984), Freeman (1987), and Hosmer and Lemeshow (1989).

Response Types and Models

Binary Response

The response, Y, of an experimental unit or an individual can take on one of two possible values, denoted for convenience by 1 and 2 (for example, Y=1 if a disease is present; otherwise Y=2). Suppose **x** is a vector of explanatory variables and $p=\Pr(Y=1 \mid \mathbf{x})$ is the response probability to be modelled. The linear logistic model has the form

$$\mathrm{logit}(p) = \log(p / (1 - p)) = \alpha + \boldsymbol{\beta}'\mathbf{x}$$

where α is the intercept parameter, and $\boldsymbol{\beta}$ is the vector of slope parameters.

The logistic model shares a common feature with a more general class of linear models that a function $g=g(\mu)$ of the mean of the response variable is assumed to be linearly related to the explanatory variables. Since the mean μ implicitly depends on the stochastic behavior of the response, and the explanatory variables are assumed fixed, the function g provides the link between the random (stochastic) component and the systematic (deterministic) component of the response variable Y. For this reason, Nelder and Wedderburn (1972) refer to $g(\mu)$ as a link function. One advantage of the logit function over other link functions is that differences on the logistic scale are interpretable regardless of whether the data are sampled prospectively or retrospectively (McCullagh and Nelder 1989, chap. 4). Other link functions that are widely used in practice are the normit function and the complementary log-log function. One of these link functions can be chosen using the LINK= option in the MODEL statement, resulting in a broader class of binary response models that the LOGISTIC procedure can fit. This class of models has the form

$$g(p) = \alpha + \beta' \mathbf{x} \quad .$$

Ordinal Response

The response, Y, of an experimental unit or an individual unit may be restricted to one of a (usually small) number, say $k+1$ ($k \geq 1$), of ordinal values, denoted for convenience by $1, \ldots, k, k+1$. For example the severity of coronary disease can be classified into three response categories as $1=$no disease, $2=$angina pectoris, and $3=$myocardial infarction. The LOGISTIC procedure fits a parallel lines regression model that is based on the cumulative distribution probabilities of the response categories, rather than on their individual probabilities. The model has the form

$$g(\Pr(Y \leq i \mid \mathbf{x})) = \alpha_i + \beta' \mathbf{x}, \qquad 1 \leq i \leq k$$

where $\alpha_1, \ldots, \alpha_k$ are k intercept parameters, and β is the vector of slope parameters.

Using the LOGISTIC Procedure

PROC LOGISTIC is similar in use to the other regression procedures in the SAS system. To demonstrate the similarity, suppose the response variable Y is binary or ordinal, and X1 and X2 are two explanatory variables of interest. To fit the logistic regression model given earlier, you can use a MODEL statement similar to those used in the REG and GLM procedures:

```
proc logistic;
   model y=x1 x2;
run;
```

The response variable Y can be either character or numeric. LOGISTIC enumerates the total number of response categories and orders the response levels according to the ORDER= option in the PROC LOGISTIC statement. The procedure also allows binary response data to be input in the form of count data from a binomial experiment as

```
proc logistic;
   model r/n=x1 x2;
run;
```

Here, N represents the number of trials and R represents the number of events.

Then, the procedure prints a profile of the response levels and prints simple statistics (including the mean, standard deviation, minimum, and maximum) for all explanatory variables in the MODEL statement.

Before estimation begins, the LOGISTIC procedure calculates the global score statistic for testing the joint significance of all explanatory variables in the MODEL statement. This is the only statistic printed if you use the NOFIT option in the MODEL statement.

The Maximum Likelihood Estimates (MLEs) of the regression parameters are computed using the Iteratively Reweighted Least Squares (IRLS) algorithm. The estimated covariance matrix of the MLEs is obtained by inverting the expected value of the hessian matrix for the last iteration. Univariate tests based on these estimates are printed. A standardized estimate for each slope parameter is also presented in the same table.

Since the LOGISTIC procedure fits a parallel lines regression model for ordinal response data, it also computes a score test for testing the parallel lines assumption.

The -2 Log Likelihood (-2 Log L) for the model is printed for these three cases:

- for fitting the intercept or intercepts only
- for fitting a model with an intercept or intercepts and explanatory variables
- for the contribution of the explanatory variables only.

The last value is in fact the likelihood ratio chi-squared test statistic for testing the joint significance of the explanatory variables included in the model. Similar profiles based on the Akaike Information Criterion (AIC) and the Schwartz Criterion (SC) are also computed. These profiles contain values for fitting models with the intercepts only and with the intercepts and explanatory variables.

Four measures of association for assessing the predictive ability of a model are calculated. They are based on the number of pairs of observations with different response values, the number of concordant pairs, and the number of discordant pairs. Formulas for these statistics are given in **Rank Correlation between the Observed Responses and Predicted Probabilities** later in this chapter.

Introductory Example: Analyzing Ingot Data

The following example illustrates the use of PROC LOGISTIC. The data, taken from Cox and Snell (1989, pp. 10-11), consist of the number, R, of ingots not ready for rolling, out of N tested, for a number of combinations of heating time and soaking time. The following statements produce **Output 27.1**:

```
data ingots;
   input heat soak r n ∂∂;
cards;
 7 1.0 0 10    7 1.7 0 17    7 2.2 0  7    7 2.8 0 12    7 4.0 0  9
14 1.0 0 31   14 1.7 0 43   14 2.2 2 33   14 2.8 0 31   14 4.0 0 19
27 1.0 1 56   27 1.7 4 44   27 2.2 0 21   27 2.8 1 22   27 4.0 1 16
51 1.0 3 13   51 1.7 0  1   51 2.2 0  1   51 4.0 0  1
;

proc logistic data=ingots;
   model r/n=heat soak;
run;
```

Output 27.1 Logistic Regression on Ingot Data

```
                              The SAS System                                  1

                           The LOGISTIC Procedure

        Data Set: WORK.INGOTS
        Response Variable (Events): R
        Response Variable (Trials): N
        Number of Observations: 19
        Link Function: Logit


                              Response Profile

                     Ordered  Binary
                     Value    Outcome      Count

                        1     EVENT          12
                        2     NO EVENT      375


             Simple Statistics for Explanatory Variables

                                    Standard
        Variable        Mean        Deviation     Minimum      Maximum

        HEAT         19.875969      9.936071      7.00000      51.0000
        SOAK          2.033333      0.942794      1.00000       4.0000


                     Criteria for Assessing Model Fit

                                   Intercept
                        Intercept     and
        Criterion         Only      Covariates    Chi-Square for Covariates

        AIC             108.988     101.346       .
        SC              112.947     113.221       .
        -2 LOG L        106.988      95.346       11.643 with 2 DF (p=0.0030)
        Score              .           .          15.109 with 2 DF (p=0.0005)


                  Analysis of Maximum Likelihood Estimates

                  Parameter   Standard     Wald        Pr >      Standardized
        Variable  Estimate     Error    Chi-Square  Chi-Square     Estimate

        INTERCEP   -5.5592     1.1197    24.6504      0.0001          .
        HEAT        0.0820     0.0237    11.9453      0.0005       0.449368
        SOAK        0.0568     0.3312     0.0294      0.8639       0.029509


          Association of Predicted Probabilities and Observed Responses

                   Concordant = 64.4%      Somers' D = 0.460
                   Discordant = 18.4%      Gamma     = 0.555
                   Tied       = 17.2%      Tau-a     = 0.028
                   (4500 pairs)            c         = 0.730
```

In the "Criteria for Assessing Model Fit" table, the Score statistic gives a test for the joint significance of the explanatory variables (sometimes called the independent variables or covariates) in the model. Thus, you conclude that the combined effect of HEAT and SOAK is significant with a p-value of 0.0005. This test considers only the independent variables, so no test is shown for the columns for "Intercept Only" and "Intercept and Covariates." The -2 LOG L row gives statistics and a test for the effects of the covariates based on -2 Log Likelihood. As with the Score statistic, the combined effects of HEAT and SOAK are significant, with $p=0.0030$. The Akaike Information Criterion (AIC) and Schwartz Criterion (SC) statistics (see **Criteria for Assessing Model Fit** later in this chapter for formulas) are primarily used for comparing different models for the same data. In general, when comparing models, lower values of these two statistics indicate a better model.

The "Analysis of Maximum Likelihood Estimates" table gives parameter estimates and tests for the estimates. Using the parameter estimates, you can calculate the estimated logit of the probability of an event (rejecting an ingot) as

$$\text{logit}(p) = -5.5592 + 0.082*\text{HEAT} + 0.0568*\text{SOAK}$$

Now, suppose HEAT=7 and SOAK=1, then logit(p)=−4.9284. Using this estimate, you can calculate p as follows:

$$p = e^{-4.9284} / (1 + e^{-4.9284})$$
$$= 0.0072$$

This value is the predicted probability that an ingot is rejected when HEAT=7 and SOAK=1. Note that LOGISTIC calculates these predicted probabilities for you when you use the P= option in the OUTPUT statement.

The final table in the output is labeled "Association of Predicted Probabilities and Observed Responses." This table gives four statistics and some information used in calculating the statistics. The statistics assess the predictive ability of the model.

Model Selection

Four model-selection methods are available. The simplest and default method is SELECTION=NONE, for which LOGISTIC fits the complete model as specified in the MODEL statement. The other three methods are FORWARD for forward selection, BACKWARD for backward elimination, and STEPWISE for stepwise selection. These methods are specified with the SELECTION= option in the MODEL statement. Intercept parameters are always forced to stay in the model unless the NOINT option is specified in the MODEL statement.

When SELECTION=FORWARD, LOGISTIC first estimates parameters for variables forced into the model. These variables are the intercept or intercepts and the first n explanatory variables in the MODEL statement, where n is the number specified by the START= or INCLUDE= option in the MODEL statement (n is zero by default). Next, the procedure computes the adjusted chi-squared statistics for all the variables not in the model and examines the largest of these statistics. If it is significant at the SLENTRY= level, the variable with this largest adjusted chi-squared statistic is entered into the model. Once a variable is entered in the model, it is never removed from the model. The process is repeated until none of the remaining variables meet the specified level for entry or until the STOP= value is reached.

When SELECTION=BACKWARD, parameters for the complete model as specified in the MODEL statement are estimated unless the START= option is specified. In that case, only the parameters for the intercepts and the first n explanatory variables in the MODEL statement are estimated, where n is the number specified by START=. The univariate tests based on the MLEs are examined. The least significant variable that does not meet the SLSTAY= level for staying in the model is removed. Once a variable is removed from the model, it remains excluded. The process is repeated until no other variable in the model meets the specified level for removal or until the STOP= value is reached.

SELECTION=STEPWISE is similar to SELECTION=FORWARD except that variables already in the model do not necessarily remain. Variables are entered into and removed from the model in such a way that each forward selection step is followed by one or more backward elimination steps. The stepwise selection process terminates if no further variable can be added to the model, or if the variable just entered into the model is the only variable removed in the subsequent backward elimination.

The LOGISTIC procedure also provides three model building options: FAST, SEQUENTIAL, and STOPRES. These options can alter the default criteria for variables to be entered into or removed from the model. See the descriptions of these options in **MODEL Statement** later in this chapter for details.

SPECIFICATIONS

These statements are available in PROC LOGISTIC:

> **PROC LOGISTIC** <*options*>;   } required statements
> **MODEL** *response=independents* < / *options*>; }
>
> **BY** *variables*;
> **OUTPUT** <OUT=*SAS-data-set*>
>   <*keyword=name . . . keyword=name*>   } optional
>   / <ALPHA =*value*>;   } statements
> **WEIGHT** *variable*;

The PROC LOGISTIC and MODEL statements are required. The rest of this section gives detailed syntax information for each of the statements above, beginning with the PROC LOGISTIC statement. The remaining statements are covered in alphabetical order.

PROC LOGISTIC Statement

> **PROC LOGISTIC** <*options*>;

The PROC LOGISTIC statement starts the LOGISTIC procedure and optionally identifies input and output data sets, or suppresses printed output. The table below summarizes the options.

Task	Options
Specify input data sets details	DATA= ORDER=
Specify output data set details*	COVOUT OUTEST=
Suppress printed output	NOPRINT NOSIMPLE

* PROC LOGISTIC also produces another output data set, OUT=, with the OUTPUT statement.

The list below gives details on these options.

   COVOUT
      adds the estimated covariance matrix to the OUTEST= data set. For COVOUT to have an effect, OUTEST= must be specified.

DATA=*SAS-data-set*
: names the SAS data set containing the data to be analyzed. If you omit the DATA= option, the procedure uses the most recently created SAS data set.

NOPRINT
: suppresses all printed output.

NOSIMPLE
: suppresses printing of simple statistics (mean, standard deviation, minimum, and maximum) for each explanatory variable in the MODEL statement.

ORDER=DATA | FORMATTED | INTERNAL
: specifies the sorting order for the levels of the response variable (specified in the MODEL statement). This ordering determines which ordered value (an integer between 1 and $k+1$ if there are $k+1$ response levels) is assigned to each level of the response variable. The table below shows how LOGISTIC interprets values of ORDER=.

Value of ORDER=	Levels sorted by
DATA	order of appearance in the input data set
FORMATTED	formatted value
INTERNAL	unformatted value

By default, ORDER=FORMATTED, if there is a user-specified format; otherwise the default is ORDER=INTERNAL. For FORMATTED and INTERNAL, the sort order is machine dependent. For more information on sorting order, see Chapter 31, "The SORT Procedure," in the *SAS Procedures Guide, Version 6, Third Edition* and "Rules of the SAS Language" in *SAS Language, Reference, Version 6, First Edition*.

OUTEST=*SAS-data-set*
: creates an output SAS data set that contains the final parameter estimates and optionally their estimated covariances (see COVOUT above). The names of the variables in this data set are the same as those of the explanatory variables in the MODEL statement plus the name INTERCEP for the intercept parameter in the case of a binary response model. For an ordinal response model with more than two response categories, if there are fewer than ten intercept parameters, the parameters are named INTERCP1, INTERCP2, and so on; otherwise the parameters are named INTERC1, INTERC2, and so on. See **OUTEST= Output Data Set** later in this chapter for more information.

BY Statement

BY *variables*;

A BY statement can be used with the LOGISTIC procedure to obtain separate analyses on observations in groups defined by the BY variables. When a BY statement appears, the procedure expects the input data set to be sorted in order of the BY variables. The *variables* are one or more variables in the input data set.

If your input data set is not sorted in ascending order, use one of the following alternatives:

- Use the SORT procedure with a similar BY statement to sort the data.
- Use the BY statement options NOTSORTED or DESCENDING in the BY statement for the LOGISTIC procedure. As a cautionary note, the NOTSORTED option does not mean that the data are unsorted, but rather means that the data are arranged in groups (according to values of the BY variables) and that these groups are not necessarily in alphabetical or increasing numeric order.
- Use the DATASETS procedure (in base SAS software) to create an index of the BY variables.

For more information on the BY statement, see the discussion in *SAS Language: Reference*. For more information on the DATASETS procedure, see the discussion in the *SAS Procedures Guide*.

MODEL Statement

MODEL *variable*=<*independents*> < / *options*>;
MODEL *events/trials* =<*independents*> < / *options*>;

The MODEL statement names the response variable and the explanatory variables (*independents*). If you omit the explanatory variables, the procedure fits an intercept-only model.

Two forms of MODEL syntax can be specified. The first form, referred to as the *actual model syntax*, is applicable to both binary response data and ordinal response data. The second form, referred to as the *events/trials model syntax*, is only applicable to binary response data. Only one MODEL statement can be used with each invocation of PROC LOGISTIC.

In the actual model syntax, you specify one variable, the variable preceding the equal sign, as the response variable. This variable can be character or numeric. Values of this variable are sorted by the ORDER= option in the PROC LOGISTIC statement.

In the events/trials model syntax, you specify two variables that contain count data for a binomial experiment. These two variables are separated by a slash. The value of the first variable, *events*, is the number of positive responses (or events). The value of the second variable, *trials*, is the number of trials. The values of both *events* and (*trials*−*events*) must be nonnegative, and the value of *trials* must be positive for the response to be valid.

For both forms of the MODEL statement, the variables following the equal sign are the explanatory variables for the model. These variables must be numeric.

The table below summarizes options available in the MODEL statement.

Task	Option
Specify model	
link function for response probabilities	LINK=
suppress intercept or intercepts	NOINT
suppress model fitting	NOFIT
specify method to select variables in model	SELECTION=
Specify model building details*	
detailed printout at each step	DETAILS
first order approximation method	FAST
variables included in every model	INCLUDE=
maximum number of moves in and out of model	MAXSTEP=
order variables added or deleted from model	SEQUENTIAL
significance level for entry in model	SLENTRY=
significance level for staying in model	SLSTAY=
number of variables in first model	START=
maximum number of variables in final model	STOP=
residual chi-square criterion for addition or deletion	STOPRES
Model fitting	
value of convergence criterion	CONVERGE=
maximum number of iterations	MAXITER=
tolerance for testing singularity	SINGULAR=
Control printing	
correlation matrix of final estimates	CORRB
covariance matrix of final estimates	COVB
iteration history	ITPRINT
Obtain classification table	
print classification table	CTABLE
specify critical probability value	PPROB=
Obtain regression diagnostics	
influence statistics	INFLUENCE
index plots	IPLOTS

* These options have no effect when SELECTION=NONE.

These options are described below.

CONVERGE=*value*
  specifies the convergence criterion. The iterations are considered to
  have converged when the maximum change (either relative or absolute)
  in parameter estimates between successive steps is less than the value
  specified. A relative change (the ratio of the change in estimate values
  to the estimate from the previous step) is used if the parameter is
  greater than 0.01 in absolute value. Otherwise, an absolute change is
  used. Values of CONVERGE= must be numeric. By default,
  CONVERGE=1E-4.

CORRB

prints the correlation matrix of final parameter estimates.

COVB

prints the covariance matrix of final parameter estimates.

CTABLE

prints a classification table for the final model. CTABLE is available only for binary response data. A jackknife approach is used to reduce the bias of classifying the same data in which the classification criterion is derived. For more information, see **Classification Table** later in this chapter.

DETAILS

produces a detailed printout at each step of the model-building process. It includes the "Analysis of Variables Not in the Model" before printing the variable selected for entry for forward or stepwise selection; and for each model fitted, it includes the "Analysis of Maximum Likelihood Estimates" and measures of association between predicted probabilities and observed responses. For the statistics printed in these tables, see items 15, 16, and 20 in **Printed Output** later in this chapter. DETAILS has no effect when SELECTION=NONE.

FAST

uses a computational algorithm of Lawless and Singhal (1978) to compute a first order approximation to the remaining slope estimates for each subsequent elimination of a variable from the model. Variables are removed from the model based on these approximate estimates. FAST is extremely efficient because the model is not refitted for every variable removed. FAST is used when SELECTION=BACKWARD and in the backward elimination steps when SELECTION=STEPWISE. FAST is ignored when SELECTION=FORWARD or SELECTION=NONE.

INCLUDE=n

includes the first n explanatory variables in the MODEL statement in every model. By default, INCLUDE=0. INCLUDE= has no effect when SELECTION=NONE.

Note that INCLUDE= and START= perform different tasks: INCLUDE= includes the first n explanatory variables in every model, whereas START= only requires that the first n explanatory variables appear in the first model.

INFLUENCE

displays diagnostic measures for identifying influential observations in the case of a binary response model. It has no effect otherwise. For each observation, INFLUENCE prints the case number (which is the observation number), the values of the explanatory variables included in the final model, and the regression diagnostic measures developed by Pregibon (1981). For a discussion of these diagnostic measures, see **Regression Diagnostics** later in this chapter.

IPLOTS

prints an index plot (a plot against the case number) for each regression diagnostic statistic.

ITPRINT

prints the iteration history of the maximum-likelihood model fitting. ITPRINT also prints the last evaluation of the gradient vector and the final change in the -2 Log Likelihood.

LINK=CLOGLOG | LOGIT | NORMIT

specifies the link function for the response probabilities. CLOGLOG is the complementary log-log function, LOGIT is the log odds function, and NORMIT is the inverse standard normal probability integral function. By default, LINK=LOGIT.

   See **Link Functions and the Corresponding Distributions** later in this chapter for details.

MAXITER=n

specifies the maximum number of iterations to perform. By default, MAXITER=25.

MAXSTEP=n

specifies the maximum number of times the explanatory variables move in and out of the model when SELECTION=STEPWISE. The default number is twice the number of explanatory variables in the MODEL statement. When the MAXSTEP= limit is reached, the stepwise model-building process is terminated. All statistics printed by the procedure (and included in output data sets) are based on the last model fitted. MAXSTEP= has no effect when SELECTION=NONE, FORWARD, or BACKWARD.

NOINT

suppresses the intercept from a binary response model, or the first intercept from an ordinal response model.

NOFIT

does not fit the model. Instead, it performs the global score test, which tests the joint significance of the explanatory variables in the model, and no further analyses are performed.

PPROB=$value$

specifies the critical probability value in classifying observations for the CTABLE option. The $value$ must be between 0 and 1. A response that has a predicted probability greater than or equal to the PPROB= value is classified as an event response. By default, PPROB=0.5. PPROB= is ignored if the CTABLE option is not specified.

SELECTION=BACKWARD | B
              | FORWARD | F
              | NONE | N
              | STEPWISE | S

specifies the method used to select the variables in the model. BACKWARD requests backward elimination, FORWARD requests forward selection, NONE fits the complete model specified in the MODEL statement, and STEPWISE requests stepwise selection. By default, SELECTION=NONE.

SEQUENTIAL
SEQ

forces variables to be added to the model in the order specified in the MODEL statement when SELECTION=FORWARD or SELECTION=STEPWISE, or eliminated from the model in the reverse order specified in the MODEL statement when SELECTION=BACKWARD. The model-building process continues until the next variable to be added has an insignificant adjusted chi-squared statistic or until the next variable to be deleted has a significant Wald chi-squared statistic. SEQUENTIAL has no effect when SELECTION=NONE.

SINGULAR=*value*

specifies the tolerance for testing the singularity of the expected value of hessian matrix (where the hessian matrix is the matrix of second partial derivatives). The test requires that a pivot for sweeping this matrix be at least this number times a norm of the matrix. Values of SINGULAR= must be numeric. By default, SINGULAR=1E-12.

SLENTRY=*value*

SLE=*value*

specifies the significance level for entry into the model used in SELECTION=FORWARD and SELECTION=STEPWISE. Values of SLENTRY should be between 0 and 1, inclusive. By default, SLENTRY=0.05. SLENTRY= has no effect when SELECTION=NONE or SELECTION=BACKWARD.

SLSTAY=*value*

SLS=*value*

specifies the significance level for staying in the model used in SELECTION=BACKWARD and SELECTION=STEPWISE. Values of SLSTAY should be between 0 and 1, inclusive. By default, SLSTAY=0.05. SLSTAY= has no effect when SELECTION=NONE or SELECTION=FORWARD.

START=*n*

begins the selection process with the first *n* explanatory variables in the MODEL statement. When SELECTION=FORWARD or SELECTION=STEPWISE, the default is START=0. When SELECTION=BACKWARD, the default value of START= is the number of explanatory variables in the MODEL statement. START= has no effect when SELECTION=NONE.

Note that START= and INCLUDE= perform different tasks: INCLUDE= includes the first *n* explanatory variables in every model, whereas START= only requires that the first *n* explanatory variables appear in the first model.

STOP=*n*

specifies the maximum number of explanatory variables included in the final model when SELECTION=FORWARD, or the minimum number included in the final model when SELECTION=BACKWARD. The LOGISTIC procedure stops the model-building process when a model with *n* explanatory variables is found. When SELECTION=BACKWARD, the default is STOP=0. When SELECTION=FORWARD, the default value of STOP= is the number of explanatory variables in the MODEL statement. STOP= has no effect when SELECTION=NONE or SELECTION=STEPWISE.

STOPRES

SR

specifies removal or entry of variables based on the value of the residual chi-square. If SELECTION=FORWARD, then STOPRES adds the explanatory variables into the model one at a time until the residual chi-square becomes insignificant (until the *p*-value of the residual chi-square exceeds the SLENTRY= value). If SELECTION=BACKWARD, then STOPRES removes variables from the model one at a time until the residual chi-square becomes significant (until the *p*-value of the residual chi-square becomes less than the SLSTAY= value). STOPRES has no effect when SELECTION=NONE or SELECTION=STEPWISE.

OUTPUT Statement

OUTPUT <OUT=*SAS-data-set*>
     <*keyword=name . . . keyword=name*>
     / <ALPHA= *value*>

The OUTPUT statement creates a new SAS data set that contains all the variables in the input data set and optionally creates the estimated linear predictor (XBETA) and its standard error estimate, the estimate of the response probability, the confidence limits for the response probability, and regression diagnostic statistics. The statistics are based on the parameter estimates of the final model produced by the procedure.

If you use the actual model syntax, the data set also contains a variable named _LEVEL_, which has values equal to those of the response variable. The probability under consideration for a given observation is the probability that the response variable is less than or equal to the *j*th response level, where *j* is the order (1,2,3,...) of the value of _LEVEL_. For details, see **OUT= Output Data Set** later in this chapter.

The list below explains specifications in the OUTPUT statement.

OUT=*SAS-data-set*
> names the output data set. If you omit the OUT=option, the output data set is created and given a default name using the DATA*n* convention.

keyword=name
> specifies the statistics included in the output data set and gives names to the new variables that contain the statistics. Specify a keyword for each desired statistic (see the following list of keywords), an equal sign, and the variable or variables to contain the statistic. With the exception of DFBETAS, you can list only one variable after the equal sign. Although you can use the OUTPUT statement without any *keyword=name* specifications, the output data set then contains only the original variables, and possibly _LEVEL_ (if you use the actual model syntax). Note that the regression diagnostics are available only for the binary model. Formulas for the statistics are given in **DETAILS** later in this chapter. The keywords allowed and the statistics they represent are as follows:

> | | |
> |---|---|
> | C | confidence interval displacement diagnostic, which measures the influence of individual observations on the regression estimates. |
> | CBAR | another confidence interval displacement diagnostic, which measures the overall change in the global regression estimates due to deleting an individual observation. |
> | DFBETAS | standardized differences in the regression estimates for assessing the effects of individual observations on the estimated regression parameters in the fitted model. A list of up to $s+1$ variable names can be specified, where s is the number of explanatory variables in the MODEL statement. The first variable contains the standardized differences in the intercept estimate, the second variable contains the standardized differences in the parameter estimate for the first explanatory variable in the MODEL statement, and so on. If an explanatory |

variable is not included in the final model, the corresponding output variable named in DFBETAS=*names* contains missing values.

DIFCHISQ   change in the chi-squared goodness-of-fit statistic attributable to deleting the individual observation.

DIFDEV   change in the deviance attributable to deleting the individual observation.

H   diagonal element of the hat matrix for detecting extreme points in the design space.

LOWER | L   lower confidence limit for the probability of an event response if the events/trials model syntax is used. If the actual model syntax is used, then the statistic is the lower confidence limit for the probability that the response variable is less than or equal to the *j*th response level, where *j* is the order (1,2,3,...) of the value of _LEVEL_. See the ALPHA= option below.

PREDICTED | PRED | PROB | P

predicted probability of an event response if the events/trials model syntax is used. If the actual model syntax is used, then the statistic is the predicted probability that the response variable is less than or equal to the *j*th response level, where *j* is the order (1,2,3,...) of the value of _LEVEL_.

RESCHI   Pearson (Chi) residual for identifying observations that are poorly accounted for by the model.

RESDEV   deviance residual for identifying poorly fitted observations.

STDXBETA   standard error estimate of XBETA (see below).

UPPER | U   upper confidence limit for the probability of an event response if the events/trials model syntax is used. If the actual model syntax is used, then the statistic is the upper confidence limit for the probability that the response variable is less than or equal to the *j*th response level, where *j* is the order (1,2,3,...) of the value of _LEVEL_. See the ALPHA= option below.

XBETA   estimate of the linear predictor $\alpha_i + \mathbf{x}'\boldsymbol{\beta}$, where *i* is the corresponding ordered value of _LEVEL_.

The following option can be specified after a slash:

ALPHA=*value*

sets the confidence level used for the confidence limits for the appropriate response probabilities. The value of *value* must be between 0 and 1. By default, ALPHA=0.05, which results in the calculation of a 95% confidence interval.

WEIGHT Statement

> **WEIGHT** *variable;*

When a WEIGHT statement appears, each observation in the input data set is weighted by the value of the WEIGHT variable. The values of the WEIGHT variable can be nonintegral and are not truncated. Observations with negative or missing values for the WEIGHT variable are excluded from the analysis.

Caution: You should exercise care when using a WEIGHT statement to specify a variable that contains the frequency of the observation. The model will be fitted correctly, but certain printed statistics will not be correct. These are the standard deviations in the "Simple Statistics for Explanatory Variables" table (and hence the standardized estimates of the slope parameters), the Schwartz Criterion, the rank correlation statistics, the classification table, and the regression diagnostics. However, note that these statistics will be correct when you use the events/trials model syntax since LOGISTIC interprets the values of events and (trials−events) as frequencies, not weights. Thus, if your data consist of frequency counts for the binomial case, the events/trials model syntax is recommended.

DETAILS

Missing Values

Any observation with missing values for the response or explanatory variables is excluded from the analysis. Also, if the WEIGHT value is negative, missing, or zero, the observation is not used. The estimated linear predictor and its standard error estimate, the fitted probabilities and confidence limits, and the regression diagnostic statistics are not computed for any observation with missing explanatory variable values.

Link Functions and the Corresponding Distributions

Three link functions are available in the LOGISTIC procedure. The logit function is the default. To specify a different link function, use the LINK= option in the MODEL statement. The link functions and the corresponding distributions are as follows:

- The logit function

$$g(p) = \log(p / (1 - p))$$

  is the inverse of the cumulative logistic distribution function, which is

$$F(x) = 1 / (1 + \exp(-x)) \quad.$$

- The normit function

$$g(p) = \Phi^{-1}(p)$$

  is the inverse of the cumulative standard normal distribution function, which is

$$F(x) = \Phi(x) = (2\pi)^{-1/2} \int_{-\infty}^{x} \exp(-z^2/2) \, dz \quad.$$

The more familiar term *probit* is often used instead of *normit*, although traditionally the probit function contains the additive constant 5.

- The complementary log-log function

$$g(p) = \log(-\log(1 - p))$$

is the inverse of the cumulative extreme-value function (also called the Gompertz distribution), which is

$$F(x) = 1 - \exp(-\exp(x)) \quad .$$

The variances of these three corresponding distributions are not all the same. Their respective means and variances are as follows:

Distribution	Mean	Variance
Normal	0	1
Logistic	0	$\pi^2/3$
Extreme-value	$-\gamma$	$\pi^2/6$

where γ is the Euler constant. In comparing parameter estimates using different link functions, you need to take into account the different scalings of the corresponding distributions and, for the complementary log-log function, a possible shift in location. For example, if the fitted probabilities are in the neighborhood of 0.1 to 0.9, then the parameter estimates using the logit function should be about $\pi/\sqrt{3}$ larger than the estimates from the normit function.

Determining Observations for Likelihood Contributions

If you use the events/trials model syntax, each observation is split into two observations. One has response value 1 with a weight equal to the weight of the original observation (which is 1 if the WEIGHT statement is not used) times the value of the variable *events*. The other observation has response value 2 and a weight equal to the weight of the original observation times the value of (*trials*−*events*). These two observations will have the same explanatory variable values as the original observation.

For either the actual or events/trials model syntax, let j index all observations. In other words, for the actual model syntax, j indexes the actual observations. And, for the events/trials model syntax, j indexes the observations after splitting (as described above). If your data set has 30 observations and you use the actual model syntax, j has values from 1 to 30; if you use the events/trials model syntax, j has values from 1 to 60.

Suppose the response variable can take on the ordered values $1, \ldots, k, k+1$ where k is an integer ≥ 1. The probability that the jth observation has response i is given by

$$\Pr(Y_j = i \mid \mathbf{x}_j) = \begin{cases} F(\alpha_1 + \boldsymbol{\beta}'\mathbf{x}_j) & i = 1 \\ F(\alpha_i + \boldsymbol{\beta}'\mathbf{x}_j) - F(\alpha_{i-1} + \boldsymbol{\beta}\mathbf{x}_j) & 1 < i \leq k \\ 1 - F(\alpha_k + \boldsymbol{\beta}'\mathbf{x}_j) & i = k+1 \end{cases}$$

where Y_j is the response variable corresponding to the known vector $\mathbf{x}'_j$ of explanatory variables; $\alpha_1, \ldots, \alpha_k$ are intercept parameters; and $\boldsymbol{\beta}$ is the slope parameter vector.

Iteratively Reweighted Least Squares (IRLS) Algorithm

PROC LOGISTIC uses iteratively reweighted least squares to compute estimates of the parameters in the model. (This is in contrast to the PROBIT procedure, which uses the Newton-Raphson method to calculate these estimates.)

Consider the multinomial variable $\mathbf{Z}_j = (Z_{1j}, \ldots, Z_{(k+1)j})'$ such that

$$Z_{ij} = 1 \qquad \text{if } Y_j = i$$
$$\phantom{Z_{ij} = } 0 \qquad \text{otherwise.}$$

With p_{ij} denoting the probability that the jth observation has response value i, the expected value of $\mathbf{Z}_j$ is $\mathbf{p}_j = (p_{1j}, \ldots, p_{(k+1)j})'$. The covariance matrix of $\mathbf{Z}_j$ is $\mathbf{V}_j$, which is the covariance matrix of a multinomial random variable for one trial with parameter vector $\mathbf{p}_j$. Let $\boldsymbol{\gamma}$ be the vector of regression parameters; in other words, $\boldsymbol{\gamma}' = (\alpha_1, \ldots, \alpha_k, \boldsymbol{\beta}')$. And, let $\mathbf{D}_j$ be the matrix of partial derivatives of $\mathbf{p}_j$ with respect to $\boldsymbol{\gamma}$. The estimating equation for the regression parameters is

$$\Sigma_j \mathbf{D}'_j \mathbf{W}_j (\mathbf{Z}_j - \mathbf{p}_j) = \mathbf{0}$$

where $\mathbf{W}_j = w_j \mathbf{V}_j^-$, w_j is the weight of the jth observation, and $\mathbf{V}_j^-$ is a generalized inverse of $\mathbf{V}_j$. LOGISTIC chooses $\mathbf{V}_j^-$ as the inverse of the diagonal matrix with $\mathbf{p}_j$ as the diagonal.

The estimates are obtained iteratively as

$$\hat{\boldsymbol{\gamma}}_{m+1} = \hat{\boldsymbol{\gamma}}_m + (\Sigma_j \hat{\mathbf{D}}'_j \hat{\mathbf{W}}_j \hat{\mathbf{D}}_j)^{-1} \Sigma_j \hat{\mathbf{D}}'_j \hat{\mathbf{W}}_j (\mathbf{Z}_j - \hat{\mathbf{p}}_j)$$

where $\hat{\mathbf{D}}_j$, $\hat{\mathbf{W}}_j$ and $\hat{\mathbf{p}}_j$ are respectively $\mathbf{D}_j$, $\mathbf{W}_j$, and $\mathbf{p}_j$ evaluated at $\hat{\boldsymbol{\gamma}}_m$. The expression after the plus sign is the step size. If the likelihood evaluated at $\hat{\boldsymbol{\gamma}}_{m+1}$ is less than that evaluated at $\hat{\boldsymbol{\gamma}}_m$, then $\hat{\boldsymbol{\gamma}}_{m+1}$ is recomputed using half the step size.

The estimated covariance matrix of $\hat{\boldsymbol{\gamma}}_{m+1}$ is

$$\text{cov}\,(\hat{\boldsymbol{\gamma}}_{m+1}) = (\Sigma_j \hat{\mathbf{D}}'_j \hat{\mathbf{W}}_j \hat{\mathbf{D}}_j)^{-1}.$$

Criteria for Assessing Model Fit

Suppose the model contains s explanatory variables. Let y_j be the response value of the jth observation. The estimate $\hat{p}_j$ of $p_j = P(Y_j = y_j)$ is obtained by replacing the regression coefficients by their maximum likelihood estimates (MLEs). The three criteria printed by the LOGISTIC procedure are calculated as follows:

- −2 Log Likelihood

$$-2 \text{ Log L} = -2\, \Sigma_j w_j \log(\hat{p}_j)$$

  where w_j is the weight of the jth observation
- Akaike Information Criterion

$$\text{AIC} = -2 \text{ Log L} + 2(k + s)$$

  where k is the number of ordered values for the response, and s is the number of explanatory variables

- Schwartz Criterion

$$SC = -2 \text{ Log } L + (k + s)\log(N)$$

where k and s are as defined above, and N is the total number of observations (for the actual model syntax) or the total number of trials (for the events/trials model syntax).

The -2 Log Likelihood statistic has a chi-square distribution under the null hypothesis (that all the explanatory variables in the model are zero), and the procedure prints a p-value for this statistic. The AIC and SC statistics give two different ways of adjusting the -2 Log Likelihood statistic for the number of terms in the model and the number of observations used. These statistics should be used when comparing different models for the same data (for example, when you use the SELECTION=STEPWISE option in the MODEL statement); lower values of the statistic indicate a more desirable model.

Score Statistics and Tests

To understand the general form of the score statistics, let $\mathbf{U}(\gamma)$ be the vector of partial derivatives of the log likelihood with respect to the parameter vector γ, and let $\mathbf{I}(\gamma)$ be the matrix of the negative second partial derivatives of the log likelihood with respect to γ. Under a hypothesized $\gamma = \gamma_0$, the chi-squared score statistic defined by

$$\mathbf{U}'(\gamma_0) \; \mathbf{I}^{-1}(\gamma_0)\mathbf{U}(\gamma_0)$$

has an asymptotic χ^2 distribution with r degrees of freedom, where r is the dimension of γ.

Residual Chi-Square

When you use SELECTION=FORWARD, BACKWARD, or STEPWISE, the procedure calculates a residual chi-square statistic and prints the statistic, its degrees of freedom, and the p-value. This section describes how the statistic is calculated.

Suppose there are s explanatory variables of interest. The full model has a parameter vector

$$\gamma = (\alpha_1, \ldots, \alpha_k, \beta_1, \ldots, \beta_s)'$$

where $\alpha_1, \ldots, \alpha_k$ are intercept parameters, and $\beta_1, \ldots, \beta_s$ are slope parameters for the explanatory variables. For a reduced model with t explanatory variables ($t<s$), let $\hat{\alpha}_1, \ldots, \hat{\alpha}_k$ be the MLEs of the unknown intercept parameters for this model, and let $\hat{\beta}_1, \ldots, \hat{\beta}_t$ be the MLEs of the unknown slope parameters for this model. The residual chi-square is the chi-squared score statistic evaluated at γ_0, which is given by

$$\gamma_0 = (\hat{\alpha}_1, \ldots, \hat{\alpha}_k, \hat{\beta}_1, \ldots, \hat{\beta}_t, 0, \ldots, 0)' \; .$$

The residual chi-square has an asymptotic chi-squared distribution with $s-t$ degrees of freedom. A special case is the global score chi-square, where the reduced model consists of the k intercepts and no explanatory variables.

Testing Individual Variables Not in the Model

These tests are performed when SELECTION=FORWARD or STEPWISE. In the output, the tests are labeled "Analysis of Variables Not in the Model." This section describes how the tests are calculated.

Suppose k intercepts and t explanatory variables (say $v_1, \ldots, v_t$) have been fitted to a model and v_{t+1} is another explanatory variable of interest. Consider a full model with the k intercepts and $t+1$ explanatory variables ($v_1, \ldots, v_t, v_{t+1}$) and a reduced model with v_{t+1} excluded. The significance of v_{t+1} adjusted for $v_1, \ldots, v_t$ can be determined by comparing the corresponding residual chi-square with a chi-squared distribution with one degree of freedom.

Testing the Parallel Lines Assumption

For an ordinal response, LOGISTIC performs a test of the parallel lines assumption. In the output, this test is labeled "Score Test for the Equal Slopes Assumption" when LINK=NORMIT or CLOGLOG. When LINK=LOGIT, the test is labeled as "Score Test for the Proportional Odds Assumption" in the output. This section describes the methods used to calculate the test.

For this test the number of response levels, $k+1$, is assumed to be strictly greater than 2. Suppose s explanatory variables are included in the model. Consider the multivariate response model

$$g(\Pr(Y \leq i \mid \mathbf{x})) = (1, \mathbf{x}')\gamma_i$$

for $i=1, \ldots, k$, where Y is the response variable, and $\gamma_i = (\gamma_{i0}, \gamma_{i1}, \ldots, \gamma_{is})'$ is a vector of unknown parameters consisting of an intercept γ_{i0} and s slope parameters. The parameter vector for this full model is

$$\gamma = (\gamma_1', \ldots, \gamma_k')'\ .$$

Under the parallel lines assumption,

$$\gamma_{1m} = \gamma_{2m} = \ldots = \gamma_{km}$$

for all $m=1, \ldots, s$. Let $\hat{\alpha}_1, \ldots, \hat{\alpha}_k$ and $\hat{\beta}_1, \ldots, \hat{\beta}_s$ be the MLEs of intercept parameters and the slope parameters under the parallel lines assumption. Then, for all i,

$$\hat{\gamma}_i = (\hat{\alpha}_i, \hat{\beta}_1, \ldots, \hat{\beta}_s)'\ .$$

The chi-squared score statistic is evaluated at

$$\gamma_0 = (\hat{\gamma}_1, \ldots, \hat{\gamma}_k)'$$

and has an asymptotic chi-squared distribution with $s(k-1)$ degrees of freedom. This tests the parallel lines assumption.

Rank Correlation between the Observed Responses and Predicted Probabilities

Define an event response as the response whose ordered value is 1. A pair of input observations (or a pair of trials for the events/trials model syntax) with different responses is said to be concordant (discordant) if the larger response has a lower (higher) predicted event probability than the smaller response. If the pair is neither concordant nor discordant, it is a tie. Enumeration of the total numbers of concordant and discordant pairs is carried out by categorizing the predicted probabilities into intervals of length 0.002.

Let N be the total number of observations in the input data set (or the total number of trials for the events/trials model syntax). Suppose there is a total of t pairs with different responses, nc of them are concordant, nd of them are discordant, and $t-nc-nd$ of them are tied. LOGISTIC computes the following four indices of rank correlation for assessing the predictive ability of a model:

$$c = (nc + 0.5(t - nc - nd)) / t$$
$$\text{Somers' } D = (nc - nd) / t$$
$$\text{Goodman-Kruskal Gamma} = (nc - nd) / (nc + nd)$$
$$\text{Kendall's Tau-a} = (nc - nd) / (0.5N(N - 1)) \quad.$$

Linear Predictor, Predicted Probability and Confidence Limits

This section describes how to calculate predicted probabilities and confidence limits using the maximum likelihood estimates (MLEs) obtained from LOGISTIC. For a specific example, see **Using the LOGISTIC Procedure** earlier in this chapter.

For a vector of explanatory variables $\mathbf{x}$, the linear predictor

$$\eta_i = g(\Pr(Y \leq i \mid \mathbf{x}))$$
$$= \alpha_i + \boldsymbol{\beta}'\mathbf{x}$$

(where $1 \leq i \leq k$) is estimated by

$$\hat{\eta}_i = \hat{\alpha}_i + \hat{\boldsymbol{\beta}}'\mathbf{x}$$

where the $\hat{\alpha}_i$ and $\hat{\boldsymbol{\beta}}$ are the MLEs of α_i and $\boldsymbol{\beta}$. The estimated standard error of η_i is $\hat{\sigma}(\hat{\eta}_i)$, which can be computed as the square root of the quadratic form $(1, \mathbf{x}')\mathbf{V_b}(1, \mathbf{x}')'$ where $\mathbf{V_b}$ is the estimated covariance matrix of the parameter estimates. The asymptotic $100(1-\alpha)\%$ confidence interval for η_i is given by

$$\hat{\eta}_i \pm z_{\alpha/2}\hat{\sigma}(\hat{\eta}_i)$$

where $z_{\alpha/2}$ is the $100(1-\alpha/2)$ percentile point of a standard normal distribution.

The predicted value and the $100(1-\alpha)\%$ confidence limits for $\Pr(Y \leq i \mid \mathbf{x})$ are obtained by back-transforming the corresponding measures for the linear predictor. For instance, if the logit link function is used, the predicted value of $\Pr(Y \leq i \mid \mathbf{x})$ is

$$1/(1 + \exp(-\hat{\eta}_i))$$

and the lower and upper confidence limits are respectively

$$1/(1 + \exp(-(\hat{\eta}_i - z_{\alpha/2}\hat{\sigma}(\hat{\eta}_i))))$$

and

$$1/(1 + \exp(-(\hat{\eta}_i + z_{\alpha/2}\hat{\sigma}(\hat{\eta}_i)))) \quad.$$

Classification Table

For binary response data, a 2×2 frequency table of observed and predicted responses can be requested by specifying the CTABLE option in the MODEL statement. This option has no effect if there are more than two response levels.

Consider a binary response model where an outcome is labeled as an EVENT if the ordered response is 1 and as NO EVENT if the ordered response is 2. Each input observation represents either a trial (an observation if the actual model syntax is used) or a number of trials (if the events/trials model syntax is used). Let **x** be the vector of explanatory variables in the fitted model. The probability of an event is

$$p = F(\alpha + \beta'\mathbf{x}) \quad .$$

The response is predicted to be an event if the estimated value of p is greater than or equal to the level specified by the PPROB= option; otherwise the response is predicted to be a nonevent. Each trial can be classified into one of the four categories.

	Observed	Predicted
1	event	event
2	event	no event
3	no event	event
4	no event	no event

The classification table is obtained by accumulating the number of trials for each category. *Sensitivity* is the proportion of EVENT responses that were predicted to be EVENT. *Specificity* is the proportion of NO EVENT responses that were predicted to be NO EVENT. The *false positive rate* is the proportion of predicted EVENT responses that were observed as NO EVENT. The *false negative rate* is the proportion of predicted NO EVENT responses that were observed as EVENT.

Calculation Method

In classifying a set of binary data, if the estimated probabilities of event responses are obtained by replacing the parameter vector $(\alpha,\beta')'$ by its MLE **b** derived from the same set of data, the resulting error-count estimate is biased. One way of reducing the bias is to remove the trial to be classified from the data, re-estimate the parameters of the model, and then classify the trial based on the new parameter estimates. However, it would be too costly to repeat the estimation every time a trial is removed. The LOGISTIC procedure provides a one-step approximation to obtain new parameter estimates. Let j index all trials, and let $\mathbf{b}_j$ denote the MLE of the parameter vector computed without the jth trial. The one-step estimate of $\mathbf{b}_j$ is given by

$$\mathbf{b}_j^1 = \mathbf{b} - \hat{\mathbf{V}}_\mathbf{b}(1,\mathbf{x}_j')'w_j(z_j - \hat{p}_j)/(1 - h_j)$$

where

z_j is 1 for an event response and 0 for a no event response.

w_j is the weight associated with the jth trial.

$\hat{\mathbf{V}}_\mathbf{b}$ is the estimated covariance matrix of **b**.

$\hat{p}_j = F((1,\mathbf{x}_j')\mathbf{b}) \quad .$

$h_j = w_j\hat{p}_j(1 - \hat{p}_j)(1,\mathbf{x}_j')\hat{\mathbf{V}}_\mathbf{b}(1,\mathbf{x}_j')' \quad .$

Regression Diagnostics

For binary response data, regression diagnostics developed by Pregibon (1981) can be requested by specifying the INFLUENCE option.

This section uses the notation below.

j index for the input observations.

w_j WEIGHT value of the jth observation; w_j is set equal to 1 if the WEIGHT statement is not used.

r_j the number of event responses out of n_j trials. If the events/trials model syntax is used, r_j is the value of *events* and n_j is the value of *trials*. For the actual model syntax, $n_j = 1$, and r_j is 1 if the ordered response is 1, and 0 if the ordered response is 2.

p_j the probability that the jth observation has an event response. This is given by

$$p_j = F(\alpha + \boldsymbol{\beta}'\mathbf{x}_j) \quad .$$

$\mathbf{b}$ the MLE of $(\alpha, \boldsymbol{\beta}')'$ obtained by the I RLS algorithm given earlier.

$\hat{\mathbf{V}}_\mathbf{b}$ the estimated covariance matrix of $\mathbf{b}$.

$\mathbf{b}_j$ the MLE of $(\alpha, \boldsymbol{\beta}')'$ when the jth observation is excluded.

Pregibon suggests using the index plots of the several diagnostic statistics to identify influential observations and to quantify the effects on various aspects of the maximum likelihood fit. The next five sections give formulas for these diagnostic statistics.

Hat Matrix Diagonal

The diagonal elements of the hat matrix are useful in detecting extreme points in the design space where they tend to have larger values. The jth diagonal element is

$$h_{jj} = w_j n_j \hat{p}_j (1 - \hat{p}_j)(1, \mathbf{x}_j')\hat{\mathbf{V}}_\mathbf{b}(1, \mathbf{x}_j')'$$

where $\hat{p}_j$ is the estimate of p_j evaluated at $\mathbf{b}$.

Pearson Residual and Deviance Residual

Pearson and deviance residuals are useful in identifying observations that are not well explained by the model. Pearson residuals are components of the Pearson chi-squared statistic; the Pearson chi-squared statistic is the sum of squares of the Pearson residuals. The Pearson residual for the jth observation is

$$\chi_j = \frac{(r_j - n_j\hat{p}_j)\sqrt{w_j}}{\sqrt{n_j\hat{p}_j(1 - \hat{p}_j)}} \quad .$$

Deviance residuals are components of the deviance. The deviance is another goodness-of-fit statistic based on the log likelihood function and is given by

$$\mathbf{D} = -2\ w_j\Sigma_j(m(\hat{p}_j) - m(r_j/n_j))$$

where

$$m(\lambda) = n_j\log(\lambda) + (n_j - r_j)\log(1 - \lambda) \quad .$$

The deviance residual for the jth observation is

$$d_j = \begin{cases} -\sqrt{-2w_jn_j\log(1 - \hat{p}_j)} & \text{if } r_j=0 \\[2ex] \pm\sqrt{2w_j(r_j\log(r_j/(n_j\hat{p}_j)) + (n_j - r_j)\log((n_j - r_j)/(n_j(1 - \hat{p}_j))))} \\[1ex] & \text{if } 0<r_j< n_j \\[2ex] \sqrt{-2w_jn_j\log(p_j)} & \text{if } r_j = n_j \end{cases}$$

where the plus (minus) in $\pm$ is used if r_j/n_j is greater (less) than $\hat{p}_j$.

DFBETAs

The procedure calculates a DFBETA diagnostic for each observation for each parameter estimate. DFBETA is the standardized difference in the parameter estimate due to deleting the corresponding observation, and it can be used to assess the effect of an individual observation on the estimated parameter of the fitted model. Instead of re-estimating the parameter every time an observation (say the jth observation) is deleted, the procedure uses the one-step estimate $\mathbf{b}_j^1 = \mathbf{b} - \Delta\mathbf{b}_j^1$ to approximate $\mathbf{b}_j$ where

$$\Delta\mathbf{b}_j^1 = \hat{\mathbf{V}}_\mathbf{b}\mathbf{x}_jw_j(r_j - n_j\hat{p}_j) / (1 - h_{jj}) \quad .$$

For the jth observation, the DFBETAs are given by

$$\text{DFBETA}i_j = \Delta_ib_j^1 / \hat{\sigma}(b_i)$$

where $i=0, 1, \ldots, s$, $\hat{\sigma}(b_i)$ is the standard error of the ith component of $\mathbf{b}$, and $\Delta_ib_j^1$ is the ith component of the one-step difference $\Delta\mathbf{b}_j^1$.

The DFBETAs are useful in detecting observations that are causing instability in the selected coefficients.

C and CBAR

C and CBAR are confidence interval displacement diagnostics that provide scalar measures of the influence of individual observations on $\mathbf{b}$. These diagnostics are based on the same idea as the Cook distance in the linear regression theory. By using the one-step estimate, $\mathbf{b}_j^1$, C and CBAR for the jth observations are computed as

$$C_j = \chi_j^2 h_{jj} / (1 - h_{jj})^2$$

and

$$\overline{C}_j = \chi_j^2 h_{jj} / (1 - h_{jj})$$

respectively.

DIFDEV and DIFCHISQ

DIFDEV and DIFCHISQ are diagnostics for detecting ill-fitted observations, that is, observations that contribute heavily to the disagreement between the data and the predicted values of the fitted model. DIFDEV is the change in the deviance due to deleting an individual observation, while DIFCHISQ is the change in the Pearson chi-squared statistic for the same deletion. By using the one-step estimate, $\mathbf{b}_j^1$, DIFDEV and DIFCHISQ for the jth observation are computed as

$$\Delta_j D = d_j^2 + \overline{C}_j$$

and

$$\Delta_j \chi^2 = \overline{C}_j / h_{jj}$$

respectively.

OUTEST= Output Data Set

The OUTEST=data set contains estimates of the regression coefficients. If you use the COVOUT option in the MODEL statement, the OUTEST=data set also contains the estimated covariance matrix of the parameter estimates.

Number of Variables and Number of Observations

The data set contains one variable for each intercept parameter and one variable for each explanatory variable in the MODEL statement.

The OUTEST= data set contains one observation for each BY group, which consists of the MLEs of the regression coefficients. If you use the COVOUT option in the MODEL statement, there are additional observations containing the rows of the estimated covariance matrix.

Variables in the Data Set

The OUTEST= data set contains the following variables:

- any BY variables specified.
- one variable for each intercept parameter. If one BY group fits a binary response model and another BY group fits an ordinal response model with more than two response levels, the data set contains the intercept variables INTERCEP (for the only intercept of the binary response model), INTERCP1, . . . , INTERCPr, where r is the largest number of intercept parameters among the BY groups. If more than nine intercepts are estimated, the variables become INTERCrr; for example, INTERC10. Any of these variables not pertinent to a specific BY group has its values set to missing.
- one variable for each explanatory variable in the MODEL statement. If an explanatory variable is not included in the final model in a model building process, the corresponding estimates of parameters and covariances are set to missing values.
- _LINK_, a character variable of length 8 with three possible values: CLOGLOG for the complementary log-log function, LOGIT for the logit function, or NORMIT for the normit function.
- _TYPE_, a character variable of length 8 with two possible values: PARMS for parameter estimates or COV for covariance estimates.

- _NAME_, a character variable of length 8 containing the name ESTIMATE for parameter estimates, the name for each intercept parameter, and the name of each explanatory variable for the covariance estimates.

OUT= Output Data Set

The OUT= data set contains all the variables in the input data set and the variables for statistics you specify using *keyword=name*.

In addition, if you use the actual model syntax, the OUT= data set contains the variable _LEVEL_. For a model with $k+1$ response categories ($k \geq 1$), each input observation generates k observations with k different values of _LEVEL_. For $k>1$ (more than two response levels), only variables named by XBETA=, STDXBETA=, PREDICTED=, LOWER=, and UPPER= have their values computed; the other variables have missing values.

Computational Resources

For each BY group, define

K = number of response levels

C = 1 + number of explanatory variables

$m_1 = K + C$

$m_2 = 1 + K + C$

$m_3 = 16m_1(m_1 + 5)$

$m_4 = 8C(C + 4) + 4m_2(m_2 + 3).$

The minimum amount of memory needed to process the BY group is m_3 bytes.

For models with more than two response levels, a test of the parallel lines assumption requires memory of m_4 bytes. However, if this additional memory is not available, the procedure skips the test and finishes the other computations.

If sufficient space is available, the input data set is also kept in memory; otherwise, the input data set is reread for each evaluation of the likelihood function and its derivatives, with the resulting execution time of the procedure substantially increased.

For binary response data, the events/trials model syntax requires one less pass of the input data set than the actual model syntax, which may result in some savings in the execution time.

Printed Output

If you use the NOPRINT option in the PROC LOGISTIC statement, the procedure does not produce any printed output. Otherwise, the printed output of the LOGISTIC procedure contains the following:

1. the two-level name of the input Data Set.

When the actual MODEL syntax is specified, the procedure prints

2. the name of the Response Variable
3. the label of the Response Variable
4. the number of Response Levels.

When the events/trials MODEL syntax is specified, the procedure prints

5. the name of the Events variable
6. the name of the Trials variable.

When the WEIGHT statement is used, the procedure prints

7. the name of the Weight Variable
8. the Sum of Weights of all the observations used in the analysis.

By default, the procedure prints

9. the Number of Observations used in the analysis.
10. the Link Function.
11. the "Response Profile" table, which gives, for each response level, the ordered value (an integer between 1 and $k+1$, inclusive, if there are $k+1$ response levels); the value of the response variable (if the actual MODEL syntax is used) or the values EVENT and NO EVENT (if the events/trials model syntax is used); the count or frequency; and the sum of weights if the WEIGHT statement is used.
12. the "Simple Statistics for Explanatory Variables" table, which gives the mean, standard deviation, minimum, and maximum for each explanatory variable in the MODEL statement. This table is not printed if you use the NOSIMPLE option in the PROC LOGISTIC statement.
13. if an ordinal response model is fitted, the score test result for testing the parallel lines assumption. If LINK=CLOGLOG or NORMIT, this is labeled as the "Score Test for the Parallel Slopes Assumption." The proportional odds assumption is a special case of the parallel lines assumption when the log odds scale is used. If LINK=LOGIT, this test is labeled as "Score Test for the Proportional Odds Assumption."
14. the "Criteria for Assessing Model Fit" table, which gives the various criteria (-2 Log L, AIC, SC) based on the likelihood for fitting a model with intercepts only and for fitting a model with intercepts and explanatory variables. If you specify NOINT, these statistics are calculated without considering the intercept parameters. The third column of the table gives the chi-square statistics and p-values for the -2 Log L statistic and for the Score statistic. These test the joint effect of the explanatory variables included in the model. The Score criterion is always missing for the models identified by the first two columns of the table. Note also that the first two rows of the Chi-Square column are always missing since the AIC and SC criteria are not meaningful in assessing the contribution of the covariates.
15. the "Analysis of Maximum Likelihood Estimates" table, which contains the following:
    - the maximum likelihood estimate of the parameter
    - the estimated standard error of the parameter estimate, computed as the square root of the corresponding diagonal element of the estimated covariance matrix
    - the Wald chi-squared statistic, computed as the square of the parameter estimate divided by its standard error estimate
    - the p-value of the Wald chi-squared statistic with respect to a chi-squared distribution with one degree of freedom
    - the standardized estimate for the slope parameter, computed by dividing the slope parameter estimate by the ratio of the standard deviation of the underlying distribution, which is the inverse of the link function, to the sample standard deviation of the explanatory variable. The standardized estimates of the intercept parameters are set to missing.

16. the table of measures of "Association between Predicted Probabilities and Observed Responses," which includes a breakdown of the number of pairs with different responses and four rank correlation indexes: Somers' D, Goodman-Kruskal Gamma, c and Kendall's Tau-a.

If you use the ITPRINT option in the MODEL statement, the procedure prints

17. the "Maximum Likelihood Iterative Phase" table, which gives the iteration number, the step size (in the scale of 1.0, .5, .25, and so on), -2 Log Likelihood, and parameter estimates for each iteration. Also printed are the last evaluation of the gradient vector and the last change in the -2 Log Likelihood (not shown).

If you use SELECTION=FORWARD, BACKWARD, or STEPWISE in the MODEL statement, the procedure prints

18. a summary of the model-building process, which gives the step number, the explanatory variable or variables entered or removed at each step, the chi-squared statistic, and the corresponding p-value in which the entry or removal of the variable is based.

If you use the FAST option in the MODEL statement, the procedure prints

19. the "Analysis of Variables Removed by Fast Backward Elimination" table, which gives the approximate chi-squared statistic for the variable removed, the corresponding p-value with respect to a chi-squared distribution with one degree of freedom, the residual chi-squared statistic for testing the joint significance of the variable and the preceding ones, the degrees of freedom, and the p-value of the residual chi-square with respect to a chi-squared distribution with the corresponding degrees of freedom.

If you use the DETAILS option in the MODEL statement, the procedure prints

20. the "Analysis of Variables Not in the Model" table, which gives the score chi-squared statistic for testing the significance of each variable not in the model after adjusting for the variables already in the model, and the p-value of the chi-squared statistic with respect to a chi-squared distribution with one degree of freedom.

If you use the COVB option in the MODEL statement, the procedure prints

21. the Estimated Covariance Matrix of the parameter estimates.

If you use the CORRB option in the MODEL statement, the procedure prints

22. the estimated correlation matrix of the parameter estimates (not shown).

If you have a binary response and use the CTABLE option in the MODEL statement, the procedure prints

23. the Classification Table, which is a 2x2 frequency table of observed and predicted responses.

If you have a binary response and use the INFLUENCE option in the MODEL statement, the procedure prints

24. the "Regression Diagnostics" table, which gives, for each observation, the case number (which is the observation number), the values of the explanatory variables included in the model, the Pearson residual, the deviance residual, the diagonal element of the hat matrix, the standardized difference in the estimate for each parameter (name Dfbeta, where name is either INTERCPT or the name of an

explanatory variable), two confidence interval displacement diagnostics (C and CBAR), the change in the Pearson chi-squared statistic (DIFCHSQ), and the change in the deviance (DIFDEV).

If you use the IPLOTS option in the MODEL statement, the procedure prints:

25. the index plot of Pearson residuals
26. the index plot of deviance residuals
27. the index plot of the diagonal elements of the hat matrix
28. index plots of the standardized differences in parameter estimates, DFBETA0 for the intercept estimate, DFBETA1 for the slope estimate of the first explanatory variable in the MODEL statement, and so on
29. the index plot of confidence interval displacement diagnostics C
30. the index plot of confidence interval displacement diagnostics CBAR
31. the index plot of the changes in the Pearson Chi-squared statistic
32. the index plot of the changes in the deviance.

The label of an explanatory variable, if it exists, is also included in the same table that contains the variable. However, due to constraints on the line size, the variable label may be suppressed in order to print the table in one panel. Use the SAS system option LINESIZE= to specify a larger line size to accommodate the printing of variable labels.

EXAMPLES

Example 1:   Multiple-Response Cheese Tasting Experiment

The data in this example were taken from McCullagh and Nelder (1989, p. 175) and were derived from an experiment concerned with the effect on taste of four cheese additives. The nine response categories range from strong dislike (1) to excellent taste (9). Let Y be the response variable. The four cheese additives are represented by three indicator variables: X1, X2, and X3. The data after the CARDS statement below are arranged like a 2-way table of additive by rating. That is, the rows are the four additives, and the columns are the nine levels of the rating scale. The following statements produce **Output 27.2**:

```
data cheese;
   drop z1-z9;
   x1=0; x2=0; x3=0;
   if _n_=1 then x1=1;
   if _n_=2 then x2=1;
   if _n_=3 then x3=1;
   array z z1-z9;
   input z1-z9;
   do over z;
      y= _i_ ;
      weight=z;
      output;
   end;
   label y='Taste Rating';
   cards;
0  0  1  7  8  8 19  8  1
6  9 12 11  7  6  1  0  0
1  1  6  8 23  7  5  1  0
0  0  0  1  3  7 14 16 11
;
```

```
proc logistic data=cheese;
   weight weight;
   model y=x1-x3 / covb;
   title1 'Multiple Response Cheese Tasting Experiment';
run;
```

Output 27.2   Cheese Tasting Experiment

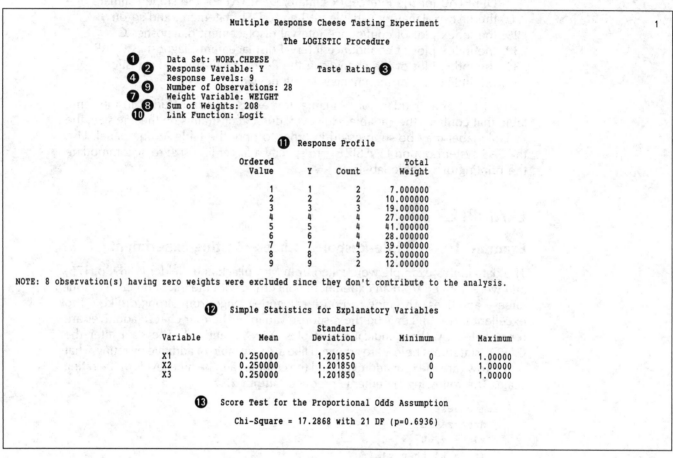

Multiple Response Cheese Tasting Experiment   1

The LOGISTIC Procedure

❶ Data Set: WORK.CHEESE
❷ Response Variable: Y   Taste Rating ❸
❹❾ Response Levels: 9
    Number of Observations: 28
❼ Weight Variable: WEIGHT
❽ Sum of Weights: 208
❿ Link Function: Logit

                    ⓫ Response Profile

              Ordered   Total
               Value   Y   Count   Weight

                 1   1   2   7.000000
                 2   2   2   10.000000
                 3   3   3   19.000000
                 4   4   4   27.000000
                 5   5   4   41.000000
                 6   6   4   28.000000
                 7   7   4   39.000000
                 8   8   3   25.000000
                 9   9   2   12.000000

NOTE: 8 observation(s) having zero weights were excluded since they don't contribute to the analysis.

             ⓬ Simple Statistics for Explanatory Variables

                                    Standard
     Variable   Mean   Deviation   Minimum   Maximum

       X1   0.250000   1.201850   0   1.00000
       X2   0.250000   1.201850   0   1.00000
       X3   0.250000   1.201850   0   1.00000

           ⓭ Score Test for the Proportional Odds Assumption

              Chi-Square = 17.2868 with 21 DF (p=0.6936)

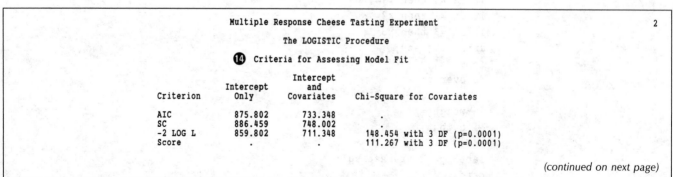

Multiple Response Cheese Tasting Experiment   2

The LOGISTIC Procedure

              ⓮ Criteria for Assessing Model Fit

                                    Intercept
                     Intercept   and
     Criterion   Only   Covariates   Chi-Square for Covariates

     AIC   875.802   733.348
     SC   886.459   748.002   .
     -2 LOG L   859.802   711.348   148.454 with 3 DF (p=0.0001)
     Score   .   .   111.267 with 3 DF (p=0.0001)
```

*(continued on next page)*
```

(continued from previous page)

⑮ Analysis of Maximum Likelihood Estimates

Variable	Parameter Estimate	Standard Error	Wald Chi-Square	Pr > Chi-Square	Standardized Estimate
INTERCP1	-7.0802	0.5624	158.4865	0.0001	.
INTERCP2	-6.0250	0.4755	160.5507	0.0001	.
INTERCP3	-4.9254	0.4272	132.9477	0.0001	.
INTERCP4	-3.8568	0.3902	97.7086	0.0001	.
INTERCP5	-2.5206	0.3431	53.9713	0.0001	.
INTERCP6	-1.5685	0.3086	25.8374	0.0001	.
INTERCP7	-0.0669	0.2658	0.0633	0.8013	.
INTERCP8	1.4930	0.3310	20.3443	0.0001	.
X1	1.6128	0.3778	18.2258	0.0001	1.068659
X2	4.9646	0.4741	109.6453	0.0001	3.289644
X3	3.3227	0.4251	61.0936	0.0001	2.201659

⑯ Association of Predicted Probabilities and Observed Responses

Concordant = 53.0%   Somers' D = 0.307
Discordant = 22.3%   Gamma   = 0.408
Tied   = 24.6%   Tau-a   = 0.280
(345 pairs)   c   = 0.654

㉑ Estimated Covariance Matrix

Variable	INTERCP1	INTERCP2	INTERCP3	INTERCP4	INTERCP5	INTERCP6	INTERCP7	INTERCP8	X1	X2	X3
INTERCP1	0.3162967	0.2195848	0.1762803	0.1476957	0.1140256	0.0910859	0.0578144	0.0413041	-0.094191	-0.186864	-0.135649
INTERCP2	0.2195848	0.2260991	0.177809	0.1479354	0.1140312	0.0910814	0.0578131	0.0413037	-0.094213	-0.181613	-0.135697
INTERCP3	0.1762803	0.177809	0.1824757	0.1488461	0.1140934	0.091075	0.0578069	0.0412999	-0.094267	-0.168699	-0.135206
INTERCP4	0.1476957	0.1479354	0.1488461	0.1522375	0.1145139	0.0911095	0.05778	0.0412768	-0.094282	-0.14717	-0.131184
INTERCP5	0.1140256	0.1140312	0.1140934	0.1145139	0.1177141	0.0918213	0.0577207	0.0411618	-0.092463	-0.114153	-0.112072
INTERCP6	0.0910859	0.0910814	0.091075	0.0911095	0.0918213	0.095221	0.0583118	0.0413235	-0.085208	-0.091127	-0.091218
INTERCP7	0.0578144	0.0578131	0.0578069	0.05778	0.0577207	0.0583118	0.0706399	0.0487801	-0.060413	-0.057811	-0.058016
INTERCP8	0.0413041	0.0413037	0.0412999	0.0412768	0.0411618	0.0413235	0.0487801	0.1095627	-0.044356	-0.041297	-0.04143
X1	-0.094191	-0.094213	-0.094267	-0.094282	-0.092463	-0.085208	-0.060413	-0.044356	0.1427148	0.0940722	0.0921275
X2	-0.186864	-0.181613	-0.168699	-0.14717	-0.114153	-0.091127	-0.057811	-0.041297	0.0940722	0.2247944	0.1328787
X3	-0.135649	-0.135697	-0.135206	-0.131184	-0.112072	-0.091218	-0.058016	-0.04143	0.0921275	0.1328787	0.1807099

The score chi-square for testing the proportional odds assumption is 17.287, which is nonsignificant with respect to a chi-squared distribution with 21 degrees of freedom ($p = 0.694$). This indicates that a proportional odds model is appropriate for the data. The positive value (1.6128) for the parameter estimate of X1 indicates a tendency towards the lower-numbered categories of the first cheese additive relative to the fourth; in other words, the fourth additive is better in taste than the first additive. Each of the second and the third additives is less favorable than the fourth additive. The relative magnitudes of these slope estimates imply this preference ordering: fourth, first, third, second.

Example 2: Stepwise Regression on Cancer Remission Data

The data, taken from Lee (1974), consist of patient characteristics and whether cancer remission occurred. The first call to the LOGISTIC procedure illustrates the use of stepwise selection to identify the prognostic factors for cancer remission. Two output SAS data sets are printed: one contains the parameter estimates and their estimated covariance matrix; the other contains the predicted values and confidence limits for the probability of cancer remission. The second call to the LOGISTIC procedure illustrates the FAST option for backward elimination. The following statements produce **Output 27.3**:

```
data remiss;
   input remiss cell smear infil li blast temp;
   label remiss='complete remission';
   cards;
```

```
1 .8 .83 .66 1.9 1.1 .996
1 .9 .36 .32 1.4 .74 .992
0 .8 .88 .7 .8 .176 .982
0 1 .87 .87 .7 1.053 .986
1 .9 .75 .68 1.3 .519 .98
0 1 .65 .65 .6 .519 .982
1 .95 .97 .92 1 1.23 .992
0 .95 .87 .83 1.9 1.354 1.02
0 1 .45 .45 .8 .322 .999
0 .95 .36 .34 .5 0 1.038
0 .85 .39 .33 .7 .279 .988
0 .7 .76 .53 1.2 .146 .982
0 .8 .46 .37 .4 .38 1.006
0 .2 .39 .08 .8 .114 .99
0 1 .9 .9 1.1 1.037 .99
1 1 .84 .84 1.9 2.064 1.02
0 .65 .42 .27 .5 .114 1.014
0 1 .75 .75 1 1.322 1.004
0 .5 .44 .22 .6 .114 .99
1 1 .63 .63 1.1 1.072 .986
0 1 .33 .33 .4 .176 1.01
0 .9 .93 .84 .6 1.591 1.02
1 1 .58 .58 1 .531 1.002
0 .95 .32 .3 1.6 .886 .988
1 1 .6 .6 1.7 .964 .99
1 1 .69 .69 .9 .398 .986
0 1 .73 .73 .7 .398 .986
;

title 'Stepwise Regression on Cancer Remission Data';
proc logistic data=remiss outest=betas covout;
   model remiss=cell smear infil li blast temp
                / selection=stepwise
                  slentry=0.3
                  slstay=0.3
                  details;
   output out=pred p=phat lower=lcl upper=ucl;
run;

proc print data=betas;
   title2 'Parameter Estimates and Covariance Matrix';
run;

proc print data=pred;
   title2 'Predicted Probabilities and 95% Confidence Limits';
run;

title 'Backward Elimination on Cancer Remission Data';
proc logistic data=remiss nosimple;
   model remiss=temp cell li smear blast
                / selection=backward
                  fast
                  slstay=0.2
                  ctable;
run;
```

Output 27.3   Using Model Selection Methods and Printing Output Data Sets

```
                      Stepwise Regression on Cancer Remission Data                    1

                               The LOGISTIC Procedure

          Data Set: WORK.REMISS
          Response Variable: REMISS        complete remission
          Response Levels: 2
          Number of Observations: 27
          Link Function: Logit


                                  Response Profile

                           Ordered
                           Value   REMISS   Count

                             1       0        18
                             2       1         9


                   Simple Statistics for Explanatory Variables

                                    Standard
           Variable      Mean      Deviation     Minimum      Maximum

           CELL       0.881481     0.186645     0.200000     1.00000
           SMEAR      0.635185     0.214052     0.320000     0.97000
           INFIL      0.570741     0.237567     0.080000     0.92000
           LI         1.003704     0.467795     0.400000     1.90000
           BLAST      0.688852     0.535804     0.000000     2.06400
           TEMP       0.997000     0.014861     0.980000     1.03800


                            Stepwise Selection Procedure


        Step  0. Intercept entered:


                      Analysis of Maximum Likelihood Estimates

                   Parameter   Standard     Wald        Pr >      Standardized
          Variable  Estimate     Error   Chi-Square  Chi-Square    Estimate

          INTERCEP   0.6931     0.4082     2.8827      0.0895

                 Residual Chi-Square = 9.4609 with 6 DF (p=0.1493)

              ⑳   Analysis of Variables Not in the Model

                                   Score       Pr >
                        Variable  Chi-Square  Chi-Square

                        CELL       1.8893      0.1693
                        SMEAR      1.0745      0.2999
                        INFIL      1.8817      0.1701
                        LI         7.9311      0.0049
                        BLAST      3.5258      0.0604
                        TEMP       0.6591      0.4169
```

```
                      Stepwise Regression on Cancer Remission Data                    2

                               The LOGISTIC Procedure

        Step  1. Variable LI entered:


                            Criteria for Assessing Model Fit

                                    Intercept
                         Intercept    and
           Criterion       Only     Covariates   Chi-Square for Covariates

           AIC            36.372      30.073        .
           SC             37.668      32.665        .
           -2 LOG L       34.372      26.073       8.299 with 1 DF (p=0.0040)
           Score            .           .          7.931 with 1 DF (p=0.0049)
```

(continued on next page)

(continued from previous page)

Analysis of Maximum Likelihood Estimates

Variable	Parameter Estimate	Standard Error	Wald Chi-Square	Pr > Chi-Square	Standardized Estimate
INTERCEP	3.7771	1.3786	7.5064	0.0061	.
LI	-2.8973	1.1868	5.9594	0.0146	-0.747230

Association of Predicted Probabilities and Observed Responses

Concordant = 84.0%		Somers' D = 0.710
Discordant = 13.0%		Gamma = 0.732
Tied = 3.1%		Tau-a = 0.328
(162 pairs)		c = 0.855

Residual Chi-Square = 3.1174 with 5 DF (p=0.6819)

Analysis of Variables Not in the Model

Variable	Score Chi-Square	Pr > Chi-Square
CELL	1.1183	0.2903
SMEAR	0.1369	0.7114
INFIL	0.5715	0.4497
BLAST	0.0932	0.7601
TEMP	1.2591	0.2618

Step 2. Variable TEMP entered:

Stepwise Regression on Cancer Remission Data   3

The LOGISTIC Procedure

Criteria for Assessing Model Fit

Criterion	Intercept Only	Intercept and Covariates	Chi-Square for Covariates
AIC	36.372	30.648	.
SC	37.668	34.535	.
-2 LOG L	34.372	24.648	9.724 with 2 DF (p=0.0077)
Score	.	.	8.365 with 2 DF (p=0.0153)

Analysis of Maximum Likelihood Estimates

Variable	Parameter Estimate	Standard Error	Wald Chi-Square	Pr > Chi-Square	Standardized Estimate
INTERCEP	-47.8559	46.4416	1.0618	0.3028	.
LI	-3.3020	1.3594	5.9005	0.0151	-0.851626
TEMP	52.4331	47.4934	1.2188	0.2696	0.429597

Association of Predicted Probabilities and Observed Responses

Concordant = 87.0%		Somers' D = 0.747
Discordant = 12.3%		Gamma = 0.752
Tied = 0.6%		Tau-a = 0.345
(162 pairs)		c = 0.873

Residual Chi-Square = 2.1431 with 4 DF (p=0.7095)

Analysis of Variables Not in the Model

Variable	Score Chi-Square	Pr > Chi-Square
CELL	1.4701	0.2253
SMEAR	0.1730	0.6775
INFIL	0.8275	0.3630
BLAST	1.1014	0.2940

Step 3. Variable CELL entered:

```
                Stepwise Regression on Cancer Remission Data                    4
                          The LOGISTIC Procedure
                       Criteria for Assessing Model Fit

                                      Intercept
                        Intercept       and
        Criterion         Only       Covariates    Chi-Square for Covariates

        AIC              36.372        29.953              .
        SC               37.668        35.137              .
        -2 LOG L         34.372        21.953       12.418 with 3 DF (p=0.0061)
        Score              .             .           9.250 with 3 DF (p=0.0261)


                    Analysis of Maximum Likelihood Estimates

                    Parameter    Standard      Wald        Pr >      Standardized
        Variable    Estimate      Error     Chi-Square  Chi-Square     Estimate

        INTERCEP    -67.6339     56.8875      1.4135      0.2345          .
        CELL         -9.6522      7.7511      1.5507      0.2130      -0.993231
        LI           -3.8671      1.7783      4.7290      0.0297      -0.997359
        TEMP         82.0738     61.7124      1.7687      0.1835       0.672450


            Association of Predicted Probabilities and Observed Responses

                   Concordant = 88.9%      Somers' D = 0.778
                   Discordant = 11.1%      Gamma     = 0.778
                   Tied       =  0.0%      Tau-a     = 0.359
                   (162 pairs)             c         = 0.889

            Residual Chi-Square = 0.1831 with 3 DF (p=0.9803)

                    Analysis of Variables Not in the Model

                                  Score        Pr >
                   Variable     Chi-Square   Chi-Square

                   SMEAR          0.0956       0.7572
                   INFIL          0.0844       0.7714
                   BLAST          0.0208       0.8852


 NOTE: No (additional) variables met the 0.3 significance level for entry into the model.
```

```
                Stepwise Regression on Cancer Remission Data                    5
                          The LOGISTIC Procedure
               ⑱   Summary of Stepwise Procedure

                         Variable        Number     Score      Wald       Pr >
        Step       Entered    Removed       In    Chi-Square Chi-Square Chi-Square

          1        LI                        1      7.9311       .        0.0049
          2        TEMP                      2      1.2591       .        0.2618
          3        CELL                      3      1.4701       .        0.2253
```

```
                Stepwise Regression on Cancer Remission Data                    6
                    Parameter Estimates and Covariance Matrix
   OBS   _LINK_   _TYPE_   _NAME_   INTERCEP    CELL    SMEAR  INFIL     LI     BLAST    TEMP

    1    LOGIT    PARMS   ESTIMATE   -67.63    -9.652     .      .     -3.8671    .     82.07
    2    LOGIT    COV     INTERCEP  3236.19   157.097     .      .     64.5726    .  -3483.23
    3    LOGIT    COV     CELL       157.10    60.079     .      .      6.9454    .   -223.67
    4    LOGIT    COV     SMEAR         .         .       .      .         .      .       .
    5    LOGIT    COV     INFIL         .         .       .      .         .      .       .
    6    LOGIT    COV     LI          64.57     6.945     .      .      3.1623    .    -75.35
    7    LOGIT    COV     BLAST         .         .       .      .         .      .       .
    8    LOGIT    COV     TEMP     -3483.23  -223.669     .      .    -75.3513    .   3808.42
```

```
                      Stepwise Regression on Cancer Remission Data
                      Predicted Probabilities and 95% Confidence Limits

 OBS   REMISS   CELL   SMEAR   INFIL    LI    BLAST    TEMP    _LEVEL_     PHAT       LCL       UCL

  1       1     0.80   0.83    0.66    1.9    1.100   0.996       0      0.27735   0.02907   0.83108
  2       1     0.90   0.36    0.32    1.4    0.740   0.992       0      0.42126   0.16238   0.73212
  3       0     0.80   0.88    0.70    0.8    0.176   0.982       0      0.89540   0.36581   0.99219
  4       0     1.00   0.87    0.87    0.7    1.053   0.986       0      0.71742   0.34317   0.92502
  5       1     0.90   0.75    0.68    1.3    0.519   0.980       0      0.28582   0.05124   0.74782
  6       0     1.00   0.65    0.65    0.6    0.519   0.982       0      0.72911   0.31049   0.94148
  7       1     0.95   0.97    0.92    1.0    1.230   0.992       0      0.67844   0.40484   0.86745
  8       0     0.95   0.87    0.83    1.9    1.354   1.020       0      0.39277   0.04713   0.89428
  9       0     1.00   0.45    0.45    0.8    0.322   0.999       0      0.83368   0.43877   0.96982
 10       0     0.95   0.36    0.34    0.5    0.000   1.038       0      0.99843   0.31038   1.00000
 11       0     0.85   0.39    0.33    0.7    0.279   0.988       0      0.92715   0.50018   0.99386
 12       0     0.70   0.76    0.53    1.2    0.146   0.982       0      0.82714   0.12794   0.99363
 13       0     0.80   0.46    0.37    0.4    0.380   1.006       0      0.99654   0.53470   0.99999
 14       0     0.20   0.39    0.08    0.8    0.114   0.990       0      0.99982   0.03518   1.00000
 15       0     1.00   0.90    0.90    1.1    1.037   0.990       0      0.42878   0.16027   0.74697
 16       1     1.00   0.84    0.84    1.9    2.064   1.020       0      0.28530   0.02811   0.84638
 17       0     0.65   0.42    0.27    0.5    0.114   1.014       0      0.99938   0.37335   1.00000
 18       0     1.00   0.75    0.75    1.0    1.322   1.004       0      0.77711   0.36330   0.95517
 19       0     0.50   0.44    0.22    0.6    0.114   0.990       0      0.99846   0.20356   1.00000
 20       1     1.00   0.63    0.63    1.1    1.072   0.986       0      0.35089   0.09445   0.73695
 21       0     1.00   0.33    0.33    0.4    0.176   1.010       0      0.98307   0.49525   0.99971
 22       0     0.90   0.93    0.84    0.6    1.591   1.020       0      0.99378   0.43938   0.99997
 23       1     1.00   0.58    0.58    1.0    0.531   1.002       0      0.74739   0.36403   0.93863
 24       0     0.95   0.32    0.30    1.6    0.886   0.988       0      0.12989   0.01519   0.59089
 25       1     1.00   0.60    0.60    1.7    0.964   0.990       0      0.06868   0.00427   0.55886
 26       1     1.00   0.69    0.69    0.9    0.398   0.986       0      0.53949   0.21471   0.83388
 27       0     1.00   0.73    0.73    0.7    0.398   0.986       0      0.71742   0.34317   0.92502
```

```
                    Backward Elimination on Cancer Remission Data

                              The LOGISTIC Procedure

          Data Set: WORK.REMISS
          Response Variable: REMISS         complete remission
          Response Levels: 2
          Number of Observations: 27
          Link Function: Logit


                                Response Profile

                          Ordered
                          Value    REMISS     Count

                            1        0         18
                            2        1          9



                          Backward Elimination Procedure

Step  0. The following variables were entered:

    INTERCEP  TEMP    CELL     LI     SMEAR     BLAST


                          Criteria for Assessing Model Fit

                                        Intercept
                            Intercept      and
            Criterion         Only      Covariates    Chi-Square for Covariates

            AIC              36.372       33.857            .
            SC               37.668       41.632            .
            -2 LOG L         34.372       21.857       12.515 with 5 DF (p=0.0284)
            Score               .           .           9.330 with 5 DF (p=0.0966)
```

(continued on next page)

(continued from previous page)

Step 1. Fast Backward Elimination:

⑲   Analysis of Variables Removed by Fast Backward Elimination

Variable Removed	Chi-Square	Pr > Chi-Square	Residual Chi-Square	DF	Pr > Residual Chi-Square
BLAST	0.0008	0.9768	0.0008	1	0.9768
SMEAR	0.0951	0.7578	0.0959	2	0.9532
CELL	1.5135	0.2186	1.6094	3	0.6573
TEMP	0.6535	0.4189	2.2629	4	0.6875

Backward Elimination on Cancer Remission Data   9

The LOGISTIC Procedure

Criteria for Assessing Model Fit

Criterion	Intercept Only	Intercept and Covariates	Chi-Square for Covariates
AIC	36.372	30.073	.
SC	37.668	32.665	.
-2 LOG L	34.372	26.073	8.299 with 1 DF (p=0.0040)
Score	.	.	7.931 with 1 DF (p=0.0049)

Residual Chi-Square = 2.8530 with 4 DF (p=0.5827)

Summary of Backward Elimination Procedure

Step	Variable Removed	Number In	Wald Chi-Square	Pr > Chi-Square
1	BLAST	4	0.000844	0.9768
1	SMEAR	3	0.0951	0.7578
1	CELL	2	1.5135	0.2186
1	TEMP	1	0.6535	0.4189

Analysis of Maximum Likelihood Estimates

Variable	Parameter Estimate	Standard Error	Wald Chi-Square	Pr > Chi-Square	Standardized Estimate
INTERCEP	3.7771	1.3786	7.5064	0.0061	.
LI	-2.8973	1.1868	5.9594	0.0146	-0.747230

Association of Predicted Probabilities and Observed Responses

Concordant = 84.0%	Somers' D	=	0.710
Discordant = 13.0%	Gamma	=	0.732
Tied = 3.1%	Tau-a	=	0.328
(162 pairs)	c	=	0.855

```
                    Backward Elimination on Cancer Remission Data                        10
                              The LOGISTIC Procedure
                    ㉓              Classification Table
                                        Predicted
                                    EVENT    NO EVENT      Total
                                 +---------------------+
                         EVENT   |    16          2    |      18
              Observed           |                     |
                      NO EVENT   |     5          4    |       9
                                 +---------------------+
                         Total         21          6          27

              Sensitivity= 88.9%  Specificity= 44.4%  Correct= 74.1%
              False Positive Rate= 23.8%  False Negative Rate= 33.3%

      NOTE: An EVENT is an outcome whose ordered response value is 1.
```

At each step of the modelling process, LOGISTIC prints the criteria for assessing model fit, an analysis of maximum-likelihood estimates, the association of predicted probabilities and observed responses, and an analysis of variables not in the model. In Step 1, the procedure adds LI to the model, which is the variable with the lowest p-value for the Step 0 analysis of variables not in the model. At the end of Step 1, both CELL and TEMP meet the specified entry criterion of 0.3 (specified with SLENTRY=). TEMP has the lower probability value, so it is entered into the model in Step 2. Similarly, CELL is added in Step 3. In the analysis of variables not in the model at the end of Step 3, none of the remaining variables meet the entry criterion, so the procedure stops.

The OUTEST= data set contains parameter estimates and the covariance matrix. Notice that all variables in the MODEL statement are included in this data set; however, variables not included in the final model have all missing values.

The OUT= data set contains all the original variables, predicted probabilities, and upper and lower confidence limits for the probabilities. Since the statements above use the actual model syntax, the PRED data set contains the variable _LEVEL_. The response variable in the MODEL statement (REMISS) has two levels, so each input observation generates only one observation in PRED, and all values of _LEVEL_ are 0. For observation 1, PHAT=0.277, which means that the probability that REMISS=0 is 0.277 for this particular combination of explanatory variable values.

The backward elimination analysis starts with all variables in the model. This analysis uses a different criterion for variables remaining in the model, 0.2. (Recall that the stepwise analysis used 0.3.) It also uses the FAST option, which is very efficient. In one step, LOGISTIC removes BLAST, SMEAR, CELL, and TEMP from the model. This leaves LI and the intercept as the only variables in the model.

Note that you can also use the FAST option when SELECTION=STEPWISE. However, FAST operates only on backward elimination steps. In this example, the stepwise process only adds variables, so FAST would not be useful.

The final portion of output shows results of the CTABLE option. LOGISTIC correctly classifies 20 of the 27 observations (74.1%). The false positive rate, false negative rate, specificity, and sensitivity are calculated and printed. (For formulas, see **Classification Table** earlier in this chapter.)

Example 3:   Analysis of Vaso-Constriction Data with Regression Diagnostics

Finney (1947) lists data on a controlled experiment to study the effect of the rate and volume of air inspired on a transient reflex vaso-constriction in the skin of the digits. Thirty-nine tests under various combinations of rate and volume of air inspired were obtained. The end point of each test is whether vaso-constriction occurred. Pregibon (1981) uses this set of data to illustrate the diagnostic measures he proposes for detecting influential observations and in quantifying their effects on various aspects of the maximum likelihood fit.

In this example, the ORDER=DATA option is specified in the PROC LOGISTIC statement. This is done so that RESPONSE values of 1 are treated as events (ordered value=1) and RESPONSE values of 0 are treated as nonevents (ordered value=2). The following statements produce **Output 27.4**:

```
data vaso;
   input volume rate response;
   logvol=log(volume);
   lograte=log(rate);
   cards;
3.7   .825  1
3.5  1.09   1
1.25 2.5    1
 .75 1.5    1
 .8  3.2    1
 .7  3.5    1
 .6   .75   0
1.1  1.7    0
 .9   .75   0
 .9   .45   0
 .8   .57   0
 .55 2.75   0
 .6  3.0    0
1.4  2.33   1
 .75 3.75   1
2.3  1.64   1
3.2  1.6    1
 .85 1.415  1
1.7  1.06   0
1.8  1.8    1
 .4  2      0
 .95 1.36   0
1.35 1.35   0
1.5  1.36   0
1.6  1.78   1
 .6  1.5    0
1.8  1.5    1
 .95 1.9    0
1.9   .95   1
1.6   .4    0
2.7   .75   1
2.35  .03   0
1.1  1.83   0
1.1  2.2    1
1.2  2.0    1
 .8  3.33   1
```

```
 .95  1.9   0
 .75  1.9   0
1.3   1.625 1
;

title 'Occurrence of Vaso-Constriction';
proc logistic data=vaso order=data;
   model response=lograte logvol / influence iplots;
run;
```

Output 27.4   Obtaining Influence Statistics and Index Plots

```
                        Occurrence of Vaso-Constriction                        1

                             The LOGISTIC Procedure

            Data Set: WORK.VASO
            Response Variable: RESPONSE
            Response Levels: 2
            Number of Observations: 39
            Link Function: Logit


                               Response Profile

                          Ordered
                           Value  RESPONSE   Count

                             1       1        20
                             2       0        19


                  Simple Statistics for Explanatory Variables

                                    Standard
            Variable      Mean      Deviation      Minimum      Maximum

            LOGRATE     0.317839    0.828558      -3.50656      1.32176
            LOGVOL      0.159636    0.537657      -0.91629      1.30833


                       Criteria for Assessing Model Fit

                                    Intercept
                         Intercept     and
            Criterion      Only     Covariates    Chi-Square for Covariates

            AIC           56.040      35.227            .
            SC            57.703      40.218            .
            -2 LOG L      54.040      29.227       24.812 with 2 DF (p=0.0001)
            Score           .           .          16.632 with 2 DF (p=0.0002)


                  Analysis of Maximum Likelihood Estimates

                       Parameter    Standard      Wald        Pr >      Standardized
            Variable    Estimate      Error    Chi-Square   Chi-Square    Estimate

            INTERCEP    -2.8754      1.3208      4.7395       0.0295         .
            LOGRATE      4.5617      1.8380      6.1597       0.0131      2.083811
            LOGVOL       5.1793      1.8648      7.7136       0.0055      1.535286


            Association of Predicted Probabilities and Observed Responses

                       Concordant = 93.7%    Somers' D = 0.874
                       Discordant =  6.3%    Gamma     = 0.874
                       Tied       =  0.0%    Tau-a     = 0.448
                       (380 pairs)           c         = 0.937
```

Occurrence of Vaso-Constriction

The LOGISTIC Procedure

㉔ Regression Diagnostics

Case Number	Covariates LOGRATE	LOGVOL	Pearson Residual Value	Deviance Residual Value	Hat Matrix Diagonal Value
1	-0.1924	1.3083	0.2205	0.3082	0.0927
2	0.0862	1.2528	0.1349	0.1899	0.0429
3	0.9163	0.2231	0.2923	0.4049	0.0612
4	0.4055	-0.2877	3.5181	2.2775	0.0867
5	1.1632	-0.2231	0.5287	0.7021	0.1158
6	1.2528	-0.3567	0.6090	0.7943	0.1524
7	-0.2877	-0.5108	-0.0328	-0.0464	0.00761
8	0.5306	0.0953	-1.0196	-1.1939	0.0559
9	-0.2877	-0.1054	-0.0938	-0.1323	0.0342
10	-0.7985	-0.1054	-0.0293	-0.0414	0.00721
11	-0.5621	-0.2231	-0.0370	-0.0523	0.00969
12	1.0116	-0.5978	-0.5073	-0.6768	0.1481
13	1.0986	-0.5108	-0.7751	-0.9700	0.1628
14	0.8459	0.3365	0.2559	0.3562	0.0551
15	1.3218	-0.2877	0.4352	0.5890	0.1336
16	0.4947	0.8329	0.1576	0.2215	0.0402
17	0.4700	1.1632	0.0709	0.1001	0.0172
18	0.3471	-0.1625	2.9062	2.1192	0.0954
19	0.0583	0.5306	-1.0718	-1.2368	0.1315
20	0.5878	0.5878	0.2405	0.3353	0.0525
21	0.6931	-0.9163	-0.1076	-0.1517	0.0373
22	0.3075	-0.0513	-0.4193	-0.5691	0.1015
23	0.3001	0.3001	-1.0242	-1.1978	0.0761
24	0.3075	0.4055	-1.3684	-1.4527	0.0717
25	0.5766	0.4700	0.3347	0.4608	0.0587
26	0.4055	-0.5108	-0.1595	-0.2241	0.0548
27	0.4055	0.5878	0.3645	0.4995	0.0661
28	0.6419	-0.0513	-0.8989	-1.0883	0.0647
29	-0.0513	0.6419	0.8981	1.0876	0.1682
30	-0.9163	0.4700	-0.0992	-0.1400	0.0507
31	-0.2877	0.9933	0.6198	0.8064	0.2459
32	-3.5066	0.8544	-0.00073	-0.00103	0.000022
33	0.6043	0.0953	-1.2062	-1.3402	0.0510
34	0.7885	0.0953	0.5447	0.7209	0.0601
35	0.6931	0.1823	0.5404	0.7159	0.0552
36	1.2030	-0.2231	0.4828	0.6473	0.1177
37	0.6419	-0.0513	-0.8989	-1.0883	0.0647
38	0.6419	-0.2877	-0.4874	-0.6529	0.1000
39	0.4855	0.2624	0.7053	0.8987	0.0531

(Pearson Residual: 1 unit = 0.44; Deviance Residual: 1 unit = 0.28; Hat Matrix Diagonal: 1 unit = 0.02)

Occurrence of Vaso-Constriction

The LOGISTIC Procedure

Regression Diagnostics

3

Case Number	INTERCEP Dfbeta Value	(1 unit = 0.13) -8 -4 0 2 4 6 8	LOGRATE Dfbeta Value	(1 unit = 0.12) -8 -4 0 2 4 6 8	LOGVOL Dfbeta Value	(1 unit = 0.13) -8 -4 0 2 4 6 8
1	-0.0165	| * |	0.0193	| * |	0.0556	| * |
2	-0.0134	| * |	0.0151	| * |	0.0261	| * |
3	-0.0492	| * |	0.0660	| |* |	0.0589	| * |
4	1.0734	| | *|	-0.9302	|* | |	-1.0180	|* | |
5	-0.0832	| *| |	0.1411	| |* |	0.0583	| * |
6	-0.0922	| *| |	0.1710	| |* |	0.0381	| * |
7	-0.00280	| * |	0.00274	| * |	0.00265	| * |
8	-0.1444	| *| |	0.0613	| |* |	0.0570	| * |
9	-0.0178	| * |	0.0173	| * |	0.0153	| * |
10	-0.00245	| * |	0.00246	| * |	0.00211	| * |
11	-0.00361	| * |	0.00358	| * |	0.00319	| * |
12	-0.1173	| *| |	0.0647	| |* |	0.1651	| |* |
13	-0.0931	| *| |	-0.00946	| * |	0.1775	| |* |
14	-0.0414	| * |	0.0538	| * |	0.0527	| * |
15	-0.0940	| *| |	0.1408	| |* |	0.0643	| |* |
16	-0.0198	| * |	0.0234	| * |	0.0307	| * |
17	-0.00630	| * |	0.00701	| * |	0.00914	| * |
18	0.9595	| | *|	-0.8279	|* | |	-0.8477	|* | |
19	-0.2591	| *| |	0.2024	| | * |	-0.00488	| * |
20	-0.0331	| * |	0.0421	| * |	0.0518	| * |
21	-0.0180	| * |	0.0158	| * |	0.0208	| * |
22	-0.1449	| *| |	0.1237	| |* |	0.1179	| |* |
23	-0.1961	| *| |	0.1275	| |* |	0.0357	| * |
24	-0.1281	| *| |	0.0410	| * |	-0.1004	| *| |
25	-0.0403	| * |	0.0570	| * |	0.0708	| |* |
26	-0.0366	| * |	0.0329	| * |	0.0373	| * |
27	-0.0327	| * |	0.0496	| * |	0.0788	| |* |
28	-0.1423	| *| |	0.0617	| |* |	0.1025	| |* |
29	0.2367	| |* |	-0.1950	| *| |	0.0286	| * |
30	-0.0224	| * |	0.0227	| * |	0.0159	| * |
31	0.1165	| |* |	-0.0996	| *| |	0.1322	| |* |
32	-3.22E-6	| * |	3.405E-6	| * |	2.48E-6	| * |
33	-0.0882	| *| |	-0.0137	| * |	-0.00216	| * |
34	-0.0425	| * |	0.0877	| |* |	0.0671	| |* |
35	-0.0340	| * |	0.0755	| * |	0.0711	| |* |
36	-0.0867	| *| |	0.1381	| |* |	0.0631	| * |
37	-0.1423	| *| |	0.0617	| |* |	0.1025	| |* |
38	-0.1395	| *| |	0.1032	| |* |	0.1397	| |* |
39	0.0326	| * |	0.0190	| * |	0.0489	| * |

Occurrence of Vaso-Constriction   4

The LOGISTIC Procedure

Regression Diagnostics

		C		CBAR			DIFDEV	
		(1 unit = 0.08)			(1 unit = 0.07)			(1 unit = 0.4)
Case Number	Value	0 2 4 6 8 12 16	Value	0 2 4 6 8 12 16		Value	0 2 4 6 8 12 16	
1	0.00548	|*	0.00497	|*		0.1000	|*	
2	0.000853	|*	0.000816	|*		0.0369	|*	
3	0.00593	|*	0.00557	|*		0.1695	|*	
4	1.2873	| *	1.1756	| *		6.3626	| *	
5	0.0414	| *	0.0366	|*		0.5296	| *	
6	0.0787	| *	0.0667	| *		0.6976	| *	
7	8.321E-6	|*	8.258E-6	|*		0.00216	|*	
8	0.0652	| *	0.0616	| *		1.4870	| *	
9	0.000322	|*	0.000311	|*		0.0178	|*	
10	6.256E-6	|*	6.211E-6	|*		0.00172	|*	
11	0.000014	|*	0.000013	|*		0.00274	|*	
12	0.0525	| *	0.0447	|*		0.5028	| *	
13	0.1395	| *	0.1168	| *		1.0577	| *	
14	0.00404	|*	0.00382	|*		0.1307	|*	
15	0.0337	|*	0.0292	|*		0.3761	|*	
16	0.00108	|*	0.00104	|*		0.0501	|*	
17	0.000089	|*	0.000088	|*		0.0101	|*	
18	0.9845	| *	0.8906	| *		5.3817	| *	
19	0.2003	| *	0.1740	| *		1.7037	| *	
20	0.00338	|*	0.00320	|*		0.1156	|*	
21	0.000465	|*	0.000448	|*		0.0235	|*	
22	0.0221	|*	0.0199	|*		0.3437	|*	
23	0.0935	| *	0.0864	| *		1.5212	| *	
24	0.1558	| *	0.1447	| *		2.2550	| *	
25	0.00741	|*	0.00698	|*		0.2193	| *	
26	0.00156	|*	0.00147	|*		0.0517	|*	
27	0.0101	|*	0.00941	|*		0.2589	| *	
28	0.0597	| *	0.0559	| *		1.2404	| *	
29	0.1961	| *	0.1631	| *		1.3460	| *	
30	0.000554	|*	0.000526	|*		0.0201	|*	
31	0.1661	| *	0.1253	| *		0.7755	| *	
32	1.18E-11	|*	1.18E-11	|*		1.065E-6	|*	
33	0.0824	| *	0.0782	| *		1.8744	| *	
34	0.0202	|*	0.0190	|*		0.5387	| *	
35	0.0180	|*	0.0170	|*		0.5295	| *	
36	0.0352	|*	0.0311	|*		0.4501	|*	
37	0.0597	| *	0.0559	| *		1.2404	| *	
38	0.0293	|*	0.0264	|*		0.4526	| *	
39	0.0295	|*	0.0279	|*		0.8355	| *	

The LOGISTIC Procedure

Regression Diagnostics

DIFCHISQ

```
                           (1 unit = 0.85)
  Case
 Number     Value        0  2  4  6  8  12  16
      1    0.0536        |*                    |
      2    0.0190        |*                    |
      3    0.0910        |*                    |
      4   13.5523        |                   * |
      5    0.3161        |*                    |
      6    0.4376        | *                   |
      7    0.00109       |*                    |
      8    1.1011        | *                   |
      9    0.00911       |*                    |
     10    0.000862      |*                    |
     11    0.00138       |*                    |
     12    0.3021        |*                    |
     13    0.7175        | *                   |
     14    0.0693        |*                    |
     15    0.2186        |*                    |
     16    0.0259        |*                    |
     17    0.00511       |*                    |
     18    9.3363        |            *        |
     19    1.3227        |  *                  |
     20    0.0610        |*                    |
     21    0.0120        |*                    |
     22    0.1956        |*                    |
     23    1.1355        | *                   |
     24    2.0171        |  *                  |
     25    0.1190        |*                    |
     26    0.0269        |*                    |
     27    0.1423        |*                    |
     28    0.8639        | *                   |
     29    0.9697        | *                   |
     30    0.0104        |*                    |
     31    0.5095        | *                   |
     32    5.324E-7      |*                    |
     33    1.5331        | *                   |
     34    0.3157        |*                    |
     35    0.3091        |*                    |
     36    0.2641        |*                    |
     37    0.8639        | *                   |
     38    0.2639        |*                    |
     39    0.5254        | *                   |
```

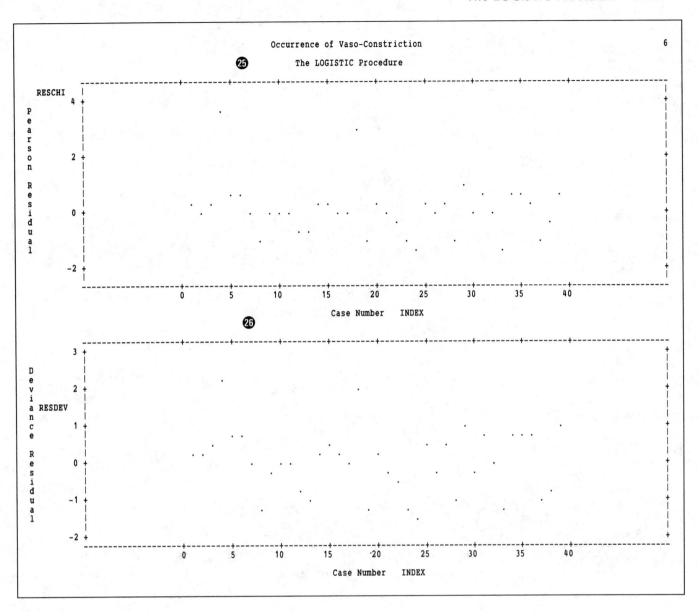

Occurrence of Vaso-Constriction

The LOGISTIC Procedure

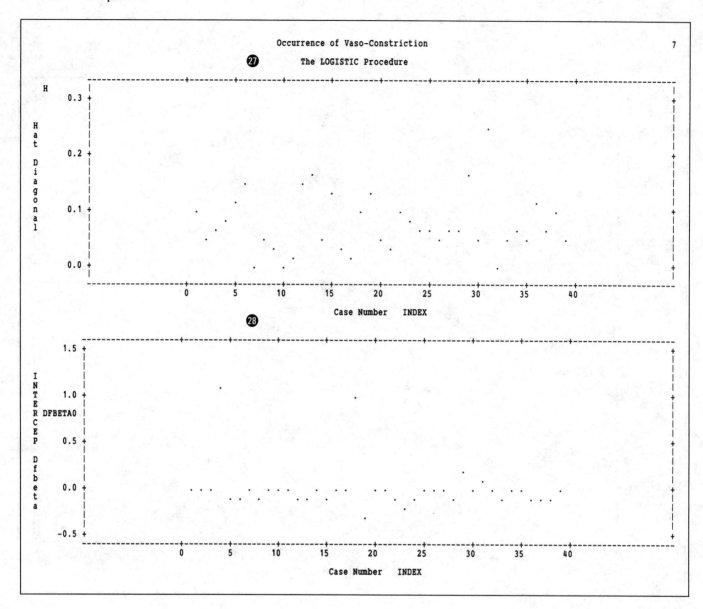

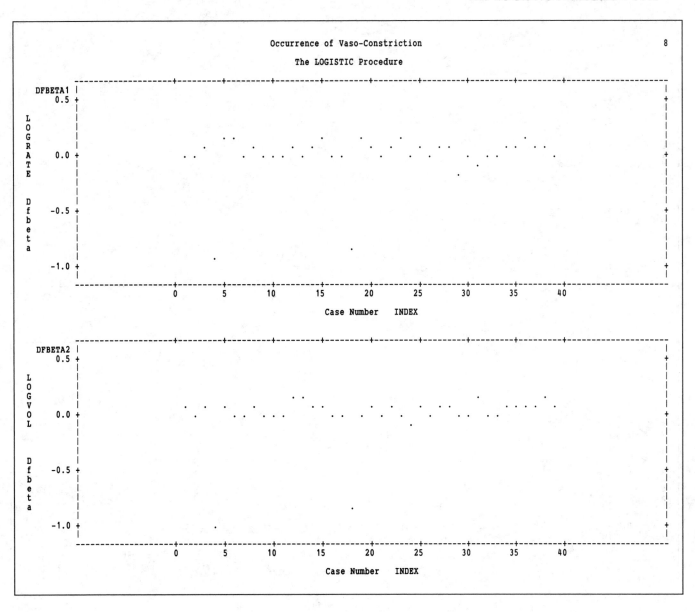

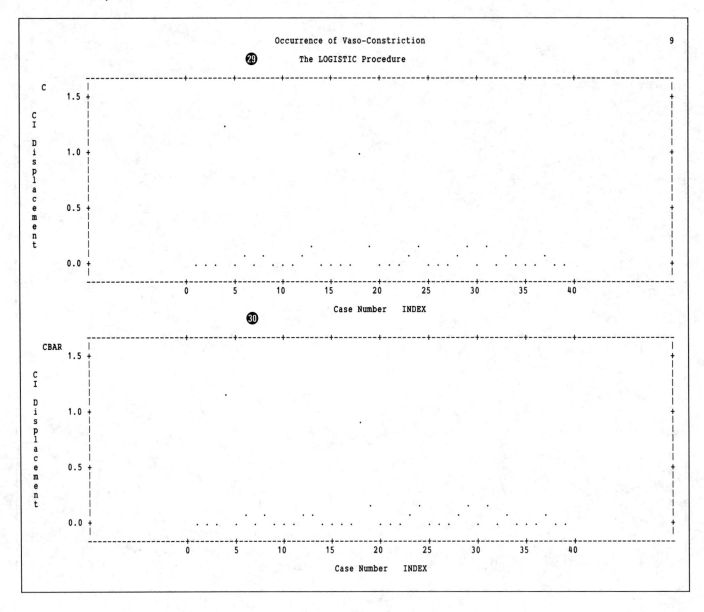

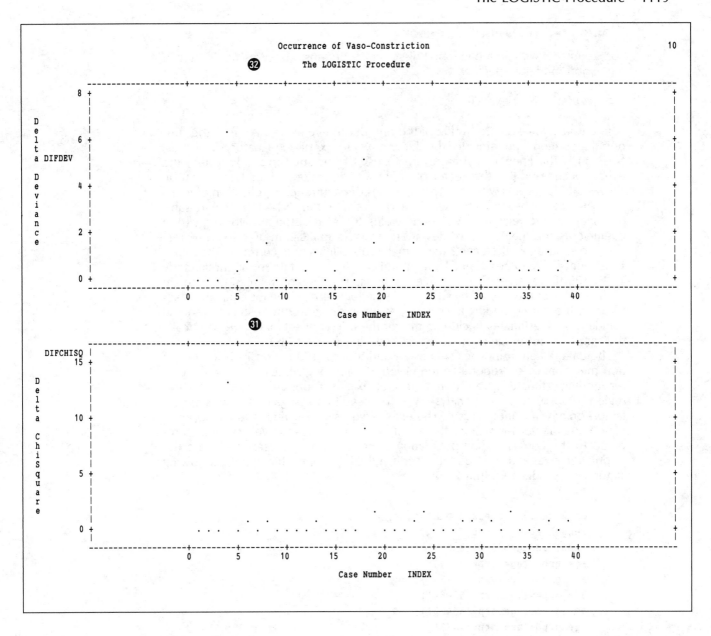

The index plots of the Pearson residuals and deviance residuals indicate that case 4 and case 18 are poorly accounted for by the model. The index plot of the diagonal elements of the hat matrix suggests that case 31 is an extreme point in the design space. The index plots of DFBETAs indicate that case 4 and case 18 are causing instability in all three parameter estimates. The other four index plots also point to these two cases as having a large impact on the coefficients and goodness-of-fit.

Example 4:   Poisson Regression

For counts n with independent Poisson distributions, the Poisson log-linear regression model is specified by

$$\mu(\mathbf{x}) = N(\mathbf{x})\, \exp(\mathbf{x}'\boldsymbol{\beta})$$

where $\mu(\mathbf{x})$ is the expected value of the number of events $n=n(\mathbf{x})$ from the subpopulation corresponding to the known vector $\mathbf{x}$ of explanatory variables, $N=N(\mathbf{x})$ is the known total exposure to risk of this subpopulation where the events occur, and $\boldsymbol{\beta}$ is the vector of unknown regression parameters. It can be shown that for events with small probabilities of occurrence, application of logistic regression to the event frequencies $\{n\}$ relative to the $\{N\}$ as if they were sample sizes for the relative populations yields the same estimates for regression coefficients and their standard deviation errors as application of Poisson regression. To ensure that the events have small probabilities of occurrence, the exposure counts have to be inflated by a multiplicative constant if they are not already 10 to 100 times larger than the event counts. The Poisson regression estimate of the intercept is obtained by subtracting the logarithm of the multiplicative factor from the corresponding logistic regression estimate. Other estimates and all standard error estimates (including that of the intercept estimate) are practically the same for both regression analyses. See Vine et al. (1989).

The data, taken from Koch, Atkinson, and Stokes (1986), consist of counts of new melanoma cases reported during 1969-1971 among white males and the corresponding estimated populations at risk for six age groups and two geographical regions. Poisson regression analysis was proposed to investigate the vital statistics factors on new melanoma cases. This example uses logistic regression to approximate Poisson regression. Since the event frequencies are relatively small as compared to the corresponding population sizes, it is not necessary to inflate the population sizes and subsequently readjust the intercept estimate. The following statements produce **Output 27.5**:

```
data;
    drop case_n case_s pop_n pop_s;
    length age_grp $ 5;
    input age_grp $ case_n case_s pop_n pop_s;
    age_grp2=(age_grp='35-44');
    age_grp3=(age_grp='45-54');
    age_grp4=(age_grp='55-64');
    age_grp5=(age_grp='65-74');
    age_grp6=(age_grp='>=75');
    case=case_n; pop=pop_n; region=0; output;
    case=case_s; pop=pop_s; region=1; output;
    label region='0=NORTHERN  1=SOUTHERN';
    cards;
<35    61 64 2880262 1074246
35-44  76 75  564535   220407
45-54  98 68  592983   198119
55-64 104 63  450740   134084
65-74  63 45  270908    70708
>=75 80 27   161850    34233
;

proc logistic;
  model case / pop=age_grp2-age_grp6 region;
run;
```

Output 27.5 Poisson Regression

```
                              The SAS System                                        1
                           The LOGISTIC Procedure

          Data Set: WORK.DATA1
  ❺       Response Variable (Events): CASE
  ❻       Response Variable (Trials): POP
          Number of Observations: 12
          Link Function: Logit


                              Response Profile

                        Ordered  Binary
                        Value    Outcome      Count

                           1     EVENT          824
                           2     NO EVENT   6652251


              Simple Statistics for Explanatory Variables

                                   Standard                           Variable
    Variable        Mean          Deviation      Minimum   Maximum    Label

    AGE_GRP2      0.117982        0.322587          0      1.00000
    AGE_GRP3      0.118908        0.323680          0      1.00000
    AGE_GRP4      0.087903        0.283154          0      1.00000
    AGE_GRP5      0.051347        0.220705          0      1.00000
    AGE_GRP6      0.029473        0.169127          0      1.00000
    REGION        0.260300        0.438798          0      1.00000    0=NORTHERN  1=SOUTHERN


                      Criteria for Assessing Model Fit

                                          Intercept
                            Intercept        and
             Criterion        Only       Covariates    Chi-Square for Covariates

             AIC           16475.997      15598.251          .
             SC            16489.707      15694.225          .
             -2 LOG L      16473.997      15584.251      889.746 with 6 DF (p=0.0001)
             Score            .              .           988.419 with 6 DF (p=0.0001)


                 Analysis of Maximum Likelihood Estimates

                 Parameter   Standard      Wald        Pr >      Standardized   Variable
    Variable     Estimate     Error     Chi-Square   Chi-Square    Estimate     Label

    INTERCEP     -10.6584     0.0952    12537.4071     0.0001         .         Intercept
    AGE_GRP2       1.7976     0.1209      220.9395     0.0001      0.319699
    AGE_GRP3       1.9133     0.1184      260.9290     0.0001      0.341437
    AGE_GRP4       2.2421     0.1183      358.9264     0.0001      0.350018
    AGE_GRP5       2.3661     0.1315      323.5880     0.0001      0.287906
    AGE_GRP6       2.9453     0.1321      497.3234     0.0001      0.274634
    REGION         0.8197     0.0710      133.1463     0.0001      0.198311     0=NORTHERN  1=SOUTHERN

NOTE: Measures of association between the observed and predicted values were not calculated because the predicted probabilities are
```

```
                              The SAS System                                        2
                           The LOGISTIC Procedure

    indistinguishable when they are classified into intervals of length 0.002 .
```

Example 5: Conditional Logistic Regression for 1–1 Matched Data

The data in this example are a subset of the data from the Los Angeles Study of the Endometrial Cancer Data described in Breslow and Day (1980). There are 63 matched pairs, each consisting of a case of endometrial cancer (OUTCOME=1) and a control (OUTCOME=0). The case and corresponding control have the same ID. The explanatory variables include GALL (an indicator variable for gall bladder disease) and HYPER (an indicator variable for hypertension). The goal of the analysis is to determine the relative risk for gall bladder disease, controlling for the effect of hypertension.

When each matched set consists of a single case and single control, the conditional likelihood is given by

$$\Pi_i(1 + exp(-\mathbf{d}_i'\boldsymbol{\beta}))^{-1}$$

where $\mathbf{d}_i = \mathbf{x}_{i1} - \mathbf{x}_{i0}$ is the difference in the two covariate vectors. This is identical to the likelihood for a linear logistic model with $\mathbf{d}_i$ as the regression variable, no intercept term and constant response variable value (Breslow 1982). Thus, the LOGISTIC procedure can be used to perform conditional logistic regression for 1–1 matched data.

Each matched pair is transformed into a single observation, where the explanatory variable value is the difference between the corresponding values for the case and the control (case−control). The response variable is OUTCOME, whose values are set to zero (although any constant, numeric or character, will do). The NOINT option is specified to obtain the conditional logistic model estimates. The following statements produce **Output 27.6**:

```
data;
    drop id1 gall1 hyper1;
    retain id1 gall1 hyper1 0;
    input id outcome gall hyper @@ ;
    if (id=id1) then do;
        gall=gall1-gall; hyper=hyper1-hyper;
        output;
    end;
    else do;
        id1=id; gall1=gall; hyper1=hyper;
    end;
    cards;
    1    1    0    0    1    0    0    0
    2    1    0    0    2    0    0    0
    3    1    0    1    3    0    0    1
    4    1    0    0    4    0    1    0
    5    1    1    0    5    0    0    1
    6    1    0    1    6    0    0    0
    7    1    1    0    7    0    0    0
    8    1    1    1    8    0    0    1
    9    1    0    0    9    0    0    0
    10   1    0    0    10   0    0    0
    11   1    1    0    11   0    0    0
    12   1    0    0    12   0    0    1
    13   1    1    0    13   0    0    1
    14   1    1    0    14   0    1    0
    15   1    1    0    15   0    0    1
    16   1    0    1    16   0    0    0
    17   1    0    0    17   0    1    1
    18   1    0    0    18   0    1    1
```

19	1	0	0	19	0	0	1
20	1	0	1	20	0	0	0
21	1	0	0	21	0	1	1
22	1	0	1	22	0	0	1
23	1	0	1	23	0	0	0
24	1	0	0	24	0	0	0
25	1	0	0	25	0	0	0
26	1	0	0	26	0	0	1
27	1	1	0	27	0	0	1
28	1	0	0	28	0	0	1
29	1	1	0	29	0	0	0
30	1	0	1	30	0	0	0
31	1	0	1	31	0	0	0
32	1	0	1	32	0	0	0
33	1	0	1	33	0	0	0
34	1	0	0	34	0	0	0
35	1	1	1	35	0	1	1
36	1	0	0	36	0	0	1
37	1	0	1	37	0	0	0
38	1	0	1	38	0	0	1
39	1	0	1	39	0	0	1
40	1	0	1	40	0	0	0
41	1	0	0	41	0	0	0
42	1	0	1	42	0	1	0
43	1	0	0	43	0	0	1
44	1	0	0	44	0	0	0
45	1	1	0	45	0	0	0
46	1	0	0	46	0	0	0
47	1	1	1	47	0	0	0
48	1	0	1	48	0	0	0
49	1	0	0	49	0	0	0
50	1	0	1	50	0	0	1
51	1	0	0	51	0	0	0
52	1	0	1	52	0	0	1
53	1	0	1	53	0	0	0
54	1	0	1	54	0	0	0
55	1	1	0	55	0	0	0
56	1	0	0	56	0	0	0
57	1	1	1	57	0	1	0
58	1	0	0	58	0	0	0
59	1	0	0	59	0	0	0
60	1	1	1	60	0	0	0
61	1	1	0	61	0	1	0
62	1	0	1	62	0	0	0
63	1	1	0	63	0	0	0

```
;

proc logistic;
   model outcome=gall / noint;
run;

proc logistic;
   model outcome=gall hyper / noint;
run;
```

Output 27.6 Conditional Logistic Regression

```
                              The SAS System                                    1
                            The LOGISTIC Procedure

          Data Set: WORK.DATA1
          Response Variable: OUTCOME
          Response Levels: 1
          Number of Observations: 63
          Link Function: Logit


                               Response Profile

                         Ordered
                          Value   OUTCOME    Count

                            1        0        63


                    Simple Statistics for Explanatory Variables

                                    Standard
          Variable       Mean       Deviation     Minimum        Maximum

          GALL        0.126984     0.523390     -1.00000        1.00000


                       Criteria for Assessing Model Fit

                      Without      With
          Criterion   Covariates   Covariates   Chi-Square for Covariates

          AIC          87.337       85.654          .
          SC           87.337       87.797          .
          -2 LOG L     87.337       83.654       3.683 with 1 DF (p=0.0550)
          Score          .            .          3.556 with 1 DF (p=0.0593)


                    Analysis of Maximum Likelihood Estimates

                    Parameter    Standard      Wald        Pr >      Standardized
          Variable  Estimate      Error     Chi-Square  Chi-Square     Estimate

          GALL       0.9555      0.5262       3.2970      0.0694      0.275723


NOTE: Measures of association between the observed and predicted values were not calculated because the predicted probabilities are
      indistinguishable when they are classified into intervals of length 0.002 .
```

```
                              The SAS System                                   2
                           The LOGISTIC Procedure

          Data Set: WORK.DATA1
          Response Variable: OUTCOME
          Response Levels: 1
          Number of Observations: 63
          Link Function: Logit


                             Response Profile

                        Ordered
                         Value   OUTCOME     Count

                           1        0         63


            Simple Statistics for Explanatory Variables

                                Standard
       Variable      Mean      Deviation     Minimum       Maximum

       GALL       0.126984     0.523390     -1.00000      1.00000
       HYPER      0.079365     0.702566     -1.00000      1.00000


                    Criteria for Assessing Model Fit

                    Without      With
       Criterion   Covariates  Covariates   Chi-Square for Covariates

        AIC          87.337      86.788           .
        SC           87.337      91.074           .
        -2 LOG L     87.337      82.788      4.549 with 2 DF (p=0.1029)
        Score           .          .         4.362 with 2 DF (p=0.1129)


                 Analysis of Maximum Likelihood Estimates

                 Parameter    Standard     Wald        Pr >      Standardized
       Variable  Estimate      Error    Chi-Square  Chi-Square    Estimate

       GALL       0.9704      0.5307     3.3432       0.0675      0.280021
       HYPER      0.3481      0.3770     0.8526       0.3558      0.134822

NOTE: Measures of association between the observed and predicted values were not calculated because the predicted probabilities are
      indistinguishable when they are classified into intervals of length 0.002 .
```

In the first call to LOGISTIC, GALL is the only predictor variable. The parameter estimate for GALL is 0.9555, so the relative risk for the gall bladder disease alone is estimated as exp(0.9555)=2.60. In the second call to LOGISTIC, the variable HYPER is added to the model as another explanatory variable. The parameter estimate for GALL is 0.9704. The relative risk for the gall bladder disease, adjusted for the effect of hypertension is exp(0.9704)=2.94. Note that the adjusted value for the gall bladder disease is not very different from the unadjusted value.

REFERENCES

Agresti, A. (1984), *Analysis of Ordinal Categorical Data*, New York: John Wiley & Sons, Inc.

Aitchison, J. and Silvey, S. D. (1957), "The Generalization of Probit Analysis to the Case of Multiple Responses," *Biometrika* 44, 131–40.

Ashford, J.R. (1959), "An Approach to the Analysis of Data for Semi-Quantal Responses in Biology Response," *Biometrics*, 15, 573–81.

Bartolucci, A.A. and Fraser, M.D. (1977), "Comparative Step-up and Composite Test for Selecting Prognostic Indicator Associated with Survival," *Biometrical Journal* 19, 437–448.

Breslow, N.E. and Day, W. (1980), *Statistical Methods in Cancer Research. Volume 1–The Analysis of Case-Control Studies*, Lyon: IARC Scientific Publication No. 32.

Breslow, N.E. (1982), "Covariance Adjustment of Relative-risk Estimates in Matched Studies," *Biometrics*, 38, 661–672.

Cook, R.D. and Weisberg, S. (1982), *Residuals and Influence in Regression*, New York: Chapman and Hall.

Cox, D.R. and Snell, E.J. (1989), *The Analysis of Binary Data*, 2d Edition, London: Chapman and Hall.

Finney, D.J. (1947), "The Estimation from Individual Records of the Relationship between Dose and Quantal Response," *Biometrika, 34*, 320–334.

Freeman, D.H., Jr. (1987), *Applied Categorical Data Analysis*, New York: Marcel Dekker, Inc.

Harrell, F.E. (1986), "The LOGIST Procedure," *SUGI Supplemental Library Guide, Version 5 Edition*, Cary, NC: SAS Institute Inc.

Hosmer, D.W, Jr. and Lemeshow, S. (1989), *Applied Logistic Regression*, New York: John Wiley & Sons, Inc.

Koch, G.G., Atkinson, S.S., and Stokes, M.E. (1986), "Poisson Regression," *Encyclopedia of Statistical Sciences*, Vol. 7, eds. S. Kotz, N.L. Johnson, and C.B. Read, New York: John Wiley & Sons, Inc.

Lawless, J.F. and Singhal, K. (1978), "Efficient Screening of Nonnormal Regression Models," *Biometrics*, 34, 318–327.

Lee, E.T. (1974), "A Computer Program for Linear Logistic Regression Analysis," *Computer Programs in Biomedicine*, 80–92.

McCullagh, P. and Nelder, J.A. (1989), *Generalized Linear Models*, 2d edition, New York: Chapman Hall.

Nelder, J.A. and Wedderburn, R.W.M. (1972), "Generalized Linear Model," *Journal of the Royal Statistical Society, Series A*, 135, 761–768.

Pregibon, D. (1981), "Logistic Regression Diagnostics," *Annals of Statistics*, 9, 705–724.

Press, S.J. and Wilson, S. (1978), "Choosing Between Logistic Regression and Discriminant Analysis," *Journal of the American Statistical Association*, 73, 699–705.

Vine, M.F., Schoenbach, V.J., Hulka, B.S., Koch, G.G., and Sampson, G. (1989), "Atypical Metaplasia and Incidence of Bronchogenic Carcinoma", *American Journal of Epidemiology*, (in preparation).

Walker, S.H. and Duncan, D.B. (1967), "Estimation of the Probability of an Event as a Function of Several Independent Variables," *Biometrika*, 54, 167–179.

Chapter 28

The NESTED
Procedure

ABSTRACT 1127
INTRODUCTION 1127
    PROC NESTED Contrasted With Other SAS Procedures 1128
SPECIFICATIONS 1128
    PROC NESTED Statement 1129
    BY Statement 1129
    CLASS Statement 1129
    VAR Statement 1130
DETAILS 1130
    Missing Values 1130
    Unbalanced Data 1130
    General Random Effects Model 1130
    Analysis of Covariance 1130
    Error Terms in F Tests 1131
    Computational Method 1131
    Printed Output 1132
EXAMPLE 1133
    Variability of Calcium Concentration in Turnip Greens 1133
    REFERENCES 1134

ABSTRACT

The NESTED procedure performs random effects analysis of variance and covariance for data from an experiment with a nested (hierarchical) structure. *

INTRODUCTION

A random effects model for data from a completely nested design with two factors has the following form:

$$y_{ijr} = \mu + \alpha_i + \beta_{ij} + \varepsilon_{ijr}$$

where

y_{ijr} is the value of the dependent variable observed at the rth replication with the first factor at its ith level and the second factor at its jth level.

μ is the overall (fixed) mean of the sampling population.

---

* PROC NESTED is modeled after the General Purpose Nested Analysis of Variance program of the Dairy Cattle Research Branch of the United States Department of Agriculture. That program was originally written by M.R. Swanson, Statistical Reporting Service, United States Department of Agriculture.

α_i, β_{ij}, ε_{ijr} are mutually uncorrelated random effects with zero means and respective variances σ_1^2, σ_2^2, and σ_ε^2 (the variance components).

This model is appropriate for an experiment with a multi-stage nested sampling design. An example of this is given in **EXAMPLE** later in this chapter, where four turnip plants were randomly chosen (the first factor), then three leaves were randomly chosen from each plant (the second factor nested within the first), and then two samples were taken from each leaf (the different replications at fixed levels of the two factors).

PROC NESTED Contrasted With Other SAS Procedures

The NESTED procedure performs a computationally efficient analysis of variance and analysis of covariance for such data, estimating the different components of variance and also testing for their significance if the design is balanced (see **Unbalanced Data** later in this chapter). Although the ANOVA, GLM, and VARCOMP procedures provide similar analyses, PROC NESTED is both easier to use and computationally more efficient for this special type of design. This is especially true when the design involves a large number of factors, levels, or observations. For example, to specify a four-factor completely nested design in the GLM, ANOVA, or VARCOMP procedures, you use the form

```
class a b c d;
model y=a b(a) c(a b) d(a b c);
```

However, to specify the same design in NESTED, you simply use the form

```
class a b c d;
var y;
```

In addition, the ANOVA and GLM procedures require TEST statements to perform appropriate tests, and the VARCOMP procedure requires that the tests be performed by hand. PROC NESTED, however, makes one assumption about the input data that the other procedures do not. **The data set that PROC NESTED uses must first be sorted by the classification or CLASS variables defining the effects.**

SPECIFICATIONS

The NESTED procedure is specified by the following statements:

PROC NESTED <*options*>;
    CLASS *variables*; — required statements

    VAR *variables*;
    BY *variables*; — optional statements

The PROC NESTED and CLASS statements are required. The BY, CLASS, and VAR statements are described in alphabetical order after the PROC NESTED statement.

PROC NESTED Statement

PROC NESTED <*options*>;

The following options can appear in the PROC NESTED statement:

AOV
: prints only the analysis of variance statistics when there is more than one dependent variable. The analysis of covariance statistics are suppressed.

DATA=*SAS-data-set*
: names the SAS data set to be used by PROC NESTED. By default, the procedure uses the most recently created SAS data set.

BY Statement

BY *variables*;

A BY statement can be used with PROC NESTED to obtain separate analyses on observations in groups defined by the BY variables. When a BY statement appears, the procedure expects the input data set to be sorted in order of the BY variables.

Note: Your data must be sorted first by the BY variables and then by the CLASS variables when using the NESTED procedure.

If your input data set is not sorted in ascending order, use one of the following alternatives:

- Use the SORT procedure with a similar BY statement to sort the data.
- Use the BY statement options NOTSORTED or DESCENDING in the BY statement for the NESTED procedure. The NOTSORTED option does not mean that the data are unsorted, but rather that the data are arranged in groups (according to values of the BY variables) and that these groups are not necessarily in alphabetical or increasing numeric order.
- Use the DATASETS procedure (in base SAS software) to create an index on the BY variables.

For more information on the BY statement, see the discussion in *SAS Language: Reference, Version 6, First Edition*. For more information on the DATASETS procedure, see the discussion in *SAS Procedures Guide, Version 6, Third Edition*.

CLASS Statement

CLASS *variables*;

A CLASS statement specifying the classification variables for the analysis must be included. **The data set must be sorted by the classification variables in the order that they are given in the CLASS statement**. Use PROC SORT to sort the data if they are not already sorted.

Values of a variable in the CLASS statement denote the levels of an effect. The name of that variable is also the name of the corresponding effect. The second effect is assumed to be nested within the first effect, the third effect is assumed to be nested within the second effect, and so on.

VAR Statement

VAR *variables;*

The VAR statement lists the dependent variables for the analysis. The dependent variables must be numeric variables. If the VAR statement is omitted, the NESTED procedure performs an analysis of variance for all numeric variables in the data set, except those already specified in the CLASS statement.

DETAILS

Missing Values

An observation with missing values for any of the variables used by the NESTED procedure is omitted from the analysis. Blank values of character CLASS variables are treated as missing values.

Unbalanced Data

A completely nested design is defined to be unbalanced if the groups corresponding to the levels of some classification variable are not all of the same size. PROC NESTED can compute unbiased estimates for the variance components in an unbalanced design, but because the sums of squares on which these estimates are based no longer have χ^2 distributions under a Gaussian model for the data, F tests for the significance of the variance components cannot be computed. PROC NESTED checks to see that the design is balanced. If it is not, a warning to that effect is placed on the log, and the columns corresponding to the F tests in the analysis of variance are left blank.

General Random Effects Model

A random effects model for data from a completely nested design with n factors has the general form

$$y_{i_1 i_2 \ldots i_n r} = \mu + \alpha_{i_1} + \beta_{i_1 i_2} + \ldots + \varepsilon_{i_1 i_2 \ldots i_n r}$$

where

$y_{i_1 i_2 \ldots i_n r}$ is the value of the dependent variable observed at the rth replication with factor j at level i_j, for $j=1, \ldots, n$.

μ is the overall (fixed) mean of the sampled population.

$\alpha_{i_1}, \beta_{i_1 i_2}, \ldots, \varepsilon_{i_1 i_2 \ldots i_n r}$

are mutually uncorrelated random effects with zero means and respective variances $\sigma_1^2, \sigma_2^2, \ldots, \sigma_\varepsilon^2$.

Analysis of Covariance

When more than one dependent variable is specified, PROC NESTED prints a descriptive analysis of the covariance between each pair of dependent variables in addition to a separate analysis of variance for each variable. The analysis of covariance is computed under the basic random effects model for each pair of dependent variables:

$$y_{i_1 i_2 \ldots i_n r} = \mu + \alpha_{i_1} + \beta_{i_1 i_2} + \ldots + \varepsilon_{i_1 i_2 \ldots i_n r}$$
$$y'_{i_1 i_2 \ldots i_n r} = \mu' + \alpha'_{i_1} + \beta'_{i_1 i_2} + \ldots + \varepsilon'_{i_1 i_2 \ldots i_n r}$$

where the notation is the same as that used in the general random effects model above. There is an additional assumption that all the random effects in the two models are mutually uncorrelated except for corresponding effects, for which

$$\text{Corr}\,(\alpha_{i_1},\,\alpha'_{i_1}) = \rho_1$$
$$\text{Corr}\,(\beta_{i_1i_2},\,\beta'_{i_1i_2}) = \rho_2$$

$$\cdot$$
$$\cdot$$
$$\cdot$$

$$\text{Corr}\,(\varepsilon_{i_1i_2\ldots\,i_nr},\,\varepsilon'_{i_1i_2\ldots\,i_nr}) = \rho_\varepsilon\quad.$$

Error Terms in *F* Tests

Random effects *ANOVA*s are distinguished from fixed effects *ANOVA*s by which error mean squares are used as the denominator for F tests. Under a fixed effects model, there is only one true error term in the model, and the corresponding mean square is used as the denominator for all tests. This is how the usual analysis is computed in PROC ANOVA, for example. However, in a random effects model for a nested experiment, mean squares are compared sequentially. The correct denominator in the test for the first factor is the mean square due to the second factor; the correct denominator in the test for the second factor is the mean square due to the third; and so on. Only the mean square due to the last factor, the one at the bottom of the nesting order, should be compared to the error mean square.

Computational Method

The building blocks of the NESTED analysis are the sums of squares for the dependent variables for each classification variable within the factors that precede it in the model, corrected for the factors that follow it. For example, for a two-factor nested design, PROC NESTED computes the following sums of squares:

Total SS	$\Sigma_{ijr}(y_{ijr} - y_{\bullet\bullet\bullet})^2$
SS for Factor 1	$\Sigma_i\, n_{i\bullet}(y_{i\bullet\bullet}/n_{i\bullet} - y_{\bullet\bullet\bullet}/n_{\bullet\bullet})^2$
SS for Factor 2 within Factor 1	$\Sigma_{ij}\, n_{ij}(y_{ij\bullet}/n_{ij} - y_{i\bullet\bullet}/n_{i\bullet})^2$
Error SS	$\Sigma_{ijr}(y_{ijr} - y_{ij\bullet}/n_{ij})^2$

where y_{ijr} is the *r*th replication, n_{ij} is the number of replications at level *i* of the first factor and level *j* of the second, and a dot as a subscript indicates summation over the corresponding index. If there is more than one dependent variable, PROC NESTED also computes the corresponding sums of crossproducts for each pair. The expected value of the sum of squares for a given classification factor is a linear combination of the variance components corresponding to this factor and to the factors that are nested within it. For each factor, the coefficients of this linear combination are computed. (The efficiency of NESTED is partly due to the fact that these various sums can be accumulated with just one pass through the data, assuming that the data have been sorted by the classification variables.) Finally, estimates of the variance components are derived as the solution to the set of linear equations that arise from equating the mean squares to their expected values.

Printed Output

The NESTED procedure prints the following items for each dependent variable:

1. Coefficients of Expected Mean Squares, the coefficients of the $n+1$ variance components making up the expected mean square. Denoting the element in the ith row and jth column of this matrix by C_{ij}, the expected value of the mean square due to the ith classification factor is

$$C_{i1}\sigma_1^2 + \ldots + C_{in}\sigma_n^2 + C_{i,n+1}\sigma_\varepsilon^2 \quad .$$

   C_{ij} is always zero for $i>j$, and if the design is balanced, C_{ij} is equal to the common size of all classification groups of the jth factor for $i\leq j$. Finally, the mean square for error is always an unbiased estimate of σ_ε^2. In other words, $C_{n+1,n+1}=1$.

For every dependent variable, PROC NESTED prints an analysis of variance table. Each table contains the following:

2. each Variance Source in the model (the different components of variance) and the total variance.
3. Degrees of Freedom for the corresponding sum of squares.
4. Sum of Squares for each classification factor. The sum of squares for a given classification factor is the sum of squares in the dependent variable within the factors that precede it in the model, corrected for the factors that follow it. (See **Computational Method** earlier in this chapter.)
5. F Value for a factor, which is the ratio of its mean square to the appropriate error mean square. The next column, labeled PR>F, gives the significance levels that result from testing the hypothesis that each variance component equals zero.
6. the appropriate Error Term for an F test, which is the mean square due to the next classification factor in the nesting order. (See **Error Terms in F Tests** earlier in this chapter.)
7. Mean Square due to a factor, which is the corresponding sum of squares divided by the degrees of freedom.
8. estimates of the Variance Component. These are computed by equating the mean squares to their expected values and solving for the variance terms. (See **Computational Method** earlier in this chapter.)
9. Percent of Total, the proportion of variance due to each source. For the ith factor, the value is

$$100 \times \frac{\text{source variance component}}{\text{total variance component}} \quad .$$

10. Mean, the overall average of the dependent variable. This gives an unbiased estimate of the mean of the population. Its variance is estimated by a certain linear combination of the estimated variance components, which is identical to the mean square due to the first factor in the model divided by the total number of observations when the design is balanced.

If there is more than one dependent variable, then PROC NESTED prints an analysis of covariance table for each pair of dependent variables (unless the AOV option is specified in the PROC NESTED statement). For each source of variation, this table includes the following (not shown):

11. Degrees of Freedom.
12. Sum of Products.

13. Mean Products.
14. Covariance Component, the estimate of the covariance component.

Items in the analysis of covariance table are computed analogously to their counterparts in the analysis of variance table. The analysis of covariance table also includes the following (not shown):

15. Variance Component Correlation for a given factor. This is an estimate of the correlation between corresponding effects due to this factor. This correlation is the ratio of the covariance component for this factor to the square root of the product of the variance components for the factor for the two different dependent variables. (See **Analysis of Covariance** earlier in this chapter.)
16. Mean Square Correlation for a given classification factor. This is the ratio of the Mean Products for this factor to the square root of the product of the Mean Squares for the factor for the two different dependent variables.

EXAMPLE

Variability of Calcium Concentration in Turnip Greens

In the following example from Snedecor and Cochran (1976), an experiment is conducted to determine the variability of calcium concentration in turnip greens. Four plants are selected at random, then three leaves are randomly selected from each plant. Two 100-mg samples are taken from each leaf. The amount of calcium is determined by microchemical methods.

Because the data are read in sorted order, it is not necessary to use PROC SORT on the CLASS variables. LEAF is nested in PLANT; SAMPLE is nested in LEAF and is left for the residual term. All the effects are random effects. The following statements read the data and invoke PROC NESTED to produce **Output 28.1**:

```
title 'CALCIUM CONCENTRATION IN TURNIP LEAVES -- NESTED RANDOM MODEL';
title2 'Snedecor and Cochran, STATISTICAL METHODS, 1976, p. 286';
data turnip;
    do plant=1 to 4;
        do leaf=1 to 3;
            do sample=1 to 2;
                input calcium @@;
                output;
                end;
            end;
        end;
    cards;
3.28 3.09 3.52 3.48 2.88 2.80
2.46 2.44 1.87 1.92 2.19 2.19
2.77 2.66 3.74 3.44 2.55 2.55
3.78 3.87 4.07 4.12 3.31 3.31
;

proc nested;
    classes plant leaf;
    var calcium;
run;
```

Output 28.1   Analysis of Calcium Concentration in Turnip Greens Using PROC NESTED

```
                    CALCIUM CONCENTRATION IN TURNIP LEAVES -- NESTED RANDOM MODEL                              1
                         Snedecor and Cochran, STATISTICAL METHODS, 1976, p. 286
                  ❶            Coefficients of Expected Mean Squares

                         Source      PLANT      LEAF      ERROR

                         PLANT         6          2          1
                         LEAF          0          2          1
                         ERROR         0          0          1
```

```
                    CALCIUM CONCENTRATION IN TURNIP LEAVES -- NESTED RANDOM MODEL                              2
                         Snedecor and Cochran, STATISTICAL METHODS, 1976, p. 286

                  Nested Random Effects Analysis of Variance for Variable CALCIUM
```

❷ Variance Source	❸ Degrees of Freedom	❹ Sum of Squares	❺ F Value	Pr > F	❻ Error Term	❼ Mean Square	❽ Variance Component	❾ Percent of Total
TOTAL	23	10.270396				0.446539	0.532938	100.0000
PLANT	3	7.560346	7.665	0.0097	LEAF	2.520115	0.365223	68.5302
LEAF	8	2.630200	49.409	0.0000	ERROR	0.328775	0.161060	30.2212
ERROR	12	0.079850				0.006654	0.006654	1.2486

```
                              Mean                        3.01208333
                              Standard error of mean      0.32404445
```

The results indicate that there is significant (nonzero) variation from plant to plant (PR>F is .0097) and from leaf to leaf within a plant (PR>F is less than .0001). Notice that the variance component for plants uses the least mean square as an error term rather than the final error term in the model.

REFERENCES

Snedecor, G.W. and Cochran, W.G. (1976), *Statistical Methods*, 6th Edition, Ames, IA: Iowa State University Press.

Steel, R.G.D. and Torrie, J.H. (1980), *Principles and Procedures of Statistics*, New York: McGraw-Hill Book Co.

Chapter 29

The NLIN Procedure

ABSTRACT   1136
INTRODUCTION   1136
SPECIFICATIONS   1137
  PROC NLIN Statement   1137
  BOUNDS Statement   1140
  BY Statement   1141
  DER Statements   1141
  ID Statement   1142
  MODEL Statement   1142
  OUTPUT Statement   1143
  PARAMETERS Statement   1145
  Other Program Statements with PROC NLIN   1146
DETAILS   1147
  Missing Values   1147
  Automatic Variables   1147
    Automatic Variables Whose Values Are Set by PROC NLIN   1147
    Automatic Variables Used to Determine Convergence Criteria   1148
    Weighted Regression with the _WEIGHT_ and _WGTJPJ_ Automatic
        Variables   1148
    Modifying the Search Direction with the _RESID_ Automatic
        Variable   1149
    Example: Using Automatic Variables to Specify Starting Values   1149
  Troubleshooting   1149
    Excessive Time   1149
    Dependencies   1150
    Unable to Improve   1150
    Divergence   1150
    Local Minimum   1151
    Discontinuities   1151
    Responding to Trouble   1151
  Computational Methods   1151
    Steepest Descent (Gradient)   1152
    Newton   1153
    Gauss-Newton   1153
    Marquardt   1154
    Secant Method (DUD)   1155
    Step-Size Search   1155
  Output Data Sets   1156
  Printed Output   1156
EXAMPLES   1156
  Example 1:   Negative Exponential Growth Curve   1156
  Example 2:   CES Production Function   1159
  Example 3:   Probit Model with Numerical Derivatives   1160
  Example 4:   Segmented Model   1162
  Example 5:   Iteratively Reweighted Least Squares   1165
  Example 6:   GLIM Models   1168
  Example 7:   Function Minimization   1174
  Example 8:   Censored Accelerated Failure Models   1175
  Example 9:   Conditional Logistic Regression and Cox Regression   1181
REFERENCES   1193

ABSTRACT

The NLIN (NonLINear regression) procedure computes least squares or weighted least squares estimates of the parameters of a nonlinear model.

INTRODUCTION

PROC NLIN fits nonlinear regression models using the least squares method. Nonlinear models are more difficult to specify and estimate than linear models. Instead of simply listing regressor variables, you must write the regression expression, declare parameter names, supply starting values for them, and possibly supply derivatives of the model with respect to the parameters. Some models are difficult to fit, and there is no guarantee that the procedure will be able to fit the model successfully.

The NLIN procedure first examines the starting value specifications of the parameters. If a grid of values is specified, NLIN evaluates the residual sum of squares at each combination of values to determine the best set of values to start the iterative algorithm. Then NLIN uses one of these five iterative methods:

- steepest-descent or gradient method
- Newton method
- modified Gauss-Newton method
- Marquardt method
- multivariate secant or false position (DUD) method.

The Gauss-Newton and Marquardt iterative methods regress the residuals onto the partial derivatives of the model with respect to the parameters until the estimates converge. The Newton iterative method regresses the residuals onto a function of the first and second derivatives of the model with respect to the parameters until the estimates converge.

For each nonlinear model to be analyzed, you must specify the following:

- the names and starting values of the parameters to be estimated
- the model (using a single dependent variable)
- partial derivatives of the model with respect to each parameter (except for the DUD method)
- the second derivatives of the model with respect to each parameter (only for the Newton method).

You can also

- confine the estimation procedure to a certain range of values of the parameters by imposing bounds on the estimates
- specify convergence criteria in terms of SSE, the parameter estimates, or both
- produce new SAS data sets containing predicted values, residuals, parameter estimates and SSE at each iteration, the asymptotic covariance matrix of parameter estimates, and other statistics
- define your own objective function to be minimized.

The NLIN procedure can be used for segmented models (see **Example 4**) or robust regression (see **Example 5**). It can also be used to compute maximum-likelihood estimates for certain models (see Jennrich and Moore 1975; Charnes, Frome, and Yu 1976).

SPECIFICATIONS

The statements available in PROC NLIN are:

PROC NLIN *<options>*;
   MODEL *dependent=expression;*
   PARAMETERS *parameter=values*
            <, . . . , parameter=values>; } required statements

   other program statements

   BOUNDS *expression <, . . . , expression>;*
   BY *variables;*
   DER.*parameter=expression;*
   DER.*parameter.parameter=expression;* } optional statements
   ID *variables;*
   OUTPUT OUT=*SAS-data-set keyword=names*
            <, . . . , keyword=names>;

The *other program statements* are valid SAS expressions that usually appear in the DATA step. NLIN allows you to create new variables within the procedure and use them in the nonlinear analysis. NLIN automatically creates several variables that are also available for use in the analysis. See **Automatic Variables** in the **DETAILS** section for more information. The PROC NLIN, PARAMETERS, and MODEL statements are required. The statements used in NLIN in addition to the PROC statement are the following (in alphabetical order):

BOUNDS   restrains the parameter estimates within specified bounds

BY   specifies variables to define subgroups for the analysis

DER   specifies the first and second partial derivatives

ID   specifies additional variables to add to the output data set

MODEL   defines the relationship between the dependent and independent variables

OUTPUT   creates an output data set containing statistics for each observation

PARAMETERS   identifies parameters to be estimated and the starting values for each parameter

other program statements
   execute assignment statements, ARRAY statements, DO loops, program control statements, and create new variables.

PROC NLIN Statement

   PROC NLIN *<options>;*

The PROC NLIN statement invokes the procedure. The table below lists the options available with the PROC NLIN statement. Explanations follow in alphabetic order.

Task	Option
Specify data sets	DATA= OUTEST=
Grid search	BEST=
Choose an iteration method	METHOD=
Control step size	NOHALVE RHO= SMETHOD= STEP= TAU=
Specify details of iteration	G4 G4SINGULAR SAVE SIGSQ=
Tuning	CONVERGEOBJ= CONVERGEPARM= EFORMAT MAXITER=

BEST=n
> prints the residual sums of squares for the best n combinations when a grid of possible starting values is given. When BEST= option is not specified, NLIN prints the residual sum of squares for all combinations of possible parameter starting values when a grid of starting values is given.

CONVERGEOBJ=c
CONVERGE=c
> uses the change in the LOSS function as the convergence criterion. The iterations are said to have converged for CONVERGEOBJ=c if

$$(LOSS^{i-1} - LOSS^i) / (LOSS^i + 10^{-6}) < c$$

> where $LOSS^i$ is the LOSS for the ith iteration. The default LOSS function is the sum of squared errors (SSE). The constant c should be a small positive number. See **Computational Methods** for more details. By default, CONVERGE=10^{-8}.

CONVERGEPARM=c
> uses the maximum change among parameter estimates as the convergence criterion. The iterations are said to have converged for CONVERGEPARM=c if

$$\max_j (\mid \beta_j^{i-1} - \beta_j^i \mid / \mid \beta_j^{i-1} \mid) < c$$

> where β_j^i is the value of the jth parameter at the ith iteration.
> The default convergence criterion for NLIN is CONVERGEOBJ. If you specify CONVERGEOBJ=c, the specified c is used instead of the default of 10^{-8}. If you specify CONVERGEPARM=c, the maximum change in parameters is used as the convergence criterion (instead of LOSS). If you specify both the CONVERGEOBJ= and CONVERGEPARM= options, NLIN continues to iterate until the decrease in LOSS is sufficiently small (as determined by CONVERGEOBJ) and the maximum change among

the parameters is sufficiently small (as determined by
CONVERGEPARM).

DATA=*SAS-data-set*

names the SAS data set containing the data to be analyzed by PROC
NLIN. By default, PROC NLIN uses the most recently created SAS data
set.

EFORMAT

prints all numeric values in scientific E-notation. This is useful if your
parameters have very different scales.

G4

uses a g4 or Moore-Penrose inverse in parameter estimation.

G4SINGULAR

uses a g4 or Moore-Penrose inverse in parameter estimation if the
Jacobian is (or becomes) of less than full rank.

MAXITER=*i*

limits the number of iterations NLIN performs before it gives up trying to
converge. The *i* value must be a positive integer. By default,
MAXITER=50.

METHOD=GAUSS | MARQUARDT | NEWTON | GRADIENT | DUD

specifies the iterative method NLIN uses. If the METHOD= option is
not specified and DER statements are present, METHOD=GAUSS is
used. If the METHOD= option is not specified and DER statements are
not present, METHOD=DUD is used. See **Computational Methods** in
the **DETAILS** section for details.

NOHALVE

turns off the step-size search during iteration. This option is used with
some types of weighted regression problems and is available only when
SMETHOD=HALVE. See **Example 5** for an example.

OUTEST=*SAS-data-set*

names an output data set to contain the parameter estimates produced
at each iteration. See **Output Data Sets** later in this chapter for details. If
you want to create a permanent SAS data set, you must specify a two-
level name. See "SAS Files" in *SAS Language: Reference, Version 6, First
Edition*, and "Introduction to DATA Step Processing" in *SAS Language
and Procedures: Usage, Version 6, First Edition* for more information on
permanent SAS data sets.

RHO=*value*

specifies a value to use in controlling the step-size search. By default,
RHO=0.1 except when METHOD=MARQUARDT, where RHO=10.
See **Computational Methods** for more details.

SAVE

specifies that, when the iteration limit is exceeded, the parameter
estimates from the final iteration are output to the OUTEST= data set.
These parameter estimates are located in the observation with
TYPE=FINAL. If the SAVE option is not specified, the parameter
estimates from the final iteration are not output to the data set.

SIGSQ=*value*

specifies a value to replace the mean square error for computing the
standard errors of the estimates. The SIGSQ= option is used with
maximum-likelihood estimation.

SMETHOD=HALVE | GOLDEN | ARMGOLD | CUBIC
> specifies the step-size search method NLIN uses. See **Computational Methods** for details. By default, SMETHOD=HALVE.

STEP=*i*
> limits the number of step-halvings. By default, STEP=20. The value of STEP must be a positive integer. The value specified in the STEP= option also becomes the initial value of the _HALVE_ automatic variable. Assigning _HALVE_ a value in a program statement overrides this initial value.

TAU=*value*
> specifies a value to use in controlling the step-size search. By default, TAU=1 except when METHOD=MARQUARDT, where TAU=0.01. See **Computational Methods** for more details.

BOUNDS Statement

> **BOUNDS** *expression* <, . . . , *expression*>;

The BOUNDS statement restrains the parameter estimates within specified bounds. In each BOUNDS statement, you can specify a series of bounds separated by commas. Each bound contains an *expression* consisting of a *parameter name*, an *inequality comparison operator*, and a *value*. In a single-bounded expression, these three elements follow one another in the order described. The following are examples of valid single-bounded expressions:

```
bounds a<=20;
bounds c>30;
bounds a<=20, c>30;
```

You can also use double-bounded expressions. In these expressions, a *value* is followed by an *inequality comparison operator*, a *parameter name*, another *inequality comparison operator*, and a final *value*, as in the following example:

```
bounds 0<=b<=10;
bounds 15<x1<=30;
```

The algorithm used to enforce inequality constraints treats the strict inequality ($<$, $>$) the same as the weak inequality ($<=$, $>=$) at boundary violations. If the inequality is used to bound the model away from a noncomputable area, allow for the effect of machine precision. Consider the following code where the variable X takes on only positive values:

```
bounds  b>0;
model y=log(x*b);
```

A better constraint on the parameter B would be

```
bounds b>1e-20;
```

If you need to restrict an expression involving several parameters, for example, A+B<1, you can reparameterize the model so that the expression becomes a parameter.

If the iteration procedure sticks at the boundary of a constrained parameter, the computational method sets that parameter at its boundary and then searches the subspace defined by the remaining parameters. If the procedure cannot perform another step in the iteration using only the remaining parameters, the procedure stops. If the procedure can perform another step in the iteration using only the remaining parameters, the procedure performs the step and then uses the entire space (defined by all parameters) to try to perform the next step in the iteration.

For more information on valid expressions, see "SAS Expressions" in *SAS Language: Reference*.

BY Statement

BY *variables*;

A BY statement can be used with PROC NLIN to obtain separate analyses on observations in groups defined by the BY variables. When a BY statement appears, the procedure expects the input data set to be sorted in order of the BY variables.

If your input data set is not sorted in ascending order, use one of the following alternatives:

- Use the SORT procedure with a similar BY statement to sort the data.
- Use the BY statement options NOTSORTED or DESCENDING in the BY statement for the NLIN procedure. As a cautionary note, the NOTSORTED option does not mean that the data are unsorted, but rather means that the data are arranged in groups (according to values of the BY variables) and that these groups are not necessarily in alphabetical or increasing numeric order.
- Use the DATASETS procedure (in base SAS software) to create an index on the BY variables.

For more information on the BY statement, see the discussion in *SAS Language: Reference*. For more information on the DATASETS procedure, see the discussion in the *SAS Procedures Guide, Version 6, Third Edition*.

DER Statements

DER.parameter=expression;
DER.parameter.parameter=expression;

The DER statement specifies first or second partial derivatives. Use the first form shown above to specify first partial derivatives, and use the second form to specify second partial derivatives.

For most of the computational methods, you must specify the first partial derivative for each parameter to be estimated. For the NEWTON method, you must specify each of the first and the second derivatives. The expression can be an algebraic representation of the partial derivative of the expression in the MODEL statement with respect to the parameter or parameters that appear in the left-hand side of the DER statement. Numerical derivatives can also be used. The expression in the DER statement must conform to the rules for a valid SAS expression and can include any quantities that the MODEL statement expression contains.

The set of statements below specifies that a model

$$Y = \beta_0(1 - e^{-\beta_1 x})$$

be fitted by the modified Gauss-Newton method, where observed values of the dependent and independent variables are contained in the SAS variables Y and X, respectively.

```
proc nlin;
   parms b0=0 to 10
         b1=.01 to .09 by .005;
   model y=b0*(1-exp(-b1*x));
   der.b0=1-exp(-b1*x);
   der.b1=b0*x*exp(-b1*x);
```

Creating a variable TEMP=EXP(-B1*X) yields a more efficient way to express the model. The following statements illustrate the use of program statements in PROC NLIN:

```
proc nlin;
   parms b0=0 to 10
         b1=.01 to .09 by .005;
   temp=exp(-b1*x);
   model y=b0*(1-temp);
   der.b0=1-temp;
   der.b1=b0*x*temp;
```

This saves computer time, since the expression EXP($-$B1*X) is evaluated only once per program execution rather than three times, as in the earlier example. Programming statements are discussed in **Other Program Statements with PROC NLIN** later in this chapter.

If necessary, numerical rather than analytical derivatives can be used (see **Example 3** later in this chapter).

To fit the model using the NEWTON method, use the following statements:

```
proc nlin method=newton;
   parms b0=0 to 10
         b1=.01 to .09 by .005;
   temp=exp(-b1*x);
   model y=b0*(1-temp);
   der.b0=1-temp;
   der.b1=b0*x*temp;
   der.b0.b0=0;
   der.b0.b1=x*temp;
   der.b1.b1=-der.b1*x;
```

Note that you do not need to specify both DER.B0.B1 and DER.B1.B0. If you do specify both, the procedure interprets this as a duplicate specification and uses whichever derivative was specified last.

ID Statement

   ID variables;

The ID statement specifies additional variables to place in the output data set created by the OUTPUT statement. Any variable on the left side of any assignment statement is eligible. Also, the automatic variables created by the procedure can be specified. Variables in the input data set do not need to be specified in the ID statement since they are automatically included in the output data set.

MODEL Statement

   MODEL dependent=expression;

The MODEL statement defines the prediction equation by declaring the dependent variable and defining an expression that evaluates predicted values. The expression can be any valid SAS expression yielding a numeric result. The expression can include parameter names, variables in the data set, and variables created by program statements in the NLIN procedure. Any operators or functions that can be used in a DATA step can also be used in the MODEL statement.

A statement such as

    model y=*expression*;

is translated into the form

    model.y=*expression*;

using the compound variable name MODEL.Y to hold the predicted value. You can use this assignment as an alternative to the MODEL statement. Either a MODEL statement or an assignment to a compound variable such as MODEL.Y must appear.

OUTPUT Statement

OUTPUT OUT=*SAS-data-set keyword=names* <, . . . , *keyword=names*>;

The OUTPUT statement creates a new SAS data set that saves diagnostic measures calculated after fitting the model. At least one specification of the form *keyword=names* is required.

All the variables in the original data set are included in the new data set, along with variables created in the OUTPUT statement. These new variables contain the values of a variety of diagnostic measures that are calculated for each observation in the data set. If you want to create a permanent SAS data set, you must specify a two-level name. See "SAS Files" in *SAS Language: Reference* and "Introduction to DATA Step Processing" in *SAS Language and Procedures* for more information on permanent SAS data sets).

If an observation includes a missing value for one of the independent variables, both the predicted value and the residual value are missing for that observation. If the iterations fail to converge, all the values of all the variables named in the OUTPUT statement are missing values.

The variables below can be calculated and output to the new data set. However, with METHOD=DUD, the following statistics are not available: H, L95, L95M, STDP, STDR, STUDENT, U95, and U95M. These statistics are all calculated using the leverage, H, as defined below. For METHOD=DUD, the Jacobian is not available because no derivatives are specified with this method.

Details on the specifications in the OUTPUT statement are given below.

OUT=*SAS-data-set*

creates a SAS data set containing all the variables in the input data set. Also included are any ID variables specified in the ID statement, plus new variables whose names are specified in the OUTPUT statement.

keyword=names   specifies the statistics to include in the output data set and gives names to the new variables that contain the statistics. Specify a keyword for each desired statistic (see the following list of keywords), an equal sign, and the variable or variables to contain the statistic.

The keywords allowed and the statistics they represent are as follows:

H=*name*

names a variable to contain the leverage, $x_i(\mathbf{X'X})^-x_i'$, where F is the expression given in the MODEL statement, relating the response to the independent variables, $\mathbf{X} = \partial F / \partial \boldsymbol{\beta}$ and x_i is the ith row of $\mathbf{X}$. If the _WEIGHT_ automatic variable is specified, the leverage is $w_i x_i (\mathbf{X'WX})^- x_i'$. See **Computational Methods** later for definitions.

L95=*name*

names a variable to contain the lower endpoint of an approximate 95% confidence interval for an individual prediction. This includes the variance of the error as well as the variance of the parameter estimates. See also U95= below.

L95M=*name*

names a variable to contain the lower endpoint of an approximate 95% confidence interval for the expected value (mean). See also U95M= below.

PARMS=*names*

names variables in the output data set to contain parameter estimates. These can be the same variable names as listed in the PARAMETERS statement; however, you can choose new names for the parameters identified in the sequence from the PARAMETERS statement. The new names should be specified in the same order as the names on the PARAMETER statement. Note that for each of these new variables, the values are the same for every observation in the new data set.

PREDICTED=*name*

P=*name*

names a variable in the output data set to contain the predicted values of the dependent variable.

RESIDUAL=*name*

R=*name*

names a variable in the output data set to contain the residuals (actual values minus predicted values).

SSE=*name*

ESS=*name*

names a variable to include in the new data set. The values for the variable are the residual sums of squares finally determined by the procedure. The values of the variable are the same for every observation in the new data set.

STDI=*name*

names a variable to contain the standard error of the individual predicted value.

STDP=*name*

names a variable to contain the standard error of the mean predicted value.

STDR=*name*

names a variable to contain the standard error of the residual.

STUDENT=*name*
> names a variable to contain the studentized residuals, which are residuals divided by their standard errors.

U95M=*name*
> names a variable to contain the upper bound of an approximate 95% confidence interval for the expected value (mean). See also L95M= above.

U95=*name*
> names a variable to contain the upper bound of an approximate 95% confidence interval for an individual prediction. See also L95= above.

WEIGHT=*name*
> names a variable in the output data set that contains the _WEIGHT_ automatic variable.

PARAMETERS Statement

> **PARAMETERS** *parameter=values* <, . . . , *parameter=values*>;
> **PARMS** *parameter=values* <, . . . , *parameter=values*>;

A PARAMETERS (or PARMS) statement must follow the PROC NLIN statement. Several parameter names and values can appear. The parameter names must all be valid SAS names and must not duplicate the names of any variables in the data set to which the NLIN procedure is applied. Only one PARMS statement is allowed.

In each *parameter=values* specification, the parameter name identifies a parameter to be estimated, both in subsequent procedure statements and in the NLIN procedure's printed output. *Values* specify the possible starting values of the parameter.

Usually, only one value is specified for each parameter. If you specify several values for each parameter, NLIN evaluates the model at each point on the grid. The value specifications can take any of several forms:

m	a single value
$m1, m2, . . . , mn$	several values
m TO n	a sequence where m equals the starting value, n equals the ending value, and the increment equals 1.
m TO n BY i	a sequence where m equals the starting value, n equals the ending value, and the increment is i.
$m1, m2$ TO $m3$	mixed values and sequences.

This PARMS statement names five parameters and sets their possible starting values as shown:

```
parms  b0=0
       b1=4 to 8
       b2=0 to .6 by .2
       b3=1, 10, 100
       b4=0, .5, 1 to 4;
```

Possible starting values				
B0	B1	B2	B3	B4
0	4	0	1	0
	5	0.2	10	0.5
	6	0.4	100	1
	7	0.6		2
	8			3
				4

Residual sums of squares are calculated for each of the 1*5*4*3*6=360 combinations of possible starting values. (This can take a long time.)

See **Automatic Variables** in the **DETAILS** section for information on programming parameter starting values.

Other Program Statements with PROC NLIN

PROC NLIN is different from many other SAS procedures in that many of the statements normally used only in a DATA step can also be used in NLIN. Several SAS program statements can be used after the PROC NLIN statement. These statements can appear anywhere in PROC NLIN, but new variables must be created before they appear in other statements. For example, the following statements are valid since they create the variable TEMP before they use it in the MODEL statement:

```
proc nlin;
   parms b0=0 to 2 by 0.5 b1=0.01 to 0.09 by 0.01;
   temp=exp(-b1*x);
   model y=b0*(1-temp);
run;
```

The following statements are not valid because the variable TEMP is referred to before it is created:

```
proc nlin;
   parms b0=0 to 2 by 0.5 b1=0.01 to 0.09 by 0.01;
   model y=b0*(1-temp);
   temp=exp(-b1*x);
run;
```

PROC NLIN can process assignment statements, explicitly or implicitly subscripted ARRAY statements, explicitly or implicitly subscripted array references, IF statements, SAS functions, and program control statements. You can use program statements to create new SAS variables for the duration of the procedure. These variables are not permanently included in the data set to which NLIN is applied. Program statements can include variables in the DATA= data set, parameter names, variables created by preceding program statements within NLIN, and automatic variables used by NLIN.

All of the following SAS program statements can be used in PROC NLIN:

- ARRAY
- assignment
- CALL
- DO
- iterative DO
- DO UNTIL
- DO WHILE
- END
- FILE
- GO TO
- IF-THEN/ELSE
- LINK-RETURN
- PUT (defaults to the log)
- RETAIN
- RETURN
- SELECT
- sum.

The statements described above can use the automatic variables created by NLIN. Consult **Automatic Variables** for more information on automatic variables.

DETAILS

Missing Values

If the value of any one of the SAS variables involved in the model is missing from an observation, that observation is omitted from the analysis. If only the value of the dependent variable is missing, that observation has a predicted value calculated for it when you use an OUTPUT statement and specify the PREDICTED= option.

If an observation includes a missing value for one of the independent variables, both the predicted value and the residual value are missing for that observation. If the iterations fail to converge, all the values of all the variables named in the OUTPUT statement are missing values.

Automatic Variables

Several automatic variables are created by PROC NLIN and can be used in PROC NLIN program statements.

Automatic Variables Whose Values Are Set by PROC NLIN

The values of the six automatic variables below are set by NLIN and should not be reset to a different value by programming statements.

ERROR   is set to 1 if a numerical error or invalid argument to a function occurs during the current execution of the program. It is reset to 0 before each new execution.

ITER   represents the current iteration number. The variable _ITER_ is set to -1 during the grid search phase and to missing ('.') when the iterations have converged. For METHOD=DUD, _ITER_ is set to very large negative numbers during the initialization phase.

MODEL   is set to 1 for passes through the data when only the predicted values are needed, not the derivatives. It is 0 when both predicted values and derivatives are needed. If your derivative calculations consume a lot of time, you can save resources by coding

```
if _model_ then return;
```

after your MODEL statement but before your derivative calculations.

_N_   indicates the number of times the NLIN step has been executed. It is never reset for successive passes through the data set.

OBS   indicates the observation number in the data set for the current program execution. It is reset to 1 to start each pass through the data set (unlike _N_).

SSE   has the error sum of squares of the last iteration. During the grid search phase, _SSE_ is set to 0. For iteration 0, _SSE_ is set to the SSE associated with the point chosen from the grid search.

Automatic Variables Used to Determine Convergence Criteria

The two automatic variables _HALVE_ and _LOSS_ can be used to determine convergence criteria.

HALVE   is an automatic variable that is checked to control step-halving during execution. The value of _HALVE_ is the maximum number of step-halvings that are done during an iteration before a nonconvergence message is printed and execution terminates. The value of _HALVE_ overrides the value of the STEP= option in the PROC NLIN statement.

LOSS   is used to determine the criterion function for convergence and step-shortening. PROC NLIN looks for the variable _LOSS_ in the program statements and, if it is defined, uses the (weighted) sum of this value instead of residual sum of squares to determine the criterion function for convergence and step-shortening. This feature is useful in certain types of maximum-likelihood estimation where the residual sum of squares is not the basic criterion.

Weighted Regression with the _WEIGHT_ and _WGTJPJ_ Automatic Variables

The _WEIGHT_ and _WGTJPJ_ automatic variables allow PROC NLIN to fit a large class of models. To get weighted least squares estimates of parameters, the _WEIGHT_ variable can be given a value in an assignment statement:

```
_weight_=expression;
```

When this statement is included, the expression on the right side of the assignment statement is evaluated for each observation in the data set to be analyzed. When a variable name is given after the equal sign, the values of the variable are taken as the weight. The larger the _WEIGHT_ value, the more importance the observation is given. The _WEIGHT_ variable is used in the calculation of the Jacobian and gradient at each point.

If the _WEIGHT_= statement is not used, the default value of 1 is used, and regular least squares estimates are obtained.

To weight the calculation of the Jacobian, use the _WGTJPJ_ variable. The value of the _WGTJPJ_ variable is assigned in the same manner as the _WEIGHT_ variable. The default value of the _WGTJPJ_ variable is the value of the _WEIGHT_ variable. For more information on the computational aspects of the _WEIGHT_ and _WGTJPJ_ variables, see the section on computational methods.

Treatment of negative and missing values in the _WEIGHT_ and _WGTJPJ_ variables is as follows:

- If either variable is missing the observation is deleted.
- When _WGTJPJ_ is negative the observation is deleted.
- If _WGTJPJ_ is nonmissing and positive, the value of _WEIGHT_ can be negative.
- If _WGTJPJ_ is not specified and _WEIGHT_ is negative, the observation is deleted.

Modifying the Search Direction with the _RESID_ Automatic Variable

The _LOSS_ variable can be used to modify the criterion function. To modify the direction, use the _RESID_ variable. See **Computational Methods** for more information.

Example: Using Automatic Variables to Specify Starting Values

For the derivative methods (GAUSS, MARQUARDT, and GRADIENT), the parameter values in the procedure are updated after the first observation of iteration 0. If you want to supply starting parameter values in your program (rather than using the values in the PARMS statement), follow this example:

```
proc nlin;
   parms b0=1 b1=1;
   if _iter_= -1 then
      do;
         b0=b0start;
         b1=b1start;
      end;
   model y=expression;
   der.b0=expression;
   der.b1=expression;
run;
```

where B0START and B1START are in the input data set or calculated with program statements.

Troubleshooting

This section describes a number of problems that can occur in your analysis with PROC NLIN.

Excessive Time

If you specify a grid of starting values that contains many points, the analysis may take excessive time since the procedure must go through the entire data set for each point on the grid.

The analysis may also take excessive time if your problem takes many iterations to converge since each iteration requires as much time as a linear regression with predicted values and residuals calculated.

Dependencies

The matrix of partial derivatives may be singular, possibly indicating an over-parameterized model. For example, if B0 starts at 0 in the following model, the derivatives for B1 are all 0 for the first iteration:

```
parms b0=0 b1=.022;
model pop=b0*exp(b1*(year-1790));
der.b0=exp(b1*(year-1790));
der.b1=(year-1790)*b0*exp(b1*(year-1790));
```

The first iteration changes a subset of the parameters; then the procedure can make progress in succeeding iterations. This singularity problem is local. The next example shows a global problem.

You may have a term B2 in the exponent that is nonidentifiable because it trades roles with B0.

```
parms b0=3.9 b1=.022 b2=0;
model pop=b0*exp(b1*(year-1790)+b2);
der.b0=exp(b1*(year-1790)+b2);
der.b1=(year-1790)*b0*exp(b1*(year-1790)+b2);
der.b2=b0*exp(b1*(year-1790)+b2);
```

In the above model, B2 and B0 actually share the same role. You should rewrite the model, omitting B2.

Unable to Improve

The method may lead to steps that do not improve the estimates even after a series of step-halvings. If this happens, the procedure issues a message stating that it was unable to make further progress, but it then prints the following warning message and prints out the results:

```
PROC NLIN failed to converge
```

This often means that NLIN has not converged at all. You should check the derivatives very closely and check the sum-of-squares error surface before proceeding. If NLIN has not converged, try a different set of starting values, a different METHOD= specification, the G4 option, or a different model.

Divergence

The iterative process may diverge, resulting in overflows in computations. It is also possible that parameters will enter a space where arguments to such functions as LOG and SQRT become illegal. For example, consider the following model:

```
parms b=1;
model y=(1/b)*x;
```

Suppose that Y happens to be all zero and X is nonzero. There is no least squares estimate for B since the SSE declines as B approaches infinity or minus infinity. The same model could be parameterized with no problem into Y=A*X, where A=1/B.

If you actually run the model, the procedure claims to converge after awhile since, by default, it measures convergence with respect to changes in the sum-of-squares error rather than to the parameter estimates. If you have divergence problems, try reparameterizing, selecting different starting values, or including a BOUNDS statement.

Local Minimum

The program may converge nicely to a local rather than a global minimum. For example, consider the following model:

```
parms a=1 b=-1;
model y=(1-a*x)*(1-b*x);
der.a=-x*(1-b*x);
der.b=-x*(1-a*x);
```

Once a solution is found, due to the symmetry of the model with respect to the parameters A and B, an equivalent solution with the same LOSS can be obtained by interchanging the roles of the parameters and switching the values of A and B.

Discontinuities

The computational methods assume that the model is a continuous and smooth function of the parameters. If this is not true, the method does not work. For example, the following models do not work:

```
model y=a+int(b*x);              /* a discontinuous model */
model y=a+b*x+4*(z>c);           /* a discontinuous model */
```

Responding to Trouble

NLIN does not necessarily produce a good solution the first time. Much depends on specifying good starting values for the parameters. You can specify a grid of values in the PARMS statement to search for good starting values. While most practical models should give you no trouble, other models may require switching to a different iteration method or an inverse computation method. METHOD=MARQUARDT sometimes works when the default method (Gauss-Newton) does not work.

Computational Methods

For the system of equations represented by the nonlinear model

$$\mathbf{Y} = \mathbf{F}(\beta_0^*, \beta_1^*, \ldots, \beta_r^*, \mathbf{Z}_1, \mathbf{Z}_2, \ldots, \mathbf{Z}_n) + \varepsilon = \mathbf{F}(\boldsymbol{\beta}^*) + \varepsilon$$

where $\mathbf{Z}$ is a matrix of the independent variables, $\boldsymbol{\beta}^*$ is a vector of the unknown parameters, ε is the error vector, and $\mathbf{F}$ is a function of the independent variables and the parameters; there are two approaches to solving for the minimum. The first method is to minimize

$$L(\boldsymbol{\beta}) = 0.5\, \mathbf{e}'\mathbf{e} \quad \text{where } \mathbf{e} = \mathbf{Y} - \mathbf{F}(\boldsymbol{\beta}) \text{ and } \quad \boldsymbol{\beta} \text{ is an estimate of } \boldsymbol{\beta}^*.$$

The second method is to solve the nonlinear "normal" equations

$$\mathbf{X}'\mathbf{F}(\boldsymbol{\beta}) = \mathbf{X}'\mathbf{e}$$

where

$$\mathbf{X} = \partial \mathbf{F} / \partial \boldsymbol{\beta} \quad .$$

In the nonlinear situation, both $\mathbf{X}$ and $\mathbf{F}(\boldsymbol{\beta})$ are functions of $\boldsymbol{\beta}$ and a closed-form solution generally does not exist. Thus NLIN uses an iterative process: a starting value for $\boldsymbol{\beta}$ is chosen and continually improved until the error sum of squares $\mathbf{e}'\mathbf{e}$ ($L(\boldsymbol{\beta})$) is minimized.

The iterative techniques NLIN uses are similar to a series of linear regressions involving the matrix $\mathbf{X}$ evaluated for the current values of $\boldsymbol{\beta}$ and $\mathbf{e}=\mathbf{Y}-\mathbf{F}(\boldsymbol{\beta})$, the residuals evaluated for the current values of $\boldsymbol{\beta}$.

The iterative process begins at some point $\boldsymbol{\beta}_0$. Then $\mathbf{X}$ and $\mathbf{Y}$ are used to compute a $\boldsymbol{\Delta}$ such that

$$L(\boldsymbol{\beta}_0 + \alpha\boldsymbol{\Delta}) < L(\boldsymbol{\beta}_0) \quad .$$

The four methods differ in how $\boldsymbol{\Delta}$ is computed to change the vector of parameters.

Steepest descent	$\boldsymbol{\Delta} = \mathbf{X}'\mathbf{e}$
Gauss-Newton	$\boldsymbol{\Delta} = (\mathbf{X}'\mathbf{X})^{-}\mathbf{X}'\mathbf{e}$
Newton	$\boldsymbol{\Delta} = \mathbf{G}^{-}\mathbf{X}'\mathbf{e}$
Marquardt	$\boldsymbol{\Delta} = (\mathbf{X}'\mathbf{X} + \lambda\,\text{diag}\,(\mathbf{X}'\mathbf{X}))^{-}\mathbf{X}'\mathbf{e}$

The default method used to compute $(\mathbf{X}'\mathbf{X})^{-}$ is the sweep operator producing a g2 inverse. In some cases it would be preferable to use a g4 or Moore-Penrose inverse. If the G4 option is specified in the PROC NLIN statement, a g4 inverse is used to calculate $\boldsymbol{\Delta}$ on each iteration. If the G4SINGULAR option is specified, a g4 inverse is used to calculate $\boldsymbol{\Delta}$ when $\mathbf{X}'\mathbf{X}$ is singular.

Steepest Descent (Gradient)

The steepest descent method is based on the gradient of $L(\boldsymbol{\beta})$.

$$0.5 \, \partial L(\boldsymbol{\beta}) / \partial \boldsymbol{\beta} = -\mathbf{X}'\mathbf{Y} + \mathbf{X}'\mathbf{F}(\boldsymbol{\beta}) = -\mathbf{X}'\mathbf{e} \quad .$$

The quantity $-\mathbf{X}'\mathbf{e}$ is the gradient along which $L(\boldsymbol{\beta})$ increases. Thus $\boldsymbol{\Delta}=\mathbf{X}'\mathbf{e}$ is the direction of steepest descent.

If the automatic variables _WEIGHT_ and _RESID_ are used, then

$$\boldsymbol{\Delta}=\mathbf{X}'\mathbf{W}^{\mathbf{G}}\mathbf{r}$$

is the direction, where

$\mathbf{W}^{\mathbf{G}}$ is an $n \times n$ diagonal matrix with elements w_i^{G} of weights from _WEIGHT_. Each element w_i^{G} contains the value of _WEIGHT_ for the i th observation.

$\mathbf{r}$ is a vector with elements r_i. Each element r_i contains the value of _RESID_ evaluated at the i th observation.

Using the method of steepest descent, let

$$\boldsymbol{\beta}_{k+1} = \boldsymbol{\beta}_k + \alpha\boldsymbol{\Delta}$$

where the scalar α is chosen such that

$$L(\boldsymbol{\beta}_k + \alpha\boldsymbol{\Delta}) < L(\boldsymbol{\beta}_k) \quad .$$

Note: The steepest descent method may converge very slowly and is therefore not generally recommended. It is sometimes useful when the initial values are poor.

Newton

The Newton method uses the second derivatives and solves the equation

$$\boldsymbol{\Delta} = \mathbf{G}^-\mathbf{X'e}$$

where

$$\mathbf{G} = (\mathbf{X'X}) + \Sigma^n_{i=1}\,\mathbf{H}_i\,(\boldsymbol{\beta})e_i$$

and $\mathbf{H}_i\,(\boldsymbol{\beta})$ is the hessian of e_i :

$$[\mathbf{H}_i]_{jk} = [\partial^2\,e_i\,/\,\partial\boldsymbol{\beta}_j\,\partial\boldsymbol{\beta}_k]_{jk}$$

If the automatic variables _WEIGHT_, _WGTJPJ_, and _RESID_ are used then

$$\boldsymbol{\Delta} = \mathbf{G}^-\mathbf{X'W}^G\mathbf{r}$$

is the direction, where

$$\mathbf{G} = \mathbf{X'W}^J\mathbf{X} + \Sigma^n_{i=1}\mathbf{H}_i\,(\boldsymbol{\beta})w_i^J r_i$$

and

$\mathbf{W}^G$ is an $n \times n$ diagonal matrix with elements w_i^G from _WEIGHT_. Each element w_i^G contains the value of _WEIGHT_ for the ith observation.

$\mathbf{W}^J$ is an $n \times n$ diagonal matrix with elements w_i^J from _WGTJPJ_. Each element w_i^J contains the value of _WGTJPJ_ for the ith observation.

$\mathbf{r}$ is a vector with elements r_i from _RESID_. Each element r_i contains the value of _RESID_ evaluated for the ith observation.

Gauss-Newton

The Gauss-Newton method uses the Taylor series

$$\mathbf{F}(\boldsymbol{\beta}) = \mathbf{F}(\boldsymbol{\beta}_0) + \mathbf{X}(\boldsymbol{\beta} - \boldsymbol{\beta}_0) + \ldots$$

where $\mathbf{X} = \partial\mathbf{F}/\partial\boldsymbol{\beta}$ is evaluated at $\boldsymbol{\beta} = \boldsymbol{\beta}_0$.

Substituting the first two terms of this series into the normal equations

$$\mathbf{X'F(\beta)} = \mathbf{X'Y}$$

$$\mathbf{X'(F(\beta_0) + X(\beta - \beta_0))} = \mathbf{X'Y}$$

$$\mathbf{(X'X)(\beta - \beta_0)} = \mathbf{X'Y} - \mathbf{X'F(\beta_0)}$$

$$\mathbf{(X'X)\Delta} = \mathbf{X'e}$$

and therefore

$$\mathbf{\Delta} = \mathbf{(X'X)^- X'e} \ .$$

Note: If $\mathbf{X'X}$ is singular or becomes singular, NLIN computes $\mathbf{\Delta}$ using a generalized inverse for the iterations after singularity occurs. If $\mathbf{X'X}$ is still singular for the last iteration, the solution should be examined.

If the automatic variables _WEIGHT_,_WGTJPJ_, and _RESID_ are used then

$$\mathbf{\Delta} = \mathbf{(X'W^J X)^- X'W^G r}$$

is the direction, where

$\mathbf{W^G}$ is an n$\times$n diagonal matrix with elements w_i^G from _WEIGHT_. Each element w_i^G contains the value of _WEIGHT_ for the i th observation.

$\mathbf{W^J}$ is an n$\times$n diagonal matrix with elements w_i^J from _WGTJPJ_. Each element w_i^J contains the value of _WGTJPJ_ for the i th observation.

$\mathbf{r}$ is a vector with elements r_i from _RESID_. Each element r_i contains the value of _RESID_ evaluated for the i th observation.

Marquardt

The Marquardt updating formula is as follows:

$$\mathbf{\Delta} = \mathbf{(X'X + \lambda diag\,(X'X))^- X'e} \ .$$

If the automatic variables _WEIGHT_,_WGTJPJ_, and _RESID_ are used then

$$\mathbf{\Delta} = \mathbf{(X'W^J X + \lambda diag\,(X'W^J X))^- X'W^G r}$$

is the direction, where

$\mathbf{W^G}$ is an n$\times$n diagonal matrix with elements w_i^G from _WEIGHT_. Each element w_i^G contains the value of _WEIGHT_ for the i th observation.

$\mathbf{W^J}$ is an n$\times$n diagonal matrix with elements w_i^J from _WGTJPJ_. Each element w_i^J contains the value of _WGTJPJ_ for the i th observation.

$\mathbf{r}$ is a vector with elements r_i from _RESID_. Each element r_i contains the value of _RESID_ evaluated for the i th observation.

The Marquardt method is a compromise between Gauss-Newton and steepest descent (Marquardt 1963). As $\lambda \to 0$, the direction approaches Gauss-Newton. As $\lambda \to \infty$, the direction approaches steepest descent.

Marquardt's studies indicate that the average angle between Gauss-Newton and steepest descent directions is about 90°. A choice of λ between 0 and infinity produces a compromise direction.

By default, PROC NLIN chooses $\lambda = 10^{-3}$ to start and computes a Δ. If $L(\beta_0 + \Delta) < L(\beta_0)$, then $\lambda = \lambda/10$ for the next iteration. Each time $L(\beta_0 + \Delta) > L(\beta_0)$, then $\lambda = \lambda*10$.

If G4 is specified in the PROC NLIN statement, λ is determined using the eigenvalues of $(X'X)$. If the smallest eigenvalue is less than 0.00001, λ is the absolute value of the smallest eigenvalue plus 0.00001. Otherwise, λ is 0. This method tries to pick the smallest value of λ such that $(X'X + \lambda\,\text{diag}(X'X))$ is positive definite. If TAU or RHO is specified, a step-size search is conducted.

If TAU or RHO is specified but G4 is not, NLIN chooses $\lambda = $TAU to start and computes a Δ. If $L(\beta_0 + \Delta) < L(\beta_0)$, then $\lambda = \lambda/$RHO for the next iteration. Each time $L(\beta + \Delta) > L(\beta_0)$, then $\lambda = \lambda*$RHO. In the Marquardt method, the default value for TAU is 0.01 and for RHO is 10.

Note: If the loss $L(\beta)$ decreases on each iteration, then $\lambda \to 0$, and you are essentially using Gauss-Newton. If the loss does not improve, then λ is increased until you are moving in the steepest descent direction.

Marquardt's method is equivalent to performing a series of ridge regressions and is useful when the parameter estimates are highly correlated or the objective function is not well approximated by a quadratic.

Secant Method (DUD)

The multivariate secant method is like Gauss-Newton, except that the derivatives are estimated from the history of iterations rather than supplied analytically. The method is also called the *method of false position* or the DUD method for Doesn't Use Derivatives (Ralston and Jennrich 1978). If only one parameter is being estimated, the derivative for iteration $i+1$ can be estimated from the previous two iterations:

$$der_{i+1} = (\hat{Y}_i - \hat{Y}_{i-1}) / (b_i - b_{i-1}) \quad .$$

When k parameters are to be estimated, the method uses the last $k+1$ iterations to estimate the derivatives.

Step-Size Search

The default method of finding the step size k is step-halving using SMETHOD=HALVE. If $L(\beta_0 + \Delta) > L(\beta_0)$, compute $L(\beta_0 + 0.5\Delta)$, $L(\beta_0 + 0.25\Delta)$, . . . , until a smaller loss L is found.

If SMETHOD=GOLDEN is specified, the step size k is determined by a golden section search. The parameter TAU determines the length of the initial interval to be searched, with the interval having length TAU or 2*TAU, depending on $L(\beta_0 + \Delta)$. The RHO parameter specifies how fine the search is to be. The loss L at each endpoint of the interval is evaluated, and a new subinterval is chosen. The size of the interval is reduced until its length is less than RHO. One pass through the data is required each time the interval is reduced. Hence, if RHO is very small relative to TAU, a large amount of time can be spent determining a step size. For more information on the GOLDEN search, see Kennedy and Gentle (1980).

If SMETHOD=ARMGOLD is specified, the step size is determined by the Goldstein-Armijo method. This method attempts to avoid premature termination caused by small step sizes. The step size used is the first term of the sequence $k=1, 0.5, 0.25, \ldots$, that satisfies the following equation:

$$L(\boldsymbol{\beta}^i + k\Delta) \leq L(\boldsymbol{\beta}^i) - \tau k \mathbf{X}'\mathbf{e}\Delta \qquad \tau \epsilon (0,0.5)$$

where τ is the default value of 0.5 or the specified TAU value. However, if you specify TAU>0.5, the default value of 0.5 is used instead.

If SMETHOD=CUBIC is specified, NLIN performs a cubic interpolation to estimate the step size. If the estimated step size does not result in a decrease in the loss L, step-halving is used.

Output Data Sets

The data set produced by the OUTEST= option in the PROC NLIN statement contains the parameter estimates on each iteration including the grid search. The variable _ITER_ contains the iteration number. The variable _TYPE_ denotes whether the observation contains iteration parameter estimates (ITER), final parameter estimates (FINAL), or covariance estimates (COVB). For the DUD method, _TYPE_ is set to DUD for iterations with _ITER_ set to a large negative number. The variable _NAME_ contains the parameter name for covariances, and the variable _SSE_ contains the objective function value for the parameter estimates.

The data set produced by the OUTPUT statement contains statistics calculated for each observation. In addition, the data set contains all the variables in the input data set and any ID variables that are specified in the ID statement.

Printed Output

In addition to the output data sets, NLIN also produces the items below:

1. the estimates of the parameters and the residual Sums of Squares determined in each iteration
2. a list of the residual Sums of Squares associated with all or some of the combinations of possible starting values of parameters.

If the convergence criterion is met, NLIN prints

3. an analysis-of-variance table including as sources of variation Regression, Residual, Uncorrected Total, and Corrected Total
4. Parameter Estimates
5. an asymptotically valid standard error of the estimate, Asymptotic Standard Error. If NLIN fails to converge, the Asymptotic Standard Error is set to zero.
6. an Asymptotic 95% Confidence Interval for the estimate of the parameter
7. an Asymptotic Correlation Matrix of the parameters.

EXAMPLES

Example 1:   Negative Exponential Growth Curve

This example demonstrates typical NLIN specifications for Marquardt's method and a grid of starting values. The predicted values and residuals are output for plotting. The following statements produce **Output 29.1**:

```
title 'NEGATIVE EXPONENTIAL: Y=B0*(1-EXP(-B1*X))';
data a;
   input x y @@;
   cards;
```

```
020 0.57 030 0.72 040 0.81 050 0.87 060 0.91 070 0.94
080 0.95 090 0.97 100 0.98 110 0.99 120 1.00 130 0.99
140 0.99 150 1.00 160 1.00 170 0.99 180 1.00 190 1.00
200 0.99 210 1.00
;

proc nlin best=10 method=marquardt;
   parms b0=0 to 2 by .5  b1=.01 to .09 by .01;
   model y=b0*(1-exp(-b1*x));
   der.b0=1-exp(-b1*x);
   der.b1=b0*x*exp(-b1*x);
   output out=b p=yhat r=yresid;
run;
proc plot data=b;
   plot y*x='a' yhat*x='p' / overlay vpos=25;
   plot yresid*x / vref=0 vpos=25;
run;
```

Output 29.1   Negative Exponential Growth Function: PROC NLIN
METHOD=MARQUARDT and PROC PLOT

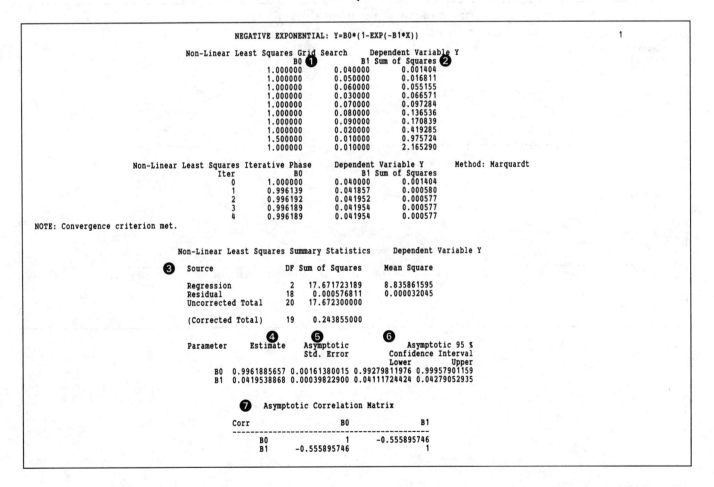

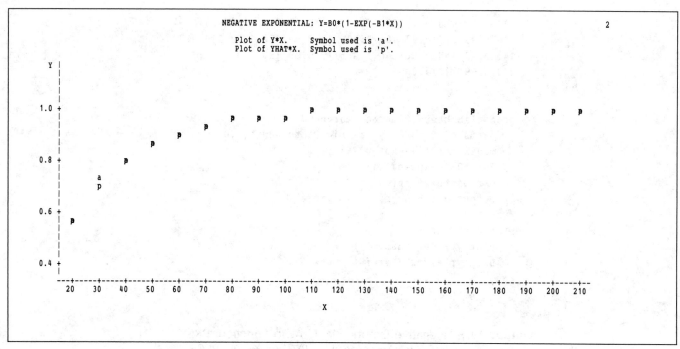

NEGATIVE EXPONENTIAL: Y=B0*(1-EXP(-B1*X))   2

Plot of Y*X.   Symbol used is 'a'.
Plot of YHAT*X. Symbol used is 'p'.

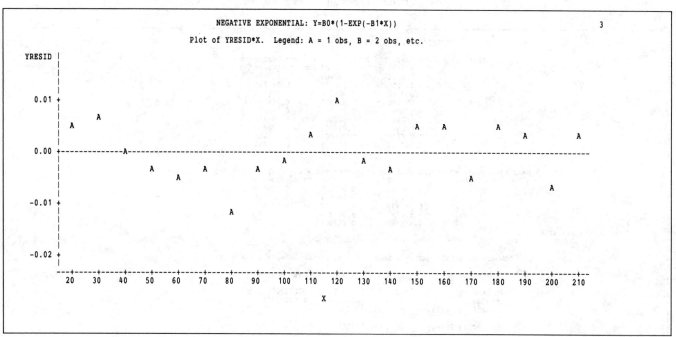

NEGATIVE EXPONENTIAL: Y=B0*(1-EXP(-B1*X))   3

Plot of YRESID*X. Legend: A = 1 obs, B = 2 obs, etc.

Example 2: CES Production Function

The CES production function in economics models the quantity produced as a function of inputs such as capital, K, and labor, L. Arrow, Chenery, Minhas, and Solow developed the CES production function and named it for its property of constant elasticity of substitution. A is the efficiency parameter, D is the distribution or factor share parameter, and R is the substitution parameter. This example was described by Lutkepohl in the work by Judge et al. (1980). The following statements produce **Output 29.2**:

```
title 'CES MODEL: LOGQ = B0 + A*LOG(D*L**R+(1-D)*K**R)';
data ces;
   input l k logq aa;
   cards;
.228 .802 -1.359   .258 .249 -1.695
.821 .771   .193   .767 .511  -.649
.495 .758  -.165   .487 .425  -.270
.678 .452  -.473   .748 .817   .031
.727 .845  -.563   .695 .958  -.125
.458 .084 -2.218   .981 .021 -3.633
.002 .295 -5.586   .429 .277  -.773
.231 .546 -1.315   .664 .129 -1.678
.631 .017 -3.879   .059 .906 -2.301
.811 .223 -1.377   .758 .145 -2.270
.050 .161 -2.539   .823 .006 -5.150
.483 .836  -.324   .682 .521  -.253
.116 .930 -1.530   .440 .495  -.614
.456 .185 -1.151   .342 .092 -2.089
.358 .485  -.951   .162 .934 -1.275
;

proc nlin data=ces;
   parms b0=1 a=-1 d=.5 r=-1;
   lr=l**r;
   kr=k**r;
   z=d*lr+(1-d)*kr;
   model logq=b0+a*log(z);
   der.b0=1;
   der.a=log(z);
   der.d=(a/z)*(lr-kr);
   der.r=(a/z)*(d*log(l)*lr+(1-d)*log(k)*kr);
run;
```

Output 29.2   CES Production Function: PROC NLIN

```
                        CES MODEL: LOGQ = B0 + A*LOG(D*L**R+(1-D)*K**R)                        1
            Non-Linear Least Squares Iterative Phase        Dependent Variable LOGQ        Method: Gauss-Newton
            Iter          B0            A            D                R     Sum of Squares
             0       1.000000    -1.000000     0.500000        -1.000000      37.096512
             1       0.533488    -0.481091     0.450601        -1.499936      35.486564
             2       0.320516    -0.307656     0.383160        -2.309682      22.690597
             3       0.124790    -0.287428     0.301408        -3.418181       1.845468
             4       0.124044    -0.307921     0.317150        -3.204351       1.833362
             5       0.122933    -0.355632     0.349730        -2.800352       1.820337
             6       0.125085    -0.324295     0.330214        -3.089113       1.774004
             7       0.124011    -0.342505     0.340530        -2.951604       1.762108
             8       0.124713    -0.332754     0.334596        -3.038983       1.761177
             9       0.124346    -0.338244     0.337849        -2.993735       1.761057
            10       0.124563    -0.335197     0.336024        -3.020171       1.761043
            11       0.124446    -0.336890     0.337035        -3.005870       1.761040
            12       0.124512    -0.335947     0.336471        -3.013966       1.761040
            13       0.124476    -0.336471     0.336785        -3.009505       1.761039
            14       0.124496    -0.336179     0.336610        -3.012002       1.761039
            15       0.124485    -0.336341     0.336707        -3.010617       1.761039
NOTE: Convergence criterion met.
```

```
            Non-Linear Least Squares Summary Statistics     Dependent Variable LOGQ

                Source            DF   Sum of Squares     Mean Square

                Regression         4    130.00369371       32.50092343
                Residual          26      1.76103929        0.06773228
                Uncorrected Total 30    131.76473300

                (Corrected Total) 29     61.28965430


                Parameter    Estimate      Asymptotic              Asymptotic 95 %
                                           Std. Error          Confidence Interval
                                                              Lower            Upper
                    B0     0.124485105   0.0783429642    -0.0365498914    0.2855201005
                     A    -0.336341238   0.2721800618    -0.8958109440    0.2231284680
                     D     0.336707458   0.1360850556     0.0569828319    0.6164320846
                     R    -3.010617415   2.3229032585    -7.7853756933    1.7641408635


                            Asymptotic Correlation Matrix

            Corr             B0              A              D              R
            --------------------------------------------------------------------
              B0              1      0.2964899511    -0.176549933    -0.32669583
               A    0.2964899511              1     -0.783557332    -0.999129892
               D   -0.176549933    -0.783557332              1      0.7833628736
               R    -0.32669583    -0.999129892     0.7833628736             1
```

Example 3:   Probit Model with Numerical Derivatives

This example fits the population of the United States across time to the cumulative normal distribution function. Numerical derivatives are coded since the analytic derivatives are messy.

The C parameter is the upper population limit. The A and B parameters scale time. The following statements produce **Output 29.3**:

```
title 'U.S. POPULATION GROWTH';
title2 'PROBIT MODEL WITH NUMERICAL DERIVATIVES';
data uspop;
   input pop :6.3 ƏƏ;
   retain year 1780;
   year=year+10;
   yearsq=year*year;
   cards;
3929 5308 7239 9638 12866 17069 23191 31443 39818 50155
62947 75994 91972 105710 122775 131669 151325 179323 203211
;
```

```
proc nlin data=uspop;
    parms a=-2.4 b=.012 c=400;
    delta=.0001;
    x=year-1790;
    pophat=c*probnorm(a+b*x);
    model pop=pophat;
    der.a=(pophat-c*probnorm((a-delta)+b*x)) / delta;
    der.b=(pophat-c*probnorm(a+(b-delta)*x)) / delta;
    der.c=pophat / c;
    output out=p p=predict;
run;
proc plot data=p;
    plot pop*year predict*year='p' / overlay vpos=30;
run;
```

Output 29.3   Probit Model with Numerical Derivatives: PROC NLIN

```
                            U.S. POPULATION GROWTH                                      1
                        PROBIT MODEL WITH NUMERICAL DERIVATIVES

        Non-Linear Least Squares Iterative Phase      Dependent Variable POP      Method: Gauss-Newton
             Iter           A              B              C Sum of Squares
                0      -2.400000       0.012000      400.000000      7174.590805
                1      -2.271908       0.012623      399.066499       209.327927
                2      -2.302425       0.012661      404.804742       177.392064
                3      -2.302788       0.012628      407.072751       177.370044
                4      -2.302819       0.012629      407.079801       177.369804
                5      -2.302818       0.012629      407.082668       177.369803
NOTE: Convergence criterion met.


        Non-Linear Least Squares Summary Statistics      Dependent Variable POP

            Source            DF Sum of Squares    Mean Square

            Regression         3   164227.89925    54742.63308
            Residual          16      177.36980       11.08561
            Uncorrected Total 19   164405.26906

            (Corrected Total)  18    71922.76175


            Parameter    Estimate     Asymptotic              Asymptotic 95 %
                                      Std. Error           Confidence Interval
                                                           Lower          Upper
                  A     -2.3028183   0.032832711    -2.37242015    -2.23321637
                  B      0.0126285   0.000956986     0.01059980     0.01465722
                  C    407.0826677  61.784898470   276.10518493   538.06015048


                            Asymptotic Correlation Matrix

            Corr                 A              B              C
            ------------------------------------------------------------
                  A              1   -0.007910181   -0.219797799
                  B   -0.007910181              1   -0.972273297
                  C   -0.219797799   -0.972273297              1
```

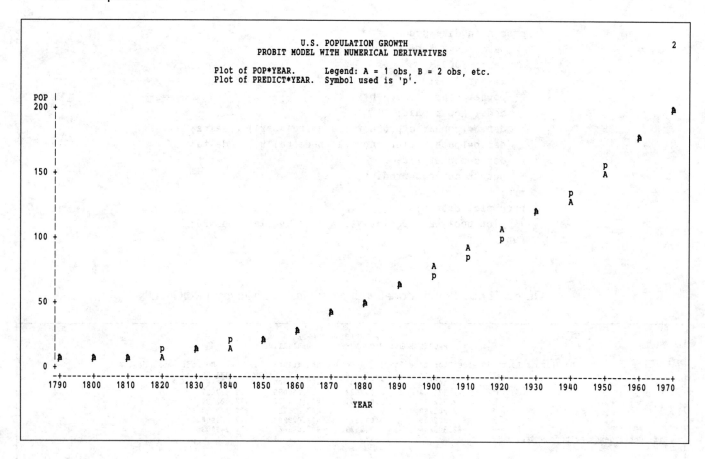

U.S. POPULATION GROWTH
PROBIT MODEL WITH NUMERICAL DERIVATIVES

Plot of POP*YEAR.   Legend: A = 1 obs, B = 2 obs, etc.
Plot of PREDICT*YEAR. Symbol used is 'p'.

Example 4: Segmented Model

From theoretical considerations you can hypothesize that

$$y = a + bx + cx^2 \quad \text{if } x < x_0$$

$$y = p \qquad\qquad\quad \text{if } x > x_0 \; .$$

That is, for values of x less than x_0, the equation relating y and x is quadratic (a parabola), and for values of x greater than x_0, the equation is constant (a horizontal line). PROC NLIN can fit such a segmented model even when the joint point, x_0, is unknown.

The curve must be continuous (the two sections must meet at x_0), and the curve must be smooth (the first derivatives with respect to x are the same at x_0).

These conditions imply that

$$x_0 = -b / 2c$$

$$p = a - b^2 / 4c \; .$$

The segmented equation includes only three parameters; however, the equation is nonlinear with respect to these parameters.

You can write program statements with PROC NLIN to conditionally execute different sections of code for the two parts of the model, depending on whether x is less than x_0.

A PUT statement is used to print the constrained parameters every time the program is executed for the first observation (where $x=1$). The following statements produce **Output 29.4**:

```
/*      FITTING A SEGMENTED MODEL USING NLIN               */
/*                                                         */
/*        |                                                */
/*     Y  | QUADRATIC               PLATEAU                */
/*        | Y=A+B*X+C*X*X           Y=P                    */
/*        |                         .....................  */
/*        |                  .      :                      */
/*        |               .         :                      */
/*        |             .           :                      */
/*        |           .             :                      */
/*        |         .               :                      */
/*        +-------------------------------------------X    */
/*                          X0                             */
/*                                                         */
/*   CONTINUITY RESTRICTION: P=A+B*X0+C*X0**2              */
/*   SMOOTHNESS RESTRICTION: 0=B+2*C*X0 SO X0=-B/(2*C)     */
/*                                                         */

title 'QUADRATIC MODEL WITH PLATEAU';
data a;
   input y x aa;
   cards;
.46 1 .47  2 .57  3 .61  4 .62  5 .68  6 .69  7
.78 8 .70  9 .74 10 .77 11 .78 12 .74 13 .80 13
.80 15 .78 16
;

proc nlin;
   parms a=.45 b=.05 c=-.0025;
   file print;
   x0=-.5*b / c;               /* Estimate Join Point    */
   db=-.5 / c;                 /* Deriv of X0 wrt B      */
   dc=.5*b / c**2;             /* Deriv of X0 wrt C      */
   if x<x0 then               /* Quadratic Part of Model */
      do;
         model y=a+b*x+c*x*x;
         der.a=1;
         der.b=x;
         der.c=x*x;
      end;
   else                        /* Plateau Part of Model */
      do;
         model y=a+b*x0+c*x0*x0;
         der.a=1;
         der.b=x0+b*db+2*c*x0*db;
         der.c=b*dc+x0*x0+2*c*x0*dc;
      end;
```

```
        if _obs_=1 & _model_=1 then          /* Print out if 1st obs */
           do;
              plateau=a+b*x0+c*x0*x0;
              put x0=plateau=;
           end;
        output out=b predicted=yp;
     run;
     proc plot;
        plot y*x yp*x='*' / overlay vpos=35;
     run;
```

Output 29.4   Segmented Model: PROC NLIN and PROC PLOT

```
                              QUADRATIC MODEL WITH PLATEAU                                    1
X0=10 PLATEAU=0.7

                 Non-Linear Least Squares Iterative Phase    Dependent Variable Y    Method: Gauss-Newton
                  Iter          A             B                  C Sum of Squares
                    0       0.450000      0.050000          -0.002500     0.056231
X0=13.165937363 PLATEAU=0.793662174
                    1       0.388118      0.061605          -0.002340     0.011764
X0=12.822300972 PLATEAU=0.7780505759
                    2       0.393040      0.060053          -0.002342     0.010068
X0=12.755624517 PLATEAU=0.7775530672
                    3       0.392216      0.060418          -0.002368     0.010066
X0=12.74846438 PLATEAU=0.7775025883
                    4       0.392126      0.060459          -0.002371     0.010066
X0=12.74774162 PLATEAU=0.7774978936
                    5       0.392116      0.060463          -0.002372     0.010066
X0=12.747669162 PLATEAU=0.7774974276
                    6       0.392115      0.060463          -0.002372     0.010066
NOTE: Convergence criterion met.


                 Non-Linear Least Squares Summary Statistics     Dependent Variable Y

                 Source            DF  Sum of Squares    Mean Square

                 Regression         3    7.7256340095    2.5752113365
                 Residual          13    0.0100659905    0.0007743070
                 Uncorrected Total 16    7.7357000000

                 (Corrected Total) 15    0.1869437500


                 Parameter   Estimate      Asymptotic            Asymptotic 95 %
                                           Std. Error         Confidence Interval
                                                               Lower         Upper
                 A     0.3921153660  0.02667414696  0.33448940946  0.44974132253
                 B     0.0604631414  0.00842304248  0.04226627534  0.07866000749
                 C    -.0023715371   0.00055131779  -.00356258609  -.00118048817


                              Asymptotic Correlation Matrix

                 Corr              A              B              C
                 -------------------------------------------------------
                    A             1        -0.90202496     0.8124326974
                    B     -0.90202496            1        -0.978795219
                    C     0.8124326974   -0.978795219           1
```

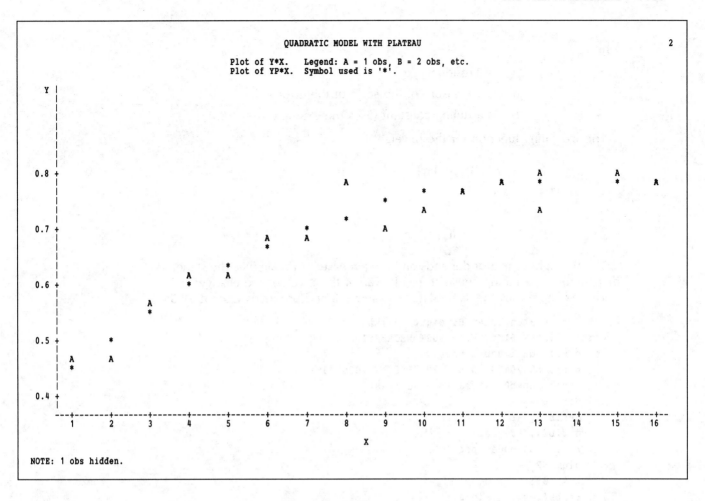

QUADRATIC MODEL WITH PLATEAU

Plot of Y*X.   Legend: A = 1 obs, B = 2 obs, etc.
Plot of YP*X.   Symbol used is '*'.

NOTE: 1 obs hidden.

Example 5:   Iteratively Reweighted Least Squares

The NLIN procedure is suited to methods that make the weight a function of the parameters in each iteration since the _WEIGHT_ variable can be computed with program statements. The NOHALVE option is used because the SSE definition is modified at each iteration and the step-shortening criteria is thus circumvented.

For many of the robust regression criteria suggested in the literature, iteratively reweighted least squares (IRLS) can produce estimates for parameters, but not their standard errors because the optimization problem is no longer least squares. These methods can act like automatic outlier rejectors since large residual values can lead to very small weights depending on the weight function. Holland and Welsch (1977) outline several of these robust methods. For example, the biweight criterion suggested by Beaton and Tukey (1974) tries to minimize

$$S_{biweight} = \Sigma \, \rho(r)$$

where

$$\rho(r) = (B^2 / 2)(1 - (1 - (r / B)^2)^2) \quad \text{if } |r| \leq B$$

or

$$\rho(r) = (B^2 / 2) \quad \text{otherwise}$$

where

r is $|residual|/\sigma$.

σ is a measure of the scale of the error.

B   is a tuning constant (uses the example B=4.685).

The weighting function for the biweight is

$$w_i = (1 - (r_i / B)^2)^2 \quad \text{if } |r_i| \leq B$$

or

$$w_i = 0 \qquad\qquad \text{if } |r_i| > B \quad .$$

The biweight estimator depends on both a measure of scale (like the standard deviation) and a tuning constant; results vary if these values are changed.

This example uses the same data as **Example 3** and produces **Output 29.5**:

```
/*    Beaton/Tukey Biweight by IRLS  */
title 'TUKEY BIWEIGHT ROBUST REGRESSION USING IRLS';
proc nlin data=uspop nohalve;
   parms b0=20450.43 b1=-22.7806 b2=.0063456;
   model pop=b0+b1*year+b2*year*year;
   der.b0=1;
   der.b1=year;
   der.b2=year*year;
   resid=pop-model.pop;
   sigma=2;
   b=4.685;
   r=abs(resid / sigma);
   if r<=b then _weight_=(1-(r / b)**2)**2;
   else _weight_=0;
   output out=c r=rbi;
run;
data c;
set c;
   sigma=2;
   b=4.685;
   r=abs(rbi / sigma);
   if r<=b then _weight_=(1-(r / b)**2)**2;
   else _weight_=0;
run;
proc print;
run;
```

Output 29.5   Iteratively Reweighted Least Squares: PROC NLIN and PROC PRINT

```
                    TUKEY BIWEIGHT ROBUST REGRESSION USING IRLS                        1

     Non-Linear Least Squares Iterative Phase    Dependent Variable POP    Method: Gauss-Newton
       Iter          B0              B1              B2          Weighted SS
        0       20450.430000     -22.780600        0.006346      57.264817
        1       20711.580896     -23.068940        0.006425      31.316348
        2       20889.771438     -23.263968        0.006478      19.794509
        3       20950.186052     -23.330292        0.006497      16.754875
        4       20966.814401     -23.348568        0.006502      16.057279
        5       20970.962721     -23.353129        0.006503      15.895348
        6       20971.960688     -23.354226        0.006503      15.857198
        7       20972.198207     -23.354487        0.006503      15.848167
        8       20972.254576     -23.354549        0.006503      15.846027
        9       20972.267943     -23.354563        0.006503      15.845520
       10       20972.271113     -23.354567        0.006503      15.845400
       11       20972.271864     -23.354568        0.006503      15.845371
       12       20972.272042     -23.354568        0.006503      15.845364
       13       20972.272084     -23.354568        0.006503      15.845363
       14       20972.272094     -23.354568        0.006503      15.845362
       15       20972.272097     -23.354568        0.006503      15.845362
NOTE: Convergence criterion met.


         Non-Linear Least Squares Summary Statistics    Dependent Variable POP

         Source            DF     Weighted SS     Weighted MS

         Regression         3    122571.96279     40857.32093
         Residual          16        15.84536         0.99034
         Uncorrected Total 19    122587.80815

         (Corrected Total)  18     59465.92678


         Parameter     Estimate      Asymptotic            Asymptotic 95 %
                                    Std. Error        Confidence Interval
                                                      Lower           Upper
               B0    20972.27210   309.61766713   20315.915225    21628.628968
               B1      -23.35457     0.32987833     -24.053875      -22.655261
               B2        0.00650     0.00008781       0.006317        0.006690


                        Asymptotic Correlation Matrix

         Corr                B0               B1               B2
         --------------------------------------------------------------
               B0             1       -0.999903521      0.9996131491
               B1    -0.999903521             1        -0.999902889
               B2     0.9996131491   -0.999902889                1
```

```
                    TUKEY BIWEIGHT ROBUST REGRESSION USING IRLS                        2

     OBS      POP     YEAR    YEARSQ       RBI     SIGMA     B         R       _WEIGHT_
       1     3.929    1790   3204100    -1.06728      2    4.685   0.53364    0.97422
       2     5.308    1800   3240000     0.38695      2    4.685   0.19347    0.99659
       3     7.239    1810   3276100     1.09250      2    4.685   0.54625    0.97300
       4     9.638    1820   3312400     0.96538      2    4.685   0.48269    0.97888
       5    12.866    1830   3348900     0.36659      2    4.685   0.18330    0.99694
       6    17.069    1840   3385600    -0.55787      2    4.685   0.27894    0.99292
       7    23.191    1850   3422500    -0.86400      2    4.685   0.43200    0.98307
       8    31.443    1860   3459600    -0.34080      2    4.685   0.17040    0.99736
       9    39.818    1870   3496900    -0.99528      2    4.685   0.49764    0.97756
      10    50.155    1880   3534400    -0.98842      2    4.685   0.49421    0.97787
      11    62.947    1890   3572100     0.17276      2    4.685   0.08638    0.99932
      12    75.994    1900   3610000     0.28827      2    4.685   0.14414    0.99811
      13    91.972    1910   3648100     2.03412      2    4.685   1.01706    0.90797
      14   105.710    1920   3686400     0.23929      2    4.685   0.11964    0.99870
      15   122.775    1930   3724900     0.47079      2    4.685   0.23539    0.99496
      16   131.669    1940   3763600    -8.76938      2    4.685   4.38469    0.01540
      17   151.325    1950   3802500    -8.54823      2    4.685   4.27411    0.02813
      18   179.323    1960   3841600    -1.28574      2    4.685   0.64287    0.96270
      19   203.211    1970   3880900     0.56608      2    4.685   0.28304    0.99271
```

The printout of the computed weights shows that the observations for 1940 and 1950 are highly discounted because of their large residuals.

The printout contains a note that missing values were propagated in 32 places. This happens when the last observation with a missing value for POP is handled. Since there are 15 iterations plus an initial iteration and the program is executed twice for each iteration (for each observation), these propagations occurred 32 times.

Example 6: GLIM Models

It is possible to fit GLIM models as described by Nelder and Wedderburn (1972). Maximum-likelihood estimates can be computed by iteratively reweighted least squares, where the weights are the reciprocals of the variances.

The following macro allows you to fit GLIM models. There are four LINK functions you can use: identity, log, normit, or logit. There are three error functions you can model: Binomial, Normal, or Poisson.

The first example analyzes the Ingot data given below to obtain MLE estimates of a probit model. The analysis uses LINK=PROBIT and ERROR=BINOMIAL. The following statements produce **Output 29.6**:

```
%macro glim(link=,error=normal,data=_last_,response=,number=,vars=,
        offset=);
  /*------------------------------------------------------------*/
  /* Variable     Function                                      */
  /* --------     --------                                      */
  /*                                                            */
  /* DATA         Input data set                                */
  /* RESPONSE     Variable containing the number of respondents */
  /* NUMBER       Variable containing the number in group       */
  /* VARS         List of independent variables                 */
  /* LINK         Name of the link function (LOGIT,PROBIT,IDENITY) */
  /* DISTRIB      Name of the probability distribution          */
  /*              (NORMAL,BINOMIAL,POISSON)                      */
  /* OFFSET       Offset for linear combination                 */
  /*------------------------------------------------------------*/
  %let n=0;       /* Split out individual names */
  %let old=;
  %if %length(&link)=0 %then
    %do;
       %if &error=binomial %then %let link=logit;
       %if &error=normal %then %let link=identity;
       %if &error=poisson %then %let link=log;
    %end;
  %do %while(%scan(&vars,&n+1)¬=);
     %let n=%eval(&n+1);
     %let var&n=%scan(&vars,&n);
     %let old=&old _old&n;
  %end;

  /* Do MLE with Nonlinear Least Squares */
  proc nlin nohalve sigsq=1
    data=&data(rename=(%do i=1 %to &n; &&var&i=_old&i %end;));
```

```
                    /* Start initial values at zero */
              parms
                 intercpt=0
                 %do i=1 %to &n; &&var&i=0 %end; ;

                 /* Compute inner product */
              _y_=intercpt %do i=1 %to &n; + &&var&i*_old&i %end;
              %if %length(&offset)¬=0 %then %str(+ &offset); ;
              /* Starting Values */
        if _iter_=-1 then
           do;
                 _mu_=0;
                 _loss_ = 0;
                 %if &error=poisson %then %str(_weight_=&response;);
                 %if &error=normal  %then %str(_weight_=&response;);
                 %if &error=binomial %then
                    %do;
                        if &response=0 then &response=0.1;
                        if &response=&number then &response=&number-0.1;
                        _weight_=&response*(&number-&response)/&number;
                    %end;
                 %if &link=log %then
                    %do;
                        if &response=0 then &response=-0.69;
                        else &response=log(&response);
                    %end;
                 %if &link=logit %then
                    %do;
                        if &response=0 then &response=0.1;
                        if &response=&number then &response=&number-0.1;
                        _weight_=&response*(&number-&response)/&number;
                        %str( &response=log(&response/(&number-&response)););
                    %end;
                 %if &link=probit %then %str(&response=probit(&response/&number););
           end;
           else do;
                 %if &link=log %then
                    %do;
                        _mu_=exp(_y_);
                        _der_=_mu_;
                    %end;
                 %if &link=identity %then
                    %do;
                        _mu_=_y_;
                        _der_=1;
                    %end;
                 %if &link=logit %then
                    %do;
                        _mu_=exp(_y_);
                        _der_=_mu_/(_mu_+1)**2;
                        _mu_=_mu_/(1+_mu_);
                    %end;
```

```
      %if &link=probit %then
          %do;
              _der_=1/sqrt(2*3.141592654)*exp((-1/2)*_y_**2);
              _mu_=probnorm(_y_);
          %end;
      %if &error=binomial %then
          %do;
              _der_=_der_*&number;
              _y_ = _mu_;
              _mu_=&number*_y_;
              _weight_=1/(&number*_y_*(1-_y_));
              _loss_=(-&response*log(_y_)-(&number-&response)
                      *log(1-_y_))/_weight_;
          %end;
      %if &error=poisson %then
          %do;
              %str(_weight_=1/_mu_; );
              %str(_loss_=(&response*log(_mu_)-_mu_)/_weight_;);
          %end;
      %if &error=normal %then
          %do;
              %str(_weight_=1/&number; );
              %str(_loss_=(&response-_mu_)**2/_weight_;);
          %end;
   end;
      /* MODEL Statement */
   model &response=_mu_;
      /* Generate the derivatives */
   der.intercpt=_der_;
   %do i=1 %to &n;
      der.&&var&i=_der_*_old&i;
   %end;
%mend;


   /*                 Ingot Data                              */
   /*  Ingots are tested for readiness to roll after different */
   /*  treatments of heating time and soaking time.           */
   /*  From Cox (1970, 67-68).                                 */
   /*                                                          */
title 'MLE ESTIMATES OF A PROBIT MODEL';
data ingots;
   input heat soak nready ntotal @@;
   cards;
7 1.0  0 10    14 1.0  0 31    27 1.0  1 56    51 1.0  3 13
7 1.7  0 17    14 1.7  0 43    27 1.7  4 44    51 1.7  0  1
7 2.2  0  7    14 2.2  2 33    27 2.2  0 21    51 2.2  0  1
7 2.8  0 12    14 2.8  0 31    27 2.8  1 22
7 4.0  0  9    14 4.0  0 19    27 4.0  1 16    51 4.0  0  1
;

%glim(link=probit,error=binomial,response=nready,number=ntotal,
      vars=%str(heat soak));
run;
```

Output 29.6   Regression Analysis of Ingot Data: PROC NLIN
                  and BINOMIAL Macro

```
                      MLE ESTIMATES OF A PROBIT MODEL                              1

      Non-Linear Least Squares Iterative Phase   Dependent Variable NREADY      Method: Gauss-Newton
            Iter      INTERCPT            HEAT          SOAK  Weighted loss
             0             0               0             0             0
             1      -1.353207        0.008697      0.002339     71.710426
             2      -2.053504        0.020274      0.007389     51.641219
             3      -2.581302        0.032626      0.018503     47.889468
             4      -2.838938        0.038763      0.030910     47.489236
             5      -2.890129        0.039889      0.035651     47.479967
             6      -2.893270        0.039953      0.036217     47.479945
             7      -2.893408        0.039955      0.036252     47.479945
NOTE: Convergence criterion met.


          Non-Linear Least Squares Summary Statistics     Dependent Variable NREADY

          Source             DF    Weighted SS      Weighted MS

          Regression          3   13.011673421     4.337224474
          Residual           16   13.850931733     0.865683233
          Uncorrected Total  19   26.862605154

          (Corrected Total)  18   25.730010271
          Sum of Loss            47.479945327

          Parameter    Estimate      Asymptotic              Asymptotic 95 %
                                      Std. Error          Confidence Interval
                                                           Lower          Upper
          INTERCPT  -2.893408210  0.50060044947  -3.9546284820  -1.8321879384
              HEAT   0.039955339  0.01184659580   0.0148418028   0.0650688757
              SOAK   0.036251825  0.14674320576  -0.2748283284   0.3473319788


                      Asymptotic Correlation Matrix

          Corr           INTERCPT            HEAT            SOAK
          --------------------------------------------------------------
          INTERCPT              1     -0.795057798    -0.753827125
              HEAT  -0.795057798               1      0.2959331155
              SOAK  -0.753827125    0.2959331155               1
```

The second example uses the macro to perform Poisson regression to analyze the number of reported damage incidents and aggregate months of service for shipping data (McCullagh and Nelder 1983). Variables included in the analysis are ship type, year of construction, and period of operation. The error is set to be POISSON.

The following statements produce **Output 29.7**:

```
/*                                                                  */
/*     MODEL: POISSON LOG                                           */
/*     NUMBER OF REPORTED DAMAGE INCIDENTS AND AGGREGATE MONTHS    */
/*     OF SERVICE BY SHIP TYPE, YEAR OF CONSTRUCTION AND PERIOD    */
/*     OF OPERATION. NOTE THAT THE AGGREGATE MONTHS OF SERVICE     */
/*     HAS BEEN INCLUDED AS AN 'OFFSET' VARIABLE.                  */
/*        MCCULLAGH,P. & NELDER,J.A. (1983).                        */
/*             GENERALISED LINEAR MODELS;                           */
/*             LONDON: CHAPMAN & HALL. PAGE 136.                    */
/*                                                                  */

data ship;
    length type $1. yr_made $7. operaton $8.;
    input type yr_made operaton service number
          x1 x2 x3 x4 x5 x6 x7 x8;
    label x1='service period 1975-79'
          x2='type B'
          x3='type C'
          x4='type D'
```

```
              x5='type E'
              x6='construction 1965-1969'
              x7='construction 1970-1974'
              x6='construction 1975-1979';
      cards;
A  1960-64  1960-74   4.8442   0  0  0  0  0  0  0  0  0
B  1960-64  1960-74  10.7118  39  0  1  0  0  0  0  0  0
C  1960-64  1960-74   7.0724   1  0  0  1  0  0  0  0  0
D  1960-64  1960-74   5.5255   0  0  0  0  1  0  0  0  0
E  1960-64  1960-74   3.8067   0  0  0  0  0  1  0  0  0
A  1960-64  1975-79   4.1431   0  1  0  0  0  0  0  0  0
B  1960-64  1975-79   9.7513  29  1  1  0  0  0  0  0  0
C  1960-64  1975-79   6.3135   1  1  0  1  0  0  0  0  0
D  1960-64  1975-79   4.6540   0  1  0  0  1  0  0  0  0
A  1965-69  1960-74   6.9985   3  0  0  0  0  0  1  0  0
B  1965-69  1960-74  10.2615  58  0  1  0  0  0  1  0  0
C  1965-69  1960-74   6.6606   0  0  0  1  0  0  1  0  0
D  1965-69  1960-74   5.6630   0  0  0  0  1  0  1  0  0
E  1965-69  1960-74   6.6708   7  0  0  0  0  1  1  0  0
A  1965-69  1975-79   6.9985   4  1  0  0  0  0  1  0  0
B  1965-69  1975-79   9.9218  53  1  1  0  0  0  1  0  0
C  1965-69  1975-79   6.5162   1  1  0  1  0  0  1  0  0
D  1965-69  1975-79   5.2575   0  1  0  0  1  0  1  0  0
E  1965-69  1975-79   6.0799   7  1  0  0  0  1  1  0  0
A  1970-64  1960-74   7.3212   6  0  0  0  0  0  0  1  0
B  1970-64  1960-74   8.8628  12  0  1  0  0  0  0  1  0
C  1970-64  1960-74   6.6631   6  0  0  1  0  0  0  1  0
D  1970-64  1960-74   5.8551   2  0  0  0  1  0  0  1  0
E  1970-64  1960-74   7.0536   5  0  0  0  0  1  0  1  0
A  1970-64  1975-79   8.1176  18  1  0  0  0  0  0  1  0
B  1970-64  1975-79   9.4803  44  1  1  0  0  0  0  1  0
C  1970-64  1975-79   7.5746   2  1  0  1  0  0  0  1  0
D  1970-64  1975-79   7.0967  11  1  0  0  1  0  0  1  0
E  1970-64  1975-79   7.6783  12  1  0  0  0  1  0  1  0
A  1975-69  1975-79   7.7160  11  1  0  0  0  0  0  0  1
B  1975-69  1975-79   8.8702  18  1  1  0  0  0  0  0  1
C  1975-69  1975-79   5.6131   1  1  0  1  0  0  0  0  1
D  1975-69  1975-79   7.6261   4  1  0  0  1  0  0  0  1
E  1975-69  1975-79   6.2953   1  1  0  0  0  1  0  0  1
;
run;

title 'POISSON REGRESSION';
%glim(error=poisson,response=number,
      vars=%str(x1 x2 x3 x4 x5 x6 x7 x8 ),offset=service);
run;
```

Output 29.7 Poisson Regression

```
                                         POISSON REGRESSION                                                 1

              Non-Linear Least Squares Iterative Phase    Dependent Variable NUMBER      Method: Gauss-Newton
  Iter    INTERCPT           X1            X2               X3            X4             X5          X6  Weighted loss
             X7           X8
   0         0             0             0                0              0             0            0           0
             0             0
   1     -0.997311      0.000835     -0.001842        -0.002168      -0.000393      0.001738     0.001091   -57409.573378
           0.001530      0.000447
   2     -1.990035      0.003096     -0.006813        -0.008024      -0.001450      0.006413     0.004047   -19772.877942
           0.005673      0.001661
   3     -2.970517      0.009166     -0.020073        -0.023658      -0.004253      0.018754     0.012011    -6146.505134
           0.016803      0.004963
   4     -3.919294      0.025131     -0.054322        -0.064141      -0.011360      0.049753     0.033157    -1343.816391
           0.046131      0.013935
   5     -4.792248      0.064833     -0.135539        -0.160801      -0.027400      0.118081     0.087084      235.193126
           0.119476      0.038177
   6     -5.515699      0.150133     -0.290310        -0.348433      -0.054123      0.226600     0.210754      674.069310
           0.280020      0.101179
   7     -6.034343      0.278110     -0.466820        -0.573160      -0.075030      0.309099     0.427443      759.370365
           0.537092      0.236677
   8     -6.329930      0.367573     -0.538464        -0.677018      -0.076631      0.324970     0.633274      767.795384
           0.755322      0.396361
   9     -6.403027      0.384110     -0.543342        -0.687306      -0.075989      0.325569     0.694512      768.012396
           0.815849      0.450943
  10     -6.405911      0.384488     -0.543354        -0.687418      -0.075980      0.325582     0.697146      768.012669
           0.818423      0.453440
  11     -6.405915      0.384488     -0.543354        -0.687418      -0.075980      0.325582     0.697150      768.012669
           0.818426      0.453444
NOTE: Convergence criterion met.
```

```
                    Non-Linear Least Squares Summary Statistics    Dependent Variable NUMBER

                    Source             DF      Weighted SS      Weighted MS

                    Regression          9      356.00000000     39.55555556
                    Residual           25       42.27694763      1.69107791
                    Uncorrected Total  34      398.27694763

                    (Corrected Total)  33      373.41338887
                    Sum of Loss               768.01266940

                    Parameter    Estimate      Asymptotic              Asymptotic 95 %
                                               Std. Error          Confidence Interval
                                                                   Lower         Upper
                    INTERCPT   -6.405914771   0.21744445374   -6.8537464220  -5.9580831194
                          X1    0.384488072   0.11827197632    0.1409043264   0.6280718172
                          X2   -0.543353982   0.17758996384   -0.9091044322  -0.1776035327
                          X3   -0.687418388   0.32904721956   -1.3650983981  -0.0097383771
                          X4   -0.075979835   0.29057889812   -0.6744334880   0.5224738189
                          X5    0.325581683   0.23587934104   -0.1602170255   0.8113803915
                          X6    0.697149667   0.14964119595    0.3889603213   1.0053390123
                          X7    0.818426343   0.16977314476    0.4687748043   1.1680778810
                          X8    0.453443532   0.23317068522   -0.0267766405   0.9336637036
```

```
                                         POISSON REGRESSION                                                 2

                                    Asymptotic Correlation Matrix

   Corr      INTERCPT         X1           X2           X3           X4           X5           X6           X7           X8
   ----------------------------------------------------------------------------------------------------------------------
   INTERCPT         1    -0.21612624  -0.81142358  -0.37836866  -0.37058118  -0.4698748   -0.48425218  -0.55013484  -0.4015435
        X1   -0.21612624         1     0.025386399 -0.00307443  -0.00472747   0.026939845 -0.12004686  -0.26358027  -0.3153469
        X2   -0.81142358   0.025386399        1     0.433164247  0.446820033   0.570660953  0.085606381  0.271421137  0.228459091
        X3   -0.37836866  -0.00307443   0.433164247        1     0.237520847   0.313616993  0.035837703  0.045511627  0.097074471
        X4   -0.37058118  -0.00472747   0.446820033  0.237520847        1       0.333772714  0.027677043  0.028587738 -0.09658764
        X5   -0.4698748    0.026939845  0.570660953  0.313616993  0.333772714         1    -0.00408579  -0.03708938   0.052791889
        X6   -0.48425218  -0.12004686   0.085606381  0.035837703  0.027677043  -0.00408579        1      0.633471017  0.475509434
        X7   -0.55013484  -0.26358027   0.271421137  0.045511627  0.028587738  -0.03708938   0.633471017        1      0.548232949
        X8   -0.4015435   -0.3153469    0.228459091  0.097074471 -0.09658764    0.052791889  0.475509434  0.548232949        1
```

Example 7:   Function Minimization

In some cases the NLIN procedure can be used to find the minimum of a function.
The following example was taken from Kennedy and Gentle (1980). The use of
arrays and METHOD=NEWTON is demonstrated. The following statements produce **Output 29.8**:

```
/*   10.6 OREN 1973                                        */
/* F(X)= sumi(sumj(((xj-1)*(xi-1))/(j+i+1))))             */
/* x=(1,1,1,1,....) x0(i)=4/i;                            */
/*                                                        */
/* minimize F(X)                                          */
/* taken from Kennedy and Gentle (1980)                   */

title 'Function Minimization Using Arrays and METHOD=NEWTON';
data oren;
   z=0;
run;

proc nlin method=newton g4 smethod=golden;
   parms x1=4 x2=2 x3=1.33333 x4=1;
   array x x1-x4;
   array dersum der.x1-der.x4;
   array der2 der.x1.x1
         der.x2.x1 der.x2.x2 der.x3.x1 der.x3.x2
         der.x3.x3 der.x4.x1 der.x4.x2 der.x4.x3 der.x4.x4;
   sum=0;
   ij=1;
   do i=1 to 4;
      dersum{i}=0;
         do j=1 to 4;
            sum=sum+((x{j}-1)*(x{i}-1)) / (j+i-1);
            dersum{i}=dersum{i}+(x{j}-1) / (j+i-1);
         end;
         dersum{i}=dersum{i}+(x{i}-1) / (i+i-1);
         do j=1 to i;
            if j<i then der2{ij}=1 / (i+j-1);
            else der2{ij}=2 / (i+i-1);
            ij=ij+1;
         end;
   end;
   model z=sum;
run;
```

Output 29.8   Function Minimization Using METHOD=NEWTON

```
                        Function Minimization Using Arrays and METHOD=NEWTON                    1
              Non-Linear Least Squares Iterative Phase     Dependent Variable Z    Method: Newton
         Iter        X1            X2             X3                  X4   Sum of Squares
          0       4.000000      2.000000      1.333330            1.000000      173.946559
          1       0.986704      0.995568      0.998523            1.000000      0.0000000671
          2       1.000059      1.000020      1.000007            1.000000      2.5894167E-17
          3       1.000004      1.000001      0.999995            0.999991      2.4269235E-22
NOTE: Convergence criterion met.


                   Non-Linear Least Squares Summary Statistics    Dependent Variable Z

                  Source            DF  Sum of Squares    Mean Square

                  Regression         4   -2.426923E-22   -6.067309E-23
                  Residual          -3   2.4269235E-22    0
                  Uncorrected Total  1    0

                  (Corrected Total)  0    0

NOTE: Negative model SS. Check model and initial parameters.


                  Parameter     Estimate    Asymptotic            Asymptotic 95 %
                                            Std. Error        Confidence Interval
                                                               Lower          Upper
                        X1     1.000004386      0         1.0000043861   1.0000043861
                        X2     1.000000732      0         1.0000007318   1.0000007318
                        X3     0.999994647      0         0.9999946469   0.9999946469
                        X4     0.999991232      0         0.9999912319   0.9999912319


                               Asymptotic Correlation Matrix

         Corr             X1             X2             X3             X4
         -----------------------------------------------------------------------
              X1           1        -0.41981168     0.0854518691    0.3227266169
              X2     -0.41981168          1        -0.268808999    -0.250510084
              X3     0.0854518691   -0.268808999         1         -0.583127447
              X4     0.3227266169   -0.250510084    -0.583127447         1
```

Example 8:   Censored Accelerated Failure Models

The NLIN procedure can be used to solve other types of optimization problems. In particular it is possible to get solutions for certain types of censored parametric accelerated failure time models. The LIFEREG procedure fits this type of model but, if special programming needs arise, the following example may be useful. One caveat is that NLIN will not use any observations for which the _WGTJPJ_ variable is less than or equal to zero. Although the _WGTJPJ_ will always be positive in the example given below, this is not the case for all distributions. For the accelerated failure time model, the function to be maximized is

$$\Sigma(f((y_i - \mathbf{x}_i'\boldsymbol{\beta})/\sigma) - \log(\sigma)) + \Sigma S((y_i - \mathbf{x}_i'\boldsymbol{\beta})/\sigma)$$

where the first sum is over uncensored events, the second sum is over right censored events, f is the log of the density function, S is the log of the survival function, $\mathbf{x}_i$ is a vector of covariates, y_i is the (possibly censored) response, and $\boldsymbol{\beta}$ and σ are the free parameters.

For the observations not censored, the contribution to the likelihood is

$$\log(g((\mathbf{y} - \mathbf{x}'\boldsymbol{\beta}) / \sigma) / \sigma) \ .$$

The regression parameters are not the usual parameterization and are multiplied by a factor of $-1/\sigma$. The parameter estimates must then be converted to the usual parameterization with their observed information-based usual standard errors.

A data set is generated to illustrate how the macro works. The macro is defined using the normal distribution. The statements assigning the loss function, gradient weight, and hessian weight can be changed if you want to specify some other distribution. The following statements generate **Output 29.9**:

```
%macro nlincen(data=_last_,var=,y=,flag=,loss=,w1=,w2=);
/*                                                           */
/* &data    the name of the data set.                        */
/* &var     the list of variables.                           */
/* &y       dependent variable                               */
/* &flag    indicator for                                    */
/*             uncensored      0                              */
/*             right censored  1                              */
/*             left  censored -1                             */
/* &loss    code section for loss function                   */
/*             put value in loss                             */
/* &wg      code section for gradient weight                 */
/*             put value in gradwt                           */
/* &wj      code section for hessian weight                  */
/*             put value in hesswgt                          */
/* Program to compute maximum likelihood estimate for        */
/* censored regression problems using nlin.                  */
/* The function to be optimized is assumed to be of the form */
/*                                                           */
/*    sum( f(x'b) )                                          */
/*                                                           */
/* where f is the -log density or -log cdf or -log sdf. NLIN */
/* then procedes to compute steps as                         */
/*                                                           */
/*    delta = (j' * wj * j)**-1 (j' * wg * r)                */
/*                                                           */
/* where r is the residual (fixed at 1 in this case)         */
/* j is the dervative matrix (set to the design matrix here) */
/* and we specify weights for (w1=) f' and (w2=) f''.        */
/* This  generates a newton-raphson iteration sequence.      */
/* The x'b is of the form                                    */
/*                                                           */
/*     (y-x'beta)/sigma                                      */
/*                                                           */
/* so the x vector is (y,x) and the parameter vector is      */
/*                                                           */
/*     (1/sigma,-beta/sigma).                                */
/*                                                           */
/* For the elements not censored, the contribution to       */
/* the likelihood is the log of g((y-x'beta)/sigma)/sigma,   */
/* so one dummy observation is added to the data set         */
/* consisting of x=(1,0) and f=(number not censored)*log.    */
/* Note that the  regression parameters are                 */
/* multiplied by -1/sigma.                                   */
/*                                                           */
```

```
      /*  A data step is added to add the dummy observation      */
      /*  of the form (y,x)=(1,0) to the end of the data set     */
      /*  the reg procedure is used to get initial parameter     */
      /*  estimates from an ols fit.                             */
      /*                                                         */
      /*  An additional data step is added at the end to recover the */
      /*  usual parameter estimates  and their observed information */
      /*  based usual standard errors.  The usual sigma is 1/scale */
      /*  and the regression parameters are  -b * sigma.         */

      /*      generate list of variables                         */
%let n=0;
%let old=;
%do %while(%scan(&var,&n+1)~=);
   %let n=%eval(&n+1);
   %let vars&n=%upcase(%scan(&var,&n));
   %let old=&old _old&n;
%end;

   /*-----Add a dummy observation to end of data set ---*/
data _nlin _nlin2; set &data(keep=&y &var &flag) end=end;
   if nmiss(of &y &var &flag)>0 then delete;
   if &flag=0 then
      do;
         output _nlin2;
         _ngood+1;
      end;
   lastobs=0;
   output _nlin;
   if end = 1 then
      do;
         &y=1;
         %do i = 1 %to &n;
            &&vars&i = 0;
         %end;
         lastobs=1;
         output _nlin;
      end;
   keep &y &var &flag lastobs _ngood;
run;

   /*--------Compute initial estimates -----*/
proc reg data=_nlin2 outest=_nlin2 noprint;
   model &y=&var/noint;
run;

data _null_;
   set _nlin2;
   %do i=1 %to &n;
      call symput("_INIT&i",-&&vars&i / _rmse_);
   %end;
   call symput("_SCALE", 1/_rmse_);
run;
```

```
    /*---Do the fit, note that sigsq is set to 1. -----*/
proc nlin data=_nlin(rename=(
        %do i=1 %to &n; &&vars&i=_old&i %end;))
        sigsq=1 outest=_nlinest method=marquardt maxiter=10;

    /* --- Set parms from ols intials ----*/
parms
    scale=&_scale
    %do i=1 %to &n; &&vars&i=&&_init&i %end;
    ;
;

    /*----Compute x b and put in the variable _z_ ----*/
_z_ =  &y * scale + (%do i=1 %to &n; +&&vars&i * _old&i %end;);

&w1;
_weight_=gradwgt;
&loss;
_loss_=loss/_weight_;

&w2 ;
_wgtjpj_=hesswgt;

    /*----Residual is identically 1. ----*/
model &y=&y-1;

%do i=1 %to &n;
    der.&&vars&i=-_old&i;
%end;
;
    der.scale=- &y;
run;

    /* Convert to usual parameterization */
data _nlinest;
    set _nlinest;
    retain varscale _loglik_ sigma %do i=1 %to &n; _old&i %end; ;

    /* Subset final parameter estimates   */
    if _type_¬='FINAL' and _type_¬='COVB' then delete;

    /* Rescale beta from beta/sigma    */
    if _type_='FINAL' then
      do;
        sigma=1/scale;
        _loglik_=_sse_;
        %do i = 1 %to &n;
            _old&i=-&&vars&i*sigma;
        %end;
      end;
```

```
            /* Convert variances        */
        else do;
           if _name_='SCALE' then
              do;
                 _value_=sigma;
                 varscale=scale;
                 _stderr_=sqrt(scale)*sigma**2;
              end;

              /* Compute standard errors of parameters   */
           %do i=1 %to &n;
              else if _name_="&&VARs&I" then
                 do;
                    _value_=_old&i;
                    _stderr_=sigma*sqrt(_old&i*_old&i*varscale
                              +2*_old&i*scale+&&vars&i);
                 end;
           %end;
           _chisq_=(_value_/_stderr_)**2;
           _prob_=1-probchi(_chisq_, 1);
           output;
        end;
        keep _name_ _value_ _stderr_ _chisq_ _prob_ _loglik_;

title 'Usual Parameter Estimates';
proc print;
    var _name_ _value_ _stderr_ _chisq_ _prob_ _loglik_;
run;

%mend;

    /* Create a data set    */
data a;
   do i=1 to 100;
      x=10*ranuni(1);
      y=10*ranuni(1);
      one=1;
      if ranuni(1)>.9 then flag=1;
      else if ranuni(1)<.1 then flag=-1;
      else flag=0;
      z=x+2*y+10*rannor(1);
      z1=.;
      z2=.;
      if flag=1 then z1=z;
      else if flag=-1 then z2=z;
      else do;
         z1=z;
         z2=z;
      end;
      output;
   end;
```

```
    /* LOSS function with normal distribution  */
%let normloss=%str(if (lastobs=1)
   then loss=-_ngood*log(scale);
   else if flag=0 then loss=_z_*_z_ / 2 + .5*log(8*atan(1));
   else if flag=1 then loss=-log(probnorm(-_z_));
   else loss=-log(probnorm(_z_));
);


    /* Gradient weights with normal distribution  */
%let normgrad=%str(if (lastobs=1)
   then gradwgt=-_ngood / scale;
   else if flag=0 then gradwgt=_z_;
   else if flag=1 then gradwgt=exp(-_z_*_z_ / 2) /
      (sqrt(8*atan(1))*probnorm(-_z_));
   else gradwgt=-exp(-_z_*_z_/2) /
      ( sqrt(8*atan(1))*probnorm(_z_));
);


    /* Hessian weights with normal distribution */
%let normhess=%str(if (lastobs=1)
   then hesswgt=_ngood / (scale*scale);
   else if flag=0 then hesswgt=1;
   else do;
      _phi=exp(-_z_*_z_/2)/sqrt(8*atan(1));
      if flag=1 then _p=probnorm(-_z_);
      else _p=probnorm(_z_);
      if flag=1 then hesswgt=_phi*(_phi-_z_*_p) / _p** 2;
      else hesswgt=_phi*(_phi+_z_*_p) / _p** 2;
   end;
);


    /*  Run macro   */
%nlincen(data=a,var=%str(one x y),y=z,flag=flag,
      loss=&normloss,w1=&normgrad,w2=&normhess);
run;
```

Output 29.9   Censored Accelerated Failure Model

```
                                    The SAS System                                        1

           Non-Linear Least Squares Iterative Phase    Dependent Variable Z    Method: Marquardt
           Iter      SCALE          ONE              X              Y       Weighted loss
             0     0.099441     -0.021727        -0.092320      -0.201739      318.269030
             1     0.100642     -0.014445        -0.084752      -0.219341      318.117413
             2     0.100652     -0.014508        -0.084747      -0.219378      318.117412
NOTE: Convergence criterion met.


              Non-Linear Least Squares Summary Statistics    Dependent Variable Z

               Source              DF      Weighted SS     Weighted MS

               Regression           4    26155.388657     6538.847164
               Residual            97     -824.624223       -8.501281
               Uncorrected Total  101    25330.764434

               (Corrected Total)  100    25330.764434
               Sum of Loss                 318.117412

               Parameter    Estimate      Asymptotic           Asymptotic 95 %
                                         Std. Error        Confidence Interval
                                                           Lower          Upper
                  SCALE   0.1006519063  0.00773718989  0.08529563848  0.11600817415
                   ONE  -.0145076299   0.28886988731  -.58783766605  0.55882240628
                     X  -.0847465335   0.04045340513  -.16503580301  -.00445726403
                     Y  -.2193779477   0.03899670663  -.29677605740  -.14197983803


                            Asymptotic Correlation Matrix

           Corr          SCALE             ONE              X              Y
           --------------------------------------------------------------------------
           SCALE             1       -0.000877457    -0.169109766    -0.410797679
            ONE      -0.000877457             1       -0.707593032    -0.560633467
              X      -0.169109766    -0.707593032             1        0.0947895133
              Y      -0.410797679    -0.560633467     0.0947895133            1
```

```
                              Usual Parameter Estimates                                   2

           OBS    _NAME_    _VALUE_    _STDERR_    _CHISQ_    _PROB_    _LOGLIK_

            1     SCALE     9.93523     0.76373    169.230    0.00000    318.117
            2     ONE       0.14414     2.87000      0.003    0.95995    318.117
            3     X         0.84198     0.39614      4.518    0.03355    318.117
            4     Y         2.17957     0.35334     38.050    0.00000    318.117
```

Example 9:   Conditional Logistic Regression and Cox Regression

The NLIN procedure can be used to fit models that are not of the form of nonlinear least squares. One device which is occasionally useful is to define a dummy response so that the residual is identically 1. When this is done the gradient, g, and the crossproducts matrix of the jacobian, $\mathbf{H}$, become

$$g = \Sigma_i \, w_i^G \, \mathbf{l_i}$$

and

$$\mathbf{H} = \Sigma_i w_i^J \mathbf{l_i} \mathbf{l_i}'$$

where $\mathbf{l_i}$ is the vector of specified derivatives, w_i^G is the value of the weight variable, _WEIGHT_, and w_i^J is the value of the weight variable, _WGTJPJ_, if specified or the value of _WEIGHT_ otherwise. The _LOSS_ variable should be specified to control the actual objective function for this approach to be meaningful.

As an example of the use of this device, consider the conditional logistic models and the Cox proportion hazard models, where the likelihood has the form of a product multinomial likelihood. Each term can be thought of as representing the probability of selection of the particular subset of a given size, say m, from a set of objects, say n of them. This probability is modeled as

$$p_i = \frac{\Pi_j z_j}{\Sigma_\pi \Pi_k z_{\pi_k}}$$

where the sum is over all subsets of size m and π represents the indexes of the subset. The sum in the denominator is one of the so-called elementary symmetric functions and can be computed using a standard recurrence. Each z_j is a weight associated with the jth object. Usually $z_j = exp(\beta x_j)$ where β is a vector of parameters and x_j is a vector of covariates.

Since the likelihood is of the multinomial form, in principle, the iterated reweighted least squares algorithm could be used. In practice, because of the large number of levels associated with each multinomial term, it is better to proceed using the device discussed earlier.

Each term of the likelihood contributes $\log(p_i)$ to the loss function. A contribution of $1/p_i \, \partial p_i / \partial \beta$ is required for the gradient and a contribution of $1/p_i^2 (\partial p_i / \partial \beta)(\partial p_i / \partial \beta)'$ is required if you are to get the usual value of the expected information. If the exact second derivative matrix are desired, second derivative terms can be specified as well.

These models can be fit then with $-\log(p_i)$ specified for the _LOSS_ variable, $1/p_i$ specified for the _WEIGHT_ variable, $1/p_i^2$ specified for the _WGTJPJ_ variable and $\partial p_i / \partial \beta$ for the derivatives.

Two macros, CONLOG, for conditional logistic regression, and CMOD, for Cox regression (see **Output 29.11**), are given in the following examples.

CONLOG is used to analyze a data set of birthweights of infants. Cases are mothers of low birthweight infants and are matched with control mothers on age.

In **Output 29.11**, CMOD fits Cox's proportional hazards model with NLIN, using the discrete hazard for ties. The macro is used to analyze a data set of lifetimes of rats exposed to the carcinogen DMBA. Groups were distinguished by pre-treatment regimen.

```
%macro condlog(strata=,case=,variable=,data=_last_);
    /*--------------------------------------------------------------*/
    /*  CONDLOG is a macro to perform conditional logistic          */
    /*  regression with the NLIN procedure.                         */
    /*  It allows for arbitrary n:m matching.                       */
    /*                                                              */
    /*     strata     names the variables which define the strata.  */
    /*                These must be numeric.                        */
    /*     case       is the name of the variable labeling          */
    /*                the cases (value must be 1) and controls (0).  */
    /*                and a control value 0.                        */
    /*     variable   lists the covariates.                         */
    /*     data       names the input dataset.                      */
    /*--------------------------------------------------------------*/


    /*----Eliminate missing values and sort the data--------------*/
```

```
data _clog1;
   set &data;
   if nmiss( of &variable &case &strata)>0 then delete;
   if &case=0 or &case=1;
   keep &variable &case &strata;
proc sort;
   by &strata &case;
run;

   /*----Generate list of variables-------------------------------*/
%let n=0;
%let old=;
%do %while(%scan(&variable,&n+1)~=);
   %let n=%eval(&n+1);
   %let var&n=%scan(&variable,&n);
   %let old=&old _old&n;
%end;

   /*----Find name of last strata variable---------------------*/
%let i=1;
%do %while(%scan(&strata,&i)~=);
   %let last=%scan(&strata,&i);
   %let i=%eval(&i+1);
%end;

   /*----Find the within strata/case counts--------------------*/

proc means noprint;
   var &variable;
   by &strata &case;
   output out=_clog2 n=n mean=&old;
run;

   /*----Throw out invalid strata and count the maximum---------*/

data _clog2;
   set _clog2;
   by &strata;
   if first.&last=last.&last then delete;
   if &case=1;

data _clog1(rename=( %do i=1 %to &n; &&var&i=_old&i %end;));
   merge _clog1 _clog2;
   by &strata;
   array c &variable;
   array m &old;
   retain casemax 0;
   if n>.;

      /* --- Zero the sum of variables over the cases --- */
   do over c;
      c=c-m;
   end;
```

```
                /* --- End of strata flag ---- */
        _sflag=last.&last;


            /* --- For array allocation --- */
        if n>casemax then
            do;
                casemax=n;
                call symput('CASEMAX',casemax);
            end;
        keep &case &variable _sflag n;
run;

proc nlin data=_clog1 sigsq=1 maxiter=20 method=marquardt;
    %let casemax=%scan(&casemax,1);

        /*----Set parms statement with initial values zero ---------*/
        parms %do i=1 %to &n; &&var&i=0 %end; ;

        array psi( &casemax );

            /* Derivatives of psi */
        %do i=1 %to &n;
            array psid&i( &casemax );
         retain psid&i.1-psid&i&casemax 0;
        %end;
        retain psi1-psi&casemax 0 ;

            /*----Compute x b and put in the variable _z_ ---- */
        _z_=exp( %do i=1 %to &n; +&&var&i*_old&i %end;) ;

            /*----Do the recurrence--------------------------------*/
        s1=1;
        do _i_=1 to n;
            s2=psi(_i_);
            psi(_i_)=psi(_i_)+_z_*s1;
            s1=s2;
        end;

        if _sflag=0 then _loss_=0;
        else  _loss_=log(psi(n)) / psi(n);

        _weight_=psi(n);

            /* --- Contribution only for each strata --- */
        if _sflag=0 then dummy=.;
        else dummy=n-1;

        model n=dummy;

        _wgtjpj_=psi(n)** 2;
```

```
        if ~_model_ then
          do;                      /* derivatives */
            %do i=1 %to &n;
              d1=0;
              s1=1;
              do _i_=1 to n;
                d2=psid&i (_i_);
                psid&i (_i_)=psid&i (_i_)+_z_*(d1+_old&i*s1);
                d1=d2;
                s1=psi(_i_);
              end;
              if _sflag=0 then der.&&var&i=0;
              else do;
                der.&&var&i=-psid&i(n) / psi(n)** 2;
                do _i_=1 to n;
                  psid&i (_i_)=0;
                end;
              end;
            %end;
          end;

        if _sflag~=0 then
          do _i_=1 to n;
            psi(_i_)=0;
          end;

run;

%mend condlog;

   /*-----------------------Birthweight Data -------------------*/
   /* Cases are mothers of low birthweight variables          */
   /* matched on age.                                         */
   /* Explanatory variables are smoking, hypertension history, */
   /* presence of uterine irritability, weight at last menstrual */
   /* period, and whether there was a previous preterm delivery. */
   /* From Hosmer and Lemeshow, ( 1989, Appendix 4 )          */
   /*---------------------------------------------------------*/

data oneto3 ;
   input str obs age low lwt smoke ht ui ptd @@;
   cards ;
1 1 16 1 130 0 0 0 0    1 2 16 0 112 0 0 0 0
1 3 16 0 135 1 0 0 0    1 4 16 0  95 0 0 0 0
2 1 17 1 130 1 0 1 1    2 2 17 0 103 0 0 0 0
2 3 17 0 122 1 0 0 0    2 4 17 0 113 0 0 0 0
3 1 17 1 120 0 0 0 0    3 2 17 0 113 0 0 0 0
3 3 17 0 119 0 0 0 0    3 4 17 0 119 0 0 0 0
4 1 18 1 148 0 0 0 0    4 2 18 0 100 1 0 0 0
4 3 18 0  90 1 0 1 0    4 4 18 0 229 0 0 0 0
5 1 18 1 110 1 0 0 1    5 2 18 0 107 1 0 1 0
5 3 18 0 100 1 0 0 0    5 4 18 0  90 1 0 1 0
6 1 19 1  91 1 0 1 1    6 2 19 0 138 1 0 0 0
6 3 19 0 189 0 0 0 0    6 4 19 0 147 1 0 0 0
7 1 19 1 102 0 0 0 0    7 2 19 0 150 0 0 0 0
```

```
 7 3 19 0 235 1 1 0 0    7 4 19 0 184 1 1 0 0
 8 1 19 1 112 1 0 1 0    8 2 19 0 182 0 0 1 0
 8 3 19 0 95  0 0 0 0    8 4 19 0 132 0 0 0 0
 9 1 20 1 150 1 0 0 0    9 2 20 0 120 0 0 1 0
 9 3 20 0 105 1 0 0 0    9 4 20 0 141 0 0 1 1
10 1 20 1 120 1 0 0 0   10 2 20 0 103 0 0 0 0
10 3 20 0 127 0 0 0 0   10 4 20 0 170 1 0 0 0
11 1 20 1 121 1 0 1 1   11 2 20 0 169 0 0 1 1
11 3 20 0 121 1 0 0 0   11 4 20 0 120 0 0 0 0
12 1 21 1 200 0 0 1 0   12 2 21 0 108 1 0 1 0
12 3 21 0 124 0 0 0 0   12 4 21 0 185 1 0 0 0
13 1 21 1 100 0 0 0 1   13 2 21 0 160 0 0 0 0
13 3 21 0 110 1 0 1 0   13 4 21 0 115 0 0 0 0
14 1 22 1 130 1 0 1 1   14 2 22 0 85  1 0 0 0
14 3 22 0 130 1 0 0 0   14 4 22 0 125 0 0 0 0
15 1 22 1 130 1 0 0 0   15 2 22 0 120 0 1 0 0
15 3 22 0 112 1 0 0 1   15 4 22 0 169 0 0 0 0
16 1 23 1 97  0 0 1 0   16 2 23 0 130 0 0 0 0
16 3 23 0 119 0 0 0 0   16 4 23 0 123 0 0 0 0
17 1 23 1 110 1 0 0 1   17 2 23 0 128 0 0 0 0
17 3 23 0 190 0 0 0 0   17 4 23 0 110 0 0 0 0
18 1 24 1 132 0 1 0 0   18 2 24 0 115 0 0 0 0
18 3 24 0 115 0 0 0 0   18 4 24 0 110 0 0 0 0
19 1 24 1 138 0 0 0 0   19 2 24 0 90  1 0 0 1
19 3 24 0 133 0 0 0 0   19 4 24 0 116 0 0 0 0
20 1 25 1 85  0 0 1 0   20 2 25 0 118 1 0 0 0
20 3 25 0 125 0 0 0 0   20 4 25 0 120 0 0 0 0
21 1 25 1 92  1 0 0 0   21 2 25 0 120 0 0 1 0
21 3 25 0 140 0 0 0 0   21 4 25 0 241 0 1 0 0
22 1 25 1 105 0 0 0 1   22 2 25 0 155 0 0 0 0
22 3 25 0 95  1 0 1 1   22 4 25 0 130 0 0 0 0
23 1 26 1 190 1 0 0 0   23 2 26 0 113 1 0 0 0
23 3 26 0 168 1 0 0 0   23 4 26 0 160 0 0 0 0
24 1 28 1 120 1 0 1 1   24 2 28 0 140 0 0 0 0
24 3 28 0 250 1 0 0 0   24 4 28 0 134 0 0 0 0
25 1 28 1 95  1 0 0 0   25 2 28 0 120 1 0 0 0
25 3 28 0 120 0 0 0 0   25 4 28 0 130 0 0 0 0
26 1 29 1 130 0 0 1 0   26 2 29 0 150 0 0 0 0
26 3 29 0 135 0 0 0 0   26 4 29 0 130 1 0 0 0
27 1 30 1 142 1 0 0 1   27 2 30 0 107 0 0 1 1
27 3 30 0 153 0 0 0 0   27 4 30 0 137 0 0 0 0
28 1 31 1 102 1 0 0 1   28 2 31 0 100 0 0 1 0
28 3 31 0 150 1 0 0 0   28 3 41 0 120 0 0 0 0
29 1 32 1 105 1 0 0 0   29 2 32 0 121 0 0 0 0
29 3 32 0 132 0 0 0 0   29 4 32 0 134 1 0 0 1
;

%condlog(strata=str,case=low, variable=smoke ht ui ptd lwt);
run;
```

Output 29.10   Conditional Logistic Regression on Birthweight Data

```
                                    The SAS System                                          1
           Non-Linear Least Squares Iterative Phase    Dependent Variable N       Method: Marquardt
    Iter       SMOKE         HT          UI          PTD       LWT   Weighted loss
     0            0           0           0            0         0     40.202536
     1       0.521256   -0.133702    0.434259    0.804132  -0.002916  33.334368
     2       0.704071   -0.210342    0.716720    1.567705  -0.003304  32.467678
     3       0.505365    0.122734    0.485699    1.429303  -0.006523  32.369836
     4       0.595931    0.019445    0.559138    1.569455  -0.004803  32.349769
     5       0.532422    0.124914    0.506889    1.506368  -0.005878  32.342885
     6       0.567254    0.075122    0.536406    1.547766  -0.005249  32.340683
     7       0.545752    0.109742    0.518709    1.523979  -0.005622  32.339879
     8       0.558340    0.090656    0.529279    1.538312  -0.005399  32.339602
     9       0.550772    0.102590    0.522998    1.529782  -0.005531  32.339501
    10       0.555269    0.095650    0.526755    1.534868  -0.005452  32.339466
    11       0.552581    0.099851    0.524518    1.531830  -0.005499  32.339454
    12       0.554183    0.097364    0.525854    1.533641  -0.005471  32.339449
    13       0.553227    0.098854    0.525058    1.532560  -0.005488  32.339447
    14       0.553798    0.097968    0.525533    1.533204  -0.005478  32.339447
    15       0.553457    0.098497    0.525250    1.532820  -0.005484  32.339447
NOTE: Convergence criterion met.


              Non-Linear Least Squares Summary Statistics    Dependent Variable N

              Source          DF    Weighted SS     Weighted MS

              Regression       5    0.00000000      0.00000000
              Residual        24  109.46755256      4.56114802
              Uncorrected Total 29 109.46755256

              (Corrected Total) 28   0.00000000
              Sum of Loss           32.33944668

         Parameter   Estimate    Asymptotic            Asymptotic 95 %
                                  Std. Error          Confidence Interval
                                                    Lower          Upper
              SMOKE  0.553457210  0.4901882258   -0.4582334173   1.5651478368
                 HT  0.098497469  1.2244363947   -2.4285946942   2.6255896325
                 UI  0.525249552  0.5524290707   -0.6148988305   1.6653979353
                PTD  1.532819663  0.6210056845    0.2511372450   2.8145020803
                LWT -0.005483938  0.0094988376   -0.0250884168   0.0141205417


                          Asymptotic Correlation Matrix

      Corr         SMOKE          HT            UI           PTD           LWT
      ---------------------------------------------------------------------------
      SMOKE            1    -0.270954798   0.1892280363   0.0750770623   0.3797566289
         HT  -0.270954798             1   -0.147535106   -0.142357042   -0.485980913
         UI   0.1892280363  -0.147535106             1    0.0182898849   0.2522734662
        PTD   0.0750770623  -0.142357042   0.0182898849             1    0.2232446973
        LWT   0.3797566289  -0.485980913   0.2522734662   0.2232446973             1
```

The following macro, CMOD, performs Cox regression, fitting proportional hazards models, and produces **Output 29.11**:

```
%macro cmod(strata=,case=,time=,covar=,data=_last_,iter=50);
   /*-------------------------------------------------------------*/
   /*  CMOD Is a macro to fit the Cox proportional hazards model   */
   /*     using NLIN.  It uses the discrete hazard for ties.       */
   /*     It accumulates the sums over the risk sets               */
   /*     from the largest time to the smallest.                   */
   /*     If time dependent covariates are desired, then the sums  */
   /*     should be reinitialized for each failure time            */
   /*     The covariates are centered for reasons of stability     */
   /*                                                              */
   /*  &strata      are the names of the variables labeling the    */
   /*               strata. These must be numeric.                 */
   /*  &time        is the name of the time variable               */
   /*  &case        is the name of the variable labeling           */
   /*               the failure and censored times. A failure      */
```

```
   /*              has a value 1 and a censored time a value   */
   /*              of 0.                                        */
   /*   &covar     names the covariates.                        */
   /*   &data      names the input dataset.                     */
   /*   &iter      gives the number of iterations to allow.     */
   /*-----------------------------------------------------------*/

   /*-----generate list of variables-----------------------------*/
%let n=0;
%let old=;
%do %while(%scan(&covar,&n+1)~=);
   %let n=%eval(&n+1);
   %let var&n=%scan(&covar,&n);
   %let old=&old _old&n;
 %end;

   /*-----Find name of last strata variable----------------------*/
%let i=1;
%do %while(%scan(&strata,&i)~=);
   %let last=%scan(&strata,&i);
   %let i=%eval(&i+1);
%end;

   /*----Eliminate missing values -------------------------------*/
data _ph1 _ph2;
set &data;
   if nmiss( of &covar &time &case &strata)>0 then delete;
   if &case=0 or &case=1 ;
   if &case=1 then output _ph2;
   output _ph1;
   keep &covar &case &strata &time;

   /*----Sort by strata and time to support later merge----------*/
proc sort data=_ph2;by &strata &time;

   /*----Count the number of tied event times--------------------*/
proc means data=_ph2 noprint;
   var &time; by &strata &time;
   output out=_ph3 n=_n;

   /*----Compute means of covariates for the events--------------*/
proc means data=_ph2 noprint;
   var &covar; by &strata;
   output out=_ph2 mean=&old;

   /*--------Center the covariates-------------------------------*/
proc sort data=_ph1;
   by &strata &time;
```

```
data _ph1(rename=( %do i=1 %to &n; &&var&i=_old&i %end; ));
   merge _ph1 _ph2;
   by &strata;
   array _c &covar;
   array _m &old;
 /* --- Center the COVARiates --- */
   do over _c;
      _c=_c-_m;
   end;
   drop &old;


 /*---------Compute the cumulative number of tied events--------*/
data _ph1;
   merge _ph1 _ph3;
   by &strata &time;
   retain _maxmaxn 0 _maxn;
   if first.&last then
      do;
         _maxn=0;
      end;
   if _maxn<_n then
      do;
         _maxn=_n;
        if _maxn>_maxmaxn then
           do;
              _maxmaxn=_maxn;
              call symput('CASEMAX',_maxmaxn);
           end;
      end;
proc sort data=_ph1;
   by &strata descending &time &case;


 /*-------Set flags for end of tied failures or new strata----*/
data _ph1;
   set _ph1;
   by &strata descending &time &case;
   if _n<=0 then _n=1;
   if first.&last then _sflag=1;
   else _sflag=0;
   if last.&CASE then _cflag=1;
   else _cflag=0;


 /*-------Fit the model -------------------------------------*/
proc nlin data=_ph1 sigsq=1 maxiter=&iter method=marquardt;

   %let casemax=%scan(&casemax,1);

      /*----Set parms statement with initial values zero ---*/
   parms %do i=1 %to &n;
      &&var&i=0
   %end; ;

   array psi{ &casemax };
```

```
          /*--- Derivatives of psi ---*/
      %do i=1 %to &n;
         array psid&i{ &casemax };
         retain psid&i.1-psid&i&casemax 0;
      %end;
   retain psi1-psi&casemax 0 ;
   retain _sum1-_sum&n 0 _zz_ 1;

   if _sflag=1 then
      do;               /* new Strata, reinitialize */
         _zz_=1;
         %do i=1 %to &n;
            _sum&i=0;
         %end;
         do _i_=1 to &casemax;
            psi{_i_}=0;
            %do i=1 %to &n;
               psid&i{_i_}=0;
            %end;
         end;
      end;


      /*----Compute x b and put in the variable _z_ ----*/
    _z_= exp( %do i=1 %to &n; +&&var&i*_old&i %end;) ;


      /*-------Do the recurrence for symmetric function-----------*/
   s1=1;
   do _i_=1 to _maxn;
      s2=psi{_i_};
      psi{_i_}=psi{_i_}+_z_*s1;
      s1=s2;
   end;


   if &case = 1 then
      do;
         _zz_=_zz_*_z_;
         %do i = 1 %to &n;
            _sum&i=_sum&i+_old&i;
         %end;
      end;


      /*------Compute the reciprocal probability----------*/
   _pp=psi{_n}/_zz_;

      /*------Use twice log(p) for convenience------*/
      /*------Do not forget the weight---*/
   if _cflag=1 & &case=1  then _loss_=2*log(_pp) /_pp;
   else  _loss_=0;

   _weight_=_pp;
```

```
    /* --- Contribution only for each STRATA --- */
if _cflag=1 & &case=1 then dummy=_maxn-1;
else dummy=.;

model _maxn=dummy;

    /*------Weight crossproducts matrix----------*/
_wgtjpj_=_pp**2;

if ~_model_ then do;   /* Derivatives */

%do i=1 %to &n;
   d1=0;
   s1=1;
   do _i_=1 to _maxn;
      d2=psid&i {_i_};
      psid&i {_i_}=psid&i {_i_}+_z_*(d1+_old&i*s1);
      d1=d2;
      s1=psi{_i_};
   end;
   if _cflag=1 & &case=1 then
   do;
      der.&&var&i=(-psid&i{_n}/psi{_n}** 2)*_zz_+_sum&i / _pp;
    end;
   else der.&&var&i=0;
%end;

end;

if _cflag=1 & &case=1 then
   do;
      _zz_=1;
      %do i=1 %to &n;
         _sum&i=0;
      %end;
   end;
run;

%mend CMOD;

   /* This data is from Kalbfleish and Prentice.         */
   /* Note that there are several ties in the data set   */
   /* and the estimates will differ from those in        */
   /* Kalbfleish and Prentice since they use a different */
   /* treatment of ties.                                 */
   /* This example uses the discrete likelihood for the  */
   /* treatment of ties.                                 */
```

```
title 'Lifetimes of Rats Exposed to DMBA';
data vagcan;
   label days='days from exposure to death'
         group='pre-treatment group';
   input days @@;
   event=(days>0);
   s=1;
   days=abs(days);
   if _n_>19 then group=1;
   else group=0;
   cards;
143 164 188 188 190 192 206 209 213 216
220 227 230 234 246 265 304  -216  -244
142 156 163 198 205 232 232 233 233 233 233 239
240 261 280 280 296 296 323 -204 -344
;

%CMOD(strata=s,case=event,time=days,covar=group);
run;
```

Output 29.11   Cox Regression on Cancer Data

```
                        Lifetimes of Rats Exposed to DMBA                                    1

        Non-Linear Least Squares Iterative Phase    Dependent Variable _MAXN    Method: Marquardt
                          Iter        GROUP    Weighted loss
                           0            0       190.785701
                           1        -0.555194   187.803656
                           2        -0.614679   187.763011
                           3        -0.621429   187.761828
                           4        -0.622311   187.761725
                           5        -0.622428   187.761713
                           6        -0.622443   187.761711
NOTE: Convergence criterion met.


              Non-Linear Least Squares Summary Statistics     Dependent Variable _MAXN

                Source           DF     Weighted SS      Weighted MS

                Regression        1     109103.94509    109103.94509
                Residual         28       8195.77610       292.70629
                Uncorrected Total 29     117299.72119

                (Corrected Total) 28       4778.58747
                Sum of Loss                 187.76171

                Parameter    Estimate     Asymptotic            Asymptotic 95 %
                                          Std. Error          Confidence Interval
                                                              Lower         Upper
                  GROUP  -.6224432532  0.31731736834  -1.2724334748  0.02754696851


                            Asymptotic Correlation Matrix

                          Corr                GROUP
                        ------------------------------
                          GROUP                 1
```

REFERENCES

Bard, J. (1970), "Comparison of Gradient Methods for the Solution of the Nonlinear Parameter Estimation Problems," *SIAM Journal of Numerical Analysis*, 7, 157–186.

Bard, J. (1974), *Nonlinear Parameter Estimation*, New York: Academic Press, Inc.

Beaton, A.E. and Tukey, J.W. (1974), "The Fitting of Power Series, Meaning Polynomials, Illustrated on Band-Spectroscopic Data," *Technometrics*, 16, 147–185.

Charnes, A., Frome, E.L., and Yu, P.L. (1976), "The Equivalence of Generalized Least Squares and Maximum Likelihood Estimates in the Exponential Family," *Journal of the American Statistical Association*, 71, 169–172.

Cox, D.R. (1970), *Analysis of Binary Data*, London: Chapman and Hall.

Finney, D.J. (1971), *Probit Analysis*, 3d Edition, Cambridge: Cambridge University Press.

Gallant, A.R. (1975), "Nonlinear Regression," *American Statistician*, 29, 73–81.

Hartley, H.O. (1961), "The Modified Gauss-Newton Method for the Fitting of Nonlinear Regression Functions by Least Squares," *Technometrics*, 3, 269–280.

Holland, P.W. and Welsch, R.E. (1977), "Robust Regression Using Iteratively Reweighted Least Squares," *Communications Statistics: Theory and Methods*, 6, 813–827.

Jennrich, R.I. (1969), "Asymptotic Properties of Nonlinear Least Squares Estimators," *Annals of Mathematical Statistics*, 40, 633–643.

Jennrich, R.I. and Moore, R.H. (1975), "Maximum Likelihood Estimation by Means of Nonlinear Least Squares," *American Statistical Association, 1975 Proceedings of the Statistical Computing Section*, 57–65.

Jennrich, R.I. and Sampson, P.F. (1968), "Application of Stepwise Regression to Nonlinear Estimation," *Technometrics*, 10, 63–72.

Judge, G.G., Griffiths, W.E., Hill, R.C., and Lee, Tsoung-Chao (1980), *The Theory and Practice of Econometrics*, New York: John Wiley & Sons, Inc.

Kennedy, W.J. and Gentle, J.E. (1980), *Statistical Computing*, New York: Marcel Dekker, Inc.

Marquardt, D.W. (1963), "An Algorithm for Least Squares Estimation of Nonlinear Parameters," *Journal for the Society of Industrial and Applied Mathematics*, 11, 431–441.

McCullagh, P. and Nelder, J.A. (1983), *Generalized Linear Models*, London: Chapman Hall.

Nelder, J.A. and Wedderburn, R.W.M. (1972), "Generalized Linear Models," *Journal of the Royal Statistical Society, Series A*, 135, 370–384.

Ralston, M.L. and Jennrich, R.I. (1978), "DUD, A Derivative-Free Algorithm for Nonlinear Least Squares," *Technometrics*, 20, 7–14.

Chapter 30

The NPAR1WAY Procedure

ABSTRACT 1195
INTRODUCTION 1196
SPECIFICATIONS 1197
  PROC NPAR1WAY Statement 1197
  BY Statement 1198
  CLASS Statement 1199
  VAR Statement 1199
DETAILS 1199
  Missing Values 1199
  Memory Requirements 1199
  Time Requirements 1199
  Resolution of Tied Values 1199
  Simple Linear Rank Statistics 1200
    Wilcoxon Scores 1200
    Median Scores 1200
    Van der Waerden Scores 1200
    Savage Scores 1200
  Statistics Based on the Empirical Distribution Function 1201
    Kolmogorov-Smirnov Statistic 1201
    Cramer-von Mises Statistic 1201
    Kuiper Statistic 1202
  Printed Output 1202
EXAMPLE 1204
  Weight Gains Data 1204
REFERENCES 1210

ABSTRACT

The NPAR1WAY procedure performs analysis of variance on ranks, and it computes several statistics based on the empirical distribution function (EDF) and certain rank scores of a response variable across a one-way classification. NPAR1WAY is a nonparametric procedure for testing that the distribution of a variable has the same location parameter across different groups or, in the case of the EDF tests, that the distribution is the same across different groups. NPAR1WAY handles the case of independent groups, not paired data. For the case of paired data, see discussion of the UNIVARIATE procedure in base SAS documentation. UNIVARIATE performs a sign test and the Wilcoxon Signed Rank test.

INTRODUCTION

Most nonparametric tests are derived by examining the distribution of the rank scores of the response variable. The rank scores are simply functions of the ranks of the response variable's values.

NPAR1WAY calculates simple linear rank statistics based on Wilcoxon scores, median scores, Savage scores, and Van der Waerden scores. These statistics are used to test if the distribution of a variable has the same location parameter across different groups. These simple linear rank statistics computed by NPAR1WAY can also be computed by calculating the rank scores using PROC RANK and analyzing these rank scores with PROC ANOVA. **Table 30.1** shows the correspondence between NPAR1WAY Wilcoxon, Median, Van der Waerden, and Savage scores and various nonparametric tests.

Table 30.1 Comparison of PROC NPAR1WAY with Nonparametric Tests

These NPAR1WAY scores . . .	correspond to these tests if data are classified in two levels, . . . *	correspond to these tests for a one-way layout or *k*-sample location test. **
Wilcoxon	Wilcoxon rank-sum test Mann-Whitney U test	Kruskal-Wallis test
Median	Median test for two samples	*k*-sample median test (Brown-Mood)
Van der Waerden	Van der Waerden test	*k*-sample Van der Waerden test
Savage	Savage test	*k*-sample Savage test

* The tests are two-tailed. For a one-tailed test, transform the significance probability by $p/2$ or $(1-p/2)$.

** NPAR1WAY provides a chi-square approximate test.

In addition to the simple linear rank statistics discussed above, NPAR1WAY also calculates three statistics that are based on the empirical distribution of the sample. These are the Kolmogorov-Smirnov statistic, the Cramer-von Mises statistic, and, if there are only two levels of the classification variable, the Kuiper statistic. These statistics are used to test if the distribution of a variable is the same across different groups. **All of the tests performed by NPAR1WAY are asymptotic and are not appropriate for small sample sizes.**

See **Simple Linear Rank Statistics** and **Statistics Based on the Empirical Distribution Function** later in this chapter for more information.

SPECIFICATIONS

The following statements are used in the NPAR1WAY procedure:

PROC NPAR1WAY <*options*>;   required statements
   CLASS *variable*;

   BY *variables*;   optional statements
   VAR *variables*;

To use PROC NPAR1WAY, you need the PROC and CLASS statements. The rest of this section gives detailed syntax information for each of the statements above, beginning with the PROC NPAR1WAY statement. The remaining statements are covered in alphabetical order.

PROC NPAR1WAY Statement

PROC NPAR1WAY <*options*>;

The PROC NPAR1WAY statement starts the NPAR1WAY procedure and optionally identifies a data set or requests particular analyses. By default, the procedure uses the most recently created SAS data set, omits missing values from the analysis, and performs all analyses available with the procedure. The table below summarizes the options.

Task	Options
Specify data set details	DATA=
	MISSING
Choose analyses	ANOVA
	EDF
	MEDIAN
	SAVAGE
	VW
	WILCOXON

The list below gives details on these options in alphabetical order. For more information, including formulas, on the analyses performed, see **Simple Linear Rank Statistics** and **Statistics Based on the Empirical Distribution Function** later in this chapter.

ANOVA
   performs a standard analysis of variance on the raw data.

DATA=*SAS-data-set*
   names the SAS data set containing the data to be analyzed. By default, the procedure uses the most recently created SAS data set.

EDF

calculates statistics based on the empirical distribution function. These always include the Kolmogorov-Smirnov and Cramer-von Mises statistics, and, if there are only two classification levels, the Kuiper statistic.

MISSING

interprets missing values of the CLASS variable as a valid class level.

MEDIAN

performs an analysis of the median scores. The median score is 1 for points above the median, and 0 otherwise. For two samples, this produces a median test. For more than two samples, this produces the Brown-Mood test.

SAVAGE

analyzes Savage scores. These are the expected order statistics for the exponential distribution, with 1 subtracted to center the scores around 0. This test is appropriate for comparing groups of data with exponential distributions.

VW

analyzes Van der Waerden scores. These are approximate normal scores derived by applying the inverse normal distribution function to the fractional ranks. For two levels, this is the standard Van der Waerden test.

WILCOXON

performs an analysis of the ranks of the data or the Wilcoxon scores. For two levels, this is the same as a Wilcoxon rank-sum test. For any number of levels, this is a Kruskal-Wallis test. For the two-sample case (where the class variable has only two levels), the procedure uses a continuity correction. The formula is given in **Printed Output** and the output is shown in **Example 1,** both later in this chapter.

BY Statement

BY *variables;*

A BY statement can be used with PROC NPAR1WAY to obtain separate analyses on observations in groups defined by the BY variables. When a BY statement appears, the procedure expects the input data set to be sorted in order of the BY variables.

If your input data set is not sorted in ascending order, use one of the following alternatives:

- Use the SORT procedure with a similar BY statement to sort the data.
- Use the BY statement options NOTSORTED or DESCENDING in the BY statement for the NPAR1WAY procedure. As a cautionary note, the NOTSORTED option does not mean that the data are unsorted, but rather means that the data are arranged in groups (according to values of the BY variables) and that these groups are not necessarily in alphabetical or increasing numeric order.
- Use the DATASETS procedure (in base SAS software) to create an index on the BY variables.

For more information on the BY statement, see the discussion in *SAS Language: Reference, Version 6, First Edition.* For more information on the DATASETS procedure, see the discussion in the *SAS Procedures Guide, Version 6, Third Edition.*

CLASS Statement

CLASS *variable*;

The CLASS statement, which is required, names one and only one classification variable. This variable identifies groups in the data. Class variables can be character or numeric.

VAR Statement

VAR *variables*;

The VAR statement names the response or dependent variables to be analyzed. If the VAR statement is omitted, the procedure analyzes all numeric variables in the data set (except for the CLASS variable, if it is numeric).

DETAILS

Missing Values

If an observation has a missing value for a response variable, that observation is excluded from the analysis. A missing value for the class variable is treated similarly unless you request the MISSING option. In that case, the procedure treats the missing value as a valid class level and analyzes the data accordingly.

Memory Requirements

The procedure must have

$$36n + 28e + 8(v + 2)$$

bytes of memory available to store the data. In the equation above,

- n is the number of nonmissing observations.
- e is the number of nonempty classes.
- v is the number of variables being processed for each BY group.

If the EDF option is requested, four temporary arrays, each of size $8e$ are allocated.

Time Requirements

The time required to run the NPAR1WAY procedure varies linearly with sample size.

Resolution of Tied Values

Although the nonparametric tests were developed for continuous distributions, tied values do occur in practice. Ties are handled in all methods by assigning the average score for the different ranks corresponding to the tied values. Adjustments to variance estimates are performed in the manner described by Hajek (1969, Ch. 7). Statistics based on the empirical distribution function are computed as usual from the definitions of the EDF. However, ties modify the exact distribution of the test statistics and may affect the quality of the large sample approximations of the probability values if they are numerous.

Simple Linear Rank Statistics

Statistics defined in the form

$$S = \Sigma_{j=1}^{n} \; c_j a(R_j)$$

are called *simple linear rank statistics*, where

R_j is the rank of the *j*th observation.

$a(R_j)$ is the rank score.

c_j is an indicator vector denoting the class to which the *j*th observation belongs.

n is the number of nonmissing values

The NPAR1WAY procedure calculates simple linear rank statistics based on the following four scores.

Wilcoxon Scores

Wilcoxon scores are the ranks

$$a(R_j) = R_j$$

and are locally most powerful for location shifts of a logistic distribution. In computing the Wilcoxon rank-sum statistic for the two-sample case, the procedure performs a continuity correction.

Median Scores

Median scores are 1 for points above the median, 0 otherwise; that is,

$$a(R_j) = 1 \quad \text{if } (R_j > (n + 1) / 2)$$
$$ = 0 \quad \text{if } (R_j \le (n + 1) / 2) \quad .$$

Median scores are locally most powerful for double exponential distributions.

Van der Waerden Scores

Van der Waerden scores are approximations of the expected values of the order statistics for a normal distribution

$$a(R_j) = \Phi^{-1}(R_j / (n + 1))$$

where Φ is the distribution function for the normal distribution. These scores are powerful for normal distributions.

Savage Scores

Savage scores are expected values of order statistics for the exponential distribution, with 1 subtracted to center the scores around 0:

$$a(R_j) = \Sigma_{i=1}^{R_j} 1 / (n - i + 1) - 1 \quad .$$

Savage scores are powerful for comparing scale differences in exponential distributions or location shifts in extreme value distributions (Hajek 1969, p. 83).

Statistics Based on the Empirical Distribution Function

The *empirical distribution function* (EDF) of a sample $\{x_j\}$, $j=1, 2, \ldots, n$ is defined as the following function:

$$F(x) = (1 / n) \text{ (number of } x_j \leq x) = (1/n) \sum_{j=1}^{n} (x_j \leq x) .$$

The NPAR1WAY procedure uses the subsample of values within the ith class level to generate an EDF, F_i. Let n_i be the number of values within the ith class level, and let n be the total number of values. Then, the EDF for the pooled sample can also be written as

$$F = (1 / n) \sum_i (n_i F_i) .$$

The k-sample analogues of the Kolmogorov-Smirnov and Cramer-von Mises statistics used by NPAR1WAY are among those studied by Kiefer (1959).

Kolmogorov-Smirnov Statistic

As computed by the NPAR1WAY procedure, the Kolmogorov-Smirnov statistic is the value

$$KS = \max_j \sqrt{\sum_i (n_i / n)[F_i(x_j) - F(x_j)]^2} \quad \text{where } j = 1, 2, \ldots, n$$

which measures the maximum deviation of the EDF within the classes to the pooled EDF. The asymptotic statistic is

$$KSa = KS \sqrt{n}$$

The values of the F_i at the maximum deviation from F, the values $(F_i - F) \sqrt{n_i}$ at the maximum deviation from F, the value of F at the maximum deviation, and the point where this maximum deviation occurs are printed by NPAR1WAY, as well as the overall Kolmogorov statistic and the asymptotic statistic. If there are only two class levels, the two-sample Kolmogorov statistic

$$D = \max_j | F_1(x_j) - F_2(x_j) | \quad \text{where } j = 1, 2, \ldots, n$$

and the probability from the asymptotic distribution of observing a larger test statistic are also computed. The quality of this approximation has been studied by Hodges (1957). For tables of the exact distribution of D where the two sample sizes are equal, see Lehman (1975, p. 413). For tables of the exact distribution for unequal sample sizes, see Kim and Jennrich (1970, pp. 79-170).

Cramer-von Mises Statistic

The Cramer-von Mises statistic is defined as

$$CM = \sum_i [(n_i/n^2) \sum_{j=1}^{p} t_j(F_i(x_j) - F(x_j))^2]$$

where t_j is the number of ties at the jth distinct value and p is the number of distinct values. CM measures the integrated deviation of the EDF within the classes to the pooled EDF. The class-specific contributions to the sum are printed by the NPAR1WAY procedure together with the sum, which is the asymptotic value formed by multiplying the Cramer-von Mises statistic by the number of observations.

Kuiper Statistic

If there are only two class levels, the Kuiper statistic, a scaled value for the asymptotic distribution, and the probability from the asymptotic distribution of observing a larger test statistic, are also computed. In this case, the Kuiper statistic is computed as

$$K = \max_j(F_1(x_j) - F_2(x_j)) - \min_j (F_1(x_j) - F_2(x_j)) \quad \text{where } j = 1, 2, \ldots, n \ .$$

The asymptotic value is

$$Ka = K\sqrt{(n_1 n_2/n)} \ .$$

Printed Output

If the ANOVA option is specified, PROC NPAR1WAY prints the following:

1. the traditional Analysis of Variance table
2. the effect mean square reported as Among MS
3. the error mean square reported as Within MS.

(These are the same values that would result from using a procedure such as ANOVA or GLM.)

NPAR1WAY produces a table for each rank score and includes the following for each level in the classification:

4. the levels of the independent variable (the CLASS variable)
5. the number of observations in each level (N)
6. the Sum of Scores
7. the Expected sum of scores Under H0, the null hypothesis that the location of the distributions is the same
8. the Std Dev Under H0, the standard deviation estimate of the sum of scores
9. the Mean Score.

For two or more levels, NPAR1WAY prints the following for each analysis of scores:

10. a chi-square statistic (CHISQ) for testing H0
11. its degrees of freedom (DF)
12. Prob > CHISQ, the asymptotic significance probability.

If there are only two levels, NPAR1WAY reports the following for each analysis of scores:

13. the sum of scores (S) corresponding to the smaller sample size.
14. the ratio (S-expected)/(Std Dev) as Z, which is approximately normally distributed under the null hypothesis. For the two-sample case, the procedure performs a continuity correction and prints Z^* (labeled as Z in the output), which is calculated as follows

$$Z^* = (Z - 0.5)/std \qquad \text{if } Z > 0$$
$$Z^* = (Z + 0.5)/std \qquad \text{if } Z < 0$$

and where no correction is performed when Z=0.
15. Prob > |Z|, the asymptotic probability of a greater observed Z value
16. T-Test approx., the significance level for an approximate t-test calculated using the formulas for Z^* above.

NPAR1WAY produces a table for each statistic dependent on the empirical data function and includes the following for each level of classification:

17. the levels of the independent variable (the CLASS variable)
18. the number of observations in the level (N).

For the Kolmogorov-Smirnov statistic, the table includes the following:

19. the value of F_i at the maximum deviation from F for each class
20. the maximum Deviation from Mean, that is, $(\sqrt{n_i})(F_i(x_j) - F(x_j))$ at the maximum deviation from F_i for each class
21. the total number of observations in each class
22. the value F of the pooled EDF at the observation where the maximum occurs
23. the point where the maximum deviation from F occurs
24. the Kolmogorov-Smirnov statistic (KS), the value for the asymptotic distribution (KSa), where $KSa = KS\sqrt{n}$
25. if there are only two levels, the two-sample Kolmogorov statistic as D, where $D = \max_j |F_1(x_j) - F_2(x_j)|$.

For the Cramer-von Mises statistic, the table includes the following:

26. the Summed Deviation from Mean $(n_i/n) \sum_{j=1}^{n} (F_i(x_j) - F(x_j))^2$
27. the Cramer-von Mises Statistic (CM) and the value for the asymptotic distribution (CMa), where $CMa = nCM$.

If there are only two classification levels, the table includes the following for the Kuiper statistic:

28. Deviation from Mean, $\max_j(F_1(x_j) - F_2 < (x_j))$ and $\max_j(F_2(x_j) - F_1(x_j))$
29. the Kuiper 2-Sample Test statistic (K), the value for the asymptotic distribution (Ka), where $Ka = K\sqrt{(n_1 n_2/n)}$, and the probability of observing a larger Ka test statistic.

EXAMPLE

Weight Gains Data

The data are read in with a variable number of observations per record. In this example, PROC NPAR1WAY first performs all six analyses on five levels of the class variable DOSE. Then the two lowest levels are output to a second data set to illustrate the two-sample tests. The following statements produce **Output 30.1:**

```
title 'Weight Gains with Gossypol Additive';
title3 'Halverson and Sherwood - 1932';
data g;
   input dose n;
   do i=1 to n;
      input gain @@;
      output;
   end;
   cards;
 0 16
    228 229 218 216 224 208 235 229 233 219 224 220 232 200 208 232
.04 11
    186 229 220 208 228 198 222 273 216 198 213
.07 12
    179 193 183 180 143 204 114 188 178 134 208 196
.10 17
    130  87 135 116 118 165 151  59 126  64  78  94 150 160 122 110 178
.13 11
    154 130 130 118 118 104 112 134  98 100 104
;

proc npar1way;
   class dose;
   var gain;
run;

proc npar1way;
   where dose <=.04;
   class dose;
   var gain;
   title4 'Doses<=.04';
run;
```

Output 30.1   Two Separate Runs of PROC NPAR1WAY: All CLASS Levels and Two Levels Only

```
                                                                          1
              Weight Gains with Gossypol Additive

                 Halverson and Sherwood - 1932
           ❶   N P A R 1 W A Y   P R O C E D U R E
              Analysis of Variance for Variable GAIN
                  Classified by Variable DOSE

                                                 ❷            ❸
   DOSE           N          Mean            Among MS      Within MS
                                             35020.7465    627.451597
   0            16       222.187500
   0.04         11       217.363636           F Value       Prob > F
   0.07         12       175.000000           55.814        0.0001
   0.1          17       120.176471
   0.13         11       118.363636
                Average Scores were used for Ties
```

```
                                                                          2
              Weight Gains with Gossypol Additive

                 Halverson and Sherwood - 1932

              N P A R 1 W A Y   P R O C E D U R E

           Wilcoxon Scores (Rank Sums) for Variable GAIN
                  Classified by Variable DOSE

  ❹              ❺           ❻            ❼            ❽            ❾
                          Sum of      Expected      Std Dev        Mean
   DOSE           N       Scores      Under H0      Under H0       Score

   0            16     890.500000      544.0      67.9789655    55.6562500
   0.04         11     555.000000      374.0      59.0635883    50.4545455
   0.07         12     395.500000      408.0      61.1366221    32.9583333
   0.1          17     275.500000      578.0      69.3807412    16.2058824
   0.13         11     161.500000      374.0      59.0635883    14.6818182
                Average Scores were used for Ties

         Kruskal-Wallis Test (Chi-Square Approximation)
      ❿ CHISQ= 52.666              ⓫ DF=  4      ⓬ Prob > CHISQ=   0.0001
```

```
                                                                          3
              Weight Gains with Gossypol Additive

                 Halverson and Sherwood - 1932

              N P A R 1 W A Y   P R O C E D U R E

           Median Scores (Number of Points above Median)
                      for Variable GAIN
                  Classified by Variable DOSE

                          Sum of      Expected      Std Dev        Mean
   DOSE           N       Scores      Under H0      Under H0       Score

   0            16        16.0      7.88059701    1.75790231    1.00000000
   0.04         11        11.0      5.41791045    1.52735508    1.00000000
   0.07         12         6.0      5.91044776    1.58096271    0.50000000
   0.1          17         0.0      8.37313433    1.79415153    0.00000000
   0.13         11         0.0      5.41791045    1.52735508    0.00000000
                Average Scores were used for Ties
         Median 1-Way Analysis (Chi-Square Approximation)
      CHISQ= 54.176              DF=  4      Prob > CHISQ=   0.0001
```

```
                        Weight Gains with Gossypol Additive                          4

                          Halverson and Sherwood - 1932

                          N P A R 1 W A Y   P R O C E D U R E

                  Van der Waerden Scores (Normal) for Variable GAIN
                            Classified by Variable DOSE

                               Sum of        Expected         Std Dev         Mean
        DOSE          N        Scores        Under H0         Under H0        Score

        0             16      16.1164737        0.0           3.32595675     1.00727961
        0.04          11       8.3408986        0.0           2.88976066     0.75826351
        0.07          12      -0.5766736        0.0           2.99118646    -0.04805613
        0.1           17     -14.6889214        0.0           3.39454039    -0.86405420
        0.13          11      -9.1917773        0.0           2.88976066    -0.83561612
                          Average Scores were used for Ties
                 Van der Waerden 1-Way (Chi-Square Approximation)
                 CHISQ=  47.297              DF= 4           Prob > CHISQ=    0.0001
```

```
                        Weight Gains with Gossypol Additive                          5

                          Halverson and Sherwood - 1932

                          N P A R 1 W A Y   P R O C E D U R E

                  Savage Scores (Exponential) for Variable GAIN
                            Classified by Variable DOSE

                               Sum of        Expected         Std Dev         Mean
        DOSE          N        Scores        Under H0         Under H0        Score

        0             16      16.0743905        0.0           3.38527520     1.00464941
        0.04          11       7.6930992        0.0           2.94129955     0.69937265
        0.07          12      -3.5849578        0.0           3.04453428    -0.29874648
        0.1           17     -11.9794882        0.0           3.45508203    -0.70467578
        0.13          11      -8.2030437        0.0           2.94129955    -0.74573125
                          Average Scores were used for Ties
                   Savage 1-Way (Chi-Square Approximation)
                 CHISQ=  39.491              DF= 4           Prob > CHISQ=    0.0001
```

```
                        Weight Gains with Gossypol Additive                          6

                          Halverson and Sherwood - 1932

                          N P A R 1 W A Y   P R O C E D U R E

                  Kolmogorov-Smirnov Test for Variable GAIN
                            Classified by Variable DOSE

                                                                        Deviation
  (17)                          (18)             (19)    EDF      (20)  from Mean
        DOSE                          N                at maximum        at maximum

        0                           16              0.00000000         -1.91044776
        0.04                        11              0.00000000         -1.58405960
        0.07                        12              0.33333333         -0.49979576
        0.1                         17              1.00000000          2.15386115
        0.13                        11              1.00000000          1.73256519
        --------                    ----            -----------
                               (21) 67         (22) 0.47761194

     (23) Maximum Deviation occurred at Observation    36
          Value of GAIN     at maximum   178.000000

          (24)    Kolmogorov-Smirnov Statistic (Asymptotic)
                  KS = 0.457928              KSa  = 3.74830
```

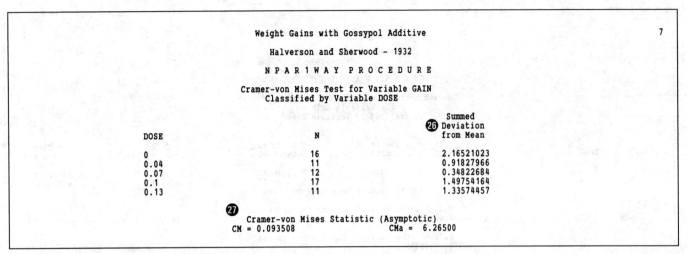

```
                    Weight Gains with Gossypol Additive                        7

                       Halverson and Sherwood - 1932

                      N P A R 1 W A Y   P R O C E D U R E

                  Cramer-von Mises Test for Variable GAIN
                        Classified by Variable DOSE

                                                         Summed
                                                    26  Deviation
        DOSE                          N                 from Mean

        0                            16                 2.16521023
        0.04                         11                 0.91827966
        0.07                         12                 0.34822684
        0.1                          17                 1.49754164
        0.13                         11                 1.33574457

              27  Cramer-von Mises Statistic (Asymptotic)
                  CM = 0.093508                CMa =  6.26500
```

```
                    Weight Gains with Gossypol Additive                        8

                       Halverson and Sherwood - 1932
                             Doses<=.04

                      N P A R 1 W A Y   P R O C E D U R E

                  Analysis of Variance for Variable GAIN
                        Classified by Variable DOSE

        DOSE          N           Mean              Among MS        Within MS
                                                    151.683712      271.479318
        0            16      222.187500
        0.04         11      217.363636             F Value         Prob > F
                                                    0.559           0.4617
                     Average Scores were used for Ties
```

```
                    Weight Gains with Gossypol Additive                        9

                       Halverson and Sherwood - 1932
                             Doses<=.04

                      N P A R 1 W A Y   P R O C E D U R E

                 Wilcoxon Scores (Rank Sums) for Variable GAIN
                        Classified by Variable DOSE

                              Sum of        Expected       Std Dev         Mean
        DOSE        N         Scores        Under H0       Under H0        Score

        0          16      253.500000        224.0       20.2215647     15.8437500
        0.04       11      124.500000        154.0       20.2215647     11.3181818
                         Average Scores were used for Ties
                    Wilcoxon 2-Sample Test (Normal Approximation)
                       (with Continuity Correction of .5)

             13  S= 124.500         14  Z= -1.43411       15  Prob > |Z| =  0.1515

             16  T-Test approx. Significance =     0.1635

                  Kruskal-Wallis Test (Chi-Square Approximation)
                  CHISQ=  2.1282             DF=  1          Prob > CHISQ=   0.1446
```

```
                     Weight Gains with Gossypol Additive                        10

                        Halverson and Sherwood - 1932
                                 Doses<=.04

                         N P A R 1 W A Y   P R O C E D U R E

                 Median Scores (Number of Points above Median)
                            for Variable GAIN
                        Classified by Variable DOSE


                              Sum of        Expected          Std Dev            Mean
     DOSE          N          Scores        Under H0          Under H0           Score

     0            16            9.0         7.70370370        1.29999472      0.562500000
     0.04         11            4.0         5.29629630        1.29999472      0.363636364
                         Average Scores were used for Ties

                    Median 2-Sample Test (Normal Approximation)
          S=  4.00000                Z= -.997155          Prob > |Z| =  0.3187

                    Median 1-Way Analysis (Chi-Square Approximation)
          CHISQ= 0.99432                DF= 1            Prob > CHISQ=   0.3187
```

```
                     Weight Gains with Gossypol Additive                        11

                        Halverson and Sherwood - 1932
                                 Doses<=.04

                         N P A R 1 W A Y   P R O C E D U R E

              Van der Waerden Scores (Normal) for Variable GAIN
                        Classified by Variable DOSE


                              Sum of        Expected          Std Dev            Mean
     DOSE          N          Scores        Under H0          Under H0           Score

     0            16        3.34651962        0.0           2.32033631      0.209157476
     0.04         11       -3.34651962        0.0           2.32033631      -.304229056
                         Average Scores were used for Ties
               Van der Waerden 2-Sample Test (Normal Approximation)
          S= -3.34652               Z= -1.44226          Prob > |Z| =  0.1492

               Van der Waerden 1-Way (Chi-Square Approximation)
          CHISQ= 2.0801                 DF= 1            Prob > CHISQ=   0.1492
```

```
                     Weight Gains with Gossypol Additive                        12

                        Halverson and Sherwood - 1932
                                 Doses<=.04

                         N P A R 1 W A Y   P R O C E D U R E

              Savage Scores (Exponential) for Variable GAIN
                        Classified by Variable DOSE


                              Sum of        Expected          Std Dev            Mean
     DOSE          N          Scores        Under H0          Under H0           Score

     0            16        1.83455386        0.0           2.40183886      0.114659616
     0.04         11       -1.83455386        0.0           2.40183886      -.166777623
                         Average Scores were used for Ties
               Savage 2-Sample Test (Normal Approximation)
          S= -1.83455               Z= -.763812          Prob > |Z| =  0.4450

               Savage 1-Way (Chi-Square Approximation)
          CHISQ= 0.58341                DF= 1            Prob > CHISQ=   0.4450
```

```
                        Weight Gains with Gossypol Additive                           13

                         Halverson and Sherwood - 1932
                                Doses<=.04

                         N P A R 1 W A Y   P R O C E D U R E

                    Kolmogorov-Smirnov Test for Variable GAIN
                         Classified by Variable DOSE

                                                                            Deviation
                                                          EDF               from Mean
        DOSE                    N                       at maximum          at maximum

        0                      16                      0.250000000        -.481481481
        0.04                   11                      0.545454545         0.580688515
        --------               ----                    ----------
                               27                      0.370370370

              Maximum Deviation occurred at Observation      4
              Value of GAIN    at maximum  216.000000

                    Kolmogorov-Smirnov 2-Sample Test (Asymptotic) 25
                     KS = 0.145172                 D = 0.295455
                    KSa = 0.754337          Prob > KSa =  0.6199
```

```
                        Weight Gains with Gossypol Additive                           14

                         Halverson and Sherwood - 1932
                                Doses<=.04

                         N P A R 1 W A Y   P R O C E D U R E

                    Cramer-von Mises Test for Variable GAIN
                         Classified by Variable DOSE

                                                         Summed
                                                        Deviation
        DOSE                    N                       from Mean

        0                      16                      0.098638419
        0.04                   11                      0.143474064


                    Cramer-von Mises Statistic (Asymptotic)
                     CM = 0.008967                CMa = 0.242112
```

```
                        Weight Gains with Gossypol Additive                           15

                         Halverson and Sherwood - 1932
                                Doses<=.04

                         N P A R 1 W A Y   P R O C E D U R E

                         Kuiper Test for Variable GAIN
                         Classified by Variable DOSE
                                              28
                                                        Deviation
        DOSE                    N                       from Mean

        0                      16                      0.090909091
        0.04                   11                      0.295454545


                         Kuiper 2-Sample Test (Asymptotic)
        29 K = 0.386364        Ka = 0.986440              Prob > Ka =    0.8383
```

REFERENCES

Conover, W.J. (1980), *Practical Nonparametric Statistics*, 2d Edition, New York: John Wiley & Sons, Inc.

Hajek, J. (1969), *A Course in Nonparametric Statistics*, San Francisco: Holden-Day.

Hodges, J.L. Jr. (1957), "The Significance Probability of the Smirnov Two-Sample Test," *Arkiv for Matematik*, 3, 469–486.

Hollander, M. and Wolfe, D.A. (1973), *Nonparametric Statistical Methods*, New York: John Wiley & Sons, Inc.

Kiefer, J. (1959), "K-Sample Analogues of the Kolmogorov-Smirnov and Cramer-von Mises Tests," *Annals of Mathematical Statistics*, 30, 420–447.

Kim, P.J. and Jennrich, R.I. (1970), "Tables of the Exact Sampling Distribution of the Two-sample Kolmogorov-Smirnov Criterion $D_{m,n}$, $m \leq n$," *Selected Tables in Mathematical Statistics* (Harter and Owen, eds.), Chicago: Markham Publishing Co.

Lehmann, E.L. (1975), *Nonparametrics: Statistical Methods Based on Ranks*, San Francisco: Holden-Day.

Quade, D. (1966), "On Analysis of Variance for the *k*-Sample Problem," *Annals of Mathematical Statistics*, 37, 1747–1758.

Chapter 31

The ORTHOREG Procedure

ABSTRACT 1211
INTRODUCTION 1211
SPECIFICATIONS 1212
    PROC ORTHOREG Statement 1212
    BY Statement 1212
    MODEL Statement 1213
    WEIGHT Statement 1213
DETAILS 1213
    Missing Values 1213
    Output Data Set 1213
    Printed Output 1213
EXAMPLES 1214
    Example 1: Longley Data 1214
    Example 2: Wampler Data 1216
REFERENCES 1219

ABSTRACT

The ORTHOREG procedure performs regression using the Gentleman-Givens method. For ill-conditioned data, PROC ORTHOREG may produce substantially more accurate estimates than other SAS procedures such as the REG procedure and the GLM procedure.

INTRODUCTION

The standard SAS regression procedures (REG and GLM) are very accurate for most problems. However, if you have very ill-conditioned data, the procedures can produce estimates that yield an error sum of squares very close to the minimum but still different from the exact least-squares estimates. Normally, this coincides with estimates that have very high standard errors. In other words, the numerical error is much smaller than the statistical standard error.

The ORTHOREG procedure can produce more accurate estimates than other regression procedures when your data is ill-conditioned. Instead of collecting crossproducts, PROC ORTHOREG uses Gentleman-Givens transformations to update and compute the upper triangular matrix **R** of the QR decomposition of the data matrix, with special care for scaling (see Gentleman 1972a; 1972b). This method has the advantage over other orthogonalization methods (for example, Householder transformations) of not requiring the data matrix to be stored in memory.

SPECIFICATIONS

The following statements are used in PROC ORTHOREG:

PROC ORTHOREG <*options*>;   } required statements
    MODEL *dependent* = *independents* < / *option*>; }

BY *variables*;   }   optional statements
WEIGHT *variable*;   }

The BY, MODEL, and WEIGHT statements are described after the PROC ORTHOREG statement in that order.

PROC ORTHOREG Statement

PROC ORTHOREG <*options*>;

The PROC ORTHOREG statement invokes the procedure. The options in the PROC ORTHOREG statement are

DATA=*SAS-data-set*
    specifies the input SAS data set to use. By default the procedure uses the most recently created SAS data set. The data set specified cannot be a TYPE=CORR, TYPE=COV, or TYPE=SSCP data set.

NOPRINT
    suppresses printing of the results.

OUTEST=*SAS-data-set*
    produces an output data set containing the parameter estimates, the BY variables, and the special variables _TYPE_ (value **PARMS**), _NAME_ (blank), _RMSE_ (root mean squared error), and INTERCEP (intercept).

SINGULAR=*s*
    specifies a singularity criterion ($s \geq 0$) for the inversion of the triangular matrix R. By default, SINGULAR=10E-12.

BY Statement

BY *variables*;

A BY statement can be used with PROC ORTHOREG to obtain separate analyses on observations in groups defined by the BY variables. When a BY statement appears, the procedure expects the input data set to be sorted in order of the BY variables.

If your input data set is not sorted in ascending order, use one of the following alternatives:

- Use the SORT procedure with a similar BY statement to sort the data.
- Use the BY statement options NOTSORTED or DESCENDING in the BY statement for the ORTHOREG procedure. As a cautionary note, the NOTSORTED option does not mean that the data are unsorted, but rather means that the data are arranged in groups (according to values of the BY variables) and that these groups are not necessarily in alphabetical or increasing numeric order.
- Use the DATASETS procedure (in base SAS software) to create an index on the BY variables.

For more information on the BY statement, see the discussion in *SAS Language: Reference, Version 6, First Edition*. For more information on the DATASETS procedure, see the discussion in *SAS Procedures Guide, Version 6, Third Edition*.

MODEL Statement

MODEL *dependent=independents < / option>;*

The MODEL statement names the dependent variable and the independent variables. The independent variables you specify in the MODEL statement must be variables in the data set being analyzed. In other words, independent variables of the form X1*X1 are not allowed in the PROC step. However, they can be created in the DATA step with assignment statements and then used in PROC ORTHOREG. Only one MODEL statement is allowed. The following option can be used in the MODEL statement:

NOINT
    omits the intercept term from in the model.

WEIGHT Statement

WEIGHT *variable;*

A WEIGHT statement names a variable in the input data set whose values are relative weights for a weighted least-squares regression. If the weight value is proportional to the reciprocal of the variance for each observation, the weighted estimates are the best linear unbiased estimates (BLUE). A more complete description of the WEIGHT statement is in Chapter 24, "The GLM Procedure."

DETAILS

Missing Values

If there is a missing value for any variable in an observation, the whole observation is dropped from the analysis.

Output Data Set

The OUTEST= option produces a TYPE=EST output SAS data set containing the BY variables, parameter estimates, and four special variables. For each new value of the BY variable or variables, PROC ORTHOREG outputs an observation to the OUTEST= data set. The variables in the data set are as follows:

- parameter estimates for all variables listed in the MODEL statement
- the BY variables
- _TYPE_, a character variable with the value **PARMS** for every observation
- _NAME_, a character variable left blank for every observation
- _RMSE_, the root mean squared error, which is the estimate of the standard deviation of the true errors
- INTERCEP, the estimated intercept, unless the NOINT option is specified.

Printed Output

PROC ORTHOREG prints the parameter estimates and associated statistics. These include the following:

1. Sum of Squared Errors.
2. Degrees of Freedom associated with error.
3. Mean Squared Error is an estimate of σ^2, the variance of the true errors.
4. Root Mean Squared Error is an estimate of the standard deviation of the true errors. It is calculated as the square root of the mean squared error.
5. R-square, a measure between 0 and 1 that indicates the portion of the total variation that is attributed to the fit.

6. Variables used as regressors, including the name INTERCEP, to identify the intercept parameter.
7. degrees of freedom (DF) for the variable. There is one degree of freedom for each parameter being estimated unless the model is not full rank.
8. Parameter Estimates.
9. Std Errors, the estimates of the standard deviations of the parameter estimates.
10. T-Ratios, the *t*-tests that the parameters are zero. This is computed as the parameter estimate divided by its standard error.
11. Prob> |t|, the probability that a *t* statistic would obtain a greater absolute value than that observed given that the true parameter is zero. This is the two-tailed significance probability.

EXAMPLES

The examples in this section apply both the ORTHOREG and GLM procedures to two sets of data noted for being ill-conditioned. (Portions of the printouts from GLM are not shown for the sake of brevity.) **The results from these examples will vary from machine to machine depending on floating-point configuration.**

Example 1:   Longley Data

The first example is from Longley (1967). The estimates in the output compare very well with the best estimates available; for additional information, see Longley (1967) and also Beaton, Rubin, and Barone (1976). The GLM procedure detects a singularity when, in fact, none exists. These statements produce **Output 31.1**:

```
data longley;
   input y x1 x2 x3 x4 x5 x6;
   cards;
60323  83.0 234289 2356 1590 107608 1947
61122  88.5 259426 2325 1456 108632 1948
60171  88.2 258054 3682 1616 109773 1949
61187  89.5 284599 3351 1650 110929 1950
63221  96.2 328975 2099 3099 112075 1951
63639  98.1 346999 1932 3594 113270 1952
64989  99.0 365385 1870 3547 115094 1953
63761 100.0 363112 3578 3350 116219 1954
66019 101.2 397469 2904 3048 117388 1955
67857 104.6 419180 2822 2857 118734 1956
68169 108.4 442769 2936 2798 120445 1957
66513 110.8 444546 4681 2637 121950 1958
68655 112.6 482704 3813 2552 123366 1959
69564 114.2 502601 3931 2514 125368 1960
69331 115.7 518173 4806 2572 127852 1961
70551 116.9 554894 4007 2827 130081 1962
;
```

```
proc orthoreg data=longley outest=longout;
   model y=x1-x6;
run;

proc print data=longout;
   format _numeric_ 20.14;
run;

proc glm data=longley;
   model y=x1-x6;
run;
```

Output 31.1 Results for Longley Example

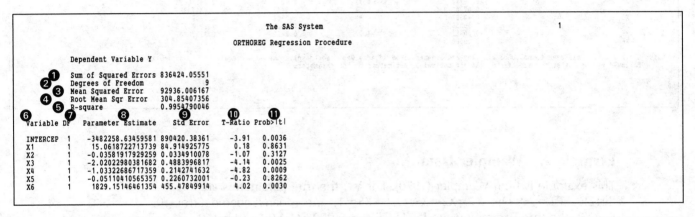

```
                                    The SAS System                                              1
                             ORTHOREG Regression Procedure

           Dependent Variable Y

①         Sum of Squared Errors  836424.05551
②         Degrees of Freedom              9
③         Mean Squared Error      92936.006167
④         Root Mean Sqr Error     304.85407356
⑤         R-square                0.9954790046
⑥        ⑦              ⑧            ⑨         ⑩        ⑪
Variable DF   Parameter Estimate    Std Error   T-Ratio  Prob>|t|

INTERCEP  1   -3482258.63459581   890420.38361    -3.91   0.0036
X1        1      15.06187227137390   84.914925775     0.18   0.8631
X2        1      -0.03581917929259    0.0334910078    -1.07   0.3127
X3        1      -2.02022980381682    0.4883996817    -4.14   0.0025
X4        1      -1.03322686717359    0.2142741632    -4.82   0.0009
X5        1      -0.05110410565357    0.2260732001    -0.23   0.8262
X6        1    1829.15146461354     455.47849914      4.02   0.0030
```

```
                                    The SAS System                                              2

OBS   _TYPE_   _NAME_           _RMSE_              INTERCEP                X1              X2

 1    PARMS             304.85407356196400   -3482258.63459581000    15.06187227137390   -0.03581917929259

OBS            X3                    X4                  X5                  X6

 1    -2.02022980381683    -1.03322686717359    -0.05110410565358    1829.15146461354000
```

```
                                    The SAS System                                              3
                             General Linear Models Procedure
                         Number of observations in data set = 16
```

```
                                    The SAS System                                              4
                             General Linear Models Procedure

Dependent Variable: Y

Source              DF      Sum of Squares         Mean Square      F Value      Pr > F

Model                5   182673588.49490500   36534717.69898110      156.45      0.0001

Error               10     2335237.50509447     233523.75050945

Corrected Total     15   185008826.00000000

            R-Square                 C.V.              Root MSE              Y Mean

            0.987378              0.739843           483.24295185       65317.00000000
```

(continued on next page)

(continued from previous page)

Source	DF	Type I SS	Mean Square	F Value	Pr > F
X1	1	174397449.77912900	174397449.77912900	746.81	0.0001
X2	1	4787181.04444727	4787181.04444727	20.50	0.0011
X3	1	2263971.10981909	2263971.10981909	9.69	0.0110
X4	1	876397.16186204	876397.16186204	3.75	0.0815
X5	1	348589.39964784	348589.39964784	1.49	0.2498
X6	0	0.00000000			

Source	DF	Type III SS	Mean Square	F Value	Pr > F
X1	1	31359.70783151	31359.70783151	0.13	0.7217
X2	0	0.00000000			
X3	0	0.00000000			
X4	1	910776.12982482	910776.12982482	3.90	0.0765
X5	0	0.00000000			
X6	0	0.00000000			

Parameter	Estimate	T for H0: Parameter=0	Pr > |T|	Std Error of Estimate
INTERCEPT	92461.30782 B	2.63	0.0252	35169.247884
X1	-48.46283	-0.37	0.7217	132.24774625
X2	0.07200 B	2.27	0.0467	0.03173387
X3	-0.40387 B	-0.92	0.3788	0.43853544
X4	-0.56050	-1.97	0.0765	0.28381275
X5	-0.40351 B	-1.22	0.2498	0.33026407
X6	0.00000 B	.	.	.

NOTE: The X'X matrix has been found to be singular and a generalized inverse was used to solve the normal equations. Estimates followed by the letter 'B' are biased, and are not unique estimators of the parameters.

Example 2:   Wampler Data

This example is from Wampler (1970). For Y1, the true parameters are INTERCEPT=−9999, X1=X2=X3=X4=X5=1, and Mean Squared Error=0. For Y2, the true parameters are INTERCEPT=−999, X1=0.1, X2=0.01, X3=0.001, X4=0.0001, X5=0.00001, and Mean Squared Error=0. For Y3, the true parameters are INTERCEPT=−9999, X1=X2=X3=X4=X5=1, and Mean Squared Error > 0. The ORTHOREG results are shown in **Output 31.2**, and the abbreviated GLM results are shown in **Output 31.3**.

```
data wampler;
   do x=0 to 20;
      input d @@;
      x1=x; x2=x*x; x3=x2*x; x4=x2*x2; x5=x3*x2;
      x1=x1+10000; x2=x2+10000; x3=x3+10000;
      x4=x4+10000; x5=x5+10000;
      y1=1+x+x2+x3+x4+x5;
      y2=1+.1*x+.01*x2+.001*x3+.0001*x4+.00001*x5;
      y3=y1+d; y4=y1+100*d; y5=y1+10000*d;
      output;
   end;
   cards;
759 -2048 2048 -2048 2523 -2048 2048 -2048 1838 -2048 2048
-2048 1838 -2048 2048 -2048 2523 -2048 2048 -2048 759
;

proc orthoreg data=wampler;
   model y1=x1 x2 x3 x4 x5;
run;
```

```
proc orthoreg data=wampler;
   model y2=x1 x2 x3 x4 x5;
run;

proc orthoreg data=wampler;
   model y3=x1 x2 x3 x4 x5;
run;

proc glm data=wampler;
   model y1-y3 = x1-x5;
run;
```

Output 31.2   PROC ORTHOREG Results for Wampler Example

```
                                        The SAS System                                       1

                                  ORTHOREG Regression Procedure

            Dependent Variable Y1

            Sum of Squared Errors           0
            Degrees of Freedom             15
            Mean Squared Error              0
            Root Mean Sqr Error             0
            R-square                        1

Variable DF    Parameter Estimate    Std Error    T-Ratio Prob>|t|

INTERCEP  1     -9999.00000029751          0     9999.99   0.0001
X1        1         1.00000000007457        0     9999.99   0.0001
X2        1         0.99999999994724        0     9999.99   0.0001
X3        1         1.00000000000846        0     9999.99   0.0001
X4        1         0.99999999999944        0     9999.99   0.0001
X5        1         1.00000000000001        0     9999.99   0.0001
```

```
                                        The SAS System                                       2

                                  ORTHOREG Regression Procedure

            Dependent Variable Y2

            Sum of Squared Errors           0
            Degrees of Freedom             15
            Mean Squared Error              0
            Root Mean Sqr Error             0
            R-square                        1

Variable DF    Parameter Estimate    Std Error    T-Ratio Prob>|t|

INTERCEP  1      -999.00000000001          0     9999.99   0.0001
X1        1                 0.1           0     9999.99   0.0001
X2        1         0.00999999999999        0     9999.99   0.0001
X3        1                 0.001         0     9999.99   0.0001
X4        1         0.00009999999999        0     9999.99   0.0001
X5        1                 0.00001       0     9999.99   0.0001
```

```
                                        The SAS System                                    3

                                  ORTHOREG Regression Procedure


          Dependent Variable Y3

              Sum of Squared Errors       83554268
              Degrees of Freedom                15
              Mean Squared Error        5570284.5333
              Root Mean Sqr Error       2360.1450238
              R-square                    0.999995559

Variable DF   Parameter Estimate      Std Error   T-Ratio Prob>|t|

INTERCEP  1   -9999.00000054495   17133638.649      -0.00   0.9995
X1        1    1.00000000009913    2363.5517347       0.00   0.9997
X2        1    0.99999999994815    779.34352433       0.00   0.9990
X3        1    1.00000000000767    101.47550755       0.01   0.9923
X4        1    0.99999999999952    5.6456651217       0.18   0.8618
X5        1    1.00000000000001    0.1123248547       8.90   0.0001
```

Output 31.3   PROC GLM Results for Wampler Example

```
                                        The SAS System                                    5

                                 General Linear Models Procedure

Dependent Variable: Y1
                                                 T for H0:                    Std Error of
Parameter                   Estimate          Parameter=0      Pr > |T|         Estimate

INTERCEPT               -9999.001069            -9999.99        0.0001               0
X1                          1.000000             9999.99        0.0001               0
X2                          1.000000             9999.99        0.0001               0
X3                          1.000000             9999.99        0.0001               0
X4                          1.000000             9999.99        0.0001               0
X5                          1.000000             9999.99        0.0001               0
```

```
                                        The SAS System                                    6

                                 General Linear Models Procedure

Dependent Variable: Y2
                                                 T for H0:                    Std Error of
Parameter                   Estimate          Parameter=0      Pr > |T|         Estimate

INTERCEPT                -998.9998280            -9999.99        0.0001               0
X1                          0.1000000             9999.99        0.0001               0
X2                          0.0100000             9999.99        0.0001               0
X3                          0.0010000             9999.99        0.0001               0
X4                          0.0001000             9999.99        0.0001               0
X5                          0.0000100             9999.99        0.0001               0
```

```
                                        The SAS System                                    7

                                 General Linear Models Procedure

Dependent Variable: Y3
                                                 T for H0:                    Std Error of
Parameter                   Estimate          Parameter=0      Pr > |T|         Estimate

INTERCEPT               -9999.001069               -0.00        0.9995      17133637.359
X1                          1.000000                0.00        0.9997      2363.5515575
X2                          1.000000                0.00        0.9990      779.34347314
X3                          1.000000                0.01        0.9923      101.47550189
X4                          1.000000                0.18        0.8618      5.64566485
X5                          1.000000                8.90        0.0001      0.11232485
```

REFERENCES

Beaton, A.E., Rubin, D. B., and Barone, J.L. (1976), "The Acceptability of Regression Solutions: Another Look at Computational Accuracy," *Journal of the American Statistical Association,* 71 , 158–168.

Gentleman, W. M. (1972a), "Basic Procedures for Large, Sparse or Weighted Least Squares Problems," Univ. of Waterloo Report CSRR-2068, Waterloo, Ontario, Canada.

Gentleman, W. M. (1972b), "Least Squares Computations by Givens Transformations without Square Roots," Univ. of Waterloo Report CSRR-2062, Waterloo, Ontario, Canada.

Lawson, C. L. and Hanson, R. J. (1974), *Solving Least Squares Problems,* Englewood Cliffs, NJ: Prentice-Hall, Inc.

Longley, J. W. (1967), "An Appraisal of Least Squares Programs for the Electronic Computer from the Point of View of the User," *Journal of the American Statistical Association,* 62, 819–841.

Wampler, R. H. (1970), "A Report of the Accuracy of Some Widely Used Least Squares Computer Programs," *Journal of the American Statistical Association,* 65, 549–563.

Chapter 32

The PLAN Procedure

ABSTRACT 1221
INTRODUCTION 1221
  Using PROC PLAN Interactively 1223
SPECIFICATIONS 1223
  PROC PLAN Statement 1224
  FACTORS Statement 1224
    Selection-Types 1225
    Syntax Examples 1225
    Handling More than One Factor-Selection 1226
  OUTPUT Statement 1227
    Factor-Value-Settings with Only an OUT= Data Set 1227
    Factor-Value-Settings with OUT= and DATA= Data Sets 1228
  TREATMENTS Statement 1229
DETAILS 1230
  Output Data Sets 1230
  Specifying Factor Structures 1231
  Randomizing Designs 1233
  Printed Output 1233
EXAMPLES 1234
  Example 1: A Completely Randomized Design for Two Treatments 1234
  Example 2: A Split-Plot Design 1235
  Example 3: A Hierarchical Design 1236
  Example 4: An Incomplete Block Design 1237
  Example 5: A Latin Square Design 1239
REFERENCES 1240

ABSTRACT

The PLAN procedure constructs designs and randomizes plans for nested and crossed experiments.

INTRODUCTION

A cell in a factorial experiment can be indexed by the levels of the various *factors* associated with it. For example, in a randomized complete block design, each cell is uniquely indexed by the block and treatment associated with the cell. In a factorial design, each cell is indexed by a combination of levels of the various factors. PROC PLAN generates designs by first generating a selection of the levels for the first factor. Then, for the second factor, PLAN generates a selection of its levels for each level of the first factor. In general, for a given factor, PLAN generates a selection of its levels for all combinations of levels for the factors that precede it. The selection can be done in three different ways:

- randomized selection, for which the levels are returned in a random order. In this case, the selection process is based on uniform pseudo-random variates generated as in the RANUNI function (see the *SAS Language: Reference, Version 6, First Edition* for a description).
- ordered selection, for which the levels are returned in a standard order every time a selection is generated.
- cyclic selection, for which the levels returned are computed by cyclically permuting the levels of the previous selection.

The randomized selection method can be used to generate randomized plans. Also, by appropriate use of cyclic selection, any of the designs in the very wide class of generalized cyclic block designs (Jarrett and Hall 1978) can be generated.

There is no limit to the depth to which the different factors can be nested, and any number of randomized plans can be generated.

You can also declare a list of factors to be selected simultaneously with the lowest (that is, the most nested) factor. The levels of the factors in this list can be seen as constituting the treatment to be applied to the cells of the design. For this reason, factors in this list are called *treatments*. With this list, you can generate and randomize plans in one run of PLAN. The following statements give an example:

```
proc plan;
   factors rep=3 ordered drug=4;
   treatments amount=4;
run;
```

These statements produce a design with three replicates of the four levels of the factor DRUG arranged in random order. The three levels of REP are arranged in order as shown in **Output 32.1** below.

Output 32.1   Using a TREATMENTS Statement

```
                                    The SAS System                                    1

Procedure PLAN

Plot Factors

Factor   Select  Levels  Order
------   ------  ------  -------
REP          3       3   Ordered
DRUG         4       4   Random


Treatment Factors

Factor   Select  Levels  Order
------   ------  ------  -------
AMOUNT       4       4   Random


     REP [ DRUG AMOUNT ]
--------  -----+-----+-----+-----+
      1  [3 1] [1 2] [4 4] [2 3]

      2  [3 1] [1 2] [4 4] [2 3]

      3  [2 2] [4 1] [1 3] [3 4]
```

Using PROC PLAN Interactively

PROC PLAN can be used interactively. After specifying a design with a FACTORS statement and running PLAN with a RUN statement, additional plans and output data sets can be generated without reinvoking PLAN.

In the PLAN procedure, all statements can be used interactively. Statements can be executed singly or in groups by following the single statement or group of statements with a RUN statement.

If you use PLAN interactively, you can end the procedure with a DATA step, another PROC step, an ENDSAS statement, or a QUIT statement. The syntax of this statement is

    quit;

When you use PLAN interactively, additional RUN statements do not end the procedure but tell PLAN to execute additional statements.

SPECIFICATIONS

The following statements are used in the PLAN procedure:

PROC PLAN <options>;   } required statements
  FACTORS factor-selections < / NOPRINT>;   }

  OUTPUT OUT=SAS-data-set   }
        <DATA=SAS-data-set>   }
        <factor-value-settings>;   } optional statements
  TREATMENTS factor-selections;   }

To use PROC PLAN, you need the PROC statement and at least one FACTORS statement before the first RUN statement. The TREATMENTS statement, OUTPUT statement, and additional FACTORS statements can appear either before the first RUN statement or after it. The rest of this section gives detailed syntax information for each of the statements above, beginning with the PROC PLAN statement. The remaining statements are covered in alphabetical order.

PROC PLAN Statement

PROC PLAN <*options*>;

The PROC PLAN statement starts the PLAN procedure and, optionally, specifies a random number seed or a default method for selecting levels of factors. By default, the procedure uses a random number seed generated from reading the time of day from the computer's clock, and randomly selects levels of factors. These defaults can be modified with the SEED= and ORDERED options, respectively. Unlike many SAS/STAT procedures, PLAN does not have a DATA= option in the PROC statement; in this procedure, both the input and output data sets are specified in the OUTPUT statement. The following options can appear in the PROC PLAN statement:

SEED=*number*
> specifies a positive integer less than $2^{31}-1$. PROC PLAN uses the value of SEED= to start the pseudo-random number generator for selecting factor levels randomly. The default is a value generated from reading the time of day from the computer's clock. However, in order to avoid the generation of artificial correlations, you should control the value of the seed explicitly rather than rely on the clock reading.

ORDERED
> selects the levels of the factor as the integers 1, 2, . . . *m* in order. For more details, see the discussion of *selection-type* in the FACTORS statement and **Specifying Factor Structures**, both later in this chapter.

FACTORS Statement

FACTORS *factor-selections* < / NOPRINT >;

The FACTORS statement specifies the factors of the plan and generates the plan. Taken together, the *factor-selections* specify the plan to be generated; more than one *factor-selection* request can be used in a FACTORS statement. The form of a *factor-selection* is

name=*m* <OF *n*> <*selection-type*>

where

name	is a valid SAS name. This gives the name of a factor in the design.
m	is a positive integer that gives the number of values to be selected. If *n* is specified, the value of *m* must be less than or equal to *n*.
n	is a positive integer that gives the number of values to be selected from.
selection-type	specifies one of three methods for selecting *m* values. Possible values are CYCLIC, ORDERED, or RANDOM. The CYCLIC *selection-type* has additional optional specifications that allow you to specify an initial block of numbers that will be cyclically permuted and an increment used to permute the numbers. By default, the *selection-type* is RANDOM unless you use the ORDERED option in the PROC PLAN statement. In this case, the default *selection-type* is ORDERED. For syntax details, see **Selection-Types** below.

The following option can appear in the FACTORS statement after the slash:

NOPRINT
> suppresses printing of the plan. This is particularly useful when you require only an output data set.

Selection-Types

PROC PLAN interprets the three *selection-types* as follows:

RANDOM
> selects the m levels of the factor randomly without replacement from the integers 1, 2, . . . , n. Or, if n is not specified, RANDOM selects levels by randomly ordering the integers 1, 2, . . . , m.

ORDERED
> selects the levels of the factor as the integers 1, 2, . . . , m, in that order.

CYCLIC <(*initial-block*)> <*increment-number*>
> selects the levels of the factor by cyclically permuting the integers 1, 2, . . . , n. Wrapping occurs at m if n is not specified, and at n if n is specified. Additional optional specifications are as follows:
>
> *initial-block*
>> specifies the block of numbers to permute. The first permutation is the block you specify, the second is the block permuted by 1 (or by the *increment-number* you specify), and so on. By default, the *initial-block* is the integers 1, 2, . . . , m. If you specify an *initial-block*, it must have m values. Values specified in *initial-block* do not have to be given in increasing order.
>
> *increment-number*
>> specifies the number by which to permute the block of numbers. By default, *increment-number* is 1.

Syntax Examples

This section gives some simple syntax examples. These examples assume you use the default random selection method and do not use the ORDERED option in the PROC PLAN statement. For more complex examples and details on how to generate various designs, see **Specifying Factor Structures** later in this chapter.

The specification

```
a=5
```

generates a random permutation of the numbers 1, 2, 3, 4, and 5. The specification

```
a=5 of 8
```

generates a random permutation of 5 of the integers from 1 to 8, selected without replacement. If you add the ORDERED *selection-type* to either specification above, the procedure generates an ordered list of the integers 1 to 5. The specification

```
a=4 cyclic
```

cyclically permutes the integers 1, 2, 3, and 4. Since this simple request generates only one permutation of the numbers, the procedure generates an ordered list of the integers 1 to 4. The specification

```
a=4 of 8 cyclic (5 6 7 8)
```

cyclically permutes the integers 5 to 8. In this case, since only one permutation is performed, the procedure generates an ordered list of the integers 5 to 8. The specification

```
a=2 ordered b=4 of 8 cyclic (5 6 7 8) 2
```

produces an ordered list for A, with values 1 and 2. The associated factor levels for B are 5, 6, 7, and 8 for level 1 of A; and 7, 8, 1, and 2 for level 2 of A.

For more detail, see **Specifying Factor Structures** later in this chapter.

Handling More than One *Factor-Selection*

For cases with more than one request in the same FACTORS statement, PROC PLAN constructs the design as follows:

1. PLAN first generates levels for the first *factor-selection* request. These levels are permutations of integers (1, 2, and so on) appropriate for the *selection-type* chosen. If you do not specify a *selection-type*, PLAN uses the default (RANDOM) unless you use the ORDERED option in the PROC PLAN statement. Then, PLAN uses selection type ORDERED.
2. For every integer generated for the first request, levels are generated for the second request. These levels are generated according to the specifications following the second equal sign.
3. This process is repeated until levels for all requests have been generated.

The statements below give an example of generating a design with two random factors:

```
proc plan;
   factors one=4 two=3;
run;
```

The procedure first generates a random permutation of the integers 1 to 4, and then for each of these, it generates a random permutation of the integers 1 to 3. You can think of factor TWO as being nested within factor ONE, where the levels of factor ONE are to be randomly assigned to 4 units.

As another example, six random permutations of the numbers 1, 2, and 3 can be generated by specifying

```
proc plan;
   factors a=6 ordered b=3;
run;
```

For more on how to use the FACTORS statement to generate different designs, see **Specifying Factor Structures** later in this chapter.

OUTPUT Statement

OUTPUT OUT=*SAS-data-set* <DATA=*SAS-data-set*>
   <*factor-value-settings*>;

The OUTPUT statement applies only to the last plan generated. If you use PROC PLAN interactively, the OUTPUT statement for a given plan must be immediately preceded by the FACTORS statement (and the TREATMENTS statement, if appropriate) for the plan. The following specifications can be used in the OUTPUT statement:

OUT=*SAS-data-set*
DATA=*SAS-data-set*

> The OUTPUT statement may be used both to output the last plan generated and to use the last plan generated to randomize another SAS data set.
>
> The first case occurs when you use only the OUT= specification in the OUTPUT statement. This creates an output SAS data set. In this case, the output data set contains one variable for each factor in the plan and one observation for each cell in the plan. The value of a variable in a given observation is the level of the corresponding factor for that cell. OUT= is required.
>
> The second case is invoked by using both the DATA= and OUT= specifications in the OUTPUT statement. In this case, the output data set (OUT=) has the same form as the input data set (DATA=) but has modified values for the variables that correspond to factors (see **Output Data Sets** later in this chapter for details). Values for variables not corresponding to factors are transferred without change.

factor-value-settings

> specify the values input or output for the factors in the design. The form for *factor-value-setting* is different when only an OUT= data set is specified, and when both OUT= and DATA= data sets are specified. Both forms are discussed below.

Factor-Value-Settings with Only an OUT= Data Set

The form for the *factor-value-setting* specification in this case is one of the following:

   factor-name <NVALS=*list-of-n-numbers*> <ORDERED | RANDOM>

or

   factor-name <CVALS=*list-of-n-strings*> <ORDERED | RANDOM>

where

   factor-name   is a factor in the FACTORS statement that immediately precedes the OUTPUT statement.

   NVALS=   lists *n* numeric values for the factor. By default, the procedure uses NVALS=(1 2 3 . . . *n*). See the example below.

   CVALS=   lists *n* character strings for the factor. Each string can be up to 40 characters in length. Enclose each string in quotes. See the example below.

Warning: When you use CVALS=, the variable created in the output data set has length equal to the length of the longest string given as a value; shorter strings are padded with trailing blanks. For example, the values output for the first level of a two-level factor with the two value specifications

```
CVALS=('String 1' 'String 2')
```

```
CVALS=('String 1' 'A longer string')
```

are not the same. The value output with the second specification is **String 1** followed by seven blanks. In order to match two such values (for example, when merging two plans), you must use the TRIM function in the DATA step (for more information see the *SAS Language: Reference, Version 6, First Edition*).

ORDERED | RANDOM

specifies how values (either those given with the NVALS= or CVALS= specification or the default values) are associated with the levels of a factor (the integers 1, 2, . . . , n). The default association type is ORDERED, for which the first value specified is output for a factor level setting of 1, the second value specified is output for a level of 2, and so on. You may also specify an association type of RANDOM, for which the levels are associated with the values in a random order. Specifying RANDOM is useful for randomizing crossed experiments (see **Randomizing Designs** later in this chapter).

The statements below give an example of using the OUTPUT statement with only an OUT= data set, and with both the NVALS= and CVALS= specifications.

```
proc plan;
   factors a=6 ordered b=3;
   output out=des1 a nvals=(10 20 30 40 50 60)
                   b cvals=('HSX' 'SB2' 'DNY');
run;
```

The DES1 data set contains two variables, A and B. The values of the variable A are 10 for the first level of the factor A in the design, 20 for the second level, and so on. Values of the variable B are **HSX** for the first level of the factor B in the design, **SB2** for the second level, and so on.

Factor-Value-Settings with OUT= and DATA= Data Sets

If you specify an input data set with the DATA= specification, then PROC PLAN assumes that each factor in the last plan generated corresponds to a variable in the input set. If the variable name is different from the name of the factor to which it corresponds, the two may be associated in the values specification by

input-variable-name=factor-name

Then, the NVALS= or CVALS= specifications can be used. The NVALS= or CVALS= values specify the input values as well as the output values for the corresponding variable.

Since the procedure assumes that the collection of input factor values constitutes a plan position description (see **Output Data Sets** later in this chapter), the values must correspond to integers less than or equal to m, the number of values selected for the associated factor. If any input values do not correspond, then the collection does not define a plan position, and the corresponding observation is output without changing the values of any of the factor variables.

For an example of using both a DATA= and OUT= data set, see **Example 1** later in this chapter.

TREATMENTS Statement

    TREATMENTS *factor-selections*;

The TREATMENTS statement specifies the *treatments* of the plan to generate, but it does not generate a plan. If you supply several FACTORS and TREATMENTS statements before the first RUN statement, the procedure uses only the last TREATMENTS specification and applies it to the plans generated by each of the FACTORS statements. The TREATMENTS statement has the same form as the FACTORS statement. The individual *factor-selections* also have the same form as in the FACTORS statement:

    name=*m* <OF *n*> <*selection-type*>

The procedure generates each *treatment* simultaneously with the lowest (that is, the most nested) factor in the last FACTORS statement. The m value for each *treatment* must be at least as large as the m for the most-nested factor because this determines how many values are selected.

The statements below give an example of using both a FACTORS and a TREATMENTS statement. First the FACTORS statement sets up the rows and columns of a 3×3 square (factors R and C). Then, the TREATMENTS statement augments the square with two cyclic treatments. The resulting design is a 3×3 Graeco-Latin square; a type of design useful in main-effects factorial experiments.

```
proc plan;
   factors r=3 ordered c=3 ordered;
   treatments a=3 cyclic
              b=3 cyclic 2;
run;
```

These statements produce the plan shown below:

```
     R   [C A B]
--------   -------+-------+-------+
     1   [1 1 1] [2 2 2] [3 3 3]

     2   [1 2 3] [2 3 1] [3 1 2]

     3   [1 3 2] [2 1 3] [3 2 1]
```

In the plan, the values for the column index C are given by the left-most number in each set of square brackets, the values for treatment factor A by the middle number, and the values for B by the right-most number. Notice how the values of R and C are ordered (1, 2, 3) as requested.

DETAILS

Output Data Sets

To understand how the PLAN procedure creates output data sets, you need to look at how the procedure represents a plan. A list of values, one for each factor, may define either the position of a cell within a plan (for example, the cell in row 3 and column 2) or the levels assigned to the factors for that cell. PLAN represents a plan as two series of such settings or lists of factor values: a *position series*, a typical element of which describes the position of the corresponding cell in the plan, and a *value series*, whose elements give the levels assigned to each factor for each cell.

If you specify only an output data set (OUT=), PLAN uses the value series by default. In other words, for each factor, the output data set contains a numeric variable with that factor's name; and the values of this numeric variable are the numbers of the successive levels selected for the factor in the plan (the corresponding elements of the value series). Alternatively, you may specify the values that are output for a factor (with the CVALS= or NVALS= specifications; see **OUTPUT Statement** earlier in this chapter). Also, you may specify that the internal values be associated with the output values in a random order (with RANDOM; see **OUTPUT Statement** earlier in this chapter).

If you also specify an input data set (DATA=), each factor is associated with a variable in the DATA= data set. This occurs either implicitly by the factor and variable having the same name, or explicitly as described in the specifications for the OUTPUT statement. When both DATA= and OUT= data sets are specified, the values of variables that correspond to factors are interpreted as a plan position description. In this case, the values of the variables corresponding to the factors are first read and then interpreted as a plan position description. Then the respective values taken by the factors at that position are assigned to the variable in the OUT= data set. When the factors are random, this has the effect of randomizing the input data set in the same manner as the plan produced (see **Randomizing Designs** and **Example 1** later in this chapter).

Specifying Factor Structures

By appropriately combining features of the PLAN procedure, you can construct an extensive set of designs. The basic tools are the *factor-selections*, which are used in the FACTORS and TREATMENTS statements. The following table summarizes how the procedure interprets various *factor-selections* (assuming the ORDERED option is not specified in the PROC PLAN statement):

Form of Request	Interpretation	Example	Results
name=*m*	produce a random permutation of the integers 1, 2, . . . , *m*	t=15	lists a random ordering of the numbers 1, 2, . . . , 15
name=*m* ordered	produce an ordered list of the integers 1, 2, . . . , *m*	t=15 ordered	lists the integers 1 to 15 in increasing order
name=*m* cyclic	cyclically permute the integers 1, 2, . . . , *m*, starting with the order 1 to *m*, then 2, 3, . . . , *m*, 1; then 3, 4, . . . , *m*, 1, 2; and so on.	t=5 cyclic	selects the integers 1 to 5. On the next iteration, selects 2, 3, 4, 5, 1; then 3, 4, 5, 1, 2; and so on.
name=*m* cyclic *increment*	cyclically permute the integers 1, 2, . . . , *m*, starting with the order 1 to *m*, then add *increment* to the first value for the second iteration and start the cycle at that value, and so on.	t=5 cyclic 2	selects the integers 1 to 5. On the next iteration, selects 3, 4, 5, 1, 2; then 5, 1, 2, 3, 4; then 2, 3, 4, 5, 1; and so on.
name=*m* of *n*	choose a random sample of *m* integers (without replacement) from the set of integers 1, 2, . . . , *n* and arrange the sample randomly. Essentially, *m* specifies the number of values to select at a time and *n* specifies the number of values to choose from.	t=5 of 15	lists a random selection of 5 numbers from 1 to 15. The procedure first selects 5 numbers and then arranges them in random order.
name=*m* of *n* ordered	has the same effect as *name*=*m* ordered	t=5 of 15 ordered	lists the integers 1 to 5 in increasing order (same as t=5 ordered)

Form of Request	Interpretation	Example	Results
name=m of *n* cyclic	permute *m* of the *n* integers. Start with 1, 2, . . . , *m*, then 2, 3, . . . , *m*, *m*+1; then 3, 4, . . . , *m*, *m*+1, *m*+2; and so on. With enough iterations, the cyclic permutation wraps at *n* to produce *n*, 1, 2, . . . , *m*−1, then 1, 2, . . . , *m*, and so on.	t=5 of 30 cyclic	selects the integers 1 to 5. On the next iteration, selects 2, 3, 4, 5, 6; then 3, 4, 5, 6, 7; and so on. The 30th iteration produces 30, 1, 2, 3, 4; the 31st iteration produces 1, 2, 3, 4, 5; and so on.
name=m of *n* cyclic *(initial-block)*	permute *m* of the *n* integers. Start with the values specified in the *initial-block*, then add 1 to each value for the second iteration, add 2 for the third iteration, and so on. With enough iterations, the cyclic permutation wraps at *n* as above.	t=5 of 30 cyclic (2 10 15 18 22)	selects the integers 2, 10, 15, 18, 22. On the next iteration, selects 3, 11, 16, 19, 23; then 4, 12, 17, 20, 24; and so on. The ninth iteration is 10, 18, 23, 26, 30; the tenth iteration is 11, 19, 24, 27, 1; and so on.
name=m of *n* cyclic *(inital-block)* *increment*	permute *m* of the *n* integers. Start with the values specified in the *initial-block*, then add the *increment* to each value for the second iteration, and add the *increment* again for the third iteration, and so on. With enough iterations, the cyclic permutation wraps at *n* as above.	t=5 of 30 cyclic (2 10 15 18 22) 2	selects the integers 2, 10, 15, 18, 22. On the next iteration, selects 4, 12, 17, 20, 24; then 6, 14, 19, 22, 26; and so on. The wrap occurs at the sixth iteration. The fifth iteration is 10, 18, 23, 26, 30; the sixth iteration is 12, 20, 25, 28, 2; and so on.

For an example of creating a completely randomized design, see **Example 1** later in this chapter. The following statements create a randomized complete block design and output the design to a data set.

```
proc plan ordered;
   factors blocks=3 cell=5;
   treatments t=5 random;
   output out=rcdb;
run;
```

See **Example 2** for statements that create a split-plot design, **Example 3** for statements that create a nested design, and **Example 5** for statements that create a Latin square design.

The statements below depict how to create an appropriately randomized generalized cyclic incomplete block design for v treatments (given by the value of T) in b blocks (given by the value of B) of size k (with values of P indexing the cells within a block) with initial block $(e_1 \; e_2 \ldots e_k)$ and increment number i.

```
treatments t=k of v cyclic (e₁ e₂ . . . eₖ) i;
factors b=b p=k;
```

For example, the specification

```
treatments t=4 of 30 cyclic (1 3 4 26) 2;
factors b=10 p=4;
```

generates the following selections for factor T, where each row is a block:

```
1    3    4   26
3    5    6   28
5    7    8   30
7    9   10    2
9   11   12    4
     .
     .
     .
```

The successive rows above constitute the generalized cyclic incomplete block design given in Example 1 of Jarrett and Hall (1978).

Randomizing Designs

In many situations, proper randomization is crucial for the validity of any conclusions to be drawn from an experiment. Randomization is used both to neutralize the effect of any systematic biases that may be involved in the design as well as to provide a basis for the assumptions underlying the analysis.

You can use the PLAN procedure to randomize an already-existing design: one produced by a previous call to the PLAN procedure, perhaps, or a more specialized design taken from a standard reference such as Cochran and Cox (1957). The method is to specify the appropriate block structure in the FACTORS statement and then to specify the data set where the design is stored with the DATA= specification in the OUTPUT statement. For an illustration of this method, see **Example 1** later in this chapter.

Two sorts of randomization are provided for, corresponding to the RANDOM factor selection and association types in the FACTORS and OUTPUT statements, respectively. Designs in which factors are completely nested (for example, block designs) should be randomized by specifying that the selection type of each factor is RANDOM in the FACTORS statement, which is the default (see **Example 4**). On the other hand, if the factors are crossed (for example, row-and-column designs), they should be randomized by one random reassignment of their values for the whole design. To do this, specify that the association type of each factor is RANDOM in the OUTPUT statement (see **Example 5**).

Printed Output

The PLAN procedure prints

1. the m value for each factor, the number of values to be selected
2. the n value for each factor, the number of values to be selected from
3. the selection type for each factor, as specified in the FACTORS statement

4. the initial block and increment number for cyclic factors
5. the factor value selections making up each plan.

In addition, notes are printed on the log giving the starting and ending values of the random number seed for each call to PLAN.

EXAMPLES

Example 1:   A Completely Randomized Design for Two Treatments

This first plan is appropriate for a completely randomized design with 12 experimental units, each to be assigned one of two treatments. Use a DATA statement to store the unrandomized design in a SAS data set and then call PROC PLAN to randomize it by specifying one RANDOM factor of 12 levels. The following statements produce **Output 32.2**:

```
title 'COMPLETELY RANDOMIZED DESIGN';
data a;
   do unit=1 to 12;
      if (unit <= 6) then treat=1;
      else                treat=2;
      output;
   end;

proc plan seed=27371;
   factors unit=12;
   output data=a out=b;
run;

proc sort;
   by unit;
run;

proc print;
run;
```

Output 32.2   A Completely Randomized Design for Two Treatments

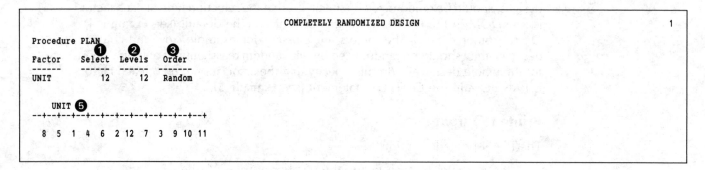

```
                              COMPLETELY RANDOMIZED DESIGN                                  2
                           OBS      UNIT     TREAT

                            1        1        1
                            2        2        1
                            3        3        2
                            4        4        1
                            5        5        1
                            6        6        1
                            7        7        2
                            8        8        1
                            9        9        2
                           10       10        2
                           11       11        2
                           12       12        2
```

You can also generate the plan without using a DATA step to set up the unrandomized plan by using a TREATMENTS statement instead. The following code generates the same plan as above:

```
proc plan seed=27371;
   factors unit=12;
   treatments treat=12 cyclic (1 1 1 1 1 1 2 2 2 2 2 2);
   output out=b;
run;
```

Example 2:   A Split-Plot Design

The second plan is appropriate for a split-plot design with main plots forming a randomized complete block design. In this example, there are three blocks, four main plots per block, and two subplots per main plot. First, three random permutations (one for each of the blocks) of the integers 1, 2, 3, and 4 are produced. The four integers correspond to the four levels of factor A; the permutation determines how the levels of A are assigned to the main plots within a block. For each of these twelve numbers (four numbers per block for three blocks), a random permutation of the integers 1 and 2 is produced. Each two-integer permutation determines the assignment of the two levels of factor B to the subplots within a main plot. The following statements produce **Output 32.3**:

```
title 'SPLIT PLOT DESIGN';
proc plan seed=37277;
   factors block=3 ordered a=4 b=2;
run;
```

Output 32.3   A Split-Plot Design

```
                                    SPLIT PLOT DESIGN                                    1

Procedure PLAN

Factor     Select   Levels   Order
------     ------   ------   -------
BLOCK         3        3     Ordered
A             4        4     Random
B             2        2     Random


    BLOCK          A        B
  --------   --------   -+-+
        1          4     2 1

                   3     2 1

                   1     2 1

                   2     2 1

        2          4     1 2

                   3     1 2

                   1     2 1

                   2     1 2

        3          4     2 1

                   2     2 1

                   3     2 1

                   1     2 1
```

Example 3:   A Hierarchical Design

The third plan is appropriate for a hierarchical design. In this example, three plants are nested within four pots, which are nested within three houses. The FACTORS statement requests a random permutation of the numbers 1, 2, and 3 to choose houses randomly and a random permutation of the numbers 1, 2, 3, and 4 for each of those first three numbers. This second step randomly assigns pots to houses. Finally, the FACTORS statement requests a random permutation of 1, 2, and 3 for each of the twelve integers in the second set of permutations. This last step randomly assigns plants to pots. The following statements produce **Output 32.4**:

```
title 'HIERARCHICAL DESIGN';
proc plan seed=17431;
    factors houses=3 pots=4 plants=3 / noprint;
    output out=nested;
run;

proc print data=nested;
run;
```

Output 32.4   A Hierarchical Design

```
                           HIERARCHICAL DESIGN                              1

                    OBS    HOUSES    POTS    PLANTS

                     1       1        3        2
                     2       1        3        3
                     3       1        3        1
                     4       1        1        3
                     5       1        1        1
                     6       1        1        2
                     7       1        2        2
                     8       1        2        3
                     9       1        2        1
                    10       1        4        3
                    11       1        4        2
                    12       1        4        1
                    13       2        4        1
                    14       2        4        3
                    15       2        4        2
                    16       2        2        2
                    17       2        2        1
                    18       2        2        3
                    19       2        3        2
                    20       2        3        3
                    21       2        3        1
                    22       2        1        2
                    23       2        1        3
                    24       2        1        1
                    25       3        4        1
                    26       3        4        3
                    27       3        4        2
                    28       3        1        3
                    29       3        1        2
                    30       3        1        1
                    31       3        2        1
                    32       3        2        2
                    33       3        2        3
                    34       3        3        3
                    35       3        3        2
                    36       3        3        1
```

Example 4:   An Incomplete Block Design

Jarrett and Hall (1978) give an example of a generalized cyclic design with good efficiency characteristics. The design consists of two replicates of 52 treatments in 13 blocks of size 8. The statements below use the PLAN procedure to generate this design in an appropriately randomized form and store it in a SAS data set. Then, the TABULATE procedure (part of base SAS software) is used to print the randomized plan. The following statements produce **Output 32.5**:

```
title 'GENERALIZED CYCLIC BLOCK DESIGN';
proc plan seed=33373;
   treatments trtmts=8 of 52 cyclic (1 2 3 4 32 43 46 49) 4;
   factors blocks=13 plots=8;
   output out=c;
quit;

proc tabulate;
   class blocks plots;
   var trtmts;
   table blocks, plots*(trtmts*f=8.) / rts=8;
run;
```

Output 32.5   A Generalized Cyclic Block Design

```
                                    GENERALIZED CYCLIC BLOCK DESIGN                                    1

Procedure PLAN

Plot Factors

Factor    Select   Levels   Order
------    ------   ------   -----
BLOCKS        13       13   Random
PLOTS          8        8   Random


Treatment Factors
                                         ❹
Factor    Select   Levels   Order    Initial block / Increment
------    ------   ------   -----    -------------------------
TRTMTS         8       52   Cyclic   (1 2 3 4 32 43 46 49) / 4


  BLOCKS [ PLOTS TRTMTS ]
-------- -------+-------+-------+-------+-------+-------+-------+-------+
      10 [ 7  1] [ 4  2] [ 8  3] [ 1  4] [ 2 32] [ 3 43] [ 5 46] [ 6 49]

       8 [ 1  5] [ 2  6] [ 4  7] [ 3  8] [ 8 36] [ 6 47] [ 5 50] [ 7  1]

       9 [ 2  9] [ 5 10] [ 4 11] [ 7 12] [ 3 40] [ 1 51] [ 8  2] [ 6  5]

       6 [ 4 13] [ 2 14] [ 6 15] [ 8 16] [ 3 44] [ 7  3] [ 1  6] [ 5  9]

       7 [ 4 17] [ 7 18] [ 6 19] [ 3 20] [ 1 48] [ 2  7] [ 8 10] [ 5 13]

       4 [ 4 21] [ 8 22] [ 1 23] [ 5 24] [ 3 52] [ 6 11] [ 7 14] [ 2 17]

       2 [ 6 25] [ 2 26] [ 3 27] [ 8 28] [ 7  4] [ 5 15] [ 1 18] [ 4 21]

       3 [ 6 29] [ 2 30] [ 3 31] [ 1 32] [ 7  8] [ 4 19] [ 5 22] [ 8 25]

       1 [ 1 33] [ 2 34] [ 7 35] [ 8 36] [ 5 12] [ 6 23] [ 3 26] [ 4 29]

       5 [ 5 37] [ 7 38] [ 6 39] [ 8 40] [ 4 16] [ 3 27] [ 1 30] [ 2 33]

      12 [ 5 41] [ 8 42] [ 1 43] [ 4 44] [ 7 20] [ 3 31] [ 6 34] [ 2 37]

      13 [ 3 45] [ 5 46] [ 1 47] [ 8 48] [ 4 24] [ 2 35] [ 6 38] [ 7 41]

      11 [ 4 49] [ 1 50] [ 5 51] [ 2 52] [ 3 28] [ 8 39] [ 6 42] [ 7 45]
```

GENERALIZED CYCLIC BLOCK DESIGN

2

	PLOTS							
	1	2	3	4	5	6	7	8
	TRTMTS SUM	TRTMTS SUM	TRTMTS SUM	TRTMTS SUM	TRTMTS SUM	TRTMTS SUM	TRTMTS SUM	TRTMTS SUM
BLOCKS								
1	33	34	26	29	12	23	35	36
2	18	26	27	21	15	25	4	28
3	32	30	31	19	22	29	8	25
4	23	17	52	21	24	11	14	22
5	30	33	27	16	37	39	38	40
6	6	14	44	13	9	15	3	16
7	48	7	20	17	13	19	18	10
8	5	6	8	7	50	47	1	36
9	51	9	40	11	10	5	12	2
10	4	32	43	2	46	49	1	3
11	50	52	28	49	51	42	45	39
12	43	37	31	44	41	34	20	42
13	47	35	45	24	46	38	41	48

Example 5:   A Latin Square Design

The preceding examples have all dealt with designs with completely nested block structures, for which PROC PLAN was especially designed. However, by appropriate coordination of its facilities a much wider class of designs may be accommodated. A Latin square design is based on experimental units that have a row-and-column block structure. The following example uses the CYCLIC option for a treatment factor TMTS to generate a simple 4×4 Latin square. Randomizing a Latin square design involves randomly permuting the row, column, and treatment values independently. In order to do this, use the RANDOM option in the OUTPUT statement of PLAN. The example also gives an example of *factor-value-settings* in the OUTPUT statement. The following statements produce **Output 32.6**:

```
title 'LATIN SQUARE DESIGN';
proc plan seed=37430;
   factors rows=4 ordered cols=4 ordered / noprint;
   treatments tmts=4 cyclic;
   output out=g
          rows cvals=('Day 1' 'Day 2' 'Day 3' 'Day 4') random
          cols cvals=('Lab 1' 'Lab 2' 'Lab 3' 'Lab 4') random
          tmts nvals=(   0       100      250      450 ) random;
quit;
proc tabulate;
   class rows cols;
   var tmts;
   table rows, cols*(tmts*f=6.) / rts=8;
run;
```

Output 32.6   A Randomized Latin Square Design

```
                          LATIN SQUARE DESIGN                              1

                 -----------------------------------------
                 |      |            COLS                 |
                 |      |----------------------------------
                 |      |Lab 1 |Lab 2 |Lab 3 |Lab 4 |
                 |      |------+------+------+------|
                 |      | TMTS | TMTS | TMTS | TMTS |
                 |      |------+------+------+------|
                 |      | SUM  | SUM  | SUM  | SUM  |
                 |------+------+------+------+------|
                 |ROWS  |      |      |      |      |
                 |------|      |      |      |      |
                 |Day 1 |    0 |  100 |  450 |  250 |
                 |------+------+------+------+------|
                 |Day 2 |  100 |  250 |    0 |  450 |
                 |------+------+------+------+------|
                 |Day 3 |  250 |  450 |  100 |    0 |
                 |------+------+------+------+------|
                 |Day 4 |  450 |    0 |  250 |  100 |
                 -----------------------------------------
```

REFERENCES

Cochran, W.G. and Cox, G.M. (1957), *Experimental Designs*, 2d Edition, New York: John Wiley & Sons, Inc.

Fishman, G.S. and Moore, L.R. (1982), "A Statistical Evaluation of Multiplicative Congruential Generators with Modulus ($2^{31}-1$)," *Journal of the American Statistical Association*, 77, 129–136.

Jarrett, R.G. and Hall, W.B. (1978), "Generalized Cyclic Incomplete Block Designs," *Biometrika*, 65, 397–401.

Chapter 33

The PRINCOMP Procedure

ABSTRACT 1241
INTRODUCTION 1241
  Background 1242
SPECIFICATIONS 1243
  PROC PRINCOMP Statement 1243
  BY Statement 1245
  FREQ Statement 1246
  PARTIAL Statement 1246
  VAR Statement 1246
  WEIGHT Statement 1247
DETAILS 1247
  Missing Values 1247
  Output Data Sets 1247
    OUT= Data Set 1247
    OUTSTAT= Data Set 1247
  Computational Resources 1249
  Printed Output 1250
EXAMPLES 1250
  Example 1: January and July Temperatures 1250
  Example 2: Crime Rates 1254
  Example 3: Basketball Data 1259
REFERENCES 1263

ABSTRACT

The PRINCOMP procedure performs principal component analysis. As input you can use raw data, a correlation matrix, a covariance matrix, or a sums of squares and crossproducts (SSCP) matrix. Output data sets containing eigenvalues, eigenvectors, and standardized or unstandardized principal component scores can be created.

INTRODUCTION

Principal component analysis is a multivariate technique for examining relationships among several quantitative variables. The choice between using factor analysis and principal component analysis depends in part upon your research objectives. You should use the PRINCOMP procedure if you are interested in summarizing data and detecting linear relationships. Plots of principal components are especially valuable tools in exploratory data analysis. Principal components can be used to reduce the number of variables in regression, clustering, and so on. Refer to Chapter 4, "Introduction to Multivariate Procedures," for a detailed comparison of the PRINCOMP and FACTOR procedures.

Background

Principal component analysis was originated by Pearson (1901) and later developed by Hotelling (1933). The application of principal components is discussed by Rao (1964), Cooley and Lohnes (1971), and Gnanadesikan (1977). Excellent statistical treatments of principal components are found in Kshirsagar (1972), Morrison (1976), and Mardia, Kent, and Bibby (1979).

Given a data set with p numeric variables, p principal components can be computed. Each principal component is a linear combination of the original variables, with coefficients equal to the eigenvectors of the correlation or covariance matrix. The eigenvectors are customarily taken with unit length. The principal components are sorted by descending order of the eigenvalues, which are equal to the variances of the components.

Principal components have a variety of useful properties (Rao 1964; Kshirsagar 1972):

- The eigenvectors are orthogonal, so the principal components represent jointly perpendicular directions through the space of the original variables.
- The principal component scores are jointly uncorrelated. Note that this property is quite distinct from the previous one.
- The first principal component has the largest variance of any unit-length linear combination of the observed variables. The jth principal component has the largest variance of any unit-length linear combination orthogonal to the first $j-1$ principal components. The last principal component has the smallest variance of any linear combination of the original variables.
- The scores on the first j principal components have the highest possible generalized variance of any set of unit-length linear combinations of the original variables.
- The first j principal components give a least-squares solution to the model

$$\mathbf{Y} = \mathbf{XB} + \mathbf{E}$$

where $\mathbf{Y}$ is an $n \times p$ matrix of the centered observed variables; $\mathbf{X}$ is the $n \times j$ matrix of scores on the first j principal components; $\mathbf{B}$ is the $j \times p$ matrix of eigenvectors; $\mathbf{E}$ is an $n \times p$ matrix of residuals; and you want to minimize trace ($\mathbf{E'E}$), the sum of all the squared elements in $\mathbf{E}$. In other words, the first j principal components are the best linear predictors of the original variables among all possible sets of j variables, although any nonsingular linear transformation of the first j principal components would provide equally good prediction. The same result is obtained if you want to minimize the determinant or the Euclidean (Schur, Frobenious) norm of $\mathbf{E'E}$ rather than the trace.
- In geometric terms, the j-dimensional linear subspace spanned by the first j principal components gives the best possible fit to the data points as measured by the sum of squared perpendicular distances from each data point to the subspace. This is in contrast to the geometric interpretation of least squares regression, which minimizes the sum of squared vertical distances. For example, suppose you have two variables. Then, the first principal component minimizes the sum of squared perpendicular distances from the points to the first principal axis. This is in contrast to least squares, which would minimize the sum of squared vertical distances from the points to the fitted line.

Principal component analysis can also be used for exploring polynomial relationships and for multivariate outlier detection (Gnanadesikan 1977) and is related to factor analysis, correspondence analysis, allometry, and biased regression techniques (Mardia, Kent, and Bibby 1979).

SPECIFICATIONS

The following statements are used in the PRINCOMP procedure:

PROC PRINCOMP <*options*>;   required statement

> **BY** *variables*;
> **FREQ** *variable*;
> **PARTIAL** *variables*;   optional statements
> **VAR** *variables*;
> **WEIGHT** *variable*;

Usually only the VAR statement is used in addition to the PROC PRINCOMP statement. The rest of this section gives detailed syntax information for each of the statements above, beginning with the PROC PRINCOMP statement. The remaining statements are covered in alphabetical order.

PROC PRINCOMP Statement

PROC PRINCOMP <*options*>;

The PROC PRINCOMP statement starts the PRINCOMP procedure and optionally identifies input and output data sets, specifies details of the analysis, or suppresses the printed output. The table below summarizes the options.

Task	Options
Specify data sets	DATA=
	OUT=
	OUTSTAT=
Specify details of analysis	COV
	N=
	NOINT
	PREFIX=
	STANDARD
	VARDEF=
Suppress printed output	NOPRINT

The list below gives details on these options.

> COVARIANCE
> COV
>> computes the principal components from the covariance matrix. If the COV option is not specified, the correlation matrix is analyzed. Use of the COV option causes variables with large variances to be more strongly associated with components with large eigenvalues and

variables with small variances to be more strongly associated with components with small eigenvalues. The COV option should not be used unless the units in which the variables are measured are comparable or the variables have been standardized in some way. If you use the COV option, the procedure calculates scores using the centered variables rather than the standardized variables.

DATA=*SAS-data-set*

names the SAS data set to be analyzed. The data set can be an ordinary SAS data set or a TYPE=CORR, COV, FACTOR, SSCP, UCORR, or UCOV data set (see Appendix 1, "Special SAS Data Sets"). Also, PRINCOMP can read the _TYPE_='COVB' matrix from a TYPE=EST data set. If you omit the DATA= option, the procedure uses the most recently created SAS data set.

N=*number*

specifies the number of principal components to be computed. The default is the number of variables. The value of N= must be an integer greater than or equal to 0.

NOINT

omits the intercept from the model. In other words, NOINT requests that the covariance or correlation matrix not be corrected for the mean. When you use PRINCOMP with the NOINT option, the covariance matrix and hence the standard deviations are not corrected for the mean. If you are interested in the standard deviations corrected for the mean, you can get them from a procedure such as PROC MEANS.

If you use a TYPE=SSCP data set as input to the PRINCOMP procedure, and list the variable INTERCEP in the VAR statement, the procedure acts as if you had also specified NOINT. If you use NOINT and also create an OUTSTAT= data set, the data set is TYPE=UCORR or UCOV rather than TYPE=CORR or COV.

NOPRINT

suppresses the printout.

OUT=*SAS-data-set*

creates an output SAS data set that contains all the original data as well as the principal component scores. If you want to create a permanent SAS data set, you must specify a two-level name. See "SAS Files" in *SAS Language: Reference, Version 6, First Edition* and "Introduction to DATA Step Processing" in *SAS Language and Procedures: Usage, Version 6, First Edition* for a discussion of permanent data sets.

OUTSTAT=*SAS-data-set*

creates an output SAS data set that contains means, standard deviations, number of observations, correlations or covariances, eigenvalues, and eigenvectors. If the COV option is specified, the data set is TYPE=COV or UCOV depending on the NOINT option, and contains covariances; otherwise, it is TYPE=CORR or UCORR depending on the NOINT option, and contains correlations. If you want to create a permanent SAS data set, you must specify a two-level name. See "SAS Files" in *SAS Language: Reference, Version 6, First Edition* and "Introduction to DATA Step Processing" in *SAS Language and Procedures: Usage, Version 6, First Edition* for a discussion of permanent data sets.

PREFIX=*name*

specifies a prefix for naming the principal components. By default the names are PRIN1, PRIN2, . . . , PRIN*n*. If PREFIX=ABC is specified, the components are named ABC1, ABC2, ABC3, and so on. The number of

characters in the prefix plus the number of digits required to designate
the components should not exceed eight.

STANDARD
STD

standardizes the principal component scores in the OUT= data set to
unit variance. If the STANDARD option is not specified, the scores have
variance equal to the corresponding eigenvalue. Note that STANDARD
has no effect on the eigenvalues themselves.

VARDEF=DF
       | N
       | WDF
       | WEIGHT | WGT

specifies the divisor used in calculating variances and standard
deviations. By default, VARDEF=DF. The values and associated divisors
are shown below.

Value	Divisor	Formula
DF	error degrees of freedom	$n - i$ (before partialling) $n - p - i$ (after partialling)
N	number of observations	n
WEIGHT | WGT	sum of weights	$\Sigma_j w_j$
WDF	sum of weights minus 1	$(\Sigma_j w_j) - i$ (before partialling) $(\Sigma_j w_j) - p - i$ (after partialling)

In the formulas for VARDEF=DF and VARDEF=WDF, p is the number
of degrees of freedom of the variables in the PARTIAL statement, and i
is 0 if the NOINT option is specified and 1 otherwise.

BY Statement

BY *variables*;

A BY statement can be used with PROC PRINCOMP to obtain separate analyses
on observations in groups defined by the BY variables. When a BY statement
appears, the procedure expects the input data set to be sorted in order of the
BY variables.

If your input data set is not sorted in ascending order, use one of the following
alternatives:

- Use the SORT procedure with a similar BY statement to sort the data.
- Use the BY statement options NOTSORTED or DESCENDING in the BY
  statement for the PRINCOMP procedure. As a cautionary note, the
  NOTSORTED option does not mean that the data are unsorted, but
  rather means that the data are arranged in groups (according to values of
  the BY variables) and that these groups are not necessarily in alphabetical
  or increasing numeric order.

- Use the DATASETS procedure (in base SAS software) to create an index on the BY variables.

For more information on the BY statement, see the discussion in *SAS Language: Reference, Version 6, First Edition*. For more information on the DATASETS procedure, see the discussion in the *SAS Procedures Guide, Version 6, Third Edition*.

FREQ Statement

FREQ *variable*;

The FREQ statement names a variable that provides frequencies for each observation in the DATA= data set. Specifically, if n is the value of the FREQ variable for a given observation, then that observation is used n times.

The analysis produced using a FREQ statement reflects the expanded number of observations. The total number of observations is considered equal to the sum of the FREQ variable. You could produce the same analysis (without the FREQ statement) by first creating a new data set that contained the expanded number of observations. For example, if the value of the FREQ variable is 5 for the first observation, the first 5 observations in the new data set would be identical. Each observation in the old data set would be replicated n_i times in the new data set, where n_i is the value of the FREQ variable for that observation.

If the value of the FREQ variable is missing or is less than one, the observation is not used in the analysis. If the value is not an integer, only the integer portion is used.

PARTIAL Statement

PARTIAL *variables*;

If you want to analyze a partial correlation or covariance matrix, specify the names of the numeric variables to be partialled out in the PARTIAL statement. PRINCOMP computes the principal components of the residuals from the prediction of the VAR variables by the PARTIAL variables. If an OUT= or OUTSTAT= data set is requested, the VAR variables should be distinguishable by the first six characters of their names so that the residual variables can be named by prefixing the characters R__.

VAR Statement

VAR *variables*;

The VAR statement lists the numeric variables to be analyzed. If the VAR statement is omitted, all numeric variables not specified in other statements are analyzed. If, however, the DATA= data set is TYPE=SSCP, the default set of variables used as VAR variables does not include INTERCEP so that the correlation or covariance matrix will be constructed correctly. If you want to analyze INTERCEP as a separate variable, you should specify it in the VAR statement.

WEIGHT Statement

> **WEIGHT** *variable*;

If you want to use relative weights for each observation in the input data set, place the weights in a variable in the data set and specify the name in a WEIGHT statement. This is often done when the variance associated with each observation is different and the values of the weight variable are proportional to the reciprocals of the variances.

The observation is used in the analysis only if the value of the WEIGHT statement variable is nonmissing and greater than zero.

DETAILS

Missing Values

Observations with missing values for any variable in the VAR, PARTIAL, FREQ, or WEIGHT statement are omitted from the analysis and are given missing values for principal component scores in the OUT= data set. If a correlation, covariance, or SSCP matrix is read, it can contain missing values as long as every pair of variables has at least one nonmissing entry.

Output Data Sets

OUT= Data Set

The OUT= data set contains all the variables in the original data set plus new variables containing the principal component scores. The N= option determines the number of new variables. The names of the new variables are formed by concatenating the value given by the PREFIX= option (or PRIN if PREFIX= is omitted) and the numbers 1, 2, 3, and so on. The new variables have mean 0 and variance equal to the corresponding eigenvalue unless the STANDARD option is specified to standardize the scores to unit variance.

If you use the COV option, the procedure calculates scores using the centered variables rather than the standardized variables.

If a PARTIAL statement is used, the OUT= data set also contains the residuals from predicting the VAR variables from the PARTIAL variables. The names of the residual variables are formed by prefixing R_ to the names of the VAR variables and possibly truncating the last one or two characters to keep the name from exceeding eight characters.

An OUT= data set cannot be created if the DATA= data set is TYPE=CORR, COV, EST, SSCP, UCORR, or UCOV.

OUTSTAT= Data Set

The OUTSTAT= data set is similar to the TYPE=CORR data set produced by the CORR procedure. The table below relates the TYPE= value for the OUTSTAT= data set to the options used in the PROC PRINCOMP statement.

Options	TYPE=
(default)	CORR
COV	COV
NOINT	UCORR
COV NOINT	UCOV

Notice that the default (neither the COV or NOINT options) produces a TYPE=CORR data set.

The new data set contains the following variables:

- the BY variables, if any.
- two new variables, _TYPE_ and _NAME_. Both are character variables of length 8.
- the variables analyzed, that is, those in the VAR statement; or, if there is no VAR statement, all numeric variables not listed in any other statement; or, if there is a PARTIAL statement, the residual variables as described under the OUT= data set.

Each observation in the new data set contains some type of statistic as indicated by the _TYPE_ variable. The values of the _TYPE_ variable are as follows:

TYPE	Contents
MEAN	mean of each variable. This observation is omitted if the PARTIAL statement is specified.
STD	standard deviations. This observation is omitted if the COV option is specified, so the SCORE procedure does not standardize the variables before computing scores. If the PARTIAL statement is used, the standard deviation of a variable is computed as its root mean squared error as predicted from the PARTIAL variables.
USTD	uncorrected standard deviations. When you specify the NOINT option in the PROC PRINCOMP statement, the OUTSTAT= data set contains standard deviations not corrected for the mean. However, if you also specify the COV option in the PROC PRINCOMP statement, this observation is omitted.
N	number of observations on which the analysis is based. This value is the same for each variable. If the PARTIAL statement is used and the VARDEF= option is DF or unspecified, then the number of observations is decremented by the degrees of freedom for the PARTIAL variables.
SUMWGT	the sum of the weights of the observations. This value is the same for each variable. If the PARTIAL statement and VARDEF=WDF are specified, then the sum of the weights is decremented by the degrees of freedom for the PARTIAL variables. This observation is output only if the value is different from that in the observation with _TYPE_='N'.
CORR	correlations between each variable and the variable named by the _NAME_ variable. The number of observations with _TYPE_='CORR' is equal to the number of variables being analyzed. If the COV option is specified, no _TYPE_='CORR' observations are produced. If the PARTIAL statement is used, the partial correlations, not the raw correlations, are output.
UCORR	uncorrected correlation matrix. When you specify the NOINT option without the COV option in the PROC PRINCOMP statement, the OUTSTAT= data set contains a matrix of correlations not corrected for the means.

However, if you also specify the COV option in the PROC PRINCOMP statement, these observations are omitted.

COV   covariances between each variable and the variable named by the _NAME_ variable. _TYPE_='COV' observations are produced only if the COV option is specified. If the PARTIAL statement is used, the partial covariances, not the raw covariances, are output.

UCOV   uncorrected covariance matrix. When you specify the NOINT and COV options in the PROC PRINCOMP statement, the OUTSTAT= data set contains a matrix of covariances not corrected for the means.

EIGENVAL   eigenvalues. If the N= option requested fewer than the maximum number of principal components, only the specified number of eigenvalues are produced, with missing values filling out the observation.

SCORE   eigenvectors. The _NAME_ variable contains the name of the corresponding principal component as constructed from the PREFIX= option. The number of observations with _TYPE_='SCORE' equals the number of principal components computed. The eigenvectors have unit length unless the STD option is used, in which case the unit-length eigenvectors are divided by the square roots of the eigenvalues to produce scores with unit standard deviations.

USCORE   scoring coefficients to be applied without subtracting the mean from the raw variables. _TYPE_='USCORE' observations are produced when you specify the NOINT option in the PROC PRINCOMP statement.

The data set can be used with the SCORE procedure to compute principal component scores, or it can be used as input to the FACTOR procedure specifying METHOD=SCORE to rotate the components. If you use the PARTIAL statement, the scoring coefficients should be applied to the residuals, not the original variables.

Computational Resources

Let

n = number of observations
v = number of VAR variables
p = number of PARTIAL variables
c = number of components.

- The minimum allocated memory required is

    $232v + 120p + 48c + \max(8cv, 8vp + 4(v + p)(v + p + 1))$

bytes.
- The time required to compute the correlation matrix is roughly proportional to $n(v + p)^2 + p(v + p)(v + p + 1)/2$.
- The time required to compute eigenvalues is roughly proportional to v^3.
- The time required to compute eigenvectors is roughly proportional to cv^2.

Printed Output

The PRINCOMP procedure prints the following items if the DATA= data set is not TYPE=CORR, COV, SSCP, UCORR, or UCOV:

1. Simple Statistics, including the Mean and Std (standard deviation) for each variable. If the NOINT option is used, the uncorrected standard deviation (Unc StD) is printed.
2. the Correlation or, if the COV option is used, the Covariance Matrix.

PRINCOMP prints the following items if the PARTIAL statement is used:

3. Regression Statistics, giving the R-square and RMSE (root mean square error) for each VAR variable as predicted by the PARTIAL variables (not shown)
4. Standardized Regression Coefficients or, if the COV option is used, Regression Coefficients for predicting the VAR variables from the PARTIAL variables (not shown)
5. the Partial Correlation Matrix or, if the COV option is used, the Partial Covariance Matrix (not shown).

PRINCOMP prints the following item if the COV option is used:

6. the Total Variance.

Unless the NOPRINT option is used, PRINCOMP prints the following items:

7. Eigenvalues of the Correlation or Covariance Matrix, as well as the Difference between successive eigenvalues, the Proportion of variance explained by each eigenvalue, and the Cumulative proportion of variance explained
8. the Eigenvectors.

EXAMPLES

Example 1:   January and July Temperatures

This example analyzes mean daily temperatures in selected cities in January and July. Both the raw data and the principal components are plotted to illustrate how principal components are orthogonal rotations of the original variables.

Note that since the COV option is used and JANUARY has a higher standard deviation than JULY, JANUARY receives a higher loading on the first component. The following statements produce **Output 33.1** through **Output 33.3**:

```
data temperat;
   title 'Mean Temperature in January and July for Selected Cities';
   input city $1-15 january july;
   cards;
Mobile          51.2 81.6
Phoenix         51.2 91.2
Little Rock     39.5 81.4
Sacramento      45.1 75.2
Denver          29.9 73.0
Hartford        24.8 72.7
Wilmington      32.0 75.8
Washington DC   35.6 78.7
Jacksonville    54.6 81.0
Miami           67.2 82.3
Atlanta         42.4 78.0
```

```
Boise               29.0 74.5
Chicago             22.9 71.9
Peoria              23.8 75.1
Indianapolis        27.9 75.0
Des Moines          19.4 75.1
Wichita             31.3 80.7
Louisville          33.3 76.9
New Orleans         52.9 81.9
Portland, ME        21.5 68.0
Baltimore           33.4 76.6
Boston              29.2 73.3
Detroit             25.5 73.3
Sault Ste Marie     14.2 63.8
Duluth               8.5 65.6
Minneapolis         12.2 71.9
Jackson             47.1 81.7
Kansas City         27.8 78.8
St Louis            31.3 78.6
Great Falls         20.5 69.3
Omaha               22.6 77.2
Reno                31.9 69.3
Concord             20.6 69.7
Atlantic City       32.7 75.1
Albuquerque         35.2 78.7
Albany              21.5 72.0
Buffalo             23.7 70.1
New York            32.2 76.6
Charlotte           42.1 78.5
Raleigh             40.5 77.5
Bismarck             8.2 70.8
Cincinnati          31.1 75.6
Cleveland           26.9 71.4
Columbus            28.4 73.6
Oklahoma City       36.8 81.5
Portland, OR        38.1 67.1
Philadelphia        32.3 76.8
Pittsburgh          28.1 71.9
Providence          28.4 72.1
Columbia            45.4 81.2
Sioux Falls         14.2 73.3
Memphis             40.5 79.6
Nashville           38.3 79.6
Dallas              44.8 84.8
El Paso             43.6 82.3
Houston             52.1 83.3
Salt Lake City      28.0 76.7
Burlington          16.8 69.8
Norfolk             40.5 78.3
Richmond            37.5 77.9
Spokane             25.4 69.7
Charleston, WV      34.5 75.0
Milwaukee           19.4 69.9
Cheyenne            26.6 69.1
;
```

```
proc plot;
   plot july*january=city / vpos=31;
run;

proc princomp cov out=prin;
   var july january;
run;

proc plot;
   plot prin2*prin1=city / vpos=19;
   title2 'Plot of Principal Components';
run;
```

Output 33.1 Plot of Raw Data

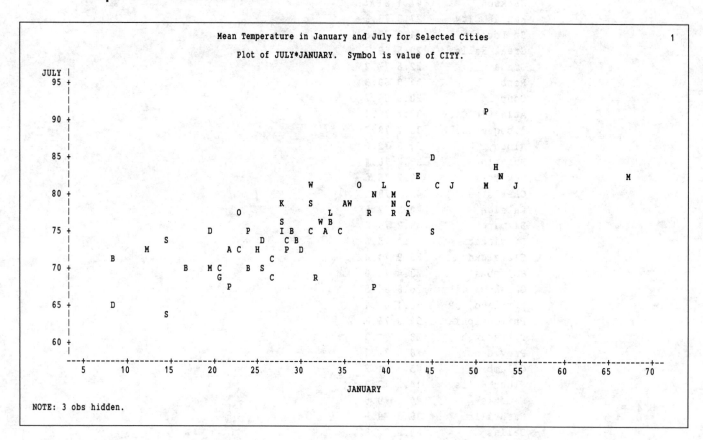

Output 33.2   Results of Principal Component Analysis

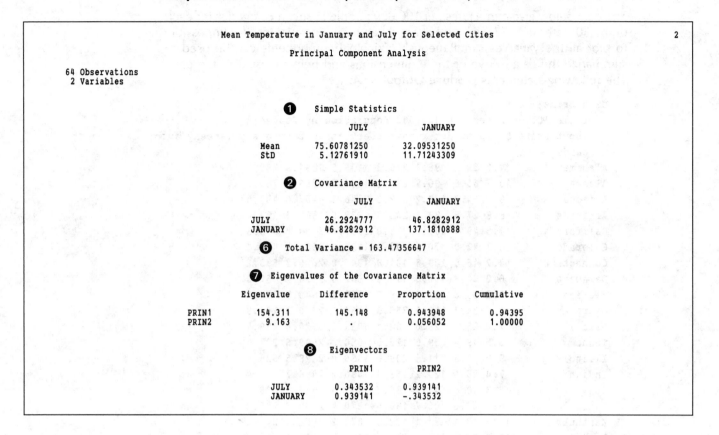

Output 33.3   Plot of Principal Components

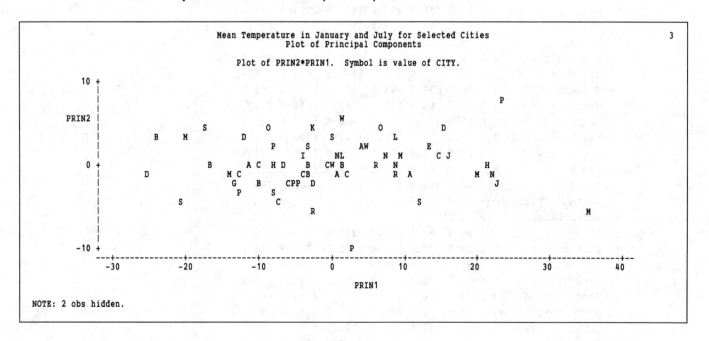

Example 2:   Crime Rates

The data below give crime rates per 100,000 people in seven categories for each of the 50 states in 1977. Since there are seven numeric variables, it is impossible to plot all the variables simultaneously. Principal components can be used to summarize the data in two or three dimensions and help to visualize the data. The following statements produce **Output 33.4**:

```
data crime;
   title 'Crime Rates per 100,000 Population by State';
   input state $1-15 murder rape robbery assault burglary larceny auto;
   cards;
Alabama         14.2 25.2  96.8 278.3 1135.5 1881.9 280.7
Alaska          10.8 51.6  96.8 284.0 1331.7 3369.8 753.3
Arizona          9.5 34.2 138.2 312.3 2346.1 4467.4 439.5
Arkansas         8.8 27.6  83.2 203.4  972.6 1862.1 183.4
California       11.5 49.4 287.0 358.0 2139.4 3499.8 663.5
Colorado         6.3 42.0 170.7 292.9 1935.2 3903.2 477.1
Connecticut      4.2 16.8 129.5 131.8 1346.0 2620.7 593.2
Delaware         6.0 24.9 157.0 194.2 1682.6 3678.4 467.0
Florida         10.2 39.6 187.9 449.1 1859.9 3840.5 351.4
Georgia         11.7 31.1 140.5 256.5 1351.1 2170.2 297.9
Hawaii           7.2 25.5 128.0  64.1 1911.5 3920.4 489.4
Idaho            5.5 19.4  39.6 172.5 1050.8 2599.6 237.6
Illinois         9.9 21.8 211.3 209.0 1085.0 2828.5 528.6
Indiana          7.4 26.5 123.2 153.5 1086.2 2498.7 377.4
Iowa             2.3 10.6  41.2  89.8  812.5 2685.1 219.9
Kansas           6.6 22.0 100.7 180.5 1270.4 2739.3 244.3
Kentucky        10.1 19.1  81.1 123.3  872.2 1662.1 245.4
Louisiana       15.5 30.9 142.9 335.5 1165.5 2469.9 337.7
Maine            2.4 13.5  38.7 170.0 1253.1 2350.7 246.9
Maryland         8.0 34.8 292.1 358.9 1400.0 3177.7 428.5
Massachusetts    3.1 20.8 169.1 231.6 1532.2 2311.3 1140.1
Michigan         9.3 38.9 261.9 274.6 1522.7 3159.0 545.5
Minnesota        2.7 19.5  85.9  85.8 1134.7 2559.3 343.1
Mississippi     14.3 19.6  65.7 189.1  915.6 1239.9 144.4
Missouri         9.6 28.3 189.0 233.5 1318.3 2424.2 378.4
Montana          5.4 16.7  39.2 156.8  804.9 2773.2 309.2
Nebraska         3.9 18.1  64.7 112.7  760.0 2316.1 249.1
Nevada          15.8 49.1 323.1 355.0 2453.1 4212.6 559.2
New Hampshire    3.2 10.7  23.2  76.0 1041.7 2343.9 293.4
New Jersey       5.6 21.0 180.4 185.1 1435.8 2774.5 511.5
New Mexico       8.8 39.1 109.6 343.4 1418.7 3008.6 259.5
New York        10.7 29.4 472.6 319.1 1728.0 2782.0 745.8
North Carolina  10.6 17.0  61.3 318.3 1154.1 2037.8 192.1
North Dakota     0.9  9.0  13.3  43.8  446.1 1843.0 144.7
Ohio             7.8 27.3 190.5 181.1 1216.0 2696.8 400.4
Oklahoma         8.6 29.2  73.8 205.0 1288.2 2228.1 326.8
Oregon           4.9 39.9 124.1 286.9 1636.4 3506.1 388.9
Pennsylvania     5.6 19.0 130.3 128.0  877.5 1624.1 333.2
Rhode Island     3.6 10.5  86.5 201.0 1489.5 2844.1 791.4
South Carolina  11.9 33.0 105.9 485.3 1613.6 2342.4 245.1
South Dakota     2.0 13.5  17.9 155.7  570.5 1704.4 147.5
Tennessee       10.1 29.7 145.8 203.9 1259.7 1776.5 314.0
Texas           13.3 33.8 152.4 208.2 1603.1 2988.7 397.6
Utah             3.5 20.3  68.8 147.3 1171.6 3004.6 334.5
```

```
Vermont          1.4 15.9  30.8 101.2 1348.2 2201.0 265.2
Virginia         9.0 23.3  92.1 165.7  986.2 2521.2 226.7
Washington       4.3 39.6 106.2 224.8 1605.6 3386.9 360.3
West Virginia    6.0 13.2  42.2  90.9  597.4 1341.7 163.3
Wisconsin        2.8 12.9  52.2  63.7  846.9 2614.2 220.7
Wyoming          5.4 21.9  39.7 173.9  811.6 2772.2 282.0
;

proc princomp out=crimcomp;
run;
```

Output 33.4   Results of Principal Component Analysis: PROC PRINCOMP

```
                        Crime Rates per 100,000 Population by State                        1
                              Principal Component Analysis

      50 Observations
       7 Variables


                                     Simple Statistics

              MURDER           RAPE         ROBBERY        ASSAULT       BURGLARY          LARCENY              AUTO
Mean     7.444000000    25.73400000    124.0920000    211.3000000    1291.904000     2671.288000      377.5260000
StD      3.866768941    10.75962995     88.3485672    100.2530492     432.455711      725.908707      193.3944175


                                     Correlation Matrix

                MURDER      RAPE    ROBBERY    ASSAULT   BURGLARY    LARCENY       AUTO

      MURDER    1.0000    0.6012     0.4837     0.6486     0.3858     0.1019     0.0688
      RAPE      0.6012    1.0000     0.5919     0.7403     0.7121     0.6140     0.3489
      ROBBERY   0.4837    0.5919     1.0000     0.5571     0.6372     0.4467     0.5907
      ASSAULT   0.6486    0.7403     0.5571     1.0000     0.6229     0.4044     0.2758
      BURGLARY  0.3858    0.7121     0.6372     0.6229     1.0000     0.7921     0.5580
      LARCENY   0.1019    0.6140     0.4467     0.4044     0.7921     1.0000     0.4442
      AUTO      0.0688    0.3489     0.5907     0.2758     0.5580     0.4442     1.0000


                             Eigenvalues of the Correlation Matrix

                       Eigenvalue    Difference    Proportion    Cumulative

             PRIN1       4.11496       2.87624       0.587851       0.58785
             PRIN2       1.23872       0.51291       0.176960       0.76481
             PRIN3       0.72582       0.40938       0.103688       0.86850
             PRIN4       0.31643       0.05846       0.045205       0.91370
             PRIN5       0.25797       0.03593       0.036853       0.95056
             PRIN6       0.22204       0.09798       0.031720       0.98228
             PRIN7       0.12406          .          0.017722       1.00000


                                       Eigenvectors

                    PRIN1      PRIN2      PRIN3      PRIN4      PRIN5      PRIN6      PRIN7

      MURDER     0.300279   -.629174   0.178245   -.232114   0.538123   0.259117   0.267593
      RAPE       0.431759   -.169435   -.244198   0.062216   0.188471   -.773271   -.296485
      ROBBERY    0.396875   0.042247   0.495861   -.557989   -.519977   -.114385   -.003903
      ASSAULT    0.396652   -.343528   -.069510   0.629804   -.506651   0.172363   0.191745
      BURGLARY   0.440157   0.203341   -.209895   -.057555   0.101033   0.535987   -.648117
      LARCENY    0.357360   0.402319   -.539231   -.234890   0.030099   0.039406   0.601690
      AUTO       0.295177   0.502421   0.568384   0.419238   0.369753   -.057298   0.147046
```

The eigenvalues indicate that two or three components provide a good summary of the data, two components accounting for 76 percent of the standardized variance (0.76=(4.11496+1.23872)/7) and three components explaining 87 percent. Subsequent components contribute less than 5 percent each.

The first component is a measure of overall crime rate since the first eigenvector shows approximately equal loadings on all variables. The second eigenvector has high positive loadings on AUTO and LARCENY and high negative loadings on MURDER and ASSAULT. There is also a small positive loading on BURGLARY and a small negative loading on RAPE. This component seems to measure the preponderance of property crime over violent crime. The interpretation of the third component is not obvious.

A simple way to examine the principal components in more detail is to print the output data set sorted by each of the large components. These statements produce **Output 33.5**:

```
proc sort;
   by prin1;
run;

proc print;
   id state;
   var prin1 prin2 murder rape robbery assault burglary larceny auto;
   title2 'States Listed in Order of Overall Crime Rate';
   title3 'As Determined by the First Principal Component';
run;

proc sort;
   by prin2;
run;

proc print;
   id state;
   var prin1 prin2 murder rape robbery assault burglary larceny auto;
   title2 'States Listed in Order of Property Vs. Violent Crime';
   title3 'As Determined by the Second Principal Component';
run;
```

Output 33.5   OUT= Data Set Sorted by Principal Components

Crime Rates per 100,000 Population by State
States Listed in Order of Overall Crime Rate
As Determined by the First Principal Component

STATE	PRIN1	PRIN2	MURDER	RAPE	ROBBERY	ASSAULT	BURGLARY	LARCENY	AUTO
North Dakota	-3.96408	0.38767	0.9	9.0	13.3	43.8	446.1	1843.0	144.7
South Dakota	-3.17203	-0.25446	2.0	13.5	17.9	155.7	570.5	1704.4	147.5
West Virginia	-3.14772	-0.81425	6.0	13.2	42.2	90.9	597.4	1341.7	163.3
Iowa	-2.58156	0.82475	2.3	10.6	41.2	89.8	812.5	2685.1	219.9
Wisconsin	-2.50296	0.78083	2.8	12.9	52.2	63.7	846.9	2614.2	220.7
New Hampshire	-2.46562	0.82503	3.2	10.7	23.2	76.0	1041.7	2343.9	293.4
Nebraska	-2.15071	0.22574	3.9	18.1	64.7	112.7	760.0	2316.1	249.1
Vermont	-2.06433	0.94497	1.4	15.9	30.8	101.2	1348.2	2201.0	265.2
Maine	-1.82631	0.57878	2.4	13.5	38.7	170.0	1253.1	2350.7	246.9
Kentucky	-1.72691	-1.14663	10.1	19.1	81.1	123.3	872.2	1662.1	245.4
Pennsylvania	-1.72007	-0.19590	5.6	19.0	130.3	128.0	877.5	1624.1	333.2
Montana	-1.66801	0.27099	5.4	16.7	39.2	156.8	804.9	2773.2	309.2
Minnesota	-1.55434	1.05644	2.7	19.5	85.9	85.8	1134.7	2559.3	343.1
Mississippi	-1.50736	-2.54671	14.3	19.6	65.7	189.1	915.6	1239.9	144.4
Idaho	-1.43245	-0.00801	5.5	19.4	39.6	172.5	1050.8	2599.6	237.6
Wyoming	-1.42463	0.06268	5.4	21.9	39.7	173.9	811.6	2772.2	282.0
Arkansas	-1.05441	-1.34544	8.8	27.6	83.2	203.4	972.6	1862.1	183.4
Utah	-1.04996	0.93656	3.5	20.3	68.8	147.3	1171.6	3004.6	334.5
Virginia	-0.91621	-0.69265	9.0	23.3	92.1	165.7	986.2	2521.2	226.7
North Carolina	-0.69925	-1.67027	10.6	17.0	61.3	318.3	1154.1	2037.8	192.1

(continued on next page)

(continued from previous page)

STATE			MURDER	RAPE	ROBBERY	ASSAULT	BURGLARY	LARCENY	AUTO
Kansas	-0.63407	-0.02804	6.6	22.0	100.7	180.5	1270.4	2739.3	244.3
Connecticut	-0.54133	1.50123	4.2	16.8	129.5	131.8	1346.0	2620.7	593.2
Indiana	-0.49990	0.00003	7.4	26.5	123.2	153.5	1086.2	2498.7	377.4
Oklahoma	-0.32136	-0.62429	8.6	29.2	73.8	205.0	1288.2	2228.1	326.8
Rhode Island	-0.20156	2.14658	3.6	10.5	86.5	201.0	1489.5	2844.1	791.4
Tennessee	-0.13660	-1.13498	10.1	29.7	145.8	203.9	1259.7	1776.5	314.0
Alabama	-0.04988	-2.09610	14.2	25.2	96.8	278.3	1135.5	1881.9	280.7
New Jersey	0.21787	0.96421	5.6	21.0	180.4	185.1	1435.8	2774.5	511.5
Ohio	0.23953	0.09053	7.8	27.3	190.5	181.1	1216.0	2696.8	400.4
Georgia	0.49041	-1.38079	11.7	31.1	140.5	256.5	1351.1	2170.2	297.9
Illinois	0.51290	0.09423	9.9	21.8	211.3	209.0	1085.0	2828.5	528.6
Missouri	0.55637	-0.55851	9.6	28.3	189.0	233.5	1318.3	2424.2	378.4
Hawaii	0.82313	1.82392	7.2	25.5	128.0	64.1	1911.5	3920.4	489.4
Washington	0.93058	0.73776	4.3	39.6	106.2	224.8	1605.6	3386.9	360.3
Delaware	0.96458	1.29674	6.0	24.9	157.0	194.2	1682.6	3678.4	467.0
Massachusetts	0.97844	2.63105	3.1	20.8	169.1	231.6	1532.2	2311.3	1140.1
Louisiana	1.12020	-2.08327	15.5	30.9	142.9	335.5	1165.5	2469.9	337.7
New Mexico	1.21417	-0.95076	8.8	39.1	109.6	343.4	1418.7	3008.6	259.5
Texas	1.39696	-0.68131	13.3	33.8	152.4	208.2	1603.1	2988.7	397.6
Oregon	1.44900	0.58603	4.9	39.9	124.1	286.9	1636.4	3506.1	388.9
South Carolina	1.60336	-2.16211	11.9	33.0	105.9	485.3	1613.6	2342.4	245.1
Maryland	2.18280	-0.19474	8.0	34.8	292.1	358.9	1400.0	3177.7	428.5
Michigan	2.27333	0.15487	9.3	38.9	261.9	274.6	1522.7	3159.0	545.5
Alaska	2.42151	0.16652	10.8	51.6	96.8	284.0	1331.7	3369.8	753.3
Colorado	2.50929	0.91660	6.3	42.0	170.7	292.9	1935.2	3903.2	477.1
Arizona	3.01414	0.84495	9.5	34.2	138.2	312.3	2346.1	4467.4	439.5
Florida	3.11175	-0.60392	10.2	39.6	187.9	449.1	1859.9	3840.5	351.4
New York	3.45248	0.43289	10.7	29.4	472.6	319.1	1728.0	2782.0	745.8
California	4.28380	0.14319	11.5	49.4	287.0	358.0	2139.4	3499.8	663.5
Nevada	5.26699	-0.25262	15.8	49.1	323.1	355.0	2453.1	4212.6	559.2

Crime Rates per 100,000 Population by State
States Listed in Order of Property Vs. Violent Crime
As Determined by the Second Principal Component

2

STATE	PRIN1	PRIN2	MURDER	RAPE	ROBBERY	ASSAULT	BURGLARY	LARCENY	AUTO
Mississippi	-1.50736	-2.54671	14.3	19.6	65.7	189.1	915.6	1239.9	144.4
South Carolina	1.60336	-2.16211	11.9	33.0	105.9	485.3	1613.6	2342.4	245.1
Alabama	-0.04988	-2.09610	14.2	25.2	96.8	278.3	1135.5	1881.9	280.7
Louisiana	1.12020	-2.08327	15.5	30.9	142.9	335.5	1165.5	2469.9	337.7
North Carolina	-0.69925	-1.67027	10.6	17.0	61.3	318.3	1154.1	2037.8	192.1
Georgia	0.49041	-1.38079	11.7	31.1	140.5	256.5	1351.1	2170.2	297.9
Arkansas	-1.05441	-1.34544	8.8	27.6	83.2	203.4	972.6	1862.1	183.4
Kentucky	-1.72691	-1.14663	10.1	19.1	81.1	123.3	872.2	1662.1	245.4
Tennessee	-0.13660	-1.13498	10.1	29.7	145.8	203.9	1259.7	1776.5	314.0
New Mexico	1.21417	-0.95076	8.8	39.1	109.6	343.4	1418.7	3008.6	259.5
West Virginia	-3.14772	-0.81425	6.0	13.2	42.2	90.9	597.4	1341.7	163.3
Virginia	-0.91621	-0.69265	9.0	23.3	92.1	165.7	986.2	2521.2	226.7
Texas	1.39696	-0.68131	13.3	33.8	152.4	208.2	1603.1	2988.7	397.6
Oklahoma	-0.32136	-0.62429	8.6	29.2	73.8	205.0	1288.2	2228.1	326.8
Florida	3.11175	-0.60392	10.2	39.6	187.9	449.1	1859.9	3840.5	351.4
Missouri	0.55637	-0.55851	9.6	28.3	189.0	233.5	1318.3	2424.2	378.4
South Dakota	-3.17203	-0.25446	2.0	13.5	17.9	155.7	570.5	1704.4	147.5
Nevada	5.26699	-0.25262	15.8	49.1	323.1	355.0	2453.1	4212.6	559.2
Pennsylvania	-1.72691	-0.19590	5.6	19.0	130.3	128.0	877.5	1624.1	333.2
Maryland	2.18280	-0.19474	8.0	34.8	292.1	358.9	1400.0	3177.7	428.5
Kansas	-0.63407	-0.02804	6.6	22.0	100.7	180.5	1270.4	2739.3	244.3
Idaho	-1.43245	-0.00801	5.5	19.4	39.6	172.5	1050.8	2599.6	237.6
Indiana	-0.49990	0.00003	7.4	26.5	123.2	153.5	1086.2	2498.7	377.4
Wyoming	-1.42463	0.06268	5.4	21.9	39.7	173.9	811.6	2772.2	282.0
Ohio	0.23953	0.09053	7.8	27.3	190.5	181.1	1216.0	2696.8	400.4
Illinois	0.51290	0.09423	9.9	21.8	211.3	209.0	1085.0	2828.5	528.6
California	4.28380	0.14319	11.5	49.4	287.0	358.0	2139.4	3499.8	663.5
Michigan	2.27333	0.15487	9.3	38.9	261.9	274.6	1522.7	3159.0	545.5
Alaska	2.42151	0.16652	10.8	51.6	96.8	284.0	1331.7	3369.8	753.3
Nebraska	-2.15071	0.22574	3.9	18.1	64.7	112.7	760.0	2316.1	249.1
Montana	-1.66801	0.27099	5.4	16.7	39.2	156.8	804.9	2773.2	309.2
North Dakota	-3.96408	0.38767	0.9	9.0	13.3	43.8	446.1	1843.0	144.7
New York	3.45248	0.43289	10.7	29.4	472.6	319.1	1728.0	2782.0	745.8
Maine	-1.82631	0.57878	2.4	13.5	38.7	170.0	1253.1	2350.7	246.9
Oregon	1.44900	0.58603	4.9	39.9	124.1	286.9	1636.4	3506.1	388.9
Washington	0.93058	0.73776	4.3	39.6	106.2	224.8	1605.6	3386.9	360.3
Wisconsin	-2.50296	0.78083	2.8	12.9	52.2	63.7	846.9	2614.2	220.7
Iowa	-2.58156	0.82475	2.3	10.6	41.2	89.8	812.5	2685.1	219.9
New Hampshire	-2.46562	0.82503	3.2	10.7	23.2	76.0	1041.7	2343.9	293.4
Arizona	3.01414	0.84495	9.5	34.2	138.2	312.3	2346.1	4467.4	439.5
Colorado	2.50929	0.91660	6.3	42.0	170.7	292.9	1935.2	3903.2	477.1
Utah	-1.04996	0.93656	3.5	20.3	68.8	147.3	1171.6	3004.6	334.5
Vermont	-2.06433	0.94497	1.4	15.9	30.8	101.2	1348.2	2201.0	265.2
New Jersey	0.21787	0.96421	5.6	21.0	180.4	185.1	1435.8	2774.5	511.5
Minnesota	-1.55434	1.05644	2.7	19.5	85.9	85.8	1134.7	2559.3	343.1
Delaware	0.96458	1.29674	6.0	24.9	157.0	194.2	1682.6	3678.4	467.0

(continued on next page)

(continued from previous page)

Connecticut	-0.54133	1.50123	4.2	16.8	129.5	131.8	1346.0	2620.7	593.2
Hawaii	0.82313	1.82392	7.2	25.5	128.0	64.1	1911.5	3920.4	489.4
Rhode Island	-0.20156	2.14658	3.6	10.5	86.5	201.0	1489.5	2844.1	791.4
Massachusetts	0.97844	2.63105	3.1	20.8	169.1	231.6	1532.2	2311.3	1140.1

Another recommended procedure is to make scatterplots of the first few components. The sorted listings help to identify observations on the plots. The following statements produce **Output 33.6**:

```
proc plot;
   plot prin2*prin1=state / vpos=31;
   title2 'Plot of the First Two Principal Components';
run;

proc plot;
   plot prin3*prin1=state / vpos=26;
   title2 'Plot of the First and Third Principal Components';
run;
```

Output 33.6   Plots of Principal Components

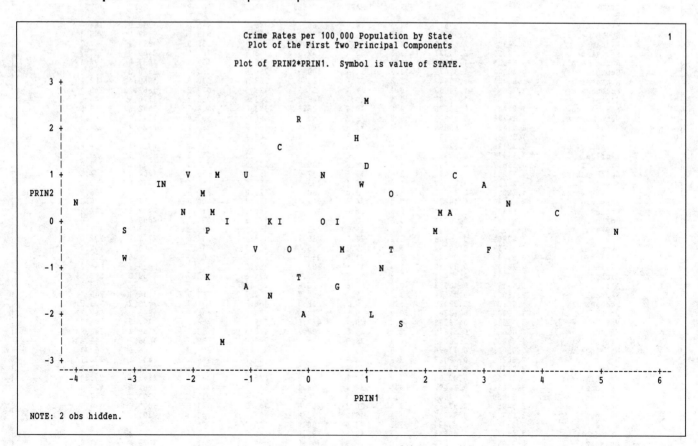

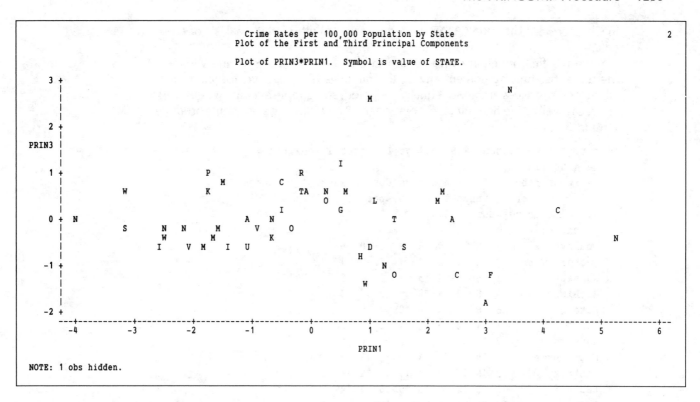

Crime Rates per 100,000 Population by State
Plot of the First and Third Principal Components

Plot of PRIN3*PRIN1. Symbol is value of STATE.

NOTE: 1 obs hidden.

It is possible to identify regional trends on the plot of the first two components. Nevada and California are at the extreme right, with high overall crime rates but an average ratio of property crime to violent crime. North and South Dakota are on the extreme left with low overall crime rates. Southeastern states tend to be in the bottom of the plot, with a higher-than-average ratio of violent crime to property crime. New England states tend to be in the upper part of the plot, with a greater-than-average ratio of property crime to violent crime.

The most striking feature of the plot of the first and third principal components is that Massachusetts and New York are outliers on the third component.

Example 3:   Basketball Data

The data in this example are rankings of 35 college basketball teams. The rankings were made before the start of the 1985–86 season by ten news services.

The purpose of the principal component analysis is to compute a single variable that best summarizes all ten of the preseason rankings.

Note that the various news services rank different numbers of teams, varying from 20 through 30 (there is a missing rank in one of the variables, WASPOST). And, of course, each service does not rank the same teams, so there are missing values in these data. Each of the 35 teams is ranked by at least one news service.

PROC PRINCOMP omits observations with missing values. To obtain principal component scores for all of the teams, it is necessary to replace the missing values. Since it is the best teams that are ranked, it is not appropriate to replace missing values with the mean of the nonmissing values. Instead, an ad hoc method is used that replaces missing values by the mean of the unassigned ranks. For example, if 20 teams are ranked by a news service, then ranks 21 through 35 are unassigned. The mean of the ranks 21 through 35 is 28, so missing values for that variable are replaced by the value 28. To prevent the method of missing-value replacement from having an undue effect on the analysis, each observation is weighted according to the number of nonmissing values it has. See **Example 2** in Chapter 34, "The PRINQUAL Procedure," for an alternative analysis of these data.

Since the first principal component accounts for 78 percent of the variance, there is substantial agreement among the rankings. The eigenvector shows that all the news services are about equally weighted, so a simple average would work almost as well as the first principal component. The following statements produce **Output 33.7**:

```
title1 'Pre-Season 1985 College Basketball Rankings';
data bballm;
   input school $13. csn dursun durher waspost usatoda
         spormag insport upi ap sporill;
   format csn--sporill 5.1;
   cards;
```

school	csn	dursun	durher	waspost	usatoda	spormag	insport	upi	ap	sporill
Louisville	1	8	1	9	8	9	6	10	9	9
Georgia Tech	2	2	4	3	1	1	1	2	1	1
Kansas	3	4	5	1	5	11	8	4	5	7
Michigan	4	5	9	4	2	5	3	1	3	2
Duke	5	6	7	5	4	10	4	5	6	5
UNC	6	1	2	2	3	4	2	3	2	3
Syracuse	7	10	6	11	6	6	5	6	4	10
Notre Dame	8	14	15	13	11	20	18	13	12	.
Kentucky	9	15	16	14	14	19	11	12	11	13
LSU	10	9	13	.	13	15	16	9	14	8
DePaul	11	.	21	15	20	.	19	.	.	19
Georgetown	12	7	8	6	9	2	9	8	8	4
Navy	13	20	23	10	18	13	15	.	20	.
Illinois	14	3	3	7	7	3	10	7	7	6
Iowa	15	16	.	.	23	.	.	14	.	20
Arkansas	16	.	.	.	25	.	.	.	.	16
Memphis State	17	.	11	.	16	8	20	.	15	12
Washington	18	.	.	.	.	.	.	17	.	.
UAB	19	13	10	.	12	17	.	16	16	15
UNLV	20	18	18	19	22	.	14	18	18	.
NC State	21	17	14	16	15	.	12	15	17	18
Maryland	22	.	.	.	19	.	.	.	19	14
Pittsburgh	23	.	.	.	.	.	.	.	.	.
Oklahoma	24	19	17	17	17	12	17	.	13	17
Indiana	25	12	20	18	21	.	.	.	.	.
Virginia	26	.	22	.	.	18	.	.	.	.
Old Dominion	27	.	.	.	.	.	.	.	.	.
Auburn	28	11	12	8	10	7	7	11	10	11
St. Johns	29	.	.	.	.	14	.	.	.	.
UCLA	30	.	.	.	.	.	19	.	.	.
St. Joseph's	.	.	19	.	.	.	.	.	.	.
Tennessee	.	.	24	.	.	16	.	.	.	.
Montana	.	.	.	20	.	.	.	.	.	.
Houston	.	.	.	.	24	.	.	.	.	.
Virginia Tech	.	.	.	.	.	.	13	.	.	.

```
;
```

```
      /* PROC MEANS is used to output a data set containing the maximum  */
      /* value of each of the newspaper and magazine rankings.  The      */
      /* output data set, maxrank, is then used to set the missing       */
      /* values to the next highest rank plus thirty-six, divided by two */
      /* (that is, the mean of the missing ranks).  This ad hoc method of*/
      /* replacing missing values is based more on intuition than on     */
      /* rigorous statistical theory.  Observations are weighted by the  */
      /* number of nonmissing values.                                    */
      /*                                                                  */
proc means data=bballm;
   output out=maxrank
         max=mcsn mdurs mdurh mwas musa mspom mins mupi map mspoi;
run;


      /* The method of filling in missing values shown below is a        */
      /* reasonable method for this specific example.  It would be       */
      /* inappropriate to use this method for other data sets.  In       */
      /* addition, any method of filling in missing values can           */
      /* result in incorrect statistics. The choice of whether to        */
      /* fill in missing values, and what method to use to do so,        */
      /* is the responsibility of the person performing the              */
      /* analysis.                                                       */
      /*                                                                  */
data bball;
   set bballm;
   if _n_=1 then set maxrank;
   array services{10} csn--sporill;
   array maxranks{10} mcsn--mspoi;
   keep school csn--sporill weight;
   weight=0;
   do i=1 to 10;
      if services{i}=. then services{i}=(maxranks{i}+36)/2;
      else weight=weight+1;
   end;
run;


      /* Use the PRINCOMP procedure to transform the observed ranks.     */
      /* Use n=1 because the data should be related to a single          */
      /* underlying variable. Sort the data and print the resulting      */
      /* component.                                                      */
      /*                                                                  */
proc princomp data=bball n=1 out=pcbball standard;
   var csn--sporill;
   weight weight;
run;


proc sort data=pcbball;
   by prin1;
run;


proc print;
   var school prin1;
   title2 'College Teams as Ordered by PROC PRINCOMP';
run;
```

Output 33.7   Basketball Rankings Using PROC PRINCOMP

```
                    Pre-Season 1985 College Basketball Rankings                        1

        Variable   N       Mean       Std Dev      Minimum       Maximum
        --------------------------------------------------------------------
        CSN        30    15.5000000   8.8034084   1.0000000    30.0000000
        DURSUN     20    10.5000000   5.9160798   1.0000000    20.0000000
        DURHER     24    12.5000000   7.0710678   1.0000000    24.0000000
        WASPOST    19    10.4210526   6.0673607   1.0000000    20.0000000
        USATODA    25    13.0000000   7.3598007   1.0000000    25.0000000
        SPORMAG    20    10.5000000   5.9160798   1.0000000    20.0000000
        INSPORT    20    10.5000000   5.9160798   1.0000000    20.0000000
        UPI        19    10.0000000   5.6273143   1.0000000    19.0000000
        AP         20    10.5000000   5.9160798   1.0000000    20.0000000
        SPORILL    20    10.5000000   5.9160798   1.0000000    20.0000000
        --------------------------------------------------------------------
```

```
                    Pre-Season 1985 College Basketball Rankings                        2

                          Principal Component Analysis

    35 Observations
    10 Variables


                                 Simple Statistics

                         CSN          DURSUN        DURHER       WASPOST        USATODA
        Mean       13.33640553   13.06451613   12.88018433   13.83410138   12.55760369
        StD        22.08036285   21.66394183   21.38091837   23.47841791   20.48207965


                       SPORMAG        INSPORT          UPI            AP          SPORILL
        Mean       13.83870968   13.24423963   13.59216590   12.83410138   13.52534562
        StD        23.37756267   22.20231526   23.25602811   21.40782406   22.93219584

                                Correlation Matrix

              CSN    DURSUN  DURHER  WASPOST USATODA SPORMAG INSPORT   UPI     AP    SPORILL
    CSN     1.0000  0.6505  0.6415  0.6121  0.7456  0.4806  0.6558  0.7007  0.6779  0.6135
    DURSUN  0.6505  1.0000  0.8341  0.7667  0.8860  0.6940  0.7702  0.9015  0.8437  0.7518
    DURHER  0.6415  0.8341  1.0000  0.7035  0.8877  0.7788  0.7900  0.7676  0.8788  0.7761
    WASPOST 0.6121  0.7667  0.7035  1.0000  0.7984  0.6598  0.8717  0.6953  0.7809  0.5952
    USATODA 0.7456  0.8860  0.8877  0.7984  1.0000  0.7716  0.8475  0.8539  0.9479  0.8426
    SPORMAG 0.4806  0.6940  0.7788  0.6598  0.7716  1.0000  0.7176  0.6220  0.8217  0.7701
    INSPORT 0.6558  0.7702  0.7900  0.8717  0.8475  0.7176  1.0000  0.7920  0.8830  0.7332
    UPI     0.7007  0.9015  0.7676  0.6953  0.8539  0.6220  0.7920  1.0000  0.8436  0.7738
    AP      0.6779  0.8437  0.8788  0.7809  0.9479  0.8217  0.8830  0.8436  1.0000  0.8212
    SPORILL 0.6135  0.7518  0.7761  0.5952  0.8426  0.7701  0.7332  0.7738  0.8212  1.0000

                         Eigenvalues of the Correlation Matrix

                    Eigenvalue    Difference    Proportion    Cumulative

        PRIN1        7.88602          .          0.788602      0.788602


                                    Eigenvectors

                                       PRIN1
                        CSN         0.270205
                        DURSUN      0.326048
                        DURHER      0.324392
                        WASPOST     0.300449
                        USATODA     0.345200
                        SPORMAG     0.293881
                        INSPORT     0.324088
                        UPI         0.319902
                        AP          0.342151
                        SPORILL     0.308570
```

```
                 Pre-Season 1985 College Basketball Rankings              3
                    College Teams as Ordered by PROC PRINCOMP

                 OBS    SCHOOL              PRIN1

                   1    Georgia Tech       -0.58068
                   2    UNC                -0.53317
                   3    Michigan           -0.47874
                   4    Kansas             -0.40285
                   5    Duke               -0.38464
                   6    Illinois           -0.33586
                   7    Syracuse           -0.31578
                   8    Louisville         -0.31489
                   9    Georgetown         -0.29735
                  10    Auburn             -0.09785
                  11    Kentucky            0.00843
                  12    LSU                 0.00872
                  13    Notre Dame          0.09407
                  14    NC State            0.19404
                  15    UAB                 0.19771
                  16    Oklahoma            0.23864
                  17    Memphis State       0.25319
                  18    Navy                0.28921
                  19    UNLV                0.35103
                  20    DePaul              0.43770
                  21    Iowa                0.50213
                  22    Indiana             0.51713
                  23    Maryland            0.55910
                  24    Arkansas            0.62977
                  25    Virginia            0.67586
                  26    Washington          0.67756
                  27    Tennessee           0.70822
                  28    St. Johns           0.71425
                  29    Virginia Tech       0.71638
                  30    St. Joseph's        0.73492
                  31    UCLA                0.73965
                  32    Pittsburgh          0.75078
                  33    Houston             0.75534
                  34    Montana             0.75790
                  35    Old Dominion        0.76821
```

REFERENCES

Cooley, W.W. and Lohnes, P.R. (1971), *Multivariate Data Analysis*, New York: John Wiley & Sons, Inc.

Gnanadesikan, R. (1977), *Methods for Statistical Data Analysis of Multivariate Observations*, New York: John Wiley & Sons, Inc.

Hotelling, H. (1933), "Analysis of a Complex of Statistical Variables into Principal Components," *Journal of Educational Psychology*, 24, 417–441, 498–520.

Kshirsagar, A.M. (1972), *Multivariate Analysis*, New York: Marcel Dekker, Inc.

Mardia, K.V., Kent, J.T., and Bibby, J.M. (1979), *Multivariate Analysis*, London: Academic Press.

Morrison, D.F. (1976), *Multivariate Statistical Methods*, 2d Edition, New York: McGraw-Hill Book Co.

Pearson, K. (1901), "On Lines and Planes of Closest Fit to Systems of Points in Space," *Philosophical Magazine*, 6(2), 559–572.

Rao, C.R. (1964), "The Use and Interpretation of Principal Component Analysis in Applied Research," *Sankhya A*, 26, 329–358.

Chapter 34

The PRINQUAL Procedure

ABSTRACT   1265
INTRODUCTION   1266
  The Three Methods of Variable Transformation   1267
    The MTV (Maximum Total Variance) Method   1267
    The MGV (Minimum Generalized Variance) Method   1267
    The MAC (Maximum Average Correlation) Method   1268
  An Introductory Example Using the MTV Method   1268
SPECIFICATIONS   1273
  PROC PRINQUAL Statement   1274
  BY Statement   1279
  ID Statement   1279
  TRANSFORM Statement   1279
    Families of Transformations   1280
      Nonoptimal Transformations   1280
      Optimal Transformations   1281
    Transformation Options (t-options)   1282
      Nonoptimal transformation t-options   1283
      Optimal transformation t-options   1283
DETAILS   1285
  Missing Values   1285
  Controlling the Number of Iterations   1286
  Performing a Principal Components Analysis of Transformed Data   1287
  Using the MAC Method   1287
  Output Data Set   1288
    Structure and Content   1288
    TYPE and _NAME_ Variables   1289
    Variable Names   1290
    Effect of the TSTANDARD= and COVARIANCE Options   1290
  Computational Resources   1291
  Printed Output   1292
EXAMPLES   1292
  Example 1:   Multidimensional Preference Analysis of Cars Data   1292
  Example 2:   Principal Components of Basketball Rankings   1302
  Example 3:   Missing Data Estimation   1310
REFERENCES   1322

ABSTRACT

The PRINQUAL procedure obtains linear and nonlinear transformations of variables using the method of alternating least squares to optimize properties of the transformed variables' covariance or correlation matrix. In addition, nonoptimal transformations for logarithm, rank, exponentiation, inverse sine, and logit are available.

INTRODUCTION

The PRINQUAL procedure (principal components of qualitative data) is a data transformation procedure that is based on the work of Kruskal and Shepard (1974); Young, Takane, and de Leeuw (1978); and Winsberg and Ramsay (1983). You can use PROC PRINQUAL to

- generalize ordinary principal component analysis to a method capable of analyzing data that are not quantitative.
- perform metric and nonmetric multidimensional preference (MDPREF) analyses (Carroll 1972).
- preprocess data, transforming variables prior to their use in other data analyses.
- estimate missing values in multivariate data prior to subsequent data analyses. When used with survey data, PROC PRINQUAL can estimate optimal scores for nominal classes of otherwise ordered variables (such as *unfamiliar with the product* in an ordered preference rating).
- summarize mixed quantitative and qualitative data, and detect nonlinear relationships.
- reduce the number of variables for subsequent use in regression analyses, cluster analyses, and other analyses.

PRINQUAL provides three methods of transforming a set of qualitative and quantitative variables to optimize the transformed variables' covariance or correlation matrix. These methods are

- the MTV or maximum total variance method
- the MGV or minimum generalized variance method
- the MAC or maximum average correlation method.

All three methods attempt to find transformations that decrease the rank of the covariance matrix computed from the transformed variables. Transforming the variables to maximize the variance accounted for by a few linear combinations (using the MTV method) locates the observations in a space whose dimensionality approximates the stated number of linear combinations as much as possible given the transformation constraints. Transforming the variables to minimize their generalized variance or maximize the sum of correlations also reduces the dimensionality. The transformed qualitative (nominal and ordinal) variables can be thought of as quantified by the analysis, with the quantification done in the context set by the algorithm. The data are quantified so that the proportion of variance accounted for by a stated number of principal components is locally maximal, the generalized variance of the variables is locally minimal, or the average of the correlations is locally maximal.

The data can contain variables with nominal, ordinal, interval, and ratio scales of measurement (Siegel 1956). Any mix is allowed with all methods:

- Nominal variables can be transformed by scoring the categories to optimize the covariance matrix (Fisher 1938).
- Ordinal variables can be transformed monotonically by scoring the ordered categories so that order is weakly preserved (adjacent categories can be merged) and the covariance matrix is optimized. Ties can be untied optimally or left tied (Kruskal 1964). Ordinal variables can also be transformed to ranks.
- Interval and ratio scale of measurement variables can be linearly transformed, or nonlinearly transformed with spline (de Boor 1978; van Rijckevorsel 1982) or monotone spline (Winsberg and Ramsay 1983) transformations. In addition, nonoptimal transformations for logarithm, exponential, power, logit, and inverse trigonometric sine are available.

- For all transformations, missing data can be estimated without constraint, with category constraints (missing values within the same group get the same value), and with order constraints (missing value estimates in adjacent groups can be tied to weakly preserve a specified ordering) (Gifi 1981; Young 1981; Kuhfeld and de Leeuw, in preparation).

The PROC PRINQUAL iterations produce a set of transformed variables. Each variable's new scoring satisfies a set of constraints based on the original scoring of the variable and the specified transformation type. First, all variables are required to satisfy standardization constraints; that is, all variables have a fixed mean and variance. The other constraints include linear constraints, weak order constraints, category constraints, and smoothness constraints. The new set of scores is selected from the sets of possible scorings that do not violate the constraints so that the method criterion is locally optimized.

The printed output from PRINQUAL is a listing of the iteration history. However, the primary output from PRINQUAL is an output data set. By default, the procedure creates an output data set that contains variables with _TYPE_='SCORE'. These observations contain original variables, transformed variables, components, or data approximations. If you use the CORRELATIONS option in the PROC PRINQUAL statement, the data set also contains observations with _TYPE_='CORR'; these observations contain correlations or component structure information.

The Three Methods of Variable Transformation

The three methods of variable transformation provided by PROC PRINQUAL are discussed in the following sections.

The MTV (Maximum Total Variance) Method

The MTV method (Young, Takane, and de Leeuw 1978) is based on the principal component model and attempts to maximize the sum of the first r eigenvalues of the covariance matrix. This method transforms variables to be (in a least-squares sense) as similar to linear combinations of r principal component score variables as possible, where r can be much smaller than the number of variables. This maximizes the total variance of the first r components (the trace of the covariance matrix of the first r principal components) (Kuhfeld, Sarle, and Young 1985).

On each iteration, the MTV algorithm alternates classical principal component analysis (Hotelling 1933) with optimal scaling (Young 1981). When all variables are ordinal preference ratings, this corresponds to Carroll's (1972) MDPREF analysis. The iterations can be initialized using the method suggested by Tenenhaus and Vachette (1977), who independently proposed the same iterative algorithm for nominal and interval scale-of-measurement variables.

The MGV (Minimum Generalized Variance) Method

The MGV method (Sarle 1984) uses an iterated multiple regression algorithm in an attempt to minimize the determinant of the covariance matrix of the transformed variables. This method transforms each variable to be (in a least-squares sense) as similar to linear combinations of the remaining variables as possible. This locally minimizes the generalized variance of the transformed variables, the determinant of the covariance matrix, the volume of the parallelepiped defined by the transformed variables, and sphericity (the extent to which a quadratic form in the optimized covariance matrix defines a sphere) (Kuhfeld, Sarle, and Young 1985).

On each iteration for each variable, the MGV algorithm alternates multiple regression with optimal scaling. The multiple regression involves predicting the selected variable from all other variables. The iterations can be initialized using a modification of the Tenenhaus and Vachette (1977) method that is appropriate with a regression algorithm. This method can be viewed as a way of investigating the nature of the linear and nonlinear dependencies in, and the rank of, a data matrix containing variables that can be nonlinearly transformed. This method tries to create a less-than-full rank data matrix. The matrix contains the transformation of each variable that is most similar to what the other transformed variables predict.

The MAC (Maximum Average Correlation) Method

The MAC method (de Leeuw 1985) uses an iterated constrained multiple regression algorithm in an attempt to maximize the average of the elements of the correlation matrix. This method transforms each variable to be (in a least-squares sense) as similar to the average of the remaining variables as possible (de Leeuw 1985).

On each iteration for each variable, the MAC algorithm alternates computing an equally weighted average of the other variables with optimal scaling. The MAC method is similar to the MGV method in that each variable is scaled to be as similar to a linear combination of the other variables as possible, given the constraints on the transformation. However, optimal weights are not computed. You can use the MAC method when all variables are positively correlated, or when no monotonicity constraints are placed on any transformations. Do not use this method with negatively correlated variables when some optimal transformations are constrained to be increasing because the signs of the correlations are not taken into account. The MAC method is useful as an initialization method for the MTV and MGV methods.

An Introductory Example Using the MTV Method

The following example illustrates PROC PRINQUAL using the MTV method. Suppose the problem is to linearize a curve through three-dimensional space. Let

$$x_1 = x^3$$
$$x_2 = x_1 - x^5$$
$$x_3 = x_2 - x^6$$

where $x = -1.00, -0.98, -0.96, \ldots, 1.0$.

These three variables define a curve in three-space. The PLOT procedure is used to show two-dimensional views of this curve. These data are completely described by three linear components, but define a single curve, which could be described as a single nonlinear component.

PROC PRINQUAL is used to straighten the curve into a one-dimensional line with a continuous transformation of each variable. Specifically, the TRANSFORM statement requests a cubic spline transformation with nine knots. Splines are curves, which are usually required to be continuous and smooth. Splines are usually defined as piecewise polynomials of degree n whose function values and first $n-1$ derivatives agree at the points where they join. The abscissa values of the join points are called *knots*. The term spline is also used for polynomials (splines with no knots) and piecewise polynomials with more than one discontinuous derivative. Splines with no knots are generally smoother than splines with knots, which are generally smoother than splines with multiple discontinuous derivatives. Splines with few knots are generally smoother than splines with many knots, however increasing the number of knots usually increases the fit of the spline function to the data. Knots give the curve freedom to bend to more closely follow the data. See Smith (1979) for an excellent introduction to splines. For another example of using splines, see **Example 2** in Chapter 40, "The TRANSREG Procedure."

One component accounts for 71 percent of the variance of the untransformed data, and after 50 iterations, over 98 percent of the variance of the transformed data is accounted for by one component.

PRINQUAL creates an output data set (which is not printed) that contains both the original and transformed variables. The original variables have the names X1, X2, and X3. Transformed variables are named TX1, TX2, and TX3. All observations in the output data set have _TYPE_='SCORE', since the CORRELATIONS option is not used in the PROC PRINQUAL statement. PROC PLOT uses this output data set, and shows the nonlinear transformations of all three variables and the nearly one-dimensional scatterplot.

PRINQUAL tries to project each variable on the first principal component. Notice that the curve in this example is closer to a circle than a function from some views and that the first component does not run approximately from one end point of the curve to the other. Since the curve has these characteristics, PROC PRINQUAL linearizes the scatterplot by collapsing the scatter around the principal axis, not by straightening the curve into a single line. PROC PRINQUAL would straighten simpler curves.

The following statements produce **Output 34.1**:

```
    /*---Generate a Three-Dimensional Curve---*/
 data x;
    do x = -1 to 1 by .02;
       x1 =       x ** 3;
       x2 = x1 - x ** 5;
       x3 = x2 - x ** 6;
       output;
    end;
    drop x;
 run;


    /*---Plot the Curve---*/
 proc plot data=x vpercent=50 hpercent=50;
    /*--- This ordering and the axis reversal serve to produce a    ---*/
    /*--- page of plots that could be folded into three cube faces ---*/
    /*--- for a three-dimensional view of the curve.               ---*/
    plot x1*x2 x1*x3 /              haxis=-1 to 1 vaxis=-1 to 1;
    plot x3*x2       / vreverse haxis=-1 to 1 vaxis=-1 to 1;
    title 'Two-Dimensional Views of a Three-Dimensional Curve';
 run;


    /*---Try to Straighten the Curve---*/
 proc prinqual data=x n=1 maxiter=50 covariance;
    title 'Iteratively Derive Variable Transformations';
    transform spline(x1-x3 / nknots=9);
 run;


    /*---Plot the Transformations---*/
 proc plot vpercent=50 hpercent=50;
    plot tx1*x1 tx2*x2 tx3*x3;
    title 'Variable Transformation Plots';
 run;
```

```
/*---Plot the Straightened Scatterplot---*/
proc plot vpercent=50 hpercent=50;
    plot tx1*tx2 tx1*tx3 /          haxis=-1 to 1 vaxis=-1 to 1;
    plot tx3*tx2          / vreverse haxis=-1 to 1 vaxis=-1 to 1;
    title 'The Nearly One-Dimensional Curve';
run;
```

Output 34.1 Three-dimensional Curved Line Example Output

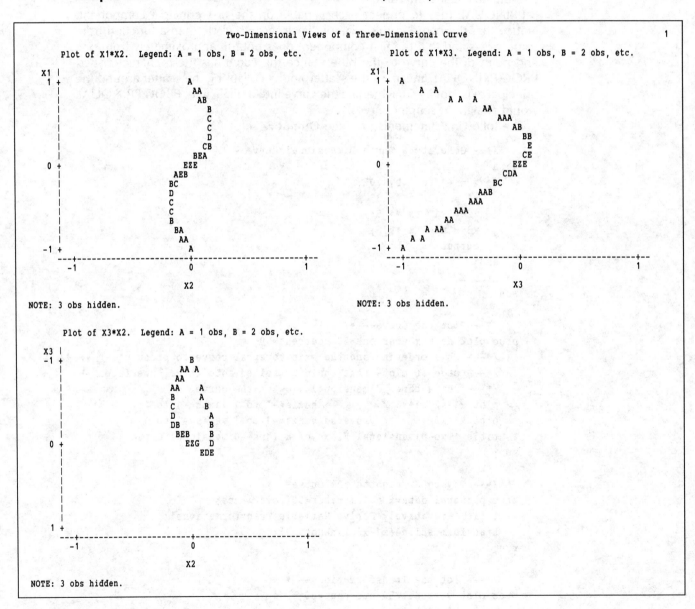

Iteratively Derive Variable Transformations   2

PRINQUAL MTV Iteration History

Iteration Number	Average Change	Maximum Change	Proportion of Variance	Variance Change
1	0.16253	1.33045	0.71369	.
2	0.07871	0.94549	0.79035	0.07667
3	0.06518	0.80219	0.86334	0.07299
4	0.05322	0.57928	0.91379	0.05045
5	0.04154	0.38404	0.94204	0.02825
6	0.03181	0.24391	0.95640	0.01436
7	0.02461	0.15397	0.96349	0.00709
8	0.01982	0.10205	0.96704	0.00355
9	0.01662	0.07393	0.96894	0.00189
10	0.01439	0.06232	0.97005	0.00112
11	0.01288	0.05436	0.97081	0.00075
12	0.01189	0.04911	0.97139	0.00058
13	0.01119	0.04531	0.97188	0.00049
14	0.01068	0.04276	0.97232	0.00044
15	0.01027	0.04115	0.97273	0.00041
16	0.00993	0.04039	0.97313	0.00040
17	0.00965	0.04249	0.97351	0.00038
18	0.00940	0.04400	0.97388	0.00037
19	0.00919	0.04509	0.97423	0.00036
20	0.00900	0.04587	0.97458	0.00034
21	0.00883	0.04643	0.97491	0.00033
22	0.00867	0.04681	0.97523	0.00032
23	0.00852	0.04705	0.97555	0.00031
24	0.00839	0.04719	0.97585	0.00031
25	0.00827	0.04724	0.97615	0.00030
26	0.00816	0.04722	0.97644	0.00029
27	0.00805	0.04713	0.97672	0.00028
28	0.00795	0.04699	0.97700	0.00027
29	0.00785	0.04680	0.97726	0.00027
30	0.00776	0.04656	0.97752	0.00026
31	0.00768	0.04629	0.97777	0.00025
32	0.00760	0.04598	0.97802	0.00025
33	0.00752	0.04564	0.97826	0.00024
34	0.00745	0.04528	0.97849	0.00023
35	0.00739	0.04489	0.97872	0.00023
36	0.00733	0.04448	0.97894	0.00022
37	0.00729	0.04405	0.97915	0.00022
38	0.00724	0.04361	0.97936	0.00021
39	0.00720	0.04315	0.97957	0.00021
40	0.00716	0.04268	0.97977	0.00020
41	0.00713	0.04219	0.97997	0.00020
42	0.00709	0.04170	0.98016	0.00019
43	0.00706	0.04120	0.98035	0.00019
44	0.00703	0.04070	0.98054	0.00019
45	0.00699	0.04019	0.98072	0.00018
46	0.00696	0.03967	0.98090	0.00018
47	0.00693	0.03916	0.98107	0.00017
48	0.00690	0.03864	0.98124	0.00017
49	0.00687	0.03812	0.98141	0.00017
50	0.00684	0.03760	0.98158	0.00017

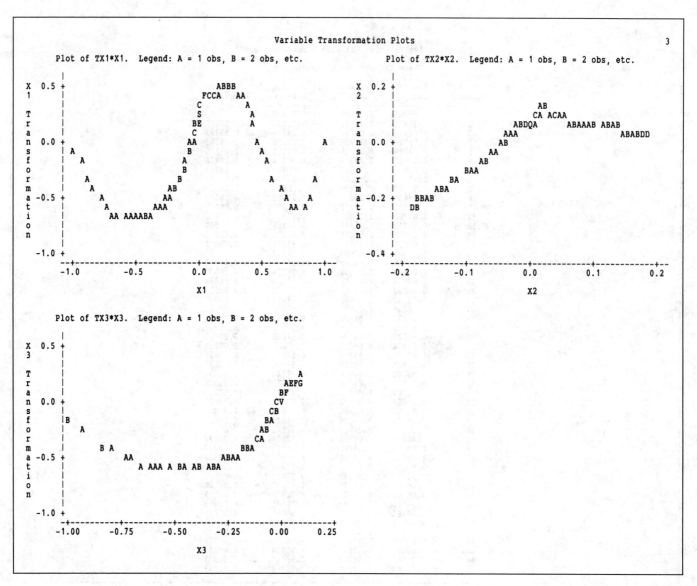

Variable Transformation Plots

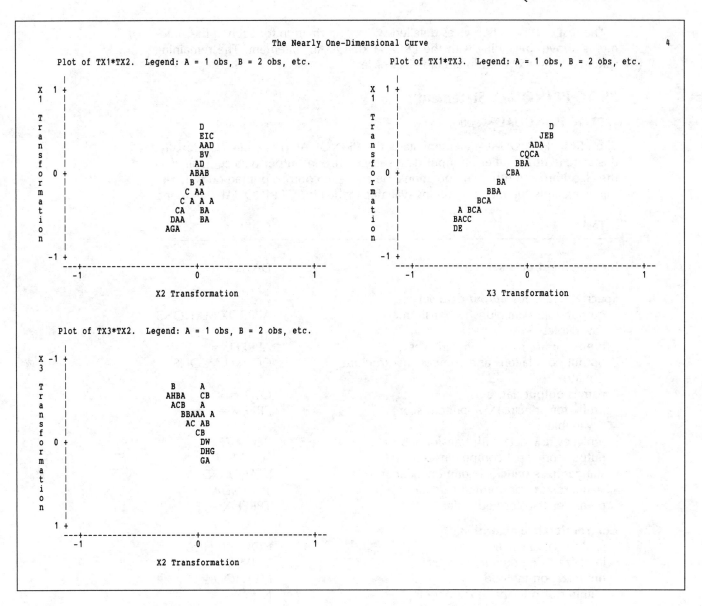

SPECIFICATIONS

The following statements are used in the PRINQUAL procedure:

PROC PRINQUAL <*options*>;
  TRANSFORM *transform(variables* < / *t-options*>) } required statements
  <. . . *transform(variables* < / *t-options*>)>;

  BY *variables;* } optional statements
  ID *variables;*

To use PROC PRINQUAL, you need the PROC and TRANSFORM statements. All *options* and *t-options* (except LOGIT) can be abbreviated to their first three letters. This is a special feature of PRINQUAL, and is not generally true of other SAS/STAT procedures.

The rest of this section gives detailed syntax information for each of the statements above, beginning with the PROC PRINQUAL statement. The remaining statements are covered in alphabetical order.

PROC PRINQUAL Statement

PROC PRINQUAL <*options*>;

The PROC PRINQUAL statement starts the PRINQUAL procedure. Optionally, this statement identifies an input data set, creates an output data set, specifies the algorithm and other computational details, and controls printed output. The following table summarizes options available in the PROC PRINQUAL statement.

Task	Options
Identify input data set	DATA=
Specify details for output data set	
output approximations to transformed variables	APPROXIMATIONS
prefix for approximation variables	APREFIX=
output correlations and component structure matrix	CORRELATIONS
names output data set	OUT=
prefix for principal component scores variables	PREFIX=
replaces raw data with transformed data	REPLACE
outputs principal component scores	SCORES
standardizes principal component scores	STANDARD
standardizes transformed variables	TSTANDARD=
prefix for transformed variables	TPREFIX=
Control iterative algorithm	
analyze covariances	COVARIANCE
initialize using dummy variables	DUMMY
optimization method	METHOD=
number of principal components	N=
suppress numerical error checking	NOCHECK
number of MGV models before refreshing	REFRESH=
effective zero	SINGULAR=
Control the number of iterations	
minimum change in criterion for convergence	CCONVERGE=
number of first iteration to be printed	CHANGE=
minimum change in standardized data for convergence	CONVERGE=
number of MAC initialization iterations	INITITER=
maximum number of iterations	MAXITER=
Specify details for handling missing values	
special values, within order and category constraints	MONOTONE=
exclude observations with missing values	NOMISS
special values, within order constraints	UNTIE=
Suppress printed output	NOPRINT

The list below describes these options in alphabetical order.

APREFIX=*name*
APR=*name*

> specifies a prefix for naming the approximation variables. By default, APREFIX=A. Specifying APREFIX= also implies the APPROXIMATIONS option.

APPROXIMATIONS
APPROX
APP

> includes principal component approximations to the transformed variables (Eckart and Young 1936) in the output data set. Variable names are constructed from the value of the APREFIX= option and the input variable names. If not specified, the approximations are not included in the output data set; however, if you specify APREFIX=, then APPROXIMATIONS are automatically included. If you specify APPROXIMATIONS and not APREFIX=, then APPROXIMATIONS uses the APREFIX= default value, A, to construct the variable names.

CCONVERGE=*n*
CCO=*n*

> specifies the minimum change in the criterion being optimized that is required to continue iterating. By default, CCONVERGE=0.0. CCONVERGE= is ignored for METHOD=MAC. For the MGV method, specify CCONVERGE=-2, an impossibly small change, to ensure data convergence.

CHANGE=*n*
CHA=*n*

> specifies the number of the first iteration to be printed in the iteration history table. The default is CHANGE=1. When you specify a larger value for *n*, the first *n*−1 iterations are not printed, thus speeding up the analysis. CHANGE= is most useful with the MGV method, which is much slower than the other methods.

CONVERGE=*n*
CON=*n*

> specifies the minimum average absolute change in standardized variable scores that is required for iteration to continue. By default, CONVERGE=0.00001. Average change is computed over only those variables that can be nontrivially transformed by the iterations, that is, all variables with missing values, and all variables specified for OPSCORE, MONOTONE, UNTIE, SPLINE, and MSPLINE transformations. For more information, see **Optimal Transformations** in the section on the TRANSFORM statement later in this chapter.

COVARIANCE
COV

> computes the principal components from the covariance matrix. For all methods, variables are centered to mean zero. If COVARIANCE is not specified, the procedure uses the correlation matrix, and the variables are standardized to variance one.

CORRELATIONS
COR

> includes correlations and the component structure matrix in the output data set. By default, this information is not included.

DATA=*SAS-data-set*
DAT=*SAS-data-set*

names the SAS data set to be analyzed. The data set must be an ordinary SAS data set; it cannot be a TYPE=CORR or TYPE=COV data set. If DATA= is omitted, the PRINQUAL procedure uses the most recently created SAS data set.

DUMMY
DUM

expands variables specified for OPSCORE optimal transformations to dummy variables for the initialization. By default, the initial values of OPSCORE variables are the actual data values. The dummy variable nominal initialization requires considerable time and memory, so it might not be possible to use DUMMY with large data sets. No separate report of the initialization is produced. Initialization results are incorporated into the first iteration shown in the iteration history table. (For more detail, see **Optimal Transformations** in the section on the TRANSFORM statement later in this chapter.

INITITER=*n*
INI=*n*

specifies the number of MAC iterations required to initialize the data before starting MTV or MGV iterations. By default, INITITER=0. INITITER= is ignored if METHOD=MAC.

MAXITER=*n*
MAX=*n*

specifies the maximum number of iterations. By default, MAXITER=30.

METHOD=MAC | MGV | MTV
MET=MAC | MGV | MTV

specifies the optimization method. By default, METHOD=MTV. Values of METHOD= are MTV for maximum total variance, MGV for minimum generalized variance, or MAC for maximum average correlation.

MONOTONE=*two-letters*
MON=*two-letters*

specifies the first and last special missing value in the list of those special missing values to be estimated using within-variable order and category constraints. By default, there are no order constraints on missing value estimates. The *two-letters* value must consist of two letters in alphabetic order. For example, MONOTONE=DF means that the estimate of .D must be less than or equal to the estimate of .E, which must be less than or equal to the estimate of .F, while no order constraints are placed on estimates of ._, .A through .C, and .G through .Z. For details, see **Missing Values** later in this chapter, and **Optimal Scaling** in Chapter 40, "The TRANSREG Procedure."

N=*n*

specifies the number of principal components to be computed. By default, N=2.

NOCHECK
NOC

turns off computationally intensive numerical error checking for the MGV method. If you do not specify NOCHECK, the procedure computes R^2 from the squared length of the predicted values vector, and compares this value to the R^2 computed from the error sum of squares that is a by-product of the sweep algorithm (Goodnight 1978). If the two values of R^2 differ by more than the square root of the value of

the SINGULAR= option, a warning is printed, the value of the
REFRESH= option is halved, and the model is refit after refreshing.
Specifying NOCHECK slightly speeds up the algorithm. Note that other
less computationally intensive error checking is always performed.

NOMISS
NOM

excludes all observations with missing values from the analysis. If you
omit NOMISS, PRINQUAL simultaneously computes the optimal
transformations of the nonmissing values and estimates the missing
values that minimize least-squares error. For details, see **Missing Values**
later in this chapter.

NOPRINT
NOP

suppresses printed output.

OUT=_SAS-data-set_

names an output SAS data set that contains results of the analysis. If
OUT= is omitted, PRINQUAL creates an output data set and names it
using the DATA*n* convention. If you want to create a permanent SAS
data set, you must specify a two-level name. (See "Introduction to DATA
Step Processing" in _SAS Language and Procedures: Usage, Version 6, First
Edition_ and "SAS Files" in _SAS Language: Reference, Version 6, First
Edition_.) You can use the REPLACE, APPROXIMATIONS, SCORES, and
CORRELATIONS options to control what information is included in the
output data set. For details, see **Output Data Set** later in this chapter.

PREFIX=_name_
PRE=_name_

specifies a prefix for naming the principal components. By default,
PREFIX=PRIN. As a result, the principal component default names are
PRIN1, PRIN2, . . . , PRIN*n*.

REFRESH=_n_
REF=_n_

specifies the number of variables to scale in the MGV method before
computing a new inverse. By default, REFRESH=5. PROC PRINQUAL
uses the REFRESH= option in the sweep algorithm of the MGV method.
Large values for REFRESH= make the method run faster, but with
increased error. Small values make the method run more slowly and
with more numerical accuracy.

REPLACE
REP

replaces the original data with the transformed data in the output data
set. The names of the transformed variables in the output data set
correspond to the names of the original variables in the input data set. If
you do not specify REPLACE, both original variables and transformed
variables (with names constructed from the TPREFIX= option and the
original variable names) are included in the output data set.

SCORES
SCO

includes principal component scores in the output data set. By default,
scores are not included.

SINGULAR=*n*

SIN=*n*

specifies the largest value within rounding error of zero. By default, SINGULAR=1E-8. SINGULAR= is used for checking $(1-R^2)$ when constructing full rank matrices of predictor variables, checking denominators before dividing, and so on. The typical range for the value of SINGULAR= is 1E-6 through 1E-10, inclusive.

STANDARD

STD

standardizes the principal component scores in the output data set to mean zero and variance one instead of the default mean zero and variance equal to the corresponding eigenvalue. See the SCORES option.

TPREFIX=*name*

TPR=*name*

specifies a prefix for naming the transformed variables. By default, TPREFIX=T. TPREFIX= is ignored if you specify the REPLACE option.

TSTANDARD=CENTER | NOMISS | ORIGINAL | Z

TST=CENTER | NOMISS | ORIGINAL | Z

specifies how to set the means and variances of the transformed variables in the output data set. By default, TSTANDARD=ORIGINAL.

For nonoptimal variable transformations, the means and variances of the original variables are actually the means and variances of the nonlinearly transformed variables, unless you specify the ORIGINAL nonoptimal variable transformation option in the TRANSFORM statement (see the next section). For example, if a variable X with no missing values is specified as LOG, by default the final transformation of X is simply LOG(X), not LOG(X) standardized to the mean of X and variance of X.

CENTER centers the output variables to mean zero, but the variances are the same as the input variables' variances.

NOMISS sets the means and variances of the transformed variables in the output data set, computed over all values in the output data set that correspond to nonmissing values in the input data set, to the means and variances computed from the nonmissing observations of the original variables. NOMISS is useful if you use PROC PRINQUAL only to estimate missing data. When a variable is linearly transformed, the final variable contains the original nonmissing values and the missing value estimates. In other words, the nonmissing values are unchanged. Thus, if your data have no missing values, NOMISS and ORIGINAL produce the same results.

ORIGINAL is the default, and sets the means and variances of the transformed variables to the means and variances of the original variables.

Z standardizes the variables to mean zero, variance one.

UNTIE=*two-letters*

UNT=*two-letters*

specifies the first and last special missing value in the list of those special missing values that are to be estimated with within-variable order constraints but no category constraints. The *two-letters* value must consist of two letters in alphabetic order. By default, there are category but no order constraints on special missing value estimates. For details, see **Missing Values** later in this chapter. Also, see **Optimal Scaling** in Chapter 40, "The TRANSREG procedure."

BY Statement

BY *variables*;

A BY statement can be used with PROC PRINQUAL to obtain separate analyses on observations in groups defined by the BY variables. When a BY statement appears, the procedure expects the input data set to be sorted in order of the BY variables.

If your input data set is not sorted in ascending order, use one of the following alternatives:

- Use the SORT procedure with a similar BY statement to sort the data.
- Use the BY statement options NOTSORTED or DESCENDING in the BY statement for the PRINQUAL procedure. As a cautionary note, the NOTSORTED option does not mean that the data are unsorted, but rather means that the data are arranged in groups (according to values of the BY variables) and that these groups are not necessarily in alphabetical or increasing numeric order.
- Use the DATASETS procedure (in base SAS software) to create an index on the BY variables.

For more information on the BY statement, see the discussion in *SAS Language: Reference, Version 6, First Edition*. For more information on the DATASETS procedure, see the discussion in the *SAS Procedures Guide, Version 6, Third Edition*.

ID Statement

ID *variables*;

The ID statement includes additional character or numeric variables in the output data set. The *variables* must be contained in the input data set.

TRANSFORM Statement

TRANSFORM *transform(variables< / t-options>)*
    < . . . transform(variables < / t-options>)>;

The TRANSFORM statement lists the variables to be analyzed (*variables*) and specifies the transformation (*transform*) to apply to each variable listed. The *variables* are variables in the data set. The *t-options* are transformation options that give details for the transformation; these depend on the *transform* chosen. The *t-options* are listed after a slash in the parentheses that enclose the variables.

For example, the following statements find a quadratic polynomial transformation of all variables in the data set:

```
proc prinqual;
    transform spline(_all_ / degree=2);
run;
```

Or, if N1 through N10 are nominal variables and M1 through M10 are ordinal variables, you can use the following statements:

```
proc prinqual;
    transform opscore(n1-n10) monotone(m1-m10);
run;
```

The next two sections discuss the transformations available (specified with *transform*) and the options available for some of the transformations (specified with *t-options*).

Families of Transformations

There are two types of transformation families: nonoptimal and optimal. Each family is summarized below:

nonoptimal transformations
> preprocess the specified variables, replacing each one with a single new nonoptimal, nonlinear transformation.

optimal transformations
> replace the specified variables with new, iteratively derived optimal transformation variables that fit the specified model better than the original variable (except for contrived cases where the transformation fits the model exactly as well as the original variable).

The table below summarizes the transformations in each family.

Family	Members of Family
Nonoptimal transformations	
inverse trigonometric sine	ARSIN
exponentiates variables	EXP
logarithm	LOG
logit	LOGIT
raises variables to specified power	POWER
transforms to ranks	RANK
Optimal transformations	
linear	LINEAR
monotonic, ties preserved	MONOTONE
monotonic B-spline	MSPLINE
optimal scoring	OPSCORE
B-spline	SPLINE
monotonic, ties not preserved	UNTIE

The *transform* is followed by a variable (or list of variables) enclosed in parentheses. Optionally, depending on the *transform*, the parentheses may also contain *t-options*, which follow the variables and a slash. For example, the statement

```
transform log(x y);
```

uses the LOG transformation of X and Y. A more complex example is

```
transform spline(y / nknots=2) log(x1 x2 x3);
```

The statement above uses the SPLINE transformation of Y and the LOG transformation of X1, X2, and X3. In addition, the NKNOTS= option is used with the SPLINE transformation and specifies two knots.

The rest of this section gives syntax details for members of both families of transformations. For more on *t-options*, see **Transformation Options (*t-options*)** later in this chapter.

Nonoptimal Transformations   Nonoptimal transformations are computed before the iterative algorithm begins. Nonoptimal transformations create a single new transformed variable that replaces the original variable. The new variable is not transformed by the subsequent iterative algorithms (except for a possible linear transformation and missing value estimation).

The PRINQUAL procedure prints error messages

- if the input values are invalid, such as negative numbers when square root or log transformations are requested.
- if the transformation would cause an arithmetic overflow, such as raising a large number to a large power.
- if the transformed values are so large that overflow is possible in subsequent calculations.

The list below gives syntax and details for nonoptimal variable transformations.

ARSIN
ARS

finds an inverse trigonometric sine transformation on the variables in the interval ($-1.0 \leq x \leq 1.0$). This transformation is performed before iterative analysis begins. Variables following ARSIN must be numeric.

EXP

exponentiates variables (x is transformed to a^x) before the iterative analysis begins. Variables following EXP must be numeric. To specify the value of a, use the PARAMETER= *t-option*. (By default, a is the mathematical constant $e = 2.718....$)

LOG

transforms variables to logarithms ($\log_a x$ for data value x) before the iterative analysis begins. Variables following LOG must be numeric and positive. To specify the base of the logarithm, use the PARAMETER= *t-option*. The default is a natural logarithm with base e (2.718 . . .).

LOGIT

finds a logit transformation on the variables in the interval ($0.0 < x < 1.0$) before the iterative analysis begins. Variables following LOGIT must be numeric. The logit of x is $\log(x/(1-x))$. Unlike other transformations, LOGIT does not have a three-letter abbreviation.

POWER
POW

raises variables to a specified power (x^a for data value x) before the iterative analysis begins. Variables following POWER must be numeric. In addition, you must specify the power parameter, a, by specifying PARAMETER= following the variables:

    power(*variables*/ parameter= *number*)

You can use POWER for squaring variables (PARAMETER=2), reciprocal transformations (PARAMETER=-1), square roots (PARAMETER=0.5), and so on.

RANK
RAN

transforms variables to ranks before the iterative analysis begins. Ranks are averaged within ties. The smallest input value is assigned the smallest rank. Variables following RANK must be numeric.

Optimal Transformations   Optimal transformations are iteratively derived. Missing values for these types of variables can be optimally estimated (see **Missing Values** later in this chapter for details). The list below gives syntax and details for optimal transformations.

LINEAR

LIN

finds an optimal linear transformation of each variable. For variables with no missing values, the transformed variable is the same as the original variable. For variables with missing values, the transformed nonmissing values have a different scale and origin from the original values. Variables following LINEAR must be numeric.

MONOTONE

MON

finds a monotonic transformation of each variable, with the restriction that ties are preserved. The Kruskal (1964) secondary least-squares monotonic transformation is used. This transformation weakly preserves order and category membership (ties). Variables following MONOTONE must be numeric and are typically discrete.

MSPLINE

MSP

finds a monotonically increasing B-spline transformation with monotonic coefficients (de Boor 1978; de Leeuw 1986) of each variable.

By default, PRINQUAL uses a quadratic spline. Knots and other degrees can be specified as *t-options*; see **Transformation Options (*t-options*)** later in this chapter.

Variables following MSPLINE must be numeric and are typically continuous.

OPSCORE

OPS

finds an optimal scoring of each variable. OPSCORE assigns scores to each class (level) of the variable. Fisher's (1938) optimal scoring method is used. Variables following OPSCORE can be either character or numeric; numeric variables should be discrete.

SPLINE

SPL

finds a B-spline transformation (de Boor 1978) of each variable. By default, PRINQUAL uses a cubic polynomial transformation. Knots and other degrees can be specified as *t-options*; see **Transformation Options (*t-options*)** below.

Variables following SPLINE must be numeric, and are typically continuous.

UNTIE

UNT

finds a monotonic transformation of each variable without the restriction that ties are preserved. TRANSREG uses the Kruskal (1964) primary least-squares monotonic transformation method. This transformation weakly preserves order but not category membership (it may untie some previously tied values).

Variables following UNTIE must be numeric and are typically discrete.

Transformation Options (*t-options*)

If you use either a nonoptimal or optimal *transform*, you can use *t-options*, which specify additional details of the transformation. The *t-options* are specified within the parentheses that enclose variables, and are listed after a slash, for example,

```
proc prinqual;
   transform spline(x y / nknots=3);
run;
```

The previous statements use an optimal variable transformation (SPLINE) of X and Y and use a *t-option* to specify the number of knots (NKNOTS=). As another example, consider the following statements:

```
proc prinqual;
    transform spline(y / nknots=3) spline(x1 x2 / nknots=6);
run;
```

These statements use the SPLINE transformation for all three variables, and use *t-options* as well; NKNOTS= specifies the number of knots for the spline.

The sections below discuss the *t-options* available for nonoptimal and optimal transformations.

Nonoptimal transformation *t-options*   Two options are available with the nonoptimal transformations.

ORIGINAL
ORI

matches the variable's final mean and variance to the mean and variance of the original variable. By default, the mean and variance are based on the transformed values. ORIGINAL is available for all of the nonoptimal transformations.

PARAMETER=*number*
PAR=*number*

specifies the transformation parameter. PARAMETER= is available for the EXP, LOG, and POWER transformations. It is required for the POWER transformation. For EXP, the parameter is the value to be exponentiated; for LOG, the parameter is the base value; for POWER, the parameter is the power. The default for PARAMETER= for LOG and EXP is e (2.718 . . .). For the POWER transformation, PARAMETER= must be specified; there is no default.

Optimal transformation *t-options*   The following options are available with SPLINE and MSPLINE optimal transformations:

DEGREE=*n*
DEG=*n*

specifies the degree of the B-spline transformation. The degree can be any nonnegative integer. The defaults are DEGREE=3 for SPLINE variables and DEGREE=2 for MSPLINE variables.

The polynomial degree must be ≥ 0, and should be a small integer, usually 0, 1, 2, or 3. Larger values are rarely useful. If you have any doubt as to what degree to specify, use the default.

KNOTS=*number-list* | *n* TO *m* BY *p*
KNO=*number-list* | *n* TO *m* BY *p*

specifies the interior knots or break points. By default, there are no knots. The first time a value is specified in the knot list, it indicates a discontinuity in the *n*th (from DEGREE=*n*) derivative of the transformation function at the value of the knot. The second mention of a value indicates a discontinuity in the (*n*−1)th derivative of the transformation function at the value of the knot. Knots can be repeated any number of times for decreasing smoothness at the break points, but the values in the knot list can never decrease.

You cannot use the KNOTS= option with the NKNOTS= option. Keep the number of knots small (see the discussion below).

NKNOTS=n
NKN=n

creates n knots, the first at the $100/(n+1)$ percentile, the second at the $200/(n+1)$ percentile, and so on. Knots are always placed at data values; there is no interpolation. For example, if NKNOTS=3, knots are placed at the 25th percentile, the median, and the 75th percentile. By default, NKNOTS=0. NKNOTS= must be ≥ 0.

You cannot use the NKNOTS= option with the KNOTS= option.

Keep the number of knots small (see the discussion below).

Keep the number of knots small (usually less than ten) although you can specify more. A degree three spline with nine knots, one at each decile, can closely follow a large variety of curves. Each spline transformation of degree p with q knots, requires that a model with $p+q$ parameters be fit. The total number of parameters should be much less than the number of observations. Usually in regression analyses, it is recommended that there be at least five or ten observations for each parameter, in order to get stable results. So, for example, when spline transformations of degree three with nine knots are requested for six variables, the number of observations in the data set should be at least five or ten times 72 (since $6*(3+9)$ is the total number of parameters). The overall model may also have one or more parameters for each non-spline variable in the model.

Increasing the number of knots gives the spline more freedom to bend and follow the data. Increasing the degree also gives the spline more freedom, but to a lesser degree. Specifying a large number of knots is much better than increasing the degree beyond three.

When NKNOTS=q is specified for a variable with n observations, then each of the $q+1$ segments of the spline will contain $(n/(q+1))$ observations on the average. When you specify KNOTS=$number$-$list$, make sure that there is a reasonable number of observations in each interval.

As an example, the following statements find a cubic polynomial transformation of Y and a linear transformation of X and Z:

```
proc prinqual;
    transform spline(y) linear(x z);
run;
```

The statements below find a linear transformation of X and Z and find a cubic spline transformation curve for Y that consists of the weighted sum of a single constant, a single straight line, a quadratic curve for the portion of the variable less than 3.0, a different quadratic curve for the portion greater than 3.0 (since the 3.0 break point is repeated), and a different cubic curve for each of the intervals: (minimum to 1.5), (1.5 to 2.4), (2.4 to 3.0), (3.0 to 4.0), (4.0 to maximum). In other words, the transformation curve is continuous everywhere, its first derivative is continuous everywhere, its second derivative is continuous everywhere except at 3.0; and its third derivative is continuous everywhere except at 1.5, 2.4, 3.0, and 4.0.

```
proc prinqual;
    transform spline(y / knots=1.5 2.4 3.0 3.0 4.0)
            linear(x z);
run;
```

The statements below again find a linear transformation of X and Z. For Y, the statements find a quadratic spline transformation that consists of a polynomial: $Y_t = b_0 + b_1 Y + b_2 Y^2$ for the range (Y<3.0), and a completely different polynomial $Y_t = b_3 + b_4 Y + b_5 Y^2$ for the range (Y>3.0). The two curves are not required to be continuous at 3.0.

```
proc prinqual;
    transform spline(y / knots=3 3 3 degree=2)
            linear(x z);
run;
```

The statements below categorize Y into 10 intervals and find a step-function transformation. One aspect of this transformation family is unlike all other optimal transformation families. The initial scaling of the data does not fit the restrictions imposed by the transformation family. This is because the initial variable can be continuous, but a discrete step function transformation is sought. Zero degree spline variables are categorized before the first iteration. Again, the statements find a linear transformation of X and Z.

```
proc prinqual;
    transform spline(y / degree=0 nknots=9)
            linear(x z);
run;
```

The statements below find a continuous, piecewise linear transformation of Y and a linear transformation of X and Z.

```
proc prinqual;
    transform spline(y / degree=1 nknots=8)
            linear(x z);
run;
```

The previous examples show various spline transformations of Y with the same linear transformation of X and Z. This is for illustrative purposes only; you could use TRANSFORM statements that requested different transformations for all three variables.

DETAILS

Missing Values

PROC PRINQUAL can estimate missing values, subject to optional constraints, so that the covariance matrix is optimized. Several approaches to missing data handling are provided. When you specify the NOMISS option (in the PROC PRINQUAL statement), observations with missing values are excluded from the analysis. Otherwise, missing data are estimated, using variable means as initial estimates. Missing values for OPSCORE character variables are treated the same as any other category during the initialization.

You can specify the OPSCORE, MONOTONE, UNTIE, LINEAR, SPLINE, MSPLINE, LOG, LOGIT, POWER, ARSIN, RANK, and EXP transformations in any combination with nonmissing values, ordinary missing values, and special missing values, as long as the nonmissing values in each variable have positive variance. No category or order restrictions are placed on the estimates of ordinary missing values (.). You can force missing value estimates within a variable to be identical by using special missing values. (See "The DATA Step" in SAS Language: Reference. You can specify up to 27 categories of missing values, where within-category estimates must be the same, by coding the missing values using .__ and .A through .Z.

You can also specify an ordering of some missing value estimates. You can use the MONOTONE= option (in the PROC PRINQUAL statement) to indicate a range of special missing values (a subset of the list from .A to .Z) whose estimates must be weakly ordered within each variable that they appear in. For example, if MONOTONE=AI, the nine classes, .A, .B, . . . , .I, are monotonically scored and optimally scaled just as MONOTONE optimal transformation values are scored. In this case, category but not order restrictions are placed on the missing values ._ and .J through .Z. You can also use the UNTIE= option (in the PROC PRINQUAL statement) to indicate a range of special missing values whose estimates must be weakly ordered within each variable that they appear in, but can be untied.

The missing value estimation facilities allow for partitioned or mixed-type variables. For example, a variable can be considered part nominal and part ordinal. Nominal classes of otherwise ordinal variables are coded with special missing values. This feature can be useful with survey research. The class "unfamiliar with the product" in the variable "Rate your preference for 'Brand X' on a 1 to 9 scale, or if you are unfamiliar with the product, check 'unfamiliar with the product'" is an example. You can code "Unfamiliar with the product" as a special missing value, such as .A. The 1s to 9s can be monotonically transformed, while no monotonic restrictions are placed on the quantification of the "unfamiliar with the product" class.

A variable specified for a LINEAR transformation, with special missing values and ordered categorical missing values, can be part interval, part ordinal, and part nominal. A variable specified for a MONOTONE transformation can have two independent ordinal parts. A variable specified for an UNTIE transformation can have an ordered categorical part and an ordered part without category restrictions. Many other mixes are possible.

Controlling the Number of Iterations

Several options in the PROC PRINQUAL statement control the number of iterations performed. Iteration terminates when any one of the following conditions becomes satisfied:

- The number of iterations equals the value of MAXITER=.
- The average absolute change in variable scores from one iteration to the next is less than the value of CONVERGE=.
- The criterion change is less than the value of CCONVERGE=.

With the MTV method, the change in the proportion of variance criterion can become negative when the data have converged so that it is numerically impossible, within machine precision, to increase the criterion. Because the MTV algorithm is convergent, a negative criterion change is the result of very small amounts of rounding error. The MGV method prints the average squared multiple correlation (which is not the criterion being optimized) so the criterion change can become negative well before convergence. The MAC method criterion (average correlation) is never computed, so CCONVERGE= is ignored for METHOD=MAC. You can specify a negative value for either convergence option if you want to define convergence only in terms of the other convergence option.

The MGV method's iterations minimize the generalized variance (determinant), but the generalized variance is not reported for two reasons. First, in most data sets, the generalized variance is almost always near zero (or will be after one or two iterations), which is its minimum. This does not mean that iteration is complete; it simply means that at least one multiple correlation is at or near one. The algorithm continues minimizing the determinant in $(m-1)$, $(m-2)$ dimensions, and so on. Because the generalized variance is almost always near zero, it does not provide a good indication of how the iterations are progressing. The mean R^2 provides a better indication of convergence. The second reason for not reporting the generalized variance is that almost no additional time is required to compute R^2 values for each step. This is because the error sum of squares is a by-product of the algorithm at each step. Computing the determinant at the end of each iteration adds more computations to an already computationally intensive algorithm.

You can increase the number of iterations to ensure convergence by increasing the value of MAXITER= and decreasing the value CONVERGE=. Because the average absolute change in standardized variable scores seldom decreases below 1E-11, you typically do not specify a value for CONVERGE= less than 1E-8 or 1E-10. Most of the data changes occur during the first few iterations, but the data can still change after 50 or even 100 iterations. You can try different combinations of values for CONVERGE= and MAXITER= to ensure convergence without extreme overiteration. If the data do not converge with the default specifications, try CONVERGE=1E-8 and MAXITER=50, or CONVERGE=1E-10 and MAXITER=200.

Performing a Principal Components Analysis of Transformed Data

PROC PRINQUAL prints an iteration history table that shows (for each iteration) the iteration number, the maximum and average absolute change in standardized variable scores computed over the iteratively transformed variables, the criterion being optimized, and the criterion change. In order to examine the results of the analysis in more detail, you can analyze the information in the output data set using other SAS procedures.

Specifically, use the PRINCOMP procedure to perform a components analysis on the transformed data. PROC PRINCOMP accepts the raw data from PROC PRINQUAL, but issues a warning because the PRINQUAL output data set has _NAME_ and _TYPE_ variables, but is not TYPE=CORR. This warning can be ignored.

If the output data set contains both scores and correlations, you must subset it for analysis with PROC PRINCOMP. Otherwise, the correlation observations are treated as ordinary observations and the PROC PRINCOMP results are incorrect. For example, consider the following statements:

```
proc prinqual data=a out=b correlations replace;
   transform spline(var1-var50 / nknots=3);
run;


proc princomp data=b;
   where _type_='SCORE';
run;
```

Also note that the proportion of variance accounted for, as reported by PRINCOMP, can exceed the proportion of variance accounted for in the last PRINQUAL iteration. This is because PRINQUAL reports the variance accounted for by the components analysis that generated the current scaling of the data, not a components analysis of the current scaling of the data.

Using the MAC Method

You can use the MAC algorithm alone by specifying METHOD=MAC, or use it as an initialization algorithm for METHOD=MTV and METHOD=MGV analyses by specifying the iteration option INITITER=. If any variables are negatively correlated, do not use the MAC algorithm with monotonic transformations (MONOTONE, UNTIE, and MSPLINE) because the signs of the correlations among the variables are not used when computing variable approximations. If an approximation is negatively correlated with the original variable, monotone constraints would make the optimally scaled variable a constant, which is not allowed. When used with other transformations, the MAC algorithm can reverse the scoring of the variables. So, for example, if variable X is designated LOG(X) with METHOD=MAC and TSTANDARD=ORIGINAL, the final transformation (for example, TX) may not be LOG(X). If TX is not LOG(X), it will have the same mean as LOG(X), the same variance as LOG(X), and it will be perfectly negatively correlated with LOG(X). PROC PRINQUAL prints a note for every variable that is reversed in this manner.

The METHOD=MAC algorithm can be used to deliberately reverse the scorings of some rating variables before a factor analysis. The correlations among bipolar ratings such as 'like - dislike', 'hot - cold', and 'fragile - monumental' are typically both positive and negative. If some items are reversed to say 'dislike - like', 'cold - hot', and 'monumental - fragile', some of the negative signs could be eliminated, and the factor pattern matrix would be cleaner. PROC PRINQUAL can be used with METHOD=MAC and LINEAR transformations to reverse some items, maximizing the average of the intercorrelations.

Output Data Set

The PRINQUAL procedure produces an output data set by default. Using the OUT=, APPROXIMATIONS, SCORES, REPLACE, and CORRELATIONS options in the PROC PRINQUAL statement, you can name this data set and control, to some extent, the contents of it.

Structure and Content

The output data set can have 16 different forms, depending on the specified combinations of the REPLACE, SCORES, APPROXIMATIONS, and CORRELATIONS options. You can specify any combination of these options. To illustrate, assume that the data matrix consists of N observations and m variables, and n components were computed. Then, define the following:

D the $N \times m$ matrix of original data with variable names that correspond to the names of the variables in the input data set. When you use the OPSCORE transformation on character variables, these variables are numeric in D and contain category numbers.

T the $N \times m$ matrix of transformed data with variable names constructed from the value of the TPREFIX= option (if REPLACE is not specified) and the names of the variables in the input data set.

S the $N \times n$ matrix of component scores with variable names constructed from the value of the PREFIX= option and integers.

A the $N \times m$ matrix of data approximations with variable names constructed from the value of the APREFIX= option and the names of the variables in the input data set.

R_{TD} the $m \times m$ matrix of correlations between the transformed variables and the original variables with variable names that correspond to the names of the variables in the input data set. When missing values exist, casewise deletion is used to compute the correlations.

R_{TT} the $m \times m$ matrix of correlations among the transformed variables with the variable names constructed from the value of the TPREFIX= option (if REPLACE is not specified) and the names of the variables in the input data set.

R_{TS} the $m \times n$ matrix of correlations between the transformed variables and the principal component scores (component structure matrix) with variable names constructed from the value of the PREFIX= option and integers.

R_{TA} the $m \times m$ matrix of correlations between the transformed variables and the variable approximations with variable names constructed from the value of the APREFIX= option and the names of the variables in the input data set.

To create a data set WORK.A that contains all information, use the following options in the PROC PRINQUAL statement

```
proc prinqual scores approximations correlations out=a;
```

and also use a TRANSFORM statement appropriate for your data. Then WORK.A contains

D   T   S   A
R_{TD} R_{TT} R_{TS} R_{TA}

To eliminate the bottom partitions that contain the correlations and component structure, do not specify CORRELATIONS. For example, use the following PROC PRINQUAL statement with an appropriate TRANSFORM statement:

```
proc prinqual scores approximations out=a;
```

Then WORK.A contains

D T S A

If you use the following PROC PRINQUAL statement (with an appropriate TRANSFORM statement)

```
proc prinqual out=a;
```

this creates a data set WORK.A of the form

D T

To output transformed data and component scores only, use the following options in the PROC PRINQUAL statement:

```
proc prinqual replace scores out=a;
```

Then WORK.A contains

T S

TYPE and _NAME_ Variables

In addition to the above information, the output data set contains two character variables, _TYPE_ and _NAME_. Both are of length 8.

TYPE has the value 'SCORE' if the observation contains variables, transformed variables, components, or data approximations; _TYPE_ has the value 'CORR' if the observation contains correlations or component structure.

NAME has values "ROW1", "ROW2", and so on, by default for the observations with _TYPE_='SCORE'. If you use an ID statement, _NAME_ contains the first eight formatted characters of the first ID variable for SCORES observations.

The values of _NAME_ for observations with _TYPE_='CORR' are the names of the transformed variables.

Certain procedures, such as PRINCOMP, which use the PRINQUAL output data set, will issue a warning that the PRINQUAL data set contains _NAME_ and _TYPE_ variables but is not TYPE=CORR. This warning can be ignored.

Variable Names

The TPREFIX=, APREFIX=, and PREFIX= options specify prefixes for the transformed and approximation variable names, and for principal component score variables, respectively. PROC PRINQUAL constructs transformed and approximation variable names from a prefix and the first characters of the original variable name. The number of characters in the prefix plus the number of characters in the original variable name (including the final digits, if any) required to uniquely designate the new variables must not exceed eight. For example, if the APREFIX= parameter you specify is one character, PROC PRINQUAL adds the first seven characters of the original variable name; if your prefix is four characters, only the first four characters of the original variable name are added.

Effect of the TSTANDARD= and COVARIANCE Options

The values in the output data set are affected by the TSTANDARD= and COVARIANCE options. If you specify TSTANDARD=NOMISS, the NOMISS standardization is performed on the transformed data, after the iterations have been completed, but before the output data set is created. The new means and variances are used in creating the output data set. Then, if you do not specify COVARIANCE, the data are transformed to mean zero and variance one. The principal component scores and data approximations are computed from the resulting matrix. The data are then linearly transformed to have the mean and variance specified by the TSTANDARD= option. The data approximations are transformed so that the means within each pair of a transformed variable and its approximation are the same. The ratio of the variance of a variable approximation to the variance of the corresponding transformed variable equals the proportion of the variance of the variable that is accounted for by the components model.

If you specify COVARIANCE and do not specify TSTANDARD=Z, you can input the transformed data to PROC PRINCOMP, again specifying COVARIANCE, to perform a components analysis of the results of PROC PRINQUAL. Similarly, if you do not specify COVARIANCE with PROC PRINQUAL, and input the transformed data to PROC PRINCOMP without COVARIANCE, you receive the same report. However, some combinations of PROC PRINQUAL options, such as COVARIANCE and TSTANDARD=Z, while valid, produce approximations and scores that cannot be reproduced by PROC PRINCOMP.

The component scores in the output data set are computed from the correlations among the transformed variables, or the covariances if you specified COVARIANCE. The component scores are computed after the TSTANDARD=NOMISS transformation, if specified. The means of the component scores in the output data set are always zero. The variances equal the corresponding eigenvalues, unless you specify STANDARD; then the variances are set to one.

Computational Resources

This section provides information on the computational resources required to run PROC PRINQUAL.

Let

N = number of observations
m = number of variables
n = number of principal components
k = maximum spline degree
p = maximum number of knots.

- For the MTV algorithm, more than

$$56m + 8Nm + 8(6N + (p + k + 2)(p + k + 11))$$

bytes of array space are required.
- For the MGV and MAC algorithms, more than $56m$ plus the maximum of the data matrix size and the optimal scaling work space bytes of array space are required. The data matrix size is $8Nm$ bytes. The optimal scaling work space requires less than $8(6N+(p+k+2)(p+k+11))$ bytes.
- For the MTV and MGV algorithms, more than $56m$ plus $4m(m+1)$ bytes of array space are required.
- PRINQUAL tries to store the original and transformed data in memory. If there is not enough memory, a utility data set is used, potentially resulting in a large increase in execution time. The amount of memory for data formulas above are underestimates of the amount of memory needed to handle most problems. These formulas give an absolute minimum amount of memory required. If a utility data set is used, and if memory could be used with perfect efficiency, then roughly the amount of memory stated above would be needed. In reality, most problems require at least two or three times the minimum.
- PRINQUAL sorts the data once. The sort time is roughly proportional to $mN^{3/2}$.
- For the MTV algorithm, the time required to compute the variable approximations is roughly proportional to $2Nm^2+5m^3+nm^2$.
- For the MGV algorithm, one regression analysis per iteration is required to compute model parameter estimates. The time required for accumulating the cross product matrix is roughly proportional to Nm^2. The time required to compute the regression coefficients is roughly proportional to m^3. For each variable for each iteration, the swept cross product matrix is updated with time roughly proportional to $m(N+m)$. The swept cross product matrix is updated for each variable with time roughly proportional to m^2, until computations are refreshed, requiring all sweeps to be performed again.
- The only computationally intensive part of the MAC algorithm is the optimal scaling, since variable approximations are simple averages.
- Each optimal scaling is a multiple regression problem, although some transformations are handled with faster special case algorithms. The number of regressors for the optimal scaling problems depends on the original values of the variable and the type of transformation. For each monotone spline transformation, an unknown number of multiple regressions is required to find a set of coefficients that satisfies the constraints. The B-spline basis is generated twice for each SPLINE and MSPLINE transformation for each iteration. The time required to generate the B-spline basis is roughly proportional to Nk^2.

Printed Output

The main output from the PRINQUAL procedure is the output data set. However, the procedure does produce printed output in the form of an iteration history table that shows the following:

1. Iteration Number
2. the criterion being optimized
3. criterion change
4. Maximum and Average absolute Change in standardized variable scores computed over variables that can be iteratively transformed.

EXAMPLES

Example 1:   Multidimensional Preference Analysis of Cars Data

This example illustrates using PROC PRINQUAL to perform a nonmetric multidimensional preference (MDPREF) analysis (Carroll 1972). MDPREF analysis is a principal component analysis of a data matrix with columns that correspond to people and rows that correspond to objects. The data are ratings or rankings of each person's preference for each object. The data are the transpose of the usual multivariate data matrix. (In other words, the columns are people instead of the more typical matrix where rows represent people.) The final result of an MDPREF analysis is a biplot (Gabriel 1981) of the resulting preference space. A biplot shows the judges and objects in a single plot by projecting them onto the plane in the transformed variable space that accounts for the most variance.

The data are ratings by 25 judges of their preference for each of 17 automobiles. The ratings were made on a 0 to 9 scale, with 0 meaning very weak preference and 9 meaning very strong preference for the automobile. These judgments were made in 1980 about that year's products. There are two additional variables that indicate the manufacturer and model of the automobile.

This example uses PROC PRINQUAL, PROC FACTOR, and PROC GPLOT. FACTOR is used before PRINQUAL to perform a principal component analysis of the raw judgments. FACTOR is also used immediately after PRINQUAL since PRINQUAL is a scoring procedure that optimally scores the data but does not report the principal component analysis. GPLOT produces the biplot.

The scree plot in the standard principal component analysis of the ratings reported by FACTOR shows that two principal components should be retained for further use. There are nine eigenvalues that are precisely zero because there are nine fewer observations than variables in the data matrix. PRINQUAL is then used to monotonically transform the raw judgments to maximize the proportion of variance accounted for by the first two principal components. The statements below create the data set and perform a principal components analysis of the original data. These statements produce **Output 34.2**.

```
title 'Preference Ratings for Automobiles Manufactured in 1980';
data carpref;
   input make $ 1-10 model $ 12-22 @25 (judge1-judge25) (1.);
   cards;
Cadillac    Eldorado     8007990491240508971093809
Chevrolet   Chevette     0051200423451043003515698
Chevrolet   Citation     4053305814161643544747795
Chevrolet   Malibu       6027400723121345545668658
Ford        Fairmont     2024006715021443530648655
Ford        Mustang      5007197705021101850657555
Ford        Pinto        0021000303030201500514078
```

```
Honda      Accord       5956897609699952998975078
Honda      Civic        4836709507488852567765075
Lincoln    Continental  7008990592230409962091909
Plymouth   Gran Fury    7006000434101107333458708
Plymouth   Horizon      3005005635461302444675655
Plymouth   Volare       4005003614021602754476555
Pontiac    Firebird     0107895613201206958265907
Volkswagen Dasher       4858696508877795377895000
Volkswagen Rabbit       4858509709695795487885000
Volvo      DL           9989998909999987989919000
;


/*---Principal Component Analysis of the Original Data---*/
proc factor data=carpref nfactors=2 scree;
   var judge1-judge25;
   title3 'Principal Components of Original Data';
run;
```

Output 34.2   Principal Components Analysis of Original Data

```
                Preference Ratings for Automobiles Manufactured in 1980                    1

                          Principal Components of Original Data

Initial Factor Method: Principal Components

                            Prior Communality Estimates: ONE

                 Eigenvalues of the Correlation Matrix:  Total = 25  Average = 1

                     1         2         3         4         5         6         7         8         9
Eigenvalue     10.8857    5.8507    2.0429    1.5222    1.2143    0.9579    0.7381    0.5884    0.3767
Difference      5.0350    3.8078    0.5208    0.3078    0.2565    0.2197    0.1497    0.2117    0.1091
Proportion      0.4354    0.2340    0.0817    0.0609    0.0486    0.0383    0.0295    0.0235    0.0151
Cumulative      0.4354    0.6695    0.7512    0.8121    0.8606    0.8989    0.9285    0.9520    0.9671

                    10        11        12        13        14        15        16        17        18
Eigenvalue      0.2676    0.1902    0.1438    0.1088    0.0481    0.0424    0.0222    0.0000    0.0000
Difference      0.0774    0.0464    0.0349    0.0607    0.0057    0.0203    0.0222    0.0000    0.0000
Proportion      0.0107    0.0076    0.0058    0.0044    0.0019    0.0017    0.0009    0.0000    0.0000
Cumulative      0.9778    0.9854    0.9911    0.9955    0.9974    0.9991    1.0000    1.0000    1.0000

                    19        20        21        22        23        24        25
Eigenvalue      0.0000    0.0000    0.0000    0.0000    0.0000    0.0000    0.0000
Difference      0.0000    0.0000    0.0000    0.0000    0.0000    0.0000
Proportion      0.0000    0.0000    0.0000    0.0000    0.0000    0.0000    0.0000
Cumulative      1.0000    1.0000    1.0000    1.0000    1.0000    1.0000    1.0000

                    2 factors will be retained by the NFACTOR criterion.
```

Preference Ratings for Automobiles Manufactured in 1980   2

Principal Components of Original Data

Initial Factor Method: Principal Components

Scree Plot of Eigenvalues

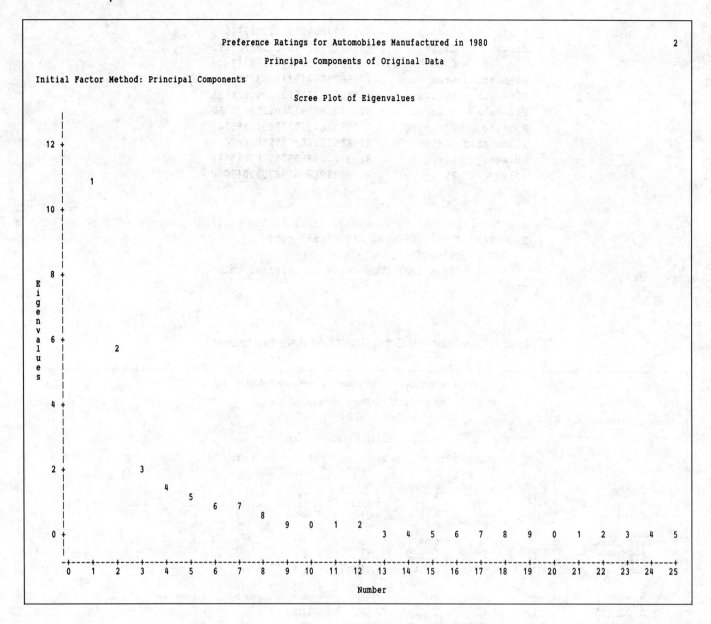

Principal Components of Original Data

Initial Factor Method: Principal Components

Factor Pattern

	FACTOR1	FACTOR2
JUDGE1	0.28769	0.62196
JUDGE2	0.95472	0.04611
JUDGE3	0.77144	-0.31847
JUDGE4	0.50731	0.73186
JUDGE5	0.48235	0.70863
JUDGE6	0.27199	0.69497
JUDGE7	0.79219	-0.16281
JUDGE8	0.51624	-0.04578
JUDGE9	-0.49910	0.72619
JUDGE10	0.93229	-0.20638
JUDGE11	0.85397	0.12460
JUDGE12	0.83323	-0.10429
JUDGE13	0.94222	-0.01972
JUDGE14	0.83153	0.18107
JUDGE15	0.85629	-0.18935
JUDGE16	0.00038	0.80219
JUDGE17	0.11363	0.65513
JUDGE18	0.72989	0.59975
JUDGE19	0.78325	0.11341
JUDGE20	0.76359	-0.58252
JUDGE21	0.08633	0.66155
JUDGE22	0.23651	-0.45238
JUDGE23	-0.75218	0.35942
JUDGE24	-0.17413	-0.74926
JUDGE25	-0.76311	0.16776

Variance explained by each factor

FACTOR1	FACTOR2
10.885720	5.850728

Final Communality Estimates: Total = 16.736448

JUDGE1	JUDGE2	JUDGE3	JUDGE4	JUDGE5	JUDGE6	JUDGE7	JUDGE8	JUDGE9	JUDGE10	JUDGE11	JUDGE12	JUDGE13
0.469601	0.913610	0.696542	0.792974	0.734808	0.556962	0.654079	0.268602	0.776445	0.911763	0.744788	0.705143	0.888174

JUDGE14	JUDGE15	JUDGE16	JUDGE17	JUDGE18	JUDGE19	JUDGE20	JUDGE21	JUDGE22	JUDGE23	JUDGE24	JUDGE25
0.724220	0.769084	0.643511	0.442104	0.892441	0.626349	0.922400	0.445100	0.260587	0.694963	0.591717	0.610480

To transform the data, use the PRINQUAL procedure. Several options are used in the PROC PRINQUAL statement. DATA=CARPREF names the input data set, OUT=RESULTS creates an output data set, and N=2 and the default METHOD=MTV transform the data to better fit a two-component model. The REPLACE option replaces the original data with the monotonically transformed data in the OUT= data set. The STANDARD option standardizes the component scores to variance one so that the geometry of the biplot is correct. The SCORES and CORRELATIONS options are used to create two variables named PRIN1 and PRIN2 in the OUT= data set that will contain the standardized principal component scores and component structure matrix, which are used to make the biplot. If the variables in data matrix $\mathbf{X}$ are standardized to mean zero and variance one, and n is the number of rows in $\mathbf{X}$, then $\mathbf{X}=(n-1)^{-1/2}(\mathbf{V})(\mathbf{\Lambda}^{1/2}\mathbf{W}')$ is the principal component model. The first two columns of $\mathbf{V}$, the standardized component scores, and $\mathbf{W}\mathbf{\Lambda}^{1/2}$, the structure matrix, are output. To simplify the algebra below, $\mathbf{X}$ will be restandardized to mean zero and variance $n-1$. That is, the new $\mathbf{X}$ is the old $\mathbf{X}$ times $(n-1)^{1/2}$. The advantage of creating a biplot based on $(n-1)^{1/2}\mathbf{X}$ instead of $\mathbf{X}$ is that coordinates do not depend on the sample size. The statements below transform the data and produce **Output 34.3**.

```
/*---Transform the Data to Better Fit a Two Component Model---*/
proc prinqual data=carpref out=results n=2
            replace standard scores correlations;
    id model;
    transform monotone(judge1-judge25);
    title2 'Multidimensional Preference (MDPREF) Analysis';
    title3 'Optimal Monotonic Transformation of Preference Data';
run;
```

Output 34.3   Transformation of Automobile Preference Data

```
              Preference Ratings for Automobiles Manufactured in 1980          1
                   Multidimensional Preference (MDPREF) Analysis
                 Optimal Monotonic Transformation of Preference Data

                        PRINQUAL MTV Iteration History

            Iteration   Average   Maximum   Proportion of   Variance
             Number     Change    Change      Variance        Change
          -----------------------------------------------------------------
                 1      0.24994   1.28017     0.66946           .
                 2      0.07223   0.36958     0.80194        0.13249
                 3      0.04522   0.29026     0.81598        0.01404
                 4      0.03096   0.25213     0.82178        0.00580
                 5      0.02182   0.23045     0.82493        0.00315
                 6      0.01602   0.19017     0.82680        0.00187
                 7      0.01219   0.14748     0.82793        0.00113
                 8      0.00953   0.11031     0.82861        0.00068
                 9      0.00737   0.06461     0.82904        0.00043
                10      0.00556   0.04469     0.82930        0.00026
                11      0.00445   0.04087     0.82944        0.00014
                12      0.00381   0.03706     0.82955        0.00011
                13      0.00319   0.03348     0.82965        0.00009
                14      0.00255   0.02999     0.82971        0.00006
                15      0.00213   0.02824     0.82976        0.00005
                16      0.00183   0.02646     0.82980        0.00004
                17      0.00159   0.02472     0.82983        0.00003
                18      0.00139   0.02305     0.82985        0.00003
                19      0.00123   0.02145     0.82988        0.00002
                20      0.00109   0.01993     0.82989        0.00002
                21      0.00096   0.01850     0.82991        0.00001
                22      0.00086   0.01715     0.82992        0.00001
                23      0.00076   0.01588     0.82993        0.00001
                24      0.00067   0.01440     0.82994        0.00001
                25      0.00059   0.00871     0.82994        0.00001
                26      0.00050   0.00720     0.82995        0.00000
                27      0.00043   0.00642     0.82995        0.00000
                28      0.00037   0.00573     0.82995        0.00000
                29      0.00031   0.00510     0.82995        0.00000
                30      0.00027   0.00454     0.82995        0.00000
```

The iteration history printed by PROC PRINQUAL indicates that the proportion of variance is increased from an initial 0.66946 to 0.82995. The proportion of variance accounted for by PROC PRINQUAL on the first iteration equals the cumulative proportion of variance shown by PROC FACTOR for the first two principal components. Unless there are nonoptimal transformations, missing data, zero degree splines, or the DUMMY option is specified, PROC PRINQUAL's initial iteration performs a standard principal component analysis of the raw data. The columns labeled "Average Change", "Maximum Change", and "Variance Change" contain values that always decrease, indicating that PROC PRINQUAL is improving the transformations at a monotonically decreasing rate over the iterations. This does not always happen, and when it does not, it suggests that the analysis may be converging to a degenerate solution. See **Example 2:   Principal Components of Basketball Ratings** for a discussion of a degenerate solution.

The second PROC FACTOR analysis is performed on the transformed data. The WHERE statement is used to retain only the monotonically transformed judgments. The scree plot shows that the first two eigenvalues are now very much larger than the remaining smaller eigenvalues. The second eigenvalue has increased markedly at the expense of the next several eigenvalues. Two principal components seem to be necessary and sufficient to adequately describe these judge's preferences for these automobiles. The cumulative proportion of variance shown by PROC FACTOR for the first two principal components is 0.83. The statements below perform the FACTOR analysis and produce **Output 34.4**.

```
/*---Final Principal Component Analysis---*/
proc factor data=results nfactors=2 scree;
    var judge1-judge25;
    where _type_='SCORE';
    title3 'Principal Components of Monotonically Transformed Data';
run;
```

Output 34.4 Principal Components of Transformed Data

```
                   Preference Ratings for Automobiles Manufactured in 1980          2
                        Multidimensional Preference (MDPREF) Analysis
                      Principal Components of Monotonically Transformed Data

Initial Factor Method: Principal Components

                          Prior Communality Estimates: ONE

               Eigenvalues of the Correlation Matrix:   Total = 25   Average = 1
```

	1	2	3	4	5	6	7	8	9
Eigenvalue	11.5959	9.1530	1.1577	0.8505	0.7221	0.4607	0.3649	0.2771	0.1520
Difference	2.4429	7.9953	0.3072	0.1284	0.2614	0.0958	0.0878	0.1251	0.0507
Proportion	0.4638	0.3661	0.0463	0.0340	0.0289	0.0184	0.0146	0.0111	0.0061
Cumulative	0.4638	0.8300	0.8763	0.9103	0.9392	0.9576	0.9722	0.9833	0.9894

	10	11	12	13	14	15	16	17	18
Eigenvalue	0.1013	0.0721	0.0520	0.0183	0.0156	0.0062	0.0007	0.0000	0.0000
Difference	0.0293	0.0201	0.0337	0.0027	0.0094	0.0056	0.0007	0.0000	0.0000
Proportion	0.0041	0.0029	0.0021	0.0007	0.0006	0.0002	0.0000	0.0000	0.0000
Cumulative	0.9934	0.9963	0.9984	0.9991	0.9997	1.0000	1.0000	1.0000	1.0000

	19	20	21	22	23	24	25
Eigenvalue	0.0000	0.0000	0.0000	0.0000	0.0000	0.0000	0.0000
Difference	0.0000	0.0000	0.0000	0.0000	0.0000	0.0000	
Proportion	0.0000	0.0000	0.0000	0.0000	0.0000	0.0000	0.0000
Cumulative	1.0000	1.0000	1.0000	1.0000	1.0000	1.0000	1.0000

```
                  2 factors will be retained by the NFACTOR criterion.
```

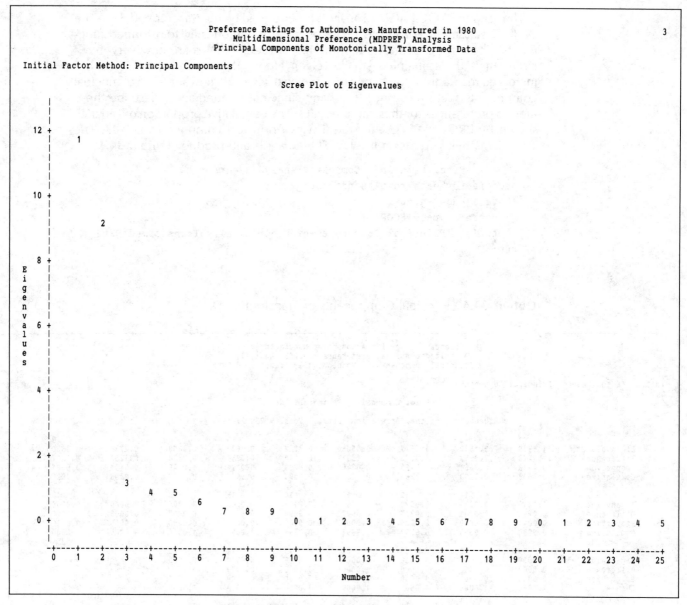

Preference Ratings for Automobiles Manufactured in 1980
Multidimensional Preference (MDPREF) Analysis
Principal Components of Monotonically Transformed Data

3

Initial Factor Method: Principal Components

Scree Plot of Eigenvalues

Preference Ratings for Automobiles Manufactured in 1980
Multidimensional Preference (MDPREF) Analysis
Principal Components of Monotonically Transformed Data

4

Initial Factor Method: Principal Components

Factor Pattern

	FACTOR1	FACTOR2
JUDGE1	0.13362	0.78412
JUDGE2	0.96471	0.12593
JUDGE3	0.85190	0.04519
JUDGE4	0.69146	0.57448
JUDGE5	0.35307	0.91622
JUDGE6	0.26747	0.70628
JUDGE7	0.85872	-0.06762
JUDGE8	0.69555	0.20109
JUDGE9	-0.49402	0.83273
JUDGE10	0.86091	-0.49123
JUDGE11	0.90132	0.30413
JUDGE12	0.95756	0.09477
JUDGE13	0.97614	-0.00054

(continued on next page)

(continued from previous page)

```
                              JUDGE14      0.96180      0.11917
                              JUDGE15      0.94460      0.09403
                              JUDGE16     -0.30510      0.94273
                              JUDGE17      0.20455      0.80338
                              JUDGE18      0.76490      0.54677
                              JUDGE19      0.92196      0.20019
                              JUDGE20      0.51883     -0.84307
                              JUDGE21     -0.15500      0.77825
                              JUDGE22      0.38429     -0.87975
                              JUDGE23     -0.54872      0.70776
                              JUDGE24     -0.24323     -0.72182
                              JUDGE25     -0.41269      0.87297

                     Variance explained by each factor

                            FACTOR1    FACTOR2
                           11.595904   9.152959


                  Final Communality Estimates: Total = 20.748863
```

JUDGE1	JUDGE2	JUDGE3	JUDGE4	JUDGE5	JUDGE6	JUDGE7	JUDGE8	JUDGE9	JUDGE10	JUDGE11	JUDGE12	JUDGE13
0.632697	0.946526	0.727768	0.808139	0.964124	0.570373	0.741969	0.524220	0.937493	0.982482	0.904874	0.925905	0.952850

JUDGE14	JUDGE15	JUDGE16	JUDGE17	JUDGE18	JUDGE19	JUDGE20	JUDGE21	JUDGE22	JUDGE23	JUDGE24	JUDGE25
0.939253	0.901107	0.981838	0.687265	0.884031	0.890088	0.979948	0.629696	0.921635	0.802009	0.580188	0.932383

The remainder of the example constructs the MDPREF biplot. A biplot is a plot that shows the relation between the row points and the columns of a data matrix. If $X=(V)(\Lambda^{1/2} W')$, then the rows of V, the standardized component scores, and $W\Lambda^{1/2}$, the structure matrix, contain enough information to reproduce X. The (i,j) element of X is the inner product of row i of V and row j of $W\Lambda^{1/2}$. If all but the first two columns of V and $W\Lambda^{1/2}$ are discarded, the (i,j) element of X is approximated by the inner product of row i of V and row j of $W\Lambda^{1/2}$.

Since the MDPREF analysis is based on a principal component model, the dimensions of the MDPREF biplot are the first two principal components. The first principal component represents the information that is most salient to the preference judgments, with one end pointing in the direction that is preferred most, on the average, by the judges. (The other end points in the least preferred direction.) The second principal component represents the direction that is most salient to the preference judgments that is orthogonal to the first principal component.

With an MDPREF biplot, it is geometrically appropriate to represent each automobile (object) by a point and each judge by a vector. The automobile points have coordinates that are the scores of the automobile on the first two principal components. The judge vectors emanate from the origin of the space and go through a point whose coordinates are the coefficients of the judge (variable) on the first two principal components.

The absolute length of a judge's vector is arbitrary. However, the relative lengths of the vectors indicate fit, with the squared lengths being proportional to the communalities in the PROC FACTOR output. The direction of the vector indicates the direction that is most preferred by the individual judge, with preference increasing as the vector moves from the origin. Let v' be row i of V, u' be row j of $U=W\Lambda^{1/2}$, $\|v\|$ be the length of v, $\|u\|$ be the length of u, and θ be the angle between v and u. The predicted degree of preference that an individual judge has for an automobile is $u'v=\|u\|\|v\|\cos\theta$. Each car point can be orthogonally projected onto the judge's vector. The projection of car i on judge vector j is $u\,((u'v)/(u'u))$ and the length of this projection is $\|v\|\cos\theta$. The automobile that projects farthest along a judge vector in the direction it points is that judge's most preferred automobile, since the length of this projection, $\|v\|\cos\theta$, differs from the predicted preference, $\|\mathbf{u}\|\|\mathbf{v}\|\cos\theta$, only by $\|\mathbf{u}\|$, which is constant within each judge.

To interpret the biplot, look for directions through the plot that show a continuous change in some attribute of the automobiles, or look for regions in the plot that contain clusters of automobile points and determine what attributes the automobiles have in common. Those points that are tightly clustered in a region of the plot represent automobiles that have the same preference patterns across the judges. Those judge vectors that point in roughly the same direction represent judges who tend to have similar preference patterns.

This example uses two steps to produce the biplot. A DATA step prepares information for the biplot and PROC GPLOT produces the biplot. The DATA step changes two details to improve the clarity of the plot: the symbols that are used to identify the points in the plot are changed, and the lengths of the judge vectors are doubled. The AXIS2 statement under PROC GPLOT specifies a length and tick range that are both 8/9 of what is specified in the AXIS1 statement, equating distances on both axes and correctly presenting the geometry of the MDPREF analysis. (See the EQUATE macro in **Example 3:   Simple Correspondence Analysis of U.S. Population** in Chapter 19, "The CORRESP Procedure," for an automatic method of generating scatterplots of point labels with axes properly equated.)

The statements below construct the biplot and produce **Output 34.5**.

```
    /*---Create Annotate Data Set---*/
    /*---SAS/GRAPH Software and a GOPTIONS Statement are Required---*/
 data biplot;
    set results;

    /*---Stretch the Judge Vectors and Remove 'JUDGE' from Names---*/
    if _type_ ne 'SCORE' then do;
      prin1=prin1*2;
      prin2=prin2*2;
      model=substr(model,6);
    end;

    y      = prin2;  /* y-axis variable                          */
    x      = prin1;  /* x-axis variable                          */
    xsys   = '2';    /* x-axis label area is axis min to axis max */
    ysys   = '2';    /* y-axis label area is axis min to axis max */
    text   = model;  /* text string to position in the plot      */
    size   = 1;      /* relative size of the text string         */
    label y = 'Dimension 2'
          x = 'Dimension 1';
    keep x y text xsys ysys size;
 run;

    /*---Plot the Results---*/
 proc gplot data=biplot;
    title3 'BiPlot of Automobiles and Judges';
    symbol1 v=none;
    /*---Lengths are Device Specific---*/
    axis1 length=7    in order=-2   to 2.5 by 0.5;
    axis2 length=6.22 in order=-1.5 to 2.5 by 0.5;
    plot y*x=1 / annotate=biplot frame haxis=axis2 vaxis=axis1
              href=0 vref=0;
 run;
```

Output 34.5   Preference Ratings for Automobiles Manufactured in 1980

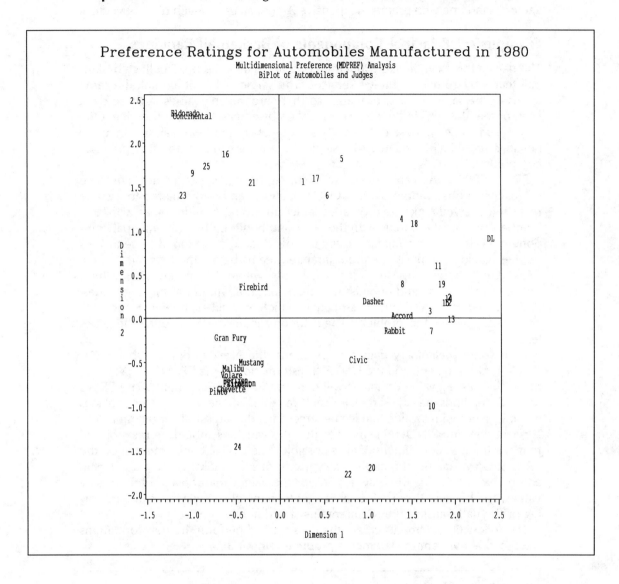

Preference Ratings for Automobiles Manufactured in 1980
Multidimensional Preference (MDPREF) Analysis
BiPlot of Automobiles and Judges

In the biplot, American automobiles are located on the left of the space, while European and Japanese automobiles are located on the right. At the top of the space are expensive American automobiles (Cadillac Eldorado, Lincoln Continental) while at the bottom are inexpensive ones (Pinto, Chevette). The first principal component differentiates American from imported automobiles, and the second arranges automobiles by price and other associated characteristics.

The two expensive American automobiles form a cluster, the sporty automobile (Firebird) is by itself, the Volvo is by itself, while the remaining imported autos form a cluster, as do the remaining American autos. It seems there are 5 prototypical automobiles in this set of 17, in terms of preference patterns among the 25 judges.

Most of the judges prefer the imported automobiles, especially the Volvo. There is also a fairly large minority that prefer the expensive cars, whether or not they are American (those whose vectors point towards one o'clock), or simply prefer expensive American automobiles (vectors toward eleven o'clock). There are two people who prefer anything except expensive American cars (five o'clock vectors), and one who prefers inexpensive American cars (seven o'clock vector).

Example 2:   Principal Components of Basketball Rankings

The data in this example are 1985-1986 preseason rankings of 35 college basketball teams by 10 different news services. The services do not all rank the same teams or the same number of teams, so there are missing values in these data. Each of the 35 teams in the data set is ranked by at least one news service. One way of summarizing these data is with a principal component analysis, since the rankings should all be related to a single underlying variable, the first principal component.

PROC PRINQUAL can be used to estimate the missing ranks and compute scores for all observations. A PRINQUAL analysis can be formulated to assume that the observed ranks are ordinal variables and to replace the ranks with new numbers that are monotonic with the ranks and better fit the one principal component model. The missing rank estimates need to be constrained since a news service would have positioned the unranked teams below the teams it ranked. PRINQUAL should impose order constraints within the nonmissing values, between the missing and nonmissing values, but not within the missing values. PRINQUAL has sophisticated missing data handling facilities; however, they will not directly handle this problem. The solution requires reformulating the problem.

With some preliminary data manipulations, the N=1 option on the PROC PRINQUAL statement, and the UNTIE transformation in the TRANSFORM statement, the missing value estimates will conform to the requirements. The PROC MEANS step finds the largest rank for each variable. The next DATA step replaces missing values with a value that is one larger than the largest observed rank. The N=1 option (in PRINQUAL) specifies that the variables should be transformed to make them as one-dimensional as possible. The UNTIE transformation on the TRANSFORM statement monotonically transforms the ranks, untying any ties in an optimal way. Since the only ties are for the values that replaced the missing values, and because these values are larger than the observed values, the rescoring of the data satisfies the requirements stated above.

The following statements create the data set and perform the transformations discussed above. These statements produce **Output 34.6**.

```
/*-------------------------------------------------------------------*/
/*                                                                   */
/* Example 2: Basketball Data                                        */
/*                                                                   */
/* Preseason 1985 College Basketball Rankings                        */
/* (rankings of 35 teams by 10 news services)                        */
/*                                                                   */
/* Note: (a) various news services rank varying numbers of teams;    */
/*       (b) not all 35 teams are ranked by all news services;       */
/*       (c) each team is ranked by at least one service; and        */
/*       (d) rank 20 is missing for UPI.                             */
/*                                                                   */
/*-------------------------------------------------------------------*/
title1 '1985 Preseason College Basketball Rankings';
data bballm;
   label csn      = 'Community Sports News (Chapel Hill NC)'
         dursun   = 'Durham Sun'
         durher   = 'Durham Morning Herald'
         waspost  = 'Washington Post'
```

```
            usatoda  = 'USA Today'
            spormag  = 'Sport Magazine'
            insport  = 'Inside Sports'
            upi      = 'United Press International'
            ap       = 'Associated Press'
            sporill  = 'Sports Illustrated'
            ;
      input school $13. csn dursun durher waspost usatoda
            spormag insport upi ap sporill;
      format csn -- sporill 5.1;
      cards;
Louisville      1  8  1  9  8  9  6 10  9  9
Georgia Tech    2  2  4  3  1  1  1  2  1  1
Kansas          3  4  5  1  5 11  8  4  5  7
Michigan        4  5  9  4  2  5  3  1  3  2
Duke            5  6  7  5  4 10  4  5  6  5
UNC             6  1  2  2  3  4  2  3  2  3
Syracuse        7 10  6 11  6  6  5  6  4 10
Notre Dame      8 14 15 13 11 20 18 13 12  .
Kentucky        9 15 16 14 14 19 11 12 11 13
LSU            10  9 13  . 13 15 16  9 14  8
DePaul         11  . 21 15 20  . 19  .  . 19
Georgetown     12  7  8  6  9  2  9  8  8  4
Navy           13 20 23 10 18 13 15  . 20  .
Illinois       14  3  3  7  7  3 10  7  7  6
Iowa           15 16  .  . 23  .  . 14  . 20
Arkansas       16  .  .  . 25  .  .  .  . 16
Memphis State  17  . 11  . 16  8 20  . 15 12
Washington     18  .  .  .  .  .  . 17  .  .
UAB            19 13 10  . 12 17  . 16 16 15
UNLV           20 18 18 19 22  . 14 18 18  .
NC State       21 17 14 16 15  . 12 15 17 18
Maryland       22  .  .  . 19  .  .  . 19 14
Pittsburg      23  .  .  .  .  .  .  .  .  .
Oklahoma       24 19 17 17 17 12 17  . 13 17
Indiana        25 12 20 18 21  .  .  .  .  .
Virginia       26  . 22  .  . 18  .  .  .  .
Old Dominion   27  .  .  .  .  .  .  .  .  .
Auburn         28 11 12  8 10  7  7 11 10 11
St. Johns      29  .  .  .  . 14  .  .  .  .
UCLA           30  .  .  .  .  .  . 19  .  .
St. Joseph's    .  . 19  .  .  .  .  .  .  .
Tennessee       .  . 24  .  . 16  .  .  .  .
Montana         .  .  . 20  .  .  .  .  .  .
Houston         .  .  .  . 24  .  .  .  .  .
Virginia Tech   .  .  .  .  .  . 13  .  .  .
      ;
```

```
      /*---------------------------------------------------------------*/
      /*                                                               */
      /* Find maximum rank for each news service and replace           */
      /* each missing value with the next highest rank.                */
      /*                                                               */
      /*---------------------------------------------------------------*/
proc means data=bballm noprint;
   output out=maxrank
          max=mcsn mdurs mdurh mwas musa mspom mins mupi map mspoi;
run;

data bball;
   set bballm;
   if _n_=1 then set maxrank;
   array services[10]  csn -- sporill;
   array maxranks[10]  mcsn -- mspoi;
   keep  school csn -- sporill;
   do i = 1 to 10;
      if services[i]=. then services[i]=maxranks[i]+1;
      end;
run;

      /*----------------------------------------------------------------*/
      /*                                                                */
      /* Assume that the ranks are ordinal and that unranked teams would */
      /* have been ranked lower than ranked teams.  Monotonically transform */
      /* all ranked teams while estimating the unranked teams.  Enforce the */
      /* constraint that the missing ranks are estimated to be less than  */
      /* the observed ranks.  Order the unranked teams optimally within  */
      /* this constraint.  Do this so as to maximize the variance accounted */
      /* for by one linear combination.  This makes the data as nearly rank */
      /* one as possible, given the constraints.                         */
      /*                                                                */
      /*----------------------------------------------------------------*/
proc prinqual data=bball out=tbball scores n=1 tstandard=z maxiter=20;
   title2 'Optimal Monotonic Transformation of Ranked Teams';
   title3 'with Constrained Estimation of Unranked Teams';
   transform untie(csn -- sporill);
   id school;
run;
```

Output 34.6   Transformation of Basketball Team Rankings

```
                    1985 Preseason College Basketball Rankings                        1
                    Optimal Monotonic Transformation of Ranked Teams
                     with Constrained Estimation of Unranked Teams

                         PRINQUAL MTV Iteration History

        Iteration    Average    Maximum    Proportion of    Variance
         Number      Change     Change       Variance        Change
      ---------------------------------------------------------------------
            1        0.18563    0.76531      0.85850            .
            2        0.03225    0.14627      0.94362         0.08512
            3        0.02126    0.10530      0.94669         0.00307
            4        0.01467    0.07526      0.94801         0.00132
            5        0.01067    0.05282      0.94865         0.00064
            6        0.00800    0.03669      0.94899         0.00034
            7        0.00617    0.02862      0.94919         0.00020
            8        0.00486    0.02636      0.94932         0.00013
            9        0.00395    0.02453      0.94941         0.00009
           10        0.00327    0.02300      0.94947         0.00006
           11        0.00275    0.02166      0.94952         0.00005
           12        0.00236    0.02041      0.94956         0.00004
           13        0.00205    0.01927      0.94959         0.00003
           14        0.00181    0.01818      0.94962         0.00003
           15        0.00162    0.01719      0.94964         0.00002
           16        0.00147    0.01629      0.94966         0.00002
           17        0.00136    0.01546      0.94968         0.00002
           18        0.00128    0.01469      0.94970         0.00002
           19        0.00121    0.01398      0.94971         0.00001
           20        0.00115    0.01332      0.94973         0.00001
```

An alternative approach is to use the pairwise deletion option of PROC CORR to compute the correlation matrix and then use PROC PRINCOMP or PROC FACTOR to perform the principal component analysis. This approach has several disadvantages. The correlation matrix may not be positive semi-definite (psd), an assumption required for principal component analysis. PROC PRINQUAL always produces a psd correlation matrix. Even with pairwise deletion, CORR removes the six observations with only a single nonmissing value from this data set. Finally, it is still not possible to calculate scores on the principal components for those teams that have missing values.

It is possible to compute the composite ranking using PROC PRINCOMP and some preliminary data manipulations, similar to those above. Chapter 33, "The PRINCOMP Procedure," contains an example where the average of the unused ranks in each poll is substituted for the missing values, and each observation is weighted by the number of nonmissing values. This method has much to recommend it. It is much faster and simpler than using PROC PRINQUAL. It is also much less prone to degeneracies and capitalization on chance. However, PRINCOMP does not allow the nonmissing ranks to be monotonically transformed and the missing values untied to optimize fit.

PROC PRINQUAL monotonically transforms the observed ranks and estimates the missing ranks (within the constraints given above) to account for almost 95 percent of the variance of the transformed data by just one dimension. PROC FACTOR is then used to report details of the principal component analysis of the transformed data. As shown by the Factor Pattern values, eight of the ten news services have a correlation of 0.94 or larger with the scores on the first principal component after the data are optimally transformed. The scores are sorted and the composite ranking is printed following the FACTOR output. More confidence can be placed in the stability of the scores for the teams that are ranked by the majority of the news services than in scores for teams that are seldom ranked.

The monotonic transformations are plotted for each of the ten news services. These plots are the values of the raw ranks (with the missing ranks replaced by the maximum rank plus one) versus the rescored (transformed) ranks. The transformations are the step functions that maximize the fit of the data to the principal component model. Smoother transformations could be found by using MSPLINE transformations, but MSPLINE transformations would not correctly handle the missing data problem.

The following statements perform the analysis discussed above and produce **Output 34.7**.

```
    /*---Perform the Final Principal Component Analysis---*/
proc factor nfactors=1;
   var tcsn -- tsporill;
   title4 'Principal-Component Analysis';
run;

proc sort;
   by prin1;
run;


    /*---Print Scores on the First Principal Component---*/
proc print;
   title4 'Teams Ordered by Scores on First Principal Component';
   var school prin1;
run;


    /*---Plot the Results---*/
proc plot nolegend vpercent=33 hpercent=50;
   plot twaspost*waspost tdursun*dursun
        tspormag*spormag tsporill*sporill
        tinsport*insport tupi*upi tap*ap /
        box haxis=1 to 21 by 5;
   plot tdurher*durher tusatoda*usatoda /
        box haxis=1 to 26 by 5;
   plot tcsn*csn / box haxis=1 to 31 by 5;
   title4 'Monotonic Transformation for Each News Service';
run;
```

Output 34.7   Alternative Approach for Analyzing Basketball Rankings

```
                     1985 Preseason College Basketball Rankings                    2
                  Optimal Monotonic Transformation of Ranked Teams
                    with Constrained Estimation of Unranked Teams
                            Principal-Component Analysis

Initial Factor Method: Principal Components

                        Prior Communality Estimates: ONE

            Eigenvalues of the Correlation Matrix:  Total = 10  Average = 1
```

	1	2	3	4	5	6	7	8	9	10
Eigenvalue	9.4974	0.2232	0.0876	0.0749	0.0423	0.0382	0.0157	0.0131	0.0042	0.0033
Difference	9.2742	0.1356	0.0127	0.0326	0.0041	0.0224	0.0026	0.0089	0.0008	
Proportion	0.9497	0.0223	0.0088	0.0075	0.0042	0.0038	0.0016	0.0013	0.0004	0.0003
Cumulative	0.9497	0.9721	0.9808	0.9883	0.9925	0.9964	0.9979	0.9992	0.9997	1.0000

```
                1 factors will be retained by the NFACTOR criterion.

                                 Factor Pattern

                                    FACTOR1

                TCSN     .   0.91065     CSN Transformation
                TDURSUN      0.98876     DURSUN Transformation
                TDURHER      0.97431     DURHER Transformation
                TWASPOST     0.97352     WASPOST Transformation
                TUSATODA     0.99049     USATODA Transformation
                TSPORMAG     0.95285     SPORMAG Transformation
                TINSPORT     0.98506     INSPORT Transformation
                TUPI         0.98494     UPI Transformation
                TAP          0.99586     AP Transformation
                TSPORILL     0.98603     SPORILL Transformation

                       Variance explained by each factor

                                    FACTOR1
                                    9.497404

                Final Communality Estimates: Total = 9.497404
```

TCSN	TDURSUN	TDURHER	TWASPOST	TUSATODA	TSPORMAG	TINSPORT	TUPI	TAP	TSPORILL
0.829285	0.977637	0.949289	0.947746	0.981063	0.907917	0.970344	0.970114	0.991747	0.972262

```
                     1985 Preseason College Basketball Rankings                    3
                  Optimal Monotonic Transformation of Ranked Teams
                    with Constrained Estimation of Unranked Teams
                   Teams Ordered by Scores on First Principal Component

                   OBS      SCHOOL              PRIN1

                     1      Georgia Tech       -6.21968
                     2      UNC                -5.94947
                     3      Michigan           -5.72634
                     4      Kansas             -4.80045
                     5      Duke               -4.77272
                     6      Illinois           -4.20342
                     7      Georgetown         -4.03951
                     8      Louisville         -3.73950
                     9      Syracuse           -3.48308
                    10      Auburn             -1.78683
                    11      LSU                -0.34948
                    12      Memphis State       0.48124
                    13      Kentucky            0.64533
                    14      Notre Dame          0.72985
                    15      Navy                0.77218
                    16      UAB                 0.99695
                    17      DePaul              1.11124
                    18      Oklahoma            1.13615
                    19      NC State            1.16673
                    20      UNLV                1.30623
                    21      Iowa                1.46728
                    22      Indiana             1.48977
                    23      Maryland            1.56294
                    24      Virginia            2.01006
                    25      Arkansas            2.03059
                    26      Washington          2.12088
                    27      Tennessee           2.29826
                    28      Virginia Tech       2.38895
                    29      St. Johns           2.40464
```

(continued on next page)

(continued from previous page)

30	Montana	2.53542
31	UCLA	2.61330
32	Pittsburg	3.01504
33	Old Dominion	3.05645
34	St. Joseph's	3.31161
35	Houston	4.41937

1985 Preseason College Basketball Rankings
Optimal Monotonic Transformation of Ranked Teams
with Constrained Estimation of Unranked Teams
Monotonic Transformation for Each News Service

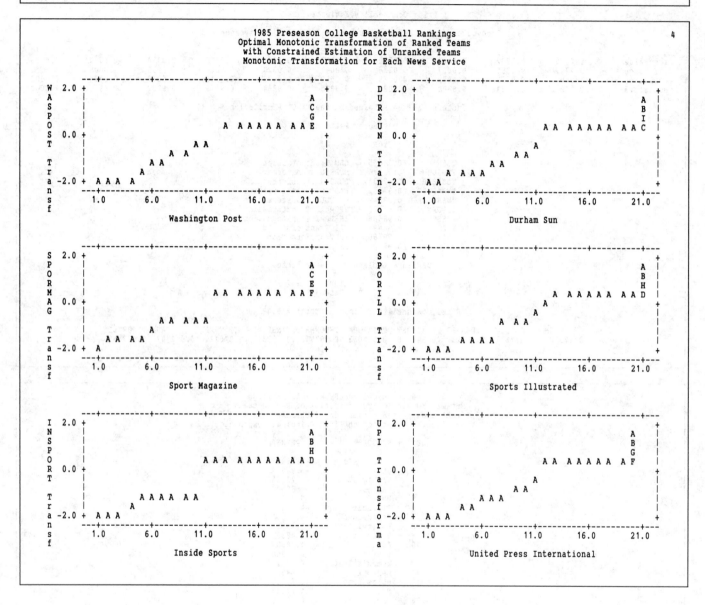

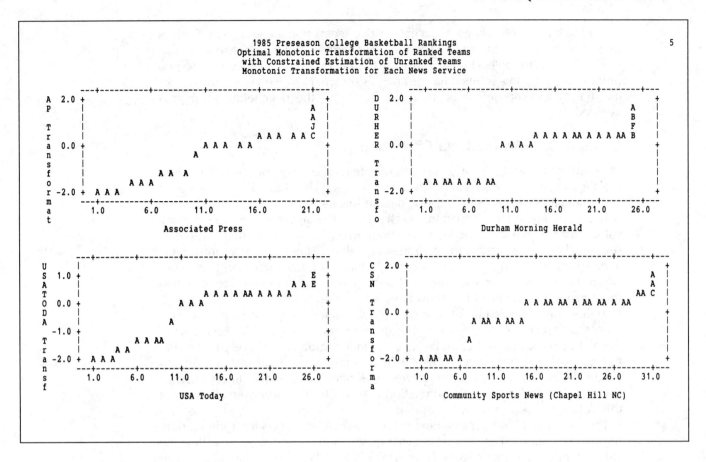

The ordinary PRINQUAL missing data handling facilities will not work for these data because they do not constrain the missing data estimates properly. If the missing ranks were coded as missing and LINEAR transformations specified, then least-squares estimates of the missing values can be computed without transforming the observed values. The first principal component then accounts for 92 percent of the variance after 20 iterations. However, Virginia Tech is ranked number 11 by its score even though it only appeared in one poll (INSPORT ranked it number 13, anchoring it firmly in the middle). Specifying MONOTONE transformations is also inappropriate since they too allow unranked teams to move in between ranked teams.

With these data, the combination of MONOTONE transformations and the freedom to score the missing ranks without constraint leads to degenerate transformations. PROC PRINQUAL tries to merge the 35 points into two points, producing a perfect fit in one dimension. There is evidence for this after 20 iterations when the Average Change, Maximum Change, and Variance Change values are all increasing, instead of the more stable decreasing change rate seen in the analysis shown. The change rates all stop increasing after 41 iterations, and it is clear by 70 or 80 iterations that one component will account for 100 percent of the transformed variables variance after sufficient iteration. While this may seem desirable (after all, it is a perfect fit), in fact you should be on guard when this happens. Whenever convergence is slow, the rates of change increase, or the final data perfectly fit the model, the solution is probably degenerating due to too few constraints on the scorings.

PROC PRINQUAL can account for 100% of the variance by scoring Montana and UCLA with one positive value on all variables, and all the other teams with one negative value on all variables. This inappropriate analysis suggests that all ranked teams are equally good except for two teams that are less good. Both of these two teams are ranked by only one news service, and their only nonmissing rank is last in the poll. This accounts for the degeneracy. This degenerate two point scoring is also a solution for the analysis shown. However, when the proper constraints are imposed throughout the iterations, the degenerate solution is avoided.

Example 3:   Missing Data Estimation

One use of the PROC PRINQUAL minimum generalized variance (MGV) method is estimating missing values in multivariate data sets. The column means are used as the initial estimates of the missing data in this iterative process. With missing data and all linear transformations, each step of the algorithm replaces missing values in a variable by their predicted values given the other variables in the data set and the current estimates of all missing values. Simultaneously, an optimal linear transformation of the nonmissing partition is found. Iteration terminates when the missing value estimates and linear transformations stabilize, or when the maximum number of iterations have been completed.

In this example, missing data estimation is illustrated with an artificial example. The IML procedure creates a 150×8 random normal data matrix. Each row of the matrix is a sample from a multivariate normal distribution with zero mean vector, and covariance matrix R where R is an equal correlation matrix with off-diagonal elements of 0.75. The first two pages of output contain sample descriptive statistics and the sample correlation matrix. The first 40 observations from this data set appear next in the output.

The DATA step that appears next creates two SAS data sets from the random normal data matrix. The data set X contains the random normal data, with some values randomly set to missing (with probability 0.05). Values that were set to missing are first stored in the MISS data set for future reference. The first 40 observations of the new data set, with random missing values, and the data set that stores the original values of the missing values are then printed.

PROC PRINQUAL estimates the missing values with the minimum generalized variance algorithm (METHOD=MGV). REPLACE specifies to replace the original variables by the new transformed variables in the output data set. DATA=X and OUT=X name the input and output data sets.

TSTANDARD=NOMISS standardizes the data at the end of the analysis so that in the output data set the mean and variance of the values that were originally nonmissing equal the mean and variance computed from the input data set values, ignoring missing values. In this particular case, TSTANDARD=NOMISS (along with the LINEAR transformation which is explained later) means that the values of the nonmissing data should not change. The means and variances of the columns in the DATA= data set will not equal the means and variances of the columns in the OUT= data set. Missing values in the DATA= data set are replaced by their estimates in the OUT= data set, and nonmissing values from the DATA= data set do not change.

CONVERGE=1E-6, CCONVERGE=-1, and MAXITER=50 specifies that iteration should stop when the average absolute change in all values is less than 0.000001, or when 50 iterations have been completed, whichever comes first. The CCONVERGE= -1 option specifies an impossibly small value of the average R^2 convergence criterion change, so R^2 convergence is not considered when convergence is evaluated. This is useful for METHOD=MGV since the average R^2 will not necessarily increase with every iteration. The default CCONVERGE=0 would cause the iterations to stop if average R^2 ever decreases.

The TRANSFORM statement names the analysis variables and their transformation types. In this case, all variables are linearly transformed. During the course of the analysis, the means and variances of the variables are maintained at zero and one. Within an iteration for a single variable, the estimates of the missing values are imputed to minimize the determinant of the correlation matrix, the values that started out nonmissing are linearly transformed, and then all values are linearly transformed to maintain the proper means and variances.

The algorithm behaves nicely with this data set. The data are changing at a monotonically decreasing rate, suggesting that the missing value estimates are converging to reasonable values. When there are too many missing values, the algorithm does not always behave this well. The missing value estimates may dominate the transformations, collapsing nonmissing values within some variables into tight groups. If the average or maximum data change increase for a few iterations, the algorithm may be trying within one or more variables to merge all nonmissing values, finding linear transformations with slopes at or near zero. Sometimes when the slope is very near zero, the algorithm succeeds in replacing nonmissing values with their mean. If the algorithm can find one observation that it can separate from the others, collapsing the others into a single point, it will try to do so, since two points define a straight line. When the slope is very near zero, the TSTANDARD=NOMISS transformation may produce a variable with all values constant. Otherwise, when the slope is near zero, the TSTANDARD=NOMISS transformation will have to use large numbers to rescale the nonmissing values back to their original values, producing outrageously large missing value estimates. If both change values do not decrease at rapid rates, or if overly large missing value estimates are produced, or if all of the nonmissing values for a variable or all of the missing and nonmissing values are scaled to a constant, you should carefully evaluate your results before using the transformed data in any other procedure. In fact, this advice applies even if nothing appears to go wrong. Whenever there are many missing values, or more generally, whenever there are few constraints on the scoring of one or more observations, constant variables and other inappropriate solutions can be a problem.

Each iteration has m steps, where m is the number of variables. The first step involves regressing variable one on all other variables. The squared multiple correlation from this step is saved. The second step regresses variable two on all other variables including the new scaling of variable one from the previous step. Again the R^2 is saved. This process continues, always using the newest values of each variable in the next set of predictor variables. After each iteration (each set of m steps), the average R^2 is reported in the iteration history table. It is important to note that this is not the mean R^2 at the end of the iteration using the current scaling of all variables. It is the mean of the R^2s saved from each step of the iteration using the current scalings of all variables at that time. These two numbers are the same when the data completely converge. The mean R^2 is not the criterion that the algorithm optimizes, so the mean R^2 will not always increase during the iterations.

The first 40 transformed observations are printed. Then the next step produces the sample correlation matrix of the transformed variables. Most of the correlations are larger than the original sample correlations and the population correlation (0.75). This is because the algorithm attempts to estimate the missing data by making the variables as collinear as possible.

The data set CHECK is created; it contains four variables and 65 observations (one for each missing value). The variable DATA contains the original value of each value that was set to missing. ESTIMATE contains PROC PRINQUAL's estimate of the value. ERROR contains the differences between the original values and their estimates. NMISS contains the number of missing values in that observation within X. This data set is then printed, summarized, plotted, and charted. The errors are approximately normally distributed around the origin, and most errors have an absolute value less than 0.5. However, some estimates are not very

accurate. While the MGV method worked well on the average, it does not necessarily work well for all missing values.

The following statements produce **Output 34.8**:

```
%let n   = 150;   /* number of rows            */
%let m   = 8;     /* number of columns         */
%let rho = 0.75;  /* population correlation     */
%let p   = 0.05;  /* proportion of missing values */

proc iml;

   /*--------------------------------------------------------------*/
   /*                                                              */
   /* The proc iml step creates a random normal data matrix X.    */
   /* The number of rows in X are specified in the %let n=        */
   /* statement, and the number of columns are specified in the   */
   /* %let m = statement, above. Each row of X is a sample from a */
   /* multivariate normal distribution with mean vector zero, and */
   /* a covariance matrix equal to an equal correlation matrix    */
   /* whose off-diagonal elements are specified in the %let rho = */
   /* statement above. This random normal data set will be output */
   /* to a SAS data set.                                          */
   /*                                                              */
   /* SAS/IML software is required to run this example.           */
   /*                                                              */
   /*--------------------------------------------------------------*/

   /*---start with each row of X being a sample from N(0,I)---*/
   X=rannor(j(&n,&m,7654321));

   one=j(&m,1,1);

   /*---Create an Equal-Correlation Matrix---*/
   R = (1 - (&rho)) * i(&m) + one * one` * (&rho);

   /*---Each Row of X is a Sample from N(0,R)---*/
   X = X * half(R);

   /*---Output X to a SAS Data Set---*/
   create x from X; append from X;
   quit;

   /*---Compute the Sample Correlation Matrix---*/
proc corr data=x noprob;
   title1 'Sample Correlation Matrix';
run;

proc print data=x(obs=40);
   title1 'The Random Normal Data Set';
   title2 'The First 40 Observations';
run;

data x(keep=x1-x&m) miss(keep=m1-m&m);
   set x;
```

```
      /*----------------------------------------------------------*/
      /*                                                          */
      /* Create two SAS data sets from X.  Each value in X will be */
      /* set to missing with probability &p.  When a value in X is */
      /* set to missing, the original value is stored in MISS.     */
      /* (Nonmissing values in X are set to missing in MISS.)     */
      /*                                                          */
      /*----------------------------------------------------------*/

      array x[&m]   x1-x&m;
      array m[&m]   m1-m&m;
      array c[&m]   col1-col&m;
      do i = 1 to &m;
         if ranuni(7654321) < &p then do;
            x[i]=.;
            m[i]=c[i];
         end;
         else do;
            m[i]=.;
            x[i]=c[i];
         end;
      end;
run;


      /*---Display the Starting Point---*/
proc print data=x(obs=40);
      title1 'Data Matrix with Random Missing Data';
      title2 'The First 40 Observations';
run;


proc print data=miss(obs=40);
      title1 'Original Values of the Random Missing Data';
      title2 'The First 40 Observations';
run;


      /*---Impute Estimates of the Missing Data---*/
proc prinqual method=mgv replace data=x out=x tstandard=nomiss
      converge=1e-6 cconverge=-1 maxiter=50;
      transform linear(x1-x&m);
      title1 'Impute Estimates of the Missing Data';
run;


proc print data=x(obs=40);
      title1 'The Random Normal Data Set with Missing Value Estimates';
      title2 'The First 40 Observations';
run;


proc corr data=x noprob;
      title1 'Correlation Matrix Recovery';
run;
```

```
   /*---Check the Results---*/
data check(keep=data estimate error nmiss);
   set x;
   set miss;
   array x[&m]  x1-x&m;
   array m[&m]  m1-m&m;
   nmiss = n(of m1-m&m);

   do i = 1 to &m;
      if m[i]  ne . then do;
         data     = m[i];
         estimate = x[i];
         error    = data - estimate;
         output;
      end;
   end;
run;


   /*---Display Results---*/
proc print data=check;
   title1 'Original Values and Their Estimates';
run;


proc means data=check mean var std min max;
   title1 'Descriptive Statistics for the Errors';
   var error;
run;


proc plot data=check;
   title1 'Plots of the Estimates and Errors';
   plot estimate*data data*data='*' / overlay box href=0 vref=0;
   plot error*data / box vref=0;
run;


proc sort data=check out=check;
   by nmiss;
run;


proc chart data=check;
   title 'Overall Errors';
   hbar error / axis=30 midpoints = -2 -1 0 1 2;
run;


proc chart data=check;
   title 'Errors, Broken Down by Number of Missings';
   hbar error / axis=30 midpoints = -2 -1 0 1 2;
   by nmiss;
run;
```

Output 34.8   Estimating Missing Data Example Output

```
                                Sample Correlation Matrix                                    1
                                  Correlation Analysis

            8 'VAR' Variables:  COL1    COL2    COL3    COL4    COL5    COL6    COL7    COL8

                                   Simple Statistics

        Variable        N          Mean      Std Dev         Sum       Minimum       Maximum

        COL1          150      0.073769     1.022212    11.065377     -2.086335      3.405589
        COL2          150      0.036049     0.955161     5.407281     -2.103785      2.469876
        COL3          150      0.054320     0.956370     8.147985     -1.865545      2.745282
        COL4          150      0.037080     0.946933     5.561942     -1.992405      2.070838
        COL5          150     -0.021583     0.919029    -3.237492     -2.307337      2.510318
        COL6          150      0.026984     1.038904     4.047654     -2.141378      2.630291
        COL7          150      0.054868     0.913432     8.230247     -2.059207      2.476295
        COL8          150      0.049398     1.013471     7.409764     -2.643983      2.630592

                          Pearson Correlation Coefficients  / N = 150

              COL1        COL2         COL3        COL4         COL5        COL6         COL7        COL8

COL1       1.00000     0.73210      0.74085     0.70824      0.74332     0.69302      0.75592     0.72523

COL2       0.73210     1.00000      0.77235     0.73562      0.70614     0.75511      0.74364     0.75414

COL3       0.74085     0.77235      1.00000     0.73337      0.73054     0.72895      0.68968     0.74582

COL4       0.70824     0.73562      0.73337     1.00000      0.70798     0.70235      0.71455     0.73075

COL5       0.74332     0.70614      0.73054     0.70798      1.00000     0.66084      0.68276     0.71668

COL6       0.69302     0.75511      0.72895     0.70235      0.66084     1.00000      0.72703     0.70017

COL7       0.75592     0.74364      0.68968     0.71455      0.68276     0.72703      1.00000     0.69529

COL8       0.72523     0.75414      0.74582     0.73075      0.71668     0.70017      0.69529     1.00000
```

```
                                The Random Normal Data Set                                   2
                                 The First 40 Observations

        OBS      COL1       COL2        COL3       COL4        COL5       COL6        COL7       COL8

          1   -0.44999   -1.02523    -0.47594   -0.38182    -0.52182   -0.00168    -0.47339   -0.10885
          2    1.28379    0.94650     1.45152    1.79287     0.70128    0.70128      0.05376    1.81926
          3    0.56390    1.11081    -0.13303    0.80755    -0.29043    2.24947      0.69691    1.35005
          4    0.41819    1.51199     0.82798    1.13793     0.86503    0.93680      0.77261    0.41907
          5    1.08506    0.25140     0.96572    0.89360     0.89272    1.02064      1.93613    0.64620
          6    1.06800    1.24536     0.56587    0.64685     0.27972    1.46482      1.11595    0.95951
          7   -0.94934   -0.79231     0.08646   -1.08471    -0.92166   -0.50763    -1.45287   -0.22889
          8   -0.39238    1.13968     0.52272    0.88968     0.38311   -0.68989     0.02786    0.23308
          9    0.94335    0.53478     1.12938    1.33400     0.32008    1.70555      1.05488    0.49779
         10   -1.84889   -1.30045     0.03226   -0.52440    -0.39773   -1.18554    -1.20208   -0.71804
         11   -1.83666   -1.12852     0.40154   -1.02303    -0.43955   -2.14138    -1.22195   -0.93282
         12    1.66774    1.36562     2.49037    1.67075     1.82240    1.35684      1.05921    1.84872
         13    0.46247    0.43474    -0.38560   -0.73884     0.03785    0.02610      0.42443    0.59761
         14   -1.11338   -1.69293    -0.73702   -1.33186    -2.00529   -1.02188    -0.07975   -1.41993
         15   -1.44930   -0.77573    -0.95005   -0.30235     0.20953   -0.32700     0.04380   -1.04877
         16    0.10162   -0.89631    -0.58041   -0.32995     0.41390    0.44086     -0.42978    1.03472
         17    2.37065    0.36634     1.24728    1.64592     1.53738    0.54326      0.92170    0.65281
         18   -0.98249   -1.19077    -1.57801   -1.99240    -0.84873   -1.36224    -0.98278   -1.95503
         19   -2.08633   -1.31964    -0.95002   -1.01853    -2.30734   -1.11977    -1.30578   -1.83739
         20    1.20120    1.40282     1.04876    0.58811     0.97029    1.51053      0.56337    1.03606
         21   -0.01434   -0.61082    -0.78706   -1.12233     0.13678   -0.61696    -0.31978   -0.02587
         22   -1.57306   -0.84960    -1.42696   -0.58650    -1.71414   -1.25847    -1.16811   -1.53975
         23    1.74062    1.57813     1.16797   -0.25059     1.49774    1.40144      2.12212    1.82125
         24    0.47305    0.36295     0.67319    0.07088     0.13374   -0.53479     0.41124    0.78186
         25   -0.16554    0.26258    -0.40989   -0.16343     0.97811    0.97261      0.24646    0.02727
         26   -0.61361   -0.51558     0.22269   -0.82414    -1.76036   -0.62158     0.09639   -0.35888
         27    0.85290   -0.13988    -0.33883   -1.16660    -0.69644   -0.82089    -0.67014   -1.00260
         28    0.18685    0.69338    -0.69857   -0.16212    -0.49488    0.32166      0.56951    1.08218
         29   -0.99356   -0.54202    -0.79953   -0.53969    -0.67123   -0.54797    -0.76378   -1.06111
         30    0.54159    1.84187     1.97339    0.86870     0.98684    2.63029      0.68271    1.86355
         31    0.28356   -0.71217    -0.17514   -0.80208     0.17852    0.57446      0.88720   -0.25011
         32   -0.41020   -0.80045    -0.10989   -0.52028    -0.18452    0.68297     -0.75025   -0.70080
         33   -0.82182   -0.03555    -0.18508    0.00430     0.45579    0.19042     -0.06275   -0.18107
         34   -0.39794   -0.62275    -0.75070   -0.27506    -0.92900   -0.14587    -0.88820    0.27017
         35   -1.25762   -1.89354    -1.74104   -1.12977    -0.91710   -1.32318    -1.31030   -1.38359
         36   -0.82779   -1.00723    -1.52540   -1.34043    -0.66833   -0.95281    -0.28946   -1.15074
         37   -0.05395    0.00971    -0.05818   -0.34099    -0.49323   -0.10835     0.53169   -0.02493
         38   -1.63515   -1.08671    -1.31831   -0.75946    -1.29862   -0.21375    -0.72100   -0.66047
         39    0.12687    1.41592     0.61340    1.28090     0.23073    1.15112      0.92924    0.98879
         40   -1.25443   -2.10379    -1.66319   -1.57269    -1.75108   -1.62040    -1.58924   -1.60855
```

Data Matrix with Random Missing Data
The First 40 Observations

3

OBS	X1	X2	X3	X4	X5	X6	X7	X8
1	-0.44999	-1.02523	-0.47594	-0.38182	-0.52182	-0.00168	-0.47339	-0.10885
2	1.28379	0.94650	1.45152	1.79287	0.07936	0.70128	0.05376	.
3	0.56390	1.11081	-0.13303	0.80755	-0.29043	2.24947	0.69691	.
4	0.41819	1.51199	0.82798	1.13793	.	0.93680	0.77261	.
5	1.08506	0.25140	0.96572	0.89360	0.89272	1.02064	1.93613	0.64620
6	1.06800	1.24536	.	0.64685	0.27972	1.46482	1.11595	0.95951
7	-0.94934	-0.79231	0.08646	-1.08471	-0.92166	-0.50763	-1.45287	-0.22889
8	-0.39238	1.13968	0.52272	0.88968	0.38311	-0.68989	0.02786	0.23308
9	0.94335	0.53478	1.12938	1.33400	0.32008	1.70555	1.05488	0.49779
10	-1.84889	-1.30045	0.03226	-0.52440	-0.39773	-1.18554	-1.20208	-0.71804
11	-1.83666	-1.12852	0.40154	-1.02303	-0.43955	-2.14138	-1.22195	-0.93282
12	1.66774	1.36562	2.49037	1.67075	1.82240	1.35684	1.05921	1.84872
13	0.46247	0.43474	-0.38560	-0.73884	0.03785	0.02610	0.42443	0.59761
14	-1.11338	-1.69293	-0.73702	-1.33186	-2.00529	-1.02188	-0.07975	-1.41993
15	.	-0.77573	-0.95005	.	0.20953	-0.32700	0.34380	-1.04877
16	0.10162	-0.89631	-0.58041	-0.32995	0.41390	0.44086	-0.42978	1.03472
17	2.37065	0.36634	1.24728	1.64592	1.53738	0.54326	0.92170	0.65281
18	-0.98249	-1.19077	-1.57801	-1.99240	-0.84873	-1.36224	-0.98278	-1.95503
19	-2.08633	-1.31964	-0.95002	-1.01853	-2.30734	-1.11977	-1.30578	-1.83739
20	1.20120	1.40282	1.04876	0.58811	0.97029	1.51053	0.56337	1.03606
21	-0.01434	-0.61082	-0.78706	-1.12233	.	.	-0.31978	-0.02587
22	-1.57306	-0.84960	.	-0.58650	-1.71414	-1.25847	-1.16811	-1.53975
23	1.74062	1.57813	1.16797	-0.25059	1.49774	.	2.12212	1.82125
24	0.47305	0.36295	0.67319	0.07088	0.13374	-0.53479	0.41124	0.78186
25	-0.16554	0.26258	.	-0.16343	0.97811	0.97261	0.24646	0.02727
26	-0.61361	-0.51558	0.22269	-0.82414	-1.76036	-0.62158	0.09639	-0.35888
27	0.85290	-0.13988	-0.33883	-1.16660	-0.69644	-0.82089	-0.67014	-1.00260
28	0.18685	0.69338	-0.69857	-0.16212	.	0.32166	0.56951	1.08218
29	-0.99356	-0.54202	-0.79953	.	-0.67123	-0.54797	-0.76378	-1.06111
30	0.54159	.	1.97339	0.86870	0.98684	2.63029	0.68271	1.86355
31	0.28356	-0.71217	-0.17514	-0.80208	0.17852	0.57446	0.88720	-0.25011
32	-0.41020	.	-0.10989	-0.52028	-0.18452	0.68297	-0.75025	-0.70080
33	.	-0.03555	.	0.00430	0.45579	0.19042	-0.06275	-0.18107
34	-0.39794	-0.62275	-0.75070	-0.27506	-0.92900	-0.14587	-0.88820	0.27017
35	-1.25762	-1.89354	-1.74104	-1.12977	-0.91710	-1.32318	-1.31030	-1.38359
36	-0.82779	-1.00723	-1.52540	-1.34043	-0.66833	-0.95281	-0.28946	-1.15074
37	-0.05395	0.00971	-0.05818	-0.34099	-0.49323	.	0.53169	-0.02493
38	-1.63515	-1.08671	-1.31831	-0.75946	-1.29862	-0.21375	-0.72100	-0.66047
39	0.12687	1.41592	0.61340	1.28090	0.23073	1.15112	0.92924	0.98879
40	-1.25443	-2.10379	-1.66319	-1.57269	-1.75108	-1.62040	-1.58924	-1.60855

Original Values of the Random Missing Data
The First 40 Observations

4

OBS	M1	M2	M3	M4	M5	M6	M7	M8
1	.	.	.	.	.	.	.	.
2	.	.	.	.	.	.	.	1.81926
3	.	.	.	.	.	.	.	1.35005
4	.	.	.	.	0.86503	.	.	0.41907
5	.	.	.	.	.	.	.	.
6	.	.	0.56587	.	.	.	.	.
7	.	.	.	.	.	.	.	.
8	.	.	.	.	.	.	.	.
9	.	.	.	.	.	.	.	.
10	.	.	.	.	.	.	.	.
11	.	.	.	.	.	.	.	.
12	.	.	.	.	.	.	.	.
13	.	.	.	.	.	.	.	.
14	.	.	.	.	.	.	.	.
15	-1.44930	.	.	-0.30235	.	.	.	.
16	.	.	.	.	.	.	.	.
17	.	.	.	.	.	.	.	.
18	.	.	.	.	.	.	.	.
19	.	.	.	.	.	.	.	.
20	.	.	.	.	.	.	.	.
21	.	.	.	.	0.13678	-0.61696	.	.
22	.	.	-1.42696	.	.	.	.	.
23	.	.	.	.	.	1.40144	.	.
24	.	.	.	.	.	.	.	.
25	.	.	-0.40989	.	.	.	.	.
26	.	.	.	.	.	.	.	.
27	.	.	.	.	.	.	.	.
28	.	.	.	.	-0.49488	.	.	.
29	.	.	.	-0.53969	.	.	.	.
30	.	1.84187	.	.	.	.	.	.
31	.	.	.	.	.	.	.	.
32	.	-0.80045	.	.	.	.	.	.
33	-0.82182	.	-0.18508	.	.	.	.	.
34	.	.	.	.	.	.	.	.
35	.	.	.	.	.	.	.	.
36	.	.	.	.	.	.	.	.
37	.	.	.	.	.	-0.10835	.	.
38	.	.	.	.	.	.	.	.
39	.	.	.	.	.	.	.	.
40	.	.	.	.	.	.	.	.

Impute Estimates of the Missing Data   5

PRINQUAL MGV Iteration History

Iteration Number	Average Change	Maximum Change	Mean Squared Multiple R	R Square Change
1	0.07725	3.33918	0.66806	.
2	0.00918	0.33438	0.71955	0.05148
3	0.00229	0.08722	0.71996	0.00041
4	0.00070	0.03130	0.72000	0.00004
5	0.00024	0.01125	0.72002	0.00002
6	0.00008	0.00405	0.72003	0.00001
7	0.00003	0.00155	0.72003	0.00000
8	0.00001	0.00060	0.72003	0.00000
9	0.00000	0.00023	0.72003	0.00000
10	0.00000	0.00009	0.72003	0.00000
11	0.00000	0.00003	0.72003	0.00000

The Random Normal Data Set with Missing Value Estimates   6
The First 40 Observations

OBS	_TYPE_	_NAME_	X1	X2	X3	X4	X5	X6	X7	X8
1	SCORE	ROW1	-0.44999	-1.02523	-0.47594	-0.38182	-0.52182	-0.00168	-0.47339	-0.10885
2	SCORE	ROW2	1.28379	0.94650	1.45152	1.79287	0.07936	0.70128	0.05376	1.46677
3	SCORE	ROW3	0.56390	1.11081	-0.13303	0.80755	-0.29043	2.24947	0.69691	0.70813
4	SCORE	ROW4	0.41819	1.51199	0.82798	1.13793	1.07725	0.93680	0.77261	1.28526
5	SCORE	ROW5	1.08506	0.25140	0.96572	0.89360	0.89272	1.02064	1.93613	0.64620
6	SCORE	ROW6	1.06800	1.24536	1.22810	0.64685	0.27972	1.46482	1.11595	0.95951
7	SCORE	ROW7	-0.94934	-0.79231	0.08646	-1.08471	-0.92166	-0.50763	-1.45287	-0.22889
8	SCORE	ROW8	-0.39238	1.13968	0.52272	0.88968	0.38311	-0.68989	0.02786	0.23308
9	SCORE	ROW9	0.94335	0.53478	1.12938	1.33400	0.32008	1.70555	1.05488	0.49779
10	SCORE	ROW10	-1.84889	-1.30045	0.03226	-0.52440	-0.39773	-1.18554	-1.20208	-0.71804
11	SCORE	ROW11	-1.83666	-1.12852	0.40154	-1.02303	-0.43955	-2.14138	-1.22195	-0.93282
12	SCORE	ROW12	1.66774	1.36562	2.49037	1.67075	1.82240	1.35684	1.05921	1.84872
13	SCORE	ROW13	0.46247	0.43474	-0.38560	-0.73884	0.03785	0.02610	0.42443	0.59761
14	SCORE	ROW14	-1.11338	-1.69293	-0.73702	-1.33186	-2.00529	-1.02188	-0.07975	-1.41993
15	SCORE	ROW15	-0.22288	-0.77573	-0.95005	-0.47311	0.20953	-0.32700	0.34380	-1.04877
16	SCORE	ROW16	0.10162	-0.89631	-0.58041	-0.32995	0.41390	0.44086	-0.42978	1.03472
17	SCORE	ROW17	2.37065	0.36634	1.24728	1.64592	1.53738	0.54326	0.92170	0.65281
18	SCORE	ROW18	-0.98249	-1.19077	-1.57801	-1.99240	-0.84873	-1.36224	-0.98278	-1.95503
19	SCORE	ROW19	-2.08633	-1.31964	-0.95002	-1.01853	-2.30734	-1.11977	-1.30578	-1.83739
20	SCORE	ROW20	1.20120	1.40282	1.04876	0.58811	0.97029	1.51053	0.56337	1.03606
21	SCORE	ROW21	-0.01434	-0.61082	-0.78706	-1.12233	-0.78935	-0.84446	-0.31978	-0.02587
22	SCORE	ROW22	-1.57306	-0.84960	-1.59867	-0.58650	-1.71414	-1.25847	-1.16811	-1.53975
23	SCORE	ROW23	1.74062	1.57813	1.16797	-0.25059	1.49774	2.19049	2.12212	1.82125
24	SCORE	ROW24	0.47305	0.36295	0.67319	0.07088	0.13374	-0.53479	0.41124	0.78186
25	SCORE	ROW25	-0.16554	0.26258	0.42900	-0.16343	0.97811	0.97261	0.24646	0.02727
26	SCORE	ROW26	-0.61361	-0.51558	0.22269	-0.82414	-1.76036	-0.62158	0.09639	-0.35888
27	SCORE	ROW27	0.85290	-0.13988	-0.33883	-1.16660	-0.69644	-0.82089	-0.67014	-1.00260
28	SCORE	ROW28	0.18685	0.69338	-0.69857	-0.16212	0.04052	0.32166	0.56951	1.08218
29	SCORE	ROW29	-0.99356	-0.54202	-0.79953	-1.02295	-0.67123	-0.54797	-0.76378	-1.06111
30	SCORE	ROW30	0.54159	2.02171	1.97339	0.86870	0.98684	2.63029	0.68271	1.86355
31	SCORE	ROW31	0.28356	-0.71217	-0.17514	-0.80208	0.17852	0.57446	0.88720	-0.25011
32	SCORE	ROW32	-0.41020	-0.24095	-0.10989	-0.52028	-0.18452	0.68297	-0.75025	-0.70080
33	SCORE	ROW33	0.16372	-0.03555	0.08745	0.00430	0.45579	0.19042	-0.06275	-0.18107
34	SCORE	ROW34	-0.39794	-0.62275	-0.75070	-0.27506	-0.92900	-0.14587	-0.88820	0.27017
35	SCORE	ROW35	-1.25762	-1.89354	-1.74104	-1.12977	-0.91710	-1.32318	-1.31030	-1.38359
36	SCORE	ROW36	-0.82779	-1.00723	-1.52540	-1.34043	-0.66833	-0.95281	-0.28946	-1.15074
37	SCORE	ROW37	-0.05395	0.00971	-0.05818	-0.34099	-0.49323	0.06721	0.53169	-0.02493
38	SCORE	ROW38	-1.63515	-1.08671	-1.31831	-0.75946	-1.29862	-0.21375	-0.72100	-0.66047
39	SCORE	ROW39	0.12687	1.41592	0.61340	1.28090	0.23073	1.15112	0.92924	0.98879
40	SCORE	ROW40	-1.25443	-2.10379	-1.66319	-1.57269	-1.75108	-1.62040	-1.58924	-1.60855

```
                          Correlation Matrix Recovery                              7
                             Correlation Analysis

            8 'VAR' Variables:  X1      X2      X3      X4      X5      X6      X7      X8

                                  Simple Statistics

        Variable        N         Mean      Std Dev         Sum       Minimum      Maximum
          X1           150       0.088060    1.016213     13.208972   -2.086335     3.405589
          X2           150       0.048266    0.960155      7.239840   -2.103785     2.469876
          X3           150       0.062669    0.975770      9.400357   -1.865545     2.745282
          X4           150       0.029296    0.970788      4.394420   -1.992405     2.070838
          X5           150      -0.035280    0.937810     -5.291963   -2.307337     2.453022
          X6           150       0.034013    1.049072      5.101959   -2.141378     2.630291
          X7           150       0.041712    0.914162      6.256784   -2.059207     2.476295
          X8           150       0.049463    1.060822      7.419523   -2.643983     3.690737

                     Pearson Correlation Coefficients  / N = 150

              X1        X2         X3         X4         X5         X6         X7         X8

   X1      1.00000    0.74023    0.74686    0.71829    0.76114    0.70819    0.77232    0.77317

   X2      0.74023    1.00000    0.79146    0.75142    0.74806    0.76727    0.73946    0.78390

   X3      0.74686    0.79146    1.00000    0.73501    0.75379    0.74106    0.71113    0.80569

   X4      0.71829    0.75142    0.73501    1.00000    0.73638    0.70402    0.72036    0.74549

   X5      0.76114    0.74806    0.75379    0.73638    1.00000    0.69384    0.69198    0.74556

   X6      0.70819    0.76727    0.74106    0.70402    0.69384    1.00000    0.73798    0.73088

   X7      0.77232    0.73946    0.71113    0.72036    0.69198    0.73798    1.00000    0.74476

   X8      0.77317    0.78390    0.80569    0.74549    0.74556    0.73088    0.74476    1.00000
```

```
                      Original Values and Their Estimates                          8
                 OBS    NMISS     DATA      ESTIMATE      ERROR
                  1       1      1.81926     1.46677      0.35249
                  2       1      1.35005     0.70813      0.64192
                  3       2      0.86503     1.07725     -0.21222
                  4       2      0.41907     1.28526     -0.86620
                  5       1      0.56587     1.22810     -0.66223
                  6       2     -1.44930    -0.22288     -1.22642
                  7       2     -0.30235    -0.47311      0.17076
                  8       2      0.13678    -0.78935      0.92613
                  9       2     -0.61696    -0.84446      0.22750
                 10       1     -1.42696    -1.59867      0.17171
                 11       1      1.40144     2.19049     -0.78906
                 12       1     -0.40989     0.42900     -0.83889
                 13       1     -0.49488     0.04052     -0.53540
                 14       1     -0.53969    -1.02295      0.48325
                 15       1      1.84187     2.02171     -0.17985
                 16       1     -0.80045    -0.24095     -0.55950
                 17       2     -0.82182     0.16372     -0.98553
                 18       2     -0.18508     0.08745     -0.27253
                 19       1     -0.10835     0.06721     -0.17557
                 20       1     -0.43857    -1.30422      0.86565
                 21       2     -0.14165    -0.52566      0.38401
                 22       2     -0.50386    -0.57154      0.06768
                 23       3     -0.18516    -0.38841      0.20324
                 24       3     -0.47629    -0.59697      0.12068
                 25       3      0.29920    -0.45021      0.74941
                 26       1      1.11536     1.38248     -0.26712
                 27       2      1.39825     2.10252     -0.70427
                 28       2      1.23553     1.92659     -0.69106
                 29       1     -0.94764    -1.44237      0.49472
                 30       1      0.94613     0.45680      0.48933
                 31       1     -0.49881    -0.85568      0.35687
                 32       1     -0.06259     0.29065     -0.35324
                 33       1      0.10070    -1.17968      1.28038
                 34       1     -0.57045     1.12842     -1.69888
                 35       1     -0.64732    -0.41491     -0.23240
                 36       1     -0.02360     0.04356     -0.06716
                 37       1      1.01398     0.99344      0.02055
                 38       2     -0.06641    -0.62553      0.55912
                 39       2     -0.05913    -0.85893      0.79979
                 40       1     -0.18906    -1.39799      1.20892
                 41       1      0.18301     0.27295     -0.08994
                 42       1     -0.44948    -0.45056      0.00108
                 43       1     -1.59331    -1.75202      0.15871
                 44       1      1.43292     3.69074     -2.25782
                 45       1     -0.62077    -0.74818      0.12741
```

(continued on next page)

(continued from previous page)

46	1	0.47338	0.84387	-0.37049
47	1	0.45885	0.37509	0.08376
48	1	0.52899	0.33042	0.19858
49	1	-0.79252	-1.33932	0.54680
50	2	0.83902	0.68985	0.14917
51	2	1.46925	0.56223	0.90702
52	1	2.51032	2.12410	0.38621
53	1	0.10111	-0.68049	0.78160
54	2	1.34932	1.49712	-0.14779
55	2	0.84294	1.79351	-0.95057
56	1	0.81981	0.88971	-0.06990

Original Values and Their Estimates   9

OBS	NMISS	DATA	ESTIMATE	ERROR
57	1	-1.56212	-0.27810	-1.28402
58	1	0.36882	-0.03585	0.40466
59	1	-0.12646	0.80073	-0.92719
60	1	0.01062	-1.69947	1.71008
61	1	-0.22062	1.10290	-1.32352
62	1	-0.49998	-1.03905	0.53907
63	1	-0.26225	0.23032	-0.49257
64	2	-0.79257	-1.23896	0.44638
65	2	-0.29062	-1.41015	1.11953

Descriptive Statistics for the Errors   10

Analysis Variable : ERROR

Mean	Std Dev	Minimum	Maximum	Variance
-0.0168790	0.7425670	-2.2578221	1.7100837	0.5514058

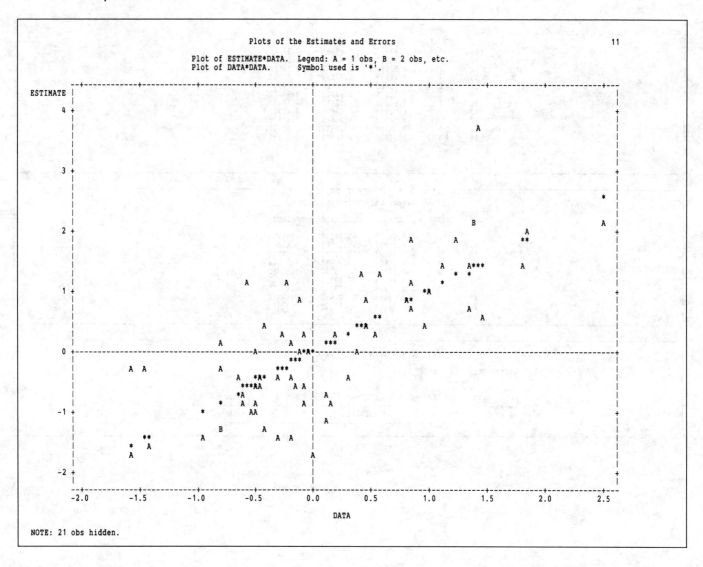

Plots of the Estimates and Errors   11

Plot of ESTIMATE*DATA.   Legend: A = 1 obs, B = 2 obs, etc.
Plot of DATA*DATA.   Symbol used is '*'.

NOTE: 21 obs hidden.

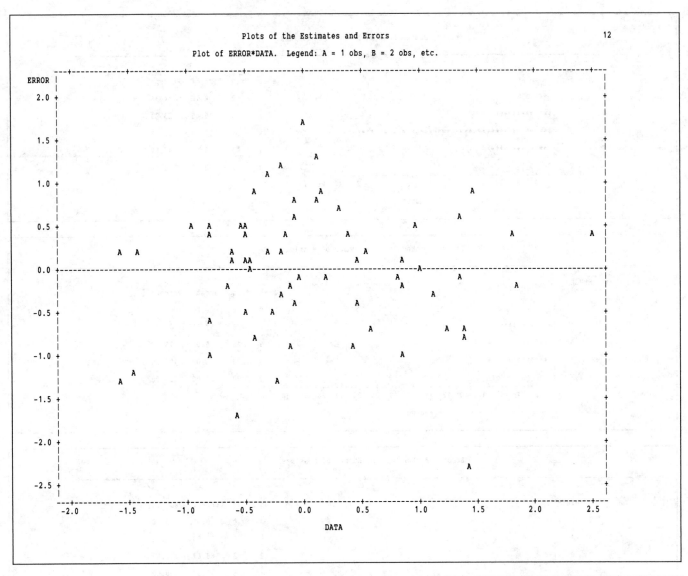

Plots of the Estimates and Errors   12

Plot of ERROR*DATA.   Legend: A = 1 obs, B = 2 obs, etc.

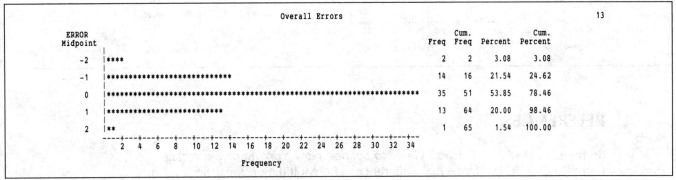

Overall Errors   13

ERROR Midpoint		Freq	Cum. Freq	Percent	Cum. Percent
-2	|****	2	2	3.08	3.08
-1	|************************	14	16	21.54	24.62
0	|***	35	51	53.85	78.46
1	|*********************	13	64	20.00	98.46
2	|**	1	65	1.54	100.00

        2 4 6 8 10 12 14 16 18 20 22 24 26 28 30 32 34

Frequency

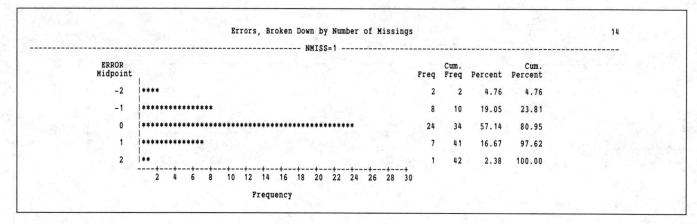

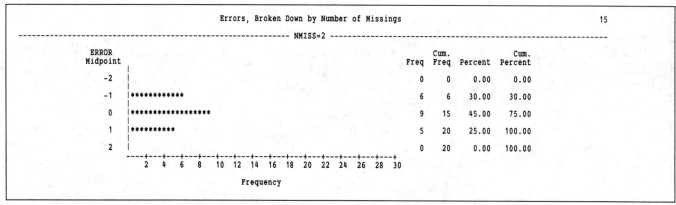

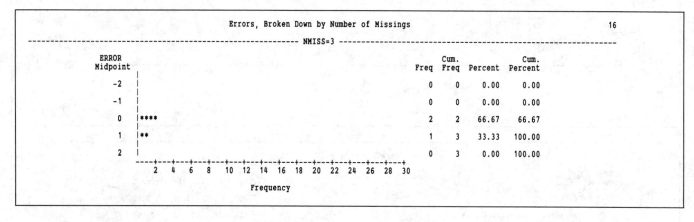

REFERENCES

de Boor, C. (1978), *A Practical Guide to Splines*, New York: Springer Verlag.

Carroll, J.D. (1972), "Individual Differences and Multidimensional Scaling," in *Multidimensional Scaling: Theory and Applications in the Behavioral Sciences (Volume 1)*, eds. R.N. Shepard, A.K. Romney, and S.B. Nerlove, New York: Seminar Press.

Eckart, C. and Young, G. (1936), "The Approximation of One Matrix by Another of Lower Rank," *Psychometrika*, 1, 211–218.

Fisher, R. (1938), *Statistical Methods for Research Workers (10th Edition)*, Edinburgh: Oliver and Boyd Press.

Gabriel, K.R. (1981), "Biplot Display of Multivariate Matrices for Inspection of Data and Diagnosis," *Interpreting Multivariate Data*, ed. V. Barnett, London: John Wiley & Sons, Inc.

Gifi, A. (1981), *Nonlinear Multivariate Analysis*, Department of Data Theory, The University of Leiden, The Netherlands.

Goodnight, J.H. (1978), SAS Technical Report R-106, *The SWEEP Operator: Its Importance in Statistical Computing*, Cary, NC: SAS Institute Inc.

Harman, H.H. (1976), *Modern Factor Analysis, 3rd Edition*, Chicago: University of Chicago Press.

Hotelling, H. (1933), "Analysis of a Complex of Statistical Variables into Principal Components," *Journal of Educational Psychology*, 24, 498–520.

Kuhfeld, W.F., Sarle, W.S., and Young, F.W. (1985), "Methods of Generating Model Estimates in the PRINQUAL Macro," *SAS Users Group International Conference Proceedings: SUGI 10*, Cary, NC: SAS Institute Inc., 962–971.

Kuhfeld, W.F., and de Leeuw, J., "Optimal Scaling of Partitioned Variables," (in preparation).

Kruskal, J.B. (1964)," Multidimensional Scaling By Optimizing Goodness of Fit to a Nonmetric Hypothesis," *Psychometrika*, 29, 1–27.

Kruskal, J.B., and Shepard, R.N. (1974), "A Nonmetric Variety of Linear Factor Analysis," *Psychometrika*, 38, 123–157.

de Leeuw, J. (1985), (Personal Conversation).

de Leeuw, J. (1986), "Regression with Optimal Scaling of the Dependent Variable," Department of Data Theory, The University of Leiden, The Netherlands.

van Rijckeveorsel, J. (1982), "Canonical Analysis with B-Splines," in *COMPUSTAT 1982*, Part I, eds. H. Caussinus, P. Ettinger, and R. Tomassone, Vienna: Wein, Physica Verlag.

Sarle, W.S. (1984), (Personal Conversation).

SAS Institute Inc. (1985), *SAS User's Guide: Statistics, Version 5 Edition*. Cary, NC: SAS Institute Inc.

SAS Institute Inc. (1985), SAS Technical Report P-135, *The Matrix Procedure: Language and Applications*, Cary, NC: SAS Institute Inc.

Siegel, S. (1956), *Nonparametric Statistics*, New York: McGraw Hill Book Co.

Smith, P.L. (1979), "Splines as a Useful and Convenient Statistical Tool," *The American Statistician*, 33, 57–62.

Tenenhaus, M. and Vachette, J.L. (1977), "PRINQUAL: Un Programme d'Analyse en Composantes Principales d'un Ensemble de Variables Nominales ou Numeriques," *Les Cahiers de Recherche #68*, CESA, Jouy-en-Josas, France.

Winsberg, S. and Ramsay, J.O. (1983), "Monotone Spline Transformations for Dimension Reduction," *Psychometrika*, 48, 575–595.

Young, F.W. (1981), "Quantitative Analysis of Qualitative Data," *Psychometrika*, 46, 357–388.

Young, F.W., Takane, Y., and deLeeuw, J. (1978), "The Principal Components of Mixed Measurement Level Multivariate Data: An Alternating Least Squares Method with Optimal Scaling Features," *Psychometrika*, 43, 279–281.

Chapter 35

The PROBIT
Procedure

ABSTRACT   1325
INTRODUCTION   1325
SPECIFICATIONS   1327
  PROC PROBIT Statement   1327
  BY Statement   1330
  CLASS Statement   1330
  MODEL Statement   1330
  OUTPUT Statement   1333
  WEIGHT Statement   1334
DETAILS   1334
  Missing Values   1334
  Computational Method   1334
  Model Specification   1335
  Distributions   1336
  Lack of Fit Tests   1336
  Tolerance Distribution   1337
  Inverse Confidence Limits   1337
  OUTEST= Data Set   1338
  Historical Notes   1339
  Printed Output   1339
EXAMPLES   1340
  Example 1:   Dosage Levels   1340
  Example 2:   Multilevel Response   1344
  Example 3:   Logistic Regression   1348
REFERENCES   1350

ABSTRACT

The PROBIT procedure calculates maximum-likelihood estimates of regression parameters and natural (threshold) response rate for biological quantal assay response data or other discrete event data. This includes probit, logit, ordinal logistic, and gompit regression models.

INTRODUCTION

Probit analysis arose from the need to analyze qualitative (dichotomous or polychotomous) dependent variables within the regression framework. Many response variables are qualitative (yes/no) by nature, while others are measured qualitatively rather than continuously (degree of agreement). Ordinary least squares (OLS) regression has been shown to be inadequate when the dependent variable is discrete. Probit or logit analyses are better suited than OLS when the response is discrete.

The PROBIT procedure computes maximum-likelihood estimates of the parameters **b** and C of the probit equation using a modified Newton-Raphson algorithm. When the response Y is binary, the probit equation is

$$p = \Pr(Y = 0) = C + (1 - C)F(\mathbf{x}'\mathbf{b})$$

where

> **b**   is a vector of parameter estimates.
>
> F   is a cumulative distribution function (the normal, logistic, or Gompertz).
>
> **x**   is a vector of independent variables.
>
> p   is the probability of a response.
>
> C   is the natural (threshold) response rate.

The choice of the distribution function F (normal for the probit model, logistic for the logit model, and Gompertz for the gompit model) determines the type of analysis. For most problems, there is relatively little difference between the normal and logistic specifications of the model. Both distributions are symmetric about the value zero. The Gompertz distribution, however, is not symmetric, approaching zero on the left more rapidly than it approaches 1 on the right. You should use the Gompertz distribution only where such asymmetry is appropriate.

As with OLS, the independent variables **x** can be random variables or fixed values, as in experimental designs. The only requirement is that they be linearly independent. Exact or near dependencies among the independent variables can lead to unstable estimates.

You can request that the natural (threshold) response rate C be estimated. If you have an initial estimate of C from a control group, it can be specified. Optionally, the natural parameter C can be set to a constant value and not estimated. The default value for C is 0.

The data set used by PROC PROBIT must include either a response variable giving the level of response for each observation or a pair of variables giving the number of subjects tested and the number of subjects responding for each vector of the independent variable values.

Two goodness of fit chi-square values are computed if requested: a Pearson chi-square test and a log-likelihood ratio chi-square test. Inverse confidence limits for one of the independent variables can also be requested. The confidence limits are computed using a critical value of 1.96, which corresponds to an approximate 95 percent confidence interval. If the Pearson goodness of fit chi-square test is requested and the p-value for the test is too small, variances and covariances are adjusted by a heterogeneity factor (the goodness of fit chi-square divided by its degrees of freedom) and a critical value from the t distribution is used to compute the fiducial limits. The p-value used for the chi-square test can be set with the HPROB= option. The default p-value is 0.10.

SPECIFICATIONS

The following statements are available in PROC PROBIT:

PROC PROBIT <*options*>;	must precede **MODEL** statement
CLASS *variables*;	optional
	must precede **MODEL** statement
MODEL *response=independents*< / *options*>;	required
BY *variables*;	
OUTPUT <**OUT**=*SAS-data-set*> <*options*>;	optional
WEIGHT *variable*;	statements

The MODEL statement is required. If a CLASS statement is used, it must precede the MODEL statement.

PROC PROBIT Statement

PROC PROBIT <*options*>;

The PROC PROBIT statement starts the procedure. The options available with the PROC PROBIT statement are listed in the table below and then described following the table in alphabetical order.

Task	Option
Name input/output data sets	
name input data set	DATA=
name an output data set for parameters	OUTEST=
request covariances be included in OUTEST	COVOUT
Specify model	
specify the order of levels of class variables	ORDER=
control the natural response rate	OPTC
	C=
replace first continuous variable (dose)	
by its natural log	LOG
replace first continuous variable (dose)	
by its common log	LOG10
request inverse confidence limits	INVERSECL
Test fit of the model	
perform a lack of fit test	LACKFIT
set probability level for goodness of fit	HPROB=
Suppress printed output	NOPRINT

COVOUT

writes the covariance estimates to the OUTEST= data set.

C=*rate*

OPTC

controls how the natural response is handled. Specify OPTC to request that the estimation of the natural (threshold) response rate C be optimized. Specify C=*rate* for the natural response rate or initial estimate of natural response rate. The natural response rate value must be a number between 0 and 1 and is determined as follows:

1. If you specify neither OPTC nor C=, a natural response rate of zero is assumed.
2. If you specify both OPTC and C=, C= should be a reasonable initial estimate of the natural response rate. For example, you could use the ratio of the number of responses to the number of subjects in a control group.
3. If you specify C= but not OPTC, the natural response rate is set to the specified value and not estimated.
4. If you specify OPTC but not C=, PROC PROBIT's action depends on the response variable as follows:
   a. If you specify either LN or LOG10 and some subjects have the first independent variable (dose) values less than or equal to zero, these subjects are treated as a control group. The initial estimate of C is then the ratio of the number of responses to the number of subjects in this group.
   b. If you do not specify LN or LOG10 or there is no control group, then
      i. If all responses are greater than zero, the initial estimate of natural rate is the minimal response rate (the ratio of the number of responses to the number of subjects in a dose group) across all dose levels.
      ii. If one or more of the responses is zero (making the response rate zero in that dose group), the initial estimate of natural rate is the reciprocal of twice the largest number of subjects in any dose group in the experiment.

DATA=*SAS-data-set*

names the SAS data set to be used by PROC PROBIT. By default, the procedure uses the most recently created SAS data set.

HPROB=*p*

specifies a probability level other than 0.10 to indicate goodness of fit. For Pearson goodness of fit chi-square values with probability greater than the HPROB= value, the fiducial limits are computed using a critical value of 1.96. For chi-square values with probability less than the HPROB= value, the critical value is a 0.95 two-sided quantile value taken from the t distribution with degrees of freedom equal to $(k-1)*m-q$, where k is the number of levels for the response variable, m is the number of different sets of independent variable values, and q is the number of parameters fit in the model. The LACKFIT option must also be specified for this option to have any effect. Note that HPROB= can also appear in the MODEL statement. When HPROB= is specified in both the PROC PROBIT and the MODEL statements, the MODEL statement option takes precedence.

INVERSECL
: computes confidence limits for the values of the first continuous independent variable (usually dose) that yield selected response values. If the algorithm fails to converge (this can happen when C is nonzero), missing values are reported for the confidence limits. See **Inverse Confidence Limits** later in this chapter for details. Note that INVERSECL can also appear in the MODEL statement.

LACKFIT
: performs two goodness of fit tests, a Pearson chi-square test, and a log-likelihood ratio chi-square test. The data set must be sorted by the independent variables before the PROBIT procedure is run if you want to perform a test of fit. This test is not appropriate if the data are very sparse, with only a few values at each set of the independent variable values. See **DETAILS** later in this chapter for a description of the test. If the Pearson chi-square test statistic is significant, then the covariance estimates and standard error estimates are adjusted. See **INTRODUCTION** for details of the adjustment. Note that LACKFIT can also appear in the MODEL statement.

LOG
LN
: analyzes the data by replacing the first continuous independent variable by its natural (Naperian) logarithm. This variable is usually the dosage level of some treatment. In addition to the usual output given by the INVERSECL option, the estimated dose values and 95 percent fiducial limits for dose are also printed if requested. If you specify OPTC, any observations with a dose value less than or equal to zero are used in the estimation as a control group.

LOG10
: specifies an analysis like that of LN or LOG above, except that the common logarithm (log to the base 10) of the dose value is used rather than the natural logarithm.

NOPRINT
: suppresses printing of the output.

OPTC
: see C= option for details.

ORDER=DATA | FORMATTED | FREQ | INTERNAL
: specifies the sorting order for the levels of the classification variables (specified in the CLASS statement). This ordering determines which parameters in the model correspond to each level in the data. The table below shows how PROBIT interprets values of ORDER=.

Value of ORDER=	Levels Sorted by
DATA	order of appearance in the input data set
FORMATTED	formatted value
FREQ	descending frequency count; levels with the most observations come first in the order
INTERNAL	unformatted value

By default, ORDER=FORMATTED. For FORMATTED and INTERNAL, the sort order is machine dependent. For more information on sorting order, see Chapter 31, "The SORT Procedure," in the *SAS Procedures Guide, Version 6, Third Edition*, and Chapter 4, "Rules of the SAS Language," in *SAS Language: Reference, Version 6, First Edition*.

OUTEST= *SAS-data-set*

names a SAS data set to contain the parameter estimates and, optionally, their estimated covariances. If this option is not specified, this output data set is not created. The contents of the data set are described in **OUTEST=Data Set** later in this chapter.

BY Statement

BY *variables*;

A BY statement can be used with PROC PROBIT to obtain separate analyses on observations in groups defined by the BY variables. When a BY statement appears, the procedure expects the input data set to be sorted in order of the BY variables.

If your input data set is not sorted in ascending order, use one of the following alternatives:

- Use the SORT procedure with a similar BY statement to sort the data.
- Use the BY statement options NOTSORTED or DESCENDING in the BY statement for the PROBIT procedure. As a cautionary note, the NOTSORTED option does not mean that the data are unsorted, but rather means that the data are arranged in groups (according to values of the BY variables) and that these groups are not necessarily in alphabetical or increasing numeric order.
- Use the DATASETS procedure (in base SAS software) to create an index on the BY variables.

For more information on the BY statement, see the discussion in *SAS Language: Reference*.

CLASS Statement

CLASS *variables*;

The CLASS statement names the classification variables to be used in the analysis. Classification variables can be either character or numeric. If a single response variable is given in the MODEL statement, it must also be listed in a CLASS statement.

Class levels are determined from the formatted values of the CLASS variables. Thus, you can use formats to group values into levels. See the discussion of the FORMAT procedure in *SAS Language: Reference*.

If the CLASS statement is used, it must appear before any of the MODEL statements.

MODEL Statement

<*label*>: **MODEL** *response=independents* < / *options*>;
<*label*>: **MODEL** *events/trials=independents* < / *options*>;

The MODEL statement names the variables to be used as the response and the independent variables. Additionally, the distribution to be used to model the response can be specified, as well as other options. More than one MODEL statement can be specified with the PROBIT procedure. The optional *label* is used to label output from the matching MODEL statement.

The *response* can be a single variable whose value is used to indicate the level of observed response. Such a response variable must be listed in the CLASS statement. For example, the response might be a variable called SYMPTOMS that takes on the values **NONE**, **MILD**, or **SEVERE**. Note that for dichotomous response variables, the probability of the lowest sorted value is modeled (see **DETAILS** later in this chapter). Because the model fit by the PROBIT procedure requires ordered response levels, you may need to use either the ORDER=DATA option in the PROC PROBIT statement or a numeric coding of the response to get the desired ordering of levels.

Alternatively, the response can be specified as a pair of variable names separated by a slash (/). Both variables must be numeric and nonnegative, and the ratio of the first variable value to the second variable value must be between 0 and 1, inclusive. For example, the variables might be HITS, a variable containing the number of hits for a baseball player, and AT_BATS, a variable containing the number of times at bat. A model for hitting proportion as a function of age could be specified as

```
model hits/at_bats=age;
```

The table below lists the options that can appear in the MODEL statement. Descriptions are given in alphabetic order following the table.

Task	Option
Specify model	
specify cumulative distribution function	D=
specify initial estimate for intercept	INTERCEPT=
specify initial estimates for regression parameters	INITIAL=
fit a no-intercept model	NOINT
Fit model	
set probability level for test of fit	HPROB=
set maximum iterations	MAXITER=
set convergence criterion	CONVERGE=
set tolerance for testing singularity	SINGULAR=
Control printing	
print estimated correlation matrix	CORRB
print estimated covariance matrix	COVB
print inverse confidence limits	INVERSECL
print iteration history	ITPRINT
print lack of fit test results	LACKFIT

CONVERGE=*value*
> gives the convergence criterion. The iterations are considered to have converged when the maximum change in the parameter estimates between Newton-Raphson steps is less than the value specified. The change is a relative change if the parameter is greater than 0.01 in absolute value; otherwise, it is an absolute change. By default, CONVERGE=0.001.

CORRB
> prints the estimated correlation matrix of the parameter estimates.

COVB
prints the estimated covariance matrix of the parameter estimates.

D=*distribution-type*
specifies the cumulative distribution function used to model the response probabilities. The distributions are described in **DETAILS** later in this chapter. Valid values for *distribution-type* are

NORMAL   the normal distribution for the probit model

LOGISTIC   the logistic distribution for the logit model

GOMPERTZ

the Gompertz distribution for the gompit model.

By default, D=NORMAL.

HPROB=*value*
specifies a probability level other than 0.10 to indicate a good fit. For Pearson goodness of fit chi-square values with probability greater than the HPROB= value, the fiducial limits are computed using a critical value of 1.96. For chi-square values with probability less than the HPROB= value, the critical value is a 0.95 two-sided quantile value taken from the t distribution with degrees of freedom equal to the $(k-1)*m-q$, where k is the number of levels for the response variable, m is the number of different sets of independent variable values, and q is the number of parameters fit in the model. The LACKFIT option must also be specified for this option to have any effect.

If HPROB= is specified in both the PROC PROBIT and MODEL statements, the MODEL statement option takes precedence.

INITIAL=*values*
sets initial values for the other parameters in the model. The values must be given in the order that the variables are listed in the MODEL statement. If some of the independent variables listed in the MODEL statement are classification variables, then there must be as many values given for that variable as there are classification levels minus 1. The INITIAL= option can be specified as follows:

Type of List	Specification
list separated by blanks	`initial=3 4 5`
list separated by commas	`initial=3,4,5`
x to y	`initial=3 to 5`
x to y by z	`initial=3 to 5 by 1`
combination of above	`initial=1,3 to 5,9`

By default, all parameters have initial estimates of zero.

INTERCEPT=*value*
initializes the intercept parameter to *value*. By default, INTERCEPT=0.

INVERSECL
computes confidence limits for the values of the first continuous independent variable (usually dose) that yield selected response values. When the algorithm fails to converge, missing values are reported for the confidence limits.

If INVERSECL is specified in both the PROC PROBIT and MODEL statements, the MODEL statement option takes precedence.

ITPRINT

prints the iteration history, the final evaluation of the gradient, and the second derivative matrix (Hessian).

LACKFIT

performs two goodness of fit tests, a Pearson chi-square test, and a log-likelihood ratio chi-square test for the fitted model. The data set must be sorted by the independent variables before the PROBIT procedure is run if you want to perform a test of fit. This test is not appropriate if the data are very sparse, with only a few values at each set of the independent variable values. See **Lack of Fit Tests** later in this chapter for a description of the test. If the Pearson chi-square test statistic is significant, then the covariance estimates and standard error estimates are adjusted. See **INTRODUCTION** for details of the adjustment.

If LACKFIT is specified in both the PROC PROBIT and MODEL statements, the MODEL statement option takes precedence.

MAXITER=*value*

gives the maximum number of iterations to be performed in estimating the parameters. By default, MAXITER=50.

NOINT

fits a model with no intercept parameter. This is most useful when the response is binary. When the response has k levels, then $k-1$ intercept parameters are fit. The NOINT option sets the intercept parameter corresponding to the lowest response level equal to zero.

SINGULAR=*value*

gives the singularity criterion for determining linear dependencies in the set of independent variables. The sum of squares and cross products matrix of the independent variables is formed and swept. If the relative size of a pivot becomes less than the value specified, then the variable corresponding to the pivot is considered to be linearly dependent on the previous set of variables considered. By default, SINGULAR=1E-12.

OUTPUT Statement

OUTPUT <OUT=*SAS-data-set*> <*keyword*=*name* . . . *keyword*=*name*>;

The OUTPUT statement creates a new SAS data set containing all variables in the input data set, the fitted probabilities, the estimate of $x'\beta$, and the estimate of its standard error. Additionally, if the *single variable response* syntax is specified in the MODEL statement, then a variable named _LEVEL_ is added to the data set. This variable contains the values of the response variable for all but the lowest response level. You can use multiple OUTPUT statements. Each OUTPUT statement creates a new data set and applies only to the preceding MODEL statement. If you want to create a permanent SAS data set, you must specify a two-level name. (See "SAS Files" in *SAS Language: Reference, Version 6, First Edition* and "Introduction to DATA Step Processing" in *SAS Language and Procedures: Usage, Version 6, First Edition*, for more information on permanent SAS data sets.)

Details on the specifications in the OUTPUT statement are given below.

keyword=name   specifies the statistics to include in the output data set and gives names to the new variables that contain the statistics. Specify a keyword for each desired statistic (see the list of keywords below), an equal sign, and the variable to contain the statistic.

The keywords allowed and the statistics they represent are as follows:

PROB | P	cumulative probability estimates
STD	standard error estimates of $a_j + x'b$
XBETA	estimates of $a_j + x'\beta$.

OUT=SAS-data-set

names the output data set. By default, the new data set is named using the DATAn convention to name the new data set.

When the *single variable response* syntax is used, the _LEVEL_ variable is added to the output data set, and there are $k-1$ output observations for each input observation, where k is the number of response levels. There is no observation output corresponding to the lowest response level. For each of the $k-1$ observations, the PROB variable contains the fitted probability of obtaining the level indicated by the _LEVEL_ variable, the XBETA variable contains $a_j + x'b$, where j references the levels and $a_1 = 0$, and the STD variable contains the standard error estimate of the XBETA variable. See **DETAILS** later in this chapter for the formulas for the parameterizations.

WEIGHT Statement

WEIGHT *variable*;

A WEIGHT statement can be used with PROC PROBIT to weight each observation by the value of the variable specified. The contribution of each observation to the likelihood function is multiplied by the value of the weight variable. Observations with zero, negative, or missing weights are not used in model estimation.

DETAILS

Missing Values

PROC PROBIT does not use any observations that have missing values for any of the independent variables or the response variables.

Computational Method

The log likelihood function is maximized by means of a ridge-stabilized Newton-Raphson algorithm. Initial parameter estimates are set to zero. The INITIAL= and INTERCEPT= options to the MODEL statement can be used to give nonzero initial estimates.

The log likelihood function, L, is computed as

$$L = \Sigma w_i \ln(p_i)$$

where the sum is over the observations in the data set, w_i is the weight for the ith observation, and p_i is the modeled probability of the observed response. In the case of the *events/trials* syntax in the MODEL statement, each observation contributes two terms corresponding to the probability of the event and the probability of its complement. This log likelihood function differs from the log likelihood function for a binomial or multinomial distribution by additive terms consisting of the log of binomial or multinomial coefficients. These terms are parameter independent and do not affect the model estimation or the standard errors and tests.

The estimated covariance matrix, **V**, of the parameter estimates is computed as the negative inverse of the information matrix of second derivatives of L with respect to the parameters evaluated at the final parameter estimates. Thus, the estimated covariance matrix is derived from the observed information matrix rather than the expected information matrix (these are generally not the same). The standard error estimates for the parameter estimates are taken as the square roots of the corresponding diagonal elements of **V**.

For a classification effect, an overall chi-square statistic is computed as

$$\chi^2 = \mathbf{b}_1'\mathbf{V}_{11}^{-1}\mathbf{b}_1$$

where $\mathbf{V}_{11}$ is the submatrix of **V** corresponding to the indicator variables for the classification effect, and $\mathbf{b}_1$ is the vector of parameter estimates corresponding to the classification effect. This chi-square statistic has degrees of freedom equal to the rank of $\mathbf{V}_{11}$.

If some of the independent variables are perfectly correlated with the response pattern, then the theoretical parameter estimates may be infinite. Although fitted probabilities of 0 and 1 are not especially pathological, infinite parameter estimates are required to yield these probabilities. Due to the finite precision of computer arithmetic, the actual parameter estimates will not be infinite. Indeed, since the tails of the distributions allowed in the PROBIT procedure become small rapidly, an argument of the nature of 20 to the cumulative distribution function becomes effectively infinite. In the case of such parameter estimates, the standard error estimates and the corresponding chi-square tests are not trustworthy.

The chi-square tests for the individual parameter values are Wald tests based on the observed information matrix and the parameter estimates. The theory behind these tests assumes large samples. If the samples are not large, it may be better to base the tests on log likelihood ratios. These changes in log likelihood can be obtained by fitting the model twice, once with all the parameters of interest and once leaving out the parameters to be tested. See Cox and Oakes (1984) for a discussion of the merits of some possible test methods.

Model Specification

For a two-level response, the probability that the lesser response occurs is modeled by the probit equation as

$$p = C + (1 - C)\, F(\mathbf{x}'\mathbf{b}) \quad .$$

The probability of the other (complementary) event is $1 - p$.

For a multilevel response with outcomes labeled l_i for $i = 1, 2, \ldots, k$, the probability, p_j, of observing level l_j is

$$p_1 = C + (1 - C)\, F(\mathbf{x}'\mathbf{b})$$

$$p_2 = (1 - C)(F(a_2 + \mathbf{x}'\mathbf{b}) - F(\mathbf{x}'\mathbf{b}))$$

$$p_j = (1 - C)(F(a_j + \mathbf{x}'\mathbf{b}) - F(a_{j-1} + \mathbf{x}'\mathbf{b}))$$

$$p_k = (1 - C)(1 - F(a_{k-1} + \mathbf{x}'\mathbf{b})) \quad .$$

Thus, for a k level response, there are $k-2$ additional parameters, $a_2, a_3, \ldots, a_{k-1}$, estimated. These parameters are denoted INTER.$j, j=2, 3, \ldots, k-1$ in the printed output.

An intercept parameter is always added to the set of independent variables as the first term in the model unless the NOINT option to the MODEL statement is specified. If a classification variable taking on k levels is used as one of the independent variables, a set of k indicator variables is generated to model the effect of this variable. Because of the presence of the intercept term, there can be at most $k-1$ degrees of freedom for this effect in the model.

Distributions

The distributions, F(x), allowed in the PROBIT procedure are specified with the D= option in the model statement. Allowable distributions are:

$$\int_{-\infty}^{x} \frac{e^{-z^2/2}}{\sqrt{2\pi}} \, dz \qquad \text{(normal)}$$

$$1/(1 + \exp(-x)) \qquad \text{(logistic)}$$

$$1 - \exp(-\exp(x)) \qquad \text{(Gompertz)}.$$

The variances of these three distributions are not all equal to 1, and their means are not all equal to 0. Their means and variances are shown below, where γ is the Euler constant.

Distribution	Mean	Variance
Normal	0	1
Logistic	0	$\pi^2/3$
Gompertz	$-\gamma$	$\pi^2/6$

In comparing parameter estimates using different distributions, you need to take into account the different scalings and, for the Gompertz, a possible shift in location. For example, if the fitted probabilities are in the neighborhood of .1 to .9, then the parameter estimates from the logistic model should be about $\pi/\sqrt{3}$ larger than the estimates from the probit model.

Lack of Fit Tests

Two goodness of fit tests can be requested from the PROBIT procedure. If there is only a single continuous independent variable, the data are internally sorted to group response values by the independent variable. Otherwise, the data are aggregated into groupings that are delimited whenever a change is observed in one of the independent variables. Because of this grouping, the data set should be sorted by the independent variables before the PROBIT procedure is run, if the LACKFIT option is requested.

The Pearson chi-square test statistic is computed as

$$\Sigma_i \Sigma_j \, (r_{ij} - n_i p_{ij})^2 / n_i p_{ij}$$

where the sum on i is over grouping, the sum on j is over levels of response, the r_{ij} is the weight of the response at the jth level for the ith grouping, n_i is the total weight at the ith grouping, and p_{ij} is the fitted probability for the jth level at the ith grouping.

The log likelihood ratio chi-square test statistic is computed as

$$2 \, \Sigma_i \Sigma_j \, r_{ij} \, \ln(r_{ij}/n_i p_{ij}) \quad .$$

If the modeled probabilities fit the data, these statistics should be approximately distributed as chi-square with degrees of freedom equal to $(k-1)*m-q$, where k is the number of levels of the multinomial or binomial response, m is the number of sets of independent variables, and q is the number of parameters fit in the model.

Tolerance Distribution

For a single independent variable representing a dosage level, the models for the probabilities can be justified on the basis of a population with mean μ and scale parameter σ of tolerances for the subjects. Then, given a dose x, the probability, P, of observing a response in a particular subject is the probability that the subject's tolerance is less than the dose, or

$$P = F((x - \mu)/\sigma) \quad .$$

Thus, in this case, the intercept parameter, b_0, and the regression parameter, b_1, are related to μ and σ by

$$b_1 = 1/\sigma$$

and

$$b_0 = -\mu/\sigma \quad .$$

Note: The parameter σ is not equal to the standard deviation of the population of tolerances for the logistic and Gompertz distributions.

Inverse Confidence Limits

In bioassay problems, estimates of the values of the independent variables that yield a desired response are often needed. The INVERSECL option requests that confidence limits be computed for the value of the independent variable that yields a specified response. These limits are computed only for the first continuous variable effect in the model. The other variables are set at either their mean values if they are continuous or at the reference level if they are discrete variables. For a discussion of inverse confidence limits, see Hubert, Bohidar, and Peace (1988).

For the PROBIT procedure, the response variable is a probability. An estimate of the dose level needed for a response of p, is given by

$$\hat{x}_1 = (F^{-1}(p) - \mathbf{x}^{*\prime} \mathbf{b}^*)/b_1$$

where F is the cumulative distribution function used to model the probability, $\mathbf{x}^*$ is the vector of independent variables excluding the first one, $\mathbf{b}^*$ is the vector of parameter estimates excluding the first one, and b_1 is the estimated regression coefficient for the independent variable of interest. This estimator is given as a ratio of random variables, say $r = a\,b$.

Confidence limits for this ratio can be computed using Fieller's theorem. A brief description of this theorem is given below. See Finney (1971) for a more complete description of Fieller's theorem.

If the random variables a and b are thought to be distributed as jointly normal, then, for any fixed value r, the following probability statement holds if $a - rb$ has mean zero:

$$\text{Prob}((a - rb)^2 > z^2(V_{aa} - 2rV_{ab} + r^2V_{bb})) = \alpha$$

if z is an $\alpha/2$ quantile from the standard normal distribution and **V** is the variance-covariance matrix of a and b. Usually the inequality can be solved for r to yield a confidence interval. The PROBIT procedure uses a value of 1.96 for z, corresponding to an α value of 0.05, unless the goodness of fit p-value is less than the specified HPROB value. When this happens, the covariance matrix used is scaled by the heterogeneity factor, and a t distribution quantile is used for z.

It is possible for the roots of the equation for r to be imaginary or for the confidence interval to be all points outside of an interval. In these cases the limits are set to missing by the PROBIT procedure.

Although the normal and logistic distributions give very comparable fitted values of p if the empirically observed proportions are not too extreme, they can give appreciably different values when extrapolated into the tails. Correspondingly, the estimates of the confidence limits and dose values can be different for the two distributions even when they agree quite well in the body of the data. Extrapolation outside of the range of the actual data is often sensitive to model assumptions, and caution is advised if this is necessary.

OUTEST= Data Set

The OUTEST= data set contains parameter estimates and the log likelihood for the specified models. A set of observations is created for each MODEL statement specified. You can use a label in the MODEL statement to distinguish between the estimates for different MODEL statements. If the COVOUT option is specified, the OUTEST= data set also contains the estimated covariance matrix of the parameter estimates.

The OUTEST= data set is not created if there are any CLASS variables in any models. If created, this data set contains each variable used as a dependent or independent variable in any MODEL statement. One observation consists of parameter values for the model with the dependent variable having the value -1. If the COVOUT option is specified, there are additional observations containing the rows of the estimated covariance matrix. For these observations the dependent variable contains the parameter estimate for the corresponding row variable. The variables listed below are also added to the data set:

MODEL   a character variable of length 8 containing the label of the MODEL statement if present, or blank otherwise

NAME   a character variable containing the name of the dependent variable for the parameter estimates observations or the name of the row for the covariance matrix estimates

TYPE   a character variable containing the type of the observation, either 'PARMS' for parameter estimates or 'COV' for covariance estimates

DIST   a character variable containing the name of the distribution modeled

LNLIKE   a numeric variable containing the last computed value of the log likelihood

INTERCEP   a numeric variable containing the intercept parameter estimates and covariances.

Any BY variables specified are also added to the OUTEST= data set.

Historical Notes

The PROBIT procedure used a different syntax in earlier releases of the SAS System. The old syntax still functions as it did in earlier releases with the exception that the plots of fitted and observed values are no longer generated. Equivalent plots can be generated by means of the OUTPUT statement and the PLOT procedure. See **Example 1** for one way to generate these plots.

Earlier releases of the PROBIT procedure defined the probit transform as $5 + \Phi^{-1}(x)$ instead of $\Phi^{-1}(x)$, where Φ is the cumulative distribution function for the standard normal distribution. This was to keep the transformed numbers positive to facilitate computational work. In order to more easily compare probit and logit models, the value 5 is no longer added as part of the probit transformation. It has become customary to refer to this newer model as the NORMIT model.

Printed Output

If the iteration history is requested (with the ITPRINT option), PROC PROBIT prints

1. the current value of the Log Likelihood
2. the ridging parameter for the modified Newton-Raphson optimization process
3. the current estimate of the parameters
4. for a natural (threshold) model, the current estimate of the parameter C (not shown)
5. the values of the Gradient and the Hessian on the last iteration.

When CLASS variables are included, PROC PROBIT prints

6. the numbers of Levels for each CLASS variable
7. the (ordered) Values of the levels
8. the Number of observations used.

After the model is fit, PROC PROBIT prints

9. the name of the input Data Set
10. the name of the Dependent Variable(s)
11. the Number of Observation used
12. the Number of Events and the number of trials
13. the final value of the Log Likelihood function
14. the parameter Estimates
15. the standard error estimates of the parameter estimates
16. approximate chi-square test statistics for the test.

If requested with the COVB or CORRB options, PROC PROBIT prints

17. the estimated covariance matrix for the parameter estimates (not shown)
18. the estimated correlation matrix for the parameter estimates (not shown).

If requested with the LACKFIT option, PROC PROBIT prints

19. a count of the number of levels of the response and the number of distinct sets of independent variables
20. a goodness of fit test based on the Pearson Chi-Square

21. a goodness of fit test based on the likelihood ratio chi-square.

If there is only one independent variable and the normal distribution is used to model the probabilities, PROC PROBIT prints

22. the mean MU of the stimulus tolerance
23. the scale parameter SIGMA of the stimulus tolerance
24. the Covariance Matrix for MU and SIGMA.

If requested with the INVERSECL options, PROC PROBIT also prints

25. the estimated dose along with the 95 percent fiducial limits for probability levels .01 to .10, .15 to .85 by .05, and .90 to .99.

EXAMPLES

Example 1:   Dosage Levels

In this example, DOSE is the level of the stimulus, N is the number of subjects tested at each level of the stimulus, and RESPONSE is the number of subjects responding to that level of the stimulus. Both probit and logit response models are fit to the data. The LOG10 option in the PROC PROBIT statement requests that the log base 10 of DOSE be used as the independent variable. Specifically, for a given level of DOSE, the probability p of a positive response is modeled as

$$p = \text{Pr(response)} = F(b_0 + b_1 * \log 10 \text{ (dose))} .$$

The probabilities are first estimated using the normal distribution function and then using the logistic distribution function. Note that in this model specification, the natural rate is assumed to be zero.

Lack of fit tests and inverse confidence limits are also requested.

In the DATA step that reads the data, a number of observations are generated that have a missing value for the response. Although the PROBIT procedure does not use the observations with the missing values to fit the model, it does give predicted values for all nonmissing sets of independent variables. These data points fill in the plot of fitted and observed values in the logistic model. The plot is that of the estimated logistic cumulative distribution function, with the observed response rates overlayed.

The following statements produce **Output 35.1**:

```
data a;
   infile cards eof=eof;
   input dose n response;
   phat= response/n;
   output;
   return;
eof: do dose=.5 to 7.5 by .25;
       output;
     end;
   cards;
1 10 1
2 12 2
3 10 4
4 10 5
5 12 8
6 10 8
7 10 10
;
```

```
proc probit log10;
  model response/n=dose / lackfit inversecl itprint;
  model response/n=dose / d=logistic inversecl;
  output out=b p=prob std=std xbeta=xbeta;
  title 'Output from Probit Procedure';
run;

proc plot;
  plot phat*dose='X' prob*dose='P' / overlay;
  title 'Plot of Observed and Fitted Probabilities';
run;
```

Output 35.1   Dosage Levels: PROC PROBIT

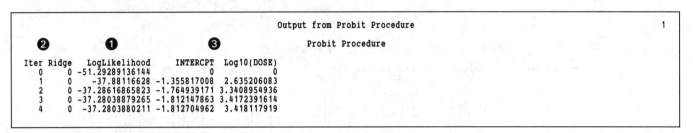

```
                          Output from Probit Procedure                                    1
                             Probit Procedure

Iter Ridge  LogLikelihood     INTERCPT    Log10(DOSE)
   0     0 -51.29289136144           0              0
   1     0    -37.88116628  -1.355817008    2.635206083
   2     0 -37.28616865823  -1.764939171    3.3408954936
   3     0 -37.28038879265  -1.812147863    3.4172391614
   4     0  -37.2803880211  -1.812704962     3.418117919
```

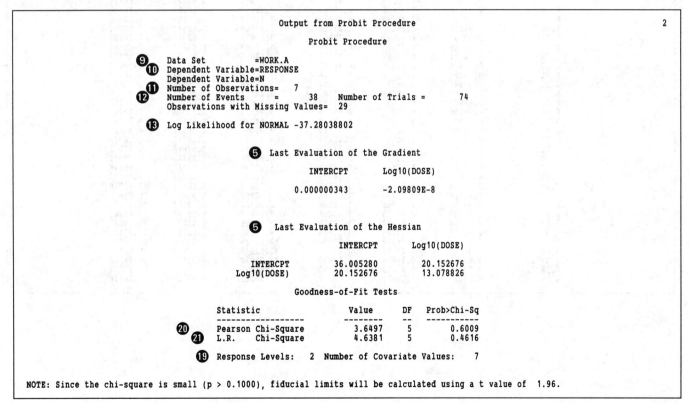

```
                          Output from Probit Procedure                                    2
                             Probit Procedure

 Data Set        =WORK.A
 Dependent Variable=RESPONSE
 Dependent Variable=N
 Number of Observations=  7
 Number of Events     =        38    Number of Trials =          74
 Observations with Missing Values=  29

 Log Likelihood for NORMAL -37.28038802


              Last Evaluation of the Gradient

                   INTERCPT        Log10(DOSE)

                0.000000343       -2.09809E-8


              Last Evaluation of the Hessian
                              INTERCPT        Log10(DOSE)

              INTERCPT       36.005280         20.152676
           Log10(DOSE)      20.152676         13.078826

                        Goodness-of-Fit Tests

        Statistic                Value    DF    Prob>Chi-Sq
        -----------------        -----    --    -----------
        Pearson Chi-Square      3.6497     5         0.6009
        L.R.    Chi-Square      4.6381     5         0.4616

        Response Levels: 2   Number of Covariate Values:    7

NOTE: Since the chi-square is small (p > 0.1000), fiducial limits will be calculated using a t value of  1.96.
```

```
                          Output from Probit Procedure                              3

                               Probit Procedure
                          ⑭          ⑮          ⑯
               Variable DF  Estimate  Std Err  ChiSquare  Pr>Chi  Label/Value

               INTERCPT  1  -1.812705 0.449341 16.27431   0.0001  Intercept
               Log10(DOS) 1  3.41811792 0.745546 21.01963 0.0001

                    Probit Model in Terms of Tolerance Distribution

                          ㉒      MU      ㉓      SIGMA
                              0.530323       0.292559


              ㉔   Estimated Covariance Matrix for Tolerance Parameters

                                        MU              SIGMA

                           MU        0.002418         -0.000409
                           SIGMA    -0.000409          0.004072
```

```
                          Output from Probit Procedure                              4

                               Probit Procedure
     ㉕                        Probit Analysis on DOSE

   Probability   Log10(DOSE) 95 Percent Fiducial Limits      DOSE 95 Percent Fiducial Limits
                              Lower      Upper
     0.01        -0.15027   -0.69520    0.07710        0.70750     0.20174    1.19428
     0.02        -0.07052   -0.55768    0.13475        0.85012     0.27690    1.36381
     0.03        -0.01992   -0.47066    0.17157        0.95517     0.33833    1.48445
     0.04         0.01814   -0.40535    0.19941        1.04266     0.39323    1.58275
     0.05         0.04911   -0.35235    0.22218        1.11971     0.44428    1.66794
     0.06         0.07546   -0.30733    0.24165        1.18976     0.49280    1.74444
     0.07         0.09857   -0.26794    0.25882        1.25478     0.53959    1.81474
     0.08         0.11926   -0.23275    0.27426        1.31600     0.58513    1.88043
     0.09         0.13807   -0.20081    0.28837        1.37427     0.62978    1.94253
     0.10         0.15539   -0.17148    0.30142        1.43019     0.67379    2.00182
     0.15         0.22710   -0.05087    0.35631        1.68696     0.88948    2.27148
     0.20         0.28410    0.04368    0.40124        1.92353     1.10582    2.51907
     0.25         0.33299    0.12342    0.44116        2.15276     1.32868    2.76162
     0.30         0.37690    0.19348    0.47857        2.38180     1.56126    3.01001
     0.35         0.41759    0.25658    0.51505        2.61573     1.80541    3.27375
     0.40         0.45620    0.31428    0.55183        2.85893     2.06198    3.56308
     0.45         0.49356    0.36754    0.58999        3.11573     2.33096    3.89040
     0.50         0.53032    0.41693    0.63057        3.39096     2.61173    4.27141
     0.55         0.56709    0.46296    0.67451        3.69051     2.90372    4.72622
     0.60         0.60444    0.50618    0.72271        4.02199     3.20757    5.28094
     0.65         0.64305    0.54734    0.77603        4.39594     3.52649    5.97082
     0.70         0.68374    0.58745    0.83551        4.82770     3.86764    6.84712
     0.75         0.72765    0.62776    0.90265        5.34134     4.24384    7.99198
     0.80         0.77655    0.66999    0.98009        5.97787     4.67723    9.55182
     0.85         0.83354    0.71675    1.07280        6.81617     5.20898   11.82500
     0.90         0.90525    0.77313    1.19192        8.03992     5.93102   15.55685
     0.91         0.92257    0.78645    1.22098        8.36704     6.11581   16.63355
     0.92         0.94139    0.80083    1.25266        8.73752     6.32162   17.89203
     0.93         0.96208    0.81653    1.28760        9.16385     6.55428   19.39079
     0.94         0.98519    0.83394    1.32673        9.66463     6.82242   21.21933
     0.95         1.01154    0.85367    1.37150       10.26925     7.13946   23.52336
     0.96         1.04250    0.87669    1.42425       11.02811     7.52812   26.56140
     0.97         1.08056    0.90479    1.48930       12.03830     8.03145   30.85292
     0.98         1.13116    0.94189    1.57603       13.52585     8.74757   37.67327
     0.99         1.21092    0.99987    1.71322       16.25233     9.99702   51.66816
```

```
                          Output from Probit Procedure                              5
                              Probit Procedure

          Data Set        =WORK.A
          Dependent Variable=RESPONSE
          Dependent Variable=N
          Number of Observations=   7
          Number of Events        =        38    Number of Trials =        74
          Observations with Missing Values=  29


          Log Likelihood for LOGISTIC -37.11065336
```

```
                          Output from Probit Procedure                              6
                              Probit Procedure

          Variable  DF   Estimate  Std Err ChiSquare  Pr>Chi Label/Value

          INTERCPT   1 -3.2246442 0.886057  13.24465  0.0003 Intercept
          Log10(DOS) 1 5.97017999 1.449172  16.97208  0.0001
```

```
                          Output from Probit Procedure                              7
                              Probit Procedure
                           Probit Analysis on DOSE

   Probability   Log10(DOSE) 95 Percent Fiducial Limits      DOSE 95 Percent Fiducial Limits
                              Lower      Upper

      0.01      -0.22955   -0.97443   0.04234    0.58945    0.10606    1.10241
      0.02      -0.11175   -0.75160   0.12404    0.77312    0.17717    1.33059
      0.03      -0.04212   -0.62020   0.17266    0.90757    0.23977    1.48818
      0.04       0.00780   -0.52620   0.20771    1.01813    0.29772    1.61328
      0.05       0.04693   -0.45266   0.23533    1.11413    0.35264    1.71923
      0.06       0.07925   -0.39207   0.25827    1.20018    0.40545    1.81245
      0.07       0.10686   -0.34039   0.27796    1.27896    0.45668    1.89655
      0.08       0.13103   -0.29522   0.29530    1.35218    0.50673    1.97380
      0.09       0.15259   -0.25503   0.31085    1.42100    0.55586    2.04573
      0.10       0.17209   -0.21876   0.32498    1.48625    0.60428    2.11340
      0.15       0.24958   -0.07553   0.38207    1.77656    0.84036    2.41031
      0.20       0.30792    0.03091   0.42645    2.03199    1.07377    2.66962
      0.25       0.35611    0.11742   0.46451    2.27043    1.31043    2.91417
      0.30       0.39820    0.19143   0.49933    2.50152    1.55391    3.15737
      0.35       0.43644    0.25684   0.53275    2.73172    1.80650    3.40997
      0.40       0.47221    0.31587   0.56619    2.96627    2.06954    3.68293
      0.45       0.50651    0.36985   0.60090    3.21006    2.34343    3.98929
      0.50       0.54013    0.41957   0.63807    3.46837    2.62766    4.34580
      0.55       0.57374    0.46559   0.67895    3.74746    2.92137    4.77469
      0.60       0.60804    0.50846   0.72475    4.05546    3.22449    5.30576
      0.65       0.64381    0.54895   0.77673    4.40366    3.53960    5.98046
      0.70       0.68205    0.58815   0.83638    4.80891    3.87389    6.86087
      0.75       0.72414    0.62752   0.90583    5.29836    4.24153    8.05054
      0.80       0.77233    0.66915   0.98877    5.92009    4.66819    9.74470
      0.85       0.83067    0.71631   1.09243    6.77126    5.20363   12.37174
      0.90       0.90816    0.77561   1.23344    8.09391    5.96506   17.11758
      0.91       0.92766    0.79014   1.26932    8.46559    6.16797   18.59179
      0.92       0.94922    0.80607   1.30913    8.89644    6.39834   20.37650
      0.93       0.97339    0.82378   1.35392    9.40575    6.66466   22.59024
      0.94       1.00100    0.84384   1.40524   10.02317    6.97974   25.42373
      0.95       1.03332    0.86713   1.46548   10.79732    7.36425   29.20649
      0.96       1.07245    0.89511   1.53866   11.81534    7.85434   34.56649
      0.97       1.12237    0.93053   1.63230   13.25466    8.52168   42.88406
      0.98       1.19200    0.97952   1.76331   15.55972    9.53935   57.98471
      0.99       1.30980    1.06166   1.98571   20.40815   11.52540   96.76344
```

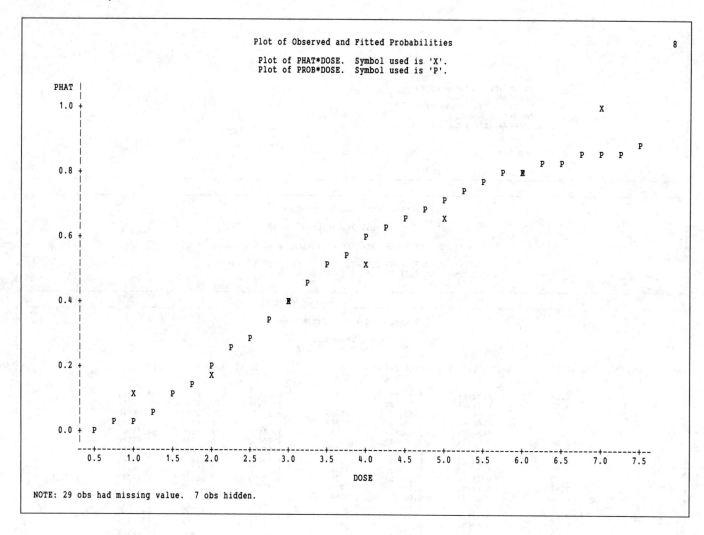

Plot of Observed and Fitted Probabilities

Plot of PHAT*DOSE.   Symbol used is 'X'.
Plot of PROB*DOSE.   Symbol used is 'P'.

NOTE: 29 obs had missing value. 7 obs hidden.

Example 2:   Multilevel Response

In this example, two preparations, a standard preparation and a test preparation, were each given at several dose levels to groups of insects. The symptoms were recorded for each insect within each group, and two multilevel probit models were fit. Because the natural sort order of the three levels is not the same as the response order, the ORDER=DATA option is specified in the PROC statement to get the desired order.

The first model uses a PREPDOSE variable to allow for nonparallelism between the dose response curves for the two preparations. The results of this first model indicate that the parameter for the PREPDOSE variable is not significant, having a Wald chi-square of 0.73. Also, since the first model is a generalization of the second, a likelihood ratio test statistic for this same parameter can be obtained by multiplying the difference in log likelihoods between the two models by 2. The value obtained, $2 \times (-345.94 - (-346.31))$, is 0.73. This is in close agreement with the Wald chi-square from the first model. The lack of fit test statistics for the two models do not indicate a problem with either fit.

The following statements produce **Output 35.2**:

```
data multi;
   input prep $ dose symptoms $ n;
   ldose=log10(dose);
   if prep='test' then prepdose=ldose;
   else prepdose=0;
   cards;
stand      10      None       33
stand      10      Mild        7
stand      10      Severe     10
stand      20      None       17
stand      20      Mild       13
stand      20      Severe     17
stand      30      None       14
stand      30      Mild        3
stand      30      Severe     28
stand      40      None        9
stand      40      Mild        8
stand      40      Severe     32
test       10      None       44
test       10      Mild        6
test       10      Severe      0
test       20      None       32
test       20      Mild       10
test       20      Severe     12
test       30      None       23
test       30      Mild        7
test       30      Severe     21
test       40      None       16
test       40      Mild        6
test       40      Severe     19
;

proc probit order=data;
   class prep symptoms;
   nonpara: model symptoms=prep ldose prepdose / lackfit;
   weight n;
   parallel: model symptoms=prep ldose / lackfit;
   weight n;
   title 'Probit Models for Symptom Severity';
run;
```

Output 35.2   Multilevel Response: PROC PROBIT

```
                        Probit Models for Symptom Severity                           1

                                 Probit Procedure
                            Class Level Information
                                 6             7
                        Class    Levels    Values

                        SYMPTOMS    3       None Mild Severe

                        PREP        2       stand test

                        Number of observations used = 23  8
```

```
                        Probit Models for Symptom Severity                           2

                                 Probit Procedure

        Data Set           =WORK.MULTI
        Dependent Variable=SYMPTOMS
        Weight Variable    =N

                Weighted Frequency Counts for the Ordered Response Categories

                                Level    Count
                                None      188
                                Mild       60
                                Severe    139


        Log Likelihood for NORMAL -345.9401767

                              Goodness-of-Fit Tests

                 Statistic                Value     DF    Prob>Chi-Sq
                 ------------------       --------   --   -----------
                 Pearson Chi-Square       12.7930    11     0.3071
                 L.R.   Chi-Square        15.7869    11     0.1492

                 Response Levels:   3   Number of Covariate Values:     8

        NOTE: Since the chi-square is small (p > 0.1000), fiducial limits will be calculated using a t value of  1.96.
```

```
                        Probit Models for Symptom Severity                           3

                                 Probit Procedure

        Variable  DF   Estimate   Std Err   ChiSquare  Pr>Chi  Label/Value

        INTERCPT  1  3.80802509  0.625166   37.10297   0.0001  Intercept

        PREP      1                          2.356826   0.1247
                  1 -1.2572764  0.818968    2.356826   0.1247  stand
                  0    0           0            .         .     test

        LDOSE     1 -2.1511952  0.390885    30.28744   0.0001
        PREPDOSE  1 -0.5072196  0.594492    0.727948   0.3935
        INTER.2   1  0.46843813 0.055912                        Mild
```

```
                        Probit Models for Symptom Severity                           4

                                 Probit Procedure
                            Class Level Information

                        Class    Levels    Values

                        SYMPTOMS    3       None Mild Severe

                        PREP        2       stand test

                        Number of observations used = 23
```

```
                      Probit Models for Symptom Severity                          5
                             Probit Procedure

     Data Set          =WORK.MULTI
     Dependent Variable=SYMPTOMS
     Weight Variable   =N

             Weighted Frequency Counts for the Ordered Response Categories

                              Level      Count
                              None        188
                              Mild         60
                              Severe      139


     Log Likelihood for NORMAL  -346.306141


                            Goodness-of-Fit Tests

            Statistic                  Value     DF    Prob>Chi-Sq
            ------------------        --------    --    -----------
            Pearson Chi-Square         12.7864    12      0.3848
            L.R.    Chi-Square         16.5189    12      0.1686

            Response Levels:  3  Number of Covariate Values:   8
```

NOTE: Since the chi-square is small (p > 0.1000), fiducial limits will be calculated using a t value of 1.96.

```
                      Probit Models for Symptom Severity                          6
                             Probit Procedure

          Variable  DF   Estimate   Std Err  ChiSquare  Pr>Chi  Label/Value

          INTERCPT   1  3.41481724  0.412605   68.4962   0.0001  Intercept

          PREP       1                         20.33039  0.0001
                     1  -0.5675155  0.125865   20.33039  0.0001  stand
                     0      0          0         .        .      test

          LDOSE      1  -2.372131   0.294948   64.68244  0.0001
          INTER.2    1  0.46780285  0.055839                     Mild
```

The negative coefficient associated with LDOSE indicates that the probability of having no symptoms (SYMPTOM='None') or no or mild symptoms (SYMPTOM='None' or 'Mild') decreases as LDOSE increases; that is, the probability of a severe symptom increases with LDOSE. This association is apparent for both treatment groups.

The negative coefficient associated with the STANDARD treatment group indicates that the STANDARD treatment is associated with more severe symptoms across all LDOSE values. The probability of having no symptoms is less for the TEST group than the STANDARD group, as is the probability of having no or mild symptoms; that is, the probability of having a severe symptom is greater for the STANDARD treatment group than it is for the TEST group, and this is true across all LDOSE levels.

Example 3:   Logistic Regression

In this example, a series of people were questioned as to whether or not they would subscribe to a new newspaper. For each person, the variables SEX, AGE, and SUBS (0=yes,1=no) were recorded. The PROBIT procedure is used to fit a logistic regression model to the probability of a positive response as a function of the variables SEX and AGE. Specifically, the probability of a positive response is modeled as

$$p = \Pr(SUBS=0) = F(b_0 + b_1{}^*SEX + b_2{}^*AGE)$$

where F is the cumulative logistic distribution function.

From **Output 35.3**, there appears to be an effect due to both the variable SEX and the variable AGE. The positive coefficient for AGE indicates that older people are more likely to subscribe than younger people. The negative coefficient for SEX indicates that females are less likely to subscribe than males.

The following statements produce **Output 35.3**:

```
data news;
   input sex $ age subs;
   cards;
Female    35    1
Male      44    1
Male      45    0
Female    47    0
Female    51    1
Female    47    1
Male      54    0
Male      47    0
Female    35    1
Female    34    1
Female    48    1
Female    56    0
Male      46    0
Female    59    0
Female    46    0
Male      59    0
Male      38    0
Female    39    1
Male      49    0
Male      42    0
Male      50    0
Female    45    1
Female    47    1
Female    30    0
Female    39    1
Female    51    1
Female    45    1
Female    43    0
Male      39    0
Male      31    1
Female    39    1
Male      34    1
Female    52    0
Female    46    1
Male      58    0
```

```
Female     50     0
Female     32     1
Female     52     0
Female     35     1
Female     51     1
;

proc probit;
   class subs sex;
   model subs=sex age / d=logistic itprint;
   title 'Logistic Regression of Subscription Status';
run;
```

Output 35.3   Logistic Regression: PROC PROBIT

```
                          Logistic Regression of Subscription Status                          1
                                       Probit Procedure
                                   Class Level Information

                           Class    Levels    Values

                           SUBS       2       0 1

                           SEX        2       Female Male

                           Number of observations used = 40
```

```
                          Logistic Regression of Subscription Status                          2
                                       Probit Procedure

Iter Ridge   LogLikelihood        INTERCPT         SEX.1           AGE
 0      0   -27.7258872224               0             0             0
 1      0   -20.14265929083   -3.634567629  -1.648455751  0.1051634384
 2      0   -19.52245047938   -5.254865196  -2.234724956  0.1506493473
 3      0   -19.4904387863    -5.728485385  -2.409827238  0.1639621828
 4      0   -19.49030280973   -5.76187293   -2.422349862  0.1649007124
 5      0   -19.49030280687   -5.7620267    -2.422407743  0.1649050312
```

```
                  Logistic Regression of Subscription Status                    3
                             Probit Procedure
    Data Set        =WORK.NEWS
    Dependent Variable=SUBS

            Weighted Frequency Counts for the Ordered Response Categories

                              Level     Count
                                0         20
                                1         20


    Log Likelihood for LOGISTIC -19.49030281


                        Last Evaluation of the Gradient

                      INTERCPT          SEX.1              AGE

                  -5.95481E-12      8.768329E-10       -1.636698E-8



                        Last Evaluation of the Hessian

                          INTERCPT          SEX.1              AGE

            INTERCPT      6.459740        4.604222         292.040518
            SEX.1         4.604222        4.604222         216.208295
            AGE         292.040518      216.208295             13487
```

```
                  Logistic Regression of Subscription Status                    4
                             Probit Procedure
    Variable  DF   Estimate   Std Err   ChiSquare  Pr>Chi  Label/Value

    INTERCPT   1  -5.7620267  2.76345   4.347576   0.0371  Intercept

    SEX        1                        6.422      0.0113
               1  -2.4224077  0.955899  6.422      0.0113  Female
               0       0         0          .        .     Male

    AGE        1   0.16490503  0.065188  6.399204   0.0114
```

REFERENCES

Cox, D.R. (1970), *Analysis of Binary Data*, London: Chapman and Hall.

Cox, D.R. and Oakes, D. (1984), *Analysis of Survival Data*, London: Chapman and Hall.

Finney, D.J. (1971), *Probit Analysis*, Third Edition, London: Cambridge University Press.

Hubert, J. J., Bohidar, N. R., and Peace, K. E. (1988), "Assessment of Pharmacological Activity," in *Biopharmaceutical Statistics for Drug Development*, ed. K. E. Peace, New York: Marcel Dekker.

Chapter 36

The REG
Procedure

ABSTRACT 1352
INTRODUCTION 1352
  Least-Squares Estimation 1354
  Using PROC REG Interactively 1356
SPECIFICATIONS 1357
  PROC REG Statement 1358
  ADD Statement 1360
  BY Statement 1360
  DELETE Statement 1361
  FREQ Statement 1361
  ID Statement 1361
  MODEL Statement 1361
    Details for MODEL Statement Options 1369
  MTEST Statement 1369
    Examples of the MTEST Statement 1370
  OUTPUT Statement 1371
    Example 1372
  PAINT Statement 1372
    Specifying Condition 1373
    Using ALLOBS 1374
    Options in the PAINT Statement 1374
    STATUS and UNDO 1375
  PLOT Statement 1375
    Specifying Yvariables, Xvariables, and Symbol 1376
    Options in the PLOT Statement 1377
  PRINT Statement 1378
  REFIT Statement 1379
  RESTRICT Statement 1379
  REWEIGHT Statement 1381
    Specifying Condition 1382
    Using ALLOBS 1383
    Options in the REWEIGHT Statement 1383
    STATUS and UNDO 1384
  TEST Statement 1384
  VAR Statement 1385
  WEIGHT Statement 1385
DETAILS 1385
  Missing Values 1385
  Input Data Set 1386
    Example Using TYPE=CORR Data Set 1386
    Example Using TYPE=SSCP Data Set 1388
  Output Data Sets 1389
    OUTEST= Data Set 1389
    OUTSSCP= Data Sets 1392

      Interactive Analysis 1393

      Model-Selection Methods 1397

        Full Model Fitted (NONE) 1397

        Forward Selection (FORWARD) 1397

        Backward Elimination (BACKWARD) 1398

        Stepwise (STEPWISE) 1398

        Maximum R^2 Improvement (MAXR) 1398

        Minimum R^2 Improvement (MINR) 1399

        R^2 Selection (RSQUARE) 1399

        Adjusted R^2 Selection (ADJRSQ) 1399

        Mallows' C_p Selection (CP) 1399

        Additional Information on Model-Selection Methods 1399

      Criteria Used in BACKWARD, FORWARD, and STEPWISE Model-
          Selection Methods 1400

      Limitations in Model-Selection Methods 1400

      Parameter Estimates and Associated Statistics 1400

      Predicted and Residual Values 1402

      Producing Scatter Plots 1404

      Painting Scatter Plots 1411

      Models of Less than Full Rank 1415

      Collinearity Diagnostics 1416

      Influence Diagnostics 1418

      Reweighting Observations in an Analysis 1426

      Testing for Heteroscedasticity 1431

      Multivariate Tests 1431

      Autocorrelation in Time Series Data 1434

      Computational Methods 1436

      Computer Resources in Regression Analysis 1436

      Printed Output 1436

    EXAMPLES 1438

      Example 1: Growth Rate Data 1438

      Example 2: Aerobic Fitness Prediction 1443

      Example 3: Predicting Weight by Height and Age 1450

    REFERENCES 1455

ABSTRACT

The REG procedure fits linear regression models by least-squares. Subsets of independent variables that "best" predict the dependent or response variable can be determined by various model-selection methods.

INTRODUCTION

PROC REG is one of many regression procedures in the SAS System. REG is a general-purpose procedure for regression, while other SAS regression procedures have more specialized applications. Other SAS/STAT procedures that perform at least one type of regression analysis are CALIS, CATMOD, GLM, LIFEREG, LOGISTIC, NLIN, ORTHOREG, PROBIT, RSREG, and TRANSREG. SAS/ETS procedures are specialized for applications in time-series or simultaneous systems. These other SAS/STAT and SAS/ETS regression procedures are summarized in Chapter 1, "Introduction to Regression Procedures," which also contains an overview of regression techniques and defines many of the statistics computed by REG and other regression procedures.

PROC REG performs the following regression techniques with flexibility:

- handles multiple MODEL statements
- provides nine model-selection methods
- allows interactive changes both in the model and the data used to fit the model
- allows linear inequality restrictions on parameters
- tests linear hypotheses and multivariate hypotheses
- generates scatter plots of data and various statistics
- "paints" or highlights scatter plots
- produces partial regression leverage plots
- computes collinearity diagnostics
- prints predicted values, residuals, studentized residuals, confidence limits, and influence statistics and can output these items to a SAS data set
- can use correlations or crossproducts for input
- writes the crossproducts matrix to an output SAS data set
- performs weighted least-squares regression.

Nine model-selection methods are available in PROC REG. The simplest method is also the default, where REG fits the complete model you specify. The other eight methods involve various ways of including or excluding variables from the model. These methods are specified with the SELECTION= option in the MODEL statement. The methods are identified below and explained in detail in **Model-Selection Methods** later in this chapter.

NONE	no model selection. This is the default. The complete model specified in the MODEL statement is fit to the data.
FORWARD	forward selection. The method starts with no variables in the model and adds variables.
BACKWARD	backward elimination. The method starts with all variables in the model and deletes variables.
STEPWISE	stepwise regression. This is similar to FORWARD except that variables already in the model do not necessarily stay there.
MAXR	forward selection to fit the best one-variable model, the best two-variable model, and so on. Variables are switched so that R^2 is maximized.
MINR	similar to MAXR, except that variables are switched so that the increase in R^2 from adding a variable to the model is minimized.
RSQUARE	finds a specified number of models with the highest R^2 in a range of model sizes.
ADJRSQ	finds a specified number of models with the highest adjusted R^2 in a range of model sizes.
CP	finds a specified number of models with the lowest C_p in a range of model sizes.

Least-Squares Estimation

Suppose that a response variable Y can be predicted by a linear combination of some regressor variables X1 and X2. You can fit the β parameters in the equation

$$Y_i = \beta_0 + \beta_1 X1_i + \beta_2 X2_i + \varepsilon_i$$

for the observations $i=1,\ldots,n$. To fit this model with the REG procedure, specify

```
proc reg;
   model y=x1 x2;
```

REG uses the principle of least squares to produce estimates that are the best linear unbiased estimates (BLUE) under classical statistical assumptions (Gauss 1809; Markov 1900).

You might use regression analysis to find out how well you can predict a child's weight if you know that child's height. Suppose you collect your data by measuring heights and weights of 19 school children. You want to estimate the intercept β_0 and the slope β_1 of a line described by the equation

$$\text{WEIGHT} = \beta_0 + \beta_1\ \text{HEIGHT} + \varepsilon$$

where

WEIGHT	is the response variable.
β_0, β_1	are the unknown parameters.
HEIGHT	is the regressor variable.
ε	is the unknown error.

The data below produce **Output 36.1**, which shows a regression analysis and a plot of the data.

```
data class;
   input name $ height weight;
   cards;
Alfred   69.0 112.5
Alice    56.5  84.0
Barbara  65.3  98.0
Carol    62.8 102.5
Henry    63.5 102.5
James    57.3  83.0
Jane     59.8  84.5
Janet    62.5 112.5
Jeffrey  62.5  84.0
John     59.0  99.5
Joyce    51.3  50.5
Judy     64.3  90.0
Louise   56.3  77.0
Mary     66.5 112.0
Philip   72.0 150.0
Robert   64.8 128.0
Ronald   67.0 133.0
Thomas   57.5  85.0
William  66.5 112.0
;
proc reg;
   model weight = height;
   plot weight*height;
run;
```

Output 36.1   Regression for Weight and Height Data

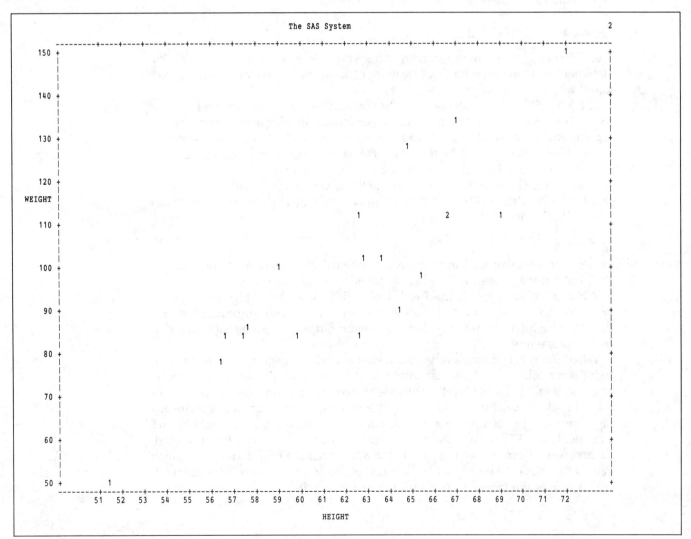

```
                                The SAS System                                    1

Model: MODEL1
Dependent Variable: WEIGHT
                              Analysis of Variance

                                  Sum of        Mean
         Source        DF        Squares       Square      F Value      Prob>F

         Model          1      7193.24912    7193.24912     57.076      0.0001
         Error         17      2142.48772     126.02869
         C Total       18      9335.73684

             Root MSE       11.22625     R-square       0.7705
             Dep Mean      100.02632     Adj R-sq       0.7570
             C.V.           11.22330

                              Parameter Estimates

                      Parameter      Standard    T for H0:
         Variable  DF   Estimate        Error    Parameter=0    Prob > |T|

         INTERCEP   1  -143.026918   32.27459130    -4.432       0.0004
         HEIGHT     1     3.899030    0.51609395     7.555       0.0001
```

The F statistic for the overall model is significant, indicating that the model explains a significant portion of the variation in the data. From the parameter estimates, the fitted model is

WEIGHT = −143.0 + 3.9*HEIGHT   .

The output also contains the t statistics and the corresponding significance probabilities to test if each parameter is significantly different from zero. The significance probabilities, or p-values, indicate that the intercept and HEIGHT parameter estimates are significant at the 95% significance level. For a complete regression analysis, you would want to try other models and, for each model, use various diagnostic techniques to examine the fit of the model. Techniques discussed later in this chapter include diagnostic plots, collinearity diagnostics, and influence statistics.

Regression is often used in an exploratory fashion to look for empirical relationships, such as the relationship between HEIGHT and WEIGHT. In this example, HEIGHT is not the cause of WEIGHT. You would need a controlled experiment to scientifically confirm the relationship. See **Comments on Interpreting Regression Statistics** in Chapter 1 for more information.

Using PROC REG Interactively

PROC REG can be used interactively. After you specify a model with a MODEL statement and run REG with a RUN statement, a variety of statements can be executed without reinvoking REG.

The **SPECIFICATIONS** section describes which statements can be used interactively. These interactive statements can be executed singly or in groups by following the single statement or group of statements with a RUN statement. Note that the MODEL statement can be repeated. This is an important difference from the GLM procedure, which allows only one MODEL statement.

If you use REG interactively, you can end the REG procedure with a DATA step, another PROC step, an ENDSAS statement, or with a QUIT statement. The syntax of the QUIT statement is

```
quit;
```

When you are using REG interactively, additional RUN statements do not end REG but tell the procedure to execute additional statements.

When a BY statement is used with PROC REG, interactive processing is not possible; that is, once the first RUN statement is encountered, processing proceeds for each BY group in the data set, and no further statements are accepted by the procedure.

When using REG interactively, you may fit a model, perform diagnostics, then refit the model, and perform diagnostics on the refitted model. Most of the interactive statements implicitly refit the model; for example, if you use the ADD statement to add a variable to the model, the regression equation is automatically recomputed. The exception to this automatic recomputing is the REWEIGHT statement. The REWEIGHT statement does not cause the model to be refitted. To do so, you can follow this statement with either a REFIT statement, which causes the model to be explicitly recomputed, or another interactive statement, which causes the model to be implicitly recomputed.

SPECIFICATIONS

Although there are numerous statements and options available in REG, many analyses use only a few of them. Often you can find the features you need by looking at an example or by scanning through this section. The statements available in REG are

PROC REG <*options*>;	required statement
<*label*>: **MODEL** *dependents*=<*regressors*> </ *options*>;	required statement for model fitting; can be used interactively

BY *variables*;
FREQ *variable*;
ID *variable*;   must appear before
VAR *variables*;   the first RUN statement
WEIGHT *variable*;

ADD *variables*;
DELETE *variables*;
<*label*>: **MTEST** <*equation*, . . . , *equation*>
          < / *options*>;
OUTPUT OUT=*SAS-data-set keyword*=*names*,
          <. . . *keyword*=*names*>;
PAINT <*condition* | ALLOBS >
          < / *options*> | <STATUS | UNDO>;   can appear
PLOT <*yvariable*xvariable*><=*symbol*>   anywhere after
          < . . . *yvariable*xvariable*><=*symbol*>   a MODEL statement
          < / *options*>;   and can be used
PRINT<*options*> <ANOVA>   interactively
          <MODELDATA>;
REFIT;
RESTRICT *equation*, . . . , *equation*;
REWEIGHT <*condition* | ALLOBS>
          < / *options*> | <STATUS | UNDO>;
<*label*>: **TEST** *equation* < , . . . , *equation*>
          < / *option* >;

In the above list, angle brackets denote optional specifications, and vertical bars denote a choice of one of the specifications separated by the vertical bars. In all cases, *label* is optional.

The PROC REG statement is required. To fit a model to the data, the MODEL statement is required. If you only want to use the options available in the PROC REG statement, you do not need a MODEL statement, but you must use a VAR statement. (See the example in **Output Data Sets** later in this chapter.) Several MODEL statements can be used. In addition, several MTEST, OUTPUT, PAINT, PLOT, PRINT, RESTRICT, and TEST statements can follow each MODEL statement. The ADD, DELETE, and REWEIGHT statements are used interactively to change the regression model and the data used in fitting the model. The ADD, DELETE, MTEST, OUTPUT, PLOT, PRINT, RESTRICT, and TEST statements implicitly refit the model; changes made to the model are reflected in the printout from these statements. The REFIT statement is used to explicitly refit the model and is most helpful when it follows a REWEIGHT statement, which does not refit the model. The BY, FREQ, ID, VAR, and WEIGHT statements are optionally specified once for the entire PROC REG step and must appear before the first RUN statement.

When TYPE=CORR, TYPE=COV, TYPE=UCORR, TYPE=UCOV, or TYPE=SSCP data sets are used as input data sets to REG, statements and options that require the original data are not available. Specifically, the FREQ, ID, OUTPUT, PAINT, PLOT, REWEIGHT, and WEIGHT statements, the MODEL and PRINT statement options ACOV, CLI, CLM, DW, INFLUENCE, P, PARTIAL, R, and SPEC are disabled.

The statements used with the REG procedure in addition to the PROC REG statement are the following (in alphabetic order):

ADD	adds independent variables to the regression model.
BY	specifies variables to define subgroups for the analysis.
DELETE	deletes independent variables from the regression model.
FREQ	specifies a frequency variable.
ID	names a variable to identify observations in the printout.
MODEL	specifies the dependent and independent variables in the regression model, requests a model selection method, prints predicted values, and provides details on the estimates (according to which options are selected).
MTEST	performs multivariate tests across multiple dependent variables.
OUTPUT	creates an output data set and names the variables to contain predicted values, residuals, and other statistics.
PAINT	paints points in scatter plots.
PLOT	generates scatter plots.
PRINT	prints information about the model and can reset options.
REFIT	refits the model.
RESTRICT	places linear equality restrictions on the parameter estimates.
REWEIGHT	excludes specific observations from analysis or changes the weights of observations used.
TEST	performs an F test on linear functions of the parameters.
VAR	lists variables for which crossproducts are to be computed, variables that can be interactively added to the model, or variables to be used in scatter plots.
WEIGHT	declares a variable to weight observations.

PROC REG Statement

PROC REG <*options*>;

The PROC REG statement is required. If you want to fit a model to the data, you must also use a MODEL statement. If you only want to use the options described below, you do not need a MODEL statement, but you must use a VAR statement. If you do not use MODEL statement, then the COVOUT and OUTEST= options are not available.

The table below gives the options you can use with the PROC REG statement.

Task	Option
Data Set Options	
name a data set to use for the regression	DATA=
output a data set that contains parameter estimates	OUTEST=
output the covariance matrix for parameter estimates to OUTEST= data set	COVOUT
output a data set that contains the sums of squares and crossproducts	OUTSSCP=
Printing and Other Options	
print simple statistics for each variable listed in MODEL or VAR statement	SIMPLE
print correlation matrix for variables listed in MODEL or VAR statement	CORR
print uncorrected sums of squares and crossproducts matrix	USSCP
print all statistics (SIMPLE, CORR, and SSCP)	ALL
suppress printing	NOPRINT
set criterion for checking for singularity	SINGULAR=

Following are explanations of the options that can be used in the PROC REG statement (in alphabetic order):

ALL

  requests many printouts. Using ALL in the PROC REG statement is equivalent to specifying ALL in every MODEL statement. ALL also implies SIMPLE, SSCP, and CORR.

CORR

  prints the correlation matrix for all variables listed in the MODEL or VAR statements.

COVOUT

  outputs the covariance matrices for the parameter estimates to the OUTEST= data set. This option is valid only if the OUTEST= option is also specified. See **Output Data Sets** later in this chapter.

DATA=*SAS-data-set*

  names the SAS data set to be used by PROC REG. The data set can be an ordinary SAS data set or a TYPE=CORR, TYPE=COV, TYPE=UCORR, TYPE=UCOV, or TYPE=SSCP data set. If one of these special TYPE= data sets is used, the FREQ, ID, OUTPUT, PAINT, PLOT, REWEIGHT, and WEIGHT statements and some options in the MODEL and PRINT statements are not available. See Appendix 1, "Special SAS Data Sets," for more information on TYPE= data sets. If the DATA= option is not specified, REG uses the most recently created SAS data set.

NOPRINT

  suppresses the printed output. Using this option in the PROC REG statement is equivalent to specifying NOPRINT in each MODEL statement.

OUTEST=*SAS-data-set*

  creates a data set that contains parameter estimates and optional statistics. See **Output Data Sets** later in this chapter for details. If you want to create a permanent SAS data set, you must specify a two-level name (see "SAS Files" in *SAS Language: Reference, Version 6, First Edition* and "Introduction to DATA Step Processing" in *SAS Language and Procedures: Usage, Version 6, First Edition* for more information on permanent SAS data sets).

OUTSSCP=*SAS-data-set*

creates a TYPE=SSCP data set that contains the sums of squares and crossproducts matrix. See **Output Data Sets** for details. If you want to create a permanent SAS data set, you must specify a two-level name (see "SAS Files" in *SAS Language: Reference* and "Introduction to DATA Step Processing" in *SAS Language and Procedures: Usage* for more information on permanent SAS data sets).

SIMPLE

prints the sum, mean, variance, standard deviation, and uncorrected sum of squares for each variable used in REG.

SINGULAR=*n*

tunes the mechanism used to check for singularities. The default value is 1E-7. This option is rarely needed. Singularity checking is described in **Computational Methods** later in this chapter.

USSCP

prints the uncorrected sums-of-squares and crossproducts matrix for all variables used in the procedure.

ADD Statement

ADD *variables*;

The ADD statement adds independent variables to the regression model. Only variables used in the VAR statement or used in MODEL statements before the first RUN statement can be added to the model. You can use the ADD statement interactively to add variables to the model or to include a variable that was previously deleted with a DELETE statement. See **Interactive Analysis** later in this chapter for an example.

BY Statement

BY *variables*;

A BY statement can be used with PROC REG to obtain separate analyses on observations in groups defined by the BY variables. When a BY statement appears, the procedure expects the input data set to be sorted in order of the BY variables.

If your input data set is not sorted in ascending order, use one of the following alternatives:

- Use the SORT procedure with a similar BY statement to sort the data.
- Use the BY statement options NOTSORTED or DESCENDING in the BY statement for the REG procedure. As a cautionary note, the NOTSORTED option does not mean that the data are unsorted, but rather means that the data are arranged in groups (according to values of the BY variables) and that these groups are not necessarily in alphabetical or increasing numeric order.
- Use the DATASETS procedure (in base SAS software) to create an index on the BY variables.

For more information on the BY statement, see the discussion in *SAS Language: Reference*. For more information on the DATASETS procedure, see the discussion in the *SAS Procedures Guide, Version 6, Third Edition*.

When a BY statement is used with PROC REG, interactive processing is not possible; that is, once the first RUN statement is encountered, processing proceeds for each BY group in the data set, and no further statements are accepted by the procedure. A BY statement that appears after the first RUN statement is ignored.

DELETE Statement

DELETE *variables*;

The DELETE statement deletes independent variables from the regression model. Use the DELETE statement to interactively delete variables from the model. The DELETE statement performs the opposite function of the ADD statement and is used in a similar manner. For an example of how the ADD statement is used (and how the DELETE statement can be used), see **Interactive Analysis** later in this chapter.

FREQ Statement

FREQ *variable*;

When a FREQ statement appears, each observation in the input data set is assumed to represent *n* observations, where *n* is the value of the FREQ variable. The analysis produced using a FREQ statement is the same as an analysis produced using a data set that contains *n* observations in place of each observation in the input data set. When the procedure determines degrees of freedom for significance tests, the total number of observations is considered to be equal to the sum of the values of the FREQ variable.

If the value of the FREQ variable is missing or is less than 1, the observation is not used in the analysis. If the value is not an integer, only the integer portion is used.

The FREQ statement must appear before the first RUN statement, or it is ignored.

ID Statement

ID *variable*;

When one of the MODEL statement options CLI, CLM, P, R, or INFLUENCE is requested, the variable listed in the ID statement is printed on the output beside each observation. If the PARTIAL option is requested in the MODEL statement, the left-most nonblank character in the value of the ID variable is used as the plotting symbol. The ID variable can be used to identify each observation. If the ID statement is omitted, the observation number is used to identify the observations.

MODEL Statement

<label>: **MODEL** *dependents=<regressors> < / options>*;

After the keyword MODEL, the dependent (response) variables are specified, followed by an equal sign and the regressor variables. Variables specified in the MODEL statement must be numeric variables in the data set being analyzed. For example, if you want to specify the quadratic term for X1 in the model, you cannot use X1*X1 in the MODEL statement but must create a new variable (say

X1SQUARE=X1*X1) in a DATA step and use the new variable in the MODEL statement. If you do not specify any regressor variables, each dependent variable is fit to a mean-only model, that is, a model with only a constant term. The label is optional.

The table below lists the options available to the MODEL statement.

Task	Option
Model Selection and Details of Selection	
model selection	SELECTION=
specify maximum number of variables selected	BEST=
print summary statistics at each step	DETAILS
provide names for groups of variables	GROUPNAMES=
include first *n* variables in the model	INCLUDE=
fit a model without the intercept term	NOINT
set criterion for entry into model	SLE=
set criterion for staying in model	SLS=
specify number of variables in model to begin the comparing and switching process	START=
stop selection criterion	STOP=
Options for RSQUARE, ADJRSQ, and CP Model Selection	
compute adjusted RSQUARE	ADJRSQ
compute AKAIKE's information criterion	AIC
compute parameter estimates for each model	B
compute Sawa's Bayesian information criterion	BIC
compute Mallow's CP statistic	CP
compute estimated MSE of prediction assuming multivariate normality	GMSEP
compute JP, the final prediction error	JP
compute MSE for each model	MSE
compute Amemiya's prediction criterion	PC
print root MSE for each model	RMSE
compute the SBC statistic	SBC
specify the true standard deviation of error term for computing CP and BIC	SIGMA=
compute SP statistic for each model	SP
compute error SS for each model	SSE
Options for Regression Calculations	
print inverse of sums-of-squares and crossproducts	I
print sums-of-squares and crossproducts matrix	XPX
Options for Details on Estimates	
print asymptotic covariance matrix of estimates assuming heteroscedasticity	ACOV
print collinearity analysis	COLLIN
print collinearity analysis with intercept adjusted out	COLLINOINT
print correlation matrix of estimates	CORRB
print covariance matrix of estimates	COVB
print squared partial correlation coefficients using Type I SS	PCORR1

Options for Details on Estimates (continued)

print squared partial correlation coefficients using Type II SS	PCORR2
print squared semi-partial correlation coefficients using Type I SS	SCORR1
print squared semi-partial correlation coefficients using Type II SS	SCORR2
print a sequence of parameter estimates during selection process	SEQB
test that first and second moments of model are correctly specified	SPEC
print the sequential sums of squares	SS1
print the partial sums of squares	SS2
print standardized parameter estimates	STB
print tolerance values for parameter estimates	TOL
print variance-inflation factors	VIF

Options for Predicted and Residual Values

compute 95% confidence limits for an individual predicted value	CLI
compute 95% confidence limits for the expected value of the dependent variable	CLM
compute a Durbin-Watson statistic	DW
compute influence statistics	INFLUENCE
compute predicted values	P
print partial regression plots for each regressor	PARTIAL
print analysis of residuals	R

Printing and Other Options

request the following options: ACOV, CLI, CLM, CORRB, COVB, I, P, PCORR1, PCORR2, R, SCORR1, SCORR2, SEQB, SPEC, SS1, SS2, STB, TOL, VIF, XPX	ALL
suppress printing	NOPRINT

The following options are available in the MODEL statement after a slash (/):

ACOV

prints the estimated asymptotic covariance matrix of the estimates under the hypothesis of heteroscedasticity. See **Testing for Heteroscedasticity** in the **DETAILS** section for more information.

ADJRSQ

computes R^2 adjusted for degrees of freedom for each model selected (Darlington 1968; Judge et al. 1980). This option is available in the RSQUARE, ADJRSQ, and CP model-selection methods only.

AIC

computes Akaike's information criterion for each model selected (Akaike 1969; Judge et al. 1980). This option is available in the RSQUARE, ADJRSQ, and CP model-selection methods only.

ALL

requests all these options: ACOV, CLI, CLM, CORRB, COVB, I, P, PCORR1, PCORR2, R, SCORR1, SCORR2, SEQB, SPEC, SS1, SS2, STB, TOL, VIF, and XPX.

B

computes estimated regression coefficients for each model selected. This option is available in the RSQUARE, ADJRSQ, and CP model-selection methods only.

BEST=n

is used with the RSQUARE, ADJRSQ, and CP model-selection methods. If SELECTION= CP or SELECTION=ADJRSQ is specified, the BEST= option specifies the maximum number of subset models to be printed or output to the OUTEST= data set. For SELECTION=RSQUARE, the BEST= option requests the maximum number of subset models for each size.

If the BEST= option is used without the B option (printing estimated regression coefficients), the variables in each MODEL are listed in order of inclusion instead of the order in which they appear in the MODEL statement.

If the BEST= option is omitted and the number of regressors is fewer than 11, all possible subsets are evaluated. If the BEST= option is omitted and the number of regressors is greater than ten, the number of subsets selected is at most equal to the number of regressors. A small value of the BEST= option greatly reduces the CPU time required for large problems.

BIC

computes Sawa's Bayesian information criterion for each model selected (Sawa 1978; Judge et al. 1980). This option is available in the RSQUARE, ADJRSQ, and CP model-selection methods only.

CLI

requests the 95% upper- and lower-confidence limits for an individual predicted value. The confidence limits reflect variation in the error, as well as variation in the parameter estimates. This option is not available when data sets of TYPE=CORR, TYPE=UCORR, TYPE=COV, TYPE=UCOV, or TYPE=SSCP are used as the input data set to PROC REG. See **Predicted and Residual Values** in the **DETAILS** section for more information.

CLM

prints the 95% upper- and lower-confidence limits for the expected value of the dependent variable (mean) for each observation. This is not a prediction interval (see the CLI option) because it takes into account only the variation in the parameter estimates, not the variation in the error term. This option is not available when data sets of TYPE=CORR, TYPE=UCORR, TYPE=COV, TYPE=UCOV, or TYPE=SSCP are used as the input data set to PROC REG. See **Predicted and Residual Values** for more information.

COLLIN

requests a detailed analysis of collinearity among the regressors. This includes eigenvalues, condition indices, and decomposition of the variances of the estimates with respect to each eigenvalue. See **Collinearity Diagnostics** in the **DETAILS** section.

COLLINOINT

requests the same analysis as the COLLIN option with the intercept variable adjusted out rather than included in the diagnostics. See **Collinearity Diagnostics**.

CORRB

prints the correlation matrix of the estimates. This is the $(X'X)^{-1}$ matrix scaled to unit diagonals.

COVB

prints the estimated covariance matrix of the estimates. This matrix is $(\mathbf{X'X})^{-1}s^2$, where s^2 is the estimated mean squared error.

CP

computes Mallows' C_p statistic for each model selected (Mallows 1973; Hocking 1976). This option is available in the RSQUARE, ADJRSQ, and CP model-selection methods only.

DETAILS

produces a table of statistics for entry and removal for each variable at each step in the model-building process. This option is available only in the BACKWARD, FORWARD, and STEPWISE methods. The statistics produced include the tolerance, R^2, and F statistic that results if each variable is added to the model, or the partial and model R^2 that results if the variable is deleted from the model.

DW

calculates a Durbin-Watson statistic to test whether or not the errors have first-order autocorrelation. (This test is only appropriate for time series data.) The sample autocorrelation of the residuals is also printed. This option is not available when data sets of TYPE=CORR, TYPE=UCORR, TYPE=COV, TYPE=UCOV, or TYPE=SSCP are used as the input data set to PROC REG. See **Autocorrelation in Time Series Data** in the **DETAILS** section.

GMSEP

computes the estimated mean square error of prediction assuming that both independent and dependent variables are multivariate normal (Stein 1960; Darlington 1969). Note that Hocking's formula (1976, eq. 4.20) contains a misprint: "$n-1$" should read "$n-2$." This option is available in the RSQUARE, ADJRSQ, and CP model-selection methods only.

GROUPNAMES='name' . . . 'name'

provides names for variable groups. This option is available only in the BACKWARD, FORWARD, and STEPWISE methods. The group name can be up to eight characters long. Subsets of independent variables listed in the MODEL statement can be designated as variable groups. This is done by enclosing the appropriate variables in braces. Variables in the same group are entered into or removed from the regression model at the same time. However, if the tolerance of a variable (see the TOL option below) in a group is less than the setting of the SINGULAR= option, then the variable is not entered into the model with the rest of its group. The group names GROUP1, GROUP2, . . . , GROUPn are assigned as groups are encountered in the MODEL statement if the GROUPNAMES= option is not used. Variables not enclosed by braces are used as groups of a single variable.

For example,

```
model y={x1 x2} x3 / selection=stepwise
  groupnames='x1 x2' 'x3';
```

As another example,

```
model y={ht wgt age} bodyfat / selection=forward
  groupnames='htwgtage' 'bodyfat';
```

I

prints the $(\mathbf{X'X})^{-1}$ matrix. The inverse of the crossproducts matrix is bordered by the parameter estimates and SSE matrices.

INCLUDE=*n*
> forces the first *n* independent variables listed in the MODEL statement
> to be included in all models. The selection methods are performed on
> the other variables in the MODEL statement. The INCLUDE= option is
> not available with SELECTION=NONE.

INFLUENCE
> requests a detailed analysis of the influence of each observation on the
> estimates and the predicted values. This option is not available when
> data sets of TYPE=CORR, TYPE=UCORR, TYPE=COV, TYPE=UCOV,
> or TYPE=SSCP are used as the input data set to PROC REG. See
> **Influence Diagnostics** in the **DETAILS** section for more detail.

JP
> computes J_p, the estimated mean square error of prediction for each
> model selected assuming that the values of the regressors are fixed and
> that the model is correct. The J_p statistic is also called the final
> prediction error (FPE) by Akaike (Nicholson 1948; Lord 1950; Mallows
> 1967; Darlington 1968; Rothman 1968; Akaike 1969; Hocking 1976;
> Judge et al. 1980). This option is available in the RSQUARE, ADJRSQ,
> and CP model-selection methods only.

MSE
> computes the mean square error for each model selected (Darlington
> 1968). This option is available in the RSQUARE, ADJRSQ, and CP
> model-selection methods only.

NOINT
> suppresses the intercept term that is otherwise included in the model.

NOPRINT
> suppresses the printout of regression results.

P
> calculates predicted values from the input data and the estimated
> model. The printout includes the observation number, the ID variable (if
> one is specified), the actual and predicted values, and the residual. If
> CLI, CLM, or R is specified, P is unnecessary. This option is not available
> when data sets of TYPE=CORR, TYPE=UCORR, TYPE=COV,
> TYPE=UCOV, or TYPE=SSCP are used as the input data set to PROC
> REG. See **Predicted and Residual Values** for more information.

PARTIAL
> requests partial regression leverage plots for each regressor. This option
> is not available when data sets of TYPE=CORR, TYPE=UCORR,
> TYPE=COV, TYPE=UCOV, or TYPE=SSCP are used as the input data
> set to PROC REG. See **Influence Diagnostics** for more information.

PC
> computes Amemiya's prediction criterion for each model selected
> (Amemiya 1976; Judge et al. 1980). This option is available in the
> RSQUARE, ADJRSQ, and CP model-selection methods only.

PCORR1
> prints the squared partial correlation coefficients using Type I sums of
> squares (SS). This is calculated as SS/(SS+SSE), where SSE is the error
> sum of squares.

PCORR2
> prints the squared partial correlation coefficients using Type II sums of
> squares. PCORR2 is calculated the same way as PCORR1, except that
> Type II SS are used instead of Type I SS.

R

requests an analysis of the residuals. The printed output includes
everything requested by the P option plus the standard errors of the
predicted and residual values, the studentized residual, and Cook's D
statistic to measure the influence of each observation on the parameter
estimates. This option is not available when data sets of TYPE=CORR,
TYPE=UCORR, TYPE=COV, TYPE=UCOV, or TYPE=SSCP are used as
the input data set to PROC REG. See **Predicted and Residual Values** for
more information.

RMSE

prints the root mean square error for each model selected. This option is
available in the RSQUARE, ADJRSQ, and CP model-selection methods
only.

SBC

computes the SBC statistic for each model selected (Schwarz 1978;
Judge et al. 1980). This option is available in the RSQUARE, ADJRSQ,
and CP model-selection methods only.

SCORR1

prints the squared semi-partial correlation coefficients using Type I sums
of squares. This is calculated as SS/SST, where SST is the corrected total
SS. If NOINT is used, the uncorrected total SS are used in the
denominator.

SCORR2

prints the squared semi-partial correlation coefficients using Type II sums
of squares. This is calculated the same way as SCORR1, except that
Type II SS are used instead of Type I SS.

SEQB

prints a sequence of parameter estimates as each variable is entered into
the model. This is printed as a matrix where each row is a set of
parameter estimates.

SELECTION=*name*

specifies the method used to select the model, where *name* can be
FORWARD (or F), BACKWARD (or B), STEPWISE, MAXR, MINR,
RSQUARE, ADJRSQ, CP, or NONE (use the full model). The default
method is NONE. Only one method can be specified in a MODEL
statement. If you want to use several methods, you must use separate
model statements for each method. See **Model-Selection Methods** for a
description of each method.

SIGMA=*n*

specifies the true standard deviation of the error term to be used in
computing CP and BIC (see above). If the SIGMA= option is not
specified, an estimate from the full model is used. This option is
available in the RSQUARE, ADJRSQ, and CP model-selection methods
only.

SLENTRY=*value*

SLE=*value*

specifies the significance level for entry into the model used in the
FORWARD and STEPWISE methods. The defaults are 0.50 for
FORWARD and 0.15 for STEPWISE.

SLSTAY=*value*

SLS=*value*

 specifies the significance level for staying in the model for the
 BACKWARD and STEPWISE methods. The defaults are 0.10 for
 BACKWARD and 0.15 for STEPWISE.

SP

 computes the S_p statistic for each model selected (Hocking 1976). This
 option is available in the RSQUARE, ADJRSQ, and CP model-selection
 methods only.

SPEC

 performs a test that the first and second moments of the model are
 correctly specified. See **Testing for Heteroscedasticity** later in this
 chapter for more information.

SS1

 prints the sequential sums of squares (Type I SS) along with the
 parameter estimates for each term in the model. See Chapter 9, "The
 Four Types of Estimable Functions," for more information on the
 different types of sums of squares.

SS2

 prints the partial sums of squares (Type II SS) along with the parameter
 estimates for each term in the model. See also SS1 above.

SSE

 computes the error sum of squares for each model selected. This option
 is available in the RSQUARE, ADJRSQ, and CP model-selection methods
 only.

START=*s*

 is used to begin the comparing-and-switching process in the MAXR,
 MINR, and STEPWISE methods for a model containing the first *s*
 independent variables in the MODEL statement, where *s* is the START
 value. For these methods, the default value of START= is 0.

 For the RSQUARE, ADJRSQ, and CP methods, START=*s* specifies the
 smallest number of regressors to be reported in a subset model. For
 these methods, the default value of START= is 1.

 The START= option cannot be used with model selection methods
 other than the six described here.

STB

 prints standardized regression coefficients. A standardized regression
 coefficient is computed by dividing a parameter estimate by the ratio of
 the sample standard deviation of the dependent variable to the sample
 standard deviation of the regressor.

STOP=*s*

 causes REG to stop when it has found the "best" *s*-variable model,
 where *s* is the STOP value. For the RSQUARE, ADJRSQ, and CP
 methods, STOP=*s* specifies the largest number of regressors to be
 reported in a subset model. For the MAXR and MINR methods, STOP=*s*
 specifies the largest number of regressors to be included in the model.

 The default setting for the STOP= option is the number of variables
 in the MODEL statement. This option can only be used with the MAXR,
 MINR, RSQUARE, ADJRSQ and CP methods.

TOL

 prints tolerance values for the estimates. Tolerance for a variable is
 defined as $1-R^2$, where R^2 is obtained from the regression of the
 variable on all other regressors in the model.

VIF
> prints variance inflation factors with the parameter estimates. Variance inflation is the reciprocal of tolerance.

XPX
> prints the **X'X** crossproducts matrix for the model. The crossproducts matrix is bordered by the **X'Y** and **Y'Y** matrices.

Details for MODEL Statement Options

The following table presents formulas and definitions used with the selection=RSQUARE, ADJRSQ, or CP option.

Table 36.1 Formulas and Definitions for Options Available Only with SELECTION=RSQUARE, ADJRSQ, or CP

Option or Statistic	Definition or Formula
n	the number of observations
p	the number of parameters including the intercept
i	1 if there is an intercept, 0 otherwise
$\hat{\sigma}^2$	the estimate of pure error variance from the SIGMA= option or from fitting the full model
SST_0	the uncorrected total sum of squares for the dependent variable
SST_1	the total sum of squares corrected for the mean for the dependent variable
SSE	the error sum of squares
MSE	$SSE/(n-p)$
R^2	$1-SSE/SST_i$
ADJRSQ	$1-[((n-i)(1-R^2))/(n-p)]$
AIC	$(n)\ln(SSE/n)+2p$
BIC	$(n)\ln(SSE/n)+2(p+2)q-2q^2$ where $q=\hat{\sigma}^2/(SSE/n)$
CP	$(SSE/\hat{\sigma}^2)+2p-n$
GMSEP	$MSE(n+1)(n-2)/(n(n-p-1))=SP(n+1)(n-2)/n$
JP	$(n+p)MSE/n$
PC	$(1-R^2)((n+p)/(n-p))=JP(n/SST_i)$
RMSE	$\sqrt{MSE}$
SBC	$(n)\ln(SSE/n)+(p)\ln(n)$
SP	$MSE/(n-p-1)$

MTEST Statement

> *<label>*: **MTEST** *<equation <, . . . ,equation>> < / options>*;

where each *equation* is a linear function composed of coefficients and variable names. *Label* is an optional name to label the statements.

The MTEST statement is used to test hypotheses in multivariate regression models where there are several dependent variables fit to the same regressors.

If no equations or options are specified, the MTEST statement tests the hypothesis that all estimated parameters except the intercept or intercepts are zero.

These options are available in the MTEST statement:

CANPRINT
: prints the canonical correlations for the hypothesis combinations and the dependent variable combinations. If you specify

```
mtest / canprint;
```

the canonical correlations between the regressors and the dependent variables are printed.

DETAILS
: prints the **M** matrix and various intermediate calculations.

PRINT
: prints the **H** and **E** matrices.

The hypotheses that can be tested with the MTEST statement are of the form

$$(\mathbf{L}\boldsymbol{\beta} - \mathbf{c}\mathbf{j})\mathbf{M} = 0$$

where **L** is a linear function on the regressor side, $\boldsymbol{\beta}$ is a matrix of parameters, **c** is a column vector of constants, **j** is a row vector of ones, and **M** is a linear function on the dependent side. The special case where the constants are zero is

$$\mathbf{L}\boldsymbol{\beta}\mathbf{M} = 0 \quad .$$

See **Multivariate Tests** later in this chapter.

Each linear function extends across either the regressor variables or the dependent variables. If the equation is across the dependent variables, then the constant term, if specified, must be zero. The equations for the regressor variables form the **L** matrix and **c** vector in the formula above; the equations for dependent variables form the **M** matrix. If no equations for the dependent variables are given, REG uses an identity matrix for **M**, testing the same hypothesis across all dependent variables. If no equations for the regressor variables are given, REG forms a linear function corresponding to a test that all the nonintercept parameters are zero.

Examples of the MTEST Statement

Consider these statements:

```
model y1 y2=x1 x2 x3;
mtest x1,x2;
mtest y1-y2,x1;
mtest y1-y2;
```

The first MTEST statement tests the hypothesis that the X1 and X2 parameters are zero for both Y1 and Y2. The second MTEST statement

```
mtest y1-y2, x1;
```

tests the hypothesis that the X1 parameter is the same for both dependent variables. For the same model, the statement

```
mtest y1-y2;
```

tests the hypothesis that all parameters except the intercept are the same for both dependent variables.

OUTPUT Statement

OUTPUT <OUT=*SAS-data-set*> *keyword*=*names* < . . . *keyword*=*names*>;

The OUTPUT statement creates a new SAS data set that saves diagnostic measures calculated after fitting the model. At least one specification of the form *keyword*=*names* is required.

All the variables in the original data set are included in the new data set, along with variables created in the OUTPUT statement. These new variables contain the values of a variety of diagnostic measures that are calculated for each observation in the data set. If you want to create a permanent SAS data set, you must specify a two-level name (see "SAS Files" in *SAS Language: Reference* for and "Introduction to DATA Step Processing" in *SAS Language and Procedures: Usage* for more information on permanent SAS data sets).

The OUTPUT statement cannot be used when a TYPE=CORR, TYPE=COV, TYPE=UCORR, TYPE=UCOV, or TYPE=SSCP data set is used as the input data set for PROC REG. See **Input Data Set** in the **DETAILS** section for more detail.

Details on the specifications in the OUTPUT statement are given below.

keyword=*names*   specifies the statistics to include in the output data set and gives names to the new variables that contain the statistics. Specify a keyword for each desired statistic (see the following list of keywords), an equal sign, and the variable or variables to contain the statistic.

In the output data set, the first variable listed after a keyword in the OUTPUT statement contains that statistic for the first dependent variable listed in the MODEL statement; the second variable contains the statistic for the second dependent variable in the MODEL statement, and so on. The list of variables following the equal sign can be shorter than the list of dependent variables in the MODEL statement. In this case, the procedure creates the new names in order of the dependent variables in the MODEL statement. See **Example** later in this section.

The keywords allowed and the statistics they represent are as follows:

COOKD=*names*
   Cook's D influence statistic.

COVRATIO=
   standard influence of observation on covariance of betas, as discussed with INFLUENCE option.

DFFITS=*names*
   standard influence of observation on predicted value.

H=*names*
   leverage, $x_i (\mathbf{X'X})^{-1} x_i'$.

L95=*names*
   lower bound of a 95% confidence interval for an individual prediction. This includes the variance of the error, as well as the variance of the parameter estimates.

L95M=*names*
   lower bound of a 95% confidence interval for the expected value (mean) of the dependent variable.

PREDICTED | P=*names*
   predicted values.

PRESS=*names*

*i*th residual divided by $(1-h)$, where h is the leverage above, and where the model has been refit without the *i*th observation.

RESIDUAL | R=*names*

residuals, calculated as ACTUAL minus PREDICTED.

RSTUDENT=*names*

a studentized residual with the current observation deleted.

STDI=*names*

standard error of the individual predicted value.

STDP=*names*

standard error of the mean predicted value.

STDR=*names*

standard error of the residual.

STUDENT=*names*

studentized residuals, which are the residuals divided by their standard errors.

U95=*names*

upper bound of a 95% confidence interval for an individual prediction.

U95M=*names*

upper bound of a 95% confidence interval for the expected value (mean) of the dependent variable.

OUT=*SASdataset*   gives the name of the new data set. By default, the procedure uses the DATA*n* convention to name the new data set.

See **Predicted and Residual Values** and **Influence Diagnostics** later in this chapter for details. Also, see Chapter 1 for definitions of these and other statistics.

Example

The following statements give the syntax for creating an output data set:

```
proc reg data=a;
   model y z=x1 x2;
   output out=b
      p=yhat zhat
      r=yresid zresid;
```

These statements create an output data set named B. In addition to the variables in the input data set, B contains the variable YHAT, whose values are predicted values of the dependent variable Y; ZHAT, whose values are predicted values of the dependent variable Z; YRESID, whose values are the residual values of Y; and ZRESID, whose values are the residual values of Z.

PAINT Statement

PAINT <*condition* | ALLOBS> < / *options*>;
PAINT <STATUS | UNDO>;

The PAINT statement selects observations to be *painted* or highlighted in a scatter plot. All observations that satisfy *condition* are painted using some specific symbol. The PAINT statement does not generate a scatter plot and must be followed by a PLOT statement, which does generate a scatter plot. However, several

PAINT statements can be used before a PLOT statement. The requests from all previous PAINT statements are applied to all PLOT statements.

Unless the NOLIST statement is specified, the PAINT statement lists the observation numbers of the observations selected, the total number of observations selected, and the plotting symbol used to paint the points.

On a plot, paint symbols take precedence over all other symbols. If any print position contains more than one painted point, the paint symbol for the observation plotted last is used.

The PAINT statement cannot be used when a TYPE=CORR, TYPE=COV, TYPE=UCORR, TYPE=UCOV, or TYPE=SSCP data set is used as the input data set for PROC REG. Note that the syntax for the PAINT statement is the same as the syntax for the REWEIGHT statement.

For detailed examples of painting scatter plots, see **Painting Scatter Plots** later in this chapter.

Specifying *Condition*

Condition is used to select observations to be painted. The syntax of *condition* is

> *variable compare value*

or

> *variable compare value   logical   variable compare value*

where

variable	is one of the following: • a variable name in the input data set. • OBS., which is the observation number. • *keyword.*, where *keyword* is a keyword for a statistic requested in the OUTPUT statement. The keyword specification is applied to all dependent variables.
compare	is an operator that compares *variable* to *value*. *Compare* can be any one of the following: $<$, $<=$, $>$, $>=$, $=$, $^=$. The operators LT, LE, GT, GE, EQ, and NE can be used instead of the symbols above. See "SAS Expressions" in *SAS Language: Reference* for more information on comparison operators.
value	gives an unformatted value of *variable*. Observations are selected to be painted if they satisfy the condition created by *variable compare value*. *Value* can be a number or a character string. If *value* is a character string, it must be eight characters or fewer and must be enclosed in quotes. In addition, *value* is case-sensitive. In other words, the statements

```
paint name='henry';
```

and

```
paint name='Henry';
```

are not the same.

logical	is one of two logical operators. Either AND or OR can be used. To specify AND, use AND or the symbol &. To specify OR, use OR or the symbol |.

Examples of the *variable compare value* form are

```
paint name='Henry';
paint residual.>=20;
paint obs.=99;
```

Examples of the *variable compare value   logical   variable compare value* form are

```
paint name='Henry'|name='Mary';
paint residual.>=20 or residual.<=20;
paint obs.>=11 and residual.<=20;
```

Note that in models with more than one dependent variable, the condition is applied to all dependent variables.

Using ALLOBS

Instead of specifying *condition*, ALLOBS can be used to select all observations. This is most useful when you want to unpaint all observations. For example,

```
paint allobs / reset;
```

resets the printing symbols for all observations.

Options in the PAINT Statement

The following options can be used when either a condition is specified, ALLOBS is specified, or when nothing is specified before the slash. If only an option is listed, the option applies to the observations selected in the previous PAINT statement, *not* to the observations selected by reapplying the condition from the previous PAINT statement. For example, with the statements

```
paint r.>0 / symbol='a';
reweight r.>0;
refit;
paint / symbol='b';
```

the second PAINT statement paints only those observations selected in the first PAINT statement. No additional observations are painted even if, after refitting the model, there are new observations that meet the condition in the first PAINT statement. Note that options are not available when either UNDO or STATUS is used.

The following options can be specified after a slash (/):

NOLIST

suppresses printing the list of observation numbers selected. If NOLIST is not specified, a list of observations selected is printed in the log. The list includes the observation numbers and painting symbol used to paint the points. The total number of observations selected to be painted is also printed.

RESET

changes the printing symbol to the current default symbol, effectively unpainting the observations selected. If you set the default symbol by using the SYMBOL= option in the PLOT statement, the RESET option in the PAINT statement changes the printing symbol to the symbol you specified. Otherwise, the default symbol of '1' is used.

SYMBOL='*character*'

specifies a printing symbol. If the SYMBOL= option is omitted, the printing symbol is either the one used in the most recent PAINT statement or, if there are no previous PAINT statements, the symbol '@'. For example,

```
paint / symbol='#';
```

changes the printing symbol for the observations selected by the most recent PAINT statement to '#'. As another example,

```
paint temp lt 22 / symbol='c';
```

changes the printing symbol to 'c' for all observations with TEMP<22. In general, the numbers 1, 2, . . . , 9 and the asterisk are not recommended as painting symbols. These symbols are used as default symbols in the PLOT statement, where they represent the number of replicates at a point. If SYMBOL='' is used, no painting is done in the current plot. If SYMBOL=' ' is used, observations are painted with a blank and are no longer seen on the plot.

STATUS and UNDO

Instead of specifying *condition* or ALLOBS, you can use STATUS or UNDO as follows:

STATUS
: lists (in the log) the observation number and plotting symbol of all currently painted observations.

UNDO
: use this to undo changes made by the most recent PAINT statement. Observations may be, but are not necessarily, unpainted. For example,

```
paint obs. <=10 / symbol='a';
other interactive statements
paint obs.=1 / symbol='b';
other interactive statements
paint undo;
```

The last PAINT statement changes the plotting symbol used for observation 1 back to 'a'. If the statement

```
paint / reset;
```

had been used instead, observation 1 would have been unpainted.

PLOT Statement

PLOT <yvariable*xvariable><=symbol>
<. . . yvariable*xvariable><=symbol> < / options>;

The PLOT statement prints scatter plots with *yvariables* on the vertical axes and *xvariables* on the horizontal axes. It uses *symbols* to mark points in the plots. The *yvariables* and *xvariables* can be any variables that appear in the VAR statement or in MODEL statements before the first RUN statement. *Yvariables* and *xvariables* can also be statistics available in the OUTPUT statement, or OBS, the observation number. The symbol can be specified as a single character enclosed in quotes or the name of any variable in the input data set.

The statement

```
plot;
```

is equivalent to respecifying the most recent PLOT statement without any options. However, the COLLECT, HPLOTS=, SYMBOL=, and VPLOTS=

options (described below) apply across PLOT statements and remain in effect if they have been previously specified.

As with most other interactive statements, the PLOT statement implicitly refits the model. If a PLOT statement is preceded by a REWEIGHT statement, the model is recomputed, and the plot reflects the new model.

The PLOT statement cannot be used when TYPE=CORR, TYPE=COV, TYPE=UCORR, TYPE=UCOV, or TYPE=SSCP data sets are used as input to PROC REG.

Several PLOT statements can be specified for each MODEL statement, and more than one plot can be specified in each PLOT statement. For detailed examples of using the PLOT statement and its options, see **Producing Scatter Plots** in the **DETAILS** section.

Specifying *Yvariables*, *Xvariables*, and *Symbol*

To specify *yvariables* and *xvariables* when you are using variables in the data set, simply use the variable name. For statistics or OBS, use

keyword.   where *keyword* is a statistic available in the OUTPUT statement, or OBS (the observation number). For example,

```
plot residual.*obs.;
```

generates one scatter plot of the residuals by the observation number for each dependent variable in the model. These plots can be useful for detecting autocorrelation. The *keyword.* specification is applied to all dependent variables.

Yvariable and *xvariable* can be replaced by a set of variables and statistics enclosed in parentheses. When this occurs, all possible combinations of *yvariable* and *xvariable* are generated. For example, the statement

```
plot (residual. student. rstudent.)*(age predicted.);
```

prints six scatter plots for each dependent variable in the model.

If a character variable is used for the symbol, the first (left-most) nonblank character in the formatted value of the variable is used as the plotting symbol. For unformatted character variables, the left-most nonblank character in the unformatted value is used as the plotting symbol. If a character in quotes is specified, that character becomes the plotting symbol. If a character is used as the plotting symbol, and if there are different plotting symbols needed at the same point, the symbol ' ?' is used at that point.

If an unformatted numeric variable is used for the symbol, the symbols '1', '2', . . . , '9' are used for variable values 1, 2, . . . , 9. For noninteger values, only the integer portion is used as the plotting symbol. For values of 10 or greater, the symbol '*' is used. For negative values, a '?' is used. If a numeric variable is used, and if there is more than one plotting symbol needed at the same point, the sum of the variable values is used at that point. If the sum exceeds 9, the symbol '*' is used.

If a symbol is not specified, the number of replicates at the point is printed. The symbol '*' is used if there are ten or more replicates.

Options in the PLOT Statement

The following options can be specified in the PLOT statement after a slash (/):

CLEAR

    clears any collected scatter plots before plotting begins but does not turn off the COLLECT option. Use this option when you want to begin a new collection with the plots in the current PLOT statement. For more information on collecting plots, see the COLLECT and NOCOLLECT options below.

COLLECT

    specifies that plots begin to be collected from one PLOT statement to the next, and that subsequent plots show an overlay of all collected plots. This option enables you to overlay plots before and after changes to the model or to the data used to fit the model. Plots collected before changes are unaffected by the changes and can be overlaid on later plots. You can request more than one plot with this option, and you do not need to request the same number of plots in subsequent PLOT statements. If you specify an unequal number of plots, plots in corresponding positions are overlaid. For example, the statements

```
plot residual.*predicted. y*x / collect;
run;
```

    produce two plots. If these statements are then followed by

```
plot residual.*x;
run;
```

two plots are again produced. The first plot shows residual against X values overlaid on residual against predicted values. The second plot is the same as produced by the first PLOT statement.

    Axes are scaled for the first plot or plots collected. The axes are not rescaled as more plots are collected.

    Once specified, the COLLECT option remains in effect until the NOCOLLECT option is specified.

HPLOTS=*number*

    sets the number of scatter plots that can be printed across the page. The procedure begins with one plot per page. The value of the HPLOTS= option remains in effect until you change it in a later PLOT statement. See the VPLOTS= option for an example.

NOCOLLECT

    specifies that the collection of scatter plots end after adding the plots in the current PLOT statement. PROC REG starts with the NOCOLLECT option in effect. After specifying the NOCOLLECT option, any following PLOT statement produces a new plot that contains only the plots requested by that PLOT statement.

    For more information, see the COLLECT option above.

OVERLAY

    allows requested scatter plots to be superimposed. The axes are scaled so that points on all plots will be shown. If the HPLOTS= or VPLOTS= option is set to more than one, the overlaid plot occupies the first position on the page. OVERLAY is similar to COLLECT in that both options produce superimposed plots. However, OVERLAY superimposes only the plots in the associated PLOT statement; COLLECT superimposes plots across PLOT statements. OVERLAY may be used when COLLECT is in effect.

SYMBOL='*character*'

changes the default plotting symbol used for all scatter plots produced in the current, and in subsequent, PLOT statements. Both SYMBOL='' and SYMBOL='' are allowed.

If the SYMBOL= option has not been specified, the default symbol is '1' for positions with one observation, '2' for positions with two observations, and so on. For positions with more than 9 observations, '*' is used. The SYMBOL= option (or a plotting symbol) is needed to avoid any confusion caused by this default convention. Specifying a particular symbol is especially important when either the OVERLAY or COLLECT option is being used.

If you specify the SYMBOL= option and use a number for *character*, that number is used for all points in the plot. For example, the statement

```
plot y*x / symbol='1';
```

produces a plot with the symbol '1' used for all points.

If you specify a plotting symbol and the SYMBOL= option, the plotting symbol overrides the SYMBOL= option. For example, in the statements

```
plot y*x y*v='.' / symbol='*';
```

the symbol used for the plot of Y against X is '*', and a '.' is used for the plot of Y against V.

If a paint symbol has been defined with a PAINT statement, the paint symbol takes precedence over both the SYMBOL= option and the default plotting symbol for the PLOT statement.

VPLOTS=*number*

sets the number of scatter plots that can be printed down the page. The procedure begins with one plot per page. The value of the VPLOTS= option remains in effect until you change it in a later PLOT statement.

For example, to specify a total of six plots per page, with two rows of three plots, use the HPLOTS= and VPLOTS= options as follows:

```
plot y1*x1 y1*x2 y1*x3 y2*x1 y2*x2 y2*x3 /
    hplots=3 vplots=2;
run;
```

PRINT Statement

PRINT <*options*> <ANOVA> <MODELDATA>;

The PRINT statement enables you to interactively print the MODEL statement options, print an *ANOVA* table, print the data for variables used in the current model, or reprint the options specified in a MODEL or a previous PRINT statement. In addition, like most other interactive statements in PROC REG, the PRINT statement implicitly refits the model; thus, effects of REWEIGHT statements are seen in the resulting printout.

You can specify any combination of *options*, ANOVA, and MODELDATA. The PRINT statement with no options uses, by default, the most recently specified options in a PRINT or MODEL statement.

The following specifications can appear in the PRINT statement:

options   interactively prints the MODEL statement options, where *option* is one or more of the following: ACOV, ALL, CLI, CLM, COLLIN, COLLINOINT, CORRB, COVB, DW, I, INFLUENCE, P, PARTIAL, PCORR1, PCORR2, R, SCORR1, SCORR2, SEQB, SPEC, SS1, SS2, STB, TOL, VIF, or XPX. See the section on the MODEL statement for a description of these options.

ANOVA   prints the *ANOVA* table associated with the current model. This is either the model specified in the last MODEL statement or the model that incorporates changes made by ADD, DELETE, or REWEIGHT statements after the last MODEL statement.

MODELDATA   prints the data for variables used in the current model.

Options that require original data values, such as R or INFLUENCE, cannot be used when a TYPE=CORR, TYPE=COV, TYPE=UCORR, TYPE=UCOV, or TYPE=SSCP data set is used as the input data set to REG. See **Input Data Set** in the **DETAILS** section for more detail.

REFIT Statement

REFIT;

The REFIT statement causes the current model and corresponding statistics to be recomputed immediately. No output is generated by this statement. REFIT is needed after one or more REWEIGHT statements to cause them to take effect before subsequent PAINT or REWEIGHT statements. This is sometimes necessary when you are using statistical conditions in REWEIGHT statements. For example, with these statements

```
paint student.>2;
plot student.*p.;
reweight student.>2;
refit;
paint student.>2;
plot student.*p.;
```

the second PAINT statement paints any additional observations that meet the condition after deleting observations and refitting the model. The REFIT statement is used because the REWEIGHT statement does not cause the model to be recomputed. In this example, the same effect could have been achieved by replacing the REFIT statement with a PLOT statement.

Most interactive statements can be used to implicitly refit the model; any plots or statistics produced by these statements reflect changes made to the model and changes made to the data used to compute the model. The exceptions are the PAINT and REWEIGHT statements, which do not cause the model to be recomputed.

RESTRICT Statement

RESTRICT *equation* <, . . . , *equation*>;

A RESTRICT statement is used to place restrictions on the parameter estimates in the MODEL statement preceding it. If you want to specify several restrictions, you can do this using a single RESTRICT statement, separating the individual restrictions by commas. Alternatively, more than one RESTRICT statement can follow each MODEL statement. If you have several RESTRICT statements, they are collected until a RUN statement is found.

If you want to print separate *ANOVA* tables for each of several RESTRICT statements, you must have a PRINT statement followed by a RUN statement for each *ANOVA* table you want to print.

After a RUN statement, any restrictions remain in effect until a new MODEL statement or another RESTRICT statement is found. To lift all restrictions on a model, submit a new MODEL statement.

For an example using the RESTRICT statement, note that the statement

```
restrict equation1=equation2=equation3;
```

is equivalent to imposing the two restrictions

```
equation1=equation2
```

and

```
equation2=equation3
```

Each restriction is written as a linear equation and can be written as

equation

or

equation = equation

The form of each equation is

$$c_1{*}variable \pm c_2{*}variable \pm \ldots \pm c_n{*}variable$$

The c_j's are constants and *variable* is any regressor variable.

When no equal sign appears, the linear combination is set equal to zero. Each variable name mentioned must be a variable in the MODEL statement to which the RESTRICT statement refers. The keyword INTERCEPT can also be used as a variable name and refers to the intercept parameter in the regression model. If you want to run a no-intercept model, use the NOINT option rather than restricting the intercept term to be zero with a RESTRICT statement.

Note that the parameters associated with the variables are restricted, not the variables themselves. Restrictions should be consistent and not redundant.

Following are some examples of valid RESTRICT statements. To restrict the parameter associated with an independent variable to be zero, use this statement:

```
restrict x1;
```

If you have two independent variables, A and B, whose parameters you know must sum to one, use this statement:

```
restrict a+b=1;
```

To restrict the parameters of three independent variables, A, B, and C, to be equal, use this statement:

```
restrict a=b=c;
```

or, equivalently,

```
restrict a=b, b=c;
```

You can use the keyword INTERCEPT when specifying restrictions, as follows:

```
restrict 2*f=a+b, intercept+f=0;
```

Do not use a restriction to fit a model with no intercept. Use the NOINT option instead. Note that you cannot specify

```
restrict f-g=0,
         f-intercept=0,
         g-intercept=1;
```

because the three restrictions are not consistent. If these restrictions are included in a RESTRICT statement, the last restricted parameter is set to zero and has zero degrees of freedom, indicating that REG is unable to apply a restriction.

The restrictions usually operate even if the model is not of full rank. Check to ensure that DF$=-1$ for each restriction. In addition, the Model DF should decrease by 1 for each restriction.

The parameter estimates are those that minimize the quadratic criterion (SSE) subject to the restrictions. If a restriction cannot be applied, its parameter value and degrees of freedom are listed as zero.

The method used for restricting the parameter estimates is to introduce a Lagrangian parameter for each restriction (Pringle and Raynor 1971). The estimates of these parameters are printed with test statistics. The Lagrangian parameter γ measures the sensitivity of the SSE to the restriction constant. If the restriction constant is changed by a small amount ε, the SSE is changed by $2\gamma\varepsilon$. The t ratio tests the significance of the restrictions. If γ is zero, the restricted estimates are the same as the unrestricted estimates, and a change in the restriction constant in either direction increases the SSE.

REWEIGHT Statement

REWEIGHT <*condition* | ALLOBS> < / *options*>;
REWEIGHT <STATUS | UNDO>;

The REWEIGHT statement interactively changes the weights of observations that are used in computing the regression equation. REWEIGHT can change observation weights or set them to zero, which causes selected observations to be excluded from the analysis. When a REWEIGHT statement sets observation weights to zero, the observations are not deleted from the data set. More than one REWEIGHT statement can be used. The requests from all REWEIGHT statements are applied to the subsequent statements.

The model and corresponding statistics are not recomputed after a REWEIGHT statement. For example, with the following statements

```
reweight r.>0;
reweight r.>0;
```

the second REWEIGHT statement does not exclude any additional observations since the model is not recomputed after the first REWEIGHT statement. Use either a REFIT statement to explicitly refit the model, or implicitly refit the model by following the REWEIGHT statement with any other interactive statement except another REWEIGHT or PAINT statement.

The REWEIGHT statement cannot be used if a TYPE=CORR, TYPE=COV, TYPE=UCORR, TYPE=UCOV, or TYPE=SSCP data set is used as an input data set to REG. Note that the syntax used in the REWEIGHT statement is the same as the syntax for the PAINT statement.

The syntax of the REWEIGHT statement is described below. For detailed examples of using this statement see **Reweighting Observations in an Analysis** in the **DETAILS** section.

Specifying *Condition*

Condition is used to find observations to be reweighted. The syntax of condition is

> *variable compare value*

or

> *variable compare value   logical   variable compare value*

where

variable is one of the following:
- a variable name in the input data set.
- OBS., which is the observation number.
- *keyword.*, where *keyword* is a keyword for a statistic requested in the OUTPUT statement. The keyword specification is applied to all dependent variables in the model.

compare is an operator that compares *variable* to *value*. *Compare* can be any one of the following: $<$, $<=$, $>$, $>=$, $=$, $\hat{}=$. The operators LT, LE, GT, GE, EQ, and NE can be used instead of the symbols above. See "SAS Expressions" in *SAS Language: Reference* for more information on comparison operators.

value gives an unformatted value of *variable*. Observations are selected to be reweighted if they satisfy the condition created by *variable compare value*. *Value* can be a number or a character string. If *value* is a character string, it must be eight characters or fewer and must be enclosed in quotes. In addition, *value* is case-sensitive. In other words, the statements

```
reweight name='steve';
```

and

```
reweight name='Steve';
```

are not the same.

logical is one of two logical operators. Either AND or OR can be used. To specify AND, use AND or the symbol &. To specify OR, use OR or the symbol |.

Examples of the *variable compare value* form are

```
reweight obs. le 10;
reweight temp=55;
reweight type='new';
```

Examples of the *variable compare value   logical   variable compare value* form are

```
reweight obs.<=10 and residual.<2;
reweight student.<-2 or student.>2;
reweight name='Mary' | name='Susan';
```

Using ALLOBS

Instead of specifying *condition*, you can use ALLOBS to select all observations. This is most useful when you want to restore the original weights of all observations. For example,

```
reweight allobs / reset;
```

resets weights for all observations and uses all observations in the subsequent analysis. Note that

```
reweight allobs;
```

specifies that all observations be excluded from analysis. Consequently, using ALLOBS is useful only if you also use one of the options discussed below.

Options in the REWEIGHT Statement

The following options can be used when either a condition, ALLOBS, or nothing is specified before the slash. If only an option is listed, the option applies to the observations selected in the previous REWEIGHT statement, not to the observations selected by reapplying the condition from the previous REWEIGHT statement. For example, with the statements

```
reweight r.>0 / weight=0.1;
refit;
reweight;
```

the second REWEIGHT statement excludes from the analysis only those observations selected in the first REWEIGHT statement. No additional observations are excluded even if there are new observations that meet the condition in the first REWEIGHT statement. Note that options are not available when either UNDO or STATUS is used.

NOLIST
> suppresses printing the list of observation numbers selected. If the NOLIST option is not specified, a list of observations selected is printed in the log.

RESET
> resets the observation weights to their original values as defined by the WEIGHT statement or to WEIGHT=1 if no WEIGHT statement is specified. For example, the statement

```
reweight / reset;
```

> resets observation weights to the original weights in the data set. If previous REWEIGHT statements have been submitted, this REWEIGHT statement applies only to the observations selected by the previous REWEIGHT statement. Note that although RESET does reset observation weights to their original values, it does not cause the model and corresponding statistics to be recomputed.

WEIGHT = value
> changes observation weights to the specified nonnegative real number. If the WEIGHT= option is not specified, then the observation weights are set to zero, and observations are excluded from the analysis. Consider this example:

```
reweight name='Alan';
other interactive statements
reweight / weight=0.5;
```

The first REWEIGHT statement changes weights to zero for all observations with NAME='Alan', effectively deleting these observations. The subsequent analysis would not include these observations. The second REWEIGHT statement applies only to those observations selected by the previous REWEIGHT statement, and changes the weights to 0.5 for all the observations with NAME='Alan'. Thus, the next analysis would include all original observations; however, those observations with NAME='Alan' would have their weights set to 0.5.

STATUS and UNDO

If *condition* or ALLOBS is not specified, then one of these two specifications can be specified:

STATUS
lists in the log the observation's number and the weight of all reweighted observations. If an observation's weight has been set to zero, it is reported as deleted. However, the observation is not deleted from the data set, only from the analysis.

UNDO
cancels the changes made by the most recent REWEIGHT statement. Weights may be, but are not necessarily, reset. For example, in these statements

```
reweight student.>2 / weight=0.1;
reweight;
reweight undo;
```

the first REWEIGHT statement sets the weights of observations that satisfy the condition to 0.1. The second REWEIGHT statement sets the weights of the same observations to zero. The third REWEIGHT statement undoes the second, changing the weights back to 0.1.

TEST Statement

label: **TEST** *equation* $<,\ldots,$ *equation*$>$ $</$ *option*$>$;

The TEST statement tests hypotheses about the parameters estimated in the preceding MODEL statement. It has the same syntax as the RESTRICT statement except that it allows an option. Each equation specifies a linear hypothesis to be tested. The rows of the hypothesis are separated by commas.

Variable names must correspond to regressors, and each variable name represents the coefficient of the corresponding variable in the model. An optional label is useful to identify each test with a name. The keyword INTERCEPT can be used instead of a variable name to refer to the model's intercept.

One option can be specified in the TEST statement after a slash (/):

PRINT
prints intermediate calculations. This includes $\mathbf{L}\ (\mathbf{X'X})^{-}\mathbf{L'}$ bordered by $\mathbf{Lb}-\mathbf{c}$, and $(\mathbf{L(X'X)}^{-}\mathbf{L'})^{-1}$ bordered by $(\mathbf{L(X'X)}^{-}\mathbf{L'})^{-1}(\mathbf{Lb}-\mathbf{c})$.

REG performs an *F* test for the joint hypotheses specified in a single TEST statement. More than one TEST statement can accompany a MODEL statement. The numerator is the usual quadratic form of the estimates; the denominator is the mean squared error. If hypotheses can be represented by

$$\mathbf{L}\boldsymbol{\beta} = \mathbf{c},$$

then the numerator of the F test is

$$Q = (\mathbf{Lb} - \mathbf{c})'(\mathbf{L}(\mathbf{X'X})^{-}\mathbf{L}')^{-1}(\mathbf{Lb} - \mathbf{c})$$

divided by degrees of freedom, where **b** is the estimate of **β**, as in this example:

```
model y=a1 a2 b1 b2;
aplus: test a1+a2=1;
b1:    test b1=0, b2=0;
b2:    test b1, b2;
```

The last two statements are equivalent; since no constant is specified, zero is assumed.

VAR Statement

VAR *list-of-variables*;

The VAR statement is used to include numeric variables in the crossproducts matrix that are not specified in the first MODEL statement.

Variables not listed in MODEL statements before the first RUN statement must be listed in the VAR statement if you want the ability to add them interactively to the model with an ADD statement, to include them in a new MODEL statement, or to plot them in a scatter plot with the PLOT statement.

In addition, if you want to use options only in the PROC REG statement and do not want to fit a model to the data (with a MODEL statement), you must use a VAR statement.

WEIGHT Statement

WEIGHT *variable*;

A WEIGHT statement names a variable in the input data set whose values are relative weights for a weighted least-squares fit. If the weight value is proportional to the reciprocal of the variance for each observation, then the weighted estimates are the best linear unbiased estimates (BLUE).

Values of the weight variable must be nonnegative. If an observation's weight is zero, the observation is deleted from the analysis. If a weight is negative or missing, it is set to zero, and the observation is excluded from the analysis. A more complete description of the WEIGHT statement can be found in Chapter 24 "The GLM Procedure."

Observation weights can be changed interactively with the REWEIGHT statement, described earlier in this chapter.

DETAILS

Missing Values

REG constructs only one crossproducts matrix for the variables in all regressions. If any variable needed for any regression is missing, the observation is excluded from all estimates. If you include variables with missing values in the VAR statement, the corresponding observations will be excluded from all analyses, even if you never include the variables in a model. PROC REG assumes that you may want to include these variables after the first RUN statement and deletes observations with missing values.

Input Data Set

REG does not compute new regressors. For example, if you want a quadratic term in your model, you should create a new variable when you prepare the input data. For example, the statement

```
model y=x1 x1*x1;
```

is not valid. Note that the MODEL statement above is valid in PROC GLM.

The input data set for most applications of PROC REG contains standard rectangular data, but special TYPE=CORR, TYPE=COV, TYPE=UCORR, TYPE=UCOV, or TYPE=SSCP data sets can also be used. TYPE=CORR, TYPE=COV, TYPE=UCORR, and TYPE=UCOV data sets created by the CORR procedure contain means and standard deviations. In addition, TYPE=CORR and TYPE=UCORR data sets contain correlations and TYPE=COV and TYPE=UCOV data sets contain covariances. TYPE=SSCP data sets created in previous runs of PROC REG that used the OUTSSCP= option contain the sums of squares and crossproducts of the variables. See Appendix 1 in this book and "SAS Files" in *SAS Language: Reference* for more information on special SAS data sets.

These summary files save CPU time. It takes nk^2 operations (where n =number of observations, k =number of variables) to calculate crossproducts; the regressions are of the order k^3. When n is in the thousands and k is in units, you can save 99 percent of the CPU time by reusing the SSCP matrix rather than recomputing it.

When you want to use a special SAS data set as input, PROC REG must determine the TYPE for the data set. PROC CORR and PROC REG automatically set the type for their output data sets. However, if you create the data set by some other means (such as a DATA step) you must specify its type with the TYPE= data set option. If the TYPE for the data set is not specified when the data set is created, you can specify TYPE= as a data set option in the DATA= option in the PROC REG statement, as in this example,

```
proc reg data=a(type=corr);
```

When TYPE=CORR, TYPE=COV, TYPE=UCORR, TYPE=UCOV, or TYPE=SSCP data sets are used with REG, statements and options that require the original data values have no effect. The FREQ, ID, OUTPUT, PAINT, PLOT, REWEIGHT, and WEIGHT statements, and the MODEL and PRINT statement options ACOV, CLI, CLM, DW, INFLUENCE, P, R, PARTIAL, and SPEC are disabled. Since the original observations needed to calculate predicted and residual values are not present, the statements and options above are inoperative.

Example Using TYPE=CORR Data Set

Here is an example using PROC CORR to produce an input data set for PROC REG. The fitness data for this analysis can be found in **Example 2** at the end of this chapter.

```
proc corr data=fitness outp=r;
   var oxy runtime age weight runpulse maxpulse rstpulse;
proc print data=r;

proc reg data=r;
   model oxy=runtime age weight;
```

Since the OUTP= data set from PROC CORR is automatically set to
TYPE=CORR, the TYPE= data set option is not required in the example above.
The data set containing the correlation matrix is printed by the PRINT procedure
as shown in **Output 36.2**. **Output 36.3** shows results from the regression using
the TYPE=CORR data as an input data set.

Output 36.2   Output Created by PROC CORR

```
                                    The SAS System                                          1
                                 Correlation Analysis

              7 'VAR' Variables:  OXY      RUNTIME  AGE     WEIGHT   RUNPULSE MAXPULSE RSTPULSE

                                    Simple Statistics

     Variable            N          Mean        Std Dev          Sum        Minimum        Maximum

     OXY                31     47.375806       5.327231    1468.650000      37.388000      60.055000
     RUNTIME            31     10.586129       1.387414     328.170000       8.170000      14.030000
     AGE                31     47.677419       5.211443    1478.000000      38.000000      57.000000
     WEIGHT             31     77.444516       8.328568    2400.780000      59.080000      91.630000
     RUNPULSE           31    169.645161      10.251986    5259.000000     146.000000     186.000000
     MAXPULSE           31    173.774194       9.164095    5387.000000     155.000000     192.000000
     RSTPULSE           31     53.451613       7.619443    1657.000000      40.000000      70.000000


              Pearson Correlation Coefficients / Prob > |R| under Ho: Rho=0 / N = 31

                    OXY        RUNTIME        AGE        WEIGHT      RUNPULSE     MAXPULSE     RSTPULSE

OXY             1.00000      -0.86219     -0.30459     -0.16275     -0.39797     -0.23674     -0.39936
                0.0           0.0001       0.0957       0.3817       0.0266       0.1997       0.0260

RUNTIME        -0.86219       1.00000      0.18875      0.14351      0.31365      0.22610      0.45038
                0.0001        0.0          0.3092       0.4412       0.0858       0.2213       0.0110

AGE            -0.30459       0.18875      1.00000     -0.23354     -0.33787     -0.43292     -0.16410
                0.0957        0.3092       0.0          0.2061       0.0630       0.0150       0.3777

WEIGHT         -0.16275       0.14351     -0.23354      1.00000      0.18152      0.24938      0.04397
                0.3817        0.4412       0.2061       0.0          0.3284       0.1761       0.8143

RUNPULSE       -0.39797       0.31365     -0.33787      0.18152      1.00000      0.92975      0.35246
                0.0266        0.0858       0.0630       0.3284       0.0          0.0001       0.0518

MAXPULSE       -0.23674       0.22610     -0.43292      0.24938      0.92975      1.00000      0.30512
                0.1997        0.2213       0.0150       0.1761       0.0001       0.0          0.0951

RSTPULSE       -0.39936       0.45038     -0.16410      0.04397      0.35246      0.30512      1.00000
                0.0260        0.0110       0.3777       0.8143       0.0518       0.0951       0.0
```

```
                                    The SAS System                                          2

 OBS    _TYPE_    _NAME_        OXY     RUNTIME      AGE      WEIGHT    RUNPULSE   MAXPULSE   RSTPULSE

  1     MEAN                  47.3758   10.5861    47.6774    77.4445    169.645    173.774    53.4516
  2     STD                    5.3272    1.3874     5.2114     8.3286     10.252      9.164     7.6194
  3     N                     31.0000   31.0000    31.0000    31.0000     31.000     31.000    31.0000
  4     CORR     OXY           1.0000   -0.8622    -0.3046    -0.1628     -0.398     -0.237    -0.3994
  5     CORR     RUNTIME      -0.8622    1.0000     0.1887     0.1435      0.314      0.226     0.4504
  6     CORR     AGE          -0.3046    0.1887     1.0000    -0.2335     -0.338     -0.433    -0.1641
  7     CORR     WEIGHT       -0.1628    0.1435    -0.2335     1.0000      0.182      0.249     0.0440
  8     CORR     RUNPULSE     -0.3980    0.3136    -0.3379     0.1815      1.000      0.930     0.3525
  9     CORR     MAXPULSE     -0.2367    0.2261    -0.4329     0.2494      0.930      1.000     0.3051
 10     CORR     RSTPULSE     -0.3994    0.4504    -0.1641     0.0440      0.352      0.305     1.0000
```

Output 36.3   Regression of Data Created by PROC CORR

```
                              The SAS System                                    1
Model: MODEL1
Dependent Variable: OXY

                           Analysis of Variance

                              Sum of        Mean
            Source      DF    Squares      Square    F Value    Prob>F

            Model        3   656.27095   218.75698    30.272    0.0001
            Error       27   195.11060     7.22632
            C Total     30   851.38154

                 Root MSE      2.68818     R-square     0.7708
                 Dep Mean     47.37581     Adj R-sq     0.7454
                 C.V.          5.67416

                           Parameter Estimates

                          Parameter     Standard    T for H0:
            Variable  DF   Estimate       Error    Parameter=0   Prob > |T|

            INTERCEP   1   93.126150    7.55915630     12.320      0.0001
            RUNTIME    1   -3.140387    0.36737984     -8.548      0.0001
            AGE        1   -0.173877    0.09954587     -1.747      0.0921
            WEIGHT     1   -0.054437    0.06180913     -0.881      0.3862
```

Example Using TYPE=SSCP Data Set

The following is an example using the saved crossproducts matrix:

```
proc reg data=fitness outsscp=sscp;
   model oxy=runtime age weight runpulse maxpulse rstpulse;
proc print data=sscp;
proc reg data=sscp;
   model oxy=runtime age weight;
```

First, all variables are used to fit the data and create the SSCP data set. **Output 36.4** shows the PROC PRINT output for the SSCP data set. The SSCP data set is then used as the input data set for PROC REG, and a reduced model is fit to the data. **Output 36.4** also shows the PROC REG output for the reduced model. (For the PROC REG output for the full model, see **Output 36.13**.)

In the example above, the TYPE= data set option is not required since PROC REG sets the OUTSSCP= data set to TYPE=SSCP.

Output 36.4   Regression Using SSCP Matrix

```
                                               The SAS System                                                        2
OBS   _TYPE_   _NAME_    INTERCEP    RUNTIME       AGE       WEIGHT    RUNPULSE    MAXPULSE    RSTPULSE        OXY

  1    SSCP    INTERCEP     31.00     328.17      1478.00     2400.78    5259.00     5387.00     1657.00     1468.65
  2    SSCP    RUNTIME     328.17    3531.80     15687.24    25464.71   55806.29    57113.72    17684.05    15356.14
  3    SSCP    AGE        1478.00   15687.24     71282.00   114158.90  250194.00   256218.00    78806.00    69767.75
  4    SSCP    WEIGHT     2400.78   25464.71    114158.90   188008.20  407745.67   417764.62   128409.28   113522.26
  5    SSCP    RUNPULSE   5259.00   55806.29    250194.00   407745.67  895317.00   916499.00   281928.00   248497.31
  6    SSCP    MAXPULSE   5387.00   57113.72    256218.00   417764.62  916499.00   938641.00   288583.00   254866.74
  7    SSCP    RSTPULSE   1657.00   17684.05     78806.00   128409.28  281928.00   288583.00    90311.00    78015.41
  8    SSCP    OXY        1468.65   15356.14     69767.75   113522.26  248497.31   254866.74    78015.41    70429.86
  9    N         31.00      31.00       31.00        31.00       31.00      31.00       31.00       31.00
```

```
                                The SAS System                                    3
Model: MODEL1
Dependent Variable: OXY

                              Analysis of Variance

                              Sum of        Mean
         Source        DF     Squares      Square     F Value    Prob>F

         Model          3    656.27095   218.75698     30.272    0.0001
         Error         27    195.11060     7.22632
         C Total       30    851.38154

              Root MSE        2.68818    R-square      0.7708
              Dep Mean       47.37581    Adj R-sq      0.7454
              C.V.            5.67416

                             Parameter Estimates

                         Parameter     Standard    T for H0:
         Variable   DF    Estimate       Error     Parameter=0   Prob > |T|

         INTERCEP    1    93.126150    7.55915630     12.320      0.0001
         RUNTIME     1    -3.140387    0.36737984     -8.548      0.0001
         AGE         1    -0.173877    0.09954587     -1.747      0.0921
         WEIGHT      1    -0.054437    0.06180913     -0.881      0.3862
```

Output Data Sets

OUTEST= Data Set

The OUTEST= specification produces a TYPE=EST output SAS data set containing estimates and optional statistics from the regression models. For each BY group on each dependent variable occurring in each MODEL statement, REG outputs an observation to the OUTEST= data set. The variables are as follows:

- the BY variables, if any.
- _MODEL_, a character variable containing the label of the corresponding MODEL statement, or MODEL*n* if no label was specified, where *n* is 1 for the first MODEL statement, 2 for the second MODEL statement, and so on.
- _TYPE_, a character variable with the value 'PARMS' for every observation (except when the COVOUT option is used; see below).
- _DEPVAR_, the name of the dependent variable.
- _RMSE_, the root mean squared error or the estimate of the standard deviation of the error term.
- INTERCEP, the estimated intercept, unless NOINT is specified.
- all the variables listed in any MODEL or VAR statement. Values of these variables are the estimated regression coefficients for the model. A variable that does not appear in the model corresponding to a given observation has a missing value in that observation. The dependent variable in each model is given a value of −1.

If the COVOUT option is used, the covariance matrix of the estimates is output after the estimates; _TYPE_ is set to the value 'COV' and the names of the rows are identified by the 8-byte character variable, _NAME_.

For the RSQUARE, ADJRSQ, and CP methods, REG outputs one observation for each subset model selected. Additional variables are as follows:

- _IN_, the number of regressors in the model not including the intercept
- _P_, the number of parameters in the model including the intercept, if any
- _EDF_, the error degrees of freedom

- _SSE_, the error sum of squares, if the SSE option is specified
- _MSE_, the mean squared error, if the MSE option is specified
- _RSQ_, the R^2 statistic
- _ADJRSQ_, the adjusted R^2, if the ADJRSQ option is specified
- _CP_, the C_p statistic, if the CP option is specified
- _SP_, the S_p statistic, if the SP option is specified
- _JP_, the J_p statistic, if the JP option is specified
- _PC_, the PC statistic, if the PC option is specified
- _GMSEP_, the GMSEP statistic, if the GMSEP option is specified
- _AIC_, the AIC statistic, if the AIC option is specified
- _BIC_, the BIC statistic, if the BIC option is specified
- _SBC_, the SBC statistic, if the SBC option is specified.

The following is an example with a printout of the OUTEST= data set. This example uses the growth data from **Example 1** at the end of this chapter. **Output 36.5** shows the regression equations and the resulting OUTEST= data set.

```
proc reg data=growth outest=est;
   m1:  model growth=dose;
   m2:  model growth=dose dosesq;
proc print data=est;
```

Output 36.5   Regression with Printout of OUTEST= Data Set

```
                                  The SAS System                                  1

Model: M1
Dependent Variable: GROWTH

                             Analysis of Variance

                              Sum of         Mean
         Source       DF     Squares        Square     F Value     Prob>F

         Model         1    24.50166      24.50166       0.286     0.6076
         Error         8   686.39834      85.79979
         C Total       9   710.90000

              Root MSE       9.26282     R-square     0.0345
              Dep Mean      82.10000     Adj R-sq    -0.0862
              C.V.          11.28236

                            Parameter Estimates

                        Parameter      Standard     T for H0:
         Variable  DF     Estimate        Error    Parameter=0    Prob > |T|

         INTERCEP   1    86.435685    8.62596597       10.020        0.0001
         DOSE       1    -0.201660    0.37736759       -0.534        0.6076
```

```
                              The SAS System                                    2

Model: M2
Dependent Variable: GROWTH

                            Analysis of Variance

                            Sum of          Mean
          Source      DF    Squares        Square     F Value    Prob>F

          Model        2   665.70617     332.85309     51.555     0.0001
          Error        7    45.19383       6.45626
          C Total      9   710.90000

               Root MSE       2.54092    R-square      0.9364
               Dep Mean      82.10000    Adj R-sq      0.9183
               C.V.           3.09491

                           Parameter Estimates

                        Parameter      Standard     T for H0:
          Variable  DF   Estimate        Error     Parameter=0    Prob > |T|

          INTERCEP   1   35.657437    5.61792724       6.347        0.0004
          DOSE       1    5.262896    0.55802206       9.431        0.0001
          DOSESQ     1   -0.127674    0.01281135      -9.966        0.0001
```

```
                              The SAS System                                    3

  OBS   _MODEL_   _TYPE_   _DEPVAR_   _RMSE_   INTERCEP    DOSE    GROWTH    DOSESQ

   1      M1      PARMS     GROWTH    9.26282   86.4357  -0.20166    -1         .
   2      M2      PARMS     GROWTH    2.54092   35.6574   5.26290    -1     -0.12767
```

Another example uses the RSQUARE method. This example requests only the "best" model for each subset size but asks for a variety of model selection statistics, as well as the estimated regression coefficients. An OUTEST= data set is created and printed. You can obtain plots of the statistics in the OUTEST= data set with PROC PLOT. See **Output 36.6** and **Output 36.7** for results.

```
proc reg data=fitness outest=est;
   model oxy=age weight runtime runpulse rstpulse maxpulse
         / selection=rsquare mse jp gmsep cp aic bic sbc b best=1;
proc print data=est;

proc print data=est;
```

Output 36.6 PROC REG Output for Physical Fitness Data: Best Models

```
                                                         The SAS System                                                    1
       N = 31      Regression Models for Dependent Variable: OXY

                                                        Parameter
              Rsq   C(p)   AIC    BIC   GMSEP  J(p)   MSE   SBC  Estimates
       In                                                        Intercept    AGE    WEIGHT   RUNTIME  RUNPULSE  RSTPULSE  MAXPULSE

        1  0.7434  13.70  64.53  65.47  8.05  8.02  7.53  67.40   82.4218      .        .     -3.3106      .         .         .
       -----------------------------------------------------------------------------------------------------------------------------
        2  0.7642  12.39  63.90  64.82  7.95  7.86  7.17  68.21   88.4623   -0.1504     .     -3.2040      .         .         .
       -----------------------------------------------------------------------------------------------------------------------------
        3  0.8111   6.960  59.04  61.31  6.86  6.73  5.96  64.77   111.7    -0.2564     .     -2.8254   -0.1309      .         .
       -----------------------------------------------------------------------------------------------------------------------------
        4  0.8368   4.880  56.50  60.40  6.40  6.21  5.34  63.67    98.1    -0.1977     .     -2.7676   -0.3481      .       0.2705
       -----------------------------------------------------------------------------------------------------------------------------
        5  0.8480   5.106  56.30  61.57  6.46  6.18  5.18  64.90   102.2    -0.2196  -0.0723  -2.6825   -0.3734      .       0.3049
       -----------------------------------------------------------------------------------------------------------------------------
        6  0.8487   7.000  58.16  64.07  6.99  6.58  5.37  68.20   102.9    -0.2270  -0.0742  -2.6287   -0.3696   -0.0215   0.3032
       -----------------------------------------------------------------------------------------------------------------------------
```

Output 36.7 PROC PRINT Output for Physical Fitness Data:
OUTEST= Data Set

```
                                                    The SAS System                                                         1
       OBS   _MODEL_   _TYPE_   _DEPVAR_   _RMSE_   INTERCEP     AGE      WEIGHT    RUNTIME   RUNPULSE   RSTPULSE   MAXPULSE

        1    MODEL1    PARMS      OXY      2.74478   82.422       .         .      -3.31056      .          .          .
        2    MODEL1    PARMS      OXY      2.67739   88.462   -0.15037      .      -3.20395      .          .          .
        3    MODEL1    PARMS      OXY      2.44063  111.718   -0.25640      .      -2.82538  -0.13091       .          .
        4    MODEL1    PARMS      OXY      2.31159   98.148   -0.19773      .      -2.76758  -0.34811       .        0.27051
        5    MODEL1    PARMS      OXY      2.27516  102.204   -0.21962  -0.072302  -2.68252  -0.37340       .        0.30491
        6    MODEL1    PARMS      OXY      2.31695  102.934   -0.22697  -0.074177  -2.62865  -0.36963   -0.021534   0.30322

       OBS    OXY    _IN_   _P_   _EDF_    _MSE_     _RSQ_     _CP_      _JP_     _GMSEP_    _AIC_     _BIC_     _SBC_

        1     -1      1     2      29    7.53384   0.74338   13.6988   8.01990   8.05462   64.5341   65.4673   67.4021
        2     -1      2     3      28    7.16842   0.76425   12.3894   7.86214   7.94778   63.9050   64.8212   68.2069
        3     -1      3     4      27    5.95669   0.81109    6.9596   6.72530   6.85833   59.0373   61.3127   64.7733
        4     -1      4     5      26    5.34346   0.83682    4.8800   6.20531   6.39837   56.4995   60.3996   63.6694
        5     -1      5     6      25    5.17634   0.84800    5.1063   6.17821   6.45651   56.2986   61.5667   64.9025
        6     -1      6     7      24    5.36825   0.84867    7.0000   6.58043   6.98700   58.1616   64.0748   68.1995
```

OUTSSCP= Data Sets

The OUTSSCP= option produces a TYPE=SSCP output SAS data set containing sums of squares and crossproducts. A special row (observation) and column (variable) of the matrix called INTERCEP contain the number of observations and sums. Observations are identified by the 8-byte character variable _NAME_. The data set contains all variables used in MODEL statements. You can specify additional variables that you want included in the crossproducts matrix with a VAR statement.

The SSCP data set is used when a large number of observations are explored in many different runs. The SSCP data set can be saved and used for subsequent runs, which are much less expensive since REG never reads the original data again. If you run PROC REG once to only create a SSCP data set, you should list all the variables that you may need in a VAR statement or include all the variables that you may need in a MODEL statement.

The example below uses the fitness data from **Example 2** to produce an output data set with the OUTSSCP= option. The resulting output is shown in **Output 36.8**.

```
proc reg data=fitness outsscp=sscp;
   var oxy runtime age weight rstpulse runpulse maxpulse;
proc print data=sscp;
```

Since a model is not fit to the data and since the only request is to create the SSCP data set, a MODEL statement is not required in the example above. However, since the MODEL statement is not used, the VAR statement is required.

Output 36.8   SSCP Data Set Created with OUTSSCP= Option: REG Procedure

```
                                      The SAS System                                                    1

 OBS  _TYPE_   _NAME_    INTERCEP      OXY    RUNTIME      AGE     WEIGHT   RSTPULSE   RUNPULSE   MAXPULSE

  1   SSCP   INTERCEP     31.00    1468.65    328.17    1478.00   2400.78    1657.00    5259.00    5387.00
  2   SSCP   OXY        1468.65   70429.86  15356.14   69767.75 113522.26   78015.41  248497.31  254866.74
  3   SSCP   RUNTIME     328.17   15356.14   3531.80   15687.24  25464.71   17684.05   55806.29   57113.72
  4   SSCP   AGE        1478.00   69767.75  15687.24   71282.00 114158.90   78806.00  250194.00  256218.00
  5   SSCP   WEIGHT     2400.78  113522.26  25464.71  114158.90 188008.20  128409.28  407745.67  417764.62
  6   SSCP   RSTPULSE   1657.00   78015.41  17684.05   78806.00 128409.28   90311.00  281928.00  288583.00
  7   SSCP   RUNPULSE   5259.00  248497.31  55806.29  250194.00 407745.67  281928.00  895317.00  916499.00
  8   SSCP   MAXPULSE   5387.00  254866.74  57113.72  256218.00 417764.62  288583.00  916499.00  938641.00
  9    N                  31.00      31.00     31.00      31.00     31.00      31.00      31.00      31.00
```

Interactive Analysis

PROC REG allows you to change interactively both the model and the data used to compute the model. See the **SPECIFICATIONS** section for information on which statements can be used interactively. All interactive features are disabled if there is a BY statement.

Other interactive features allow you to produce and highlight scatter plots. These features are discussed in **Producing Scatter Plots** and **Painting Scatter Plots** later in this chapter. In addition, a more detailed explanation of changing the data used to compute the model is given in **Reweighting Observations in an Analysis** later in this chapter.

The following example shows the usefulness of the interactive features. First the full regression model is fit, and **Output 36.9** is produced.

```
data class;
   input name $ height weight age;
   cards;
Alfred   69.0 112.5 14
Alice    56.5  84.0 13
Barbara  65.3  98.0 13
Carol    62.8 102.5 14
Henry    63.5 102.5 14
James    57.3  83.0 12
Jane     59.8  84.5 12
Janet    62.5 112.5 15
Jeffrey  62.5  84.0 13
John     59.0  99.5 12
Joyce    51.3  50.5 11
```

```
Judy      64.3   90.0 14
Louise    56.3   77.0 12
Mary      66.5  112.0 15
Philip    72.0  150.0 16
Robert    64.8  128.0 12
Ronald    67.0  133.0 15
Thomas    57.5   85.0 11
William   66.5  112.0 15
;
proc reg;
   model weight=age height;
   id name;
run;
```

Output 36.9   Interactive Analysis: Full Model

```
                                The SAS System                                1

Model: MODEL1
Dependent Variable: WEIGHT

                            Analysis of Variance

                              Sum of        Mean
      Source          DF     Squares       Square      F Value      Prob>F

      Model            2   7215.63710   3607.81855      27.228      0.0001
      Error           16   2120.09974    132.50623
      C Total         18   9335.73684

         Root MSE        11.51114      R-square       0.7729
         Dep Mean       100.02632      Adj R-sq       0.7445
         C.V.            11.50811

                            Parameter Estimates

                        Parameter     Standard     T for H0:
      Variable    DF     Estimate       Error     Parameter=0    Prob > |T|

      INTERCEP     1   -141.223763   33.38309350     -4.230       0.0006
      AGE          1      1.278393    3.11010374      0.411       0.6865
      HEIGHT       1      3.597027    0.90546072      3.973       0.0011
```

Next, the regression model is reduced by the following statements, and **Output 36.10** is produced.

```
delete age;
print;
run;
```

Output 36.10   Interactive Analysis: Reduced Model

```
                              The SAS System                                    2

Model: MODEL1
Dependent Variable: WEIGHT

                           Analysis of Variance

                              Sum of          Mean
     Source          DF      Squares        Square    F Value    Prob>F

     Model            1    7193.24912    7193.24912     57.076    0.0001
     Error           17    2142.48772     126.02869
     C Total         18    9335.73684

            Root MSE       11.22625     R-square       0.7705
            Dep Mean      100.02632     Adj R-sq       0.7570
            C.V.           11.22330

                           Parameter Estimates

                      Parameter      Standard    T for H0:
     Variable   DF     Estimate         Error   Parameter=0    Prob > |T|

     INTERCEP    1   -143.026918   32.27459130       -4.432    0.0004
     HEIGHT      1      3.899030    0.51609395        7.555    0.0001
```

Next, the following statements generate a scatter plot of the residuals against the predicted values from the full model. **Output 36.11** is produced. The scatter plot shows a possible outlier.

```
add age;
plot r.*p.;
run;
```

Output 36.11   Interactive Analysis: Scatter Plot

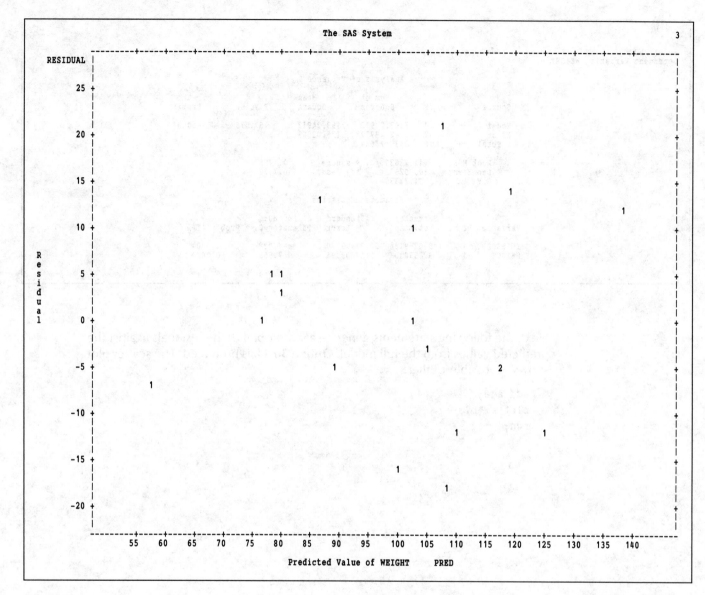

The following statements delete the observation with the largest residual, refit the regression model, and produce a scatter plot of residuals against predicted values for the refitted model. **Output 36.12** shows the new scatter plot.

```
reweight r.>20;
plot;
run;
```

Output 36.12   Interactive Analysis: Scatter Plot for Refitted Model

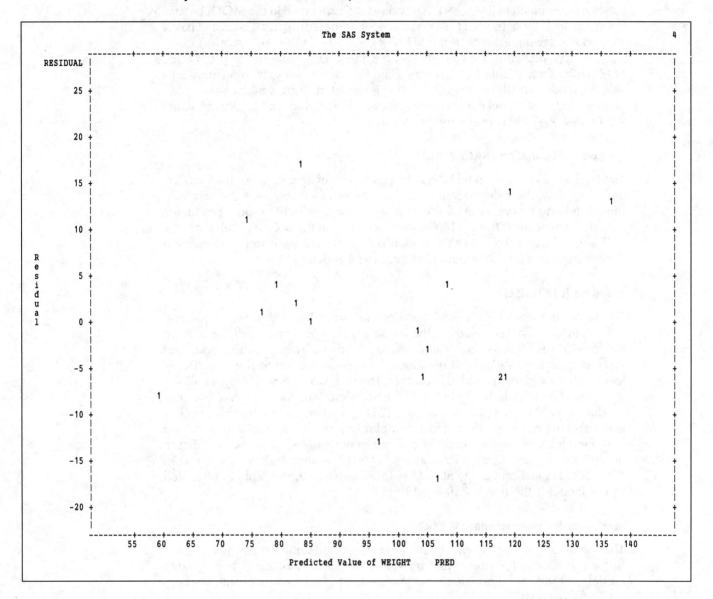

Model-Selection Methods

The nine methods of model selection implemented in PROC REG are specified with the SELECTION= option in the MODEL statement. Each method is discussed below.

Full Model Fitted (NONE)

This method is the default and provides no model selection capability. The complete model specified in the MODEL statement is used to fit the model. For many regression analyses, this may be the only method you need.

Forward Selection (FORWARD)

The forward-selection technique begins with no variables in the model. For each of the independent variables, FORWARD calculates F statistics that reflect the variable's contribution to the model if it is included. The p-values for these F statistics are compared to the SLENTRY= value that is specified in the MODEL statement (or to 0.50 if the SLENTRY= option is omitted). If no F statistic has a significance level greater than the SLENTRY= value, FORWARD stops. Otherwise, FORWARD adds the variable that has the largest F statistic to the model. FORWARD then calculates F statistics again for the variables still remaining outside the model, and the evaluation process is repeated. Thus, variables are added one by one to the model until no remaining variable produces a significant F statistic. Once a variable is in the model, it stays.

Backward Elimination (BACKWARD)

The backward-elimination technique begins by calculating statistics for a model, including all of the independent variables. Then the variables are deleted from the model one by one until all the variables remaining in the model produce F statistics significant at the SLSTAY= level specified in the MODEL statement (or at the 0.10 level if the SLSTAY= option is omitted). At each step, the variable showing the smallest contribution to the model is deleted.

Stepwise (STEPWISE)

The stepwise method is a modification of the forward-selection technique and differs in that variables already in the model do not necessarily stay there. As in the forward-selection method, variables are added one by one to the model, and the F statistic for a variable to be added must be significant at the SLENTRY= level. After a variable is added, however, the stepwise method looks at all the variables already included in the model and deletes any variable that does not produce an F statistic significant at the SLSTAY= level. Only after this check is made and the necessary deletions accomplished can another variable be added to the model. The stepwise process ends when none of the variables outside the model has an F statistic significant at the SLENTRY= level and every variable in the model is significant at the SLSTAY= level, or when the variable to be added to the model is the one just deleted from it.

Maximum R^2 Improvement (MAXR)

The maximum R^2 improvement technique does not settle on a single model. Instead, it tries to find the "best" one-variable model, the "best" two-variable model, and so forth, although it is not guaranteed to find the model with the largest R^2 for each size.

The MAXR method begins by finding the one-variable model producing the highest R^2. Then another variable, the one that yields the greatest increase in R^2, is added. Once the two-variable model is obtained, each of the variables in the model is compared to each variable not in the model. For each comparison, MAXR determines if removing one variable and replacing it with the other variable increases R^2. After comparing all possible switches, MAXR makes the switch that produces the largest increase in R^2. Comparisons begin again, and the process continues until MAXR finds that no switch could increase R^2. Thus, the two-variable model achieved is considered the "best" two-variable model the technique can find. Another variable is then added to the model, and the comparing-and-switching process is repeated to find the "best" three-variable model, and so forth.

The difference between the STEPWISE method and the MAXR method is that all switches are evaluated before any switch is made in MAXR. In the STEPWISE method, the "worst" variable can be removed without considering what adding the "best" remaining variable might accomplish. MAXR may require much more computer time than STEPWISE.

Minimum R^2 Improvement (MINR)

The MINR method closely resembles MAXR, but the switch chosen is the one that produces the smallest increase in R^2. For a given number of variables in the model, MAXR and MINR usually produce the same "best" model, but MINR considers more models of each size.

R^2 Selection (RSQUARE)

The RSQUARE method finds subsets of independent variables that best predict a dependent variable by linear regression in the given sample. You can specify the largest and smallest number of independent variables to appear in a subset and the number of subsets of each size to be selected. The RSQUARE method can efficiently perform all possible subset regressions and print the models in decreasing order of R^2 magnitude within each subset size. Other statistics are available for comparing subsets of different sizes. These statistics, as well as estimated regression coefficients, can be printed or output to a SAS data set.

The subset models selected by RSQUARE are optimal in terms of R^2 for the given sample, but they are not necessarily optimal for the population from which the sample was drawn or for any other sample for which you may want to make predictions. If a subset model is selected on the basis of a large R^2 value or any other criterion commonly used for model selection, then all regression statistics computed for that model under the assumption that the model is given a priori, including all statistics computed by REG, are biased.

While the RSQUARE method is a useful tool for exploratory model building, no statistical method can be relied on to identify the "true" model. Effective model building requires substantive theory to suggest relevant predictors and plausible functional forms for the model.

The RSQUARE method differs from the other selection methods in that RSQUARE always identifies the model with the largest R^2 for each number of variables considered. The other selection methods are not guaranteed to find the model with the largest R^2. RSQUARE requires much more computer time than the other selection methods, so a different selection method such as STEPWISE is a good choice when there are many independent variables to consider.

Adjusted R^2 Selection (ADJRSQ)

This method is similar to RSQUARE, except that the adjusted R^2 statistic is used as the criterion for selecting models, and the method finds the models with the highest adjusted R^2 within the range of sizes.

Mallows' C_p Selection (CP)

This method is similar to ADJRSQ, except that Mallow's C_p statistic is used as the criterion for model selection.

Additional Information on Model-Selection Methods

If the RSQUARE or STEPWISE procedure (as documented in *SAS User's Guide: Statistics, Version 5 Edition*) is requested, PROC REG with the appropriate model-selection method is actually used.

Reviews of model-selection methods by Hocking (1976) and Judge et al. (1980) describe these and other variable-selection methods.

Criteria Used in BACKWARD, FORWARD, and STEPWISE Model-Selection Methods

When many significance tests are performed, each at a level of, say 5 percent, the overall probability of rejecting at least one true null hypothesis is much larger than 5 percent. If you want to guard against including any variables that do not contribute to the predictive power of the model in the population, you should specify a very small significance level. In most applications many of the variables considered have some predictive power, however small. If you want to choose the model that provides the best prediction using the sample estimates, you need only guard against estimating more parameters than can be reliably estimated with the given sample size, so you should use a moderate significance level, perhaps in the range of 10 percent to 25 percent.

In addition to R^2, the C_p statistic is printed for each model generated in the model-selection methods. C_p was proposed by Mallows (1973) as a criterion for selecting a model. It is a measure of total squared error defined as

$$C_p = (SSE_p / s^2) - (N - 2{*}p)$$

where s^2 is the MSE for the full model, and SSE_p is the error sum of squares for a model with p parameters including the intercept, if any. If C_p is plotted against p, Mallows recommends the model where C_p first approaches p. When the right model is chosen, the parameter estimates are unbiased, and this is reflected in C_p near p. For further discussion, see Daniel and Wood (1980).

The adjusted R^2 statistic is an alternative to R^2 that is adjusted for the number of parameters in the model. The adjusted R^2 statistic is calculated as

$$ADJRSQ = 1 - [((n - i)(1 - R^2)) / (n - p)]$$

where n is the number of observations used in fitting the model, and i is an indicator variable that is 1 if the model includes an intercept, and 0 otherwise.

Limitations in Model-Selection Methods

The use of model-selection methods can be time-consuming in some cases because there is no built-in limit on the number of independent variables, and the calculations for a large number of independent variables can be lengthy. The recommended limit on the number of independent variables for the MINR method is $20+i$, where i is the value of the INCLUDE= option.

For the RSQUARE, ADJRSQ, or CP methods, with a large value of the BEST= option, adding one more variable to the list from which regressors are selected may significantly increase the CPU time. Also, the time required for the analysis is highly dependent on the data and on the values of the BEST=, START=, and STOP= options.

Parameter Estimates and Associated Statistics

The following example uses the fitness data from **Example 2** later in this chapter. **Output 36.13** shows the parameter estimates and the printout from the SS1, SS2, STB, COVB, and CORRB options.

```
proc reg data=fitness;
   model oxy=runtime age weight runpulse maxpulse rstpulse
      / ss1 ss2 stb covb corrb;
```

Output 36.13 Regression Using the SS1, SS2, STB, COVB, and CORRB Options

```
                                    The SAS System                                      1

Model: MODEL1
Dependent Variable: OXY

                                 Analysis of Variance

                                    Sum of        Mean
          Source        DF        Squares       Square     F Value     Prob>F

          Model          6      722.54361    120.42393      22.433     0.0001
          Error         24      128.83794      5.36825
          C Total       30      851.38154

              Root MSE        2.31695      R-square       0.8487
              Dep Mean       47.37581      Adj R-sq       0.8108
              C.V.            4.89057

                                 Parameter Estimates

                     Parameter     Standard     T for H0:                                        Standardized
    Variable   DF     Estimate        Error    Parameter=0   Prob > |T|    Type I SS    Type II SS    Estimate

    INTERCEP    1   102.934479   12.40325810        8.299       0.0001        69578    369.728311   0.00000000
    RUNTIME     1    -2.628653    0.38456220       -6.835       0.0001   632.900100    250.822101  -0.68460149
    AGE         1    -0.226974    0.09983747       -2.273       0.0322    17.765633     27.745771  -0.22204052
    WEIGHT      1    -0.074177    0.05459316       -1.359       0.1869     5.605217      9.910588  -0.11596863
    RUNPULSE    1    -0.369628    0.11985294       -3.084       0.0051    38.875742     51.058058  -0.71132998
    MAXPULSE    1     0.303217    0.13649519        2.221       0.0360    26.826403     26.491424   0.52160512
    RSTPULSE    1    -0.021534    0.06605428       -0.326       0.7473     0.570513      0.570513  -0.03079918


                                 Covariance of Estimates

COVB            INTERCEP        RUNTIME           AGE          WEIGHT       RUNPULSE       MAXPULSE       RSTPULSE

INTERCEP    153.84081152   0.7678373769   -0.902049478   -0.178237818   0.280796516   -0.832761667   -0.147954715
RUNTIME       0.7678373769   0.1478880839   -0.014191688   -0.004417672  -0.009047784    0.0046249498  -0.010915224
AGE          -0.902049478   -0.014191688    0.009967521    0.0010219105  -0.001203914    0.0035823843   0.0014897532
WEIGHT       -0.178237818   -0.004417672    0.0010219105   0.0029804131   0.0009644683  -0.001372241    0.0003799295
RUNPULSE      0.280796516   -0.009047784   -0.001203914    0.0009644683   0.0143647273  -0.014952457   -0.000764507
MAXPULSE     -0.832761667    0.0046249498   0.0035823843  -0.001372241   -0.014952457    0.0186309364   0.0003425724
RSTPULSE     -0.147954715   -0.010915224    0.0014897532   0.0003799295  -0.000764507    0.0003425724   0.0043631674


                                 Correlation of Estimates

CORRB           INTERCEP        RUNTIME           AGE          WEIGHT       RUNPULSE       MAXPULSE       RSTPULSE

INTERCEP          1.0000         0.1610        -0.7285        -0.2632        0.1889        -0.4919        -0.1806
RUNTIME           0.1610         1.0000        -0.3696        -0.2104       -0.1963         0.0881        -0.4297
AGE              -0.7285        -0.3696         1.0000         0.1875       -0.1006         0.2629         0.2259
WEIGHT           -0.2632        -0.2104         0.1875         1.0000        0.1474        -0.1842         0.1054
RUNPULSE          0.1889        -0.1963        -0.1006         0.1474        1.0000        -0.9140        -0.0966
MAXPULSE         -0.4919         0.0881         0.2629        -0.1842       -0.9140         1.0000         0.0380
RSTPULSE         -0.1806        -0.4297         0.2259         0.1054       -0.0966         0.0380         1.0000
```

The output above first shows an Analysis of Variance table. The *F* statistic for the overall model is significant, indicating that the model explains a significant portion of the variation in the data.

The second portion of output shows Parameter Estimates and some associated statistics. First, the estimates are shown, followed by their Standard Errors. The next two columns of the table contain the *t* statistics and the corresponding probabilities for testing the null hypothesis that the parameter is not significantly different from zero. These probabilities are usually referred to as *p*-values. For example, in the output above, the INTERCEP (or intercept) term in the model is estimated to be 102.9 and is significantly different from zero (at the 5% significance level). The next two columns of the table are the result of requesting the SS1 and SS2 options and show sequential and partial Sums of Squares (SS) associated with each variable. The Standardized Estimates (produced by the STB option) are the parameter estimates that result when all variables are standardized to a mean of 0 and a variance of 1. These estimates are computed by multiplying the original estimates by the standard deviation of the regressor (independent) variable and then dividing by the standard deviation of the dependent variable.

The final two sections of output are produced as a result of requesting the COVB and CORRB options. These sections show the estimated covariance matrix of the parameter estimates and the estimated correlation matrix of the estimates.

For further discussion of the parameters and statistics, see **Printed Output** later in this chapter, and **Parameter Estimates and Associated Statistics** and **Comments on Interpreting Regression Statistics** in Chapter 1.

Predicted and Residual Values

The printout of the predicted values and residuals is controlled by the P, R, CLM, and CLI options in the MODEL statement. The P option causes REG to print the observation number, the ID value (if an ID statement is used), the actual value, the predicted value, and the residual. The R, CLI, and CLM options also produce the items under the P option. Thus, P is unnecessary if you use one of the other options.

The R option requests more detail, especially about the residuals. The standard errors of the predicted value and the residual are printed. The studentized residual, which is the residual divided by its standard error, is both printed and plotted. A measure of influence, Cook's D, is printed. Cook's D measures the change to the estimates that results from deleting each observation. See Cook (1977, 1979). (This statistic is very similar to DFFITS.)

The CLM option requests that REG print the 95% lower and upper confidence limits for the predicted mean values. This accounts for the variation due to estimating the parameters only. If you want a 95% confidence interval for individual predicted values (future values of the dependent variable at the observed values of the regressor variables), you can use the CLI option, which adds in the estimated variability of the error term.

You can use these statistics in PLOT and PAINT statements. This is useful in performing a variety of regression diagnostics. For definitions of the statistics produced by these options, see Chapter 1.

Here is an example using the growth data found in **Example 1** later in this chapter. These statements produce **Output 36.14**:

```
proc reg data=growth;
   id dose;
   model growth=dose dosesq / p r cli clm;
```

Output 36.14   Regression Using the P, R, CLI, and CLM Options

```
                                    The SAS System                                          1

Model: MODEL1
Dependent Variable: GROWTH

                               Analysis of Variance

                                    Sum of         Mean
        Source          DF        Squares        Square      F Value      Prob>F

        Model            2      665.70617     332.85309       51.555      0.0001
        Error            7       45.19383       6.45626
        C Total          9      710.90000

               Root MSE        2.54092      R-square       0.9364
               Dep Mean       82.10000      Adj R-sq       0.9183
               C.V.            3.09491

                               Parameter Estimates

                         Parameter       Standard      T for H0:
        Variable    DF    Estimate          Error     Parameter=0     Prob > |T|

        INTERCEP     1    35.657437     5.61792724          6.347       0.0004
        DOSE         1     5.262896     0.55802206          9.431       0.0001
        DOSESQ       1    -0.127674     0.01281135         -9.966       0.0001
```

```
                                    The SAS System                                          2

                 Dep Var  Predict  Std Err  Lower95%  Upper95%  Lower95%  Upper95%            Std Err   Student
Obs   DOSE       GROWTH     Value   Predict     Mean      Mean   Predict   Predict  Residual  Residual  Residual    -2-1-0 1 2

 1      10      73.0000   75.5190    1.691   71.5198   79.5182   68.3014   82.7366   -2.5190     1.896    -1.328    |  **|   |
 2      10      78.0000   75.5190    1.691   71.5198   79.5182   68.3014   82.7366    2.4810     1.896     1.308    |   |**  |
 3      15      85.0000   85.8742    1.077   83.3280   88.4204   79.3486   92.3998   -0.8742     2.301    -0.380    |   |    |
 4      20      90.0000   89.8457    1.108   87.2258   92.4657   83.2910   96.4       0.1543     2.287     0.067    |   |    |
 5      20      91.0000   89.8457    1.108   87.2258   92.4657   83.2910   96.4       1.1543     2.287     0.505    |   |*   |
 6      25      87.0000   87.4335    1.070   84.9042   89.9629   80.9145   93.9526   -0.4335     2.305    -0.188    |   |    |
 7      25      86.0000   87.4335    1.070   84.9042   89.9629   80.9145   93.9526   -1.4335     2.305    -0.622    |  *|   |
 8      25      91.0000   87.4335    1.070   84.9042   89.9629   80.9145   93.9526    3.5665     2.305     1.547    |   |*** |
 9      30      75.0000   78.6377    1.204   75.7896   81.4857   71.9885   85.2868   -3.6377     2.237    -1.626    |***|   |
10      35      65.0000   63.4581    2.269   58.0916   68.8245   55.4021   71.5141    1.5419     1.143     1.349    |   |**  |
11      40       .        41.8948    4.208   31.9439   51.8456   30.2707   53.5189    .          .         .
12      45       .        13.9478    6.860   -2.2725   30.1681   -3.3496   31.2452    .          .         .

                 Cook's
Obs   DOSE         D

 1      10       0.468
 2      10       0.454
 3      15       0.011
 4      20       0.000
 5      20       0.020
 6      25       0.003
 7      25       0.028
 8      25       0.172
 9      30       0.255
10      35       2.393
11      40        .
12      45        .

Sum of Residuals                    0
Sum of Squared Residuals       45.1938
Predicted Resid SS (Press)    145.7300
```

After printing the usual Analysis of Variance and Parameter Estimates tables, the procedure prints the results of requesting the options for predicted and residual values. For each observation, the requested information is shown. Note that the ID variable is used to identify each observation. Also, note that for observations with missing dependent variables, the predicted value, standard error of the predicted value, and confidence intervals for the predicted value are still available.

The plot of studentized residuals and the Cook's D statistics are printed as a result of requesting the R option. In general, in the plot of studentized residuals, a large number of observations with absolute values greater than two indicates an inadequate model.

Producing Scatter Plots

The interactive PLOT statement available in REG allows you to look at scatter plots of data and diagnostic statistics. These plots can help you to evaluate the model and detect outliers in your data. Several options enable you to place multiple plots on a single page, superimpose plots, and collect plots to be overlayed by later plots. The PAINT statement can be used to highlight points on a plot. See **Painting Scatter Plots** later in this chapter for more information on painting.

The CLASS data set introduced in **Interactive Analysis** is used in the examples below.

You can superimpose several plots with the OVERLAY option. With the statements below, a plot of WEIGHT against HEIGHT is overlaid with plots of the predicted values and the 95% prediction intervals. The model on which the statistics are based is the full model including HEIGHT and AGE. These statements produce **Output 36.15**:

```
proc reg data=class;
   model weight=height age / noprint;
   plot (u95. l95. p.)*height='-' weight*height
        / overlay symbol='o';
run;
```

Output 36.15 Scatter Plot Showing Data, Predicted Values, and Confidence Limits

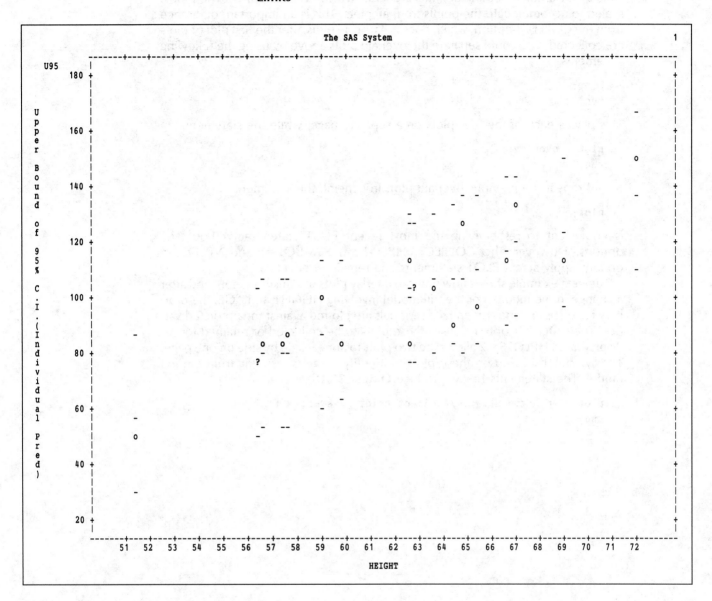

On this plot, the data values are marked with the symbol 'o' and the predicted values and prediction interval limits are labeled with the symbol '-'. The plot is scaled to accommodate the points from all plots. This is an important difference from the COLLECT option, which does not rescale plots after the first plot or plots are collected. You could separate the overlaid plots above by using the following statements:

```
plot;
run;
```

This places each of the four plots on a separate page, while the statements

```
plot / overlay;
run;
```

would repeat the previous overlaid plot. In general, the statement

```
plot;
```

is equivalent to respecifying the most recent PLOT statement without any options. However, the COLLECT, HPLOTS=, SYMBOL=, and VPLOTS= options apply across PLOT statements and remain in effect.

The next example shows how you can overlay plots of statistics before and after a change in the model. For the full model involving HEIGHT and AGE, the ordinary residuals and the studentized residuals are plotted against the predicted values. The COLLECT option causes these plots to be collected or retained for redisplay later. HPLOTS=2 allows the two plots to appear side by side on one page. The symbol 'f' is used on these plots to identify them as resulting from the full model. The statements below produce **Output 36.16**:

```
plot r.*p. student.*p. / collect hplots=2 symbol='f';
run;
```

Output 36.16   Collecting Residual Plots for the Full Model

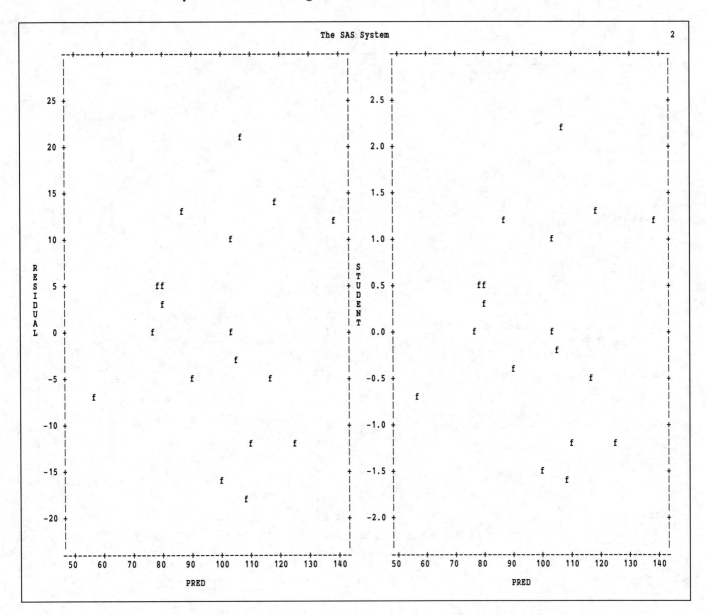

Note that these plots are not overlaid. The COLLECT option does not overlay the plots in one PLOT statement but retains them so they can be overlaid by later plots. When the COLLECT option appears in a PLOT statement, the plots in that statement become the first plots in the collection.

Next, the model is reduced by deleting the AGE variable. The PLOT statement requests the same plots as before but labels the points with the symbol 'r' denoting the reduced model. The statements below produce **Output 36.17**:

```
delete age;
plot r.*p. student.*p. / symbol='r';
run;
```

Output 36.17   Overlaid Residual Plots for Full and Reduced Models

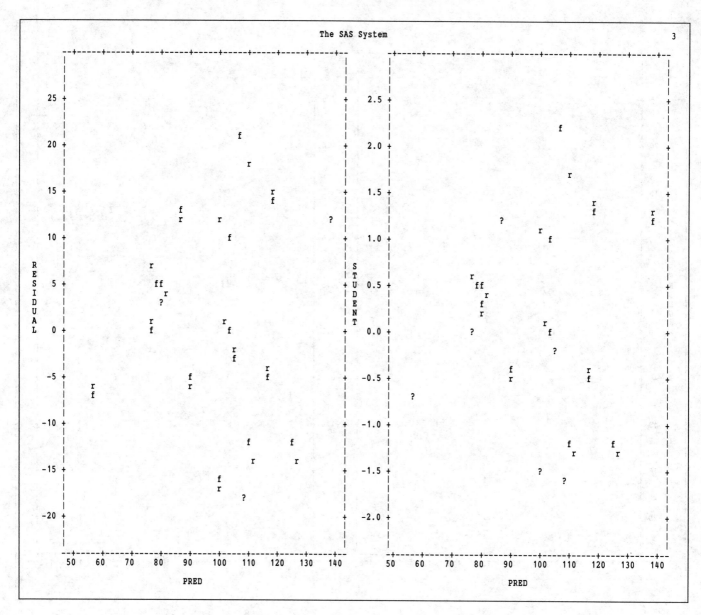

Notice that the COLLECT option caused the corresponding plots to be overlaid. The points labeled 'f' are from the full model, and points labeled 'r' are from the reduced model. Positions labeled '?' contain at least one point from each model. In this example, OVERLAY could not be used because all of the plots to be overlaid could not be specified in one PLOT statement. With the COLLECT option, any changes to the model or the data used to fit the model do not affect plots collected before the changes. Collected plots are always reproduced exactly as they first appeared. (Similarly, a PAINT statement does not affect plots collected before the PAINT statement was issued.)

The previous example overlaid the residual plots for two different models. You may prefer to see them side by side on the same page. This can also be done with the COLLECT option by using a blank plot. Continuing from the last example, COLLECT, HPLOTS=2 and SYMBOL='r' are still in effect. In the PLOT statement below, the CLEAR option deletes the collected plots and allows the specified plot to begin a new collection. The plot created is the residual plot for the reduced model. The statements below produce **Output 36.18**:

```
plot r.*p. / clear;
run;
```

Output 36.18   Residual Plot for Reduced Model Only

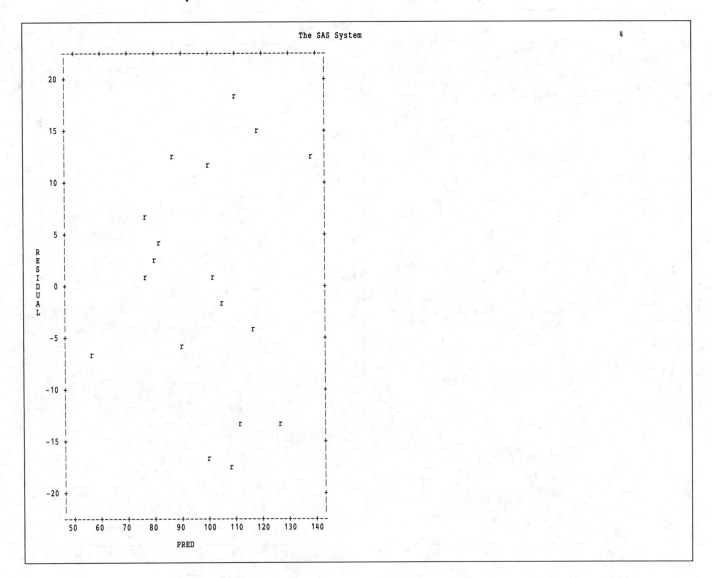

The next statements add AGE to the model and place the residual plot for the full model next to the plot for the reduced model. Notice that a blank plot is created in the first plot request by placing nothing between the quotes. Since COLLECT is in effect, this plot is superimposed on the residual plot for the

reduced model. The residual plot for the full model is created by the second
request. The result is the desired side-by-side plots. The NOCOLLECT option
turns off the collection process after the specified plots are added and displayed.
Any PLOT statements that follow show only the newly specified plots. These
statements produce **Output 36.19**:

```
add age;
plot r.*p.='' r.*p.='f' / nocollect;
run;
```

Output 36.19   Side-by-Side Residual Plots for the Full and Reduced Models

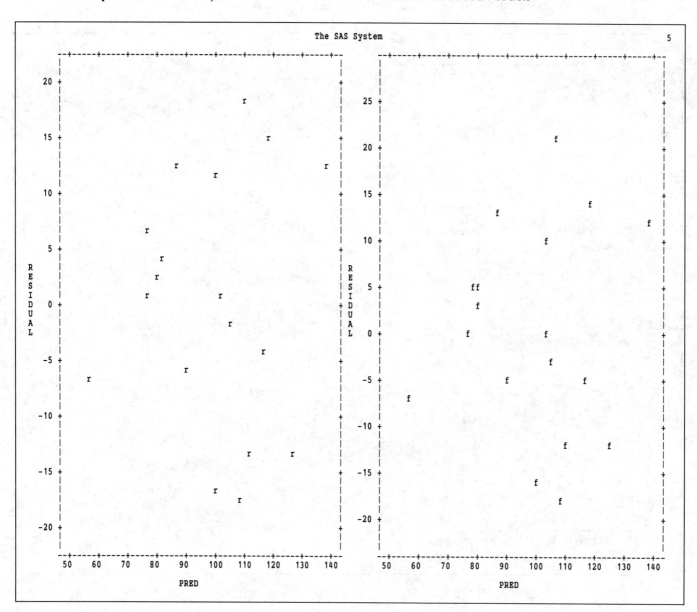

Frequently, when COLLECT is in effect, you will want the current and following PLOT statements to show only the specified plots. To do this, use both the CLEAR and NOCOLLECT options in the current PLOT statement.

Painting Scatter Plots

Painting scatter plots is a useful interactive tool that allows you to mark points of interest in scatter plots. Painting can be used to identify extreme points in scatter plots or to reveal the relationship between two scatter plots. The CLASS data (from **Interactive Analysis** earlier in this chapter) is used to illustrate some of these applications. First, a scatter plot of the studentized residuals against the predicted values is generated. This plot is shown in **Output 36.20**.

```
proc reg data=class;
   model weight=age height / noprint;
   id name;
   plot student.*p.;
run;
```

Output 36.20   Plotting Studentized Residuals Against Predicted Values

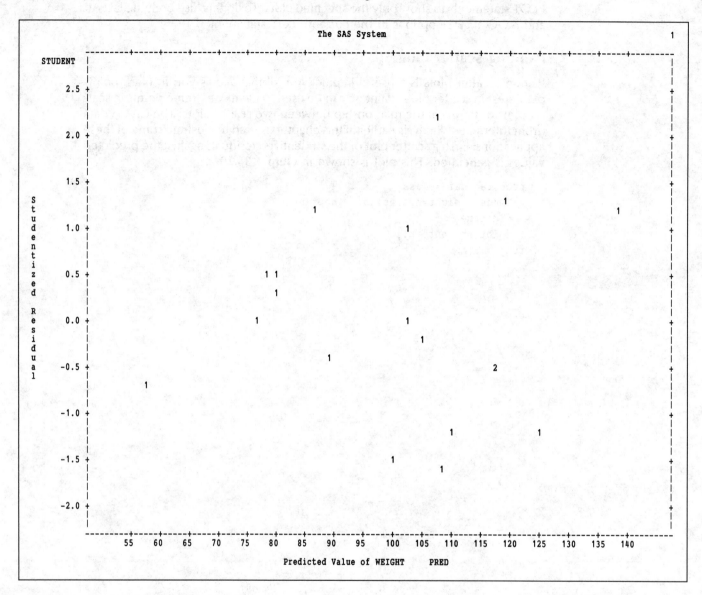

Then, the following statements identify the observation **Henry** in the scatter plot and produce **Output 36.21**:

```
paint name='Henry' / symbol = 'H';
plot;
run;
```

Output 36.21 Painting One Observation

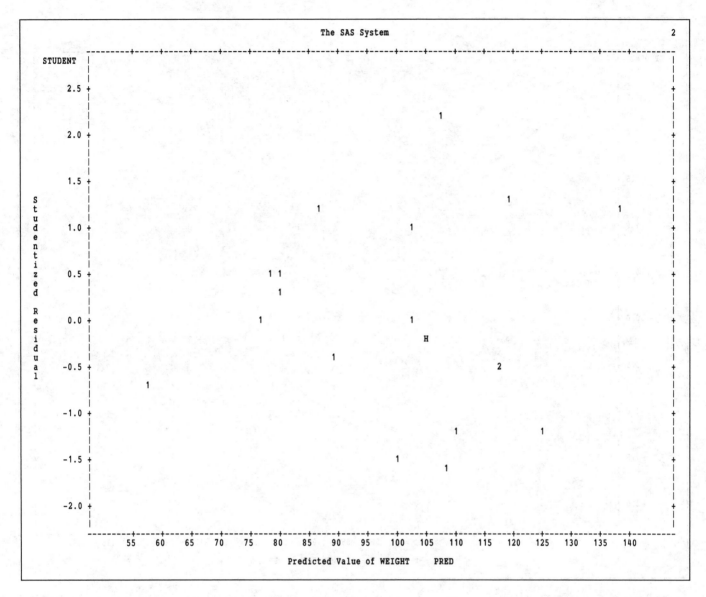

Then, use the following statements to identify observations with large absolute residuals:

```
paint student.>=2 or student.<=-2 / symbol='s';
plot;
run;
```

The log shows the observation numbers found with the above condition and gives the printing symbol and the number of observations found. Note that the previous PAINT statement is also used in the PLOT statement. **Output 36.22** shows the scatter plot produced by the statements above.

Output 36.22   Painting Several Observations

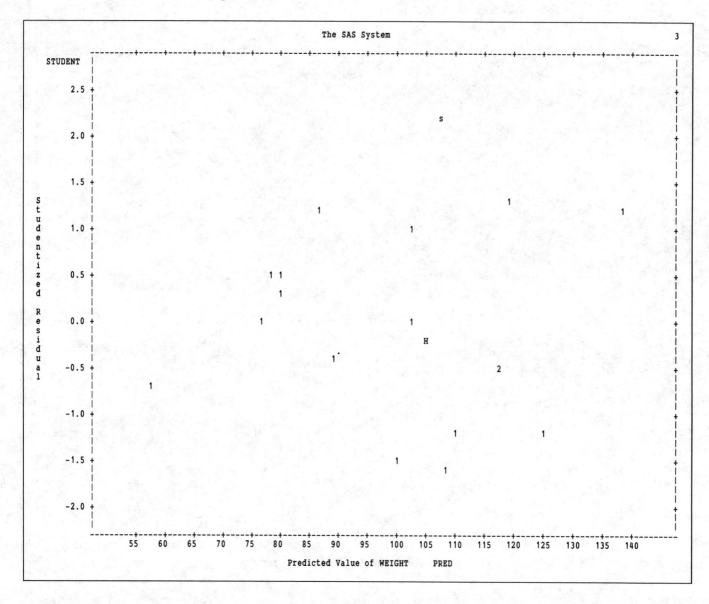

Use the following statements to relate two different scatter plots. These statements produce **Output 36.23**:

```
paint student.>=1 / symbol='p';
paint student.<1 and student.>-1 / symbol='s';
paint student.<=-1 / symbol='n';
plot student. * p. cookd. * h. / hplots=2;
run;
```

Output 36.23 Painting Observations on More than One Plot

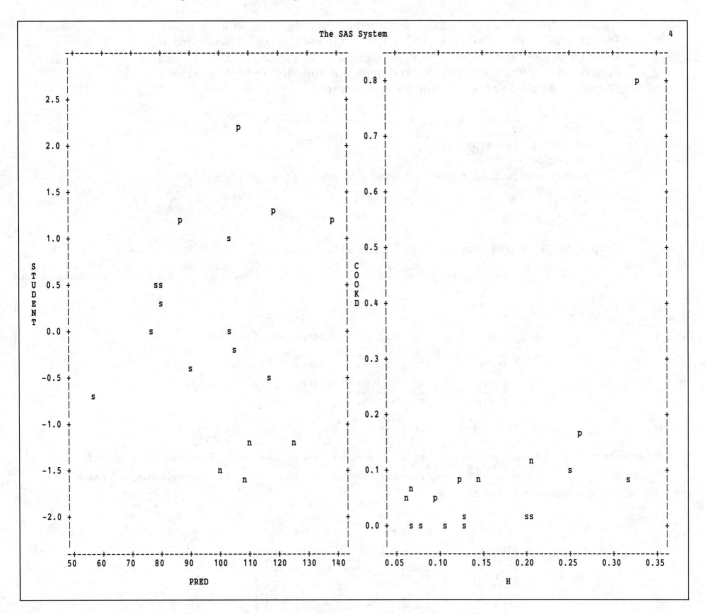

Models of Less than Full Rank

If the model is not full rank, there are an infinite number of least-squares solutions for the estimates. REG chooses a nonzero solution for all variables that are linearly independent of previous variables and a zero solution for other variables. This solution corresponds to using a generalized inverse in the normal equations, and the expected values of the estimates are the Hermite normal form of **X** multiplied by the true parameters:

$$E(\mathbf{b}) = (\mathbf{X'X})^-(\mathbf{X'X})\boldsymbol{\beta} \quad .$$

Degrees of freedom for the estimates set to zero are reported as zero. The hypotheses that are not testable have *t* tests printed as missing. The message that the model is not full rank includes a printout of the relations that exist in the matrix.

The example below uses the fitness data from **Example 2** later in this chapter. The variable DIF=RUNPULSE−RSTPULSE is created. When this variable is included in the model along with RUNPULSE and RSTPULSE, there is a linear dependency (or exact collinearity) between the dependent variables. **Output 36.24** shows how this problem is diagnosed.

```
data fit2;
   set fitness;
   dif=runpulse-rstpulse;
proc reg data=fit2;
   model oxy=runtime age weight runpulse maxpulse rstpulse dif;
run;
```

Output 36.24   Model That Is Not Full Rank: REG Procedure

```
                                 The SAS System                                          1

Model: MODEL1
Dependent Variable: OXY

                              Analysis of Variance

                                 Sum of        Mean
         Source        DF       Squares       Square     F Value      Prob>F

         Model          6     722.54361    120.42393      22.433      0.0001
         Error         24     128.83794      5.36825
         C Total       30     851.38154

              Root MSE      2.31695     R-square     0.8487
              Dep Mean     47.37581     Adj R-sq     0.8108
              C.V.          4.89057

NOTE: Model is not full rank. Least-squares solutions for the parameters are not unique. Some statistics will be misleading. A
      reported DF of 0 or B means that the estimate is biased.
      The following parameters have been set to 0, since the variables are a linear combination of other variables as shown.

   DIF      = +1.0000 * RUNPULSE -1.0000 * RSTPULSE
                              Parameter Estimates

                        Parameter      Standard      T for H0:
         Variable  DF    Estimate         Error     Parameter=0     Prob > |T|

         INTERCEP   1   102.934479   12.40325810        8.299         0.0001
         RUNTIME    1    -2.628653    0.38456220       -6.835         0.0001
         AGE        1    -0.226974    0.09983747       -2.273         0.0322
         WEIGHT     1    -0.074177    0.05459316       -1.359         0.1869
         RUNPULSE   B    -0.369628    0.11985294       -3.084         0.0051
         MAXPULSE   1     0.303217    0.13649519        2.221         0.0360
         RSTPULSE   B    -0.021534    0.06605428       -0.326         0.7473
         DIF        0     0               .              .              .
```

Note that PROC REG prints a message informing you that the model is less than full rank. Parameters with DF=0 are not estimated, and parameters with DF=B are biased. In addition, the form of the linear dependency among the regressors is printed.

Collinearity Diagnostics

When a regressor is nearly a linear combination of other regressors in the model, the affected estimates are unstable and have high standard errors. This problem is called *collinearity* or *multicollinearity*. It is a good idea to find out which variables are nearly collinear with which other variables. The approach in PROC REG follows that of Belsley, Kuh, and Welsch (1980). REG provides several methods for detecting collinearity with the COLLIN, COLLINOINT, TOL, and VIF options.

The COLLIN option in the MODEL statement requests that a collinearity analysis be done. First, **X'X** is scaled to have 1s on the diagonal. If COLLINOINT is specified, the intercept variable is adjusted out first. Then the eigenvalues and eigenvectors are extracted. The analysis in REG is reported with eigenvalues of **X'X** rather than values from the singular decomposition of **X**. The singular values of **X** are the square roots of the eigenvalues of **X'X**.

The condition indices are the square roots of the ratio of the largest eigenvalue to each individual eigenvalue. The largest condition index is the condition number of the scaled **X** matrix. When this number is large, the data are said to be ill-conditioned. When this number is extremely large, the estimates may have a fair amount of numerical error (although the statistical standard error almost always is much greater than the numerical error).

For each variable, REG prints the proportion of the variance of the estimate accounted for by each principal component. A collinearity problem occurs when a component associated with a high condition index contributes strongly to the variance of two or more variables.

The VIF option in the MODEL statement provides the variance inflation factors. These factors measure the inflation in the variances of the parameter estimates due to collinearities that exist among the regressor (dependent) variables. There are no formal criteria for deciding if a VIF is large enough to affect the predicted values.

The TOL option requests the tolerance values for the parameter estimates.

For a complete discussion of the methods discussed above, see Belsley, Kuh, and Welsch (1980). For a more detailed explanation of using the methods with PROC REG, see Freund and Littell (1986).

Here is an example using the COLLIN option on the fitness data found in **Example 2** later in this chapter. The statements below produce **Output 36.25**:

```
proc reg data=fitness;
   model oxy=runtime age weight runpulse maxpulse rstpulse
        / tol vif collin;
run;
```

Output 36.25   Regression Using the TOL, VIF, and COLLIN Options

```
                            The SAS System                                    1
Model: MODEL1
Dependent Variable: OXY

                         Analysis of Variance

                            Sum of         Mean
        Source      DF     Squares        Square    F Value    Prob>F

        Model        6   722.54361     120.42393     22.433    0.0001
        Error       24   128.83794       5.36825
        C Total     30   851.38154

           Root MSE       2.31695     R-square       0.8487
           Dep Mean      47.37581     Adj R-sq       0.8108
           C.V.           4.89057
```

(continued on next page)

(continued from previous page)

Parameter Estimates

Variable	DF	Parameter Estimate	Standard Error	T for H0: Parameter=0	Prob > |T|	Tolerance	Variance Inflation
INTERCEP	1	102.934479	12.40325810	8.299	0.0001	.	0.00000000
RUNTIME	1	-2.628653	0.38456220	-6.835	0.0001	0.62858771	1.59086788
AGE	1	-0.226974	0.09983747	-2.273	0.0322	0.66101010	1.51283618
WEIGHT	1	-0.074177	0.05459316	-1.359	0.1869	0.86555401	1.15532940
RUNPULSE	1	-0.369628	0.11985294	-3.084	0.0051	0.11852169	8.43727418
MAXPULSE	1	0.303217	0.13649519	2.221	0.0360	0.11436612	8.74384843
RSTPULSE	1	-0.021534	0.06605428	-0.326	0.7473	0.70641990	1.41558865

Collinearity Diagnostics

Number	Eigenvalue	Condition Number	Var Prop INTERCEP	Var Prop RUNTIME	Var Prop AGE	Var Prop WEIGHT	Var Prop RUNPULSE	Var Prop MAXPULSE	Var Prop RSTPULSE
1	6.94991	1.00000	0.0000	0.0002	0.0002	0.0002	0.0000	0.0000	0.0003
2	0.01868	19.29087	0.0022	0.0252	0.1463	0.0104	0.0000	0.0000	0.3906
3	0.01503	21.50072	0.0006	0.1286	0.1501	0.2357	0.0012	0.0012	0.0281
4	0.00911	27.62115	0.0064	0.6090	0.0319	0.1831	0.0015	0.0012	0.1903
5	0.00607	33.82918	0.0013	0.1250	0.1128	0.4444	0.0151	0.0083	0.3648
6	0.00102	82.63757	0.7997	0.0975	0.4966	0.1033	0.0695	0.0056	0.0203
7	0.0001795	196.78560	0.1898	0.0146	0.0621	0.0228	0.9128	0.9836	0.0057

Influence Diagnostics

The INFLUENCE option requests the statistics proposed by Belsley, Kuh, and Welsch (1980) to measure the influence of each observation on the estimates. Influential observations are those that, according to various criteria, appear to have a large influence on the parameter estimates. Let $\mathbf{b}(i)$ be the parameter estimates after deleting the ith observation; let $s(i)^2$ be the variance estimate after deleting the ith observation; let $\mathbf{X}(i)$ be the $\mathbf{X}$ matrix without the ith observation; let $\hat{y}(i)$ be the ith value predicted without using the ith observation; let $r_i = y_i - \hat{y}_i$ be the ith residual; and let h_i be the ith diagonal of the projection matrix for the predictor space, also called the *hat matrix*:

$$h_i = \mathbf{x}_i(\mathbf{X'X})^{-1}\mathbf{x}_i' \quad .$$

Belsley, Kuh, and Welsch propose a cutoff of 2*p/n, where n is the number of observations used to fit the model, and p is the number of parameters in the model. Observations with h_i values above this cutoff should be investigated.

For each observation, REG first prints the residual, the studentized residual, and the h_i. The studentized residual differs slightly from that in the previous section since the error variance is estimated by $s(i)^2$ without the ith observation, not by s^2, for example,

$$\text{RSTUDENT} = r_i / \left(s(i) \sqrt{(1-h_i)} \right) \quad .$$

Observations with RSTUDENT larger than 2 in absolute value may need some attention.

The COVRATIO statistic measures the change in the determinant of the covariance matrix of the estimates by deleting the ith observation:

$$\text{COVRATIO} = \det \left(s^2(i)(\mathbf{X}(i)'\mathbf{X}(i))^{-1} \right) / \det \left(s^2(\mathbf{X}'\mathbf{X})^{-1} \right) \quad .$$

Belsley, Kuh, and Welsch suggest observations with

$$|\,\text{COVRATIO} - 1\,| \geq 3p\,/\,n$$

where p is the number of parameters in the model, and n is the number of observations used to fit the model, are worth investigation.

The DFFITS statistic is a scaled measure of the change in the predicted value for the ith observation and is calculated by deleting the ith observation. A large value indicates that the observation is very influential in its neighborhood of the $\mathbf{X}$ space.

$$\text{DFFITS} = (\hat{y}_i - \hat{y}(i)) / \left(s(i)\sqrt{h_i} \right) \quad .$$

Large values of DFFITS indicate influential observations. A general cutoff to consider is 2; a size-adjusted cutoff recommended by Belsley, Kuh, and Welsch is $2\sqrt{p/n}$, where n and p are as defined above.

DFFITS is very similar to Cook's D, defined in **Predicted and Residual Values** earlier in this chapter.

DFBETAS are the scaled measures of the change in each parameter estimate and are calculated by deleting the ith observation:

$$\text{DFBETAS}_j = (b_j - b_j(i)) / (s(i)\sqrt{(\mathbf{X}'\mathbf{X})^{jj}})$$

where

$$(\mathbf{X}'\mathbf{X})^{jj} \quad \text{is the } (j, j)\text{th element of } (\mathbf{X}'\mathbf{X})^{-1} \quad .$$

In general, large values of DFBETAS indicate observations that are influential in estimating a given parameter. Belsley, Kuh, and Welsch recommend 2 as a general cutoff value to indicate influential observations and $2/\sqrt{n}$ as a size-adjusted cutoff.

Output 36.26 shows the portion of output produced by the INFLUENCE option for the growth rate example (**Example 1**). See **Output 36.14** for the fitted regression equation.

```
proc reg data=growth;
   model growth=dose dosesq / influence;
run;
```

Output 36.26   Regression Using the INFLUENCE Option

```
                                      The SAS System                                         2

                           Hat Diag      Cov             INTERCEP    DOSE     DOSESQ
      Obs  Residual  Rstudent      H     Ratio   Dffits   Dfbetas   Dfbetas  Dfbetas

        1   -2.5190   -1.4221   0.4430   1.1928  -1.2683   -1.0473    0.8237  -0.6697
        2    2.4810    1.3936   0.4430   1.2293   1.2430    1.0263   -0.8072   0.6563
        3   -0.8742   -0.3554   0.1796   1.8183  -0.1663   -0.0243   -0.0182   0.0382
        4    0.1543    0.0625   0.1901   1.9570   0.0303   -0.0137    0.0193  -0.0204
        5    1.1543    0.4761   0.1901   1.7544   0.2307   -0.1043    0.1468  -0.1555
        6   -0.4335   -0.1746   0.1772   1.9009  -0.0810    0.0438   -0.0502   0.0459
        7   -1.4335   -0.5924   0.1772   1.6274  -0.2750    0.1486   -0.1703   0.1558
        8    3.5665    1.7662   0.1772   0.5497   0.8197   -0.4431    0.5078  -0.4644
        9   -3.6377   -1.9081   0.2247   0.4937  -1.0272    0.0636    0.0078  -0.1496
       10    1.5419    1.4523   0.7977   3.1802   2.8841    1.2837   -1.6654   2.0301
       11       .         .     2.7429      .        .         .         .        .
       12       .         .     7.2880      .        .         .         .        .

Sum of Residuals                    0
Sum of Squared Residuals      45.1938
Predicted Resid SS (Press)   145.7300
```

In the output above, none of the observations exceed the cutoff value of 2 for RSTUDENT. Observation 10 exceeds the HAT cutoff of 0.60 as well as the cutoff of 2 for DFFITS and DFBETAS for the squared term. Observations 4, 6, and 10 exceed the COVRATIO cutoff of .90. Taken together, these statistics indicate that observation 10 should be investigated further to try to understand why it is as influential as it is.

The PARTIAL option produces partial regression leverage plots. One plot is printed for each regressor in the full, current model. For example, plots are produced for regressors included by using ADD statements; plots are not produced for interim models in the various model-selection methods but only for the full model. If you use a model-selection method and the final model contains only a subset of the original regressors, the PARTIAL option still produces plots for all regressors in the full model.

For a given regressor, the partial regression leverage plot is the plot of the dependent variable and the regressor after they have been made orthogonal to the other regressors in the model. These can be obtained by plotting the residuals for the dependent variable against the residuals for the selected regressor, where the residuals for the dependent variable are calculated with the selected regressor omitted, and the residuals for the selected regressor are calculated from a model where the selected regressor is regressed on the remaining regressors. A line fit to the points has a slope equal to the parameter estimate in the full model.

On the plot, points are marked by the number of replicates appearing at one print position. The symbol '*' is used if there are ten or more replicates. If an ID statement is specified, the left-most nonblank character in the value of the ID variable is used as the plotting symbol.

The following statements use the fitness data in **Example 2** with the PARTIAL option to produce **Output 36.27**:

```
proc reg data=fitness;
   model oxy=runtime weight age / partial;
run;
```

Output 36.27   Regression Using the PARTIAL Option

```
                              The SAS System                                    1

Model: MODEL1
Dependent Variable: OXY

                          Analysis of Variance

                             Sum of          Mean
     Source       DF        Squares        Square     F Value     Prob>F

     Model         3      656.27095     218.75698      30.272     0.0001
     Error        27      195.11060       7.22632
     C Total      30      851.38154

             Root MSE       2.68818     R-square       0.7708
             Dep Mean      47.37581     Adj R-sq       0.7454
             C.V.           5.67416

                          Parameter Estimates

                      Parameter      Standard     T for H0:
     Variable   DF     Estimate         Error    Parameter=0    Prob > |T|

     INTERCEP    1    93.126150    7.55915630        12.320        0.0001
     RUNTIME     1    -3.140387    0.36737984        -8.548        0.0001
     WEIGHT      1    -0.054437    0.06180913        -0.881        0.3862
     AGE         1    -0.173877    0.09954587        -1.747        0.0921
```

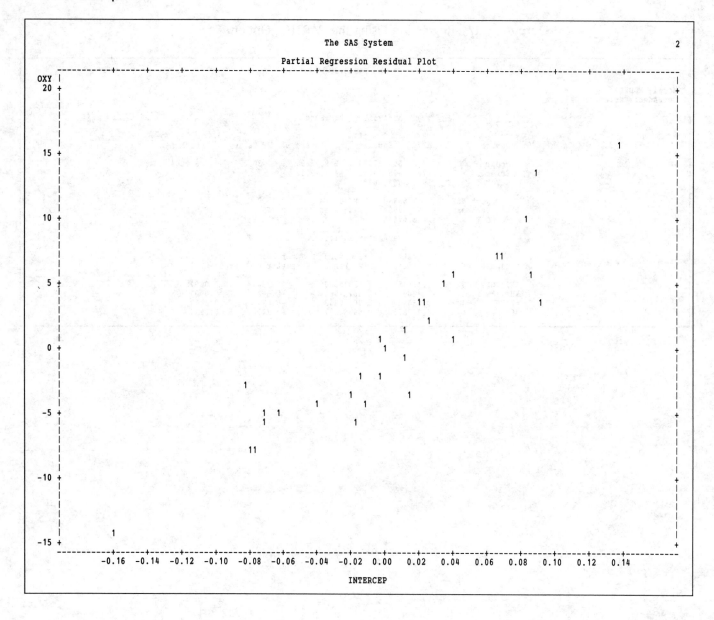

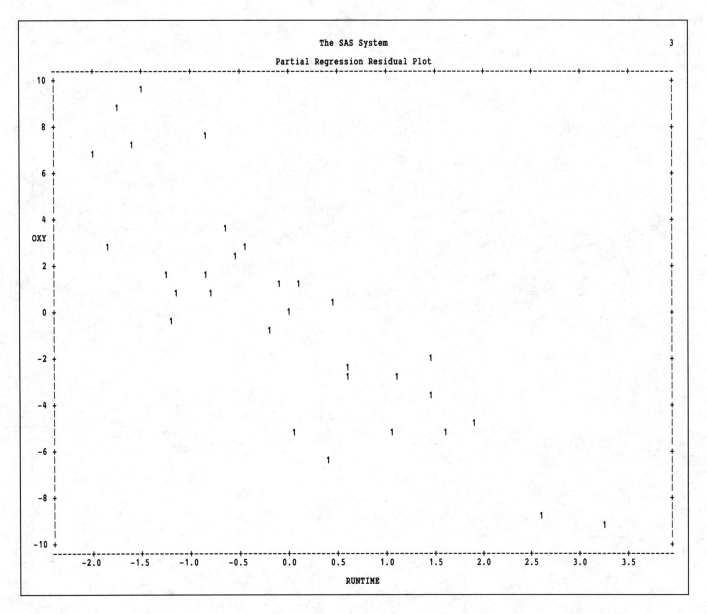

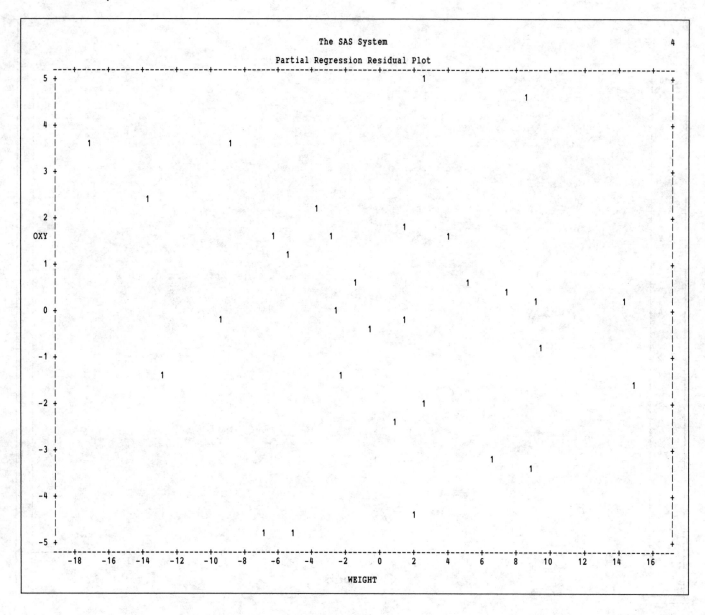

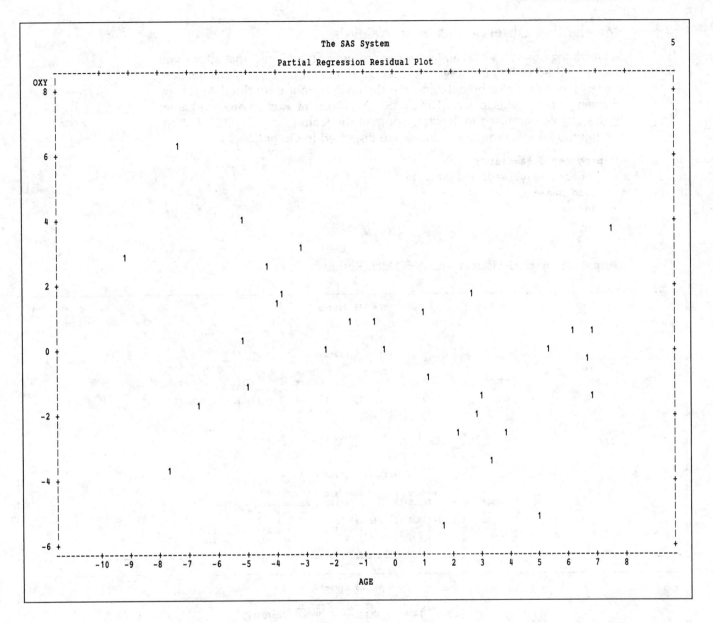

Partial Regression Residual Plot

Reweighting Observations in an Analysis

Reweighting observations is an interactive feature of PROC REG that allows you to change the weights of observations used in computing the regression equation. Observations may also be deleted from the analysis (not from the data set) by changing their weights to zero. The CLASS data (from **Interactive Analysis** earlier in this chapter) are used to illustrate some of the features of REWEIGHT. First, the full model is fit, and the residuals are displayed in **Output 36.28**.

```
proc reg data=class;
   model weight=age height / p;
   id name;
run;
```

Output 36.28   Full Model for CLASS Data, Residuals Shown

```
                                    The SAS System                                        1

Model: MODEL1
Dependent Variable: WEIGHT

                              Analysis of Variance

                                   Sum of          Mean
         Source        DF        Squares        Square      F Value     Prob>F

         Model          2     7215.63710    3607.81855       27.228     0.0001
         Error         16     2120.09974     132.50623
         C Total       18     9335.73684

              Root MSE       11.51114     R-square       0.7729
              Dep Mean      100.02632     Adj R-sq       0.7445
              C.V.           11.50811

                              Parameter Estimates

                        Parameter      Standard     T for H0:
         Variable  DF    Estimate         Error    Parameter=0    Prob > |T|

         INTERCEP   1  -141.223763   33.38309350        -4.230     0.0006
         AGE        1     1.278393    3.11010374         0.411     0.6865
         HEIGHT     1     3.597027    0.90546072         3.973     0.0011
```

```
                                    The SAS System                                        2

                               Dep Var    Predict
              Obs    NAME      WEIGHT       Value    Residual

                1    Alfred     112.5      124.9    -12.3686
                2    Alice     84.0000     78.6273    5.3727
                3    Barbara    98.0       110.3    -12.2812
                4    Carol     102.5       102.6     -0.0670
                5    Henry     102.5       105.1     -2.5849
                6    James     83.0000     80.2266    2.7734
                7    Jane      84.5000     89.2191   -4.7191
                8    Janet     112.5       102.8      9.7337
                9    Jeffrey   84.0000    100.2     -16.2095
               10    John       99.5       86.3415   13.1585
               11    Joyce     50.5000     57.3660   -6.8660
               12    Judy      90.0000    108.0     -17.9625
               13    Louise    77.0000     76.6295    0.3705
               14    Mary      112.0       117.2     -5.1544
               15    Philip    150.0       138.2     11.7836
               16    Robert    128.0       107.2     20.7957
               17    Ronald    133.0       119.0     14.0471
               18    Thomas    85.0000     79.6676    5.3324
               19    William   112.0       117.2     -5.1544

Sum of Residuals                     0
Sum of Squared Residuals     2120.0997
Predicted Resid SS (Press)   3272.7219
```

Upon examining the data and residuals, you realize that observation 17 (`Ronald`) was mistakenly included in the analysis. Also, you would like to examine the effect of reweighting to 0.5 observations whose residuals have absolute values greater than or equal to 17.

```
reweight obs.=17;
reweight r. le -17 or r. ge 17 / weight=0.5;
print p;
run;
```

At this point, a message (in the log) appears that tells you which observations have been reweighted and what the new weights are. **Output 36.29** is produced.

Output 36.29   Model with Reweighted Observations

```
                                 The SAS System                                3

                                      Dep Var    Predict
            Obs    NAME     Weight    WEIGHT      Value   Residual

             1    Alfred    1.0000    112.5      121.6     -9.1250
             2    Alice     1.0000     84.0000    79.9296    4.0704
             3    Barbara   1.0000     98.0      107.5     -9.5484
             4    Carol     1.0000    102.5      102.2      0.3337
             5    Henry     1.0000    102.5      104.4     -1.8632
             6    James     1.0000     83.0000    79.9762    3.0238
             7    Jane      1.0000     84.5000    87.8225   -3.3225
             8    Janet     1.0000    112.5      103.7      8.8111
             9    Jeffrey   1.0000     84.0000    98.8     -14.7606
            10    John      1.0000     99.5       85.3117   14.1883
            11    Joyce     1.0000     50.5000    58.6811   -8.1811
            12    Judy      0.5000     90.0000   106.9     -16.8740
            13    Louise    1.0000     77.0000    76.8377    0.1623
            14    Mary      1.0000    112.0      116.2     -4.2429
            15    Philip    1.0000    150.0      136.0      14.0312
            16    Robert    0.5000    128.0      103.5      24.4850
            17    Ronald         0    133.0      117.8      15.1879
            18    Thomas    1.0000     85.0000    78.1398    6.8602
            19    William   1.0000    112.0      116.2     -4.2429

Sum of Residuals                     0
Sum of Squared Residuals       1500.6119
Predicted Resid SS (Press)     2287.5762
NOTE: The above statistics use observation weights or frequencies.
```

The first REWEIGHT statement excluded observation 17 and the second reweighted observations 12 and 16 to 0.5. An important feature to note from this example is that the model was not refit until after the PRINT statement. REWEIGHT statements do not cause the model to be refit. This is so that multiple REWEIGHT statements can be applied to a subsequent model.

In this example, since the intent is to reweight observations with large residuals, the observation that was mistakenly included in the analysis should be deleted, the model should be fit for those remaining observations, and then the observations with large residuals should be reweighted. To accomplish this, you must first set all observation weights back to their original values of 1 before deleting the erroneous value and refitting the model with the REFIT statement. These statements produce **Output 36.30**:

```
reweight allobs / weight=1.0;
reweight obs.=17;
refit;
reweight r. le -17 or r. ge 17 / weight=.5;
print;
run;
```

Output 36.30   Observations Excluded from Analysis, Model Refitted and Observations Reweighted

```
                              The SAS System                              4
                               Dep Var    Predict
        Obs   NAME    Weight   WEIGHT      Value    Residual

          1  Alfred   1.0000   112.5      121.0     -8.4716
          2  Alice    1.0000   84.0000    79.5342    4.4658
          3  Barbara  1.0000   98.0       107.1     -9.0746
          4  Carol    1.0000   102.5      101.6      0.9319
          5  Henry    1.0000   102.5      103.8     -1.2588
          6  James    1.0000   83.0000    79.7204    3.2796
          7  Jane     1.0000   84.5000    87.5443   -3.0443
          8  Janet    1.0000   112.5      102.9      9.5533
          9  Jeffrey  1.0000   84.0000    98.3     -14.3117
         10  John     1.0000   99.5       85.0407   14.4593
         11  Joyce    1.0000   50.5000    58.6253   -8.1253
         12  Judy     1.0000   90.0000    106.3    -16.2625
         13  Louise   1.0000   77.0000    76.5908    0.4092
         14  Mary     1.0000   112.0      115.5     -3.4651
         15  Philip   1.0000   150.0      135.0     15.0047
         16  Robert   0.5000   128.0      103.2     24.8077
         17  Ronald   0        133.0      117.0     15.9701
         18  Thomas   1.0000   85.0000    78.0288    6.9712
         19  William  1.0000   112.0      115.5     -3.4651

Sum of Residuals                     0
Sum of Squared Residuals       1637.8188
Predicted Resid SS (Press)     2473.8798
NOTE: The above statistics use observation weights or frequencies.
```

Notice that this results in a slightly different model than the previous set of statements: only observation 16 is reweighted to 0.5.

Another important feature of REWEIGHT is the ability to nullify the effect of a previous or all REWEIGHT statements. First, assume that you have several REWEIGHT statements in effect and you want to restore the original weights of all the observations. The following REWEIGHT statement accomplishes this and produces **Output 36.31**:

```
reweight allobs / reset;
print;
run;
```

Output 36.31   Restoring Weights of All Observations

```
                              The SAS System                              5
                          Dep Var    Predict
            Obs   NAME    WEIGHT      Value    Residual

              1  Alfred   112.5      124.9    -12.3686
              2  Alice    84.0000    78.6273    5.3727
              3  Barbara  98.0       110.3    -12.2812
              4  Carol    102.5      102.6     -0.0670
              5  Henry    102.5      105.1     -2.5849
              6  James    83.0000    80.2266    2.7734
              7  Jane     84.5000    89.2191   -4.7191
              8  Janet    112.5      102.8      9.7337
              9  Jeffrey  84.0000    100.2    -16.2095
```

(continued on next page)

(continued from previous page)

```
10   John       99.5     86.3415   13.1585
11   Joyce      50.5000  57.3660   -6.8660
12   Judy       90.0000  108.0     -17.9625
13   Louise     77.0000  76.6295   0.3705
14   Mary       112.0    117.2     -5.1544
15   Philip     150.0    138.2     11.7836
16   Robert     128.0    107.2     20.7957
17   Ronald     133.0    119.0     14.0471
18   Thomas     85.0000  79.6676   5.3324
19   William    112.0    117.2     -5.1544
```

```
Sum of Residuals                          0
Sum of Squared Residuals          2120.0997
Predicted Resid SS (Press)        3272.7219
```

The resulting model is identical to the original model specified at the beginning of this section. Note that the Weight column does not appear.

Now suppose you only want to undo the changes made by the most recent REWEIGHT statement. Use REWEIGHT UNDO for this. These statements produce **Output 36.32**:

```
reweight r. le -12 or r. ge 12 / weight=.75;
reweight r. le -17 or r. ge 17 / weight=.5;
reweight undo;
print;
run;
```

Output 36.32 Example of UNDO in REWEIGHT Statement

```
                              The SAS System                                6

                                     Dep Var   Predict
         Obs   NAME     Weight   WEIGHT     Value   Residual

          1   Alfred   0.7500   112.5    125.1   -12.6152
          2   Alice    1.0000   84.0000  78.7691   5.2309
          3   Barbara  0.7500   98.0     110.3   -12.3236
          4   Carol    1.0000   102.5    102.9    -0.3836
          5   Henry    1.0000   102.5    105.4    -2.8936
          6   James    1.0000   83.0000  80.1133   2.8867
          7   Jane     1.0000   84.5000  89.0776   -4.5776
          8   Janet    1.0000   112.5    103.3    9.1678
          9   Jeffrey  0.7500   84.0000  100.3   -16.2835
         10   John     0.7500   99.5     86.2090   13.2910
         11   Joyce    1.0000   50.5000  57.0745   -6.5745
         12   Judy     0.7500   90.0000  108.3   -18.2622
         13   Louise   1.0000   77.0000  76.5275   0.4725
         14   Mary     1.0000   112.0    117.7    -5.6752
         15   Philip   1.0000   150.0    138.9    11.0789
         16   Robert   0.7500   128.0    107.0    20.9937
         17   Ronald   0.7500   133.0    119.5    13.5319
         18   Thomas   1.0000   85.0000  79.3061   5.6939
         19   William  1.0000   112.0    117.7    -5.6752
```

```
Sum of Residuals                          0
Sum of Squared Residuals          1694.8711
Predicted Resid SS (Press)        2547.2275
NOTE: The above statistics use observation weights or frequencies.
```

The resulting model reflects changes made only by the first REWEIGHT statement since the third REWEIGHT statement negates the effect of the second REWEIGHT statement. Observations 1, 3, 9, 10, 12, 16, and 17 have their weights changed to 0.75.

Now suppose you want to reset the observations selected by the most recent REWEIGHT statement to their original weights. Use the REWEIGHT statement with the RESET option to do this. These statements produce **Output 36.33**:

```
reweight r. le -12 or r. ge 12 / weight=.75;
reweight r. le -17 or r. ge 17 / weight=.5;
reweight / reset;
print;
run;
```

Output 36.33   REWEIGHT Statement with RESET option

```
                                 The SAS System                                    7

                                      Dep Var    Predict
        Obs     NAME     Weight     WEIGHT       Value    Residual

          1   Alfred     0.7500      112.5       126.0    -13.5076
          2   Alice      1.0000       84.0000     77.8727    6.1273
          3   Barbara    0.7500       98.0       111.3    -13.2805
          4   Carol      1.0000      102.5       102.5      0.0297
          5   Henry      1.0000      102.5       105.1     -2.6278
          6   James      1.0000       83.0000     80.2290    2.7710
          7   Jane       1.0000       84.5000     89.7199   -5.2199
          8   Janet      1.0000      112.5       102.0     10.4878
          9   Jeffrey    0.7500       84.0000    100.7    -16.6507
         10   John       0.7500       99.5        86.6828   12.8172
         11   Joyce      1.0000       50.5000     56.7703   -6.2703
         12   Judy       1.0000       90.0000    108.2    -18.1649
         13   Louise     1.0000       77.0000     76.4327    0.5673
         14   Mary       1.0000      112.0       117.2     -5.1975
         15   Philip     1.0000      150.0       138.8     11.2419
         16   Robert     1.0000      128.0       108.7     19.2984
         17   Ronald     0.7500      133.0       119.1     13.9043
         18   Thomas     1.0000       85.0000     80.3076    4.6924
         19   William    1.0000      112.0       117.2     -5.1975

Sum of Residuals                        0
Sum of Squared Residuals        1879.0898
Predicted Resid SS (Press)      2959.5728
NOTE: The above statistics use observation weights or frequencies.
```

Note that observations that meet the condition of the second REWEIGHT statement (residuals with an absolute value greater than or equal to 17) now have weights reset to their original value of 1. Observations 1, 3, 9, 10, and 17 have weights of 0.75, but observations 12 and 16 (which met the condition of the second REWEIGHT statement) have their weights reset to 1.

Notice how the last three examples show three ways to change weights back to a previous value. In the first example, ALLOBS and the RESET option were used to change weights for all observations back to their original values. In the second example, the UNDO option was used to negate the effect of a previous REWEIGHT statement, thus changing weights for observations selected in the previous REWEIGHT statement to the weights specified in still another REWEIGHT statement. In the third example, the RESET option was used to change weights for observations selected in a previous REWEIGHT statement back to their original values.

Testing for Heteroscedasticity

The regression model is specified as $y_i = \mathbf{x}_i\boldsymbol{\beta} + \varepsilon_i$, where the ε_i's are identically and independently distributed: $E(\varepsilon) = 0$ and $E(\varepsilon'\varepsilon) = \sigma^2\mathbf{I}$. If the ε_i's are not independent or their variances are not constant, the parameter estimates are unbiased, but the estimate of the covariance matrix is inconsistent. In the case of heteroscedasticity, the ACOV option provides a consistent estimate of the covariance matrix. If the regression data are from a simple random sample, the ACOV option produces the covariance matrix. This matrix is

$$(\mathbf{X'X})^{-1}(\mathbf{X'}\ \mathrm{diag}(e_i{}^2)\mathbf{X})(\mathbf{X'X})^{-1}$$

where

$$e_i = y_i - \mathbf{x}_i\mathbf{b}\quad .$$

The SPEC option performs a test for heteroscedasticity. When the SPEC option has been specified, tests with both the usual covariance matrix and the heteroscedasticity consistent covariance matrix are performed. Tests performed with the consistent covariance matrix are asymptotic. For more information, see White (1980).

Both the ACOV and SPEC options can be specified in a MODEL or PRINT statement.

Multivariate Tests

The MTEST statement described above can test hypotheses involving several dependent variables in the form

$$(\mathbf{L}\boldsymbol{\beta} - \mathbf{cj})\mathbf{M} = 0$$

where $\mathbf{L}$ is a linear function on the regressor side, $\boldsymbol{\beta}$ is a matrix of parameters, $\mathbf{c}$ is a column vector of constants, $\mathbf{j}$ is a row vector of ones, and $\mathbf{M}$ is a linear function on the dependent side. The special case where the constants are zero is

$$\mathbf{L}\boldsymbol{\beta}\mathbf{M} = 0\quad .$$

To test this hypothesis, REG constructs two matrices called $\mathbf{H}$ and $\mathbf{E}$ that correspond to the numerator and denominator of a univariate F test:

$$\mathbf{H} = \mathbf{M'}(\mathbf{LB} - \mathbf{cj})'(\mathbf{L}(\mathbf{X'X})^{-}\mathbf{L'})^{-1}(\mathbf{LB} - \mathbf{cj})\mathbf{M}$$

$$\mathbf{E} = \mathbf{M'}(\mathbf{Y'Y} - \mathbf{B'}(\mathbf{X'X})\mathbf{B})\mathbf{M}\quad .$$

These matrices are printed for each MTEST statement if the PRINT option is specified.

Four test statistics based on the eigenvalues of $\mathbf{E}^{-1}\mathbf{H}$ or $(\mathbf{E}+\mathbf{H})^{-1}\mathbf{H}$ are formed. These are Wilks' Lambda, Pillai's Trace, the Hotelling-Lawley Trace, and Roy's maximum root. These are discussed in Chapter 1.

The following statements perform a multivariate analysis of variance and produce **Output 36.34**:

```
/* Manova Data from Morrison (1976, 190) */
data a;
    input sex $ drug $ @;
    do rep=1 to 4;
        input y1 y2 @;
        output;
    end;
    cards;
m a  5  6  5  4  9  9  7  6
m b  7  6  7  7  9 12  6  8
m c 21 15 14 11 17 12 12 10
f a  7 10  6  6  9  7  8 10
f b 10 13  8  7  7  6  6  9
f c 16 12 14  9 14  8 10  5
;
data b;
    set a;
    sexcode=(sex='m')-(sex='f');
    drug1=(drug='a')-(drug='c');
    drug2=(drug='b')-(drug='c');
    sexdrug1=sexcode*drug1;
    sexdrug2=sexcode*drug2;
proc reg;
    model y1 y2=sexcode drug1 drug2 sexdrug1 sexdrug2;
y1y2drug: mtest y1=y2, drug1,drug2;
drugshow: mtest drug1, drug2 / print canprint;
run;
```

Output 36.34   Multivariate Analysis of Variance: REG Procedure

```
                              The SAS System                                  1

Model: MODEL1
Dependent Variable: Y1

                         Analysis of Variance

                              Sum of       Mean
       Source        DF     Squares      Square    F Value    Prob>F

       Model          5   316.00000    63.20000     12.038    0.0001
       Error         18    94.50000     5.25000
       C Total       23   410.50000

           Root MSE      2.29129     R-square     0.7698
           Dep Mean      9.75000     Adj R-sq     0.7058
           C.V.         23.50039

                         Parameter Estimates

                       Parameter    Standard    T for H0:
       Variable   DF    Estimate       Error   Parameter=0    Prob > |T|

       INTERCEP    1    9.750000   0.46770717      20.846        0.0001
       SEXCODE     1    0.166667   0.46770717       0.356        0.7257
       DRUG1       1   -2.750000   0.66143783      -4.158        0.0006
       DRUG2       1   -2.250000   0.66143783      -3.402        0.0032
       SEXDRUG1    1   -0.666667   0.66143783      -1.008        0.3269
       SEXDRUG2    1   -0.416667   0.66143783      -0.630        0.5366
```

The SAS System   2

Dependent Variable: Y2

Analysis of Variance

Source	DF	Sum of Squares	Mean Square	F Value	Prob>F
Model	5	69.33333	13.86667	2.189	0.1008
Error	18	114.00000	6.33333		
C Total	23	183.33333			

Root MSE	2.51661	R-square 0.3782
Dep Mean	8.66667	Adj R-sq 0.2055
C.V.	29.03782	

Parameter Estimates

Variable	DF	Parameter Estimate	Standard Error	T for H0: Parameter=0	Prob > |T|
INTERCEP	1	8.666667	0.51370117	16.871	0.0001
SEXCODE	1	0.166667	0.51370117	0.324	0.7493
DRUG1	1	-1.416667	0.72648316	-1.950	0.0669
DRUG2	1	-0.166667	0.72648316	-0.229	0.8211
SEXDRUG1	1	-1.166667	0.72648316	-1.606	0.1257
SEXDRUG2	1	-0.416667	0.72648316	-0.574	0.5734

The SAS System   3

Multivariate Test: Y1Y2DRUG

Multivariate Statistics and Exact F Statistics

S=1   M=0   N=8

Statistic	Value	F	Num DF	Den DF	Pr > F
Wilks' Lambda	0.28053917	23.0811	2	18	0.0001
Pillai's Trace	0.71946083	23.0811	2	18	0.0001
Hotelling-Lawley Trace	2.56456456	23.0811	2	18	0.0001
Roy's Greatest Root	2.56456456	23.0811	2	18	0.0001

The SAS System   4

Multivariate Test: DRUGSHOW

E, the Error Matrix

94.5	76.5
76.5	114

H, the Hypothesis Matrix

301	97.5
97.5	36.333333333

	Canonical Correlation	Adjusted Canonical Correlation	Approx Standard Error	Squared Canonical Correlation	Eigenvalue	Eigenvalues of INV(E)*H = CanRsq/(1-CanRsq) Difference	Proportion	Cumulative
1	0.905903	0.899927	0.040101	0.820661	4.5760	4.5125	0.9863	0.9863
2	0.244371	.	0.210254	0.059717	0.0635	.	0.0137	1.0000

(continued on next page)

(continued from previous page)

```
                    Test of H0: The canonical correlations in the
                      current row and all that follow are zero

                Likelihood
                  Ratio      Approx F     Num DF     Den DF    Pr > F

            1   0.16862952     12.1991        4          34    0.0001
            2   0.94028273      1.1432        1          18    0.2991

                   Multivariate Statistics and F Approximations

                          S=2     M=-0.5     N=7.5

         Statistic                Value        F      Num DF   Den DF   Pr > F

         Wilks' Lambda          0.16862952   12.1991      4       34    0.0001
         Pillai's Trace         0.88037810    7.0769      4       36    0.0003
         Hotelling-Lawley Trace 4.63953666   18.5581      4       32    0.0001
         Roy's Greatest Root    4.57602675   41.1842      2       18    0.0001

             NOTE: F Statistic for Roy's Greatest Root is an upper bound.
               NOTE: F Statistic for Wilks' Lambda is exact.
```

The first MTEST statement tests the hypothesis that the DRUG1 and DRUG2 parameters are the same for both of the dependent variables Y1 and Y2. This hypothesis is rejected based on any of the multivariate test statistics reported.

The second MTEST statement tests the hypothesis that the DRUG1 and DRUG2 parameters are zero for both dependent variables. This hypothesis is also rejected based on any of the multivariate test statistics reported.

Autocorrelation in Time Series Data

When regression is done on time series data, the errors may not be independent. Often errors are autocorrelated; that is, each error is correlated with the error immediately before it. Autocorrelation is also a symptom of systematic lack of fit. The DW option provides the Durbin-Watson d statistic to test that the auto-correlation is zero:

$$d = \Sigma_{i=2}^{n} (e_i - e_{i-1})^2 / \Sigma e_i^2 \quad .$$

The value of d is close to 2 if the errors are uncorrelated. The distribution of d is reported by Durbin and Watson (1950, 1951). Tables of the distribution are found in most econometrics textbooks, such as Johnston (1972) and Pindyck and Rubinfeld (1976).

The sample autocorrelation estimate is shown after the Durbin-Watson statistic on the printout. The sample is computed as

$$r = \Sigma_{i=2}^{n} e_i e_{i-1} / \Sigma e_i^2 \quad .$$

This autocorrelation of the residuals may not be a very good estimate of the autocorrelation of the true errors, especially if there are few observations and the independent variables have certain patterns. If there are missing observations in the regression, these measures are computed as though the missing observations did not exist.

Positive autocorrelation of the errors generally tends to make the estimate of the error variance too small, so confidence intervals are too narrow and true null hypotheses are rejected with a higher probability than the stated significance level. Negative autocorrelation of the errors generally tends to make the estimate of the error variance too large, so confidence intervals are too wide and the power of significance tests is reduced. With either positive or negative autocorrelation, least-squares parameter estimates are usually not as efficient as generalized least-squares parameter estimates. For more details see Judge et al. (1985, chap. 8) and the *SAS/ETS User's Guide, Version 6, First Edition.*

In the following example, the population of the United States from 1790 to 1970 is fit to linear and quadratic functions of time. The following SAS statements request the DW option for the US population data (see **Output 36.35**):

```
data uspop;
   input pop @@;
   retain year 1780;
   year=year+10;
   yearsq=year*year;
   pop=pop/1000;
   cards;
3929 5308 7239 9638 12866 17069 23191 31443 39818 50155
62947 75994 91972 105710 122775 131669 151325 179323 203211
. . .
;
proc reg data=uspop;
   model pop=year yearsq / dw;
```

Output 36.35 Regression Using DW Option

```
                              The SAS System                                       1

Model: MODEL1
Dependent Variable: POP

                          Analysis of Variance

                              Sum of         Mean
   Source          DF       Squares        Square     F Value      Prob>F

   Model            2   71799.01619   35899.50810    4641.719      0.0001
   Error           16     123.74556       7.73410
   C Total         18   71922.76175

           Root MSE      2.78102     R-square       0.9983
           Dep Mean     69.76747     Adj R-sq       0.9981
           C.V.          3.98613

                          Parameter Estimates

                     Parameter      Standard      T for H0:
   Variable   DF      Estimate         Error    Parameter=0     Prob > |T|

   INTERCEP    1         20450   843.47532063        24.245         0.0001
   YEAR        1    -22.780606     0.89784903       -25.372         0.0001
   YEARSQ      1      0.006346     0.00023877        26.576         0.0001
```

```
                              The SAS System                                       2

Durbin-Watson D                 1.264
(For Number of Obs.)               19
1st Order Autocorrelation       0.299
```

From the printout above, you see that the Durbin-Watson statistic is 1.264 and the estimate for the first-order autocorrelation coefficient is .299. Because the D-W statistic is close to 2 when the errors are uncorrelated, there appears to be little evidence to suggest that there is significant autocorrelation present, and so time series methods are not necessarily needed.

Computational Methods

The REG procedure first composes a crossproducts matrix. The matrix can be calculated from input data, reformed from an input correlation matrix, or read in from an SSCP data set. For each model, the procedure selects the appropriate crossproducts from the main matrix. The normal equations formed from the crossproducts are solved using a sweep algorithm (Goodnight 1979). The method is accurate for data that are reasonably scaled and not too collinear.

The mechanism PROC REG uses to check for singularity involves the diagonal (pivot) elements of $\mathbf{X'X}$ as it is being swept. If a pivot is less than SINGULAR*CSS, then a singularity is declared and the pivot is not swept (where CSS is the corrected sum of squares for the regressor, and SINGULAR is 1E-8 or reset in the PROC statement).

The sweep algorithm is also used in many places in model-selection methods. The RSQUARE method uses the leaps and bounds algorithm by Furnival and Wilson (1974).

Computer Resources in Regression Analysis

The REG procedure is efficient for ordinary regression; however, requests for optional features can greatly increase the amount of time required.

The major computational expense in the regression analysis is the collection of the crossproducts matrix. For p variables and n observations, the time required is proportional to np^2. For each model run, REG needs time roughly proportional to k^3, where k is the number of regressors in the model. Add an additional nk^2 for one of the R, CLM, or CLI options and another nk^2 for the INFLUENCE option.

Most of the memory REG needs to solve large problems is used for crossproducts matrices. PROC REG requires $4p^2$ bytes for the main crossproducts matrix plus $4k^2$ bytes for the largest model. If several output data sets are requested, memory is also needed for buffers.

See **Input Data Set** earlier in this chapter for information on how to use TYPE=SSCP data sets to reduce computing time.

Printed Output

Many of the more specialized printouts are described in detail in the sections above. Most of the formulas for the statistics are in Chapter 1.

The analysis-of-variance table is printed and contains

1. the Source of the variation, Model for the fitted regression, Error for the residual error, and C Total for the total variation after correcting for the mean. The Uncorrected Total Variation is printed when the NOINT option is used.
2. the degrees of freedom (DF) associated with the source.
3. the Sum of Squares for the term.
4. the Mean Square, the sum of squares divided by the degrees of freedom.
5. the F Value for testing the hypothesis that all parameters are zero except for the intercept. This is formed by dividing the mean square for Model by the mean square for Error.
6. the Prob>F, the probability of getting a greater F statistic than that observed if the hypothesis is true. This is the significance probability.

These statistics are also printed:

7. Root MSE is an estimate of the standard deviation of the error term. It is calculated as the square root of the mean square error.
8. Dep Mean is the sample mean of the dependent variable.
9. C.V. is the coefficient of variation, computed as 100 times Root MSE divided by Dep Mean. This expresses the variation in unitless values.
10. R-Square is a measure between 0 and 1 that indicates the portion of the (corrected) total variation that is attributed to the fit rather than left to residual error. It is calculated as SS(Model) divided by SS(Total). It is also called the *coefficient of determination*. It is the square of the multiple correlation; in other words, the square of the correlation between the dependent variable and the predicted values.
11. Adj R-Sq, the adjusted R^2, is a version of R^2 that has been adjusted for degrees of freedom. It is calculated as

$$\overline{R}^2 = 1 - [((n - i)(1 - R^2)) / (n - p)]$$

where i is equal to 1 if there is an intercept, 0 otherwise; n is the number of observations used to fit the model; and p is the number of parameters in the model.

The parameter estimates and associated statistics are then printed, and they contain the following:

12. the Variable used as the regressor, including the name INTERCEP to represent the estimate of the intercept parameter.
13. the degrees of freedom (DF) for the variable. There is one degree of freedom unless the model is not full rank.
14. the Parameter Estimate.
15. the Standard Error, the estimate of the standard deviation of the parameter estimate.
16. T for H0: Parameter=0, the t test that the parameter is zero. This is computed as the Parameter Estimate divided by the Standard Error.
17. the Prob $> |T|$, the probability that a t statistic would obtain a greater absolute value than that observed given that the true parameter is zero. This is the two-tailed significance probability.

If model-selection methods other than NONE, RSQUARE, ADJRSQ, or CP are used, the analysis-of-variance table and the parameter estimates with associated statistics are printed at each step. Also printed are

18. C(p), which is Mallows' C_p statistic
19. Bounds on the condition number of the correlation matrix for the variables in the model (Berk 1977).

After statistics for the final model have been printed, the following is printed when the method chosen is FORWARD, BACKWARD, or STEPWISE:

20. a Summary table listing Step number, Variable Entered or Removed, Partial and Model R**2, and C(p) and F statistics.

The RSQUARE method prints its results beginning with the model containing the fewest independent variables and producing the largest R^2. Results for other models with the same number of variables are then printed in order of decreasing R^2, and so on, for models with larger numbers of variables. The ADJRSQ and CP methods group models of all sizes together and print results beginning with the model having the optimal value of adjusted R^2 and C_p, respectively.

For each model considered, the RSQUARE, ADJRSQ, and CP methods print the following:

21. Number in Model or IN, the number of independent variables used in each model
22. R-Square or RSQ, the squared multiple correlation coefficient

If the B option is specified, RSQUARE, ADJRSQ, and CP print the following:

23. Parameter Estimates, the estimated regression coefficients (not shown).

If the B option is not specified, RSQUARE, ADJRSQ, and CP print the following:

24. Variables in Model, the names of the independent variables included in the model.

EXAMPLES

Example 1:   Growth Rate Data

In the following example, the use of linear regression is demonstrated with growth rate data for experimental rats fed differing doses of a dietary supplement. Note that the quadratic term must be created in the DATA step; this is done because polynomial effects such as X*X cannot be used in PROC REG. The statements that follow begin by fitting the linear term and requesting residuals and confidence intervals. Next, a plot of the residuals versus the predicted values is requested. The quadratic term is added to the model and the fit is again analyzed with the residual plot. A final plot of the predicted curve with upper and lower confidence intervals is requested. The statements shown below generate **Output 36.36** and **Output 36.37**:

```
data growth;
   input dose growth @@;
   dosesq=dose*dose;
   cards;
10 73 10 78 15 85 20 90 20 91 25 87 25 86 25 91 30 75 35 65
40 . 45 .
;
proc reg data=growth;
   var dosesq;
   model growth=dose / r cli clm;
   plot r.*p.;
   add dosesq;
   print;
   plot;
   run;

plot growth*dose='a' predicted.*dose='p' u95.*dose='u'
     l95.*dose='l' / overlay;
   run;
```

Output 36.36   Growth Rate Data: PROC REG

```
                                    The SAS System                                          1

Model: MODEL1
Dependent Variable: GROWTH

                                  Analysis of Variance

            ❶           ❷    ❸  Sum of    ❹  Mean        ❺           ❻
            Source      DF      Squares      Square      F Value      Prob>F

            Model        1     24.50166    24.50166       0.286       0.6076
            Error        8    686.39834    85.79979
            C Total      9    710.90000

                 ❼  Root MSE      9.26282  ❿ R-square     0.0345
              ❽     Dep Mean     82.10000  ⓫ Adj R-sq    -0.0862
                 ❾  C.V.         11.28236

                                  Parameter Estimates

            ⓬        ⓭  ⓮ Parameter   ⓯ Standard   ⓰ T for H0:   ⓱
            Variable  DF    Estimate       Error    Parameter=0    Prob > |T|

            INTERCEP   1    86.435685   8.62596597     10.020        0.0001
            DOSE       1    -0.201660   0.37736759     -0.534        0.6076
```

```
                                    The SAS System                                          2

       Dep Var  Predict  Std Err  Lower95%  Upper95%  Lower95%  Upper95%           Std Err  Student                     Cook's
Obs    GROWTH    Value   Predict    Mean      Mean     Predict   Predict  Residual Residual Residual  -2-1-0 1 2          D

  1   73.0000  84.4191   5.236    72.3453    96.5    59.8826    109.0   -11.4191   7.641   -1.494  |    **|         |   0.524
  2   78.0000  84.4191   5.236    72.3453    96.5    59.8826    109.0    -6.4191   7.641   -0.840  |     *|         |   0.166
  3   85.0000  83.4108   3.821    74.6005  92.2211   60.3049    106.5     1.5892   8.438    0.188  |      |         |   0.004
  4   90.0000  82.4025   2.983    75.5228  89.2822   59.9616    104.8     7.5975   8.769    0.866  |      |*        |   0.043
  5   91.0000  82.4025   2.983    75.5228  89.2822   59.9616    104.8     8.5975   8.769    0.980  |      |*        |   0.056
  6   87.0000  81.3942   3.213    73.9845  88.8038   58.7852    104.0     5.6058   8.688    0.645  |      |*        |   0.028
  7   86.0000  81.3942   3.213    73.9845  88.8038   58.7852    104.0     4.6058   8.688    0.530  |      |*        |   0.019
  8   91.0000  81.3942   3.213    73.9845  88.8038   58.7852    104.0     9.6058   8.688    1.106  |      |**       |   0.084
  9   75.0000  80.3859   4.344    70.3689  90.4029   56.7935    104.0    -5.3859   8.181   -0.658  |     *|         |   0.061
 10   65.0000  79.3776   5.877    65.8262  92.9290   54.0813    104.7   -14.3776   7.160   -2.008  |  ****|         |   1.358
 11      .     78.3693   7.571    60.9106    95.8    50.7818    106.0       .        .        .                        .
 12      .     77.3610   9.339    55.8242    98.9    47.0279    107.7       .        .        .                        .

Sum of Residuals                    0
Sum of Squared Residuals       686.3983
Predicted Resid SS (Press)    1352.0466
```

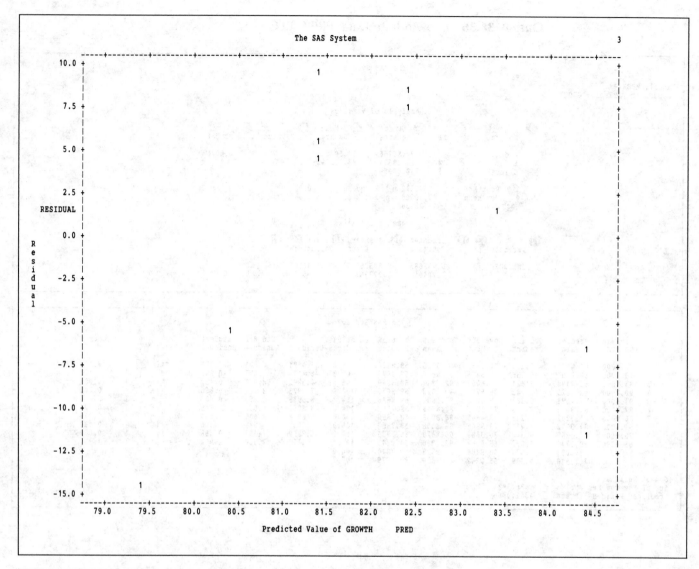

The SAS System   4

Model: MODEL1
Dependent Variable: GROWTH

Analysis of Variance

Source	DF	Sum of Squares	Mean Square	F Value	Prob>F
Model	2	665.70617	332.85309	51.555	0.0001
Error	7	45.19383	6.45626		
C Total	9	710.90000			

Root MSE	2.54092	R-square	0.9364	
Dep Mean	82.10000	Adj R-sq	0.9183	
C.V.	3.09491			

Parameter Estimates

Variable	DF	Parameter Estimate	Standard Error	T for H0: Parameter=0	Prob > |T|
INTERCEP	1	35.657437	5.61792724	6.347	0.0004
DOSE	1	5.262896	0.55802206	9.431	0.0001
DOSESQ	1	-0.127674	0.01281135	-9.966	0.0001

```
                                          The SAS System                                                    5

             Dep Var   Predict   Std Err  Lower95%  Upper95%  Lower95%  Upper95%           Std Err  Student                    Cook's
      Obs    GROWTH     Value    Predict    Mean      Mean     Predict   Predict  Residual Residual Residual   -2-1-0 1 2        D

       1    73.0000   75.5190    1.691    71.5198   79.5182   68.3014   82.7366   -2.5190   1.896   -1.328   |    **|     |    0.468
       2    78.0000   75.5190    1.691    71.5198   79.5182   68.3014   82.7366    2.4810   1.896    1.308   |      |**   |    0.454
       3    85.0000   85.8742    1.077    83.3280   88.4204   79.3486   92.3998   -0.8742   2.301   -0.380   |      |     |    0.011
       4    90.0000   89.8457    1.108    87.2258   92.4657   83.2910   96.4       0.1543   2.287    0.067   |      |     |    0.000
       5    91.0000   89.8457    1.108    87.2258   92.4657   83.2910   96.4       1.1543   2.287    0.505   |      |*    |    0.020
       6    87.0000   87.4335    1.070    84.9042   89.9629   80.9145   93.9526   -0.4335   2.305   -0.188   |      |     |    0.003
       7    86.0000   87.4335    1.070    84.9042   89.9629   80.9145   93.9526   -1.4335   2.305   -0.622   |     *|     |    0.028
       8    91.0000   87.4335    1.070    84.9042   89.9629   80.9145   93.9526    3.5665   2.305    1.547   |      |***  |    0.172
       9    75.0000   78.6377    1.204    75.7896   81.4857   71.9885   85.2868   -3.6377   2.237   -1.626   |   ***|     |    0.255
      10    65.0000   63.4581    2.269    58.0916   68.8245   55.4021   71.5141    1.5419   1.143    1.349   |      |**   |    2.393
      11     .        41.8948    4.208    31.9439   51.8456   30.2707   53.5189    .         .        .
      12     .        13.9478    6.860    -2.2725   30.1681   -3.3496   31.2452    .         .        .

Sum of Residuals                    0
Sum of Squared Residuals      45.1938
Predicted Resid SS (Press)   145.7300
```

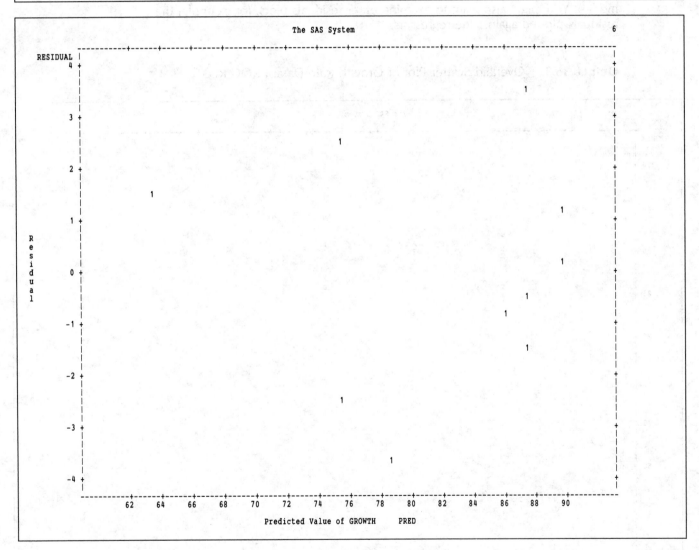

The fitted equation for the first model is

GROWTH = 86.44 −.20*DOSE

The first plot of residuals by predicted values indicates an inadequate model; perhaps additional terms (such as the quadratic) are needed, or perhaps the data need to be transformed before analysis. The second model adds the quadratic term. The fitted equation is

GROWTH = 35.66 + 5.26*DOSE −.13*DOSESQ

The plot of residuals by predicted values is improved and no longer indicates the need for additional terms in the model. To complete an analysis of these data, you would want to examine influence statistics (and perhaps then refit the model). You might also want to examine other residuals plots, for example, the residuals plotted against the regressors.

Output 36.37 Overlaid Scatter Plot of Growth Rate Data: PROC REG

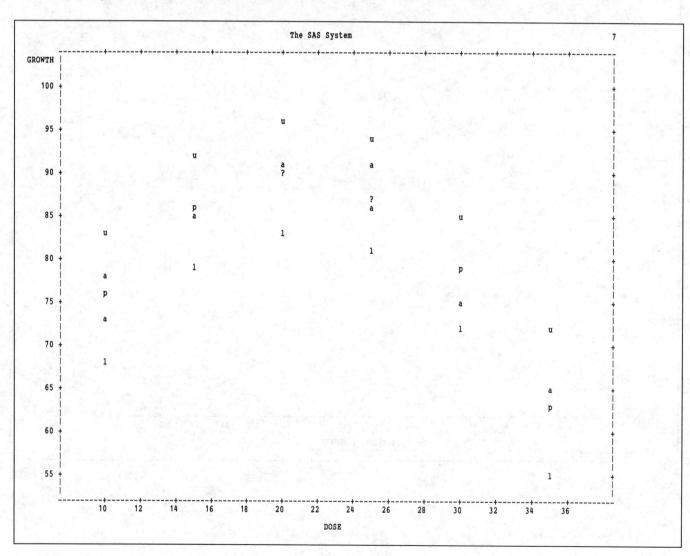

This plot shows the actual data as a's, the predicted values as p's, and the upper and lower 95% confidence limits for an individual value (sometimes called a *prediction interval*) as u's and l's, respectively.

Example 2:   Aerobic Fitness Prediction

Aerobic fitness (measured by the ability to consume oxygen) is fit to some simple exercise tests. The goal is to develop an equation to predict fitness based on the exercise tests rather than on expensive and cumbersome oxygen consumption measurements. Three model-selection methods are used: forward selection, backward selection, and MAXR selection. The statements below produce **Output 36.38** through **Output 36.40**. (Collinearity diagnostics for the full model are shown in **Output 36.25** earlier in this chapter.)

```
    /*              Data on Physical Fitness              */
    /* These measurements were made on men involved in a physical */
    /* fitness course at N.C. State Univ. The variables are        */
    /* age (years), weight (kg), oxygen intake rate                */
    /* (ml per kg body weight per minute),                         */
    /* time to run 1.5 miles (minutes), heart rate while resting,  */
    /* heart rate while running (same time oxygen rate measured),  */
    /* and maximum heart rate recorded while running.              */
    /*  ***Certain values of maxpulse were changed for this        */
    /*  analysis.                                                  */
    /*                                                             */
data fitness;
    input age weight oxy runtime rstpulse runpulse maxpulse;
    cards;
44 89.47  44.609 11.37 62 178 182
40 75.07  45.313 10.07 62 185 185
44 85.84  54.297  8.65 45 156 168
42 68.15  59.571  8.17 40 166 172
38 89.02  49.874  9.22 55 178 180
47 77.45  44.811 11.63 58 176 176
40 75.98  45.681 11.95 70 176 180
43 81.19  49.091 10.85 64 162 170
44 81.42  39.442 13.08 63 174 176
38 81.87  60.055  8.63 48 170 186
44 73.03  50.541 10.13 45 168 168
45 87.66  37.388 14.03 56 186 192
45 66.45  44.754 11.12 51 176 176
47 79.15  47.273 10.60 47 162 164
54 83.12  51.855 10.33 50 166 170
49 81.42  49.156  8.95 44 180 185
51 69.63  40.836 10.95 57 168 172
51 77.91  46.672 10.00 48 162 168
48 91.63  46.774 10.25 48 162 164
49 73.37  50.388 10.08 67 168 168
57 73.37  39.407 12.63 58 174 176
54 79.38  46.080 11.17 62 156 165
52 76.32  45.441  9.63 48 164 166
50 70.87  54.625  8.92 48 146 155
51 67.25  45.118 11.08 48 172 172
54 91.63  39.203 12.88 44 168 172
51 73.71  45.790 10.47 59 186 188
57 59.08  50.545  9.93 49 148 155
```

```
49 76.32  48.673   9.40 56 186 188
48 61.24  47.920  11.50 52 170 176
52 82.78  47.467  10.50 53 170 172
;
proc reg;
   model oxy=age weight runtime runpulse rstpulse maxpulse
      / selection=forward;

   model oxy=age weight runtime runpulse rstpulse maxpulse
      / selection=backward;

   model oxy=age weight runtime runpulse rstpulse maxpulse
      / selection=maxr;
   run;
```

Output 36.38   Forward Selection Method: PROC REG

```
                                   The SAS System                                           1

                       Forward Selection Procedure for Dependent Variable OXY
                                                                 ⑱
Step 1   Variable RUNTIME Entered   R-square = 0.74338010   C(p) = 13.69884048

                              DF      Sum of Squares       Mean Square      F    Prob>F

                 Regression    1       632.90009985      632.90009985   84.01   0.0001
                 Error        29       218.48144499        7.53384293
                 Total        30       851.38154484

                          Parameter       Standard         Type II
                 Variable   Estimate        Error      Sum of Squares      F    Prob>F

                 INTERCEP   82.42177268    3.85530378   3443.36654076  457.05   0.0001
                 RUNTIME    -3.31055536    0.36119485    632.90009985   84.01   0.0001
⑲
Bounds on condition number:          1,           1
---------------------------------------------------------------------------------------------

Step 2   Variable AGE Entered      R-square = 0.76424693   C(p) = 12.38944895

                              DF      Sum of Squares       Mean Square      F    Prob>F

                 Regression    2       650.66573237      325.33286618   45.38   0.0001
                 Error        28       200.71581247        7.16842187
                 Total        30       851.38154484

                          Parameter       Standard         Type II
                 Variable   Estimate        Error      Sum of Squares      F    Prob>F

                 INTERCEP   88.46228749    5.37263885   1943.41070877  271.11   0.0001
                 AGE        -0.15036567    0.09551468     17.76563252    2.48   0.1267
                 RUNTIME    -3.20395056    0.35877488    571.67750579   79.75   0.0001

Bounds on condition number:    1.036941,     4.147763
---------------------------------------------------------------------------------------------

Step 3   Variable RUNPULSE Entered  R-square = 0.81109446   C(p) =  6.95962673

                              DF      Sum of Squares       Mean Square      F    Prob>F

                 Regression    3       690.55085627      230.18361876   38.64   0.0001
                 Error        27       160.83068857        5.95669217
                 Total        30       851.38154484

                          Parameter       Standard         Type II
                 Variable   Estimate        Error      Sum of Squares      F    Prob>F

                 INTERCEP   111.71806443   10.23508836    709.69013814  119.14   0.0001
                 AGE        -0.25639826    0.09622892     42.28867438    7.10   0.0129
                 RUNTIME    -2.82537867    0.35828041    370.43528607   62.19   0.0001
                 RUNPULSE   -0.13090870    0.05059011     39.88512390    6.70   0.0154

Bounds on condition number:    1.354763,     11.59745
---------------------------------------------------------------------------------------------
```

The SAS System   2

Step 4   Variable MAXPULSE Entered   R-square = 0.83681815   C(p) = 4.87995808

	DF	Sum of Squares	Mean Square	F	Prob>F
Regression	4	712.45152692	178.11288173	33.33	0.0001
Error	26	138.93001792	5.34346223		
Total	30	851.38154484			

Variable	Parameter Estimate	Standard Error	Type II Sum of Squares	F	Prob>F
INTERCEP	98.14788797	11.78569002	370.57373243	69.35	0.0001
AGE	-0.19773470	0.09563662	22.84231496	4.27	0.0488
RUNTIME	-2.76757879	0.34053643	352.93569605	66.05	0.0001
RUNPULSE	-0.34810795	0.11749917	46.90088674	8.78	0.0064
MAXPULSE	0.27051297	0.13361978	21.90067065	4.10	0.0533

Bounds on condition number: 8.4182,   76.85135

Step 5   Variable WEIGHT Entered   R-square = 0.84800181   C(p) = 5.10627546

	DF	Sum of Squares	Mean Square	F	Prob>F
Regression	5	721.97309402	144.39461880	27.90	0.0001
Error	25	129.40845082	5.17633803		
Total	30	851.38154484			

Variable	Parameter Estimate	Standard Error	Type II Sum of Squares	F	Prob>F
INTERCEP	102.20427520	11.97928972	376.78934930	72.79	0.0001
AGE	-0.21962138	0.09550245	27.37429100	5.29	0.0301
WEIGHT	-0.07230234	0.05331009	9.52156710	1.84	0.1871
RUNTIME	-2.68252297	0.34098544	320.35967836	61.89	0.0001
RUNPULSE	-0.37340085	0.11714109	52.59623720	10.16	0.0038
MAXPULSE	0.30490783	0.13393642	26.82640270	5.18	0.0316

Bounds on condition number: 8.731225,   104.8254

No other variable met the 0.5000 significance level for entry into the model.

(20)   Summary of Forward Selection Procedure for Dependent Variable OXY

Step	Variable Entered	Number In	Partial R**2	Model R**2	C(p)	F	Prob>F
1	RUNTIME	1	0.7434	0.7434	13.6988	84.0076	0.0001
2	AGE	2	0.0209	0.7642	12.3894	2.4783	0.1267
3	RUNPULSE	3	0.0468	0.8111	6.9596	6.6959	0.0154
4	MAXPULSE	4	0.0257	0.8368	4.8800	4.0986	0.0533
5	WEIGHT	5	0.0112	0.8480	5.1063	1.8394	0.1871

The FORWARD model-selection method begins with no variables in the model and adds RUNTIME, then AGE, then RUNPULSE, then MAXPULSE, and finally, WEIGHT. The final variable available to add to the model, RSTPLSE, is not added since it does not meet the 0.50 significance-level criterion for entry into the model.

Output 36.39 Backward Selection Method: PROC REG

```
                                    The SAS System                                          1

                     Backward Elimination Procedure for Dependent Variable OXY

Step 0    All Variables Entered      R-square = 0.84867192   C(p) = 7.00000000

                              DF      Sum of Squares     Mean Square       F     Prob>F

             Regression        6       722.54360701     120.42393450     22.43   0.0001
             Error            24       128.83793783       5.36824741
             Total            30       851.38154484

                           Parameter        Standard        Type II
             Variable        Estimate         Error      Sum of Squares    F     Prob>F

             INTERCEP      102.93447948     12.40325810    369.72831073   68.87   0.0001
             AGE            -0.22697380      0.09983747     27.74577148    5.17   0.0322
             WEIGHT         -0.07417741      0.05459316      9.91058836    1.85   0.1869
             RUNTIME        -2.62865282      0.38456220    250.82210090   46.72   0.0001
             RUNPULSE       -0.36962776      0.11985294     51.05805832    9.51   0.0051
             RSTPULSE       -0.02153364      0.06605428      0.57051299    0.11   0.7473
             MAXPULSE        0.30321713      0.13649519     26.49142405    4.93   0.0360

Bounds on condition number:    8.743848,     137.1345
---------------------------------------------------------------------------------------------

Step 1    Variable RSTPULSE Removed  R-square = 0.84800181   C(p) = 5.10627546

                              DF      Sum of Squares     Mean Square       F     Prob>F

             Regression        5       721.97309402     144.39461880     27.90   0.0001
             Error            25       129.40845082       5.17633803
             Total            30       851.38154484

                           Parameter        Standard        Type II
             Variable        Estimate         Error      Sum of Squares    F     Prob>F

             INTERCEP      102.20427520     11.97928972    376.78934930   72.79   0.0001
             AGE            -0.21962138      0.09550245     27.37429100    5.29   0.0301
             WEIGHT         -0.07230234      0.05331009      9.52156710    1.84   0.1871
             RUNTIME        -2.68252297      0.34098544    320.35967836   61.89   0.0001
             RUNPULSE       -0.37340085      0.11714109     52.59623720   10.16   0.0038
             MAXPULSE        0.30490783      0.13393642     26.82640270    5.18   0.0316

Bounds on condition number:    8.731225,     104.8254
---------------------------------------------------------------------------------------------

Step 2    Variable WEIGHT Removed    R-square = 0.83681815   C(p) = 4.87995808

                              DF      Sum of Squares     Mean Square       F     Prob>F

             Regression        4       712.45152692     178.11288173     33.33   0.0001
             Error            26       138.93001792       5.34346223
             Total            30       851.38154484

                           Parameter        Standard        Type II
             Variable        Estimate         Error      Sum of Squares    F     Prob>F

             INTERCEP       98.14788797     11.78569002    370.57373243   69.35   0.0001
             AGE            -0.19773470      0.09563662     22.84231496    4.27   0.0488
```

```
                                    The SAS System                                          2

             RUNTIME        -2.76757879      0.34053643    352.93569605   66.05   0.0001
             RUNPULSE       -0.34810795      0.11749917     46.90088674    8.78   0.0064
             MAXPULSE        0.27051297      0.13361978     21.90067065    4.10   0.0533

Bounds on condition number:    8.4182,     76.85135
---------------------------------------------------------------------------------------------

All variables in the model are significant at the 0.1000 level.

              Summary of Backward Elimination Procedure for Dependent Variable OXY

                  Variable    Number   Partial    Model
         Step     Removed       In      R**2      R**2      C(p)         F     Prob>F

           1      RSTPULSE       5      0.0007    0.8480    5.1063     0.1063   0.7473
           2      WEIGHT         4      0.0112    0.8368    4.8800     1.8394   0.1871
```

The BACKWARD model-selection method begins with the full model. RSTPLSE is the first variable deleted, followed by WEIGHT. No other variables are deleted from the model since the variables remaining (AGE, RUNTIME, RUNPULSE, and MAXPULSE) are all significant at the 0.10 significance level.

Output 36.40   Maximum R-Square Improvement Selection Method: PROC REG

```
                                  The SAS System                                                    1

                      Maximum R-square Improvement for Dependent Variable OXY

Step 1   Variable RUNTIME Entered   R-square = 0.74338010   C(p) = 13.69884048

                              DF      Sum of Squares     Mean Square        F    Prob>F

             Regression       1       632.90009985      632.90009985    84.01    0.0001
             Error           29       218.48144499        7.53384293
             Total           30       851.38154484

                          Parameter        Standard         Type II
             Variable       Estimate          Error      Sum of Squares       F    Prob>F

             INTERCEP     82.42177268      3.85530378     3443.36654076   457.05    0.0001
             RUNTIME      -3.31055536      0.36119485      632.90009985    84.01    0.0001

Bounds on condition number:         1,            1
-----------------------------------------------------------------------------------------------------

The above model is the best  1-variable model found.

Step 2   Variable AGE Entered      R-square = 0.76424693   C(p) = 12.38944895

                              DF      Sum of Squares     Mean Square        F    Prob>F

             Regression       2       650.66573237      325.33286618    45.38    0.0001
             Error           28       200.71581247        7.16842187
             Total           30       851.38154484

                          Parameter        Standard         Type II
             Variable       Estimate          Error      Sum of Squares       F    Prob>F

             INTERCEP     88.46228749      5.37263885     1943.41070877   271.11    0.0001
             AGE          -0.15036567      0.09551468       17.76563252     2.48    0.1267
             RUNTIME      -3.20395056      0.35877488      571.67750579    79.75    0.0001

Bounds on condition number:     1.036941,     4.147763
-----------------------------------------------------------------------------------------------------

The above model is the best  2-variable model found.

Step 3   Variable RUNPULSE Entered  R-square = 0.81109446   C(p) = 6.95962673

                              DF      Sum of Squares     Mean Square        F    Prob>F

             Regression       3       690.55085627      230.18361876    38.64    0.0001
             Error           27       160.83068857        5.95669217
             Total           30       851.38154484

                          Parameter        Standard         Type II
             Variable       Estimate          Error      Sum of Squares       F    Prob>F

             INTERCEP    111.71806443     10.23508836      709.69013814   119.14    0.0001
             AGE          -0.25639826      0.09622892       42.28867438     7.10    0.0129
             RUNTIME      -2.82537867      0.35828041      370.43528607    62.19    0.0001
             RUNPULSE     -0.13090870      0.05059011       39.88512390     6.70    0.0154

Bounds on condition number:     1.354763,     11.59745
```

```
                                          The SAS System                                              2
------------------------------------------------------------------------------------------------------

The above model is the best  3-variable model found.

Step 4    Variable MAXPULSE Entered  R-square = 0.83681815   C(p) =  4.87995808

                          DF        Sum of Squares        Mean Square         F     Prob>F

        Regression         4         712.45152692        178.11288173     33.33     0.0001
        Error             26         138.93001792          5.34346223
        Total             30         851.38154484

                          Parameter         Standard          Type II
        Variable          Estimate            Error       Sum of Squares        F     Prob>F

        INTERCEP        98.14788797       11.78569002        370.57373243     69.35     0.0001
        AGE             -0.19773470        0.09563662         22.84231496      4.27     0.0488
        RUNTIME         -2.76757879        0.34053643        352.93569605     66.05     0.0001
        RUNPULSE        -0.34810795        0.11749917         46.90088674      8.78     0.0064
        MAXPULSE         0.27051297        0.13361978         21.90067065      4.10     0.0533

Bounds on condition number:      8.4182,      76.85135
------------------------------------------------------------------------------------------------------

The above model is the best  4-variable model found.

Step 5    Variable WEIGHT Entered    R-square = 0.84800181   C(p) =  5.10627546

                          DF        Sum of Squares        Mean Square         F     Prob>F

        Regression         5         721.97309402        144.39461880     27.90     0.0001
        Error             25         129.40845082          5.17633803
        Total             30         851.38154484

                          Parameter         Standard          Type II
        Variable          Estimate            Error       Sum of Squares        F     Prob>F

        INTERCEP       102.20427520       11.97928972        376.78934930     72.79     0.0001
        AGE             -0.21962138        0.09550245         27.37429100      5.29     0.0301
        WEIGHT          -0.07230234        0.05331009          9.52156710      1.84     0.1871
        RUNTIME         -2.68252297        0.34098544        320.35967836     61.89     0.0001
        RUNPULSE        -0.37340085        0.11714109         52.59623720     10.16     0.0038
        MAXPULSE         0.30490783        0.13393642         26.82640270      5.18     0.0316

Bounds on condition number:     8.731225,     104.8254
------------------------------------------------------------------------------------------------------

The above model is the best  5-variable model found.

Step 6    Variable RSTPULSE Entered  R-square = 0.84867192   C(p) =  7.00000000

                          DF        Sum of Squares        Mean Square         F     Prob>F

        Regression         6         722.54360701        120.42393450     22.43     0.0001
        Error             24         128.83793783          5.36824741
        Total             30         851.38154484

                          Parameter         Standard          Type II
```

```
                                          The SAS System                                              3

        Variable          Estimate            Error       Sum of Squares        F     Prob>F

        INTERCEP       102.93447948       12.40325810        369.72831073     68.87     0.0001
        AGE             -0.22697380        0.09983747         27.74577148      5.17     0.0322
        WEIGHT          -0.07417741        0.05459316          9.91058836      1.85     0.1869
        RUNTIME         -2.62865282        0.38456220        250.82210090     46.72     0.0001
        RUNPULSE        -0.36962776        0.11985294         51.05805832      9.51     0.0051
        RSTPULSE        -0.02153364        0.06605428          0.57051299      0.11     0.7473
        MAXPULSE         0.30321713        0.13649519         26.49142405      4.93     0.0360

Bounds on condition number:     8.743848,     137.1345
------------------------------------------------------------------------------------------------------

The above model is the best  6-variable model found.

No further improvement in R-square is possible.
```

The MAXR method tries to find the "best" one-variable model, the "best" two-variable model, and so on. For the fitness data, the one-variable model contains RUNTIME; the two-variable model contains RUNTIME and AGE; and the three-variable model contains RUNTIME, AGE, and RUNPULSE. The four-variable model contains AGE, RUNTIME, RUNPULSE, and MAXPULSE. The five-variable model contains AGE, WEIGHT, RUNTIME, RUNPULSE, and MAXPULSE. Finally, the six-variable model contains all the variables in the MODEL statement.

Note that for all three of the above methods, RSTPULSE contributes least to the model. In the case of forward selection, it is not added to the model. In the case of backward selection, it is the first variable to be removed from the model. In the case of MAXR selection, RSTPULSE is included only for the full model.

Next, the RSQUARE model-selection method is used to request R^2 and C_p statistics for all possible combinations of the six independent variables. The statements below produce **Output 36.41**:

```
model oxy=age weight runtime runpulse rstpulse maxpulse
      / selection=rsquare cp;
title 'Physical fitness data: all models';
run;
```

Output 36.41   All Models by the RSQUARE Method: PROC REG

```
                         Physical fitness data: all models                      1

         N = 31    Regression Models for Dependent Variable: OXY

         Number in    R-square         C(p)    Variables in Model
         Model

              1       0.74338010    13.69884   RUNTIME
              1       0.15948531   106.30211   RSTPULSE
              1       0.15838344   106.47686   RUNPULSE
              1       0.09277653   116.88184   AGE
              1       0.05604592   122.70716   MAXPULSE
              1       0.02648849   127.39485   WEIGHT
         ------------------------------------------------------
              2       0.76424693    12.38945   AGE RUNTIME
              2       0.76142381    12.83718   RUNTIME RUNPULSE
              2       0.74522106    15.40687   RUNTIME MAXPULSE
              2       0.74493479    15.45227   WEIGHT RUNTIME
              2       0.74353296    15.67460   RUNTIME RSTPULSE
              2       0.37599543    73.96451   AGE RUNPULSE
              2       0.30027026    85.97420   AGE RSTPULSE
              2       0.28941948    87.69509   RUNPULSE MAXPULSE
              2       0.25998174    92.36380   AGE MAXPULSE
              2       0.23503072    96.32092   RUNPULSE RSTPULSE
              2       0.18060672   104.95234   WEIGHT RSTPULSE
              2       0.17403933   105.99390   RSTPULSE MAXPULSE
              2       0.16685536   107.13325   WEIGHT RUNPULSE
              2       0.15063534   109.70568   AGE WEIGHT
              2       0.06751590   122.88807   WEIGHT MAXPULSE
         ------------------------------------------------------
              3       0.81109446     6.95963   AGE RUNTIME RUNPULSE
              3       0.80998844     7.13504   RUNTIME RUNPULSE MAXPULSE
              3       0.78173017    11.61668   AGE RUNTIME MAXPULSE
              3       0.77083060    13.34531   AGE WEIGHT RUNTIME
              3       0.76734943    13.89741   AGE RUNTIME RSTPULSE
              3       0.76189848    14.76190   RUNTIME RUNPULSE RSTPULSE
              3       0.76182904    14.77292   WEIGHT RUNTIME RUNPULSE
              3       0.74615485    17.25878   WEIGHT RUNTIME MAXPULSE
              3       0.74522683    17.40596   RUNTIME RSTPULSE MAXPULSE
              3       0.74511138    17.42427   WEIGHT RUNTIME RSTPULSE
              3       0.46664844    61.58732   AGE RUNPULSE RSTPULSE
              3       0.42227346    68.62501   AGE RUNPULSE MAXPULSE
              3       0.40912553    70.71021   AGE WEIGHT RUNPULSE
              3       0.39000680    73.74237   AGE RSTPULSE MAXPULSE
              3       0.35684729    79.00132   AGE WEIGHT RSTPULSE
              3       0.35377183    79.48908   RUNPULSE RSTPULSE MAXPULSE
              3       0.32077932    84.72155   WEIGHT RUNPULSE MAXPULSE
```

(continued on next page)

(continued from previous page)

```
          3    0.29021246    89.56933    AGE WEIGHT MAXPULSE
          3    0.24465116    96.79516    WEIGHT RUNPULSE RSTPULSE
          3    0.18823207   105.74299    WEIGHT RSTPULSE MAXPULSE
         ------------------------------------------------------------------
          4    0.83681815     4.87996    AGE RUNTIME RUNPULSE MAXPULSE
          4    0.81649255     8.10351    AGE WEIGHT RUNTIME RUNPULSE
          4    0.81584902     8.20557    WEIGHT RUNTIME RUNPULSE MAXPULSE
          4    0.81167015     8.86832    AGE RUNTIME RUNPULSE RSTPULSE
          4    0.81040041     9.06970    RUNTIME RUNPULSE RSTPULSE MAXPULSE
          4    0.78622430    12.90393    AGE WEIGHT RUNTIME MAXPULSE
          4    0.78343214    13.34675    AGE RUNTIME RSTPULSE MAXPULSE
          4    0.77503285    14.67885    AGE WEIGHT RUNTIME RSTPULSE
```

```
                      Physical fitness data: all models                            2

    Number in    R-square       C(p)   Variables in Model
      Model

          4    0.76225238    16.70578    WEIGHT RUNTIME RUNPULSE RSTPULSE
          4    0.74617854    19.25502    WEIGHT RUNTIME RSTPULSE MAXPULSE
          4    0.50339774    57.75904    AGE WEIGHT RUNPULSE RSTPULSE
          4    0.50245083    57.90921    AGE RUNPULSE RSTPULSE MAXPULSE
          4    0.47171966    62.78305    AGE WEIGHT RUNPULSE MAXPULSE
          4    0.42560710    70.09631    AGE WEIGHT RSTPULSE MAXPULSE
          4    0.38579687    76.41004    WEIGHT RUNPULSE RSTPULSE MAXPULSE
         ------------------------------------------------------------------
          5    0.84800181     5.10628    AGE WEIGHT RUNTIME RUNPULSE MAXPULSE
          5    0.83703132     6.84615    AGE RUNTIME RUNPULSE RSTPULSE MAXPULSE
          5    0.81755611     9.93484    AGE WEIGHT RUNTIME RUNPULSE RSTPULSE
          5    0.81608280    10.16850    WEIGHT RUNTIME RUNPULSE RSTPULSE MAXPULSE
          5    0.78870109    14.51112    AGE WEIGHT RUNTIME RSTPULSE MAXPULSE
          5    0.55406593    51.72328    AGE WEIGHT RUNPULSE RSTPULSE MAXPULSE
         ------------------------------------------------------------------
          6    0.84867192     7.00000    AGE WEIGHT RUNTIME RUNPULSE RSTPULSE MAXPULSE
         ------------------------------------------------------------------
```

The models in the output above are arranged first by the number of variables in the model, and second by the magnitude of R^2 for the model. Before making a final decision about which model to use, you would want to perform collinearity diagnostics. Note that when many different models are fit and the choice of a final model is based on R^2, the statistics are biased and the p values for the parameter estimates are not valid.

Example 3:   Predicting Weight by Height and Age

In this example, the weights of school children are modeled as a function of their heights and ages. Modeling is performed separately for boys and girls. The example shows the use of a BY statement with PROC REG; multiple MODEL statements; and the OUTEST= and OUTSSCP= options, which create data sets. Since the BY statement is used, interactive processing is not possible in this example; no statements can appear after the first RUN statement. The statements below produce **Output 36.42**:

```
/* Data on Age, Weight, and Height of Children     */
/* Age (months), height (inches), and weight (pounds) */
/* were recorde for a group of school children.    */
/* From Lewis and Taylor (1967).                   */
/*                                                 */

data htwt;
   input sex $ age :3.1 height weight @@;
   cards;
f 143 56.3  85.0 f 155 62.3 105.0 f 153 63.3 108.0 f 161 59.0  92.0
f 191 62.5 112.5 f 171 62.5 112.0 f 185 59.0 104.0 f 142 56.5  69.0
```

```
f 160 62.0  94.5 f 140 53.8  68.5 f 139 61.5 104.0 f 178 61.5 103.5
f 157 64.5 123.5 f 149 58.3  93.0 f 143 51.3  50.5 f 145 58.8  89.0
f 191 65.3 107.0 f 150 59.5  78.5 f 147 61.3 115.0 f 180 63.3 114.0
f 141 61.8  85.0 f 140 53.5  81.0 f 164 58.0  83.5 f 176 61.3 112.0
f 185 63.3 101.0 f 166 61.5 103.5 f 175 60.8  93.5 f 180 59.0 112.0
f 210 65.5 140.0 f 146 56.3  83.5 f 170 64.3  90.0 f 162 58.0  84.0
f 149 64.3 110.5 f 139 57.5  96.0 f 186 57.8  95.0 f 197 61.5 121.0
f 169 62.3  99.5 f 177 61.8 142.5 f 185 65.3 118.0 f 182 58.3 104.5
f 173 62.8 102.5 f 166 59.3  89.5 f 168 61.5  95.0 f 169 62.0  98.5
f 150 61.3  94.0 f 184 62.3 108.0 f 139 52.8  63.5 f 147 59.8  84.5
f 144 59.5  93.5 f 177 61.3 112.0 f 178 63.5 148.5 f 197 64.8 112.0
f 146 60.0 109.0 f 145 59.0  91.5 f 147 55.8  75.0 f 145 57.8  84.0
f 155 61.3 107.0 f 167 62.3  92.5 f 183 64.3 109.5 f 143 55.5  84.0
f 183 64.5 102.5 f 185 60.0 106.0 f 148 56.3  77.0 f 147 58.3 111.5
f 154 60.0 114.0 f 156 54.5  75.0 f 144 55.8  73.5 f 154 62.8  93.5
f 152 60.5 105.0 f 191 63.3 113.5 f 190 66.8 140.0 f 140 60.0  77.0
f 148 60.5  84.5 f 189 64.3 113.5 f 143 58.3  77.5 f 178 66.5 117.5
f 164 65.3  98.0 f 157 60.5 112.0 f 147 59.5 101.0 f 148 59.0  95.0
f 177 61.3  81.0 f 171 61.5  91.0 f 172 64.8 142.0 f 190 56.8  98.5
f 183 66.5 112.0 f 143 61.5 116.5 f 179 63.0  98.5 f 186 57.0  83.5
f 182 65.5 133.0 f 182 62.0  91.5 f 142 56.0  72.5 f 165 61.3 106.5
f 165 55.5  67.0 f 154 61.0 122.5 f 150 54.5  74.0 f 155 66.0 144.5
f 163 56.5  84.0 f 141 56.0  72.5 f 147 51.5  64.0 f 210 62.0 116.0
f 171 63.0  84.0 f 167 61.0  93.5 f 182 64.0 111.5 f 144 61.0  92.0
f 193 59.8 115.0 f 141 61.3  85.0 f 164 63.3 108.0 f 186 63.5 108.0
f 169 61.5  85.0 f 175 60.3  86.0 f 180 61.3 110.5 m 165 64.8  98.0
m 157 60.5 105.0 m 144 57.3  76.5 m 150 59.5  84.0 m 150 60.8 128.0
m 139 60.5  87.0 m 189 67.0 128.0 m 183 64.8 111.0 m 147 50.5  79.0
m 146 57.5  90.0 m 160 60.5  84.0 m 156 61.8 112.0 m 173 61.3  93.0
m 151 66.3 117.0 m 141 53.3  84.0 m 150 59.0  99.5 m 164 57.8  95.0
m 153 60.0  84.0 m 206 68.3 134.0 m 250 67.5 171.5 m 176 63.8  98.5
m 176 65.0 118.5 m 140 59.5  94.5 m 185 66.0 105.0 m 180 61.8 104.0
m 146 57.3  83.0 m 183 66.0 105.5 m 140 56.5  84.0 m 151 58.3  86.0
m 151 61.0  81.0 m 144 62.8  94.0 m 160 59.3  78.5 m 178 67.3 119.5
m 193 66.3 133.0 m 162 64.5 119.0 m 164 60.5  95.0 m 186 66.0 112.0
m 143 57.5  75.0 m 175 64.0  92.0 m 175 68.0 112.0 m 175 63.5  98.5
m 173 69.0 112.5 m 170 63.8 112.5 m 174 66.0 108.0 m 164 63.5 108.0
m 144 59.5  88.0 m 156 66.3 106.0 m 149 57.0  92.0 m 144 60.0 117.5
m 147 57.0  84.0 m 188 67.3 112.0 m 169 62.0 100.0 m 172 65.0 112.0
m 150 59.5  84.0 m 193 67.8 127.5 m 157 58.0  80.5 m 168 60.0  93.5
m 140 58.5  86.5 m 156 58.3  92.5 m 156 61.5 108.5 m 158 65.0 121.0
m 184 66.5 112.0 m 156 68.5 114.0 m 144 57.0  84.0 m 176 61.5  81.0
m 168 66.5 111.5 m 149 52.5  81.0 m 142 55.0  70.0 m 188 71.0 140.0
m 203 66.5 117.0 m 142 58.8  84.0 m 189 66.3 112.0 m 188 65.8 150.5
m 200 71.0 147.0 m 152 59.5 105.0 m 174 69.8 119.5 m 166 62.5  84.0
m 145 56.5  91.0 m 143 57.5 101.0 m 163 65.3 117.5 m 166 67.3 121.0
m 182 67.0 133.0 m 173 66.0 112.0 m 155 61.8  91.5 m 162 60.0 105.0
m 177 63.0 111.0 m 177 60.5 112.0 m 175 65.5 114.0 m 166 62.0  91.0
m 150 59.0  98.0 m 150 61.8 118.0 m 188 63.3 115.5 m 163 66.0 112.0
m 171 61.8 112.0 m 162 63.0  91.0 m 141 57.5  85.0 m 174 63.0 112.0
m 142 56.0  87.5 m 148 60.5 118.0 m 140 56.8  83.5 m 160 64.0 116.0
m 144 60.0  89.0 m 206 69.5 171.5 m 159 63.3 112.0 m 149 56.3  72.0
m 193 72.0 150.0 m 194 65.3 134.5 m 152 60.8  97.0 m 146 55.0  71.5
m 139 55.0  73.5 m 186 66.5 112.0 m 161 56.8  75.0 m 153 64.8 128.0
m 196 64.5  98.0 m 164 58.0  84.0 m 159 62.8  99.0 m 178 63.8 112.0
```

```
       m 153 57.8  79.5 m 155 57.3  80.5 m 178 63.5 102.5 m 142 55.0  76.0
       m 164 66.5 112.0 m 189 65.0 114.0 m 164 61.5 140.0 m 167 62.0 107.5
       m 151 59.3  87.0
       ;
       title '-------- Data on age, weight, and height of children ---------';
       proc reg outest=est1 outsscp=sscp1;
          by sex;
          eq1: model  weight=height;
          eq2: model  weight=height age;
       proc print data=sscp1;
          title2 'SSCP type data set';
       proc print data=est1;
          title2 'EST type data set';
       run;
```

Output 36.42   Height and Weight Data: PROC REG

```
                 -------- Data on age, weight, and height of children ---------                          1
--------------------------------------------------------- SEX=f -----------------------------------------------------
Model: EQ1
Dependent Variable: WEIGHT

                                    Analysis of Variance

                                  Sum of         Mean
             Source        DF     Squares       Square      F Value      Prob>F

             Model          1   21506.52309   21506.52309   141.094      0.0001
             Error        109   16614.58502     152.42739
             C Total      110   38121.10811

                 Root MSE      12.34615     R-square     0.5642
                 Dep Mean      98.87838     Adj R-sq     0.5602
                 C.V.          12.48620

                                  Parameter Estimates

                          Parameter     Standard     T for H0:
             Variable  DF   Estimate       Error     Parameter=0    Prob > |T|

             INTERCEP   1  -153.128910   21.24814273     -7.207      0.0001
             HEIGHT     1     4.163612    0.35052308     11.878      0.0001
```

```
-------- Data on age, weight, and height of children ---------                    2
--------------------------------------------------- SEX=f -----------------------------------------------------

Model: EQ2
Dependent Variable: WEIGHT

                              Analysis of Variance

                              Sum of         Mean
Source            DF         Squares        Square      F Value      Prob>F

Model              2       22432.27243   11216.13621     77.210      0.0001
Error            108       15688.83568     145.26700
C Total          110       38121.10811

            Root MSE        12.05268      R-square       0.5884
            Dep Mean        98.87838      Adj R-sq       0.5808
            C.V.            12.18939

                              Parameter Estimates

                         Parameter      Standard     T for H0:
Variable   DF            Estimate         Error     Parameter=0    Prob > |T|

INTERCEP    1          -150.596982     20.76729993     -7.252       0.0001
HEIGHT      1             3.603780      0.40776801      8.838       0.0001
AGE         1             1.907026      0.75542849      2.524       0.0130
```

```
-------- Data on age, weight, and height of children ---------                    3
--------------------------------------------------- SEX=m -----------------------------------------------------

Model: EQ1
Dependent Variable: WEIGHT

                              Analysis of Variance

                              Sum of         Mean
Source            DF         Squares        Square      F Value      Prob>F

Model              1       31126.05991   31126.05991    206.239      0.0001
Error            124       18714.35477     150.92222
C Total          125       49840.41468

            Root MSE        12.28504      R-square       0.6245
            Dep Mean       103.44841      Adj R-sq       0.6215
            C.V.            11.87552

                              Parameter Estimates

                         Parameter      Standard     T for H0:
Variable   DF            Estimate         Error     Parameter=0    Prob > |T|

INTERCEP    1          -125.698066     15.99362486     -7.859       0.0001
HEIGHT      1             3.689771      0.25692946     14.361       0.0001
```

```
-------- Data on age, weight, and height of children ---------                    4
--------------------------------------------------- SEX=m -----------------------------------------------------

Model: EQ2
Dependent Variable: WEIGHT

                              Analysis of Variance

                              Sum of         Mean
Source            DF         Squares        Square      F Value      Prob>F

Model              2       32974.75022   16487.37511    120.241      0.0001
Error            123       16865.66447     137.11922
C Total          125       49840.41468

            Root MSE        11.70979      R-square       0.6616
            Dep Mean       103.44841      Adj R-sq       0.6561
            C.V.            11.31945
```

(continued on next page)

(continued from previous page)

```
                           Parameter Estimates

                      Parameter      Standard     T for H0:
    Variable    DF     Estimate        Error    Parameter=0    Prob > |T|

    INTERCEP    1     -113.713465   15.59021361     -7.294        0.0001
    HEIGHT      1        2.680749    0.36809058      7.283        0.0001
    AGE         1        3.081672    0.83927355      3.672        0.0004
```

```
          -------- Data on age, weight, and height of children ---------          5
                           SSCP type data set

    OBS   SEX   _TYPE_   _NAME_    INTERCEP      HEIGHT       WEIGHT        AGE

     1     f    SSCP    INTERCEP     111.0      6718.40     10975.50     1824.90
     2     f    SSCP    HEIGHT      6718.4    407879.32    669469.85   110818.32
     3     f    SSCP    WEIGHT     10975.5    669469.85   1123360.75   182444.95
     4     f    SSCP    AGE         1824.9    110818.32    182444.95    30363.81
     5     f    N          111.0      111.00       111.00      111.00
     6     m    SSCP    INTERCEP     126.0      7825.00     13034.50     2072.10
     7     m    SSCP    HEIGHT      7825.0    488243.60    817919.60   129432.57
     8     m    SSCP    WEIGHT     13034.5    817919.60   1398238.75   217717.45
     9     m    SSCP    AGE         2072.1    129432.57    217717.45    34515.95
    10     m    N          126.0      126.00       126.00      126.00
```

```
          -------- Data on age, weight, and height of children ---------          6
                           EST type data set

    OBS  SEX  _MODEL_  _TYPE_  _DEPVAR_  _RMSE_  INTERCEP   HEIGHT  WEIGHT    AGE

     1    f    EQ1     PARMS   WEIGHT   12.3461  -153.129   4.16361   -1        .
     2    f    EQ2     PARMS   WEIGHT   12.0527  -150.597   3.60378   -1     1.90703
     3    m    EQ1     PARMS   WEIGHT   12.2850  -125.698   3.68977   -1        .
     4    m    EQ2     PARMS   WEIGHT   11.7098  -113.713   2.68075   -1     3.08167
```

For both females and males, the overall *F* statistics for both models are significant, indicating that the model explains a significant portion of the variation in the data. For females, the full model is

$$\text{WEIGHT} = -150.57 + 3.60*\text{HEIGHT} + 1.91*\text{AGE}$$

and, for males, the full model is

$$\text{WEIGHT} = -113.71 + 2.68*\text{HEIGHT} + 3.08*\text{AGE} \ .$$

The OUTSSCP= data set is printed. Note how the BY groups are separated. Observations with _TYPE_='N' contain the number of observations in the associated BY group. Observations with _TYPE_='SSCP' contain the rows of the uncorrected sums of squares and crossproducts matrix. The observations with _NAME_='INTERCEP' contain crossproducts for the intercept.

The OUTEST= data set is printed, and again, the BY groups are separated. Observations with _MODEL_ contain the labels for models from MODEL statements. If no labels had been specified, the defaults MODEL1 and MODEL2 would appear as values for _MODEL_. Note that _TYPE_='PARMS' for all observations, indicating that all observations contain parameter estimates. _DEPVAR_ gives the dependent variable, and _RMSE_ gives the Root Mean Square Error for the associated model. INTERCEP gives the estimate for the intercept for the associated model, and variables with the same name as variables in the original data set (HEIGHT, AGE) give parameter estimates for those variables. Note that the dependent variable, WEIGHT, is shown with a value of −1.

REFERENCES

Akaike, H. (1969), "Fitting Autoregressive Models for Prediction," *Annals of the Institute of Statistical Mathematics*, 21, 243–247.

Allen, D.M. (1971), "Mean Square Error of Prediction as a Criterion for Selecting Variables," *Technometrics*, 13, 469–475.

Allen, D.M. and Cady, F.B. (1982), *Analyzing Experimental Data by Regression*, Belmont, CA: Lifetime Learning Publications.

Amemiya, T. (1976), "Selection of Regressors," Technical Report No. 225, Stanford, CA: Stanford University.

Belsley, D.A., Kuh, E., and Welsch, R.E. (1980), *Regression Diagnostics*, New York: John Wiley & Sons, Inc.

Berk, K.N. (1977), "Tolerance and Condition in Regression Computations," *Journal of the American Statistical Association*, 72, 863–866.

Bock, R.D. (1975), *Multivariate Statistical Methods in Behavioral Research*, New York: McGraw-Hill Book Co.

Box, G.E.P. (1966), "The Use and Abuse of Regression," *Technometrics*, 8, 625–629.

Cook, R.D. (1977), "Detection of Influential Observations in Linear Regression," *Technometrics*, 19, 15–18.

Cook, R.D. (1979), "Influential Observations in Linear Regression," *Journal of the American Statistical Association*, 74, 169–174.

Daniel, C. and Wood, F. (1980), *Fitting Equations to Data*, Revised Edition, New York: John Wiley & Sons, Inc.

Darlington, R.B. (1968), "Multiple Regression in Psychological Research and Practice," *Psychological Bulletin*, 69, 161–182.

Draper, N. and Smith, H. (1981), *Applied Regression Analysis*, 2d Edition, New York: John Wiley & Sons, Inc.

Durbin, J. and Watson, G.S. (1951), "Testing for Serial Correlation in Least Squares Regression," *Biometrika*, 37, 409–428.

Freund, R.J. and Littell, R.C. (1986), *SAS System for Regressions, 1986 Edition*, Cary, NC: SAS Institute Inc.

Furnival, G.M. and Wilson, R.W. (1974), "Regression by Leaps and Bounds," *Technometrics*, 16, 499–511.

Gauss, K.F. (1809), *Werke*, 4, 1–93.

Goodnight, J.H. (1979), "A Tutorial on the SWEEP Operator," *The American Statistician*, 33, 149–158. (Also available as *The Sweep Operator: Its Importance in Statistical Computing*, SAS Technical Report R-106.)

Grunfeld, Y. (1958), "The Determinants of Corporate Investment," Unpublished Thesis, Chicago, discussed in Boot, J.C.G. (1960), "Investment Demand: An Empirical Contribution to the Aggregation Problem," *International Economic Review*, 1, 3–30.

Hocking, R.R. (1976), "The Analysis and Selection of Variables in Linear Regression," *Biometrics*, 32, 1–50.

Johnston, J. (1972), *Econometric Methods*, New York: McGraw-Hill Book Co.

Judge, G.G., Griffiths, W.E., Hill, R.C., and Lee, T. (1980), *The Theory and Practice of Econometrics*, New York: John Wiley & Sons, Inc.

Judge, G.G., Griffiths, W.E., Hill, R.C., Lutkepohl, H., and Lee, T.C. (1985) *The Theory and Practice of Econometrics*, 2d edition, New York: John Wiley & Sons, Inc.

Kennedy, W.J. and Gentle, J.E. (1980), *Statistical Computing*, New York: Marcel Dekker, Inc.

Lewis, T. and Taylor, L.R. (1967), *Introduction to Experimental Ecology*, New York: Academic Press, Inc.

Lord, F.M. (1950), "Efficiency of Prediction when a Progression Equation from One Sample is Used in a New Sample," Research Bulletin No. 50-40, Princeton, NJ: Educational Testing Service.

Mallows, C.L. (1967), "Choosing a Subset Regression," unpublished report, Bell Telephone Laboratories.

Mallows, C.L. (1973), "Some Comments on Cp," *Technometrics*, 15, 661–675.

Mardia, K.V., Kent, J.T., and Bibby, J.M. (1979), *Multivariate Analysis*, London: Academic Press, Inc.

Markov, A.A. (1900), *Wahrscheinlichkeitsrechnung*, Tebrer, Leipzig.

Morrison, D.F. (1976), *Multivariate Statistical Methods*, 2d Edition, New York: McGraw-Hill, Inc.

Mosteller, F. and Tukey, J.W. (1977), *Data Analysis and Regression*, Reading, MA: Addison-Wesley Publishing Co., Inc.

Neter, J. and Wasserman, W. (1974), *Applied Linear Statistical Models*, Homewood, IL: Irwin.

Nicholson, G.E., Jr. (1948), "The Application of a Regression Equation to a New Sample," unpublished Ph.D. dissertation, University of North Carolina at Chapel Hill.

Pillai, K.C.S. (1960), *Statistical Table for Tests of Multivariate Hypotheses*, Manila: The Statistical Center, University of the Philippines.

Pindyck, R.S. and Rubinfeld, D.L. (1981), *Econometric Models and Econometric Forecasts*, 2d Edition, New York: McGraw-Hill Book Co.

Pringle, R.M. and Raynor, A.A. (1971), *Generalized Inverse Matrices with Applications to Statistics*, New York: Hafner Publishing Company.

Rao, C.R. (1973), *Linear Statistical Inference and Its Applications*, 2d Edition, New York: John Wiley & Sons, Inc.

Rawlings, J.O. (1988), *Applied Regression Analysis: A Research Tool*, Pacific Grove, California: Wadsworth & Brooks/Cole Advanced Books and Software.

Rothman, D. (1968), Letter to the editor, *Technometrics*, 10, 432.

Sall, J.P. (1981), *SAS Regression Applications*, Revised Edition, SAS Technical Report A-102, Cary, NC: SAS Institute Inc.

Sawa, T. (1978), "Information Criteria for Discriminating Among Alternative Regression Models," *Econometrica*, 46, 1273–1282.

Schwarz, G. (1978), "Estimating the Dimension of a Model," *Annals of Statistics*, 6, 461–464.

Stein, C. (1960), "Multiple Regression," in *Contributions to Probability and Statistics*, eds. I. Olkin et al., Stanford, CA: Stanford University Press.

Timm, N.H. (1975), *Multivariate Analysis with Applications in Education and Psychology*, Monterey, CA: Brooks-Cole Publishing Co.

Weisberg, S. (1980), *Applied Linear Regression*, New York: John Wiley & Sons, Inc.

White, H. (1980), "A Heteroskedasticity-Consistent Covariance Matrix Estimator and a Direct Test for Heteroskedasticity," *Econometrics*, 48, 817–838.

Chapter 37

The RSREG
Procedure

ABSTRACT   1457
INTRODUCTION   1458
   Response Surface Experiments   1458
   Model Fitting and Analysis of Variance   1458
   Canonical Analysis   1458
   Ridge Analysis   1459
   Coding the Factor Variables   1459
   Comparison to PROC GLM   1459
   Terminology   1460
SPECIFICATIONS   1460
   PROC RSREG Statement   1461
   BY Statement   1461
   ID Statement   1461
   MODEL Statement   1462
   RIDGE Statement   1464
   WEIGHT Statement   1465
DETAILS   1465
   Missing Values   1465
   Output Data Sets   1465
     OUT= Data Sets   1465
     OUTR= Data Sets   1466
   Lack-of-Fit Test   1466
   Interpreting the Canonical Analysis   1466
   Plotting the Surface   1467
   Searching for Multiple Response Conditions   1467
   Handling of the Covariates   1468
   Computational Method   1468
   Printed Output   1469
EXAMPLES   1471
   Example 1:   A Response Surface with a Simple Optimum   1471
   Example 2:   A Saddle-Surface Response Using the Ridge Analysis   1475
REFERENCES   1477

ABSTRACT

The RSREG procedure fits the parameters of a complete quadratic response surface and analyzes the fitted surface to determine the factor levels of optimum response.

INTRODUCTION

Response Surface Experiments

Many industrial experiments are conducted to discover which values of factor variables optimize a response. If each factor variable is measured at three or more values, a quadratic response surface can be estimated by least-squares regression. The predicted optimal value can be found from the estimated surface if the surface is shaped like a simple hill or a valley. If the estimated surface is more complicated, or if the predicted optimum is far from the region of experimentation, then the shape of the surface can be analyzed to indicate the directions in which new experiments should be performed.

Suppose that a response variable y is measured at combinations of values of two factor variables, x_1 and x_2. The quadratic response-surface model for this variable is written:

$$y = \beta_0 + \beta_1 x_1 + \beta_2 x_2 + \beta_3 x_1^2 + \beta_4 x_2^2 + \beta_5 x_1 x_2 + \varepsilon \quad .$$

The steps in the analysis for such data are

1. model fitting and analysis of variance to estimate parameters
2. canonical analysis to investigate the shape of the predicted response surface
3. ridge analysis to search for the region of optimum response.

Model Fitting and Analysis of Variance

The first task in analyzing the response surface is to estimate the parameters of the model by least-squares regression and to obtain information about the fit in the form of an analysis of variance. This is accomplished using the statements

```
proc rsreg;
   model y = x1 x2;
run;
```

The estimated surface will typically be curved: a "hill" whose peak occurs at the unique estimated point of maximum response, a "valley", or a "saddle-surface" with no unique minimum or maximum. Use the results of this phase of the analysis to answer the following questions:

- What is the contribution of each type of effect to the statistical fit? (The types of effects are linear, quadratic, and crossproduct.)
- What part of the residual error is due to lack of fit? Does the quadratic response model adequately represent the true response surface?
- What is the contribution of each factor variable to the statistical fit? Can the response be predicted as well if the variable is removed?
- What are the predicted responses for a grid of factor values? (See **Plotting the Surface** and **Searching for Multiple Response Conditions** later in this chapter.)

Canonical Analysis

The second task in analyzing the response surface is to examine the overall shape of the curve and determine whether the estimated stationary point is a maximum, a minimum, or a saddle-point. This canonical analysis of the response surface is performed by the PROC and MODEL statements above. The canonical analysis can be used to answer the following:

- Is the surface shaped like a hill, a valley, a saddle-surface, or a flat surface?
- If there is a unique optimum combination of factor values, where is it?
- To which factor or factors are the predicted responses most sensitive?

Because the eigenvalues and eigenvectors are based on parameter estimates from fitting the response to the coded data, they will in general be different from those computed by PROC RSREG in Version 5. (See Coding the Factor Variables below.)

Ridge Analysis

If the estimated surface is found to have a simple optimum well within the range of experimentation, the analysis performed by the two steps above may be sufficient. In more complicated situations, further search for the region of optimum response is required. The method of ridge analysis computes the estimated ridge of optimum response for increasing radii from the center of the original design. The ridge analysis answers the following question:

- If there is not a unique optimum of the response surface within the range of experimentation, in which direction should further searching be done in order to locate the optimum?

For example, the ridge of maximum response is computed using the following statements:

```
proc rsreg;
   model y=x1 x2;
   ridge max;
run;
```

Coding the Factor Variables

For the results of the canonical and ridge analyses to be interpretable, the values of different factor variables should be comparable. This is because the canonical and ridge analyses of the response surface are not invariant with respect to differences in scale and location of the factor variables. The analysis of variance is not affected by these changes. Although the actual predicted surface does not change, its parameterization does. The usual solution to this problem is to code each factor variable so that its minimum in the experiment is -1 and its maximum is 1 and to carry through the analysis with the coded values instead of the original ones. This practice has the added benefit of making 1 a reasonable boundary radius for the ridge analysis since 1 represents approximately the edge of the experimental region. By default, PROC RSREG computes the linear transformation to perform this coding as the data are initially read in, and the canonical and ridge analyses are performed on the model fit to the coded data. The actual form of the coding operation for each value of a variable is

$$coded\ value = (original\ value - M)/S$$

where M is the average of the highest and lowest values for the variable in the design and S is half their difference.

Comparison to PROC GLM

Other SAS/STAT procedures can be used to fit the response surface, but PROC RSREG is more specialized. The following statements for modeling a three factor response surface in RSREG are more compact than the statements for other regression procedures in SAS/STAT software:

```
proc rsreg;
   model y=x1 x2 x3;
run;
```

For example, the equivalent statements for PROC GLM are

```
proc glm;
   model y=x1 x1*x1
            x2 x1*x2 x2*x2
            x3 x1*x3 x2*x3 x3*x3;
run;
```

Terminology

Variables are used according to the following conventions:

factor variables
: independent variables used in constructing the quadratic response surface. To estimate the necessary parameters, each variable must have at least three distinct values in the data. Independent variables must be numeric.

response variables
: the dependent variables to which the quadratic response surface is fit. Dependent variables must be numeric.

covariates
: additional independent variables for use in the regression but not in the formation of the quadratic response surface. Covariates must be numeric.

WEIGHT variable
: a variable for weighting the observations in the regression. WEIGHT variables must be numeric.

ID variables
: variables not in the above lists that are transferred to an output data set containing statistics for each observation in the input data set. This data set is created using the OUT= option in the PROC RSREG statement. ID variables can be either character or numeric.

BY variables
: variables for grouping observations. Separate analyses are obtained for each BY group. BY variables can be either character or numeric.

SPECIFICATIONS

The RSREG procedure allows one of each of the following statements:

> **PROC RSREG** <options>;
> **MODEL** responses=independents / <options>;   } required statements

> **RIDGE** <options>;
> **WEIGHT** variable;
> **ID** variables;
> **BY** variables;   } optional statements

The PROC RSREG and MODEL statements are required. The BY, ID, MODEL, RIDGE, and WEIGHT statements are described after the PROC RSREG statement below and can appear in any order.

PROC RSREG Statement

PROC RSREG <*options*>;

The PROC RSREG statement invokes the procedure. The following options are allowed with the PROC RSREG statement:

DATA=*SAS-data-set*
specifies the input SAS data set that contains the data to be analyzed. By default, PROC RSREG uses the most recently created SAS data set.

NOPRINT
suppresses all printed results when only the output data set is required. For more information, see the description of the NOPRINT option in the MODEL and RIDGE statements.

OUT=*SAS-data-set*
creates an output SAS data set that contains statistics for each observation in the input data set. In particular, this data set contains the BY variables, ID variables, the WEIGHT variable, variables in the MODEL statement, and the OUTPUT options requested in the MODEL statement. You must specify OUTPUT options in the MODEL statement. Otherwise, the output data set is created but contains no observations. To create a permanent SAS data set, you must specify a two-level name (see "SAS Files" in *SAS Language: Reference, Version 6, First Edition*, and "Introduction to DATA Step Processing" in *SAS Language and Procedures: Usage, Version 6, First Edition* for more information on permanent SAS data sets). For details on the data set created by PROC RSREG, see **Output Data Sets** later in this chapter.

BY Statement

BY *variables*;

A BY statement can be used with PROC RSREG to obtain separate analyses on observations in groups defined by the BY variables. When a BY statement appears, the procedure expects the input data set to be sorted in order of the BY variables.

If your input data set is not sorted in ascending order, use one of the following alternatives:

- Use the SORT procedure with a similar BY statement to sort the data.
- Use the BY statement options NOTSORTED or DESCENDING in the BY statement for the RSREG procedure. As a cautionary note, the NOTSORTED option does not mean that the data are unsorted, but rather means that the data are arranged in groups (according to values of the BY variables) and that these groups are not necessarily in alphabetical or increasing numeric order.
- Use the DATASETS procedure (in base SAS software) to create an index on the BY variables.

For more information on the BY statement, see the discussion in *SAS Language: Reference*. For more information on the DATASETS procedure, see the discussion in *SAS Procedures Guide, Version 6, Third Edition*.

ID Statement

ID *variables*;

The ID statement names variables that are to be transferred to the data set created by the OUT= option in the PROC RSREG statement.

MODEL Statement

MODEL *responses=independents* / *<options>*;

The MODEL statement lists response (dependent) variables followed by an equal sign and then lists independent variables, some of which may be covariates. Independent variables specified in the MODEL statement must be variables in the data set being analyzed. In other words, independent variables of the form X1*X1 or X1(X2) are not valid. To use variables of this form, you must create them in a prior DATA step. The output options to the MODEL statement specify which statistics are output to the data set created using the OUT= option in the PROC RSREG statement. If none of the options are selected, the data set is created but contains no observations. The option keywords become values of the special variable _TYPE_ in the output data set. The table below illustrates the tasks performed by the options that may be specified in the MODEL statement.

Task	Options
analyze original data	NOCODE
fit model to first BY group only	BYOUT
declare covariates	COVAR=
request additional statistics	PRESS
request additional tests	LACKFIT
suppress printed output	NOANOVA
	NOOPTIMAL
	NOPRINT
output statistics	ACTUAL
	PREDICT
	RESIDUAL
	L95
	U95
	L95M
	U95M
	D

Any of the following options may be specified in the MODEL statement:

ACTUAL
  specifies the actual values from the input data set.

BYOUT
  uses only the first BY group to estimate the model. Subsequent BY groups have scoring statistics computed in the output data set only. BYOUT is used only when a BY statement is specified.

COVAR=*n*
  declares that the first *n* variables on the independent side of the model are simple linear regressors (covariates) rather than factors in the quadratic response surface. By default, PROC RSREG forms quadratic and crossproduct effects for all regressor variables in the MODEL statement.

D
  specifies Cook's *D* influence statistic. See Chapter 1, "Introduction to Regression Procedures," for details and formulas.

LACKFIT
   performs a lack-of-fit test. To specify the LACKFIT option, your data
   must first be sorted by the independent variables so that repeated
   observations are grouped together. See Draper and Smith (1981) for a
   discussion of lack-of-fit tests.

L95
   specifies the lower bound of a 95% confidence interval for an individual
   prediction. The variance used in calculating this bound is a function of
   both the mean square error and the variance of the parameter estimates.
   See Chapter 1 for details and formulas.

L95M
   specifies the lower bound of a 95% confidence interval for the expected
   value, or mean, of the dependent variable. The variance used in
   calculating this bound is a function of the variance of the parameter
   estimates. See Chapter 1 for details and formulas.

NOANOVA
NOAOV
   suppresses printing the analysis of variance and parameter estimates
   from the model fit.

NOCODE
   performs the canonical and ridge analyses with the parameter estimates
   derived from fitting the response to the original values of the factors
   variables, rather than their coded values (see **INTRODUCTION** for
   details). Use this option if the data are already stored in a coded form
   that does not have -1 and 1 as the lowest and highest values,
   respectively, for each factor variable. This is the case, for example, for
   some central composite designs (see Myers (1976)).

NOOPTIMAL
NOOPT
   suppresses printing the canonical analysis for the quadratic response
   surface.

NOPRINT
   suppresses printing both the analysis of variance and the canonical
   analysis.

PREDICT
   specifies the values predicted by the model.

PRESS
   computes and prints the predicted residual sum of squares (PRESS)
   statistic for each dependent variable in the model. The PRESS statistic is
   added to the summary information at the beginning of the analysis of
   variance, so if NOANOVA or NOPRINT is specified, PRESS has no
   effect. See Chapter 1 for details and formulas.

RESIDUAL
   specifies the residuals, calculated as ACTUAL$-$PREDICTED.

U95
   specifies the upper bound of a 95% confidence interval for an individual
   prediction. See Chapter 1 for details and formulas.

U95M
   specifies the upper bound of a 95% confidence interval for the
   expected value, or mean, of the dependent variable. See Chapter 1 for
   details and formulas.

RIDGE Statement

RIDGE <*options*>;

A RIDGE statement computes the ridge of optimum response. The ridge starts at a given point x_0, and the point on the ridge at radius r from x_0 is the collection of factor settings that optimizes the predicted response at this radius. You can think of the ridge as climbing or falling as fast as possible on the surface of predicted response. Thus, the ridge analysis can be used as a tool to help interpret an existing response surface or to indicate the direction in which further experimentation should be performed.

The default starting point, x_0, has each coordinate equal to the point midway between the highest and lowest values of the factor in the design. The default radii at which the ridge is computed are 0, 0.1, . . . , 0.9, 1. If, as usual, the ridge analysis is based on the response surface fit to coded values for the factor variables (see **INTRODUCTION** for details), then this results in a ridge that starts at the point with a coded zero value for each coordinate and extends toward, but not beyond, the edge of the range of experimentation. Alternatively, both the center point for the ridge and the radii at which it is to be computed may be specified.

The following options can be specified in the RIDGE statement:

CENTER=*uncoded-factor-values*
> gives the coordinates of the point x_0 from which to begin the ridge. The coordinates should be given in the original (uncoded) factor variable values. There must be as many coordinates specified as there are factors in the model, and the order of the coordinates must be the same as that used in the MODEL statement. If the number of coordinates in the list exceeds the number of factors in the model, the extra coordinates are ignored. This starting point should be well inside the range of experimentation. The default sets each coordinate equal to the value midway between the highest and lowest values for the associated factor. The list of coordinates can take any of the following forms or can be composed of mixtures of them:

> $m_1, m_2, . . . , m_n$ several values.

> m TO n a sequence where m equals the starting value, n equals the ending value, and the increment equals 1.

> m TO n BY i a sequence where m equals the starting value, n equals the ending value, and i equals the increment.

> Mixtures of the above forms should be separated by commas. The default list runs from 0 to 1 by increments of 0.1. Below are several examples of valid lists.

```
center=0 to 5 by .5;
center=0, .2, .25, .3, .5 to 1.0 by .1;
```

MAXIMUM
MAX
> computes the ridge of maximum response. Both the MIN and MAX options can be specified; at least one must be specified.

MINIMUM
MIN
> computes the ridge of minimum response. Both the MIN and MAX options can be specified; at least one must be specified.

NOPRINT
   suppresses printing the ridge analysis when only an output data set is
   required.

OUTR=*SAS-data-set*
   creates an output SAS data set containing the computed optimum ridge.
   For details, see **Output Data Sets** later in this chapter.

RADIUS=*coded-radii*
   gives the distances from the ridge starting point at which to compute the
   optimum. The values in the list represent distances between coded
   points. The list can take any of the following forms or can be composed
   of mixtures of them (see CENTER= option):

   $m_1, m_2, \ldots, m_n$ several values.

   m TO *n*   a sequence where *m* equals the starting value, *n*
               equals the ending value, and the increment equals
               1.

   m TO *n* BY *i*   a sequence where *m* equals the starting value,
               n equals the ending value, and *i* equals the
               increment.

Mixtures of the above forms should be separated by commas. The default list
runs from 0 to 1 by increments of 0.1.

WEIGHT Statement

   WEIGHT *variable*;

When a WEIGHT statement is used, a weighted residual sum of squares

$$\Sigma_i\, w_i(y_i - \hat{y}_i)^2$$

is minimized, where w_i is the value of the variable specified in the WEIGHT statement, y_i is the observed value of the response variable, and $\hat{y}_i$ is the predicted
value of the response variable.

   The observation is used in the analysis only if the value of the WEIGHT statement variable is greater than zero. The WEIGHT statement has no effect on
degrees of freedom or number of observations. If the weights for the observations
are proportional to the reciprocals of the error variances, then the weighted least-
squares estimates are BLUE (best linear unbiased estimators).

DETAILS

Missing Values

If an observation has missing data for any of the variables used by the procedure,
then that observation is not used in the estimation process. If one or more
response variables are missing, but no factor or covariate variables are missing,
then predicted values and confidence limits are computed for the output data
set, but the residual and Cook's D statistic are missing.

Output Data Sets

OUT= Data Sets

An output data set containing statistics requested with options in the model statement for each observation in the input data set is created whenever the OUT=

option is specified in the PROC RSREG statement. The data set contains the following variables:

- the BY variables.
- the ID variables.
- the WEIGHT variable.
- the independent variables in the MODEL statement.
- the variable _TYPE_, which identifies the observation type in the output data set. _TYPE_ is a character variable with a length of eight, and it takes on the values ACTUAL, PREDICT, RESIDUAL, U95M, L95M, U95, L95, and D, corresponding to the options specified.
- the response variables containing special output values identified by the _TYPE_ variable.

All confidence limits use the two-tailed Student's t-value.

OUTR= Data Sets

An output data set containing the optimum response ridge is created when the OUTR= option is specified in the RIDGE statement. The data set contains the following variables:

- the current values of the BY variables.
- a character variable _DEPVAR_ containing the name of the dependent variable.
- a character variable _TYPE_ identifying the type of ridge being computed, MINIMUM or MAXIMUM. If both MAXIMUM and MINIMUM are specified, the data set contains observations for the minimum ridge followed by observations for the maximum ridge.
- a numeric variable _RADIUS_, giving the distance from the ridge starting point.
- the values of the model factors at the estimated optimum point at distance _RADIUS_ from the ridge starting point.
- a numeric variable _PRED_, the estimated expected value of the dependent variable at the optimum.
- a numeric variable _STDERR_, the standard error of the estimated expected value.

Lack-of-Fit Test

If you specify the LACKFIT option in the MODEL statement, the data must be sorted so that repeated observations appear together. If the data are not sorted, the procedure cannot find these repeats. Since all other test statistics for the model are tested by total error rather than pure error, you may want to hand-calculate the tests with respect to pure error if the lack-of-fit is significant.

Interpreting the Canonical Analysis

The eigenvalues and eigenvectors in the matrix of second-order parameters characterize the shape of the response surface. The eigenvectors point in the directions of principle orientation for the surface, and the signs and magnitudes of the associated eigenvalues give the shape of the surface in these directions. Positive eigenvalues indicate directions of upward curvature, and negative eigenvalues indicate directions of downward curvature. The larger an eigenvalue is in absolute value, the more pronounced is the curvature of the response surface in the associated direction. Often, all of the coefficients of an eigenvector except for one are relatively small, indicating that the vector points roughly along the axis associated with the factor corresponding to the single large coefficient. In this case, the canonical analysis can be used to determine the relative sensitivity of the predicted response surface to variations in that factor. (See **EXAMPLES** later in the chapter.)

Plotting the Surface

You can generate predicted values for a grid of points with the PREDICT option (see **Example 1** later in this chapter) and then use these values to create a contour plot of the response surface over a two-dimensional grid. Any two factor variables can be chosen to form the grid for the plot. Several plots can be generated by using different pairs of factor variables.

Searching for Multiple Response Conditions

Suppose you want to find the factor setting that produces responses in a certain region. For example, you want to find the values of x_1 and x_2 *that maximize* y_1 subject to $y_2 < 2$ and $y_3 < y_2 + y_1$. The exact answer is not easy to obtain analytically, but the following method can be applied. Approach the problem by checking conditions across a grid of values in the range of interest.

```
data b;
   set a end=eof;
   output;
   if eof then
      do;
         y1=.;
         y2=.;
         y3=.;
            do x1=1 to 5 by .1;
               do x2=1 to 5 by .1;
                  output;
               end;
            end;
      end;

proc rsreg data=b out=c;
   model y1 y2 y3=x1 x2 / predict;
run;

data d;
   set c;
   if y2<2;
   if y3<y2+y1;

proc sort data=d;
   by descending y1;
run;

proc print;
run;
```

Handling of the Covariates

Covariate regressors are added to a response surface model because they are believed to account for a sizable yet relatively uninteresting portion of the variation in the data. What the experimenter is really interested in is the response corrected for the effect of the covariates. A common example is the block effect in a block design. In the canonical and ridge analyses of a response surface, which estimate responses at hypothetical levels of the factor variables, the actual value of the predicted response is computed using the average values of the covariates. The estimated response values do optimize the estimated surface of the response corrected for covariates, but true prediction of the response requires actual values for the covariates.

Computational Method

For each response variable, the model can be written in the form

$$y_i = x_i' A x_i + b' x_i + c' z_i + \varepsilon_i$$

where

y_i is the ith observation of the response variable.

$x_i = (x_{i1}, x_{i2}, \ldots, x_{ik})'$
   are the k factor variables for the ith observation.

$z_i = (z_{i1}, z_{i2}, \ldots, z_{iL})'$
   are the L covariates, including the intercept term.

A is the $k \times k$ symmetrized matrix of quadratic parameters, with diagonal elements equal to the coefficients of the pure quadratic terms in the model and off-diagonal elements equal to half the coefficient of the corresponding cross-product.

b is the $k \times 1$ vector of linear parameters.

c is the $L \times 1$ vector of covariate parameters, one of which is the intercept.

ε_i is the error associated with the ith observation. Tests performed by RSREG assume that errors are independently and normally distributed with mean zero and variance σ^2.

The parameters in A, b, and c are estimated by least squares. To optimize y with respect to x, take partial derivatives, set them to zero, and solve:

$$\partial y / \partial x = 2x'A + b' = 0$$
$$x = -0.5A^{-1}b .$$

To determine if the solution is a maximum or minimum, find out if A is negative or positive definite by looking at the eigenvalues of A:

If eigenvalues	then solution is
are all negative	a maximum
are all positive	a minimum
have mixed signs	a saddle-point
contain zeros	in a flat area

The eigenvector for the largest eigenvalue gives the direction of steepest ascent from the stationary point, if positive, or steepest descent, if negative. The eigenvectors corresponding to small or zero eigenvalues point in directions of relative flatness.

The point on the optimum response ridge at a given radius R from the ridge origin is found by optimizing

$$(\mathbf{x}_o + \mathbf{d})'\mathbf{A}(\mathbf{x}_o + \mathbf{d}) + \mathbf{b}'(\mathbf{x}_o + \mathbf{d})$$

over $\mathbf{d}$ satisfying $\mathbf{d}'\mathbf{d} = R^2$, where $\mathbf{x}_o$ is the $k \times 1$ vector containing the ridge origin and $\mathbf{A}$ and $\mathbf{b}$ are as above. By the method of Lagrange multipliers, the optimal $\mathbf{d}$ has the form

$$\mathbf{d} = -(\mathbf{A} - \mu\mathbf{I})^{-1}(\mathbf{A}\mathbf{x}_o + 0.5\mathbf{b})$$

where $\mathbf{I}$ is the $k \times k$ identity matrix and μ is chosen so that $\mathbf{d}'\mathbf{d} = R^2$. There may be several values of μ that satisfy this constraint; the right one depends on which sort of response ridge is of interest. If you are searching for the ridge of maximum response, then the appropriate μ is the unique one that satisfies the constraint and is greater than all the eigenvalues of $\mathbf{A}$. Similarly, the appropriate μ for the ridge of minimum response satisfies the constraint and is less than all the eigenvalues of $\mathbf{A}$. (See Myers (1976) for details.)

Printed Output

All estimates and hypothesis tests assume the model is correctly specified and the errors are distributed according to classical statistical assumptions.

The output for RSREG contains the following:

Estimation and Analysis of Variance

1. The actual form of the coding operation for each value of a variable is

   coded value = (*original value* − M)/S

   where M is the average of the highest and lowest values for the variable in the design and S is half their difference. The Subtracted off column contains the M values for this formula for each factor variable, and S is found in the Divided by column.

2. The Response Mean is the mean of the response variable in the sample. When a WEIGHT statement is used, the mean is calculated by

   $$\Sigma_i w_i y_i \ / \ \Sigma_i w_i$$

3. The Root MSE estimates the standard deviation of the response variable and is calculated as the square root of the total error mean square.

4. The R-Square value is R^2, or the coefficient of determination. R^2 measures the proportion of the variation in the response that is attributed to the model rather than to random error.

5. The Coef. of Variation is 100 times the ratio of the Root MSE to the Response Mean.

6. Terms are brought into the regression in four steps: (1) the intercept and any covariates in the model (not shown), (2) Linear terms like X1 and X2, (3) pure Quadratic terms like X1*X1 or X2*X2, and (4) Crossproduct terms like X1*X2.

7. The Degrees of Freedom should be the same as the number of corresponding parameters unless one or more of the parameters are not estimable.

8. Type I Sums of Squares, also called the sequential sums of squares, measure the reduction in the error sum of squares as sets of terms (Linear, Quadratic, and so forth) are added to the model.

9. These R-Squares measure the portion of total R^2 contributed as each set of terms (Linear, Quadratic, and so forth) is added to the model.

10. Each F-Ratio tests the null hypothesis that all parameters in the term are zero using the Total Error mean square as the denominator. This item is a test of a Type I hypothesis, containing the usual F test numerator, conditional on the effects of subsequent variables not being in the model.

11. Prob > F is the significance value or probability of obtaining at least as great an F ratio given that the null hypothesis is true.

12. The Total Error Sum of Squares can be partitioned into Lack of Fit and Pure Error. When Lack of Fit is significant, there is variation in the model other than random error (such as cubic effects of the factor variables).

13. The Total Error Mean Square estimates σ^2, the variance.

14. The Parameter Estimates are the parameter estimates based on the *uncoded* values of the factor variables. If an effect is a linear combination of previous effects, the parameter for the effect is not estimable. When this happens, the degrees of freedom are zero, the parameter estimate is set to zero, and the estimates and tests on other parameters are conditional on this parameter being zero (not shown).

15. The Standard Error column contains the estimated standard deviations of the parameter estimates based on *uncoded* data.

16. The column headed T for H0: Parameter=0 contains t values of a test of the null hypothesis that the true parameter is zero when the *uncoded* values of the factor variables are used.

17. Prob > |T| gives the significance value or probability of a greater absolute t ratio given that the true parameter is zero.

18. The Parameter Estimates from Coded Data are the parameter estimates based on the *coded* values of the factor variables. These are the estimates used in the subsequent canonical and ridge analyses.

19. The test on a Factor, say X1, is a joint test on all the parameters involving that factor. For example, the test for X1 tests the null hypothesis that the true parameters for X1, X1*X1, and X1*X2 are all zero.

Canonical Analysis

20. The Critical Values are the values of the factor variables that correspond to the stationary point of the fitted response surface. The critical values can be at a minimum, maximum, or saddle point.

21. The Eigenvalues and Eigenvectors are from the matrix of quadratic parameter estimates based on the coded data. They characterize the shape of the response surface. **Because the eigenvalues and eigenvectors are based on parameter estimates from fitting the response to the coded data, they will in general be different from those computed by PROC RSREG in Version 5.**

Ridge Analysis

22. The Coded Radius is the distance from the coded version of the associated point to the coded version of the origin of the ridge. The origin is given by the point at radius zero.
23. The Estimated Response is the estimated value of the response variable at the associated point. The Standard Error of this estimate is also given. This quantity is useful for assessing the relative credibility of the prediction at a given radius. Typically, this standard error increases rapidly as the ridge moves up to and beyond the design perimeter, reflecting the inherent difficulty of making predictions beyond the range of experimentation.
24. The Uncoded Factor Values are the values of the uncoded factor variables that give the optimum response at this radius from the ridge origin.

EXAMPLES

Example 1:   A Response Surface with a Simple Optimum

This example uses the three-factor quadratic model discussed in John (1971). The objective is to minimize the unpleasant odor of a chemical. The following statements read the data and invoke PROC RSREG. These statements produce **Output 37.1**:

```
/*                                                              */
/*  Schneider and Stockett (1963) performed an experiment aimed */
/*  at reducing the unpleasant odor of a chemical produced with */
/*  several factors.  From John (1971).                         */
/*                                                              */
data a;
   input y x1-x3 @@;
   label y="ODOR"
      x1="TEMPERATURE"
      x2="GAS-LIQUID RATIO"
      x3="PACKING HEIGHT";
   cards;
66 -1 -1  0      39  1 -1  0      43 -1  1  0      49  1  1  0
58 -1  0 -1      17  1  0 -1      -5 -1  0  1     -40  1  0  1
65  0 -1 -1       7  0  1 -1      43  0 -1  1     -22  0  1  1
-31  0  0  0     -35  0  0  0     -26  0  0  0
;

proc sort;
   by x1-x3;
run;

proc rsreg;
   model y=x1-x3 / lackfit;
run;
```

Output 37.1   A Response Surface with a Simple Optimum, Using the
LACKFIT Option

The SAS System   1

Coding Coefficients for the Independent Variables

Factor	Subtracted off	Divided by
X1	0	1.000000
X2	0	1.000000
X3	0	1.000000

The SAS System   2

Response Surface for Variable Y: ODOR

Response Mean	15.200000
Root MSE	22.478508
R-Square	0.8820
Coef. of Variation	147.8849

Regression	Degrees of Freedom	Type I Sum of Squares	R-Square	F-Ratio	Prob > F
Linear	3	7143.250000	0.3337	4.712	0.0641
Quadratic	3	11445	0.5346	7.550	0.0264
Crossproduct	3	293.500000	0.0137	0.194	0.8965
Total Regress	9	18882	0.8820	4.152	0.0657

Residual	Degrees of Freedom	Sum of Squares	Mean Square	F-Ratio	Prob > F
Lack of Fit	3	2485.750000	828.583333	40.750	0.0240
Pure Error	2	40.666667	20.333333		
Total Error	5	2526.416667	505.283333		

Parameter	Degrees of Freedom	Parameter Estimate	Standard Error	T for H0: Parameter=0	Prob > |T|	Parameter Estimate from Coded Data
INTERCEPT	1	-30.666667	12.977973	-2.363	0.0645	-30.666667
X1	1	-12.125000	7.947353	-1.526	0.1876	-12.125000
X2	1	-17.000000	7.947353	-2.139	0.0854	-17.000000
X3	1	-21.375000	7.947353	-2.690	0.0433	-21.375000
X1*X1	1	32.083333	11.698187	2.743	0.0407	32.083333
X2*X1	1	8.250000	11.239254	0.734	0.4959	8.250000
X2*X2	1	47.833333	11.698187	4.089	0.0095	47.833333
X3*X1	1	1.500000	11.239254	0.133	0.8990	1.500000
X3*X2	1	-1.750000	11.239254	-0.156	0.8824	-1.750000
X3*X3	1	6.083333	11.698187	0.520	0.6252	6.083333

Factor	Degrees of Freedom	Sum of Squares	Mean Square	F-Ratio	Prob > F	
X1	4	5258.016026	1314.504006	2.602	0.1613	TEMPERATURE
X2	4	11045	2761.150641	5.465	0.0454	GAS-LIQUID RATIO
X3	4	3813.016026	953.254006	1.887	0.2510	PACKING HEIGHT

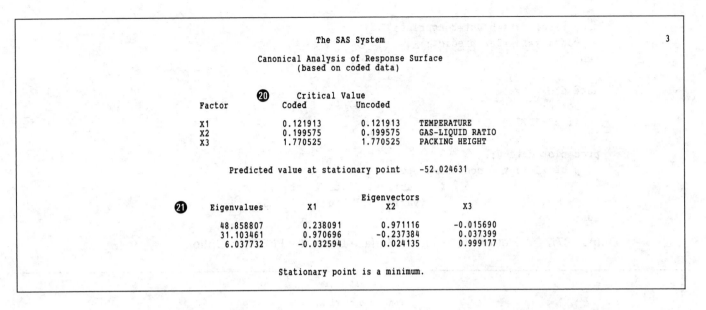

```
                            The SAS System                                      3

                   Canonical Analysis of Response Surface
                            (based on coded data)

                 ⑳         Critical Value
         Factor          Coded        Uncoded

         X1            0.121913      0.121913     TEMPERATURE
         X2            0.199575      0.199575     GAS-LIQUID RATIO
         X3            1.770525      1.770525     PACKING HEIGHT


             Predicted value at stationary point    -52.024631


                                          Eigenvectors
   ㉑                                 X1           X2            X3
         Eigenvalues

           48.858807            0.238091     0.971116      -0.015690
           31.103461            0.970696    -0.237384       0.037399
            6.037732           -0.032594     0.024135       0.999177


                     Stationary point is a minimum.
```

The canonical analysis indicates that the directions of principle orientation for the predicted response surface are along the axes associated with the three factors. The largest component of the eigenvector corresponding to the largest eigenvalue (48.8588) is associated with X2 and the second largest eigenvalue (31.1035) is associated with X1. The third eigenvalue (6.0377), associated with X3, is quite a bit smaller than the other two, indicating that the response surface is relatively insensitive to changes in this factor. The canonical analysis also finds a minimum for the estimated response surface when X1 and X2 are both near the middle of their respective ranges and X3 is relatively high. However, the lack-of-fit for the data is significant and further experimentation should be performed before firm statements are made concerning the underlying process. Since the data are stored in coded form, the coding operation within the procedure has no effect. The estimates based on coded and uncoded data are identical.

To plot the response surface with respect to two of the factor variables, first fix X3, the least significant factor variable, at its estimated optimum value and generate a grid of points for X1 and X2. To ensure that the grid data do not affect parameter estimates, the response variable (Y) is set to missing. (See **Missing Values** earlier in this chapter.) PROC RSREG computes the predicted values, which are output and plotted using the CONTOUR feature of PROC PLOT. The following statements produce **Output 37.2**:

```
data b;
    /*    GET THE ACTUAL VALUES                */
    set a end=eof;
    output;
    /*    CREATE AN X1*X2 GRID FOR PLOTTING    */
    if eof then
      do;
          y=.;
          x3=1.77;
              do x1=-1.5 to 1.5 by .1;
                  do x2=-2 to 2 by .1;
                      output;
                  end;
              end;
      end;
```

```
proc rsreg data=b out=c noprint;
   model y=x1-x3 / predict;
run;

data d;
   set c;
   if x3=1.77;

proc plot data=d;
   plot x1*x2=y / contour=6 hpos=100  vpos=36  hspace=10
                           haxis=-2   to 2   by .5
                           vaxis=-1.5 to 1.5 by .5;
run;
```

Output 37.2 A Plot of the Response Surface Using the PREDICT Option

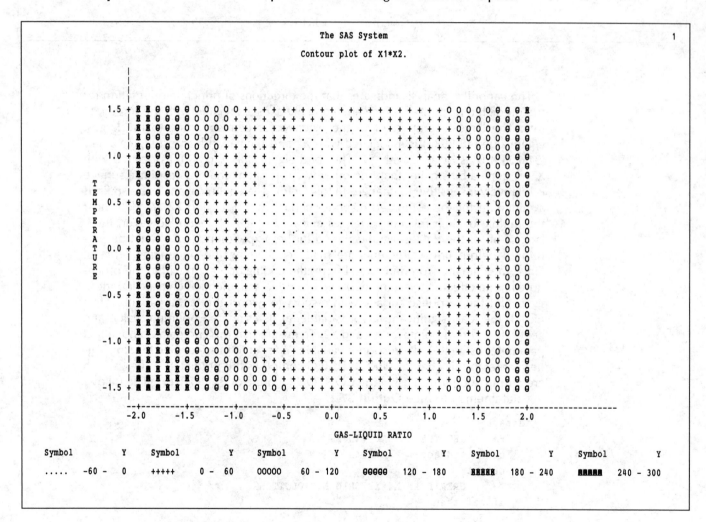

Example 2:   A Saddle-Surface Response Using the Ridge Analysis

This is an example of a two-factor model in which the estimated surface does not have a unique optimum. A ridge analysis is used to determine the region in which the optimum lies. The objective is to find the settings of time and temperature in the processing of a chemical that maximize the yield. The following statements read the data and invoke PROC RSREG. These statements produce **Output 37.3**:

```
/* Frankel (1961) reports an experiment aimed at maximizing the   */
/* yield of mercaptobenzothiazole (MBT) by varying processing time */
/* and temperature.  From Myers (1976).                           */
/*                                                                */
data d;
  input time temp mbt;
  label
    time="REACTION TIME (HOURS)"
    temp="TEMPERATURE (DEGREES CENTIGRADE)"
     mbt="PERCENT YIELD MERCAPTOBENZOTHIAZOLE";
  cards;
 4.0    250    83.8
20.0    250    81.7
12.0    250    82.4
12.0    250    82.9
12.0    220    84.7
12.0    280    57.9
12.0    250    81.2
 6.3    229    81.3
 6.3    271    83.1
17.7    229    85.3
17.7    271    72.7
 4.0    250    82.0
;

proc sort;
   by time temp;
run;

proc rsreg;
  model mbt=time temp / lackfit;
  ridge max;
run;
```

Output 37.3 A Saddle-Surface Response, with Ridge Analysis

```
                             The SAS System                                        1

                 Coding Coefficients for the Independent Variables

                     Factor      Subtracted off     Divided by

                     TIME          12.000000         8.000000
                     TEMP         250.000000        30.000000
```

```
                             The SAS System                                        2

           Response Surface for Variable MBT: PERCENT YIELD MERCAPTOBENZOTHIAZOLE

                          Response Mean          79.916667
                          Root MSE                4.615964
                          R-Square                0.8003
                          Coef. of Variation      5.7760
```

	Degrees of Freedom	Type I Sum of Squares	R-Square	F-Ratio	Prob > F
Regression					
Linear	2	313.585803	0.4899	7.359	0.0243
Quadratic	2	146.768144	0.2293	3.444	0.1009
Crossproduct	1	51.840000	0.0810	2.433	0.1698
Total Regress	5	512.193947	0.8003	4.808	0.0410

	Degrees of Freedom	Sum of Squares	Mean Square	F-Ratio	Prob > F
Residual					
Lack of Fit	3	124.696053	41.565351	39.628	0.0065
Pure Error	3	3.146667	1.048889		
Total Error	6	127.842720	21.307120		

Parameter	Degrees of Freedom	Parameter Estimate	Standard Error	T for H0: Parameter=0	Prob > |T|	Parameter Estimate from Coded Data
INTERCEPT	1	-545.867976	277.145373	-1.970	0.0964	82.173110
TIME	1	6.872863	5.004928	1.373	0.2188	-1.014287
TEMP	1	4.989743	2.165839	2.304	0.0608	-8.676768
TIME*TIME	1	0.021631	0.056784	0.381	0.7164	1.384394
TEMP*TIME	1	-0.030075	0.019281	-1.560	0.1698	-7.218045
TEMP*TEMP	1	-0.009836	0.004304	-2.285	0.0623	-8.852519

Factor	Degrees of Freedom	Sum of Squares	Mean Square	F-Ratio	Prob > F	
TIME	3	61.290957	20.430319	0.959	0.4704	REACTION TIME (HOURS)
TEMP	3	461.250925	153.750308	7.216	0.0205	TEMPERATURE (DEGREES CENTIGRADE)

```
                        The SAS System                                    3

                Canonical Analysis of Response Surface
                        (based on coded data)


                       Critical Value
         Factor       Coded       Uncoded

         TIME       -0.441758     8.465935    REACTION TIME (HOURS)
         TEMP       -0.309976   240.700718    TEMPERATURE (DEGREES CENTIGRADE)


              Predicted value at stationary point    83.741940


                                           Eigenvectors
                 Eigenvalues           TIME           TEMP

                   2.528816          0.953223      -0.302267
                  -9.996940          0.302267       0.953223


                  Stationary point is a saddle point.
```

```
                        The SAS System                                    4

     Estimated Ridge of Maximum Response for Variable MBT: PERCENT YIELD MERCAPTOBENZOTHIAZOLE


    ㉒  Coded   ㉓ Estimated  ㉓ Standard   ㉔ Uncoded Factor Values
       Radius     Response      Error        TIME           TEMP

        0.0      82.173110    2.665023    12.000000      250.000000
        0.1      82.952909    2.648671    11.964493      247.002956
        0.2      83.558260    2.602270    12.142790      244.023941
        0.3      84.037098    2.533296    12.704153      241.396084
        0.4      84.470454    2.457836    13.517555      239.435227
        0.5      84.914099    2.404616    14.370977      237.919138
        0.6      85.390012    2.410981    15.212247      236.624811
        0.7      85.906767    2.516619    16.037822      235.449230
        0.8      86.468277    2.752355    16.850813      234.344204
        0.9      87.076587    3.130961    17.654321      233.284652
        1.0      87.732874    3.648568    18.450682      232.256238
```

The canonical analysis indicates that the predicted response surface is shaped like a saddle. The eigenvalue of 2.5 shows that the valley orientation of the saddle is less curved than the hill orientation, with eigenvalue of -9.99. The coefficients of the associated eigenvectors show that the valley is more aligned with TIME and the hill with TEMP. Because the canonical analysis resulted in a saddle point, the estimated surface does not have a unique optimum. However, the ridge analysis indicates that maximum yields will result from relatively high reaction times and low temperatures. Note from the analysis of variance for the model that the test for the time factor is not significant. If further experimentation is undertaken, it might be best to fix time at a moderate to high value and to concentrate on the effect of temperature. Finally, the test for lack of fit for the model is highly significant. The quadratic model does not fit the data very well, so firm statements about the underlying process should not be based only on the above analysis. In the actual experiment discussed here, extra runs were made that confirmed the above conclusions.

REFERENCES

Box, G.E.P. (1954), "The Exploration and Exploitation of Response Surfaces: Some General Considerations," *Biometrics* 10, 16.

Box, G.E.P. (1987), *Empirical Model Building and Response Surfaces*, New York: John Wiley & Sons, Inc.

Box, G.E.P. and Draper, N.R. (1982), "Measures of Lack of Fit for Response Surface Designs and Predictor Variable Transformations," *Technometrics* 24, 1-8.

Box, G.E.P. and Hunter, J.S. (1957), "Multifactor Experimental Designs for Exploring Response Surfaces," *Annals of Mathematical Statistics*, 28, 195–242.

Box, G.E.P. and Hunter, J.S. (1978), *Statistics for Experimentors* , New York: John Wiley & Sons, Inc.

Box, G.E.P. and Wilson, K.J. (1951), "On the Experimental Attainment of Optimum Conditions," *Journal of the Royal Statistical Society*, Ser. B, 13, 1–45.

Cochran, W.G. and Cox, G.M. (1957), *Experimental Designs*, 2d Edition, New York: John Wiley & Sons, Inc.

Draper, N.R. (1963), "Ridge Analysis of Response Surfaces," *Technometrics* 5, 469-479.

Draper, N.R. and John, J.A. (1988), "Response Surface Designs for Quantative and Qualitative Variables," *Technometrics* 30, no. 4, 423-428.

Draper, N.R. and Smith, H. (1981), *Applied Regression Analysis, Second Edition*, New York: John Wiley & Sons, Inc.

John, P.W.M. (1971), *Statistical Design and Analysis of Experiments*, New York: Macmillan Publishing Co., Inc.

Mead, R. and Pike, D.J. (1975), "A Review of Response Surface Metholody from a Biometric Point of View," *Biometrics* 31, 803.

Meyer, D.C. (1963), "Response Surface Methodology in Education and Psychology," *Journal of Experimental Education* 31, 329.

Myers, R.H. (1976), *Response Surface Methodology*, Blacksburg, VA: Virginia Polytechnic Institute and State University.

Chapter 38

The SCORE Procedure

ABSTRACT   1479
INTRODUCTION   1479
  Raw Data Set   1480
  Scoring Coefficients Data Set   1480
  Standardization of Raw Data   1480
SPECIFICATIONS   1480
  PROC SCORE Statement   1481
  BY Statement   1482
  ID Statement   1482
  VAR Statement   1482
DETAILS   1483
  Missing Values   1483
  Regression Parameter Estimates from PROC REG   1483
  Output Data Set   1483
  Computational Resources   1483
    Memory   1484
    Time   1484
EXAMPLES   1484
  Example 1:   Factor Scoring Coefficients   1484
  Example 2:   Regression Parameter Estimates   1487
  Example 3:   Custom Scoring Coefficients   1490

ABSTRACT

The SCORE procedure multiplies values from two SAS data sets, one containing coefficients (for example, factor-scoring coefficients or regression coefficients) and the other containing raw data to be scored using the coefficients from the first data set. The result of this multiplication is a SAS data set containing linear combinations of the coefficients and the raw data values.

INTRODUCTION

Many statistical procedures output coefficients that PROC SCORE can apply to raw data to produce scores. The new score variable is formed as a linear combination of raw data and scoring coefficients. For each observation in the raw data set, PROC SCORE multiplies the value of a variable in the raw data set by the matching scoring coefficient from the data set of scoring coefficients. This multiplication process is repeated for each variable in the VAR statement. The resulting products are then summed to produce the value of the new score variable. This entire process is repeated for each observation in the raw data set. In other words, SCORE cross multiplies part of one data set with another.

Raw Data Set

The raw data set can contain the original data used to calculate the scoring coefficients, or it can contain an entirely different data set. The raw data set must contain all the variables needed to produce scores. In addition, the scoring coefficients and the variables in the raw data set that are used in scoring must have the same names. See the **EXAMPLES** section for further illustration.

Scoring Coefficients Data Set

The data set containing scoring coefficients must contain two special variables: the _TYPE_ variable and the _NAME_ or _MODEL_ variable. The _TYPE_ variable identifies the observations that contain scoring coefficients. The _NAME_ or _MODEL_ variable provides a SAS name for the new score variable.

For example, the FACTOR procedure produces an output data set that contains factor-scoring coefficients. In this output data set, the scoring coefficients are identified by _TYPE_='SCORE'. For _TYPE_='SCORE', the _NAME_ variable has values of 'FACTOR1', 'FACTOR2', and so forth. PROC SCORE gives the new score variables the names FACTOR1, FACTOR2, and so forth.

As another example, the REG procedure produces an output data set that contains parameter estimates. In this output data set, the parameter estimates are identified by _TYPE_='PARMS'. The _MODEL_ variable contains the label used in the MODEL statement in PROC REG, or MODELn if no label is specified. This label is the name PROC SCORE gives to the new score variable.

Standardization of Raw Data

If the scoring coefficients data set contains observations with _TYPE_='MEAN' and _TYPE_='STD', then the raw data are standardized before scoring. If the scoring coefficients data set does not contain observations with _TYPE_='MEAN' and _TYPE_='STD', or if you use the NOSTD option, the raw data are not standardized. See the **EXAMPLES** section for further illustration.

If the scoring coefficients are obtained from observations with _TYPE_='USCORE', the raw data are standardized using the uncorrected standard deviations identified by _TYPE_='USTD', and the means are not subtracted from the raw data. For more information on _TYPE_='USCORE' scoring coefficients in TYPE=UCORR or UCOV output data sets, see Appendix 1, "Special SAS Data Sets."

SPECIFICATIONS

You can invoke PROC SCORE with the following statements:

> **PROC SCORE** DATA=*SAS-data-set* <*options*>;   required statement
>
> > **BY** *variables*; ⎫
> > **ID** *variables*; ⎬   optional statements
> > **VAR** *variables*; ⎭

The only required statement is the PROC SCORE statement. The BY, ID, and VAR statements are described after the PROC SCORE statement below.

PROC SCORE Statement

PROC SCORE DATA=*SAS-data-set* <*options*>;

The PROC SCORE statement starts the procedure. The following options can be specified in the PROC SCORE statement:

DATA=*SAS-data-set*
  names the input SAS data set containing the raw data to score. This specification is required.

NOSTD
  suppresses centering and scaling of the raw data. Ordinarily, if PROC SCORE finds _TYPE_='MEAN', _TYPE_='USCORE', _TYPE_='USTD', and _TYPE_='STD' observations in the SCORE= data set, the procedure uses these to standardize the raw data before scoring.

OUT=*SAS-data-set*
  specifies the name of the SAS data set created by PROC SCORE. If you want to create a permanent SAS data set, you must specify a two-level name. (See "SAS Files" in *SAS Language: Reference, Version 6, First Edition* and "Introduction to DATA Step Processing" in *SAS Language and Procedures: Usage, Version 6, First Edition* for more information on permanent SAS data sets.) If the OUT= option is omitted, PROC SCORE still creates an output data set and automatically names it according to the DATA*n* convention, just as if you omitted a data set name in a DATA statement.

PREDICT
  specifies that PROC SCORE should treat coefficients of −1 in the SCORE= data set as 0. In regression applications, the dependent variable is coded with a coefficient of −1. Applied directly to regression results, PROC SCORE produces negative residuals (see RESIDUAL below); the PREDICT option changes this so that predicted values are produced instead.

RESIDUAL
  reverses the sign of each score. Applied directly to regression results, PROC SCORE produces negative residuals (PREDICT−ACTUAL); the RESIDUAL option produces positive residuals (ACTUAL−PREDICT) instead.

SCORE=*SAS-data-set*
  names the data set containing the scoring coefficients. If the SCORE= option is omitted, the most recently created SAS data set is used. This data set must have two special variables: _TYPE_ and either _NAME_ or _MODEL_.

TYPE=*name*
  specifies the observations in the SCORE= data set that contain scoring coefficients. The TYPE= procedure option is unrelated to the data set option that has the same name. PROC SCORE examines the values of the special variable _TYPE_ in the SCORE= data set. When the value of _TYPE_ matches TYPE=*name*, the observation in the SCORE= data set is used to score the raw data in the DATA= data set.

  If TYPE= is not specified, scoring coefficients are read from observations with either _TYPE_= 'SCORE' or _TYPE_= 'USCORE'. Because a default for PROC SCORE is TYPE=SCORE, you need not specify TYPE= for factor scoring or for computing scores from OUTSTAT= data sets from the CANCORR, CANDISC, PRINCOMP, or

VARCLUS procedures. When you use regression coefficients from PROC REG, specify TYPE=PARMS.

BY Statement

BY *variables*;

A BY statement can be used with PROC SCORE to obtain separate scoring for observations in groups defined by the BY variables. A BY statement can also be used to apply separate groups of scoring coefficients to the entire DATA= data set.

If your SCORE= input data set is not sorted in ascending order of the BY variables, use one of the following alternatives:

- Use the SORT procedure with a similar BY statement to sort the data.
- Use the BY statement options NOTSORTED or DESCENDING in the BY statement for the SCORE procedure. The NOTSORTED option does not mean that the data are unsorted, but rather that the data are arranged in groups (according to values of the BY variables) and that these groups are not necessarily in alphabetical or increasing numeric order.
- Use the DATASETS procedure (in base SAS software) to create an index on the BY variables.

For more information on the BY statement, see the discussion in *SAS Language: Reference*. For more information on the DATASETS procedure, see the discussion in *SAS Procedures Guide, Version 6, Third Edition*.

If the DATA= data set does not contain any of the BY variables, the entire DATA= data set is scored by each BY group of scoring coefficients in the SCORE= data set.

If the DATA= data set contains some but not all of the BY variables , or if some BY variables do not have the same type or length in the DATA= data set as in the SCORE= data set, then PROC SCORE prints an error message and stops.

If all of the BY variables appear in the DATA= data set with the same type and length as in the SCORE= data set, then each BY group in the DATA= data set is scored using scoring coefficients from the corresponding BY group in the SCORE= data set. The BY groups in the DATA= data set must be in the same order as in the SCORE= data set. All BY groups in the DATA= data set must also appear in the SCORE= data set. If you do not specify the NOTSORTED option, some BY groups can appear in the SCORE= data set but not in the DATA= data set; such BY groups are not used in computing scores.

ID Statement

ID *variables*;

The ID statement identifies variables from the DATA= data set to be included in the OUT= data set. If there is no ID statement, all variables from the DATA= data set are included in the OUT= data set. The ID variables can be character or numeric.

VAR Statement

VAR *variables*;

The VAR statement specifies the variables to be used in computing scores. These variables must be in both the DATA= and SCORE= input data sets and must be numeric. If no VAR statement is given, the procedure uses all numeric variables in the SCORE= data set. You should almost always use a VAR statement with PROC SCORE because you would rarely use all the numeric variables in your data set to compute scores.

DETAILS

Missing Values

If one of the scoring variables in the DATA= data set has a missing value for an observation, all the scores have missing values for that observation. The exception to this criterion is if the PREDICT option is specified, the variable with a coefficient of -1 can tolerate a missing value and still produce a prediction score. Also, a variable with a coefficient of 0 can tolerate a missing value.

If a scoring coefficient in the SCORE= data set has a missing value for an observation, the coefficient is not used in creating the new score variable for the observation. In other words, missing values of scoring coefficients are treated as zeros. This treatment affects only the observation in which the missing value occurs.

Regression Parameter Estimates from PROC REG

When the SCORE= data set is an OUTEST= data set produced by PROC REG, and when TYPE=PARMS is specified, the interpretation of the new score variables depends on the PROC SCORE options chosen and the variables listed in the VAR statement. If the VAR statement contains only the independent variables used in a model in PROC REG, the new score variables give the predicted values. If the VAR statement contains the dependent variable and the independent variables used in a model in PROC REG, the interpretation of the new score variables depends on the PROC SCORE options chosen. If neither the PREDICT option nor the RESIDUAL option is specified, the new score variables give negative residuals (PREDICT−ACTUAL). If the RESIDUAL option is chosen, the new score variables give positive residuals (ACTUAL−PREDICT). If the PREDICT option is chosen, the new score variables give predicted values.

Unless you specify the NOINT option for PROC REG, the OUTEST= data set contains the variable INTERCEP. PROC SCORE adds the INTERCEP value in computing the scores.

Output Data Set

PROC SCORE produces an output data set but no printed output. The output OUT= data set contains the following:

- the ID variables (if any)
- all variables from the DATA= data set (if no ID variables are specified)
- the BY variables (if any)
- the new score variables (named from the _NAME_ or _MODEL_ values in the SCORE= data set).

Computational Resources

In the equations below, let

v = number of variables used in computing scores
s = number of new score variables
b = maximum number of new score variables in a BY group
n = number of observations.

Memory

The array storage required is approximately $8(4v+(3+v)b+s)$ bytes.

When you do not use BY processing, the array storage required is approximately $8(4v+(4+v)s)$ bytes.

Time

The time required to construct the scoring matrix is roughly proportional to vs and the time needed to compute the scores is roughly proportional to nvs.

EXAMPLES

The following three examples use a subset of the FITNESS data set. The complete data set is given in **Example 2: Aerobic Fitness Prediction** in Chapter 36, "The REG Procedure."

Example 1:   Factor Scoring Coefficients

This example shows how to use PROC SCORE with factor scoring coefficients. First, PROC FACTOR produces an output data set containing scoring coefficients in observations identified by _TYPE_='SCORE'. These data, together with the original data set FITNESS, are supplied to PROC SCORE, resulting in a data set containing scores FACTOR1 and FACTOR2. The following statements produce **Output 38.1** through **Output 38.3**:

```
/* This data set contains only the first 12 observations */
/* from the full data set used in the chapter on PROC REG. */
data fitness;
   input age weight oxy runtime rstpulse runpulse @@;
   cards;
44 89.47  44.609 11.37 62 178     40 75.07  45.313 10.07 62 185
44 85.84  54.297  8.65 45 156     42 68.15  59.571  8.17 40 166
38 89.02  49.874  9.22 55 178     47 77.45  44.811 11.63 58 176
40 75.98  45.681 11.95 70 176     43 81.19  49.091 10.85 64 162
44 81.42  39.442 13.08 63 174     38 81.87  60.055  8.63 48 170
44 73.03  50.541 10.13 45 168     45 87.66  37.388 14.03 56 186
;

proc factor data=fitness outstat=factout
            method=prin rotate=varimax score;
   var age weight runtime runpulse rstpulse;
   title 'FACTOR SCORING EXAMPLE';
   run;

proc print data=factout;
   title2 'Data Set from PROC FACTOR';
run;
proc score data=fitness score=factout out=fscore;
   var age weight runtime runpulse rstpulse;
   run;

proc print data=fscore;
   title2 'Data Set from PROC SCORE';
run;
```

Output 38.1 shows the PROC FACTOR output. The scoring coefficients for the two factors are shown at the end of the PROC FACTOR output.

Output 38.1   Creating an OUTSTAT= Data Set with PROC FACTOR

```
                              FACTOR SCORING EXAMPLE                               1

Initial Factor Method: Principal Components

                        Prior Communality Estimates: ONE

              Eigenvalues of the Correlation Matrix:  Total = 5  Average = 1

                          1          2          3          4          5
             Eigenvalue   2.3093     1.1922     0.8822     0.5026     0.1137
             Difference   1.1171     0.3100     0.3797     0.3889
             Proportion   0.4619     0.2384     0.1764     0.1005     0.0227
             Cumulative   0.4619     0.7003     0.8767     0.9773     1.0000

                  2 factors will be retained by the MINEIGEN criterion.

                                 Factor Pattern

                               FACTOR1     FACTOR2

                    AGE        0.29795     0.93675
                    WEIGHT     0.43282    -0.17750
                    RUNTIME    0.91983     0.28782
                    RUNPULSE   0.72671    -0.38191
                    RSTPULSE   0.81179    -0.23344

                      Variance explained by each factor

                             FACTOR1     FACTOR2
                             2.309306    1.192200

              Final Communality Estimates: Total = 3.501506

                 AGE      WEIGHT    RUNTIME   RUNPULSE   RSTPULSE
              0.966284  0.218834  0.928933  0.673962   0.713493
```

```
                              FACTOR SCORING EXAMPLE                               2

Rotation Method: Varimax

                          Orthogonal Transformation Matrix

                                    1          2

                         1       0.92536     0.37908
                         2      -0.37908     0.92536

                             Rotated Factor Pattern

                               FACTOR1     FACTOR2

                    AGE       -0.07939     0.97979
                    WEIGHT     0.46780    -0.00018
                    RUNTIME    0.74207     0.61503
                    RUNPULSE   0.81725    -0.07792
                    RSTPULSE   0.83969     0.09172

                      Variance explained by each factor

                             FACTOR1     FACTOR2
                             2.148775    1.352731

              Final Communality Estimates: Total = 3.501506

                 AGE      WEIGHT    RUNTIME   RUNPULSE   RSTPULSE
              0.966284  0.218834  0.928933  0.673962   0.713493

                    Scoring Coefficients Estimated by Regression

           Squared Multiple Correlations of the Variables with each Factor
```

(continued on next page)

(continued from previous page)

```
                        FACTOR1   FACTOR2
                        1.000000  1.000000

                     Standardized Scoring Coefficients

                              FACTOR1   FACTOR2

                  AGE        -0.17846   0.77600
                  WEIGHT      0.22987  -0.06672
                  RUNTIME     0.27707   0.37440
                  RUNPULSE    0.41263  -0.17714
                  RSTPULSE    0.39952  -0.04793
```

Output 38.2 lists the OUTSTAT= data set from PROC FACTOR. Note that observations 18 and 19 have _TYPE_='SCORE'. Observations 1 and 2 have _TYPE_='MEAN' and _TYPE_='STD', respectively. These four observations will be used by PROC SCORE.

Output 38.2   OUTSTAT= Data Set from PROC FACTOR Reproduced with PROC PRINT

```
                             FACTOR SCORING EXAMPLE                                3
                            Data Set from PROC FACTOR

    OBS   _TYPE_     _NAME_       AGE     WEIGHT   RUNTIME  RUNPULSE  RSTPULSE

     1    MEAN                  42.4167  80.5125  10.6483  172.917    55.6667
     2    STD                    2.8431   6.7660   1.8444    8.918     9.2769
     3    N                     12.0000  12.0000  12.000   12.000    12.0000
     4    CORR       AGE         1.0000   0.0128   0.5005   -0.095    -0.0080
     5    CORR       WEIGHT      0.0128   1.0000   0.2637    0.173     0.2396
     6    CORR       RUNTIME     0.5005   0.2637   1.0000    0.556     0.6620
     7    CORR       RUNPULSE   -0.0953   0.1731   0.5555    1.000     0.4853
     8    CORR       RSTPULSE   -0.0080   0.2396   0.6620    0.485     1.0000
     9    COMMUNAL               0.9663   0.2188   0.9289    0.674     0.7135
    10    PRIORS                 1.0000   1.0000   1.0000    1.000     1.0000
    11    EIGENVAL               2.3093   1.1922   0.8822    0.503     0.1137
    12    UNROTATE   FACTOR1     0.2980   0.4328   0.9198    0.727     0.8118
    13    UNROTATE   FACTOR2     0.9368  -0.1775   0.2878   -0.382    -0.2334
    14    TRANSFOR   FACTOR1     0.9254  -0.3791     .         .         .
    15    TRANSFOR   FACTOR2     0.3791   0.9254     .         .         .
    16    PATTERN    FACTOR1    -0.0794   0.4678   0.7421    0.817     0.8397
    17    PATTERN    FACTOR2     0.9798  -0.0002   0.6150   -0.078     0.0917
    18    SCORE      FACTOR1    -0.1785   0.2299   0.2771    0.413     0.3995
    19    SCORE      FACTOR2     0.7760  -0.0667   0.3744   -0.177    -0.0479
```

Since the PROC SCORE statement does not contain the NOSTD option, the data in FITNESS are standardized before scoring. For each variable specified in the VAR statement, the mean and standard deviation are obtained from FACTOUT. For each observation in FITNESS, the variables are then standardized. For example, for observation 1 in FITNESS, AGE is standardized to $0.5569 = [(44 - 42.4167)/2.8431]$.

After the data in FITNESS are standardized, the standardized values of the variables in the VAR statement are multiplied by the matching coefficients in FACTOUT, and the resulting products are summed. This sum is output as a value of the new score variable.

Output 38.3 prints the FSCORE data set produced by PROC SCORE. This data set contains AGE, WEIGHT, OXY, RUNTIME, RSTPULSE, and RUNPULSE from FITNESS. It also contains FACTOR1 and FACTOR2, the two new score variables.

Output 38.3 OUT= Data Set from PROC SCORE Reproduced with PROC PRINT

```
                            FACTOR SCORING EXAMPLE                                    4
                            Data Set from PROC SCORE

  OBS   AGE   WEIGHT    OXY    RUNTIME   RSTPULSE   RUNPULSE   FACTOR1    FACTOR2
   1    44    89.47   44.609    11.37      62         178      0.82129    0.35663
   2    40    75.07   45.313    10.07      62         185      0.71173   -0.99605
   3    44    85.84   54.297     8.65      45         156     -1.46064    0.36508
   4    42    68.15   59.571     8.17      40         166     -1.76087   -0.27657
   5    38    89.02   49.874     9.22      55         178      0.55819   -1.67684
   6    47    77.45   44.811    11.63      58         176     -0.00113    1.40715
   7    40    75.98   45.681    11.95      70         176      0.95318   -0.48598
   8    43    81.19   49.091    10.85      64         162     -0.12951    0.36724
   9    44    81.42   39.442    13.08      63         174      0.66267    0.85740
  10    38    81.87   60.055     8.63      48         170     -0.44496   -1.53103
  11    44    73.03   50.541    10.13      45         168     -1.11832    0.55349
  12    45    87.66   37.388    14.03      56         186      1.20836    1.05948
```

Example 2:   Regression Parameter Estimates

In this example, PROC REG computes regression parameter estimates for the FITNESS data. (See **Example 1** to create the FITNESS data set.) The parameter estimates are output to a data set and used as scoring coefficients. For the first part of this example, PROC SCORE is used to score the FITNESS data, which are the same data used in the regression. In the second part of this example, PROC SCORE is used to score a new data set, FITNESS2. For PROC SCORE, the TYPE= specification is PARMS, and the names of the score variables are found in the variable _MODEL_, which gets its values from the label of a model. The following statements produce **Output 38.4** through **Output 38.6**:

```
proc reg data=fitness outest=regout;
oxyhat: model oxy=age weight runtime runpulse rstpulse;
   title 'REGRESSION SCORING EXAMPLE';
run;

proc print data=regout;
   title2 'OUTEST= Data Set from PROC REG';
run;

proc score data=fitness score=regout out=rscorep type=parms;
   var age weight runtime runpulse rstpulse;
run;

proc print data=rscorep;
   title2 'Predicted Scores for Regression';
run;

proc score data=fitness score=regout out=rscorer type=parms;
   var oxy age weight runtime runpulse rstpulse;
run;

proc print data=rscorer;
   title2 'Residual Scores for Regression';
run;
```

Output 38.4 shows the PROC REG output. The column labeled "Parameter Estimate" lists the parameter estimates. These estimates are output to the REGOUT data set.

Output 38.4   Creating an OUTEST= Data Set with PROC REG

```
                          REGRESSION SCORING EXAMPLE                          1

Model: OXYHAT
Dependent Variable: OXY

                            Analysis of Variance

                              Sum of        Mean
         Source      DF      Squares       Square    F Value    Prob>F

         Model        5    509.62201    101.92440     15.802    0.0021
         Error        6     38.70060      6.45010
         C Total     11    548.32261

              Root MSE       2.53970    R-square      0.9294
              Dep Mean      48.38942    Adj R-sq      0.8706
              C.V.           5.24847

                            Parameter Estimates

                       Parameter     Standard    T for H0:
         Variable  DF   Estimate        Error   Parameter=0    Prob > |T|

         INTERCEP   1  151.915500   31.04737619      4.893    0.0027
         AGE        1   -0.630450    0.42502668     -1.483    0.1885
         WEIGHT     1   -0.105862    0.11868838     -0.892    0.4068
         RUNTIME    1   -1.756978    0.93844085     -1.872    0.1103
         RUNPULSE   1   -0.228910    0.12168627     -1.881    0.1090
         RSTPULSE   1   -0.179102    0.13005008     -1.377    0.2176
```

Output 38.5 lists the REGOUT data set. Notice that _TYPE_='PARMS' and _MODEL_='OXYHAT', the label in the MODEL statement in PROC REG.

Output 38.5   OUTEST= Data Set from PROC REG Reproduced with PROC PRINT

```
                          REGRESSION SCORING EXAMPLE                          2
                         OUTEST= Data Set from PROC REG

OBS  _MODEL_  _TYPE_  _DEPVAR_  _RMSE_  INTERCEP    AGE    WEIGHT   RUNTIME   RUNPULSE  RSTPULSE   OXY

 1   OXYHAT   PARMS    OXY     2.53970  151.916  -0.63045  -0.10586  -1.75698  -0.22891  -0.17910   -1
```

Output 38.6 lists the data sets created by PROC SCORE. Since the SCORE= data set does not contain observations with _TYPE_='MEAN' or _TYPE_='STD', the data in FITNESS are not standardized before scoring. The SCORE= data set contains the variable INTERCEP, so this intercept value is used in computing the score. To produce RSCOREP, the VAR statement in PROC SCORE includes only the independent variables from the model in PROC REG. As a result, OXYHAT gives predicted values. To produce RSCORER, the VAR statement in PROC SCORE includes both the dependent variable and the independent variables from the model in PROC REG. As a result, OXYHAT gives negative residuals (PREDICT−ACTUAL). If the RESIDUAL option is specified, OXYHAT gives positive residuals (ACTUAL−PREDICT). If the PREDICT option had been specified, OXYHAT would have given predicted values.

Output 38.6 Predicted and Residual Scores from the OUT= Data Set
Created by PROC SCORE and Reproduced Using PROC PRINT

```
                         REGRESSION SCORING EXAMPLE                              3
                        Predicted Scores for Regression

   OBS    AGE    WEIGHT     OXY     RUNTIME    RSTPULSE    RUNPULSE    OXYHAT

    1      44     89.47    44.609    11.37       62         178       42.8771
    2      40     75.07    45.313    10.07       62         185       47.6050
    3      44     85.84    54.297     8.65       45         156       56.1211
    4      42     68.15    59.571     8.17       40         166       58.7044
    5      38     89.02    49.874     9.22       55         178       51.7386
    6      47     77.45    44.811    11.63       58         176       42.9756
    7      40     75.98    45.681    11.95       70         176       44.8329
    8      43     81.19    49.091    10.85       64         162       48.6020
    9      44     81.42    39.442    13.08       63         174       41.4613
   10      38     81.87    60.055     8.63       48         170       56.6171
   11      44     73.03    50.541    10.13       45         168       52.1299
   12      45     87.66    37.388    14.03       56         186       37.0080
```

```
                         REGRESSION SCORING EXAMPLE                              4
                        Residual Scores for Regression

   OBS    AGE    WEIGHT     OXY     RUNTIME    RSTPULSE    RUNPULSE    OXYHAT

    1      44     89.47    44.609    11.37       62         178      -1.73195
    2      40     75.07    45.313    10.07       62         185       2.29197
    3      44     85.84    54.297     8.65       45         156       1.82407
    4      42     68.15    59.571     8.17       40         166      -0.86657
    5      38     89.02    49.874     9.22       55         178       1.86460
    6      47     77.45    44.811    11.63       58         176      -1.83542
    7      40     75.98    45.681    11.95       70         176      -0.84811
    8      43     81.19    49.091    10.85       64         162      -0.48897
    9      44     81.42    39.442    13.08       63         174       2.01935
   10      38     81.87    60.055     8.63       48         170      -3.43787
   11      44     73.03    50.541    10.13       45         168       1.58892
   12      45     87.66    37.388    14.03       56         186      -0.38002
```

The second part of this example uses the parameter estimates to score a new data set. The following statements produce **Output 38.7** and **Output 38.8**:

```
    /* The FITNESS2 data set contains observations 13-16 from the */
    /* FITNESS data set used in EXAMPLE 2 in the PROC REG chapter. */
data fitness2;
   input age weight oxy runtime rstpulse runpulse;
   cards;
45  66.45   44.754  11.12  51  176
47  79.15   47.273  10.60  47  162
54  83.12   51.855  10.33  50  166
49  81.42   49.156   8.95  44  180
;

proc print data=fitness2;
   title 'REGRESSION SCORING EXAMPLE';
   title2 'New Raw Data Set to be Scored';
run;

proc score data=fitness2 score=regout out=newpred type=parms
        nostd predict;
   var oxy age weight runtime runpulse rstpulse;
run;
```

```
proc print data=newpred;
   title2 'Predicted Scores for Regression';
   title3 'for Additional Data from FITNESS2';
run;
```

Output 38.7 lists the FITNESS2 data set.

Output 38.7 FITNESS2 Data Set

```
                    REGRESSION SCORING EXAMPLE                              1
                    New Raw Data Set to be Scored

         OBS    AGE    WEIGHT    OXY     RUNTIME    RSTPULSE    RUNPULSE

          1      45    66.45    44.754   11.12        51         176
          2      47    79.15    47.273   10.60        47         162
          3      54    83.12    51.855   10.33        50         166
          4      49    81.42    49.156    8.95        44         180
```

PROC SCORE scores the FITNESS2 data set using the parameter estimates in REGOUT. These parameter estimates are from fitting a regression equation to FITNESS. The NOSTD option is specified, so the raw data are not standardized before scoring. (However, the NOSTD option is not necessary here. The SCORE= data set does not contain observations with _TYPE_='MEAN' or _TYPE_='STD', so standardization is not performed.) The VAR statement contains the dependent variable and the independent variables used in PROC REG. In addition, the PREDICT option is specified. This combination gives predicted values for the new score variable. The name of the new score variable is OXYHAT, from the value of _MODEL_ in the SCORE= data set. **Output 38.8** shows the data set produced by PROC SCORE.

Output 38.8 Predicted Scores from the OUT= Data Set Created by PROC SCORE and Reproduced Using PROC PRINT

```
                    REGRESSION SCORING EXAMPLE                              3
                    Predicted Scores for Regression
                    for Additional Data from FITNESS2

     OBS   AGE   WEIGHT    OXY     RUNTIME   RSTPULSE   RUNPULSE   OXYHAT

      1     45   66.45    44.754   11.12       51        176     47.5507
      2     47   79.15    47.273   10.60       47        162     49.7802
      3     54   83.12    51.855   10.33       50        166     43.9682
      4     49   81.42    49.156    8.95       44        180     47.5949
```

Example 3: Custom Scoring Coefficients

This example uses a specially created custom scoring data set and produces **Output 38.9**. The first scoring coefficient creates a variable that is AGE−WEIGHT; the second evaluates RUNPULSE−RSTPULSE; and the third totals all six variables. Because the scoring coefficients data set (data set A) does not contain any observations with _TYPE_='MEAN' or _TYPE_='STD', the data in FITNESS (see **Example 1**) are not standardized before scoring.

```
data a;
   input _type_ $ _name_ $
         age weight runtime runpulse rstpulse;
   cards;
SCORE   AGE_WGT  1 -1  0  0  0
SCORE   RUN_RST  0  0  0  1 -1
SCORE   TOTAL    1  1  1  1  1
;

proc print data=a;
   title 'CONSTRUCTED SCORING EXAMPLE';
   title2 'Scoring Coefficients';
run;

proc score data=fitness score=a out=b;
   var age weight runtime runpulse rstpulse;
run;

proc print data=b;
   title2 'Scored Data';
run;
```

Output 38.9   Custom Scoring Data Set and Scored Fitness Data Reproduced Using PROC PRINT

```
                          CONSTRUCTED SCORING EXAMPLE                                    1
                              Scoring Coefficients

        OBS   _TYPE_   _NAME_    AGE   WEIGHT   RUNTIME   RUNPULSE   RSTPULSE

         1    SCORE    AGE_WGT    1      -1        0         0          0
         2    SCORE    RUN_RST    0       0        0         1         -1
         3    SCORE    TOTAL      1       1        1         1          1
```

```
                          CONSTRUCTED SCORING EXAMPLE                                    2
                                  Scored Data

   OBS  AGE  WEIGHT   OXY    RUNTIME  RSTPULSE  RUNPULSE  AGE_WGT  RUN_RST  TOTAL
    1    44  89.47   44.609   11.37      62       178     -45.47     116    384.84
    2    40  75.07   45.313   10.07      62       185     -35.07     123    372.14
    3    44  85.84   54.297    8.65      45       156     -41.84     111    339.49
    4    42  68.15   59.571    8.17      40       166     -26.15     126    324.32
    5    38  89.02   49.874    9.22      55       178     -51.02     123    369.24
    6    47  77.45   44.811   11.63      58       176     -30.45     118    370.08
    7    40  75.98   45.681   11.95      70       176     -35.98     106    373.93
    8    43  81.19   49.091   10.85      64       162     -38.19      98    361.04
    9    44  81.42   39.442   13.08      63       174     -37.42     111    375.50
   10    38  81.87   60.055    8.63      48       170     -43.87     122    346.50
   11    44  73.03   50.541   10.13      45       168     -29.03     123    340.16
   12    45  87.66   37.388   14.03      56       186     -42.66     130    388.69
```

1492

Chapter 39

The STEPDISC Procedure

ABSTRACT   1493
INTRODUCTION   1493
SPECIFICATIONS   1495
  PROC STEPDISC Statement   1496
  BY Statement   1499
  CLASS Statement   1499
  FREQ Statement   1499
  VAR Statement   1499
  WEIGHT Statement   1499
DETAILS   1500
  Missing Values   1500
  Input Data Set   1500
  Computational Resources   1501
    Memory Requirements   1501
    Time Requirements   1501
  Printed Output   1501
EXAMPLE   1503
  Performing a Stepwise Discriminant Analysis   1503
REFERENCES   1509

ABSTRACT

The STEPDISC procedure performs a stepwise discriminant analysis by forward selection, backward elimination, or stepwise selection of quantitative variables that can be useful for discriminating among several classes.

INTRODUCTION

The STEPDISC procedure selects a subset of quantitative variables to produce a good discrimination model using forward selection, backward elimination, or stepwise selection (Klecka 1980). The set of variables that make up each class is assumed to be multivariate normal with a common covariance matrix.

Variables are chosen to enter or leave the model according to one of two criteria:

- the significance level of an *F* test from an analysis of covariance, where the variables already chosen act as covariates and the variable under consideration is the dependent variable
- the squared partial correlation for predicting the variable under consideration from the CLASS variable, controlling for the effects of the variables already selected for the model.

The significance level and the squared partial correlation criteria select variables in the same order, although they may select different numbers of variables. Increasing the sample size tends to increase the number of variables selected when using significance levels but has little effect on the number selected using squared partial correlations.

It is important to remember that when many significance tests are performed, each at a level of, for example, 5 percent, the overall probability of rejecting at least one true null hypothesis is much larger than 5 percent. If you want to guard against including any variables that do not contribute to the discriminatory power of the model in the population, you should specify a very small significance level. In most applications, all variables considered have some discriminatory power, however small. To choose the model that provides the best discrimination using the sample estimates, you need only guard against estimating more parameters than can be reliably estimated with the given sample size; hence, a moderate significance level is appropriate.

Costanza and Afifi (1979) use Monte Carlo studies to compare alternative stopping rules that can be used with the forward selection method in the two-group multivariate normal classification problem. Five different numbers of variables, ranging from 10 to 30, are considered in the studies. The comparison is based on conditional and estimated unconditional probabilities of correct classification. They conclude that the use of a moderate significance level, in the range of 10 percent to 25 percent, often performs better than the use of a much larger or a much smaller significance level.

Forward selection begins with no variables in the model. At each step the variable is entered that contributes most to the discriminatory power of the model as measured by Wilks' lambda, the likelihood ratio criterion. When none of the unselected variables meet the entry criterion, the forward selection process stops.

Backward elimination begins with all variables in the model except those that are linearly dependent on previous variables in the VAR statement. At each step the variable that contributes least to the discriminatory power of the model as measured by Wilks' lambda is removed. When all remaining variables meet the criterion to stay in the model, the backward elimination process stops.

Stepwise selection begins like forward selection with no variables in the model. At each step the model is examined. If the variable in the model that contributes least to the discriminatory power of the model as measured by Wilks' lambda fails to meet the criterion to stay, then that variable is removed. Otherwise, the variable not in the model that contributes most to the discriminatory power of the model is entered. When all variables in the model meet the criterion to stay and none of the other variables meets the criterion to enter, the stepwise selection process stops.

It is important to realize that in the selection of variables for entry, only one variable can be entered into the model at each step. The selection process does not take into account the relationships between variables that have not yet been selected. Thus, some important variables could be excluded in the process.

The models selected by the STEPDISC procedure are not necessarily the best possible models, and Wilks' lambda may not be the best measure of discriminatory power for your application. However, if STEPDISC is used carefully, in combination with your knowledge of the data and careful cross-validation, it can be a valuable aid in selecting a discrimination model.

See Chapter 5, "Introduction to Discriminant Procedures," for more information on discriminant analysis.

SPECIFICATIONS

The following statements are used with the STEPDISC procedure:

PROC STEPDISC <*options*>;   required statements
    CLASS *variable*;

    BY *variables*;
    FREQ *variable*;
    VAR *variables*;   optional statements
    WEIGHT *variable*;

The BY, CLASS, FREQ, VAR, and WEIGHT statements are described after the PROC STEPDISC statement.

PROC STEPDISC Statement

PROC STEPDISC <*options*>;

This statement invokes the STEPDISC procedure. The following options can appear in the PROC STEPDISC statement.

Task	Option
Specify data set	DATA=
Select method	METHOD=
Specify selection criterion	SLENTRY=
	SLSTAY=
	PR2ENTRY=
	PR2STAY=
Specify selection process	INCLUDE=
	MAXSTEP=
	START=
	STOP=
Determine singularity	SINGULAR=
Control printed output	
Correlations	BCORR
	PCORR
	TCORR
	WCORR
Covariances	BCOV
	PCOV
	TCOV
	WCOV
SSCP matrix	BSSCP
	PSSCP
	TSSCP
	WSSCP
Miscellaneous	ALL
	SIMPLE
	STDMEAN
Suppress printing	SHORT

ALL

activates all of the printing options.

BCORR

prints between-class correlations.

BCOV

prints between-class covariances. The between-class covariance matrix equals the between-class SSCP matrix divided by $n(c-1)/c$, where n is the number of observations and c is the number of classes. The between-class covariances should be interpreted in comparison with the total-sample and within-class covariances, not as formal estimates of population parameters.

BSSCP

prints the between-class SSCP matrix.

DATA=*SAS-data-set*

specifies the data set to be analyzed. The data set can be an ordinary SAS data set or one of several specially structured data sets created by statistical procedures available with SAS/STAT software. These specially structured data sets include TYPE=CORR, COV, CSSCP, and SSCP. If the DATA= option is omitted, the procedure uses the most recently created SAS data set.

INCLUDE=*n*

includes the first *n* variables in the VAR statement in every model. By default, INCLUDE=0.

MAXSTEP=*n*

specifies the maximum number of steps. By default, MAXSTEP= two times the number of variables in the VAR statement.

METHOD=BACKWARD | BW
         | FORWARD | FW
         | STEPWISE | SW

specifies the method used to select the variables in the model. BACKWARD specifies backward elimination, FORWARD specifies forward selection, and STEPWISE specifies stepwise selection. By default, METHOD=STEPWISE.

PCORR

prints pooled within-class correlations (partial correlations based on the pooled within-class covariances).

PCOV

prints pooled within-class covariances.

PR2ENTRY=*p*
PR2E=*p*

specifies the partial R^2 for adding variables in the forward selection mode, where $p \leq 1$.

PR2STAY=*p*
PR2S=*p*

specifies the partial R^2 for retaining variables in the backward elimination mode, where $p \leq 1$.

PSSCP

prints the pooled within-class corrected SSCP matrix.

SHORT

suppresses the printed output from each step.

SIMPLE
: prints simple descriptive statistics for the total sample and within each class.

SINGULAR=p
: specifies the singularity criterion for entering variables, where $0<p<1$. PROC STEPDISC precludes the entry of a variable if the squared multiple correlation of the variable with the variables already in the model exceeds $1-p$. With more than one variable already in the model, STEPDISC also excludes a variable if it would cause any of the variables already in the model to have a squared multiple correlation (with the entering variable and the other variables in the model) exceeding $1-p$. By default, SINGULAR=1E-8.

SLENTRY=p
SLE=p
: specifies the significance level for adding variables in the forward selection mode, where $0 \leq p \leq 1$. The default value is 0.15.

SLSTAY=p
SLS=p
: specifies the significance level for retaining variables in the backward elimination mode, where $0 \leq p \leq 1$. The default value is 0.15.

START=n
: specifies that the first n variables in the VAR statement be used to begin the selection process. The default value is 0 when METHOD=FORWARD or METHOD=STEPWISE is used and is the number of variables in the VAR statement when METHOD=BACKWARD is used.

STDMEAN
: prints total-sample and pooled within-class standardized class means.

STOP=n
: specifies the number of variables in the final model. The STEPDISC procedure stops the selection process when a model with n variables is found. This option applies only when METHOD=FORWARD or METHOD=BACKWARD is used. The default value is the number of variables in the VAR statement when METHOD=FORWARD is used and is 0 when METHOD=BACKWARD is used.

TCORR
: prints total-sample correlations.

TCOV
: prints total-sample covariances.

TSSCP
: prints the total-sample corrected SSCP matrix.

WCORR
: prints within-class correlations for each class level.

WCOV
: prints within-class covariances for each class level.

WSSCP
: prints the within-class corrected SSCP matrix for each class level.

BY Statement

> **BY** *variables*;

A BY statement can be used with PROC STEPDISC to obtain separate analyses on observations in groups defined by the BY variables. When a BY statement appears, the procedure expects the input data set to be sorted in order of the BY variables.

If your input data set is not sorted in ascending order, use one of the following alternatives:

- Use the SORT procedure with a similar BY statement to sort the data.
- Use the BY statement options NOTSORTED or DESCENDING in the BY statement for the STEPDISC procedure. As a cautionary note, the NOTSORTED option does not mean that the data are unsorted, but rather means that the data are arranged in groups (according to values of the BY variables) and that these groups are not necessarily in alphabetical or increasing numeric order.
- Use the DATASETS procedure (in base SAS software) to create an index on the BY variables.

For more information on the BY statement, see the discussion in *SAS Language: Reference, Version 6, First Edition*. For more information on the DATASETS procedure, see the discussion in the *SAS Procedures Guide, Version 6, Third Edition*.

CLASS Statement

> **CLASS** *variable*;

The values of the CLASS variable define the groups for analysis. Class levels are determined by the formatted values of the CLASS variable. The CLASS variable can be numeric or character. **A CLASS statement is required**.

FREQ Statement

> **FREQ** *variable*;

If a variable in the data set represents the frequency of occurrence for the other values in the observation, include the variable's name in a FREQ statement. The procedure then treats the data set as if each observation appears *n* times, where *n* is the value of the FREQ variable for the observation. The total number of observations is considered to be equal to the sum of the FREQ variable when the procedure determines degrees of freedom for significance probabilities.

If the value of the FREQ variable is missing or less than one, the observation is not used in the analysis. If the value is not an integer, the value is truncated to an integer.

VAR Statement

> **VAR** *variables*;

The VAR statement specifies the quantitative variables eligible for selection. The default is all numeric variables not listed in other statements.

WEIGHT Statement

> **WEIGHT** *variable*;

To use relative weights for each observation in the input data set, place the weights in a variable in the data set and specify the name in a WEIGHT statement.

This is often done when the variance associated with each observation is different and the values of the WEIGHT variable are proportional to the reciprocals of the variances. If the value of the WEIGHT variable is missing or less than zero, then a value of zero for the weight is assumed.

The WEIGHT and FREQ statements have a similar effect except that the WEIGHT statement does not alter the degrees of freedom.

DETAILS

Missing Values

Observations containing missing values are omitted from the analysis.

Input Data Set

The input data set can be an ordinary SAS data set or one of several specially structured data sets created by statistical procedures available with SAS/STAT software. For more information on these data sets, see Appendix 1, "Special SAS Data Sets." The BY variable in these data sets becomes the CLASS variable in PROC STEPDISC. These specially structured data sets include

- TYPE=CORR data sets created by the CORR procedure using a BY statement
- TYPE=COV data sets created by the PRINCOMP procedure using both the COV option and a BY statement
- TYPE=CSSCP data sets created by PROC CORR using the CSSCP option and a BY statement, where the OUT= data set is assigned TYPE=CSSCP with the TYPE= data set option
- TYPE=SSCP data sets created the REG procedure using both the OUTSSCP= option and a BY statement.

When the input data set is TYPE=CORR, TYPE=COV, or TYPE=CSSCP, STEPDISC reads the number of observations for each class from the observations with _TYPE_='N' and the variable means in each class from the observations with _TYPE_='MEAN'. STEPDISC then reads the within-class correlations from the observations with _TYPE_='CORR', the standard deviations from the observations with _TYPE_='STD' (data set TYPE=CORR), the within-class covariances from the observations with _TYPE_='COV' (data set TYPE=COV), or the within-class corrected sums of squares and crossproducts from the observations with _TYPE_='CSSCP' (data set TYPE=CSSCP).

When the data set does not include any observations with _TYPE_='CORR' (data set TYPE=CORR), _TYPE_='COV' (data set TYPE=COV), or _TYPE_='CSSCP' (data set TYPE=CSSCP) for each class, STEPDISC reads the pooled within-class information from the data set. In this case, STEPDISC reads the pooled within-class correlations from the observations with _TYPE_='PCORR', the pooled within-class standard deviations from the observations with _TYPE_='PSTD' (data set TYPE=CORR), the pooled within-class covariances from the observations with _TYPE_='PCOV' (data set TYPE=COV), or the pooled within-class corrected SSCP matrix from the observations with _TYPE_='PSSCP' (data set TYPE=CSSCP).

When the input data set is TYPE=SSCP, STEPDISC reads the number of observations for each class from the observations with _TYPE_='N', the sum of weights of observations from the variable INTERCEP in observations with

TYPE='SSCP' and _NAME_='INTERCEP', the variable sums from the variable=*variablenames* in observations with _TYPE_='SSCP' and _NAME_='INTERCEP', and the uncorrected sums of squares and crossproducts from the variable=*variablenames* in observations with _TYPE_='SSCP' and _NAME_=*variablenames*.

Computational Resources

In the following discussion, let

n = number of observations
c = number of class levels
v = number of variables in the VAR list
l = length of the CLASS variable
$t = v+c-1$.

Memory Requirements

The amount of memory in bytes for temporary storage needed to process the data is

$$c(4v^2 + 28v + 3l + 4c + 72) + 16v^2 + 92v + 4t^2 + 20t + 4l \ .$$

Additional temporary storage of 72 bytes at each step is also required to store the results.

Time Requirements

The following factors determine the time requirements of a stepwise discriminant analysis:

1. The time needed for reading the data and computing covariance matrices is proportional to nv^2. STEPDISC must also look up each class level in the list. This is faster if the data are sorted by the CLASS variable. The time for looking up class levels is proportional to a value ranging from n to $n \log(c)$.
2. The time needed for stepwise discriminant analysis is proportional to the number of steps required to select the set of variables in the discrimination model. The number of steps required depends on the data set itself and the selection method and criterion used in the procedure. Each forward or backward step takes time proportional to $(v+c)^2$.

Printed Output

The STEPDISC procedure prints the following output:

1. Class Level Information, including the values of the classification variable, the Frequency of each value, the Weight of each value, and its Proportion in the total sample.

Optional output includes

2. Within-Class SSCP Matrices for each group (not shown)
3. Pooled Within-Class SSCP Matrix (not shown)
4. Between-Class SSCP Matrix
5. Total-Sample SSCP Matrix
6. Within-Class Covariance Matrices for each group (not shown)
7. Pooled Within-Class Covariance Matrix (not shown)

8. Between-Class Covariance Matrix, equal to the between-class SSCP matrix divided by $n(c-1)/c$, where n is the number of observations and c is the number of classes (not shown)
9. Total-Sample Covariance Matrix (not shown)
10. Within-Class Correlation Coefficients and Prob $> |R|$ to test the hypothesis that the within-class population correlation coefficients are zero (not shown)
11. Pooled Within-Class Correlation Coefficients and Prob $> |R|$ to test the hypothesis that the partial population correlation coefficients are zero (not shown)
12. Between-Class Correlation Coefficients and Prob $> |R|$ to test the hypothesis that the between-class population correlation coefficients are zero (not shown)
13. Total-Sample Correlation Coefficients and Prob $> |R|$ to test the hypothesis that the total population correlation coefficients are zero (not shown)
14. Simple Statistics, including N (the number of observations), Sum, Mean, Variance, and Standard Deviation for the total sample and within each class (not shown)
15. Total-Sample Standardized Class Means, obtained by subtracting the grand mean from each class mean and dividing by the total-sample standard deviation (not shown)
16. Pooled Within-Class Standardized Class Means, obtained by subtracting the grand mean from each class mean and dividing by the pooled within-class standard deviation (not shown).

At each step, the following statistics are printed:

17. for each variable considered for entry or removal: (Partial) R**2, the squared (partial) correlation, the F statistic, and Prob $> F$, the probability level, from a one-way analysis of covariance.
18. the minimum Tolerance for entering each variable. Tolerance for the entering variable is one minus the squared multiple correlation of the variable with the other variables already in the model. Tolerance for a variable already in the model is one minus the squared multiple correlation of the variable with the entering variable and other variables already in the model. A variable is entered only if its tolerance and the tolerances for variables in the model are greater than the value specified in the SINGULAR= option.

    The tolerance is computed using the total-sample correlation matrix. It is customary to compute tolerance using the pooled within-class correlation matrix (Jennrich 1977), but it is possible for a variable with excellent discriminatory power to have a high total-sample tolerance and a low pooled within-class tolerance. For example, PROC STEPDISC enters a variable that yields perfect discrimination (that is, produces a canonical correlation of one), but a program using pooled within-class tolerance does not.
19. the variable Label, if any.
20. the name of the variable chosen.
21. the variable or variables already selected or removed.
22. Wilks' Lambda and the associated F approximation with degrees of freedom and Prob $< F$, the associated probability level after the selected variable has been entered or removed. Wilks' lambda is the likelihood ratio statistic for testing the hypothesis that the means of

the classes on the selected variables are equal in the population (see **Multivariate Tests** in Chapter 1, "Introduction to Regression Procedures"). Lambda is close to zero if any two groups are well separated.

23. Pillai's Trace and the associated F approximation with degrees of freedom and Prob > F, the associated probability level after the selected variable has been entered or removed. Pillai's trace is a multivariate statistic for testing the hypothesis that the means of the classes on the selected variables are equal in the population (see **Multivariate Tests** in Chapter 1).

24. Average Squared Canonical Correlation (ASCC). The ASCC is Pillai's trace divided by the number of groups minus one. The ASCC is close to one if all groups are well separated and if all or most directions in the discriminant space show good separation for at least two groups.

25. A Summary is printed to give statistics associated with the variable chosen at each step. The Summary includes the following:
   - Step number
   - Variable Entered or Removed
   - Number of variables In the model
   - Partial R**2
   - F Statistic for entering or removing the variable
   - Prob > F, the probability level for the *F* statistic
   - Wilks' Lambda
   - Prob < Lambda based on the *F* approximation to Wilks' lambda
   - Average Squared Canonical Correlation
   - Prob > ASCC based on the *F* approximation to Pillai's trace
   - the variable Label, if any.

EXAMPLE

Performing a Stepwise Discriminant Analysis

The iris data published by Fisher (1936) have been widely used for examples in discriminant analysis and cluster analysis. The sepal length, sepal width, petal length, and petal width were measured in millimeters on 50 iris specimens from each of three species: *Iris setosa, I. versicolor,* and *I. virginica.* A stepwise discriminant analysis is performed using stepwise selection.

In the PROC STEPDISC statement, the BSSCP and TSSCP options print the between-class SSCP matrix and the total-sample corrected SSCP matrix. By default, the significance level of an *F* test from an analysis of covariance is used as the selection criterion. The variable under consideration is the dependent variable, and the variables already chosen act as covariates. In Step 1, the tolerance is 1.0 for each variable under consideration because no variables have yet been in the model. Variable PETALLEN is selected because its F statistic, 1180.161, is the largest among all variables. In Step 2, with variable PETALLEN already in the model, PETALLEN is tested for removal before selecting a new variable for entry. Since PETALLEN meets the criterion to stay, it is used as a covariate in the analysis of covariance for variable selection. Variable SEPALWID is selected because its

F statistic, 43.035, is the largest among all variables not in the model and its associated tolerance, 0.8164, meets the criterion to enter. The process is repeated in Steps 3 and 4. Variable PETALWID is entered in Step 3, and variable SEPALLEN is entered in Step 4. The following SAS statements produce **Output 39.1**:

```
proc format;
   value specname
      1='SETOSA    '
      2='VERSICOLOR'
      3='VIRGINICA ';
run;

data iris;
   title 'Fisher (1936) Iris Data';
   input sepallen sepalwid petallen petalwid species @@;
   format species specname.;
   label sepallen='Sepal Length in mm.'
         sepalwid='Sepal Width  in mm.'
         petallen='Petal Length in mm.'
         petalwid='Petal Width  in mm.';
   cards;
50 33 14 02 1 64 28 56 22 3 65 28 46 15 2 67 31 56 24 3
63 28 51 15 3 46 34 14 03 1 69 31 51 23 3 62 22 45 15 2
59 32 48 18 2 46 36 10 02 1 61 30 46 14 2 60 27 51 16 2
65 30 52 20 3 56 25 39 11 2 65 30 55 18 3 58 27 51 19 3
68 32 59 23 3 51 33 17 05 1 57 28 45 13 2 62 34 54 23 3
77 38 67 22 3 63 33 47 16 2 67 33 57 25 3 76 30 66 21 3
49 25 45 17 3 55 35 13 02 1 67 30 52 23 3 70 32 47 14 2
64 32 45 15 2 61 28 40 13 2 48 31 16 02 1 59 30 51 18 3
55 24 38 11 2 63 25 50 19 3 64 32 53 23 3 52 34 14 02 1
49 36 14 01 1 54 30 45 15 2 79 38 64 20 3 44 32 13 02 1
67 33 57 21 3 50 35 16 06 1 58 26 40 12 2 44 30 13 02 1
77 28 67 20 3 63 27 49 18 3 47 32 16 02 1 55 26 44 12 2
50 23 33 10 2 72 32 60 18 3 48 30 14 03 1 51 38 16 02 1
61 30 49 18 3 48 34 19 02 1 50 30 16 02 1 50 32 12 02 1
61 26 56 14 3 64 28 56 21 3 43 30 11 01 1 58 40 12 02 1
51 38 19 04 1 67 31 44 14 2 62 28 48 18 3 49 30 14 02 1
51 35 14 02 1 56 30 45 15 2 58 27 41 10 2 50 34 16 04 1
46 32 14 02 1 60 29 45 15 2 57 26 35 10 2 57 44 15 04 1
50 36 14 02 1 77 30 61 23 3 63 34 56 24 3 58 27 51 19 3
57 29 42 13 2 72 30 58 16 3 54 34 15 04 1 52 41 15 01 1
71 30 59 21 3 64 31 55 18 3 60 30 48 18 3 63 29 56 18 3
49 24 33 10 2 56 27 42 13 2 57 30 42 12 2 55 42 14 02 1
49 31 15 02 1 77 26 69 23 3 60 22 50 15 3 54 39 17 04 1
66 29 46 13 2 52 27 39 14 2 60 34 45 16 2 50 34 15 02 1
44 29 14 02 1 50 20 35 10 2 55 24 37 10 2 58 27 39 12 2
47 32 13 02 1 46 31 15 02 1 69 32 57 23 3 62 29 43 13 2
74 28 61 19 3 59 30 42 15 2 51 34 15 02 1 50 35 13 03 1
56 28 49 20 3 60 22 40 10 2 73 29 63 18 3 67 25 58 18 3
49 31 15 01 1 67 31 47 15 2 63 23 44 13 2 54 37 15 02 1
56 30 41 13 2 63 25 49 15 2 61 28 47 12 2 64 29 43 13 2
51 25 30 11 2 57 28 41 13 2 65 30 58 22 3 69 31 54 21 3
54 39 13 04 1 51 35 14 03 1 72 36 61 25 3 65 32 51 20 3
61 29 47 14 2 56 29 36 13 2 69 31 49 15 2 64 27 53 19 3
68 30 55 21 3 55 25 40 13 2 48 34 16 02 1 48 30 14 01 1
```

```
45 23 13 03 1 57 25 50 20 3 57 38 17 03 1 51 38 15 03 1
55 23 40 13 2 66 30 44 14 2 68 28 48 14 2 54 34 17 02 1
51 37 15 04 1 52 35 15 02 1 58 28 51 24 3 67 30 50 17 2
63 33 60 25 3 53 37 15 02 1
;

proc stepdisc data=iris bsscp tsscp;
   class species;
   var sepallen sepalwid petallen petalwid;
run;
```

Output 39.1   Iris Data: PROC STEPDISC

```
                        Fisher (1936) Iris Data                              1

                      Stepwise Discriminant Analysis

        150 Observations           4 Variable(s) in the Analysis
          3 Class Levels           0 Variable(s) will be included

        The Method for Selecting Variables will be: STEPWISE

        Significance Level to Enter = 0.1500
        Significance Level to Stay  = 0.1500
                    ❶   Class Level Information

        SPECIES         Frequency        Weight       Proportion

        SETOSA                 50       50.0000         0.333333
        VERSICOLOR             50       50.0000         0.333333
        VIRGINICA              50       50.0000         0.333333
```

```
                        Fisher (1936) Iris Data                              2

                      Stepwise Discriminant Analysis
                    ❹   Between-Class SSCP Matrix

Variable        SEPALLEN        SEPALWID        PETALLEN        PETALWID

SEPALLEN      6321.21333    -1995.26667     16524.84000      7127.93333    Sepal Length in mm.
SEPALWID     -1995.26667     1134.49333     -5723.96000     -2293.26667    Sepal Width  in mm.
PETALLEN     16524.84000    -5723.96000     43710.28000     18677.40000    Petal Length in mm.
PETALWID      7127.93333    -2293.26667     18677.40000      8041.33333    Petal Width  in mm.


                    ❺   Total-Sample SSCP Matrix

Variable        SEPALLEN        SEPALWID        PETALLEN        PETALWID

SEPALLEN     10216.83333     -632.26667     18987.30000      7692.43333    Sepal Length in mm.
SEPALWID      -632.26667     2830.69333     -4911.88000     -1812.42667    Sepal Width  in mm.
PETALLEN     18987.30000    -4911.88000     46432.54000     19304.58000    Petal Length in mm.
PETALWID      7692.43333    -1812.42667     19304.58000      8656.99333    Petal Width  in mm.
```

```
                          Fisher (1936) Iris Data                                    3
                       Stepwise Discriminant Analysis

Stepwise Selection:  Step 1

              ⑰       Statistics for Entry, DF = 2, 147

            Variable    R**2        F       Prob > F    Tolerance   Label
                                                        ⑱          ⑲
            SEPALLEN    0.6187    119.265    0.0001      1.0000    Sepal Length in mm.
            SEPALWID    0.4008     49.160    0.0001      1.0000    Sepal Width  in mm.
            PETALLEN    0.9414   1180.161    0.0001      1.0000    Petal Length in mm.
            PETALWID    0.9289    960.007    0.0001      1.0000    Petal Width  in mm.

                   ⑳      Variable PETALLEN will be entered

                 ㉑  The following variable(s) have been entered:
                              PETALLEN

                          Multivariate Statistics

     ㉒  Wilks' Lambda  = 0.05862828   F( 2, 147) = 1180.161    Prob > F = 0.0001
     ㉓  Pillai's Trace =  0.941372    F( 2, 147) = 1180.161    Prob > F = 0.0001

          ㉔  Average Squared Canonical Correlation = 0.47068586
-------------------------------------------------------------------------------------------

Stepwise Selection:  Step 2

                       Statistics for Removal,  DF = 2, 147

            Variable    R**2         F        Prob > F   Label

            PETALLEN    0.9414    1180.161    0.0001     Petal Length in mm.


                          No variables can be removed

                          ---------------------------

                       Statistics for Entry, DF = 2, 146

                       Partial
            Variable    R**2         F       Prob > F   Tolerance   Label

            SEPALLEN    0.3198     34.323    0.0001      0.2400    Sepal Length in mm.
            SEPALWID    0.3709     43.035    0.0001      0.8164    Sepal Width  in mm.
            PETALWID    0.2533     24.766    0.0001      0.0729    Petal Width  in mm.

                       Variable SEPALWID will be entered

                 The following variable(s) have been entered:
                            SEPALWID PETALLEN
```

Fisher (1936) Iris Data   4

Stepwise Discriminant Analysis

Stepwise Selection: Step 2

Multivariate Statistics

Wilks' Lambda = 0.03688411   F(4, 292) = 307.105   Prob > F = 0.0001
Pillai's Trace = 1.119908   F(4, 294) = 93.528   Prob > F = 0.0001

Average Squared Canonical Correlation = 0.55995394

Stepwise Selection: Step 3

Statistics for Removal, DF = 2, 146

Variable	Partial R**2	F	Prob > F	Label
SEPALWID	0.3709	43.035	0.0001	Sepal Width in mm.
PETALLEN	0.9384	1112.954	0.0001	Petal Length in mm.

No variables can be removed

Statistics for Entry, DF = 2, 145

Variable	Partial R**2	F	Prob > F	Tolerance	Label
SEPALLEN	0.1447	12.268	0.0001	0.1323	Sepal Length in mm.
PETALWID	0.3229	34.569	0.0001	0.0662	Petal Width in mm.

Variable PETALWID will be entered

The following variable(s) have been entered:
SEPALWID PETALLEN PETALWID

Multivariate Statistics

Wilks' Lambda = 0.02497554   F(6, 290) = 257.503   Prob > F = 0.0001
Pillai's Trace = 1.189914   F(6, 292) = 71.485   Prob > F = 0.0001

Average Squared Canonical Correlation = 0.59495691

```
                              Fisher (1936) Iris Data                              5
                          Stepwise Discriminant Analysis

Stepwise Selection:  Step 4

                        Statistics for Removal,  DF = 2, 145

                        Partial
           Variable     R**2         F        Prob > F     Label

           SEPALWID     0.4295     54.577      0.0001     Sepal Width  in mm.
           PETALLEN     0.3482     38.724      0.0001     Petal Length in mm.
           PETALWID     0.3229     34.569      0.0001     Petal Width  in mm.


                          No variables can be removed

                        ---------------------------

                        Statistics for Entry, DF = 2, 144

                      Partial
          Variable    R**2         F       Prob > F    Tolerance    Label

          SEPALLEN    0.0615      4.721     0.0103      0.0320    Sepal Length in mm.

                        Variable SEPALLEN will be entered

                        All variables have been entered

                             Multivariate Statistics

         Wilks' Lambda =  0.02343863   F( 8, 288) = 199.145     Prob > F = 0.0001
         Pillai's Trace =  1.191899     F( 8, 290) =  53.466     Prob > F = 0.0001

                  Average Squared Canonical Correlation = 0.59594941
----------------------------------------------------------------------------------------
Stepwise Selection:  Step 5

                        Statistics for Removal,  DF = 2, 144

                        Partial
           Variable     R**2         F        Prob > F     Label

           SEPALLEN     0.0615      4.721      0.0103     Sepal Length in mm.
           SEPALWID     0.2335     21.936      0.0001     Sepal Width  in mm.
           PETALLEN     0.3308     35.590      0.0001     Petal Length in mm.
           PETALWID     0.2570     24.904      0.0001     Petal Width  in mm.


                          No variables can be removed

No further steps are possible
```

```
                              Fisher (1936) Iris Data                              6
                   ㉕      Stepwise Discriminant Analysis

Stepwise Selection:  Summary

                                                             Average
                                                             Squared
          Variable     Number Partial    F      Prob >  Wilks'   Prob <  Canonical   Prob >
     Step Entered Removed  In   R**2   Statistic   F     Lambda  Lambda  Correlation  ASCC   Label
     ----------------------------------------------------------------------------------------------------
       1  PETALLEN          1  0.9414  1180.161  0.0001  0.05862828  0.0001  0.47068586  0.0001  Petal Length in mm.
       2  SEPALWID          2  0.3709    43.035  0.0001  0.03688411  0.0001  0.55995394  0.0001  Sepal Width  in mm.
       3  PETALWID          3  0.3229    34.569  0.0001  0.02497554  0.0001  0.59495691  0.0001  Petal Width  in mm.
       4  SEPALLEN          4  0.0615     4.721  0.0103  0.02343863  0.0001  0.59594941  0.0001  Sepal Length in mm.
```

REFERENCES

Costanza, M.C. and Afifi, A.A. (1979), "Comparison of Stopping Rules in Forward Stepwise Discriminant Analysis," *Journal of the American Statistical Association*, 74, 777–785.

Fisher, R.A. (1936), "The Use of Multiple Measurements in Taxonomic Problems," *Annals of Eugenics*, 7, 179–188.

Jennrich, R.I. (1977), "Stepwise Discriminant Analysis," in *Statistical Methods for Digital Computers*, eds. K. Enslein, A. Ralston, and H. Wilf, New York: John Wiley & Sons, Inc.

Klecka, W.R. (1980), *Discriminant Analysis*, Sage University Paper Series on Quantitative Applications in the Social Sciences, Series No. 07-019, Beverly Hills: Sage Publications.

Rencher, A.C. and Larson, S.F. (1980), "Bias in Wilks's Λ in Stepwise Discriminant Analysis," *Technometrics*, 22, 349–356.

ABSTRACT   1512
INTRODUCTION   1512
  Background   1513
  Introductory Examples   1514
    Generating the Output Data Set   1514
    Detecting Nonlinear Relationships   1516
    Nonlinear Transformations   1518
SPECIFICATIONS   1520
  PROC TRANSREG Statement   1521
  BY Statement   1523
  ID Statement   1523
  MODEL Statement   1523
    Families of Transformations   1524
      Variable expansions   1525
      Nonoptimal transformations   1526
      Optimal transformations   1527
    Transformation Options (t-options)   1528
      Nonoptimal transformation t-options   1528
      Optimal transformation t-options   1529
    Options in the MODEL Statement   1531
    Using the MODEL Statement   1534
  OUTPUT Statement   1535
DETAILS   1540
  Missing Values   1540
  Centering of Variables   1541
  Controlling the Iteration Process   1541
  Point Models   1542
  Optimal Scaling   1542
    OPSCORE, MONOTONE, UNTIE, and LINEAR Transformations   1543
    SPLINE and MSPLINE Transformations   1544
  Output Data Set   1546
    Examples   1546
    Matrices   1548
      Details for the UNIVARIATE method   1551
      Details for MORALS method   1552
      Details for the CANALS and REDUNDANCY methods   1552
    Variable Names   1552
      TYPE and _NAME_ variables   1553
      MORALS method variables   1554
    Using Options to Produce the Coefficient Partition   1554
  Computational Resources   1556
  Convergence and Degeneracies   1557
  Solving Standard Least-squares Problems   1558
    Nonlinear Regression Functions   1558

        Simultaneously Fitting Two Regression Functions   1562
        Unbalanced ANOVA without Dummy Variables   1565
    Printed Output   1566
  EXAMPLES   1567
    Example 1:   Using Splines and Knots   1567
    Example 2:   Transformed Variables as Input to Other Procedures   1575
    Example 3:   Simple Conjoint Analysis   1578
    Example 4:   Conjoint Analyses of Tea-tasting Data   1581
    Example 5:   Transformation Regression of Exhaust Emissions Data   1598
    Example 6:   Preference Mapping of Cars Data   1603
  REFERENCES   1610

ABSTRACT

The TRANSREG procedure obtains linear and nonlinear transformations of variables using the method of alternating least squares to fit the data to linear regression, canonical correlation, and analysis-of-variance models. Also, nonoptimal transformations for logarithm, rank, exponentiation, inverse sine, and logit are available.

INTRODUCTION

The TRANSREG (transformation regression) procedure is a data transformation procedure that lets you perform many types of analyses.

The TRANSREG procedure's optimal transformation capabilities should never be used as a preliminary step in hypothesis testing. The usual assumptions that must be made to test hypotheses in general linear model analyses are violated when the variables are optimally transformed. The usual test statistics reported by the REG and GLM procedures are not valid for optimally transformed variables. TRANSREG should be used only for descriptive analyses. Sometimes there is a direct correspondence between fitting a model with the TRANSREG procedure's nonlinear transformations and fitting a model with the REG procedure and a larger set of variables. However, even in this situation, all test statistics, except possibly R^2, are not correct when the TRANSREG output data set is directly used as an input data set for the REG procedure. See **Example 2** for an illustration.

TRANSREG fits many types of linear models including

- simple and generalized conjoint analysis and other ANOVA models with optional variable transformations (de Leeuw, Young, and Takane 1976; Green and Wind 1975)
- metric and nonmetric vector and ideal point preference regression (Carroll 1972)
- simple, multiple, and multivariate regression with optional variable transformations (Young, de Leeuw, and Takane 1976; Winsberg and Ramsay 1980; Breiman and Friedman 1985)
- redundancy analysis (Stewart and Love 1968) with optional variable transformations (Israels 1984)
- canonical correlation analysis with optional variable transformations (van der Burg and de Leeuw 1983)
- response surface regression (Myers 1976; Khuri and Cornell 1987) with a variety of response surface models and optional variable transformations.

The data can contain variables with nominal, ordinal, interval, and ratio scales of measurement (Siegel 1956). Any mix of these variable types is allowed for the dependent and independent variables. For example,

- Nominal variables can be transformed by scoring the categories to minimize squared error (Fisher 1938) or they can be expanded into dummy variables.
- Ordinal variables can be transformed monotonically by scoring the ordered categories so that order is weakly preserved (adjacent categories can be merged) and squared error is minimized. Ties can be untied optimally or left tied (Kruskal 1964). Ordinal variables can also be transformed to ranks.
- Interval and ratio scale of measurement variables can be linearly transformed or nonlinearly transformed with spline (de Boor 1978; van Rijckevorsel 1982) or monotone spline (Winsberg and Ramsay 1980) transformations. In addition, nonoptimal transformations for logarithm, exponential, power, logit, and inverse trigonometric sine are available.
- For all transformations, missing data can be estimated without constraint, with category constraints (that is, missing values within the same group get the same value), and with order constraints (that is, missing value estimates in adjacent groups can be tied to weakly preserve a specified ordering) (Gifi 1981; Young 1981; Kuhfeld and de Leeuw, in preparation).

PROC TRANSREG is a scoring procedure. It generates only a small amount of printed output. It creates an output data set containing the transformed (optimally scaled) variables. You can then input these variables to other SAS procedures for further analysis. For example, you can use the PROC TRANSREG output data set as

- input to procedures such as PLOT, GPLOT, or G3D in order to obtain preference biplots, transformation plots, and so on
- input to procedures such as REG, CANCORR, ANOVA, or GLM in order to obtain final analyses; however, all p-values and significance tests should be ignored. The usual p-values computed from optimally transformed variables are generally much too small. TRANSREG should be used as an exploratory data analysis procedure, but never as a method of "maximizing significance" or "proving the alternative hypothesis."

Transformations produced by the PROC TRANSREG multiple regression algorithm, requesting spline transformations, are often similiar to transformations produced by the ACE smooth regression method of Breiman and Friedman (1985). However, ACE does not explicitly optimize a loss function (de Leeuw 1986), while PROC TRANSREG always explicitly optimizes a squared-error loss function.

Background

PROC TRANSREG extends the ordinary general linear model by providing optimal variable transformations that are iteratively derived using the method of alternating least squares (Young 1981). The ordinary regression model assumes that the variables are all measured on an equal interval scale and, therefore, can be geometrically represented as vectors in an n (the number of observations) dimensional space. In analysis of variance, the independent variables are nominal variables, so they are not correctly represented as single vectors. Nominal independent variables are expanded to design matrices, each column of which can be treated as a vector. Nominal dependent variables can also be handled within the framework of the ordinary general linear model (discriminant analysis).

An ordinary general linear model analysis can be cursorily described as taking a set of interval and nominal variables, expanding the nominal variables to a set of variables that can be treated as vectors, then fitting a regression (or canonical correlation) model to the expanded set of variables. The alternating least-squares algorithm adds one additional capability to the general linear model; it allows variables whose full representation is a matrix consisting of more than one vector to be represented by a single vector, which is an optimal linear combination of the columns of the matrix. For any type of linear model, an alternating least-squares program can solve for an optimal vector representation of any number of variables simultaneously.

Because the alternating least-squares algorithm can replace a matrix with a vector, it can be used for fitting a linear model for many types of variables, including

- interval variables
- ordinal variables with or without category constraints (Kruskal 1964)
- nominal variables within the space of a single vector (Fisher 1938)
- interval variables that should be nonlinearly transformed (van Rijckevorsel 1982)
- interval variables that should be nonlinearly but monotonically transformed (Winsberg and Ramsay 1980)
- any type of variable with some additional ordered or unordered categories (Kuhfeld and de Leeuw, in preparation)
- any type of variable with any mixture of missing value types that should be scored with or without category constraints (Gifi 1981; Young 1981)
- variables that consist of more than one measurement partition (Kuhfeld and de Leeuw, in preparation).

TRANSREG can handle any mixture of these cases. It iterates until convergence, alternating these two steps:

- finding least-squares estimates of the parameters of the model (given the current scoring of the data, that is, the current set of vectors)
- finding least-squares estimates of the scoring parameters (given the current set of model parameters).

For more background on alternating least-squares optimal scaling methods and transformation regression methods, see Young, de Leeuw, and Takane (1976), Winsberg and Ramsay (1980), Young (1981), Gifi (1981), Schiffman, Reynolds, and Young (1981), van der Burg and de Leeuw (1983), Israels (1984), de Leeuw (1986), Kuhfeld and de Leeuw (in preparation), Breiman and Friedman (1985), and Hastie and Tibshirani (1986). (These are just a few of the many relevant sources.)

Introductory Examples

This section gives several examples that illustrate features of the TRANSREG procedure.

Generating the Output Data Set

The following statements perform a simple conjoint analysis, monotonically transforming the variable Y to better fit a main effects analysis of variance model with factors X1 and X2:

```
title 'Introductory Conjoint Analysis Example';
data a;
    input y x1 $ x2 $;
    cards;
8 a a
7 a a
4 a b
3 a b
```

```
5 b a
4 b a
2 b b
1 b b
;

   /* Monotonically transform Y to better fit   */
   /* a main-effects ANOVA model.               */
proc transreg noprint;
   model monotone(Y) = class(X1 X2) / intercept;
   output coefficients;
run;

   /* Display TRANSREG output data set          */
proc print;
   format ty -- x2b 5.2;
run;
```

The input data set contains the variables Y, X1, and X2 and eight observations. TRANSREG produces the data set shown in **Output 40.1**.

Output 40.1 Output Data Set from PROC TRANSREG

```
                        Introductory Conjoint Analysis Example                              1

 OBS    _TYPE_    _NAME_    Y     TY    INTERCEP    X1A    X1B    X2A    X2B    X1    X2

  1     SCORE     ROW1      8    7.39     1.00       .     0.00    .     0.00    a     a
  2     SCORE     ROW2      7    7.39     1.00       .     0.00    .     0.00    a     a
  3     SCORE     ROW3      4    4.25     1.00       .     0.00    .     1.00    a     b
  4     SCORE     ROW4      3    4.25     1.00       .     0.00    .     1.00    a     b
  5     SCORE     ROW5      5    4.25     1.00       .     1.00    .     0.00    b     a
  6     SCORE     ROW6      4    4.25     1.00       .     1.00    .     0.00    b     a
  7     SCORE     ROW7      2    1.11     1.00       .     1.00    .     1.00    b     b
  8     SCORE     ROW8      1    1.11     1.00       .     1.00    .     1.00    b     b
  9     M COEFFI  TY        .      .      7.39       .    -3.14    .    -3.14
 10     MEAN      TY        .      .       .        5.82   2.68   5.82   2.68
```

The output data set has three kinds of observations, identified by values of _TYPE_.

- When _TYPE_='M COEFFI', the observation contains coefficients of the final linear model.
- When _TYPE_='MEAN', the observation contains the marginal means.
- When _TYPE_='SCORE', the observation contains information on the dependent and independent variables as follows:
  - Y is the original dependent variable, and TY contains the monotone transformation. The transformed variable has the same total sum of squares as the original, but the within-cell and interaction sums of squares have been minimized to zero.
  - X1 and X2 are the independent classification variables, and INTERCEP through X2B contain the main effects design matrix that TRANSREG creates.
  - X1B and X2B contain binary variables.
  - X1A and X2A contain missing values since by default a full rank parameterization is performed. (The X1A dummy variable would be

the difference INTERCEP−X1B, and the X2A dummy variable would be the difference INTERCEP−X2B.)
- By default, TRANSREG corrects variables for their mean by centering. Specifying the INTERCEPT option includes an intercept column of ones (another variable, named INTERCEP) in the output data set.

The observations with _TYPE_='M COEFFI' and _TYPE_='MEAN' form the *coefficient partition* of the data set, and the observations with _TYPE_='SCORE' form the *score partition* of the data set.

Detecting Nonlinear Relationships

TRANSREG can detect nonlinear relationships among variables. For example, suppose 400 observations are generated from the following function:

$$y = x / 4 + \sin(x) \quad .$$

The following statements find cubic spline transformations of both variables with four knots. Splines are curves, which are usually required to be continuous and smooth. Splines are usually defined as piecewise polynomials of degree n whose function values and first $n-1$ derivatives agree at the points where they join. The abscissa values of the join points are called *knots*. The term spline is also used for polynomials (splines with no knots) and piecewise polynomials with more than one discontinuous derivative. Splines with no knots are generally smoother than splines with knots, which are generally smoother than splines with multiple discontinuous derivatives. Splines with few knots are generally smoother than splines with many knots, however increasing the number of knots usually increases the fit of the spline function to the data. Knots give the curve freedom to bend to more closely follow the data. See Smith (1979) for an excellent introduction to splines.

The following statements produce **Output 40.2**:

```
title 'Curve Straightening Example';
   /*---Create Artificial Nonlinear Scatterplot---*/
data curve;
   pi=3.14159265359;
   pi4=4*pi;
   inc=pi4/400;
   do x=inc to pi4 by inc;
      y=x/4 + sin(x);
      output;
   end;
run;

   /*---Request Spline Transformations of Both Variables---*/
proc transreg data=curve;
   model spline(y / nknots=4)=spline(x / nknots=4);
   output;
run;

   /*---Plot the Results---*/
proc plot vpercent=50 hpercent=50;
   plot y*x ty*tx tx*x ty*y / box;
run;
```

TRANSREG increases the squared multiple correlation from the original value of 0.48447 to 0.99847. The resulting plot of Y by X shows the original function, and the plot of TY by TX shows the relationship between the transformed variables. The plots show how TRANSREG linearizes the relationship by finding an almost linear transformation of Y and a nonlinear transformation of X.

This problem is particularly well suited for TRANSREG because the data perfectly fit a curve, and portions of sine curves can be closely approximated by cubic polynomials. The large change in the squared correlation shows that transforming the variables before fitting the final linear model is very effective.

Output 40.2 Curve Straightening

```
                        Curve Straightening Example                             1

            TRANSREG MORALS Algorithm Iteration History For Dependent Variable Y

              Iteration    Average    Maximum    Squared    Criterion
              Number       Change     Change     Multiple R  Change
              -----------------------------------------------------------
                 1         0.45937    0.95564    0.48447       .
                 2         0.16190    0.60153    0.88264     0.39817
                 3         0.10561    0.26743    0.94403     0.06139
                 4         0.07334    0.25623    0.97098     0.02695
                 5         0.05021    0.18980    0.98516     0.01418
                 6         0.03407    0.13134    0.99218     0.00702
                 7         0.02305    0.08965    0.99553     0.00335
                 8         0.01559    0.06107    0.99710     0.00157
                 9         0.01055    0.04162    0.99784     0.00073
                10         0.00715    0.02838    0.99818     0.00034
                11         0.00485    0.01937    0.99833     0.00016
                12         0.00329    0.01323    0.99841     0.00007
                13         0.00224    0.00903    0.99844     0.00003
                14         0.00152    0.00617    0.99846     0.00002
                15         0.00103    0.00421    0.99846     0.00001
                16         0.00070    0.00287    0.99847     0.00000
                17         0.00048    0.00196    0.99847     0.00000
                18         0.00032    0.00134    0.99847     0.00000
                19         0.00022    0.00091    0.99847     0.00000
                20         0.00015    0.00062    0.99847     0.00000
                21         0.00010    0.00042    0.99847     0.00000
                22         0.00007    0.00029    0.99847     0.00000
                23         0.00005    0.00020    0.99847     0.00000
                24         0.00003    0.00013    0.99847     0.00000
                25         0.00002    0.00009    0.99847     0.00000
                26         0.00001    0.00006    0.99847     0.00000
                27         0.00001    0.00004    0.99847     0.00000
                28         0.00001    0.00003    0.99847     0.00000
```

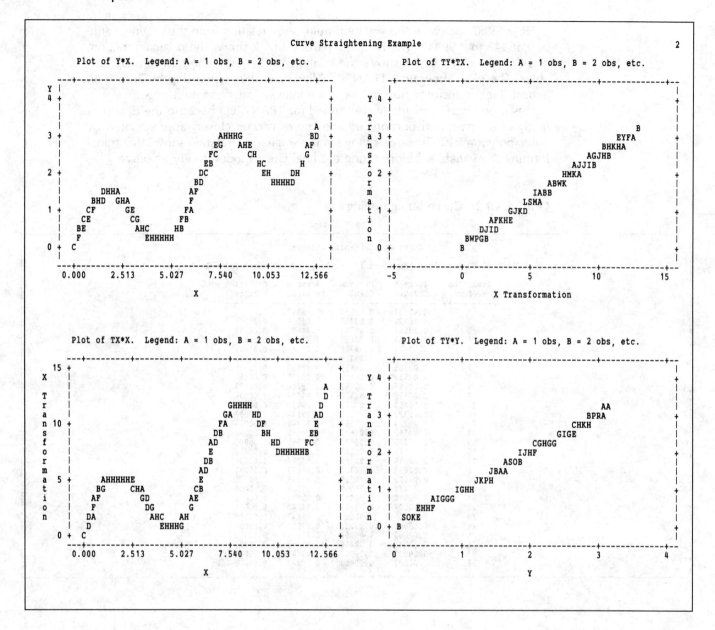

Nonlinear Transformations

This example illustrates a case where the variables do not define a nonlinear function. A sample of 400 observations is drawn from a bivariate normal population with mean vector zero, variances one, and correlation zero. The same TRANSREG statements as those shown above increase the sample squared correlation from 0.00350 to 0.04204. The plots below show that TRANSREG finds nonlinear transformations of both variables, but cannot linearize the relationship because no linear or nonlinear relationship exists. Thus, neither the plots of transformed variables nor plots of untransformed variables show a linear relationship.

The following statements produce **Output 40.3**:

```
title 'Introductory Bivariate Normal Example';
   /*---Create Bivariate Normal Scatterplot---*/
data normal;
   do i = 1 to 400;
      y = rannor(7654321);
      x = rannor(7654321);
      output;
   end;
   drop i;
run;

   /*---Spline Transformations of Both Variables---*/
proc transreg data=normal maxiter=20;
   model spline(y / nknots=4)=spline(x / nknots=4);
   output;
run;

   /*---Plot the Results---*/
proc plot vpercent=50 hpercent=50;
   plot y*x ty*tx tx*x ty*y / box;
run;
```

Output 40.3   Bivariate Normal Example Output

```
                    Introductory Bivariate Normal Example                      1

        TRANSREG MORALS Algorithm Iteration History For Dependent Variable Y

           Iteration   Average   Maximum   Squared     Criterion
           Number      Change    Change    Multiple R  Change
           ----------------------------------------------------------
               1       0.76791   2.11605   0.00350        .
               2       0.13754   3.48314   0.03546     0.03197
               3       0.08105   0.95359   0.03940     0.00394
               4       0.06597   0.61896   0.04033     0.00092
               5       0.05417   0.48264   0.04091     0.00058
               6       0.04374   0.40275   0.04131     0.00040
               7       0.03486   0.32614   0.04157     0.00027
               8       0.02758   0.26034   0.04175     0.00017
               9       0.02175   0.20623   0.04186     0.00011
              10       0.01711   0.16268   0.04193     0.00007
              11       0.01345   0.12804   0.04197     0.00004
              12       0.01057   0.10066   0.04200     0.00003
              13       0.00830   0.07909   0.04201     0.00002
              14       0.00652   0.06214   0.04203     0.00001
              15       0.00512   0.04881   0.04203     0.00001
              16       0.00403   0.03835   0.04204     0.00000
              17       0.00316   0.03014   0.04204     0.00000
              18       0.00249   0.02368   0.04204     0.00000
              19       0.00195   0.01861   0.04204     0.00000
              20       0.00154   0.01463   0.04204     0.00000
```

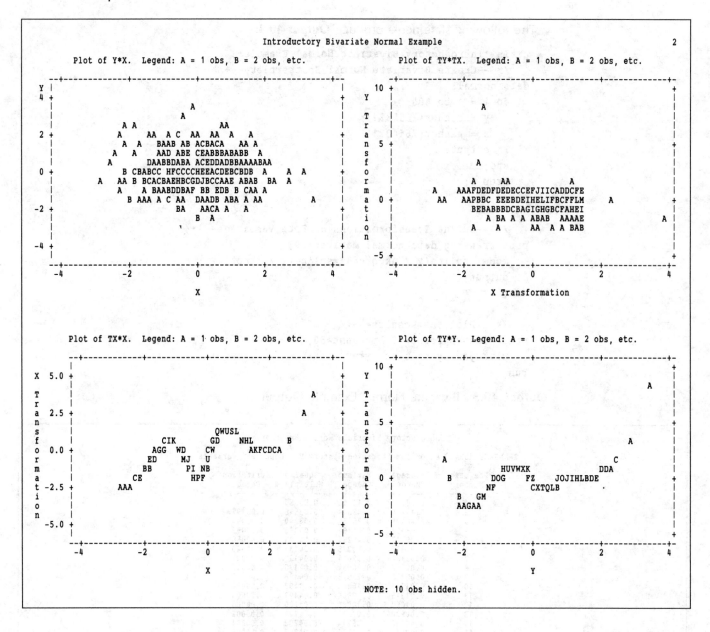

SPECIFICATIONS

The following statements are used in the TRANSREG procedure:

PROC TRANSREG <*option*>;
   MODEL *transform(dependents* < / *t-options*>)
      < . . . *transform(dependents*< / *t-options*>)>=
      transform(independents < / *t-options*>)
      < . . . *transform(independents*< / *t-options*>)>
      < / *options*>;

} required statements

   BY *variables*;
   ID *variables*;
   OUTPUT <OUT=*SAS-data-set*> <*options*>;

} optional statements

To use PROC TRANSREG, you need the PROC and MODEL statements. To produce an output data set, the OUTPUT statement is required. Unlike most procedures, TRANSREG allows you to specify the same options in more than one statement. All the *options* in the MODEL statement and all the *options* in the OUTPUT statement can also be specified in the PROC TRANSREG statement. (However, this is not true of the *t-options* nor the OUT= specification.) All *options* and *t-options* can be abbreviated to their first three letters. This is a special feature of TRANSREG, and is not generally true of other SAS/STAT procedures.

The options most frequently needed are DATA=, METHOD=, MAXITER=, CONVERGE=, TSTANDARD=, ADDITIVE, REPLACE, INTERCEPT, APPROXIMATIONS, COEFFICIENTS, and COORDINATES. You can specify all of these in the PROC TRANSREG statement.

The rest of this section gives detailed syntax information for each of the statements above, beginning with the PROC TRANSREG statement. The remaining statements are covered in alphabetical order.

PROC TRANSREG Statement

PROC TRANSREG <*options*>;

The PROC TRANSREG statement starts the TRANSREG procedure. Optionally, this statement identifies an input data set, specifies the algorithm and other computational details, and identifies variables to be included in the output data set (which is created with the OUTPUT statement). The table below summarizes options available in the PROC TRANSREG statement. All options except DATA= are described in sections on either the MODEL or OUTPUT statements.

Task	Option	Statement Where Described
Identify input data set	DATA=	PROC
Specify analysis method and control iterations	CCONVERGE=	MODEL
	CONVERGE=	MODEL
	MAXITER=	MODEL
	METHOD=	MODEL
	NCAN=	MODEL
	SINGULAR=	MODEL
Control how missing data handled	MONOTONE=	MODEL
	NOMISS	MODEL
	UNTIE=	MODEL
Control intercept and binary variables in design matrix	ALLCATS	MODEL
	INTERCEPT	MODEL
	NOINT	MODEL
Suppress printed output	NOPRINT	MODEL
Control contents for _TYPE_='SCORE' in output data set	ADDITIVE	OUTPUT
	NOSCORES	OUTPUT
	TSTANDARD=	OUTPUT
Control approximations for _TYPE_='SCORE' in output data set	APPROXIMATIONS	OUTPUT
	DAPPROXIMATIONS	OUTPUT
	IAPPROXIMATIONS	OUTPUT
Control replacement when _TYPE_='SCORE in output data set	DREPLACE	OUTPUT
	IREPLACE	OUTPUT
	REPLACE	OUTPUT
Control contents for coefficients and means in output data set	COEFFICIENTS	OUTPUT
	COORDINATES	OUTPUT
	MEANS	OUTPUT
Control details for coefficients and means in output data set	CCC	OUTPUT
	CEC	OUTPUT
	CPC	OUTPUT
	CQC	OUTPUT
	MEC	OUTPUT
	MPC	OUTPUT
	MQC	OUTPUT
	MRC	OUTPUT
Control prefixes for variable names in output data set	ADPREFIX=	OUTPUT
	AIPREFIX=	OUTPUT
	CPREFIX=	OUTPUT
	TDPREFIX=	OUTPUT
	TIPREFIX=	OUTPUT
Specify output data set	OUT=	OUTPUT

The DATA= option is described below.

DATA=*SAS-data-set*
> names the SAS data set to be analyzed. If you do not specify the DATA= option, PROC TRANSREG uses the most recently created SAS data set.

BY Statement

> **BY** *variables*;

A BY statement can be used with PROC TRANSREG to obtain separate analyses on observations in groups defined by the BY variables. When a BY statement appears, the procedure expects the input data set to be sorted in order of the BY variables.

If your input data set is not sorted in ascending order, use one of the following alternatives:

- Use the SORT procedure with a similar BY statement to sort the data.
- Use the BY statement options NOTSORTED or DESCENDING in the BY statement for the TRANSREG procedure. As a cautionary note, the NOTSORTED option does not mean that the data are unsorted, but rather means that the data are arranged in groups (according to values of the BY variables) and that these groups are not necessarily in alphabetical or increasing numeric order.
- Use the DATASETS procedure (in base SAS software) to create an index on the BY variables.

For more information on the BY statement, see the discussion in *SAS Language: Reference, Version 6, First Edition*. For more information on the DATASETS procedure, see the discussion in *SAS Procedures Guide, Release 6.06 Edition*.

ID Statement

> **ID** *variables*;

The ID statement includes additional character or numeric variables in the output data set. The *variables* must be contained in the input data set.

MODEL Statement

> **MODEL** *transform(dependents < / t-options>)*
> *< . . . transform(dependents < / t-options>)>=*
> *transform(independents < / t-options>)*
> *< . . . transform(independents < / t-options>)>*
> *< / options>*;

The MODEL statement names the dependent and independent variables (*dependents* and *independents*, respectively) and specifies the transformation (*transform*) to apply to each variable. The *t-options* are transformation options that give details for the transformation; these depend on the *transform* chosen. The *t-options* are listed after a slash in the parentheses that enclose the variable list (either dependents or independents). The *options* control the algorithm used, details of iteration, details of how the intercept and binary class variables are generated in the design matrix, and printed output details. The *options* are listed after the entire model specification (the dependents, independents, transformations, and *t-options*) and after a slash. These *options* can also be specified in the PROC TRANSREG statement.

The next three sections discuss the transformations available (specified with *transform*), the options available for some of the transformations (specified with *t-options*), and the options available regardless of the transformation (specified with *options*).

Families of Transformations

In the MODEL statement, *transform* specifies a transformation in one of three families.

variable expansions
> preprocess the specified variables, replacing them with more variables.

nonoptimal transformations
> preprocess the specified variables, replacing each one with a single new nonoptimal, nonlinear transformation.

optimal transformations
> replace the specified variables with new iteratively derived optimal transformation variables that fit the specified model better than the original variable (except for contrived cases where the transformation fits the model exactly as well as the original variable).
>
> NOTE: The optimal transformation capabilities should never be used as a preliminary step in hypothesis testing. The usual assumptions that must be made to test hypotheses in general linear model analyses are violated after variables are optimally transformed. The usual test statistics reported by PROC REG and PROC GLM are not valid for optimally transformed variables. For more detail, see **Example 2** later in this chapter.

The table below summarizes the transformations in each family.

Family	Members of Family
Variable expansions	
create set of dummy variables	CLASS
create elliptical response surface	EPOINT
create circular response surface	POINT
create quadratic response surface	QPOINT
Nonoptimal transformations	
inverse trignonometric sine	ARSIN
exponentiates variables	EXP
logarithm	LOG
logit	LOGIT
raises variables to specified power	POWER
transforms to ranks	RANK
Optimal transformations	
linear	LINEAR
monotonic, ties preserved	MONOTONE
monotonic B-spline	MSPLINE
optimal scoring	OPSCORE
B-spline	SPLINE
monotonic, ties not preserved	UNTIE

Any transformation can be used with either dependent or independent variables. However, the variable expansions are generally more appropriate for independent variables.

The *transform* is followed by a variable (or list of variables) enclosed in parentheses. Optionally, depending on the *transform*, the parentheses may also contain *t-options*, which follow the variables and a slash. For example,

```
model log(y)=class(x);
```

uses the LOG transformation of Y and the CLASS *transform* of X. A more complex example is

```
model spline(y / nknots=3)=log(x1 x2 x3);
```

The statement above uses the SPLINE transformation of Y and the LOG transformation of X1, X2, and X3. In addition, the NKNOTS= *t-option* is used with the SPLINE transformation, and specifies three knots.

The rest of this section gives syntax details for members of the three families of transformations. For more on *t-options*, see **Transformation Options (*t-options*)**, which follows this section.

Variable expansions   TRANSREG performs variable expansions before iteration begins. Variable expansions expand the original variables into a larger set of new variables. The *original variables* are those that are listed in parentheses after *transform*, and are sometimes referred to as *POINT variables*, *EPOINT variables*, or *QPOINT variables*. The variables following a CLASS *transform* are referred to as *CLASS expansion variables*, and the expanded variables are referred to as *dummy variables*.

The resulting variables are not transformed by the iterative algorithms after the initial preprocessing. Observations with missing values for these types of variables are excluded from the analysis.

POINT, EPOINT, and QPOINT are used in preference mapping analyses (also called PREFMAP, external unfolding, ideal point regression) (Carroll 1972) and for response surface regressions. These three expansions create circular, elliptical, and quadratic response or preference surfaces (see **Point Models** later in this chapter). CLASS is used for main effects *ANOVA*.

The list below gives syntax and details for the variable expansion *transforms*.

CLASS
CLA

> expands each variable to a set of dummy variables. The column for the first category is set to missing unless you use the ALLCATS option (listed after a slash after the entire model specification).
>
> Variables following CLASS can be character or numeric, but should be categorical. To determine class membership, TRANSREG uses the first eight characters of the formatted values of the variable.

EPOINT
EPO

> expands the variables to create an elliptical response or preference surface. EPOINT is used for elliptical response surface regression or for elliptical ideal point regression.
>
> Each axis of the ellipse (or ellipsoid) is oriented in the same direction as one of the variables. EPOINT creates a new variable for each original variable. The value of each new variable is the square of each observed value for the corresponding parenthesized variable. The regression analysis then uses both sets of variables (original and squared).
>
> Variables following EPOINT must be numeric.

POINT
POI

expands the variables to create a circular response or preference surface. POINT is used for a circular response surface regression or circular ideal point regression.

POINT creates a new variable whose value for each observation is the sums of squares of all the POINT variables. This new variable is added to the set of variables and used in the regression analysis. For more on ideal point regression, see Carroll (1972).

Variables following POINT must be numeric.

QPOINT
QPO

expands the variables to create a quadratic response or preference surface. QPOINT is used for a quadratic response surface regression or quadratic ideal point regression.

For m QPOINT variables, $m(m+1)/2$ new variables are created containing the squares and crossproducts of the original variables. The regression analysis uses both sets (original and crossed).

Variables following QPOINT must be numeric.

Nonoptimal transformations   Like variable expansions, nonoptimal transformations are computed before the iterative algorithm begins. Nonoptimal transformations create a single new transformed variable that replaces the original variable. The new variable is not transformed by the subsequent iterative algorithms (except for a possible linear transformation and missing value estimation).

TRANSREG prints error messages

- if the input values are invalid, such as negative numbers when square root or log transformations are requested
- if the transformation would cause an arithmetic overflow, such as raising a large number to a large power
- if the transformed values are so large that overflow is possible in subsequent calculations.

The list below gives syntax and details for nonoptimal variable transformations.

ARSIN
ARS

finds an inverse trigonometric sine transformation on the variables in the interval $(-1.0 \leq x \leq 1.0)$. This transformation is performed before iterative analysis begins. Variables following ARSIN must be numeric.

EXP

exponentiates variables (x is transformed to a^x) before the iterative analysis begins. Variables following EXP must be numeric. To specify the value of a, use the PARAMETER= t-option. (By default, a is the mathematical constant e (2.718. . .).

LOG

transforms variables to logarithms ($log_a x$ for data value x) before the iterative analysis begins. Variables following LOG must be numeric and positive. To specify the base of the logarithm, use the PARAMETER= t-option. The default is a natural logarithm with base e (2.718. . .).

LOGIT

finds a logit transformation on the variables in the interval $(0.0 < x < 1.0)$ before the iterative analysis begins. Variables following LOGIT must be numeric. The logit of x is $log(x/(1-x))$. Unlike other transformations, LOGIT does not have a three-letter abbreviation.

POWER
POW

raises variables to a specified power (x^a for data value x) before the iterative analysis begins. Variables following POWER must be numeric. In addition, you must specify the power parameter a by specifying PARAMETER= following the variables:

```
power(variables / parameter=number);
```

You can use POWER for squaring variables (PARAMETER=2), reciprocal transformations (PARAMETER= -1), square roots (PARAMETER=0.5), and so on.

RANK
RAN

transforms variables to ranks before the iterative analysis begins. Ranks are averaged within ties. The smallest input value is assigned the smallest rank. Variables following RANK must be numeric.

Optimal transformations   Optimal transformations are iteratively derived. Missing values for these types of variables can be optimally estimated (see **Missing Values** later in this chapter).

The optimal transformation capabilities should never be used as a preliminary step in hypothesis testing. The usual assumptions that must be made to test hypotheses in general linear model analyses are violated after variables are optimally transformed. The usual test statistics reported by PROC REG and PROC GLM are not valid for optimally transformed variables. Sometimes there is a direct correspondence between fitting a model with the TRANSREG procedure's nonlinear transformation and fitting a model with the REG procedure and a larger set of variables. However, even in this situation, all test statistics, except possibly R^2, are incorrect when the TRANSREG output data set is directly used as an input data set for the REG procedure. See **Example 2** for an illustration.

The list below gives syntax and details for optimal transformations.

LINEAR
LIN

finds an optimal linear transformation of each variable. For variables with no missing values, the transformed variable is the same as the original variable. For variables with missing values, the transformed nonmissing values have a different scale and origin from the original values. Variables following LINEAR must be numeric.

MONOTONE
MON

finds a monotonic transformation of each variable, with the restriction that ties are preserved. The Kruskal (1964) secondary least-squares monotonic transformation is used. This transformation weakly preserves order and category membership (ties). Variables following MONOTONE must be numeric and are typically discrete.

MSPLINE
MSP

finds a monotonically increasing B-spline transformation with monotonic coefficients (de Boor 1978; de Leeuw 1986) of each variable.

By default, TRANSREG uses a quadratic spline. Knots and other degrees can be specified as *t-options*; see **Transformation Options (*t-options*)** below.

Variables following MSPLINE must be numeric and are typically discrete.

OPSCORE
OPS

> finds an optimal scoring of each variable. OPSCORE assigns scores to each class (level) of the variable. Fisher's (1938) optimal scoring method is used. Variables following OPSCORE can be either character or numeric; numeric variables should be discrete.

SPLINE
SPL

> finds a B-spline transformation (de Boor 1978) of each variable. By default, TRANSREG uses a cubic polynomial transformation. Knots and other degrees can be specified as *t-options*; see **Transformation Options (*t-options*)** below.
>
> Variables following SPLINE must be numeric, and are typically continuous.

UNTIE
UNT

> finds a monotonic transformation of each variable without the restriction that ties are preserved. TRANSREG uses the Kruskal (1964) primary least-squares monotonic transformation method. This transformation weakly preserves order but not category membership (it may untie some previously tied values).
>
> Variables following UNTIE must be numeric, and are typically discrete.

For more detail on splines, see **Optimal Scaling** and **Example 1** later in this chapter. For information on the algorithms used, see SAS Technical Report: R-108, *Algorithms for the PRINQUAL and TRANSREG Procedures*.

Transformation Options (*t-options*)

If you use either a nonoptimal or optimal *transform*, you can use *t-options*, which specify additional details of the transformation. The *t-options* are specified within the parentheses that enclose variables, and are listed after a slash. They can be used with both dependent and independent variables, for example:

```
proc transreg;
   model spline(y / nknots=3)=linear(x);
   output;
run;
```

The statements above use an optimal variable transformation (SPLINE) of the dependent variable, and use a *t-option* to specify the number of knots (NKNOTS=). Below is a more complex example:

```
proc transreg;
   model spline(y / nknots=3)=spline(x1 x2 / nknots=2);
   output;
run;
```

These statements use the SPLINE transformation for both the dependent variable and the independent variables, and use *t-options* for both; NKNOTS= specifies the number of knots for the spline.

The sections below discuss the *t-options* available for nonoptimal and optimal transformations.

Nonoptimal transformation *t-options*   Two options are available with the nonoptimal transformations.

ORIGINAL
ORI

   matches the variable's final mean and variance to the mean and variance
   of the original variable. By default, the mean and variance are based on
   the transformed values. ORIGINAL is available for all of the nonoptimal
   transformations.

PARAMETER=*number*
PAR=*number*

   specifies the transformation parameter. PARAMETER= is available for
   the EXP, LOG, and POWER transformations. It is required for the
   POWER transformation. For EXP, the parameter is the value to be
   exponentiated; for LOG, the parameter is the base value; for POWER,
   the parameter is the power. The default for PARAMETER= for LOG and
   EXP is e (2.718. . .). For the POWER transformation, PARAMETER= must
   be specified; there is no default.

Optimal transformation *t-options* The following options are available with
SPLINE and MSPLINE transformations:

DEGREE=*n*
DEG=*n*

   specifies the degree of the B-spline transformation. The degree can be
   any nonnegative integer. The defaults are DEGREE=3 for SPLINE
   variables and DEGREE=2 for MSPLINE variables.
      The polynomial degree must be ≥ 0, and should be a small integer,
   usually 0, 1, 2, or 3. Larger values are rarely useful. If you have any
   doubt as to what degree to specify, use the default.

KNOTS=*number-list* | *n* TO *m* BY *p*
KNO=*number-list* | *n* TO *m* BY *p*

   specifies the interior knots or break points. By default, there are no
   knots. The first time a value is specified in the knot list, it indicates a
   discontinuity in the *n*th (from DEGREE=*n*) derivative of the
   transformation function at the value of the knot. The second mention of
   a value indicates a discontinuity in the $(n-1)$th derivative of the
   transformation function at the value of the knot. Knots can be repeated
   any number of times for decreasing smoothness at the break points, but
   the values in the knot list can never decrease.
      You cannot use the KNOTS= option with the NKNOTS= option.
   Keep the number of knots small (see discussion below).

NKNOTS=*n*
NKN=*n*

   creates *n* knots, the first at the $100/(n+1)$ percentile, the second at the
   $200/(n+1)$ percentile, and so on. Knots are always placed at data
   values; there is no interpolation. For example, if NKNOTS=3, knots are
   placed at the twenty-fifth percentile, the median, and the seventy-fifth
   percentile. By default, NKNOTS=0. NKNOTS= must be ≥ 0.
      You cannot use the NKNOTS= option with the KNOTS= option.
   Keep the number of knots small (see discussion below).

Keep the number of knots small (usually less than 10) although you can specify
more. A degree three spline with nine knots, one at each decile, can closely follow a large variety of curves. Each spline transformation of degree *p* with *q* knots
requires that a model with *p*+*q* parameters be fit. The total number of parameters
should be much less than the number of observations. Usually in regression analyses, it is recommended that there be at least five or ten observations for each

parameter, in order to get stable results. For example, when spline transformations of degree three with nine knots are requested for six variables, the number of observations in the data set should be at least five or ten times 72 (since 6*(3+9) is the total number of parameters). The overall model may also have a parameter for the intercept and one or more parameters for each non-spline variable in the model.

Increasing the number of knots gives the spline more freedom to bend and follow the data. Increasing the degree also gives the spline more freedom, but to a lesser degree. Specifying a large number of knots is much better than increasing the degree beyond three.

When NKNOTS=q is specified for a variable with n observations, then each of the $q+1$ segments of the spline will contain ($n/(q+1)$) observations on the average. When you specify KNOTS=*number-list*, make sure that there is a reasonable number of observations in each interval.

As an example, the following statements find a cubic polynomial transformation of Y and a linear transformation of X:

```
proc transreg;
   model spline(y)=linear(x);
   output;
run;
```

The statements below find a linear transformation of X and a cubic spline transformation curve for Y that consists of the weighted sum of a single constant, a single straight line, a quadratic curve for the portion of the variable less than 3.0, a different quadratic curve for the portion greater than 3.0 (since the 3.0 break point is repeated), and a different cubic curve for each of the intervals: (minimum to 1.5), (1.5 to 2.4), (2.4 to 3.0), (3.0 to 4.0), (4.0 to maximum). In other words, the transformation curve is continuous everywhere, its first derivative is continuous everywhere, its second derivative is continuous everywhere except at 3.0; and its third derivative is continuous everywhere except at 1.5, 2.4, 3.0, and 4.0.

```
proc transreg;
   model spline(y / knots=1.5 2.4 3.0 3.0 4.0)=linear(x);
   output;
run;
```

The statements below find a quadratic spline transformation that consists of a polynomial: $Y_t=b_0+b_1Y+b_2Y^2$ for the range (Y<3.0) and a completely different polynomial $Y_t=b_3+b_4Y+b_5Y^2$ for the range (Y>3.0). The two curves are not required to be continuous at 3.0. Again, the statements find a linear transformation of X.

```
proc transreg;
   model spline(y / knots=3 3 3 degree=2)=linear(x);
   output;
run;
```

The statements below categorize Y into 10 intervals and find a step-function transformation. One aspect of this transformation family is unlike all other optimal transformation families. The initial scaling of the data does not fit the restrictions imposed by the transformation family. This is because the initial variable can be continuous, but a discrete step function transformation is sought. Zero degree spline variables are categorized before the first iteration. The statements below also find a linear transformation of X.

```
proc transreg;
   model spline(y / degree=0 nknots=9)=linear(x);
   output;
run;
```

The statements below find a continuous, piecewise linear transformation of Y and a linear transformation of X.

```
proc transreg;
   model spline(y / degree=1 nknots=8)=linear(x);
   output;
run;
```

The examples above show various spline transformations of Y with the same linear transformation of X. This is for illustrative purposes only; you could perform different transformations for several dependent and independent variables.

Options in the MODEL Statement

This section discusses the *options* in the MODEL statement. These are listed after the entire model specification and after a slash, for example,

```
proc transreg;
   model spline(y / nknots=3)=log(x1 x2 / parameter=2)
         / nomiss maxiter=50;
   output;
run;
```

In the statements above, NOMISS and MAXITER= are *options*. (SPLINE and LOG are *transforms*, and NKNOTS= and PARAMETER= are *t-options*.) The statements find a spline transformation with 3 knots on Y and a base 2 logarithmic transformation on X1 and X2. NOMISS excludes all observations with missing values and MAXITER= specifies the maximum number of iterations.

The table below summarizes the options available in the MODEL statement.

Task	Options
Specify analysis method and control iterations	
minimum change in criterion optimized	CCONVERGE=
minimum average absolute change	CONVERGE=
maximum number of iterations	MAXITER=
iterative algorithm	METHOD=
number of canonical variables used	NCAN=
effective zero	SINGULAR=
Control how missing data handled	
special values, within order and category constraints	MONOTONE=
exclude observations with missing values	NOMISS
special values, within order constraints	UNTIE=
Control intercept and binary variables in design matrix	
one binary variable per class category	ALLCATS
include intercept	INTERCEPT
omit intercept, do not center variables	NOINT
Suppress printed output	NOPRINT

The list below gives details on these options.

ALLCATS
ALL
creates one binary dummy variable for each category of each CLASS expansion variable. By default, a binary dummy variable is not created for the first category found. When you specify the CLASS *transform*, the output data set always includes a column for each category to allow for different categories across BY groups and for the output of marginal means. ALLCATS controls whether one column per CLASS expansion variable contains a zero/one dummy variable, or contains missing values that are ignored when the linear model is fit.

If you specify ALLCATS and also specify COEFFICIENTS in the OUTPUT statement, the model is less-than-full-rank, and the procedure issues a warning message to that effect.

CCONVERGE=*n*
CCO=*n*
specifies the minimum change in the criterion being optimized (squared multiple correlation for MORALS and UNIVARIATE, average squared multiple correlation for REDUNDANCY, average squared canonical correlation for CANALS) that is required to continue iterating. By default, CCONVERGE=0.0.

CONVERGE=*n*
CON=*n*
specifies the minimum average absolute change in standardized variable scores that is required to continue iterating.
By default, CONVERGE=0.00001.

Average change is computed over only those variables that can be nontrivially transformed by the iterations; that is, all variables with missing values, and all variables specified for OPSCORE, MONOTONE, UNTIE, SPLINE, and MSPLINE transformations.

INTERCEPT
INT
includes a variable, INTERCEP, which usually is a column of ones in the output data set. Internally, during the iterations, the variables are centered to correct for their means.

MAXITER=*n*
MAX=*n*
specifies the maximum number of iterations. By default, MAXITER=30.

METHOD=CANALS | CAN
        | MORALS | MOR
        | REDUNDANCY | RED
        | UNIVARIATE | UNI
MET=CANALS | CAN
    | MORALS | MOR
    | REDUNDANCY | RED
    | UNIVARIATE | UNI
specifies the iterative algorithm. By default, METHOD=UNIVARIATE, unless you specify options that cannot be handled by UNIVARIATE. Specifically, the default is METHOD=MORALS for the following situations:

- if you specify MONOTONE, UNTIE, OPSCORE, SPLINE, or MSPLINE transformations for the independent variables

- if you specify the ADDITIVE option (in the PROC TRANSREG or OUTPUT statement) with more than one dependent variable
- if you specify IAPPROXIMATIONS.

CANALS specifies canonical correlation with alternating least squares. This jointly transforms all dependent and independent variables to maximize the average of the first n-squared canonical correlations, where n is the value of the NCAN= option.

MORALS specifies multiple optimal regression with alternating least squares. This transforms each dependent variable, along with the set of independent variables, to maximize the squared multiple correlation.

REDUNDANCY jointly transforms all dependent and independent variables to maximize the average of the squared multiple correlations.

UNIVARIATE transforms each dependent variable to maximize the squared multiple correlation, while the independent variables are not transformed.

MONOTONE=*two-letters*

MON=*two-letters*

specifies the first and last special missing value in the list of those special missing values to be estimated using within-variable order and category constraints. By default there are no order constraints on missing value estimates. The *two-letters* value must consist of two letters in alphabetical order. For example, MONOTONE=DF means that the estimate of .D must be less than or equal to the estimate of .E, which must be less than or equal to the estimate of .F, while no order constraints are placed on estimates of .__, .A through .C, and .G through .Z. For details, see **Missing Values** later in this chapter.

NCAN=*n*

NCA=*n*

specifies the number of canonical variables to use in the METHOD=CANALS algorithm. By default, NCAN=1. The value of NCAN= must be ≥ 1.

When canonical coefficients and coordinates are included in the output data set, NCAN= also controls the number of rows of the canonical coefficient matrices in the data set. If you specify an NCAN= value larger than the minimum of the number of dependent variables and the number of independent variables, TRANSREG prints a warning and sets NCAN= to the maximum allowable value.

NOINT

NOI

omits the intercept from the output data set, and suppresses centering of data. By default, the variables are centered during the iterations.

NOMISS

NOM

excludes all observations with missing values from the analysis. If you omit NOMISS, TRANSREG simultaneously computes the optimal transformations of the nonmissing values and estimates the missing values that minimize least-squares error. For details, see **Missing Values** later in this chapter.

NOPRINT

NOP

suppresses printed output.

SINGULAR=*n*
SIN=*n*

    specifies the largest value within rounding error of zero. By default, SINGULAR=1E–8. SINGULAR= is used for checking $(1-R^2)$ when constructing full rank matrices of predictor variables, checking denominators before dividing, and so on. The typical range for the value of SINGULAR= is 1E–6 through 1E–10, inclusive.

UNTIE=*two-letters*
UNT=*two-letters*

    specifies the first and last special missing value in the list of those special missing values that are to be estimated with within-variable constraints but no category order constraints. The *two-letters* value must consist of two letters in alphabetical order. By default, there are category but no order constraints on special missing value estimates. For details, see **Missing Values** and **Optimal Scaling** later in this chapter.

Using the MODEL Statement

PROC TRANSREG allows you to easily perform ordinary and monotone multiple regression analyses, conjoint analyses, and ideal point analyses by constructing your MODEL statement as shown in the following examples. (Note that METHOD=UNIVARIATE for each of these statements.)

MODEL Statement	Performs
`model linear(y1-y5) = linear(x1-x4);`	ordinary multivariate multiple regression analysis.
`model monotone(y1-y5) = linear(x1-x4);`	monotone multivariate multiple regression analysis.
`model monotone(y1) = class(x1-x2);`	simple conjoint analysis.

`model monotone(y1) = point(x1-x3);`
`model monotone(y1) = epoint(x1-x3);`
`model monotone(y1) = qpoint(x1-x3);`
	PREFMAP or ideal point regression analyses (Carroll 1972) of increasing complexity.

    You cannot specify interaction terms in *ANOVA* analyses directly. Also, you cannot specify regression models with knots, multiple intercepts, multiple slopes, and so on, in a direct way. However, you can run these models in TRANSREG by coding the dummy variables directly and inputting them for LINEAR optimal variable transformations.

    You can also run models with main effects and interactions by creating a single cell membership indicator variable in a DATA step. If you specify that variable in a CLASS expansion and also specify the NOINT and ALLCATS options, a full rank cell means model (a model with main effects and interactions) is fit. If you specify that variable in a CLASS expansion, and specify INTERCEPT, a full rank reference cell model (also a model with main effects and interactions) is fit.

There are many typical MODEL statement forms. You can use any mix of the OPSCORE, LINEAR, MONOTONE, and UNTIE optimal variable transformations to fit a mixed measurement level model. Often, you may need to specify only one transformation or expansion for all the independent variables. Usually it is either the LINEAR optimal variable transformation, or one of the variable expansions CLASS, POINT, QPOINT, or EPOINT. When you specify one of these, the independent variables are not transformed. Rather, they are expanded and then remain unchanged throughout the analysis. Usually, you specify one of the optimal or nonoptimal transformations for the dependent variables, although any mix is allowed. Use complicated mixes with caution.

OUTPUT Statement

OUTPUT <OUT=*SAS-data-set*> <*options*>;

The OUTPUT statement creates a new SAS data set that contains coefficients, marginal means, and information on original and transformed variables. The information on original and transformed variables composes the *score partition* of the data set; observations have _TYPE_='SCORE'. The coefficients and marginal means compose the *coefficient partition* of the data set; observations have _TYPE_='M COEFFI' or _TYPE_='MEAN'. Other values of _TYPE_ are possible; for details, see **_TYPE_ and _NAME_ Variables** later in this chapter. For details on data set structure, see **Output Data Set** later in this chapter.

To name the data set, use the OUT= specification.

OUT=*SAS-data-set*

names the output data set. When you use an OUTPUT statement but do not use the OUT= specification, TRANSREG creates a data set and uses the DATA*n* convention. If you want to create a permanent SAS data set, you must specify a two-level name (see "SAS Files" in *SAS Language: Reference, Version 6, First Edition* and "Introduction to DATA Step Processing" in *SAS Language and Procedures: Usage, Version 6, First Edition* for details).

To control the contents of the data set and variable names use one or more of the options available. These options can also be specified in the PROC TRANSREG statement.

The default contents of the data set depend on the transformations and options specified in the MODEL statement.

By default, TRANSREG constructs variable names from a prefix and the first characters of the original variable name. The number of characters in the prefix plus the number of characters in the original variable name required to uniquely designate the new variables should not exceed eight. By default, TRANSREG uses the prefix 'A' for approximations for dependent and independent variables, the prefix 'T' for transformed dependent and independent variables, and the first 7 letters of a CLASS expansion variable (specified with the CLASS *transform* in the MODEL statement). For example, if you specify ADPREFIX=X, TRANSREG adds the first seven characters of the original variable name to the prefix X; if the original variable name is TEMPERAT, the new variable name is XTEMPERA. If you specify ADPREFIX=APRX and the original variable name is TEMPERAT, the new variable name is APRXTEMP.

The table below provides a summary of options in the OUTPUT statement.

Task	Option
Control contents for _TYPE_='SCORE' in output data set	
scale independent variables for additive model	ADDITIVE
standardization of means and variances of transformed variables	TSTANDARD=
exclude _TYPE_='SCORE' observations	NOSCORE
Control approximations for _TYPE_='SCORE' in output data set	
approximations to transformed variables	APPROXIMATIONS
approximations to transformed dependents	DAPPROXIMATIONS
approximations to transformed independents	IAPPROXIMATIONS
Control replacement when _TYPE_='SCORE' in output data set	
replace dependents with transformed variables	DREPLACE
replace independents with transformed variables	IREPLACE
replace variables with transformed variables	REPLACE
Control contents for coefficients and means in output data set	
canonical or multiple regression coefficients	COEFFICIENTS
external unfolding ideal point coordinates	COORDINATES
marginal means	MEANS
Control details for coefficients and means in output data set	
canonical correlation coefficients	CCC
canonical elliptical point model coordinates	CEC
canonical point model coordinates	CPC
canonical quadratic point model coordinates	CQC
multiple regression elliptical point model coordinates	MEC
multiple regression point model coordinates	MPC
multiple regression quadratic point model coordinates	MQC
multiple regression coefficients	MRC
Control prefixes for variable names in output data set	
dependent variable approximations	ADPREFIX=
independent variable approximations	AIPREFIX=
binary CLASS expansion variables	CPREFIX=
transformed dependent variables	TDPREFIX=
transformed independent variables	TIPREFIX=

For the coefficients partition, the COEFFICIENTS, COORDINATES, and MEANS options provide appropriate coefficients information, which depends on the transformation chosen. For more explicit control of the coefficient partition, use the options that control details and prefixes.

The list below gives details on these options.

ADDITIVE
ADD

> creates an additive model by multiplying the value of each independent variable (after the TSTANDARD= standardization) by that variable's corresponding multiple regression coefficient. This process scales the independent variables so that the predicted-values variable for the final

dependent variable is simply the sum of the final independent variables. An additive model is a univariate multiple regression model. As a result, ADDITIVE is not valid if METHOD=CANALS, or if METHOD=REDUNDANCY or UNIVARIATE with more than one dependent variable.

ADPREFIX=name

ADP=name

specifies a prefix for naming the dependent variable approximations. The default is ADPREFIX=A. Specifying ADPREFIX= also implies the output data set score partition option DAPPROXIMATIONS.

AIPREFIX=name

AIP=name

specifies a prefix for naming the independent variable approximations. The default is AIPREFIX=A. Specifying AIPREFIX= also implies the IAPPROXIMATIONS option.

APPROXIMATIONS

APPROX

APP

is equivalent to specifying both DAPPROXIMATIONS and IAPPROXIMATIONS. If METHOD=UNIVARIATE, then APPROXIMATIONS implies only DAPPROXIMATIONS.

CCC

includes canonical correlation coefficients.

CEC

includes canonical elliptical point model coordinates.

COEFFICIENTS

COE

includes either raw canonical coefficients or multiple regression coefficients.

If you specify METHOD=CANALS (in the MODEL or PROC TRANSREG statement), then COEFFICIENTS outputs the first n canonical variables, where n is the value of the NCAN= option (specified in the MODEL or PROC TRANSREG statement).

Otherwise, COEFFICIENTS includes multiple regression coefficients in the output data set. In addition, when you specify the CLASS *transform* for any independent variable, COEFFICIENTS outputs marginal means.

COORDINATES

COO

includes external unfolding ideal point coordinates in the output data set. When METHOD=CANALS, these coordinates are computed from canonical coefficients; otherwise, the coordinates are computed from multiple regression coefficients. For details, see **Point Models** later in this chapter.

CPC

includes canonical point model coordinates.

CPREFIX=n

CPR=n

specifies the number of first characters of a CLASS expansion variable's name to use in constructing names for binary variables in the output data set. The default is CPREFIX=7, except when a format is specified for a CLASS expansion variable; then the default for that variable is $8 - min(7, max(1, f))$, where f is the format length. Dummy variable names are constructed by appending the first $(8-n)$ characters of the formatted CLASS expansion variable's value to the n character prefix. If n is greater than a CLASS expansion variable name's length, n is decremented accordingly for that CLASS expansion variable. When CPREFIX=0, dummy variable names are created entirely from the CLASS expansion variable's formatted values.

You must ensure that CPREFIX= and the CLASS expansion variable values will combine to uniquely identify the dummy variable. For example, when VAR1 and VAR2 both have the values *1* and *2*, the statements

```
proc transreg;
    model monotone(y) = class(var1-var2);
    output cprefix=2;
run;
```

produce warning messages that VA1 and VA2 are already in the output data set and then the procedure quits. This example works correctly if CPREFIX=4.

CQC
   includes canonical quadratic point model coordinates.

DAPPROXIMATIONS
DAPPROX
DAP
   includes the approximations to the transformed dependent variables in the output data set. These are ordinary regression predicted values. The names of the approximation variables are constructed from the ADPREFIX= option and the original dependent variable names. Specifying ADPREFIX= also implies DAPPROXIMATIONS.

DREPLACE
DRE
   replaces the original dependent variables with the transformed dependent variables in the output data set. The names of the transformed variables in the output data set correspond to the names of the original dependent variables in the input data set. By default, both the original dependent variables and transformed dependent variables (with names constructed from the TDPREFIX= option and the original dependent variable names) are included in the output data set.

IAPPROXIMATIONS
IAPPROX
IAP
   includes the approximations to the transformed independent variables in the output data set. The names of the approximation variables are constructed from the AIPREFIX= option and the original independent variable names. Specifying AIPREFIX= also implies IAPPROXIMATIONS. IAPPROXIMATIONS is not valid when METHOD=UNIVARIATE.

IREPLACE
IRE
   replaces the original independent variables with the transformed independent variables in the output data set. The names of the transformed variables in the output data set correspond to the names of the original independent variables in the input data set. If you do not specify IREPLACE, both original independent variables and transformed independent variables (with names constructed from the TIPREFIX=

option and the original independent variable names) are included in the output data set, unless the transformed independent variables cannot possibly differ from the untransformed variables. In this case, the replacement occurs in the output data set even if you do not specify IREPLACE. Such cases occur when all independent variables are named as expansions (CLASS, POINT, EPOINT, and QPOINT), or when METHOD=UNIVARIATE and all independent variables are named either as expansions or specified as LINEAR optimal transformations. However, if TSTANDARD= is not ORIGINAL, the original and transformed variables are different, so you must specify IREPLACE to achieve replacement.

MEANS
MEA

includes marginal means for the binary columns created from CLASS variable expansions in the output data set.

MEC

includes multiple regression elliptical point model coordinates.

MPC

includes multiple regression point model coordinates.

MQC

includes multiple regression quadratic point model coordinates.

MRC

includes multiple regression coefficients.

NOSCORES
NOS

excludes original variables, transformed variables, and approximations. You can use NOSCORES with various other options to create an output data set that contains only a coefficient partition (for example, a data set consisting entirely of coefficients and coordinates).

REPLACE
REP

is equivalent to specifying both DREPLACE and IREPLACE.

TDPREFIX=name
TDP=name

specifies a prefix for naming the transformed dependent variables. By default, TDPREFIX=T. TDPREFIX= is ignored when you specify the DREPLACE option.

TIPREFIX=name
TIP=name

specifies a prefix for naming the transformed independent variables. By default, TIPREFIX=T. TIPREFIX= is ignored when you specify the IREPLACE option.

TSTANDARD=CENTER | NOMISS | ORIGINAL | Z
TST=CENTER | NOMISS | ORIGINAL | Z

specifies how to set the means and variances of the transformed variables in the output data set. By default, TSTANDARD=ORIGINAL.

However, the final standardization is affected by other options. If you also specify the ADDITIVE option, the TSTANDARD= option specifies an intermediate step in computing the final means and variances. The final independent variables, along with their means and standard deviations, are scaled by the regression coefficients, creating an additive model with all coefficients equal to one.

For nonoptimal variable transformations, the means and variances of the original variables are actually the means and variances of the nonlinearly transformed variables, unless you specify the ORIGINAL nonoptimal variable transformation option in the MODEL statement. For example, if a variable X with no missing values is specified as LOG, by default the final transformation of X is simply LOG(X), not LOG(X) standardized to the mean of X and variance of X.

CENTER centers the output variables to mean zero, but the variances are the same as the input variables' variances.

NOMISS sets the means and variances of the transformed variables in the output data set, computed over all values in the output data set that correspond to nonmissing values in the input data set, to the means and variances computed from the nonmissing observations of the original variables. NOMISS is useful if you use PROC TRANSREG only to estimate missing data. When a variable is linearly transformed, the final variable contains the original nonmissing values and the missing value estimates. In other words, the nonmissing values are unchanged. Thus, if your data have no missing values, NOMISS and ORIGINAL produce the same results.

ORIGINAL is the default, and sets the means and variances of the transformed variables to the means and variances of the original variables.

Z standardizes the variables to mean zero, variance one.

DETAILS

Missing Values

PROC TRANSREG can estimate missing values, subject to optional constraints, so that the variance accounted for by the regression model is optimized. Several approaches to missing data handling are provided. All observations with missing values in CLASS, POINT, EPOINT, and QPOINT expansion variables are excluded from the analysis. When METHOD=UNIVARIATE (specified in the PROC TRANSREG or MODEL statement), observations with missing values in any of the independent variables are excluded from the analysis. When you specify the NOMISS option (in the PROC TRANSREG or MODEL statement), observations with missing values in the other analysis variables are excluded. Otherwise, missing data are estimated, using variable means as initial estimates. The procedure then generates final estimates.

You can specify the OPSCORE, MONOTONE, UNTIE, LINEAR, SPLINE, MSPLINE, LOG, LOGIT, POWER, ARSIN, RANK, and EXP transformations in any combination with nonmissing values, ordinary missing values, and special missing values, as long as the nonmissing values in each variable have positive variance. No category or order restrictions are placed on the estimates of ordinary missing values. You can force missing value estimates within a variable to be identical by using special missing values (see "The DATA Step" in *SAS Language: Reference, Version 6, First Edition*) You can specify up to 27 categories of missing values, where within-category estimates must be the same, by coding the missing values using ._ and .A through .Z.

You can also specify an ordering of some missing value estimates. You can use the MONOTONE= option in the PROC TRANSREG or MODEL statement to indicate a range of special missing values (a subset of the list from .A to .Z) whose estimates must be weakly ordered within each variable that they appear. For example, if MONOTONE=AI, the nine classes, .A, .B, . . . , .I, are monotonically scored and optimally scaled just as MONOTONE transformation values are scored. In this case, category but not order restrictions are placed on the missing values ._ and .J through .Z. You can also use the UNTIE= option (in the PROC TRANSREG or MODEL statement) to indicate a range of special missing values whose estimates must be weakly ordered within each variable that they appear, but can be untied.

The missing value estimation facilities allow for partitioned or mixed type variables. For example, a variable can be considered part nominal and part ordinal. Nominal classes of otherwise ordinal variables are coded with special missing values. This feature can be useful with survey research. The class "unfamiliar with the product" in the variable "Rate your preference for 'Brand X' on a 1 to 9 scale, or if you are unfamiliar with the product, check 'unfamiliar with the product'" is an example. You can code "unfamiliar with the product" as a special missing value, such as .A. The 1's to 9's can be monotonically transformed, while no monotonic restrictions are placed on the quantification of the "unfamiliar with the product" class.

A variable specified for a LINEAR transformation, with special missing values and ordered categorical missing values, can be part interval, part ordinal, and part nominal. A variable specified for a MONOTONE transformation can have two independent ordinal parts. A variable specified for an UNTIE transformation can have an ordered categorical part and an ordered part without category restrictions. Many other mixes are possible.

Centering of Variables

By default, variables are centered during the iterations to correct for their mean, but you can override this default with the NOINT and INTERCEPT options in the PROC TRANSREG or MODEL statement. The only constant variable permitted is the intercept variable. When there is no intercept, the squared multiple correlations in the iteration history table (of the output) are redefined to be ratios of uncorrected sums of squares instead of the usual ratios of sums of squares around the mean. A redefined R^2 is not invariant under linear transformations of the variables, so the values reported in the iteration history table (which are computed from the internally standardized variables) do not always match the redefined R^2 values reported by PROC REG (which are computed from the final standardized variables).

When you specify METHOD=CANALS in the PROC TRANSREG or MODEL statement, the average of the largest eigenvalues is always reported under the "Average Squared R" column. By default, when the variables are centered, the eigenvalues are squared canonical correlations.

Controlling the Iteration Process

Iteration terminates when any one of the following conditions becomes satisfied:

- the number of iterations equals the value of the MAXITER= option (specified in the PROC TRANSREG or MODEL statement)
- the average absolute change in variable scores from one iteration to the next is less than the value of the CONVERGE= option (specified in the PROC TRANSREG or MODEL statement)
- the criterion change is less than the value of the CCONVERGE= option (specified in the PROC TRANSREG or MODEL statement).

The criterion change can become negative when the data have converged so that it is numerically impossible, within machine precision, to increase the criterion. Because the algorithms are convergent, a negative criterion change is the result of very small amounts of rounding error. Negative values can be specified for either convergence option if you wish to define convergence only in terms of the other option.

You can increase the number of iterations to ensure convergence by increasing the value of MAXITER= and decreasing the value CONVERGE=. Since the average absolute change in standardized variable scores seldom decreases below 1E–11, you should not specify a value for CONVERGE= less than 1E–8 or 1E–10. Most of the data changes occur during the first few iterations, but the data can still change after 50 or even 100 iterations. You can try different combinations of values for CONVERGE= and MAXITER= to ensure convergence without extreme overiteration. If the data do not converge with the default specifications, try CONVERGE=1E–8 and MAXITER=50, or CONVERGE=1E–10 and MAXITER=200.

Point Models

The expanded set of independent variables generated from the POINT, EPOINT, and QPOINT expansions can be used to perform ideal point regressions (Carroll 1972) and compute ideal point coordinates for plotting in a biplot (Gabriel 1981). The three types of ideal point coordinates can all be described as transformed coefficients. Assume that m independent variables are specified in one of the three point expansions. Let $\mathbf{b}'$ be a $(1 \times m)$ row vector of coefficients for these variables and one of the dependent variables. Let $\mathbf{R}$ be a matrix created from the coefficients of the extra variables. When MPC, MEC, or MQC coordinates are requested (with the respective options in the OUTPUT or PROC TRANSREG statement), $\mathbf{b}'$ and $\mathbf{R}$ are created from multiple regression coefficients. When CPC, CEC, or CQC coordinates are requested (again, with the respective options in the OUTPUT or PROC TRANSREG statement), $\mathbf{b}'$ and $\mathbf{R}$ are created from canonical coefficients.

If you specify the POINT transform in the MODEL statement, $\mathbf{R}$ is an $(m \times m)$ identity matrix times the coefficient for the sums of squares (_ISSQ_) variable. If you specify the EPOINT transform, $\mathbf{R}$ is an $(m \times m)$ diagonal matrix of coefficients from the squared variables. If you specify the QPOINT transform, $\mathbf{R}$ is an $(m \times m)$ symmetric matrix of coefficients from the squared variables on the diagonal and crossproduct variables off the diagonal. The MPC, MEC, MQC, CPC, CEC, and CQC ideal point coordinates are defined as $-0.5\mathbf{b}'\mathbf{R}^{-1}$. When $\mathbf{R}$ is singular, the ideal point coordinates are infinitely far away and are set to missing, so a simpler version of the model should be tried. The version that is simpler than the POINT model is the vector model where no extra variables are created. In the vector model, designate all independent variables for LINEAR transformations, and then specify the COEFFICIENTS option (in either the OUTPUT or PROC TRANSREG statement). Then draw vectors from the origin to the COEFFICIENTS points.

Typically, when you request ideal point coordinates, the MODEL statement should consist of a single transformation for the dependent variables (usually MONOTONE, MSPLINE, or LINEAR) and a single expansion for the independent variables (one of POINT, EPOINT, or QPOINT).

Optimal Scaling

An alternating least-squares optimal scaling algorithm can be divided into two major stages. The first stage estimates the parameters of the linear model. These parameters are used to create the predicted values or target for each variable that can be transformed. Each target minimizes squared error (as shown in the discussion of the algorithms in SAS Technical Report R-108). The definition of the target depends on many factors, such as whether a variable is independent or dependent, which algorithm is used (for example, regression, redundancy, CANALS, principal components), and so on. The definition of the target is independent of the transformation family you specify for the variable. However, the target values for a variable typically do not fit the prescribed transformation family for the variable. They might not have the right category structure; they might not have the right order; they might not be a linear combination of the columns of a B-spline basis; and so on.

The second major stage is optimal scaling. Optimal scaling can be defined as a possibly constrained, least-squares regression problem. When you specify an optimal transformation family other than LINEAR for a variable, or when missing data are estimated for any variable, the full representation of the variable is not simply a vector; it is a matrix with more than one column. The optimal scaling phase finds the vector that is a linear combination of the columns of this matrix, is closest to the target (in terms of least-squares error), and does not violate any of the constraints imposed by the transformation family. Optimal scaling methods are independent of the data analysis method that generated the target. In all cases, optimal scaling can be accomplished by creating a design matrix based on the original scaling of the variable and the transformation family specified for that variable. The optimally scaled variable is a linear combination of the columns of the design matrix. The coefficients of the linear combination are found using the method of possibly constrained, least squares. Many optimal scaling problems are solved without actually constructing design and projection matrices. The following sections describe the algorithms used by PROC TRANSREG for optimal scaling. The first section below discusses optimal scaling for OPSCORE, MONOTONE, UNTIE, and LINEAR transformations, including how missing values are handled. The second section addresses SPLINE and MSPLINE transformations.

OPSCORE, MONOTONE, UNTIE, and LINEAR Transformations

Two vectors of information are needed to produce the optimally scaled variable: the initial variable scaling vector $\mathbf{x}$ and the target vector $\mathbf{y}$. For convenience, both vectors are first sorted on the values of the initial scaling vector. If you request an UNTIE transformation, the target vector is sorted within ties in the initial scaling vector. The normal SAS System collating sequence for missing and nonmissing values is used. Sorting simply allows constraints to be specified in terms of relations among adjoining coefficients. The sorting partitions $\mathbf{x}$ and $\mathbf{y}$ into missing and nonmissing parts $(\mathbf{x}_m' \quad \mathbf{x}_n')'$, and $(\mathbf{y}_m' \quad \mathbf{y}_n')'$.

Next, PROC TRANSREG determines category membership. Every ordinary missing value (.) forms a separate category. (Three ordinary missing values form three categories.) Every special missing value within the range specified in the UNTIE= option forms a separate category. (If UNTIE= BC and there are three .B and two .C missing values, five categories are formed from them.) For all other special missing values, a separate category is formed for each different value. (If there are four .A missing values, one category is formed from them.)

Each distinct nonmissing value forms a separate category for OPSCORE and MONOTONE transformations (1 1 1 2 2 3 form three categories). Each nonmissing datum forms a separate category for all other transformations (1 1 1 2 2 3 form six categories). Once category membership is determined, category means are computed, for example:

x:	(.	.	.A	.A	.B	1	1	1	2	2	3	3	3	4)'
y:	(5	6	2	4	2	1	2	3	4	6	4	5	6	7)'
OPSCORE and MONOTONE means:	(5	6	3		2	2			5	5				7)'
other means:	(5	6	3		2	1	2	3	4	6	4	5	6	7)'

The category means are the coefficients of a category indicator design matrix. The category means are the Fisher (1938) optimal scores. For MONOTONE and

UNTIE transformations, order constraints are imposed on the category means for the nonmissing partition by merging categories that are out of order. The algorithm checks upward until an order violation is found, then averages downward until the order violation is averaged away. (The average of $\bar{x}_1$ computed from n_1 observations and $\bar{x}_2$ computed from n_2 observations is $(n_1\bar{x}_1 + n_2\bar{x}_2)/(n_1 + n_2)$.) The MONOTONE algorithm (Kruskal 1964, secondary approach to ties) for this example with means for the nonmissing values $(2\ 5\ 5\ 7)'$ would do the following checks: $2<5$:OK, $5=5$:OK, $5<7$:OK. The means are in the proper order so no work is needed.

The UNTIE transformation (Kruskal 1964, primary approach to ties) uses the same algorithm on the means of the nonmissing values $(1\ 2\ 3\ 4\ 6\ 4\ 5\ 6\ 7)'$ but with different results for this example: $1<2$:OK, $2<3$:OK, $3<4$:OK, $4<6$:OK, $6>4$:average 6 and 4 and replace 6 and 4 by the average. The new means of the nonmissing values are $(1\ 2\ 3\ 4\ 5\ 5\ 5\ 6\ 7)'$. The check resumes: $4<5$:OK, $5=5$:OK, $5=5$:OK, $5<6$:OK, $6<7$:OK. If some of the special missing values are ordered, the upward checking, downward averaging method is applied to them too, independently of the other missing and nonmissing partitions. Once the means conform to any required category or order constraints, an optimally scaled vector is produced from the means. The following example results from a MONOTONE transformation:

```
x:        (.    .    .A   .A   .B   1    1    1    2    2    3    3    3    4)'
y:        (5    6    2    4    2    1    2    3    4    6    4    5    6    7)'
result:   (5    6    3    3    2    2    2    2    5    5    5    5    5    7)'
```

The upward checking, downward averaging algorithm is equivalent to creating a category indicator design matrix, solving for least-squares coefficients with order constraints, then computing the linear combination of design matrix columns.

For the optimal transformation LINEAR, and for nonoptimal transformations, missing values are handled as just described. The nonmissing target values are regressed onto the matrix defined by the nonmissing initial scaling values and an intercept. In this example, the target vector $\mathbf{y}_n = (1\ 2\ 3\ 4\ 6\ 4\ 5\ 6\ 7)'$ is regressed onto the design matrix

$$\begin{bmatrix} 1 & 1 & 1 & 1 & 1 & 1 & 1 & 1 & 1 \\ 1 & 1 & 1 & 2 & 2 & 3 & 3 & 3 & 4 \end{bmatrix}'$$

Although only a linear transformation is performed, the effect of a linear regression optimal scaling is not eliminated by the later standardization step (except if the variable has no missing values). In the presence of missing values, the linear regression is necessary to minimize squared error.

SPLINE and MSPLINE Transformations

The missing portions of variables subjected to SPLINE or MSPLINE transformations are handled the same way as for OPSCORE, MONOTONE, UNTIE, and LINEAR transformations (see the previous section). The nonmissing partition is handled by first creating a B-spline basis of the specified degree with the specified knots for the nonmissing partition of the initial scaling vector, and then regressing the target onto the basis. The optimally scaled vector is a linear combination of the B-spline basis vectors using least-squares regression coefficients. An algorithm for generating the B-spline basis is given in de Boor (1978, pp. 134–135). B-splines are both a computationally accurate and efficient way of constructing a basis for piecewise polynomials; however, they are not the most natural method of describing splines.

Consider an initial scaling vector $\mathbf{x} = (1\ 2\ 3\ 4\ 5\ 6\ 7\ 8\ 9)'$ and a degree three spline with interior knots at 3.5 and 6.5. The B-spline basis for the transformation is the left matrix below, and the natural piecewise polynomial spline basis is the right matrix below. The two matrices span the same column space. The natural basis has an intercept, a linear term, a quadratic term, a cubic term, and two more terms since there are two interior knots. These terms are generated (for knot k and $\mathbf{x}$ element x) by the formula: $(x-k)^3*(x>k)$. The logical expression $(x>k)$ evaluates to 1.0 if x is greater than k and 0.0 otherwise. If knot k had been repeated, there would be a $(x-k)^2*(x>k)$ term also. Notice that the fifth column makes no contribution to the curve before 3.5, makes zero contribution at 3.5 (the transformation is continuous), and makes an increasing contribution beyond 3.5. The same pattern of results holds for the last term with knot 6.5. The coefficient of the fifth column represents the change in the cubic portion of the curve after 3.5. The coefficient of the sixth column represents the change in the cubic portion of the curve after 6.5.

$$
\begin{array}{c}
\text{B-Spline Basis} \\
\text{Piecewise Polynomial}
\end{array}
\qquad
\begin{array}{c}
\text{Piecewise Polynomial} \\
\text{Splines}
\end{array}
$$

$$
\begin{bmatrix}
.171 & .557 & .250 & .022 & 0 & 0 \\
.037 & .447 & .443 & .073 & 0 & 0 \\
.001 & .251 & .576 & .172 & 0 & 0 \\
0 & .093 & .572 & .334 & .001 & 0 \\
0 & .020 & .437 & .517 & .027 & 0 \\
0 & .001 & .253 & .623 & .123 & 0 \\
0 & 0 & .108 & .557 & .332 & .003 \\
0 & 0 & .032 & .341 & .548 & .079 \\
0 & 0 & .004 & .109 & .523 & .364
\end{bmatrix}
\begin{bmatrix}
1 & 1 & 1 & 1 & 0 & 0 \\
1 & 2 & 4 & 8 & 0 & 0 \\
1 & 3 & 9 & 27 & 0 & 0 \\
1 & 4 & 16 & 64 & 0.125 & 0 \\
1 & 5 & 25 & 125 & 3.375 & 0 \\
1 & 6 & 36 & 216 & 15.625 & 0 \\
1 & 7 & 49 & 343 & 42.875 & 0.125 \\
1 & 8 & 64 & 512 & 91.125 & 3.375 \\
1 & 9 & 81 & 729 & 166.375 & 15.625
\end{bmatrix}
$$

The numbers in the B-spline basis do not have a simple interpretation like the numbers in the natural piecewise polynomial basis. The B-spline basis has a diagonally banded structure. The band shifts to the right one column after every knot. The number of nonzero elements in a row is one greater than the degree. The elements within a row always sum to one. The B-spline basis is accurate because of the smallness of the numbers and the lack of extreme collinearity inherent in the natural polynomials. B-splines are efficient because PROC TRANSREG can take advantage of the sparseness of the B-spline basis when it accumulates crossproducts. The number of required multiplications and additions to accumulate the crossproduct matrix does not increase with the number of knots, but does increase with the degree of the spline, so it is much more computationally efficient to increase the number of knots than to increase the degree of the polynomial.

MSPLINE transformations are handled like SPLINE transformations except constraints are placed on the coefficients to ensure monotonicity. When the coefficients of the B-spline basis are monotonically increasing, the transformation is monotonically increasing. When the polynomial degree is two or less, monotone coefficient splines, integrated splines (Winsberg and Ramsay 1980), and the general class of all monotone splines are equivalent.

Output Data Set

The organization and content of the output data set can be very complicated. However, in most cases, the output data set contains a small portion of the entire range of information given below and is organized for direct input into procedures such as PLOT, GPLOT, or G3D for graphical analysis of the transformed variables, or input into procedures such as REG, CANCORR, ANOVA, and GLM for a final analysis of the transformed variables. **However, all *p*-values and significance tests should be ignored.** The usual *p*-values computed from optimally transformed variables are generally much too small. You should use TRANSREG as an exploratory data analysis procedure, never as a method of "maximizing significance" or "proving the alternative hypothesis".

Examples

The next section gives a complete list of matrices that can appear in the output data set. But before presenting complete details, this section gives two brief examples.

The first example shows the output data set from a full rank reference cell parameterization of a two-way *ANOVA* model. The following statements produce **Output 40.4**:

```
title 'ANOVA Output Data Set Example';
data refcell;
   input y x1 $ x2 $;
   c = compress(x1||x2);
      /*---Note, x1 and x2 are level indicators and---*/
      /*---c is a cell indicator                  ---*/
   cards;
11  a  a
12  a  a
10  a  a
 4  a  b
 5  a  b
 3  a  b
 5  b  a
 6  b  a
 4  b  a
 2  b  b
 3  b  b
 1  b  b
;

   /*---Fit Reference Cell Two-Way ANOVA Model---*/
proc transreg;
   model linear(y)=class(c) / intercept;
   id x1 x2;
   output coefficients;
run;

   /*---Print the Results---*/
proc print;
run;
```

Output 40.4 *ANOVA* Example Output Data Set

```
                              ANOVA Output Data Set Example                                1

  OBS   _TYPE_     _NAME_   Y    TY   INTERCEP   CAA   CAB   CBA   CBB   C    X1   X2

   1    SCORE       a       11   11      1        .     0     0     0    aa    a    a
   2    SCORE       a       12   12      1        .     0     0     0    aa    a    a
   3    SCORE       a       10   10      1        .     0     0     0    aa    a    a
   4    SCORE       a        4    4      1        .     1     0     0    ab    a    b
   5    SCORE       a        5    5      1        .     1     0     0    ab    a    b
   6    SCORE       a        3    3      1        .     1     0     0    ab    a    b
   7    SCORE       b        5    5      1        .     0     1     0    ba    b    a
   8    SCORE       b        6    6      1        .     0     1     0    ba    b    a
   9    SCORE       b        4    4      1        .     0     1     0    ba    b    a
  10    SCORE       b        2    2      1        .     0     0     1    bb    b    b
  11    SCORE       b        3    3      1        .     0     0     1    bb    b    b
  12    SCORE       b        1    1      1        .     0     0     1    bb    b    b
  13    M COEFFI    TY       .    .      11             -7    -6    -9
  14    MEAN        TY       .    .       .       11     4     5     2
```

TYPE indicates observation type: score, multiple regression coefficient (parameter estimates), and marginal means (which are actually cell means with this parameterization). _NAME_ contains the observation name, which is formed from the first eight characters of the first ID variable for score observations and is the transformed dependent variable name (TY) for the remaining observations. Y is the original variable, and TY is the transformed variable. In this data set, Y and TY are the same since the MODEL statement requests a linear transformation with no missing value estimation. The variables INTERCEP through CBB contain the design matrix created from the category variable C. C in turn is created in a DATA step from the ID variables (which are factor level indicators) with the statement: C=COMPRESS(X1 || X2);. In this two-way design, C indicates cell membership. The table below shows the relationships between the cell means and the reference cell parameter estimates.

		a	X2	b
X_1	a	$\bar{y} = 11 = 11 + 0$		$\bar{y} = 4 = 11 + -7$
	b	$\bar{y} = 5 = 11 + -6$		$\bar{y} = 2 = 11 + -9$

You can directly input this data set to PROC GLM or PROC REG for hypothesis tests because you did not request any optimal nonlinear transformations and because the missing values in Y and TY for both the 'M COEFFI' and 'MEAN' observations cause those observations to be excluded from the GLM or REG analysis.

The next example illustrates a data set with variable approximations. The scatterplot of the original input variables Y and X is one-quarter of a unit circle. The following statements request a two-piece continuous linear transformation of each variable:

```
title 'Output Data Set with Approximations Example';
    /*---Create a Quarter of a Circle---*/
data a;
    do i=1 to 200;
        x=ranuni(7654321);
        y=sqrt(1-x*x);
        output;
    end;
run;

    /*---Attempt to Straighten Scatterplot, Output Approximations---*/
proc transreg noprint;
    model spline(y / degree=1 nknots=1)=spline(x / degree=1 nknots=1);
    output approximations out=b;
run;

    /*---Print the First Five Observations---*/
proc print data=b(obs=5);
    format _numeric_ 5.2;
run;
```

These statements produce **Output 40.5**. The NOPRINT option suppresses any output from the TRANSREG procedure; and the OBS=5 data set option in the PROC PRINT statement causes only the first 5 observations to be printed.

Output 40.5   Approximations Example Output Data Set

```
                       Output Data Set with Approximations Example                        1

    OBS    _TYPE_    _NAME_      Y      TY      AY      X      TX      AX

      1    SCORE     ROW1      0.47    0.52    0.50    0.88    0.87    0.85
      2    SCORE     ROW2      0.90    0.79    0.82    0.43    0.45    0.49
      3    SCORE     ROW3      0.81    0.69    0.71    0.58    0.60    0.61
      4    SCORE     ROW4      0.87    0.72    0.76    0.50    0.52    0.57
      5    SCORE     ROW5      0.26    0.41    0.44    0.97    0.95    1.00
```

The resulting data set contains a _TYPE_ variable, along with a _NAME_ variable that now contains the default observation labels, "ROW1", "ROW2", and so on (because no ID statement is present). Y is the original dependent variable, TY is the transformed dependent variable, and AY is the approximation to TY (ordinary regression predicted values). X is the original independent variable, TX is the transformed independent variable, and AX is the approximation of TX.

Matrices

This section presents the various matrices that can result from TRANSREG processing and appear in the output data set. The way TRANSREG generates these matrices is a result of the transformation method you specify in the MODEL statement. **Table 40.1** shows each matrix that TRANSREG can generate, gives a brief description, and names the methods that can produce the matrix. The following scalars are used in the matrix table:

a the number of EPOINT independent variables
b the number of QPOINT independent variables
c the number of CLASS independent variables
d the number of POINT independent variables
$e[i]$ the number of categories in the ith CLASS independent variable
f the number of EPOINT dependent variables
g the number of QPOINT dependent variables
h the number of CLASS dependent variables
j the number of POINT dependent variables
$k[i]$ the number of categories in the ith CLASS dependent variable
l the number of canonical variables
m the number of dependent variables
n the number of observations
p the number of independent variables
q the number of expanded independent variables
$$q = p+a+b(b+1)/2 +e[1]+e[2]+ \ldots +e[c]-c+$$
$$\text{(1 if } d>0 \text{ or 0 otherwise)}+$$
$$\text{(1 if INT is specified or 0 otherwise)}$$
r the number of expanded dependent variables
$$r = m+f+g(g+1)/2+k[1]+k[2]+ \ldots +k[h]-h+$$
$$\text{(1 if } j>0 \text{ or 0 otherwise)}.$$

The matrices shown below in **Table 40.1** can appear in the output data set.

Table 40.1   PROC TRANSREG Matrix Table

Matrix	Description	Method
$\mathbf{A}(n \times q)$	the independent variables	UNIVARIATE, CANALS, REDUNDANCY
$\mathbf{B}(n \times r)$	the dependent variables	UNIVARIATE, CANALS, REDUNDANCY
$\mathbf{C}(nr \times 1)$	the dependent variables	MORALS
$\mathbf{D}(nr \times q)$	the repeated independent variables	MORALS
$\mathbf{E}(n \times q)$	the transformed independent variables	UNIVARIATE, CANALS, REDUNDANCY

(continued)

Table 40.1 (*continued*)

Matrix	Description	Method
$\mathbf{F}(n \times r)$	the transformed dependent variables	UNIVARIATE, CANALS, REDUNDANCY
$\mathbf{G}(nr \times 1)$	the transformed dependent variables	MORALS
$\mathbf{H}(nr \times q)$	the transformed independent variables	MORALS
$\mathbf{I}(n \times q)$	the approximations to independent variables	CANALS, REDUNDANCY
$\mathbf{J}(n \times r)$	the approximations to dependent variables	UNIVARIATE, CANALS, REDUNDANCY
$\mathbf{K}(nr \times 1)$	the approximations to dependent variables	MORALS
$\mathbf{L}(nr \times q)$	the approximations to independent variables	MORALS
$\mathbf{M}(r \times q)$	the independent variable MRC coefficients	UNIVARIATE, MORALS, CANALS, REDUNDANCY
$\mathbf{N}(r \times q)$	the independent variable MPC coordinates	UNIVARIATE, CANALS, REDUNDANCY
$\mathbf{O}(r \times q)$	the independent variable MEC coordinates	UNIVARIATE, CANALS, REDUNDANCY
$\mathbf{P}(r \times q)$	the independent variable MQC coordinates	UNIVARIATE, CANALS, REDUNDANCY
$\mathbf{Q}(l \times q)$	the independent variable CCC coefficients	UNIVARIATE, CANALS, REDUNDANCY
$\mathbf{R}(l \times r)$	the dependent variable CCC coefficients	UNIVARIATE, CANALS, REDUNDANCY
$\mathbf{S}(l \times q)$	the independent variable CPC coordinates	UNIVARIATE, CANALS, REDUNDANCY

(*continued*)

Table 40.1 (*continued*)

Matrix	Description	Method
T(*l*×*q*)	the independent variable CEC coordinates	UNIVARIATE, CANALS, REDUNDANCY
U(*l*×*q*)	the independent variable CQC coordinates	UNIVARIATE, CANALS, REDUNDANCY
.	a matrix of missing values; the order is deduced from context	UNIVARIATE, MORALS, CANALS, REDUNDANCY

The values in the last column, labeled "Method", are values of the METHOD= option, which you can specify in the MODEL or PROC TRANSREG statement.

The expanded but untransformed variables (matrices **A**, **B**, **C**, and **D**) are created from the original input data. Several potential differences exist between these matrices and the input data. An intercept variable can be added, new variables can be added for POINT, EPOINT, QPOINT, and CLASS variables, and category numbers are substituted for character OPSCORE variables. These matrices are not always what is input to the first iteration. After the expanded data set is stored for inclusion in the output data set, several things happen to the data before they are input to the first iteration: column means are substituted for missing values; zero degree SPLINE and MSPLINE variables are transformed so that the iterative algorithms get step function data as input, which conform to the zero degree transformation family restrictions; and the nonoptimal transformations are performed.

The **N**, **O**, **P**, **S**, **T**, and **U** matrices (from the point models) contain both ideal point coordinates and regression coefficients. Columns corresponding to variables named in the POINT, EPOINT, and QPOINT expansions contain ideal point coordinates and the other columns contain regression coefficients.

Details for the UNIVARIATE method   When you specify METHOD=UNIVARIATE (in the MODEL or PROC TRANSREG statement), TRANSREG can perform several analyses, one for each dependent variable. While each dependent variable can be transformed, their independent variables are not transformed. Thus, the output data set can contain the following matrices, all optional:

```
B F J A E
. . . . . M
. . . . . N
. . . . . O
. . . . . P
. R . . . Q
. . . . . S
. . . . . T
. . . . . U
```

The missing value partitions allow the output data set to be used in two very different ways without further manipulation. The data set can be input to PROC REG for a final report of the results, regressing the transformed dependent variables on the expanded independent variables; however, all p-values and significance tests should be ignored. The missing values on the dependent variables cause the coefficient observations to be excluded so only the correct observations are input to PROC REG. Also, the independent variable columns can be input to a plotting procedure to produce a biplot of both independent variable scores and ideal point coordinates, again without further manipulation.

Details for MORALS method   When you specify METHOD=MORALS (in the MODEL or PROC TRANSREG statement), successive analyses are performed, one for each dependent variable. Each analysis transforms one dependent variable and the entire set of the independent variables. Thus, the output data set can contain the following matrices, all optional:

```
C G K D H L
. . . . M .
```

However, the observations in the output data set do not appear in the order shown here. In fact, all information for the first dependent variable (scores followed by coefficients) appear first. Then all information for the second dependent variable (scores followed by coefficients) appear next. This arrangement is repeated for all dependent variables. (See **Variable Names** later in this section for additional details when METHOD=MORALS.)

Details for the CANALS and REDUNDANCY methods   For METHOD=CANALS and METHOD=REDUNDANCY (specified in either the MODEL or PROC statement), one analysis is performed that simultaneously transforms all dependent and independent variables. Thus, the output data set can contain the following matrices, all optional:

```
B F J A E I
. . . . M .
. . . . N .
. . . . O .
. . . . P .
. R . . Q .
. . . . S .
. . . . T .
. . . . U .
```

Variable Names

As shown in the examples above, some variables in the output data set directly correspond to input variables, and some are created. If you specify INTERCEPT, the variable INTERCEP is added to the output data set. All optimal and nonoptimal transformation variable names are unchanged.

POINT, QPOINT, and EPOINT expansion variable names are also left unchanged, but new variables are created. When independent POINT variables are present, the sum-of-squares variable _ISSQ_ is added to the output data set. When dependent POINT variables are present, the sum-of-squares variable _DSSQ_ is added to the output data set. For each EPOINT variable, a new squared variable is created by appending "_2". Up to the first six variable name characters are used. For each QPOINT variable, a new squared variable is created by appending "_2". In addition, for each unique combination of different

QPOINT variables, a new crossproduct variable is created from combining up to the first four characters of each name. While the following example does not represent a typical analysis, for purposes of MODEL statement construction, note that the statement

```
model monotone(v1) = point(p1-p2) epoint(e1-e3) qpoint(q1-q3);
```

produces the following independent variables: P1, P2, E1, E2, E3, Q1, Q2, Q3, _ISSQ_, E1_2, E2_2, E3_2, Q1_2, Q2_2, Q3_2, Q1Q2, Q1Q3, Q2Q3. An equivalent MODEL statement is

```
model monotone(v1) = point(p1) point(p2) epoint(e1) epoint(e2)
       epoint(e3) qpoint(q1) qpoint(q2) qpoint(q3);
```

If you use a CLASS *transform* in the MODEL statement, one variable is added to the output data set for each unique value of each CLASS expansion variable, even if you did not specify ALLCATS. This allows for the possibility of different reference cells and different class values across BY groups. It also provides enough columns for marginal means to be output. When a dummy variable would not have any ones because it is one of the reference cell levels or it does not appear in the current BY group, its values in the output data set are set to missing. The name is constructed by appending up to the first $(8-n)$ (where n is specified in CPREFIX=n) characters from the formatted class value to the first n characters from the CLASS expansion variable name. If the CLASS expansion variable name has fewer than n characters, n is decremented accordingly. The resulting character string is converted to a valid SAS name using the method described in the TRANSPOSE procedure (see the *SAS Procedures Guide, Version 6, Third Edition*).

PROC TRANSREG then uses these variable names when creating the transformed variable names and approximations variable names, by affixing the relevant prefix and possibly dropping extra characters. If this process leads to duplicate output data set variable names, warnings appear for each duplicate variable, and TRANSREG issues an error and stops processing.

TYPE and _NAME_ variables   The output data set also contains two character variables, _TYPE_ and _NAME_.

TYPE has the following variable values and contents:

Value of _TYPE_	Content of observation
SCORE	scores
M COEFFI	multiple regression coefficients
M POINT	MPC POINT variable ideal point coordinates
M EPOINT	MEC EPOINT variable ideal point coordinates
M QPOINT	MQC QPOINT variable ideal point coordinates
C COEFFI	canonical coefficients
C POINT	CPC POINT ideal point coordinates
C EPOINT	CEC EPOINT ideal point coordinates
C QPOINT	CQC QPOINT ideal point coordinates
MEAN	marginal means

NAME has values ROW1, ROW2, and so on, by default for the SCORES observations. If you use an ID statement, _NAME_ contains the first eight formatted characters of the first ID variable for observations with _TYPE_='SCORE'. The coefficient observations contain the transformed variable names as the values of the _NAME_ variable. In addition, if any ID variables or CLASS expansion variables exist, they are included in the output data set. The CLASS expansion variables in the output data set are character variables (length of 8) containing the first eight characters of the formatted input CLASS variables, which are the values that PROC TRANSREG uses to determine category membership.

MORALS method variables   When you specify METHOD=MORALS and only one dependent variable is present, the output data set is structured exactly as if METHOD=REDUNDANCY (see **Details for CANALS and REDUNDANCY methods** earlier in this chapter). When more than one dependent variable is present, the dependent variables are output in the variable _DEPEND_, transformed dependent variables are output in the variable _DTRANS_, and dependent variable approximations are output in the variable _DAPPRO_. You can partition the data set into BY groups, one per dependent variable by referring to the character variable _VAR_, which contains the original dependent variable names.

Using Options to Produce the Coefficient Partition

The COEFFICIENTS and COORDINATES options provide a simple method of letting PROC TRANSREG decide what should be included in the coefficient partition of the data set:

- COEFFICIENTS specifies that the set of coefficients suggested by the model be placed in the output data set:
  - When METHOD=CANALS, specifying COEFFICIENTS is the same as specifying CCC.
  - Otherwise, COEFFICIENTS is the same as MRC.
  - When there are independent CLASS expansion variables, COEFFICIENTS also specifies MEANS.

- When METHOD=CANALS, specifying COORDINATES is the same as
  - specifying CPC when the MODEL statement contains the POINT *transform* for some variables (called POINT variables)
  - specifying CEC when the MODEL statement contains the EPOINT *transform* for some variables (called EPOINT variables)
  - specifying CQC when the MODEL statement contains the QPOINT *transform* for some variables (called QPOINT variables).

- When METHOD= is not CANALS, specifying COORDINATES is the same as
  - specifying MPC when there are POINT variables
  - specifying MEC when there are EPOINT variables
  - specifying MQC when there are QPOINT variables.

You can specify MRC and COEFFICIENTS anytime. When METHOD=MORALS, there is exactly one dependent variable in each model, so the canonical options (CCC, CPC, CEC, and CQC) are not allowed. Further, you cannot specify MPC, MEC, MQC, and COORDINATES when METHOD=MORALS. Otherwise, both canonical and multiple-regression-based information can be output. You can specify MPC and CPC only when there are independent POINT variables; specify MEC and CEC only when there are independent EPOINT variables; and specify MQC and CQC only when there are independent QPOINT variables. You can use the COORDINATES option only when there are POINT, EPOINT, or QPOINT independent variables. You can specify MEANS only when there are independent CLASS expansion variables.

You can specify all valid options in any combination. The examples below illustrate some properties of the coefficient partition options. The following statements perform a simple conjoint analysis outputting the design matrix, transformed dependent variable, model parameter estimates, and marginal means:

```
proc transreg; /* allowed and reasonable */
   model monotone(y1) = class(x1-x2) / intercept;
   output coefficients;
run;
```

The following statements create an output data set with both multiple regression and canonical correlation coefficients:

```
proc transreg; /* allowed and reasonable */
   model linear(y1-y10) = linear(x1-x15);
   output noscores ccc mrc;
run;
```

The following statements perform nonmetric external unfolding analysis with the configuration and ideal point coordinates being output to create a biplot. The ID statement names variables to be used in a biplot:

```
proc transreg; /* allowed and reasonable */
   model monotone(y1-y10) = qpoint(x1-x5);
   output out=biplot coordinates;
   id name;
run;
```

The following statements perform metric external unfolding analysis with the configuration, ideal point coordinates, and first canonical ideal point being output to create a biplot:

```
proc transreg; /* allowed and reasonable */
   model linear(y1-y10) = point(x1-x5);
   output out=biplot cpc mpc;
   id name;
run;
```

The following statements perform nonmetric external unfolding analysis finding monotonic transformations of the dependent variables in the context of a regression algorithm (METHOD=UNIVARIATE by default in this case), but asks for both multiple regression-based and canonical-based coordinates:

```
proc transreg; /* allowed but perhaps unreasonable */
   model monotone(y1-y10) = point(x1-x5);
   output out=biplot cpc mpc mrc;
   id name;
run;
```

In addition, multiple regression coefficients, which do not belong in a biplot, are requested.

In the following statements, POINT, EPOINT, and QPOINT independent variables are specified, and all sets of coordinates are requested:

```
proc transreg; /* allowed but perhaps unreasonable */
   model linear(y1-y10) = point(x1-x5) epoint(x6-x10)
                          qpoint(x11-x15);
   output out=biplot coordinates;
   id name;
run;
```

Typically, if POINT, EPOINT, or QPOINT appear on the right of the equal sign, you should specify only that one expansion name on the right. Note in this case that specifying COORDINATES is equivalent to specifying MPC, MEC, and MQC.

The following statements request multiple regresssion-based transformations and canonical coefficients:

```
proc transreg; /* allowed but perhaps unreasonable */
   model monotone(y1-y10) = linear(x1-x15);
   output ccc;
run;
```

The following sets of statements show combinations of options that are not valid, since the statistics requested in the OUTPUT statement cannot be obtained for the transformations requested.

The following statements request METHOD=MORALS and canonical coefficients (which cannot be output for METHOD=MORALS):

```
proc transreg method=morals; /* not allowed */
   model monotone(y1-y10) = monotone(x1-x5);
   output ccc;
run;
```

The following statements request no EPOINT variables, but MEC is specified:

```
proc transreg; /* not allowed */
   model monotone(y1-y10) = qpoint(x1-x5);
   id name;
   output mec;
run;
```

Computational Resources

This section provides information on the computational resources required to use PROC TRANSREG.

Let

n = number of observations
q = number of expanded independent variables
r = number of expanded dependent variables
k = maximum spline degree
p = maximum number of knots.

- More than $56(q+r)$ plus the maximum of the data matrix size, the optimal scaling work space, and the covariance matrix size bytes of array space are required. The data matrix size is $8n(q+r)$ bytes. The optimal scaling work space requires less than $8(6n+(p+k+2)(p+k+11))$ bytes. The covariance matrix size is $4(q+r)(q+r+1)$ bytes.

- TRANSREG tries to store the original and transformed data in memory. If there is not enough memory, a utility data set is used, potentially resulting in a large increase in execution time. The amount of memory for data formulas above are underestimates of the amount of memory needed to handle most problems. These formulas give an absolute minimum amount of memory required. If a utility data set is used, and if memory could be used with perfect efficiency, then roughly the amount of memory stated above would be needed. In reality, most problems require at least two or three times the minimum.

- TRANSREG sorts the data once. The sort time is roughly proportional to $(q+r)n^{3/2}$.

- One regression analysis per iteration is required to compute model parameters (or two canonical correlation analyses per iteration for METHOD=CANALS). The time required for accumulating the cross-product matrix is roughly proportional to $n(q+r)^2$. The time required to compute the regression coefficients is roughly proportional to q^3.
- Each optimal scaling is a multiple regression problem, although some transformations are handled with faster special case algorithms. The number of regressors for the optimal scaling problems depends on the original values of the variable and the type of transformation. For each monotone spline transformation, an unknown number of multiple regressions is required to find a set of coefficients that satisfies the constraints. The B-spline basis is generated twice for each SPLINE and MSPLINE transformation for each iteration. The time required to generate the B-spline basis is roughly proportional to nk^2.

Convergence and Degeneracies

For all the methods available in PROC TRANSREG, the algorithms are convergent, both in terms of the criterion being optimized and the parameters being estimated. The value of the criterion being maximized (squared multiple correlation, average squared multiple correlation, or average squared canonical correlation) can theoretically never decrease from one iteration to the next. The values of the parameters being solved for (the scores and weights of the transformed variables) become stable after sufficient iteration.

In practice, the criterion being maximized can decrease with overiteration. When the statistic has very nearly reached its maximum, further iterations might report a decrease in the criterion in the last few decimal places. This is a normal result of very small amounts of rounding error. By default, iteration terminates when this occurs because by default CCONVERGE=0.0. Specifying CCONVERGE=−1, an impossible change, turns off this check for convergence.

Even though the algorithms are convergent, they might not converge to a global optimum. Also, the solution might degenerate. TRANSREG detects and avoids degenerate variable transformations (merging all categories to create a constant variable). When the optimal scaling phase tries to produce a constant variable (for example, for variable X), the message

```
WARNING: A constant transformation was avoided for variable X.
```

is written to the iteration history table, and the previous scaling of the variable is not replaced by the constant scaling. This can happen with very contrived, rank deficient, and unconstrained data. For example, if all variables are uncorrelated, the regression-predicted values for the dependent variables are the column means.

With extreme collinearity, small amounts of rounding error might interact with the instability of the coefficients to produce target vectors that are not positively correlated with the original scaling. If a regression coefficient for a variable is zero, the formula for the target for that variable contains a zero divide. In a multiple regression model, after many iterations, one independent variable can be scaled the same way as the current scaling of the dependent variable, so the other independent variables will have coefficients of zero. When the constant transformation warning appears, you should interpret your results with extreme caution, and recheck your model.

Because two points always form a straight line, the algorithms sometimes try to reach this degenerate optimum. This sometimes occurs when one observation is an ordinal outlier (when one observation has the extreme rank on all variables).

The algorithm can reach an optimal solution that ties all other categories producing two points. Similar results can occur when there are many missing values. More generally, whenever there are very few constraints on the scoring of one or more points, degeneracies can be a problem. In a well-behaved analysis, the maximum data change, average data change, and criterion change all decrease at a rapid rate with each iteration. When the rate of change increases for several iterations, the solution might be degenerating.

Solving Standard Least-squares Problems

This section illustrates how to solve some ordinary least-squares problems and generalizations of those problems by formulating them as transformation regression problems. One problem involves finding linear and nonlinear regression functions in a scatterplot. The next problem involves simultaneously fitting two lines or curves through a scatterplot. The last problem involves finding the overall fit of a multi-way main-effects and interactions analysis-of-variance model.

Nonlinear Regression Functions

This example illustrates using PROC TRANSREG in simple regression to find the optimal linear regression line, a nonlinear but monotone regression function, and a nonlinear nonmonotone regression function. A linear regression line can be found by specifying

```
proc transreg;
   model linear(y) = linear(x);
   output approximations;
run;
```

A monotone regression function (in this case a monotonically decreasing regression function, since the correlation coefficient is negative) can be found by requesting an MSPLINE transformation of the independent variable as shown below.

```
proc transreg;
   model linear(y) = mspline(x / nknots=9);
   output approximations;
run;
```

The monotonicity restriction can be relaxed by requesting a SPLINE transformation of the independent variable as shown below.

```
proc transreg;
   model linear(y) = spline(x / nknots=9);
   output approximations;
run;
```

In all cases, the results can be displayed by running PROC PLOT with the following PLOT statement:

```
plot ay*x='r' y*x='*' / overlay;
```

In this example, it is not useful to plot the transformation TX, since TX is just an intermediate result used in finding a regression function through the original X and Y scatterplot.

The following statements give a specific example of using the TRANSREG procedure for a nonlinear regression function. These statements produce **Output 40.6**.

```
title 'Generate Plots for the Nonlinear Regression Function Example';
   /*---Generate an Artificial Nonlinear Scatterplot---*/
   /*---SAS/IML Software is Required for this Example---*/
proc iml;
   n   = 500;
   x   = (1:n)`;
   x   = x/(n/200);
   y   = -((x/50)-1.5)##2 + sin(x/8) + sqrt(x)/5 + 2*log(x) + cos(x);
   x   = x - x[:,];
   x   = -x / sqrt(x[##,]/(n-1));
   y   = y - y[:,];
   y   = y / sqrt(y[##,]/(n-1));
   all = y || x;
   create outset from all;
   append        from all;
   quit;


data a;
   set outset(rename=(col1=y col2=x));
   if y<-2 then y=-2 + ranuni(7654321)/2;
   x1=x; x2=x; x3=x; x4=x;
   run;


   /*---Predicted Values for the Linear Regression Line---*/
proc transreg data=a;
   title 'A Linear Regression Line';
   model linear(y)=linear(x);
   output out=a approximations;
   id x1-x4;
   run;


   /*---Predicted Values for the Monotone Regression Function---*/
proc transreg data=a(rename=(ay=ly));
   title 'A Monotone Regression Function';
   model linear(y)=mspline(x / nknots=9);
   output out=a approximations;
   id x1-x4 ly;
   run;


   /*---Predicted Values for the Nonmonotone Regression Function---*/
proc transreg data=a(rename=(ay=my));
   title 'A Nonmonotone Regression Function';
   model linear(y)=spline(x / nknots=9);
   output out=a approximations;
   id x1-x4 ly my;
   run;


   /*---Plot the Results---*/
proc plot data=a vpercent=50 hpercent=50 nolegend;
   title 'Linear, Monotone, and Nonmonotone Regression Functions';
   plot y*x1='*' / box
```

```
          haxis=-2 to 2 by 2 vaxis=-2 to 2 by 2;
    plot ly*x2='r' y*x2='*' / box overlay
          haxis=-2 to 2 by 2 vaxis=-2 to 2 by 2;
    plot my*x3='r' y*x3='*' / box overlay
          haxis=-2 to 2 by 2 vaxis=-2 to 2 by 2;
    plot ay*x4='r' y*x4='*' / box overlay
          haxis=-2 to 2 by 2 vaxis=-2 to 2 by 2;
    label ly = 'Linear Regression'
          my = 'Monotone Regression'
          ay = 'Nonmonotone Regression'
          x1 = 'Nonlinear Scatterplot'
          x2 = 'r**2 = 0.14580'
          x3 = 'r**2 = 0.60576'
          x4 = 'r**2 = 0.89634';
    run;
```

In the plots below, the ordinate values of the regression line are contained in the dependent variable approximation and are indicated by the 'r' characters in the plots.

Output 40.6   Nonlinear Regression Functions

```
                      A Monotone Regression Function                              1

         TRANSREG MORALS Algorithm Iteration History For Dependent Variable Y

              Iteration   Average    Maximum    Squared    Criterion
              Number      Change     Change     Multiple R  Change
              --------------------------------------------------------
                 1        0.62131    1.34209    0.14580       .
                 2        0.00000    0.00000    0.60576    0.45995
```

```
                      A Nonmonotone Regression Function                           2

         TRANSREG MORALS Algorithm Iteration History For Dependent Variable Y

              Iteration   Average    Maximum    Squared    Criterion
              Number      Change     Change     Multiple R  Change
              --------------------------------------------------------
                 1        0.83948    2.78984    0.14580       .
                 2        0.00000    0.00000    0.89634    0.75054
```

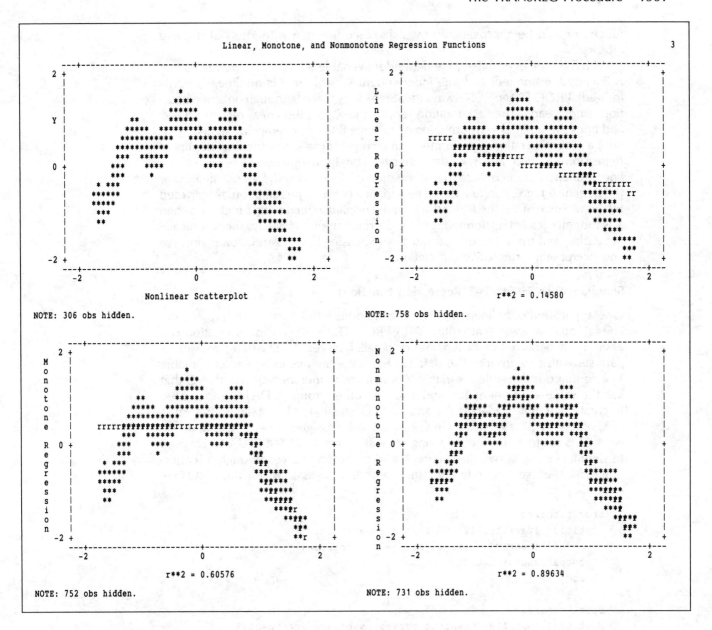

Linear, Monotone, and Nonmonotone Regression Functions

NOTE: 306 obs hidden.

Nonlinear Scatterplot

r**2 = 0.14580

NOTE: 758 obs hidden.

r**2 = 0.60576

NOTE: 752 obs hidden.

r**2 = 0.89634

NOTE: 731 obs hidden.

The squared correlation is only 0.15 for the linear regression, showing that a simple linear regression model is not appropriate for these data. By relaxing the constraints placed on the regression line, the proportion of variance accounted for increases from 0.15 (linear) to 0.61 (monotone) to 0.90 (nonmonotone). Relaxing the linearity constraint allows the regression function to bend and more closely follow the right portion of the scatterplot. Relaxing the monotonicity constraint allows the regression function to follow the periodic portion of the left side of the plot more closely. The nonlinear MSPLINE transformation is a quadratic spline with knots at the deciles. The nonlinear nonmonotonic SPLINE transformation is a cubic spline with knots at the deciles.

Different knots and different degrees would produce slightly different results. The two nonlinear regression functions could be closely approximated by simpler piecewise linear regression functions. The monotone function could be approximated by a two-piece line with a single knot at the elbow. The nonmonotone function could be approximated by a six-piece function with knots at the five elbows.

With this type of problem (one dependent variable with no missing values that is linearly transformed, and one independent variable that is nonlinearly transformed), PROC TRANSREG always iterates exactly twice (although only one iteration is necessary). The first iteration reports the R^2 for the linear regression line and finds the optimal transformation of X. Since the data change in the first iteration, a second iteration is performed, which reports the R^2 for the final nonlinear regression function, and zero data change. The approximation of Y, which is a linear function of the optimal transformation of X, contains the y-coordinates for the nonlinear regression function. The variance of the approximation of Y divided by the variance of Y is the R^2 for the fit of the nonlinear regression function. When X is monotonically transformed, the transformation of X is always monotonically increasing, but the approximation to Y is increasing if the correlation is positive and decreasing for negative correlations.

Simultaneously Fitting Two Regression Functions

One application of ordinary multiple regression is fitting two or more regression lines through a single scatterplot. With PROC TRANSREG, this application can easily be generalized to fit separate or parallel curves. To illustrate, consider a data set with two groups. The data set has a continuous independent variable X, a continuous dependent variable Y, and a group membership variable G that has the value 1 for one group and 2 for the other group. A DATA step is used to create two more variables, X1 and X2. If G equals 1, X1 is assigned the value of X, otherwise X1 is set to zero. If G equals 2, X2 is assigned the value of X, otherwise X2 is set to zero. The following code shows how TRANSREG can be used to simultaneously fit two lines, curves, and monotone curves through a scatterplot. You can use this code with an appropriate *number-list* for the KNOTS= option.

```
proc transreg;
    title1 'parallel lines, separate intercepts';
    model linear(y)=class(g) spline(x / degree=1);
    output approximations;
    run;

proc transreg;
    title1 'parallel monotone curves, separate intercepts';
    model linear(y)=class(g) mspline(x / knots=number-list);
    output approximations;
    run;

proc transreg;
    title1 'parallel curves, separate intercepts';
    model linear(y)=class(g) spline(x / knots=number-list);
    output approximations;
    run;

proc transreg;
    title1 'separate slopes, same intercept';
    model linear(y)=spline(x1-x2 / degree=1);
    id x;
    output approximations;
    run;
```

```
proc transreg;
    title1 'separate monotone curves, same intercept';
    model linear(y)=mspline(x1-x2 / knots=number-list);
    id x;
    output approximations;
    run;

proc transreg;
    title1 'separate curves, same intercept';
    model linear(y)=spline(x1-x2 / knots=number-list);
    id x;
    output approximations;
    run;

proc transreg;
    title1 'separate slopes, separate intercepts';
    model linear(y)=class(g) spline(x1-x2 / degree=1);
    id x;
    output approximations;
    run;

proc transreg;
    title1 'separate monotone curves, separate intercepts';
    model linear(y)=class(g) mspline(x1-x2 / knots=number-list);
    id x;
    output approximations;
    run;

proc transreg;
    title1 'separate curves, separate intercepts';
    model linear(y)=class(g) spline(x1-x2 / knots=number-list);
    id x;
    output approximations;
    run;
```

Since the variables X1 and X2 both will have a large partition of zeros, KNOTS= is used instead of NKNOTS=. The following example generates an artificial data set with two curves. In the interest of space, only the separate curves, separate intercepts example from above will be run.

```
data a;
    do x=-2 to 3 by 0.025;
        g=1;   x1=x; x2=0;
        y=8*(x*x + 2*cos(x*6)) + 15*normal(7654321);
        output;
        g=2;   x1=0; x2=x;
        y=4*(-x*x + 4*sin(x*4)) - 40 + 15*normal(7654321);
        output;
    end;
run;
```

```
proc transreg data=a;
   title1 'separate curves, separate intercepts';
   model linear(y)=class(g) spline(x1-x2 / knots=-1.5 to 2.5 by 0.5);
   id x;
   output approximations;
   run;

proc plot;
   plot ay*x='r' y*x='*' / box overlay href=0 vref=0;
   run;
```

The following statements produce **Output 40.7**. Alternatively, PROC GPLOT could have been used to plot the results.

```
proc gplot;
   symbol1 v=dot;
   symbol2 v=plus;
   plot y*x=1 ay*x=2 / frame overlay href=0 vref=0;
   run;
```

Output 40.7 Fitting Models: Separate Curves, Separate Intercepts

```
                        separate curves, separate intercepts                      1

          TRANSREG MORALS Algorithm Iteration History For Dependent Variable Y

              Iteration   Average    Maximum    Squared     Criterion
              Number      Change     Change     Multiple R  Change
              -----------------------------------------------------------
                 1        0.61693    4.52229    0.71020      .
                 2        0.01972    0.05497    0.86574     0.15554
                 3        0.01573    0.04362    0.86586     0.00012
                 4        0.01252    0.03421    0.86593     0.00007
                 5        0.00994    0.02653    0.86597     0.00004
                 6        0.00787    0.02033    0.86600     0.00003
                 7        0.00620    0.01538    0.86601     0.00002
                 8        0.00488    0.01146    0.86602     0.00001
                 9        0.00381    0.00838    0.86603     0.00001
                10        0.00297    0.00599    0.86603     0.00000
                11        0.00230    0.00451    0.86603     0.00000
                12        0.00177    0.00382    0.86604     0.00000
                13        0.00135    0.00323    0.86604     0.00000
                14        0.00102    0.00273    0.86604     0.00000
                15        0.00076    0.00231    0.86604     0.00000
                16        0.00062    0.00195    0.86604     0.00000
                17        0.00060    0.00166    0.86604     0.00000
                18        0.00057    0.00140    0.86604     0.00000
                19        0.00053    0.00119    0.86604     0.00000
                20        0.00049    0.00101    0.86604     0.00000
                21        0.00045    0.00085    0.86604     0.00000
                22        0.00041    0.00084    0.86604     0.00000
                23        0.00037    0.00081    0.86604     0.00000
                24        0.00034    0.00078    0.86604     0.00000
                25        0.00030    0.00073    0.86604     0.00000
                26        0.00027    0.00068    0.86604     0.00000
                27        0.00024    0.00063    0.86604     0.00000
                28        0.00021    0.00057    0.86604     0.00000
                29        0.00019    0.00052    0.86604     0.00000
                30        0.00017    0.00047    0.86604     0.00000
```

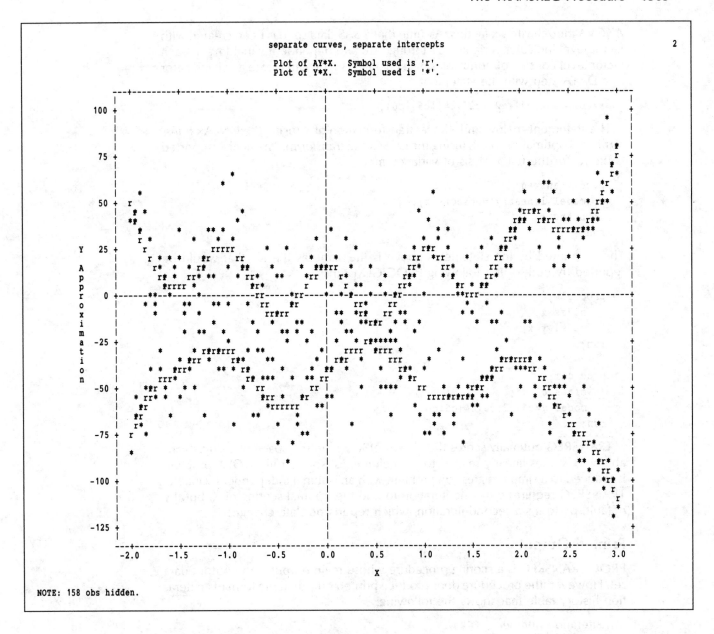

Unbalanced *ANOVA* without Dummy Variables

This example illustrates that an analysis-of-variance model can be formulated as a simple regression model. The purpose of the example is to explain one aspect of how TRANSREG works, not to propose a better way of performing an analysis of variance.

Finding the overall fit of a large, unbalanced analysis-of-variance model can be handled as an optimal scoring problem without creating large, sparse design matrices. For example, consider an unbalanced full main effects and interactions

ANOVA model with six factors. Assume that a SAS data set has been created with factor level indicator variables C1 through C6 and dependent variable Y. If each factor level consists of nonblank single characters, you can create a cell indicator in a DATA step with the statement

```
x=compress(c1||c2||c3||c4||c5||c6);
```

The statements below find a linear transformation of Y (using the LINEAR *transform*) and optimally score X (using the OPSCORE *transform*). The final R^2 reported is the R^2 for the full analysis-of-variance model.

```
proc transreg;
   model linear(y)=opscore(x);
   output;
run;
```

The R^2 printed by the statements above is the same as the R^2 that would be reported by both of the following PROC GLM runs:

```
proc glm;
   class x;
   model y=x;
run;
```

```
proc glm;
   class c1-c6;
   model y=c1|c2|c3|c4|c5|c6;
run;
```

TRANSREG optimally scores the classes of X, within the space of a single variable with values linearly related to the cell means, so the full *ANOVA* problem is reduced to a simple regression problem with an optimal independent variable. TRANSREG requires only one iteration to find the optimal scoring of X, but, by default, performs a second iteration, which reports no data changes.

Printed Output

PROC TRANSREG is a scoring procedure whose main output is the output data set. However, the procedure does produce printed output in the form of an iteration history table that shows the following:

1. iteration number
2. the criterion being optimized
3. criterion change
4. maximum and average absolute change in standardized variable scores computed over variables that can be iteratively transformed.

In addition, if multiple regression coefficients or any coordinates are requested for inclusion in the output data set, TRANSREG reports any linear dependencies in the independent variables. If dependencies are found, TRANSREG prints a model that can be used to construct variables from a linear combination of preceding variables.

EXAMPLES

Example 1:   Using Splines and Knots

This example illustrates some properties of splines. Splines are curves, which are usually required to be continuous and smooth. Splines are usually defined as piecewise polynomials of degree n whose function values and first $n-1$ derivatives agree at the points where they join. The abscissa values of the join points are called *knots*. The term spline is also used for polynomials (splines with no knots) and piecewise polynomials with more than one discontinuous derivative. Splines with no knots are generally smoother than splines with knots, which are generally smoother than splines with multiple discontinuous derivatives. Splines with few knots are generally smoother than splines with many knots, however, increasing the number of knots usually increases the fit of the spline function to the data. Knots give the curve freedom to bend to more closely follow the data. See Smith (1979) for an excellent introduction to splines.

In this example, an artificial data set is created with a variable Y that is a discontinuous function of X. See the first plot in **Output 40.14** below. Notice that the function has four unconnected parts, each of which is a curve. Notice too that there is an overall quadratic trend, that is, ignoring the shapes of the individual curves; at first the Y values tend to decrease as X increases, then Y values tend to increase.

The first TRANSREG analysis fits a linear regression model by finding a degree one spline transformation of the variable X. The predicted values of Y given the transformation of X are output and plotted to form the linear regression line. A linear transformation of X would have produced the same regression line, but less printed output. TRANSREG would not have printed an iteration history if the model statement MODEL LINEAR(Y) = LINEAR(X); had been specified since no iterations are necessary with all linear transformations and no missing data. When there are spline transformations, an iteration history is always printed. The R^2 for the linear regression is 0.10061, and it can be seen from the second plot in **Output 40.14** that the linear regression model is not appropriate for these data. The following statements create the data set and perform the first TRANSREG analysis. These statements produce **Output 40.8**.

```
options ls=120;
title 'An Illustration of Splines and Knots';
   /*----------------------------------------------------------*/
   /*                                                          */
   /* Create in Y a discontinuous function of X.               */
   /*                                                          */
   /* Store copies of X in V1-V7 for use in PROC PLOT.         */
   /* These variables are only necessary so that each          */
   /* plot can have its own x-axis label while putting         */
   /* four plots on a page.                                    */
   /*                                                          */
   /*----------------------------------------------------------*/
data a;
   array v[7] v1-v7;
   x=-0.000001;
   do i=0 to 199;
      if mod(i,50)=0 then do;
         c=((x/2)-5)**2;
         if i=150 then c=c+5;
         y=c;
      end;
```

```
      x=x+0.1;
      y=y-sin(x-c);
      do j=1 to 7;
         v[j]=x;
      end;
      output;
   end;
run;


   /*-------------------------------------------------------*/
   /*                                                       */
   /* Each of the PROC TRANSREG steps fits a                */
   /* different spline model to the data set created        */
   /* above.  The TRANSREG steps build up a data set with   */
   /* various regression functions.  All of the functions   */
   /* are then plotted with the final PROC PLOT step.       */
   /*                                                       */
   /* The OUTPUT statements add new predicted values        */
   /* variables to the data set, while the ID statements    */
   /* save all of the previously created variables that     */
   /* are needed for the plots.                             */
   /*                                                       */
   /*-------------------------------------------------------*/
proc transreg data=a;
   model linear(y)=spline(x / degree=1);
   title2 'A Linear Regression Function';
   output out=a adprefix=linear;
   id v1-v7;
   run;
```

Output 40.8   Fitting a Linear Regression Model with TRANSREG

```
                     An Illustration of Splines and Knots                    1
                     A Linear Regression Function

         TRANSREG MORALS Algorithm Iteration History For Dependent Variable Y

           Iteration   Average   Maximum   Squared    Criterion
           Number      Change    Change    Multiple R Change
           ------------------------------------------------------
              1        0.00000   0.00000   0.10061    .
```

The second TRANSREG analysis finds a degree two spline transformation with no knots, which is a quadratic polynomial. The spline is a weighted sum of a single constant, a single straight line, and a single quadratic curve. The R^2 increases from 0.10061, which is the linear fit value from before, to 0.40720. It can be seen from the third plot in **Output 40.14** that the quadratic regression function does not fit any of the individual curves well, but it does follow the overall trend in the data.

Since the overall trend is quadratic, a degree three spline with no knots (not shown) increases R^2 by only a small amount. The following statements perform this analysis and produce **Output 40.9**:

```
proc transreg data=a;
   model linear(y)=spline(x / degree=2);
   title2 'A Quadratic Polynomial Regression Function';
   output out=a adprefix=quad;
   id v1-v7 lineary;
   run;
```

Output 40.9   Fitting a Quadratic Polynomial

```
                 An Illustration of Splines and Knots                    2
                 A Quadratic Polynomial Regression Function

        TRANSREG MORALS Algorithm Iteration History For Dependent Variable Y

              Iteration   Average   Maximum   Squared     Criterion
              Number      Change    Change    Multiple R  Change
              -------------------------------------------------------
                 1        0.82127   2.77121   0.10061       .
                 2        0.00000   0.00000   0.40720     0.30659
```

The next step uses the default degree of three for a piecewise cubic polynomial, and requests knots at the known break points, $x=5$, 10, and 15. This requests a spline that is continuous, has continuous first and second derivatives, and has a third derivative that is discontinuous at 5, 10, and 15. The spline is a weighted sum of a single constant, a single straight line, a single quadratic curve, a cubic curve for the portion of X less than 5, a different cubic curve for the portion of X between 5 and 10, a different cubic curve for the portion of X between 10 and 15, and another cubic curve for the portion of X greater than 15. The new R^2 is 0.61730, and it can be seen from the fourth plot (in **Output 40.14**) that the spline is less smooth than the quadratic polynomial and it follows the data more closely than the quadratic polynomial. The following statements perform this analysis and produce **Output 40.10**:

```
proc transreg data=a;
   model linear(y) = spline(x / knots=5 10 15);
   title2 'A Cubic Spline Regression Function';
   title3 'The Third Derivative is Discontinuous at X=5, 10, 15';
   output out=a adprefix=cub1;
   id v1-v7 lineary quady;
   run;
```

Output 40.10 Fitting a Piecewise Cubic Polynomial

```
                          An Illustration of Splines and Knots                        3
                          A Cubic Spline Regression Function
                       The Third Derivative is Discontinuous at X=5, 10, 15

                  TRANSREG MORALS Algorithm Iteration History For Dependent Variable Y

           ❶ Iteration ❹ Average ❹ Maximum ❷ Squared ❸ Criterion
             Number      Change    Change    Multiple R  Change
           ----------------------------------------------------------
                1        0.85367   3.88449   0.10061      .
                2        0.00000   0.00000   0.61730     0.51670
```

The same model could be fit with a DATA step and PROC REG as follows. (The output from the code below is not shown.)

```
data b;                 /* a is the data set used for transreg */
   set a(keep=x y);
   x1=x;                    /* x                            */
   x2=x**2;                 /* x squared                    */
   x3=x**3;                 /* x cubed                      */
   x4=(x> 5)*((x-5)**3);    /* change in x**3 after  5 */
   x5=(x>10)*((x-10)**3);   /* change in x**3 after 10 */
   x6=(x>15)*((x-15)**3);   /* change in x**3 after 15 */
   run;

proc reg;
   model y=x1-x6;
run;
```

In the next step each knot is repeated three times, so the first, second, and third derivatives are discontinuous at $x=5$, 10, and 15, but the spline is required to be continuous at the knots. The spline is a weighted sum of

- a single constant
- a line for the portion of X less than 5
- a quadratic curve for the portion of X less than 5
- a cubic curve for the portion of X less than 5
- a different line for the portion of X between 5 and 10
- a different quadratic curve for the portion of X between 5 and 10
- a different cubic curve for the portion of X between 5 and 10
- a different line for the portion of X between 10 and 15
- a different quadratic curve for the portion of X between 10 and 15
- a different cubic curve for the portion of X between 10 and 15
- another line for the portion of X greater than 15
- another quadratic curve for the portion of X greater than 15
- and another cubic curve for the portion of X greater than 15.

The spline is continuous since there is not a separate constant in the formula for the spline for each knot. Now the R^2 is 0.95542, and the spline closely follows the data, except at the knots. The following statements perform this analysis and produce **Output 40.11**:

```
proc transreg data=a;
   model linear(y) = spline(x / knots=5 5 5 10 10 10 15 15 15);
   title2 'A Cubic Spline Regression Function';
   title3 'First - Third Derivatives Discontinuous at X=5, 10, 15';
   output out=a adprefix=cub3;
   id v1-v7 lineary quady cub1y;
run;
```

Output 40.11   Piecewise Polynomial with Discontinuous Derivatives

```
                     An Illustration of Splines and Knots                    4
                     A Cubic Spline Regression Function
            First - Third Derivatives Discontinuous at X=5, 10, 15

TRANSREG MORALS Algorithm Iteration History For Dependent Variable Y

     Iteration   Average   Maximum   Squared    Criterion
     Number      Change    Change    Multiple R Change
     ---------------------------------------------------------
         1       0.92492   3.50038   0.10061        .
         2       0.00000   0.00000   0.95542    0.85481
```

The same model could be fit with a DATA step and PROC REG as follows. (The output from the code below is not shown.)

```
data b;
   set a(keep=x y);
   x1=x;                          /* x                          */
   x2=x**2;                       /* x squared                  */
   x3=x**3;                       /* x cubed                    */
   x4=(x>5)  * (x- 5);            /* change in x      after  5 */
   x5=(x>10) * (x-10);            /* change in x      after 10 */
   x6=(x>15) * (x-15);            /* change in x      after 15 */
   x7=(x>5)  * ((x-5)**2);        /* change in x**2 after  5 */
   x8=(x>10) * ((x-10)**2);       /* change in x**2 after 10 */
   x9=(x>15) * ((x-15)**2);       /* change in x**2 after 15 */
   x10=(x>5)  * ((x-5)**3);       /* change in x**3 after  5 */
   x11=(x>10) * ((x-10)**3);      /* change in x**3 after 10 */
   x12=(x>15) * ((x-15)**3);      /* change in x**3 after 15 */
run;

proc reg;
   model y=x1-x12;
run;
```

When the knots are repeated four times in the next step, the spline function is discontinuous at the knots, and follows the data even more closely, with an R^2 of 0.99254. In this step, each separate curve is approximated by a cubic polynomial (with no knots within the separate polynomials). The following statements perform this analysis and produce **Output 40.12**:

```
proc transreg data=a;
   model linear(y) = spline(x / knots=5 5 5 5 10 10 10 10 15 15 15 15);
   title2 'A Cubic Spline Regression Function';
   title3 'Discontinuous Function and Derivatives';
   output out=a adprefix=cub4;
   id v1-v7 lineary quady cub1y cub3y;
run;
```

Output 40.12   Discontinuous Function and Derivatives

```
                      An Illustration of Splines and Knots                    5
                       A Cubic Spline Regression Function
                      Discontinuous Function and Derivatives

           TRANSREG MORALS Algorithm Iteration History For Dependent Variable Y

              Iteration   Average    Maximum    Squared     Criterion
              Number      Change     Change     Multiple R  Change
              ------------------------------------------------------------
                 1        0.90271    3.29184    0.10061        .
                 2        0.00000    0.00000    0.99254     0.89193
```

To solve this problem with a DATA step and PROC REG, all of the variables in the DATA step above (the B data set for the piecewise polynomial with discontinuous third derivatives), plus the following three variables would need to be created:

```
x13=(x >  5); /* intercept change after  5 */
x14=(x > 10); /* intercept change after 10 */
x15=(x > 15); /* intercept change after 15 */
```

The last two steps use the NKNOTS= option to specify the number of knots but not their location. NKNOTS=4 places knots at the quintiles while NKNOTS=9 places knots at the deciles. The spline and its first two derivatives are continuous. The R^2 values are 0.74450 and 0.95256. Even though the knots were placed in the wrong places, the spline can closely follow the data with NKNOTS=9. The following statements produce **Output 40.13**:

```
proc transreg data=a;
   model linear(y) = spline(x / nknots=4);
   title2 'A Cubic Spline Regression Function';
   title3 'Four Knots';
   output out=a adprefix=cub4k;
   id v1-v7 lineary quady cub1y cub3y cub4y;
run;
```

```
proc transreg data=a;
   model linear(y) = spline(x / nknots=9);
   title2 'A Cubic Spline Regression Function';
   title3 'Nine Knots';
   output out=a adprefix=cub9k;
   id v1-v7 lineary quady cub1y cub3y cub4y cub4ky;
run;
```

Output 40.13   Specifying Number of Knots instead of Knot Location

```
                    An Illustration of Splines and Knots                        6
                    A Cubic Spline Regression Function
                              Four Knots

   TRANSREG MORALS Algorithm Iteration History For Dependent Variable Y

        Iteration   Average   Maximum   Squared    Criterion
         Number     Change    Change    Multiple R  Change
        -----------------------------------------------------
            1       0.90305   4.46027   0.10061       .
            2       0.00000   0.00000   0.74450     0.64389
```

```
                    An Illustration of Splines and Knots                        7
                    A Cubic Spline Regression Function
                              Nine Knots

   TRANSREG MORALS Algorithm Iteration History For Dependent Variable Y

        Iteration   Average   Maximum   Squared    Criterion
         Number     Change    Change    Multiple R  Change
        -----------------------------------------------------
            1       0.94832   3.03488   0.10061       .
            2       0.00000   0.00000   0.95256     0.85196
```

The following statements produce plots that show the data and fit at each step of the analysis. These statements produce **Output 40.14.**

```
proc plot data=a vpercent=50 hpercent=50 nolegend;
   title2;
   plot                y*x='*' / box;
   plot lineary *v1='r' y*x='*' / box overlay;
   plot quady   *v2='r' y*x='*' / box overlay;
   plot cub1y   *v3='r' y*x='*' / box overlay;
   plot cub3y   *v4='r' y*x='*' / box overlay;
   plot cub4y   *v5='r' y*x='*' / box overlay;
   plot cub4ky  *v6='r' y*x='*' / box overlay;
   plot cub9ky  *v7='r' y*x='*' / box overlay;
   label v1      = 'Linear Regression';
   label v2      = 'Quadratic Regression Function';
   label v3      = '1 Discontinuous Derivative';
   label v4      = '3 Discontinuous Derivatives';
   label v5      = 'Discontinuous Function';
   label v6      = '4 Knots';
   label v7      = '9 Knots';
   label y       = 'Y';
   label lineary = 'Y';
   label quady   = 'Y';
   label cub1y   = 'Y';
```

```
      label cub3y   = 'Y';
      label cub4y   = 'Y';
      label cub4ky  = 'Y';
      label cub9ky  = 'Y';
   run;
```

Output 40.14 Plots Summarizing Analysis for Spline Example

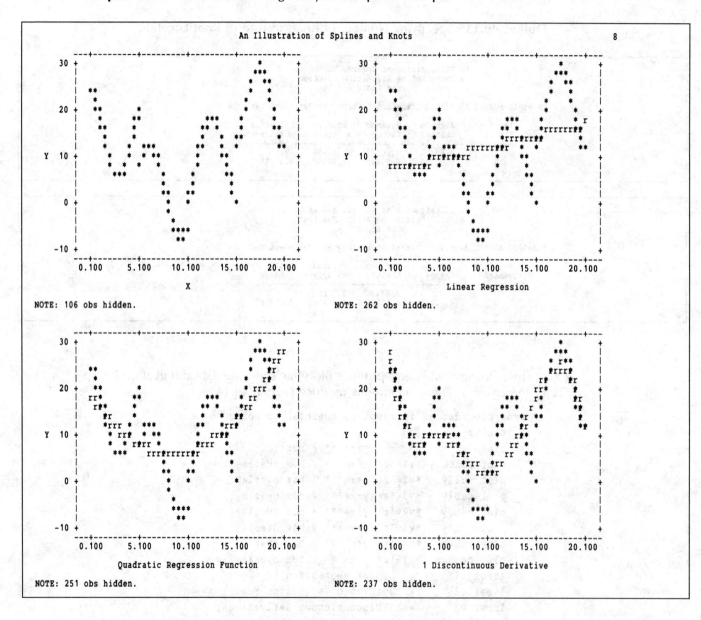

NOTE: 106 obs hidden.

NOTE: 262 obs hidden.

NOTE: 251 obs hidden.

NOTE: 237 obs hidden.

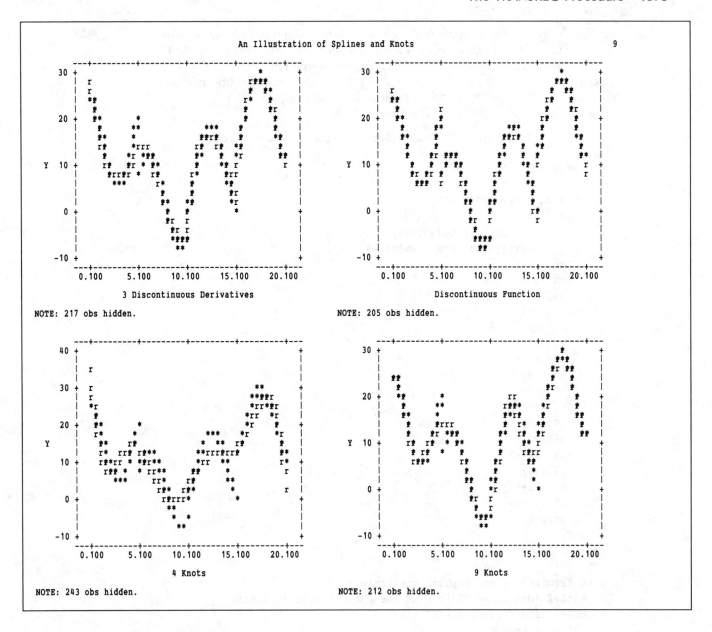

An Illustration of Splines and Knots 9

3 Discontinuous Derivatives

NOTE: 217 obs hidden.

Discontinuous Function

NOTE: 205 obs hidden.

4 Knots

NOTE: 243 obs hidden.

9 Knots

NOTE: 212 obs hidden.

Example 2: Transformed Variables as Input to Other Procedures

This example illustrates why you should not use variables that are output from PROC TRANSREG as input to the REG and GLM procedures. A DATA step creates a random data set with dependent variable Y and independent variables X1 through X5. In addition, X1, X1 squared, X1 cubed, . . . , X5 cubed, are created and stored in X11 through X53. PROC TRANSREG is run requesting cubic polynomial transformations of X1 through X5, then these transformations are input for PROC REG. The next PROC REG step fits the same overall model that TRANSREG fit using X11 through X53 as independent variables. In both PROC REG regression tables, the model, error, and total sums of squares are the same, and all three regression analyses produce the same R^2. The first (incorrect use of) PROC REG reports an F statistic for overall fit of $F = 3.048$ ($p < 0.0136$). This is not correct for these data because it does not allow for the fact that three, not one, degrees of freedom were used up for each transformation. PROC REG has no way of knowing that a previous procedure has already used up degrees of freedom. The second PROC REG reports an F statistic for overall fit of $F=0.908$ ($p < 0.5584$). This is correct because there are 15 model degrees of freedom (three per original independent variable) 99 total degrees of freedom (the number of observations minus one for the intercept) and 84 error degrees of freedom (99-15).

The following statements produce **Output 40.15**:

```
title 'Why Transformed Variables Should Not be Input to Reg';
data a;
   array x[5] x1-x5;
   do i=1 to 100;
      y=normal(7654321)*20;
      do j=1 to 5;
         x[j]=normal(7654321)*20;
         y=y+x[j]*(uniform(7654321)-0.5);
      end;
      x11=x1;
      x12=x1**2;
      x13=x1**3;
      x21=x2;
      x22=x2**2;
      x23=x2**3;
      x31=x3;
      x32=x3**2;
      x33=x3**3;
      x41=x4;
      x42=x4**2;
      x43=x4**3;
      x51=x5;
      x52=x5**2;
      x53=x5**3;
      output;
   end;
run;

proc transreg data=a replace converge=1e-10;
   title2 'Use TRANSREG to Find the Optimal Transformations';
   model linear(y)=spline(x1-x5);
   output out=b;
run;
```

```
proc reg data=b;
    title2 'Inappropriate Use of PROC REG';
    title3 'Degrees of Freedom are Not Correct';
    model y=x1-x5;
run;

proc reg data=a;
    title2 'Use REG to Fit the Same Model that TRANSREG Fit';
    model y=x11--x53;
run;
```

Output 40.15 Using Transformed Variables with Other Procedures

```
                 Why Transformed Variables Should Not be Input to Reg                        1
                   Use TRANSREG to Find the Optimal Transformations

        TRANSREG MORALS Algorithm Iteration History For Dependent Variable Y

             Iteration    Average    Maximum    Squared    Criterion
              Number      Change     Change     Multiple R  Change
            ---------------------------------------------------------------
                 1        0.50212    7.73656    0.07939       .
                 2        0.09544    0.52635    0.13724     0.05784
                 3        0.01778    0.25385    0.13941     0.00218
                 4        0.00233    0.04300    0.13950     0.00009
                 5        0.00028    0.00397    0.13950     0.00000
                 6        0.00004    0.00030    0.13950     0.00000
                 7        0.00001    0.00006    0.13950     0.00000
                 8        0.00000    0.00001    0.13950     0.00000
                 9        0.00000    0.00000    0.13950     0.00000
                10        0.00000    0.00000    0.13950     0.00000
                11        0.00000    0.00000    0.13950     0.00000
                12        0.00000    0.00000    0.13950     0.00000
                13        0.00000    0.00000    0.13950    -.00000
```

```
                 Why Transformed Variables Should Not be Input to Reg                        2
                         Inappropriate Use of PROC REG
                         Degrees of Freedom are Not Correct

Model: MODEL1
Dependent Variable: Y

                              Analysis of Variance

                               Sum of         Mean
          Source      DF      Squares        Square     F Value    Prob>F

          Model        5    6187.82574    1237.56515      3.048    0.0136
          Error       94   38167.83968     406.04085
          C Total     99   44355.66541

              Root MSE      20.15046     R-square     0.1395
              Dep Mean      -5.18395     Adj R-sq     0.0937
              C.V.        -388.70867

                             Parameter Estimates

                         Parameter     Standard     T for H0:
          Variable  DF    Estimate       Error     Parameter=0    Prob > |T|

          INTERCEP   1   -4.975607    2.04700495     -2.431       0.0170
          X1         1    0.126584    0.10474534      1.208       0.2299
          X2         1   -0.203687    0.09580665     -2.126       0.0361
          X3         1    0.151360    0.10079509      1.502       0.1365
          X4         1   -0.235753    0.11778763     -2.002       0.0482
          X5         1    0.133616    0.10602784      1.260       0.2107
```

```
                    Why Transformed Variables Should Not be Input to Reg                    3
                       Use REG to Fit the Same Model that TRANSREG Fit

Model: MODEL1
Dependent Variable: Y

                              Analysis of Variance

                           Sum of          Mean
      Source       DF      Squares        Square      F Value     Prob>F

      Model        15    6187.82574     412.52172      0.908      0.5584
      Error        84   38167.83968     454.37904
      C Total      99   44355.66541

             Root MSE      21.31617     R-square      0.1395
             Dep Mean      -5.18395     Adj R-sq     -0.0142
             C.V.        -411.19565

                            Parameter Estimates

                       Parameter     Standard     T for H0:
      Variable   DF     Estimate       Error     Parameter=0    Prob > |T|

      INTERCEP    1     2.430260     4.62409805     0.526        0.6006
      X11         1     0.053714     0.20374119     0.264        0.7927
      X12         1     0.000269     0.00445118     0.060        0.9519
      X13         1  0.000059727     0.00016389     0.364        0.7165
      X21         1    -0.194656     0.20434586    -0.953        0.3435
      X22         1    -0.002743     0.00488236    -0.562        0.5758
      X23         1  0.000016139     0.00017997     0.090        0.9288
      X31         1     0.006730     0.16797764     0.040        0.9681
      X32         1    -0.005354     0.00456436    -1.173        0.2441
      X33         1  0.000080456     0.00010364     0.776        0.4397
      X41         1    -0.209554     0.20315539    -1.031        0.3053
      X42         1    -0.012529     0.00702642    -1.783        0.0782
      X43         1     0.000300     0.00019849     1.512        0.1344
      X51         1     0.136559     0.19848421     0.688        0.4933
      X52         1    -0.003830     0.00452028    -0.847        0.3993
      X53         1  -0.000048433    0.00014514    -0.334        0.7394
```

Example 3:   Simple Conjoint Analysis

This example (inspired by Carroll 1972) illustrates using PROC TRANSREG to perform a conjoint analysis of a set of tea-tasting data. Conjoint analysis tries to
decompose rank ordered evaluation judgments of objects into components
based on qualitative object attributes. For each attribute of interest, a numerical
"utility" value is computed. The goal is to compute utilities such that the rank
ordering of the sums of each object's set of utilities is the same as the original
rank ordering, or violates the ordering as little as possible. (This example is a
greatly simplified variation of **Example 4**.)

The stimuli for the experiment were 18 hypothetical cups of tea. The stimuli
differed in temperature (hot, room temperature, cold), sweetness (no sugar, one
teaspoon sugar, two teaspoons sugar), strength (very strong, moderate strength,
very weak), and lemon (with lemon, without lemon) composing a $(3\times3\times3\times2)$
design. Of the 54 possible combinations, 18 were selected in an orthogonal array
(all pairs of zero/one dummy variables, where each dummy variable is from a
different factor, are uncorrelated). The combinations were then ranked from 1
(most preferred) to 18 (least preferred).

First, PROC FORMAT is used to specify the meanings of the factor variables,
which are entered as numbers in the data step along with the ranks. The input
data set is then printed. Then PROC TRANSREG is used to peform the conjoint
analysis. A maximum of 50 iterations are requested. The MODEL statement specifies that the dependent variable RANK should be monotonically transformed
while the classification or factor variables are optimally scored. The OUTPUT
statement creates an output data set. TSTANDARD=CENTER centers the transformed variables to mean zero. ADDITIVE specifies that the independent variables are to be multiplied by their regression coefficients producing an additive
model. In an additive model, the regression coefficients for the final transformed
variables are all one, so the predicted values of the transformed dependent

variable are simply the sum of the optimal independent variables. In this case, the final optimal independent variable scores are the utility values, which are measures of how influential the attributes are in determining subject preference. Negative utilities are associated with preferred levels and positive utilities with less preferred levels since small ranks are associated with preferred combinations. The results show that the most preferred combination, which is not actually in the data set, is hot tea, of moderate strength, with no lemon and no sugar. The sum of the utilities for this combination is

$$-9.03 = -3.02 + -3.77 + -1.16 + -1.08 \ .$$

The relative importance of attributes is indicated by the magnitude of the difference between the utilities at the lowest and highest levels of an attribute. Sweetness is the most important attribute with a difference of 8.56 ($=4.79 - (-3.77)$), with temperature close behind at 8.0 ($=4.98 - (-3.02)$). Strength (2.3) and lemon (1.62) are relatively unimportant attributes.

The following statements produce **Output 40.16**:

```
proc format;
   value temf
                 1 = 'Hot        '
                 2 = 'Room Temp'
                 3 = 'Cold       ';
   value swef
                 1 = 'No Sugar '
                 2 = '1 Spoon  '
                 3 = '2 Spoons ';
   value strf
                 1 = 'Strong   '
                 2 = 'Moderate '
                 3 = 'Weak       ';
   value lemf
                 1 = 'Lemon     '
                 2 = 'No Lemon ';
   run;

data combos;
   input temp sweet strength lemon rank;
   format temp temf. sweet swef. strength strf. lemon lemf.;
   cards;
1 1 1 1   2
1 2 2 1   4
1 3 3 2  10
2 1 2 2   8
2 2 3 1  16
2 3 1 1  17
3 1 3 1   6
3 2 1 2   7
3 3 2 1  11
1 1 3 2   1
1 2 1 1   5
1 3 2 1  12
2 1 1 1  15
2 2 2 2  14
2 3 3 1  18
3 1 2 1   3
```

```
3 2 3 1   9
3 3 1 2  13
;
proc print;
   run;

proc transreg maxiter=50;
   model monotone(rank)=opscore(temp sweet strength lemon);
   output tstandard=center additive;
   run;

proc print;
   format trank ttemp tsweet tstrengt tlemon 6.2;
   run;
```

Output 40.16 Simple Conjoint Analysis

```
                              The SAS System                                    1

     OBS    TEMP        SWEET      STRENGTH    LEMON      RANK

      1    Hot        No Sugar    Strong      Lemon        2
      2    Hot        1 Spoon     Moderate    Lemon        4
      3    Hot        2 Spoons    Weak        No Lemon    10
      4    Room Temp  No Sugar    Moderate    No Lemon     8
      5    Room Temp  1 Spoon     Weak        Lemon       16
      6    Room Temp  2 Spoons    Strong      Lemon       17
      7    Cold       No Sugar    Weak        Lemon        6
      8    Cold       1 Spoon     Strong      No Lemon     7
      9    Cold       2 Spoons    Moderate    Lemon       11
     10    Hot        No Sugar    Weak        No Lemon     1
     11    Hot        1 Spoon     Strong      Lemon        5
     12    Hot        2 Spoons    Moderate    Lemon       12
     13    Room Temp  No Sugar    Strong      Lemon       15
     14    Room Temp  1 Spoon     Moderate    No Lemon    14
     15    Room Temp  2 Spoons    Weak        Lemon       18
     16    Cold       No Sugar    Moderate    Lemon        3
     17    Cold       1 Spoon     Weak        Lemon        9
     18    Cold       2 Spoons    Strong      No Lemon    13
```

```
                              The SAS System                                    2

   TRANSREG MORALS Algorithm Iteration History For Dependent Variable RANK

      Iteration   Average   Maximum    Squared    Criterion
      Number      Change    Change     Multiple R  Change
      -----------------------------------------------------------
          1       0.32165   1.27613    0.41108      .
          2       0.15969   0.68147    0.90536     0.49428
          3       0.04996   0.16387    0.98119     0.07583
          4       0.01808   0.08129    0.99100     0.00981
          5       0.01472   0.04944    0.99361     0.00261
          6       0.01277   0.04256    0.99478     0.00117
          7       0.00949   0.03945    0.99555     0.00076
          8       0.00823   0.03593    0.99609     0.00055
          9       0.00759   0.03319    0.99655     0.00045
         10       0.00713   0.03071    0.99692     0.00038
         11       0.00675   0.02845    0.99725     0.00032
         12       0.00644   0.02638    0.99752     0.00027
         13       0.00615   0.02449    0.99776     0.00024
         14       0.00572   0.02277    0.99796     0.00021
         15       0.00461   0.02038    0.99814     0.00017
         16       0.00353   0.01200    0.99823     0.00009
         17       0.00189   0.00777    0.99829     0.00006
         18       0.00102   0.00387    0.99831     0.00002
         19       0.00068   0.00274    0.99832     0.00001
         20       0.00052   0.00255    0.99832     0.00000
         21       0.00044   0.00251    0.99832     0.00000
         22       0.00041   0.00252    0.99833     0.00000
```

(continued on next page)

(continued from previous page)

23	0.00039	0.00253	0.99833	0.00000
24	0.00038	0.00254	0.99834	0.00000
25	0.00037	0.00255	0.99834	0.00000
26	0.00037	0.00256	0.99834	0.00000
27	0.00037	0.00257	0.99835	0.00000
28	0.00036	0.00257	0.99835	0.00000
29	0.00036	0.00257	0.99836	0.00000
30	0.00036	0.00258	0.99836	0.00000
31	0.00036	0.00258	0.99836	0.00000
32	0.00034	0.00206	0.99837	0.00000
33	0.00023	0.00124	0.99837	0.00000
34	0.00015	0.00078	0.99837	0.00000
35	0.00010	0.00050	0.99837	0.00000
36	0.00007	0.00032	0.99837	0.00000
37	0.00004	0.00020	0.99837	0.00000
38	0.00003	0.00013	0.99837	0.00000
39	0.00002	0.00008	0.99837	0.00000
40	0.00001	0.00005	0.99837	0.00000
41	0.00001	0.00003	0.99837	0.00000

```
                                          The SAS System                                                3
OBS    _TYPE_    _NAME_    RANK    TRANK    TEMP        SWEET       STRENGTH    LEMON       TTEMP    TSWEET    TSTRENGT    TLEMON

  1    SCORE     ROW1       2      -6.35    Hot         No Sugar    Strong      Lemon       -3.02    -3.77     -0.07        0.54
  2    SCORE     ROW2       4      -4.66    Hot         1 Spoon     Moderate    Lemon       -3.02    -1.02     -1.16        0.54
  3    SCORE     ROW3      10       1.73    Hot         2 Spoons    Weak        No Lemon    -3.02     4.79      1.23       -1.08
  4    SCORE     ROW4       8      -1.12    Room Temp   No Sugar    Moderate    No Lemon     4.98    -3.77     -1.16       -1.08
  5    SCORE     ROW5      16       5.74    Room Temp   1 Spoon     Weak        Lemon        4.98    -1.02      1.23        0.54
  6    SCORE     ROW6      17      10.26    Room Temp   2 Spoons    Strong      Lemon        4.98     4.79     -0.07        0.54
  7    SCORE     ROW7       6      -3.90    Cold        No Sugar    Weak        Lemon       -1.97    -3.77      1.23        0.54
  8    SCORE     ROW8       7      -3.90    Cold        1 Spoon     Strong      No Lemon    -1.97    -1.02     -0.07       -1.08
  9    SCORE     ROW9      11       1.73    Cold        2 Spoons    Moderate    Lemon       -1.97     4.79     -1.16        0.54
 10    SCORE     ROW10      1      -6.65    Hot         No Sugar    Weak        No Lemon    -3.02    -3.77      1.23       -1.08
 11    SCORE     ROW11      5      -3.90    Hot         1 Spoon     Strong      Lemon       -3.02    -1.02     -0.07        0.54
 12    SCORE     ROW12     12       1.73    Hot         2 Spoons    Moderate    Lemon       -3.02     4.79     -1.16        0.54
 13    SCORE     ROW13     15       1.73    Room Temp   No Sugar    Strong      Lemon        4.98    -3.77     -0.07        0.54
 14    SCORE     ROW14     14       1.73    Room Temp   1 Spoon     Moderate    No Lemon     4.98    -1.02     -1.16       -1.08
 15    SCORE     ROW15     18      11.56    Room Temp   2 Spoons    Weak        Lemon        4.98     4.79      1.23        0.54
 16    SCORE     ROW16      3      -6.35    Cold        No Sugar    Moderate    Lemon       -1.97    -3.77     -1.16        0.54
 17    SCORE     ROW17      9      -1.12    Cold        1 Spoon     Weak        Lemon       -1.97    -1.02      1.23        0.54
 18    SCORE     ROW18     13       1.73    Cold        2 Spoons    Strong      No Lemon    -1.97     4.79     -0.07       -1.08
```

Example 4:   Conjoint Analyses of Tea-tasting Data

This example (inspired by Carroll 1972) illustrates using PROC TRANSREG to perform conjoint analyses of a set of tea-tasting data. Conjoint analysis tries to decompose rank-ordered evaluation judgments of objects into components based on qualitative object attributes. For each attribute of interest, a numerical "utility" value is computed. The goal is to compute utilities such that the rank ordering of the sums of each object's set of utilities is the same as the original rank ordering, or violates the ordering as little as possible.

This example has three parts. In the first part, a DATA step creates descriptions of the stimuli for the experiment: eighteen hypothetical cups of tea. The stimuli differed in temperature (hot, room temperature, cold), sweetness (no sugar, one teaspoon sugar, two teaspoons sugar), strength (very strong, moderate strength, very weak), and lemon (with lemon, without lemon) composing a ($3\times3\times3\times2$) design. Of the 54 possible combinations, 18 were selected in an orthogonal array (all pairs of 0/1 dummy variables, where each dummy variable is from a different factor, are uncorrelated). The descriptions were printed, then cut into two-inch by three-inch stimuli. Subjects were given the papers and were asked to imagine small styrofoam cups of tea with these characteristics. They were then asked to sort the combinations from the most preferred to the least preferred. The subjects were not given any real tea to drink. The six subjects were SAS Institute employees who were originally from five different countries.

The following statements produce **Output 40.17**. This output is abbreviated; the statements produce stimuli for all combinations.

```
data _null_;
    /*---------------------------------------------------------*/
    /*                                                         */
    /* Create the stimuli for the tea-tasting conjoint         */
    /* analysis example.                                       */
    /*                                                         */
    /* The data values are factor levels in this               */
    /* 3 x 3 x 3 x 2 fractional factorial design.              */
    /*                                                         */
    /*---------------------------------------------------------*/
title;
input ntemp nsweet nstrengt nlemon;
if       ntemp   = 1 then temp     = 'Hot                ';
else if ntemp   = 2 then temp     = 'Room Temperature   ';
else if ntemp   = 3 then temp     = 'Cold               ';
if       nsweet  = 1 then sweet    = 'No Sugar           ';
else if nsweet  = 2 then sweet    = '1 Teaspoon Sugar   ';
else if nsweet  = 3 then sweet    = '2 Teaspoons Sugar  ';
if       nstrengt = 1 then strength = 'Very Strong        ';
else if nstrengt = 2 then strength = 'Moderate Strength  ';
else if nstrengt = 3 then strength = 'Very Weak          ';
if       nlemon  = 1 then lemon    = 'With Lemon         ';
else if nlemon  = 2 then lemon    = 'Without Lemon      ';
file print;
if mod(_n_,4) eq 1 then put _page_;
put // 'Combination Number ' _n_
    // 'Temperature = ' temp
    // 'Sweetness = ' sweet
    // 'Strength = ' strength
    // lemon;
cards;
1 1 1 1
1 2 2 1
1 3 3 2
2 1 2 2
2 2 3 1
2 3 1 1
3 1 3 1
3 2 1 2
3 3 2 1
1 1 3 2
1 2 1 1
1 3 2 1
2 1 1 1
2 2 2 2
2 3 3 1
3 1 2 1
3 2 3 1
3 3 1 2
;
```

Output 40.17   Conjoint Analysis Stimuli Descriptions

```
                                                                    1

Combination Number 1

Temperature = Hot

Sweetness = No Sugar

Strength = Very Strong

With Lemon


Combination Number 2

Temperature = Hot

Sweetness = 1 Teaspoon Sugar

Strength = Moderate Strength

With Lemon


Combination Number 3

Temperature = Hot

Sweetness = 2 Teaspoons Sugar

Strength = Very Weak

Without Lemon


Combination Number 4

Temperature = Room Temperature

Sweetness = No Sugar

Strength = Moderate Strength

Without Lemon
```

The second part of the example performs the conjoint analyses. The first DATA step reads the factor levels and creates abbreviated level names. The next DATA step reads the data. Only the combination numbers are entered, one row per subject. The DO loop and assignment statement convert the raw data to ranks. For subject one, combination 11 was the most preferred, so the eleventh rank variable (R11) is set to 1; combination 2 was the second most preferred, so R2 is set to 2; and so on. PROC TRANSPOSE transposes this (6×18) data set into an (18×6) data set that can be merged with the factor level data set COMBOS. The next DATA step does the merge, creates the average rank for each combination, and creates the variable COMBO that contains the factor levels. PROC PRINT displays some of these variables.

The PROC TRANSREG METHOD=MORALS algorithm individually fits seven different conjoint models, one for each subject and one for the average ranks. IREPLACE replaces the original independent variables with the transformed independent variables in the output data set. Specifying MAXITER=20 and using the defaults CONVERGE=0.00001, and CCONVERGE=0.0 cause the iterations to stop when the first of three events occurs: the number of iterations reaches 20, the average absolute change in standardized variable scores is less than 0.00001, or the squared multiple correlation can no longer increase within machine precision.

The MODEL statement specifies that the dependent variables should be monotonically transformed with a quadratic monotone spline transformation with a knot at the median, while the classification or factor variables are optimally scored. Typically, the optimal monotonic transformation family (MONOTONE) is used with conjoint analysis. There is no reason why MONOTONE must be used, however. If one of these models were fit with MONOTONE, 25 parameters would be "estimated" in a model with 18 available degrees of freedom. The dependent variable mean is the first parameter. There are 18 dependent variable scoring parameters, but only 17 are free to vary. There are 11 factor levels, but four (one per independent variable) are not free to vary, given the estimate of the mean. Some parameters are not free to vary due to the constraints imposed that all optimally scored variables in this analysis have a fixed mean. A quadratic spline transformation has three parameters, plus as many additional parameters as there are knots. This monotone quadratic spline has one knot for a total of four parameters. For ranked data, MSPLINE transformations with a small number of knots will not over-fit the data as much as MONOTONE transformations, and MSPLINE transformations will be smoother than MONOTONE transformations.

Since the OUT= option is not specified in the OUTPUT statement, the default WORK.DATA*n* naming convention is used to name the output data set. Specifying TSTANDARD=CENTER centers the transformed variables to mean zero. ADDITIVE specifies that the independent variables are then to be multiplied by their regression coefficients producing an additive model. In an additive model, the regression coefficients for the final transformed variables are all one, so the predicted values of the transformed dependent variable are simply the sum of the optimal independent variables. In this case, the final optimal independent variable scores are the utility values, which are measures of how influential the attributes are in determining subject preference. Negative utilities are associated with preferred levels and positive utilities with less preferred levels since small ranks are associated with preferred combinations. The ID statement copies the variable COMBO into the output data set. The next two steps print the PROC TRANSREG output data set and plot the dependent variable transformations.

The MORALS algorithm produces one iteration history table for each dependent variable. The squared multiple correlation from the first iteration in each table may be small. These values have no meaning since the independent variables are character variables. They are simply the squared multiple correlations for regression models with untransformed ranks as the dependent variable and category numbers (0, 1, 2, . . .) for the character input variables. The final squared multiple correlations are large, meaning that the monotonically transformed ranks are highly related to the independent variables, which are optimally scored with utilities. Equivalently, the monotonically transformed ranks closely fit a main effects analysis-of-variance model.

Only the interpretation of the average ranks (observations 109 to 126 in the output data set) will be discussed. The first observation contains the second most preferred combination. The −3.61785 transformed average rank is approximately the sum of the utilities

$$-3.62 \cong -2.23 + -1.49 + 0.23 + 0.48 = -3.01$$

Hot tea is preferred over cold tea, which is preferred over room temperature tea. No sugar is preferred over one teaspoon, which is preferred over two teaspoons. Moderate strength tea is preferred over strong tea, which is preferred over weak tea. No lemon is preferred over lemon. Each column sums to zero, so the average utility in a factor, weighted by the number of observations in each category, is zero, which is the mean transformed rank. (The values of the utilities are different if a different standardization is requested.) The values of the utilities depend on what other factors appear in the model. A factor could be highly related to the dependent variable, but have all utilities at or near zero if it is highly related to a different factor. The values of the utilities depend on what other factors appear in the model, even if an orthogonal design is used, because the dependent variable transformation depends on the independent variables, and the final coefficients depend on the transformation. The utilities are coefficients of a constrained less-than-full rank analysis-of-variance model, so all of the usual problems with interpreting regression coefficients are problems with interpreting utilities. Also, one of the utility values for each factor is completely determined given the other utilities, since the weighted average of each factor's utilities must be zero.

Analyses could have been run requesting a linear transformation of the ranks instead of a monotone transformation. Then, because the combinations of the independent variables form an orthogonal array, the utilities for a factor would not depend on the other factors in the analysis. The linear transformation analysis typically will not fit the data as well as the monotone analysis. With an orthogonal array of independent variables and a linearly transformed dependent variable, the conjoint analysis is much faster. The first iteration does all of the work, but a second iteration is performed that finds it cannot improve on the solution.

PROC TRANSREG allows you to formulate conjoint analyses in many different ways. You can include an intercept in the model or not; you can use TSTANDARD=ORIGINAL, TSTANDARD=CENTER, or TSTANDARD=Z standardizations; you can construct an additive model or allow nonunit coefficients; you can optimally score categories or expand to dummy variables; with CLASS expansion variables, you can fit full rank or less than full rank models. Another possibility, if you prefer positive utilities to correspond to high preference and negative utilities to correspond to low preference, is to reverse the ranks in a DATA step before PROC TRANSREG is run. Just subtract each rank from one plus the highest rank: in this example, RANK=19−RANK. This example illustrates just one combination of the available options.

This example also illustrates a macro that is useful with both PROC TRANSREG and PROC PRINQUAL. When given abbreviated variable lists of numbered names like SUBJ1–SUBJ6, these procedures produce transformed variables with names like TSUBJ1–TSUBJ6. Often, the transformations are plotted. If there are a large number of variables it becomes tedious to type

```
plot tsubj1*subj1 tsubj2*subj2 tsubj3*subj3 . . . ;
```

The macro MATCH provides a convenient way of producing these plot requests. This macro could be simplified by assuming that &START is always 1, &SYMBOL is always an asterisk, and the prefix 'T' is always used for the transformations. The following statements produce **Output 40.18**:

```
data combos;
    /*--------------------------------------------------------*/
    /*                                                        */
    /* Read in the design variables with abbreviated          */
    /* category labels.                                       */
    /*                                                        */
    /*--------------------------------------------------------*/
    input ntemp nsweet nstrengt nlemon;
    drop  ntemp nsweet nstrengt nlemon;
    if       ntemp   = 1 then temp    = 'Hot      ';
    else if ntemp   = 2 then temp    = 'Room Temp';
    else if ntemp   = 3 then temp    = 'Cold     ';
    if       nsweet  = 1 then sweet   = 'No Sugar ';
    else if nsweet  = 2 then sweet   = '1 Spoon  ';
    else if nsweet  = 3 then sweet   = '2 Spoons ';
```

```
    if       nstrengt = 1 then strength = 'Strong   ';
    else if nstrengt = 2 then strength = 'Moderate ';
    else if nstrengt = 3 then strength = 'Weak     ';
    if       nlemon   = 1 then lemon    = 'Lemon    ';
    else if nlemon   = 2 then lemon    = 'No Lemon ';
    cards;
 1 1 1 1
 1 2 2 1
 1 3 3 2
 2 1 2 2
 2 2 3 1
 2 3 1 1
 3 1 3 1
 3 2 1 2
 3 3 2 1
 1 1 3 2
 1 2 1 1
 1 3 2 1
 2 1 1 1
 2 2 2 2
 2 3 3 1
 3 1 2 1
 3 2 3 1
 3 3 1 2
 ;

data sorts;
    /*-------------------------------------------------------*/
    /*                                                       */
    /* Subjects were asked to order combinations from most   */
    /* preferred to least preferred.  Each observation in    */
    /* this data set corresponds to a subject.  The first    */
    /* number in each row is the combination number of the   */
    /* most preferred combination.  The second number is     */
    /* the combination number of the second most preferred   */
    /* combination, and so on.  This DATA step transforms    */
    /* these data to ranks.                                  */
    /*                                                       */
    /*-------------------------------------------------------*/
    input c1-c18;
    drop i c1-c18;
    array c[18]  c1-c18;
    array r[18]  r1-r18;

    /*---Assign Ranks---*/
    do i = 1 to 18;
       r[c [i]]=i;
    end;
    drop i c1-c18;
    cards;
 11 02 10 01 12 03 07 16 17 09 08 18 04 05 06 15 13 14
 10 01 07 16 17 08 11 02 18 03 09 12 04 13 14 05 15 06
 02 11 12 01 08 09 18 16 14 04 10 06 03 07 17 13 05 15
```

```
16  07  01  10  04  13  08  17  02  11  14  05  09  18  06  15  12  03
14  04  08  18  03  10  11  06  12  02  13  09  01  16  15  05  17  07
16  07  17  10  01  03  09  02  05  15  14  04  12  11  18  06  08  13
;

   /*---Create an Object by Subject Data Matrix---*/
proc transpose data=sorts out=sorts prefix=subj;
run;

   /*---Merge the Factor Levels With the Data Matrix---*/
data both;
   merge combos sorts;
   average = mean(of subj1 - subj6);
   length combo $ 40;
   combo = trim(temp)      || ', ' ||
           trim(sweet)     || ', ' ||
           trim(strength)  || ', ' ||
           trim(lemon);
run;

   /*---Print Input Data Set---*/
proc print;
   title 'Data Set for Conjoint Analysis';
   var combo subj1-subj6 average;
run;

   /*---Fit The Average Rank and Each Subject Individually---*/
proc transreg data=both method=morals ireplace maxiter=20;
   title 'Individual Conjoint Analyses';
   model mspline(subj1-subj6 average / nknots=1)=
         opscore(temp sweet strength lemon);
   output tstandard=center additive;
   id combo;
run;

   /*---Print Results---*/
proc print;
   var combo _dtrans_ temp sweet strength lemon;
   by notsorted _var_;
run;

   /*---Rearrange Data Set so Proc Plot Can Fit Six Plots Per Page---*/
data tposed;
   set _last_(keep=_depend_ _dtrans_ _var_);
   by notsorted _var_;
   retain count;
   if first._var_ then count=0;
   count=count+1;
run;

proc sort data=tposed out=tposed;
   by count _var_;
run;
```

```
data tposed;
   set tposed;
   retain i 0;
   retain average subj1-subj6 taverage tsubj1-tsubj6;
   array v[14] average subj1-subj6 taverage tsubj1-tsubj6;
   keep average subj1-subj6 taverage tsubj1-tsubj6;
   i = i + 1;
   v[i]=_depend_;
   v[i+7]=_dtrans_;
   if i=7 then do;
      output;
      i=0;
   end;
run;

%macro match(prefix1,prefix2,symbol,start,stop);
   /*----------------------------------------------------------*/
   /* This macro can be used to combine matching variable */
   /* lists for PLOT statements and renaming variables.   */
   /*                                                     */
   /* For example,                                        */
   /* plot %match(tsubj,subj,*,1,6);                       */
   /* produces                                            */
   /*                                                     */
   /* plot tsubj1 * subj1 tsub2 * subj2 tsubj3 * subj3    */
   /*      tsubj4 * subj4 tsub5 * subj5 tsubj6 * subj6;   */
   /*                                                     */
   /*----------------------------------------------------------*/

   %do i = &start %to &stop;
       &prefix1.&i &symbol &prefix2.&i
   %end;

   %mend match;

   /*---Plot the Individual and Average Monotone Transformations---*/
proc plot vpercent=33 hpercent=50;
   plot %match(tsubj,subj,*,1,6) taverage*average / box;
run;
```

Output 40.18   Conjoint Analysis

```
                            Data Set for Conjoint Analysis                                    1
  OBS   COMBO                              SUBJ1   SUBJ2   SUBJ3   SUBJ4   SUBJ5   SUBJ6   AVERAGE

   1    Hot, No Sugar, Strong, Lemon         4       2       4       3      13       5     5.1667
   2    Hot, 1 Spoon, Moderate, Lemon        2       8       1       9      10       8     6.3333
   3    Hot, 2 Spoons, Weak, No Lemon        6      10      13      18       5       6     9.6667
   4    Room Temp, No Sugar, Moderate, No Lemon  13  13      10       5       2      12     9.1667
   5    Room Temp, 1 Spoon, Weak, Lemon     14      16      17      12      16       9    14.0000
   6    Room Temp, 2 Spoons, Strong, Lemon  15      18      12      15       8      16    14.0000
```

(continued on next page)

(continued from previous page)

7	Cold, No Sugar, Weak, Lemon	7	3	14	2	18	2	7.6667
8	Cold, 1 Spoon, Strong, No Lemon	11	6	5	7	3	17	8.1667
9	Cold, 2 Spoons, Moderate, Lemon	10	11	6	13	12	7	9.8333
10	Hot, No Sugar, Weak, No Lemon	3	1	11	4	6	4	4.8333
11	Hot, 1 Spoon, Strong, Lemon	1	7	2	10	7	14	6.8333
12	Hot, 2 Spoons, Moderate, Lemon	5	12	3	17	9	13	9.8333
13	Room Temp, No Sugar, Strong, Lemon	17	14	16	6	11	18	13.6667
14	Room Temp, 1 Spoon, Moderate, No Lemon	18	15	9	11	1	11	10.8333
15	Room Temp, 2 Spoons, Weak, Lemon	16	17	18	16	15	10	15.3333
16	Cold, No Sugar, Moderate, Lemon	8	4	8	1	14	1	6.0000
17	Cold, 1 Spoon, Weak, Lemon	9	5	15	8	17	3	9.5000
18	Cold, 2 Spoons, Strong, No Lemon	12	9	7	14	4	15	10.1667

Individual Conjoint Analyses   2

TRANSREG MORALS Algorithm Iteration History For Dependent Variable SUBJ1

Iteration Number	Average Change	Maximum Change	Squared Multiple R	Criterion Change
1	0.49248	1.15862	0.26643	.
2	0.30900	0.96766	0.73547	0.46905
3	0.11866	0.44423	0.91752	0.18204
4	0.03072	0.13999	0.96764	0.05013
5	0.00000	0.00000	0.97470	0.00706

Individual Conjoint Analyses   3

TRANSREG MORALS Algorithm Iteration History For Dependent Variable SUBJ2

Iteration Number	Average Change	Maximum Change	Squared Multiple R	Criterion Change
1	0.15747	0.62398	0.82095	.
2	0.02472	0.17501	0.98081	0.15986
3	0.01156	0.06119	0.98848	0.00767
4	0.00443	0.02161	0.98953	0.00105
5	0.00140	0.00757	0.98968	0.00015
6	0.00052	0.00321	0.98970	0.00002
7	0.00046	0.00178	0.98970	0.00000
8	0.00035	0.00155	0.98970	0.00000
9	0.00025	0.00118	0.98970	0.00000
10	0.00017	0.00084	0.98970	0.00000
11	0.00012	0.00057	0.98970	0.00000
12	0.00008	0.00038	0.98970	0.00000
13	0.00005	0.00025	0.98970	0.00000
14	0.00003	0.00017	0.98970	0.00000
15	0.00002	0.00011	0.98970	0.00000
16	0.00001	0.00007	0.98970	0.00000
17	0.00001	0.00005	0.98970	0.00000

Individual Conjoint Analyses   4

TRANSREG MORALS Algorithm Iteration History For Dependent Variable SUBJ3

Iteration Number	Average Change	Maximum Change	Squared Multiple R	Criterion Change
1	0.45060	1.62283	0.57757	.
2	0.01589	0.11930	0.94166	0.36409
3	0.01101	0.09094	0.94516	0.00350
4	0.00859	0.07049	0.94737	0.00220
5	0.00681	0.05486	0.94875	0.00139
6	0.00537	0.04277	0.94962	0.00087
7	0.00423	0.03338	0.95016	0.00054
8	0.00332	0.02608	0.95050	0.00034
9	0.00262	0.02040	0.95071	0.00021
10	0.00206	0.01597	0.95084	0.00013
11	0.00162	0.01252	0.95092	0.00008
12	0.00127	0.00982	0.95097	0.00005
13	0.00100	0.00770	0.95100	0.00003
14	0.00079	0.00605	0.95102	0.00002
15	0.00062	0.00475	0.95103	0.00001
16	0.00049	0.00373	0.95104	0.00001
17	0.00038	0.00293	0.95104	0.00000
18	0.00030	0.00231	0.95104	0.00000
19	0.00024	0.00181	0.95105	0.00000
20	0.00019	0.00143	0.95105	0.00000

Individual Conjoint Analyses   5

TRANSREG MORALS Algorithm Iteration History For Dependent Variable SUBJ4

Iteration Number	Average Change	Maximum Change	Squared Multiple R	Criterion Change
1	0.19256	1.03429	0.96526	.
2	0.01154	0.04598	0.97732	0.01206
3	0.00404	0.01346	0.97750	0.00018
4	0.00153	0.00530	0.97753	0.00003
5	0.00066	0.00285	0.97754	0.00001
6	0.00040	0.00167	0.97754	0.00000
7	0.00028	0.00103	0.97754	0.00000
8	0.00019	0.00065	0.97754	0.00000
9	0.00013	0.00042	0.97754	0.00000
10	0.00009	0.00028	0.97754	0.00000
11	0.00006	0.00018	0.97754	0.00000
12	0.00004	0.00012	0.97754	0.00000
13	0.00003	0.00008	0.97754	0.00000
14	0.00002	0.00005	0.97754	0.00000
15	0.00001	0.00004	0.97754	0.00000
16	0.00001	0.00002	0.97754	0.00000

Individual Conjoint Analyses   6

TRANSREG MORALS Algorithm Iteration History For Dependent Variable SUBJ5

Iteration Number	Average Change	Maximum Change	Squared Multiple R	Criterion Change
1	0.27349	1.17339	0.87289	.
2	0.02869	0.09424	0.98155	0.10865
3	0.02243	0.07494	0.98318	0.00163
4	0.01702	0.05715	0.98395	0.00078
5	0.01270	0.04266	0.98435	0.00040
6	0.00939	0.03151	0.98456	0.00021
7	0.00692	0.02316	0.98467	0.00011
8	0.00508	0.01699	0.98473	0.00006
9	0.00373	0.01245	0.98476	0.00003
10	0.00273	0.00912	0.98478	0.00002
11	0.00200	0.00669	0.98479	0.00001
12	0.00147	0.00490	0.98479	0.00001
13	0.00108	0.00359	0.98479	0.00000
14	0.00079	0.00264	0.98480	0.00000
15	0.00058	0.00193	0.98480	0.00000
16	0.00043	0.00142	0.98480	0.00000
17	0.00031	0.00104	0.98480	0.00000
18	0.00023	0.00076	0.98480	0.00000
19	0.00017	0.00056	0.98480	0.00000
20	0.00012	0.00041	0.98480	0.00000

Individual Conjoint Analyses   7

TRANSREG MORALS Algorithm Iteration History For Dependent Variable SUBJ6

Iteration Number	Average Change	Maximum Change	Squared Multiple R	Criterion Change
1	0.34789	1.18171	0.36154	.
2	0.04072	0.15642	0.80578	0.44424
3	0.02497	0.10358	0.82301	0.01723
4	0.01511	0.06857	0.82966	0.00665
5	0.00910	0.04326	0.83211	0.00245
6	0.00547	0.02665	0.83300	0.00089
7	0.00328	0.01622	0.83332	0.00032
8	0.00197	0.00980	0.83343	0.00011
9	0.00118	0.00590	0.83347	0.00004
10	0.00071	0.00354	0.83349	0.00001
11	0.00042	0.00212	0.83349	0.00001
12	0.00025	0.00127	0.83349	0.00000
13	0.00015	0.00076	0.83349	0.00000
14	0.00009	0.00046	0.83349	0.00000
15	0.00005	0.00027	0.83349	0.00000
16	0.00003	0.00016	0.83349	0.00000
17	0.00002	0.00010	0.83349	0.00000
18	0.00001	0.00006	0.83349	0.00000
19	0.00001	0.00004	0.83349	0.00000

Individual Conjoint Analyses   8

TRANSREG MORALS Algorithm Iteration History For Dependent Variable AVERAGE

Iteration Number	Average Change	Maximum Change	Squared Multiple R	Criterion Change
1	0.23432	0.83170	0.63432	.
2	0.01895	0.11414	0.95310	0.31878
3	0.00846	0.04868	0.95585	0.00275
4	0.00412	0.02317	0.95646	0.00061
5	0.00207	0.01155	0.95662	0.00016
6	0.00106	0.00586	0.95666	0.00004
7	0.00054	0.00300	0.95667	0.00001
8	0.00028	0.00154	0.95667	0.00000
9	0.00014	0.00079	0.95667	0.00000
10	0.00007	0.00040	0.95667	0.00000
11	0.00004	0.00021	0.95667	0.00000
12	0.00002	0.00011	0.95667	0.00000
13	0.00001	0.00005	0.95667	0.00000

Individual Conjoint Analyses   9

-- _VAR_=SUBJ1 --

OBS	COMBO	_DTRANS_	TEMP	SWEET	STRENGTH	LEMON
1	Hot, No Sugar, Strong, Lemon	-5.92498	-5.98891	-1.09806	0.89209	-0.50428
2	Hot, 1 Spoon, Moderate, Lemon	-6.84548	-5.98891	-0.04404	-0.35229	-0.50428
3	Hot, 2 Spoons, Weak, No Lemon	-4.39082	-5.98891	1.14210	-0.53980	1.00857
4	Room Temp, No Sugar, Moderate, No Lemon	4.35389	6.12954	-1.09806	-0.35229	1.00857
5	Room Temp, 1 Spoon, Weak, Lemon	5.29143	6.12954	-0.04404	-0.53980	-0.50428
6	Room Temp, 2 Spoons, Strong, Lemon	6.05851	6.12954	1.14210	0.89209	-0.50428
7	Cold, No Sugar, Weak, Lemon	-3.39362	-0.14063	-1.09806	-0.53980	-0.50428
8	Cold, 1 Spoon, Strong, No Lemon	1.96742	-0.14063	-0.04404	0.89209	1.00857
9	Cold, 2 Spoons, Moderate, Lemon	0.51849	-0.14063	1.14210	-0.35229	-0.50428
10	Hot, No Sugar, Weak, No Lemon	-6.46194	-5.98891	-1.09806	-0.53980	1.00857
11	Hot, 1 Spoon, Strong, Lemon	-7.07560	-5.98891	-0.04404	0.89209	-0.50428
12	Hot, 2 Spoons, Moderate, Lemon	-5.23461	-5.98891	1.14210	-0.35229	-0.50428
13	Room Temp, No Sugar, Strong, Lemon	7.08129	6.12954	-1.09806	0.89209	-0.50428
14	Room Temp, 1 Spoon, Moderate, No Lemon	7.33698	6.12954	-0.04404	-0.35229	1.00857
15	Room Temp, 2 Spoons, Weak, Lemon	6.65513	6.12954	1.14210	-0.53980	-0.50428
16	Cold, No Sugar, Moderate, Lemon	-2.24300	-0.14063	-1.09806	-0.35229	-0.50428
17	Cold, 1 Spoon, Weak, Lemon	-0.93896	-0.14063	-0.04404	-0.53980	-0.50428
18	Cold, 2 Spoons, Strong, No Lemon	3.24589	-0.14063	1.14210	0.89209	1.00857

-- _VAR_=SUBJ2 --

OBS	COMBO	_DTRANS_	TEMP	SWEET	STRENGTH	LEMON
19	Hot, No Sugar, Strong, Lemon	-6.2850	-2.93382	-2.87825	-0.07070	0.38008
20	Hot, 1 Spoon, Moderate, Lemon	-2.3443	-2.93382	-0.25305	0.41835	0.38008
21	Hot, 2 Spoons, Weak, No Lemon	-0.5861	-2.93382	3.13130	-0.34766	-0.76015
22	Room Temp, No Sugar, Moderate, No Lemon	2.7051	6.34986	-2.87825	0.41835	-0.76015
23	Room Temp, 1 Spoon, Weak, Lemon	6.9706	6.34986	-0.25305	-0.34766	0.38008
24	Room Temp, 2 Spoons, Strong, Lemon	10.3554	6.34986	3.13130	-0.07070	0.38008
25	Cold, No Sugar, Weak, Lemon	-5.7672	-3.41604	-2.87825	-0.34766	0.38008
26	Cold, 1 Spoon, Strong, No Lemon	-3.8802	-3.41604	-0.25305	-0.07070	-0.76015
27	Cold, 2 Spoons, Moderate, Lemon	0.4028	-3.41604	3.13130	0.41835	0.38008
28	Hot, No Sugar, Weak, No Lemon	-6.7473	-2.93382	-2.87825	-0.34766	-0.76015
29	Hot, 1 Spoon, Strong, Lemon	-3.1401	-2.93382	-0.25305	-0.07070	0.38008
30	Hot, 2 Spoons, Moderate, Lemon	1.4998	-2.93382	3.13130	0.41835	0.38008
31	Room Temp, No Sugar, Strong, Lemon	4.0187	6.34986	-2.87825	-0.07070	0.38008
32	Room Temp, 1 Spoon, Moderate, No Lemon	5.4405	6.34986	-0.25305	0.41835	-0.76015
33	Room Temp, 2 Spoons, Weak, Lemon	8.6089	6.34986	3.13130	-0.34766	0.38008
34	Cold, No Sugar, Moderate, Lemon	-5.1938	-3.41604	-2.87825	0.41835	0.38008
35	Cold, 1 Spoon, Weak, Lemon	-4.5648	-3.41604	-0.25305	-0.34766	0.38008
36	Cold, 2 Spoons, Strong, No Lemon	-1.4930	-3.41604	3.13130	-0.07070	-0.76015

--- _VAR_=SUBJ3 ---

OBS	COMBO	_DTRANS_	TEMP	SWEET	STRENGTH	LEMON
37	Hot, No Sugar, Strong, Lemon	-5.18852	-4.01100	0.88445	-1.77087	0.20833
38	Hot, 1 Spoon, Moderate, Lemon	-8.87223	-4.01100	-1.32399	-3.28999	0.20833
39	Hot, 2 Spoons, Weak, No Lemon	2.87914	-4.01100	0.43955	5.06086	-0.41665
40	Room Temp, No Sugar, Moderate, No Lemon	0.27995	4.25315	0.88445	-3.28999	-0.41665
41	Room Temp, 1 Spoon, Weak, Lemon	7.89394	4.25315	-1.32399	5.06086	0.20833
42	Room Temp, 2 Spoons, Strong, Lemon	1.90209	4.25315	0.43955	-1.77087	0.20833
43	Cold, No Sugar, Weak, Lemon	3.96686	-0.24215	0.88445	5.06086	0.20833
44	Cold, 1 Spoon, Strong, No Lemon	-4.10128	-0.24215	-1.32399	-1.77087	-0.41665
45	Cold, 2 Spoons, Moderate, Lemon	-3.08437	-0.24215	0.43955	-3.28999	0.20833
46	Hot, No Sugar, Weak, No Lemon	1.03569	-4.01100	0.88445	5.06086	-0.41665
47	Hot, 1 Spoon, Strong, Lemon	-7.57399	-4.01100	-1.32399	-1.77087	0.20833
48	Hot, 2 Spoons, Moderate, Lemon	-6.34609	-4.01100	0.43955	-3.28999	0.20833
49	Room Temp, No Sugar, Strong, Lemon	6.47426	4.25315	0.88445	-1.77087	0.20833
50	Room Temp, 1 Spoon, Moderate, No Lemon	-0.45563	4.25315	-1.32399	-3.28999	-0.41665
51	Room Temp, 2 Spoons, Weak, Lemon	9.42429	4.25315	0.43955	5.06086	0.20833
52	Cold, No Sugar, Moderate, Lemon	-1.26155	-0.24215	0.88445	-3.28999	0.20833
53	Cold, 1 Spoon, Weak, Lemon	5.16523	-0.24215	-1.32399	5.06086	0.20833
54	Cold, 2 Spoons, Strong, No Lemon	-2.13779	-0.24215	0.43955	-1.77087	-0.41665

--- _VAR_=SUBJ4 ---

OBS	COMBO	_DTRANS_	TEMP	SWEET	STRENGTH	LEMON
55	Hot, No Sugar, Strong, Lemon	-6.62179	0.46190	-6.10419	-0.29066	-0.11140
56	Hot, 1 Spoon, Moderate, Lemon	-0.45307	0.46190	0.14030	-0.09623	-0.11140
57	Hot, 2 Spoons, Weak, No Lemon	7.70532	0.46190	5.96389	0.38689	0.22280
58	Room Temp, No Sugar, Moderate, No Lemon	-4.73533	1.41975	-6.10419	-0.09623	0.22280
59	Room Temp, 1 Spoon, Weak, Lemon	2.95681	1.41975	0.14030	0.38689	-0.11140
60	Room Temp, 2 Spoons, Strong, Lemon	5.69690	1.41975	5.96389	-0.29066	-0.11140
61	Cold, No Sugar, Weak, Lemon	-7.50134	-1.88165	-6.10419	0.38689	-0.11140
62	Cold, 1 Spoon, Strong, No Lemon	-2.67909	-1.88165	0.14030	-0.29066	0.22280
63	Cold, 2 Spoons, Moderate, Lemon	3.95147	-1.88165	5.96389	-0.09623	-0.11140
64	Hot, No Sugar, Weak, No Lemon	-5.69978	0.46190	-6.10419	0.38689	0.22280
65	Hot, 1 Spoon, Strong, Lemon	0.72360	0.46190	0.14030	-0.29066	-0.11140
66	Hot, 2 Spoons, Moderate, Lemon	7.11714	0.46190	5.96389	-0.09623	-0.11140
67	Room Temp, No Sugar, Strong, Lemon	-3.72843	1.41975	-6.10419	-0.29066	-0.11140
68	Room Temp, 1 Spoon, Moderate, No Lemon	1.88086	1.41975	0.14030	-0.09623	0.22280
69	Room Temp, 2 Spoons, Weak, Lemon	6.44767	1.41975	5.96389	0.38689	-0.11140
70	Cold, No Sugar, Moderate, Lemon	-8.33846	-1.88165	-6.10419	-0.09623	-0.11140
71	Cold, 1 Spoon, Weak, Lemon	-1.58731	-1.88165	0.14030	0.38689	-0.11140
72	Cold, 2 Spoons, Strong, No Lemon	4.86483	-1.88165	5.96389	-0.29066	0.22280

--- _VAR_=SUBJ5 ---

OBS	COMBO	_DTRANS_	TEMP	SWEET	STRENGTH	LEMON
73	Hot, No Sugar, Strong, Lemon	2.3208	-0.47420	0.93887	-1.50589	2.95764
74	Hot, 1 Spoon, Moderate, Lemon	0.6997	-0.47420	-0.64585	-2.18116	2.95764
75	Hot, 2 Spoons, Weak, No Lemon	-3.2578	-0.47420	-0.29302	3.68705	-5.91528
76	Room Temp, No Sugar, Moderate, No Lemon	-8.4180	-1.29512	0.93887	-2.18116	-5.91528
77	Room Temp, 1 Spoon, Weak, Lemon	5.9170	-1.29512	-0.64585	3.68705	2.95764
78	Room Temp, 2 Spoons, Strong, Lemon	-0.1869	-1.29512	-0.29302	-1.50589	2.95764
79	Cold, No Sugar, Weak, Lemon	9.4117	1.76932	0.93887	3.68705	2.95764
80	Cold, 1 Spoon, Strong, No Lemon	-6.4658	1.76932	-0.64585	-1.50589	-5.91528
81	Cold, 2 Spoons, Moderate, Lemon	1.5610	1.76932	-0.29302	-2.18116	2.95764
82	Hot, No Sugar, Weak, No Lemon	-2.0020	-0.47420	0.93887	3.68705	-5.91528
83	Hot, 1 Spoon, Strong, Lemon	-0.9784	-0.47420	-0.64585	-1.50589	2.95764
84	Hot, 2 Spoons, Moderate, Lemon	0.3725	-0.47420	-0.29302	-2.18116	2.95764
85	Room Temp, No Sugar, Strong, Lemon	1.0206	-1.29512	0.93887	-1.50589	2.95764
86	Room Temp, 1 Spoon, Moderate, No Lemon	-10.6023	-1.29512	-0.64585	-2.18116	-5.91528
87	Room Temp, 2 Spoons, Weak, Lemon	4.4988	-1.29512	-0.29302	3.68705	2.95764
88	Cold, No Sugar, Moderate, Lemon	3.3001	1.76932	0.93887	-2.18116	2.95764
89	Cold, 1 Spoon, Weak, Lemon	7.5546	1.76932	-0.64585	3.68705	2.95764
90	Cold, 2 Spoons, Strong, No Lemon	-4.7457	1.76932	-0.29302	-1.50589	-5.91528

--- _VAR_=SUBJ6 ---

OBS	COMBO	_DTRANS_	TEMP	SWEET	STRENGTH	LEMON
91	Hot, No Sugar, Strong, Lemon	-3.5657	-0.32628	-3.45934	3.56096	-0.76258
92	Hot, 1 Spoon, Moderate, Lemon	0.4752	-0.32628	1.22742	-0.21922	-0.76258
93	Hot, 2 Spoons, Weak, No Lemon	-2.0349	-0.32628	2.23193	-3.34174	1.52516
94	Room Temp, No Sugar, Moderate, No Lemon	3.5009	3.42695	-3.45934	-0.21922	1.52516
95	Room Temp, 1 Spoon, Weak, Lemon	1.4545	3.42695	1.22742	-3.34174	-0.76258
96	Room Temp, 2 Spoons, Strong, Lemon	5.0645	3.42695	2.23193	3.56096	-0.76258
97	Cold, No Sugar, Weak, Lemon	-9.2610	-3.10067	-3.45934	-3.34174	-0.76258
98	Cold, 1 Spoon, Strong, No Lemon	5.2599	-3.10067	1.22742	3.56096	1.52516
99	Cold, 2 Spoons, Moderate, Lemon	-0.6880	-3.10067	2.23193	-0.21922	-0.76258
100	Hot, No Sugar, Weak, No Lemon	-5.2803	-0.32628	-3.45934	-3.34174	1.52516
101	Hot, 1 Spoon, Strong, Lemon	4.4390	-0.32628	1.22742	3.56096	-0.76258

(continued on next page)

(continued from previous page)

102	Hot, 2 Spoons, Moderate, Lemon	4.0091	-0.32628	2.23193	-0.21922	-0.76258
103	Room Temp, No Sugar, Strong, Lemon	5.3772	3.42695	-3.45934	3.56096	-0.76258
104	Room Temp, 1 Spoon, Moderate, No Lemon	2.9146	3.42695	1.22742	-0.21922	1.52516
105	Room Temp, 2 Spoons, Weak, Lemon	2.2500	3.42695	2.23193	-3.34174	-0.76258
106	Cold, No Sugar, Moderate, Lemon	-11.5271	-3.10067	-3.45934	-0.21922	-0.76258
107	Cold, 1 Spoon, Weak, Lemon	-7.1788	-3.10067	1.22742	-3.34174	-0.76258
108	Cold, 2 Spoons, Strong, No Lemon	4.7908	-3.10067	2.23193	3.56096	1.52516

```
                              Individual Conjoint Analyses                            12
-------------------------------------- _VAR_=AVERAGE --------------------------------------
```

OBS	COMBO	_DTRANS_	TEMP	SWEET	STRENGTH	LEMON
109	Hot, No Sugar, Strong, Lemon	-3.61785	-2.22858	-1.49033	0.22622	0.48266
110	Hot, 1 Spoon, Moderate, Lemon	-2.82364	-2.22858	-0.32276	-1.07801	0.48266
111	Hot, 2 Spoons, Weak, No Lemon	-0.37479	-2.22858	1.81308	0.85179	-0.96532
112	Room Temp, No Sugar, Moderate, No Lemon	-0.75909	3.42036	-1.49033	-1.07801	-0.96532
113	Room Temp, 1 Spoon, Weak, Lemon	4.71884	3.42036	-0.32276	0.85179	0.48266
114	Room Temp, 2 Spoons, Strong, Lemon	4.71884	3.42036	0.22622	0.48266
115	Cold, No Sugar, Weak, Lemon	-1.87604	-1.19178	-1.49033	0.85179	0.48266
116	Cold, 1 Spoon, Strong, No Lemon	-1.50971	-1.19178	-0.32276	0.22622	-0.96532
117	Cold, 2 Spoons, Moderate, Lemon	-0.24313	-1.19178	1.81308	-1.07801	0.48266
118	Hot, No Sugar, Weak, No Lemon	-3.83878	-2.22858	-1.49033	0.85179	-0.96532
119	Hot, 1 Spoon, Strong, Lemon	-2.47328	-2.22858	-0.32276	0.22622	0.48266
120	Hot, 2 Spoons, Moderate, Lemon	-0.24313	-2.22858	1.81308	-1.07801	0.48266
121	Room Temp, No Sugar, Strong, Lemon	4.20368	3.42036	-1.49033	0.22622	0.48266
122	Room Temp, 1 Spoon, Moderate, No Lemon	0.65480	3.42036	-0.32276	-1.07801	-0.96532
123	Room Temp, 2 Spoons, Weak, Lemon	6.98507	3.42036	1.81308	0.85179	0.48266
124	Cold, No Sugar, Moderate, Lemon	-3.05388	-1.19178	-1.49033	-1.07801	0.48266
125	Cold, 1 Spoon, Weak, Lemon	-0.50356	-1.19178	-0.32276	0.85179	0.48266
126	Cold, 2 Spoons, Strong, No Lemon	0.03562	-1.19178	1.81308	0.22622	-0.96532

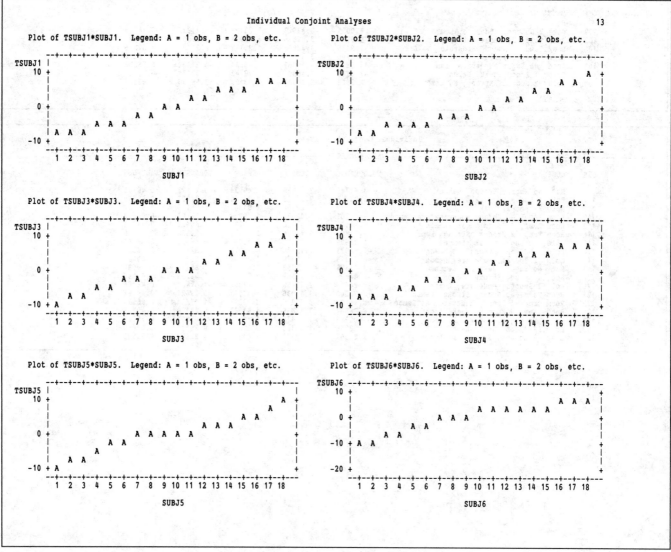

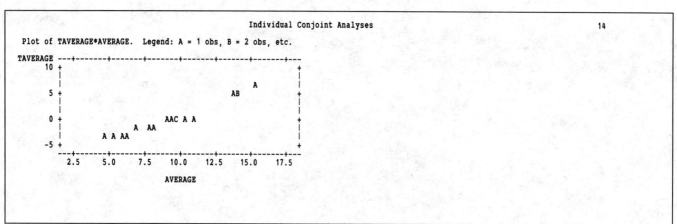

The third part of this example is a continuation of the second part. The input data set BOTH from the second part is analyzed by PROC TRANSREG with the METHOD=REDUNDANCY option. Just the subject's ranks, not the average ranks, are analyzed. This analysis simultaneously finds monotone transformations of the dependent variables and optimal scorings of the independent variables that maximize the average of the six squared multiple correlations. It can be seen from the final average R^2 of 0.88140 that it is not possible to fit each subject as well as in the previous analyses where each subject's model was fit separately. Each subject has a different set of utilities that are the products of the optimally scored independent variables and the subject's regression coefficients. For example, subject one's utilities for the last combination are -0.40927 times 5.83124, 0.93175 times 0.92957, -0.63230 times -0.56130, and 0.66667 times 1.36971. (See **Output 40.19**, page 2, the 6th and 7th lines from the bottom for the last four columns.) Some subjects weight the optimal scores positively and some weight them negatively.

The following statements produce **Output 40.19**:

```
    /*---Simultaneously Fit All Subjects                    ---*/
    /*---Allow Each Subject to Weight the Factors Differently---*/
proc transreg data=both method=redundancy ireplace maxiter=20;
    title 'Multivariate Conjoint Analysis';
    model mspline(subj1-subj6 / nknots=1)=
         opscore(temp sweet strength lemon);
    output tstandard=center coefficients;
    id combo;
run;

    /*---Print Results---*/
proc print;
    id  combo;
    var tsubj1-tsubj6 temp sweet strength lemon;
run;

    /*---Plot Results---*/
proc plot vpercent=33 hpercent=50;
    plot %match(tsubj,subj,*,1,6) / box;
run;
```

Output 40.19   Multivariate Conjoint Analysis Output

Multivariate Conjoint Analysis   1

TRANSREG Redundancy Analysis Algorithm Iteration History

Iteration Number	Average Change	Maximum Change	Average Squared R	Criterion Change
1	0.23363	1.00992	0.64411	.
2	0.07171	0.40285	0.84943	0.20532
3	0.03267	0.22637	0.87367	0.02424
4	0.01714	0.10705	0.87922	0.00555
5	0.00994	0.06458	0.88069	0.00147
6	0.00586	0.03814	0.88115	0.00047
7	0.00346	0.02243	0.88131	0.00016
8	0.00205	0.01321	0.88137	0.00006

(continued on next page)

(continued from previous page)

9	0.00122	0.00780	0.88139	0.00002
10	0.00072	0.00461	0.88140	0.00001
11	0.00043	0.00273	0.88140	0.00000
12	0.00025	0.00162	0.88140	0.00000
13	0.00015	0.00096	0.88140	0.00000
14	0.00009	0.00057	0.88140	0.00000
15	0.00005	0.00034	0.88140	0.00000
16	0.00003	0.00020	0.88140	0.00000
17	0.00002	0.00012	0.88140	0.00000
18	0.00001	0.00007	0.88140	0.00000
19	0.00001	0.00004	0.88140	0.00000

Multivariate Conjoint Analysis   2

COMBO	TSUBJ1	TSUBJ2	TSUBJ3	TSUBJ4	TSUBJ5	TSUBJ6	TEMP	SWEET	STRENGTH	LEMON
Hot, No Sugar, Strong, Lemon	-5.47428	-7.1924	-5.2063	-6.78383	2.8668	-4.1686	-0.73044	-1.05654	-0.63231	-0.33333
Hot, 1 Spoon, Moderate, Lemon	-6.19929	-1.2882	-5.9879	-0.22188	1.3614	-0.4034	-0.73044	0.12479	-0.52059	-0.33333
Hot, 2 Spoons, Weak, No Lemon	-4.26593	-0.3061	2.7141	6.85418	-3.2417	-2.8367	-0.73044	0.93175	1.15290	0.66667
Room Temp, No Sugar, Moderate, No Lemon	3.26297	1.9613	-0.8295	-4.80738	-8.9461	3.4754	1.13971	-1.05654	-0.52059	0.66667
Room Temp, 1 Spoon, Weak, Lemon	4.50022	6.5565	8.7375	3.37544	5.5374	0.6980	1.13971	0.12479	1.15290	-0.33333
Room Temp, 2 Spoons, Strong, Lemon	5.74572	10.9133	1.4402	5.76708	0.2558	5.6666	1.13971	0.93175	-0.63231	-0.33333
Cold, No Sugar, Weak, Lemon	-3.48051	-5.9003	4.0809	-7.69297	7.9651	-8.6258	-0.40927	-1.05654	1.15290	-0.33333
Cold, 1 Spoon, Strong, No Lemon	0.81325	-2.7633	-4.7374	-2.62007	-6.7994	5.9405	-0.40927	0.12479	-0.63231	0.66667
Cold, 2 Spoons, Moderate, Lemon	-0.39922	0.1910	-4.1642	4.31760	2.2355	-1.5816	-0.40927	0.93175	-0.52059	-0.33333
Hot, No Sugar, Weak, No Lemon	-5.89720	-8.6078	0.2589	-5.82196	-1.8306	-5.5775	-0.73044	-1.05654	1.15290	0.66667
Hot, 1 Spoon, Strong, Lemon	-6.38054	-1.9642	-5.8316	1.05629	-0.6648	4.7901	-0.73044	0.12479	-0.63231	-0.33333
Hot, 2 Spoons, Moderate, Lemon	-4.93053	0.9468	-5.5711	6.63676	0.9312	4.1875	-0.73044	0.93175	-0.52059	-0.33333
Room Temp, No Sugar, Strong, Lemon	8.26150	3.2344	7.0925	-3.74008	1.7337	6.1048	1.13971	-1.05654	-0.63231	-0.33333
Room Temp, 1 Spoon, Moderate, No Lemon	9.53178	4.7661	-1.8195	2.28834	-11.3381	2.6537	1.13971	0.12479	-0.52059	0.66667
Room Temp, 2 Spoons, Weak, Lemon	6.99948	8.6056	10.4752	6.27439	4.5177	1.7225	1.13971	0.93175	1.15290	-0.33333
Cold, No Sugar, Moderate, Lemon	-2.57425	-4.7314	-2.7053	-8.54940	3.6275	-10.2653	-0.40927	-1.05654	-0.52059	-0.33333
Cold, 1 Spoon, Weak, Lemon	-1.54715	-3.6857	5.5403	-1.44733	6.6865	-7.0632	-0.40927	0.12479	1.15290	-0.33333
Cold, 2 Spoons, Strong, No Lemon	2.03398	-0.7356	-3.4869	5.11481	-4.8979	5.2831	-0.40927	0.93175	-0.63231	0.66667
	.	.	.	.	.	.	5.83124	0.92957	-0.56130	1.36971
	.	.	.	.	.	.	5.14455	3.40963	-0.47938	-1.42135
	.	.	.	.	.	.	3.76472	-0.17029	4.53561	-1.97505
	.	.	.	.	.	.	1.13609	6.03264	0.22623	0.25198
	.	.	.	.	.	.	-1.04813	-0.54661	2.80804	-9.26347
							2.73035	2.71269	-3.24368	2.23462

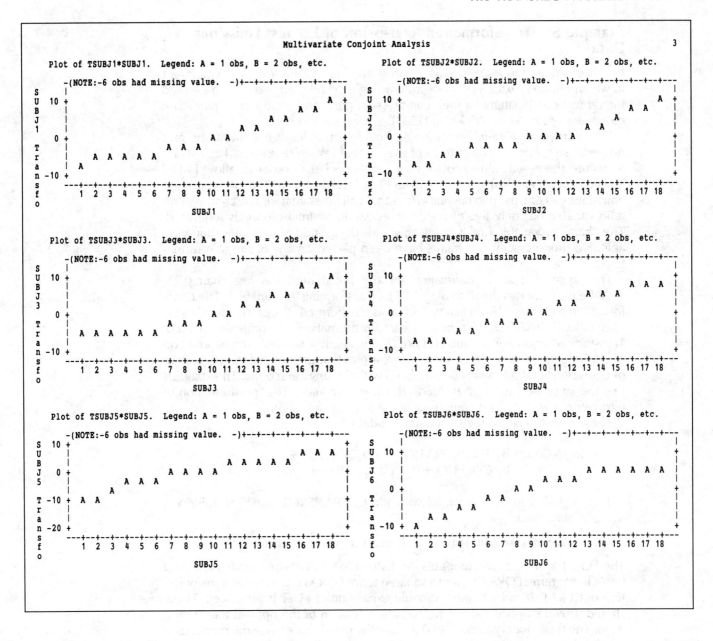

Multivariate Conjoint Analysis

Example 5:   Transformation Regression of Exhaust Emissions Data

In this example, the MORALS algorithm is applied to data from an experiment in which nitrogen oxide emissions from a single cylinder engine were measured for various combinations of fuel, compression ratio, and equivalence ratio. The data were provided by Brinkman (1981).

The equivalence ratio and nitrogen oxide variables are continuous and numeric, so spline transformations of these variables are requested. Each spline is degree three with nine knots (one at each decile) in order to allow PROC TRANSREG a great deal of freedom in finding transformations. The nitrogen oxide emissions variable has two missing values that will be estimated. The compression ratio variable has only five discrete values, so an optimal scoring is requested. The character variable fuel is nominal, so it is designated as a classification variable. No monotonicity constraints have been placed on any of the transformations.

The squared multiple correlation for the initial model is less than 0.25. TRANSREG increases the R^2 to over 0.95 by transforming the variables. The transformation plots show how each variable was transformed. Transformed compression ratio (TCPRATIO) is a near linear transformation of compression ratio. Transformed equivalence ratio (TEQRATIO) is nearly a parabolic transformation of equivalence ratio. It can be seen from this plot that the optimal transformation of equivalence ratio is nearly uncorrelated with the original scoring. This suggests that the large increase in R^2 is due to this transformation. The transformation of nitrogen oxide (TNOX) is something like a log transformation.

These results suggest the parametric model

$$\log(NOX) = b_0 + b_1 * EQRATIO + b_2 * EQRATIO^2 + b_3 * CPRATIO + \Sigma b_j * class_j (FUEL) + error \quad .$$

This analysis can be performed with PROC TRANSREG using the following MODEL statement:

```
model log(nox)=epoint(eqratio) linear(cpratio) class(fuel);
```

The LOG transformation computes the natural log. EPOINT expands EQRATIO into a linear term, EQRATIO, and a squared term, EQRATI_2. A linear transformation of CPRATIO and a dummy variable expansion of FUEL is requested. These should provide a good parametric operationalization of the optimal transformations. The final model has an R^2 of 0.91 (smaller than before since the model uses many fewer degrees of freedom, but still quite good).

The following statements produce **Output 40.20**:

```
title 'Gasoline Example';
data gas;
   input fuel :$8. cpratio eqratio nox @@;
   label fuel    = 'Fuel'
         cpratio = 'Compression Ratio (CR)'
         eqratio = 'Equivalence Ratio (PHI)'
         nox     = 'Nitrogen Oxide (NOX)';
   cards;
ETHANOL  12.0 0.907 3.741 ETHANOL  12.0 0.761 2.295 ETHANOL  12.0 1.108 1.498
ETHANOL  12.0 1.016 2.881 ETHANOL  12.0 1.189 0.760 ETHANOL   9.0 1.001 3.120
ETHANOL   9.0 1.231 0.638 ETHANOL   9.0 1.123 1.170 ETHANOL  12.0 1.042 2.358
ETHANOL  12.0 1.215 0.606 ETHANOL  12.0 0.930 3.669 ETHANOL  12.0 1.152 1.000
ETHANOL  15.0 1.138 0.981 ETHANOL  18.0 0.601 1.192 ETHANOL   7.5 0.696 0.926
ETHANOL  12.0 0.686 1.590 ETHANOL  12.0 1.072 1.806 ETHANOL  15.0 1.074 1.962
```

```
ETHANOL   15.0 0.934 4.028 ETHANOL    9.0 0.808 3.148 ETHANOL    9.0 1.071 1.836
ETHANOL    7.5 1.009 2.845 ETHANOL    7.5 1.142 1.013 ETHANOL   18.0 1.229 0.414
ETHANOL   18.0 1.175 0.812 ETHANOL   15.0 0.568 0.374 ETHANOL   15.0 0.977 3.623
ETHANOL    7.5 0.767 1.869 ETHANOL    7.5 1.006 2.836 ETHANOL    9.0 0.893 3.567
ETHANOL   15.0 1.152 0.866 ETHANOL   15.0 0.693 1.369 ETHANOL   15.0 1.232 0.542
ETHANOL   15.0 1.036 2.739 ETHANOL   15.0 1.125 1.200 ETHANOL    9.0 1.081 1.719
ETHANOL    9.0 0.868 3.423 ETHANOL    7.5 0.762 1.634 ETHANOL    7.5 1.144 1.021
ETHANOL    7.5 1.045 2.157 ETHANOL   18.0 0.797 3.361 ETHANOL   18.0 1.115 1.390
ETHANOL   18.0 1.070 1.947 ETHANOL   18.0 1.219 0.962 ETHANOL    9.0 0.637 0.571
ETHANOL    9.0 0.733 2.219 ETHANOL    9.0 0.715 1.419 ETHANOL    9.0 0.872 3.519
ETHANOL    7.5 0.765 1.732 ETHANOL    7.5 0.878 3.206 ETHANOL    7.5 0.811 2.471
ETHANOL   15.0 0.676 1.777 ETHANOL   18.0 1.045 2.571 ETHANOL   18.0 0.968 3.952
ETHANOL   15.0 0.846 3.931 ETHANOL   15.0 0.684 1.587 ETHANOL    7.5 0.729 1.397
ETHANOL    7.5 0.911 3.536 ETHANOL    7.5 0.808 2.202 ETHANOL    7.5 1.168 0.756
INDOLENE   7.5 0.831 4.818 INDOLENE   7.5 1.045 2.849 INDOLENE   7.5 1.021 3.275
INDOLENE   7.5 0.970 4.691 INDOLENE   7.5 0.825 4.255 INDOLENE   7.5 0.891 5.064
INDOLENE   7.5 0.710 2.118 INDOLENE   7.5 0.801 4.602 INDOLENE   7.5 1.074 2.286
INDOLENE   7.5 1.148 0.970 INDOLENE   7.5 1.000 3.965 INDOLENE   7.5 0.928 5.344
INDOLENE   7.5 0.767 3.834 ETHANOL    7.5 0.749 1.620 ETHANOL    7.5 0.892 3.656
ETHANOL    7.5 1.002 2.964 82RONGAS   7.5 0.873 6.021 82RONGAS   7.5 0.987 4.467
82RONGAS   7.5 1.030 3.046 82RONGAS   7.5 1.101 1.596 82RONGAS   7.5 1.173 0.835
82RONGAS   7.5 0.931 5.498 82RONGAS   7.5 0.822 5.470 82RONGAS   7.5 0.749 4.084
82RONGAS   7.5 0.625 0.716 94%ETH     7.5 0.818 2.382 94%ETH     7.5 1.128 1.004
94%ETH     7.5 1.191 0.623 94%ETH     7.5 1.132 1.030 94%ETH     7.5 0.993 2.593
94%ETH     7.5 0.866 2.699 94%ETH     7.5 0.910 3.177 94%ETH    12.0 1.139 1.151
94%ETH    12.0 1.267 0.474 94%ETH    12.0 1.017 2.814 94%ETH    12.0 0.954 3.308
94%ETH    12.0 0.861 3.031 94%ETH    12.0 1.034 2.537 94%ETH    12.0 0.781 2.403
94%ETH    12.0 1.058 2.412 94%ETH    12.0 0.884 2.452 94%ETH    12.0 0.766 1.857
94%ETH     7.5 1.193 0.657 94%ETH     7.5 0.885 2.969 94%ETH     7.5 0.915 2.670
ETHANOL   18.0 0.812 3.760 ETHANOL   18.0 1.230 0.672 ETHANOL   18.0 0.804 3.677
ETHANOL   18.0 0.712 .     ETHANOL   12.0 0.813 3.517 ETHANOL   12.0 1.002 3.290
ETHANOL    9.0 0.696 1.139 ETHANOL    9.0 1.199 0.727 ETHANOL    9.0 1.030 2.581
ETHANOL   15.0 0.602 0.923 ETHANOL   15.0 0.694 1.527 ETHANOL   15.0 0.816 3.388
ETHANOL   15.0 0.896 .     ETHANOL   15.0 1.037 2.085 ETHANOL   15.0 1.181 0.966
ETHANOL    7.5 0.899 3.488 ETHANOL    7.5 1.227 0.754 INDOLENE   7.5 0.701 1.990
INDOLENE   7.5 0.807 5.199 INDOLENE   7.5 0.902 5.283 INDOLENE   7.5 0.997 3.752
INDOLENE   7.5 1.224 0.537 INDOLENE   7.5 1.089 1.640 ETHANOL    9.0 1.180 0.797
ETHANOL    7.5 0.795 2.064 ETHANOL   18.0 0.990 3.732 ETHANOL   18.0 1.201 0.586
METHANOL   7.5 0.975 2.941 METHANOL   7.5 1.089 1.467 METHANOL   7.5 1.150 0.934
METHANOL   7.5 1.212 0.722 METHANOL   7.5 0.859 2.397 METHANOL   7.5 0.751 1.461
METHANOL   7.5 0.720 1.235 METHANOL   7.5 1.090 1.347 METHANOL   7.5 0.616 0.344
GASOHOL    7.5 0.712 2.209 GASOHOL    7.5 0.771 4.497 GASOHOL    7.5 0.959 4.958
GASOHOL    7.5 1.042 2.723 GASOHOL    7.5 1.125 1.244 GASOHOL    7.5 1.097 1.562
GASOHOL    7.5 0.984 4.468 GASOHOL    7.5 0.928 5.307 GASOHOL    7.5 0.889 5.425
GASOHOL    7.5 0.827 5.330 GASOHOL    7.5 0.674 1.448 GASOHOL    7.5 1.031 3.164
METHANOL   7.5 0.871 3.113 METHANOL   7.5 1.026 2.551 METHANOL   7.5 0.598 0.204
INDOLENE   7.5 0.973 5.055 INDOLENE   7.5 0.980 4.937 INDOLENE   7.5 0.665 1.561
ETHANOL    7.5 0.629 0.561 ETHANOL    9.0 0.608 0.563 ETHANOL   12.0 0.584 0.678
ETHANOL   15.0 0.562 0.370 ETHANOL   18.0 0.535 0.530 94%ETH     7.5 0.674 0.900
GASOHOL    7.5 0.645 1.207 ETHANOL   18.0 0.655 1.900 94%ETH     7.5 1.022 2.787
94%ETH     7.5 0.790 2.645 94%ETH     7.5 0.720 1.475 94%ETH     7.5 1.075 2.147
;
```

```
      /*---Fit the Nonparametric Model---*/
proc transreg data=gas;
   model spline(nox / nknots=9)=spline(eqratio / nknots=9)
                                 opscore(cpratio) class(fuel);
   title2 'Iteratively Estimate NOX, CPRATIO and EQRATIO';
   title3 'Transformations and Missing Data';
   output out=results;
run;

      /*---Plot the Results                                ---*/
      /*---SAS/GRAPH Software and a GOPTIONS Statement are Required---*/
proc gplot data=results;
   title4 'Transformation Plots';
   symbol1 v=plus;
   /*---Lengths are Device Specific---*/
   axis1 length=6 IN;
   plot tcpratio*cpratio teqratio*eqratio tnox*nox
        / frame haxis=axis1 vaxis=axis1;
run;

      /*-Fit the Parametric Model Suggested by the Nonparametric Analysis-*/
proc transreg data=gas;
   title2 'Now fit log(NOX) = b0 + b1*EQRATIO + b2*EQRATIO**2 +';
   title3 'b3*CPRATIO + Sum b(j)*FUEL(j) + error';
   title4 'and Estimate Missing Data';
   model log(nox)=epoint(eqratio) linear(cpratio) class(fuel);
   output out=results2;
run;
```

Output 40.20   Transformation Regression Example Output

```
                              Gasoline Example                                    1
                 Iteratively Estimate NOX, CPRATIO and EQRATIO
                        Transformations and Missing Data

        TRANSREG MORALS Algorithm Iteration History For Dependent Variable NOX

             Iteration    Average    Maximum    Squared    Criterion
             Number       Change     Change     Multiple R Change
             --------------------------------------------------------------
                 1        1.05958    2.88478    0.24547     .
                 2        0.33833    1.31152    0.61698    0.37151
                 3        0.11944    0.71822    0.81844    0.20146
                 4        0.07515    0.28129    0.89850    0.08007
                 5        0.05050    0.18612    0.93194    0.03343
                 6        0.03579    0.12143    0.94644    0.01451
                 7        0.02604    0.08314    0.95284    0.00640
                 8        0.01926    0.05760    0.95576    0.00292
                 9        0.01438    0.04035    0.95717    0.00141
                10        0.01094    0.03001    0.95790    0.00073
                11        0.00842    0.02462    0.95830    0.00040
                12        0.00656    0.01999    0.95854    0.00024
                13        0.00516    0.01615    0.95868    0.00014
                14        0.00409    0.01302    0.95877    0.00009
                15        0.00327    0.01049    0.95883    0.00006
                16        0.00263    0.00846    0.95887    0.00004
                17        0.00212    0.00683    0.95889    0.00002
                18        0.00172    0.00552    0.95891    0.00002
                19        0.00139    0.00451    0.95892    0.00001
                20        0.00113    0.00368    0.95893    0.00001
                21        0.00092    0.00300    0.95893    0.00000
                22        0.00074    0.00244    0.95894    0.00000
                23        0.00060    0.00199    0.95894    0.00000
                24        0.00049    0.00162    0.95894    0.00000
                25        0.00040    0.00132    0.95894    0.00000
```

(continued on next page)

(continued from previous page)

26	0.00032	0.00107	0.95894	0.00000
27	0.00026	0.00087	0.95894	0.00000
28	0.00021	0.00071	0.95894	0.00000
29	0.00017	0.00058	0.95894	0.00000
30	0.00014	0.00047	0.95894	0.00000

Gasoline Example
Now fit log(NOX) = b0 + b1*EQRATIO + b2*EQRATIO**2 +
b3*CPRATIO + Sum b(j)*FUEL(j) + error
and Estimate Missing Data

2

TRANSREG Univariate Algorithm Iteration History For Dependent Variable NOX

Iteration Number	Average Change	Maximum Change	Squared Multiple R	Criterion Change
1	0.01444	1.09493	0.90803	.
2	0.00062	0.02977	0.91478	0.00675
3	0.00003	0.00174	0.91479	0.00001
4	0.00000	0.00010	0.91479	0.00000

Output 40.21   Compression Ratio Plot

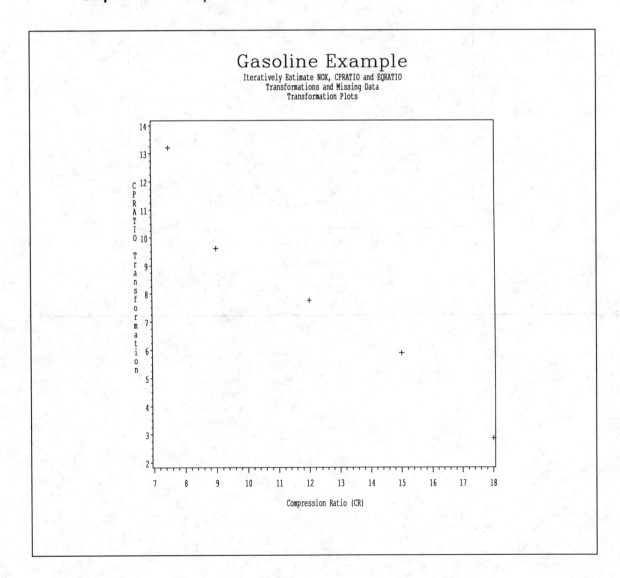

Output 40.22   Equivalence Ratio Plot

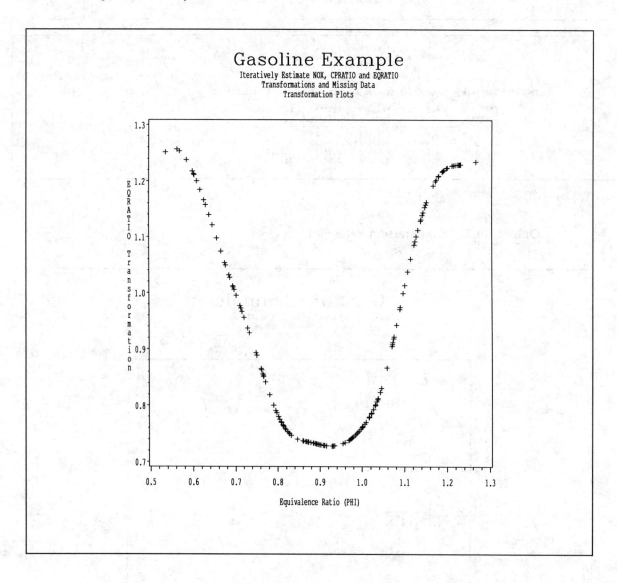

Output 40.23   Nitrogen Oxide Plot

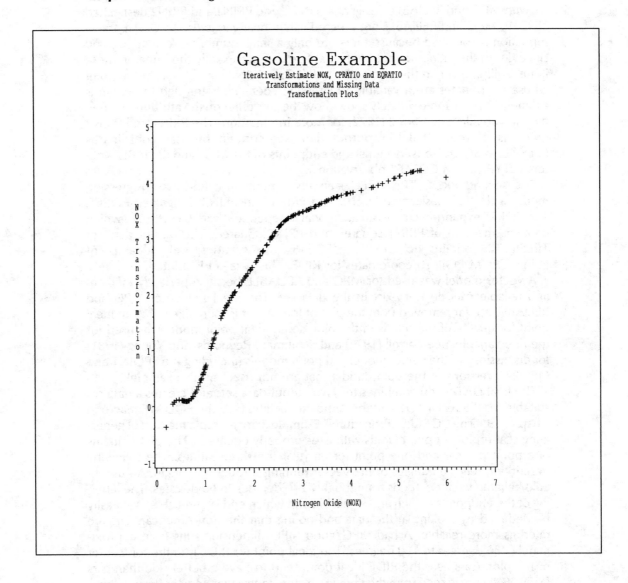

Gasoline Example
Iteratively Estimate NOX, CPRATIO and EQRATIO
Transformations and Missing Data
Transformation Plots

Example 6:   Preference Mapping of Cars Data

This example illustrates using PROC TRANSREG to perform a nonmetric preference mapping (PREFMAP) analysis (Carroll 1972) of car preference data after a
PROC PRINQUAL nonmetric principal component analysis. PREFMAP analysis
is a response surface regression that locates ideal points for each dependent variable in a space defined by the independent variables.

Twenty-five judges rated 17 automobiles. The ratings were made on a zero
(very weak preference) to nine (very strong preference) scale. These judgments
were made in 1980 about that year's products. There are two character variables
indicating the manufacturer and model of the automobile. The data set also contains three ratings: miles per gallon (MPG), projected reliability (RELIABLE), and
quality of the ride (RIDE). These ratings are on a one (bad) to five (good) scale.
PROC PRINQUAL finds monotonic transformations of the 25 judges' ratings to
maximize the fit of the data to a two principal-component model, and creates
an output data set containing standardized observation scores on the first two
components (PRIN1 and PRIN2), along with the ID variables MODEL, MPG,
RELIABLE, and RIDE.

The first PROC TRANSREG step fits two nonmetric univariate regression models with MPG and RELIABLE designated UNTIE and PRIN1 and PRIN2 designated LINEAR. MPG and RELIABLE are ordered categorical variables. An UNTIE transformation is specified because there are only a small number of categories, and since ties in the ratings do not imply that tied cars are exactly the same on these items. A line drawn in the plot of the PRIN1 and PRIN2 variables from the point whose coordinates are a variable's regression coefficients through the origin is a dimension that approximately shows how the cars differ on the attribute defined by that variable. See Carroll (1972) for more information. The PRIN1 and PRIN2 columns of the TRESULT1 output data set contain the car coordinates (_TYPE_='SCORE' observations) and endpoints of the MPG and RELIABLE vectors (_TYPE_='M COEFFI' observations).

The second PROC TRANSREG step fits a nonmetric univariate regression model with RIDE designated UNTIE, and PRIN1 and PRIN2 designated POINT. The POINT expansion creates an additional independent variable _ISSQ_ which contains the sum of PRIN1 squared and PRIN2 squared. The output data set TRESULT2 contains no _TYPE_='SCORE' observations, only ideal point (_TYPE_='M POINT') coordinates for RIDE. This data set is printed.

A vector model was used for MPG and RELIABLE because perfectly efficient and reliable cars do not exist in the data set. The ideal points for MPG and RELIABLE are far removed from the plot of the cars. It is more likely that an ideal point for quality of the ride is in the plot, so an ideal point model was used for the ride variable. See Carroll (1972) and Schiffman, Reynolds, and Young (1981) for discussions of the vector model and point models (including the EPOINT and QPOINT versions of the point model that are not used in this example).

The final DATA step combines the two output data sets and creates a data set suitable for PROC GPLOT and the Annotate facility. (See the EQUATE macro in Chapter 19, "The CORRESP Procedure," **Example 3**, for a simple method of generating scatterplots of point labels with axes properly equated.) The plot contains one point per car and one point for each of the three ratings. The following description relies on angles of the vector running through the origin. An unreliable/reliable vector extends from roughly 240 degrees to 60 degrees. The labeling of the endpoints (which end is reliable and which end is unreliable) can easily be deduced by looking at the data and noting that the non-American cars are rated as more reliable. A bad MPG/good MPG dimension runs from approximately 280 degrees to 100 degrees. The ideal point for RIDE is in the top center of the plot. Cars near the RIDE ideal point tend to have a better ride than cars far away. It can be seen from the iteration history tables that none of these ratings, even after the UNTIE transformation, perfectly fits the model, so all of the interpretations are approximate.

The RIDE point is a "negative-negative" ideal point. The point models assume that small ratings mean that the object (car) is similar to the rating name and large ratings imply dissimilarity to the rating name. Because the opposite scoring is used, the interpretation of the RIDE point must be reversed to a negative ideal point (bad ride). However, the coefficient for the _ISSQ_ variable is negative, so the interpretation is reversed again, back to the original interpretation. Any mix of positive and negative ideal points may be produced, so the coefficients for the _ISSQ_ variable should always be examined. When COEFFICIENTS is specified in the OUTPUT statement, raw regression coefficients are output for all independent variables. When COORDINATES is specified, original raw regression coefficients are output for variables not named in the POINT expansion, and the coordinates are output for the POINT expansion variables, so you do not have to specify COEFFICIENTS to check for negative ideal points.

The following statements produce **Output 40.24**:

```
title 'Preference Ratings for Automobiles Manufactured in 1980';
data carpref;
    input make $ 1-10 model $ 12-22 @25 (judge1-judge25) (1.)
          mpg reliable ride;
    cards;
Cadillac   Eldorado    8007990491240508971093809 3 2 4
Chevrolet  Chevette    0051200423451043003515698 5 3 2
Chevrolet  Citation    4053305814161643544747795 4 1 5
Chevrolet  Malibu      6027400723121345545668658 3 3 4
Ford       Fairmont    2024006715021443530648655 3 3 4
Ford       Mustang     5007197705021101850657555 3 2 2
Ford       Pinto       0021000303030201500514078 4 1 1
Honda      Accord      5956897609699952998975078 5 5 3
Honda      Civic       4836709507488852567765075 5 5 3
Lincoln    Continental 7008990592230409962091909 2 4 5
Plymouth   Gran Fury   7006000434101107333458708 2 1 5
Plymouth   Horizon     3005005635461302444675655 4 3 3
Plymouth   Volare      4005003614021602754476555 2 1 3
Pontiac    Firebird    0107895613201206958265907 1 1 5
Volkswagen Dasher      4858696508877795377895000 5 3 4
Volkswagen Rabbit      4858509709695795487885000 5 4 3
Volvo      DL          9989998909999987989919000 4 5 5
;

    /*---Compute Coordinates for a 2-Dimensional Scatterplot of Cars---*/
proc prinqual data=carpref out=presults(drop=judge1-judge25) n=2
              replace standard scores;
    id model mpg reliable ride;
    transform monotone(judge1-judge25);
    title2 'Multidimensional Preference (MDPREF) Analysis';
    title3 'Optimal Monotonic Transformation of Preference Data';
run;

    /*---Compute Endpoints for MPG and Reliability Vectors---*/
proc transreg data=presults;
    model untie(mpg reliable)=linear(prin1 prin2);
    output tstandard=center coefficients replace out=tresult1;
    id model;
    title2 'Preference Mapping (PREFMAP) Analysis';
run;

    /*---Compute Ride Ideal Point Coordinates---*/
proc transreg data=presults;
    model untie(ride)=point(prin1 prin2);
    output tstandard=center coordinates replace noscores out=tresult2;
    id model;
    title2 'Preference Mapping (PREFMAP) Analysis';
run;

    /*---Print Results---*/
proc print data=tresult2;
    title2 'Ideal Point Coordinates';
run;
```

```
          /*---Create Annotate Data Set---*/
     data biplot;
        set tresult1 tresult2;
        y     = prin2;  /* y-axis variable                           */
        x     = prin1;  /* x-axis variable                           */
        xsys  = '2';     /* x-axis label area is axis min to axis max */
        ysys  = '2';     /* y-axis label area is axis min to axis max */
        size  = 1;       /* relative size of the text string          */
        xsys  = '2';
        ysys  = '2';

                          /* text string to position in the plot      */
        if _type_ = 'SCORE' then text = model;
                            else text = _name_;
        label y = 'Dimension 2'
              x = 'Dimension 1';
        keep x y text xsys ysys size;
     run;


          /*---Plot the Results                                   ---*/
          /*---SAS/GRAPH Software and a GOPTIONS Statement are Required---*/
     proc gplot data=biplot;
        title3 'Plot of Automobiles and Ratings';
        symbol1 v=none;
        /*---Lengths are Device Specific---*/
        axis1 length=6 IN order=-2 to 2.5 by 0.5;
        plot y*x=1 / annotate=biplot frame haxis=axis1 vaxis=axis1
                     href=0 vref=0;
     run;
```

Output 40.24   Preference Ratings Example Output

Preference Ratings for Automobiles Manufactured in 1980   1
Multidimensional Preference (MDPREF) Analysis
Optimal Monotonic Transformation of Preference Data

PRINQUAL MTV Iteration History

Iteration Number	Average Change	Maximum Change	Proportion of Variance	Variance Change
1	0.24994	1.28017	0.66946	.
2	0.07223	0.36958	0.80194	0.13249
3	0.04522	0.29026	0.81598	0.01404
4	0.03096	0.25213	0.82178	0.00580
5	0.02182	0.23045	0.82493	0.00315
6	0.01602	0.19017	0.82680	0.00187
7	0.01219	0.14748	0.82793	0.00113
8	0.00953	0.11031	0.82861	0.00068
9	0.00737	0.06461	0.82904	0.00043
10	0.00556	0.04469	0.82930	0.00026
11	0.00445	0.04087	0.82944	0.00014
12	0.00381	0.03706	0.82955	0.00011
13	0.00319	0.03348	0.82965	0.00009
14	0.00255	0.02999	0.82971	0.00006
15	0.00213	0.02824	0.82976	0.00005
16	0.00183	0.02646	0.82980	0.00004
17	0.00159	0.02472	0.82983	0.00003
18	0.00139	0.02305	0.82985	0.00003
19	0.00123	0.02145	0.82988	0.00002
20	0.00109	0.01993	0.82989	0.00002
21	0.00096	0.01850	0.82991	0.00001
22	0.00086	0.01715	0.82992	0.00001
23	0.00076	0.01588	0.82993	0.00001
24	0.00067	0.01440	0.82994	0.00001
25	0.00059	0.00871	0.82994	0.00001
26	0.00050	0.00720	0.82995	0.00000
27	0.00043	0.00642	0.82995	0.00000
28	0.00037	0.00573	0.82995	0.00000
29	0.00031	0.00510	0.82995	0.00000
30	0.00027	0.00454	0.82995	0.00000

Preference Ratings for Automobiles Manufactured in 1980   2
Preference Mapping (PREFMAP) Analysis

TRANSREG Univariate Algorithm Iteration History For Dependent Variable MPG

Iteration Number	Average Change	Maximum Change	Squared Multiple R	Criterion Change
1	0.31994	0.63374	0.40085	.
2	0.05608	0.10046	0.70472	0.30387
3	0.03529	0.06620	0.70957	0.00485
4	0.02203	0.04250	0.71150	0.00193
5	0.01371	0.02692	0.71226	0.00076
6	0.00853	0.01693	0.71255	0.00029
7	0.00531	0.01061	0.71266	0.00011
8	0.00331	0.00663	0.71271	0.00004
9	0.00206	0.00414	0.71273	0.00002
10	0.00128	0.00258	0.71273	0.00001
11	0.00080	0.00161	0.71274	0.00000
12	0.00050	0.00100	0.71274	0.00000
13	0.00031	0.00062	0.71274	0.00000
14	0.00019	0.00039	0.71274	0.00000
15	0.00012	0.00024	0.71274	0.00000
16	0.00007	0.00015	0.71274	0.00000
17	0.00005	0.00009	0.71274	0.00000
18	0.00003	0.00006	0.71274	0.00000
19	0.00002	0.00004	0.71274	0.00000
20	0.00001	0.00002	0.71274	0.00000
21	0.00001	0.00001	0.71274	0.00000

Preference Ratings for Automobiles Manufactured in 1980
Preference Mapping (PREFMAP) Analysis   3

TRANSREG Univariate Algorithm Iteration History For Dependent Variable RELIABLE

Iteration Number	Average Change	Maximum Change	Squared Multiple R	Criterion Change
1	0.47019	1.17139	0.51858	.
2	0.01238	0.03852	0.92113	0.40255
3	0.00388	0.01201	0.92151	0.00038
4	0.00121	0.00375	0.92155	0.00004
5	0.00038	0.00117	0.92155	0.00000
6	0.00012	0.00037	0.92155	0.00000
7	0.00004	0.00011	0.92155	0.00000
8	0.00001	0.00004	0.92155	0.00000
9	0.00000	0.00001	0.92155	0.00000

Preference Ratings for Automobiles Manufactured in 1980
Preference Mapping (PREFMAP) Analysis   4

TRANSREG Univariate Algorithm Iteration History For Dependent Variable RIDE

Iteration Number	Average Change	Maximum Change	Squared Multiple R	Criterion Change
1	0.42936	1.15921	0.29136	.
2	0.06045	0.12263	0.66657	0.37521
3	0.02118	0.03325	0.67035	0.00378
4	0.00791	0.01610	0.67083	0.00048
5	0.00348	0.00934	0.67090	0.00008
6	0.00185	0.00584	0.67092	0.00002
7	0.00117	0.00381	0.67093	0.00001
8	0.00079	0.00255	0.67093	0.00000
9	0.00054	0.00173	0.67094	0.00000
10	0.00037	0.00119	0.67094	0.00000
11	0.00025	0.00083	0.67094	0.00000
12	0.00017	0.00057	0.67094	0.00000
13	0.00012	0.00039	0.67094	0.00000
14	0.00008	0.00027	0.67094	0.00000
15	0.00006	0.00018	0.67094	0.00000
16	0.00004	0.00013	0.67094	0.00000
17	0.00003	0.00009	0.67094	0.00000
18	0.00002	0.00006	0.67094	0.00000
19	0.00001	0.00004	0.67094	0.00000
20	0.00001	0.00003	0.67094	0.00000

Preference Ratings for Automobiles Manufactured in 1980
Ideal Point Coordinates   5

OBS	_TYPE_	_NAME_	RIDE	PRIN1	PRIN2	_ISSQ_	MODEL
1	M POINT	RIDE	.	0.16142	2.01640	-0.44321	

Output 40.25   Preference Ratings for Automobiles Manufactured in 1980

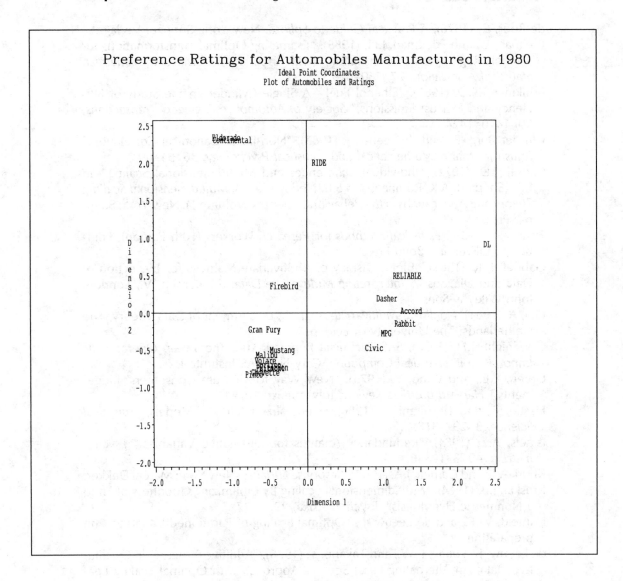

REFERENCES

de Boor, C. (1978), *A Practical Guide to Splines*, New York: Springer Verlag.

Breiman, L., and Friedman, J.H. (1985), "Estimating Optimal Transformations for Multiple Regression and Correlation," (with discussion), *Journal of the American Statistical Association*, 77, 580–619.

Brinkman, N.D. (1981), "Ethanol Fuel—A Single-Cylinder Engine Study of Efficiency and Exhaust Emissions," *Society of Automotive Engineers Transactions*, 90, 1410–1424.

van der Burg, E., and de Leeuw, J. (1983), "Non-linear Canonical Correlation," *British Journal of Mathematical and Statistical Psychology*, 36, 54–80.

Carroll, J.D. (1972), "Individual Differences and Multidimensional Scaling," in R.N. Shepard, A.K. Romney, and S.B. Nerlove (eds.), *Multidimensional Scaling: Theory and Applications in the Behavioral Sciences* (Volume 1), New York: Seminar Press.

Fisher, R. (1938), *Statistical Methods for Research Workers* (10th Edition), Edinburgh: Oliver and Boyd Press.

Gabriel, K.R. (1981), "Biplot Display of Multivariate Matrices for Inspection of Data and Diagnosis," *Interpreting Multivariate Data*, ed. Barnett, V., London: John Wiley & Sons.

Gifi, A. (1981), *Nonlinear Multivariate Analysis*, Department of Data Theory, The Netherlands: The University of Leiden.

Goodnight, J.H. (1978), SAS Technical Report R-106, *The Sweep Operator: Its Importance in Statistical Computing*, Cary NC: SAS Institute Inc.

Green, P.E., and Wind, Y. (1975), "New Way to Measure Consumers' Judgements," *Harvard Business Review*, July-August, 107–117.

Hastie, T., and Tibshirani, R. (1986), "Generalized Additive Models," *Statistical Science*, 3, 297–318.

Israels, A.Z. (1984), "Redundancy Analysis for Qualitative Variables," *Psychometrika*, 49, 331–346.

Khuri, A.I., and Cornell, J.A. (1987), *Response Surfaces*, New York: Marcel Dekker.

Kruskal, J.B. (1964), "Multidimensional Scaling By Optimizing Goodness of Fit to a Nonmetric Hypothesis," *Psychometrika*, 29, 1–27.

Kuhfeld, W.F., and de Leeuw, J., "Optimal Scaling of Partitioned Variables," (in preparation).

de Leeuw, J., Young, F.W., and Takane, Y. (1976), "Additive Structure in Qualitative Data: An Alternating Least Squares Approach with Optimal Scaling Features," *Psychometrika*, 41, 471–503.

de Leeuw, J. (1986), "Regression with Optimal Scaling of the Dependent Variable," Department of Data Theory, The Netherlands: The University of Leiden.

Meyers, R.H. (1976), *Response Surface Methodology*, Blacksburg, VA: Virginia Polytechnic Institute and State University.

van Rijckevorsel, J. (1982), "Canonical Analysis with B-Splines," in H. Caussinus, P. Ettinger, and R. Tomassone (ed.), *COMPUSTAT 1982*, Part I, Wein, Physica Verlag.

Schiffman, S.S., Reynolds, M.L., and Young, F.W. (1981), *Introduction to Multidimensional Scaling*, New York: Academic Press.

Siegel, S. (1956), *Nonparametric Statistics*, New York: McGraw-Hill.

Smith, P.L. (1979), "Splines as a Useful and Convenient Statistical Tool," *The American Statistician*, 33, 57–62.

Stewart, D., and Love, W. (1968), "A General Canonical Correlation Index," *Psychological Bulletin*, 70, 160–163.

Winsberg, S., and Ramsay, J.O. (1980), "Monotonic Transformations to Additivity Using Splines," *Biometrika*, 67, 669–674.

Young, F.W. (1981), "Quantitative Analysis of Qualitative Data," *Psychometrika*, 46, 357–388.

Young, F.W., de Leeuw, J., and Takane, Y. (1976), "Regression with Qualitative and Quantitative Variables: An Alternating Least Squares Approach with Optimal Scaling Features," *Psychometrika*, 41, 505–529.

Chapter 41

The TREE
Procedure

ABSTRACT   1613
INTRODUCTION   1613
SPECIFICATIONS   1614
   PROC TREE Statement   1614
   BY Statement   1618
   COPY Statement   1618
   FREQ Statement   1618
   HEIGHT Statement   1619
   ID Statement   1619
   NAME Statement   1619
   PARENT Statement   1619
DETAILS   1619
   Missing Values   1619
   Output Data Set   1620
   Printed Output   1620
EXAMPLES   1620
   Example 1:   Mammals' Teeth   1620
   Example 2:   Iris Data   1626
REFERENCES   1631

ABSTRACT

The TREE procedure prints a tree diagram, also known as a dendrogram or phenogram, using a data set created by the CLUSTER or VARCLUS procedure. PROC TREE can also create an output data set identifying disjoint clusters at a specified level in the tree.

INTRODUCTION

The CLUSTER and VARCLUS procedures create output data sets giving the results of hierarchical clustering as a tree structure. The TREE procedure uses the output data set to print a diagram of the tree structure in the style of Johnson (1967), with the root at the top. Alternatively, the diagram can be oriented horizontally, with the root at the left. Any numeric variable in the output data set can be used to specify the heights of the clusters. PROC TREE can also create an output data set containing a variable to indicate the disjoint clusters at a specified level in the tree.

Trees are discussed in the context of cluster analysis by Duran and Odell (1974), Hartigan (1975), and Everitt (1980). Knuth (1973) provides a general treatment of trees in computer programming.

The literature on trees contains a mixture of botanical and genealogical terminology. The objects that are clustered are *leaves*. The cluster containing all objects is the *root*. A cluster containing at least two objects but not all of them is a *branch*. The general term for leaves, branches, and roots is *node*. If a cluster A is the union of clusters B and C, then A is the *parent* of B and C, and B and C are *children* of A. A leaf is thus a node with no children, and a root is a node with no parent. If every cluster has at most two children, the tree is a *binary tree*. The CLUSTER procedure always produces binary trees. The VARCLUS procedure can produce trees with clusters that have many children.

SPECIFICATIONS

The TREE procedure is invoked by the following statements:

PROC TREE <*options*>;   required statement

    NAME *variables*;
    HEIGHT *variables*;
    PARENT *variables*;
    BY *variables*;   optional statements
    COPY *variables*;
    FREQ *variable*;
    ID *variable*;

If the input data set has been created by CLUSTER or VARCLUS, the only statement required is the PROC TREE statement. The BY, COPY, FREQ, HEIGHT, ID, NAME, and PARENT statements are described after the PROC TREE statement.

PROC TREE Statement

    PROC TREE <*options*>;

The PROC TREE statement starts the TREE procedure. The options that can appear in the PROC TREE statement are summarized in the table below.

Task	Options
Specify data sets	DATA= DOCK= LEVEL= NCLUSTERS= OUT= ROOT=
Specify cluster heights	HEIGHT= DISSIMILAR SIMILAR
Print horizontal trees	HORIZONTAL
Control the height axis	INC= MAXHEIGHT= MINHEIGHT= NTICK= PAGES= POS= SPACES= TICKPOS=

Control characters printed in trees	FILLCHAR=
	JOINCHAR=
	LEAFCHAR=
	TREECHAR=
Control sort order	DESCENDING
	SORT
Control output	LIST
	NOPRINT
	PAGES=

These options are listed in alphabetical order below.

DATA=*SAS-data-set*

names the input data set defining the tree. If the DATA= option is omitted, the most recently created SAS data set is used.

DESCENDING
DES

reverses the sorting order for the SORT option.

DISSIMILAR
DIS

implies that the values of the HEIGHT variable are dissimilarities; that is, a large height value means that the clusters are very dissimilar or far apart.

If neither the SIMILAR nor the DISSIMILAR option is specified, TREE attempts to infer from the data whether the height values are similarities or dissimilarities. If TREE cannot tell this from the data, it issues an error message and does not print a tree diagram.

DOCK=*n*

in the OUT= data set, causes observations assigned to output clusters with a frequency of *n* or less to be given missing values for the output variables CLUSTER and CLUSNAME. If the NCLUSTERS= option is also specified, DOCK= also prevents clusters with a frequency of *n* or less from being counted toward the number of clusters requested by the NCLUSTERS= option. By default, DOCK=0.

FILLCHAR='*c*'
FC='*c*'

specifies the character to print between leaves that have not been joined into a cluster. The character should be enclosed in single quotes. The default is a blank.

HEIGHT=*name*
H=*name*

specifies certain conventional variables to be used for the height axis of the tree diagram. For many situations, the only option you will need is HEIGHT=. Valid values for *name* and their meanings are

HEIGHT | H   specifies the _HEIGHT_ variable.

LENGTH | L   defines the height of each node as its path length from the root. This can also be interpreted as the number of ancestors of the node.

MODE|M   specifies the _MODE_ variable.

NCL|N   specifies the _NCL_ (number of clusters) variable.

RSQ|R   specifies the _RSQ_ variable.

See also the HEIGHT statement, which can specify any variable in the input data set to be used for the height axis. In rare cases, you may need to use either the DISSIMILAR option or the SIMILAR option.

HORIZONTAL
HOR

orients the tree diagram with the height axis horizontal and the root at the left. If this option is not used, the height axis will be vertical, with the root at the top. If the tree takes up more than one page and will be viewed on a screen, horizontal orientation can make the tree diagram considerably easier to read.

INC=n

specifies the increment between tick values on the height axis. If the HEIGHT variable is _NCL_, the default is usually 1, although a different value can be used for consistency with other options. For any other HEIGHT variable, the default is some power of 10 times 1, 2, 2.5, or 5.

JOINCHAR='c'
JC='c'

specifies the character to print between leaves that have been joined into a cluster. The character should be enclosed in single quotes. The default is **x**.

LEAFCHAR='c'
LC='c'

specifies a character to represent clusters having no children. The character should be enclosed in single quotes. The default is a period.

LEVEL=n

for the OUT= data set, specifies the level of the tree defining disjoint clusters. The LEVEL= option also causes only clusters between the root and a height of n to be printed. The clusters in the output data set are those that exist at a height of n on the tree diagram. For example, if the HEIGHT variable is _NCL_ (number of clusters) and LEVEL=5 is specified, then the OUT= data set contains 5 disjoint clusters. If the HEIGHT variable is _RSQ_ (R^2) and LEVEL=0.9 is specified, then the OUT= data set contains the smallest number of clusters that yields an R^2 of at least 0.9.

LIST

lists all the nodes in the tree, printing the height, parent, and children of each node.

MAXHEIGHT=n
MAXH=n

specifies the maximum value printed on the height axis.

MINHEIGHT=n
MINH=n

specifies the minimum value printed on the height axis.

NCLUSTERS=n
NCL=n
N=n

specifies the number of clusters desired in the OUT= data set. The number of clusters obtained may not equal the number specified if

(1) there are fewer than *n* leaves in the tree, (2) there are more than *n* unconnected trees in the data set, (3) a multi-way tree does not contain a level with the specified number of clusters, or (4) the DOCK= option eliminates too many clusters.

The NCLUSTERS= option uses the _NCL_ variable to determine the order in which the clusters were formed. If there is no _NCL_ variable, the height variable (as determined by the HEIGHT statement or HEIGHT= option) is used instead.

NTICK=*n*

specifies the number of tick intervals on the height axis. The default depends on the values of other options.

NOPRINT

suppresses printing the tree if you only want to create an OUT= data set.

OUT=*SAS-data-set*

creates an output data set that contains one observation for each object in the tree or subtree being processed and variables called CLUSTER and CLUSNAME showing cluster membership at any specified level in the tree. If the OUT= option is used, then either NCLUSTERS= or LEVEL= must be specified to define the output partition level. If you want to create a permanent SAS data set you must specify a two-level name (see "SAS Files" in the *SAS Language: Reference, Version 6, First Edition* and "Introduction to Data Step Processing" in *SAS Language and Procedures: Usage, Version 6, First Edition*).

PAGES=*n*

specifies the number of pages over which the tree diagram (from root to leaves) is to extend. The default is 1.

POS=*n*

specifies the number of print positions on the height axis. The default depends on the value of the PAGES= option, the orientation of the tree diagram, and the values specified by the PAGESIZE= and LINESIZE= options.

ROOT=*'name'*

specifies the value of the NAME variable for the root of a subtree to be printed if you do not want to print the entire tree. If the OUT= option is also specified, the output data set contains only objects belonging to the subtree specified by the ROOT= option.

SIMILAR
SIM

implies that the values of the HEIGHT variable are similarities; that is, a large height value means that the clusters are very similar or close together.

If neither the SIMILAR nor the DISSIMILAR option is specified, TREE attempts to infer from the data whether the height values are similarities or dissimilarities. If TREE cannot tell this from the data, it issues an error message and does not print a tree diagram.

SORT

sorts the children of each node by the HEIGHT variable, in the order of cluster formation. See the DESCENDING option.

SPACES=*s*
S=*s*

specifies the number of spaces between objects on the printout. The default depends on the number of objects, the orientation of the tree diagram, and the values specified by the PAGESIZE= and LINESIZE= options.

TICKPOS=*n*

specifies the number of print positions per tick interval on the height axis. The default value is usually between 5 and 10, although a different value may be used for consistency with other options.

TREECHAR='*c*'

TC='*c*'

specifies a character to represent clusters with children. The character should be enclosed in single quotes. The default is **x**.

BY Statement

BY *variables*;

A BY statement can be used with PROC TREE to obtain separate analyses on observations in groups defined by the BY variables. When a BY statement appears, the procedure expects the input data set to be sorted in order of the BY variables.

If your input data set is not sorted in ascending order, use one of the following alternatives:

- Use the SORT procedure with a similar BY statement to sort the data.
- Use the BY statement options NOTSORTED or DESCENDING in the BY statement for the TREE procedure. The NOTSORTED option does not mean that the data are unsorted, but rather means that the data are arranged in groups (according to values of the BY variables) and that these groups are not necessarily in alphabetical or increasing numeric order.
- Use the DATASETS procedure (in base SAS software) to create an index on the BY variables.

For more information on the BY statement, see the discussion in *SAS Language: Reference, Version 6, First Edition*. For more information on the DATASETS procedure, see the discussion in *SAS Procedures Guide, Version 6, Third Edition*.

COPY Statement

COPY *variables*;

The COPY statement lists one or more character or numeric variables to be copied to the OUT= data set.

FREQ Statement

FREQ *variable*;

The FREQ statement lists one numeric variable that tells how many clustering observations belong to the cluster. If the FREQ statement is omitted, TREE looks for a variable called _FREQ_ to specify the number of observations per cluster. If neither the FREQ statement nor the _FREQ_ variable is present, each leaf is assumed to represent one clustering observation, and the frequency for each internal node is found by summing the frequencies of its children.

HEIGHT Statement

HEIGHT *variable;*

The HEIGHT statement specifies the name of a numeric variable to define the height of each node (cluster) in the tree. The height variable can also be specified by the HEIGHT= option in the PROC TREE statement. If both the HEIGHT statement and the HEIGHT= option are omitted, TREE looks for a variable called _HEIGHT_. If the data set does not contain _HEIGHT_, TREE looks for a variable called _NCL_. If _NCL_ is not found either, the height of each node is defined to be its path length from the root.

ID Statement

ID *variable;*

The ID variable is used to identify the objects (leaves) in the tree on the printout. The ID variable can be a character or numeric variable of any length. If the ID statement is omitted, the variable in the NAME statement is used instead. If both ID and NAME are omitted, TREE looks for a variable called _NAME_. If the _NAME_ variable is not found in the data set, TREE issues an error message and stops. The ID variable is copied to the OUT= data set.

NAME Statement

NAME *variable;*

The NAME statement specifies a character or numeric variable identifying the node represented by each observation. The NAME variable and PARENT variable jointly define the tree structure. If the NAME statement is omitted, TREE looks for a variable called _NAME_. If the _NAME_ variable is not found in the data set, TREE issues an error message and stops.

PARENT Statement

PARENT *variable;*

The PARENT statement specifies a character or numeric variable identifying the node in the tree that is the parent of each observation. The PARENT variable must have the same formatted length as the NAME variable. If the PARENT statement is omitted, TREE looks for a variable called _PARENT_. If the _PARENT_ variable is not found in the data set, TREE issues an error message and stops.

DETAILS

Missing Values

An observation with a missing value for the NAME variable is omitted from processing. If the PARENT variable has a missing value but the NAME variable is present, the observation is treated as the root of a tree. A data set can contain several roots and, hence, several trees.

Missing values of the HEIGHT variable are set to upper or lower bounds determined from the nonmissing values under the assumption that the heights are monotonic with respect to the tree structure.

Missing values of the FREQ variable are inferred from nonmissing values where possible; otherwise, they are treated as zero.

Output Data Set

The OUT= data set contains one observation for each leaf in the tree or subtree being processed. The variables are

- the BY variables, if any.
- the ID variable, or the NAME variable if the ID statement is not used.
- the COPY variables.
- a numeric variable CLUSTER taking values from 1 to c, where c is the number of disjoint clusters. The cluster to which the first observation belongs is given the number 1, the cluster to which the next observation belongs that does not belong to cluster 1 is given the number 2, and so on.
- a character variable CLUSNAME giving the value of the NAME variable of the cluster to which the observation belongs.

The CLUSTER and CLUSNAME variables are missing if the corresponding leaf has a nonpositive frequency.

Printed Output

The printed output from the TREE procedure includes the following:

1. the names of the objects in the tree.
2. the height axis.
3. the tree diagram. The root (the cluster containing all the objects) is indicated by a solid line of the character specified by TREECHAR= (the default character is **x**). At each level of the tree, clusters are shown by unbroken lines of the TREECHAR= symbol with the FILLCHAR= symbol (the default is a blank) separating the clusters. The LEAFCHAR= symbol (the default character is a period) represents single-member clusters.

By default, the tree diagram is oriented with the height axis vertical and the object names at the top of the diagram. If the HORIZONTAL option is used, then the height axis is horizontal and the object names are on the left.

EXAMPLES

Example 1:   Mammals' Teeth

The data below give the numbers of different kinds of teeth for a variety of mammals. The mammals are clustered by average linkage using PROC CLUSTER. The first PROC TREE uses the average-linkage distance as the height axis, which is the default. The second PROC TREE sorts the clusters at each branch in order of formation and uses the number of clusters for the height axis. The third PROC TREE produces no printed output but creates an output data set indicating the cluster to which each observation belongs at the 6-cluster level in the tree; this data set is reproduced by PROC PRINT. The following statements produce **Output 41.1** through **Output 41.4**:

```
data teeth;
    title 'Mammals'' Teeth';
    input mammal $ 1-16 @21 (v1-v8) (1.);
    label V1='Right Top Incisors'
          V2='Right Bottom Incisors'
          V3='Right Top Canines'
          V4='Right Bottom Canines'
```

```
                V5='Right Top Premolars'
                V6='Right Bottom Premolars'
                V7='Right Top Molars'
                V8='Right Bottom Molars';
        cards;
Brown Bat          23113333
Mole               32103333
Silver Hair Bat    23112333
Pigmy Bat          23112233
House Bat          23111233
Red Bat            13112233
Pika               21002233
Rabbit             21003233
Beaver             11002133
Groundhog          11002133
Gray Squirrel      11001133
House Mouse        11000033
Porcupine          11001133
Wolf               33114423
Bear               33114423
Raccoon            33114432
Marten             33114412
Weasel             33113312
Wolverine          33114412
Badger             33113312
River Otter        33114312
Sea Otter          32113312
Jaguar             33113211
Cougar             33113211
Fur Seal           32114411
Sea Lion           32114411
Grey Seal          32113322
Elephant Seal      21114411
Reindeer           04103333
Elk                04103333
Deer               04003333
Moose              04003333
;
options pagesize=60 linesize=110;

proc cluster method=average std pseudo noeigen outtree=tree;
    id mammal;
    var v1-v8;
run;

proc tree;
run;

proc tree sort height=n;
run;

proc tree noprint out=part nclusters=6;
    id mammal;
    copy v1-v8;
run;
```

```
proc sort;
   by cluster;
run;

proc print label uniform;
   id mammal;
   var v1-v8;
   format v1-v8 1.;
   by cluster;
run;
```

Output 41.1   Clustering of Mammals: PROC CLUSTER

```
                                    Mammals' Teeth                                        1

                                Average Linkage Cluster Analysis

                    The data have been standardized to mean 0 and variance 1
                    Root-Mean-Square Total-Sample Standard Deviation =        1
                    Root-Mean-Square Distance Between Observations   =        4

    Number                                    Frequency                        Normalized
      of                                       of New      Pseudo   Pseudo        RMS
    Clusters   Clusters Joined                 Cluster       F       t**2      Distance   Tie

       31      Beaver          Groundhog          2         .         .        0.000000    T
       30      Gray Squirrel   Porcupine          2         .         .        0.000000    T
       29      Wolf            Bear               2         .         .        0.000000    T
       28      Marten          Wolverine          2         .         .        0.000000    T
       27      Weasel          Badger             2         .         .        0.000000    T
       26      Jaguar          Cougar             2         .         .        0.000000    T
       25      Fur Seal        Sea Lion           2         .         .        0.000000    T
       24      Reindeer        Elk                2         .         .        0.000000    T
       23      Deer            Moose              2         .         .        0.000000
       22      Pigmy Bat       Red Bat            2       281.19      .        0.228930
       21      CL28            River Otter        3       138.67      .        0.229221
       20      Brown Bat       Silver Hair Bat    2       109.35      .        0.235702    T
       19      Pika            Rabbit             2        95.13      .        0.235702    T
       18      CL31            CL30               4        73.24      .        0.235702
       17      CL27            Sea Otter          3        67.37      .        0.246183
       16      CL22            House Bat          3        62.89     1.75      0.285937
       15      CL21            CL17               6        47.42     6.81      0.332845
       14      CL25            Elephant Seal      3        45.04      .        0.336177
       13      CL20            CL16               5        40.83     3.50      0.367188
       12      CL15            Grey Seal          7        38.90     2.78      0.407838
       11      CL29            Raccoon            3        38.02      .        0.422997
       10      CL19            CL18               6        34.51    10.27      0.433918
        9      CL12            CL26               9        30.01     7.27      0.507122
        8      CL24            CL23               4        28.69      .        0.547281
        7      CL9             CL14              12        25.74     6.99      0.566841
        6      CL10            House Mouse        7        28.32     4.12      0.579239
        5      CL11            CL7               15        26.83     6.87      0.662106
        4      CL13            Mole               6        31.93     7.23      0.715610
        3      CL4             CL8               10        30.98    12.67      0.879851
        2      CL3             CL6               17        27.83    16.12      1.031622
        1      CL2             CL5               32         .       27.83      1.193815
```

Output 41.2 Clustering of Mammals: PROC TREE

Output 41.3   Clustering of Mammals: PROC TREE with SORT and HEIGHT= Options

```
                                          Mammals' Teeth                                            3

                                    Average Linkage Cluster Analysis

                                     Name of Observation or Cluster

                                                                              S
                                                                              i
                                                                              l
                     E                                                        v
                     l                                                        e
                     e                                         G              r
                     p                              R          r
                     h                              i          a              B       H
                     a      F  S                 G  v          y              r       o    P
                     n      u  e                 r  e       W  S           R  o       u    i
            R        t      r  a     J  C        e  r    W  o  e           e  w       s    g     R
            a        r      a  l     a  o        y  O  M  v  a     W  B  M  i  n      B     e    m  e
            c   W  B  S  S  L  i  C  g  u  S  M  a  e  o  e  t  H  a  o  b  b  n  R  D  M  r  H  y  d
            o   o  e  e  e  i  o  y  u  g  e  v  r  t  r  t  a  o  d  a  u  v  e  o  o  o  o  H  g  e
            o   e  a  a  a  o  u  p  a  e  t  e  t  t  r  i  d  u  g  s  i  h  i  e  e  o  w  a  m  e
            n   f  r  l  l  n  r  r  l  r  e  r  e  n  e  t  e  s  u  k  e  o  n  r  s  l  n  r  y  d
    1 +XXXXXXXXXXXXXXXXXXXXXXXXXXXXXXXXXXXXXXXXXXXXXXXXXXXXXXXXXXXXXXXXXXXXXXXXXXXXXXX
    2 +XXXXXXXXXXXXXXXXXXXXXXXXXXXXXXXXXXXXXX  XXXXXXXXXXXXXXXXXXXXXXXXXXXXXXXXXXXXXXXX
    3 +XXXXXXXXXXXXXXXXXXXXXXXXXXXXXXXXXXXXXX  XXXXXXXXXXXXXXXXXX  XXXXXXXXX  XXXXXXXXXX
    4 +XXXXXXXXXXXXXXXXXXXXXXXXXXXXXXXXXXXXXX  XXXXXXXXXXXXXXXXXX  XXXXXXXXX  XXXXXXXXXX
    5 +XXXXXXXXXXXXXXXXXXXXXXXXXXXXXXXXXXXXXX  XXXXXXXXXXXXXXXXXX  XXXXXXXXX  .  XXXXXXXXXX
    6 +XXXXXXX  XXXXXXXXXXXXXXXXXXXXXXXXXXXXX  XXXXXXXXXXXXXXXXXX  XXXXXXXXX  .  XXXXXXXXXX
    7 +XXXXXXX  XXXXXXXXXXXXXXXXXXXXXXXXXXXXX  .  XXXXXXXXXXXXXXX  XXXXXXXXX  .  XXXXXXXXXX
N   8 +XXXXXXX  XXXXXXX  XXXXXXXXXXXXXXXXXXXX  .  XXXXXXXXXXXXXXX  XXXXXXXXX  .  XXXXXXXXXX
u   9 +XXXXXXX  XXXXXXX  XXXXXXXXXXXXXXXXXXXX  .  XXXXXXXXXXXXXXX  XXXX  XXXX  .  XXXXXXXXXX
m  10 +XXXXXXX  XXXXXXX  XXXX  XXXXXXXXXXXXXX  .  XXXXXXXXXXXXXXX  XXXX  XXXX  .  XXXXXXXXXX
b  11 +XXXXXXX  XXXXXXX  XXXX  XXXXXXXXXXXXXX  .  XXXX  XXXXXXXXX  XXXX  XXXX  .  XXXXXXXXXX
e  12 +.  XXXX  XXXXXXX  XXXX  XXXXXXXXXXXXXX  .  XXXX  XXXXXXXXX  XXXX  XXXX  .  XXXXXXXXXX
r  13 +.  XXXX  XXXXXXX  XXXX  .  XXXXXXXXXXX  .  XXXX  XXXXXXXXX  XXXX  XXXX  .  XXXXXXXXXX
   14 +.  XXXX  XXXXXXX  XXXX  .  XXXXXXXXXXX  .  XXXX  XXXXXXXXX  XXXX  XXXX  .  XXXX  XXXXXXX
o  15 +.  XXXX  .  XXXX  XXXX  .  XXXXXXXXXXX  .  XXXX  XXXXXXXXX  XXXX  XXXX  .  XXXX  XXXXXXX
f  16 +.  XXXX  .  XXXX  XXXX  .  XXXXXXX  XXXXXXX  .  XXXX  XXXXXXXXX  XXXX  XXXX  .  XXXX  XXXXXXX
   17 +.  XXXX  .  XXXX  XXXX  .  XXXXXXX  XXXXXXX  .  XXXX  XXXXXXXXX  XXXX  XXXX  .  XXXX  XXXX
C  18 +.  XXXX  .  XXXX  XXXX  .  XXXXXXX  .  XXXX  .  XXXX  XXXXXXXXX  XXXX  XXXX  .  XXXX  .  XXXX
l  19 +.  XXXX  .  XXXX  XXXX  .  XXXXXXX  .  XXXX  .  XXXX  XXXXXXXXX  XXXX  XXXX  .  XXXX  .  XXXX
u  20 +.  XXXX  .  XXXX  XXXX  .  XXXXXXX  .  XXXX  .  XXXX  XXXX  XXXX  XXXX  XXXX  .  XXXX  .  XXXX
s  21 +.  XXXX  .  XXXX  XXXX  .  XXXXXXX  .  XXXX  .  XXXX  XXXX  XXXX  XXXX  XXXX  .  .  .  XXXX
t  22 +.  XXXX  .  XXXX  XXXX  .  .  XXXX  .  XXXX  .  XXXX  XXXX  XXXX  XXXX  XXXX  .  .  .  XXXX
e  23 +.  XXXX  .  XXXX  XXXX  .  .  XXXX  .  XXXX  .  XXXX  XXXX  XXXX  XXXX  XXXX  .  .  .  .
r  24 +.  XXXX  .  XXXX  XXXX  .  .  XXXX  .  XXXX  .  XXXX  XXXX  XXXX  XXXX  .  .  .  .  .
s  25 +.  XXXX  .  XXXX  XXXX  .  .  XXXX  .  XXXX  .  XXXX  XXXX  XXXX  .  .  .  .  .
   26 +.  XXXX  .  .  XXXX  .  .  XXXX  .  XXXX  .  XXXX  XXXX  .  .  .  .  .
   27 +.  XXXX  .  .  .  .  .  XXXX  .  XXXX  .  XXXX  XXXX  .  .  .  .  .
   28 +.  XXXX  .  .  .  .  .  XXXX  .  .  .  XXXX  XXXX  .  .  .  .  .
   29 +.  XXXX  .  .  .  .  .  .  .  .  .  XXXX  XXXX  .  .  .  .  .
   30 +.  .  .  .  .  .  .  .  .  .  .  XXXX  XXXX  .  .  .  .  .
   31 +.  .  .  .  .  .  .  .  .  .  .  XXXX  .  .  .  .  .  .
   32 +.  .  .  .  .  .  .  .  .  .  .  .  .  .  .  .  .  .
```

Output 41.4   Clustering of Mammals: PROC PRINT

Mammals' Teeth   4

-- CLUSTER=1 --

MAMMAL	Right Top Incisors	Right Bottom Incisors	Right Top Canines	Right Bottom Canines	Right Top Premolars	Right Bottom Premolars	Right Top Molars	Right Bottom Molars
Beaver	1	1	0	0	2	1	3	3
Groundhog	1	1	0	0	2	1	3	3
Gray Squirrel	1	1	0	0	1	1	3	3
Porcupine	1	1	0	0	1	1	3	3
Pika	2	1	0	0	2	2	3	3
Rabbit	2	1	0	0	3	2	3	3
House Mouse	1	1	0	0	0	0	3	3

-- CLUSTER=2 --

MAMMAL	Right Top Incisors	Right Bottom Incisors	Right Top Canines	Right Bottom Canines	Right Top Premolars	Right Bottom Premolars	Right Top Molars	Right Bottom Molars
Wolf	3	3	1	1	4	4	2	3
Bear	3	3	1	1	4	4	2	3
Raccoon	3	3	1	1	4	4	3	2

-- CLUSTER=3 --

MAMMAL	Right Top Incisors	Right Bottom Incisors	Right Top Canines	Right Bottom Canines	Right Top Premolars	Right Bottom Premolars	Right Top Molars	Right Bottom Molars
Marten	3	3	1	1	4	4	1	2
Wolverine	3	3	1	1	4	4	1	2
Weasel	3	3	1	1	3	3	1	2
Badger	3	3	1	1	3	3	1	2
Jaguar	3	3	1	1	3	2	1	1
Cougar	3	3	1	1	3	2	1	1
Fur Seal	3	2	1	1	4	4	1	1
Sea Lion	3	2	1	1	4	4	1	1
River Otter	3	3	1	1	4	3	1	2
Sea Otter	3	2	1	1	3	3	1	2
Elephant Seal	2	1	1	1	4	4	1	1
Grey Seal	3	2	1	1	3	3	2	2

-- CLUSTER=4 --

MAMMAL	Right Top Incisors	Right Bottom Incisors	Right Top Canines	Right Bottom Canines	Right Top Premolars	Right Bottom Premolars	Right Top Molars	Right Bottom Molars
Reindeer	0	4	1	0	3	3	3	3
Elk	0	4	1	0	3	3	3	3
Deer	0	4	0	0	3	3	3	3
Moose	0	4	0	0	3	3	3	3

Mammals' Teeth   5

-- CLUSTER=5 --

MAMMAL	Right Top Incisors	Right Bottom Incisors	Right Top Canines	Right Bottom Canines	Right Top Premolars	Right Bottom Premolars	Right Top Molars	Right Bottom Molars
Pigmy Bat	2	3	1	1	2	2	3	3
Red Bat	1	3	1	1	2	2	3	3
Brown Bat	2	3	1	1	3	3	3	3
Silver Hair Bat	2	3	1	1	2	3	3	3
House Bat	2	3	1	1	1	2	3	3

-- CLUSTER=6 --

MAMMAL	Right Top Incisors	Right Bottom Incisors	Right Top Canines	Right Bottom Canines	Right Top Premolars	Right Bottom Premolars	Right Top Molars	Right Bottom Molars
Mole	3	2	1	0	3	3	3	3

To see how the tree diagram is interpreted, consider the first tree diagram. As you look up from the bottom of the diagram, objects and clusters are progressively joined until a single, all-encompassing cluster is formed at the top (or root) of the diagram. Clusters exist at each level of the diagram. For example, the unbroken line of Xs at the left-most side of the 0.6 level indicates that the five bats have formed a cluster. The next cluster is represented by a period because it contains only one mammal, MOLE. REINDEER, ELK, DEER, and MOOSE form the next cluster, indicated by Xs again. The mammals PIKA through HOUSE MOUSE are in the fourth cluster. WOLF, BEAR, and RACCOON form the fifth cluster, while the last cluster contains MARTEN through ELEPHANT SEAL. The same clusters can be seen at the 6-cluster level of the second tree diagram, although they appear in a different order.

Example 2: Iris Data

Fisher's (1936) iris data are clustered by kth-nearest-neighbor density linkage using the CLUSTER procedure with K=8. Observations are identified by species in the tree diagram, which is oriented with the height axis horizontal. The following statements produce **Output 41.5** and **Output 41.6**:

```
data iris;
    title 'Fisher''s Iris Data';
    input sepallen sepalwid petallen petalwid spec_no @@;
    if spec_no=1 then species='Setosa     ';
    else if spec_no=2 then species='Versicolor';
    else if spec_no=3 then species='Virginica ';
    cards;
50 33 14 02 1 64 28 56 22 3 65 28 46 15 2 67 31 56 24 3
63 28 51 15 3 46 34 14 03 1 69 31 51 23 3 62 22 45 15 2
59 32 48 18 2 46 36 10 02 1 61 30 46 14 2 60 27 51 16 2
65 30 52 20 3 56 25 39 11 2 65 30 55 18 3 58 27 51 19 3
68 32 59 23 3 51 33 17 05 1 57 28 45 13 2 62 34 54 23 3
77 38 67 22 3 63 33 47 16 2 67 33 57 25 3 76 30 66 21 3
49 25 45 17 3 55 35 13 02 1 67 30 52 23 3 70 32 47 14 2
64 32 45 15 2 61 28 40 13 2 48 31 16 02 1 59 30 51 18 3
55 24 38 11 2 63 25 50 19 3 64 32 53 23 3 52 34 14 02 1
49 36 14 01 1 54 30 45 15 2 79 38 64 20 3 44 32 13 02 1
67 33 57 21 3 50 35 16 06 1 58 26 40 12 2 44 30 13 02 1
77 28 67 20 3 63 27 49 18 3 47 32 16 02 1 55 26 44 12 2
50 23 33 10 2 72 32 60 18 3 48 30 14 03 1 51 38 16 02 1
61 30 49 18 3 48 34 19 02 1 50 30 16 02 1 50 32 12 02 1
61 26 56 14 3 64 28 56 21 3 43 30 11 01 1 58 40 12 02 1
51 38 19 04 1 67 31 44 14 2 62 28 48 18 3 49 30 14 02 1
51 35 14 02 1 56 30 45 15 2 58 27 41 10 2 50 34 16 04 1
46 32 14 02 1 60 29 45 15 2 57 26 35 10 2 57 44 15 04 1
50 36 14 02 1 77 30 61 23 3 63 34 56 24 3 58 27 51 19 3
57 29 42 13 2 72 30 58 16 3 54 34 15 04 1 52 41 15 01 1
71 30 59 21 3 64 31 55 18 3 60 30 48 18 3 63 29 56 18 3
49 24 33 10 2 56 27 42 13 2 57 30 42 12 2 55 42 14 02 1
49 31 15 02 1 77 26 69 23 3 60 22 50 15 3 54 39 17 04 1
66 29 46 13 2 52 27 39 14 2 60 34 45 16 2 50 34 15 02 1
44 29 14 02 1 50 20 35 10 2 55 24 37 10 2 58 27 39 12 2
47 32 13 02 1 46 31 15 02 1 69 32 57 23 3 62 29 43 13 2
74 28 61 19 3 59 30 42 15 2 51 34 15 02 1 50 35 13 03 1
56 28 49 20 3 60 22 40 10 2 73 29 63 18 3 67 25 58 18 3
49 31 15 01 1 67 31 47 15 2 63 23 44 13 2 54 37 15 02 1
```

```
56 30 41 13 2 63 25 49 15 2 61 28 47 12 2 64 29 43 13 2
51 25 30 11 2 57 28 41 13 2 65 30 58 22 3 69 31 54 21 3
54 39 13 04 1 51 35 14 03 1 72 36 61 25 3 65 32 51 20 3
61 29 47 14 2 56 29 36 13 2 69 31 49 15 2 64 27 53 19 3
68 30 55 21 3 55 25 40 13 2 48 34 16 02 1 48 30 14 01 1
45 23 13 03 1 57 25 50 20 3 57 38 17 03 1 51 38 15 03 1
55 23 40 13 2 66 30 44 14 2 68 28 48 14 2 54 34 17 02 1
51 37 15 04 1 52 35 15 02 1 58 28 51 24 3 67 30 50 17 2
63 33 60 25 3 53 37 15 02 1
;
options pagesize=60 linesize=110;

proc cluster data=iris method=twostage print=10 k=8 noeigen;
   var sepallen sepalwid petallen petalwid;
   copy species;
run;

proc tree horizontal pages=1;
   id species;
run;
```

Output 41.5   Fisher's Iris Data: PROC CLUSTER with METHOD=DENSITY

```
                              Fisher's Iris Data                                    1

                        Two-Stage Density Linkage Clustering

                                    K = 8

        Root-Mean-Square Total-Sample Standard Deviation = 10.69224
```

					Normalized Maximum Density in Each Cluster		
Number of Clusters	Clusters	Joined	Frequency of New Cluster	Normalized Fusion Density	Lesser	Greater	Tie
10	CL11	OB98	48	0.2879	0.1479	8.3678	
9	CL13	OB24	46	0.2802	0.2005	3.5156	
8	CL10	OB25	49	0.2699	0.1372	8.3678	
7	CL8	OB121	50	0.2586	0.1372	8.3678	
6	CL9	OB45	47	0.1412	0.0832	3.5156	
5	CL6	OB39	48	0.1070	0.0605	3.5156	
4	CL5	OB21	49	0.0969	0.0541	3.5156	
3	CL4	OB90	50	0.0715	0.0370	3.5156	

```
                       3 modal clusters have been formed.
```

					Normalized Maximum Density in Each Cluster		
Number of Clusters	Clusters	Joined	Frequency of New Cluster	Normalized Fusion Density	Lesser	Greater	Tie
2	CL3	CL7	100	2.6277	3.5156	8.3678	

Output 41.6   Fisher's Iris Data: PROC TREE with HORIZONTAL Option

```
                                 Fisher's Iris Data                                    2

                          Two-Stage Density Linkage Clustering

                                Cluster Fusion Density

                0    5   10   15   20   25   30   35   40   45   50   55   60   65   70   75
                +----+----+----+----+----+----+----+----+----+----+----+----+----+----+----+
S    Virginica X...............................................................................
P             X
E    Virginica X...............................................................................
C             X
I    Virginica X...............................................................................
E             X
S    Virginica X...............................................................................
              X
     Virginica XX..............................................................................
              XX
   Versicolor XX..............................................................................
              XX
     Virginica XX..............................................................................
              XX
     Virginica XX..............................................................................
              XX
     Virginica XXX.............................................................................
              XXX
     Virginica XXX.............................................................................
              XXX
     Virginica XXX.............................................................................
              XXX
     Virginica XXX.............................................................................
              XXX
     Virginica XXXX............................................................................
              XXXX
     Virginica XXXX............................................................................
              XXXX
     Virginica XXXX............................................................................
              XXXX
     Virginica XXXX............................................................................
              XXXX
     Virginica XXXX............................................................................
              XXXX
     Virginica XXXX............................................................................
              XXXX
     Virginica XXXX............................................................................
              XXXX
   Versicolor XXXXX...........................................................................
              XXXXX
     Virginica XXXXX...........................................................................
              XXXX
     Virginica XXXX............................................................................
              XXXX
     Virginica XXXX............................................................................
              XXXX
     Virginica XXXXX...........................................................................
              XXXXX
     Virginica XXXXX...........................................................................
              XXXXX
     Virginica XXXXX...........................................................................
              XXXXX
     Virginica XXXXX...........................................................................
              XXXXX
     Virginica XXXXX...........................................................................
              XXXXX
     Virginica XXXXX...........................................................................
              XXXX
     Virginica XXXX............................................................................
              XXXX
     Virginica XXXX............................................................................
              XXXX
   Versicolor XXXX............................................................................
              XXXX
     Virginica XXXX............................................................................
              XXXX
     Virginica XXXX............................................................................
              XXXX
     Virginica XXXX............................................................................
              XXX
     Virginica XXX.............................................................................
              XXX
     Virginica XXX.............................................................................
              XXX
     Virginica XXX.............................................................................
              XXX
```

(continued on next page)

(continued from previous page)

```
    Virginica XXX.....................................................................
              XX
    Virginica XX......................................................................
              XX
    Virginica XX......................................................................
              XX
    Virginica XX......................................................................
              XX
    Virginica XX......................................................................
              XX
    Virginica XX......................................................................
              XX
    Virginica XX......................................................................
              XX
    Virginica XX......................................................................
              XX
    Virginica XX......................................................................
              X
    Virginica X.......................................................................
              X
    Virginica X.......................................................................
              X
    Virginica X.......................................................................
              X
    Virginica X.......................................................................
              X
   Versicolor X.......................................................................
              X
   Versicolor XX......................................................................
              XX
   Versicolor XXX.....................................................................
              XXX
   Versicolor XXX.....................................................................
              XXX
   Versicolor XXX.....................................................................
              XXX
   Versicolor XXX.....................................................................
              XXX
   Versicolor XXXX....................................................................
              XXXX
   Versicolor XXXX....................................................................
              XXXX
   Versicolor XXXX....................................................................
              XXXX
   Versicolor XXXX....................................................................
              XXXX
    Virginica XXXX....................................................................
              XXXX
   Versicolor XXXXX...................................................................
              XXXXX
   Versicolor XXXXX...................................................................
              XXXXX
   Versicolor XXXXX...................................................................
              XXXXX
   Versicolor XXXXXXX.................................................................
              XXXXXXX
   Versicolor XXXXXXX.................................................................
              XXXXXXX
   Versicolor XXXXXXX.................................................................
              XXXXXXX
   Versicolor XXXXXXXX................................................................
              XXXXXXXX
   Versicolor XXXXXXXX................................................................
              XXXXXXXX
   Versicolor XXXXXXXXX...............................................................
              XXXXXXXXX
   Versicolor XXXXXXXXX...............................................................
              XXXXXXXXXX
   Versicolor XXXXXXXXXX..............................................................
              XXXXXXXX
   Versicolor XXXXXXXXXX..............................................................
              XXXXXXXX
   Versicolor XXXXXXXX................................................................
              XXXXXXX
   Versicolor XXXXXXX.................................................................
              XXXXXXX
   Versicolor XXXXXXX.................................................................
              XXXXX
   Versicolor XXXXX...................................................................
              XXXXX
   Versicolor XXXXX...................................................................
              XXXXX
   Versicolor XXXXX...................................................................
              XXXX
```

(continued on next page)

(continued from previous page)

```
 Versicolor XXXX...................................................................................
            XXXX
 Versicolor XXXX...................................................................................
            XXXX
 Versicolor XXXXX..................................................................................
            XXXXX
 Versicolor XXXXX..................................................................................
            XXXXX
 Versicolor XXXXXX.................................................................................
            XXXXXX
 Versicolor XXXXXX.................................................................................
            XXXXX
 Versicolor XXXXX..................................................................................
            XXXXX
 Versicolor XXXXX..................................................................................
            XXXX
 Versicolor XXXX...................................................................................
            XXXX
 Versicolor XXXX...................................................................................
            XXX
 Versicolor XXX....................................................................................
            XXX
 Versicolor XXX....................................................................................
            XXX
 Versicolor XXX....................................................................................
            XXX
  Virginica XXX....................................................................................
            XXX
 Versicolor XXX....................................................................................
            XX
 Versicolor XX.....................................................................................
            X
 Versicolor X......................................................................................
            X
 Versicolor X......................................................................................
            X
 Versicolor X......................................................................................

     Setosa XXX....................................................................................
            XXX
     Setosa XXXX...................................................................................
            XXXX
     Setosa XXXXX..................................................................................
            XXXXX
     Setosa XXXXXXX................................................................................
            XXXXXXX
     Setosa XXXXXXX................................................................................
            XXXXXXX
     Setosa XXXXXXX................................................................................
            XXXXXXX
     Setosa XXXXXXX................................................................................
            XXXXXXX
     Setosa XXXXXXX................................................................................
            XXXXXXXX
     Setosa XXXXXXXXXXX............................................................................
            XXXXXXXXXXX
     Setosa XXXXXXXXXXXX...........................................................................
            XXXXXXXXXXXX
     Setosa XXXXXXXXXXXXXX.........................................................................
            XXXXXXXXXXXXXX
     Setosa XXXXXXXXXXXXXXXXXX.....................................................................
            XXXXXXXXXXXXXXXXXX
     Setosa XXXXXXXXXXXXXXXXXXX....................................................................
            XXXXXXXXXXXXXXXXXXX
     Setosa XXXXXXXXXXXXXXXXXXXXXX.................................................................
            XXXXXXXXXXXXXXXXXXXXXX
     Setosa XXXXXXXXXXXXXXXXXXXXXX.................................................................
            XXXXXXXXXXXXXXXXXXXXXXX
     Setosa XXXXXXXXXXXXXXXXXXXXXXX................................................................
            XXXXXXXXXXXXXXXXXXXXXXXX
     Setosa XXXXXXXXXXXXXXXXXXXXXXXXXX.............................................................
            XXXXXXXXXXXXXXXXXXXXXXXXXX
     Setosa XXXXXXXXXXXXXXXXXXXXXXXXXXXXXX.........................................................
            XXXXXXXXXXXXXXXXXXXXXXXXXXXXXXX
     Setosa XXXXXXXXXXXXXXXXXXXXXXXXXXXXXXXXXX.....................................................
            XXXXXXXXXXXXXXXXXXXXXXXXXXXXXXXXXXXX
     Setosa XXXXXXXXXXXXXXXXXXXXXXXXXXXXXXXXXXXXXXXXXX.............................................
            XXXXXXXXXXXXXXXXXXXXXXXXXXXXXXXXXXXXXXXXXX
     Setosa XXXXXXXXXXXXXXXXXXXXXXXXXXXXXXXXXXXXXXXXXXXXXXXXXX......................................
            XXXXXXXXXXXXXXXXXXXXXXXXXXXXXXXXXXXXXXXXXXXXXXXX
     Setosa XXXXXXXXXXXXXXXXXXXXXXXXXXXXXXXXXXXXXXXXXXXXXXXXXXXXXXXXXXXXXXXXXX...........
            XXXXXXXXXXXXXXXXXXXXXXXXXXXXXXXXXXXXXXXXXXXXXXXXXXXXXXXXXXXXXXX
     Setosa XXXXXXXXXXXXXXXXXXXXXXXXXXXXXXXXXXXXXXXXXXXXXXXXXXXXXXXXXXXXXXXXXXXXXXXXXXXXXXXX
            XXXXXXXXXXXXXXXXXXXXXXXXXXXXXXXXXXXXXXXXXXXXXXXXXXXXXXXXXXXXXXXXXXXXXXXXXXXXXXXXX
```

(continued on next page)

(continued from previous page)

```
Setosa XXXXXXXXXXXXXXXXXXXXXXXXXXXXXXXXXXXXXXXXXXXXXXXXXXXXXXXXXXXXXXXXXXXXXXXXXXXXXXXXXXXXXX
       XXXXXXXXXXXXXXXXXXXXXXXXXXXXXXXXXXXXXXXXXXXXXXXXXXXXXXX
Setosa XXXXXXXXXXXXXXXXXXXXXXXXXXXXXXXXXXXXXXXXXXXXXXXXXXXXX...............................
       XXXXXXXXXXXXXXXXXXXXXXXXXXXXXXXXXXXXXXXXXXXXXXXX
Setosa XXXXXXXXXXXXXXXXXXXXXXXXXXXXXXXXXXXXXXXXXXXXXXX.................................
       XXXXXXXXXXXXXXXXXXXXXXXXXXXXXXXXXXXXXXXXXX
Setosa XXXXXXXXXXXXXXXXXXXXXXXXXXXXXXXXXXXXXXXXXX...................................
       XXXXXXXXXXXXXXXXXXXXXXXXXXXXXXXXXXXXX
Setosa XXXXXXXXXXXXXXXXXXXXXXXXXXXXXXXXXXXXX...................................
       XXXXXXXXXXXXXXXXXXXXXXXXXXXXXXXXXX
Setosa XXXXXXXXXXXXXXXXXXXXXXXXXXXXXXXX..................................
       XXXXXXXXXXXXXXXXXXXXXXXXXXXXXX
Setosa XXXXXXXXXXXXXXXXXXXXXXXXXXXXX.................................
       XXXXXXXXXXXXXXXXXXXXXXXXXX
Setosa XXXXXXXXXXXXXXXXXXXXXXXX....................................
       XXXXXXXXXXXXXXXXXXXXXX
Setosa XXXXXXXXXXXXXXXXXXXXXX.....................................
       XXXXXXXXXXXXXXXXXXXX
Setosa XXXXXXXXXXXXXXXXXXXX.......................................
       XXXXXXXXXXXXXXXXXX
Setosa XXXXXXXXXXXXXXXXXX.........................................
       XXXXXXXXXXXXXXXXX
Setosa XXXXXXXXXXXXXXXXX..........................................
       XXXXXXXXXXXXX
Setosa XXXXXXXXXXXXX..............................................
       XXXXXXXXXXXX
Setosa XXXXXXXXXXXX...............................................
       XXXXXXXXXXXX
Setosa XXXXXXXXXXXX...............................................
       XXXXXXX
Setosa XXXXXXX....................................................
       XXXXXXX
Setosa XXXXXXX....................................................
       XXXXXXX
Setosa XXXXXXX....................................................
       XXXXXX
Setosa XXXXXX.....................................................
       XXXX
Setosa XXXX.......................................................
       XXX
Setosa XXX........................................................
       XXX
Setosa XXX........................................................
       XXX
Setosa XXX........................................................
       XX
Setosa XX.........................................................
       XX
Setosa XX.........................................................
       X
Setosa X..........................................................
```

REFERENCES

Duran, B.S. and Odell, P.L. (1974), *Cluster Analysis*, New York: Springer-Verlag.

Everitt, B.S. (1980), *Cluster Analysis,* 2d Edition, London: Heineman Educational Books Ltd.

Fisher, R.A. (1936), "The Use of Multiple Measurements in Taxonomic Problems," *Annals of Eugenics*, 7, 179–188.

Hartigan, J.A. (1975), *Clustering Algorithms*, New York: John Wiley & Sons, Inc.

Johnson, S.C. (1967), "Hierarchical Clustering Schemes," *Psychometrika*, 32, 241–254.

Knuth, D.E. (1973), *The Art of Computer Programming, Volume 1, Fundamental Algorithms*, Reading, MA: Addison-Wesley Publishing Co., Inc.

1632

Chapter 42

The TTEST
Procedure

ABSTRACT 1633
INTRODUCTION 1633
SPECIFICATIONS 1634
   PROC TTEST Statement 1634
   BY Statement 1634
   CLASS Statement 1635
   VAR Statement 1635
DETAILS 1635
   Missing Values 1635
   Computational Method 1635
      The t Statistic 1635
      The Folded Form F Statistic 1636
      The Approximate t Statistic 1636
      The Cochran and Cox Approximation 1636
      Satterthwaite's Approximation 1636
   Printed Output 1636
EXAMPLES 1637
   Example 1: Comparing Group Means 1637
   Example 2: Paired Comparisons Using PROC MEANS 1638
REFERENCES 1639

ABSTRACT

The TTEST procedure performs a two sample t-test for testing the hypothesis that the means of two groups of independent and normally distributed observations are equal.

INTRODUCTION

PROC TTEST computes sample means for each of two groups of observations identified by levels of a CLASS variable and tests the hypothesis that the population means are the same. This analysis can be considered a special case of a one-way analysis of variance with two levels of classification.

PROC TTEST computes the t statistic based on the assumption that the variances of the two groups are equal, and it computes an approximate t based on the assumption that the variances are unequal (the Behrens-Fisher problem). The degrees of freedom and probability level are given for each; Satterthwaite's (1946) approximation is used to compute the degrees of freedom associated with the approximate t. In addition, you can request the Cochran and Cox (1950) approximation of the probability level for the approximate t. An F' (folded) statistic is computed to test for equality of the two variances (Steel and Torrie 1980).

The TTEST procedure is not designed for paired comparisons. See **Example 2** for a description of a method for a paired-comparisons t-test.

Note that the underlying assumption of the *t*-test is that the observations are random samples drawn from two independent and normally distributed populations. If the assumptions for the *t*-test are not satisfied, you should analyze your data using PROC NPAR1WAY.

SPECIFICATIONS

The following statements are available in PROC TTEST:

> **PROC TTEST** <*options*>; ⎫
> **CLASS** *variable*;   ⎬ required statements
>   ⎭

> **BY** *variables*; ⎫   optional statements
> **VAR** *variables*; ⎭

No statement may be used more than once. There is no restriction on the order of the statements after the PROC statement. The CLASS statement is required.

PROC TTEST Statement

> **PROC TTEST** <COCHRAN> <DATA=*SAS-data-set*>;

The following options can appear in the PROC TTEST statement:

COCHRAN
> requests the Cochran and Cox (1950) approximation of the probability level of the approximate *t* statistic for the unequal variances situation.

DATA=*SAS-data-set*
> names the SAS data set for the procedure to use. By default, PROC TTEST uses the most recently created SAS data set.

BY Statement

> **BY** *variables*;

A BY statement can be used with PROC TTEST to obtain separate analyses on observations in groups defined by the BY variables. When a BY statement appears, the procedure expects the input data set to be sorted in order of the BY variables.

If your input data set is not sorted in ascending order, use one of the following alternatives:

- Use the SORT procedure with a similar BY statement to sort the data.
- Use the BY statement options NOTSORTED or DESCENDING in the BY statement for the TTEST procedure. As a cautionary note, the NOTSORTED option does not mean that the data are unsorted, but rather means that the data are arranged in groups (according to values of the BY variables) and that these groups are not necessarily in alphabetical or increasing numeric order.
- Use the DATASETS procedure (in base SAS software) to create an index on the BY variables.

For more information on the BY statement, see the discussion in *SAS Language: Reference, Version 6, First Edition*. For more information on the DATASETS procedure, see the discussion in the *SAS Procedures Guide, Version 6, Third Edition*.

CLASS Statement

> **CLASS** *variable*;

A CLASS statement giving the name of the grouping variable must accompany the PROC TTEST statement. The grouping variable must have two, and only two, levels. PROC TTEST divides the observations into the two groups for the *t*-test using the levels of this variable.

You can use either a numeric or a character variable in the CLASS statement. If you use a character variable longer than 16 characters, the values are truncated and a warning message is issued.

Class levels are determined from the formatted values of the CLASS variable. Thus, you can use formats to define group levels. See the discussion of the FORMAT procedure, the FORMAT statement, and "SAS Informats and Formats" in *SAS Language: Reference, Version 6, First Edition*.

VAR Statement

> **VAR** *variables*;

The VAR statement names the variables whose means are to be compared. If the VAR statement is omitted, all numeric variables in the input data set (except a numeric variable appearing in the CLASS statement) are included in the analysis.

DETAILS

Missing Values

An observation is omitted from the calculations if it has a missing value for either the CLASS variable or for the variable to be tested.

If more than one variable is listed in the VAR statement, an observation is included in calculations for all variables for which the observation has nonmissing values. In other words, if an observation has a missing value for one of the variables, the observation is omitted only from the calculations for that variable. The observation is still included in calculations for other variables.

Computational Method

The *t* Statistic

The *t* statistic for testing the equality of means from two independent samples with n_1 and n_2 observations is

$$t = (\bar{x}_1 - \bar{x}_2) / \sqrt{s^2(1/n_1 + 1/n_2)}$$

where s^2 is the pooled variance

$$s^2 = [(n_1 - 1)s_1^2 + (n_2 - 1)s_2^2] / (n_1 + n_2 - 2)$$

and where s_1^2 and s_2^2 are the sample variances of the two groups. The use of this *t* statistic depends on the assumption that $\sigma_1^2 = \sigma_2^2$, where σ_1^2 and σ_2^2 are the population variances of the two groups.

The Folded Form F Statistic

The folded form of the F statistic, F', tests the hypothesis that the variances are equal, where

$$F' = (\text{larger of } s_1^2, s_2^2) \,/\, (\text{smaller of } s_1^2, s_2^2) \quad.$$

A test of F' is a two-tailed F test because you do not specify which variance you expect to be larger. The printout value of Prob > F gives the probability of a greater F value under the null hypothesis that $\sigma_1^2 = \sigma_2^2$.

The Approximate t Statistic

Under the assumption of unequal variances, the approximate t statistic is computed as

$$t' = (\bar{x}_1 - \bar{x}_2) \,/\, \sqrt{w_1 + w_2}$$

where

$$w_1 = s_1^2/n_1, \qquad w_2 = s_2^2/n_2 \quad.$$

The Cochran and Cox Approximation

The Cochran and Cox (1950) approximation of the probability level of the approximate t statistic is the value of p such that

$$t' = (w_1 t_1 + w_2 t_2) \,/\, (w_1 + w_2)$$

where t_1 and t_2 are the critical values of the t distribution corresponding to a significance level of p and sample sizes of n_1 and n_2, respectively. The number of degrees of freedom is between n_1-1 and n_2-1. In general, the Cochran and Cox test tends to be conservative (Lee and Gurland 1975).

Satterthwaite's Approximation

The formula for Satterthwaite's (1946) approximation for the degrees of freedom for the approximate t statistic is

$$df = \frac{(w_1 + w_2)^2}{w_1^2 \,/\, (n_1 - 1) + w_2^2 \,/\, (n_2 - 1)} \quad.$$

Refer to Steel and Torrie (1980) or Freund, Littell, and Spector (1986) for more information.

Printed Output

For each variable in the analysis, the TTEST procedure prints the following statistics for each group:

1. the name of the dependent variable
2. the levels of the classification variable
3. N, the number of nonmissing values
4. the Mean or average
5. Std Dev, the standard deviation
6. Std Error, the standard error of the mean

7. the Minimum value, if the line size allows
8. the Maximum value, if the line size allows.

Under the assumption of unequal variances, the TTEST procedure prints the following:

9. T, an approximate t statistic for testing the null hypothesis that the means of the two groups are equal.
10. DF, the approximate degrees of freedom. The approximate degrees of freedom for Satterthwaite's approximation are always shown. If $n_1 = n_2$, then the approximate degrees of freedom for the Cochran and Cox approximation are also shown.
11. Prob > |T|, the probability of a greater absolute value of t under the null hypothesis. This probability results from using Satterthwaite's approximation for the degrees of freedom. This is the two-tailed significance probability.
12. the Cochran and Cox approximation of Prob > |T| if the COCHRAN option is specified. This is the two-tailed significance probability.

Under the assumption of equal variances, the TTEST procedure prints the following:

13. T, the t statistic for testing the null hypothesis that the means of the two groups are equal.
14. DF, the degrees of freedom.
15. Prob > |T|, the probability of a greater absolute value of t under the null hypothesis. This is the two-tailed significance probability. For a one-tailed test halve this probability.

PROC TTEST then gives the results of the test of equality of variances:

16. the F' (folded) statistic (see **DETAILS** earlier in this chapter)
17. the degrees of freedom, DF, in each group
18. Prob > F', the probability of a greater F value. This is the two-tailed significance probability.

Note that the TTEST procedure prints all the items in the list above. You need to decide which are appropriate for your data.

EXAMPLES

Example 1:   Comparing Group Means

The data for this example consist of golf scores for a physical education class. You can use a t-test to determine if the mean golf score for the men in the class differs significantly from the mean score for the women. The output is shown in **Output 42.1**.

The grouping variable is GENDER, and it appears in the INPUT statement and the CLASS statement.

The circled numbers on the sample output correspond to the statistics described above.

```
options linesize=110;
data scores;
   input gender $ score @@;
   cards;
f 75  f 76  f 80  f 77  f 80  f 77  f 73
m 82  m 80  m 85  m 85  m 78  m 87  m 82
;

proc ttest cochran;
   class gender;
   var score;
   title 'GOLF SCORES';
run;
```

Output 42.1   Comparing Group Means with PROC TTEST

```
                                GOLF SCORES                                                     1

                               TTEST PROCEDURE

Variable: SCORE ❶

GENDER ❷  N ❸         Mean ❹        Std Dev ❺      Std Error ❻      Minimum ❼       Maximum ❽
--------------------------------------------------------------------------------------------------
f         7      76.85714286     2.54483604      0.96185761      73.00000000     80.00000000
m         7      82.71428571     3.14718317      1.18952343      78.00000000     87.00000000

Variances      T   Method          DF    Prob>|T|
--------------------------------------------------------------
Unequal ❾  -3.8288  Satterthwaite ❿ 11.5  0.0026 ⓫
                    Cochran          6.0   0.0087 ⓬
Equal ⓭   -3.8288                  12.0 ⓮ 0.0024 ⓯

For H0: Variances are equal, F' = 1.53 ⓰  DF = (6,6) ⓱   Prob>F' = 0.6189 ⓲
```

The results from the test of equality of variances show that the assumption of equal variances is reasonable for these data. If the assumption of normality is also reasonable, the appropriate test is the usual *t*-test, which shows that the average golf scores for men and women are significantly different. The *p*-value associated with this test is 0.0024. If the assumptions of normality or equality of variances are not reasonable, you should analyze the data with the nonparametric Wilcoxon Rank Sum test using PROC NPAR1WAY.

Example 2:   Paired Comparisons Using PROC MEANS

When there is a natural pairing of the data, you need to use an analysis that takes the correlation into account. For example, if you have both PRETEST and POSTTEST scores for each observation in the data set, then you may want to test whether the mean change from PRETEST to POSTTEST is significantly different from zero.

For paired comparisons such as these, use PROC MEANS rather than PROC TTEST. Create a new variable containing the differences between the paired variables, and use the T and PRT options of PROC MEANS to test whether the mean difference is significantly different from zero.

Following the INPUT statement in the DATA step is an assignment statement creating a new variable, DIFF, made by subtracting PRETEST from POSTTEST. PROC MEANS is used with the T and PRT options to get a *t* statistic and a probability value for the null hypothesis that DIFF's mean is equal to zero. This example produces **Output 42.2**.

```
options linesize=110;
data a;
   input id pretest posttest @@;
   diff=posttest-pretest;
   cards;
1   80  82    2  73   71    3  70  95
4   60  69    5  88  100    6  84  71
7   65  75    8  37   60    9  91  95
10  98  99   11  52   65   12  78  83
13  40  60   14  79   86   15  59  62
;
proc means n mean stderr t prt;
   var diff;
   title 'PAIRED-COMPARISONS T TEST';
run;
```

Output 42.2   Making Paired Comparisons with PROC MEANS

```
                   PAIRED-COMPARISONS T TEST                                1

Analysis Variable : DIFF


N       Mean      Std Error        T   Prob>|T|
-------------------------------------------------------
15   7.9333333    2.5643465   3.0937057   0.0079
-------------------------------------------------------
```

The results of the paired comparison show that the average DIFF is significantly different from zero. The associated *p*-value is 0.0079.

Note that this test of hypothesis assumes that the variable DIFF is normally distributed, an assumption which can be investigated using PROC UNIVARIATE with the NORMAL option. If the differences are skewed, you may want to analyze percent change (PCTCHG=(POSTTEST−PRETEST)/PRETEST) to standardize the changes relative to the PRETEST value.

REFERENCES

Best, D.I. and Rayner, C.W. (1987), "Welch's Approximate Solution for the Behren's-Fisher problem," *Technometrics* 29, 205–210.

Cochran, W.G. and Cox, G.M. (1950), *Experimental Designs*, New York: John Wiley & Sons, Inc.

Freund, R.J., Littell, R.C., and Spector, P.C. (1986), *SAS System for Linear Models, 1986 Edition*, Cary, NC: SAS Institute Inc.

Lee, A.F.S. and Gurland, J. (1975), "Size and Power of Tests for Equality of Means of Two Normal Populations with Unequal Variances," *Journal of the American Statistical Association*, 70, 933–941.

Posten, H.O., Yeh, Y.Y., and Owen, D.B. (1982), "Robustness of the two-sample t test under violations of the homogeneity of variance assumption," *Communications in Statistics*, 11, 109–126.

Ramsey, P.H. (1980), "Exact Type I error rates for robustness of Student's t test with unequal variances," *Journal of Educational Statistics*, 5, 337–349.

Robinson, G.K. (1976), "Properties of Student's t and of the Behrens- Fisher solution to the two mean problem," *Annals of Statistics*, 4, 963–971.

Satterthwaite, F.W. (1946), "An Approximate Distribution of Estimates of Variance Components," *Biometrics Bulletin*, 2, 110–114.

Scheffe, H. (1970), "Practical solutions of the Behrens-Fisher problem," *Journal of the American Statistical Association*, 65, 1501–1508.

Steel, R.G.D. and Torrie, J.H. (1980), *Principles and Procedures of Statistics*, 2d Edition, New York: McGraw-Hill Book Company.

Wang, Y.Y. (1971), "Probabilities of the Type I error of the Welch tests for the Behren's-Fisher problem," *Journal of the American Statistical Association* 66, 605–608.

Yuen, K.K. (1974), "The two-sample trimmed t for unequal population variances," *Biometrika*, 61, 165–170.

Chapter 43

The VARCLUS Procedure

ABSTRACT   1641
INTRODUCTION   1641
  Background   1642
SPECIFICATIONS   1643
  PROC VARCLUS Statement   1643
  BY Statement   1647
  FREQ Statement   1648
  PARTIAL Statement   1648
  SEED Statement   1648
  VAR Statement   1648
  WEIGHT Statement   1648
DETAILS   1649
  Missing Values   1649
  Using PROC VARCLUS   1649
    Execution Time   1649
  Output Data Sets   1649
    OUTSTAT= Data Set   1649
    OUTTREE= Data Set   1650
  Computational Resources   1651
    Time   1651
    Memory   1651
  Interpreting VARCLUS Procedure Output   1651
  Printed Output   1652
EXAMPLE   1653
  Correlations among Physical Variables   1653
REFERENCES   1659

ABSTRACT

The VARCLUS procedure performs either disjoint or hierarchical clustering of variables based on a correlation or covariance matrix. The clusters are chosen to maximize the variation accounted for by either the first principal component or the centroid component of each cluster, so VARCLUS can be used to reduce the number of variables. An output data set containing the results of the analysis can be created and used with the SCORE procedure to compute cluster component scores. A second output data set can be used by the TREE procedure to draw a tree diagram of hierarchical clusters.

INTRODUCTION

The VARCLUS procedure divides a set of numeric variables into either disjoint or hierarchical clusters. Associated with each cluster is a linear combination of the variables in the cluster, which may be either the first principal component or the centroid component.

The first principal component is a weighted average of the variables that explains as much variance as possible. See Chapter 33, "The PRINCOMP Procedure" for further details.

Use centroid components (the CENTROID option) if you want the cluster components to be (unweighted) averages of the standardized variables (the default) or the unstandardized variables (if you use the COV option).

PROC VARCLUS tries to maximize the sum across clusters of the variance of the original variables that is explained by the cluster components.

Either the correlation or the covariance matrix can be analyzed. If correlations are used, all variables are treated as equally important. If covariances are used, variables with larger variances have more importance in the analysis.

PROC VARCLUS creates an output data set that can be used with the SCORE procedure to compute component scores for each cluster. A second output data set can be used by the TREE procedure to draw a tree diagram of hierarchical clusters.

Background

The VARCLUS procedure attempts to divide a set of variables into non-overlapping clusters in such a way that each cluster can be interpreted as essentially unidimensional. For each cluster, VARCLUS computes a component that can be either the first principal component or the centroid component and tries to maximize the sum across clusters of the variation accounted for by the cluster components. VARCLUS is a type of oblique component analysis related to multiple group factor analysis (Harman 1976).

VARCLUS can be used as a variable-reduction method. A large set of variables can often be replaced by the set of cluster components with little loss of information. A given number of cluster components does not generally explain as much variance as the same number of principal components on the full set of variables, but the cluster components are usually easier to interpret than the principal components, even if the latter are rotated.

For example, an educational test might contain 50 items. VARCLUS could be used to divide the items into, say, five clusters. Each cluster could be treated as a subtest, and the subtest scores would be given by the cluster components. If the cluster components were centroid components of the covariance matrix, each subtest score would simply be the sum of the item scores for that cluster.

By default, VARCLUS begins with all variables in a single cluster. It then repeats the following steps:

1. A cluster is chosen for splitting. Depending on the options specified, the selected cluster has either the smallest percentage of variation explained by its cluster component (use the PERCENT= option) or the largest eigenvalue associated with the second principal component (use the MAXEIGEN= option).

2. The chosen cluster is split into two clusters by finding the first two principal components, performing an orthoblique rotation (raw quartimax rotation on the eigenvectors), and assigning each variable to the rotated component with which it has the higher squared correlation.

3. Variables are iteratively reassigned to clusters to maximize the variance accounted for by the cluster components. The reassignment may be required to maintain a hierarchical structure.

The procedure stops when each cluster satisfies a user-specified criterion involving either the percentage of variation accounted for or the second eigenvalue of each cluster. By default, VARCLUS stops when each cluster has only a single eigenvalue greater than one, thus satisfying the most popular criterion for determining the sufficiency of a single underlying factor dimension.

The iterative reassignment of variables to clusters proceeds in two phases. The first is a nearest component sorting (NCS) phase, similar in principle to the nearest centroid sorting algorithms described by Anderberg (1973). In each iteration the cluster components are computed, and each variable is assigned to the component with which it has the highest squared correlation. The second phase involves a search algorithm in which each variable in turn is tested to see if assigning it to a different cluster increases the amount of variance explained. If a variable is reassigned during the search phase, the components of the two clusters involved are recomputed before the next variable is tested. The NCS phase is much faster than the search phase but is more likely to be trapped by a local optimum.

You can have the iterative reassignment phases restrict the reassignment of variables such that hierarchical clusters are produced. In this case, when a cluster is split, a variable in one of the two resulting clusters can be reassigned to the other cluster resulting from the split, but not to a cluster that was not part of the original cluster (the one that was split).

If principal components are used, the NCS phase is an alternating least-squares method and converges rapidly. The search phase is very time consuming for a large number of variables and is omitted by default. If the default initialization method is used, the search phase is rarely able to improve the results of the NCS phase. If random initialization is used, the NCS phase may be trapped by a local optimum from which the search phase can escape.

If centroid components are used, the NCS phase is not an alternating least-squares method and may not increase the amount of variance explained; therefore, it is limited, by default, to one iteration.

SPECIFICATIONS

PROC VARCLUS<*options*>;   required statement

VAR *variable*;
SEED *variables*;
PARTIAL *variables*;
WEIGHT *variable*;   optional statements
FREQ *variable*;
BY *variable*;

Usually you need only the VAR statement in addition to the PROC VARCLUS statement. The following section gives detailed syntax information for each of the statements above, beginning with the PROC VARCLUS statement. The remaining statements are listed in alphabetical order.

PROC VARCLUS Statement

PROC VARCLUS <*options*>;

The PROC VARCLUS statement starts the VARCLUS procedure and optionally identifies a data set or requests particular cluster analyses. By default, the procedure uses the most recently created SAS data set, and omits observations with missing values from the analysis. The table below summarizes the options available on the PROC VARCLUS statement.

Task	Options
Specify data sets	DATA= OUTSTAT= OUTTREE=
Determine the number of clusters	MAXCLUSTERS= MINCLUSTERS= MAXEIGEN= PROPORTION=
Specify cluster formation	CENTROID COVARIANCE HIERARCHY INTITIAL= MAXITER= MAXSEARCH= MULTIPLEGROUP RANDOM=
Control output	CORR NOPRINT SHORT SIMPLE SUMMARY TRACE
Omit intercept	NOINT
Specify divisor for variances	VARDEF=

The following list gives details on these options. The list is in alphabetical order.

CENTROID
uses centroid components rather than principal components. You should use centroid components if you want the cluster components to be unweighted averages of the standardized variables (the default) or the unstandardized variables (if you specify the COV option). It is possible to obtain locally optimal clusterings in which a variable is not assigned to the cluster component with which it has the highest squared correlation. You cannot use the CENTROID option with the MAXEIGEN= option.

CORR
C
prints the correlation matrix.

COVARIANCE
COV
analyzes the covariance matrix rather than the correlation matrix.

DATA=SAS-data-set
names the input data set to be analyzed. The data set can be an ordinary SAS data set or TYPE=CORR, UCORR, COV, UCOV, FACTOR,

or SSCP. If you do not specify the DATA= option, the most recently created SAS data set is used. Refer to Appendix 1, "Special SAS Data Sets" for more information on types of SAS data sets.

HIERARCHY
HI

requires the clusters at different levels to maintain a hierarchical structure.

INITIAL=GROUP
     | INPUT
     | RANDOM
     | SEED

specifies the method for initializing the clusters. If the INITIAL= option is omitted and MINCLUSTERS= is greater than 1, the initial cluster components are obtained by extracting the required number of principal components and performing an orthoblique rotation. The values for the INITIAL= option are explained below.

GROUP	can be used if the input data set is a TYPE=CORR, UCORR, COV, UCOV, or FACTOR data set. The cluster membership of each variable is obtained from an observation with _TYPE_='GROUP', which contains an integer for each variable ranging from one to the number of clusters. You can use a data set created either by a previous run of VARCLUS or in a DATA step.
INPUT	can be used if the input data set is a TYPE=CORR, UCORR, COV, UCOV, or FACTOR data set, in which case scoring coefficients are read from observations where _TYPE_='SCORE'. Scoring coefficients from the FACTOR procedure or a previous run of VARCLUS can be used, or you can enter other coefficients in a DATA step.
RANDOM	assigns variables randomly to clusters. If you specify INITIAL=RANDOM without the CENTROID option, it is recommended that you specify MAXSEARCH=5, although the CPU time required is substantially increased.
SEED	initializes clusters according to the variables named in the SEED statement. Each variable listed in the SEED statement becomes the sole member of a cluster, and the other variables remain unassigned. If you do not specify the SEED statement, the first MINCLUSTERS= variables in the VAR statement are used as seeds.

MAXCLUSTERS=n
MAXC=n

specifies the largest number of clusters desired. The default value is the number of variables.

MAXEIGEN=n

specifies the largest permissible value of the second eigenvalue in each cluster. If you do not specify either the PROPORTION= or the MAXCLUSTERS= options, the default value is the average of the diagonal elements of the matrix being analyzed. This value is either the average variance if a covariance matrix is analyzed, or 1 if the correlation matrix is analyzed (unless some of the variables are constant, in which case the value will be the number of non-constant variables divided by the number of variables). Otherwise, the default is 0. The MAXEIGEN= option cannot be used with the CENTROID option.

MAXSEARCH=*n*

specifies the maximum number of iterations during the search phase. The default is 10 if you specify CENTROID; the default is 0 otherwise.

MINCLUSTERS=*n*

MINC=*n*

specifies the smallest number of clusters desired. The default value is 2 if INITIAL=RANDOM or INITIAL=SEED; otherwise, the procedure begins with one cluster and tries to split it in accordance with the PROPORTION= or MAXEIGEN= options.

MULTIPLEGROUP

MG

performs a multiple group component analysis (see Harman 1976). The input data set must be TYPE=CORR, UCORR, COV, UCOV, FACTOR, or SSCP and must contain an observation with _TYPE_='GROUP' defining the variable groups. Specifying MULTIPLEGROUP is equivalent to specifying all of the following options: MINC=1, MAXITER=0, MAXSEARCH=0, MAXEIGEN=0, PROPORTION=0, and INITIAL=GROUP.

NOINT

requests that no intercept be used; covariances or correlations are not corrected for the mean. If you use the NOINT option, the OUTSTAT= data set will be TYPE=UCORR.

NOPRINT

suppresses the printout.

OUTSTAT=*SAS-data-set*

creates an output data set to contain statistics including means, standard deviations, correlations, cluster scoring coefficients, and the cluster structure. If you want to create a permanent SAS data set, you must specify a two-level name. The OUTSTAT= data set will be TYPE=UCORR if the NOINT option is specified. See "SAS Files" in *SAS Language: Reference, Version 6, First Edition* and "Introduction to DATA Step Processing" in *SAS Language and Procedures: Usage, Version 6, First Edition*, for more information on permanent SAS data sets. See Appendix 1, "Special SAS Data Sets," for information on types of SAS data sets.

OUTTREE=*SAS-data-set*

creates an output data set to contain information on the tree structure that can be used by the TREE procedure to print a tree diagram. OUTTREE= implies the HIERARCHY option. See **EXAMPLE** for use of the OUTTREE= option. If you want to create a permanent SAS data set, you must specify a two-level name. See "SAS Files" in *SAS Language: Reference, Version 6, First Edition* and "Introduction to DATA Step Processing" in *SAS Language and Procedures: Usage, Version 6, First Edition*, for more information on permanent SAS data sets.

PROPORTION=*n*

PERCENT=*n*

gives the proportion or percentage of variation that must be explained by the cluster component. Values greater than 1.0 are considered to be percentages, so PROPORTION=0.75 and PERCENT=75 are equivalent.

If you specify the CENTROID option, the default value is 0.75; otherwise, the default value is 0.

MAXITER=*n*

specifies the maximum number of iterations during the alternating least-squares phase. The default value is 1 if you specify CENTROID; the default is 10 otherwise.

RANDOM=*n*

specifies a positive integer as a starting value for use with REPLACE=RANDOM. If you do not specify the RANDOM= option, the time of day is used to initialize the pseudo-random number sequence.

SHORT

suppresses printing of the cluster structure, scoring coefficient, and intercluster correlation matrices.

SIMPLE
S

prints means and standard deviations.

SUMMARY

suppresses all default printout except the final summary table.

TRACE

lists the cluster to which each variable is assigned during the iterations.

VARDEF=DF
      | N
      | WDF
      | WEIGHT | WGT

specifies the divisor to be used in the calculation of variances and covariances. The default value is VARDEF=DF. The values and associated divisors are shown below:

Value	Divisor	Formula
DF	degrees of freedom	$n-i$
N	number of observations	n
WDF	sum of weights minus one	$(\Sigma_j w_j) - i$
WEIGHT | WGT	sum of weights	$\Sigma_j w_j$

where $i=0$ if the NOINT option is specified, and is $i=1$ otherwise.

BY Statement

BY *variables*;

A BY statement can be used with PROC VARCLUS to obtain separate analyses on observations in groups defined by the BY variables. When a BY statement appears, the procedure expects the input data set to be sorted in order of the BY variables.

If your input data set is not sorted in ascending order, use one of the following alternatives:

- Use the SORT procedure with a similar BY statement to sort the data.
- Use the BY statement options NOTSORTED or DESCENDING in the BY statement for the VARCLUS procedure. The NOTSORTED option does

not mean that the data are unsorted, but rather that the data are arranged in groups (according to values of the BY variables) and that these groups are not necessarily in alphabetical or increasing numeric order.
- Use the DATASETS procedure (in base SAS software) to create an index on the BY variables.

For more information on the BY statement, see the discussion in *SAS Language: Reference*. For more information on the DATASETS procedure, see the discussion in *SAS Procedures Guide, Version 6, Third Edition*.

FREQ Statement

FREQ *variable*;

If a variable in your data set represents the frequency of occurrence for the other values in the observation, include the variable's name in a FREQ statement. The procedure then treats the data set as if each observation appears *n* times, where *n* is the value of the FREQ variable for the observation. If the value of the FREQ variable is less than 1, the observation is not used in the analysis. Only the integer portion of the value is used. The total number of observations is considered equal to the sum of the FREQ variable.

PARTIAL Statement

PARTIAL *variables*;

If you want to base the clustering on partial correlations, list the variables to be partialled out in the PARTIAL statement.

SEED Statement

SEED *variables*;

The SEED statement specifies variables to be used as seeds to initialize the clusters. It is not necessary to use INITIAL=SEED if the SEED statement is present, but if any other INITIAL= option is specified, the SEED statement is ignored.

VAR Statement

VAR *variables*;

The VAR statement specifies the variables to be clustered. If you do not specify the VAR statement, and do not specify TYPE=SSCP, all numeric variables not listed in other statements (except the SEED statement) are processed. The default VAR variable list does not include INTERCEP if the DATA= data set is TYPE=SSCP. If the INTERCEP option is explicitly specified in the VAR statement with a TYPE=SSCP data set, the NOINT option is turned on.

WEIGHT Statement

WEIGHT *variable*;

If you want to use relative weights for each observation in the input data set, place the weights in a variable in the data set and specify the name in a WEIGHT statement. This is often done when the variance associated with each observation is different and the values of the weight variable are proportional to the reciprocals of the variances. The WEIGHT variable can take nonintegral values. An observation is used in the analysis only if the value of the WEIGHT variable is greater than zero.

DETAILS

Missing Values

Observations containing missing values are omitted from the analysis.

Using PROC VARCLUS

Default options for PROC VARCLUS often provide satisfactory results. If you want to change the final number of clusters, use the MAXCLUSTERS=, MAXEIGEN=, or PROPORTION= options. The MAXEIGEN= and PROPORTION= options usually produce similar results but occasionally cause different clusters to be selected for splitting. The MAXEIGEN= option tends to choose clusters with a large number of variables, while the PROPORTION= option is more likely to select a cluster with a small number of variables.

Execution Time

VARCLUS usually requires more computer time than principal factor analysis but can be faster than some of the iterative factoring methods. If you have more than 30 variables, you may want to reduce execution time by one or more of the following methods:

- Use the MINCLUSTERS= and MAXCLUSTERS= options if you know how many clusters you want.
- Use the HIERARCHY option.
- Use the SEED statement if you have some prior knowledge of what clusters to expect.

If computer time is not a limiting factor, you may want to try one of the following methods to obtain a better solution:

- Use the MAXSEARCH= option with principal components and specify a value of 5 or 10.
- Try several factoring and rotation methods with FACTOR to use as input to VARCLUS.
- Run VARCLUS several times specifying INITIAL=RANDOM.

Output Data Sets

OUTSTAT= Data Set

The OUTSTAT= data set is TYPE=CORR and can be used as input to the SCORE procedure or a subsequent run of VARCLUS. The variables it contains are

- BY variables
- _NCL_, a numeric variable giving the number of clusters
- _TYPE_, a character variable indicating the type of statistic the observation contains
- _NAME_, a character variable containing a variable name or a cluster name, which is of the form CLUSn where n is the number of the cluster
- the variables that were clustered.

The values of _TYPE_ are listed here:

TYPE	Contents
MEAN	means
STD	standard deviations
USTD	uncorrected standard deviations, produced when NOINT is specified
N	number of observations
CORR	correlations
UCORR	uncorrected correlation matrix, produced when NOINT is specified
MEMBERS	number of members in each cluster
VAREXP	variance explained by each cluster
PROPOR	proportion of variance explained by each cluster
GROUP	number of the cluster to which each variable belongs
RSQUARED	squared multiple correlation of each variable with its cluster component
SCORE	standardized scoring coefficients
USCORE	scoring coefficients to be applied without subtracting the mean from the raw variables, produced when NOINT is specified
STRUCTUR	cluster structure
CCORR	correlations between cluster components.

The observations with _TYPE_='MEAN', 'STD', 'N', and 'CORR' have missing values for _NCL_. All other values of _TYPE_ are repeated for each cluster solution, with different solutions distinguished by the value of _NCL_. If you want to use the OUTSTAT= data set with the SCORE procedure, you can use a DATA step to select observations with _NCL_ missing or equal to the desired number of clusters or use a where clause, for example:

```
proc score score=s (where=(_ncl_ =3)) data=newscore;
```

OUTTREE= Data Set

The OUTTREE= data set contains one observation for each variable clustered plus one observation for each cluster of two or more variables, that is, one observation for each node of the cluster tree. The total number of output observations is between n and $2n-1$, where n is the number of variables clustered.

The variables in the OUTTREE= data set are

- the BY variables, if any.
- _NAME_, a character variable giving the name of the node. If the node is a cluster, the name is CLUSn where n is the number of the cluster. If the node is a single variable, the variable name is used.
- _PARENT_, a character variable giving the value of _NAME_ of the parent of the node.
- _NCL_, the number of clusters.
- _VAREXP_, the total variance explained by the clusters at the current level of the tree.

- _PROPOR_, the total proportion of variance explained by the clusters at the current level of the tree.
- _MINPRO_, the minimum proportion of variance explained by a cluster component.
- _MAXEIG_, the maximum second eigenvalue of a cluster.

Computational Resources

Let

n = number of observations
v = number of variables
c = number of clusters.

It is assumed that at each stage of clustering, the clusters all contain the same number of variables.

Time

The time required for VARCLUS to analyze a given data set varies greatly depending on the number of clusters requested, the number of iterations in both the alternating least-squares and search phases, and whether centroid or principal components are used.

The time required to compute the correlation matrix is roughly proportional to nv^2.

Default cluster initialization requires time roughly proportional to v^3. Any other method of initialization requires time roughly proportional to cv^2.

In the alternating least-squares phase, each iteration requires time roughly proportional to cv^2 if centroid components are used, or

$$(c + 5v/c^2)v^2$$

if principal components are used.

In the search phase, each iteration requires time roughly proportional to v^3/c if centroid components are used, or v^4/c^2 if principal components are used. The HIERARCHY option speeds up each iteration after the first split by as much as $c/2$.

Memory

The amount of memory, in bytes, needed by PROC VARCLUS is approximately

$$v^2 + 2vc + 20v + 15c .$$

Interpreting VARCLUS Procedure Output

Because PROC VARCLUS is a type of oblique component analysis, its output is similar to the output from PROC FACTOR for oblique rotations. The scoring coefficients have the same meaning in both VARCLUS and FACTOR; they are coefficients applied to the standardized variables to compute component scores. The cluster structure is analogous to the factor structure containing the correlations between each variable and each cluster component. A cluster pattern is not printed because it would be the same as the cluster structure, except that zeros would appear in the same places that zeros appear in the scoring coefficients. The intercluster correlations are analogous to interfactor correlations; they are the correlations among cluster components.

VARCLUS also prints a cluster summary and a cluster listing. The cluster summary gives the number of variables in each cluster and the variation explained by the cluster component. The latter is similar to the variation explained by a factor but includes contributions from only the variables in that cluster rather than from all variables, as in FACTOR. The proportion of variance explained is obtained by dividing the variance explained by the total variance of variables in the cluster. If the cluster contains two or more variables and the CENTROID option is not used, the second largest eigenvalue of the cluster is also printed.

The cluster listing gives the variables in each cluster. Two squared correlations are printed for each cluster. The column labeled "Own Cluster" gives the squared correlation of the variable with its own cluster component. This value should be higher than the squared correlation with any other cluster unless an iteration limit has been exceeded or the CENTROID option has been used. The larger the squared correlation is, the better. The column labeled "Next Closest" contains the next highest squared correlation of the variable with a cluster component. This value is low if the clusters are well separated. The column headed "$1-R**2$ Ratio" gives the ratio of one minus the "Own Cluster" R^2 to one minus the "Next Closest" R^2. A small "$1-R**2$ Ratio" indicates a good clustering.

Printed Output

The items described below are printed for each cluster solution unless NOPRINT or SUMMARY is specified. The CLUSTER SUMMARY table includes

1. the Cluster number.
2. Members, the number of members in the cluster.
3. Cluster Variation of the variables in the cluster.
4. Variation Explained by the cluster component. This statistic is based only on the variables in the cluster rather than all variables.
5. Proportion Explained, the result of dividing the variation explained by the cluster variation.
6. Second Eigenvalue, the second largest eigenvalue of the cluster. This is printed if the cluster contains more than one variable and the CENTROID option is not specified.

VARCLUS also prints

7. Total variation explained, the sum across clusters of the variation explained by each cluster
8. Proportion, the total explained variation divided by the total variation of all the variables.

The cluster listing includes

9. Variable, the variables in each cluster.
10. R-squared with Own Cluster, the squared correlation of the variable with its own cluster component; and R-squared with Next Closest, the next highest squared correlation of the variable with a cluster component. Own Cluster values should be higher than the R^2 with any other cluster unless an iteration limit has been exceeded or you specified the CENTROID option. Next Closest should be a low value if the clusters are well separated.
11. $1-R**2$ Ratio, the ratio of one minus the value in the Own Cluster column to one minus the value in the Next Closest column. The occurrence of low ratios indicates well-separated clusters.

If the SHORT option is not specified, VARCLUS also prints

12. Standardized Scoring Coefficients, standardized regression coefficients for predicting cluster components from variables

13. Cluster Structure, the correlations between each variable and each cluster component
14. Inter-Cluster Correlations, the correlations between the cluster components.

If the analysis includes partitions for two or more numbers of clusters, a final summary table is printed. Each row of the table corresponds to one partition. The columns include

15. Number of Clusters
16. Total Variation Explained by Clusters
17. Proportion of Variation Explained by Clusters
18. Minimum Proportion (of variation) Explained by a Cluster
19. Maximum Second Eigenvalue in a Cluster
20. Minimum R-squared for a Variable
21. Maximum $1-R**2$ Ratio for a Variable.

EXAMPLE

Correlations among Physical Variables

The data are correlations among eight physical variables as given by Harman (1976). The first VARCLUS run uses principal cluster components, the second uses centroid cluster components. The third analysis is hierarchical, and the TREE procedure is used to print a tree diagram. The following statements produce **Output 43.1** through **Output 43.4**:

```
data phys8(type=corr);
    title 'Eight Physical Variables Measured on 305 School Girls';
    title2 'See Page 22 of Harman: Modern Factor Analysis, 3rd Ed';
    label height='Height'
          arm_span='Arm Span'
          forearm='Length of Forearm'
          low_leg='Length of Lower Leg'
          weight='Weight'
          bit_diam='Bitrochanteric Diameter'
          girth='Chest Girth'
          width='Chest Width';
    input _name_ $ 1-8
          (height arm_span forearm low_leg weight bit_diam girth width)
          (8.);
    _type_='corr';
    cards;
height  1.0     .846    .805    .859    .473    .398    .301    .382
arm_span.846    1.0     .881    .826    .376    .326    .277    .415
forearm .805    .881    1.0     .801    .380    .319    .237    .345
low_leg .859    .826    .801    1.0     .436    .329    .327    .365
weight  .473    .376    .380    .436    1.0     .762    .730    .629
bit_diam.398    .326    .319    .329    .762    1.0     .583    .577
girth   .301    .277    .237    .327    .730    .583    1.0     .539
width   .382    .415    .345    .365    .629    .577    .539    1.0
;

proc varclus data=phys8;
run;
```

```
proc varclus data=phys8 centroid;
run;

proc varclus data=phys8 maxc=8 summary outtree=tree;
run;

proc tree;
   height _propor_;
run;
```

Output 43.1   Principal Cluster Components: PROC VARCLUS

Eight Physical Variables Measured on 305 School Girls
See Page 22 of Harman: Modern Factor Analysis, 3rd Ed   1

Oblique Principal Component Cluster Analysis

10000 Observations   PROPORTION =   0
8 Variables   MAXEIGEN   =   1

Cluster summary for 1 cluster(s)

❶ Cluster	❷ Members	❸ Cluster Variation	❹ Variation Explained	❺ Proportion Explained	❻ Second Eigenvalue
1	8	8.00000	4.67288	0.5841	1.7710

❼ Total variation explained = 4.67288 Proportion = 0.5841 ❽

Cluster 1 will be split.

Eight Physical Variables Measured on 305 School Girls
See Page 22 of Harman: Modern Factor Analysis, 3rd Ed   2

Oblique Principal Component Cluster Analysis

Cluster summary for 2 cluster(s)

Cluster	Members	Cluster Variation	Variation Explained	Proportion Explained	Second Eigenvalue
1	4	4.00000	3.50922	0.8773	0.2361
2	4	4.00000	2.91728	0.7293	0.4764

Total variation explained = 6.426502 Proportion = 0.8033

	❿ R-squared with		⓫	
❾ Variable	Own Cluster	Next Closest	1-R**2 Ratio	
Cluster 1				
HEIGHT	0.8777	0.2088	0.1545	Height
ARM_SPAN	0.9002	0.1658	0.1196	Arm Span
FOREARM	0.8661	0.1413	0.1560	Length of Forearm
LOW_LEG	0.8652	0.1829	0.1650	Length of Lower Leg
Cluster 2				
WEIGHT	0.8477	0.1974	0.1898	Weight
BIT_DIAM	0.7386	0.1341	0.3019	Bitrochanteric Diameter
GIRTH	0.6981	0.0929	0.3328	Chest Girth
WIDTH	0.6329	0.1619	0.4380	Chest Width

(continued on next page)

(continued from previous page)

⓬ Standardized Scoring Coefficients

Cluster	1	2	
HEIGHT	0.266977	0.000000	Height
ARM_SPAN	0.270377	0.000000	Arm Span
FOREARM	0.265194	0.000000	Length of Forearm
LOW_LEG	0.265057	0.000000	Length of Lower Leg
WEIGHT	0.000000	0.315597	Weight
BIT_DIAM	0.000000	0.294591	Bitrochanteric Diameter
GIRTH	0.000000	0.286407	Chest Girth
WIDTH	0.000000	0.272710	Chest Width

⓭ Cluster Structure

Cluster	1	2	
HEIGHT	0.936881	0.456908	Height
ARM_SPAN	0.948813	0.407210	Arm Span
FOREARM	0.930624	0.375865	Length of Forearm
LOW_LEG	0.930142	0.427715	Length of Lower Leg
WEIGHT	0.444281	0.920686	Weight
BIT_DIAM	0.366201	0.859404	Bitrochanteric Diameter
GIRTH	0.304779	0.835529	Chest Girth
WIDTH	0.402430	0.795572	Chest Width

Eight Physical Variables Measured on 305 School Girls
See Page 22 of Harman: Modern Factor Analysis, 3rd Ed

Oblique Principal Component Cluster Analysis

⓮ Inter-Cluster Correlations

Cluster	1	2
1	1.00000	0.44513
2	0.44513	1.00000

No cluster meets the criterion for splitting.

Eight Physical Variables Measured on 305 School Girls
See Page 22 of Harman: Modern Factor Analysis, 3rd Ed

Oblique Principal Component Cluster Analysis

⓯ Number of Clusters	⓰ Total Variation Explained by Clusters	⓱ Proportion of Variation Explained by Clusters	⓲ Minimum Proportion Explained by a Cluster	⓳ Maximum Second Eigenvalue in a Cluster	⓴ Minimum R-squared for a Variable	㉑ Maximum 1-R**2 Ratio for a Variable
1	4.672880	0.5841	0.5841	1.770983	0.3810	.
2	6.426502	0.8033	0.7293	0.476418	0.6329	0.4380

Output 43.2   Centroid Cluster Components: PROC VARCLUS

```
              Eight Physical Variables Measured on 305 School Girls              5
               See Page 22 of Harman: Modern Factor Analysis, 3rd Ed

                    Oblique Centroid Component Cluster Analysis

             10000 Observations      PROPORTION  =      0.75
                8 Variables          MAXEIGEN    =         0


                        Cluster summary for 1 cluster(s)

                                   Cluster      Variation    Proportion
             Cluster    Members    Variation    Explained    Explained
             ------------------------------------------------------------
                1          8        8.00000      4.63100       0.5789

             Total variation explained =     4.631 Proportion = 0.5789
```
Cluster 1 will be split.

```
              Eight Physical Variables Measured on 305 School Girls              6
               See Page 22 of Harman: Modern Factor Analysis, 3rd Ed

                    Oblique Centroid Component Cluster Analysis

                        Cluster summary for 2 cluster(s)

                                   Cluster      Variation    Proportion
             Cluster    Members    Variation    Explained    Explained
             ------------------------------------------------------------
                1          4        4.00000      3.50900       0.8772
                2          4        4.00000      2.91000       0.7275

             Total variation explained =     6.419 Proportion = 0.8024


                               R-squared with
                         ------------------------
                          Own       Next     1-R**2
               Variable   Cluster   Closest  Ratio
  Cluster   1---------------------------------------
               HEIGHT     0.8778    0.2075   0.1543   Height
               ARM_SPAN   0.8994    0.1669   0.1208   Arm Span
               FOREARM    0.8663    0.1410   0.1557   Length of Forearm
               LOW_LEG    0.8658    0.1824   0.1641   Length of Lower Leg
  Cluster   2---------------------------------------
               WEIGHT     0.8368    0.1975   0.2033   Weight
               BIT_DIAM   0.7335    0.1341   0.3078   Bitrochanteric Diameter
               GIRTH      0.6988    0.0929   0.3321   Chest Girth
               WIDTH      0.6473    0.1618   0.4207   Chest Width


                         Standardized Scoring Coefficients

               Cluster          1           2
               ------------------------------------
               HEIGHT      0.266918    0.000000   Height
               ARM_SPAN    0.266918    0.000000   Arm Span
               FOREARM     0.266918    0.000000   Length of Forearm
               LOW_LEG     0.266918    0.000000   Length of Lower Leg
               WEIGHT      0.000000    0.293105   Weight
               BIT_DIAM    0.000000    0.293105   Bitrochanteric Diameter
               GIRTH       0.000000    0.293105   Chest Girth
               WIDTH       0.000000    0.293105   Chest Width


                               Cluster Structure

               Cluster          1           2
               ------------------------------------
               HEIGHT      0.936883    0.455485   Height
               ARM_SPAN    0.948361    0.408589   Arm Span
               FOREARM     0.930744    0.375468   Length of Forearm
               LOW_LEG     0.930477    0.427054   Length of Lower Leg
               WEIGHT      0.444419    0.914781   Weight
               BIT_DIAM    0.366212    0.856453   Bitrochanteric Diameter
               GIRTH       0.304821    0.835936   Chest Girth
               WIDTH       0.402246    0.804574   Chest Width
```

```
                Eight Physical Variables Measured on 305 School Girls          7
                See Page 22 of Harman: Modern Factor Analysis, 3rd Ed

                     Oblique Centroid Component Cluster Analysis

                              Inter-Cluster Correlations

                     Cluster              1              2

                        1            1.00000        0.44484
                        2            0.44484        1.00000
```

Cluster 2 will be split.

```
                Eight Physical Variables Measured on 305 School Girls          8
                See Page 22 of Harman: Modern Factor Analysis, 3rd Ed

                     Oblique Centroid Component Cluster Analysis

                           Cluster summary for 3 cluster(s)

                                     Cluster    Variation    Proportion
             Cluster    Members     Variation   Explained    Explained
             ------------------------------------------------------------
                1          4         4.00000      3.50900      0.8772
                2          3         3.00000      2.38333      0.7944
                3          1         1.00000      1.00000      1.0000

            Total variation explained = 6.892333 Proportion = 0.8615
```

```
                             R-squared with
                           ------------------
                           Own       Next      1-R**2
             Variable     Cluster    Closest    Ratio
Cluster  1-----------------------------------------------
             HEIGHT       0.8778    0.1921    0.1513    Height
             ARM_SPAN     0.8994    0.1722    0.1215    Arm Span
             FOREARM      0.8663    0.1225    0.1524    Length of Forearm
             LOW_LEG      0.8658    0.1668    0.1611    Length of Lower Leg
Cluster  2-----------------------------------------------
             WEIGHT       0.8685    0.3956    0.2175    Weight
             BIT_DIAM     0.7691    0.3329    0.3461    Bitrochanteric Diameter
             GIRTH        0.7482    0.2905    0.3548    Chest Girth
Cluster  3-----------------------------------------------
             WIDTH        1.0000    0.4259    0.0000    Chest Width
```

```
                        Standardized Scoring Coefficients

             Cluster          1          2          3
             ------------------------------------------------
             HEIGHT       0.26692    0.00000    0.00000    Height
             ARM_SPAN     0.26692    0.00000    0.00000    Arm Span
             FOREARM      0.26692    0.00000    0.00000    Length of Forearm
             LOW_LEG      0.26692    0.00000    0.00000    Length of Lower Leg
             WEIGHT       0.00000    0.37398    0.00000    Weight
             BIT_DIAM     0.00000    0.37398    0.00000    Bitrochanteric Diameter
             GIRTH        0.00000    0.37398    0.00000    Chest Girth
             WIDTH        0.00000    0.00000    1.00000    Chest Width
```

```
                    Eight Physical Variables Measured on 305 School Girls                    9
                    See Page 22 of Harman: Modern Factor Analysis, 3rd Ed

                           Oblique Centroid Component Cluster Analysis

                                     Cluster Structure

         Cluster            1            2            3
         --------------------------------------------------------
         HEIGHT         0.93688      0.43830      0.38200     Height
         ARM_SPAN       0.94836      0.36613      0.41500     Arm Span
         FOREARM        0.93074      0.35004      0.34500     Length of Forearm
         LOW_LEG        0.93048      0.40838      0.36500     Length of Lower Leg
         WEIGHT         0.44442      0.93196      0.62900     Weight
         BIT_DIAM       0.36621      0.87698      0.57700     Bitrochanteric Diameter
         GIRTH          0.30482      0.86501      0.53900     Chest Girth
         WIDTH          0.40225      0.65259      1.00000     Chest Width


                               Inter-Cluster Correlations

         Cluster            1            2            3

            1           1.00000      0.41716      0.40225
            2           0.41716      1.00000      0.65259
            3           0.40225      0.65259      1.00000

No cluster meets the criterion for splitting.
```

```
                    Eight Physical Variables Measured on 305 School Girls                   10
                    See Page 22 of Harman: Modern Factor Analysis, 3rd Ed

                           Oblique Centroid Component Cluster Analysis

                       Total        Proportion      Minimum      Minimum       Maximum
         Number      Variation     of Variation   Proportion    R-squared    1-R**2 Ratio
           of        Explained      Explained      Explained      for a         for a
         Clusters   by Clusters    by Clusters    by a Cluster   Variable      Variable
         ------------------------------------------------------------------------------------
            1         4.631000        0.5789         0.5789        0.4306          .
            2         6.419000        0.8024         0.7275        0.6473        0.4207
            3         6.892333        0.8615         0.7944        0.7482        0.3548
```

Output 43.3 Hierarchical Clusters: PROC VARCLUS Specifying the
SUMMARY Option

```
                    Eight Physical Variables Measured on 305 School Girls                   11
                    See Page 22 of Harman: Modern Factor Analysis, 3rd Ed

                           Oblique Principal Component Cluster Analysis

                       10000 Observations      PROPORTION   =          1
                           8 Variables         MAXEIGEN     =          0


                    Total      Proportion     Minimum      Maximum     Minimum     Maximum
         Number    Variation  of Variation  Proportion     Second     R-squared  1-R**2 Ratio
           of      Explained   Explained     Explained   Eigenvalue     for a       for a
         Clusters by Clusters by Clusters  by a Cluster  in a Cluster  Variable    Variable
         --------------------------------------------------------------------------------------
            1      4.672880     0.5841       0.5841       1.770983      0.3810         .
            2      6.426502     0.8033       0.7293       0.476418      0.6329       0.4380
            3      6.895347     0.8619       0.7954       0.418369      0.7421       0.3634
            4      7.271218     0.9089       0.8773       0.238000      0.8652       0.2548
            5      7.509218     0.9387       0.8773       0.236135      0.8652       0.1665
            6      7.740000     0.9675       0.9295       0.141000      0.9295       0.2560
            7      7.881000     0.9851       0.9405       0.119000      0.9405       0.2093
            8      8.000000     1.0000       1.0000       0.000000      1.0000       0.0000
```

Output 43.4   TREE Diagram: PROC TREE

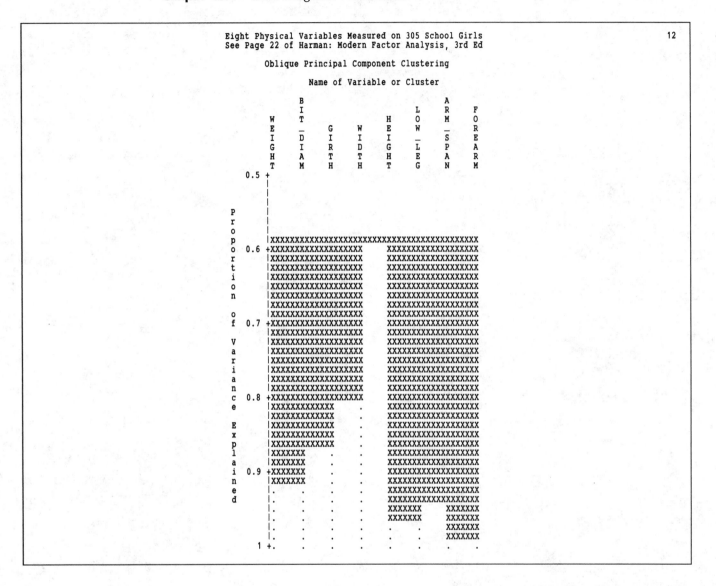

REFERENCES

Anderberg, M.R. (1973), *Cluster Analysis for Applications*, New York: Academic Press, Inc.

Harman, H.H. (1976), *Modern Factor Analysis*, 3d Edition, Chicago: University of Chicago Press.

Chapter 44

The VARCOMP Procedure

ABSTRACT   1661
INTRODUCTION   1661
SPECIFICATIONS   1662
   PROC VARCOMP Statement   1662
   BY Statement   1663
   CLASS Statement   1663
   MODEL Statement   1663
DETAILS   1664
   Missing Values   1664
   Fixed and Random Effects   1664
   Negative Variance Component Estimates   1665
   Computational Methods   1665
      The Type I Method   1665
      The MIVQUE0 Method   1665
      The Maximum-Likelihood Method   1666
      The Restricted Maximum-Likelihood Method   1666
   Printed Output   1666
EXAMPLES   1667
   Example 1:   Using the Four Estimation Methods   1667
   Example 2:   Analyzing the Cure Rate of Rubber   1670
REFERENCES   1672

ABSTRACT

The VARCOMP procedure estimates the variance components in a general linear model.

INTRODUCTION

The VARCOMP procedure handles models that have random effects. Random effects are classification effects where the levels of the effect are assumed to be randomly selected from an infinite population of possible levels. The VARCOMP procedure estimates the contribution of each of the random effects to the variance of the dependent variable. For more information on random effects and the kind of models that can be analyzed with PROC VARCOMP, see **Fixed and Random Effects** later in this chapter.

A single MODEL statement specifies the dependent variables and the effects: main effects, interactions, and nested effects. The effects must be composed of class variables; no continuous variables are allowed on the right side of the equal sign. See **Specification of Effects** in the chapter on the ANOVA procedure for information on how to specify effects in the MODEL statement.

You can specify certain effects as fixed (nonrandom) by putting them first in the MODEL statement and indicating the number of fixed effects with the FIXED= option. An intercept is always fitted and assumed fixed. Except for the effects specified as fixed, all other effects are assumed to be random, and their contribution to the model can be thought of as an observation from a distribution that is normally and independently distributed.

The dependent variables are grouped based on the similarity of their missing values. Each group of dependent variables is then analyzed separately. The columns of the design matrix **X** are formed in the same order as the effects are specified in the MODEL statement. No reparameterization is done. Thus, the columns of **X** contain only 0s and 1s.

Four methods of estimation can be specified in the PROC VARCOMP statement using the METHOD= option. They are TYPE1 (based on computation of type I sum of squares for each effect), MIVQUE0, Maximum Likelihood (METHOD=ML), and Restricted Maximum Likelihood (METHOD=REML).

SPECIFICATIONS

The following statements are used in the VARCOMP procedure:

> **PROC VARCOMP** <options>;   required, must be
>   **CLASS** variables;   in this order
>   **MODEL** dependents=effects < / option>;
>
>   **BY** variables;   optional statement

Only one MODEL statement is allowed. The BY, CLASS, and MODEL statements are described after the PROC VARCOMP statement.

PROC VARCOMP Statement

PROC VARCOMP <options>;

This statement invokes the VARCOMP procedure. The options below can appear in the PROC VARCOMP statement:

DATA=SAS-data-set
  specifies the input SAS data set to use. If this option is omitted, the most recently created SAS data set is used.

EPSILON=number
  specifies the convergence value of the objective function for METHOD=ML or REML. By default, EPSILON=1E-8.

MAXITER=number
  specifies the maximum number of iterations for METHOD=ML or REML. By default, MAXITER=50.

METHOD=TYPE1 | MIVQUE0 | ML | REML
  specifies which of the four methods (TYPE1, MIVQUE0, ML, or REML) you want to use. By default, METHOD=MIVQUE0. For more information on these methods, see **Computational Methods** later in this chapter.

BY Statement

BY *variables*;

A BY statement can be used with PROC VARCOMP to obtain separate analyses on observations in groups defined by the BY variables. When a BY statement appears, the procedure expects the input data set to be sorted in order of the BY variables.

If your input data set is not sorted in ascending order, use one of the following alternatives:

- Use the SORT procedure with a similar BY statement to sort the data.
- Use the BY statement options NOTSORTED or DESCENDING in the BY statement for the VARCOMP procedure. As a cautionary note, the NOTSORTED option does not mean that the data are unsorted, but rather means that the data are arranged in groups (according to values of the BY variables) and that these groups are not necessarily in alphabetical or increasing numeric order.
- Use the DATASETS procedure (in base SAS software) to create an index on the BY variables.

For more information on the BY statement, see the discussion in *SAS Language: Reference, Version 6, First Edition*. For more information on the DATASETS procedure, see the discussion in the *SAS Procedures Guide, Version 6, Third Edition*.

CLASS Statement

CLASS *variables*;

The CLASS statement specifies the classification variables to be used in the analysis. All effects in the MODEL statement must be composed of effects that appear in the CLASS statement. Class variables may be either numeric or character; if they are character, only the first 16 characters will be used.

Numeric class variables are not restricted to integers since a variable's format determines the levels. For more information, see the discussion of the FORMAT statement in the chapter "SAS Statements Used in the Proc Step" in the *SAS Language: Reference*.

MODEL Statement

MODEL *dependents=effects < / option>*;

The MODEL statement gives the dependent variables and independent effects. If more than one dependent variable is specified, a separate analysis is performed for each one. The independent effects are limited to main effects, interactions, and nested effects; no continuous effects are allowed. All independent effects must be composed of effects that appear in the CLASS statement. Effects are specified in the VARCOMP procedure in the same way as described for the ANOVA procedure. Only one MODEL statement is allowed.

Only one option is available in the MODEL statement:

FIXED=n
> tells VARCOMP that the first *n* effects in the MODEL statement are fixed effects. The remaining effects are assumed to be random. By default, PROC VARCOMP assumes that all effects are random in the model. Keep in mind that if you use bar notation and, for example, specify Y=A│B / FIXED=2, then A*B is considered a random effect.

DETAILS

Missing Values

If an observation has a missing value for any variable used in the independent effects, then the analyses of all dependent variables omit this observation. An observation will be deleted from the analysis of a given dependent variable if the observation's value for that dependent variable is missing. Note that a missing value in one dependent variable does not eliminate an observation from the analysis of the other dependent variables.

During processing, the VARCOMP procedure groups the dependent variables on their missing values across observations so that sums of squares and crossproducts can be computed in the most efficient manner.

Fixed and Random Effects

Central to the idea of variance components models is the idea of fixed and random effects. Each effect in a variance components model must be classified as either a fixed or a random effect. Fixed effects arise when the levels of an effect constitute the entire population about which you are interested. For example, if a plant scientist is comparing the yields of three varieties of soybeans, then VARIETY would be a fixed effect, providing that the scientist was concerned about making inferences on only these three varieties of soybeans. Similarly, if an industrial experiment focused on the effectiveness of two brands of a machine, MACHINE would be a fixed effect only if the experimenter's interest did not go beyond the two machine brands.

On the other hand, an effect is classified as a random effect when you want to make inferences on an entire population, and the levels in your experiment represent only a sample from that population. Psychologists comparing test results between different groups of subjects would consider SUBJECT as a random effect. Depending on the psychologists' particular interest, the GROUP effect might be either fixed or random. For example, if the groups were based on the sex of the subject, then SEX would be a fixed effect. But if the psychologists were interested in the variability in test scores due to different teachers, then they might choose a random sample of teachers as being representative of the total population of teachers, and TEACHER would be a random effect. Note that, in the soybean example presented earlier, if the scientist were interested in making inferences on the entire population of soybean varieties and randomly chose three varieties for testing, then VARIETY would be a random effect.

If all the effects in a model (except for the intercept) are considered random effects, then the model is called a *random effects model*; likewise a model with only fixed effects is called a *fixed effects model*. The more common case, where some factors are fixed and others are random, is called a *mixed model*. In PROC VARCOMP, by default, effects are assumed to be random. You specify which effects are fixed by using the FIXED= option in the MODEL statement. In general, if an interaction or nested effect contains any effect that is random, then the interaction or nested effect should be considered as a random effect as well.

In the linear model, each level of a fixed effect contributes a fixed amount to the expected value of the dependent variable. What makes a random effect different is that each level of a random effect contributes an amount that is viewed as a sample from a population of normally distributed variables, each with mean 0, and an unknown variance, much like the usual random error term that is a part of all linear models. The estimate of the variance associated with the random effect is known as the *variance component* because it is measuring the part of the overall variance contributed by that effect. Thus, PROC VARCOMP estimates the variance of the random variables that are associated with the random effects in your model, and the variance components tell you how much each of the random factors contributes to the overall variability in the dependent variable.

Negative Variance Component Estimates

The variance components estimated by PROC VARCOMP should always be positive because they are assumed to represent the variance of a random variable. Nevertheless, when you are using METHOD=MIVQUE0 (the default) or METHOD=TYPE1, some estimates of variance components may become negative. (Due to the nature of the algorithms used for METHOD=ML and METHOD=REML, negative estimates are constrained to zero.) These negative estimates may arise for a variety of reasons:

- The variability in your data may be large enough to produce a negative estimate, even though the true value of the variance component is positive.
- Your data may contain outliers. See Hocking (1983) for a graphical technique for detecting outliers in variance components models using the SAS System.
- A different model for interpreting your data may be appropriate. Under some statistical models for variance components analysis, negative estimates are an indication that observations in your data are negatively correlated. See Hocking (1984) for further information about these models.

Assuming that you are satisfied that the model PROC VARCOMP is using is appropriate for your data, it is common practice to treat negative variance components as if they were zero.

Computational Methods

Four methods of estimation can be specified in the PROC VARCOMP statement using the METHOD= option. They are described below.

The Type I Method

This method (METHOD=TYPE1) computes the Type I sum of squares for each effect, equates each mean square involving only random effects to its expected value, and solves the resulting system of equations (Gaylor, Lucas, and Anderson 1970). The $\mathbf{X'X} \mid \mathbf{X'Y}$ matrix is computed and adjusted in segments whenever memory is not sufficient to hold the entire matrix.

The MIVQUE0 Method

Based on the technique suggested by Hartley, Rao, and LaMotte (1978), the MIVQUE0 method (METHOD=MIVQUE0) produces unbiased estimates that are invariant with respect to the fixed effects of the model and are locally best quadratic unbiased estimates given that the true ratio of each component to the residual error component is zero. The technique is similar to TYPE1 except that the random effects are adjusted only for the fixed effects. This affords a considerable timing advantage over the TYPE1 method; thus, MIVQUE0 is the default method used in PROC VARCOMP. The $\mathbf{X'X} \mid \mathbf{X'Y}$ matrix is computed and adjusted in segments whenever memory is not sufficient to hold the entire matrix. Each element (i,j) of the form

$$\text{SSQ}\ (\mathbf{X}_i'\mathbf{M}\mathbf{X}_j)$$

is computed, where

$$\mathbf{M} = \mathbf{I} - \mathbf{X}_0(\mathbf{X}_0'\mathbf{X}_0)^-\mathbf{X}_0'$$

$\mathbf{X}_0$ is part of the design matrix for the fixed effects, $\mathbf{X}_i$ is part of the design matrix for one of the random effects, and SSQ is an operator that takes the sum of squares of the elements. For more information see Rao (1971, 1972).

The Maximum-Likelihood Method

The ML method (METHOD=ML) computes maximum-likelihood estimates of the variance components using the W-transformation developed by Hemmerle and Hartley (1973). The procedure then iterates until the log-likelihood objective function converges. The objective function for METHOD=ML is $\ln(|\mathbf{V}|)$, where

$$\mathbf{V} = \sigma_0^2 \mathbf{I} + \Sigma_{i=1}^{n_r} \sigma_i^2 \, \mathbf{X}_i\mathbf{X}_i'$$

σ_0^2 is the residual variance, n_r is the number of random effects in the model, σ_i^2 represents the variance components, and $\mathbf{X}_i$ is part of the design matrix for one of the random effects.

The Restricted Maximum-Likelihood Method

The Restricted Maximum-Likelihood Method (METHOD=REML) is similar to the maximum-likelihood method, but it first separates the likelihood into two parts: one that contains the fixed effects and one that does not (Patterson and Thompson 1971). This is an iterated version of MIVQUE0. The procedure iterates until convergence is reached for the log-likelihood objective function of the portion of the likelihood that does not contain the fixed effects. The objective function for METHOD=REML is $\ln(|\mathbf{MVM'}|)$ where

$$\mathbf{V} = \sigma_0^2 \mathbf{I} + \Sigma_{i=1}^{n_r} \sigma_i^2 \, \mathbf{X}_i\mathbf{X}_i'$$

σ_0^2 is the residual variance, n_r is the number of random effects in the model, σ_i^2 represents the variance components, and $\mathbf{X}_i$ is part of the design matrix for one of the random effects, and

$$\mathbf{M} = \mathbf{I} - \mathbf{X}_0(\mathbf{X}_0'\mathbf{X}_0)^-\mathbf{X}_0' \quad .$$

Printed Output

The VARCOMP procedure prints the following items:

1. Class Level Information for verifying the levels and number of observations in your data
2. for METHOD=TYPE1, an analysis-of-variance table with Source, DF, Type I SS, Type I MS, and Expected Mean Square
3. for METHOD=MIVQUE0, the SSQ Matrix containing sums of squares of partitions of the $\mathbf{X'X}$ crossproducts matrix adjusted for the fixed effects
4. for METHOD=ML and METHOD=REML, the iteration history, including the objective function, as well as variance component estimates
5. for METHOD=ML and METHOD=REML, the estimated Asymptotic Covariance Matrix of the variance components.

EXAMPLES

Example 1:   Using the Four Estimation Methods

In this example, A and B are classification variables and Y is the dependent variable. A is declared fixed, and B and A*B are random. Note that this design is unbalanced because the cell sizes are not all the same. PROC VARCOMP is invoked four times, once for each of the estimation methods. The data are from Hemmerle and Hartley (1973). The following statements produce **Output 44.1**:

```
data a;
   input a b y @@;
   cards;
1 1 237 1 1 254 1 1 246
1 2 178 1 2 179
2 1 208 2 1 178 2 1 187
2 2 146 2 2 145 2 2 141
3 1 186 3 1 183
3 2 142 3 2 125 3 2 136
;

proc varcomp method=type1;
   class a b;
   model y=a|b / fixed=1;
run;

proc varcomp method=mivque0;
   class a b;
   model y=a|b / fixed=1;
run;

proc varcomp method=ml;
   class a b;
   model y=a|b / fixed=1;
run;

proc varcomp method=reml;
   class a b;
   model y=a|b / fixed=1;
run;
```

Output 44.1 VARCOMP Procedure Invoked Once for Each Estimation
Method

```
                              The SAS System                                    1

                   Variance Components Estimation Procedure
                            Class Level Information
               ❶ Class     Levels     Values

                   A           3       1 2 3

                   B           2       1 2


               Number of observations in data set = 16
```

```
                              The SAS System                                    2
                   ❷ Variance Components Estimation Procedure

Dependent Variable: Y

Source            DF        Type I SS         Type I MS      Expected Mean Square

A                  2     11736.43750000    5868.21875000     Var(Error) + 2.725 Var(A*B) + 0.1 Var(B) + Q(A)

B                  1     11448.12564103   11448.12564103     Var(Error) + 2.6308 Var(A*B) + 7.8 Var(B)

A*B                2       299.04102564     149.52051282     Var(Error) + 2.5846 Var(A*B)

Error             10       786.33333333      78.63333333     Var (Error )

Corrected Total   15     24269.93750000



Variance Component              Estimate

Var(B)                       1448.37683150

Var(A*B)                       27.42658730

Var(Error)                     78.63333333
```

```
                              The SAS System                                    3

                   Variance Components Estimation Procedure
                            Class Level Information

                   Class     Levels     Values

                   A           3       1 2 3

                   B           2       1 2


               Number of observations in data set = 16
```

```
                               The SAS System                                    4

                   MIVQUE(0) Variance Component Estimation Procedure
                          ❸   SSQ Matrix

        Source              B               A*B             Error              Y

        B            60.84000000      20.52000000       7.80000000      89295.38000000
        A*B          20.52000000      20.52000000       7.80000000      30181.30000000
        Error         7.80000000       7.80000000      13.00000000      12533.50000000

                                                    Estimate
                         Variance Component             Y

                          Var(B)               1466.12301587
                          Var(A*B)              -35.49170274
                          Var(Error)            105.73659674
```

```
                               The SAS System                                    5

                     Variance Components Estimation Procedure
                            Class Level Information

                     Class     Levels    Values

                       A          3      1 2 3

                       B          2      1 2


              Number of observations in data set = 16
```

```
                               The SAS System                                    6

              ❹ Maximum Likelihood Variance Components Estimation Procedure

Dependent Variable: Y


     Iteration       Objective          Var(B)          Var(A*B)         Var(Error)

         0         78.38503712     1031.49069751  1.6518113942E-11      74.39097179
         1         78.26504142      750.94298641          0             77.13600689
         2         78.26357008      726.97149749          0             77.48091619
         3         78.26354743      724.05329274          0             77.52465553
         4         78.26354712      723.71413514          0             77.52976467
         5         78.26354712      723.67188758          0             77.53040147

                        Convergence criteria met.

              ❺   Asymptotic Covariance Matrix of Estimates

                           Var(B)         Var(A*B)        Var(Error)

          Var(B)        537843.87287          0          -107.4056356
          Var(A*B)             0              0                0
          Var(Error)     -107.4056356         0           858.7090218
```

```
                                     The SAS System                                         7

                          Variance Components Estimation Procedure
                                 Class Level Information

                          Class      Levels      Values

                          A             3        1 2 3

                          B             2        1 2


                     Number of observations in data set = 16
```

```
                                     The SAS System                                         8

               Restricted Maximum Likelihood Variance Components Estimation Procedure

Dependent Variable: Y


       Iteration        Objective          Var(B)          Var(A*B)        Var(Error)

           0          63.41341449     1269.52701231    2.032998639E-11     91.55811913
           1          63.06193968     1298.52859523      18.97866174       82.05999526
           2          63.03324297     1418.29754241      24.74967982       79.64434229
           3          63.03129780     1450.83757616      26.32528557       79.06768297
           4          63.03113719     1460.93943800      26.80063541       78.89842549
           5          63.03112712     1463.54704841      26.92110055       78.85574362
           6          63.03112655     1464.17389143      26.94995430       78.84553606
           7          63.03112651     1464.32183190      26.95676177       78.84312905
           8          63.03112651     1464.35660462      26.95836175       78.84256339

                               Convergence criteria met.


                       Asymptotic Covariance Matrix of Estimates
                                    Var(B)         Var(A*B)        Var(Error)

                  Var(B)         4401576.446         1.230          -273.227
                  Var(A*B)             1.230      3559.011          -502.847
                  Var(Error)        -273.227      -502.847         1249.704
```

Example 2: Analyzing the Cure Rate of Rubber

This example using data from Hicks (1973) is concerned with an experiment to
determine the sources of variability in cure rates of rubber. The goal of the experiment was to find out if different laboratories had more of an effect on the variance
of cure rates than did different batches of raw materials. This information would
be useful in trying to control the cure rate of the final product because it would
provide insights into the sources of the variability in cure rates. The rubber used
was cured at three temperatures, which were taken to be fixed. Three laboratories
were chosen at random, and three different batches of raw material were tested
at each combination of temperature and laboratory.

The SAS statements to produce the data set and perform the restricted
maximum-likelihood variance component analysis are given below. The output
is shown in **Output 44.2**.

```
data cure;
   input lab temp batch $ cure @@;
   cards;
1 145 A 18.6    1 145 A 17.0    1 145 A 18.7    1 145 A 18.7
1 145 B 14.5    1 145 B 15.8    1 145 B 16.5    1 145 B 17.6
1 145 C 21.1    1 145 C 20.8    1 145 C 21.8    1 145 C 21.0
1 155 A  9.5    1 155 A  9.4    1 155 A  9.5    1 155 A 10.0
1 155 B  7.8    1 155 B  8.3    1 155 B  8.9    1 155 B  9.1
```

```
1 155 C 11.2    1 155 C 10.0    1 155 C 11.5    1 155 C 11.1
1 165 A  5.4    1 165 A  5.3    1 165 A  5.7    1 165 A  5.3
1 165 B  5.2    1 165 B  4.9    1 165 B  4.3    1 165 B  5.2
1 165 C  6.3    1 165 C  6.4    1 165 C  5.8    1 165 C  5.6
2 145 A 20.0    2 145 A 20.1    2 145 A 19.4    2 145 A 20.0
2 145 B 18.4    2 145 B 18.1    2 145 B 16.5    2 145 B 16.7
2 145 C 22.5    2 145 C 22.7    2 145 C 21.5    2 145 C 21.3
2 155 A 11.4    2 155 A 11.5    2 155 A 11.4    2 155 A 11.5
2 155 B 10.8    2 155 B 11.1    2 155 B  9.5    2 155 B  9.7
2 155 C 13.3    2 155 C 14.0    2 155 C 12.0    2 155 C 11.5
2 165 A  6.8    2 165 A  6.9    2 165 A  6.0    2 165 A  5.7
2 165 B  6.0    2 165 B  6.1    2 165 B  5.0    2 165 B  5.2
2 165 C  7.7    2 165 C  8.0    2 165 C  6.6    2 165 C  6.3
3 145 A 19.7    3 145 A 18.3    3 145 A 16.8    3 145 A 17.1
3 145 B 16.3    3 145 B 16.7    3 145 B 14.4    3 145 B 15.2
3 145 C 22.7    3 145 C 21.9    3 145 C 19.3    3 145 C 19.3
3 155 A  9.3    3 155 A 10.2    3 155 A  9.8    3 155 A  9.5
3 155 B  9.1    3 155 B  9.2    3 155 B  8.0    3 155 B  9.0
3 155 C 11.3    3 155 C 11.0    3 155 C 10.9    3 155 C 11.4
3 165 A  6.7    3 165 A  6.0    3 165 A  5.0    3 165 A  4.8
3 165 B  5.7    3 165 B  5.5    3 165 B  4.6    3 165 B  5.4
3 165 C  6.6    3 165 C  6.5    3 165 C  5.9    3 165 C  5.8
;

proc varcomp method=reml;
    class temp lab batch;
    model cure=temp|lab batch(lab temp) / fixed=1;
run;
```

Output 44.2   REML Analysis of Rubber Cure Data

```
                          The SAS System                                    1

                  Variance Components Estimation Procedure
                          Class Level Information

                    Class     Levels     Values

                    TEMP         3        145 155 165

                    LAB          3        1 2 3

                    BATCH        3        A B C


           Number of observations in data set = 108
```

```
                                    The SAS System                                            2
                    Restricted Maximum Likelihood Variance Components Estimation Procedure
Dependent Variable: CURE


   Iteration      Objective           Var(LAB)       Var(TEMP*LAB)   Var(BATCH(TEMP*LAB))      Var(Error)
       0        13.45000603          0.50944643            0              2.40048886           0.57871852
       1        13.10436765          0.32772214            0              2.14611933           0.59715947
       2        13.09007928          0.31984352            0              2.08988267           0.60137455
       3        13.08934862          0.31808589            0              2.07732774           0.60235179
       4        13.08931440          0.31771107            0              2.07464989           0.60256200
       5        13.08931265          0.31762664            0              2.07404666           0.60260944
       6        13.08931256          0.31760741            0              2.07390923           0.60262026
       7        13.08931256          0.31760301            0              2.07387785           0.60262273

                                  Convergence criteria met.


                           Asymptotic Covariance Matrix of Estimates

                                    Var(LAB)        Var(TEMP*LAB)   Var(BATCH(TEMP*LAB))      Var(Error)
Var(LAB)                          0.3245255861           0             -0.049985752         -1.936581E-8
Var(TEMP*LAB)                          0                 0                   0                    0
Var(BATCH(TEMP*LAB))              -0.049985752           0              0.4504323062         -0.002241828
Var(Error)                       -1.936581E-8           0             -0.002241828          0.0089667691
```

The results of the analysis show that the variance attributable to BATCH(TEMP*LAB) (with a variance component of 2.0739) is considerably larger than the variance attributable to LAB (0.3177). Therefore, attempts to reduce the variability of cure rates should concentrate on improving the homogeneity of the batches of raw material used rather than standardizing the practices or equipment within the laboratories. It is also of interest to note that since the BATCH(TEMP*LAB) variance is considerably larger than the experimental error (Var(Error)=0.6026), the BATCH(TEMP*LAB) variability plays an important part in the overall variability of the cure rates.

REFERENCES

Gaylor, D.W., Lucas, H.L., and Anderson, R.L. (1970), "Calculation of Expected Mean Squares by the Abbreviated Doolittle and Square Root Methods," *Biometrics*, 26, 641–655.

Goodnight, J.H. (1978), *Computing MIVQUE0 Estimates of Variance Components*, SAS Technical Report R-105. Cary, NC: SAS Institute Inc.

Goodnight, J.H. and Hemmerle, W.J. (1979), "A Simplified Algorithm for the W-Transformation in Variance Component Estimation," *Technometrics*, 21, 265–268.

Hartley, H.O., Rao, J.N.K., and LaMotte, L. (1978), "A Simple Synthesis-Based Method of Variance Component Estimation," *Biometrics*, 34, 233–244.

Hemmerle, W.J. and Hartley, H.O. (1973), "Computing Maximum Likelihood Estimates for the Mixed AOV Model Using the W-Transformation," *Technometrics*, 15, 819–831.

Hicks, C.R. (1973), *Fundamental Concepts in the Design of Experiments*, New York: Holt, Rinehart and Winston, Inc.

Hocking, R.R. (1983), "A Diagnostic Tool for Mixed Models with Applications to Negative Estimates of Variance Components," *SAS Users Group International Conference Proceedings*, Cary, NC: SAS Institute Inc., 711–716.

Hocking, R.R. (1984), *The Analysis of Linear Models*, Monterey, CA: Brooks-Cole Publishing Co.

Patterson, H.D. and Thompson, R. (1971), "Recovery of Inter-Block Information When Block Sizes Are Unequal," *Biometrika*, 58, 545–554.

Rao, C.R. (1971), "Minimum Variance Quadratic Unbiased Estimation of Variance Components," *Journal of Multivariate Analysis*, 1, 445–456.

Rao, C.R. (1972), "Estimation of Variance and Covariance Components in Linear Models," *Journal of the American Statistical Association*, 67, 112–115.

Special
SAS®
Data Sets

Introduction to Special SAS Data Sets   1675
TYPE=CORR Data Sets   1678
   Example 1:   A TYPE=CORR Data Set Produced by PROC CORR   1680
   Example 2:   Creating a TYPE=CORR Data Set in a DATA Step   1681
TYPE=UCORR Data Sets   1681
TYPE=COV Data Sets   1682
TYPE=UCOV Data Sets   1682
TYPE=SSCP Data Sets   1682
   Example 3:   A TYPE=SSCP Data Set Produced by PROC REG   1683
TYPE=CSSCP Data Sets   1683
TYPE=EST Data Sets   1683
   Example 4:   A TYPE=EST Data Set Produced by PROC REG   1684
TYPE=RAM Data Sets   1684
TYPE=DISTANCE Data Sets   1684
TYPE=FACTOR Data Sets   1685
TYPE=LINEAR Data Sets   1685
TYPE=QUAD Data Sets   1685
TYPE=MIXED Data Sets   1685
TYPE=TREE Data Sets   1685
TYPE=ACE Data Sets   1686
Definitional Formulas   1686

Introduction to Special SAS Data Sets

Many SAS/STAT procedures create SAS data sets containing various statistics. Some of these data sets are organized according to certain conventions that allow them to be read by a SAS/STAT procedure for further analysis. Such specially organized data sets are recognized by the TYPE= attribute of the data set.

For example, the CORR procedure (See the *SAS Procedures Guide, Version 6, Third Edition*) can create a data set with the attribute TYPE=CORR containing a correlation matrix. This TYPE=CORR data set can be read by the REG or FACTOR procedures, among others. If the original data set is large, using a special SAS data set in this way can save a great deal of computer time by avoiding the recomputation of the correlation matrix in each of several analyses.

As another example, the REG procedure can create a TYPE=EST data set containing estimated regression coefficients. If you need to make predictions for new observations, you can have the SCORE procedure read both the TYPE=EST data set and a data set containing the new observations. PROC SCORE can then compute predicted values or residuals without repeating the entire regression analysis. See Chapter 38, "The SCORE Procedure," for an example.

A special SAS data set may contain different kinds of statistics. A special variable called _TYPE_ is used to distinguish the various statistics. For example, in a TYPE=CORR data set, an observation in which _TYPE_='MEAN' contains the means of the variables in the analysis, and an observation in which _TYPE_='STD' contains the standard deviations. Correlations appear in observations with _TYPE_='CORR'. Another special variable, _NAME_, is needed to identify the row of the correlation matrix. Thus, the correlation between variables X and Y would be given by the value of the variable X in the observation for which _TYPE_='CORR' and _NAME_='Y', or by the value of the variable Y in the observation for which _TYPE_='CORR' and _NAME_='X'.

You can create special SAS data sets directly in a DATA step. You must specify the data set TYPE= option in parentheses after the data set name in the DATA statement. Examples are given later in this appendix.

The special data sets created by SAS/STAT procedures can generally be used directly by other procedures without modification. However, if you create an output data set with PROC CORR and use the NOCORR option to omit the correlation matrix from the output data set, you need to set the data set TYPE= option either in parentheses following the output data set name in the PROC CORR statement, or in parentheses following the DATA= option in any other procedure that recognizes the special data set TYPE= attribute. In either case, the TYPE= option should be set to COV, CSSCP, or SSCP according to what type of matrix is stored in the data set and what data set types are accepted as input by the other procedures you plan to use. If you do not follow these steps, and you use the TYPE=CORR data set with no correlation matrix as input to another procedure, the procedure may issue an error message indicating that the correlation matrix is missing from the data set.

If you use a DATA step with a SET statement to modify a special SAS data set, you must specify the TYPE= option in the DATA statement. The TYPE= of the data set in the SET statement is *not* automatically copied to the data set being created.

You can find out the TYPE= of a data set by using the CONTENTS procedure (see the *SAS Procedures Guide* for details).

Table A1.1 summarizes the TYPE= data sets that may be used as input to SAS/STAT procedures and the TYPE= data sets that are created by SAS/STAT procedures. The essential parts of the statements each procedure uses to create its output data set or data sets are shown.

Formulas useful for illustrating differences between corrected and uncorrected matrices in some special SAS data sets are shown in **Definitional Formulas** at the end of this appendix.

Table A1.1 SAS/STAT Procedures and Types of Data Sets

Procedure	Accepts Input Data Set(s) TYPE= as shown*	Creates Output Data Set(s) (TYPE=null or as shown)	Created by the Statement and Specification
ACECLUS	ACE, CORR, COV, SSCP, UCORR, UCOV	ACE	PROC ACECLUS OUTSTAT= PROC ACECLUS OUT=
ANOVA			PROC ANOVA OUTSTAT=
CALIS	CORR, COV, FACTOR, RAM, SSCP, UCORR, UCOV	CORR COV EST UCORR UCOV RAM	PROC CALIS OUTSTAT= PROC CALIS COV OUTSTAT= PROC CALIS OUTEST= PROC CALIS NOINT OUTSTAT= PROC CALIS NOINT COV OUTSTAT= PROC CALIS OUTRAM=
CANCORR	CORR, COV, FACTOR, SSCP, UCORR, UCOV	CORR UCORR	PROC CANCORR OUTSTAT= PROC CANCORR NOINT OUTSTAT= PROC CANCORR OUT=
CANDISC	CORR, COV, SSCP, CSSCP	CORR	PROC CANDISC OUTSTAT= PROC CANDISC OUT=
CATMOD	EST	EST	RESPONSE / OUTEST= RESPONSE / OUT=
CLUSTER	DISTANCE	TREE	PROC CLUSTER OUTTREE=
CORRESP			PROC CORRESP OUTC= PROC CORRESP OUTF=
DISCRIM	CORR, COV, SSCP, CSSCP, LINEAR, QUAD, MIXED	LINEAR QUAD MIXED CORR	PROC DISCRIM POOL=YES OUTSTAT= PROC DISCRIM POOL=NO OUTSTAT= PROC DISCRIM POOL=TEST OUTSTAT= PROC DISCRIM METHOD=NPAR OUTSTAT= PROC DISCRIM OUTCROSS PROC DISCRIM OUTD PROC DISCRIM TESTOUT PROC DISCRIM TESTOUTD
FACTOR	ACE, CORR, COV, FACTOR, SSCP, UCORR, UCOV	FACTOR	PROC FACTOR OUTSTAT= PROC FACTOR OUT=
FASTCLUS			PROC FASTCLUS OUT= PROC FASTCLUS MEAN=
FREQ			TABLES / OUT=
GLM			PROC GLM OUTSTAT= LSMEANS / OUT= OUTPUT OUT=
LIFEREG		EST	PROC LIFEREG OUTEST= OUTPUT OUT=
LIFETEST			PROC LIFETEST OUTSURV= PROC LIFETEST OUTTEST=

(continued)

*If no TYPE= shown, the procedure does not recognize any special data set types except possibly to issue an error message for inappropriate values of TYPE=.

Table A1.1 (*continued*)

Procedure	Accepts Input Data Set(s) TYPE= as shown*	Creates Output Data Set(s) (TYPE=null or as shown)	Created by the Statement and Specification
LOGISTIC		EST	PROC LOGISTIC OUTEST= OUTPUT OUT=
NESTED		none	
NLIN		EST	PROC NLIN OUTEST= OUTPUT OUT=
NPAR1WAY		none	
ORTHOREG		EST	PROC ORTHOREG OUTEST=
PLAN			OUTPUT OUT=
PRINCOMP	CORR, COV, EST, FACTOR, SSCP, UCORR, UCOV	CORR COV UCORR UCOV	PROC PRINCOMP OUTSTAT= PROC PRINCOMP COV OUTSTAT= PROC PRINCOMP NOINT OUTSTAT= PROC PRINCOMP NOINT COV OUTSTAT= PROC PRINCOMP OUT=
PRINQUAL			PROC PRINQUAL OUT=
PROBIT		EST	PROC PROBIT OUTEST= OUTPUT OUT=
REG	CORR, COV, SSCP, UCORR, UCOV	EST SSCP	PROC REG OUTEST= PROC REG OUTSSCP= OUTPUT OUT=
RSREG			PROC RSREG OUT= RIDGE OUTR=
SCORE	any		PROC SCORE OUT=
STEPDISC	CORR, COV, SSCP, CSSCP	none	
TRANSREG			OUTPUT OUT=
TREE	TREE		PROC TREE OUT=
TTEST		none	
VARCLUS	CORR, COV, FACTOR, SSCP, UCORR, UCOV	CORR UCORR TREE	PROC VARCLUS OUTSTAT= PROC VARCLUS NOINT OUTSTAT= PROC VARCLUS OUTTREE=
VARCOMP		none	

*If no TYPE= shown, the procedure does not recognize any special data set types except possibly to issue an error message for inappropriate values of TYPE=.

TYPE=CORR Data Sets

A TYPE=CORR data set usually contains a correlation matrix and possibly other statistics including means, standard deviations, and the number of observations in the original SAS data set from which the correlation matrix was computed.

Using PROC CORR with an output data set option (OUTP=, OUTS=, OUTK=, OUTH=, or OUT=) produces a TYPE=CORR data set. (For a complete description of the CORR procedure, see the *SAS Procedures Guide, Version 6, Third Edition.*)

The CALIS, CANCORR, CANDISC, DISCRIM, PRINCOMP, and VARCLUS procedures can also create a TYPE=CORR data set with additional statistics.

A TYPE=CORR data set containing a correlation matrix can be used as input for the ACECLUS, CALIS, CANCORR, CANDISC, DISCRIM, FACTOR, PRINCOMP, REG, SCORE, STEPDISC, and VARCLUS procedures.

The variables in a TYPE=CORR data set are

- the BY variable or variables, if a BY statement is used with the procedure.
- _TYPE_, a character variable of length eight whose values identify the type of statistic in each observation, such as **MEAN**, **STD**, **N**, and **CORR**.
- _NAME_, a character variable of length eight whose values identify the variable with which a given row of the correlation matrix is associated. _NAME_ is blank for observations in which a row name is not needed.
- other variables that were analyzed by the CORR procedure or another procedure.

The usual values of the _TYPE_ variable are as follows:

TYPE	Contents
MEAN	mean of each variable analyzed.
STD	standard deviation of each variable.
N	number of observations used in the analysis. PROC CORR records the number of nonmissing values for each variable unless the NOMISS option is used. If NOMISS is specified, or if the CALIS, CANCORR, CANDISC, PRINCOMP, or VARCLUS procedures are used to create the data set, observations with one or more missing values are omitted from the analysis, so this value is the same for each variable and gives the number of observations with no missing values. If a FREQ statement was used with the procedure that created the data set, the number of observations is taken to be the sum of the relevant values of the variable in the FREQ statement. Procedures that read a TYPE=CORR data set use the smallest value in the observation with _TYPE_='N' as the number of observations in the analysis.
SUMWGT	sum of the observation weights if a WEIGHT statement was used with the procedure that created the data set. The values are determined analogously to those of the _TYPE_='N' observation.
CORR	correlations with the variable named by the _NAME_ variable.

There may be additional observations in a TYPE=CORR data set depending on the particular procedure and options used.

If you create a TYPE=CORR data set yourself, the data set need not contain the observations with _TYPE_='MEAN', 'STD', 'N', or 'SUMWGT' unless you intend to use one of the discriminant procedures. Procedures assume that all of the means are 0.0 and that the standard deviations are 1.0 if this information is not in the TYPE=CORR data set. If _TYPE_='N' does not appear, most procedures assume that the number of observations is 10,000; significance tests and other statistics that depend on the number of observations are, of course, meaningless. In the CALIS and CANCORR procedures, you can use the EDF= option instead of including a _TYPE_='N' observation.

A correlation matrix is symmetric; that is, the correlation between X and Y is the same as the correlation between Y and X. The CALIS, CANCORR, CANDISC, CORR, DISCRIM, PRINCOMP, and VARCLUS procedures output the entire correlation matrix. If you create the data set yourself, you need to include only one of the two occurrences of the correlation between two variables; the other may be given a missing value.

If you create a TYPE=CORR data set yourself, the _TYPE_ and _NAME_ variables are not necessary except for use with the discriminant procedures and PROC SCORE. If there is no _TYPE_ variable, then all observations are assumed to contain correlations. If there is no _NAME_ variable, the first observation is assumed to correspond to the first variable in the analysis, the second observation to the second variable, and so on. However, if you omit the _NAME_ variable, you will not be able to analyze arbitrary subsets of the variables or list the variables in a VAR or MODEL statement in a different order.

Example 1:   A TYPE=CORR Data Set Produced by PROC CORR

See **Output A1.1** for an example of a TYPE=CORR data set produced by the following statements:

```
title 'Five Socioeconomic Variables';
data socecon;
   title2 'see page 14 of Harman (1976), Modern Factor Analysis, 3rd ed';
   input pop school employ services house;
   cards;
5700    12.8    2500    270    25000
1000    10.9    600     10     10000
3400    8.8     1000    10     9000
3800    13.6    1700    140    25000
4000    12.8    1600    140    25000
8200    8.3     2600    60     12000
1200    11.4    400     10     16000
9100    11.5    3300    60     14000
9900    12.5    3400    180    18000
9600    13.7    3600    390    25000
9600    9.6     3300    80     12000
9400    11.4    4000    100    13000
;
proc corr noprint outp=corrcorr;
proc print;
   title3 'A TYPE=CORR Data Set Produced by PROC CORR';
run;
```

Output A1.1   A TYPE=CORR Data Set Produced by PROC CORR

```
                            Five Socioeconomic Variables                                    1
                  see page 14 of Harman (1976), Modern Factor Analysis, 3rd ed
                         A TYPE=CORR Data Set Produced by PROC CORR

        OBS    _TYPE_    _NAME_      POP      SCHOOL    EMPLOY    SERVICES    HOUSE

         1     MEAN                6241.67   11.4417   2333.33    120.833   17000.00
         2     STD                 3439.99    1.7865   1241.21    114.928    6367.53
         3     N                     12.00   12.0000     12.00     12.000      12.00
         4     CORR    POP            1.00    0.0098      0.97      0.439       0.02
         5     CORR    SCHOOL         0.01    1.0000      0.15      0.691       0.86
         6     CORR    EMPLOY         0.97    0.1543      1.00      0.515       0.12
         7     CORR    SERVICES       0.44    0.6914      0.51      1.000       0.78
         8     CORR    HOUSE          0.02    0.8631      0.12      0.778       1.00
```

Example 2:   Creating a TYPE=CORR Data Set in a DATA Step

This example creates a TYPE=CORR data set by reading a correlation matrix in a DATA step. **Output A1.2** shows the resulting data set.

```
    title 'Five Socioeconomic Variables';
    data datacorr(type=corr);
       infile cards missover;
       _type_='corr';
       input _name_ $ pop school employ services house;
       cards;
    POP         1.00000
    SCHOOL      0.00975   1.00000
    EMPLOY      0.97245   0.15428   1.00000
    SERVICES    0.43887   0.69141   0.51472   1.00000
    HOUSE       0.02241   0.86307   0.12193   0.77765   1.00000
    ;
    proc print;
       title2 'A TYPE=CORR Data Set Created by a DATA Step';
    run;
```

Output A1.2   A TYPE=CORR Data Set Created by a DATA Step

```
                            Five Socioeconomic Variables                                    1
                      A TYPE=CORR Data Set Created by a DATA Step

        OBS    _TYPE_    _NAME_       POP      SCHOOL    EMPLOY    SERVICES    HOUSE

         1     corr      POP        1.00000      .         .         .          .
         2     corr      SCHOOL     0.00975   1.00000      .         .          .
         3     corr      EMPLOY     0.97245   0.15428   1.00000      .          .
         4     corr      SERVICES   0.43887   0.69141   0.51472   1.00000       .
         5     corr      HOUSE      0.02241   0.86307   0.12193   0.77765       1
```

TYPE=UCORR Data Sets

A TYPE=UCORR data set is almost identical to a TYPE=CORR data set, except that the correlations are uncorrected for the mean. The corresponding value of the _TYPE_ variable is UCORR instead of CORR. Uncorrected standard deviations are in observations with _TYPE_='USTD'.

A TYPE=UCORR data set can be used as input for every SAS/STAT procedure that uses a TYPE=CORR data set, except for the CANDISC, DISCRIM, and STEPDISC procedures. TYPE=UCORR data sets can be created by the CALIS, CANCORR, PRINCOMP, AND VARCLUS procedures.

TYPE=COV Data Sets

A TYPE=COV data set is similar to a TYPE=CORR data set except that it has _TYPE_='COV' observations containing covariances instead of or in addition to _TYPE_='CORR' observations containing correlations. The CALIS and PRINCOMP procedures create a TYPE=COV data set if the COV option is used. You can also create a TYPE=COV data set by using PROC CORR with the COV and NOCORR options and specifying the data set option TYPE=COV in parentheses following the name of the output data set. You may use only the OUTP= or OUT= options to create a TYPE=COV data set with PROC CORR.

Another way to create a TYPE=COV data set is to read a covariance matrix in a DATA step, as shown in **Example 2** for a TYPE=CORR data set.

TYPE=COV data sets are used by the same procedures that use TYPE=CORR data sets.

TYPE=UCOV Data Sets

A TYPE=UCOV data set is similar to a TYPE=COV data set, except that the covariances are uncorrected for the mean. Also, the corresponding value of the _TYPE_ variable is UCOV instead of COV.

A TYPE=UCOV data set can be used as input for every SAS/STAT procedure that uses a TYPE=COV data set, except for the CANDISC, DISCRIM, and STEPDISC procedures. TYPE=UCOV data sets can be created by the CALIS and PRINCOMP procedures.

TYPE=SSCP Data Sets

A TYPE=SSCP data set contains an uncorrected sum of squares and crossproducts (SSCP) matrix. TYPE=SSCP data sets are produced by PROC REG when the OUTSSCP= option is specified in the PROC REG statement. You can also create a TYPE=SSCP data set by using PROC CORR with the SSCP option and specifying the data set option TYPE=SSCP in parentheses following the name of the OUTP= or OUT= data set.

You can also create TYPE=SSCP data sets in a DATA step; in this case TYPE=SSCP must be specified as a data set option.

The variables in a TYPE=SSCP data set include those found in a TYPE=CORR data set. In addition there is a variable called INTERCEP that contains crossproducts for the intercept (sums of the variables). The SSCP matrix is stored in observations with _TYPE_='SSCP', including a row with _NAME_='INTERCEP'. PROC REG also outputs an observation with _TYPE_='N'. PROC CORR includes _TYPE_='MEAN' and _TYPE_='STD' as well.

TYPE=SSCP data sets are used by the same procedures that use TYPE=CORR data sets.

Example 3: A TYPE=SSCP Data Set Produced by PROC REG

Output A1.3 shows a TYPE=SSCP data set produced by PROC REG from the SOCECON data set created in **Example 1**.

```
proc reg data=socecon outsscp=regsscp;
   model house=pop school employ services / noprint;
proc print;
   title2 'A TYPE=SSCP SAS Data Set Produced by PROC REG';
run;
```

Output A1.3   A TYPE=SSCP Data Set Produced by PROC REG

```
                                      The SAS System                                              1
                            A TYPE=SSCP SAS Data Set Produced by PROC REG

 OBS   _TYPE_   _NAME_    INTERCEP        POP        SCHOOL       EMPLOY     SERVICES        HOUSE

  1    SSCP    INTERCEP      12.0       74900       137.30        28000         1450       204000
  2    SSCP    POP        74900.0   597670000    857640.00    220440000     10959000   1278700000
  3    SSCP    SCHOOL       137.3      857640      1606.05       324130        18152      2442100
  4    SSCP    EMPLOY     28000.0   220440000    324130.00     82280000      4191000    486600000
  5    SSCP    SERVICES    1450.0    10959000     18152.00      4191000       320500     30910000
  6    SSCP    HOUSE     204000.0  1278700000   2442100.00    486600000     30910000   3914000000
  7    N                     12.0          12        12.00           12           12           12
```

TYPE=CSSCP Data Sets

A TYPE=CSSCP data set contains a corrected sum of squares and crossproducts (CSSCP) matrix. TYPE=CSSCP data sets are created by using the CORR procedure with the CSSCP option and specifying the data set option TYPE=CSSCP in parentheses following the name of the OUTP= or OUT= data set.

You can also create TYPE=CSSCP data sets in a DATA step; in this case TYPE=CSSCP must be specified as a data set option.

The variables in a TYPE=CSSCP data set are the same as those found in a TYPE=SSCP data set, except that there is not a variable called INTERCEP, nor is there a row with _NAME_='INTERCEP'.

TYPE=CSSCP data sets are read by only the CANDISC, DISCRIM, and STEPDISC procedures.

TYPE=EST Data Sets

A TYPE=EST data set contains parameter estimates. The CALIS, CATMOD, LIFEREG, LOGISTIC, NLIN, ORTHOREG, PROBIT, and REG procedures create TYPE=EST data sets when the OUTEST= option is specified. A TYPE=EST data set produced by LIFEREG, ORTHOREG, or REG can be used with PROC SCORE to compute residuals or predicted values.

The variables in a TYPE=EST data set include

- the BY variables, if a BY statement is used.
- _TYPE_, a character variable of length eight, that indicates the type of estimate. The values depend on which procedure created the data set. Usually **PARM** or **PARMS** indicates estimated regression coefficients, and **COV** or **COVB** indicates estimated covariances of the parameter estimates. Some procedures, such as NLIN, have other values of _TYPE_ for special purposes.
- _NAME_, a character variable of length eight, appears if the procedure outputs the covariance matrix of the parameter estimates. The values are

the names of the rows of the covariance matrix or are blank for observations that do not contain covariances.

- variables that contain the parameter estimates, usually the same variables that appear in the VAR statement or in any MODEL statement. See Chapter 14, "The CALIS Procedure," Chapter 17, "The CATMOD Procedure," and Chapter 29, "The NLIN Procedure," for details on the variable names used in output data sets created by those procedures.

Other variables may be included depending on the particular procedure and options used.

Example 4: A TYPE=EST Data Set Produced by PROC REG

Output A1.4 shows the TYPE=EST data set produced by the following statements:

```
proc reg data=socecon outest=regest covout;
   full:   model house=pop school employ services / noprint;
   empser: model house=employ services / noprint;
proc print;
   title 'A TYPE=EST Data Set Produced by PROC REG';
run;
```

Output A1.4   A TYPE=EST Data Set Produced by PROC REG

A TYPE=EST Data Set Produced by PROC REG   1

OBS	_MODEL_	_TYPE_	_NAME_	_DEPVAR_	_RMSE_	INTERCEP	POP	SCHOOL	EMPLOY	SERVICES	HOUSE
1	FULL	PARMS		HOUSE	3122.03	-8074.21	0.65	2140.10	-2.92	27.81	-1
2	FULL	COV	INTERCEP	HOUSE	3122.03	109408014.44	-9157.04	-9784744.54	20612.49	102764.89	.
3	FULL	COV	POP	HOUSE	3122.03	-9157.04	2.32	852.86	-6.20	-5.20	.
4	FULL	COV	SCHOOL	HOUSE	3122.03	-9784744.54	852.86	907886.36	-2042.24	-9608.59	.
5	FULL	COV	EMPLOY	HOUSE	3122.03	20612.49	-6.20	-2042.24	17.44	6.50	.
6	FULL	COV	SERVICES	HOUSE	3122.03	102764.89	-5.20	-9608.59	6.50	202.56	.
7	EMPSER	PARMS		HOUSE	3789.96	15021.71	.	.	-1.94	53.88	-1
8	EMPSER	COV	INTERCEP	HOUSE	3789.96	5824096.19	.	.	-1915.99	-1294.94	.
9	EMPSER	COV	EMPLOY	HOUSE	3789.96	-1915.99	.	.	1.15	-6.41	.
10	EMPSER	COV	SERVICES	HOUSE	3789.96	-1294.94	.	.	-6.41	134.49	.

TYPE=RAM Data Sets

The CALIS procedure creates and accepts as input a TYPE=RAM data set. This data set contains the model specification and the computed parameter estimates. A TYPE=RAM data set is intended to be reused as an input data set to specify good initial values in a subsequent analysis by PROC CALIS. See Chapter 14, "The CALIS Procedure," for details.

TYPE=DISTANCE Data Sets

A TYPE=DISTANCE data set is created only in a DATA step by reading or computing a lower triangular or symmetric matrix of dissimilarity values, such as a chart of mileage between cities. The number of observations must be equal to the number of variables used in the analysis. This type of data set is used as input only by the CLUSTER procedure. PROC CLUSTER ignores the upper triangular portion of a TYPE= DISTANCE data set, and assumes that all main diagonal values are zero, even if they are missing. See **Example 1** in Chapter 18, "The CLUSTER Procedure," for an example and details.

TYPE=FACTOR Data Sets

A TYPE=FACTOR data set is created by PROC FACTOR when the OUTSTAT= option is specified. PROC FACTOR and PROC SCORE can use TYPE=FACTOR data sets as input. The variables are the same as in a TYPE=CORR data set. The statistics include means, standard deviations, sample size, correlations, eigenvalues, eigenvectors, factor pattern, residual correlations, scoring coefficients, and others depending on the options specified. See Chapter 21, "The FACTOR Procedure," for details.

When the NOINT option is used with the OUTSTAT= option in PROC FACTOR, the value of the _TYPE_ variable is set to USCORE instead of SCORE to indicate that the scoring coefficients have not been corrected for the mean. If this data set is used with the SCORE procedure, the value of the _TYPE_ variable tells PROC SCORE whether or not to subtract the mean from the scoring coefficients.

TYPE=LINEAR Data Sets

A TYPE=LINEAR data set contains the coefficients of a linear function of the variables in observations with _TYPE_='LINEAR'.

The DISCRIM procedure stores linear discriminant function coefficients in a TYPE=LINEAR data set when METHOD=NORMAL (the default method), POOL=YES, and OUTSTAT= are specified; the data set can be used in a subsequent invocation of DISCRIM to classify additional observations. Many other statistics may be included depending on the options used. See **Output Data Sets** in Chapter 20, "The DISCRIM Procedure," for details.

TYPE=QUAD Data Sets

A TYPE=QUAD data set contains the coefficients of a quadratic function of the variables in observations with _TYPE_='QUAD'.

The DISCRIM procedure stores quadratic discriminant function coefficients in a TYPE=QUAD data set when METHOD=NORMAL (the default method), POOL=NO, and OUTSTAT= are specified; the data set can be used in a subsequent invocation of DISCRIM to classify additional observations. Many other statistics may be included depending on the options used. See **Output Data Sets** in Chapter 20 for details.

TYPE=MIXED Data Sets

A TYPE=MIXED data set contains coefficients of either a linear or a quadratic function, or both if there are BY groups.

The DISCRIM procedure produces a TYPE=MIXED data set when METHOD=NORMAL (the default method), POOL=TEST, and OUTSTAT= are specified. See **Output Data Sets** in Chapter 20 for details.

TYPE=TREE Data Sets

A TYPE=TREE data set is created by the CLUSTER procedure and is used as input to the TREE procedure. PROC TREE uses the TYPE=TREE data set to draw a tree diagram or output clusters at a specified level of the tree. See Chapter 18, "The CLUSTER Procedure," and Chapter 41, "The TREE Procedure," describing the CLUSTER and TREE procedures for details.

TYPE=ACE Data Sets

A TYPE=ACE data set is created by the ACECLUS procedure and contains the approximate within-cluster covariance estimate, as well as eigenvalues and eigenvectors from a canonical analysis, among other statistics. It can be used as input to the ACECLUS procedure to initialize another execution of PROC ACECLUS. It can also be used to compute canonical variable scores with the SCORE procedure, and as input to the FACTOR procedure, specifying METHOD=SCORE, to rotate the canonical variables. See Chapter 12, "The ACECLUS Procedure," for details.

Definitional Formulas

This section contrasts corrected and uncorrected SSCP, COV, and CORR matrices by showing how these matrices can be computed.

In the following formulas, assume that the data consist of two variables, X and Y, with n observations.

$$SSCP = \begin{bmatrix} n & \Sigma X & \Sigma Y \\ \Sigma X & \Sigma X^2 & \Sigma XY \\ \Sigma Y & \Sigma XY & \Sigma Y^2 \end{bmatrix}$$

$$CSSCP = \begin{bmatrix} \Sigma(X - \overline{X})^2 & \Sigma(X - \overline{X})(Y - \overline{Y}) \\ \Sigma(X - \overline{X})(Y - \overline{Y}) & \Sigma(Y - \overline{Y})^2 \end{bmatrix}$$

$$COV = CSSCP / (n - 1) = \begin{bmatrix} \Sigma(X - \overline{X})^2 / (n - 1) & \Sigma(X - \overline{X})(Y - \overline{Y}) / (n - 1) \\ \Sigma(X - \overline{X})(Y - \overline{Y}) / (n - 1) & \Sigma(Y - \overline{Y})^2 / (n - 1) \end{bmatrix}$$

$$UCOV = \begin{bmatrix} \Sigma X^2 / n & \Sigma XY / n \\ \Sigma XY / n & \Sigma Y^2 / n \end{bmatrix}$$

$$CORR = \begin{bmatrix} 1 & \dfrac{\Sigma(X - \overline{X})(Y - \overline{Y})}{\sqrt{\Sigma(X - \overline{X})^2 \Sigma(Y - \overline{Y})^2}} \\ \dfrac{\Sigma(X - \overline{X})(Y - \overline{Y})}{\sqrt{\Sigma(X - \overline{X})^2 \Sigma(Y - \overline{Y})^2}} & 1 \end{bmatrix}$$

$$UCORR = \begin{bmatrix} 1 & \dfrac{\Sigma XY}{\sqrt{\Sigma X^2 \Sigma Y^2}} \\ \dfrac{\Sigma XY}{\sqrt{\Sigma X^2 \Sigma Y^2}} & \end{bmatrix}$$

Index

A

a priori zeros 463
ABSOLUTE option
  ACECLUS procedure 196
  PROC ACECLUS statement 196
ABSORB statement
  and BY statement (ANOVA) 215
  and BY statement (GLM) 903, 904
  and INT option (ANOVA) 215
  and INT option (GLM) 903
  ANOVA procedure 214, 215
  GLM procedure 900, 903
absorbing variables in models 903
absorption
  GLM procedure 937–939
  memory requirements 938
accelerated failure time models 106,
    997–998
ACECLUS procedure 189–207
  See also "Changes and Enhancements"
  ABSOLUTE option 196
  BY statement 198
  compared with other procedures 54, 193
  computational resources 201
  controlling iterations 191, 197
  CONVERGE= option 196
  DATA= option 196
  example 202–207
  FREQ statement 199
  INITIAL= option 196
  initial estimates 191, 196
  MAXITER= option 196
  memory requirements 201
  methods 190
  METRIC option 196
  missing values 200
  N= option 196
  NOPRINT option 196
  OUT= option 196
  output data sets 197, 200
  OUTSTAT= option 196
  PP option 196
  PREFIX= option 196
  printed output 201–202
  PROC ACECLUS statement 195
  QQ option 196
  SHORT option 196
  SINGULAR= option 196
  syntax summary 195
  time requirements 201
  VAR statement 199
  WEIGHT statement 199

ACOV option
  MODEL statement (REG) 1363
actual model syntax
  defined, LOGISTIC procedure 1079
ACTUAL option
  MODEL statement (RSREG) 1462
actuarial estimates
  See life table estimates
ADD statement
  REG procedure 1357, 1358, 1360
ADDCELL= option
  and output, CATMOD procedure 473
  MODEL statement (CATMOD) 426
  using, CATMOD procedure 463
ADDITIVE option
  OUTPUT statement (TRANSREG)
    1536–1537
adjacent-category logits
  See also response functions
  specifying in CATMOD procedure 433
  using, CATMOD procedure 446
adjacent-level contrasts
  repeated measurements (ANOVA) 225
  repeated measurements (GLM) 925
ADJRSQ option
  MODEL statement (REG) 1363
ADJRSQ selection method, REG procedure
    1399
adjusted chi-square value (CALIS) 303
adjusted goodness-of-fit index (CALIS) 303
adjusted means 908–909, 948–949
adjusted R-square statistic
  CANCORR procedure 376
adjusted sums of squares
  See Type II SS
  See also Type III SS
  See also Type IV SS
ADPREFIX= option
  OUTPUT statement (TRANSREG) 1536,
    1537
agglomerative hierarchical clustering
    analysis 520
AIC option
  MODEL statement (REG) 1363
AIPREFIX= option
  OUTPUT statement (TRANSREG) 1536,
    1537
Akaike's Information criterion (AIC)
  CALIS procedure 304
  FACTOR procedure 798
  LOGISTIC procedure 1088–1089
algorithms
  LOGISTIC procedure 1088

ALL option
  CORRESP procedure 622
  FACTOR procedure 780
  MODEL statement (REG) 1363
  PROC CALIS statement 261
  PROC CANCORR statement 370
  PROC CANDISC statement 390
  PROC CORRESP statement 621
  PROC DISCRIM statement 687
  PROC FACTOR statement 781
  PROC REG statement 1359
  PROC STEPDISC statement 1497
  TABLES statement (FREQ) 858
ALL
  in H= specification, MANOVA statement
    (GLM) 910
  in H= specification, MANOVA statement
    (ANOVA) 216–217
ALL_PARMS
  CONTRAST statement (CATMOD) 419
ALLCATS option
  and COEFFICIENTS option (TRANSREG)
    1532
  MODEL statement (TRANSREG) 1531,
    1532
  with NOINT and CLASS, TRANSREG
    procedure 1534
ALOGITS function
  RESPONSE statement (CATMOD) 433
ALPHA= option
  MEANS statement (ANOVA) 220
  MEANS statement (GLM) 914
  MODEL statement (GLM) 918
  OUTPUT statement (LOGISTIC) 1085
  PROC LIFETEST statement 1038
  TABLES statement (FREQ) 859
alpha factor analysis 774, 782
alternating least squares
  TRANSREG procedure 1513–1514
alternating least squares
  VARCLUS procedure 1643
analyse des correspondances 616
analysis of covariance
  See also least-squares means
  adjusted means 908–909, 948–949
  MODEL statements (GLM) 896
  NESTED procedure 1130
  with GLM procedure 973–975
analysis-of-median scores 1198
analysis of variance
  See also ANOVA procedure
  See also NPAR1WAY procedure
  See also TTEST procedure
  analysis of covariance (GLM) 973–975
  and linear models 22
  categorical data 407
  CATMOD procedure 409
  definition 22
  description of analysis 22
  doubly-multivariate repeated measures,
    using GLM 988–993
  mixed models (GLM) 986–988

MODEL statements (ANOVA) 213–214
MODEL statements (GLM) 896
multivariate (ANOVA) 216–219
multivariate (GLM) 910–913, 949–951,
  978–982
nested design 1127–1133
nominal data, with CATMOD procedure
  26
nonparametric 26–27
nonparametric analogues 25
of proportions, with CATMOD procedure
  26
ordinal data, with CATMOD procedure 26
overview of SAS procedures for 21–28
PROC ANOVA for balanced designs 23
PROC CATMOD for categorical variables
  26
PROC GLM for unbalanced designs 23–24
quadratic response surfaces 1458
reduction notation 111
repeated measures (GLM) 951–958,
  982–986
repeated measures, in CATMOD
  procedure 449–452
three-way design (GLM) 976–978
two-way design (GLM) 972–973
using GLM procedure 898–899
with TRANSREG procedure 1513,
  1565–1566
within-subject factors (GLM) 926
within-subject factors, repeated
  measurements 226
analysis-of-variance procedures 21–28
analyzing binary response data
  PROBIT procedure 1325–1326, 1335, 1340
analyzing data in groups
  ACECLUS procedure 198
  ANOVA procedure 215
  CALIS procedure 273
  CANCORR procedure 373
  CANDISC procedure 393
  CATMOD procedure 417
  DISCRIM procedure 693
  FACTOR procedure 788–789
  FASTCLUS procedure 829
  GLM procedure 904
  LOGISTIC procedure 1078–1079
  NESTED procedure 1129
  NPAR1WAY procedure 1198
  ORTHOREG procedure 1212
  PRINCOMP procedure 1245
  PRINQUAL procedure 1279
  SCORE procedure 1482
  STEPDISC procedure 1499
  TRANSREG procedure 1523
  TREE procedure 1618
  VARCLUS procedure 1647–1648
  VARCOMP procedure 1663
analyzing multilevel response data
  PROBIT procedure 1325–1326, 1335, 1344

ANOVA option
    PRINT statement (REG) 1378–1379
    PROC CANDISC statement 390
    PROC DISCRIM statement 687
    PROC NPAR1WAY statement 1197
ANOVA procedure 209–244
    See also "Changes and Enhancements"
    ABSORB statement 214, 215
    and GLM procedure 894
    at (@) notation 212
    automatic pooling 213
    bar (|) notation 212
    BY statement 210, 214, 215
    CLASS statement 214, 216
    compared with other procedures 21–22
    computational methods 228
    examples 229–243
    FREQ statement 214, 216
    interactivity, and missing values 210, 227
    MANOVA statement 214, 216–219
    MEANS statement 214, 219–223
    memory requirements 228
    missing values 227
    MODEL statement 214, 223
    output data sets 227–228
    positional requirements for statements 214
    printed output 228–229
    PROC ANOVA statement 214
    repeated measurements analysis 223–226
    REPEATED statement 214, 223–226
    specification of effects 211–213
    summary of statistical method 23
    syntax summary 214
    TEST statement 214, 226–227
    using interactively 210
    WHERE statement 210
ANOVA statistic 874
AOV option
    PROC NESTED statement 1129
appropriate scoring 616
approximate covariance estimation
    clustering 189
approximate t statistic 1636
approximations
    Cochran and Cox 1633, 1634, 1636
    Satterthwaite's 1633, 1636
APPROXIMATIONS option
    and output data set (PRINQUAL) 1288
    OUTPUT statement (TRANSREG) 1536,
        1537
    PROC PRINQUAL statement 1275
APREFIX= option
    and output data set (PRINQUAL) 1291
    PROC PRINQUAL statement 1275
ARSIN transform
    and missing values (PRINQUAL) 1285
    and missing values (TRANSREG) 1540
    MODEL statement (TRANSREG) 1524,
        1526
    TRANSFORM statement (PRINQUAL)
        1280, 1281

arcsine transformation
    PRINQUAL procedure 1280, 1281
    TRANSREG procedure 1524, 1526
association
    rows and columns 616
asymptotic standard errors 860
at (@) notation
    See also "Changes and Enhancements"
    ANOVA procedure 212
    CATMOD procedure 412
    GLM procedure 897
AUGMENT option
    PROC CALIS statement 261
automatic pooling in ANOVA procedure 213
automatic variables
    NLIN procedure 1147–1149
average linkage
    compared with other clustering methods
        56–97
    with CLUSTER procedure 522, 530
AVERAGED models
    CATMOD procedure 456–459
AVERAGED option
    MODEL statement (CATMOD) 426

B

B option
    MODEL statement (REG) 1364
    PROC CANCORR statement 370
B-splines
    See spline transformations
backward selection
    LOGISTIC procedure 1076
    REG procedure 1398
balanced data, definition 210
balanced designs 1128
    and ANOVA procedure 23
    definition 23
bar (|) notation
    ANOVA procedure 212
    CATMOD procedure 412–413
    GLM procedure 897
Bayes' theorem
    DISCRIM procedure 680
BCORR option
    PROC CANDISC statement 390
    PROC DISCRIM statement 687
    PROC STEPDISC statement 1497
BCOV option
    PROC CANDISC statement 391
    PROC DISCRIM statement 687
    PROC STEPDISC statement 1497
Behrens-Fisher problem 1633
Bentler & Bonnett's normed coefficient
    (CALIS) 304
Bentler's comparative fit index (CFI) (CALIS)
    304
BEST= option
    MODEL statement (REG) 1364
    PROC NLIN statement 1138

BEST variables
    CORRESP procedure 648-649
BETA= option
    PROC CLUSTER statement 523
beta distribution
    testing for fit of 126
between-subject effects
    repeated measures analysis 953
between-subject factors
    repeated measures analysis 923
BFGS update method specification
    PROC CALIS statement 271
BIASKUR option
    PROC CALIS statement 261
BIC option
    MODEL statement (REG) 1364
bimodality coefficient
    formula, for CLUSTER procedure 561
    printed in CLUSTER procedure 527
binary design matrix, definition 646
binary indicator variable 645
binomial distribution
    for contingency tables 31
biological assay data 1325, 1337
biplots
    creating 1292-1302
    interpreting 1300
biweight kernel method
    DISCRIM procedure 678, 682
    formulas 682
blocked analysis
    for contingency tables 33
Bollen's nonnormed index Delta2 (CALIS)
        305
Bollen's normed index Rho1 (CALIS) 305
BON option
    MEANS statement (ANOVA) 220
    MEANS statement (GLM) 914, 943
Bonferroni t-tests 220, 914, 943
    and Scheffe's multiple comparison
            method 944
botryology
    See clustering
BOUNDS statement
    CALIS procedure 272
    NLIN procedure 1140-1141
Box's epsilon 954
Breslow's test for homogeneity 859, 877
Brown-Mood test 1196, 1198
BSSCP option
    PROC CANDISC statement 391
    PROC DISCRIM statement 688
    PROC STEPDISC statement 1497
Burt tables
    CORRESP procedure 628
    definition 625
    illustration 642
BY statement
    ACECLUS procedure 198-199
    and ABSORB statement (ANOVA) 215
    and ABSORB statement (GLM) 903, 904
    ANOVA procedure 210, 214, 215

CALIS procedure 273
CANCORR procedure 369, 373-374
CANDISC procedure 389, 393
CATMOD procedure 415, 417
CLUSTER procedure 521, 527-528
CORRESP procedure 627-628
DISCRIM procedure 686, 693
FACTOR procedure 779, 788-789
FASTCLUS procedure 829
FREQ procedure 857
GLM procedure 895, 900, 904
LIFEREG procedure 1001
LIFETEST procedure 1041
LOGISTIC procedure 1077, 1078-1079
NESTED procedure 1129
NLIN procedure 1141
NPAR1WAY procedure 1197, 1198
ORTHOREG procedure 1212
PRINCOMP procedure 1243, 1245-1246
PRINQUAL procedure 1273, 1279
PROBIT procedure 1330
REG procedure 1357, 1358, 1360-1361
RSREG procedure 1461
SCORE procedure 1482
STEPDISC procedure 1495, 1499
TRANSREG procedure 1520, 1523
TREE procedure 1618
TTEST procedure 1634
VARCLUS procedure 1647-1648
VARCOMP procedure 1662, 1663
BYOUT option
    MODEL statement (RSREG) 1462

C

C= option, PROC PROBIT statement 1328
C option
    PROC CANCORR statement 370
    PROC VARCLUS statement 1644
C specification
    OUTPUT statement (LOGISTIC) 1084
calibration data set
    DISCRIM procedure 678
calibration information
    DISCRIM procedure 698
CALIS procedure 245-365
    See also regression procedures
    See also "Changes and Enhancements"
    BOUNDS statement 272
    BY statement 273
    compared with PRINCOMP procedure
        774
    compared with SYSLIN 138
    COSAN Model statement 273
    COV statement 275-276
    examples 307-363
    FACTOR statement 276
    FREQ statement 278
    introduction 137-187
    LINEQS statement 278
    MATRIX statement 279

missing values   291
    PARAMETERS statement   281
    PARTIAL statement   281
    printed output   302-306
    PROC CALIS statement   260
    RAM statement   283
    STD statement   284
    VAR statement   285
    VARNAMES statement   285
    WEIGHT statement   286
CANALS method
    and output data sets (TRANSREG)   1552
    specifying in TRANSREG procedure   1532
CANCORR procedure   39, 367-385
    See also "Changes and Enhancements"
    BY statement   369, 373-374
    computational resources   376
    example   379-384
    FREQ statement   369, 374
    missing values   375
    output data sets   371, 375-376
    PARTIAL statement   369, 374
    printed output   377-379
    PROC CANCORR statement   369-373
    statistical methods used   368-369
    statistics computed   369-373, 377-379
    syntax summary   369
    time requirements   376
    VAR statement   369, 374
    WEIGHT statement   369, 374
    WITH statement   369, 375
CANDISC procedure   45, 46, 387-404
    See also "Changes and Enhancements"
    BY statement   389, 393
    CLASS statement   389, 393
    computational resources   397
    example   399-404
    FREQ statement   389, 393
    input data sets   394-395
    memory requirements   397
    methods   387-389
    missing values   394
    OUT= data sets   391, 395
    output data sets   395-397
    OUTSTAT= data sets   391, 395-397
    printed output   398-399
    PROC CANDISC statement   390
    syntax summary   389
    time requirements   397
    VAR statement   389, 394
    WEIGHT statement   389, 394
canonical analysis
    for MANOVA statement (ANOVA)   218
    MANOVA statement (GLM)   911
    repeated measurements (ANOVA)   225
    repeated measurements (GLM)   925
    response surfaces, RSREG procedure
        1458-1459, 1466
canonical coefficients
    printing   377
    raw, TRANSREG procedure   1537

standardized and unstandardized   368,
    376, 378
canonical correlation   1533
canonical correlation analysis
    definition   40
    using TRANSREG procedure   1512
canonical correlation coefficients
    TRANSREG procedure   1537
canonical correlations   367, 368
    CANCORR procedure   377
canonical discriminant analysis   46, 387-404,
    678
canonical elliptical coordinates
    TRANSREG procedure   1537
canonical factor solution   778
CANONICAL option
    MANOVA statement (ANOVA)   218
    MANOVA statement (GLM)   911
    PROC DISCRIM statement   688
    REPEATED statement (ANOVA)   225
    REPEATED statement (GLM)   925, 954
canonical point model coordinates
    TRANSREG procedure   1537
canonical quadratic coordinates
    TRANSREG procedure   1538
canonical redundancy analysis   368, 369,
    372, 378
CANPREFIX= option
    PROC DISCRIM statement   688
CANPRINT option
    MTEST statement (REG)   1370
CAPABILITY procedure
    using to test for distributions   126
case-control studies
    logit confidence interval   876
    logit estimator   876
    Mantel-Haenszel confidence interval
        875-876
    Mantel-Haenszel estimator   875-876
    relative risk estimates   871
categorical analysis
    procedures for   29-38
categorical data analysis
    See also CATMOD procedure
categorical variable
    definition   26
categorical variables
    See classification variables
CATMOD procedure   29, 46, 405-517
    See also "Changes and Enhancements"
    See also regression procedures
    analysis of variance   26
    at (@) notation   412, 413
    AVERAGED models   456-459
    bar (|) notation   412
    BY statement   415, 417
    cautions   462-465
    compared with other procedures   21-22
    compared with FREQ procedure   35
    compared with LOGISTIC procedure
        35-38, 446
    compared with PROBIT procedure   35-38

CATMOD procedure (continued)
  computational method 465–466
  CONTRAST statement 415, 417–420
  direct input of design matrix 428–429
  DIRECT statement 415, 420–421
  effective sample sizes 462
  estimation methods 413–414
  examples 473–516
  FACTORS statement 415, 421–424
  formulas 467–470
  generating design matrix 452–462
  hypothesis testing 411, 464–465
  input data sets 441
  interactive use 414–415
  log-linear analysis 447–449
  logistic analysis 446–447
  LOGLIN statement 415, 424
  memory requirements 471
  missing values 441
  MODEL statement 415, 425
  modelling methods, compared 414
  notation 466
  ordering of parameters 456
  ordering of populations 443–444
  ordering of responses 443–444
  output data sets 434, 444–445
  parameter estimation 411
  parameterization, compared with GLM
      procedure 931
  POPULATION statement 415, 429–431
  positional requirements for statements 415
  printed output 471–473
  PROC CATMOD statement 415, 417
  relaxing sampling assumptions 34–35
  repeated measurement factors 431–433
  repeated measures analysis 449–452
  REPEATED statement 415, 431–433
  response functions and estimation
      methods 433
  RESPONSE statement 415, 433–440
  RESTRICT statement 415, 440
  restrictions on parameters 440
  singular covariance matrix 463
  specification of effects 411–413
  specifying response functions 433–440
  syntax summary 415
  time requirements 471
  types of analysis 407, 408–411
  types of input data 408
  underlying model 413–414
  WEIGHT statement 415, 440
  zeros, structural and sampling 463
causal model 144
CBAR specification
  OUTPUT statement (LOGISTIC) 1084
CCC option
  and output data sets (TRANSREG) 1554
  OUTPUT statement (TRANSREG) 1536,
      1537
  PROC CLUSTER statement 523

CCONVERGE= option
  and iterations (PRINQUAL) 1286
  and iterations (TRANSREG) 1541
  MODEL statement (TRANSREG) 1531,
      1532
  PROC PRINQUAL statement 1275
CD update method specification
  PROC CALIS statement 272
CDF= option
  OUTPUT statement (LIFEREG) 1006
CDF
  See cumulative distribution function
CEC option
  and output data sets (TRANSREG) 1554
  OUTPUT statement (TRANSREG) 1536,
      1537
cell in a design
  as represented by PLAN procedure 1230
  definition 1221
CELLCHI2 option
  CORRESP procedure 622
  PROC CORRESP statement 623
  TABLES statement (FREQ) 859
cells, in a contingency table
  definition 30
CENSORED= option
  OUTPUT statement (LIFEREG) 1006
censored accelerated failure models
  example of (NLIN) 1175–1181
censored data 997
censoring 997, 1009, 1028, 1043
  interval 105
  left 105
  LIFEREG procedure 1002
  right 105, 1027
CENTER= option
  RIDGE statement (RSREG) 1464
centroid cluster components example 1653
centroid components 1641–1643
  definition 1641
  VARCLUS procedure 1642
centroid method
  with CLUSTER procedure 522, 530
CENTROID option
  PROC VARCLUS statement 1644
centroid sorting
  See centroid method
CER, definition 943
CES production function
  example of (NLIN) 1159–1160
chaining, reducing when clustering 527
CHANGE= option
  PROC PRINQUAL statement 1276
characteristic roots and vectors
  printing in ANOVA procedure 216–217,
      226
  printing in GLM procedure 910, 926
chi-square statistic 865, 1326, 1328, 1329,
      1332, 1333, 1335, 1337, 1339
  CORRESP procedure 620
  FREQ procedure 855

chi-square test   128
   FREQ procedure   859
CHISQ option
   TABLES statement (FREQ)   859
circular ideal point regression
   TRANSREG procedure   1526
circular response surface
   with POINT (TRANSREG)   1526
CLASS expansion variables
   definition, TRANSREG procedure   1525
CLASS statement
   See also "Changes and Enhancements"
      (PROBIT)
   ANOVA procedure   214, 216
   CANDISC procedure   389, 393
   DISCRIM procedure   686, 694
   GLM procedure   900, 904
   LIFEREG procedure   1001
   NESTED procedure   1129
   NPAR1WAY procedure   1197, 1199
   PROBIT procedure   1330
   STEPDISC procedure   1495, 1499
   TTEST procedure   1635
   VARCOMP procedure   1662, 1663
CLASS transform
   and CPREFIX= option (TRANSREG)   1537
   and output data sets (TRANSREG)   1537
   MODEL statement (TRANSREG)   1524,
      1525
   with ALLCATS and NOINT, TRANSREG
      procedure   1534
   with INTERCEPT, TRANSREG procedure
      1535
classification clumping
   See clustering
classification criterion
   DISCRIM procedure   678
classification error-rate estimates
   DISCRIM procedure   684-685
classification variables
   definition   22, 30, 210, 211, 895
   for fixed or random effects   22
classificatory discriminant analysis   45
classifying observations
   LOGISTIC procedure   1091-1092
CLDIFF option
   MEANS statement (ANOVA)   220, 234
   MEANS statement (GLM)   914
CLEAR option
   PLOT statement (REG)   1377
CLI option
   MODEL statement (GLM)   918
   MODEL statement (REG)   1364
CLM option
   MEANS statement (ANOVA)   220
   MEANS statement (GLM)   914
   MODEL statement (GLM)   918, 970
   MODEL statement (REG)   1364
CLOGITS function
   RESPONSE statement (CATMOD)   433
CLUSTER= option
   FASTCLUS procedure   826
   PROC FASTCLUS statement   826

cluster analysis   46
   disjoint   823
   tree diagrams   1613-1614
cluster formation
   FASTCLUS procedure   823
CLUSTER procedure   519-614
   See also TREE procedure
   See also "Changes and Enhancements"
   algorithms   562
   and FASTCLUS procedure   520
   and TREE procedure   520
   BY statement   521, 527-528
   clustering methods   520, 529-536
   compared with FASTCLUS procedure   55
   compared with other procedures   54
   computational resources   563-564
   COPY statement   521, 528
   examples   568-613
   FREQ statement   521, 528
   ID statement   521, 528
   input data sets   524
   memory requirements   563
   missing values   564
   output data sets   526, 564-566
   printed output   566-568
   PROC CLUSTER statement   521-527
   RMSSTD statement   521, 529
   syntax summary   521
   test statistics   523, 526, 527
   ties   564
   time requirements   563
   types of data sets   520
   using macros for many analyses   589-613
   VAR statement   521, 529
cluster seeds   824
cluster structure   1653
clustering
   See also CLUSTER procedure
   and outliers   520, 527
   and smoothing parameters   532
   average linkage   522, 530
   centroid method   522, 530
   complete linkage method   522, 531
   deciding on number of clusters   97-99
   density linkage methods   522, 524, 525,
      526, 527, 531-533, 535
   disjoint   1641
   flexible-beta method   522, 523
   Gower's method   522, 534
   hierarchical   1641
   large data sets   823
   maximum-likelihood method   522, 526,
      533, 534
   McQuitty's similarity analysis   522, 534
   median method   522, 534
   methods affected by frequencies   528
   methods compared, clusters with varying
      dispersion   70-80
   methods compared, elongated multinormal
      clusters   80-91
   methods compared, multinormal clusters
      70-80

clustering (*continued*)
  methods compared, nonconvex clusters
      91–97
  methods compared, poorly-separated
      clusters 59–70
  methods compared, unequal-sized clusters
      70–80
  methods compared, well-separated clusters
      57–59
  methods for clustering observations 56–97
  nonparametric probability density
      estimation 133
  of observations 55–56, 519–614
  of variables 55
  overview of 53–101
  procedures for 54–55
  single linkage 522, 534–535
  standardizing variables 527
  transforming variables for 520
  two-stage density linkage 522
  types of clusters 53
  types of input data 54
  Ward's method 522, 535
  weighted average linkage 522, 534
clustering methods
  FASTCLUS procedure 824–825
clusters
  covariance estimation 189
  elliptical 189–190
  spherical 189–190
CMH option
  TABLES statement (FREQ) 859
CMH statistics 33, 35
CMH1 option
  TABLES statement (FREQ) 859
CMH2 option
  TABLES statement (FREQ) 859
Cochran and Cox approximation (TTEST)
      1633, 1634, 1636
  See also "Changes and Enhanceemnts"
COCHRAN option
  PROC TTEST statement 1634
Cochran-Mantel-Haenszel statistics 859,
      873–874
  See CMH statistics
coefficient alpha
  FACTOR procedure 799
coefficient partition
  output data sets (TRANSREG) 1516
COEFFICIENTS option
  and ALLCATS option (TRANSREG) 1532
  and output data sets (TRANSREG)
      1554–1556
  OUTPUT statement (TRANSREG) 1536,
      1537
cohort studies
  logit confidence interval 876
  logit estimator 876
  Mantel-Haenszel confidence interval 876
  Mantel-Haenszel estimator 876
  relative risk estimates 871

COLLECT option
  PLOT statement (REG) 1377
COLLIN option
  MODEL statement (REG) 1364
collinearity
  and TRANSREG procedure 1557
COLLINOINT option
  MODEL statement (REG) 1364
COLUMN= option
  CORRESP procedure 622
  PROC CORRESP statement 623, 639–641
common factor
  defined for factor analysis 775
common factor analysis 39
  common factor rotation 776
  Harris component analysis 776
  image component analysis 776
  interpreting 776
comparisons
  between means 1633, 1637–1638
  of variances 1633, 1636, 1637–1638
comparisons of proportions 865
comparisonwise error rate
  controlling 942
complementary log-log function
  LOGISTIC procedure 1087
complete linkage
  with CLUSTER procedure 522, 531
completely randomized design
  analyzing with ANOVA procedure 229–234
  estimable functions for 112–113
  generating with PLAN procedure
      1234–1235
COMPONENT option
  FACTOR statement (CALIS) 276
computational formulas
  LIFETEST procedure 1044
computational methods
  ANOVA procedure 228
  GLM procedure 961
  LIFEREG procedure 1008
  NESTED procedure 1131
  NLIN procedure 1151–1156
  REG procedure 1436
  RSREG procedure 1468–1469
computational resources
  ACECLUS procedure 201
  CANCORR procedure 376
  CLUSTER procedure 563
  CORRESP procedure 638
  DISCRIM procedure 703–704
  FACTOR procedure 797
  FASTCLUS procedure 831–832
  FREQ procedure 863
  GLM procedure 960–961
  LIFEREG procedure 1013
  LIFETEST procedure 1049–1050
  PRINQUAL procedure 1291
  REG procedure 1436
  STEPDISC procedure 1501
  TRANSREG procedure 1556–1557
  VARCLUS procedure 1651

conditional logistic analysis
CATMOD procedure 410
examples, CATMOD procedure 510–514
conditional logistic regression 1181
example of (NLIN) 1182–1187
confidence intervals
displacement diagnostics, LOGISTIC
procedure 1094
for event response (LOGISTIC) 1085, 1091
for mean, RSREG procedure 1463
from regression 16
hazard function 1046, 1048, 1049
in LOGISTIC procedure 1084
individual observation, RSREG procedure
1463
individual prediction (GLM) 921
mean prediction (GLM) 921
means 220, 914
NLIN procedure 1144, 1145
pairwise differences between means 220,
914
PDF 1046–1048
predicted values (GLM) 918
R-square, in CANCORR procedure 376,
378
SDF 1046, 1048
confidence limits
mean predicted values (GLM) 918
survival analysis 1046
CONGRA optimization technique
specification
PROC CALIS statement 266
conjoint analysis 42, 1512
example (TRANSREG) 1514–1516
syntax example 1534
TRANSREG procedure 1578–1597
connectedness method
See single linkage
consistent information criterion (CIC)
(CALIS) 304
constrained estimation
NLIN procedure 1140
contained effect 117
definition 117
contingency coefficient 859, 866
contingency tables
CORRESP procedure 617, 628
definition 30
FREQ procedure 854
measures of association 864–877
represented in CATMOD procedure 30
represented in FREQ procedure 30
continuity correction, Wilcoxon rank-sum
test 1202
continuity-adjusted chi-square 865
continuous variables
GLM procedure 895
continuous-by-class effects
GLM procedure 896
model parameterization in GLM
procedure 930

continuous-nesting-class effects
GLM procedure 896
model parameterization in GLM procedure
930–931
CONTRAST specification
REPEATED statement (ANOVA) 225
CONTRAST statement
and MANOVA statement (GLM) 910
and RANDOM statement (GLM) 922–923
and REPEATED statement (GLM) 924
CATMOD procedure 415, 417–420
examples (GLM) 964, 976
examples, CATMOD procedure 487–491,
498–501, 506–509
GLM procedure 900, 905–906
options (GLM) 905
CONTRAST transformation
REPEATED statement (GLM) 955
contrasts
comparing for CATMOD and GLM 419
repeated measurements (GLM) 924
repeated measurements, tables for (GLM)
926
contrasts, repeated measurements
analysis of variance tables for 226
contrasts, single-degree-of-freedom
for repeated measurements (ANOVA)
224–225
contrasts, specifying
CATMOD procedure 417–420
CONTROL= option
OUTPUT statement (LIFEREG) 1006
CONVERGE= option
ACECLUS procedure 196
and iterations (PRINQUAL) 1286
and iterations (TRANSREG) 1541
FACTOR procedure 780
FASTCLUS procedure 826
MODEL statement (LIFEREG) 1003
MODEL statement (LOGISTIC) 1080
MODEL statement (PROBIT) 1331
MODEL statement (TRANSREG) 1531,
1532
PROC ACECLUS statement 196
PROC FACTOR statement 781
PROC FASTCLUS statement 826
PROC NLIN statement 1138
PROC PRINQUAL statement 1275
convergence
TRANSREG procedure 1557–1558
convergence criterion
ACECLUS procedure 196
CATMOD procedure 427
FASTCLUS procedure 826
NLIN procedure 1138
TRANSREG procedure 1532
convergence, defining
PRINQUAL procedure 1286
TRANSREG procedure 1542
CONVERGEOBJ= option
PROC NLIN statement 1138

CONVERGEPARM= option
  PROC NLIN statement 1138–1139
COOKD= option
  OUTPUT statement (REG) 1371
COOKD specification
  OUTPUT statement (GLM) 921
Cook's *D* 17
Cook's D statistic 1463
  saving in GLM procedure 921
COORDINATES option
  and output data sets (TRANSREG)
      1554–1556
  OUTPUT statement (TRANSREG) 1536,
      1537
COPY statement
  CLUSTER procedure 521, 528
  TREE procedure 1618
CORR data sets
  CLUSTER procedure 524
CORR option
  FACTOR procedure 780
  PROC CALIS statement 262
  PROC CANCORR statement 370
  PROC FACTOR statement 781
  PROC REG statement 1359
  PROC VARCLUS statement 1644
CORR procedure
  See also "Changes and Enhancements"
  and PRINQUAL procedure 1305
CORRB option
  and output, CATMOD procedure 472
  MODEL statement (CATMOD) 426
  MODEL statement (LIFEREG) 1003
  MODEL statement (LOGISTIC) 1081
  MODEL statement (PROBIT) 1331
  MODEL statement (REG) 1364
  PROC CANCORR statement 371
correlation matrix 246
  estimated, CATMOD procedure 426
  fitting a model (CALIS) 140
  of parameter estimates, LOGISTIC
      procedure 1081
correlation statistic (df=1) 874
correlations
  CANCORR procedure 370, 371, 375, 376
CORRELATIONS option
  and output data set (PRINQUAL) 1288
  and principal components 1250
  PROC PRINQUAL statement 1275
CORRESP procedure 29, 39, 615–674
  See also "Changes and Enhancements"
  algorithm 639
  ALL option 622
  BY statement 627–628
  CELLCHI2 option 622
  chi-square statistic 620
  COLUMN= option 622
  compared with others 41–42
  computational resources 638
  CP option 622, 623
  creating data sets 635–636
  CROSS= option 622, 629

DATA= option 622
DEVIATION option 622, 624
DIMENS= option 622, 629
examples 652–673
EXPECTED option 622, 624
FREQOUT option 622, 624, 632
ID statement 628
ID statement cautions 621
input data sets 634–635
introductory example 616–620
invalid data 634
MCA option 622, 625
MININERTIA= option 622, 625
missing data 634
MISSING option 622, 625
multiple correspondence analysis 625,
    641–644
multiple correspondence analysis, example
    659–665
NOCOLUMN option 622, 625
NOPRINT option 622, 625
NOROW option 622, 625
NVARS= option 622, 625
OBSERVED option 622, 625
OUTC= option 622, 625
OUTF= option 622, 626
output data sets 636–637
plotting cautions 617
plotting symbols 620
PRINT= option 622, 626
printed output 650–652
printing options 622
PROC CORRESP statement 621
PROFILE= option 622, 626
ROW= option 622, 626
RP option 622, 627
scaling axes 617–618
SHORT option 622, 627, 629
simple correspondence analysis, examples
    652–659, 665–673
SINGULAR= option 622, 627
statistics that aid interpretation 648–649
SUPPLEMENTARY statement 628, 631
syntax abbreviations 621
syntax summary 621
TABLES statement 621, 628–632
VAR statement 621, 632–633
variable specification 628
WEIGHT statement 633–634
correspondence analysis 39, 41–42
  definition of 616
COSAN Model statement
  CALIS procedure 273
COSAN statement
  CALIS procedure 273–275
COV option
  and output, CATMOD procedure 471
  LSMEANS statement (GLM) 909
  MODEL statement (CATMOD) 426
  PROC PRINCOMP statement 1243–1244
COV statement
  CALIS procedure 275–276

COVAR= option
  MODEL statement (RSREG) 1462
covariance
  betas GLM procedure 921
covariance matrix 246
  fitting a model (CALIS) 140
  for parameter estimates, CATMOD
      procedure 426
  for response functions, CATMOD
      procedure 426
  for parameter estimates, LOGISTIC
      procedure 1081
  singular, in CATMOD procedure 463
COVARIANCE option
  and output data set (PRINQUAL) 1290
  FACTOR procedure 781
  PROC CALIS statement 262
  PROC FACTOR statement 781
  PROC PRINCOMP statement 1243-1244
  PROC PRINQUAL statement 1276
  PROC VARCLUS statement 1644
covariance structure analysis 137-187, 246
  See also CALIS procedure
  definition 137
  specification 141-145
covariances, and principal components
      1249, 1250
covariates
  GLM procedure 928
  LIFETEST procedure 1034-1037,
      1046-1048
  RSREG procedure 1459
COVB option
  and output, CATMOD procedure 472
  MODEL statement (CATMOD) 426
  MODEL statement (LIFEREG) 1004
  MODEL statement (LOGISTIC) 1081
  MODEL statement (PROBIT) 1332
  MODEL statement (REG) 1365
COVOUT option
  PROC LIFEREG statement 1000
  PROC LOGISTIC statement 1077
  PROC PROBIT statement 1328
  PROC REG statement 1359
COVRATIO= option
  OUTPUT statement (REG) 1371
COVRATIO specification
  OUTPUT statement (GLM) 921
Cox regression 1181
  example of (NLIN) 1187-1192
CP option
  CORRESP procedure 622
  MODEL statement (REG) 1365
  PROC CORRESP statement 623
CP selection method, REG procedure 1399
CPC option
  and output data sets (TRANSREG) 1554
  OUTPUT statement (TRANSREG) 1536,
      1537
CPREFIX= option
  OUTPUT statement (TRANSREG)
      1537-1538

CQC option
  and output data sets (TRANSREG) 1554
  OUTPUT statement (TRANSREG) 1536,
      1538
Cramer-von Mises statistic 126, 1196, 1201
Cramer's V 859, 866
creating data sets
  CORRESP procedure 635-636
CROSS= option
  CORRESP procedure 622, 629
  PROC CORRESP statement 623
crossed effects
  and design matrix, CATMOD procedure
      453
  model parameterization in GLM procedure
      928-929
  specifying in ANOVA procedure 211
  specifying in GLM procedure 411, 895
CROSSLIST option
  PROC DISCRIM statement 688
CROSSLISTERR option
  PROC DISCRIM statement 688
crossproducts matrix
  printing in GLM procedure 920
crosstabulation tables
  FREQ procedure 852-889
CROSSVALIDATE option
  PROC DISCRIM statement 688
CTABLE option
  MODEL statement (LOGISTIC) 1081
cubic clustering criterion 525, 527
  CLUSTER procedure 523
  definition 98
cubic polynomial transformation
  example 1284, 1530
cubic spline transformation
  example 1284, 1530
CUMCOL option
  TABLES statement (FREQ) 859
cumulative distribution function 1009-1010,
      1011, 1012, 1028, 1050, 1326, 1332,
      1336
cumulative logistic distribution function
  LOGISTIC procedure 1086
cumulative logits
  See also response functions
  examples, CATMOD procedure 447
  specifying in CATMOD procedure 433
  using, CATMOD procedure 446
Cureton-Mulaik technique
  example 813
custom scoring coefficients, example
      1490-1491
CVALS= option
  OUTPUT statement (PLAN) 1227
CYCLIC selection-type
  FACTORS statement (PLAN) 1225
  increment-number specification, PLAN
      procedure 1225
  initial-block specification, PLAN
      procedure 1225
  TREATMENTS statement (PLAN) 1229

D

D= option, MODEL statement (PROBIT)
1332
D option
MODEL statement (RSREG) 1463
DAPPROXIMATIONS option
OUTPUT statement (TRANSREG) 1536,
1538
DATA= data set
and OUT= data sets, PRINCOMP
procedure 1247
DATA= option
ACECLUS procedure 196
CORRESP procedure 622
FACTOR procedure 781
FASTCLUS procedure 826
OUTPUT statement (PLAN) 1227, 1230
PROC ACECLUS statement 196
PROC ANOVA statement 214
PROC CALIS statement 262
PROC CANCORR statement 371
PROC CANDISC statement 391
PROC CATMOD statement 417
PROC CLUSTER statement 524
PROC CORRESP statement 624
PROC FACTOR statement 781
PROC FASTCLUS statement 827
PROC FREQ statement 856
PROC GLM statement 902
PROC LIFEREG statement 1000
PROC LIFETEST statement 1038
PROC LOGISTIC statement 1077, 1078
PROC NESTED statement 1129
PROC NLIN statement 1139
PROC NPAR1WAY statement 1197
PROC ORTHOREG statement 1212
PROC PRINCOMP statement 1244
PROC PRINQUAL statement 1276
PROC PROBIT statement 1328
PROC REG statement 1359
PROC RSREG statement 1461
PROC SCORE statement 1481
PROC STEPDISC statement 1497
PROC TRANSREG statement 1523
PROC TREE statement 1615
PROC TTEST statement 1634
PROC VARCLUS statement 1644-1645
PROC VARCOMP statement 1662
TREE procedure 1615
data set indexing
See "Changes and Enhancements"
DBFGS update method specification
PROC CALIS statement 271
DDFP update method specification
PROC CALIS statement 271
DEGREE= t-option
MODEL statement (TRANSREG) 1529
TRANSFORM statement (PRINQUAL)
1284

degrees of freedom
CALIS procedure 293-294
FACTOR procedure 788
models with class variables (GLM) 931-932
DELETE= option
FASTCLUS procedure 826
PROC FASTCLUS statement 827
DELETE statement
REG procedure 1357, 1358, 1361
DEMPHAS= option
PROC CALIS statement 262
dendogram, definition 1613
dendritic method
See single linkage
density estimation 678
nonparametric 133
density linkage
compared with other clustering methods
56-97
with CLUSTER procedure 522, 524, 525,
526, 527, 531-533, 535
dependent effect, definition 211
dependent variable
in analysis of variance, definition 22, 210
DEPONLY option
MEANS statement (GLM) 915
DER statement
NLIN procedure 1141-1142
derivatives
NLIN procedure 1141-1142
DESCENDING option
TREE procedure 1615
design matrix
formulas, CATMOD procedure 469
design matrix generation, CATMOD
procedure 452-462
design of experiments
See experimental design
DETAILS option
MODEL statement (LOGISTIC) 1081
MODEL statement (REG) 1365
MTEST statement (REG) 1370
deviance residual
formulas, LOGISTIC procedure 1093-1094
DEVIATION option
CORRESP procedure 622
PROC CORRESP statement 624
TABLES statement (FREQ) 859
DFBETAs
formulas, LOGISTIC procedure 1094
DFBETAS specification
OUTPUT statement (LOGISTIC)
1084-1085
DFFITS= option
OUTPUT statement (REG) 1371
DFFITS specification
OUTPUT statement (GLM) 921
DFP update method specification
PROC CALIS statement 271
DFREDUCE= option
PROC CALIS statement 262

DIA specification
    COSAN Model statement (CALIS)   274
diagnostics
    for logistic regression, LOGISTIC
        procedure   1081, 1093
diameter method
    See complete linkage
DIFCHISQ specification
    OUTPUT statement (LOGISTIC)   1085
DIFDEV specification
    OUTPUT statement (LOGISTIC)   1085
DIM= option
    PROC CLUSTER statement   524
DIMENS= option
    CORRESP procedure   622, 629
    PROC CORRESP statement   624
direct effects
    and design matrix, CATMOD procedure
        455
    specifying in CATMOD procedure   455
DIRECT statement
    and logistic regression (CATMOD)   447
    CATMOD procedure   415, 420-421
discontinuities
    NLIN procedure   1151
discrete variables
    See classification variables
DISCRIM procedure   45-46, 677-771
    See also "Changes and Enhancements"
    analyzing data in groups   693
    BY statement   693
    calibration information   698
    CLASS statement   694
    computational resources   703-704
    examples   707-770
    FREQ statement   694
    ID statement   694
    input data sets   699-700
    memory requirements   704
    methods   678-685
    missing values   696
    nonparametric methods   681-684
    OUT= data sets   700-701
    output data sets   700-703
    output, printed   705-707
    OUTSTAT= data sets   701-703
    parametric methods   680
    PRIORS statement   694-695
    PROC DISCRIM statement   686
    syntax summary   686
    TESTCLASS statement   695
    TESTFREQ statement   695
    TESTID statement   695
    time requirements   704
    VAR statement   695
    WEIGHT statement   696
discriminant analysis
    assumptions   46
    canonical   46, 387-404
    classificatory   45
    compared with cluster analysis   46
    compared with logistic regression   46

definition   45
    nonparametric   133
    nonparametric methods in   45-46
    parametric methods in   45
    stepwise   46, 1493-1509
discriminant functions   388
discriminant procedures
    introduction   45-51
    references   50-51
disjoing clusters, definition   53
disjoint clustering   823-850, 1641
dissection, definition   53
DISSIMILAR option
    PROC TREE statement   1615
    TREE procedure   1615
DIST variable
    PROBIT procedure   1338
DISTANCE data sets
    CLUSTER procedure   524
DISTANCE option
    FASTCLUS procedure   826, 835
    PROC CANDISC statement   391
    PROC DISCRIM statement   688
    PROC FASTCLUS statement   827
DISTRIBUTION= option
    MODEL statement (LIFEREG)   1004
distributions
    binomial   31
    comparing for different groups   126
    exponential   1029
    extreme value   997-998, 1004, 1010-1011
    frequency tables, FREQ procedure   852
    gamma   997-998, 1004, 1010-1011
    Gompertz   1326, 1332, 1336
    hypergeometric   33
    logistic   997-998, 1004, 1010-1011, 1326,
        1332, 1336
    loglogistic   997-998, 1004, 1010-1011
    lognormal   997-998, 1004, 1010-1011
    multinomial   31
    multiple hypergeometric   33-34
    normal   997-998, 1004, 1010-1011, 1326,
        1332, 1336
    product multinomial   32
    testing a single sample for   126-127
    Weibull   997-998, 1004, 1010-1011, 1029
distributions allowed
    LIFEREG procedure   1010-1011
    PROBIT procedure   1336
divergence
    NLIN procedure   1150
DIVISOR= option
    ESTIMATE statement (GLM)   907
DOCK= option
    PROC TREE statement   1615
    TREE procedure   1615
dosage levels, example
    PROBIT procedure 1340-1344
DOT product   1479
double exponential distributions   1200
DREPLACE option
    OUTPUT statement (TRANSREG)   1536,
        1538

DRIFT option
  FASTCLUS procedure   826, 832
  PROC FASTCLUS statement   827
dual scaling   616
DUMMY option
  PROC PRINQUAL statement   1276
dummy variables
  and ALLCATS option (TRANSREG)   1532
  definition for TRANSREG procedure   1525
  use in TRANSREG procedure   1525
DUNCAN option
  MEANS statement (ANOVA)   221, 233
  MEANS statement (GLM)   915, 946
Duncan-Waller multiple comparison test
    223, 917, 947–948
Duncan's multiple-range test   221, 915, 946
DUNNETT option
  MEANS statement (ANOVA)   221
  MEANS statement (GLM)   915
DUNNETTL option
  MEANS statement (ANOVA)   221
  MEANS statement (GLM)   915
Dunnett's multiple comparison methods   945
Dunnett's test
  See also "Changes and Enhancements"
      (GLM)
  one-tailed lower   221, 915
  one-tailed upper   221, 915
  two-tailed   221, 915
DUNNETTU option
  MEANS statement (ANOVA)   221
  MEANS statement (GLM)   915
Durbin-Watson statistic
  formula   1434
DW option
  MODEL statement (REG)   1365

E

E= option
  CONTRAST statement (GLM)   905
  LSMEANS statement (GLM)   909
  MEANS statement (ANOVA)   221
  MEANS statement (GLM)   915
E= specification
  MANOVA statement (ANOVA)   217
  MANOVA statement (GLM)   910
  TEST statement (ANOVA)   226–227
  TEST statement (GLM)   927
E option
  CONTRAST statement (GLM)   905
  ESTIMATE statement (GLM)   907
  LSMEANS statement (GLM)   909
  MODEL statement (GLM)   918
EDF= option
  PROC CALIS statement   262
  PROC CANCORR statement   371
EDF
  See empirical distribution function

EDF option
  and memory requirements (NPAR1WAY)
      1199
  PROC NPAR1WAY statement   1198
EERC, definition   943
EERP, definition   943
effect, definition   895
effective sample size
  LIFETEST procedure   1044
effective zero
  PRINQUAL procedure   1278
  TRANSREG procedure   1534
effects
  contained in another   117
  definition   211
  definition, CATMOD procedure   411
  fixed   1661–1662, 1663, 1664–1665
  random   1661–1662, 1663, 1664–1665
EFORMAT option
  PROC NLIN statement   1139
eigenvalues
  and principal components   1242, 1249,
      1250
  RSREG procedure   1468–1469
  VARCLUS procedure   1643
EIGENVECTORS option
  FACTOR procedure   780
  PROC FACTOR statement   781
eigenvectors
  and principal components   1242, 1249,
      1250
  RSREG procedure   1468–1469
Einot and Gabriel multiple comparison tests
      222, 916, 947
elementary linkage analysis
  See single linkage
elliptical ideal point regression
  TRANSREG procedure   1525
elliptical preference surface
  with EPOINT (TRANSREG)   1525
elliptical response surface regression
  TRANSREG procedure   1525
empirical distribution function (EDF),
      definition   1201
endogenous variables   143, 150
  definition   138
Epanechnikov kernel method
  DISCRIM procedure   678, 682
  formulas   682
EPOINT transform
  MODEL statement (TRANSREG)   1524,
      1525
EPOINT variables, definition   1525
EPSILON= option
  MODEL statement (CATMOD)   427
  PROC VARCOMP statement   1662
EQS (equations) model   248
equality
  of means   1633, 1637–1638
  of variances   1633, 1636, 1637–1638
equamax method   774
equamax rotation   786

error rate estimation, discriminant analysis
    679
error sum-of-squares clustering method
    See Ward's method
ESS= option
    OUTPUT statement (NLIN)   1144
estimability 109–115, 894
    definition 109–110
estimability checking
    GLM procedure   905, 907, 909, 919, 941
estimability of hypotheses
    See estimable functions
estimable functions 109–124
    definition 110–111
    for Type I SS 115–116
    for Type II SS 116–120
    for Type III SS 120–122
    for Type IV SS 122–124
    form of Type II 117
    four types 109–124
    general form 110–115
    general form for main-effects model
        113–114
    general form for one-way model 112–113
    general form for regression 114–115
    generating set for 110–111
    GLM procedure 932–937
    printing (GLM) 918–919
    two-way design 932–933
    Type I 115–116
    Type II 116–120
    Type III 120–122
    Type IV 122–124
ESTIMATE statement
    GLM procedure   900, 907, 939–941
    options (GLM) 907
estimating missing values
    PRINQUAL procedure   1278, 1285,
        1302–1322
    TRANSREG procedure   1533, 1540
ETYPE= option
    CONTRAST statement (GLM)   905
    LSMEANS statement (GLM)   909
    MANOVA statement (GLM)   911
    MEANS statement (GLM)   915
    TEST statement (GLM)   927
Euclidean distances   525, 526, 823
    DISCRIM procedure   678
    in clustering   520
events/trials model syntax
    defined, LOGISTIC procedure   1079
EXACT option
    TABLES statement (FREQ)   859–860
exogenous variables   143, 149
    definition   138
EXP transform
    and missing values (PRINQUAL) 1285
    and missing values (TRANSREG) 1540
    MODEL statement (TRANSREG) 1524,
        1526
    TRANSFORM statement (PRINQUAL)
        1280, 1281

expected mean squares
    random effects 958–959
EXPECTED option
    CORRESP procedure   622
    PROC CORRESP statement   624
    TABLES statement (FREQ)   860
experimental design
    See also factors in a design
    See also PLAN procedure
    See also treatments in a design
    SAS software for   27
experimentwise error rate
    controlling   942
    definition   942
exponential distributions
    and comparing groups 1198
    double 1200
    LIFEREG procedure 1004
    testing for fit of 126
exponential scores test 133
exponential transformation
    PRINQUAL procedure 1280, 1281
    TRANSREG procedure 1524, 1526
external unfolding analysis 1525
extreme value distributions
    LIFEREG procedure 997–998, 1004, 1010
    location shifts 1200
extreme-value function
    LOGISTIC procedure 1087
E1 option
    MODEL statement (GLM)   918
E2 option
    MODEL statement (GLM)   919
E3 option
    MODEL statement (GLM)   919
E4 option
    MODEL statement (GLM)   919

F

F statistics
    in CLUSTER procedure   526, 561–562
_F_
    MODEL statement (CATMOD)   425
factor
    defined for factor analysis 774
factor analysis
    and MAC algorithm, PRINQUAL
        procedure 1288
    CALIS procedure 276–277
    compared with component analysis 774
    definition 39
    multiple group 1642
    rotation methods 786
FACTOR procedure   39, 773–821
    See also "Changes and Enhancements"
    See also common factor analysis
    ALL option 780
    and PRINQUAL procedure 1305
    BY statement   779, 788–789

FACTOR procedure (*continued*)
  compared with PRINCOMP procedure
    40–41
  computational resources 797
  CONVERGE= option 780
  CORR option 780
  COVARIANCE option 780
  DATA= option 780
  EIGENVECTORS option 780
  examples 800–820, 1293–1303
  factor scores 794
  FLAG= option 780
  FREQ statement 779, 789
  FUZZ= option 780
  GAMMA= option 780
  Heywood cases 796
  HEYWOOD option 780
  HKPOWER= option 780
  input data sets 790
  MAXITER= option 780
  METHOD= option 780
  MINEIGEN= option 780
  missing values 793
  MSA option 780
  NFACTORS= option 780
  NOCORR option 780
  NOINT option 780
  NORM= option 780
  NPLOT= option 780
  number of factors extracted 783
  OUT= option 780
  output data sets 779, 785, 792
  OUTSTAT= option 780
  PARTIAL statement 779, 789
  PLOT option 780
  POWER= option 780
  PREPLOT option 780
  PREROTATE= option 780
  principal component analysis 776
  principal factor analysis 778
  PRINT option 780
  printed output 774, 797–800
  PRIORS= option 780
  PRIORS statement 779, 789
  PROC FACTOR statement 779
  PROPORTION= option 780
  RANDOM= option 780
  REORDER option 780
  RESIDUALS option 780
  ROTATE= option 780
  rotation method 786
  ROUND option 780
  SCORE option 780
  SCREE option 780
  SIMPLE option 780
  SINGULAR= option 780
  syntax summary 779
  TARGET= option 780
  time requirements 794, 797
  ULTRAHEYWOOD option 780
  use with VARCLUS procedure 55
  VAR statement 789

  VARDEF= option 780
  variances 788
  warning messages 819–820
  WEIGHT option 780
  WEIGHT statement 779, 790
  weighting variables 795
factor rotation methods 774
factor scores
  FACTOR procedure 794–795
  indeterminancy 776
factor scoring coefficients, example
    1484–1487
FACTOR statement
  CALIS procedure 276–277
  VAR statement 779
factor structure, common factor analysis 776
factor-selection specification
  FACTORS statement (PLAN) 1224–1225
  TREATMENTS statement (PLAN)
    1229–1230
factor-value-settings
  OUTPUT statement (PLAN) 1227–1228
factorial designs
  analyzing 897–899
  estimable functions for 118–120
  generating in PLAN procedure 1221–1222
factors in a design
  definition 1221–1222
  selecting levels for 1224–1226, 1231–1233
FACTORS statement
  See also "Changes and Enhancements"
  See also PLAN procedure, examples
  CATMOD procedure 415, 421–424
  examples (CATMOD) 422–424, 506–509
  examples (PLAN) 1222, 1223, 1224–1226,
    1229
  options (CATMOD) 422
failure time 997, 1028
  example using PROC LIFEREG 1014
false negative rate
  in LOGISTIC procedure 1092
false positive rate
  in LOGISTIC procedure 1092
FAST option
  MODEL statement (LOGISTIC) 1081
FASTCLUS procedure 850
  See also "Changes and Enhancements"
  BY statement 829
  CLUSTER option 826
  compared with CLUSTER procedure 55
  compared with other procedures 54, 832
  computational resources 831–832
  controlling iterations 827
  CONVERGE= option 826
  DATA= option 826
  DELETE= option 826
  DISTANCE option 826
  DRIFT option 826
  examples 832, 835–849
  FREQ statement 829
  ID statement 830
  IMPUTE option 826

initialization method   824
LIST option   826
MAXITER= option   826
MEAN= option   826
memory requirements   831
methods   824–825
missing values   827, 830
NOMISS option   826
NOPRINT option   826
OUT= option   826
outliers   833
output data sets   827, 828, 830
printed output   834–835
PROC FASTCLUS statement   825
RANDOM= option   826
REPLACE= option   826
SEED= option   826
SHORT option   826
STRICT option   826
SUMMARY option   826
syntax summary   825, 826
time requirements   831–832
use   823
VAR statement   830
VARDEF option   826
WEIGHT statement   830
FCONV= option
   PROC CALIS statement   263
fiducial limits   1326, 1328, 1329, 1332
Fieller's Theorem   1338
FILLCHAR= option
   PROC TREE statement   1615
   TREE procedure   1615
Fisher sign test
   See sign test
Fisher's Exact test   35, 127, 859, 865–866
   See also "Changes and Enhancements"
   examples   882–885
Fisher's LSD test   222, 917, 942
   protected   942
FIXED= option
   MODEL statement (VARCOMP)   1663
fixed effects (VARCOMP)   1661–1662, 1663,
      1664–1665
fixed zeros   463
fixed-effects models
   statistical summary   23
FLAG= option
   FACTOR procedure   780
   PROC FACTOR statement   781
flexible-beta method
   with CLUSTER procedure   522, 523
folded form F' statistic   1633, 1636
FORMCHAR= option
   PROC FREQ statement   856
   PROC LIFETEST statement   1038
formulas
   CATMOD procedure   467–470
   matrices in special SAS data sets   1686
   NESTED procedure   1131
   NPAR1WAY procedure   1200–1202
   regression influence diagnostics   1418–1425

formulas, TTEST procedure   1635–1636
forward selection
   LOGISTIC procedure   1076
   REG procedure   1397–1398
Forward-Dolittle transformation   934
FR update method specification
   PROC CALIS statement   272
FREQ option
   and output, CATMOD procedure   471
   MODEL statement (CATMOD)   427
FREQ procedure   29, 852–889
   See also "Changes and Enhancements"
   ANOVA statistic   874
   Breslow-Day test   859, 877
   BY statement   857
   chi-square statistic   855, 865
   chi-square test   859
   Cochran-Mantel-Haenszel statistics
      873–874
   compared with CATMOD procedure   35
   compared with other procedures   855
   computational resources   863
   confidence intervals   859
   contingency coefficent   866
   contingency tables   854
   continuity-adjusted chi-square   865
   correlation statistic (def=1)   874
   Cramer's V   866
   customizing table outlines   856
   definitions of statistics   864–877
   examples   878–888
   Fisher's exact test   865–866
   formatted values   863
   gamma   866
   general association statistic   874–875
   grouping variables   863–864
   Kendall's tau-b   867
   lambda asymmetric   870
   likelihood ratio chi-square   865
   limitations   862–863
   logit estimator   876
   Mantel-Haenszel chi-square   865
   Mantel-Haenszel statistic   874
   measures of association   854, 860, 864
   memory requirements   859
   missing values   862
   one-way frequency tables   852–853
   output data set   861, 862
   Pearson chi-square   865
   Pearson correlation coefficients   868
   Phi coefficent   866
   printed output   855, 862, 877–878
   PROC FREQ statement   856–857
   RANK scores   872
   references   888–889
   relative risk estimates   875–876
   requesting tables   857–860
   ridit scores   872
   selecting measures   854
   Somers' D   867–868
   Spearman rank correlation coefficient
      868–869

FREQ procedure (*continued*)
  statistical notation 864
  statistics produced 859, 864–877
  Stuart's tau-c 867
  summary statistics 872–877
  tables produced 852–854
  TABLES statement 857–858
  tests 864
  two-way crosstabulations 853–854
  uncertainty coefficient (U) 870–871
  uncertainty coefficient C | R 870
  WEIGHT statement 861–862
FREQ statement
  ACECLUS procedure 199
  and RMSSTD statement, CLUSTER
    procedure 528, 529
  ANOVA procedure 214, 216
  CALIS procedure 278
  CANCORR procedure 369, 374
  CANDISC procedure 389, 393
  CLUSTER procedure 521, 528
  DISCRIM procedure 686, 694
  FACTOR procedure 779, 789
  FASTCLUS procedure 829
  GLM procedure 900, 908
  LIFETEST procedure 1042
  PRINCOMP procedure 1243, 1246
  REG procedure 1357, 1358, 1361
  STEPDISC procedure 1495, 1499
  TREE procedure 1618
  VARCLUS procedure 1648
FREQOUT option
  CORRESP procedure 622
  PROC CORRESP statement 624, 632
frequency tables
  as input to CATMOD procedure 442
  FREQ procedure 852–889
  generating with CATMOD procedure 427
Friedman's chi-square 132, 874
  FREQ procedure, example 887–888
FUNCAT 415
furthest neighbor clustering
  See complete linkage
FUZZ= option
  FACTOR procedure 780
  PROC FACTOR statement 781
fuzzy clusters, definition 53
fuzzy-coding, definition 646

G

G-G epsilon
  See Greenhouse-Geisser epsilon
Gabriel (*i, u*)-intervals 945
GABRIEL option
  MEANS statement (ANOVA) 221
  MEANS statement (GLM) 915, 945
Gabriel's multiple-comparison procedure
  221, 915
GAMMA= option
  FACTOR procedure 780
  PROC FACTOR statement 781

gamma 860, 866
gamma distribution 997–998, 1004, 1010
  LIFEREG procedure 1004
  testing for fit of 126
Gauss-Newton method
  NLIN procedure 1136, 1141, 1153
GCONV= option
  PROC CALIS statement 263
GEN specification
  COSAN Model statement (CALIS) 274
general association statistic 874–875
general linear models
  hypothesis tests 24–25
  summary of 23–25
general random effects model 1130
Generalized COSAN Model 247
generalized cyclic incomplete block design
  generating with PLAN procedure
    1232–1233, 1236–1239
generalized inverse
  printing in GLM procedure 919
generalized least squares
  See weighted least squares
generalized logits
  See also response functions
  examples, CATMOD procedure 446
  formulas, CATMOD procedure 468
  specifying in CATMOD procedure 434
  using, CATMOD procedure 446
generalized Savage test 133
generalized Wilcoxon test 133
generating set for estimable functions
  110–111
Gentleman-Givens method 1211
GLIM models
  example of (NLIN) 1168–1171
GLM procedure 891–996
  See also "Changes and Enhancements"
  See also regression procedures
  ABSORB statement 900, 903–904
  absorption 937–939
  analyzing data in groups 903–904
  and TRANSREG procedure 1575–1578
  at (@) notation 897
  bar(|) notation 897
  BY statement 895, 900, 904
  CLASS statement 900, 904
  compared with other procedures 21–22,
    1460
  computational methods 961
  computational resources 960–961
  CONTRAST statement 900, 905–906
  contrasted with others 894
  estimability checking 905, 907, 909, 919,
    941
  ESTIMATE statement 900, 907, 939–941
  examples 964–993
  FREQ statement 900, 908
  hypothesis testing 932–937
  ID statement 900, 908
  influence statistics 920
  interactivity and BY statement 904

interactivity, and missing values   895, 959
leverage statistics   922
LSMEANS statement   900, 908–909
MANOVA statement   900, 910–913
MEANS statement   900, 913–917
memory requirements   903
missing values   959–960
mixed-model analysis of variance   986–988
MODEL statement   900, 917–920
multivariate analysis of variance   949–951
output data sets   961–963
OUTPUT statement   900, 920–922
parameterization   928–932
positional requirements for statements   901
predicted values   922
press statistic   919
printed output   963–964, 966–968,
      969–970, 971–973, 974–975, 977–978,
      979–982, 983–985, 987–988, 990–993
PROC GLM statement   900, 902–903
random effects   958–959
RANDOM statement   900, 922–923
repeated measurements analysis   923–926
repeated measures analysis of variance
      951–958, 982–986
REPEATED statement   900, 923–926
singularity checking   919, 920
specifying effects   895
sphericity tests   926, 954, 986
summary of features   893–894
syntax summary   900–902
TEST statement   900, 926–927
use for unbalanced designs   23–24
using interactively   894–895
WEIGHT statement   900, 927, 941
weighted analyses   927
WHERE statement   895
global score statistic
   LOGISTIC procedure   1089
GLS estimation method specification
   PROC CALIS statement   264
GLS option
   MODEL statement (CATMOD)   428
GMSEP option
   MODEL statement (REG)   1365
Gompertz distribution   1326, 1332, 1336
   LOGISTIC procedure   1087
goodness-of-fit tests
   CALIS procedure   303
   LOGISTIC procedure   1085
   PROBIT procedure   1326, 1328, 1329,
      1332, 1333, 1336–1337
   structural equation modeling   140
Gower's method
   See also median method
   with CLUSTER procedure   522, 534
Graeco-Latin square
   generating with PLAN procedure   1229
Greenhouse-Geisser epsilon   954
group average clustering
   See average linkage

GROUPNAMES= option
   MODEL statement (REG)   1365
growth curve analysis
   examples, CATMOD procedure   498–501
GSK models
   See methods comparison, CATMOD
      procedure
GT2 option
   MEANS statement (ANOVA)   221, 222
   MEANS statement (GLM)   916, 917, 944
G4= option
   PROC CALIS statement   263
G4 option
   PROC NLIN statement   1139
G4SINGULAR option
   PROC NLIN statement   1139

H

H= option
   OUTPUT statement (NLIN)   1143–1144
   OUTPUT statement (REG)   1371
H= specification
   MANOVA statement (ANOVA)   216–217
   MANOVA statement (GLM)   910
   TEST statement (ANOVA)   226–227
   TEST statement (GLM)   927
H specification
   OUTPUT statement (GLM)   921
   OUTPUT statement (LOGISTIC)   1085
H-F epsilon
   See Huynh-Feldt epsilon
Harris component analysis   774, 776, 782
Harris-Kaiser method   774
Harris-Kaiser rotation   786
HARVEY procedure   121
Harvey's fixed-effects linear models   121
hat matrix
   formulas, LOGISTIC procedure   1093
   in LOGISTIC procedure   1085
hazard function   1028, 1045, 1046, 1051
HEIGHT= option
   PROC TREE statement   1615–1616
   TREE procedure   1615
HEIGHT statement
   TREE procedure   1619
heirarchical clusters, definition   53
HELMERT transformation
   REPEATED statement (ANOVA)   225
   REPEATED statement (GLM)   925, 956–957
HESSALG= option
   PROC CALIS statement   263
Heywood cases
   FACTOR procedure   796–797
HEYWOOD option
   FACTOR procedure   780
   FACTOR statement (CALIS)   277
   PROC FACTOR statement   781
HIER procedure   54
hierarchical clustering   1641

hierarchical design
  generating with PLAN procedure
    1236–1237
Hierarchical Factor Analysis Models 250
HIERARCHY option
  PROC VARCLUS statement 1645
histograms, obtaining 126
historical notes, PROBIT procedure 1339
HKPOWER= option
  FACTOR procedure 780
  PROC FACTOR statement 781–782
Hochberg's pairwise comparison methods
    944
Hoelter's critical N (CALIS) 305
homogeneity analysis 616
homogeneity of survival curves
  LIFETEST procedure 1028–1034, 1046
homogeneity of variance, test for 690–691
honestly significant difference tests 222, 917,
    944
  See also HSD test
HORIZONTAL option
  PROC TREE statement 1616
  TREE procedure 1614
Hotelling-Lawley trace 19, 953
  CANCORR procedure 378
  printing in ANOVA 216
  printing in GLM 910
Howe's solution 778
HPLOTS= option
  PLOT statement (REG) 1377
HPROB= option
  MODEL statement (PROBIT) 1332
  PROBIT procedure 1326
  PROC PROBIT statement 1328
HSD test 222, 917, 944
HTYPE= option
  MANOVA statement (GLM) 911, 982
  MEANS statement (GLM) 916
  REPEATED statement (GLM) 925
  TEST statement (GLM) 927
Huynh-Feldt condition 954
Huynh-Feldt epsilon 954
HYBRID option
  and FREQ statement, CLUSTER
      procedure 528
  and other options (CLUSTER) 525, 526,
      527
  and RMSSTD statement, CLUSTER
      procedure 529
  PROC CLUSTER statement 524, 532
hypergeometric distribution
  and contingency tables 33
hypothesis tests
  See also estimable functions
  and transformations (TRANSREG) 1512
  canonical correlation 367
  CATMOD procedure 411
  comparing adjusted means 909
  construction of from estimable functions
      112–115
  contrasts (GLM) 905–906

contrasts in CATMOD procedure 417–420
custom tests (GLM) 926–927
custom tests in ANOVA procedure 226
estimable functions in GLM procedure
    932–937
for intercept in ANOVA procedure 223
in cluster analysis 97–99
incorrect hypotheses, CATMOD procedure
    464–465
intercept (GLM) 919
lack of fit 1466
multivariate ANOVA 949–951
multivariate, regression 17–19
nested designs 1130
nested effects 923
nonparametric, comparing means
    1195–1210
nonparametric, for independent
    distributions 1195–1210
parametric, comparing means (TTEST)
    1633, 1637–1638
parametric, comparing variances (TTEST)
    1633, 1637–1638
random effects (GLM) 923, 958–959
repeated measures analysis of variance
    953–955
Type I SS (GLM) 934

I

I option
  MODEL statement (GLM) 919
  MODEL statement (REG) 1365
IAPPROXIMATIONS option
  OUTPUT statement (TRANSREG) 1536,
      1538
ID statement
  CLUSTER procedure 521, 528
  CORRESP procedure 628
  DISCRIM procedure 686, 694
  FASTCLUS procedure 830
  GLM procedure 900, 908
  LIFETEST procedure 1042
  NLIN procedure 1142
  PRINQUAL procedure 1273, 1280
  REG procedure 1357, 1358, 1361
  RSREG procedure 1462
  SCORE procedure 1482
  TRANSREG procedure 1520, 1523
  TREE procedure 1619
ID statement cautions
  CORRESP procedure 621
IDE specification
  COSAN Model statement (CALIS) 274
ideal point coordinates
  TRANSREG procedure 1537
ideal point regression 1512, 1525
  TRANSREG procedure 1542
ill-conditioned data
  ORTHOREG procedure 1211
image component analysis 774, 776, 782

IMI specification
  COSAN Model statement (CALIS)   274
IMPUTE option
  FASTCLUS procedure   826
  PROC FASTCLUS statement   827
INC= option
  PROC TREE statement   1616
  TREE procedure   1614
INCLUDE= option
  MODEL statement (LOGISTIC)   1081
  MODEL statement (REG)   1366
  PROC STEPDISC statement   1497
incomplete block design
  generating with PLAN procedure
    1237–1239
independent variables
  definition for analysis of variance   22
index plots
  in LOGISTIC procedure   1081
indicator matrix   644
inertia, in correspondence analysis   617
influence diagnostics
  with LOGISTIC procedure   1081
INFLUENCE option
  MODEL statement (LOGISTIC)   1081
  MODEL statement (REG)   1366
influence statistics
  GLM procedure   921
information matrix   998, 999, 1009–1010,
    1335
INITIAL= option
  ACECLUS procedure   196
  and SEED statement   1648
  MODEL statement (LIFEREG)   1004
  MODEL statement (PROBIT)   1332
  PROC ACECLUS statement   196
  PROC VARCLUS statement   1645
initial estimates
  ACECLUS procedure   196
initialization method
  FASTCLUS procedure   824
INITITER= option
  and MAC method (PRINQUAL)   1287
  PROC PRINQUAL statement   1276
input data sets
  CALIS procedure   286–287
  CANDISC procedure   394–395
  CATMOD procedure   441
  CORRESP procedure   634–635
  DISCRIM procedure   699–700
  FACTOR procedure   790
  LOGISTIC procedure   1078–1079
  PLAN procedure   1227–1229, 1230
  REG procedure   1386–1389
  STEPDISC procedure   1500–1501
  TYPE=, all procedures   1675–1686
INRAM= option
  PROC CALIS statement   263
INT option
  and ABSORB statement (GLM)   903–904
  MODEL statement (GLM)   919
  PROC CANCORR statement   371

inter-cluster correlations   1653
interactions
  model parameterization in GLM procedure
    928–929
  specifying in ANOVA procedure   211
  specifying in CATMOD procedure   411
  specifying in GLM procedure   895
  terms for, TRANSREG procedure   1534
interactive procedures
  See also "Changes and Enhancements"
  CATMOD procedure   414–415
  PLAN procedure   1223
  REG procedure   1393–1397
INTERCEPT= option
  MODEL statement (LIFEREG)   1005
  MODEL statement (PROBIT)   1332
intercept
  hypothesis tests for (GLM)   919
  hypothesis tests for (ANOVA)   223
  in GLM models   928
  omitting from models (GLM)   919
INTERCEPT
  in H= specification, MANOVA statement
    (ANOVA) 216–217
  in H= specification, MANOVA statement
    (GLM)   910
INTERCEPT argument
  CONTRAST statement (CATMOD)   418
  CONTRAST statement (GLM)   905
  ESTIMATE statement (GLM)   907
INTERCEPT option
  and ABSORB statement (ANOVA)   215
  MODEL statement (ANOVA)   223
  MODEL statement (GLM)   919
  MODEL statement (TRANSREG)   1531,
    1532
  with CLASS transform (TRANSREG)   1535
interpretation
  factor analysis   776
  score variables   1483
interpreting factors, elements to consider
    776
interval determination, LIFETEST procedure
    1045
interval scale
  definition   30
interval-censoring   105
INTERVALS= option
  and BY statement   1041
  LIFETEST procedure   1045
  PROC LIFETEST statement   1039
intitial seeds
  FASTCLUS procedure   828
introductory example
  CORRESP procedure   616–620
  correspondence analysis   616–620
INV specification
  COSAN Model statement (CALIS)   274
inverse confidence limits
  PROBIT procedure   1329, 1337–1338
INVERSE option
  MODEL statement (GLM)   919

INVERSECL option, PROBIT procedure
    1329, 1332
IPFPHC procedure 54
IPLOTS option
    MODEL statement (LOGISTIC) 1081
IREPLACE option
    OUTPUT statement (TRANSREG) 1536,
    1538
IRLS algorithm
    LOGISTIC procedure 1088
iterated factor analysis 774
iterative methods (NLIN)
    DUD 1136
    Gauss-Newton 1136, 1152
    Marquardt 1136, 1152
    Newton 1136, 1152
    steepest-descent 1136, 1152
iterative reassignment
    VARCLUS procedure 1643
iteratively reweighted least squares
    example of (NLIN) 1165–1167
ITPRINT option
    MODEL statement (LIFEREG) 1005
    MODEL statement (LOGISTIC) 1081
    MODEL statement (PROBIT) 1333

J

Jacobian (NLIN) 1148–1149
JOINCHAR= option
    PROC TREE statement 1616
    TREE procedure 1615
JOINT function
    RESPONSE statement (CATMOD) 434
joint plot
    constructing 616
joint response probabilities
    See response functions
JP option
    MODEL statement (REG) 1366

K

K= option
    and other options (CLUSTER) 524, 526,
    527
    PROC CLUSTER statement 525, 531, 532
    PROC DISCRIM statement 688
k-means method
    algorithm 824
    compared to other clustering methods
    56–97
k-nearest-neighbor methods
    See also kth nearest-neighbor methods
    cluster analysis 133
    density estimation 133
    DISCRIM procedure 678
    discriminant analysis 133
Kaiser's measure of sampling adequacy
    example 803

Kaplan-Meier estimates 106, 1039
    See product-limit estimates
Kendall's tau-b 860, 867
KERNEL= option
    PROC DISCRIM statement 689
kernel
    density estimates 133
    discriminant analysis 133
kernel method
    DISCRIM procedure 678
KNOTS= t-option
    MODEL statement (TRANSREG) 1529
    TRANSFORM statement (PRINQUAL)
    1283
knots
    See splines
Kolmogorov-Smirnov tests
    comparing distributions 126
    for normality 126
    statistic 1196, 1201
KRATIO= option
    MEANS statement (ANOVA) 221
    MEANS statement (GLM) 916
Kruskal-Wallis test 35, 130–132, 874, 1196,
    1198
kth-nearest neighbor
    See also density linkage
    See also single linkage
kth-nearest neighbor estimation
    CLUSTER procedure 525, 527, 531
Kuiper statistic 126, 1196, 1202
kurtosis
    printed in CLUSTER procedure 527
KURTOSIS option
    PROC CALIS statement 264

L

lack-of-fit tests
    See goodness of fit tests
    RSREG procedure 1466
LACKFIT option
    MODEL statement (PROBIT) 1333
    MODEL statement (RSREG) 1463
    PROC PROBIT statement 1329
Lagrange Multiplier test statistics 1009
lambda 860
    asymmetric 869–870
    symmetric 870
Lance-Williams flexible-beta method
    See flexible-beta method
latent variables
    definition 138
Latin square design
    generating with PLAN procedure
    1239–1240
Latin square split-plot design
    analyzing with ANOVA procedure 238–239
LEAFCHAR= option
    PROC TREE statement 1616
    TREE procedure 1615

least-squares method
  estimation   1008
  nonlinear regression   1136
  solving in TRANSREG procedure
    1558-1566
least-significant-difference test   222, 917
least-squares means   908-909, 948-949
left-censoring   105
LEVEL= option
  PROC TREE statement   1616
  TREE procedure   1614
leverage   16
leverage (NLIN)   1143
leverage statistic
  GLM procedure   921
LEVMAR optimization technique
  specification
  PROC CALIS statement   266
life table estimates   106, 1028, 1039,
    1044-1045, 1050-1051, 1062-1068
LIFEREG procedure   106, 997-1025
  See also "Changes and Enhancements"
  See also regression procedures
  BY statement   1001
  CLASS statement   1001
  compared with LIFETEST procedure   106
  computational method   1008
  computational resources   1013
  distributions allowed   1010-1011
  examples   1014-1024
  main effects   1008
  missing values   1008
  model specifications   1009-1010
  MODEL statement   1002-1006
  OUTPUT statement   1006-1007
  predicted values   1011-1012
  printed output   1013-1014
  PROC LIFEREG statement   1000-1001
  syntax summary   999-1000
  WEIGHT statement   1008
LIFETEST procedure   106, 1027-1069
  See also "Changes and Enhancements"
  BY statement   1037, 1041
  compared with LIFEREG procedure   106
  computational formulas   1044
  computer resources   1049-1050
  confidence limits   1046
  examples   1052-1068
  FREQ statement   1037, 1042
  ID statement   1037, 1042
  interpreting plots   1029-1034
  interval determination   1045
  life table estimates, example   1062-1068
  life table method   1044-1045
  MISSING option   1040
  missing values   1043-1044
  output data sets   1040, 1048-1050
  printed output   1050-1052
  PROC LIFETEST statement   1038-1043
  product-limit estimates, example
    1052-1062
  product-limit method   1044

STRATA statement   1037, 1042
syntax summary   1037
TEST statement   1037, 1043
tests performed   1028
TIME statement   1037, 1043
likelihood function   1334
likelihood ratio test   859, 865, 1051
  Bartlett's modification of   690-691
  LIFETEST procedure   1028, 1034, 1046
limitations
  NPAR1WAY procedure   1199
limitations in model-selection methods
  REG procedure   1400
linear discriminant function   678
linear models
  CATMOD procedure   408
  compared with log-linear models   414
linear rank statistics   106
linear structural equation models   246
LINEAR *transform*
  and missing values (PRINQUAL)   1285,
    1286
  and missing values (TRANSREG)   1540
  MODEL statement (TRANSREG)   1524,
    1527
  TRANSFORM statement (PRINQUAL)
    1282
  TRANSREG procedure   1543-1544
linear transformation
  example   1285, 1530
  PRINQUAL procedure   1280, 1282
  TRANSREG procedure   1524, 1527
LINEQS statement
  CALIS procedure   278-279
LINES option
  MEANS statement (ANOVA)   221-222
  MEANS statement (GLM)   916
LINK= option
  MODEL statement (LOGISTIC)   1082
link functions
  definition   1072-1073
  formulas for, LOGISTIC procedure
    1086-1087
  specifying in LOGISTIC procedure   1082
LISREL (Linear Structural Relationship)
  model   249
LIST option
  FASTCLUS procedure   826
  PROC DISCRIM statement   689
  PROC FASTCLUS statement   827
  PROC TREE statement   1616
  TABLES statement (FREQ)   860
  TREE procedure   1615
LISTERR option
  PROC DISCRIM statement   689
LN option, PROC PROBIT statement   1329
LNLIKE variable
  PROBIT procedure   1339
local minimum (NLIN)   1151
log likelihood function   999, 1009
  LOGISTIC procedure   1088-1089

log likelihood ratio chi-square test 999,
    1326, 1335, 1337, 1340, 1344
LOG option, PROC PROBIT statement 1329
log rank scores 106
log rank test 1051
    LIFETEST procedure 1028, 1034, 1037,
        1046
LOG *transform*
    and missing values (PRINQUAL) 1285
    and missing values (TRANSREG) 1540
    MODEL statement (TRANSREG) 1524,
        1526
    TRANSFORM statement (PRINQUAL)
        1280, 1281
log-linear analyses
    CATMOD procedure 447-449
    examples, CATMOD procedure 485-492
    multiple populations, CATMOD procedure
        448-449
    one population, CATMOD procedure 448
log-linear models
    and design matrix, CATMOD procedure
        459-462
    CATMOD procedure 409
    compared with linear models 414
logarithmic transformation
    PRINQUAL procedure 1280, 1281
    TRANSREG procedure 1524, 1526
LOGIST procedure 446
logistic analysis
    CATMOD procedure 410, 446-447
    examples, CATMOD procedure 498-501,
        510-514
logistic analysis, ordinal data 410
logistic distribution 997-998, 1004, 1011,
        1326, 1332, 1336
    LIFEREG procedure 1004
    testing for location shift 1200
LOGISTIC procedure 29, 46, 1071-1126
    See also "Changes and Enhancements"
    See also regression procedures
    BY statement 1077, 1078-1079
    calculation methods 1092
    classification table 1091-1092
    compared with CATMOD and PROBIT
        procedures 35-38
    compared with CATMOD procedure 446
    convergence criterion 1080
    criteria for assessing fit 1088-1089
    examples 1074-1075, 1099-1125
    input data sets 1078-1079
    iteratively reweighted least squares
        algorithm 1088
    link functions and distributions 1086-1087
    memory requirements 1096
    missing values 1086
    model selection methods 1076, 1082
    MODEL statement 1077, 1079-1083
    number of observations, input data set
        1087-1088
    output data sets 1078, 1095-1096
    OUTPUT statement 1077, 1084-1085

    printed output 1077-1078, 1081,
        1096-1099
    PROC LOGISTIC statement 1077-1078
    regression diagnostics 1093-1095
    response types and models 1072-1073
    score statistics and tests 1089-1090
    syntax summary 1077
    time requirements 1096
    WEIGHT statement 1077, 1086
logistic regression 1325
    See also CATMOD procedure
    See also LOGISTIC procedure
    See also PROBIT procedure
    See also regression
    and continuous variables 447
    CATMOD procedure 409, 446-447
    example, PROBIT procedure 1348-1350
    examples, CATMOD procedure 481-484
logit estimator 876
logit function
    LOGISTIC procedure 1086
LOGIT *transform*
    and missing values (PRINQUAL) 1285
    and missing values (TRANSREG) 1540
    MODEL statement (TRANSREG) 1524,
        1526
    TRANSFORM statement (PRINQUAL)
        1280, 1281
logit transformation
    PRINQUAL procedure 1280, 1281
    TRANSREG procedure 1524, 1526
logits
    See adjacent-category logits
    See also cumulative logits
    See also generalized logits
LOGITS *function*
    RESPONSE statement (CATMOD) 434
LOGLIN statement (CATMOD) 415, 424
    See also "Changes and Enhancements"
loglogistic distribution 997-998, 1004, 1011
    LIFEREG procedure 1004
lognormal distribution 997-998, 1004, 1011
    LIFEREG procedure 1004
    testing for fit of 126
LOG10 option, PROC PROBIT statement
        1329
LOW specification
    COSAN Model statement (CALIS) 274
LOWER specification
    OUTPUT statement (LOGISTIC) 1085
LSD option
    MEANS statement (ANOVA) 222, 234
    MEANS statement (GLM) 916, 917
LSD test
    See Fisher's LSD test
LSGLS estimation method specification
    PROC CALIS statement 264
LSMEANS statement (GLM) 900, 908-909
    See also "Changes and Enhancements"
    options (GLM) 909
LSML estimation method specification
    PROC CALIS statement 265

L95= option
OUTPUT statement (NLIN)   1144
OUTPUT statement (REG)   1371
L95 option
MODEL statement (RSREG)   1463
L95 specification
OUTPUT statement (GLM)   921
L95M= option
OUTPUT statement (NLIN)   1144
OUTPUT statement (REG)   1371
L95M option
MODEL statement (RSREG)   1463
L95M specification
OUTPUT statement (GLM)   921

M

M= specification
MANOVA statement (ANOVA)   217
MANOVA statement (GLM)   910
MAC method   1268
PRINQUAL procedure   1266-1268, 1287
PRINQUAL procedure, specifying   1276
Mahalanobis distances   392
DISCRIM procedure   678
main effects
and design matrix, CATMOD procedure
452
LIFEREG procedure   1008
model parameterization in GLM
procedure   928
specifying in ANOVA procedure   211
specifying in CATMOD procedure   411
specifying in GLM procedure   895
main-effects model
estimable functions for   113-114
manifest variables
definition   138
Mann-Whitney U test   127, 1196
MANOVA option
PROC ANOVA statement   214
PROC DISCRIM statement   689
PROC GLM statement   902
MANOVA statement
See also "Changes and Enhancements"
(ANOVA)
See also "Changes and Enhancements"
(GLM)
and CONTRAST statement (GLM)   910
ANOVA procedure   214, 216-219
GLM procedure   900, 910-913
options (ANOVA)   218
options (GLM)   911-912
Mantel-Haenszel chi-square   859, 865
FREQ procedure   855
Mantel-Haenszel statistic   874
marginal means   908-909
TRANSREG procedure   1539
marginal probabilities
See also response functions
specifying in CATMOD procedure   434

MARGINALS function
RESPONSE statement (CATMOD)   434
Marquardt method   1136, 1154
matched analysis
for contingency tables   33
matched comparisons
See paired comparisons
matched pairs, definition   127
matrix decompositions   623, 627, 640
matrix factor
defined for factor analysis   774
matrix multiplication   1479
MATRIX statement
CALIS procedure   279
MAXCLUSTERS= option
PROC FASTCLUS statement   826
PROC VARCLUS statement   1645
using, VARCLUS procedure   1649
MAXCLUSTERS= option, use   824
MAXEIGEN= option
PROC VARCLUS statement   1645
using, VARCLUS procedure   1649
MAXFUNC= option
PROC CALIS statement   264
MAXHEIGHT= option
PROC TREE statement   1616
TREE procedure   1614
maximum average correlation method
See MAC method
maximum generalized variance method
See MGV method
maximum likelihood hierarchical clustering
with CLUSTER procedure   522, 533, 534
maximum method
See complete linkage
MAXIMUM option
RIDGE statement (RSREG)   1464
maximum rank hypothesis, definition   114
maximum total variance method
See MTV method
maximum-likelihood estimates   998, 1136
CATMOD procedure   427
PROBIT procedure   1325
maximum-likelihood factor analysis   774,
778-779, 782
with FACTOR procedure   778-779
maximum-likelihood method
CATMOD procedure   413
formulas, CATMOD procedure   470
VARCOMP procedure   1666
MAXITER= option
ACECLUS procedure   196
and iterations (PRINQUAL)   1286
and iterations (TRANSREG)   1541
FACTOR procedure   780
FASTCLUS procedure   826
MODEL statement (CATMOD)   427
MODEL statement (LIFEREG)   1005
MODEL statement (LOGISTIC)   1082
MODEL statement (PROBIT)   1333
MODEL statement (TRANSREG)   1531,
1532

MAXITER= option (continued)
  PROC ACECLUS statement 197
  PROC CALIS statement 264
  PROC FACTOR statement 782
  PROC FASTCLUS statement 827
  PROC NLIN statement 1139
  PROC PRINQUAL statement 1276
  PROC VARCLUS statement 1647
  PROC VARCOMP statement 1662
MAXSEARCH= option
  PROC VARCLUS statement 1646
MAXSTEP= option
  MODEL statement (LOGISTIC) 1082
  PROC STEPDISC statement 1497
MAXTIME= option, PROC LIFETEST
    statement 1039
MCA
  See multiple correspondence analysis
MCA option
  CORRESP procedure 622
  PROC CORRESP statement 625, 641–644
McDonald's measure of centrality (CALIS)
    304
McNemar's test 128, 129–130
McQuitty's similarity analysis
  with CLUSTER procedure 522
MDPREF analysis
  See multidimensional preference (MDPREF)
    analysis
MEAN= data sets
  FASTCLUS procedure 827, 831, 842
MEAN= option
  FASTCLUS procedure 826
  PROC FASTCLUS statement 827
mean separation tests
  See multiple comparison methods
MEAN specification
  REPEATED statement (ANOVA) 225
MEAN transformation
  REPEATED statement (GLM) 925, 957
means
  for effects in models (ANOVA) 219
  for effects in models (GLM) 913
  printed in CLUSTER procedure 527
MEANS function
  RESPONSE statement (CATMOD) 434
MEANS option
  and output data sets (TRANSREG) 1554
  OUTPUT statement (TRANSREG) 1536,
    1539
MEANS statement
  See also "Changes and Enhancements"
    (ANOVA)
  See also "Changes and Enhancements"
    (GLM)
  ANOVA procedure 214, 219–223
  GLM procedure 900, 913–917
  options (ANOVA) 219–223
  options (GLM) 913–917
means, differences between
  independent samples 1633, 1637–1638
  paired observations 1633

measurement model 144
measures of association
  for contingency tables 864–877
  FREQ procedure 854
MEASURES option
  TABLES statement (FREQ) 860
MEC option
  and output data sets (TRANSREG) 1554
  OUTPUT statement (TRANSREG) 1536,
    1539
median method
  with CLUSTER procedure 522, 534
MEDIAN option
  PROC NPAR1WAY statement 1198
median scores, definition 1200
median tests 127, 1196, 1197, 1198, 1200
MEER, definition 943
memory requirements
  See also absorption
  ACECLUS procedure 201
  and absorption (GLM) 937–938
  ANOVA procedure 228
  CATMOD procedure 471
  CLUSTER procedure 563
  FACTOR procedure 797
  FASTCLUS procedure 831
  FREQ procedure 859
  GLM procedure 960–961
  LOGISTIC procedure 1096
  NPAR1WAY procedure 1199
  PRINCOMP procedure 1249
  PRINQUAL procedure 1291
  TRANSREG procedure 1556
  VARCLUS procedure 1651
METHOD= option
  and output data sets (TRANSREG) 1554
  and printed output, TRANSREG
    procedure 1541
  FACTOR procedure 780
  MODEL statement (TRANSREG) 1531
  PROC CALIS statement 264
  PROC DISCRIM statement 689
  PROC FACTOR statement 782
  PROC LIFETEST statement 1039
  PROC NLIN statement 1139
  PROC PRINQUAL statement 1276
  PROC STEPDISC statement 1497
  PROC VARCOMP statement 1662
METHOD= specification
  PROC CLUSTER statement 522
methods comparison
  CATMOD procedure 414
METRIC= option
  ACECLUS procedure 196
  PROC ACECLUS statement 197
  PROC DISCRIM statement 689
MGV method 1267
  PRINQUAL procedure 1266–1268, 1286
  PRINQUAL procedure, specifying 1277
MINCLUSTERS= option
  PROC VARCLUS statement 1646

MINEIGEN= option
  FACTOR procedure   780
  PROC FACTOR statement   782–783
MINHEIGHT= option
  PROC TREE statement   1616
  TREE procedure   1614
minimization
  example of (NLIN)   1174–1175
Minimum Generalized Variance method
  See MGV method
minimum method
  See single linkage
MINIMUM option
  RIDGE statement (RSREG)   1465
MININERTIA= option
  CORRESP procedure   622
  PROC CORRESP statement   625
MISSING option
  CORRESP procedure   622
  LIFETEST procedure   1042
  PROC CORRESP statement   625
  PROC LIFETEST statement   1040
  PROC NPAR1WAY statement   1198, 1199
  TABLES statement (FREQ)   860
missing values
  ACECLUS procedure   200
  and interactivity, ANOVA procedure   210,
    227
  and interactivity, GLM procedure   895, 959
  and output data sets (TRANSREG)   1551
  ANOVA procedure   214, 227
  CALIS procedure   291
  CANCORR procedure   375
  CANDISC procedure   394
  CATMOD procedure   441
  CLUSTER procedure   564
  CORRESP procedure   634
  DISCRIM procedure   696
  estimating in multivariate data   1266
  estimating, PRINQUAL procedure   1285,
    1302–1322
  estimating, TRANSREG procedure   1533,
    1540
  FACTOR procedure   793
  FASTCLUS procedure   827, 830
  FREQ procedure   860, 862
  GLM procedure   902, 959–960
  LIFEREG procedure   1008
  LIFETEST procedure   1043–1044
  LOGISTIC procedure   1086
  NESTED procedure   1130
  NLIN procedure   1147
  NPAR1WAY procedure   1198, 1199
  ORTHOREG procedure   1213
  output data sets   827
  PRINCOMP procedure   1247, 1259
  PRINQUAL procedure, options for
    1275–1278
  PROBIT procedure   1334
  REG procedure   1385
  RSREG procedure   1465
  SCORE procedure   1483

special missing values, PRINQUAL
  procedure   1285
special missing values, TRANSREG
  procedure   1533, 1540–1541, 1543
STEPDISC procedure   1500
TRANSREG procedure   1543, 1544
TRANSREG procedure, options for   1533,
  1534
TREE procedure   1619
TTEST procedure   1635
VARCLUS procedure   1649
VARCOMP procedure   1664
MISSPRINT option
  TABLES statement (FREQ)   860
MIVQUE0 method, VARCOMP procedure
  1665
MIVQUE0 option
  PROC VARCOMP statement   1662
mixed-model analysis of variance
  GLM procedure   986–988
  SAS procedures for   26
ML estimation method specification
  PROC CALIS statement   265
ML factor analysis
  and computer time   779
  and multivariate normal distribution   779
ML option
  and output, CATMOD procedure   472
  MODEL statement (CATMOD)   427
  PROC VARCOMP statement   1662
MNAMES= specification
  MANOVA statement (ANOVA)   217
  MANOVA statement (GLM)   911
modal clusters
  in density estimation, CLUSTER
    procedure   525
MODE= option
  PROC CLUSTER statement   525
MODECLUS procedure   54, 134
model selection
  LOGISTIC procedure   1076
model specifications
  LIFEREG procedure   1009–1010
  PROBIT procedure   1335–1336
MODEL statement
  See also "Changes and Enhancements"
    (PROBIT)
  ANOVA procedure   214, 223
  CATMOD procedure   415, 425
  examples for repeated measures
    (CATMOD)   451–452
  examples, CATMOD procedure   425
  GLM procedure   900, 917–920
  LIFEREG procedure   1002–1006
  LOGISTIC procedure   1077, 1079–1083
  NLIN procedure   1142–1143
  options (ANOVA)   223
  options (CATMOD)   426–429
  options (GLM)   918–920
  options (LIFEREG)   1003–1006
  options (LOGISTIC)   1080–1083
  options (ORTHOREG)   1213

MODEL statement (*continued*)
  options (PROBIT) 1330–1333
  options (REG) 1357, 1358, 1361–1369
  options (RSREG) 1462
  options (TRANSREG) 1531–1535
  t-options for transformations (TRANSREG) 1528–1531
  transformations available (TRANSREG) 1524–1528
  TRANSREG procedure 1521, 1523–1535
  TRANSREG procedure, printed output option 1533
  VARCOMP procedure 1662, 1663
MODEL variable
  PROBIT procedure 1338
MODELDATA option
  PRINT statement (REG) 1379
MODIFICATION option
  PROC CALIS statement 265
modified ridit scores 872
MONOTONE= option
  and missing values (PRINQUAL) 1285
  MODEL statement (TRANSREG) 1533–1534
  PROC PRINQUAL statement 1277
MONOTONE *transform*
  and missing values (PRINQUAL) 1285, 1286
  and missing values (TRANSREG) 1540
  MODEL statement (TRANSREG) 1524, 1527
  TRANSFORM statement (PRINQUAL) 1282
  TRANSREG procedure 1543–1544
monotonic splines
  See MSPLINE *transform*
  See also splines
monotonic transformations
  PRINQUAL procedure 1280, 1282
  TRANSREG procedure 1524, 1527, 1528
monotonically increasing B-spline transformation 1527
MORALS method
  and output data sets (TRANSREG) 1552
  specifying in TRANSREG procedure 1532
morphometrics
  See clustering
MPC option
  and output data sets (TRANSREG) 1554
  OUTPUT statement (TRANSREG) 1536, 1539
MQC option
  and output data sets (TRANSREG) 1554
  OUTPUT statement (TRANSREG) 1536, 1539
MRANK procedure 134
MRC option
  and output data sets (TRANSREG) 1554
  OUTPUT statement (TRANSREG) 1536, 1539
MSA option
  FACTOR procedure 780
  PROC FACTOR statement 783

MSE option
  MODEL statement (REG) 1366
MSPLINE *transform*
  MODEL statement (TRANSREG) 1524, 1527
  options (PRINQUAL) 1283–1285
  options (TRANSREG) 1529–1531
  TRANSFORM statement (PRINQUAL) 1280, 1282
  TRANSREG procedure 1544–1545
MTEST statement
  REG procedure 1357, 1358, 1369–1370
MTV method 1267
  PRINQUAL procedure 1266–1268, 1287
  PRINQUAL procedure, example 1268–1273
  PRINQUAL procedure, specifying 1277
multi-stage nested design 1127
multidimensional contingency table
  definition 30
multidimensional preference (MDPREF)
    analyses 40, 41, 1266
  example 1292–1302
multilevel response 1335
  example, PROBIT procedure 1344–1347
multinomial distribution 31
MULTIPASS option
  PROC ANOVA statement 214
  PROC GLM statement 902
multiple comparison methods 25, 913–917, 941–948
  and confidence intervals 941
  and unequal cell sizes 944–945
  and weighted means 941
  ANOVA procedure 219
  Bayesian approach 947–948
  comparing treatments to control 945
  definition 941
  interpreting results 941
  multiple-stage tests 946–947
  pairwise comparisons 942
  recommendations 948
multiple correspondence analysis (MCA)
    625, 641–644
  example, CORRESP procedure 659–665
multiple group component analysis
  PROC VARCLUS statement 1646
multiple group factor analysis 1642
multiple hypergeometric distribution
  for contingency tables 33
multiple optimal regression 1533
multiple regression
  with TRANSREG procedure 1562–1565
multiple-stage tests
  See multiple comparison methods
  See also multiple comparison procedures
MULTIPLEGROUP option
  PROC VARCLUS statement 1646
multivariate analyses
  contrasting with univariate analysis 46–50
  overview of procedures 39

multivariate analysis of variance
   See MANOVA statement
   GLM procedure 949–951
   performing with GLM procedure 978–982
multivariate general linear hypothesis
   definition 950
multivariate normal null hypothesis
   in clustering 97
multivariate tests
   between-subject effects, repeated
      measures 953
   repeated measures analysis (GLM) 951
   within-subject effects, repeated measures
      953–954

N

N= option
   ACECLUS procedure 196
   FACTOR statement (CALIS) 277
   PROC ACECLUS statement 197
   PROC PRINCOMP statement 1244
   PROC PRINQUAL statement 1276
NAME statement
   TREE procedure 1619
NAME variable
   PROBIT procedure 1338
natural response rate 1325, 1326, 1328,
   1339
NCAN= option
   MODEL statement (TRANSREG) 1531,
      1533
   PROC CANCORR statement 371
   PROC CANDISC statement 391
   PROC DISCRIM statement 689
NCLUSTERS= option
   PROC TREE statement 1616
   TREE procedure 1614
nearest component sorting 1643
nearest neighbor
   See also single linkage
   cluster analysis 133
   density estimation 133
   discriminant analysis 133
negative exponential growth curve
   example of (NLIN) 1156–1158
negative variance component estimates
   VARCOMP procedure 1665
NEIGHBOR procedure
   See "Changes and Enhancements"
   See also DISCRIM procedure
nested designs 1127
   error terms 1131
   generating with PLAN procedure
      1236–1237
nested effects
   and design matrix, CATMOD procedure
      454
   model parameterization in GLM procedure
      929–930
   specifying in ANOVA procedure 211, 212

specifying in CATMOD procedure 411
specifying in GLM procedure 896
NESTED procedure 1127–1134
   See also "Changes and Enhancements"
   analysis of covariance 1130–1131
   and GLM procedure 894
   BY statement 1129
   CLASS statement 1129
   compared with other procedures 21–22
   computational method 1131
   example 1133–1134
   formulas 1131
   missing values 1130
   printed output 1131–1133
   PROC NESTED statement 1129
   unbalanced data 1130
   VAR statement 1130
nested-by-value effects
   and design matrix, CATMOD procedure
      454
   specifying in CATMOD procedure 411
Newman-Keuls multiple range test 222, 917,
   946–947
NEWRAP optimization technique
   specification
   PROC CALIS statement 266
Newton's method (NLIN) 1141, 1142, 1153
Newton-Raphson algorithm 998
NFACTORS= option
   FACTOR procedure 780, 782
   PROC FACTOR statement 783
NINTERVAL= option, PROC LIFETEST
   statement 1040
NKNOTS= option, MODEL statement
   (TRANSREG) 1529
NKNOTS= t-option
   MODEL statement (TRANSREG) 1529
   TRANSFORM statement (PRINQUAL)
      1285
NLIN procedure 1135–1193
   See also "Changes and Enhancements"
   See also regression procedures
   automatic variables 1147–1149
   BOUNDS statement 1140–1141
   BY statement 1141
   computational methods 1151–1156
   confidence intervals 1144, 1145
   constrained estimation 1140
   convergence criterion 1138
   DER statements 1141–1142
   derivatives 1141–1142
   divergence 1150–1151
   Gauss-Newton method 1141, 1153–1154
   ID statement 1142
   Marquardt method 1154–1155
   missing values 1147
   MODEL statement 1142–1143
   Newton method 1141, 1142, 1153
   normal equations 1151
   OUT= data sets 1143, 1156
   OUTEST= data set 1156
   output data sets 1156

NLIN procedure (*continued*)
  OUTPUT statement 1143–1145
  PARAMETERS statement 1145–1146
  printed output 1156
  PROC NLIN statement 1137–1140
  steepest-descent method 1152
  syntax summary 1137
  system of equations 1151–1152
  weighted least squares 1136, 1148–1149
NOANOVA option
  MODEL statement (RSREG) 1463
NOCENTER option
  TRANSREG procedure, see INT option
    1532
NOCHECK option
  PROC PRINQUAL statement 1276–1277
NOCLASSIFY option
  PROC DISCRIM statement 690
NOCODE option
  MODEL statement (RSREG) 1463
NOCOL option
  TABLES statement (FREQ) 860
NOCOLLECT option
  PLOT statement (REG) 1377
NOCOLUMN option
  CORRESP procedure 622
  PROC CORRESP statement 625
NOCORR option
  FACTOR procedure 780
  PROC FACTOR statement 783
NOCUM option
  TABLES statement (FREQ) 860
NODESIGN option
  and output, CATMOD procedure 471
  MODEL statement (CATMOD) 427
NODIAG option
  PROC CALIS statement 265
NOEIGEN option
  PROC CLUSTER statement 525
NOFIT option
  MODEL statement (LOGISTIC) 1082
NOFREQ option
  TABLES statement (FREQ) 860
NOHALVE option
  PROC NLIN statement 1139
NOID option
  PROC CLUSTER statement 525
NOINT option
  FACTOR procedure 780
  MODEL statement (CATMOD) 427
  MODEL statement (GLM) 919, 928
  MODEL statement (LIFEREG) 1005
  MODEL statement (LOGISTIC) 1082
  MODEL statement (ORTHOREG) 1213
  MODEL statement (PROBIT) 1333
  MODEL statement (REG) 1366
  MODEL statement (TRANSREG) 1531,
    1533
  PROC CALIS statement 265
  PROC CANCORR statement 371
  PROC FACTOR statement 783
  PROC PRINCOMP statement 1244

PROC VARCLUS statement 1646
  with ALLCATS and CLASS, TRANSREG
    procedure 1534
NOITER option
  MODEL statement (CATMOD) 427
NOLIST option
  PAINT statement (REG) 1374
  REWEIGHT statement (REG) 1383
NOLOG option
  MODEL statement (LIFEREG) 1005
NOM option
  REPEATED statement (ANOVA) 225
  REPEATED statement (GLM) 925
nominal scale, definition 26, 30
nominal variables
  See classification variables
NOMISS option
  FASTCLUS procedure 826
  MODEL statement (TRANSREG) 1531,
    1533
  PROC FASTCLUS statement 827
  PROC PRINQUAL statement 1277
NOMOD option
  PROC CALIS statement 265
NONE estimation method specification
  PROC CALIS statement 265
NONE optimization technique specification
  PROC CALIS statement 266
nonlinear regression 1136
  DUD method 1155
  Gauss-Newton method 1153–1154
  least-squares method 1136
  Marquardt method 1154–1155
  maximum-likelihood estimates 1136
  Newton method 1153
  residual sum of squares 1136
  robust regression 1136
  secant method 1155
  segmented models 1136
  specifying derivatives 1141–1142
  specifying parameters and starting values
    1145–1146
  steepest-descent method 1152–1153
  step-size search 1155–1156
  weighted least squares 1136, 1148
  with TRANSREG procedure 1558–1562
nonlinear transformations
  TRANSREG procedure 1518–1520
nonoptimal transformations
  defined, TRANSREG procedure 1524
  options for (PRINQUAL) 1283
  options for (TRANSREG) 1528–1529
  PRINQUAL procedure 1281–1282
  TRANSREG procedure 1526–1527
NONORM option
  PROC CLUSTER statement 525
nonparametric analyses
  See also categorical analysis
  See also "Changes and Enhancements"
  See also density linkage
  See also NPAR1WAY procedure
  analysis of variance 26–27

and clustering 133
and discriminant analysis 133
available SAS procedures 125–135
DISCRIM procedure 681–684
estimates of survival curves 133–134
with FREQ procedure 35
nonparametric density estimation 133, 681
nonparametric tests
  compared with NPAR1WAY procedure
    1196
  definition 125
NOOPTIMAL option
  MODEL statement (RSREG) 1463
NOPARM option
  MODEL statement (CATMOD) 427
NOPERCENT option
  TABLES statement (FREQ) 860
NOPRINT option
  ACECLUS procedure 196
  CORRESP procedure 622
  FACTORS statement (PLAN) 1225
  FASTCLUS procedure 826
  LSMEANS statement (GLM) 909
  MODEL statement (REG) 1366
  MODEL statement (RSREG) 1463
  MODEL statement (TRANSREG) 1531,
    1533
  PROC ACECLUS statement 197
  PROC CALIS statement 265
  PROC CANCORR statement 371
  PROC CANDISC statement 391
  PROC CLUSTER statement 525
  PROC CORRESP statement 625
  PROC DISCRIM statement 690
  PROC FASTCLUS statement 828
  PROC GLM statement 902
  PROC LIFEREG statement 1000
  PROC LIFETEST statement 1040
  PROC LOGISTIC statement 1078
  PROC ORTHOREG statement 1212
  PROC PRINCOMP statement 1244
  PROC PRINQUAL statement 1277
  PROC PROBIT statement 1329
  PROC REG statement 1359
  PROC RSREG statement 1461
  PROC TREE statement 1617
  PROC VARCLUS statement 1646
  RIDGE statement (RSREG) 1465
  TABLES statement (FREQ) 861
  TREE procedure 1615
NOPROFILE option
  and output, CATMOD procedure 471
  MODEL statement (CATMOD) 427
NORESPONSE option
  MODEL statement (CATMOD) 427
NORM= option
  FACTOR procedure 780
  PROC FACTOR statement 784
NORM option
  FACTOR statement (CALIS) 277

normal distribution 997–998, 1004, 1010,
    1326, 1332, 1336
  LIFEREG procedure 1004
  testing for fit of 126
normal kernel
  formulas 682
normal kernel method
  DISCRIM procedure 678, 682
Normal theory reweighted LS chi-square
    (CALIS) 304
normalizing data 103
normit function
  LOGISTIC procedure 1086
NOROW option
  CORRESP procedure 622
  PROC CORRESP statement 625
  TABLES statement (FREQ) 861
NOSCALE option
  MODEL statement (LIFEREG) 1005
NOSCORES option
  OUTPUT statement (TRANSREG) 1536,
    1539
NOSHAPE1 option
  MODEL statement (LIFEREG) 1005
NOSIMPLE option
  PROC LOGISTIC statement 1078
nosography
  See clustering
nosology
  See clustering
NOSORT option
  MEANS statement (ANOVA) 222
  MEANS statement (GLM) 916
NOSQUARE option
  and algorithms used, CLUSTER procedure
    562
  PROC CLUSTER statement 524, 525
NOSTD option
  PROC SCORE statement 1481
NOSTDERR option
  PROC CALIS statement 265
NOTABLE option
  LIFETEST procedure 1035
  PROC LIFETEST statement 1040
NOTIE option
  PROC CLUSTER statement 526
NOU option
  REPEATED statement (ANOVA) 225
  REPEATED statement (GLM) 925
NOUNI option
  MODEL statement (ANOVA) 223
  MODEL statement (GLM) 919, 982, 983
NPAR1WAY procedure 1195–1210
  and GLM procedure 894
  and UNIVARIATE procedure 1195
  BY statement 1197, 1198
  CLASS statement 1197, 1199
  compared with nonparametric tests 1196
  compared with other procedures 21–22
  defaults for 1197
  example 1204–1209
  formulas for 1200–1202

NPAR1WAY procedure (*continued*)
  memory requirements 1199
  missing values 1198, 1199
  output 1202–1203
  PROC NPAR1WAY statement 1197–1198
  resolution of tied values 1199
  syntax summary 1197
  tests performed 1196
  VAR statement 1197, 1199
NPLOT= option
  FACTOR procedure 780
  PROC FACTOR statement 784
NTICK= option
  PROC TREE statement 1617
  TREE procedure 1614
numerical taxonomy
  See clustering
NVALS= option
  OUTPUT statement (PLAN) 1227
NVARS= option
  CORRESP procedure 622, 632
  PROC CORRESP statement 625

O

oblique component analysis 1642
oblique Procrustean method 774
oblique transformations
  common factor analysis 776, 786
OBSERVED option
  CORRESP procedure 622, 629
  PROC CORRESP statement 625
odds ratios 860, 877
OMETHOD= option
  PROC CALIS statement 266
ONEWAY option
  and output, CATMOD procedure 471
  MODEL statement (CATMOD) 427
OPSCORE *transform*
  and missing values (PRINQUAL) 1285
  and missing values (TRANSREG) 1540
  MODEL statement (TRANSREG) 1524,
    1528
  TRANSFORM statement (PRINQUAL)
    1281, 1283
  TRANSREG procedure 1543–1544
OPTC option, PROC PROBIT statement
    1328, 1329
optimal scaling 616
  TRANSREG procedure 1542–1545
optimal scoring 616
  PRINQUAL procedure 1281, 1283
  TRANSREG procedure 1524, 1528
optimal transformations
  defined, TRANSREG procedure 1524
  options for (TRANSREG) 1529
  PRINQUAL procedure 1281
  TRANSFORM statement (PRINQUAL)
    1281–1282
  TRANSREG procedure 1524–1528
optimization techniques 266, 295–298

ORDER= option
  examples, CATMOD procedure 443–444,
    478–481, 498–501
  PROBIT procedure 1331
  PROC CATMOD statement 417
  PROC FREQ statement 856
  PROC GLM statement 903, 928, 931, 940,
    964
  PROC LIFEREG statement 1000–1001
  PROC LOGISTIC statement 1078
order statistics
  exponential distribution 1200
  normal distribution 1200
ORDERED option
  OUTPUT statement (PLAN) 1228
  PROC PLAN statement 1224
ORDERED *selection-type*
  FACTORS statement (PLAN) 1225
  TREATMENTS statement (PLAN)
    1229–1230
ordinal scale, definition 26, 30
origin and scale changes
  See linear transformation
Original COSAN Model 248
ORIGINAL *t-option*
  MODEL statement (TRANSREG) 1529
  TRANSFORM statement (PRINQUAL)
    1283
ORTH option
  MANOVA statement (ANOVA) 218
  MANOVA statement (GLM) 911
orthoblique rotation 1642
orthogonal polynomial contrasts
  repeated measurements (ANOVA) 225
  repeated measurements (GLM) 925
orthogonal transformations
  common factor analysis 776, 786
orthomax method 774
orthomax rotation 786
orthonormalizing transformation matrix
  ANOVA procedure 218
  GLM procedure 911
ORTHOREG procedure 1211–1219
  See also "Changes and Enhancements"
  See also regression procedures
  BY statement 1212
  compared with GLM and REG
    procedures 1211
  examples 1214–1219
  missing values 1213
  MODEL statement 1213
  output data sets 1213
  output, printed 1213
  PROC ORTHOREG statement 1212
  WEIGHT statement 1213
OUT= data sets
  ACECLUS procedure 197, 200
  CANCORR procedure 371, 375
  FACTOR procedure 784, 792
  FASTCLUS procedure 830
  NLIN procedure 1156

PRINCOMP procedure 1247
TREE procedure 1620
OUT= option
  ACECLUS procedure 196
  FACTOR procedure 780
  FASTCLUS procedure 826
  LSMEANS statement (GLM) 909
  OUTPUT statement (GLM) 922
  OUTPUT statement (LIFEREG) 1007
  OUTPUT statement (LOGISTIC)
      1084–1085
  OUTPUT statement (PROBIT) 1334
  OUTPUT statement (REG) 1372
  OUTPUT statement (TRANSREG) 1535
  PROC ACECLUS statement 197
  PROC CANCORR statement 371
  PROC CANDISC statement 391
  PROC DISCRIM statement 690
  PROC FACTOR statement 784
  PROC FASTCLUS statement 828
  PROC PRINCOMP statement 1244
  PROC PRINQUAL statement 1277
  PROC RSREG statement 1461
  PROC SCORE statement 1481
  PROC TREE statement 1617
  RESPONSE statement (CATMOD) 434
  TABLES statement (FREQ) 861
  TREE procedure 1614
OUT= specification
  OUTPUT statement (PLAN) 1227, 1230
OUTC= data set
  CORRESP procedure 636–637
OUTC= option
  CORRESP procedure 622
  PROC CORRESP statement 625
OUTD= option
  PROC DISCRIM statement 690
OUTEST= data set
  LIFEREG procedure 1012–1013
  NLIN procedure 1156
OUTEST= option
  PROC CALIS statement 266
  PROC LIFEREG statement 1001
  PROC LOGISTIC statement 1078
  PROC NLIN statement 1139
  PROC ORTHOREG statement 1212
  PROC PROBIT statement 1330, 1338
  PROC REG statement 1359–1360
  RESPONSE statement (CATMOD) 434
OUTF= data set
  CORRESP procedure 637–638
OUTF= option
  CORRESP procedure 622
  PROC CORRESP statement 626
outliers 521, 522, 523
  FASTCLUS procedure 833
output data sets
  ACECLUS procedure 197, 200
  ANOVA procedure 227–228
  CALIS procedure 288–291
  CANCORR procedure 371
  CANDISC procedure 395–397

CATMOD procedure 434, 444–445
CLUSTER procedure 526, 564–566
CORRESP procedure 636–637
DISCRIM procedure 700–703
FACTOR procedure 779, 785, 792
FASTCLUS procedure 827, 828, 830
FREQ procedure 862
GLM procedure 961–963
LIFETEST procedure 1048–1049
LOGISTIC procedure 1078, 1095–1096
NLIN procedure 1156
ORTHOREG procedure 1213
PLAN procedure 1227–1229, 1230
PRINCOMP procedure 1247–1249
PRINQUAL procedure 1267, 1277,
    1288–1290
REG procedure 1389–1393
RSREG procedure 1466
SCORE procedure 1483
TRANSREG procedure 1514–1516, 1532,
    1546–1551
TREE procedure 1615, 1616, 1617, 1620
TYPE=, all procedures 1675–1686
VARCLUS procedure 1646, 1649
OUTPUT statement
  GLM procedure 900, 920–922
  LIFEREG procedure 1006–1007
  LOGISTIC procedure 1077, 1084–1085
  NLIN procedure 1143–1145
  options, TRANSREG procedure 1536–1540
  PLAN procedure 1223, 1227–1229
  PROBIT procedure 1333–1334
  REG procedure 1357, 1358, 1371–1372
  TRANSREG procedure 1521, 1535–1540
output, printed
  ACECLUS procedure 201–202
  ANOVA procedure 228–229
  CALIS procedure 302–307
  CANCORR procedure 377–379
  CANDISC procedure 398–399
  CATMOD procedure 471–473
  CLUSTER procedure 566–568
  DISCRIM procedure 705–707
  GLM procedure 963–964, 966–968,
      969–970, 971, 972–973, 974–975,
      977–978, 979–982, 983–985, 987–988,
      990–993
  LIFEREG procedure 1013–1014
  LOGISTIC procedure 1077–1078, 1081,
      1096–1099
  NLIN procedure 1156
  NPAR1WAY procedure 1202–1203
  ORTHOREG procedure 1213
  PLAN procedure 1233–1234
  PRINCOMP procedure 1250
  PRINQUAL procedure 1267, 1277, 1292
  REG procedure 1436–1438
  RSREG procedure 1469–1471
  STEPDISC procedure 1501–1503
  TRANSREG procedure 1566
  TTEST procedure 1636–1637
  VARCOMP procedure 1666

OUTR= option
  RIDGE statement (RSREG) 1465
OUTRAM= option
  PROC CALIS statement 267
OUTSSCP= option
  PROC REG statement 1360
OUTSTAT= data set
  PRINCOMP procedure 1247–1249
OUTSTAT= data sets
  ACECLUS procedure 200–201
  CANCORR procedure 371–372, 375–376
  FACTOR procedure 784, 792
  VARCLUS procedure 1646, 1649
OUTSTAT= option
  ACECLUS procedure 196
  FACTOR procedure 780
  PROC ACECLUS statement 198
  PROC ANOVA statement 214
  PROC CALIS statement 267
  PROC CANCORR statement 371–372
  PROC CANDISC statement 391
  PROC DISCRIM statement 690
  PROC FACTOR statement 784
  PROC GLM statement 903
  PROC PRINCOMP statement 1244
  PROC VARCLUS statement 1646
OUTSURV= data set
  LIFETEST procedure 1048
OUTSURV= option
  PROC LIFETEST statement 1040
OUTTEST= data set
  LIFETEST procedure 1049
OUTTEST= option
  PROC LIFETEST statement 1040
OUTTREE= data sets
  VARCLUS procedure 1646, 1650
OUTTREE= option
  PROC CLUSTER statement 526
  PROC VARCLUS statement 1646
over-parameterization
  See parameterization of models
OVERCLUS procedure 54
overlapping clusters, definition 53
OVERLAY option
  PLOT statement (REG) 1377

P

P= option
  OUTPUT statement (REG) 1371
P option
  MODEL statement (GLM) 919, 970
  MODEL statement (REG) 1366
P specification
  OUTPUT statement (GLM) 921
p-value
  definition 23
PAGE option
  PROC FREQ statement 857
PAGES= option
  PROC TREE statement 1617
  TREE procedure 1614

PAINT statement (REG) 1357, 1358,
    1372–1375
  See also "Changes and Enhancements"
painting plots
  PAINT statement (REG) 1372–1375
paired comparisons 1633, 1638–1639
  example using PROC MEANS 1638–1639
paired samples, definition 127
paired-difference *t*-test 1633
pairwise comparisons of means 942–945
parallel lines assumption
  testing for, LOGISTIC procedure 1090
PARAMETER= *t-option*
  MODEL statement (TRANSREG) 1529
  TRANSFORM statement (PRINQUAL)
    1283
parameter estimates
  printing for GLM procedure 919
parameter estimates and associated statistics
  REG procedure 1400–1402
parameterization of models
  GLM procedure 928–932
PARAMETERS statement
  CALIS procedure 281
  NLIN procedure 1145–1146
parametric methods
  DISCRIM procedure 680
parametric tests, definition 125
PARENT statement
  TREE procedure 1619
PARMS= option
  OUTPUT statement (NLIN) 1144
parsimax method 774
parsimax rotation 787
Parsimonious index (CALIS) 305
partial canonical correlation 367, 369
partial contributions to inertia table 648
partial correlations
  and principal components 1250
  CANCORR procedure 374, 376, 379
  multivariate analysis of variance, printing
    950
  printing in CANCORR procedure 372
PARTIAL option
  MODEL statement (REG) 1366
PARTIAL statement
  CALIS procedure 281–283
  CANCORR procedure 369, 374
  FACTOR procedure 779, 789
  PRINCOMP procedure 1243, 1246
  VARCLUS procedure 1648
partitioning
  See clustering
path analysis 137–187
  See also CALIS procedure
  definition 137
PB update method specification
  PROC CALIS statement 272
PC option
  MODEL statement (REG) 1366

PCORR option
   PROC CANCORR statement   372
   PROC CANDISC statement   391
   PROC DISCRIM statement   690
   PROC STEPDISC statement   1497
PCORR1 option
   MODEL statement (REG)   1366
PCORR2 option
   MODEL statement (REG)   1366
PCOV option
   PROC CANDISC statement   391
   PROC DISCRIM statement   690
   PROC STEPDISC statement   1497
PDF
   See probability density function
PDIFF option
   LSMEANS statement (GLM)   909, 975
Pearson chi-square   859, 865
   FREQ procedure   855
Pearson chi-square test statistic   1326, 1328,
      1337
Pearson correlation coefficients   860, 868
Pearson residual
   formulas, LOGISTIC procedure   1093-1094
   OUTPUT statement (LOGISTIC)   1085
PENALTY= option
   PROC CLUSTER statement   526
PERCENT= option
   PROC ACECLUS statement   195
   PROC FACTOR statement   785
   PROC VARCLUS statement   1646-1647
permutation null hypothesis, in clustering   97
PESTIM option
   PROC CALIS statement   267
phenogram, definition   1613
phi coefficient   859, 866
piecewise linear transformation
   example   1285, 1531
Pillai's trace   18, 953
   CANCORR procedure   378
   printing in ANOVA   217
   printing in GLM   910
PINITIAL option
   PROC CALIS statement   267
PLAN procedure   1221-1240
   See also "Changes and Enhancements"
   compared to other procedures   21-22
   defaults   1224, 1225
   examples   1226, 1229, 1232-1233,
      1234-1240
   FACTORS statement   1223, 1224-1226
   factors, selecting levels for   1224-1226
   input data set   1227-1229, 1230
   methods   1221-1223, 1226
   output data sets   1227-1229, 1230
   OUTPUT statement   1223, 1227-1229
   printed output   1230, 1233-1234
   PROC PLAN statement   1223
   randomizing designs   1230, 1233
   specifying factor structures   1231-1233
   syntax summary   1223
      TREATMENTS statement   1223, 1229-1230
      using interactively   1223
PLATCOV option
   PROC CALIS statement   267
PLOT option
   FACTOR procedure   780
   PROC FACTOR statement   784
PLOT procedure
   using with PRINCOMP procedure   1252,
      1258
PLOT statement (REG)   1357, 1358,
      1375-1378
   See also "Changes and Enhancements"
PLOTS= option
   PROC LIFETEST statement   1029, 1040
plotting cautions
   CORRESP procedure   617-618
plotting symbols
   CORRESP procedure   620
point models
   See variable expansions
point preference regression   1512
POINT transform
   MODEL statement (TRANSREG)   1524,
      1526
Poisson regression
   example of (NLIN)   1171-1173
polynomial effects, in GLM procedure   895
POLYNOMIAL specification
   REPEATED statement (ANOVA)   225
polynomial terms, in GLM models   928
POLYNOMIAL transformation
   REPEATED statement (GLM)   925, 956, 983
POOL= option
   PROC DISCRIM statement   690-691
pooled variance   1635
population marginal means   948-949
population profiles, definition   30
POPULATION statement
   CATMOD procedure   415, 429-431
POS= option
   PROC TREE statement   1617
   TREE procedure   1614
position series for a design, definition   1230
posterior probability error-rate estimates
   DISCRIM procedure   696-698
POSTERR option
   PROC DISCRIM statement   691
POWER= option
   FACTOR procedure   780
   PROC FACTOR statement   784
POWER transform
   and missing values (PRINQUAL)   1285
   and missing values (TRANSREG)   1540
   MODEL statement (TRANSREG)   1524,
      1527
   TRANSFORM statement (PRINQUAL)
      1280, 1281
power transformation
   PRINQUAL procedure   1280, 1281
   TRANSREG procedure   1524, 1527

PP option
ACECLUS procedure 196
PROC ACECLUS statement 198
PPROB= option
MODEL statement (LOGISTIC) 1082
PR update method specification
PROC CALIS statement 272
PRED= option
MODEL statement (CATMOD) 427
PREDET option
PROC CALIS statement 267
PREDICT option
MODEL statement (CATMOD) 427
MODEL statement (RSREG) 1463
PROC SCORE statement 1481
PREDICTED= option
OUTPUT statement (LIFEREG) 1006
OUTPUT statement (NLIN) 1144
OUTPUT statement (REG) 1371
predicted probabilities
example, CATMOD procedure 514–516
PREDICTED specification
OUTPUT statement (GLM) 921
OUTPUT statement (LOGISTIC) 1085
predicted values
for response functions, CATMOD
procedure 427
GLM procedure 922
LIFEREG procedure 1011–1012
predicted values from regression 15–17
preference analysis 1525
preference mapping
TRANSREG procedure 1603–1609
PREFIX= option
ACECLUS procedure 196
and output data set (PRINQUAL) 1290
PROC ACECLUS statement 198
PROC CANDISC statement 392
PROC PRINCOMP statement 1244–1245
PROC PRINQUAL statement 1277
PREFIX= specification
MANOVA statement (ANOVA) 217
MANOVA statement (GLM) 911
PREFMAP analysis 1525
preliminary analysis
FASTCLUS procedure 833
preliminary clusters
definition 532
using in CLUSTER procedure 524
PREPLOT option
FACTOR procedure 780
PROC FACTOR statement 784
PREROTATE= option
FACTOR procedure 780
PROC FACTOR statement 784
PRESS= option
OUTPUT statement (REG) 1372
PRESS option
MODEL statement (RSREG) 1463
PRESS specification
OUTPUT statement (GLM) 921

PRESS statistic 17
GLM procedure 919
PRIMAT option
PROC CALIS statement 268
principal cluster components example 1653
principal component analysis 774
definition 39
example 800–801
FACTOR procedure 782
with FACTOR procedure 777
principal components
See also PRINCOMP procedure
definition 1241–1242
interpreting eigenvalues 1255
partialling out variables 1246
properties of 1242–1243
rotating 1249
using weights 1247
principal components analysis
See also PRINQUAL procedure
transformed data (PRINQUAL) 1287
using PRINQUAL procedure 1292–1310
principal factor analysis 778, 782
example 803
with FACTOR procedure 778
PRINCOMP procedure 39, 1241–1263
See also "Changes and Enhancements"
and PRINQUAL procedure 1287, 1305
and SCORE procedure 1249
BY statement 1243, 1245–1246
compared with other procedures 55
compared with CALIS procedure 774
compared with CORRESP procedure 41
compared with FACTOR procedure 40–41
compared with PRINQUAL procedure 41
computational resources 1249
examples 1250–1263
FREQ statement 1243, 1246
input data set 1244
memory requirements 1249
missing values 1247, 1259
output data sets 1244, 1247–1249
PARTIAL statement 1243, 1246
printed output 1250
PROC PRINCOMP statement 1243
suppressing output 1244
syntax summary 1243
time requirements 1249
VAR statement 1243, 1246
WEIGHT statement 1243, 1247
weights 1247
PRINQUAL procedure 39, 1265–1323
See also "Changes and Enhancements"
and factor analysis 1288
and FACTOR procedure 1305
and PRINCOMP procedure 1287, 1305
BY statement 1273, 1279
compared with CORRESP procedure 41–42
compared with PRINCOMP procedure 41
compared with TRANSREG procedure 42
computational resources 1291
controlling number of iterations 1286–1287

error messages 1281
examples 1268–1273, 1292–1322
families of transformations 1280–1285
ID statement 1273, 1279
memory requirements 1291
missing values 1285–1286
missing values, estimating 1285,
    1302–1322
missing values, options for 1275, 1276,
    1277, 1278
options for controlling algorithm 1275,
    1276, 1277, 1278
options for controlling iterations 1275,
    1276
output 1267
output data set 1288–1290
output data set, options for 1275, 1277,
    1278
principal components analysis 1287
printed output 1292
PROC PRINQUAL statement 1274
suppressing output 1277
syntax summary 1273
time requirements 1291
TRANSFORM statement 1273, 1279–1285
transformation methods 1266–1268
PRINT= option
    CORRESP procedure 622
    PROC CLUSTER statement 526
    PROC CORRESP statement 626
PRINT option
    FACTOR procedure 780
    MTEST statement (REG) 1369–1370
    PROC CALIS statement 268
    PROC FACTOR statement 784
PRINT statement
    REG procedure 1357, 1358, 1378–1379
PRINTE option
    MANOVA statement (ANOVA) 218
    MANOVA statement (GLM) 911, 950, 982
    REPEATED statement (ANOVA) 225
    REPEATED statement (GLM) 925, 954, 986
printed output
    ANOVA procedure 228–229
    CORRESP procedure 650–652
    FACTOR procedure 774, 797–800
    LIFEREG procedure 1013–1014
    LIFETEST procedure 1050–1052
    NESTED procedure 1131–1133
    NLIN procedure 1156
printed output options
    PROC CORRESP statement 622–627
PRINTH option
    MANOVA statement (ANOVA) 218
    MANOVA statement (GLM) 911, 982
    REPEATED statement (ANOVA) 225
    REPEATED statement (GLM) 925
printing options
    CORRESP procedure 622
PRINTM option
    REPEATED statement (ANOVA) 226
    REPEATED statement (GLM) 926, 954

PRINTRV option
    REPEATED statement (ANOVA) 226
    REPEATED statement (GLM) 926
prior communality estimates 785
PRIORS= option
    FACTOR procedure 780
    PROC FACTOR statement 785
PRIORS statement
    DISCRIM procedure 686, 694–695
    FACTOR procedure 779, 789
PRIVEC option
    PROC CALIS statement 268
PROB= option, OUTPUT statement
    (PROBIT) 1334
PROB option
    and output, CATMOD procedure 471
    MODEL statement (CATMOD) 427
PROB specification
    OUTPUT statement (LOGISTIC) 1085
probability density function 1028, 1045,
    1046, 1051
    nonparametric estimation 133
probit equation 1326, 1335
probit model
    example of (NLIN) 1160–1162
PROBIT procedure 30, 1325–1350
    See also "Changes and Enhancements"
    See also regression procedures
    CLASS statement 1330
    compared with LOGISTIC and CATMOD
        procedures 35–38
    distributions 1336
    examples 1340–1350
    historical notes 1339
    inverse confidence limits 1337–1338
    lack-of-fit tests 1336–1337
    missing values 1334
    MODEL statement 1330–1333
    models 1335–1336
    OUTPUT statement 1333–1334
    printed output 1339–1340
    PROC PROBIT statement 1327–1330
    syntax summary 1327
    tolerance distribution 1337
    WEIGHT statement 1334
PROBT option
    PROC CANCORR statement 372
PROC ACECLUS statement
    ACECLUS procedure 195
PROC ANOVA statement 214
PROC CALIS statement 260
PROC CANCORR statement
    CANCORR procedure 369–373
PROC CANDISC statement
    CANDISC procedure 390
    options 390–393
PROC CATMOD statement 415
    CATMOD procedure 417
PROC CLUSTER statement 521
    CLUSTER procedure 521–527
    options 523–527

PROC CORRESP statement
  CORRESP procedure 621
  other options 622
  printed output options 622-627
  table construction options 622-627
PROC DISCRIM statement
  DISCRIM procedure 686
  options 686-693
PROC FACTOR statement
  FACTOR procedure 779
PROC FASTCLUS statement
  FASTCLUS procedure 825
PROC FREQ statement 856-857
  FREQ procedure 856-857
PROC GLM statement 900, 902-903
  options 902-903
PROC LIFEREG statement
  LIFEREG procedure 1000-1001
  options 1000-1001
PROC LIFETEST statement 1038-1043
PROC LOGISTIC statement 1077-1078
  LOGISTIC procedure 1077
  options 1077-1078
PROC NESTED statement
  NESTED procedure 1129
PROC NLIN statement
  NLIN procedure 1137
  options 1138-1140
PROC NPAR1WAY statement 1197-1198
  options 1197-1198
PROC ORTHOREG statement
  ORTHOREG procedure 1212
PROC PLAN statement 1224
PROC PRINCOMP statement 1243
  options 1243-1245
PROC PRINQUAL statement 1273, 1274
  options 1274-1278
PROC PROBIT statement 1327-1330
PROC REG statement
  options 1359
  REG procedure 1358-1360
PROC RSREG statement
  RSREG procedure 1461
PROC SCORE statement
  SCORE procedure 1481-1482
PROC STEPDISC statement
  options 1496-1500
PROC TRANSREG statement 1521-1523
  options 1521-1523
PROC TREE statement
  TREE procedure 1614
PROC TTEST statement
  TTEST procedure 1634
PROC VARCLUS statement
  VARCLUS procedure 1643
  VARCLUS statement options 1643
PROC VARCOMP statement
  VARCOMP procedure 1662
procrustes rotation 787
producing plots
  PLOT statement (REG) 1375-1378

product multinomial distribution
  See multinomial distribution
product-limit estimates 106, 1028, 1039,
    1044, 1050, 1052-1062
PROFILE= option
  CORRESP procedure 622
  FACTORS statement (CATMOD) 422-424
  PROC CORRESP statement 626, 639-641
  REPEATED statement (CATMOD) 432
PROFILE specification
  REPEATED statement (ANOVA) 225
PROFILE transformation
  REPEATED statement (GLM) 925, 957-958
profiles in contingency tables, definition 30
promax 774
promax rotation 787
PROPORTION= option
  FACTOR procedure 780
  PROC ACECLUS statement 195
  PROC FACTOR statement 785
  PROC VARCLUS statement 1646
  using, VARCLUS procedure 1649
proportional hazards model 106, 1010, 1029
  LIFETEST procedure 1029
  regression (NLIN) 1181
proportional odds assumption
  testing for, LOGISTIC procedure 1090
proportions, comparisons of 865
PR2ENTRY=option
  PROC STEPDISC statement 1497
PR2STAY=option
  PROC STEPDISC statement 1497
pseudo F and t statistics
  in CLUSTER procedure 526
PSEUDO option
  PROC CLUSTER statement 526
PSSCP option
  PROC CANDISC statement 392
  PROC DISCRIM statement 691
  PROC STEPDISC statement 1497

Q

Q option
  RANDOM statement (GLM) 923, 958
Q-analysis
  See clustering
QPOINT transform
  MODEL statement (TRANSREG) 1524,
    1526
QPOINT variables, definition 1525
QQ option
  ACECLUS procedure 196
  PROC ACECLUS statement 198
quadratic discriminant function 678
quadratic forms for fixed effects
  printing in GLM procedure 923
quadratic ideal point regression
  TRANSREG procedure 1526
quadratic polynomial transformation
  example 1279

quadratic response surface
   with QPOINT (TRANSREG)   1526
quadratic spline transformation
   example   1284, 1530
qualitative variables
   See also classification variables
   definition   30
QUANEW optimization technique
      specification
   PROC CALIS statement   266
quantal response data   1325
quantification method
   CORRESP procedure   616
QUANTILES= option
   OUTPUT statement (LIFEREG)   1007
quartimax method   774
quartimax rotation   787
QUIT statement
   and PLAN procedure   1223

R

R= option
   and other options (CLUSTER)   524, 525,
      527
   FACTOR statement (CALIS)   277
   OUTPUT statement (REG)   1372
   PROC CLUSTER statement   526, 532
   PROC DISCRIM statement   691
R option
   MODEL statement (REG)   1367
R specification
   OUTPUT statement (GLM)   921
R-notation   895-896, 934
R-square statistic
   CANCORR procedure   376
   CLUSTER procedure   527
RADIUS= option
   PROC CALIS statement   268
   PROC FASTCLUS statement   826
   RIDGE statement (RSREG)   1465
RADIUS= option, use   824, 825
radius of sphere of support   526
RAM Model   248
RAM statement
   CALIS procedure   283-284
RANDOM= option
   FACTOR procedure   780
   FASTCLUS procedure   826
   PROC CALIS statement   268
   PROC FACTOR statement   785-786
   PROC FASTCLUS statement   828
   PROC VARCLUS statement   1647
random effects model
   See also nested designs
   definition   25-26
   expected mean squares (GLM)   958-959
   GLM procedure   922
   SAS procedures for   26
   VARCOMP procedure   1661-1662, 1663,
      1664-1665

random number generators
   and PLAN procedure   1224
RANDOM option
   OUTPUT statement (PLAN)   1228
RANDOM selection-type
   FACTORS statement (PLAN)   1225
   TREATMENTS statement (PLAN)
      1229-1230
RANDOM statement
   See also "Changes and Enhancements"
      (GLM)
   and CONTRAST statement   922
   GLM procedure   900-901, 922-923
random zeros   463
randomization model test statistics
   See CMH statistics
randomization of designs
   using PLAN procedure   1233
randomized complete block design
   analyzing with ANOVA procedure   234-235
   analyzing with GLM procedure   964-969
   generating with PLAN procedure   1232
rank order typal analysis
   See complete linkage
RANK procedure   103
   See also "Changes and Enhancements"
   and the ANOVA procedure   1196
RANK scores   872
   See also simple linear rank statistics
rank tests   126-132, 133
   See Wilcoxon rank sum test
   LIFETEST procedure   1046-1048
RANK transform
   and missing values (PRINQUAL)   1285
   and missing values (TRANSREG)   1540
   MODEL statement (TRANSREG)   1524,
      1527
   TRANSFORM statement (PRINQUAL)
      1281, 1282
rank transformation
   PRINQUAL procedure   1280, 1281
   TRANSREG procedure   1524, 1527
ranking data   103
ranks, obtaining   132
RANUNI function
   and PLAN procedure   1222
Rao's approximation, for likelihood ratio
   CANCORR procedure   377
ratios
   odds   877
RDF= option
   PROC CALIS statement   269
   PROC CANCORR statement   372
READ function
   RESPONSE statement (CATMOD)   434
reciprocal averaging   616
RED option
   PROC CANCORR statement   372
reduction notation   111-112, 895-896, 934
redundancy analysis   1512
   See canonical redundancy analysis

REDUNDANCY method
    and output data sets (TRANSREG) 1552
    specifying in TRANSREG procedure 1532
REDUNDANCY option
    PROC CANCORR statement 372
reference structure, common factor analysis
    776
REFIT statement (REG) 1357, 1358, 1379
    See also "Changes and Enhancements"
REFRESH= option
    PROC PRINQUAL statement 1277
REG procedure 1351-1456
    See also "Changes and Enhancements"
    See also regression procedures
    ADD statement 1360
    ADJRSQ selection method 1400
    and GLM procedure 894
    and TRANSREG procedure 1575-1578
    backward elimination technique 1398
    BY statement 1360-1361
    computational methods 1436
    computational resources 1436
    CP selection method 1399
    DELETE statement 1361
    forward selection technique 1397-1398
    FREQ statement 1361
    ID statement 1361
    input data sets 1386-1389
    interactive analysis 1393-1397
    limitations in model-selection methods
        1400
    missing values 1385
    MODEL statement 1361-1369
    MTEST statement 1369-1370
    output data sets 1389-1393
    OUTPUT statement 1371-1372
    OUTSSCP= data sets 1392-1393
    PAINT statement 1372-1375
    parameter estimates and associated
        statistics 1400
    PLOT statement 1375-1378
    PRINT statement 1378-1379
    printed output 1436-1438
    PROC REG statement 1358-1360
    REFIT statement 1379
    RESTRICT statement 1379-1381
    REWEIGHT statement 1381-1384
    RSQUARE selection method 1399
    SSCP data set 1392
    TEST statement 1384-1385
    TYPE=CORR data set 1386-1388
    TYPE=SSCP data set 1386, 1388-1389
    VAR statement 1385
    WEIGHT statement 1385
regression
    associated statistics 10-12
    assumptions 9-10
    autocorrelation, time-series 1434-1436
    background 9-12
    CATMOD procedure 410
    coefficients, TRANSREG procedure 1537
    collinearity diagnostics 1416-1418

coordinates, TRANSREG procedure 1539
diagnostics, in LOGISTIC procedure
    1093-1095
example 4-5
general form of estimable functions
    114-115
grouping variables 1365
ill-conditioned data 1211
influence diagnostics 1418-1425
interpreting 12-15
less-than-full-rank models 1415-1416
logistic regression 1071-1126
MODEL statements (GLM) 896
model-selection methods 1397-1399
multivariate tests 17-19, 1431-1434
ORTHOREG procedure 1211
parameter estimates 10, 1400-1402
performing with GLM procedure 969-971
predicted and residual values 15-17,
    1402-1404
reduction notation 111-112
test of hypotheses 17-19
testing for heteroscedasticity 1431
using GLM procedure 898
using transformations, TRANSREG
    procedure 1598-1603
regression coefficients
    CANCORR procedure 370
regression effects, in GLM models 928
regression parameter estimates, example
    1487-1490
regression procedures 1-20
    See also "Changes and Enhancements"
    See also CALIS procedure
    See also CATMOD procedure
    See also GLM procedure
    See also LIFEREG procedure
    See also LOGISTIC procedure
    See also NLIN procedure
    See also ORTHOREG procedure
    See also PROBIT procedure
    See also REG procedure
    See also RSREG procedure
    See also TRANSREG procedure
    CATMOD procedure, summary 9
    comparing 1-3
    GLM procedure, summary 8
    interpreting regression statistics 12-15
    LIFEREG procedure, summary 8
    nonlinear with NLIN procedure 7-8
    predicted and residual values 15-17
    REG procedure, summary 7
    statistical background 9-10
regression, painting plots
    detailed examples 1411-1415
regression, producing plots
    detailed examples 1404-1411
regression, reweighting observations
    detailed examples 1426-1430
regressors (GLM) 895
REGWF option
    MEANS statement (ANOVA) 222
    MEANS statement (GLM) 916, 947

REGWQ option
  MEANS statement (ANOVA)   222
  MEANS statement (GLM)   916, 947
relative risk estimates   871, 875–877
  case-control studies   871, 872
  cohort studies   871–872
  FREQ procedure   875–877
REML option
  PROC VARCOMP statement   1662
REORDER option
  FACTOR procedure   780
  PROC FACTOR statement   786
repeated measurement factors
  CATMOD procedure   431–433
  example   224
  specifying in REPEATED statement
      (ANOVA)   224
  specifying in REPEATED statement
      (CATMOD)   431–433
  specifying in REPEATED statement (GLM)
      924
repeated measures analysis
  See also absorbing variables in models
  adjusted F values   954
  ANOVA procedure   223–226
  CATMOD procedure   409, 449–452
  doubly-multivariate (GLM)   988–993
  examples, CATMOD procedure   492–506
  GLM procedure   923–926, 951–958
  hypothesis testing   953–955
  more than one factor in ANOVA procedure
      223–226
  more than one factor in GLM procedure
      926
  more than one repeated factor   954
  multiple populations (CATMOD)   451–452
  one population (CATMOD)   449–451
  organization of data for   951–953
  performing with GLM procedure   982–986
  transformations   955–958
REPEATED statement
  and CONTRAST statement (GLM)   924
  and design matrix, CATMOD procedure
      457–459
  and TEST statement (GLM)   924
  ANOVA procedure   214, 223–226
  CATMOD procedure   415, 431–433
  examples, CATMOD procedure   449–452
  GLM procedure   900, 923–926
  options (ANOVA)   225–226
  options (GLM)   925–926
  options, CATMOD procedure   432–433
REPLACE= option
  FASTCLUS procedure   826
  PROC FASTCLUS statement   828
REPLACE= option, use   825
REPLACE option
  and output data set (PRINQUAL)
      1288–1289
  FASTCLUS procedure   832

OUTPUT statement (TRANSREG)   1536,
    1539
  PROC PRINQUAL statement   1277
RESCHI specification
  OUTPUT statement (LOGISTIC)   1085
RESDEV specification
  OUTPUT statement (LOGISTIC)   1085
RESET option
  PAINT statement (REG)   1374
  REWEIGHT statement (REG)   1383
RESIDUAL= option
  OUTPUT statement (NLIN)   1144
  OUTPUT statement (REG)   1372
residual chi-square
  LOGISTIC procedure   1089
residual correlation
  factor analysis   775
RESIDUAL option
  MODEL statement (RSREG)   1463
  PROC CALIS statement   268
  PROC SCORE statement   1481
RESIDUAL specification
  OUTPUT statement (GLM)   921
residual sum of squares
  nonlinear regression   1136
residual values from regression   15–17
residuals
  GLM procedure   921
residuals and partial correlation   1246, 1247
RESIDUALS option
  FACTOR procedure   780
  PROC FACTOR statement   786
resource usage
  FREQ procedure   859
response functions
  customized (CATMOD)   437–439
  direct input of, example (CATMOD)
      506–509
  examples   442–443
  examples, CATMOD procedure   437–439
  formulas   467
  identifying with FACTORS statement
      (CATMOD)   421
  inverse variance of, formulas   468
  number of and formulas for   436
  reading directly into CATMOD procedure
      442–443
  related to design matrix (CATMOD)
      452–462
  specifying in CATMOD procedure   433–440
  standard functions, CATMOD procedure
      439–440
  using transformations (CATMOD)   437–439
  variance of, formulas   468
response profiles, definition   30
RESPONSE statement
  CATMOD procedure   415, 433–440
  examples, CATMOD procedure   437–439,
      442–443, 474–477, 478–481, 492–498,
      506–509

RESPONSE statement (*continued*)
  in repeated measures analysis (CATMOD)
    449, 498–501, 502–506
  options, CATMOD procedure   434
response surface regression
  using TRANSREG procedure   1512
response surfaces
  canonical analysis, interpreting   1466
  contour plots   1467
  covariates   1468
  examples   1471–1477
  experiments   1458
  ridge analysis   1459
response variable, definition   211
RESPONSE= option
  FACTORS statement (CATMOD)   422
  REPEATED statement (CATMOD)   432
RESPONSE
  and AVERAGED models, CATMOD
    procedure   457
  and LOGLIN statement (CATMOD)   424
  MODEL statement (CATMOD)   425
RESTRICT statement
  See also "Changes and Enhancements"
    (REG)
  CATMOD procedure   415, 440
  REG procedure   1357, 1358, 1379–1381
restricted maximum likelihood method
  VARCOMP procedure   1666
restrictions
  in models, CATMOD procedure   440
reticular action model (RAM)   150
REWEIGHT statement (REG)   1357, 1358,
    1381–1384
  See also "Changes and Enhancements"
reweighting observations
  REWEIGHT statement (REG)   1381–1384
RHO= option
  PROC NLIN statement   1139
ridge analysis   1459
RIDGE option
  PROC CALIS statement   269
RIDGE statement (RSREG)   1464
  See also "Changes and Enhancements"
ridit scores   872
right-censoring   105
risk ratios   860
RMSE option
  MODEL statement (REG)   1367
RMSSTD option
  PROC CLUSTER statement   526
RMSSTD statement
  and FREQ statement, CLUSTER
    procedure   528, 529
  CLUSTER procedure   521, 529
robust parameter estimates   999
robust regression   1136
  example of (NLIN)   1165–1168
ROOT= option
  PROC TREE statement   1617
  TREE procedure   1614
root mean square residual (CALIS)   304

root-mean-square standard deviation
    formula, for CLUSTER procedure   561
ROTATE= option
  FACTOR procedure   780
  FACTOR statement (CALIS)   277
  PROC FACTOR statement   786–787
rotating principal components   1249
rotation methods
  FACTOR procedure   786–787
rotation option
  FACTOR procedure   786–787
rotation, definition   40
ROUND option
  FACTOR procedure   780
  PROC FACTOR statement   787
ROW= option
  CORRESP procedure   622
  PROC CORRESP statement   626, 639–641
Roy's greatest root
  CANCORR procedure   378
Roy's maximum root   19, 953
Roy's maximum root criterion
  printing in ANOVA   217
  printing in GLM   910
RP option
  CORRESP procedure   622
  PROC CORRESP statement   627
RSQ option
  PROC CLUSTER statement   527
RSQUARE option
  PROC CLUSTER statement   527
RSQUARE procedure
  See "Changes and Enhancements"
  See also REG procedure
RSQUARE selection method, REG
    procedure   1399
RSREG procedure   1457–1478
  See also "Changes and Enhancements"
  See also regression procedures
  and GLM procedure   894
  BY statement   1461
  computational methods   1468
  examples   1471–1477
  ID statement   1462
  missing values   1465
  MODEL statement   1462
  output data sets   1466
  printed output   1469–1471
  PROC RSREG statement   1461
  RIDGE statement   1464
  syntax summary   1460
  WEIGHT statement   1465
RSTUDENT= option
  OUTPUT statement (REG)   1372
RSTUDENT specification
  OUTPUT statement (GLM)   921
RUN statement
  and PLAN procedure   1223
Ryan multiple comparison tests   222, 916,
    947

S

S option
  PROC CANCORR statement   372
  PROC CLUSTER statement   527
SALPHA= option
  PROC CALIS statement   269
sample sizes
  and categorical analyses   35
  required, for CATMOD procedure   462
sample survey analysis, ordinal data   410
sampling
  simple random, in contingency tables   31
  stratified random, in contingency tables
    31–33
sampling assumptions, CATMOD procedure
  34–35
sampling zeros   463
  and log-linear analyses (CATMOD)   448
  and structural zeros (CATMOD)   463
SAS/ETS procedures   3
Satterthwaite's approximation   1633, 1636
  testing random effects   959
SAVAGE option
  PROC NPAR1WAY statement   1198
Savage scores   1200
Savage tests   127, 1196, 1198, 1200
  generalized   133
  LIFETEST procedure   1028
SAVE option
  PROC NLIN statement   1139
SBC option
  MODEL statement (REG)   1367
SCALE= option
  MODEL statement (LIFEREG)   1005
scale and origin changes
  See linear transformation
scaling axes
  CORRESP procedure   618
scalogram analysis   616
SCHEFFE option
  MEANS statement (ANOVA)   222
  MEANS statement (GLM)   916, 944
Scheffe's multiple comparison method   222,
  916
  contrasted with Bonferroni   944
  contrasted with Sidak's   944
Schwartz Criterion
  LOGISTIC procedure   1089
Schwarz's Bayesian criterion
  CALIS procedure   304
  FACTOR procedure   798
SCORE= option
  PROC SCORE statement   1481
SCORE option
  FACTOR procedure   780
  PROC FACTOR statement   787
score partition
  output data sets (TRANSREG)   1516
SCORE procedure   103, 1479–1491
  See also "Changes and Enhancements"
  analyzing data in groups   1482

and PRINCOMP procedure   1249
  BY statement   1482
  ID statement   1482
  missing values   1483
  output data set   1483
  PROC SCORE statement   1481–1482
  syntax summary   1480
  VAR statement   1482–1483
score statistics
  global, in LOGISTIC procedure   1082
  LOGISTIC procedure   1089–1090
score variables, interpretation   1483
SCORES= option
  TABLES statement (FREQ)   861
SCORES option
  and output data set (PRINQUAL)   1290
  PROC PRINQUAL statement   1277
scoring coefficients   1479
scoring procedures   103
scoring, optimal
  See optimal scoring
SCORR1 option
  MODEL statement (REG)   1367
SCORR2 option
  MODEL statement (REG)   1367
SCREE option
  FACTOR procedure   780
  PROC FACTOR statement   787
scree plot   774, 787, 798
  interpreting   1292, 1297
SDF
  See survival distribution function
SEB option
  PROC CANCORR statement   372
Secant (DUD) method   1136
SEED= option
  FASTCLUS procedure   826
  PROC FASTCLUS statement   828
  PROC PLAN statement   1224
seed replacement
  FASTCLUS procedure   824, 825, 828
SEED statement
  VARCLUS procedure   1648
segmented models   1136
  example of (NLIN)   1163–1165
SELECTION= option
  MODEL statement (LOGISTIC)   1082
  MODEL statement (REG)   1367
selection-type specification
  FACTORS statement (PLAN)   1225
semipartial correlation
  formula, for CLUSTER procedure   561
semipartial correlations
  CANCORR procedure   372, 376, 379
sensitivity
  in LOGISTIC procedure   1092
sensitivity to linear dependencies
  GLM procedure   919, 920
SEQB option
  MODEL statement (REG)   1367
SEQUENTIAL option
  MODEL statement (LOGISTIC)   1082

sequential sums of squares
  See Type I SS
SHAPE1= option
  MODEL statement (LIFEREG) 1005
SHORT option
  ACECLUS procedure 196, 198
  CORRESP procedure 622, 629
  FASTCLUS procedure 826, 834, 835
  PROC ACECLUS statement 198
  PROC CALIS statement 269
  PROC CANCORR statement 372
  PROC CANDISC statement 392
  PROC CORRESP statement 627
  PROC DISCRIM statement 691
  PROC FASTCLUS statement 828
  PROC STEPDISC statement 1497
  PROC VARCLUS statement 1647
SIDAK option
  MEANS statement (ANOVA) 222
  MEANS statement (GLM) 917, 943
Sidak t-test 943
Sidak's inequality
  using for multiple comparison tests 222,
    917
Sidak's multiple comparison method
  contrasted with Scheffe's 944
SIGMA= option
  MODEL statement (REG) 1367
sign test 126-127, 128, 1195
signed rank test
  See Wilcoxon signed rank test
significance probability value
  definition 23
SIGSQ= option
  PROC NLIN statement 1139
SIMILAR option
  PROC TREE statement 1617
  TREE procedure 1614
simple cluster-seeking algorithm 825
simple correspondence analysis
  example, CORRESP procedure 652-659,
    665-673
simple linear rank statistics
  See also NPAR1WAY procedure
  definition 1200
  formulas for 1200
SIMPLE option
  FACTOR procedure 780
  PROC CALIS statement 269
  PROC CANCORR statement 372
  PROC CANDISC statement 392
  PROC CLUSTER statement 527
  PROC DISCRIM statement 691
  PROC FACTOR statement 787
  PROC REG statement 1360
  PROC STEPDISC statement 1498
  PROC VARCLUS statement 1647
simultaneous inference methods, definition
    942
simultaneous test procedure, definition 942

single linkage
  compared to other clustering methods
    56-97
  with CLUSTER procedure 522, 534-535
SINGULAR= option
  ACECLUS procedure 196
  CONTRAST statement (GLM) 905
  CORRESP procedure 622, 627
  ESTIMATE statement (GLM) 907
  FACTOR procedure 780
  LSMEANS statement (GLM) 909
  MODEL statement (GLM) 919
  MODEL statement (LIFEREG) 1006
  MODEL statement (LOGISTIC) 1083
  MODEL statement (PROBIT) 1333
  MODEL statement (TRANSREG) 1531,
    1534
  PROC ACECLUS statement 198
  PROC CALIS statement 269
  PROC CANCORR statement 372
  PROC CANDISC statement 392
  PROC DISCRIM statement 691-692
  PROC FACTOR statement 787
  PROC LIFETEST statement 1041
  PROC ORTHOREG statement 1212
  PROC PRINQUAL statement 1278
  PROC REG statement 1360
  PROC STEPDISC statement 1498
singularity checking
  CANCORR procedure 372
  GLM procedure 919, 920
  LIFETEST procedure 1041
  STEPDISC procedure 1498
skewness
  printed in CLUSTER procedure 527
SLENTRY= option
  MODEL statement (LOGISTIC) 1083
  MODEL statement (REG) 1367
  PROC STEPDISC statement 1498
SLMW= option
  PROC CALIS statement 269
SLPOOL= option
  PROC DISCRIM statement 692
SLSTAY= option
  MODEL statement (LOGISTIC) 1083
  MODEL statement (REG) 1368
  PROC STEPDISC statement 1498
SMC option
  PROC CANCORR statement 372
SMETHOD= option
  PROC CALIS statement 270
  PROC NLIN statement 1140
SMM option
  MEANS statement (ANOVA) 222
  MEANS statement (GLM) 917, 944
smoothing parameters
  in cluster analysis 532
SNK option
  MEANS statement (ANOVA) 222
  MEANS statement (GLM) 917, 946
SOLUTION option
  MODEL statement (GLM) 919, 931, 964

Somers' D 860, 867–868
SORT option
  PROC TREE statement 1617
  TREE procedure 1615
SP option
  MODEL statement (REG) 1368
SPACES= option
  PROC TREE statement 1617–1618
  TREE procedure 1614
SPARSE option
  TABLES statement (FREQ) 861
SPCORR option
  PROC CANCORR statement 372
Spearman rank correlation coefficient 860,
    868–869
Spearman's correlation 35
SPEC option
  MODEL statement (REG) 1368
special SAS data sets 1675–1686
specification of effects
  CATMOD procedure 411–413
specificity
  in LOGISTIC procedure 1092
sphericity tests 954, 986
  ANOVA procedure 225
  GLM procedure 925
SPLINE transform
  and missing values (PRINQUAL) 1285
  and missing values (TRANSREG) 1540
  MODEL statement (TRANSREG) 1524,
    1528
  options (PRINQUAL) 1283–1285
  options (TRANSREG) 1529–1531
  TRANSFORM statement (PRINQUAL)
    1281, 1283
  TRANSREG procedure 1544–1545
spline transformations
  PRINQUAL procedure 1280, 1282
  TRANSREG procedure 1524, 1527, 1528
splines
  definition 1516, 1567
  details of use 1544–1545
  examples 1516–1518, 1567–1575
  examples, TRANSREG procedure 1528,
    1530–1531
split-plot design
  See also repeated measures analysis
  analyzing with ANOVA procedure
    236–237, 238–239, 240–243
  analyzing with TEST statements (ANOVA)
    227
  analyzing with TEST statements (GLM) 927
  generating with PLAN procedure
    1235–1236
SPRECISION= option
  PROC CALIS statement 270
SQPCORR option
  PROC CANCORR statement 372
SQSPCORR option
  PROC CANCORR statement 372
squared multiple correlations
  CANCORR procedure 372

squared partial correlations
  CANCORR procedure 379
squared semipartial correlations
  CANCORR procedure 372, 376, 379
  formula, for CLUSTER procedure 561
SS
  See sums of squares
SSCP data set, REG procedure 1392–1393
SSCP matrix
  printing for multivariate tests (GLM) 910,
    911, 925
  printing for multivariate tests in ANOVA
    procedure 216–217, 218, 225
SSE= option
  OUTPUT statement (NLIN) 1144
SSE option
  MODEL statement (REG) 1368
SS1 option
  MODEL statement (GLM) 919
  MODEL statement (REG) 1368
SS2 option
  MODEL statement (GLM) 920
  MODEL statement (REG) 1368
SS3 option
  MODEL statement (GLM) 920
SS4 option
  MODEL statement (GLM) 920
standard deviations
  printed in CLUSTER procedure 527
standard errors
  individual predicted value (GLM) 921
  mean predicted value (GLM) 921
  residuals (GLM) 921
STANDARD option
  PROC CLUSTER statement 527
  PROC PRINCOMP statement 1245
  PROC PRINQUAL statement 1278
STANDARD procedure 103
  use in cluster analysis 55
standard response functions
  defined, CATMOD procedure 439
standardization 1480
standardized scoring coefficients 1652
standardizing variables
  in CLUSTER procedure 527
START= option
  MODEL statement (LOGISTIC) 1083
  MODEL statement (REG) 1368
  PROC CALIS statement 270
  PROC STEPDISC statement 1498
statistical tests for contingency tables
    864–877
statistics
  descriptive, FREQ procedure 852–889
  FREQ procedure 864–877
  measures of association 854–855
statistics in FREQ procedure 864–877
STATUS option
  PAINT statement (REG) 1375
  REWEIGHT statement (REG) 1384
STB option
  MODEL statement (REG) 1368
  PROC CANCORR statement 373

STD= option, OUTPUT statement
      (PROBIT) 1334
STD _ERR= option
   OUTPUT statement (LIFEREG) 1007
STD option
   PROC CLUSTER statement 527
   PROC PRINCOMP statement 1245
STD statement
   CALIS procedure 284-285
STDERR option
   LSMEANS statement (GLM) 909, 975
   PROC CALIS statement 271
STDI= option
   OUTPUT statement (NLIN) 1144
   OUTPUT statement (REG) 1372
STDI specification
   OUTPUT statement (GLM) 921
STDMEAN option
   PROC CANDISC statement 392
   PROC DISCRIM statement 692
   PROC STEPDISC statement 1498
STDP= option
   OUTPUT statement (NLIN) 1144
   OUTPUT statement (REG) 1372
STDP specification
   OUTPUT statement (GLM) 921
STDR= option
   OUTPUT statement (NLIN) 1144
   OUTPUT statement (REG) 1372
STDR specification
   OUTPUT statement (GLM) 921
STDXBETA specification
   OUTPUT statement (LOGISTIC) 1085
steepest-descent method 1136, 1152
STEP= option
   PROC NLIN statement 1140
step-down methods
   See multiple comparison methods
step-down multiple-stage test, definition 941
step-down test
   See multiple comparison methods
STEPDISC procedure 45, 46, 1493-1508
   See also "Changes and Enhancements"
   BY statement 1495, 1499
   CLASS statement 1495, 1499
   computational resources 1501
   example 1503-1508
   FREQ statement 1495, 1499
   input data sets 1500-1501
   memory requirements 1501
   methods 1493-1495
   missing values 1500
   printed output 1501-1503
   syntax summary 1495
   time requirements 1501
   TYPE= data sets 1500-1501
   VAR statement 1495, 1499
   WEIGHT statement 1495, 1499-1500
stepwise discriminant analysis 46,
      1493-1508
STEPWISE procedure
   See "Changes and Enhancements"
   See also REG procedure

stepwise selection
   LOGISTIC procedure 1076
stepwise technique, REG procedure 1398
STOP= option
   MODEL statement (LOGISTIC) 1083
   MODEL statement (REG) 1368
   PROC STEPDISC statement 1498
STOPRES option
   MODEL statement (LOGISTIC) 1083
stored data algorithm 562
stored distance algorithm 562
STRATA statement, LIFETEST procedure
      1042
stratified analysis
   for contingency tables 33
   FREQ procedure 852-889
stratified random sampling
   and contingency tables 31-33
stratum, definition 33
STRICT= option
   FASTCLUS procedure 842
   PROC FASTCLUS statement 828
STRICT option
   FASTCLUS procedure 826
strip-split plot design
   analyzing with ANOVA procedure 240-243
structural equation modeling 137-187
   See also CALIS procedure
   definition 137
   estimation methods 139
   goodness-of-fit statistics 140-141
   identification of models 145-149
   optimization methods 141
   path diagrams 149-154
   RAM model 149-154
   specification 141-145
   statistical inference 139-140
structural model 145
structural zeros 463
Stuart's tau-c 860, 867
STUDENT= option
   OUTPUT statement (NLIN) 1145
   OUTPUT statement (REG) 1372
Student-Newman-Keuls multiple range test
      946-947
studentized maximum modulus
   using in multiple comparison tests 222,
      917
studentized residuals 16
   GLM procedure 921
Student's multiple range test 222, 917
SUMMARY option
   FASTCLUS procedure 826, 834
   MANOVA statement (ANOVA) 218
   MANOVA statement (GLM) 912
   PROC CALIS statement 271
   PROC FASTCLUS statement 828
   PROC VARCLUS statement 1647
   REPEATED statement (ANOVA) 226
   REPEATED statement (GLM) 926, 954,
      983, 986

sums of squares
    printing in GLM procedure 919-920
sums of squares, types of
    estimable functions for Type I 115-116
    estimable functions for Type II 116-120
    estimable functions for Type III 120-122
    estimable functions for Type IV 122-124
supplementary rows and columns 647
SUPPLEMENTARY statement
    CORRESP procedure 628, 631-632
survival analysis 105-107
    comparing curves (LIFETEST) 1028-1034,
        1046
    comparing procedures 106
    example (LIFEREG) 1016-1023
    nonparametric estimates 133
    rank tests 133
survival data 107, 1028
    definition 105
survival distribution function 998,
        1009-1010, 1028, 1044-1045, 1051
survival models
    accelerated failure time 106
    loglogistic 106
    lognormal 106
    nonparametric 106, 1027
    parametric 106, 997-998
    proportional hazards 106
    Weibul 106
survival time 1028
SYM specification
    COSAN Model statement (CALIS) 274
SYMBOL= option
    PAINT statement (REG) 1374-1375
    PLOT statement (REG) 1378
syntax abbreviations
    CORRESP procedure 621
syntax summary
    ACECLUS procedure 196
    CORRESP procedure 621
    FACTOR procedure 779
    FASTCLUS procedure 825, 826
    NESTED procedure 1128
    TREE procedure 1614-1615
syntax summary, REG procedure 1357
SYSLIN procedure
    compared with CALIS 138
system of equations
    NLIN procedure 1151-1152
systematics
    See clustering

T

T option
    MEANS statement (ANOVA) 222
    MEANS statement (GLM) 917, 942
    PROC CANCORR statement 373
t statistic
    for equality of means 1635

t-options
    MODEL statement (TRANSREG) 1528-1531
    TRANSFORM statement (PRINQUAL)
        1279, 1282-1285
t-square statistics
    in CLUSTER procedure 526, 561-562
t-tests
    ORTHOREG procedure 1214
    with NPAR1WAY procedure 25
    with TTEST procecure 25
table construction options
    CORRESP procedure 622
    PROC CORRESP statement 622-627
table of summary options
    PROC FREQ 858
tables
    contingency, FREQ procedure 854
    frequency and crosstabulation, FREQ
        procedure 852-889
    n-way, FREQ procedure 854
    one-way frequency, FREQ procedure
        852-853
    two-way crosstabulations, FREQ procedure
        853-854
TABLES statement
    CORRESP procedure 621, 628-632
    FREQ procedure 857
TARGET= option
    FACTOR procedure 780
    PROC FACTOR statement 787
TAU= option
    PROC NLIN statement 1140
taximetrics
    See clustering
taxonorics
    See clustering
TCORR option
    PROC CANDISC statement 392
    PROC DISCRIM statement 692
    PROC STEPDISC statement 1498
TCOV option
    PROC CANDISC statement 392
    PROC DISCRIM statement 692
    PROC STEPDISC statement 1498
TDIFF option
    LSMEANS statement (GLM) 909
TDPREFIX= option
    OUTPUT statement (TRANSREG) 1536,
        1539
TEST option
    RANDOM statement (GLM) 923, 958,
        959, 986
TEST statement
    and REPEATED statement (GLM) 924
    ANOVA procedure 214, 226-227
    GLM procedure 900, 926-927
    LIFETEST procedure 1043
    REG procedure 1358, 1384-1385
TESTCLASS statement
    DISCRIM procedure 686, 695
TESTDATA= option
    PROC DISCRIM statement 692

TESTFREQ statement
  DISCRIM procedure 686, 695
TESTID statement
  DISCRIM procedure 686, 695
TESTLIST option
  PROC DISCRIM statement 692
TESTLISTERR option
  PROC DISCRIM statement 692
TESTOUT= data set, DISCRIM procedure
  701
TESTOUT= option
  PROC DISCRIM statement 692
TESTOUTD= data set, DISCRIM procedure
  701
TESTOUTD= option
  PROC DISCRIM statement 692
tests of association (LIFETEST) 1046-1048
  example 1052-1062
THRESHOLD= option
  PROC ACECLUS statement 195
  PROC DISCRIM statement 692
threshold response rate 1325, 1326, 1328,
  1339
TICKPOS= option
  PROC TREE statement 1618
  TREE procedure 1614
tied values
  and NPAR1WAY procedure 1199
ties
  and transformations, PRINQUAL
    procedure 1282
  and transformations, TRANSREG
    procedure 1527, 1528
  checking for in CLUSTER procedure 526
  CLUSTER procedure 564
time requirements
  ACECLUS procedure 201
  CANCORR procedure 377
  CATMOD procedure 471
  CLUSTER procedure 563
  FACTOR procedure 794, 797
  FASTCLUS procedure 831-832
  LOGISTIC procedure 1096
  PRINCOMP procedure 1249
  PRINQUAL procedure 1291
  TRANSREG procedure 1556
  VARCLUS procedure 1649, 1651
TIME statement, LIFETEST procedure 1043
TIPREFIX= option
  OUTPUT statement (TRANSREG) 1536,
    1539
TITLE= option
  FACTORS statement (CATMOD) 422
  LOGLIN statement (CATMOD) 424
  MODEL statement (CATMOD) 428
  REPEATED statement (CATMOD) 433
  RESPONSE statement (CATMOD) 434
Tobit model 999, 1024
TOL option
  MODEL statement (REG) 1368
tolerance 12

tolerance distribution, PROBIT procedure
  1337
TOLERANCE option
  MODEL statement (GLM) 920
TOTEFF option
  PROC CALIS statement 271
TPREFIX= option
  and output data set (PRINQUAL) 1290
  PROC PRINQUAL statement 1278
TRACE option
  PROC VARCLUS statement 1647
trace W method
  See Ward's method
training data set
  DISCRIM procedure 678
TRANSFORM statement
  MSPLINE transformation option
    (PRINQUAL) 1283
  nonoptimal transformation options
    (PRINQUAL) 1283
  options for transformations (PRINQUAL)
    1283-1286
  PRINQUAL procedure 1273, 1279-1285
  SPLINE transformation option
    (PRINQUAL) 1283
  transformations available (PRINQUAL)
    1280-1282
transformation families
  PRINQUAL procedure 1280-1285
  TRANSREG procedure 1524-1528
  TRANSREG procedure, nonoptimal 1526
transformation matrices
  printing in ANOVA procedure 226
  printing in GLM procedure 926
transformation regression
  See TRANSREG procedure
transformations
  See also PRINQUAL procedure
  See also TRANSREG procedure
  examples with PRINQUAL procedure
    1284-1285
  examples with TRANSREG procedure
    1530-1531
  for multivariate *ANOVA* (GLM) 217, 910
  for single-degree-of-freedom contrasts
    (ANOVA) 224-225
  for single-degree-of-freedom contrasts
    (GLM) 924-925
  in cluster analysis 520
  MAC method 1268
  MGV method 1267
  MTV method 1267
  repeated measures analysis of variance
    (GLM) 955-958
  RESPONSE statement (CATMOD) 434
transforming data 103
TRANSPOSE procedure
  See also "Changes and Enhancements"
  using for repeated measures data (GLM)
    952

TRANSREG procedure   103, 1511–1611
  See also "Changes and Enhancements"
  See also regression procedures
  and GLM procedure   1575–1578
  and REG procedure   1575–1578
  BY statement   1520, 1523
  centering variables   1541
  compared with other procedures   1513
  compared with PRINQUAL procedure   42
  computational resources   1556–1557
  controlling iterations   1531, 1541
  convergence and degeneracies   1557–1558
  dummy variables in design matrix   1532
  error messages   1526
  examples   1514–1520, 1567–1609
  ID statement   1520, 1523
  iteration method   1514
  memory requirements   1556
  missing values   1531, 1533, 1540, 1543,
      1544
  missing values and output data sets   1551
  missing values, estimating   1540
  MODEL statement   1521, 1523–1535
  optimal transformations, methods
      1542–1545
  output data sets   1546–1551, 1575–1578
  OUTPUT statement   1521, 1535–1540
  printed output   1566
  PROC TRANSREG statement   1521–1523
  specifying analysis methods   1531
  statistical background   1513–1514
  suppressing output   1531
  syntax summary   1521
  time requirements   1556
  transformations and hypothesis testing
      1512
  transformations available   1524–1531
treatments in a design
  See also factors in a design
  defined for PROC PLAN   1222
  specifying in PLAN procedure   1229–1230
TREATMENTS statement (PLAN)   1223, 1229
  See also "Changes and Enhancements"
  See also PLAN procedure, examples
  examples   1222, 1229
tree diagrams
  binary tree   1614
  branch   1614
  children   1614
  definitions   1613
  horizontal   1616
  leaves   1613
  node   1614
  parent   1614
tree diagram examples   1620–1631
TREE procedure   1613–1631
  See also "Changes and Enhancements"
  BY statement   1618
  compared to other procedures   54
  COPY statement   1618
  DATA= option   1614
  DESCENDING option   1615

DISSIMILAR option   1614
DOCK= option   1614
FILLCHAR= option   1615
FREQ statement   1618
HEIGHT= option   1614
HEIGHT statement   1619
HORIZONTAL option   1614
ID statement   1619
INC= option   1614
JOINCHAR= option   1615
LEAFCHAR= option   1615
LEVEL= option   1614
LIST option   1615
MAXHEIGHT= option   1614
MINHEIGHT= option   1614
missing values   1619
NAME statement   1619
NCLUSTERS= option   1614
NOPRINT option   1615
NTICK= option   1614
OUT= option   1614
output data sets   1615, 1616, 1617, 1620
PAGES= option   1615
PARENT statement   1619
POS= option   1614
printed output   1620
PROC TREE statement   1614
ROOT= option   1614
SIMILAR option   1614
SORT option   1615
SPACES= option   1614
syntax summary   1614–1615
TICKPOS= option   1614
TREECHAR= option   1615
TREECHAR= option
  PROC TREE statement   1618
  TREE procedure   1615
TRIM= option
  and other options (CLUSTER)   524, 525,
      526, 527
  PROC CLUSTER statement   524, 527
triweight kernel
  formulas   682
triweight kernel method
  DISCRIM procedure   678, 682
TSSCP option
  PROC CANDISC statement   392
  PROC DISCRIM statement   693
  PROC STEPDISC statement   1498
TSTANDARD= option
  and MAC method (PRINQUAL)   1287–1288
  and output data set (PRINQUAL)   1291
  OUTPUT statement (TRANSREG)   1536,
      1539
  PROC PRINQUAL statement   1278
TTEST procedure   1633–1640
  See also "Changes and Enhancements"
  and GLM procedure   894
  BY statement   1634
  CLASS statement   1635
  compared with other procedures   21–22
  computational method   1635

TTEST procedure (*continued*)
  examples 1637-1639
  missing values 1635
  printed output 1636-1637
  PROC TTEST statement 1634
  summary of 25
  VAR statement 1635
Tucker and Lewis's Reliability Coefficient
    799
TUKEY option
  MEANS statement (ANOVA) 222, 234
  MEANS statement (GLM) 917, 944
Tukey-Kramer criterion 944
Tukey's studentized range test 222, 917
two-sample *t*-test 1633, 1637-1638
two-stage density linkage
  with CLUSTER procedure 522, 535
TYPE= data sets
  See also "Changes and Enhancements"
  described 1675-1686
  FACTOR procedure 792
  STEPDISC procedure 1500-1501
TYPE= option
  PROC SCORE statement 1481-1482
TYPE=ACE data sets 1686
TYPE=CORR data sets 1678-1681
  REG procedure 1386-1388
  VARCLUS procedure 1649
TYPE=COV data sets 1682
TYPE=CSSCP data sets 1683
TYPE=DISTANCE data sets 1684
TYPE=EST data sets 1683-1684
TYPE=FACTOR data sets 1685
TYPE=LINEAR data sets 1685
TYPE=MIXED data sets 1685
TYPE=QUAD data sets 1685
TYPE=RAM data sets 1684
TYPE=SSCP data set, REG procedure
    1388-1389
TYPE=SSCP data sets 1682-1683
TYPE=TREE data sets 1685
TYPE=UCORR data sets 1681-1682
TYPE=UCOV data sets 1682
Type H covariance structure 954
Type I
  estimable functions 115-116
  hypotheses, appropriate models 115-116
  sums of squares 115
Type I method, VARCOMP procedure 1665
Type I SS
  estimable functions for 115-116, 934-935
  models appropriate for 116
Type II
  estimable functions 116-120
  estimable functions, examples 118-120
  hypotheses, appropriate models 119-120
  sums of squares 116-120
Type II SS
  estimable functions for 116-120, 935-936
  models appropriate for 120

Type III
  estimable functions 120-122
  hypotheses 120-122
  hypotheses, compared with Type IV 124
  hypotheses, construction 120-122
  sums of squares 120
Type III SS
  estimable functions for 120-122, 936-937
  hypotheses, compared with Type IV 124
  hypotheses, construction 120-122
Type IV
  estimable functions 122-124
  hypotheses 122-124
  hypotheses, compared with Type III 124
  hypotheses, construction 123-124
Type IV SS
  estimable functions for 122-124, 936-937
  hypotheses, compared with Type III 124
  hypotheses, construction 123-124
Type 1 error rate
  and repeated multiple comparison tests
    942
TYPE variable
  PROBIT procedure 1338
types of sums of squares (GLM) 932-937
typology
  See clustering

U

UCORR option
  PROC CALIS statement 271
UCOV option
  PROC CALIS statement 271
ULS estimation method specification
  PROC CALIS statement 265
ultra-Heywood cases, FACTOR procedure
    796-797
ULTRAHEYWOOD option
  FACTOR procedure 780
  PROC FACTOR statement 787
ultrametric, definition 562
unbalanced designs
  and GLM procedure 23-25
  and multiple comparison methods 944-945
  definition 23, 898
  NESTED procedure 1130
uncertainty coefficients 860, 870
  uncertainty coefficient (U) 870-871
  uncertainty coefficient C|R 870
UNDO option
  PAINT statement (REG) 1375
  REWEIGHT statement (REG) 1381-1384
unequal variances
  testing for 25
uniform kernel
  formulas 682
uniform kernel method
  DISCRIM procedure 678, 682
uniform null hypothesis, in clustering 97

uniform kernel estimation
  CLUSTER procedure   526, 527, 532
unique factor
  defined for factor analysis   775
univariate analysis
  contrasting with multivariate analysis   46–50
UNIVARIATE method
  and output data sets (TRANSREG)   1551
  specifying in TRANSREG procedure   1532
UNIVARIATE procedure
  See also "Changes and Enhancements"
  and NPAR1WAY procedure   1195
univariate tests
  between-subject effects, repeated
      measures   953
  repeated measures analysis (GLM)   951
  within-subject effects, repeated measures
      953
unsquared Euclidean distances   524, 526
unsupervised pattern recognition
  See clustering
UNTIE= option
  MODEL statement (TRANSREG)   1531,
      1534
  PROC PRINQUAL statement   1278
UNTIE transform
  and missing values (PRINQUAL)   1285,
      1286
  and missing values (TRANSREG)   1540
  MODEL statement (TRANSREG)   1524,
      1528
  TRANSFORM statement (PRINQUAL)
      1280, 1282
  TRANSREG procedure   1544
unweighted least-squares factor analysis   774
unweighted pair-group clustering
  See average linkage
  See also centroid method
UPDATE= option
  PROC CALIS statement   271
UPGMA
  See average linkage
UPGMC
  See centroid method
UPP specification
  COSAN Model statement (CALIS)   274
UPPER specification
  OUTPUT statement (LOGISTIC)   1085
USSCP option
  PROC REG statement   1360
U95= option
  OUTPUT statement (NLIN)   1145
  OUTPUT statement (REG)   1372
U95 option
  MODEL statement (RSREG)   1463
U95 specification
  OUTPUT statement (GLM)   921
U95M= option
  OUTPUT statement (NLIN)   1145
  OUTPUT statement (REG)   1372
U95M option
  MODEL statement (RSREG)   1464

U95M specification
  OUTPUT statement (GLM)   921

V

value series for a design, definition   1230
Van der Waerden tests   127, 1196, 1198,
      1200
VAR statement
  ACECLUS procedure   199
  CALIS procedure   285
  CANCORR procedure   369, 374
  CANDISC procedure   389, 394
  CLUSTER procedure   521, 529
  CORRESP procedure   621, 632–633
  DISCRIM procedure   686, 695
  FACTOR procedure   779, 789
  FASTCLUS procedure   830
  NESTED procedure   1130
  NPAR1WAY procedure   1197, 1199
  PRINCOMP procedure   1243, 1246
  REG procedure   1357, 1358, 1385
  SCORE procedure   1482–1483
  STEPDISC procedure   1495, 1499
  TTEST procedure   1635
  VARCLUS procedure   1648
VARCLUS procedure   1641–1659
  See also "Changes and Enhancements"
  See also TREE procedure
  BY statement   1647
  compared with other procedures   54
  computational resources   1651
  controlling number of clusters   1645–1646
  controlling number of iterations   1646,
      1647
  example   1653–1659
  FREQ statement   1648
  how to choose options   1649
  initializing clusters   1645
  memory requirements   1651
  missing values   1649
  output data sets   1646
  PARTIAL statement   1648
  printed output   1647, 1652–1653
  PROC VARCLUS statement   1643
  PROC VARCLUS statement options   1643
  SEED statement   1648
  syntax summary   1643
  time requirements   1649, 1651
  use with FACTOR procedure   55
  VAR statement   1648
  WEIGHT statement   1648
VARCOMP procedure   1661–1673
  See also "Changes and Enhancements"
  and GLM procedure   894
  BY statement   1662, 1663
  CLASS statement   1662, 1663
  compared with other procedures   21–22
  examples   1667–1672
  missing values   1664
  MODEL statement   1662, 1663

VARCOMP procedure (*continued*)
  printed output 1666
  PROC VARCOMP statement 1662
VARDEF= option
  FACTOR procedure 780
  FASTCLUS procedure 826
  PROC CALIS statement 272
  PROC FACTOR statement 788
  PROC FASTCLUS statement 828
  PROC PRINCOMP statement 1245
  PROC VARCLUS statement 1647
variable expansions (TRANSREG)
  definition 1524
  models generated 1542
  syntax 1525
variable selection
  discriminant analysis 1493
  regression analysis 1353
variable specification
  CORRESP procedure 628
variable transformations
  See transformations
variable-reduction method 1642
variance components 1128, 1661, 1664
  negative 1665
variance inflation 12
variances
  FACTOR procedure 788
  ratio of 1633, 1636, 1637–1638
  test for equal 690–691
varimax method 774
varimax rotation 787
VARNAMES statement
  CALIS procedure 285–286
VDEP option
  PROC CANCORR statement 373
VIF option
  MODEL statement (REG) 1369
VN= option
  PROC CANCORR statement 373
VNAME= option
  PROC CANCORR statement 373
VP= option
  PROC CANCORR statement 373
VPLOTS= option
  PLOT statement (REG) 1378
VPREFIX= option
  PROC CANCORR statement 373
VREG option
  PROC CANCORR statement 373
VW option
  PROC NPAR1WAY statement 1198

W

Wald statistics 1010
  definition 33
Wald tests 1335, 1344
WALLER option
  MEANS statement (ANOVA) 223, 233
  MEANS statement (GLM) 917, 947

Waller-Duncan multiple comparison test
    223, 917, 947–948
Ward's minimum variance method
    compared with other clustering methods
    56–97
Ward's minimum-variance method
  with CLUSTER procedure 522, 535
WCORR option
  PROC CANDISC statement 393
  PROC DISCRIM statement 693
  PROC STEPDISC statement 1498
WCOV option
  PROC CANDISC statement 393
  PROC DISCRIM statement 693
  PROC STEPDISC statement 1498
WDEP option
  PROC CANCORR statement 373
Weibull distribution 997–998, 1004, 1011,
    1029
  LIFEREG procedure 1004
  testing for fit of 126
WEIGHT= option
  OUTPUT statement (NLIN) 1145
  REWEIGHT statement (REG) 1383–1384
WEIGHT option
  See also "Changes and Enhancements"
      (PROBIT)
  See also "Changes and Enhancements"
      (LIFEREG)
  FACTOR procedure 780
  PROC FACTOR statement 788
WEIGHT statement
  ACECLUS procedure 199
  and missing values (LOGISTIC) 1086
  and multiple comparison methods, GLM
      procedure 941
  CALIS procedure 286
  CANCORR procedure 369, 374
  CANDISC procedure 389, 394
  CATMOD procedure 415, 440
  CORRESP procedure 633–634
  DISCRIM procedure 686, 696
  FACTOR procedure 779, 790
  FASTCLUS procedure 830
  FREQ procedure 861–862
  GLM procedure 900, 927
  LIFEREG procedure 1008
  LOGISTIC procedure 1077, 1086
  ORTHOREG procedure 1213
  PRINCOMP procedure 1243, 1247
  PROBIT procedure 1334
  REG procedure 1357, 1358, 1385
  RSREG procedure 1465
  STEPDISC procedure 1495, 1499–1500
  VARCLUS procedure 1648
weighted analyses
  GLM procedure 927
weighted average linkage
  with CLUSTER procedure 522, 534
weighted least squares
  CATMOD procedure 413–414
  formulas, CATMOD procedure 469

NLIN procedure   1136, 1148–1149
normal equations (GLM)   927
weighted pair-group methods
   See McQuitty's similarity analysis
   See median method
weighted principal component analysis   616
weighted product-moment correlation
   coefficients   374
weighted-group method
   See centroid method
weighting variables
   FACTOR procedure   795
Welsch's multiple-comparison tests   222,
   916, 947
WHERE statement
   See also "Changes and Enhancements"
   ANOVA procedure   210
   example   1650
   GLM procedure   895
WIDTH= option, PROC LIFETEST
   statement   1041, 1045
WILCOXON option
   PROC NPAR1WAY statement   1198
Wilcoxon rank-sum test   127, 1196, 1198
   continuity correction   1200, 1202
Wilcoxon scores   106
   definition   1200
Wilcoxon signed-rank test   126–127, 128,
   1195
Wilcoxon test
   generalized   133
   LIFETEST procedure   1028, 1034, 1037,
      1046–1048, 1051, 1052
Wilk-Shapiro test   126
Wilks' criterion
   printing in ANOVA procedure   217
   printing in GLM procedure   910
Wilks' Lambda   18, 953
   CANCORR procedure   377, 378
WITH statement
   CANCORR procedure   369, 375
within-subject effects
   repeated measures analysis of variance
      953–954
within-subject factors
   defined for repeated measures analysis
      923
WLS option
   MODEL statement (CATMOD)   428
WN= option
   PROC CANCORR statement   373
WNAME= option
   PROC CANCORR statement   373
Wong's hybrid method
   CLUSTER procedure   524, 532
WP= option
   PROC CANCORR statement   373
WPGMA
   See McQuitty's similarity analysis
WPGMC
   See median method

WPREFIX= option
   PROC CANCORR statement   373
WREG option
   PROC CANCORR statement   373
WSSCP option
   PROC CANDISC statement   393
   PROC DISCRIM statement   693
   PROC STEPDISC statement   1498

X

XBETA= option
   OUTPUT statement (LIFEREG)   1007
   OUTPUT statement (PROBIT)   1334
XBETA specification
   OUTPUT statement (LOGISTIC)   1085
XPX option
   and output, CATMOD procedure   471
   MODEL statement (CATMOD)   428
   MODEL statement (GLM)   920
   MODEL statement (REG)   1369

Y

Yates' weights squares-of-means   121

Z

Z-test of Wilson and Hilferty (CALIS)   305
ZDI specification
   COSAN Model statement (CALIS)   274
zeros, structural and random   463
   examples, CATMOD procedure   487–492
ZETA= option
   MODEL statement (GLM)   920
ZID specification
   COSAN Model statement (CALIS)   274

Special Characters

(@) operator
   ANOVA procedure   212
   CATMOD procedure   412
   GLM procedure   897
(|) operator
   ANOVA procedure   212
   CATMOD procedure   412
   GLM procedure   897

Your Turn

If you have comments or suggestions about the *SAS/STAT User's Guide, Version 6, Fourth Edition* or SAS/STAT software, please send them to us on a photocopy of this page.

Please return the photocopy to the Publications Division (for comments about this book) or the Technical Support Department (for suggestions about the software) at SAS Institute Inc., SAS Circle, Box 8000, Cary, NC 27512-8000.